Ki Baruch Hu

Baruch A. Levine

Ki Baruch Hu

Ancient Near Eastern, Biblical, and Judaic Studies in Honor of Baruch A. Levine

edited by

ROBERT CHAZAN
WILLIAM W. HALLO
and
LAWRENCE H. SCHIFFMAN

Eisenbrauns
Winona Lake, Indiana
1999

Printed in the United States of America.

Library of Congress Cataloging-in-Publication Data

Ki Baruch hu : ancient Near Eastern, biblical, and Judaic studies in honor of Baruch A. Levine / edited by Robert Chazan, William W. Hallo, and Lawrence H. Schiffman.

p. cm.

English, French, and Hebrew; includes English abstracts of the Hebrew essays.

Includes bibliographical references and index.

Added title page title: Ki Barukh hu.

ISBN 1-57506-030-2 (cloth : alk. paper)

1. Bible. O.T.—Criticism, interpretation, etc. 2. Middle East—History—To 622. 3. Jews—History. 4. Judaism—History. I. Levine, Baruch A. II. Chazan, Robert. III. Hallo, William W. IV. Schiffman, Lawrence H. V. Title: Ki Barukh hu.

BS1151.2.K5 1999

296′.09—dc21 99-11847

CIP

The paper used in this publication meets the minimum requirements of the American National Standard for Information Sciences—Permanence of Paper for Printed Library Materials, ANSI Z39.48-1984.⊗™

Contents

PART III: JUDAICA

INDEXES

HEBREW ESSAYS

Baruch A. Levine: A Brief Biography

LAWRENCE H. SCHIFFMAN
New York University

Baruch A. Levine was the elder of two sons of Benjamin B. and Helen K. Levine. He was born on July 10, 1930, in Cleveland, Ohio and had a younger brother, Joseph H. Levine.

In Cleveland Heights, Baruch Levine attended the public schools and graduated from Heights High School in 1948. In 1951 he earned a B.A. in Comparative Literature with an emphasis on French literature from Adelbert College of Western Reserve University. It was here that he acquired the sensitivity to literary issues that would play so great a role in his analysis of biblical texts.

Baruch Levine was raised in a family for which Jewish education, including all phases of Judaic culture and Modern Hebrew language and literature, was extremely important and in which traditional Jewish learning in the Bible and Talmud was considered a mainstay of Jewish life. Concurrent with his general education, Baruch Levine attended various Hebrew schools and, from eleven through eighteen years of age, he received private Hebrew instruction from Zvi Shuster, who used Modern Hebrew as his language of instruction for a curriculum of Bible, Rashi, Aggadah, and Modern Hebrew literature. He also attended two Hebrew-speaking camps, Camp Massad (1944) and Camp Yavneh (1945–46), that greatly aided him in the mastery of spoken Hebrew. From eighth grade through high school graduation, he attended the Telshe Yeshivah in the afternoons, Monday through Thursday and all day Sunday. Here the main course of study was the Babylonian Talmud and its commentaries. This left a rich and variegated imprint on him in terms of his dedication to full-time Judaic learning and his legendary facility in traditional Jewish texts.

In his pre-teens, Baruch Levine had already joined a Zionist youth movement, and his ongoing participation in Zionist activities continued through college and attendance at Jewish Theological Seminary from 1951 to 1955.

He constantly expressed (and lived) the centrality of Israel to the Jewish people as a national, cultural, and religious fact. He was a member of Habonim and Hashomer Hadati, now called Bene Akiva. His ability to be a participant in two Zionist youth groups so different in their religious ideologies stemmed from the overriding zeal of Levine and his friends that resulted from the emergence of the state of Israel. This zeal united them, irrespective of their religious differences. The Hillel House at Western Reserve was a beehive of student activity, and Levine participated fully in programs such as end-of-the-summer retreats.

Levine signed up as a pretheological student at Jewish Theological Seminary at age nineteen with the stipulation that he do military service as a Jewish chaplain after graduation. The four years at the Seminary were years of intense immersion in Judaic and Hebraic studies under such masters as H. L. Ginsberg, Saul Lieberman, Salo Baron, Shalom Spiegel, and others. Ginsberg was to become his model of a biblical scholar, pursuing critical biblical research while maintaining his strong commitments to Judaism and the Jewish people. Their relationship would deepen greatly in later years when Levine came to live in New York. Ginsberg's comparativist approach to the Bible would remain with Levine and form a basic pillar of his research and teaching. From Saul Lieberman Levine learned how to meld the deep traditional learning he had acquired in the Yeshivah with modern philological analysis of rabbinic literature. Despite his concentration on biblical studies, he never lost his dedication to the study of the Talmud, and he never stopped transmitting the Lieberman tradition. From Mordecai Kaplan Levine came to understand the challenges posed to Judaism by the modern era and the freedom of American society.

During the school term Levine taught Hebrew high school, and during the summers he served as a counselor and unit head at Camp Ramah in the Poconos and as director of Camp Yavneh in 1960 and 1961.

Upon ordination in June 1955, he enlisted in the U.S. Army Reserve as a First Lieutenant and was assigned to Fort Benjamin Harrison, just outside Indianapolis, until May, 1957. Here he realized the unprecedented degree of acceptance of American Jews and Judaism that had become the norm in American society but came also to fear the tug toward assimilation due to that acceptance. As a chaplain he devoted much of his time to teaching, which added immeasurably to his teaching experience.

After completing his service in the military, Levine briefly entered the active congregational rabbinate. From 1957 to 1959, he served as Assistant Rabbi at Temple Emanuel, Newton Center, Massachusetts, under senior Rabbi Albert Gordon. By the middle of his second year, he realized that his true calling was to a life of scholarship, and so he enrolled as a doctoral student at Brandeis University in the Department of Mediterranean Studies under Cyrus H. Gordon. Gordon would bequeath to Levine the skills and languages needed to bring to bear the vast array of ancient Near Eastern sources on the study of the biblical and rabbinic literature. He completed his M.A. in 1959 and his doctorate in 1962 with a dissertation entitled *Survivals of Ancient Canaanite in the Mishnah.* This work demonstrated the need to access the influence of ancient Near Eastern materials on talmudic texts, an area in which Levine pioneered.

Levine soon began teaching at Brandeis, where between 1962 and 1969 he reached the rank of Associate Professor in the Department of Near Eastern and Judaic Studies. During this period he came under the spell of Thorkild Jacobsen and learned much from William Hallo. In these years, he began to specialize in the study of the biblical sacrificial cult and the relevant ancient Near Eastern evidence. He laid the groundwork for what would eventually be a lifetime project. He also began his pattern of spending long periods of time in Israel, helping to build the Israeli academic and intellectual climate, while at the same time imbibing the wisdom of the land and its scholars. In 1968, he served as Visiting Lecturer at Brown University. In 1969, just as he was leaving Brandeis, he married Corinne Godfrey, a painter and graphic artist, originally from Toronto.

Levine was appointed Professor of Hebrew and Near Eastern Languages in the Department of Near Eastern Languages and Literatures at New York University in 1969, beginning a new chapter in his personal and academic life. In the environment of the Department of Near Eastern Languages and Literature and the Kevorkian Center for Near Eastern Studies, Levine strove to make sure that Israel and Judaic Studies were given their proper representation and that they were fully integrated into the general field of Near Eastern studies. Levine's commitment to participation in Israeli academic life deepened greatly during these years, leading him to spend more and more time in Israel, where he was also a frequent visitor to archaeological sites. Further, Levine championed the notion that Judaic studies had to be integrated intellectually with other related disciplines and that the same academic standards applying in other disciplines had to be applied here. His tireless support of these notions was an important part of the process that led up to the reorganization of Judaic studies into the Skirball Department of Hebrew and Judaic Studies in 1986.

It was during his early years at NYU that Levine participated in the founding of the Association for Jewish Studies. Here he was motivated by the same principles regarding the academic character of university Judaic studies, as well as by the desire to make clear that the study of the Hebrew Bible had to be seen as part of the growing American academic study of Judaism. He was elected president of the association and served from 1971 to 1972. As its second president, his role in defining the young organization was significant. This activity took place even while he was active in the Society of Biblical Literature and the American Oriental Society. In 1979 he was honored with election as a fellow of the American Academy for Jewish Research. Levine has also participated actively in the Columbia University

Seminar for the Study of the Hebrew Bible and in the Biblical Colloquium. Throughout his scholarly career he has cultivated close intellectual relations with Christian biblical scholars, helping to develop a common language of discourse across confessional lines. He has continued to participate in the work of all of these organizations.

In the Skirball Department Levine flourished anew, deriving great satisfaction in the rounding out and expansion of the offerings in biblical and ancient Near Eastern studies. Levine worked with colleagues to create a premier center for Judaic studies in the American university ambience. In 1987, his contributions to the field as a whole and to New York University in particular were recognized when he was appointed Skirball Professor of Bible and Ancient Near Eastern Studies in the Skirball Department of Hebrew and Judaic Studies, where he still serves. His contribution to the training of the next generation of scholars, an activity in which he already engaged in his Brandeis years and which was continued extensively at NYU, has given him great satisfaction.

During his years at NYU he received numerous academic invitations, testifying to the respect in which his work is held. He was Visiting Lecturer at Sarah Lawrence College in 1969–70 and at Drew University in 1977, and Visiting Professor at Hebrew University in 1983 and at Ben Gurion University of the Negev in 1984–85 and 1988–90. Levine has held research fellowships from the National Endowment for the Humanities and the John Simon Guggenheim Foundation. He was a fellow of the Institute for Advanced Studies of the Hebrew University of Jerusalem in 1979–80.

In 1987, he received a Doctor of Hebrew Letters, Honoris Causa, from Jewish Theological Seminary of America. He was recently honored with the Distinguished Scholar Award by the National Foundation for Jewish Culture, recognizing his lifetime of biblical and Judaic scholarship. He serves as editor of the *Israel Exploration Journal* (Jerusalem) and *Handbuch der Orientalistik* (Leiden). He has contributed to the most important Jewish encyclopedias and biblical dictionaries, among them *Encyclopaedia Judaica, Interpreters' Dictionary of the Bible*, *Encyclopaedia of Religion*, and the *Anchor Bible Dictionary.*

For the past thirty-five years or so, Baruch Levine has been writing original works principally on the Hebrew Bible and ancient Near Eastern epigraphy, especially Ugaritic ritual texts and Aramaic inscriptions, often reaching into cuneiform literature. He has written several articles specifically on the recently discovered Balaam inscriptions form Deir ʿAlla in Transjordan.

In biblical studies, he represents the comparativist school, applying ancient Near Eastern evidence to biblical interpretation. In this approach, his knowledge of Semitic languages comes into play. He is also a phenomenologist who seeks to comprehend the inner meanings as well as the outward manifestations of religious rites and celebrations. His first monograph, *In the Presence of the Lord* (1974), dealt with the Israelite sacrificial system, and since then he has published the JPS Torah Commentary *Leviticus* (1989) and one of two projected volumes on Numbers for the Anchor Bible (1993). In press is the second volume of the Anchor Bible Commentary on Numbers 21–36, and he is presently working on an edition of Hebrew, Aramaic, and Nabataean-Aramaic Naḥal Ḥever papyri from the Dead Sea region.

Baruch A. Levine: An Appreciation

R. Chazan
New York University

Baruch Levine, as both scholar and teacher, is impressive in many ways. Indeed, the dominant feature of his academic career is the multiple dimensions of his interest, his expertise, and his achievement. These diversified interests and abilities are manifest in his writing, his teaching, and in his flowing everyday conversation.

Baruch is first and foremost a philologist. He has long been interested in the languages of the ancient Near East, Hebrew predominantly but far from exclusively. The notes to his two outstanding commentaries—on Leviticus in the Jewish Publication Society Commentary and on Numbers in the Anchor Bible—are filled with keen linguistic observations, often directing the reader to enlightening cognate expressions in one or another of the languages of the ancient world. This awareness of language lies at the core of many of his most innovative insights into the biblical text and its thinking. Baruch's teaching is similarly rich in careful clarification of terms and their meaning. This sharp sense of the languages of the Bible and its environs is paralleled by a fine feel for English idiom as well, making him a translator par excellence.

Beyond the linguistic—or over and above the linguistic—Baruch has an abiding interest in the everyday realities of ancient Near Eastern life. He has long been concerned with the fruits of archaeological research in Israel and the Near East; he has organized a series of international convocations on the economies of the ancient world; legal terminology and practice have fascinated him; cult and cultic practices have been at the center of his work from the very beginning of his scholarly journey. His concern with the realities of the ancient Near East has always been paralleled by a passionate interest in patterns of thinking—in the ways in which both the elites and the common folk understood the world around them and attempted to control their fate.

A voracious reader, Baruch weaves the widest possible range of findings into his work. This is once again true of his writing, his teaching, and his informal conversation. This last is particularly striking. Never at a loss for words, Baruch is an extraordinary conversationalist, whose wide-ranging knowledge makes him comfortable in nearly all circles. Not surprisingly, he is much sought after as a teacher of teachers, lecturing regularly to his fellow faculty at New York University.

Baruch has the historian's concern with the provenance and objectives of the literary documents with which he deals. He has long been an adherent of the documentary hypothesis in biblical studies. For him, without acknowledgment by the reader of the multiplicity of literary sources out of which the biblical record was composed, this record becomes utterly incomprehensible. His sense of sources and their goals is highlighted in the introduction to his commentary on Numbers 1–20:

> The commentator must decide how best to present the content of Numbers. Instead of offering a detailed outline of the book, chapter by chapter, it would be more fruitful to discuss what the major contributors to Numbers, the historiographers of the source JE and the writers of P (= the Priestly source), sought, in accordance with their respective agenda, to communicate to succeeding generations.

Throughout the commentary and his oeuvre more generally, awareness of sources and their agenda deepens our understanding of the texts and its intricacies.

A word about Baruch's teaching. Baruch Levine is a gifted lecturer, at every level of instruction. He has long taught broad introductory courses on the Bible and biblical Israel. He is genuinely excited about the opportunity to open up the texts and realities that have captivated him to the diverse undergraduate population at New York University. His broad knowledge and his gift for conversation very much enhance his classroom charisma.

At the more advanced graduate levels, Baruch exhibits similar enthusiasm and a parallel interest in the widest possible range of students. His students from around the world—Jewish, Christian, and Muslim—are a source of great pride. His trips abroad at the invitation of these disciples are among the high points of his scholarly experience. For all of his advanced students, the essential approach is the same approach found in his writings—careful philology, an unremitting concern with the widest range of realities, a concern to illuminate the thinking of those whose literary remains he studies.

Baruch A Levine: A Personal Reflection

William W. Hallo
Yale University

I first encountered Baruch Levine in April, 1962, at the meeting of the American Oriental Society in Cambridge, where he gave a paper entitled "A Ugaritic-Rabbinic Cultic Parallel." I still have my abstract of the paper, with the marginal notation ("Brother of Little Joe L."). The late Joseph Levine was well known to me at Hebrew Union College in Cincinnati, where I was teaching at the time. Baruch's paper was based on the dissertation that he was then completing at Brandeis under Cyrus Gordon. It ran into the kind of crossfire reserved for "maiden-speeches" at the AOS by some of its older members including, in this case, the late Moshe Held. But Baruch, as was far less usual in these situations, held his ground. I was impressed and invited him to New Haven, where I was ready to take up duties in the fall. He was eager to continue publishing, his first article, "The Netinim," having appeared in the *Journal of Biblical Literature* in May, 1963. I encouraged him to publish in the *Journal of Cuneiform Studies*, where his "Ugaritic Descriptive Rituals" appeared in December of the same year.

The title reflected our discussions of what I considered "archival" texts, abundant in Mesopotamia but rare at Ugarit. They had been the subject of his thesis, and they contained cultic information often overlooked by historians of religion. Thus began a lengthy and fruitful collaboration between us. It involved among other projects his "Descriptive Tabernacle Texts of the Pentateuch," which he published in the *Journal of the American Oriental Society* in 1965, while I was Associate Editor. Here he extended the concept of archival texts, or at least archival prototypes, to the Bible, a notion that I have gratefully exploited every since. He in turn made good use there of my concept of the two-dimensional account. (I remember having occasion to correct the arithmetic of one of his charts.) By 1967, we were combining forces to apply all of these insights to two large Old Babylonian texts, which we edited together in the *Hebrew Union College Annual* under the title of "Offerings to the Temple Gates at Ur." The fold-out charts that accompanied this article must have taxed the ingenuity of the printer, not to mention the budget of the *Annual.*

The collaboration continued with Baruch's undertaking to edit for me the volume of neo-Sumerian texts left unfinished by their owner and copyist, Carl H. Lager. Although he eventually had to abandon the effort under the pressure of other commitments, his notes proved helpful to D. C. Snell in the final preparation of the material, which appeared as volume 18 of Yale Oriental Series in 1991. As recently as 1995, he flattered me by asking for my critique of his essay on "The Balaam Inscriptions from Deir ʿAlla" for his forthcoming commentary, *Numbers 21–36.*

Besides these professional contacts, I have enjoyed a life-long friendship with Baruch and Corinne, cemented by their admiration for my late wife. I have fond memories of gourmet meals served by Baruch in New York, Jerusalem, and Lakeridge (Connecticut), and in the last location am happy to have become his neighbor. He is one of those rare scholars who, for all their academic attainments, retain their good humor, their love of life, and their capacity for the human touch. It can truly be said of him, as it was said of Israel to Balaam, "Surely he is blessed!"

Bibliography of the Writings of Baruch A. Levine

compiled by
Marlene R. Schiffman

1960

1. "The Language of the Magical Bowls." Appendix, pp. 343–75 in Volume 5 of *A History of the Jews of Babylonia*. Edited by J. Neusner. Leiden: Brill.

1963

2. "The Netînîm." *Journal of Biblical Literature* 82: 207–12.
3. "Ugaritic Descriptive Rituals." *Journal of Cuneiform Studies* 17: 105–11.

1964

4. "Notes on an Aramaic Dream Text from Egypt." *Journal of the American Oriental Society* 84: 18–22.

1965

5. "A Biblical Legacy." Review of *Genesis* (Anchor Bible 1), translation, with an introduction and notes by E. A. Speiser. *Judaism* 14: 373–77.
6. "Divisiveness in American Jewry: A Case in Point." *Judaism* 14: 224–29.
7. "The Descriptive Tabernacle Texts of the Pentateuch." *Journal of the American Oriental Society* 85: 307–18.
8. Review of *A Commentary on the Book of Genesis, Part One: From Adam to Noah*, by Umberto Cassuto. Translated by I. Abrahams. *Journal of the American Oriental Society* 85: 253–54.
9. "Comments on Some Technical Terms of the Biblical Cult." *Lešonénu* 30: 3–11. [Hebrew]

1967

10. "Offerings to the Temple Gates at Ur." *Hebrew Union College Annual* 38: 17–58. [with W. W. Hallo]

11. "The Pesikta." Review of *Pesikta de Rav Kahana: A Critical Edition*, by Bernard Mandelbaum. *Judaism* 16: 246–50.
12. Review of *Hebrew Union College Annual, Volume* 37. Edited by E. L. Epstein. *Journal of Biblical Literature* 86: 359–61.

1968

13. "*Melūgu/melûg*: The Origin of a Talmudic Legal Institution." *Journal of the American Oriental Society* 88: 271–85.
14–15. Articles in Volume 5 of *Encyclopaedia Biblica* (*Encyclopaediyah Mikra'it*). Jerusalem: Bialik Institute. [Hebrew]
14. "Nisrok." P. 887.
15. "Nergal." Pp. 924–26.

1969

16. "Kippûrîm." [Leviticus 16]. *Eretz-Israel* 9 (Albright Volume): 88–95. [Hebrew]
17. "Notes on a Hebrew Ostracon from Arad." *Israel Exploration Journal* 19: 49–51.

1970

18. "On the Presence of the Lord in Biblical Religion." Pp. 71–87 in *Religions in Antiquity: Essays in Memory of Erwin Ramsdell Goodenough*. Edited by J. Neusner. Studies in the History of Religions / Supplements to Numen 14. Leiden: Brill.

1971

19–24. Articles in *Encyclopaedia Judaica*. Jerusalem: Keter.
19. "Cult." 5.1155–62.
20. "Cult Places, Israelite." 5.1162–69.
21. "Firstfruits in the Bible." 6.1312–14.
22. "Firstborn in the Bible." 6.1306–8.
23. "Gibeonites and Nethinim." 7.552–55.
24. "Solomon, Servants of." 15.116–17.
25–27. Articles in Volume 6 of *Encyclopaedia Biblica* (*Encyclopaediyah Mikra'it*). Jerusalem: Bialik Institute. [Hebrew]
25. "ʿAbdê Šelômô." Pp. 25–26.
26. "Piggûl, Piggûlîm." Pp. 435–36.
27. "Paḥad Yiṣḥaq." Pp. 451–52.
28. "Prolegomenon." Pp. vii–xliv in *Sacrifice in the Old Testament: Its Theory and Practice*, by George Buchanan Gray. Library of Biblical Studies. New York: Ktav.

1972

29. "Aramaic Texts from Persepolis." Review of *Aramaic Ritual Texts from Persepolis*, by Raymond A. Bowman. *Journal of the American Oriental Society* 92: 70–79.

1973

30. "Damascus Document IX, 17–22: A New Translation and Comments." *Revue de Qumran* 8: 195–96.
31. "Later Sources on the Netînîm." Pp. 101–7 in *Orient and Occident: Essays Presented to Cyrus H. Gordon on the Occasion of His Sixty-Fifth Birthday*. Edited by H. Hoffner. Alter Orient und Altes Testament 22. Neukirchen-Vluyn: Neukirchener Verlag.

1974

32. *In the Presence of the Lord: A Study of the Cult and Some Cultic Terms in Ancient Israel*. Studies in Judaism in Late Antiquity 5. Leiden: Brill.
33. *Talmudic Thought: Course Syllabus*. New York: The Academy for Jewish Studies without Walls; American Jewish Committee in association with the University of Haifa.
34. Review of *Documents araméens d'Égypte*, by Pierre Grelot. *Journal of Biblical Literature* 93: 605–6.

1975

35. "Ha-Naviʾ Yeshaʿyahu ve-Yaḥaso le-Vet ha-Miqdash." Pp. 145–67 in *ʿIyunim be-Sefer Yeshaʿyahu*, Ḥeleq 1: Mi-Divre ha-Ḥug ba-Tanakh be-Vet ha-Nasi. Edited by B. T. Lurya. Jerusalem: Ha-Ḥevrah le-Ḥeqer ha-Miqra be-Yisraʾel be-Shituf ʿim ha-Makhlaqah le-Ḥinukh ule-Tarbut ba-Golah shel ha-Histadrut ha-Tsiyonit.
36. "On the Origins of the Aramaic Legal Formulary at Elephantine." Pp. 37–54 in Volume 3 of *Christianity, Judaism, and Other Greco-Roman Cults: Studies for Morton Smith at Sixty*. Edited by J. Neusner. Leiden: Brill.
37. Review of *The Hebrew Bible—Latter Prophets: The Babylonian Codex of Petrograd*. Edited with preface and critical annotations by Hermann L. Strack; Prolegomenon by P. Wernberg-Møller. *Journal of the American Oriental Society* 95: 111–12.

1976

38. "Critical Note: More on the Inverted *Nuns* of Num. 10: 35–36." *Journal of Biblical Literature* 95: 122–24.

39–41. Articles in *Interpreter's Dictionary of the Bible, Supplementary Volume*. Nashville: Abingdon.

39. "Numbers, Book of." Pp. 631–35.

40. "Priestly Writers." Pp. 683–87.
41. "Priests." Pp. 687–90.

1977

42. "The Role of the Bible in the Spiritual Development of Soviet Jewry." *Association for Jewish Studies Newsletter* 20: 4.
43. Review of *A Synoptic Concordance of Aramaic Inscriptions (according to H. Donner and W. Röllig)*. Edited by Walter Aufrecht; programming by John C. Hurd. *Journal of Biblical Literature* 96: 575–76.

1978

44. "Chapters in the History of Spoken Hebrew." *Eretz-Israel* 14 (H. L. Ginsberg Volume): 155–60. [Hebrew]
45. "On the Arad Inscriptions." *Šnat Miqra: Šnaton la-Miqra ule-Ḥeqer ha-Mizraḥ ha-Qadum* 3: 283–94 [Hebrew], xxvi [English summary].
46. "The Temple Scroll: Aspects of Its Historical Provenance and Literary Character." *Bulletin of the American Schools of Oriental Research* 232: 5–23.

1979

47. "Comparative Perspectives on Jewish and Christian History." Review of *Studies in Jewish and Christian History*, Part One, by Elias Bickerman. *Journal of the American Oriental Society* 99: 81–86.
48. "Major Directions in Contemporary Biblical Research." *Journal of Jewish Studies* 30: 179–91.
49. Review of *Temples and Temple-Service in Ancient Israel*, by Menahem Haran. *Journal of Biblical Literature* 99: 448–51.

1981

50. "The Deir ʿAlla Plaster Inscriptions." Review of *Aramaic Texts from Deir ʿAlla*, by J. Hoftijzer and G. van der Kooij. *Journal of the American Oriental Society* 101: 195–205.
51. Review of *Le culte à Ugarit d'après les textes de la pratique en cunéiformes alphabétiques*, by Jean-Michel de Tarragon. *Revue Biblique* 88: 245–50.

1982

52. "Assyriology and Hebrew Philology: A Methodological Re-examination." Pp. 521–30 in *Mesopotamien und seine Nachbarn: Politische und kulturelle Wechselbeziehungen im alten Vorderasien vom 4. bis 1. Jt. v. Chr.* Edited by H.-J. Nissen and J. Renger. Berlin: Reimer.
53. "From the Aramaic Enoch Fragments: The Semantics of Cosmography." *Journal of Jewish Studies* 33 (Yadin Volume): 311–26.
54. "Research in the Priestly Source: The Linguistic Factor." *Eretz-Israel* 16 (H. M. Orlinsky Volume): 124–31. [Hebrew]

1983

55. "The Descriptive Ritual Texts from Ugarit: Some Formal and Functional Features of the Genre." Pp. 467–75 in *The Word of the Lord Shall Go Forth: Essays in Honor of David Noel Freedman in Celebration of His Sixtieth Birthday*. Edited by C. L. Meyers and M. O'Connor. Winona Lake, Ind.: Eisenbrauns / American Schools of Oriental Research.
56. "In Praise of the Israelite *Mišpaḥâ*: Legal Themes in the Book of Ruth." Pp. 96–106 in *The Quest for the Kingdom of God: Studies in Honor of George E. Mendenhall*. Edited by H. B. Huffmon, F. A. Spina, and A. R. W. Green. Winona Lake, Ind.: Eisenbrauns.
57. "Late Language in the Priestly Source: Some Literary and Historical Observations." Pp. 69–82 in *Proceedings of the Eighth World Congress of Jewish Studies, Panel Sessions: Bible Studies and Hebrew Language*. Jerusalem: Magnes.
58. "*Miṣwāh*." Pp. 1085–95 in *Theologisches Wörterbuch zum Alten Testament*. Edited by G. J. Botterweck, H. Ringgren, and H.-J. Fabry. Stuttgart: Kohlhammer. [German]
59. Review of *Leviticus: An Introduction and Commentary*, by R. K. Harrison. *Journal of Biblical Literature* 102: 130–31.

1984

60. "The Role of Language in Graduate Programs of Jewish Studies." Pp. 106–20 in *New Humanities and Academic Disciplines: The Case of Jewish Studies*. Edited by J. Neusner. Madison Wis.: University of Wisconsin Press.
61. Review of *I testi rituali di Ugarit, I: Testi*, by Paolo Xella. *Israel Exploration Journal* 34: 66–67.
62. Review of *The Torah, the Prophets, the Writings: A New Translation of the Holy Scriptures according to the Masoretic Text*, Jewish Publication Society of America. *Journal of Reform Judaism* 31: 70–73.
63. "Dead Kings and 'Rephaim': the Patrons of the Ugaritic Dynasty [KTU 1.161 (=RS 34:126)" [transcription, English translation]. *Journal of the American Oriental Society* 104: 649–59. [with J.-M. de Tarragon]

1985

64. "René Girard on Job: The Question of the Scapegoat." *Semeia* 33: 125–33.
65. "The Balaam Text from Deir ʿAlla: Historical Aspects." Pp. 326–39 in *Biblical Archaeology Today: Proceedings of the International Congress on Biblical Archaeology, Jerusalem, April 1984*. Edited by Joseph Aviram. Jerusalem: Israel Exploration Society and Israel Academy of Sciences and Humanities in Cooperation with the American Schools of Oriental Research.

66. "The Pronoun Še in Biblical Hebrew in the Light of Ancient Epigraphy." *Eretz-Israel* 18 (Avigad Volume): 147–52. [Hebrew]

1986

67. Review of *Les Écoles et la formation de la Bible dans l'ancien Israël*, by André Lemaire. *Journal of Near Eastern Studies* 45: 67–69.
68. Review of *The Balaam Text from Deir ʿAlla*, by Jo Ann Hackett. *Journal of the American Oriental Society* 106: 364–65.
69. [Editor]. *The Early Biblical Period: Historical Studies*, by Benjamin Mazar, edited by S. Aḥituv and B. A. Levine. Jerusalem: Israel Exploration Society.

1987

70–71. Articles in *The Encyclopedia of Religion*. Editor-in-chief M. Eliade. New York: Macmillan.
70. "Biblical Temple." 2.202–17.
71. "Levites." 8.523–32.
72. "The Epilogue to the Holiness Code: A Priestly Statement on the Destiny of Israel." Pp. 9–34 in *Judaic Perspectives on Ancient Israel*. Edited by J. Neusner, B. A. Levine, and E. S. Frerichs. Philadelphia: Fortress.
73. [Editor]. *Judaic Perspectives on Ancient Israel*. Edited by J. Neusner, B. A. Levine, and E. S. Frerichs. Philadelphia: Fortress.
74. "The Language of Holiness: Perceptions of the Sacred in the Hebrew Bible." Pp. 241–55 in *Backgrounds for the Bible*. Edited by M. P. O'Connor and D. N. Freedman. Winona Lake, Ind.: Eisenbrauns.
75. Review of *The Israelian Heritage of Judaism*, by H. L. Ginsberg. *Association for Jewish Studies Review* 12: 143–57.

1988

76. "'Shapsu Cries Out in Heaven': Dealing with Snake-Bites at Ugarit (KTU 1.100, 1.107)." *Revue Biblique* 95: 481–518. [with J.-M. de Tarragon]

1989

77. "The Triumphs of the Lord." *Eretz-Israel* 20 (Yadin Memorial Volume): 202–14. [Hebrew]
78. *Leviticus*. The Jewish Publication Society Torah Commentary. Philadelphia: Jewish Publication Society.
79. Review of *La péricope de Balaam (Nombres 22–24)*, by Hedwige Rouillard. *Journal of the American Oriental Society* 109: 678–79.

1990

80. "A Further Look at the 'Môʿadîm' of the Temple Scroll." Pp. 53–66 in *Archaeology and History in the Dead Sea Scrolls: The New York University*

Conference in Memory of Yigael Yadin. Edited by L. H. Schiffman. Sheffield: JSOT Press.

81. "On Translating a Key Passage." *S'vara* 1/1: 71–73.
82. "The Impure Dead and the Cult of the Dead: Polarization and Opposition in Israelite Religion." *Bitzaron* n.s. 10/45–48 (Anniversary Volume, 1990–1991) 80–89. [Hebrew]

1991

83. "The Plaster Inscriptions from Deir ʿAlla: A General Interpretation." Pp. 58–72 in *The Balaam Text from Deir ʿAlla Re-evaluated*. Edited by J. Hoftijzer and G. van der Kooij. Leiden: Brill.
84. Review of *Property Rights in the Eighth Century Prophets*, by John Andrew Dearman. *Journal of the American Oriental Society* 111: 644–45.

1992

85. "Leviticus, Book of." Pp. 311–21 in Volume 4 of *Anchor Bible Dictionary*. Editor-in-chief D. N. Freedman. New York: Doubleday.
86. "The European Background." Pp. 15–32 in *Students of the Covenant: A History of Jewish Biblical Scholarship in North America*. Edited by S. D. Sperling. Society of Biblical Literature Confessional Perspectives Series. Atlanta: Scholars Press.
87. "The Second Wave." Pp. 89–113 in *Students of the Covenant: A History of Jewish Biblical Scholarship in North America*. Edited by S. D. Sperling. Society of Biblical Literature Confessional Perspectives Series. Atlanta: Scholars Press.
88. Review of *Textes ougaritiques, Vol. II: Textes, rituels, correspondance*, by A. Caquot, Jean-Michel de Tarragon, and Jesus-Luis Cunchillos. *Journal of the American Oriental Society* 112: 125–27.

1993

89. "'The Lord Your God Accept You' (2 Samuel 24:13): The Altar Erected by David on the Threshing Floor of Araunah." *Eretz-Israel* 24 (Malamat Volume): 122–29. [Hebrew]
90. "An Essay on Prophetic Attitudes toward Temple and Cult in Biblical Israel." Pp. 202–25 in *Minḥah le-Naḥum: Biblical and Other Studies Presented to Nahum M. Sarna in Honour of His 70th Birthday*. Edited by M. Brettler and M. Fishbane. Journal for the Study of the Old Testament Supplement Series 154. Sheffield: Sheffield Academic Press.
91. "LPNY YHWH: Phenomenology of the Open-Air Altar." Pp. 196–205 in *Biblical Archaeology Today, 1990: Proceedings of the Second International Congress on Biblical Archaeology*. Edited by J. Aviram. Jerusalem: Israel Exploration Society and The Israel Academy of Sciences and Humanities.

92. "On the Semantics of Land Tenure in Biblical Israel: The Term ʾAhuzzah." Pp. 134–39 in *The Tablet and the Scroll: Near Eastern Studies in Honor of William W. Hallo*. Edited by M. E. Cohen, D. Snell, and D. Weisberg. Bethesda, Md.: CDL Press.
93. "Silence, Sound, and the Phenomenology of Mourning in Biblical Israel." *Journal of the Ancient Near Eastern Society (of Columbia University)* 22 (Comparative Studies in Honor of Yohanan Muffs): 89–106.
94. Review of *Leviticus 1–16: A New Translation with Commentary*, by Jacob Milgrom. *Biblica* 74: 280–85.
95. *Numbers 1–20: A New Translation with Introduction and Commentary.* Anchor Bible 4A. New York: Doubleday.
96. "The King Proclaims the Day: Ugaritic Rites for the Vintage (KTU 1.41//1.87)." *Revue Biblique* 100: 75–115. [with J.-M. de Tarragon]

1994

97. Review of *I Have Built You an Exalted House: Temple Building in the Bible in Light of Mesopotamian and Northwest Semitic Writings*, by Victor (Avigdor) Hurowitz. *Hebrew Studies* 35: 154–56.

1995

98. " 'Tanakh': A Shared Field." Pp. 96–103 in *Teaching Jewish Civilization: A Global Approach to Higher Education*. Edited by M. Davis. New York: New York University Press.
99. "The Semantics of Loss: Two Exercises in Biblical Hebrew Lexicography." Pp. 137–58 in *Solving Riddles and Untying Knots: Biblical, Epigraphic, and Semitic Studies in Honor of Jonas C. Greenfield*. Edited by Z. Zevit, S. Gitin, and M. Sokoloff. Winona Lake, Ind.: Eisenbrauns.
100. "The ʿ*Edah* as the Popular Assembly of an Empowered Religious Community." Pp. 1–24 in *Signs of Democracy in the Bible*. The Resnick Lectures, Temple Beth-El of Northern Westchester, Chappaqua, N.Y.
101. "The Balaam Inscriptions from Deir ʿAlla." *Qadmoniot* 28: 90–96. [Hebrew]

1996

102. " 'What's in a Name?' The Onomasticon of the Biblical Period and the Religious Beliefs of Israelites." *Eretz-Israel* 25 (Joseph Aviram Volume): 202–9. [Hebrew]
103. "Farewell to the Ancient Near East: Evaluating Biblical References to Ownership of Land in Comparative Perspective." Pp. 223–42 in *"Privatization" in the Ancient Near East and the Classical World*. Edited by M. Hudson and B. A. Levine. Cambridge, Mass.: Peabody Museum.
104. [Editor]. *"Privatization" in the Ancient Near East and the Classical World.* Edited by B. A. Levine and M. Hudson. Cambridge, Mass.: Peabody Museum.

105. "Offerings Rejected by God: Numbers 16:15 in Comparative Perspective." Pp. 107–16 in *Go to the Land I will Show You: Studies in Honor of Dwight W. Young*. Edited by J. E. Coleson and V. H. Matthews. Winona Lake, Ind.: Eisenbrauns.

106. Review of *The Invention of Ancient Israel: The Silencing of Palestinian History*, by Keith W. Whitelam. *Israel Exploration Journal* 46: 284–88. [with A. Malamat]

107. Review of *You Shall Not Abhor an Edomite for He Is Your Brother: Edom and Seir in History and Tradition*, edited by D. V. Edelman. *Israel Exploration Journal* 46: 290–91.

1997

108. "The Next Phase in Jewish Religion: The Land of Israel as Sacred Space." Pp. 245–57 in *Tehillah le-Moshe: Biblical and Judaic Studies in Honor of Moshe Greenberg*. Edited by M. Cogan, B. L. Eichler, and J. H. Tigay. Winona Lake, Ind.: Eisenbrauns.

Editorial

Israel Exploration Journal. Jerusalem: Israel Exploration Society. Co-editor, with M. Tadmor.

Handbuch der Orientalistik. Leiden: Brill. [with others]

Abbreviations

General

AV	Authorized Version (King James Version)
BH	Biblical Hebrew
BM	Bronze Moyen
BR	Bronze Récent
CH	Code of Hammurabi
EA	El-Amarna (tablet)
JPSV	Jewish Publication Society Version
LXX	Septuagint
MAL	Middle Assyrian Laws
MT	Masoretic Text
NAB	New American Bible
NASB	New American Standard Bible
NEB	New English Bible
NIV	New International Version
NJPSV	New Jewish Publication Society Version
NKJV	New King James Version
NRSV	New Revised Standard Version
NT	New Testament
Pap.	Papyrus
REB	Revised English Bible (Revised NEB)
RS	Ras Shamra
RSV	Revised Standard Version
RV	Revised Version
TEV	Today's English Version (Good News Bible)

Museum Sigla

A.	Preliminary Louvre Museum sigla for Mari tablets
AO	Tablets in the collections of the Musée du Louvre
BM	Tablets in the collections of the British Museum
K.	Tablets in the Kouyunjik collection of the British Museum
MFA	Museum of Fine Arts, Boston
NBC	Nies Babylonian Collection, Yale University
PAM	Palestinian Archaeological Museum photograph number
RS	Field numbers of tablets excavated at Ras Shamra
TLB	Tabulae Cuneiformes a F. M. Th. de Liagre Böhl collectae
YBC	Tablets in the Babylonian Collection, Yale University Library

Reference works

AAT	Ägypten und Altes Testament
AB	Anchor Bible
ABD	*The Anchor Bible Dictionary*. Edited by D. N. Freedman. 6 vols. Garden City, N.Y.: Doubleday, 1992
AEM	Archives épistolaires de Mari
AfO	*Archiv für Orientforschung*
AfO Beiheft	Archiv für Orientforschung Beiheft
AHw	W. von Soden. *Akkadisches Handwörterbuch*. 3 vols. Wiesbaden: Harrassowitz, 1965–81
AJP	*American Journal of Philology*
AJSL	*American Journal of Semitic Languages and Literatures*
AJS Review	*Association for Jewish Studies Review*
AKA	E. A. W. Budge and L. W. King. *The Annals of the Kings of Assyria*. London: British Museum, 1902
AnBib	Analecta Biblica
ANEP	*The Ancient Near East in Pictures Relating to the Old Testament*. 2d ed. Edited by J. B. Pritchard. Princeton: Princeton University Press, 1969
ANET	*Ancient Near Eastern Texts Relating to the Old Testament*. 3d ed. Edited by J. B. Pritchard. Princeton: Princeton University Press, 1969
ANETS	Ancient Near Eastern Texts and Studies
AnOr	Analecta Orientalia
ANRW	Aufstieg und Niedergang der römischen Welt
AOAT	Alter Orient und Altes Testament
APOT	*The Apocrypha and Pseudepigrapha of the Old Testament*. Edited by R. H. Charles. Oxford: Clarendon, 1913
ARAB	D. D. Luckenbill (ed.), *Ancient Records of Assyria and Babylonia*
ARM	Archives royales de Mari
ArOr	*Archiv Orientální*
ATD	Das Alte Testament Deutsch
ATR	*Anglican Theological Review*
BA	*Biblical Archaeologist*
BaM	Baghdader Mitteilungen
BARev	*Biblical Archaeology Review*
BASOR	*Bulletin of the American Schools of Oriental Research*
BBET	Beiträge zur biblischen Exegese und Theologie
BBR	*Bulletin for Biblical Research*
BDB	F. Brown, S. R. Driver, and C. A. Briggs, *Hebrew and English Lexicon of the Old Testament*. Oxford: Clarendon, 1907
BETL	Bibliotheca ephemeridum theologicarum lovaniensium
BHS	*Biblia Hebraica Stuttgartensia*
Bib	*Biblica*
BIFAO	Bulletin de l'Institut Français d'Archéologie Orientale
BIN	Babylonian Inscriptions in the Collection of J. B. Nies. New Haven: Yale University.
BJS	Brown Judaic Studies
BK	*Bibel und Kirche*

BKAT	Biblischer Kommentar: Altes Testament
BO	*Bibliotheca Orientalis*
BSOAS	*Bulletin of the School of Oriental and African Studies*
BZ	*Biblische Zeitschrift*
BZAW	Beihefte zur ZAW
CAD	*The Assyrian Dictionary of the Oriental Institute of the University of Chicago*. Edited by A. L. Oppenheim et al. Chicago: The Oriental Institute of the University of Chicago, 1956–
CBQ	*Catholic Biblical Quarterly*
CG	Catalogue général des antiquités égyptiennes du Musée du Caire
ConBOT	Coniectanea Biblica, Old Testament
CRAIBL	*Comptes rendus de l'Académie des Inscriptions et Belles-Lettres*
CRRAI	Compte rendu de la Rencontre Assyriologique Internationale
CT	Cuneiform Texts from the British Museum
CTA	A. Herdner. *Corpus des tablettes en cunéiformes alphabétiques*. Paris: Imprimerie Nationale, 1963
DBSup	*Dictionnaire de la Bible, Supplément*
DJD	Discoveries in the Judaean Desert
EB	Echter Bibel
EncBib	*Encyclopaedia Biblica*. Edited by E. L. Sukenik et al. 9 vols. Jerusalem: Bialik, 1950–88
EncJud	*Encyclopaedia Judaica*. Edited by Cecil Roth. 16 vols. Jerusalem: Keter, 1972
ErIsr	Eretz-Israel
FOTL	Forms of the Old Testament Literature
GAG	W. von Soden, *Grundriss der akkadischen Grammatik*
GB	[Wilhelm Gesenius and] Gotthelf Bergsträsser. *Hebräische Grammatik*. 29th ed. 2 vols. Leipzig: Hinrichs, 1918–29. Reprinted, Hildesheim: Olms, 1962.
HALAT	L. Koehler and W. Baumgartner et al. *Hebräisches und aramäisches Lexikon zum Alten Testament*. 4 vols. Leiden: Brill, 1967–90
HAR	*Hebrew Annual Review*
HAT	Handbuch zum Alten Testament
HBD	*Harper's Bible Dictionary*. Edited by P. J. Achtemeier et al. San Francisco: Harper & Row, 1985
HR	*History of Religions*
HSM	Harvard Semitic Monographs
HSS	Harvard Semitic Studies
HTR	*Harvard Theological Review*
HTS	Harvard Theological Studies
HUCA	*Hebrew Union College Annual*
IB	*Interpreter's Bible*
ICC	International Critical Commentary
IDB	*Interpreter's Dictionary of the Bible*. Edited by G. A. Buttrick. 4 vols. Nashville: Abingdon, 1962
IDBSup	*IDB Supplementary Volume*. Edited by K. Crim. Nashville: Abingdon, 1976
IEJ	*Israel Exploration Journal*

Int	*Interpretation*
IOS	*Israel Oriental Studies*
JAAR	*Journal of the American Academy of Religion*
JANES(CU)	*Journal of the Ancient Near Eastern Society (of Columbia University)*
JAOS	*Journal of the American Oriental Society*
JARCE	*Journal of the American Research Center in Egypt*
JBL	*Journal of Biblical Literature*
JCS	*Journal of Cuneiform Studies*
JEA	*Journal of Egyptian Archaeology*
JESHO	*Journal of Economic and Social History of the Orient*
JHNES	Johns Hopkins Near Eastern Studies
JJS	*Journal of Jewish Studies*
JNES	*Journal of Near Eastern Studies*
JNSL	*Journal of Northwest Semitic Languages*
JPS Torah Commentary	Jewish Publication Society Torah Commentary
JQR	*Jewish Quarterly Review*
JRelS	*Journal of Religious Studies*
JSJ	*Journal for the Study of Judaism*
JSOT	*Journal for the Study of the Old Testament*
JSOTSup	Journal for the Study of the Old Testament Supplement Series
JSS	*Journal of Semitic Studies*
JTS	*Journal of Theological Studies*
KAT	Kommentar zum Alten Testament
KB	Keilinschriftliche Bibliothek
KHAT	Kurzer Hand-Commentar zum Alten Testament
KTU	M. Dietrich, O. Loretz, and J. Sanmartín. *Die Keilalphabetischen Texte aus Ugarit*. Alter Orient und Altes Testament 24. Kevelaer: Butzon & Bercker / Neukirchen-Vluyn: Neukirchener Verlag, 1976
LÄ	*Lexikon der Ägyptologie*. Edited by W. Helck and W. Westendorf. 7 vols. Wiesbaden: Harrassowitz, 1975–89
LAPO	Littératures anciennes du Proche-Orient
LCL	Loeb Classical Library
Leš	*Lešonénu*
LSJ	H. G. Liddell and R. Scott. *Greek-English Lexicon*. Revised by H. S. Jones. Oxford: Clarendon, 1968
MAL	Middle Assyrian Laws
MARI	*Mari: Annales de recherches interdisciplinaires*
MDAIK	Mitteilungen des Deutschen Archäologischen Instituts, Abteilung Kairo
Mém. de N.A.B.U.	Mémoires de Nouvelles assyriologiques brèves et utilitaires
MGWJ	*Monatsschrift für Geschichte und Wissenschaft des Judentums*
MIFAO	Mitteilungen des Instituts für Orientforschung
MRS	Mission de Ras Shamra
MSL	Materialien zum sumerischen Lexikon. Edited by B. Landsberger et al. Rome: Pontifical Biblical Institute, 1937–
MVN	Materiali per il vocabulario neosumerico
NCB	New Century Bible
NCC	New Century Commentary

NICOT	New International Commentary on the Old Testament
NJBC	*The New Jerome Biblical Commentary*. Edited by R. E. Brown et al. Englewood, N.J.: Prentice Hall, 1989
OBO	Orbis biblicus et orientalis
OBT	Overtures to Biblical Theology
OECT	Oxford Editions of Cuneiform Texts
OIP	Oriental Institute Publications
OLZ	*Orientalische Literaturzeitung*
Or	*Orientalia*
OTL	Old Testament Library
OTP	*The Old Testament Pseudepigrapha*. Edited by J. H. Charlesworth. Garden City, N.Y.: Doubleday, 1983–85
OTS	*Oudtestamentische Studiën*
PDT	A. Salonen et al. *Die Puzriš-Dagan Texte der Istanbuler Archäologischen Museen*. Helsinki: Academia Scientiarum Fennica
PG	Patrologia Graeca (ed. Migne)
PEQ	*Palestine Exploration Quarterly*
QDAP	*Quarterly of the Department of Antiquities in Palestine*
RA	*Revue d'assyriologie et d'archéologie orientale*
RB	*Revue biblique*
RdÉ	*Revue d'Égyptologie*
REJ	*Revue des études juives*
RevQ	*Revue de Qumran*
RHR	*Revue de l'histoire des religions*
RlA	*Reallexikon der Assyriologie*. Edited by E. Ebeling et al. Berlin: de Gruyter, 1932–
RSF	*Rivista di Studi Fenici*
SBLDS	SBL Dissertation Series
SBLMS	SBL Monograph Series
SBTS	Sources for Biblical and Theological Study
SCM Bulletin	*La Société canadienne des études Mésopotamiennes: Bulletin*
ScrHier	Scripta hierosolymitana
SEL	*Studi epigrafici et linguistici*
Sem	*Semitica*
SET	T. B. Jones and J. W. Snyder. *Sumerian Economic Texts from the Third Ur Dynasty*. Minneapolis: University of Minnesota Press, 1961
SJLA	Studies in Judaism in Late Antiquity
SJOT	*Scandinavian Journal of the Old Testament*
StudOr	*Studia Orientalia*
SWBA	Social World of Biblical Antiquity
TDNT	*Theological Dictionary of the New Testament*. Edited by G. Kittel and G. Friedrich. 10 vols. Grand Rapids, Mich.: Eerdmans, 1964–76
TDOT	*Theological Dictionary of the Old Testament*. Edited by G. J. Botterweck and H. Ringgren. 8 vols–. Grand Rapids, Mich.: Eerdmans, 1990–
THAT	*Theologisches Handwörterbuch zum Alten Testament*. Edited by E. Jenni and C. Westermann. 2 vols. Munich: Kaiser / Zürich: Theologischer Verlag, 1971–76
Thompson Gilg.	R. C. Thompson. *The Epic of Gilgamish*. Oxford: Clarendon, 1930

TLZ	*Theologische Literaturzeitung*
TRU	L. Legrain. *Le temps des rois d'Ur*. Paris: Bibliothèque de l'École des Hautes Études, 1912
TWAT	*Theologisches Wörterbuch zum Alten Testament*. Edited by G. J. Botterweck and H. Ringgren. Stuttgart: Kohlhammer, 1973
TynBul	*Tyndale Bulletin*
UF	*Ugarit-Forschungen*
Urk.	Urkunden des ägyptischen Altertums
UT	C. H. Gordon. *Ugaritic Textbook*. Analecta Orientalia 38. Rome: Pontifical Biblical Institute, 1965
VAB	Vorderasiatische Bibliothek
VT	*Vetus Testamentum*
VTSup	Vetus Testamentum Supplements
Wb.	A. Erman and H. Grapow. *Wörterbuch der ägyptischen Sprache*. 5 vols. Leipzig: Akademie, 1926–31. Reprinted 1963
WBC	Word Biblical Commentary
WZKM	*Wiener Zeitschrift für die Kunde des Morgenlandes*
YNER	Yale Near Eastern Researches
ZA	*Zeitschrift für Assyriologie*
ZAH	*Zeitschrift für Althebräistik*
ZÄS	*Zeitschrift für ägyptische Sprache und Altertumskunde*
ZAW	*Zeitschrift für die Alttestamentliche Wissenschaft*
ZDPV	*Zeitschrift des deutschen Palästina-Vereins*
ZTK	*Zeitschrift für Theologie und Kirche*

Part I

Ancient Near East

Introducing the Witnesses in Neo-Babylonian Documents

EVA VON DASSOW
New York University and The City College of New York

Several terms and phrases are used to designate or introduce witnesses in Neo-Babylonian contracts and records. In this period, the most common term for 'witness' is *mukinnu*, from the verb *kânu* 'to be firm, secure', the D-stem of which is used to mean 'to attest, testify' (among other meanings); *šību*, the standard term for 'witness' since the Old Akkadian period, occurs relatively seldom. The other phrases used to introduce witnesses are (*ina*) *maḫar* 'before' (usually following a formula such as *ina kanāk ṭuppi šuāti* 'at the sealing of this tablet'), *ina ušuzzu* (*ša*) 'in the presence of' (based on *i/uzuzzu* → *ušuzzu* 'to stand'), and *ina ašābi* (*ša*), also 'in the presence of' (based on

Author's note: It is an honor to dedicate the present contribution to my teacher Baruch Levine in affection and in gratitude for his intellectual guidance and unflagging support.

An earlier paper on this theme was presented at the 202d Meeting of the American Oriental Society in Cambridge, Massachusetts, March 29–April 1, 1992. For their critiques of that paper I thank Martha T. Roth, Stephen A. Kaufman, and Raymond Westbrook. I am also grateful to Ira Spar and S. David Sperling for reading a draft of the present article, and special thanks are due to Ira Spar for his generous loan of several books. Responsibility for errors of fact or interpretation remains my own.

The term *Neo-Babylonian* is here applied, for convenience, to the entire period from the late 8th–early 5th century B.C.E. (as described in the second paragraph). All dates referred to are B.C.E. Dates by a king's regnal years are given in the form of a number followed by the king's name (for example, "3 Nabonidus" means "Year 3 of Nabonidus's reign"). The abbreviations PN and FPN are sometimes used to indicate masculine and feminine personal names. The reader unfamiliar with the dialect of Neo-Babylonian documents is asked to excuse the inconsistent use of case endings; particularly for stock phrases, I have tried to follow attested spellings.

A list of bibliographic abbreviations and sigla other than those used by *JBL* is appended at the end of this paper.

ašābu 'to sit'). In certain documents, two or more of these expressions may be used to introduce different (groups of) witnesses.

The plethora of terms invites us to ask why so many were necessary: do the various ways of introducing witnesses denote different functions or capacities? Moreover, on what basis were individuals chosen to serve in these capacities—were there guidelines for the selection of certain people as witnesses and the exclusion of others, or did one just grab anyone who was hanging around? While the use of distinct phrases to introduce witnesses in different types of documents, or to introduce different types of witnesses, has hardly gone unnoticed, the topic has not yet been the object of a comprehensive examination. The brief study that follows is limited essentially to the period from Neo-Assyrian domination of Babylonia through the reign of Darius I, that is, the late 8th century through the early 5th century B.C.E. The large number of documents from this period both facilitates the investigation proposed here and (since complete coverage of the documentation would overrun the available space) curtails its scope in the present context; this *esquisse* may at least delineate the answers to the questions posed above.[1]

1. This study is based on a survey, by no means exhaustive, of published Neo-Babylonian documents and records from the period indicated (after Darius I, significant changes in documentary practice occur, so the later Achaemenid and Seleucid periods are not examined); a bibliography of tablets published up to 1983 may be found in M. Dandamayev, *Slavery in Babylonia* (De Kalb, Ill.: Northern Illinois University Press, 1984) 7–16.

To reduce the burden of the notes, statements made in this paper will often be documented by sample citations only or by reference to the following collections of texts and archival studies: *NRV* contains translations of the documents published in *VS* 3–6, arranged chronologically within subdivisions defined by the type of transaction (or record) involved; San Nicolò's editions and translations of various documents in *BR* 8/7 and 6 are ordered according to the same principles. J. Krecher catalogued the published documents of the Egibi archive, together with an analysis of the archive, in "Das Geschäftshaus Egibi in Babylon in neubabylonischer und achämenidischer Zeit" (unpubl. Habilitationsschrift, Münster, 1970). More recent archival studies, which include new tablets and editions of previously published tablets, are: F. Joannès, *Archives de Borsippa: La famille Ea-ilûta-bâni* (Geneva: Droz, 1989), containing editions of 264 tablets pertaining to a group of family archives (hereafter Joannès, *Archives*); K. Kessler, *Uruk. Urkunden aus Privathäusern: Die Wohnhäuser westlich des Eanna-Tempelbereichs* (Ausgrabungen aus Uruk/Warka, Endbericht 8/1; Mainz: von Zabern, 1991), vol. 1, in which tablets from private archives excavated in Uruk are published (hereafter Kessler, AUWE 8/1); C. Wunsch, *Die Urkunden des babylonischen Geschäftsmannes Iddin-Marduk: Zum Handel mit Naturalien im 6. Jahrhundert v. Chr.* (2 vols.; Cuneiform Monographs 3a and 3b; Groningen: Styx, 1993), with editions of 387 documents assigned to the Iddin-Marduk "dossier" in the Egibi archive in vol. 2 and copies of newly published documents in vol. 1 (hereafter Wunsch, *UIM* 1 and 2).

After a synopsis of previous discussion concerning the role of witnesses in Mesopotamia, I shall survey the terminology associated with witnessing in Neo-Babylonian documents.

In the literary work entitled by Lambert "Counsels of Wisdom," there occurs a passage exhorting the reader or listener not to frequent a law court (or 'assembly' *puḫru*), "for you will be made to serve as their witness (*ana šībūtī-šunu*), they will bring you to testify (*kunnu*) in a case which is not your concern."[2] This piece of advice assumes that people who just happened to be around were indeed liable to be called upon to be witnesses. At the same time, however, the exhortation makes it clear that the role of a witness was sufficiently burdensome to be worth avoiding. Though the cited passage has to do with serving as a witness in a court proceeding rather than witnessing a transaction or document, it reminds us that being a witness was not simply a passive function but carried some responsibility.

San Nicolò linked the function of witnesses in Mesopotamian documents to the function of the document itself: the document is primarily evidentiary rather than dispositive, serving to record that a certain transaction or process has taken place, and the recorded presence of witnesses serves to authenticate that document. The witnesses would be expected to testify concerning the documented transaction, in case of litigation, but they are not in the first instance witnesses of the transaction, elements of which could have taken place outside of their presence.[3] This conception of the witnesses' role is reiterated by Cardascia, who emphasizes that "les témoins ne garantissent pas la sincérité de tout le contenu de l'acte."[4] On the other hand, in the case of undocumented transactions, the witnesses' role was to attest to the transaction itself; a witnessed transaction or agreement could be considered valid without documentation.[5] Either witnessed documents or

2. W. G. Lambert, *Babylonian Wisdom Literature* (Oxford: Clarendon, 1960; repr., Winona Lake, Ind.: Eisenbrauns, 1996) 100–101, lines 34–35; for translation compare CAD K 168, s.v. *kânu* 4a; CAD Š/2 402, s.v. *šībūtu* 2c.

3. M. San Nicolò, *Beiträge zur Rechtsgeschichte im Bereiche der keilschriftlichen Rechtsquellen* (Oslo: Aschehoug, 1931) 133–34, 162–63. J. Renger ("Legal Aspects of Sealing in Ancient Mesopotamia," *Seals and Sealing in Ancient Mesopotamia* [ed. R. D. Biggs and M. Gibson; Bibliotheca Mesopotamica 6; Malibu, Calif.: Undena, 1977] 75–88) likewise defines the Mesopotamian legal document as fundamentally an instrument of evidence, which exhibits some dispositive elements, in contrast to a modern contract: "the Mesopotamian document attests that a legal agreement has been concluded, while a modern contract creates a legal agreement" (p. 76). The dispositive or constitutive aspects of Mesopotamian documents are emphasized by M. Malul, *Studies in Mesopotamian Legal Symbolism* (AOAT 221; Neukirchen-Vluyn: Neukirchener Verlag, 1988) 450–52.

4. G. Cardascia, *Les Archives des Murašû* (Paris: Imprimerie Nationale, 1951) 23.

5. See San Nicolò, *Beiträge*, 133 n. 2; and Renger, "Legal Aspects of Sealing in Ancient Mesopotamia," 76.

the witnesses themselves were required in order to press a claim or prove a case. The witnessing of an action or declaration could be separately documented if necessary (see the discussion below of documents formulated with *mārē banî/mukinnē ša ina panīšunu*).

In spite of the passage cited above from the "Counsels of Wisdom," the persons who performed the function of witnesses were not typically selected for this role at random. As described by Hallo for the Old Babylonian period, many of the witnesses to contracts and legal proceedings were "chosen for their previous acquaintance with the contracting or contending parties or with the case at issue, and some of these were themselves interested parties;" this principle is upheld for the Neo-Babylonian period by Weisberg.[6] Martha Roth, succinctly defining witnesses to a transaction as "those persons in whose presence the transaction was concluded," states that while those persons could be "the people who happened to be at hand at the moment," the presence of certain individuals as witnesses was "conditioned by legal necessity."[7] The recording of certain witnesses' names connoted more than simply authentication of the document: an individual potentially entitled to an appeal or claim with regard to the transaction relinquished, through being present as a witness, any such right.[8] The presence of such witnesses thus signified consent to the transaction as well as attestation thereof. That witnessing may carry the secondary function of consent or agreement is widely recognized (see further below, in the discussion of the phrase *ina ašābi*). Other secondary functions have been postulated for certain witnesses, for instance confirming the borders of a field as described in a document of sale, on the part of a neigboring property-owner;[9] and confirming an heir's right to cede his father's credit claim, on the part of relatives.[10]

6. William W. Hallo, "The Slandered Bride," in *Studies Presented to A. Leo Oppenheim* (ed. R. D. Biggs and J. A. Brinkman; Chicago: University of Chicago Press, 1964) 103–4; see also idem, review of *Reallexikon der Assyriologie*, vol. 3, fasc. 1, ed. E. Ebeling and E. Weidner, *JAOS* 87 (1967) 65; and see David B. Weisberg, *Guild Structure and Political Allegiance in Early Achaemenid Mesopotamia* (YNER 1; New Haven: Yale University Press, 1967) 25.

7. M. T. Roth, *Babylonian Marriage Agreements, 7th–3rd Centuries* B.C. (AOAT 222; Neukirchen-Vluyn: Neukirchener Verlag, 1989) 20 [hereafter Roth, *BMA*]. In view of the foregoing paragraph, the definition could be modified thus: "those persons in whose presence the transaction was concluded or the document thereof was issued."

8. Roth, *BMA*, 20–22; San Nicolò, *Beiträge*, 134.

9. Roth, *BMA*, 21, without reference to a specific example; she posits alternatively that such a person might have been chosen as a witness because he was "readily available."

10. H. Petschow, "Zur Forderungsabtretung im neubabylonischen Recht," *Symbolae Raphaeli Taubenschlag dedicatae* (Eos; Commentari Societatis Philologae Polonorum 48/2; ed. I. Biezunska-Malowist; Bratislava and Warsaw: Ossolineum, 1957) 27. This is in addition to the function of renouncing potential claims. I thank Maynard P. Maidman for providing me with a copy of this article.

It has often been observed that the same individuals appear repeatedly as witnesses in the documents of a given family archive. Such individuals may also appear as scribes or transacting parties in other documents of the same archive, and they may be members of the family to which the archive belonged. The witnesses to the documents of Iddin-Marduk of the Nūr-Sîn family, for example, are often Iddin-Marduk's relatives, partners, or business agents, or are scribes of other documents of his (and they may be all of the above).[11] Prominent businessmen such as Itti-Marduk-balāṭu of the Egibi family and, in the second half of the fifth century, the sons of Murašû were evidently accompanied by a retinue of business associates, whether at home or out of town.[12] These people would be on hand to be witnesses of the principals' documents, besides serving as their scribes, agents, or proxies. The presence of relatives or business associates as witnesses can be due either to their availability or to their having an interest in the transaction or process described in the document.

I shall now survey how the various words or phrases listed in the first paragraph of this paper are used to introduce or designate witnesses. Which phrase is chosen depends on the role of the persons so introduced with respect to the transaction or document and on the type of transaction or document being witnessed.

From the mid–7th century onward, the word *mukinnu* (preceded by the determinative LÚ) introduces the list of witnesses in the majority of contracts and records of transactions, including the following types: sales of slaves and mobilia; contracts for lease, rent, or hire; and promissory notes and quittances.[13] One of the earliest discrete "archives" of the period examined in the present study is the tablet hoard of Bēl-ušallim, descendant of

11. Such instances are regularly noted by Wunsch; e.g., *UIM* 1.12, 14 n. 58, 15, 16 n. 67, 18 n. 76, 28 n. 111, 41 n. 154, 73–75 nn. 279–80, 281, and 285. Iddin-Marduk witnesses documents of transactions conducted by his associates and relatives or of transactions in which he had an interest (ibid., 1.76, 82 n. 309).

12. See Cardascia, *Archives des Murašû*, 20; M. Stolper, "The Murašû Texts from Susa," *RA* 86 (1992) 69–77, esp. p. 72; L. B. Bregstein, *Seal Use in Fifth Century* B.C. *Nippur, Iraq: A Study of Seal Selection and Sealing Practices in the Murašû Archive* (unpublished Ph.D. dissertation, University of Pennsylvania, 1993) 338–39 n. 55. The Murašû archive, being one of the most thoroughly analyzed of first-millennium Babylonian archives, is a useful source of comparative data, although it falls outside the time frame of this paper.

13. For confirmation of this statement regarding the use of the term *mukinnu* (supporting citations would be too numerous to list), one may consult the collections of text editions cited in n. 1 above. In *NRV*, *mukinnū* is rendered 'Zeugen' (while other phrases introducing witnesses are rendered differently). In the editions of 387 documents presented by Wunsch in *UIM* 2, 'Zeugen' translates *mukinnū* in all cases but nos. 167 (Nbn 356) and 292 (Cyr 161) and the documents with *ina ušuzzu* (see below).

Lēʾēa, consisting entirely of promissory notes dated to the mid-to-late 7th century, in each of which the witnesses are introduced by the term *mukinnu*.[14] In general, the witnesses to documents wherein obligations are incurred by one or more of the parties and to documents wherein obligations are outstanding are termed *mukinnu*.

However, *mukinnu* does *not* introduce the witnesses of contracts for the purchase of real estate or prebends. In these types of transactions, the formula (usually set off by ruled lines) *ina kanāk/šaṭār kanki/ṭuppi šuāti* 'at the sealing/writing of this sealed document/tablet', followed by *maḫar*, introduces the witnesses.[15] This usage continues the normal practice attested by kudurrus from the Middle Babylonian period through the mid–7th century. In witnessed documents recorded on kudurrus, the list of witnesses, who are usually officials, characteristically opens with *ina kanāk kanki šuāti* 'at the sealing of this sealed document' (or a similar formula) and closes with *izzazzū* '(these persons) are present'.[16] The principal formulaic difference in Neo-Babylonian real estate sales is that the list of witnesses is regularly preceded by *maḫar* and does not close with *izzazzū*.[17]

14. L. Jakob-Rost, "Ein neubabylonisches Tontafelarchiv aus dem 7. Jh. v. u. Z.," *Forschungen und Berichte* 10 (1968) 39–62.

15. See the documents in the relevant sections in *NRV* (Part 1 D. I: a–c), *BR* 8/7 (nos. 3–20, 22–36) and *BR* 6 (IV A). Documents recording sales of real estate in Joannès, *Archives*, are (in chronological order) A 131, *TuM* 2/3 17, TCL 12–13 6, *TuM* 2/3 14, A 98, and NBC 8395; in the Egibi archive, Nbn 164, 193, 203, 477 (among others; see Krecher, *Das Geschäftshaus Egibi*, 28–29, 42, 44–45, 70–71, 74); among Iddin-Marduk's documents, the duplicates Cyr 160 and 161 (Wunsch, *UIM* 2.292; IGI is omitted, Cyr 160:rev. 10–11′, 161:52) are the sole instances of a transfer of real estate (on the absence of such documents from Iddin-Marduk's extant dossier, see Wunsch, *UIM* 1.58–60).

16. E.g., *BBSt* 4 ii:1–11; 9 top, 14–23 (*izzazzū* omitted); 10 rev. 41–50; 25 rev. 25–36; 27 rev. 14–bottom edge 2; 28 rev. 18–25. Not all kudurrus record witnesses; in those that do, formulas mentioning sealing refer to sealed clay tablets documenting transactions, which were copied onto the kudurrus (F. X. Steinmetzer, *Die babylonischen Kudurru [Grenzsteine] als Urkundenform* [Paderborn: Ferdinand Schöningh, 1922; reprinted, New York: Johnson Reprint, 1968] 101–12, esp. 109–10; J. Oelsner, "Zur Siegelung mittelbabylonischer Rechtsurkunden," *Rocznik Orientalistyczny* 41 [1980] 94). The wording is adjusted to the content of the document, so, for instance, the witnesses of the final settlement recorded on *BBSt* 9 are introduced with *ina šâmi šaṭāri u barāmi* 'at the purchase, writing, and sealing' (iv A:29); and in *BBSt* 6, in which Nebuchadnezzar I grants exemptions to Šitti-Marduk as a reward for his service on the campaign against Elam (recently studied by V. Hurowitz, "Some Literary Observations on the Šitti-Marduk Kudurru [BBSt. 6]," ZA 82 [1992] 39–59), the list of witnesses opens with *ina zakût ālāni šuātu* (ii:11).

17. Since these alterations disrupt the syntax, it is likely that the formula *ina kanāk* . . . (names of witnesses) *izzazzū* has been conflated with the formula *maḫar* (followed by names), as suggested by San Nicolò and Ungnad in *NRV*, where they

In certain types of documents, *ina kanāk . . . maḫar* is interchangeable with *mukinnu*. Tablets documenting exchanges of real estate may have either phrase (e.g., *NRV* nos. 109–12, *TuM* 2/3 23, and *BR* 8/7 40). The witnesses to marriage agreements are introduced by *ina kanāk . . . maḫar* more often than by *mukinnu*; no other formal difference seems to be correlated with this variation.[18] In other documents concerning family affairs, such as testamentary dispositions and other intrafamilial property divisions and bequests, either the term *mukinnu* or the formula *ina kanāk . . . maḫar* may be employed.[19]

The term *mukinnu* also denotes the witnesses to documents of judicial proceedings.[20] As well as introducing the list of persons witnessing the document or the proceeding itself, *mukinnu* is used to denote witnesses summoned to give testimony; what they do is *kunnu* 'testify, prove, convict'. For example, YOS 7 7 documents the conviction of Gimillu, an oblate of Ištar of Uruk, on twelve counts of embezzlement and theft.[21] The text opens with a summary of the charges against him and the statement *mukinnū ukinnūšuma eli ramnīšu ukīn* 'witnesses testified against him, and he testified against

---

read IGI as *maḫar* (p. 6, no. 2 n. 15). The same syntactical difficulty later inclined both scholars to read IGI as *šību* (see *BR* 8/7 p. 3, note on no. 1:rev. x + 4, with further references). However, since in this position IGI is sometimes preceded by *ana* or *ina* (e.g., *TuM* 2/3 14, 17, 23) and occasionally written syllabically *ma-ḫar* (e.g., L 1663, Joannès, *Archives*, 251–52, in addition to the citations in CAD M/1 107, s.v. *maḫru* 2a2′), the reading *maḫar* is preferable; differently, J. Oelsner, "Zur neu- und spätbabylonischen Siegelpraxis," *Festschrift Lubor Matouš zum 70. Geburtstag* (Assyriologia 5; ed. B. Hruška and G. Komoróczy; Budapest, 1978) 2.168 n. 5.

18. See the documents in Roth, *BMA*. Anomalously, instead of the expected *maḫar*, the term *mukinnu* follows the formula *ina kunuk nudunnî šuāti* in Roth, *BMA* no. 42:26–27, dated in Year 108 of the Seleucid era.

19. The witnesses are introduced by *mukinnu* in the following examples: *TuM* 2/3 5 and NBC 8360 (Joannès, *Archives*, 168, 343), two documents from the same family archive concerning the division of inherited property; TCL 12–13 174 (Joannès, *Archives*, 317), a woman's assignment of her dower property (divided between her son and her husband, part of whose share is designated for her daughter); Nbn 697 (Wunsch, *UIM* 2 no. 211), a man's bequest of a slave to his daughter-in-law; and OECT 10:161 (Wunsch, *UIM* 2 no. 354) and Wunsch, *UIM* 2 no. 355 (copy Wunsch, *UIM* 1.123), two bequests made by a woman to her granddaughter. Other examples may be found in *NRV*, in the categories "Schenkungen" and "Nachlaßregelungen," nos. 11–32. In *VS* 5 21 (*NRV* no. 12), wherein a man bequeathes his prebends and other property to his daughter (while she undertakes to care for him for the rest of his life), the witnesses are introduced by *ina kanāk . . . maḫar*.

20. See for instance the documents recording judicial hearings or interrogations studied by San Nicolò, "Parerga Babylonica XI: Die *maš'altu*-Urkunden im neubabylonischen Strafverfahren," *ArOr* 5 (1933) 287–302; and below, nn. 22 and 29.

21. Edited by San Nicolò, "Parerga Babylonica IX: Der Monstreprozeß des Gimillu, eines širku von Eanna," *ArOr* 5 (1933) 61–77.

himself' (or, 'witnesses convicted him [= proved (the charge) against him], and he convicted himself'); nearly every one of the charges itemized concludes with *ina puḫri ukinnuš* '(PN) testified against him' or *eli ramnišu ukīn* 'he testified against himself', followed by the prescription of a 30-fold penalty. The formulation *ina ūmu mukinnu (ana)* PN *uktinnu ša* 'should a witness testify against PN that (he committed thus-and-such a deed)' occurs in several documents that prescribe a penalty in case the defendant is convicted.[22] Nbk 183 elaborates alternative outcomes of such a situation: on a certain day, Imbiya is to bring his witness (*mukinnu*) to the canal administrator to testify (*kunnu*) against Arrabi that the latter took the garments of Imbiya; if the witness so testifies (or 'convicts him' *kî uktinnuš*), Arrabi must give Imbiya the garments, and if not, he is 'clear' (*zaki*); should Arrabi fail to appear on the specified day, he must give him the garments *ša la mukinnūtu* 'in the absence of witnessing' (or 'without testimony').[23]

It may be noted that none of these examples refers to witnesses of documents, but to witnesses who could attest to the performance of deeds or whose testimony could establish the facts. In the case of documented transactions or acts, one consulted the documents without necessarily summoning the witnesses to those documents. For instance, the judges examined the tablets and contracts pertaining to a widow's suit in Nbn 356:29–30 (Wunsch, *UIM* 2 no. 167), but did not call witnesses. In Nbn 13, in order to settle a suit in which the seller of a slave claimed that the purchaser had not paid the price, the judges were shown the contract of sale and took testimony from the seller's sons (who confirmed, *ukinnū*, that the price was paid), but they did not call the witnesses of the contract. A document could even be referred to—if only rhetorically—as a 'witness' *mukinnu* (e.g., CT 22 176:18, and see CAD M/2 186, s.v. *mukinnu* 1b). If documents were unavailable, one had to have recourse to live witnesses. In this context it is pertinent to mention UET 4 327, a rather hysterical letter from one Sîn-uballiṭ to his mother concerning his house which he insists has been unjustly taken from him; witnesses (*mukinnē*) must be found whose statements would support his claim (lines 4–12), but it turns out that one of his potential witnesses is dead (lines 6–7).

Finally, a specific type of document, consisting of a résumé of an action or declaration and a list of the witnesses (equivocally termed *mukinnu* or *mār banî* 'citizen') who would attest to the performance of that action or to the making of that declaration, is formulated as follows: *(annûtu) mārē banî/*

22. E.g., YOS 6 122 and 148, TCL 12 70 and 106, and YOS 7 141, treated by San Nicolò in "Parerga Babylonica VII: Der §8 des Gesetzbuches Hammurapis in den neubabylonischen Urkunden," *ArOr* 4 (1932) 327–44; and YOS 6 203:14–16 *mimma mala . . . mukinnū (ana)* PN *u* PN_2 *ukannū* 'as much (stolen goods) as witnesses prove against PN and PN_2' (see San Nicolò, "Parerga Babylonica XI," 296–97).

23. This text is edited by E. Salonen, *Neubabylonische Urkunden verschiedenen Inhalts* 3 (Annales Academiae Scientiarum Fennicae B/206; Helsinki, 1980) no. 5.

mukinnē ša ina panīšunu '(these are) the witnesses/citizens before whom (PN declared as follows, or thus-and-such an action was performed)'.[24]

The content and purpose of these documents, found in both private and temple archives, is quite varied and cannot be discussed in any depth here. Tablets formulated in this way could be issued in the course of judicial proceedings: CT 2 2, for instance, records an investigation conducted by the *šangû* (chief temple administrator) of Sippar and the Ebabbara temple personnel (*ērib bīt Šamaš*) into the disappearance of linen from temple stores and its possible theft by a member of the temple 'college' (*kiništu*); from the Eanna temple in Uruk, TCL 12 117 records the witnesses before whom the oblate Ibni-Ištar drew a dagger against a royal official, the dagger being then 'tied and sealed' by the assembly.[25] Such documents could also be issued in the course of the resolution of private disputes (see *NRV* no. 704 with remarks p. 610). The summons to which Arrabi was expected to respond, according to Nbk 183 (see above), may have resulted in the issuance of a "declaration before witnesses" of this sort, recording the content of Imbiya's witness's testimony and the names of the persons in whose presence it was heard.

In sum, witnesses to documents of both transactions and judicial proceedings are normally termed *mukinnu*. The term *šību* in the meaning 'witness' is unequivocally attested in only a few Neo-Babylonian documents (excluding possibly ambiguous uses of the logogram IGI). It introduces the witnesses in two documents from the 7th century, *BR* 8/7 15:28 (*ši-i-bi*), a contract for the purchase of a house, and *BR* 8/7 44:11 (^{lú}AB.BA^{meš}), a fragment of a contract probably involving alienation of property. Also, the

24. On this type of document, see *NRV*, 607–9 and nos. 703–16. TCL 12 117, which opens with *mārē banî ša ina panīšunu* and then introduces the list of those *mārē banî* with the word *mukinnū* (line 9), demonstrates that in this context the two terms are interchangeable; a document of this type recently published by M. W. Stolper ("Late Achaemenid Legal Texts from Uruk and Larsa," *Baghdader Mitteilungen* 21 [1990] no. 10) includes the phrase *mārē banî šunu mukinnū* (line 11), translated by Stolper 'the freemen are the witnesses'.

Recent discussions of the term *mār banî* may be found in M. Roth, "Women in Transition and the *bīt mār banî*," *RA* 82 (1988) 131–38; idem, "A Case of Contested Status," in *DUMU-E$_2$-DUB-BA-A: Studies in Honor of Åke W. Sjöberg* (Occasional Publications of the Samuel Noah Kramer Fund 11; ed. H. Behrens, D. Loding, and M. T. Roth; Philadelphia: University of Pennsylvania Museum, 1989) 481–89; and by M. Dandamayev, "The Neo-Babylonian Popular Assembly," in *ŠULMU: Papers on the Ancient Near East Presented at International Conference of Socialist Countries (Prague, Sept. 30–Oct. 3, 1986)* (ed. P. Vavroušek and V. Souček; Prague: Charles University Press, 1988) 63–71.

25. CT 2 2 is treated briefly by A. L. Oppenheim in "Essay on Overland Trade in the First Millennium B.C.," *JCS* 21 (1967) 236–54; a translation is given on p. 250 n. 77. TCL 12 117 is edited by San Nicolò, "Parerga Babylonica IX," 77; see also Dandamayev, "The Neo-Babylonian Popular Assembly," 67–68.

abstract noun $^{(lú)}$*šībūtu* (written syllabically or ^{lú}AB.BA^{meš}) occasionally interchanges with $^{(lú)}$*mukinnūtu* in the formula *ana šībūtu/mukinnūtu (ina libbi) ašābu* 'to be present at the witnessing'.[26] Otherwise, *mukinnu* has replaced *šību* as the standard term for witnesses.

The preference in certain types of documents for the formula *ina kanāk . . . maḫar*, derived from an older prototype, may reflect the greater weight assigned to the transactions concerned (alienation of real property and alteration of family relationships), as well as the conservatism of scribal practice. For documents of another comparably solemn type, documents recording decisions of lawsuits, the similarly structured formula *ina purussê dīni šuāti* 'at the decision of this case' (without *maḫar*) was created for the purpose of introducing the list of judges (e.g., Nbn 13:13, 64:2, and 356:41). This formula was not uniformly employed, however: in TCL 13 219 (duplicate of Nbn 720), a tablet of the Egibi archive in which Itti-Marduk-balāṭu calls for a *purussû* (line 10) and gets a judgment against the defendants (lines 25–27), the judges are introduced with the phrase *ina šaṭār ṭuppi šuāti* 'at the writing of this tablet' (line 29); judges may also be introduced with *ina maḫar* alone.[27] Two further examples illustrate the flexibility even of conservative scribal practice. In the tablet of the inheritance division among the 3 sons of Itti-Marduk-balāṭu, descendant of Egibi, the list of witnesses consists of 6 judges and 21 more individuals and is introduced by *ina šaṭār ṭuppi zitti šuāti* 'at the writing of this tablet of inheritance division' (Dar 379:70; *maḫar* is omitted); the presence of judges and an unusually large number of witnesses can be accounted for by the likelihood of contention among the heirs (see Wunsch, *UIM* 1.69 and 84 n. 316) and the exceptional size of the property being divided. On the other hand, *ina purussê dīni šuāti* introduces the list of witnesses in a tablet of the division of inherited property that included several prebends, AUWE 8/1 no. 89 rev. 31′; Kessler attributes the use of this formula to the fact that the division of the prebends among the heirs was overseen by the temple administration (AUWE 8/1 34). Evidently scribes were able to adapt formulas to the circumstances.

The phrase *ina ušuzzu* (*šā*) 'in the presence of' is used in two contexts: to introduce witnesses in "internal" accounting records and memoranda of transactions, that is, documents produced for the accounting purposes of the household or administration of the archive to which they pertained; and to

26. This formula is discussed below in connection with the phrase *ina ašābi*. In most other attestations, *šībūtu* means 'elders'; see CAD Š/2, s.v. *šību* A2 and 3k; M. Dandamayev, "The Neo-Babylonian Elders," *Societies and Languages of the Ancient Near East: Studies in Honor of I. M. Diakonoff* (ed. J. N. Postgate et al.; Warminster: Aris & Phillips, 1982) 38–41.

27. E.g., L 1663 (Joannès, *Archives*, 251–52); from the Egibi archive, note Nbn 359:6–7, *u'iltim ina ma-ḫar dayyānê ina muḫḫi* PN *ēlet* 'the document was issued to the debit of PN before the judges' and a similar clause in lines 14–16 in the related document Nbn 355. See also *NRV* Glossar 87, s.v. *maḫru*.

introduce officials as witnesses in documents of transactions, or records of procedures, overseen or authorized by them. This phrase is usually written *ina* GUB^{zu} *ša* (PN) but is spelled syllabically in TCL 13 177:16 and YOS 7 141:12; *ušuzzu* is the Neo(/Late)-Babylonian form of the G-stem infinitive of the irregular verb *i/uzuzzu* 'to stand' (GAG §107d).

That *ina ušuzzu* refers to persons acting in a capacity different from persons designated *mukinnu* and therefore that the two phrases denote different legal functions is demonstrated by documents in which both are employed. In numerous contracts between individuals and the temple administration, *ina ušuzzu* precedes the names of officials overseeing the transaction, following which *mukinnu* precedes a list of persons identified by name and filiation but usually not by official titles. For instance, Nbn 637 is a promissory note for goods owed by an individual to the Ebabbara temple in Sippar, drawn up *ina ušuzzu* the *qīpu* (administrative overseer) of the temple and the *šangû* of Sippar; Nbn 636, a promissory note, and Cyr 310, a contract for the sale of a ship, are similar examples; and in leases of temple property, *ina ušuzzu* introduces the officials responsible for granting the lease.[28] After the names of the supervising officials, the term *mukinnu* introduces the remaining witnesses of these documents. Likewise, in many documents of judicial proceedings, the authorities responsible for conducting the proceeding are introduced by *ina ušuzzu*, followed by the list of *mukinnu*.[29] The *mukinnu* of these types of documents may indeed have administrative positions without being identified thereby; the criterion for using official titles in legal documents was not whether a person could act in an official capacity, but whether that person was acting in an official capacity with respect to the particular document or transaction.

The category of texts in which *ina ušuzzu* is most extensively attested is the administrative archives of the temples, consisting of records of deliveries and expenditures and other types of accounting records. In these texts the persons introduced by *ina ušuzzu* are those responsible for registering deliveries, authorizing disbursements, and keeping accounts: that is, the action

28. E.g., YOS 6 33 and 67, and YOS 7 169, a promissory note for payment on a lease; such leases may instead have *mukinnu* alone (YOS 7 47 and 51) or *ina ušuzzu* alone (YOS 6 150). These and other documents from the Eanna temple having to do with the management of temple lands and their produce are edited in D. Cocquerillat, *Palmeraies et Cultures de l'Eanna d'Uruk (559–520)* (Ausgrabungen der Deutschen Forschungsgemeinschaft in Uruk-Warka 8; Berlin: Mann, 1967) 108–35.

29. See the documents mentioned above, n. 20; also YOS 7 161, in which the defendant has been convicted and the penalty is decided; and the court hearing conducted the morning after an attempted escape from the Eanna's prison, YOS 7 97, treated by San Nicolò in "Eine kleine Gefängnismeuterei in Eanna zur Zeit des Kambyses," *Festschrift für Leopold Wenger* (Münich: Beck, 1945) 2.1–17. TCL 12 117, described above (p. 11), was drawn up *ina ušuzzu* a royal official; the second of the *mukinnu* (= *mār banî*) is identified by his job title, *sepīru*.

recorded took place in the presence of the person indicated because it was that person's job to supervise those actions and records. Such persons may be identified by their official titles, although, especially in the case of lower-ranking functionaries, administrative records (as distinct from documents of contracts and legal proceedings, above paragraph) often dispense with titles. To give a few examples from the Ebabbara archive in Sippar, CT 55 743 and 745 are records of the receipt of tithes *ina ušuzzu ša* the *qīpu*, and Nbn 321 records a disbursement made *ina ušuzzu ša* the *qīpu* and the *šangû*. These are the same persons *ina qībi ša* 'by the order of' whom such actions were performed, as recorded in other administrative records: again from the Ebabbara archive, Nbn 728 records an expenditure made *ina qībi ša* the *šangû* of Sippar, Cyr 71 records a disbursement made *ina qībi ša* the *qīpu*, and Nbn 558 lists vessels brought to Sippar *ina qībi ša* the *bēl piqitti* ('commissioner') of Esagila and PN_2 the *zazakku* ('secretary').[30] Authorization for an action is recorded in the "active voice" with *ina qībi* and in the "passive voice" with *ina ušuzzu*. In accord with its literal meaning 'with (so-and-so) standing (there)', *ina ušuzzu ša* (PN) is also used to record the presence of persons merely observing or overseeing the transaction in question; from 'in the presence of', the phrase developed the connotation 'under the oversight of', then 'under the authorization of'.

San Nicolò and Ungnad were no doubt correct to state that the phrase *ina ušuzzu* originated in legal and administrative documents of the public sphere (*NRV*, 620). The use of a phrase derived from *i/uzuzzu* 'to stand' to indicate the presence of supervisory authorities is reminiscent of the use of the same verb in the witness formula attested in kudurrus, *ina kanāk kanki šuāti* (PN, PN_2, . . .) *izzazzū* (and variations, see above, p. 8 and n. 16). The witnesses listed in such a formula are usually officials, and the transaction recorded would have been effected under their supervision. The practice of issuing documents of land transfer under the oversight of local authorities continued through the 7th century and, sporadically, later. Several contracts for the purchase of real estate are drawn up *ina ušuzzu* one or two officials (usually the *šākin ṭēmi* and the *šatammu*); this phrase is preceded by the witness formula customary in documents of real estate purchases, *ina kanāk ṭuppi šuāti*, and followed by *maḫar* and the remaining witnesses.[31] Instead of *ina*

30. Other administrative texts of various types drafted *ina ušuzzu* one or more persons: Nbn 548, 784, 898, 911, 939, 941 1010, 1017, Cyr 28, 47, 73; *ina qībi*: Nbn 864, 868, 1034, 1036, 1099. Both phrases are used, predicated of different individuals, in Nbn 1100 and Cyr 96. This small number of examples could easily be multiplied *ad nauseam*.

31. See *BR* 8/7 nos. 11, 13, 15, 26, 27, 28, 30, 33; also no. 36, documenting the purchase of a prebend; no. 41, an exchange of real estate; and from the 6th century, *BR* 6 nos. 12 and 13. The formulation is retrospective in *BR* 8/7 no. 14, a "Sammeltafel" bearing copies of six real estate purchases, in three of which the presiding official is introduced by the phrase *ina ūmīšu* (lit. 'in its day'; cf. San Nicolò, ibid. p. 38, note on no. 14 i:35); the sixth transaction has *ina ušuzzu*.

ušuzzu, the phrase *ana maḫar* is used to introduce the presiding officials in some documents from Borsippa.[32]

As San Nicolò and Ungnad observed, in addition to introducing the officials under whose authority a transaction was undertaken or a document was issued, *ina ušuzzu* is also used to introduce private individuals as witnesses in certain types of records pertaining to private archives—in contrast to the use of *mukinnu* in most contracts (*NRV*, 619–21). In private archives, *ina ušuzzu* typically introduces witnesses in receipts, records of expenditures, various types of accounting records, and documents labeled 'memoranda' (*taḫsistu*).[33] This usage derives from the use of the same phrase in the same type of documents in "public" (temple or state) archives. However, in private archival records, *ina ušuzzu* does not indicate an "authorizing" function on the part of the persons so introduced, but rather indicates merely the presence of those persons, observing or overseeing the action recorded.

One other use of *ina ušuzzu* may be identified: to refer to the witnesses of undocumented transactions. During the judicial investigation recorded in CT 2 2, described above, an undergarment of Egyptian linen was found in the possession of Uballissu-Gula; in order to determine whether or not this undergarment was stolen from the wardrobe of the gods, the wardrobe personnel were questioned, and then Uballissu-Gula was questioned about how he obtained it. He responded that he had purchased it from an Egyptian *ina ušuzzu ša* 'in the presence of' four individuals, whom he names (lines 16–18). These four individuals then testified or confirmed, *ukinnū*, that Uballissu-Gula had indeed purchased the garment as he said, *ina ušuzzīni* 'in our presence' (lines 20–24). No document of sale is mentioned, nor would a cash purchase of

32. *BR* 8/7 7, 8, 9, 18, and the real estate exchange no. 42; this is also noted in Oelsner, "Zur neu- und spätbabylonischen Siegelpraxis," n. 5. In the later Achaemenid period, the phrase *ina maḫar* characteristically introduces judges and other authorizing officials (Cardascia, *Archives des Murašû*, 19–22; Bregstein, "Seal Use in Fifth Century B.C. Nippur, Iraq," 340).

33. On the use of this phrase in receipts and other records in private archives, see *NRV*, 317, no. 344 n. 4; 318, no. 345 n. 4; 491, no. 576 n. 5 (correcting the reading *nazāzu* to *ušuzzu*); and p. 608. Among Iddin-Marduk's documents, *ina ušuzzu* introduces witnesses in the following documents (in chronological order): Nbk 402 and 406; Lab 3; Nbn 134, 160; Moldenke 1 18 and 19 (= MMA 79.7.35 and 79.7.3); Nbn 466, 562, 657, 741, 872; TCL 12 126; Cyr 65 and 212; Camb 135 (Wunsch, *UIM* 2.47–48, 85, 121, 132, 160, 174, 180, 190, 204, 218, 236, 277, 279, 297, 329); and in Joannès, *Archives*: A 85, A 132, A 99, L 1636, NBC 8335, A 154 (restored), NBC 8324, *TuM* 2/3 218, and NBC 8329. C. Wunsch considers the introduction of witnesses with *ina ušuzzu* to be a distinctive feature of internal documents in private archives (*UIM* 1.41 n. 156, 73 n. 277); according to Krecher, a private archive document wherein *ina ušuzzu* (instead of *mukinnu*, *ina maḫar*, or *ina ašābi*) introduces the witnesses should be understood as "eine 'interne' Urkunde . . . ausgestellt durch die Verwaltung des Geschäftshauses in Abwesenheit der Kontrahenten" (*Das Geschäftshaus Egibi*, 119).

clothing require documentation. The phrase *ina ušuzzu* also occurs in YOS 7 7 (described above), with reference to persons in whose presence Gimillu's criminal acts took place (ii:66 and iii:129); it is used in the negative in relating that he led away animals from the herd at the disposal of Šumaya, *illa ušuzzu ša* 'in the absence of' Šumaya (who is thus exonerated; ii:52).

The specialized usage of the phrase *ina ašābi*, as well as related formulas constructed with the verb *ašābu* 'to be present' (literally, 'to sit'), was recognized early on in the study of Neo-Babylonian legal documents and has been thoroughly described in the literature. P. Koschaker examined the meaning and function of the clauses *ina ašābi ša* PN/FPN 'in the presence of PN/FPN' and *ana mukinnūtu* (/*šībūtu*) PN/FPN (*ina libbi*) *ašib* 'PN/FPN was present at the witnessing', appended to some documents, as expressions signifying a person's renunciation of a potential claim or right of appeal affecting the transaction in question.[34] Various other clauses occur in which the person renouncing a right is the subject of the verb *ašābu*, often with reference to the document or contract at which the person is said to be present and sometimes without the term 'witnessing' (*mukinnūtu* or *šībūtu*); for example: *ina kanāk kunukki* FPN *ašbat* 'at the sealing of the sealed document FPN was present' (*BR* 8/7 no. 3:38–39); PN *ina libbi ašib* 'PN was there present' (Nbn 755:7–8, with reference to the contract [*riksu*] mentioned in line 6).[35]

As used in these formulas, *ašābu* connotes in effect 'consent'. The recorded presence of a potential claimant indicates that that person renounces the right to exercise his or her claim (through 'concealment' [*Verschweigung*] of such rights, according to Koschaker's analysis) in regard to the transaction concerned and thus consents to the transaction. *Ina ašābi* and other clauses formulated with *ašābu* were used to signify the 'consent' of both males and females. A man's presence and renunciation of rights could also be signified through recording his name among the witnesses, introduced by *mukinnu* or (*ina*) *maḫar*, to the transaction; since women could not serve as witnesses, a woman's renunciation of rights had to be signified through a clause using the verb *ašābu* to indicate her presence. The phrase *ina la ašābi* 'in the absence of' likewise signifies 'without the consent of', as in Nbn 65, one of two documents cited by Eugène and Victor Revillout to demonstrate that the phrase *ina ašābi* 'avec l'acception juridique d'assistance comportant consentement' was not exclusively employed with women.[36] According to Nbn 65, which documents an agreement between ^{f}Gugūa and her eldest son, Ea-zēra-ibni,

34. P. Koschaker, *Babylonisch-Assyrisches Bürgschaftsrecht* (Leipzig: Teubner, 1911) 201–8.

35. On Nbn 755:6–8 (Wunsch, *UIM* 2 no. 222); see Wunsch, *UIM* 1.78 n. 297; and M. Roth, "The Dowries of the Women of the Itti-Marduk-balāṭu Family," *JAOS* 111 (1991) 22 n. 6.

36. E. Revillout and V. Revillout, "Les Dépôts et les confiements en droit égyptien et en droit babylonien," *Proceedings of the Society for Biblical Archaeology* 9 (1887) 267–310 (the quotation is from p. 287).

regarding the disposition of her dower property, ᶠGugūa had assigned the property to Ea-zēra-ibni but then divided some of it among her four younger sons *ina la ašābi ša* 'without the consent of' Ea-zēra-ibni.[37]

San Nicolò discussed the clauses formulated with *ašābu* in the context of his investigation of supplementary payments made to relatives of the seller in some contracts for the alienation of property: persons potentially able to exercise a claim to the property might receive compensation for their renunciation of such rights, and these persons may be listed among the witnesses of the contract, or a separate clause may indicate their presence (*ašābu*) at (the witnessing of) the contract.[38] Both Koschaker and San Nicolò drew attention to documents issued with the sole object of declaring one or more persons to be 'present' at (the witnessing of) a contract that had already, or had not yet, been concluded.[39] The purpose of these fictive "declarations of presence" is to document the renunciation of rights by the persons said to be "present," subsequent to or in advance of the transaction affected by their (potential) claims, like the statement of a person's actual presence in the case of an *ašābu*-clause incorporated into the contract itself. One such document discussed by San Nicolò, YOS 6 18, concerns the settlement of a claim (*paqāru*) raised by a relative of the seller against the sale of a property more than 30 years after the sale was concluded.[40] Upon receiving a compensatory gift from the purchaser, the claimant is declared to be 'present at the witnessing' of the sale tablet (I. [the claimant] . . . *ina ṭuppi ša* G. [the purchaser] *ana mukinnūtu ašib*, lines 8–13), that is, he renounces his claim; following the list of witnesses (*mukinnu*), the claimant's mother is introduced by *ina ašābi*, signifying that she agrees to the settlement and will not exercise any claim (lines 20–22). In another example, *VS* 5 57/58 (*NRV*, no. 26), the owner of a prebend obtains a previous owner's agreement not to contest any future disposition of that prebend: should the present owner sell or lease the prebend, the previous owner 'is present at the witnessing' (*ana mukinnūtu ina libbi ašib*).[41]

37. For other citations of *ina la ašābi*, as well as *ina ašābi* and related *ašābu*-clauses, see CAD A/2 391, s.v. *ašābu* 1d7′b′. With regard to the documents of the Murašû archive, Cardascia understands *ina ašābi* to convey "authorization" for a transaction (*Archives des Murašû*, 23 n. 4).

38. San Nicolò, "Zum *atru* und anderen Nebenleistungen des Käufers beim neubabylonischen Immobiliarkauf," *Or* n.s. 16 (1947) 273–302, esp. pp. 290–99. See further Y. Muffs, *Studies in the Aramaic Legal Papyri from Elephantine* (Studia et Documenta ad Iura Orientalis Antiqui Pertinentia 8; Leiden: Brill, 1969; repr., New York: Ktav, 1973) 169.

39. Koschaker, *Babylonisch-Assyrisches Bürgschaftsrecht*, 203–7 (examples listed p. 204 n. 14); San Nicolò, "Zum *atru*," 293–99. See also the remarks of San Nicolò and Ungnad on *VS* 5 35 and *VS* 6 97 and 101/102 (*NRV*, nos. 67, 68, and 69), *NRV*, 108.

40. San Nicolò, "Zum *atru*," 297–99.

41. Lines 10–15; see the remarks of San Nicolò and Ungnad, *NRV*, 39–40, and on the related tablet, *VS* 6 89 (*NRV*, 711), p. 615; also San Nicolò, "Zum *atru*," 293 n. 1.

A somewhat different context for this usage of *ašābu* is found in MMA 86.11.167 + BM 77856, a tablet styled as a "dialogue" between Bēl-kāṣir and his father Nādin, in which Bēl-kāṣir proposes to adopt his wife's son by her previous husband as his own heir.[42] Bēl-kāṣir's address to his father reads in part (lines 4–10): *Bēl-usāt . . . ana mārūti lulqē-ma lu mārūā šū ina ṭuppi mārūtišu tišab-ma isqētīni u mimmûni mala bašû kunuk-ma panīšu šudgil* 'let me adopt Bēl-usāt, let him be my son; be present at the tablet of his adoption and transfer to him under seal our prebends and our property, as much as exists'. By means of the clause *ina ṭuppi mārūtišu tišab*, Bēl-kāṣir requests his father's consent to the adoption and the consequent transfer of family property, as recognized by F. E. Peiser in his 1888 edition of the text.[43] Nādin, however, refuses his consent (*la imgur*, line 12).

The function of witnesses in general is attestation, and the recorded presence of witnesses constitutes authentication of a document (see above, p. 5). As stated by M. Roth, a witness's presence indicates his tacit agreement to the transaction and thus renunciation of any claims pertaining thereto (*BMA* 20). The phrase *ina ašābi*, or another of the formulas constructed with *ašābu* discussed here, was employed to separate the signification 'renunciation of rights or claims, agreement, consent' from the signification 'attestation, authentication'.

Each of the phrases and terms discussed above has a specific field of usage in the formulary of Neo-Babylonian documents. The participle *mukinnu* has become the general term for 'witness', meaning both witnesses of events and witnesses of documents. But a phrase preserved from an older formulaic tradition, (*ina*) *maḫar*, is preferred for introducing the witnesses to certain types of documents, particularly documents of transactions whose effects are more profound or durable. The phrase *ina ušuzzu*, also derived from an earlier formula, connotes authorization or oversight of the transaction or proceeding on the part of the person(s) so introduced; and *ina ašābi* signifies a person's renunciation of rights or claims potentially affecting the transaction. 'Witnessing', in the sense of 'attesting' or 'authenticating', is not in all cases the primary function of persons introduced by (*ina*) *maḫar*, *ina ušuzzu*, and *ina ašābi*.

We should ask how and when the legal capacity of 'witnessing' came to be denoted by the verb *kunnu*. In the G-stem, the semantic range of *kânu* in-

42. BM 77856 was first published as Nbn 380; MMA 86.11.167 was published as Moldenke 2 no. 54. Prior to the latter publication, the joined text was published by T. Pinches, "The Law of Inheritance in Ancient Babylonia," *Hebraica* 3 (1886–87) 13–21; and an edition was offered by F. E. Peiser, "Eine babylonische Verfügung von Todes wegen," ZA 3 (1888) 365–71. See also the translation and discussion in M. Roth, "The Neo-Babylonian Widow," *JCS* 43–45 (1991–93) 23–24. A new edition of MMA 86.11.167 + BM 77856 will be published as Text 102 in I. Spar and E. von Dassow, *Cuneiform Texts in the Metropolitan Museum of Art*, vol. 3: *Private Archive Texts from the First Millennium* B.C. (in preparation).

43. F. E. Peiser, ZA 3 (1888) 369.

cludes the meaning 'to be true', in opposition with *sarāru* 'to be false'.[44] The semantic range of the D-stem *kunnu* 'to establish' therefore includes the meaning 'to establish as true or valid, confirm, prove', which is what witnesses do: a witness 'attests' to the performance of an action (for instance) or 'authenticates' a document, establishes it as valid and legally binding. *Kunnu* is used to mean 'to testify, act as a witness, prove by means of witnesses' in the Old Babylonian period (see CAD K 168–69, s.v. *kânu* 4a), but it is only in the Neo-Babylonian period that *mukinnu* comes into use as a term for 'witness' in legal documents.[45] It is difficult to know how early this usage was introduced because of the paucity of Babylonian documents from the 12th–8th centuries. In witnessed Middle Babylonian tablets, each witness's name is preceded by IGI (= *maḫar* or *šību*).[46] The type of formula characteristically used to introduce witnesses in kudurrus through the mid–7th century, *ina kanāk . . . izzazzū*, is discussed above (p. 8 and n. 16). Some kudurrus have less elaborate formulas for recording witnesses: in *BBSt* 8, a royal land grant, each witness's name is introduced by *ina ušuzzu*, and all the witnesses have official titles (one being the king's son, i:29–ii:30); in *BBSt* 30, which records the transfer of land by purchase, IGI precedes the name of each of the witnesses, none of whom bears an official title (rev. 11–21).

Some early examples of the usage of *mukinnu* for witnesses of documents are the following, dating to the late 8th and early 7th century:

- *BRM* 1.22, a fragmentary document of obscure content, dated 4 Nabû-mukīn-zēri (728?[47]); the list of witnesses, the beginning of which is broken, closes with the words *annûtu mukinnū* (line 11)

44. On the opposition *kênu* 'true' vs. *sarru* 'false', see T. Jacobsen, "The Graven Image," in *Ancient Israelite Religion: Essays in Honor of Frank Moore Cross* (ed. P. D. Miller et. al.; Philadelphia: Fortress, 1987) 18–20 (with observations on the semantics of *kunnu* 'prove [an accusation]', p. 20); also M. Stol, "Eine Prozeßurkunde über 'falsches Zeugnis,'" in *Marchands, Diplomates et Empereurs: Études sur la civilisation mésopotamienne offertes à Paul Garelli* (ed. D. Charpin and F. Joannès; Paris: Éditions Recherche sur les Civilisations, 1991) 333–39, esp. 335.

45. The sole Old Babylonian citation for *mukinnu* given by the CAD (M/2 186, s.v.) occurs not in a legal document but in a letter. Contrary to San Nicolò's translation, 'Bezeuger der Grenze' (*Beiträge*, 119 n. 2), the phrase *mukīn kudurri* in the title of a kudurru from the time of Marduk-nādin-aḫḫē (1098–1081; *BBSt* no. 7, title line 2) probably is related to the common meaning of *kunnu* 'to establish (a boundary)'; see CAD K 165, s.v. *kânu* 3d.

46. E.g., H. Petschow, *Mittelbabylonische Rechts- und Wirtschaftsurkunden der Hilprecht-Sammlung Jena* (Abhandlungen der Sächsischen Akademie der Wissenschaften zu Leipzig, Phil.-hist. Klasse 64/4; Berlin: Akademie, 1974) nos. 1–11; Petschow renders IGI as 'vor' (thus reading *maḫar*), but the witnesses as a group are termed *šībūtu* (no. 13:5, 11, 20; no. 1:42, LÚ.INIM.INIM.MA; no. 2:33, LÚ.INIM.INIM.MA.E.NE).

47. The date is problematic; see J. A. Brinkman, A *Political History of Post-Kassite Babylonia*, *1158–722* B.C. (AnOr 43; Rome: Pontifical Biblical Institute, 1968) 239

- *VS* 1 70, a kudurru from the time of Sargon II; in the last transaction recorded, dated 11 Sargon (710; v:4), the witnesses are introduced by *ina kanāk ṭuppi šuāti; maḫar* (v:12) and summed up with the words *napḫaru annûtu mukinnū* (v:20)
- UET 4 8 (*BR* 8/7 no. 26), a house sale in dialogue form (date formula missing; end of 8th century[48]); after two officials introduced by *ina ušuzzu*, the list of witnesses opens with *maḫar* and closes with *an-na-t*[*im* ^{lú}*mu-kin*]*-nu-ú* (line 35, as restored by San Nicolò, *BR* 8/7 p. 63)
- UET 4 27 (*BR* 8/7 no. 37), a slave sale in dialogue form dated to Year 8 of Ningal-Iddin, governor of Ur (early 7th century);[49] the list of witnesses is introduced by *mukinnu* (line 7) and concludes with *napḫaru annûtu mukinnū* (line 14)

In these four examples, the word *mukinnu* occurs in a phrase concluding the witness list, (*napḫaru*) *annûtu mukinnū* '(all) these are the witnesses'.[50] Possibly the inconsistent use of this concluding phrase, together with various introductory phrases, reflects the recent introduction of *mukinnu* as a designation for the witnesses of a document. Regarding UET 4 8, San Nicolò remarks on how unusual it is to close the witness list with this phrase, and observes that it resembles the opening phrase of the 'declarations before witnesses' described above (*BR* 8/7 64, note on no. 26:35).

By the 8th century, the usage of *mukinnu* to denote witnesses of documents developed from the judicial usage of *kunnu* to mean 'prove, convict', thus 'testify, attest'. While (*ina*) *maḫar*, *ina ušuzzu*, and *ina ašābi* explicitly refer to the presence of the person(s) introduced by those phrases, the term *mukinnu* refers to their legal capacity as witnesses, namely to 'attest' that an event took place, or to 'authenticate' a document.

This overview of the terminology of witnessing in the Neo-Babylonian period and of the functions or capacities associated with the various terms leaves several questions largely unexamined. For instance, the possibility of

n. 1530; J. A. Brinkman and D. A. Kennedy, "Documentary Evidence for the Economic Base of Early Neo-Babylonian Society: A Survey of Dated Babylonian Economic Texts, 721–626 B.C.," *JCS* 35 (1983) 65 (AI.1); Brinkman, *Prelude to Empire: Babylonian Society and Politics, 747–626* B.C. (Occasional Publications of the Babylonian Fund 7; Philadelphia, 1984) 14 n. 53.

48. For the date, see J. A. Brinkman, "Merodach-Baladan II," *Studies Presented to A. Leo Oppenheim* (ed. R. D. Biggs and J. A. Brinkman; Chicago: University of Chicago Press, 1964) 17 and 26 n. 144; Brinkman and Kennedy, "Documentary Evidence," 12 (An. 3, 5).

49. On the dates of this text and of Ningal-iddin's governorship, see G. Frame, *Babylonia 689–627* B.C.*: A Political History* (Istanbul: Nederlands Historisch-Archaeologisch Instituut te Istanbul, 1992) 61 and 285.

50. There are also documents from the same period in which *mukinnu* simply opens the list of witnesses and there is no closing formula; for instance *BR* 8/7 40 and 51.

geographical variation in documentary practice has not been investigated here. There are numerous exceptions to the general rules derived above for the use of the terminology under discussion, and only a far more intensive study could determine whether such exceptions are, by and large, the result of random variation and scribal error or of geographical and temporal variation, or whether instead they are conditioned by substantive differences in the documents and functional differences in the roles of the individuals to whom the terms and formulas refer. Furthermore, I have not discussed the matter of whether and when witnesses seal documents.[51] The presence or absence of witnesses' sealings is in part conditioned by the type of transaction documented and in part a function of the sealer's role in respect to the transaction; thus sealing or not sealing by witnesses, which is also subject to significant temporal variation, can be correlated to some extent with the terminology wherewith the witnesses are introduced. These are issues for future research.

51. See, for now, Oelsner, "Zur neu- und spätbabylonischen Siegelpraxis," 167–86; and Bregstein, "Seal Use in Fifth Century B.C. Nippur, Iraq," 354–63.

Abbreviations

- A — Siglum of tablets in the collection of the Bodleian Library at the Ashmolean Museum
- AUWE 8/1 — K. Kessler, *Uruk: Urkunden aus Privathäusern: Die Wohnhäuser westlich des Eanna-Tempelbereichs*, vol. 1 (Ausgrabungen aus Uruk/Warka, Endbericht 8/I; Mainz: von Zabern, 1991).
- BBSt — King, L. W. *Babylonian Boundary Stones and Memorial-Tablets in the British Museum*. London: British Museum, 1912.
- BMA — M. Roth, *Babylonian Marriage Agreements, 7th–3rd Centuries* B.C. (AOAT 222; Neukirchen-Vluyn: Neukirchener Verlag, 1989) 20.
- BR 6 — San Nicolò, M., and H. Petschow. *Babylonische Rechtsurkunden aus dem 6. Jahrhunderts v. Chr.* Abhandlungen der Bayerischen Akademie der Wissenschaften, Philosophisch-Historische Klasse n.s. 51. Munich, 1960.
- BR 8/7 — San Nicolò, M. *Babylonische Rechtsurkunden des ausgehenden 8. und des 7. Jahrhunderts v. Chr.* Abhandlungen der Bayerischen Akademie der Wissenschaften, Philosophisch-Historische Klasse n.s. 34. Munich, 1951.
- BRM — Clay, A. T. *Babylonian Records in the Library of J. Pierpont Morgan*. New York, 1912.
- Camb — Straßmaier, J. N. *Inschriften von Cambyses, König von Babylon (529–521 v. Chr.)*. Leipzig: Pfeiffer, 1890.
- Cyr — Straßmaier, J. N. *Inschriften von Cyrus, König von Babylon (538–529 v. Chr.)*. Leipzig: Pfeiffer, 1890.
- Dar — Straßmaier, J. N. *Inschriften von Darius, König von Babylon (521–485 v. Chr.)*. Leipzig: Pfeiffer, 1897.

Joannès, *Archives* F. Joannès, *Archives de Borsippa: La famille Ea-ilûta-bâni* (Geneva: Droz, 1989).
L Siglum of tablets in the collection of the Istanbul Museum of the Ancient Orient
Lab Evetts, B. *Inscriptions of the Reigns of Evil-Merodach (B.C. 562–559), Neriglissar (B.C. 559–555), and Laborosoarchod (B.C. 555)*. Leipzig: Pfeiffer, 1892. [Texts from the reign of Lābāši-Marduk]
MMA Siglum of tablets in the collection of The Metropolitan Museum of Art
Moldenke Moldenke, A. B. *Babylonian Contract Tablets in The Metropolitan Museum of Art*, Parts 1 and 2. New York, 1893.
Nbk Straßmaier, J. N. *Inschriften von Nabuchodonosor, König von Babylon (604–561 v. Chr.)*. Leipzig: Pfeiffer, 1889.
Nbn Straßmaier, J. N. *Inschriften von Nabonidus, König von Babylon (555–538 v. Chr.)*. Leipzig: Pfeiffer, 1889.
NRV San Nicolò, M., and Ungnad, A. *Neubabylonische Rechts- und Verwaltungsurkunden*. Leipzig: Hinrichs, 1935. Reprinted, 1974.
NRV Glossar Ungnad, A. *Beiheft zu Band I: Neubabylonische Rechts- und Verwaltungsurkunden—Glossar*. Leipzig: Hinrichs, 1937.
OECT Oxford Editions of Cuneiform Texts
TCL Textes cunéiformes du Louvre
TuM 2/3 Krückmann, O. *Texte und Materialen der Frau Professor Hilprecht Collection of Babylonian Antiquities im Eigentum der Universität Jena 2/3: Neubabylonische Rechts- und Verwaltungs-Texte*. Leipzig: Hinrichs, 1933.
UET Ur Excavations, Texts
UIM 1, 2 C. Wunsch, *Die Urkunden des babylonischen Geschäftsmannes Iddin-Marduk. Zum Handel mit Naturalien im 6. Jahrhundert v. Chr.* (2 vols.; Cuneiform Monographs 3a and 3b; Groningen: Styx, 1993).
VS *Vorderasiatische Schriftdenkmäler*
YOS Yale Oriental Series, Babylonian Texts

Kemet and Other Egyptian Terms for Their Land

Ogden Goelet
New York University

It would be, as the expression goes, "reinventing the wheel" to demonstrate that such familiar words as *Kmt* and *Tꜣ-mry* meant 'Egypt' to the inhabitants of that land. Instead, the purpose of this study is to examine how the ancient Egyptians used the words for their country and what it might reveal about their sense of a nation. Here the expression *reinvent the wheel* is ironically apropos, for, just as the wheel functioned awkwardly in the sandy environment of Egypt, such modern notions as nationality and fixed legal borders work poorly within what seems to have been ancient Egypt's concept of itself. Because the history of Egypt comprises such a vast expanse of time, in this paper I will discuss only how the Egyptians' terminology for their country developed over the course of the Old and Middle Kingdoms.

The Egyptian Concepts of Limits and the "Natural" Borders of Egypt

In order to understand how the ancient Egyptians conceived the relationship of their land to the rest of the world, it would be helpful first to discuss

Author's note: There are few experiences in my academic life that I enjoy more than a meeting with Baruch Levine. Within a few minutes we are exchanging as many stories as footnotes and telling each other stories as long and detailed as most bibliographies—yet he has a way of making all wonderfully relevant to the matter at hand. Baruch has a unique ability to impart great wisdom filled with wit and warmth. By the end of our encounter, I always come away realizing the many ways in which this humane individual inspires those about him but also having been reminded that I am in the profession of the humanities, a discipline best enriched by exchange. The topic of this paper, in fact, is the result of an idea which grew out of one of our many discussions.

briefly both their terminology for borders and the way these words reflected Egypt's natural setting. The two most common words for 'borders' or 'limits' normally exhibit a preference for the plural:  *ḏrw* and 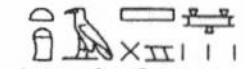 *tꜣšw*. *Ḏrw* tends to be used more often in cases where the limits of indefinite, unquantifiable things such as time and the universe are involved; *tꜣšw*, by contrast, is the word used for borders of political or geographical entities and frequently occurs in texts describing the extent of Egypt and the countries surrounding it.[1] If most references to Egypt's extent seem rather unspecific to our modern legal sensibilities, that vagueness is, on closer examination, due to the distinctness of its natural borders. In both ancient and modern times, any viable country in the northeastern corner of Africa will by necessity coincide largely with "livable Egypt," to use Napoleon's apt description—essentially the fertile areas of the Nile Valley and the Delta, along with a smattering of the outlying oases. As clear as this definition may appear from a quick glance at a map, the Egyptians often changed their views concerning the extent of their land.

Perhaps the clearest information about the ancient Egyptians' concept of their natural borders are nome lists, a genre of geographical texts found on temple pediments and votive cubits.[2] As these and other sources demonstrate, the names, the boundaries, and the sequence of the 22 southern nomes became fixed at an earlier date than their northern counterparts. Certainly the geography of Upper Egypt, essentially the Nile Valley between Memphis and the First Cataract, can be divided into discrete units more readily than the fan-shaped Delta with its two river branches. For Upper Egypt, the greatest uncertainty seems to have been at the southern border, formed naturally by the First Cataract. This region was called *Tꜣ-sty*, a somewhat ambiguous term that can refer just to Egypt's southernmost nome or

1. This distinction between *tꜣšw* and *ḏrw*, which holds true with few exceptions, is derived from two general discussions of the Egyptian concept of limits; see E. Hornung, "Limits and Symmetries," chap. 4 in *Idea into Image: Essays on Ancient Egyptian Thought* (trans. E. Bredeck; New York: Timken, 1992) 73–92; and W. Helck, "Grenze, Grenzsicherung," *LÄ* 2.896–97. There are a number of apparent exceptions in which *ḏrw* is used in political contexts as well, nearly all of which involve the expression *ỉn ḏrw* 'to reach, acquire the limits' of a land. In discussing this phrase, D. Lorton (*The Juridicial Terminology of International Relations in Egyptian Texts through Dyn. XVIII* [JHNES; Baltimore: Johns Hopkins University Press, 1974] 73–76) has raised the possibility that: "*tꜣš*(*w*), when applied to foreign relations, undergoes a transformation from a juridicial to a metaphorical term and that expressions formulated with it relate to religious rather than to legal concepts, or at any rate divine rather than positive law" (p. 75).

2. For a discussion of the borders of Egypt in both the north and south, see A. Schlott-Schwab, *Die Ausmässe Ägyptens nach altägyptischen Texten* (Ägypten und Altes Testament 3; Wiesbaden: Harrassowitz, 1981) 66–100; and E. Otto, "Ägypten im Selbstbewusstsein des Ägypters," *LÄ* 1.76–78.

more broadly to 'Nubia'.[3] As A. Schlott-Schwab has pointed out,[4] the Egyptians applied the term *Tꜣ-sty* to any part of the region south of Gebel Silsile, so it is not always clear which of these two meanings is intended. It was not until the early Middle Kingdom that the toponym *Tꜣ-sty* was written on a standard, the normal form of a nome name.[5] On the other hand, excavations have revealed that Elephantine was settled by the Egyptians as early as Dynasty I and that a temple was constructed in the region sometime in that period.[6] The town of Elephantine soon became the capital of the nome, and the region about was recognized as the southern limit of Egypt. During Dynasty IV, Elephantine was fortified, an indication that this outpost had become a border town in every sense of the word. In Dynasty XII, when an extensive string of fortresses had been constructed south of Elephantine, it can be quite unclear whether the word *Tꜣ-sty* refers to the First Nome or to

3. The term has been variously interpreted. One common translation is 'Bow-land = the land of the Nubians'; see P. Montet, "L'arc nubien  et ses emplois dans l'écriture," *Kêmi: Revue de philologie et d'archéologie égyptiennes et coptes* 6 (1936) 43–62; T. Säve-Söderbergh, *Ägypten und Nubien: Ein Beitrag zur Geschichte altägyptischer Aussenpolitik* (Lund: Ohlssons, 1941) 6. The alternative explanation, 'the *Sty*-mineral land', was also proposed by P. Montet, *Géographie de l'Égypte ancienne* (Paris: Klincksieck, 1961) 2.13. The mineral in question is a type of yellow ochre that was apparently mined in the region and was used frequently in medical recipes; see W. Helck, *Materialien zur Wirtschaftsgeschichte des Neuen Reiches* (6 vols.; Akademie der Wissenschaften und der Literatur in Mainz; Abhandlungen der Geistes- und sozialwiss. Klasse; Wiesbaden: Franz Steiner, 1961–69) 436, 437, 993, 994, 1002, 1003, 1004. The possibility of a relationship between the mineral and the place-name is not mentioned in recent study of ancient Egyptian minerals; see S. Aufrère, *L'univers minéral dans la pensée égyptienne* (Bibliothèque d'Étude 105/1–2; Cairo: Institut Français d'Archéologie Orientale, 1991) 652–53, with notes on p. 659.

4. Schlott-Schwab, *Die Ausmässe Ägyptens*, 70–71.

5. On an offering table from the pyramid of Sesostris I, Cairo CG 23001, see H. Gauthier and G. Jéquier, *Mémoires sur les fouilles de Licht* (Mémoires publiés par les Membres de l'Institut Français d'Archéologie Orientale 6; Paris: Institut Français d'Archéologie Orientale, 1902) 24. On the other hand, *Tꜣ-sty* appears without a standard in the nome list on the "White Chapel" of Sesostris I at Karnak; see P. Lacau and H. Chevrier, *Une chapelle de Sésostris* 1er *à Karnak* (Cairo: Institut Français d'Archéologie Orientale, 1956) 220, §617. In fact, of the citations gathered by F. Gomaà (*Die Besiedlung Ägyptens während des Mittleren Reiches*, vol. 1: *Oberägypten und das Fayyum* [Beihefte zum Tübinger Atlas des Vorderen Orients, series B, 66/1; Wiesbaden: Reichert, 1986] 9–11), only the Licht offering table has the name written with the nome standard.

6. For good summaries of Egyptian activity in the First Nome before the Middle Kingdom, see M. Ziermann, *Befestigungsanlagen und Stadtentwicklung in der Frühzeit und im frühen Alten Reich: Elephantine XVI* (Archäologischen Veröffentlichungen, Deutsches Archäologisches Institut, Abteilung Kairo 87; Mainz am Rhein: Zabern, 1993) 132–38; Säve-Söderbergh, *Ägypten und Nubien*, 6–10; and J. Baines and J. Málek, *Atlas of Ancient Egypt* (New York: Facts on File, 1980) 72–73.

the Nubian lands north of the Second Cataract.[7] The territory between the two cataracts was at that time considered Egyptian enough for Egyptians to choose to be buried there, a striking fact, if one bears in mind the fear of foreign burial implicit in the *Tale of Sinuhe*.[8]

The extent of the land in the north was far more uncertain, both geographically and politically. The Mediterranean coastline may have formed a more distinct natural border than the cataract region, but, during the Old Kingdom, the Delta regions apparently were never as thoroughly settled and administered as Upper Egypt. From this period and into the New Kingdom, the northern limits of the country seem to have been along the coast in the 7th, 6th, 16th and 14th nomes. By the New Kingdom, however, the nome lists placed the northern limit at the town of *Bḥdt* in the 17th Lower Egyptian nome; *Bḥdt* appears in classical sources as Diospolis inferior and was located near the modern site of Tell el-Balamun. The length of Egypt was considered to be the distance along the Nile between *Bḥdt* and the nome of Elephantine in the south.[9] Political considerations, however, meant that the town at the northern end-point could be shifted from time to time. In such cases, the southern end of Egypt would remain at Elephantine, but the northeastern limit could be moved to such residential cities as Pi-Ramesses, Tanis, or Alexandria, or to the garrison town *Ṯȝrw* 'Sile'.[10] Like Elephantine, Sile served as a jumping-off place for military expeditions into the "Asiatic" territories to Egypt's northeast.[11] Unlike Elephantine, however, Sile was not established as a fortified border town until Dynasty XVIII following the expulsion of the Hyksos. In the western half of the Delta, the situation was more uncertain, but the evidence indicates that the border was felt to lie along the desert edge of the 3d Lower Egyptian nome called, significantly, the "Western."[12]

Like other civilizations of the ancient Near East, the Egyptians believed their land had been created before all other lands and lay at the center of the world. From the earliest written records on, the chief terms for Egypt were based on the word 𓇾𓏤 *tȝ* 'land', which not only meant 'the earth', but also 'the world'. The hieroglyph employed in this word itself conveys what the Egyptians felt was the chief characteristic of their country—its flatness. For-

7. On this problem in Egyptian usage, see A. H. Gardiner, "Inscriptions from the Tomb of Si-renpowet I., Prince of Elephantine," *ZÄS* 45 (1908) 139 n. 1.

8. See below in the discussion of terms for 'Egypt' in this story, pp. 37–39. The nature and intent of Middle Kingdom activity in Nubia has long been debated. A discussion of some of the problems involved can be found in P. J. Frandsen, "Egyptian Imperialism," in *Power and Propaganda* (ed. M. T. Larsen; Mesopotamia 7; Copenhagen, 1979) 168 with n. 9 on p. 182.

9. Schlott-Schwab, *Die Ausmässe Ägyptens* (1981) 82–83.

10. Ibid., 88–100.

11. See the discussion of the use of *Kmt* in *The Satire on the Trades* below, p. 39.

12. Schlott-Schwab, *Die Ausmässe Ägyptens*, 91.

eign countries, by contrast, were thought to be eminently hilly, as shown by the word *ḫꜣst* 'hill country', which is also the generic word for 'foreign land'. Significantly, the same 'hill-country' logogram (Sign-list N25) appears as well in most Egyptian words connected with the desert. Except where *tꜣ* 'land' is further qualified by an adjective like 'this', it is not always clear whether an Egyptian is speaking of his land or the entire world. Indeed, closed in as the country was from the outside world, the distinction between inside and outside often had little importance for the average Egyptian.

From the king's point of view, however, Egypt's limits were hardly a matter of indifference. The gods had charged him with keeping order in the world at large and, particularly, with the critical responsibility of maintaining Egypt's borders safe from foreigners and other representatives of the forces of chaos.[13] These fundamental elements of Egyptian royal ideology bear directly on the question of what precisely the king ruled. If we are interested in the question of dominion, then we should look to royal titulary for guidance. In royal inscriptions, where there is frequently a need to emphasize the monarch's role as the unifying ruler of a country comprised of two quite disparate regions, both geographically and ecologically, his dominion was called *Tꜣwy* 'the Two Lands'. This dual noun was always the most common term for Egypt in both private and royal contexts. Several kings used the term as an element of their Horus names.[14] The only other reference to the land or its duality to appear in Old Kingdom royal titularies is the phrase *n-sw-bỉt* 'King of Upper and Lower Egypt', placed before the king's first cartouche or "nomen."

Terms for Egypt during the Old Kingdom

Terms referring to Egypt alone such as *Kmt* or *Tꜣ-mry*, ironically enough, occur neither in titularies nor in any other type of text during the Old Kingdom. The lack of a special name for their land during this period is particularly interesting, since Egypt certainly exhibited a strong interest, both commercial and military, in the territories beyond its natural borders from very earliest written history onwards. Enough Egyptian material bearing royal names of Dynasties "0" through II has been found in the lower reaches

13. These theoretical concepts, which lie at the very heart of Egypt's imperial policies in the New Kingdom, have been conveniently discussed by B. Kemp, "Imperialism and Empire in New Kingdom Egypt (c. 1575–1087 B.C.)," in *Imperialism in the Ancient World* (ed. P. D. A. Garnsey and C. R. Whittaker; Cambridge: Cambridge University Press, 1978) 5–20; S. Morenz, "Der Kreis der Verehrer," chap. 3 in *Ägyptische Religion* (Die Religionen der Menschheit 8; Stuttgart: Kohlhammer, 1960) 44–59.

14. Niusserre, Dyn. V: *St-ỉb-Tꜣwy* 'the Pleasure of the Two Lands'; Unas, Dyn. V: *Wꜣḏ-Tꜣwy* 'the Two Lands are Green'; Teti, Dyn. VI: *Sḥtp-Tꜣwy* 'the One who Pleases the Two Lands'; Pepi I, Dyn. VI: *Mry-Tꜣwy* 'the Beloved of the Two Lands'.

of Palestine to suggest that Egypt may have even briefly sporadically attempted to colonize that region.[15] Farther up the Palestinian coast there is much evidence to show that Egypt and Byblos maintained friendly trade relations throughout the Old Kingdom. In the East, the area around the Wadi Mughara on the Sinai Peninsula has revealed evidence of sporadic mining activity throughout this period. Reliefs dating to Dynasty V show that its kings conducted military expeditions against Libyans on the northwest frontiers of Egypt. To the south, following the establishment of a firm grip on the first two nomes of Upper Egypt by the early pharaohs, later monarchs continued an aggressive policy toward the Nubian regions south of the First Cataract. That this activity may not have been entirely successful in pacifying the region is shown by the mention of fortresses in the region as early as Dynasties III and IV. Even as late as Dynasty VI, the name for Elephantine was occasionally still written with a sign indicating that it was a defensive outpost placed so that it could control river traffic.[16]

Nevertheless, despite Egypt's constant, if somewhat low-level, interest in the world about it, there is an apparent absence of a specialized terminology distinguishing Egypt from the outside world in Old Kingdom texts, except for occasional toponyms, most of which are compounds of the word *tꜣ* 'land'. Such terms as *Kmt* and *Tꜣ-mry* remain unattested in Old Kingdom sources. Since both trade and travel to such places beyond Egypt's limits were normally done only at royal request during the Old Kingdom, the destination given by most voyagers when returning from abroad was often simply 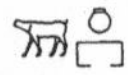 *Ḫnw* 'the Residence', literally, 'the Interior'.[17] In travel or campaign narratives of this period, the words for 'borders'—*tꜣšw* and *ḏrw*—are strikingly absent.[18] An interesting example of this phenomenon occurs in the titulary of a Dynasty V official who held the unusual title *ḥry-sštꜣ n rꜣ-ꜥꜣ ḫꜣswt m gswy* 'Privy Counselor of the Doorway (to) the Foreign Lands

15. A good summary of Egypt's interconnections with Palestine in this period can be found in D. B. Redford, *Egypt, Canaan, and Israel in Ancient Times* (Princeton: Princeton University Press, 1992) 27–37, with extensive references.

16. See Schlott-Schwab, *Die Ausmässe Ägyptens*, 71–72.

17. For example, Herkhuf, apparently while still in Nubia, receives a letter from the young Pepi II, exhorting him: "come north immediately to the *ḫnw*" (K. Sethe, *Urkunden des ägyptischen Altertums*, vol. 1: *Urkunden des Alten Reiches* [2d ed.; Leipzig: Hinrichs, 1933] 129, 1; henceforth *Urk.* I). Similarly, when another Dynasty VI official named Pepinakht is in Nubia, he states that he sent people back "to the *ḫnw*" (*Urk.* I 133, 14). This recalls the somewhat ambigous passage in the Middle Kingdom literary work, *The Tale of the Shipwrecked Sailor*, which speaks of returning *r ḫnw*, which can be interpreted either as '(back) home' or 'to the Residence'; see A. de Buck, *Egyptian Readingbook* (Leiden: Nederlandsch Archaeologisch-Philologisch Instituut voor het Nabije Oosten, 1948) 103, 105.

18. On the absence of these terms in Old Kingdom texts, see D. B. Redford, "Egypt and Western Asia in the Old Kingdom,' *JARCE* 23 (1986) 132.

in the Delta'.[19] The substitution of the term 'doorway' for 'border' at the southern limit of the land as well is attested first during the Old Kingdom and becomes more frequent in the Middle Kingdom.[20]

The Terms for 'Egypt' in the First Intermediate Period and Middle Kingdom

During the First Intermediate Period, the lack of a strong central government combined with a heightened sense of provincial pride seems to have produced many changes in the Egyptian geographical terminology. Perhaps in light of this new spirit, such time-honored phrases as 'this land' lost some of their original force and the Egyptians felt a need to define their country more distinctly. Somewhere around the period when Egypt was once more reunified under the rule of the Dynasty XI monarch Nebhepetre Menthuhotep (II), the terms  *Kmt* 'the Black (Land)'[21] and 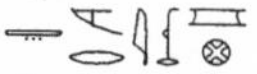 *Tꜣ-mry* 'the Beloved Land'[22] first made their appearance. Unfortunately, the study of virtually all aspects of the First Intermediate Period is greatly hampered by the enormous difficulty in dating the texts ascribed to it. This is particularly true of several major literary texts that either were first written

19. H. Kees, *Beiträge zur altägyptischen Provinzialverwaltung und der Geschichte des Feudalismus II: Unterägypten* (Nachrichten von der Gesellschaft der Wissenschaften zu Göttingen, Phil.-Hist. Klasse; Berlin, 1933) 590. The expression *gswy* 'the Two Sides' in this title has generally been considered a reference to the Delta; see H. G. Fischer, "An Old Kingdom Monogram," ZÄS 93 (1966) 66 n. 38.

20. This is the title *ỉmy-rꜣ ꜥꜣ gꜣw Šmꜥw* 'Overseer of the Narrow Door of Upper Egypt'; see H. G. Fischer, *Dendera in the Third Millennium* B.C. *down to the Theban Domination of Upper Egypt* (New York: Augustin, 1968) 12 n. 56. However, the same title has been read by H. Kees ("Beiträge zur altägyptischen Provinzialverwaltung und der Geschichte des Feudalismus I: Oberägypten" [*Nachrichten von der Gesellschaft der Wissenschaften zu Göttingen*, Phil.-Hist. Klasse; Berlin, 1932] 95; and idem, "Zu einigen Fachausdrücken der altägyptischen Provinzialverwaltung," ZÄS 70 [1934] 83–86) as 'Vorsteher des Südtores von Elephantine'. In "Zu einigen Fachausdrücken," Kees demonstrates that during the Middle Kingdom there were several titles mentioning a "Southern Doorway" at Elephantine. Places designated *rꜣ-ꜥꜣ* acted as checkpoints for traffic into an area that the king wished to control; see H. G. Fischer, "The Inscription of *ꜣIn-ỉt.f*, Born of *Ṯ fi*," *JNES* 19 (1960) 261–62. For titles of this sort during the Middle Kingdom, see D. Franke, "The Career of Khnumhotep III. of Beni Hasan and the So-Called 'Decline of the Nomarchs'," in *Middle Kingdom Studies* (ed. S. Quirke; New Malden, Surrey: SIA, 1991) 57 n. 14; and E. Edel, "Zur Lesung und Bedeutung einiger Stellen in der biographischen Inschrift *Sꜣ-rnpwt*'s I. (*Urk.* VII 1, 20; 2, 1; 2, 4)," ZÄS 87 (1962) 96–97. A stela of the Dynasty XII monarch Sesostris III mentioning the construction of a *rꜣ-ꜥꜣ* 'doorway' has been found at Elephantine; see below in the discussion of the term *Kmt* in nonliterary texts of the Middle Kingdom.

21. A. Erman and H. Grapow (eds.), *Wörterbuch der ägyptischen Sprache* 5 (Leipzig: Hinrichs, 1931) 5.126, 7–127, 20 [hereafter *Wb.* 5].

22. *Wb.* 5.223, 1–15.

during the First Intermediate Period or else were later set in those years, most likely because, as an era, it offered an admonitory example of the chaos that might arise in the absence of strong kingship. Nonetheless, there are a few rare examples of *Kmt* and *Tꜣ-mry* in nonliterary sources of Dynasty XI, so that the literary evidence appears to be in keeping with the vocabulary of material of unquestioned First Intermediate Period date.

As intimated above, the words *Kmt* and *Tꜣ-mry* are considerably more common in literary texts. Since the dating of much Middle Kingdom literature, particularly the works supposedly set in the First Intermediate Period, has long puzzled scholars, it seemed wise to defer any discussion of this large corpus of citations until after the nonliterary material had been treated. Many "Middle Kingdom" works may have actually been largely composed at a much later date. Certainly, many of the hieratic manuscripts of the most important Middle Kingdom literary texts actually date to the New Kingdom and may not always accurately represent Middle Kingdom orthography and terminology.[23]

The first nonliterary sources mentioning *Kmt* seldom employ ⊗, the 'town' sign (Sign-list O49) associated with cities and settlements. Most of these early examples of *Kmt* either write the word with no determinative or else with the 'cultivated land' sign ⌶ (Sign-list N23) and frequently have *Kmt* in parallelism with some word for the *Dšrt* 'the Red Land', thus setting a pattern followed throughout Egyptian history.[24] The contrast implied in this common usage is between the blackish soil of the fertile Nile Valley and the red-yellow sand of the upland deserts beyond the cultivation.[25] In other words, many of the earlier examples of *kmt* appear to refer to a type of land rather than to the political and geographic entity we call *Egypt*. Accordingly

23. An extensive discussion of the questions surrounding the dating of Middle Kingdom literary texts is far beyond the scope of this paper. For an admirable survey of the problems involved, see R. B. Parkinson, "Teachings, Discourses and Tales from the Middle Kingdom," in *Middle Kingdom Studies* (ed. S. Quirke; New Malden, Surrey: SIA, 1991) 92–104, with numerous references.

24. *Wb.* 5.126, 7–11. The association of this word with the black land that is cultivated in contrast with the red soil of the desert persisted into Coptic times as well; see W. E. Crum, A *Coptic Dictionary* (Oxford: Clarendon, 1939) 110, s.v.

25. For discussions of colors and their symbolic value in Egyptian society, see J. Baines, "Color Terminology and Color Classification: Ancient Egyptian Color Terminology and Polychromy," *American Anthropologist* 87 (1985) 282–97; H. Kees, *Farbensymbolik in ägyptischen religiösen Texten* (Nachrichten von der Gesellschaft der Wissenschaften zu Göttingen, Phil.-Hist. Klasse; Göttingen: Vandenhoeck & Ruprecht, 1943) 413–79; and W. Schenkel, "Die Farben in ägyptischer Kunst und Sprache," ZÄS 88 (1963) 131–47. For the association of the color black with death and its use for funerary objects of all kinds, see A. Niwinski, "Ritual Protection of the Dead or Symbolic Reflection of His Special Status in Society?" in *The Intellectual Heritage of Egypt* (Kákosy Festschrift; ed. U. Luft; Studia Aegyptiaca 14; Budapest: Innova, 1992) 468.

we shall adopt an uncapitalized transliteration *kmt* in transcribing these examples. The parallelism of red and black occurs in one of the earliest datable examples of *kmt* in Egyptian texts on a stela of an official at Dendera named *Mn-ꜥnḫ-Ppy*, also called *Mnỉ*. This monument is hard to date with certainty, but H. G. Fischer has made a strong case that this official should be dated later than the Old Kingdom, most likely to Dynasty XI or later.[26] In *Mnỉ*'s titulary there is an instructive juxtaposition of the two phrases: *ỉmy-rꜣ kmt ỉmy-rꜣ dšrt nbt*, which Fischer plausibly renders 'Overseer of the black (cultivated) place, overseer of every red (desert) place'. The contrast between the Nile Valley and the desert is certainly at hand in two obscure and unique titles found in a roughly contemporaneous graffito in Wadi Hammamat (Hammamat 1, temp. Menthuhotep IV):[27]

ỉmy-rꜣ mšꜥw ḥr ḫꜣswt ỉmy-rꜣ pr ḥr  *kmt*

troop-leader in the hill countries, steward (?) in the black land

One of the most informative uses of the term in this respect appears in the Hammamat graffito of an early Dynasty XII official named Antef. Although this text never specifically contrasts *kmt* with the high desert, it shows that the word referred primarily to the Nile Valley as the place where people dwelled (Hammamat 199, temp. Amenemhat I):[28]

26. The stela is illustrated in W. M. F. Petrie (*Dendereh* [Egyptian Exploration Fund, Memoir 17; London: Egypt Exploration Fund, 1900] pl. 2a) and is cited among the *Belegstellen* as an object of "D 6"; see A. Erman and H. Grapow, *Wörterbuch der ägyptischen Sprache: Die Belegstellen* (Berlin: Hinrichs, 1953) 5.19, s.v. "Seite 126, 6." The reasons for placing this individual later than the Old Kingdom have been discussed at length by Fischer, *Dendera*, 85–91. In his discussion of *Mn-ꜥnḫ-Ppy/Mnỉ*, Fischer groups *Mni* with officials of Dyn. XI or later.

27. J. Couyat and P. Montet, *Les inscriptions hiéroglyphiques et hiératiques du Ouâdi Hammâmât* (MIFAO 34; Cairo: Institut Français d'Archéologie Orientale, 1912) 32–33 and pl. 3. This text has often been translated, e.g.: J. H. Breasted, *Ancient Records of Egypt* (Chicago: University of Chicago Press, 1906) vol. 1, §§454–56; W. Schenkel, *Memphis-Herakleopolis-Theben: Die epigraphischen Zeugnisse der 7.–11. Dynastie Ägyptens* (Ägyptologische Abhandlungen 12; Wiesbaden: Harrassowitz, 1965) 269–70; C. Vandersleyen, "Les inscriptions 114 et 1 du Ouadi Hammamât (11e dynastie)," *Chronique d'Égypt* 64 (1989) 156–58. For a discussion of the two titles involved, see O. Goelet, "*Wꜣḏ-wr* and Lexicographical Method," in *The Intellectual Heritage of Egypt* (Kákosy Festschrift; ed. U. Luft; Studia Aegyptiaca 14; Budapest: Innova, 1992) 210.

28. Couyat and Montet, *Ouâdi Hammâmât*, 100–102; see also H. Goedicke, "Some Remarks on Stone Quarrying in the Egyptian Middle Kingdom," *JARCE* 3 (1964) 43–45. For the significance of the two verbs *hꜣỉ* and *prỉ* in texts connected with quarrying inscriptions, see Goelet, "*Wꜣḏ-wr*," 209.

> *ꜥḥꜥ.n hꜣi.kwi r*  *kmt mšꜥw r ḏr.f nn ẖt šms n(n) mwt wr nḏs pḥ(.i)*  *kmt m ḥtp ḥr spd(.i)m prt n st*
>
> Then I and the entire force descended to the black land without there being any retreating of any follower or the death of a great person or a little person, I reaching the black land safely, because of my skill in ascending to (this) place.[29]

Of course, both instances of *kmt* in this passage could have been interpreted as *Kmt* 'Egypt' instead, but the shift in determinatives used in the two writings of the term makes it uncertain what the scribe had in mind. The reversal of the  *km*-sign (Sign-list I 6) in several other texts associated with quarrying expeditions may arise either from a shift between an Old Kingdom and a Middle Kingdom form of the hieroglyph or else may be due to the influence of hieratic.[30]

Given the number of citations of *kmt* deriving from Wadi Hammamat, it is not surprising that the two nonliterary sources containing the word spelled in its classical form should derive from expeditionary records as well. However, in these texts the word seems to refer to 'Egypt' rather than to the 'black land'. In the much-discussed stela of Herwerre at Serâbît el-Khadim in

29. The expression *hꜣi r kmt* may also appear in a Wadi Hammamat graffito dating to the reign of Sesostris I; see G. Goyon, *Nouvelles inscriptions rupestres du Wadi Hammamat* (Paris: Adrien-Maisonneuve, 1957), inscription 61, lines 15–16: *n sp hꜣw mitt irt* (?) *r kmt*(?) *ḏr rk nṯr* 'Never had the like thereof(?) descended to the black land(?) since the time of the god'. For a study of this inscription, see D. Farout, "Le carrière du *wḥmw* Ameny et l'organisation des expéditions au ouadi Hammamat au Moyen Empire," *BIFAO* 94 (1994) 145–48.

30. The sign (Sign-list I 6) represents a piece of crocodile skin; see A. H. Gardiner, *Egyptian Grammar* (3d rev. ed.; London: Oxford University Press, 1957) 475; and H. G. Fischer, *Ancient Egyptian Calligraphy: A Beginner's Guide to Writing Hieroglyphs* (3d ed.; New York: Metropolitan Museum of Art, 1988) 21. Recently A. Nibbi ("The Hieroglyph Signs *gs* and *km* and Their Relationship," *Göttinger Miszellen* 52 [1981] 43–54) has proposed that the sign represents a mound of black soil with vegetation growing on it. Her suggestion that the Arabic word *kôm* 'mound, tell' may be thus related to the ancient word *km* is much less plausible than a derivation from the Arabic root KWM 'to pile up'; see H. Wehr, *A Dictionary of Modern Written Arabic* (ed. J. M. Cowan; Ithaca, N.Y.: Cornell University Press, 1961) 846. W. Vycichl (*Dictionnaire étymologique de la langue copte* [Louvain: Peeters, 1983] 81, s.v. **ⲔⲘⲞⲘ**) sees no immediate Arabic etymology for the Egyptian word and its Coptic derivatives.

Unlike most Old Kingdom hieroglyphic forms of this sign, the hieratic versions are always oriented so that the serrate portion faces opposite to the direction of the writing, but during the Middle Kingdom both the hieratic and hieroglyphic forms faced forward; see G. Möller, *Hieratische Paläographie*, vol. 1: *Bis zum Beginn der Achtzehnten Dynastie* (2d ed.; Leipzig: Hinrichs, 1927) 37 (#392); and H. Goedicke, *Old Hieratic Paleography* (Baltimore: HALGO, 1988) 18.

the Sinai, the word appears in an obscure passage describing his arrival at Sinai (Sinai 90, temp. Amenemhet II):[31]

 *ỉwt.ỉ ḥr Kmt bdš.ỉ štꜣ ḥr.ỉ*

When I arrived from Egypt, I was discouraged.

Similarly in a stela probably dating to the reign of Sesostris III found at Semna, a functionary by the name of Menthuemhat has two remarkable epithets at the end of his stela:[32]

mḥ-ỉb n nswt m srwḏ mnnw.f m ỉrt rꜣ-ꜥꜣ  *ḥr Kmt*

the confidant of the king in maintaining his fortress and in making the doorway for Egypt

Although it would be tempting to locate this 'doorway for Egypt' somewhere in the vicinity of the fortress at Semna, it seems more likely to connect this construction with the one mentioned on a royal stela erected by Sesostris III at the island of Elephantine that speaks of making a *rꜣ-ꜥꜣ* 'doorway' at the fortress there.[33]

The two instances of *Kmt* in nonliterary texts may employ variant writings of the term in its classical form with the 'town' determinative. An apparent plural occurs on the stela of Sesostris I's vizier Menthuhotep, definitely one of the best-executed objects of its kind made in Dynasty XII. Since this stela was certainly given to its owner as a royal reward, it also seems likely that the text would reflect the official phraseology and orthography of the time. In a lengthy string of Menthuhotep's titles and laudatory epithets we find the unique phrase:[34]

31. Both the form of the verb and the use of the preposition *ḥr* in this passage has long puzzled scholars. For a discussion of some of the problems involved with the translation, see E. Iversen, "The Inscription of Herwerre at Serâbit-al-Kâdem," in *Studien zu Sprache und Religion Ägyptens* (Westendorf Festschrift; ed. F. Junge; 2 vols.; Göttingen: Hubert, 1984) 1.511; and H. Goedicke, "The Inscription of *Ḥr-wr-rꜥ* (Sinai no. 90)," *MDAIK* 18 (1962) 17–19.

32. Boston MFA 29.1130: R. J. Leprohon, *Museum of Fine Arts Boston: Stelae*, vol. 1: *The Early Dynastic Period to the Late Middle Kingdom* (Corpus Antiquitatum Aegyptiacarum; Mainz am Rhein: von Zabern, 1985) 153–55; J. M. A. Janssen, "La stèle de Montouemhat trouvée à Semna," *ArOr* 20 (1952) 442–45; and J.W. Wells, "Sesostris III's First Nubian Campaign," in *Essays in Egyptology in Honor of Hans Goedicke* (ed. B. M. Bryan and D. Lorton; San Antonio: Van Siclen, 1994) 339–47.

33. BM 857: E. A. W. Budge, *Hieroglyphic Texts from Egyptian Stelae, &c., in the British Museum* (London, 1913) vol. 4, pl. 10; and Wells, "Sesostris III's First Nubian Campaign," 339–47.

34. Cairo CG 20539: H. O. Lange and H. Schäfer, *Catalogue général des antiquités égyptiens du Musée du Caire, Nos. 20001–20780: Grab- und Denksteine des Mittleren Reichs im Museum von Kairo*, vol. 2: *Text zu 20400–20780* (Berlin: Reichsdrückerei,

 *ḥry-tp n kmtwt dšrtwt*

chieftain of the black (inhabited) places and the red (desert) places

which is reminiscent of a similar expression on the stela of *Mnỉ* quoted above. The difference between the Nile Valley and the upland deserts is emphasized by the contrasting determinatives used in Menthuhotep's text. The two epithets directly following—*dd wḏw n Šmꜥw ỉp rỉdr n Tꜣ-mḥw* 'the one who gives commands to Upper Egypt and reckons the cattle-count for Lower Egypt'—indicate that the word *kmtwt* most likely was a nominalized nisbe-adjective referring to the Nile Valley as opposed to the desert, rather than to Egypt as a totality.

On a crude stela of a "steward" named Amenemhet from Abydos, the word appears in a passage describing the rule of Amenemhet II, his king and namesake:[35]

sꜣḳ.n.f tꜣ pn rdỉ.n n.f Rꜥ-Ḥr ḥḳꜣt  *Kmt*

He has seized this land. Re-Horus has given him the rule of Egypt.

In this instance *Kmt* is employed simply as a synonym for the word 'land' without drawing any parallel with the desert or foreign territories.

Significantly, the first datable nonliterary references to *Tꜣ-mry* also occur in the late inscriptions of Dynasty XI in the Wadi Hammamat, the same place and time when the term *Kmt* is first attested. The *Tꜣ-mry* appears in two graffiti incised within a few days of each other by Menthuhotep IV's vizier, Amenhotep, almost certainly the same man as the founder of Dynasty XII, King Sehetepibre Amenemhet I. In one of Amenemhet's graffiti, *Tꜣ-mry* occurs in an interesting parallel with *Kmt* that is in turn explicitly connected with the entirety of Egypt (Hammamat 191):[36]

sḏm st ntyw m 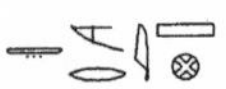 *Tꜣ-mry rḫyt ntt ḥr*  *Kmt Šmꜥw ḥnꜥ Tꜣ-mḥw*

Hear this, O (you) who are in the Beloved Land, (you) common people who are in Egypt, (namely) Upper Egypt and Lower Egypt.

1908) 153, line 11. On this title, see also W. K. Simpson, "Mentuhotep, Vizier of Sesostris I, Patron of Art and Architecture," *MDAIK* 47 (1991) 333, where it is translated 'chief of the cities of Egypt and of the desert'.

35. The form of the *km*-sign is rather awkward; see Cairo CG 20541: H. O. Lange and H. Schäfer, *Grab- und Denksteine* (Berlin, 1902–25) 2.161–62. The rare word *ḥḳꜣt* has been explained by E. Blumenthal (*Untersuchungen zum ägyptischen Königtum des Mittleren Reiches*, vol. 1: *Die Phraseologie* [Abhandlungen der Sächsischen Akademie der Wissenschaften zu Leipzig 61/1; Berlin: Akademie, 1970] 29–30) as an abstract formation from the noun *ḥḳꜣ* 'ruler'.

36. Couyat and Montet, *Ouâdi Hammâmât*, 98. As with the inscription mentioned in the previous note, this text has been frequently discussed. A convenient translation with references and a commentary appears in Schenkel, *Memphis-Herakleopolis-Theben*, 265–67.

In the concluding lines of a nearby graffito left by the same quarrying expedition, *Tȝ-mry* is named as the ultimate destination of the force (Hammamat 192):[37]

> *ỉsṯ mšʿ n ḫȝw m ẖnw spȝwt Tȝ-mḥw ḥr šms.f m ḥtp r* 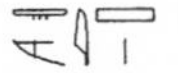 *Tȝ-mry*
>
> Lo, a force of thousands of oarsmen of the nomes of Lower Egypt are accompanying it safely to the Beloved Land.

Like *Kmt*, the term *Tȝ-mry* is rarely encountered on stelae of the Middle Kingdom. The only such example known to me appears on a late Middle Kingdom stela of a "Steward" named Hetep. The stela was found at Abydos and is now in the Cairo Museum. An odd writing of the term appears in an *appel aux vivants* in parallel with the word *tȝ* 'earth' (Cairo 20014):[38]

> *ʾI ʿnḫw tpy(w) tȝ*  *sš nb n Tȝ-mry*
>
> O living ones upon earth and every scribe of the Beloved Land. . . .

Tȝ-mry seems to be used here not just as a term for Egypt but for the land of the living as well.

Although there are a great many toponyms found both in Middle Kingdom official documents and among the vast number of titles of the period, the terms *Kmt* and *Tȝ-mry* are rarely encountered in those sources. In fact, the same absence of these two words applies even when we examine material found in Nubia, where the Egyptians were quite active. The simplest explanation for this phenomenon might lie in a natural tendency not to incorporate a modifier in situations where it would be applicable in nearly every case. For example, officials appearing in the Abusir Papyri almost never employ the name of Neferirkare's funerary establishment as a component of their titles, yet they mention that institution prominently in the titularies inscribed in their Saqqara tombs.[39]

"Egypt" in Literary Texts

In contrast with the small number of citations of *Kmt* and *Tȝ-mry* in the inscriptional evidence discussed above, the two words are found in a much

37. Couyat and Montet, *Ouâdi Hammâmât*, 100; and Schenkel, *Memphis-Herakleopolis-Theben*, 268–69.

38. Cairo CG 20014: H. O. Lange and H. Schäfer, *Catalogue général des antiquités égyptiens du Musée du Caire, Nos. 20001–20780: Grab- und Denksteine des Mittleren Reichs im Museum von Kairo*, vol. 1: *Text zu 20001–20399* (Berlin: Reichsdrückerei, 1902) 14, line 4.

39. On this point, see O. Goelet, "The Nature of the Term *pr-ʿȝ* in the Old Kingdom," *Bulletin of the Egyptological Seminar of New York* 10 (1989–90) 83; and A. M. Roth, "The Distribution of the Old Kingdom Title *ḫnty-š*," *Studien zur altägyptischen Kultur, Beihefte* 4 (1990) 179–82.

greater proportion of literary sources. Many of these texts underwent subsequent editing and accretions long after their original composition during the Middle Kingdom. Unfortunately, the problems of dating literary materials often leave one uncertain as to whether a citation is representative of Middle Egyptian usage or whether it might not have been influenced by later orthography and phraseology. Even if the dating of many literary hieratic texts whose action is set in the First Intermediate Period remains questionable, this is less true of other classics of Middle Kingdom literature. It must be admitted, furthermore, that in literary material the use of both *Kmt* and *Tꜣ-mry* conforms well with the evidence from the nonliterary sources treated above. In respect to its orthography, the only minor difference *Kmt* shows in literary sources is that the word nearly always has 𓊖, the 'town' sign, as its determinative and *never* uses 𓈅, the 'cultivated land' sign. At the risk of an overly broad generalization, we can describe the literary passages in which *Kmt* and *Tꜣ-mry* are apt to occur as contexts requiring a distinction between (1) the Nile Valley where the Egyptians lived and the desert, or (2) a distinction between Egypt and the peoples beyond its borders, particularly in the Asiatic lands. Otherwise, however, when speaking of conditions within Egypt itself, literary texts tend to prefer terms such as 'the Two Lands' or 'this land'. In discussing the use of *Kmt* and *Tꜣ-mry* in literary texts, we shall concentrate on *The Tale of Sinuhe* because it contains the greatest number of examples of these terms and because the usage of the two terms in this text is typical of their usage in other literary sources.

One of the most important literary texts to use *Kmt* is the *Hymns to Sesostris III*, since the work not only is of undoubted Dynasty XII origin but it is also one of the few Middle Kingdom literary papyri to derive from an excavation. This text is particularly interesting because a form of *Kmt* occurs twice, apparently as a collective term for the people of Egypt. In the fourth poem, the following lines appear (pl. III, 3–5):[40]

> *ỉỉ.n.f n.n ḥkꜣ.n.f* [hieroglyphs] *Kmt*(?) *rdỉ .n.f dšrt m ꜥb.f ỉỉ.n.f n.n mkỉ.n.f tꜣwy sgrḥ.n.f ỉdbwy ỉỉ.n.f n.n sꜥnḫ.n.f* [hieroglyphs] *Kmt*(?) *ẖsr.n.f šnww.s*
>
> It was (after) he had ruled the (people of ?) Egypt (lit., the Black Land), and (after) he had put the Red Land in his company, that he came to us. It was (after) he had protected the Two Lands, and (after) he had pacified the Two Banks, that he came to us. It was (after) he had caused (the people of?) Egypt to live and (after) he had removed its needs, that he came to us.

40. F. L. Griffith, *The Petrie Papyri: Hieratic Papyri from Kahun and Gurob (Principally of the Middle Kingdom)*, vol. 2: *Plates* (London: Quaritch, 1898) pl. 3; a facsimile appears in G. Möller, *Hieratische Lesestücke für den akademischen Gebrauch*, vol. 1: *Alt- und Mittelhieratische Texte* (2d ed.; Leipzig: Hinrichs, 1927) pl. 5; conveniently transcribed in K. Sethe, *Ägyptische Lesestücke zum Gebrauch im akademischen Unterricht* (Leipzig: Hinrichs, 1928) 37.

A major problem in interpreting this passage is whether to consider the two instances of as a nisbe-adjective *Kmtyw* 'those of the Black Land' or simply as the same word *Kmt* personified with the appropriate determinatives. In the first occurrence of the word, the presence of 'the Red Land', 'the Two Lands', and 'the Two Banks' in the following clauses, all without the personal determinatives, makes it more probable that the personified country was intended in both cases.[41] In the second phrase containing *Kmt*, furthermore, the sentence following it refers back to that word by means of the third-person singular feminine suffix pronoun *s*. Although these poems certainly represent a rather rarefied literary usage, it is still interesting to note that *Kmt* could personify Egypt and its inhabitants by the end of Dynasty XII.

It is only fitting that the *Tale of Sinuhe*, the most famous of all Egyptian literary tales, should also contain the most references to 'Egypt' and the 'Beloved Land'. In addition, this piece offers us the Egyptian terms for 'Egyptian people' and 'Egyptian language'. Since *Sinuhe* takes its protagonist far beyond the borders of Egypt, then back home again, this tale is of particular importance to the question of the terminology for the country during Dynasty XII. As with the *Hymns* discussed above, there are more than paleographic grounds for dating the major papyri—archaeological evidence indicates that at least one of the two major manuscripts of *Sinuhe* was contemporaneous with Dynasty XII or the early part of Dynasty XIII.

The first references to Egypt appear in the description of the hero's flight, when he first encounters a group of Asiatic herdsmen, presumably at a point in the far reaches of Egypt if not beyond its borders: "I heard the sound of cattle lowing and saw Asiatics, one of their leaders who had been in Egypt. . . ."[42] That the word *Kmt* should be used here is not surprising, but it is significant that, as in the quarrying inscriptions above, this word normally occurs throughout *Sinuhe* in those contexts in which a contrast between Egypt and the rest of the world is drawn. Shortly after this passage, the narration takes Sinuhe to the land of Qedem, whose ruler Ammunenshi invites Sinuhe to stay with him because "you will hear *rꜣ n Kmt* 'the Egyptian language'."[43] Furthermore, Sinuhe encounters other *rmṯ Kmt*

41. On this point, see also M. Lichtheim, *Ancient Egyptian Literature*, vol. 1: *The Old and Middle Kingdoms* (Berkeley: University of California Press, 1973) 201 n. 6.

42. *Sinuhe* B 26. As a rule, the Ramesseum (R) variant writes the word without the complementary *m*, whereas the Berlin manuscript has the fuller writing with one exception. All citations below will use the recent text edition of R. Koch, *Die Erzählung des Sinuhe* (Bibliotheca Aegyptiaca 17; Brussels: Éditions de la Fondation Égyptologique Reine Elisabeth, 1990).

43. Literally, 'the speech of Egypt', *Sinuhe* B 31–32. The term for the Egyptian language in Coptic is ⲙⲛⲧⲣⲙⲛⲕⲙⲉ (S.), lit., 'that which pertains to the people of Egypt'; see Vycichl, *Dictionaire étymologique*, 81. Crum (*Coptic Dictionary*, 110) notes that this Coptic expression can also mean 'Egyptian nationality'.

'Egyptians' with Ammunenshi in Qedem.[44] Yet, in the midst of the first of Sinuhe's lengthy encomnia to Sesostris I shortly after this passage, Egypt is called simply 'the land'; it is left to the Asiatic chieftain to comment, "Now, indeed Egypt is happy. . . ."[45] After a successful life abroad, Sinuhe eventually yearns to return to Egypt and live again as one of its people, yet he is reluctant to do so without first obtaining royal permission, saying to himself "may  the king of (*Kmt*) Egypt be pleased with me. . . ."[46] It is only by returning to Egypt that the exiled hero can hope to achieve a proper burial and insure an eternal place for himself in the company of his monarch. Fortunately, his merciful ruler has a "decree brought to this humble servant concerning his being brought back to Egypt."[47] In this letter, the king promises Sinuhe readmission to the court he once served, as well as a proper Egyptian burial, imploring him: "Make a return to Egypt!" In his reply to the king, Sinuhe invokes the blessing of several deities: "Amun, lord of the thrones of the Two Lands, Sobek-Re, lord of Semenu, Horus, Hathor, all the gods of the Beloved Land (*Tꜣ-mry*), and the totality of the Ennead of the Great Gods."[48] It should be pointed out, however, that the reference to Egypt in this form appears only in the Ashmolean Ostracon of *Sinuhe*, an object that probably dates to the Ramesside period. In Sinuhe's account of his return home, there is no specific mention of Egypt, nor is there a description of crossing its borders. *The Tale of Sinuhe* ends with a lengthy passage describing Sinuhe's transformation from an Asiatic back into an Egyptian. When he is presented to the court, in his identity as an Asiatic and still in his outlandish costume, the prodigal Sinuhe is called

 *pdty msw m Tꜣ-mry*

a bowman who was born in Egypt,

the sole occurrence of this term in the Middle Kingdom manuscripts of the tale.[49] The passage following this reveals much about the Egyptians' concept of what made a person Egyptian, since Sinuhe's transformation is essentially

44. *Sinuhe* B 33–34. The use of *rmṯ* 'people' to mean 'Egyptians' in contrast with foreigners is rather common in Egyptian sources throughout their history. During the Middle Kingdom *rmṯ* occurs by itself in the Execration Texts in the heading of the section listing the names of cursed Egyptians. The expression *rmṯ n Kmt* is preserved in Sahidic Coptic as **ⲣⲙⲛⲕⲏⲙⲉ** 'Egyptian' employed as a noun and adjective; see Vycichl, *Dictionnaire étymologique*, 81.

45. *Sinuhe* B 76.

46. Ibid., B 165.

47. This line occurs only in ibid., B 178. In this instance the letter *m* is not written.

48. *Sinuhe* AOS 23–24; see Koch, *Sinuhe*, 23–24.

49. *Sinuhe* B 276. The two parallel versions, both dating later than Dynasty XII, apparently write 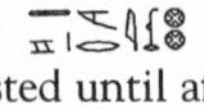 *Tꜣ-mry* as a dual with two town-signs (Sign-list O49), a writing not attested until after the Middle Kingdom.

a *transvestiture*—the casting off of Asiatic customs, clothing, and language and adopting their Egyptian equivalent.

Although there is little surprising or unusual in these quotations, the terms for 'Egypt' appear here more frequently than in any other Middle Kingdom text. The word *Kmt* appears to have taken on the quality of an official term for the land, yet occurs only when there is a need to contrast Egypt with the rest of the world. In *The Satire on the Trades*, for example, *Kmt* occurs only in the description of the travails of the *śḫꜣḫꜣty* 'courier' when he is sent on a mission (P. Sallier II, VII, 6–8):[50] "The courier goes forth into the (*ḫꜣst*) foreign land (or: desert), having transferred his property over to his children, fearing lions and Asiatics. He comes to his senses (lit., knows himself) (only) when he is in (*Kmt*) Egypt (again)." All other geographical references in this text are either to specific sites, such as the Delta, or more generally, to "the land." However, unlike the remaining sources for the word *Kmt*, *The Satire* is set firmly within a Middle Kingdom context.

The use of *Kmt* in other Middle Kingdom literary texts is often subtle and complex, yet none of these works introduces a usage not already encountered among the examples from literary and nonliterary sources discussed above. Accordingly, we shall examine only those instances that seem particularly noteworthy. It has long been recognized that such works as *The Admonitions of Ipuwer*, *The Tale of the Eloquent Peasant*, *The Prophecy of Neferty*, and *The Instruction for King Merikare* were composed partially with the political intent of contrasting the disorder of the First Intermediate Period with the stability and prosperity of Dynasty XII.[51] It is not surprising, then, that in this politicized literature *Kmt* appears most often in contexts involving struggles between Egyptians and Asiatics and appears to be used as a generic term for the entire land. Only rarely, as in one instance in the *Eloquent Peasant*, does *Kmt* appear in the more political literature in contrasts involving the desert.[52]

50. W. Helck, *Die Lehre des Dwꜣ-Ḫtjj* (Kleine Ägyptische Texte; Wiesbaden: Harrassowitz, 1970) 93–95. A discussion of this passage with a slightly different translation can be found in A. G. McDowell, *Hieratic Ostraca in the Hunterian Museum Glasgow (The Colin Campbell Ostraca)* (Oxford: Griffith Institute, 1993) 17 and pl. 16. All versions of this passage write *Kmt* with the town-sign, but none of these manuscripts is of a Middle Kingdom origin. Since the author of this piece purportedly came from the border town of Sile, he may actually have known something about travel abroad.

51. On this point see, for example, F. Junge, "Die Welt der Klagen," in *Fragen an die altägyptische Literatur* (Otto Gedenkschrift; ed. J. Assmann et. al.; Wiesbaden: Reichert, 1977) 275–88.

52. The Peasant, who is an inhabitant of Wadi Tumilat, descends from those upland desert regions into Egypt (*hꜣt r* *Kmt*) at the beginning of the story; see R. B. Parkinson, *The Tale of the Eloquent Peasant* (Oxford: Griffith Institute, 1991) 1.

Kmt occurs in *Merikare* in a passage in which the king describes how he expelled Asiatics from the Delta:[53] "I captured their underlings, I seized their cattle, until the Asiatics abhorred (*Kmt*) Egypt." In this context it seems more likely that *Kmt* is a generic term for the entirety of Egypt rather than a word referring to its fertile regions alone. The most intriguing of all passages in this "Instruction" employs *Kmt* as a term for the entire country as well as for its *personification:*[54] "The affairs of the enemy are miserable and destroyed. The enemy has not been quiet in (*Kmt*) Egypt. Troops shall fight troops, as the ancestors foretold concerning it. Egypt (*Kmt*) shall fight in the necropolis." In the first instance *Kmt* is the familiar toponym; in the second, the word personifies the nation.

The *Admonitions of Ipuwer* uses the term *Kmt* more often than any other literary work except for *Sinuhe*. In all cases the term appears as , the same form that is also used throughout *Merikare*. For the most part *Kmt* occurs in *Ipuwer* as a term for the entire land, almost always in situations in which foreign nations are besetting the land.[55] However, a passage that speaks of Egypt's "not being given over ⟨to⟩ sand"[56] may imply a contrast between fertile and desert soil. In addition to this standard usage, *Kmt* performs an activity of human beings:[57] "See, Egypt has fallen into pouring water," a type of personification paralleled elsewhere for other parts of the country.[58] As in the *Hymns to Sesostris III* and *Merikare*, *Kmt* has an uncommon role in *Ipuwer* as a personification of the country.

It is easy to find similar instances in which other Middle Kingdom literary works use *Kmt* as a generic term for the whole country. In *Neferty* the inter-

---

Except for the choice of the determinative, this could be interpreted as an example of *kmt* 'black land'. This is the sole mention of *Kmt* in the entire text, which otherwise prefers to use 'the land', 'the Two Lands', and so on, as the terms for Egypt.

53. Pap. Petersburg 1116A, IX, 4–5; see W. Helck (*Die Lehre für König Merikare* [Kleine Ägyptische Texte; Wiesbaden: Harrassowitz, 1977] 58), restoring partially from the Pap. Carlsberg VI version.

54. Pap. Petersburg 1116A, VI, 11–VII, 1, with the ememendation suggested by Helck, *Merikare*, 41–42.

55. Pap. Leiden 344, recto, III, 1; see A. H. Gardiner, *The Admonitions of an Egyptian Sage from a Hieratic Papyrus in Leiden (Pap. Leiden 344 recto)* (Leipzig: Hinrichs, 1909) 30–31. This passage speaks of a foreign tribe coming to Egypt (*ỉỉ.tỉ n Kmt*), but uses the preposition *n* instead of the more correct *r*, encountered in other examples of this phrase. If the term *Kmt* is interpreted as a personification, however, the preposition *n* might be acceptable. Otherwise, another plausible interpretation of *n* here has been offered by H. Goedicke (*The Protocol of Neferyt [The Prophecy of Neferti]* [JHNES; Baltimore: Johns Hopkins University Press, 1977] 33, 47 n. 118): 'alien foreigners have come for arable land'.

56. Pap. Leiden 344, recto, XV, 3; see Gardiner, *Admonitions*, 90.

57. Pap. Leiden 344, recto, VII, 4–5; see Gardiner, *Admonitions*, 55.

58. "Lower Egypt weeps," Pap. Leiden 344, recto, X, 3; see Gardiner, *Admonitions*, 72.

esting phrase *ỉtrw nw Kmt* 'the River of Egypt', that is, the Nile, appears twice.[59] Two other passages in this text containing *Kmt* employ it similarly as the word for the entire land, both of which, significantly, involve Asiatics.[60]

Some Conclusions concerning the Development of the Terminology for 'Egypt' in the Middle Kingdom

At this juncture it is possible to see a few unifying threads in the discussion of *Kmt* and *Tꜣ-mry*. Certainly, the difference between the evidence drawn from literary and nonliterary sources seems to lie more in the realm of frequency than usage per se. The sole exception to this observation appears to be the use of *Kmt* as a personification of the entire land, in any case an uncommon usage during the Middle Kingdom. It is striking, furthermore, how often both words in question occur when there seems to be a need to draw a sharp distinction between Egypt and the outside world. This distinction, furthermore, could involve either the difference between the fertile land and the desert or else a difference between Egypt and foreign lands and peoples. The latter usage eventually evolved into the employment of *Kmt* as the country's official name. Except for activity mostly in the nearby desert regions, Old Kingdom Egypt seldom had much need to concern itself with that outside world, so it is not surprising that there does not seem to be much in the way of a specialized terminology for the country during that period.

Some Remarks on the Use of Kmt and Tꜣ-mry after the Middle Kingdom

On the one hand, it is impossible to give a brief yet comprehensive account of *Kmt* and *Tꜣ-mry* in texts following Dynasty XII; on the other hand, there are surprisingly few new developments in their usage after the Middle Kingdom. Indeed, if there is any marked change in the way these words are employed in texts of the New Kingdom, Ramesside period, and later, it would be that the terms are encountered much more frequently. The most important development, one already presaged during the Middle Kingdom, is that *Kmt* became the *official* name for the country. For instance, during the New Kingdom, the term *Kmt* is occasionally a component of pharaonic titularies. Similarly, in the Peace Treaty between Ramesses II and the Hittite

59. Pap. Petersburg 1116B, 26 and 35–36; see W. Helck, *Die Prophezeihung des Nft.tj* (Kleine Ägyptische Texte; Wiesbaden: Harrassowitz, 1970) 24 and 31. The genitival adjective *nw*, of course, is an error since *ỉtrw* is actually singular.

60. Pap. Petersburg 1116B, 33; for which, see Helck, *Prophezeihung des Nft.tj*, 28, for the expression *hꜣỉ r Kmt*, used to describe the descent of Asiatics but without an apparent connection with the desert; also for the description of the 'Walls-of-the-Ruler', which were constructed to prevent Asiatics from entering (*r Kmt*) into Egypt, Pap. Petersburg 1116B, 67; see Helck, *Prophezeihung des Nft.tj*, 56.

monarch Hattusilis III, the two rulers are respectively called "the Great Ruler of Egypt" and "the Great Prince of Ḫatti,"[61] and their countries are called "the land of Egypt" and "the land of Ḫatti."[62] In the Coptic translations of the Greek New Testament, the term **ⲔⲎⲘⲈ**, a clear derivation from the ancient *Kmt*, is used consistently to translate Αἴγυπτος.[63]

Perhaps the only other major addition to Middle Kingdom usage encountered in later sources are instances in which *Kmt* appears as the land of the living. A typical example of this occurs in the late Dynasty XVIII tomb of an individual named Neferhotep in a Harper's Song that praises the land of Eternity:[64] "Those who shall be born to millions (of people) upon millions, they will all come to it (the land of Eternity), for no one tarries in (*tꜣ n Kmt*) the land of Egypt." This expression may be simply a development of the often-made contrast between the fertile land of the living and the sandy soil of the desert, the underlying sense of *Kmt* that seems to have been retained throughout Egyptian history.

61. *Ḥkꜣ ꜥꜣ n Kmt* and *wr ꜥꜣ n Ḫtꜣ*. The two rulers are so named in many places in this document (for example, line 12); see K. A. Kitchen, *Ramesside Inscriptions: Historical and Biographical* (Oxford: Blackwell, 1971) 2.227, 11–12.

62. *Pꜣ tꜣ n Kmt* and *pꜣ tꜣ n Ḫtꜣ*; see *Wb.* 5.216, 2–3. In the Treaty these two expressions are found in a number of parallel clauses and occasionally contiguously, as in line 31; see Kitchen, *Ramesside Inscriptions*, 2.230, 13.

63. Crum, *Coptic Dictionary*, 110.

64. See M. Lichtheim, "The Songs of the Harpers," *JNES* 4 (1945) 197–98.

A Ugaritic Cognate for Akkadian *ḫitpu*?

William W. Hallo
Yale University

"The Babylonian Sabbath" once exercised a considerable hold on the Assyriological imagination and sparked an extended controversy which I reviewed briefly in 1977.[1] It was originally reconstructed by Albert T. Clay on the basis of cuneiform texts of Achaemenid date in the Yale Babylonian Collection. But he chose to publish only 6 of the 23 relevant texts then at Yale, and others have since been acquired there or published from other collections, so that a new review of the evidence was clearly called for. When Ellen Robbins, a student of Baruch Levine who had just completed a doctoral dissertation on the cultic calendar of Israel, came to me in 1989 with a request for a postdoctoral project, it seemed only natural to suggest such a review to her. She has since copied or recopied all of the Yale texts in question which, together with the material elsewhere, now adds up to more than 40 texts dating from the reign of Nabonidus to that of Cambyses. Her exhaustive study will appear elsewhere in due course. [See now *JCS* 48 (1996) 61–87.]

All the texts in question are tabular or two-dimensional in their basic format.[2] They come from the Eanna temple in Uruk and are characterized by the recurrence of an offering of sacrificial animals described as *ḫi-it-pi* or, occasionally, *ḫi-it-pu* at intervals of six, seven, or eight days in each lunar month.[3] In later (Seleucid) times, the offering is "always associated with the

Author's note: The nature of the *ḫitpu*-offering and, more particularly, the etymology of the term will here be studied in light of the comparative evidence as a tribute to Baruch Levine, with whom I have collaborated formally and informally for many fruitful years (cf. especially below, n. 2).

1. W. W. Hallo, "New Moons and Sabbaths: A Case-Study in the Contrastive Approach," *HUCA* 48 (1977) 1–18, esp. 8–9. Reprinted in *Essential Papers on Israel and the Ancient Near East* (ed. F. E. Greenspahn; New York: New York University Press, 1991) 313–32, esp. 319.

2. For the "two-dimensional" concept, see B. A. Levine and W. W. Hallo, "Offerings to the Temple Gates at Ur," *HUCA* 38 (1967) 17–58, esp. 20 and n. 16, with previous literature.

3. See most recently P.-A. Beaulieu, "The Impact of Month-Lengths on the Neo-Babylonian Cultic Calendar," ZA 83 (1993) 66–87, esp. 80–81.

clothing ceremony (*lubuštu*)."[4] A particularly noteworthy example of this association speaks of a share "in the sheep of the *ḫitpu*-offerings which pertain to the clothing ceremonies" of various deities at Uruk, using what appears to be the plural of *ḫitpu* (*ḫi-ta-pat*.MEŠ or perhaps *ḫi-it*(!)-*pat*.MEŠ).[5] In the time of the tabular *ḫitpu*-texts, the clothing ceremony was still the subject of separate texts.[6]

In 1977, I stated:

> The root *ḥtp* is familiar in Arabic, Hebrew and Aramaic in connection with slaughtering or hunting and occurs already in a Ugaritic text in the specific context of a sacrifice. We read, in a prayer to Baʿal, "A bull, oh Baʿal, we consecrate (to you), a votive offering, oh Baʿal, we dedicate (to you), the first fruits, oh Baʿal, we consecrate (to you), the booty, oh Baʿal, we offer (to you), a tithe, oh Baʿal, we tithe (to you)." The word translated 'booty' here is *ḥtp*, comparable to the *ḥetep* ('prey') of Proverbs 23:28. Given the context, however, the word may already foreshadow the connotation of a kind of sacrifice. That is surely the meaning of Akkadian *ḫitpu* which occurs in monthly sacrificial lists of the late first millennium.[7]

The Ugaritic text in question is RS 24.266 = KTU 1.119, cited then from the partial edition by Herdner.[8] In an addendum,[9] I cited a new study of the text by Spalinger and a proposed Egyptian cognate in the approximate sense of '(food) offering'.[10] Since then, several new attempts have been made to explain the Ugaritic text.

Herdner herself published the full text in 1978.[11] Dietrich, Loretz, and Sanmartín included it in their authoritative corpus of Ugaritic texts of 1976, indicating that the *p* of *ḥtp* was damaged.[12] Xella dealt with the root *ḥtp* in

4. Ibid. and n. 34.

5. OECT 9:50:6. Cf. the edition by L. T. Doty, "Akkadian *bīt pirišti*," in *The Tablet and the Scroll: Near Eastern Studies in Honor of William W. Hallo* (ed. M. E. Cohen, D. C. Snell, and D. B. Weisberg; Bethesda, Md.: CDL, 1993) 87–89, esp. p. 88.

6. E. Matsushima, "On the Material Related to the Clothing Ceremony: *lubuštu* in the Later Periods in Babylonia," *Acta Sumerologica* 16 (1994) 177–200; eadem, "Some Remarks on the Divine Garments: *kusītu* and *naḫlaptu*," *Acta Sumerologica* 17 (1995) 233–49, esp. 237–39 and n. 12.

7. Hallo, "New Moons and Sabbaths," 8; repr. in *Essential Papers*, 319.

8. A. Herdner, "Une prière à Baal de Ugaritains en danger," *CRAIBL* (1962) 694; cited in my "New Moons and Sabbaths," 8 n. 37; repr. in *Essential Papers*, 319 and 328 n. 37.

9. "New Moons and Sabbaths," 17–18; repr. *Essential Papers*, 328 n. 37.

10. A. J. Spalinger, "A Canaanite Ritual Found in Egyptian Reliefs," *Society for the Study of Egyptian Antiquities* 9 (1978) 47–60, esp. 55 and nn. 40–45.

11. A. Herdner, "Nouveaux textes alphabétiques de Ras Shamra," *Ugaritica* 7 (1978) 31–39.

12. M. Dietrich, O. Loretz, and J. Sanmartín, *Die keilalphabetischen Texte aus Ugarit* (AOAT 24/1; Neukirchen-Vluyn: Neukirchener Verlag, 1976) [KTU].

1977 and with the whole text in 1978 and again in 1981.[13] Avishur translated the text into Hebrew and provided a new commentary.[14] He rendered Ugaritic *ḥtp* by Hebrew *qorban* 'offering' on the basis of Akkadian *ḫitpu*, rejecting an emendation to *ḥtk* proposed by Margalit (below). Avishur compared the five synonyms for offering found in the Ugaritic text to the five or six such terms found in Deut 12:6 where, by a kind of process of elimination, the Ugaritic *ḥtp* corresponds to Hebrew *zbḥ* 'sacrifice'.

Margalit dealt with *ḥtp* and the problem of equating it with *ḫitpu* in 1981.[15] His proposal to emend the text to *ḥtk* 'son' rests in part on the assumed parallel with *bkr* 'firstborn' in the preceding line and in part on the orthographic similarity between the Ugaritic signs for P and K. De Moor included the text in his "selection of liturgical texts from Ugarit" in 1983.[16] He translated the crucial word into Dutch as 'de *ḫitpu*-verplichtingen', the *ḫitpu*-obligations. In the same year, Saracino rendered it 'a *ḫitpu*-sacrifice', while invoking the whole prayer as a parallel to Mic 5:4–5.[17] The following year, Watson translated the term by 'the crush-sacrifice', noting that "like the Akkadian *ḫitpu*-sacrifice this apparently involved destruction of the victim by repeated blows with a stick," and referring to Xella's study of 1977.[18]

In 1987, Sasson took issue with Margalit's emendation and with other elements of his proposal, paraphrasing the passage as follows:

> We shall sacrifice a bull // We shall fulfill a pledge
> We shall sacrifice a (?)*kr* // We shall fulfill a *ḥtp*
> We shall (therefore/furthermore) pay a tithe.[19]

The following year, Miller, citing with approval my claim that the Ugaritic texts known in 1968 "are neither hymns nor prayers" and therefore not

13. P. Xella, "ḥtp = 'uccidere, annientare' in Giobbe 9, 12," *Henoch* 1 (1977) 337–41; idem, "Un testo ugaritico recente (RS 24:266, verso, 9–19) e il 'sacrificio dei primi nati'," *Rivista di Studi Fenici* 6 (1978) 127–36; idem, *I Testi Rituali di Ugarit, I: Testi* (Studi Semitici 54; Rome: Herder, 1981) 25–34.

14. Y. Avishur, "Prayer to Baal," *Shnaton* 3 (1978–79) 254–62 [Heb.; Eng. summary, pp. xxv–xxvi].

15. B. Margalit, "A Ugaritic Prayer for a City under Siege," *Proceedings of the Seventh World Congress of Jewish Studies: Studies in the Bible and the Ancient Near East* (Jerusalem: World Union of Jewish Studies, 1981) 63–83, esp. 76–77 and 83 [Heb.; based on his lecture of 1977].

16. J. C. de Moor, "Enkele liturgische teksten uit Ugarit," *Schrijvend Verleden: Documenten uit het oude Nabije Oosten vertaald en toegelicht* (ed. K. R. Veenhof; Leiden: Ex Oriente Lux / Zutphen: Terra, 1983) 247–52, esp. 251–52.

17. F. Saracino, "A State of Siege: Mi 5:4–5 and an Ugaritic Prayer," ZAW 93 (1983) 263–69.

18. W. G. E. Watson, *Classical Hebrew Poetry: A Guide to Its Techniques* (JSOTSup 26; Sheffield: JSOT Press, 1984) 360–26, esp. 361 and n. 9. Cf. above, n. 13.

19. J. M. Sasson, "Human Sacrifice and Circumcision," *BARev* 13/2 (1987) 12–15, 60, esp. 60.

prima facie bases for comparison with biblical Psalms,[20] welcomed the newly-published prayer to Baal as "all the more important." His study of the text is particularly valuable because it is based on collations made with a binocular microscope by Dennis Pardee that support the reading *ḥtp*, albeit with some doubt implied for the third letter.[21] The same collation, it may be added, leaves a restoration *⸢d⸣kr* quite as plausible as *⸢b⸣kr* in the preceding line which, as in Sasson's scansion of the text (above), is parallel to *ḥtp*.[22] Hence a translation 'a male animal' is possible here, in preference to the 'firstborn son' (of a human being) that had been suggested by those invoking the Moabite and Egyptian parallels.[23] Miller translated *ḥtp* by 'a sacrifice' without further comment.

Pardee and Bordreuil rendered the Ugaritic term as 'food-offering' in 1992, Avishur as 'sacrifice' in 1994.[24] Dietrich, Loretz, and Sanmartín read *ḥtp* in 1995, leaving no doubt about the first letter and some about the third.[25]

The Egyptian reliefs adduced by Spalinger in connection with the Ugaritic prayer have also come in for renewed attention. Stager identified the relief in Spalinger's fig. 2 as a stele of Merneptah, not of Rameses II, and as picturing the Egyptian siege of Ashkelon, with the king of Ashkelon sacrificing his own son in a gesture of ultimate desperation.[26] He was basing himself on the work of Yurco, who has since given his own reasons for assigning the stele to Merneptah, and reproduced the relief showing the siege of Ashkelon.[27]

Spalinger had noted three children shown in three different positions on the relief. Hoffmeier added the interesting suggestion that "these depictions represent a sequence of events. A child is shown to the besiegers, it is slain

20. W. W. Hallo, "Individual Prayer in Sumerian," *JAOS* 88 (1968) 71–89, esp. 72.

21. P. D. Miller, Jr., "Prayer and Sacrifice in Ugarit and Israel," in *Text and Context: Old Testament and Semitic Studies for F. C. Fensham* (ed. W. Classen; JSOTSup 48; Sheffield: JSOT Press, 1988) 139–55.

22. Ibid., 147.

23. Cf. especially above, n. 15; below, at nn. 28–31.

24. D. Pardee and P. Bordreuil, "Ugarit: Texts and Literature," *ABD* 6.706–21, esp. 708; Y. Avishur, *Studies in Hebrew and Ugaritic Psalms* (Jerusalem: Magnes, 1994) 253–67, esp. 255, 261–62 and nn. 44–46. Cf. the review-article by O. Loretz, "Zur Zitat-Vernetzung zwischen Ugarit-Texten und Psalmen," *UF* 26 (1994) 225–43, esp. 239. See also below, n. 47.

25. M. Dietrich, O. Loretz, and J. Sanmartín, *The Cuneiform Alphabetic Texts from Ugarit, Ras ibn Hani and Other Places* (KTU; 2d. enlarged ed.; Abhandlungen zur Literatur Alt-Syrien–Palästinas 8; Münster: Ugarit-Verlag, 1995) 134.

26. L. E. Stager, "Merenptah, Israel and Sea Peoples: New Light on an Old Relief," *ErIsr* 18 (Avigad Volume; 1985) 56*–64*, esp. 57*.

27. Frank J. Yurco, "3,200-Year-Old Picture of Israelites Found in Egypt," *BARev* 16/5 (1990) 20–38, esp. 28–29.

in full view, and then the corpse is thrown down for the enemy to see."[28]

Spalinger had sought to buttress his arguments by appeal to 2 Kgs 3:26–27a:

> Seeing that the battle was going against him, the king of Moab led an attempt of seven hundred swordsmen to break through to the king of Edom; but they failed. So he took his firstborn son, who was to succeed him as king, and offered him up on the wall as a burnt offering. (NJPSV)

In this he was preceded by Derchain and followed by Margalit.[29] But it is worth noting the rabbinic view (Qimḥi, Gersonides, Abarbanel), according to which the biblical passage means that Mesha sacrificed not his own son but the son of the king of Edom, whom he had previously captured; this would justify the prophetic condemnation of Moab as the one who "burned the bones of the king of Edom to lime" (Amos 2:1).[30] The resultant "great wrath . . . upon Israel" (2 Kgs 3:27b) has also been variously interpreted and attributed.[31]

Finally, Spalinger had called attention to a possible Egyptian cognate, *ḥtp*(*w*). This word occurs in the "cuneiform vocabulary of Egyptian words" from El Amarna first published in 1925 by Smith and Gadd and now numbered EA 368 by Rainey.[32] This lexical text has been described by Artzi as a "practical vocabulary"[33] dealing (in lines 5–11) with "the (royal) house and its furniture."[34] In line 11, Egyptian *ḫa-tà*(DA)*-pu* is equated with Sumerian GIŠ.BANŠUR 'table'. The table as offering table recurs both in Akkadian and in Biblical Hebrew.[35]

28. James K. Hoffmeier, "Further Evidence for Infant Sacrifice in the Ancient Near East," *BARev* 13/2 (1987) 60–61.

29. P. Derchain, "Les plus ancients témoignages de sacrifices d'enfants chez les Sémites occidentaux," *VT* 20 (1970) 351–55; Margalit, "A Ugaritic Prayer," 72–73; idem, "Why King Mesha of Moab Sacrificed His Eldest Son," *BARev* 12/6 (1986) 62–64, 76.

30. Cf. M. Cogan and H. Tadmor, *II Kings: A New Translation with Introduction and Commentary* (AB 11; Garden City, N.Y.: Doubleday, 1988) 47–48. Cf. also B. Aaronson, "Whose Son Was Sacrificed?" *BARev* 16/3 (1990) 62, 67.

31. Cogan and Tadmor, *II Kings,* 47–48; J. J. M. Roberts, "Nebuchadnezzar's Elamite Crisis in Theological Perspective," in *Essays in Memory of Jacob J. Finkelstein* (ed. M. de-J. Ellis; Hamden, Conn.: Archon, 1977) 183–87, esp. 184–85 n. 25.

32. S. Smith and C. J. Gadd, "A Cuneiform Vocabulary of Egyptian Words," *JEA* 11 (1925) 230–39; A. F. Rainey, *El Amarna Tablets 359–379* (AOAT 8; Neukirchen-Vluyn: Neukirchener Verlag, 1970) 34–35.

33. P. Artzi, "Observations on the 'Library' of the Amarna Archives," in *Cuneiform Archives and Libraries* (ed. K. R. Veenhof; CRRAI 30; Leiden: Nederlands Historisch-Archaeologisch Instituut te Istanbul, 1986) 210–12, esp. 211.

34. Idem, "Studies in the Library of the Amarna Archive," *Bar-Ilan Studies in Assyriology Dedicated to Pinḥas Artzi* (ed. J. Klein and A. Skaist; Ramat Gan: Bar-Ilan University Press, 1990) 139–56, esp. 141–42.

35. AHw, s.v. *paššūru*; W. W. Hallo, *The Book of the People* (BJS 225; Atlanta: Scholars Press, 1991) 64–65.

To the extent that these parallels, both Egyptian and biblical, truly illustrate a situation as described in the Ugaritic prayer, they may be said to lend support to Margalit's reading of the latter text. But its context, both the wider one and the immediate one, militates against the emendation. The rest of the text deals in ordinary rather than extraordinary sacrifices, and even the poem that concludes the text concerns the not overly uncommon contingency of a siege.[36] Moreover, the strict parallelism of the verbs suggests a rough equivalence of the first image with the third and of the second with the fourth, as in Sasson's paraphrase (above), not of the first with the second and the third with the fourth, as in Margalit's translation. One does not 'pay' a son as one would a vow, yet that is the sense of *mlʾ* in the second and fourth images, comparable to Hebrew *šlm* used of paying vows. And if the 'firstborn' of the third image is correctly restored and is parallel to the 'bull' of the first, then a firstling of the flock is more likely than a firstborn of a human being. Finally, moving from bull to vow to (firstborn) son, the fifth image would be anticlimactic, even if we understood it, with Margalit, as 'a tenth (of our wealth)'. Thus it is not surprising that the consensus of Ugaritic scholarship accepts the reading *ḥtp* and the comparison with Akkadian *ḫitpu*.

One question that has barely been addressed in all these discussions is the phonemic one. Only Margalit pointed out that "attempts to interpret Ugaritic Ḥ-T-P as the equivalent of Akkadian Ḫ-T-P are highly improbable on purely phonological grounds," and Xella noted the difficulties involved.[37] These difficulties may be stated simply. Normally, Ugaritic (and proto-Semitic) Ḫ is reflected by Akkadian Ḫ, while Ugaritic Ḥ is reflected by Akkadian zero or, more precisely, by an ablaut *e* for original *a* and, in Assyrian, also for original *i*. This is particularly evident in initial position. The following examples will illustrate the correspondences:

Ugaritic	Akkadian
ḫdw	*ḫadû* ('to rejoice')
ḫṭ	*ḫaṭṭu* ('scepter')
ḫṭʾ	*ḫaṭû* ('to sin')
ḫlq	*ḫalāqu* ('to perish')
ḫmš	*ḫamiš* ('five')
ḫnzr	*ḫuzīru* ('pig')
ḫss	*ḫasāsu* ('to bethink')
ḫpṯ	*ḫupšu* ('a class of soldiers')

36. Cf. Xella, "Un testo ugaritico," 135.

37. Margalit, "Why King Mesha of Moab. . . ," 76 n. 3; cf. idem, "A Ugaritic Prayer," 76–77 and 83 n. 4; Xella, "Un testo ugaritico," 135.

ḥbr	*ibru* (Ass. *ebru*) ('friend')
ḥdṯ	*edēšu* ('to be or become new')
ḥmr	*imēru* (Ass. *emāru*) ('donkey')
ḥnn	*enēnu* ('to be gracious')
ḥrr	*erēru* ('to be scorched'; cf. the divine name Erra)
ḥrṯ	*erēšu* ('to plow, cultivate')

But there are also occasional examples of a correspondence between Ugaritic Ḥ and Akkadian Ḫ, as in *ḥwš* for *ḫiāšu* 'hurry' or in *rḥṣ* 'wash' for *raḫāṣu* 'flood'.[38] In the case of *ḥkm* for *ḫakāmu* and *ḥrm* for *ḫarāmu*, the possibility of Amorite influence has been suggested by Lambert in connection with Akkadian *ḫarimtu* 'prostitute',[39] while the whole subject has been reviewed by Stern from a comparative Semitic point of view in connection with Hebrew *ḥerem* 'ban'.[40]

There is also the possibility of a late or learned loanword from West Semitic into Akkadian.[41] The existence of an Akkadian root *ḫatāpu* in Old Babylonian texts from Elam makes this a less likely solution. There may even be such a root already in the North Semitic dialect of Ebla, to judge by entry no. 252 in the great Vocabulary of Ebla.[42]

A subsidiary question is that of the second root letter. Several Semitic languages have a root *ḥṭp* with a meaning close to that of *ḥtp*. If the root with emphatic dental is original, the loss of this emphatic may represent a special case of "Geers' Law," according to which Akkadian, and to some extent other Semitic languages, cannot tolerate two emphatics in one root.[43] It

38. P. Fronzaroli, *La Fonetica Ugaritica* (Sussidi Eruditi 7; Rome: Edizioni di Storia e Letteratura, 1955) 18; M. Held, "The Action-Result (Factitive-Passive) Sequence of Identical Verbs in Biblical Hebrew and Ugaritic," *JBL* 84 (1967) 272–82, esp. 277 n. 26; references courtesy Mark S. Smith. Cf. in general E. Salonen, "Über den Laut H im Akkadischen," *StudOr* 46 (1975) 291–99.

39. W. G. Lambert, "Prostitution," *Aussenseiter und Randgruppen: Beiträge zu einer Sozialgeschichte des Alten Orients* (ed. V. Haas; Xenia 32; Konstanz: Universitätsverlag, 1992) 127–61, esp. 138.

40. P. D. Stern, *The Biblical* ḥerem: *A Window on Israel's Religious Experience* (BJS 211; Atlanta: Scholars Press, 1991) chap. 1: pp. 5–17 .

41. Avishur (*Studies*, 261 n. 45) notes that "*ḥ*/*ḫ* interchanges are occasionally attested, particularly in Northwest Semitic terms which were absorbed into Akkadian" (citing Xella, "Un testo," 135).

42. G. Pettinato, *Testi lessicali bilingui della biblioteca L. 2769* (Materiali Epigrafici di Ebla 4; Naples: Istituto Universitario Orientale, 1982) 227; cf. Joachim Krecher, in *Il Bilinguismo à Ebla* (ed. L. Cagni; Naples: Istituto Universitario Orientale, 1984) 154 n. 109.

43. F. W. Geers, "The Treatment of Emphatics in Akkadian," *JNES* 4 (1945) 65–67; cf. E. E. Knudsen, "Cases of Free Variants in the Akkadian *q* Phoneme," *JCS* 15 (1961) 84–90.

must be added at once, however, that /ḫṭp/ contains only one emphatic, and that the sequences /ḫṭ/ and /ṭp/ can both occur in Akkadian.[44]

More recent research has illuminated both phonological questions. Tropper has identified additional examples of Proto-Semitic and Ugaritic *ḥ* cognate with Akkadian *ḫ* and the phonological environments in which the correspondence occurs.[45] Cohen has tried to apply Geers's Law to certain anomalous items in the Hebrew lexicon.[46]

All in all, the existence of a Ugaritic *ḥtp* and its possible relationship to (late) Akkadian *ḫitpu* remain somewhat uncertain. But the importance of both terms in their respective cultic contexts would seem to justify the persistent attention they have received in the scholarly literature.[47]

44. Cf. E. Reiner, *A Linguistic Analysis of Akkadian* (The Hague: Mouton, 1966) 39–41, 50–51, for nonoccurring "consonant clusters."

45. J. Tropper, "Akkadisch *nuḫḫutu* und die Repräsentierung des Phonems /ḥ/ im Akkadischen," ZA 85 (1995) 58–66.

46. C. Cohen, "The Law of Dissimilation in Akkadian (the Geers Law) and Its Ramifications for Biblical Hebrew Lexicography," lecture at Yale University, February 19, 1996, now published in *Hebrew through the Ages: In Memory of Shoshanna Bahat* (ed. M. Bar-Asher; Studies in Language 2; Jerusalem: Academy of the Hebrew Language, 1997) 29–45 [Heb.].

47. Cf. most recently G. del Olmo Lete, "The Sacrificial Vocabulary at Ugarit," *SEL* 12 (1995) 37–49; del Olmo Lete, however, regards the conclusion of KTU 1.119 as a psalm, not a ritual text, and therefore relegates ḤTP to "the general vocabulary" (p. 48 and n. 69). Pardee offers new translations of the prayer in "Poetry in Ugaritic Ritual Texts," in *Verse in Ancient Near Eastern Prose* (ed J. C. de Moor and W. G. E. Watson; AOAT 42; Neukirchen-Vluyn: Neukirchener Verlag, 1993) 207–18, esp. 213–17, and in *The Context of Scripture, vol. I: Canonical Compositions from the Biblical World* (ed. W. W. Hallo and K. L. Younger, Jr.; Leiden: Brill, 1997) 283–85, rendering the word 'a *ḥtp*-offering'.

Un anneau inscrit du Bronze Récent à Megiddo

Émile Puech
CNRS—École Biblique et Archéologique Française de Jérusalem

Au milieu de poteries du BM II et du BR II et d'objets en bronze, cuivre, or, argent, fer et pierre trouvés en 1931 dans la tombe 912 B au sud-est de Tell el-Mutesellim—Megiddo (carré V 17), fut découvert un anneau en or (ou en électrum mais à haute proportion en or), n° M 2992.[1]

En guise de chaton, cet anneau d'environ 1,9 à 2 cm de diamètre porte une surface étalée, oblongue et courbe, divisée en trois registres par des lignes gravées (voir figure 1). Contrairement au registre central délimité par des lignes sensiblement parallèles, les deux registres latéraux sont bordés sur l'extérieur par des lignes en arc de cercle. On remarque cependant que la partie centrale de la ligne extérieure du registre inférieur (ou gauche) fait défaut, apparemment à cause d'une usure plus fortement marquée de ce côté.[2] Chacun des deux registres supérieurs mesure environ 4 mm de largeur, alors que le registre inférieur légèrement plus large mesure un peu plus de 5 mm malgré l'usure dans sa partie centrale. De prime abord, il est difficile de s'assurer de l'ordre de gravure des registres. En effet, comme les lignes qui les délimitent ne sont pas gravées dans les prolongements de la largeur de l'anneau lui-même, on peut se demander si le graveur n'a pas justement commencé par

1. Voir P. L. O. Guy, with contributions by R. M. Engberg, *Megiddo Tombs* (OIP 33; Chicago: University of Chicago Press, 1938). Plan général du tell, p. 3, plan et section de la tombe 912, p. 63, description de la tombe, pp. 69–72, poteries et objets, pls 32–36 et 123–134. Pour l'anneau M 2992, voir pl 128:15 et p. 174, fig. 177 (échelle 2:1). L'objet est exposé au Palestine Archaeological Museum—Rockefeller Museum, salle nord, vitrine LL, n° 1228.

2. On peut comparer la description donnée dans le catalogue, pl. 128:15: "intact," et celle des éditeurs, W. A. Irwin et R. A. Bowman, dans Guy, *Megiddo Tombs*, 173–76, en particulier p. 174: ". . . part of the lower edge of the bezel is entirely worn away."

FIGURE 1. Dessin de l'anneau de Megiddo (d'après Guy, *Megiddo Tombs*, p. 174).

graver le registre "inférieur" en remplissant les deux autres à l'aide de motifs divers. Dans le cas contraire, il aurait réservé une surface de largeur légèrement plus grande pour le registre devant porter l'inscription. Mais vu l'orientation des motifs des autres registres, on désigne arbitrairement comme registre supérieur le registre extérieur non inscrit.

Le registre médian est composé d'un décor floral stylisé, une série de sept palmettes(?), où les trois motifs centraux sont composés de 6 à 7 traits ou branches, et les deux latéraux de 4 traits ou branches, le graveur disposant aux extrêmes des traits parallèles isolés (on sait en effet l'*horror vacui* des graveurs) et des traits perpendiculaires de délimitation du/es registre(s) (2,5 cm entre ces deux traits). Le petit trait, à gauche, perpendiculaire à la ligne inférieure et à la ligne délimitant les deux registres, a sûrement cette signification. Il devrait en être de même à droite avec le ou les deux trait(s) perpendiculaire(s) aux lignes du registre médian. On ne peut donc aucunement y lire une lettre isolée, à plus forte raison comme étant la première d'une inscription, ainsi que l'ont tenté les éditeurs pour qui l'interprétation semble l'avoir emporté sur l'observation.[3]

3. Ibid., 174:

> At first glance the legend appears to be confined to the lowest register, but faint ladder-like traces at the extreme right in the second register, almost on the band of the ring, look very much like worn remains of the letter ח. It seems clear in the enlarged photograph (see Fig. 177) but, perhaps due to faulty impression, is so faint as to be almost invisible in the cast. Since these lines do not resemble the characteristic 'floral' motif of the second register it is possible that they represent a letter. If this be the case the reading of the legend is aided, for it begins otherwise with a meaningless single letter followed by what is probably a word divider. Just why the first letter should be in the line above the rest of the legend is uncertain. If the legend read from left to right it could easily be explained by the hypothesis of crowding at the end, but it is unlikely that the legend, if semitic, is to be read in that direction.

Et p. 176: "The interpretation is aided if ח is to be read before the first letter (ג) in the bottom register, for then one might find in the חג some word for 'ring,' related perhaps to Hebrew חוּג, 'circle.'"

Le registre supérieur est très difficilement identifiable étant donné la gravure et sans doute aussi en partie l'usure de la surface, il s'agit probablement d'un décor animalier, un quadrupède: genre de crocodile(?) ou un insecte: sauterelle(?), passant à gauche.[4] En faveur de la sauterelle, on peut invoquer le trait oblique indiquant la tête, les pattes et les deux élytres ou/et ailes dont l'épaisseur serait signifiée par les deux traits au-dessus des deux palmettes à droite qui coupent la ligne de séparation des registres.

Dans le registre inférieur, des lettres sont nettement gravées à l'aide d'un poinçon ou burin, sans que bien souvent les segments ne se touchent. Cela pourrait être dû, en partie du moins, à l'usure de la surface pour des traits faiblement gravés autant qu'à la qualité de la gravure d'une surface restreinte (longueur maximale 2,2 cm). La méthode de gravure pourrait rappeler quelque peu celle de la coupe de Tekke (Cnossos) en Crète,[5] quoique le bronze de la coupe soit en métal plus résistant que l'or et qu'il nécessite l'usage d'un burin. Il est clair que cet art de la gravure auquel semble s'ajouter une certaine usure de la surface peut dérouter le lecteur ou déchiffreur.

Convaincus de lire une inscription sémitique, les éditeurs ont proposé un déchiffrement de droite à gauche en incluant, malgré les apparences graphiques qu'ils ont relevées (voir n. 3), une première lettre à droite dans le registre médian, *ḥet*. Ce *ḥet*, à rapprocher du *gimel* qui est préférable à une lecture *pe* ou même *dalet* si on y joignait le trait séparateur, permettrait de lire un premier mot, חוג. Puis ils lisent un *lamed* presque certain, *nun*, *šin* et *taw* suivi d'un trait séparateur ou d'un trait accidentel. Le mot suivant est plus difficile. Plutôt que *nun* précédé d'un (deuxième?) trait séparateur, ils ont retenu *reš* suivi d'un autre *reš* avec un autre trait séparateur ou mieux *bet* et enfin un *ʾalep* certain. Ne tenant pas compte des probables traits séparateurs, écrivent-ils, il est alors possible de lire de gauche à droite au registre inférieur: גלנשתרבא. Mais lue en dextrograde, cette séquence ne donne aucune combinaison vraisemblable en sémitique. Puisque on s'attend à lire le nom du propriétaire, le *lamed* introduirait ce nom "appartenant à NP." D'une part, comme la tombe a fourni des scarabées égyptiens, un sceau hurrite (de type

4. Cela serait d'autant plus vraisemblable que le wadi ez-Zarqa qui se dirige vers l'ouest mais qui avec le wadi Ara assure le passage vers Leǧǧun—Megiddo, se nomme "wadi des crocodiles," *naḥal Tanninîm* qui, au dire des Anciens, était infesté de crocodiles, voir Pseudo-Scylax, Strabon, Pline l'Ancien, etc. Une ville au nord de Césarée, située sur les rives du wadi (*fuit oppidum Crocodilon, est flumen*—Pline) est identifiée soit à Tell Mubarak—Mevorak, soit à Tell el-Malat—Tanninîm, voir F. M. Abel, *Géographie de la Palestine* (Paris: Lecoffre, 1933–38) 1.470–71 et carte IV, 2.143; E. Stern, *Excavations at Tel Mevorak (1973–1976)*, part 1: *From the Iron Age to the Roman Period* (Qedem 9; Jerusalem: Israel Exploration Society, 1978) 1–2. Pour une sauterelle, voir le sceau de *ḥmn* de Megiddo, D. Diringer, *Le iscrizioni antico-ebraiche palestinesi* (Firenze: Università degli studi di Firenze, 1934) 165–67 et tav. xix:3.

5. Voir É. Puech, "Origine de l'alphabet," *RB* 93 (1986) 161–213, en particulier 168–170 avec la bibliographie.

Nuzi), de la poterie mycénienne et cananéenne, la possibilité est trop grande d'avoir affaire à des noms d'origine non sémitiques. D'autre part, la gravure aussi grossière des lettres à laquelle s'ajoute la distribution singulière des traits séparateurs[6] rend la lecture finale très incertaine. Toutefois, l'interprétation serait facilitée si on lisait un *ḥet* avant le *gimel.*[7] Le *lamed* est encore probablement la préposition indiquant le propriétaire suivi de l'anthroponyme, ou moins vraisemblablement d'un titre. En définitive, écrivent-ils, l'anneau défie toute traduction et doit rester, du moins pour le moment, dans le domaine des conjectures.[8]

Trente ans plus tard, Albright a fait une nouvelle proposition. Lire probablement *l-ʾšt bky* 'à la femme de Bikay', en acceptant toujours une lecture de droite à gauche mais sans expliquer ses choix pour le moins surprenants, ni se poser des questions de vraisemblance.[9] Sans doute, une bague en or ne déparerait pas le doigt d'une femme, mais la dimension paraît un peu grande. Aussi, ses disciples qui n'ont pas relevé cet argument ou détail, se sont-ils contentés de retenir la seule lettre qui soit de lecture vraisemblable, *šin*,[10] que d'aucun par la suite n'ose même pas retenir, préférant considérer l'ensemble comme une pseudo-inscription.[11]

On peut toutefois ne pas partager un tel jugement et essayer tout de même de comprendre le message que le graveur a voulu signifier et transmettre, comme nous l'avons tenté pour les deux autres registres.[12] Le sens de lecture et donc de gravure pourrait nous être donné par l'orientation du *šin*

6. Ces traits isolent la première lettre, *gimel*, rendent invraisemblable la séquence *bet-ʾalep*, et laissent isolé le *reš*: ג.לנשת.ר.בא.

7. Voir ci-dessus, note 3, et nos remarques sur la gravure du registre médian, mettant en doute une telle lecture.

8. Irwin and Bowman, dans Guy, *Megiddo Tombs*, 176.

9. W. F. Albright, *The Proto-Sinaitic Inscriptions and Their Decipherment* (HTS 22; Cambridge: Harvard University Press, 1966) 11: "(. . . found with pottery from final phase of Late Bronze II, second half of 13th century). Read probably *l-ʾšt Bky*, 'belonging to the wife of Bikay' ('Man of the Mastix Tree'; the tree is Heb. *bākāʾ*, Eg. *bikaʾ*, with the personal name *Bikaʾi*, etc. well attested in 13th century Egyptian)."

10. Voir F. M. Cross et P. K. McCarter, "Two Archaic Inscriptions on Clay Objects from Byblus," *Rivista di Studi Fenici* 1 (1973) 3–8, en particulier p. 8 et p. 7, fig. 2: "M?".

11. B. Sass, *The Genesis of the Alphabet and Its Development in the Second Millenium* [sic] B.C. (Ägypten und Altes Testament 13; Wiesbaden: Harrassowitz, 1988) 101 et fig. 264–66. "The form of one of the signs is identical to the Proto-Canaanite vertical *shin* (Cross and McCarter), but since the rest of the signs cannot be identified, there is no way of knowing whether this resemblance is accidental or not. For this reason, I prefer to regard these signs as a pseudo-inscription." Les meilleures pages du livre restent les reproductions photographiques.

12. Nous n'avions pas retenu cette inscription dans notre étude en *RB* ("Origine de l'alphabet," n. 5) parce que, bien que conscient d'avoir affaire à une inscription, nous n'avions pas alors de solution pertinente à proposer. L'utilisation des signes restait donc insignifiante pour notre propos.

vers la droite. Dans les inscriptions cananéennes passées de l'écriture verticale à l'écriture horizontale, on remarque que lorsque la lettre n'est pas restée couchée sur les deux arcs de cercle ou sur ses deux pointes comme elle l'était dans l'écriture verticale, elle a adopté la direction de l'écriture—lecture: soit vers la droite dans les inscriptions de l'aiguière de Lakish, du bol de Qubur el-Walaydah,[13] soit vers la gauche dans les inscriptions des bols de Lakish ou de l'ostracon de Beth Shemesh (verso, si on lit horizontalement en suivant le bord supérieur du tesson). Dans ce cas, nous aurions affaire à une inscription horizontale à lire de gauche à droite selon une écriture dextrograde. Sinon nous avons affaire à une écriture verticale comme il arrive sur les anses d'objets par exemple et, dans ce cas encore, l'écriture et la lecture allant de haut en bas, on retrouve la même direction. Il reste donc à exploiter ce sens de la gravure qui est juste à l'opposé des deux précédentes tentatives de déchiffrement.

La première lettre ressemble à un *ʾalep* des XIIIe–XIe siècles (ostracon de Beth Shemesh, flèches d'el-Khadr ou cônes de Byblos par exemple); pour cette lettre on accepte donc l'identification des éditeurs et non celle d'Albright. Il semble même que le trait de la bordure externe du registre ait été tracé après la gravure de la lettre, ce qui favoriserait la thèse de la gravure de ce registre en dernier. La deuxième lettre, en triangle 'couché' avec un des côtés un peu plus long que les deux autres, doit être un *dalet* comparable à l'ensemble des *dalet* de cette période. La lettre suivante est formée de trois traits en zigzag et non jointifs, en dessous et à droite (ou à gauche et légèrement en dessous dans une écriture verticale). Il ne peut s'agir que d'un *nun* que ce soit dans une écriture horizontale ou verticale. La lettre suivante composée d'une tête triangulaire à peu près fermée et d'une longue haste est un *bet* dans l'une ou l'autre écriture, horizontale ou verticale, comparer le *bet* de l'ostracon de Beth Shemesh (recto) et du sceau-cylindre d'Arqa, ou des bols de Lakish.[14] Jouxtant la tête triangulaire du *bet*, est gravé très probablement un trait séparateur.

Vient ensuite un signe en forme de X (non une croix ou "+") mais dont l'axe principal est nettement plus long et qu'accompagne un trait oblique non entièrement conservé en dessous ou à sa gauche. Cette lettre semble devoir être lue *yod*, comparer les *yod* de l'inscription de l'aiguière de Lakish, en dextrograde, avec la partie du bras en haut, non en bas à gauche comme dans ce cas (image inversée) ou ceux de l'ostracon d'Izbet Ṣarṭah en écriture semi-verticale. Mais la rotation de 180° ne saurait changer la valeur du signe.[15] La

13. Voir ibid., 173–80. Ajouter peut-être le tesson de Tell eṣ-Ṣarem (support fénestré), si on adopte une écriture horizontale au-dessus du bord de la fenêtre.

14. Voir ibid., 173–84 et 191. On peut lire le recto de cet ostracon en écriture verticale ou horizontale de gauche à droite et le verso en écriture verticale ou horizontale de droite à gauche, voir *infra* n. 32.

15. En *RB*, ibid., nous avons montré que les XIIIe–XIIe siècles englobent la période pendant laquelle on assiste au passage de l'alphabet long (de 27 + 3 ou de 28

lecture *yod* semble préférable à celle d'un *nun* qu'on pourrait imaginer en ne tenant pas compte du "trait séparateur," mais le trait inférieur serait encore en surnombre et le trait médian coupant la haste (X) serait bien gauchement tracé. Après le *šin* à droite, de lecture certaine, la lettre à traits en zigzag doit être un *mem* qui, à première vue, peut paraître incomplet. Mais comme le graveur ne peut imiter exactement le tracé du *šin* précédent sous peine de totale confusion, il semble avoir, par faute d'espace,[16] astucieusement compensé les deux traits manquants du 'zigzag' par un trait vertical et un appendice, tout contre, à droite (ou en dessous); le *mem* serait ainsi en partie désarticulé.[17] Par ailleurs, un tel tracé ne déparerait pas trop l'image mentale du *mem* qu'en avaient les scribes des inscriptions en cunéiformes alphabétiques, deux coins perpendiculaires ou à angle légèrement obtus. La dernière lettre est faite de quatre traits formant losange mais dont l'un d'entre eux se confond avec le tracé discontinu de la bordure externe, et d'un petit trait en forme de bissectrice de l'angle obtus supérieur. Cette lettre ne peut être qu'un *ʿaïn* dans lequel la pupille est signifiée par ce petit trait.[18] On obtient alors une lecture tout à fait acceptable, pour ne pas dire certaine: אדן ב(ן) וישמע.

Ce déchiffrement permet d'affirmer que le registre inscrit a bien été gravé en dernier. On peut invoquer pour cela: la disposition du *nun* légèrement décalé en dessous, ou à gauche, du *dalet*, l'espace disponible trop restreint cause de dislocation du *mem*, un trait du *ʿaïn* faisant double emploi avec la ligne de bordure, ainsi que le tracé discontinu de la bordure inférieure gravé dans les intervalles (voir *ʾalep* et *ʿaïn*) comparé à celui en continu du registre supérieur, ou enfin la gravure des autres motifs indiquant un haut et un bas.[19]

---

lettres) à l'alphabet court (22 lettres) et où se cherche la direction de l'écriture, que ce soit en écriture linéaire ou en cunéiformes alphabétiques. Voir aussi F. M. Cross, "The Evolution of the Proto-Canaanite Alphabet," *BASOR* 134 (1954) 15–24, en particulier, pp. 21–22.

16. Pour des *mem* incomplets faute d'espace, voir par exemple ceux de l'inscription de la coupe de Tekke (Cnossos), Puech, "Origine de l'alphabet," 168–71.

17. Sur le cône B de Byblos, le trait inférieur (ou cinquième trait) du *mem* est aussi quelque peu déplacé à gauche et, avec le quatrième, il ne serait pas sans rappeler le 'trait avec son appendice' de Megiddo, voir J. Teixidor, "An Archaic Inscription from Byblos," *BASOR* 225 (1977) 70–71. (A la figure 2, nous avons ajouté dans la case du *mem* la disposition que nous pensons être l'image mentale originelle de la lettre non gravée en tant que telle, faute d'espace.)

18. Comparer le *ʿaïn* de l'inscription de la coupe de Tekke (Cnossos), voir Puech, "Origine de l'alphabet," 168–71.

19. Le déchiffrement récemment proposé de cet anneau par B. E. Colless, dans "The Syllabic Inscriptions of Byblos: Miscellaneous Texts," *Abr-Nahrain* 34 (1997) 42–57, spécialement 45–46, comme inscription pseudo-hiéroglyphique utilisant l'écriture même des textes de Byblos, est totalement inacceptable. Non seulement il lit tous les trois registres sens dessus dessous, mais encore le résultat obtenu tient de l'invraisemblance. Le signes aux valeurs hypothétiques seraient à lire *nu ḥu ta ma*

Ainsi lue, cette courte inscription gravée sur le chaton de la bague fait bien connaître son propriétaire, mais sans un *lamed* d'appartenance, ainsi que son patronyme et le terme de filiation, אדן ב(ן) | ישמע, lecture paléographiquement préférable à אדן בן(?) שמע. L'assimilation du *nun* de l'élément de filiation *bn*, quand il est exprimé, n'est pas un phénomène rare. Citons par exemple l'inscription en cunéiformes alphabétiques de la lamelle du Tabor vers 1200, *lṣlbˁl b*(*n*) *plṣbˁl* (sans trait séparateur) ou l'ugaritique *bǵlmt* pour *bn ǵlmt* (UT 51 = CTA 4 VII 54).[20] L'assimilation est même un phénomène assez fréquent dans les inscriptions de Byblos, site qui a fourni la plupart des inscriptions connues de cette époque dans la région: voir *b*(*n*) *bd* (cône B),[21] *b*(*n*) *klby* (vase du potier ʿAbdo)[22], *b*(*n*) *yḥymlk* (inscription d'Elibaʿal, ligne 1, et de Shipṭibaʿal, ligne 3).[23] L'assimilation du *nun* devant le *yod* rappelle précisément celle de la lettre dans *b*(*n*) *yḥymlk*, bien que le trait séparateur puisse surprendre dans le cas de l'anneau de Megiddo à une place où on ne l'attendrait apparemment pas. Plus tard, les scribes auront plutôt tendance à mettre une marque de séparation après l'anthroponyme ou, si l'on veut, avant l'élément de filiation que, parfois, ils ne séparent pas du patronyme. Le graveur aurait-il été gauche ou distrait dans la gravure du trait séparateur? Le trait séparateur est-il un signe d'abréviation? Il faut avouer notre ignorance dans ces hautes périodes pour lesquelles nous disposons de trop peu d'éléments de comparaison. Mais une lecture *bn* est paléographiquement difficile à accepter, à plus forte raison une lecture *bt*. Par ailleurs, vu sa dimension, l'anneau a très vraisemblablement appartenu à un homme.

L'anthroponyme אדן 'Adon' est déjà attesté plusieurs fois en cananéo-phénicien, sur une anse de cruche de Sarepta (fin du XIIIe siècle),[24] sur une tablette d'el-Amarna (fin du XIVe siècle), "Aduna roi d'Irqata,"[25] à Ugarit,

---

| *šu ša /mi ma ga du*(?) *da*(?) et à comprendre 'Seal of the name/sceptre of Megiddo'. La conclusion "Accordingly, this gold ring could have been the royal seal of Megiddo, perhaps declaring: 'Sealed. The sceptre of Megiddo', montre l'inanité de cette dernière tentative dont il est inutile de discuter le déchiffrement.

20. La lecture de l'expression a été discutée: C. H. Gordon, *Ugaritic Textbook* (Rome: Pontificium Istitutum Biblicum, 1965) 373, a compris *b(n) ǵlmt* 'son of Ǵalmat' = (the young woman), tandis que *Textes ougaritiques, I: Mythes et légendes* (par A. Caquot, M. Sznycer, et A. Herdner; LAPO 7; Paris: du Cerf, 1974) 219 note w, ont lu *b*(*n*) *ǵlmt* '*des ténébreux*' comme variante et parallèle de *bn ẓlmt* en CTA 8,7–8.

21. Voir M. Dunand, *Fouilles de Byblos* (Paris: Maisonneuve, Texte 1954–58; Atlas 1950) vol. 2, pl. 144, n° 11687.

22. Voir idem, *Biblia Grammata* (Beyrouth: Direction des Antiquités, 1945) 152–53.

23. Voir ibid., 146–47; et idem, *Fouilles de Byblos* (Paris: Geuthner, 1939) 1.17–18.

24. Voir É. Puech, "Nouvelle inscription en alphabet cunéiforme court à Sarepta," *RB* 96 (1989) 338–44.

25. Tablettes E.A. 75,25 et 140,10, voir *Les lettres d'el-Amarna* (traduction de W. L. Moran et al.; LAPO 13; Paris: du Cerf, 1987) 253 et 369.

ʾadn, bn ʾdn,[26] ou encore "Adon, roi d'Eqron"(?), sur un papyrus araméen (fin du 7e siècle) adressé au Pharaon.[27]

Le patronyme n'est pas inconnu, voir en composition *yšmʿʾl, yšmʿyh(w)*, etc., pas même déjà en cananéen et en forme brève, *bn yšmʿ* et *yašmu*.[28] On notera aussi un certain *šmʿ*, serviteur de Jéroboam, gravé sur un sceau retrouvé à Megiddo, **לשמע עבד ירבעם**,[29] que l'on identifie à Jéroboam II.[30]

Quoi qu'il en soit, la lecture de cette inscription nous a ramené dans le milieu sémitique cananéen dominant, à l'exclusion des sphères d'influence égyptienne, hurrite et mycénienne présentes dans la tombe. Cette indication n'est pas sans intérêt pour apprécier et étudier le reste du matériel si riche et varié de la tombe 912 et déterminer l'appartenance ethnique des défunts.

L'étude paléographique de cette courte inscription gravée, comparée à celle du cylindre d'Arqa (milieu du XIVe s.), de l'ostracon de Beth Shemesh (XIIIe s.), des inscriptions de Lakish (XIVe–XIIIe s.), du bol de Qubur el-Walaydah (fin du XIIIe s.), de l'ostracon d'Izbet Ṣarṭah (début du XIIe s.), des flèches inscrites d'el-Khadr (XIIe–XIe s.), des cônes de Byblos (XIe s.),[31] ou même de la coupe de Tekke (XIe s.) donne déjà une datation relative, au mieux entre 1250 et 1150 environ[32] (voir figure 2).[33]

Sans doute le contexte archéologique de la chambre B de la tombe 912 donne-t-il une longue période d'utilisation: matériel du BM II et du BR II.

26. F. Gröndahl, *Die Personennamen der Texte aus Ugarit* (Studia Pohl 1; Rome: Pontificium Istitutum Biblicum, 1967) 361.

27. Voir B. Porten, "The Identity of King Adon," *BA* 44 (1981) 36–52.

28. Voir F. Gröndahl, *Die Personennamen*, 194 et 58; et Gordon, UT, 492 (*s.v.*): *bn yšmʿ*, ^p^*ia-aš-me*[.

29. Voir G. Schumacher et C. Steuernagel, *Tell el-Mutesellim, I. Band: Fundbericht*, A. *Text* (Leipzig: Haupt, 1908) 99–100, fig. 147.

30. Voir Diringer, *Le iscrizioni*, 224–28. G. W. Ahlström, "The Seal of Shemaʿ," *SJOT* 7 (1993) 208–15, essaie de montrer, par le contexte archéologique et la paléographie, que ce sceau a appartenu à un serviteur de Jéroboam I, mais en l'état actuel des données épigraphiques, la paléographie n'autorise certainement pas une datation aussi haute, et le contexte archéologique n'est pas d'un grand secours pour dater un si petit objet quand on sait par l'expérience du terrain le travail souterrain des taupes et autres animaux.

31. Voir Puech, "Origine de l'alphabet," 190–91 (tableau comparatif). Pour les inscriptions de Lakish, voir maintenant idem, "The Canaanite Inscriptions of Lachish and Their Religious Background," *Tel Aviv* 13–14 (1986–87) 13–25.

32. Ces conclusions abaissent d'un siècle celles données par les éditeurs Irwin et Bowman (dans Guy, *Megiddo Tombs*, 175–76), mais la datation proposée pour les inscriptions de référence est beaucoup trop haute, et a été révisée depuis longtemps.

33. Que ce soit pour l'ostracon de Beth-Shemesh ou l'anneau de Megiddo, il est difficile de trancher entre une écriture/gravure verticale ou horizontale. Les deux sont théoriquement possibles et acceptables. C'est pourquoi la figure 2 présente côte à côte les deux possibilités. Les décors floral et animalier des deux autres registres ne peuvent imposer en toute certitude une gravure à l'horizontale, de gauche à droite.

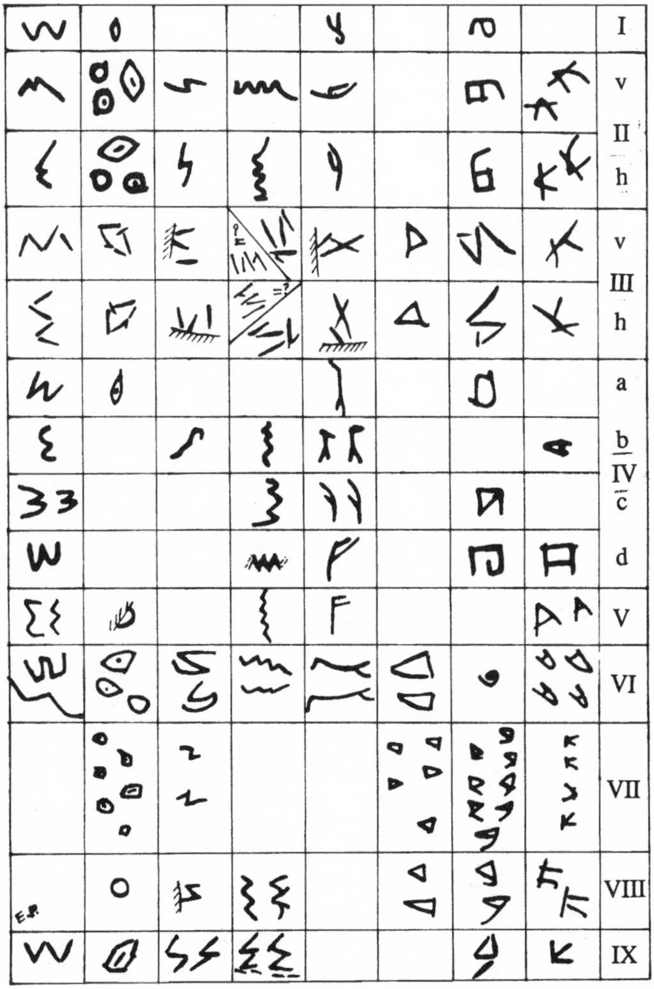

FIGURE 2. Tableau comparatif des huit lettres attestées sur l'anneau de Megiddo: I = cylindre-sceau d'Arqa; II = ostracon de Beth Shemesh (en écriture verticale [v], horizontale [h]); III = anneau de Megiddo (en écriture verticale [v], horizontale [h]), IV = Lakish, bol (a), aiguière (b), bol (c), fragment de bol (d); V = bol de Qubur el-Walaydah; VI = ostracon d'Izbet Ṣarṭah; VII = flèches inscrites d'el-Khadr; VIII = Byblos (cônes a–b); IX = coupe de Tekke.

Comme le contexte du Bronze Moyen II ne peut être pris en considération, reste celui du Bronze Récent II. Les éditeurs acceptent aussi cette solution mais, ajoutent-ils, pas plus tard que le règne de Ramsès II.

Quelques éléments de céramique peuvent cependant permettre de cerner un peu plus précisément la date de fin d'utilisation du locus 912 B (*terminus ad quem*). Le vase à étrier (Guy, pl. 34:22), au décor lustré avec la présence d'une spirale peinte sur le faux goulot et un décor linéaire sur la panse, doit être rangé dans le "style simple" de la classification de Furumark,[34] style qui n'est pas antérieur à Ramsès II et qui est plus ou moins contemporain du Chypriote Récent II C 2 à Enkomi. Postérieur à la destruction du palais de Mycènes (Myc III B 1), ce vase appartient à la phase d'occupation hors les murs ou Mycénien III B 2. Par ailleurs, la production chypriote de la Planche 34 (tombe 912 B) est contemporaine du Myc III B 2, grosso modo pas antérieure aux dernières années du règne de Ramsès II, voire même contemporaine du règne de Merneptah, soit environ de 1230 à 1200.[35] C'est dire que la tombe 912 B a été utilisée dans le XIIIe s. et au moins jusqu'à la fin du siècle, peut-être même un peu après.

Ces indications chronologiques par la céramique correspondent parfaitement aux conclusions obtenues par la paléographie qui, vu la gravure pas très soignée et le nombre limité d'inscriptions pour la comparaison, suggérait déjà une datation vers 1250–1150, de préférence dans le XIIIe siècle. Dans ce cas, l'anneau a appartenu à un Cananéen de Megiddo dans la deuxième moitié du XIIIe siècle, plus probablement même vers la fin du siècle.

Ce déchiffrement de l'anneau de Megiddo apporte une indication non sans importance. D'une part, il fait connaître la première inscription cananéenne trouvée sur le site,[36] et vient ainsi grossir le nombre très restreint des témoignages de l'écriture sémitique en alphabet linéaire au deuxième millénaire dans le nord Canaan, lequel deviendra, dans les Xe–VIIIe siècles avant J.-C., le royaume d'Israël.[37] D'autre part, il permet d'attribuer

34. Voir A. Furumark, *Mycenaean Pottery, I: Analysis and Classification*, et *II: Chronology* (2e ed.; Stockholm: Svenska Institutet i Athen, 1972) 1.522–23, 2.116–18.

35. Je remercie Mme. J. Balensi pour la discussion et le traitement de ces aspects de chronologie de la céramique mycénienne. Ces conclusions abaissent quelque peu la datation retenue par les éditeurs et par l'étude d'Albright, *The Proto-Sinaitic Inscriptions*.

36. Pour des inscriptions du premier millénaire, voir le sceau de "Shéma, serviteur de Jéroboam (II)," et dans Diringer, *Le iscrizioni*: sceaux n° 3 (p. 165); n° 7 (p. 168); inscription n° 12 (p. 301), et S. Moscati, *L'epigrafia ebraica antica 1935–1950* (Rome: Pontificium Institutum Biblicum, 1951) inscription n° 1 (p. 111) mais lire *lyw*, avec H. G. May, "An Inscribed Jar from Megiddo," *AJSL* 50 (1933–34) 10–14.

37. Voir Puech, "Origine de l'alphabet": Ḥaṣor]*lt*[(p. 173, fig. 4:2), Tell eṣ-Ṣarem (p. 183, fig. 6:2), Sichem (non déchiffrées, p. 183, fig. 6: 8 et 9), l'anse de Raddana, *ʾḥl*[(p. 173, fig. 4:4), Izbet Ṣarṭah, alphabet et séquences de lettres (p. 171, fig. 3) et Gezer,]*klb*[(p. 183:6). Mais on ne peut rien tirer des sceaux dernièrement qualifiés de "philistins," O. Keel, "Philistine 'Anchor' Seals," *IEJ* 44 (1994) 21–35, n°s 2 et 6 à Megiddo et 9–10 à Akko et Tell Keisân. Le n° 2 semble imiter grossièrement une palette de jeu, le n° 6 porte le dessin d'un personnage dans la position de l'"image-hiéroglyphe" de la lettre *he* en proto-cananéen, mais il est impossible de dater correctement ce type d'objet en stratigraphie (strat. VIA–XIe s. étant le *terminus ad*

avec certitude à une famille cananéenne, Adon, fils d'Yišmaʿ, la jouissance de la tombe 912 B à la fin du XIIIe s.

Il nous est agréable de dédier cette modeste contribution à un ami qui a consacré tant d'énergie à déchiffrer et à interpréter des inscriptions sémitiques du deuxième millénaire notamment.

---

quem?). Les n°s 9 et 10 portent la gravure identique à un *taw* quelque peu déformé (en X, non la croix) dont la signification est celle d'une "marque," sans plus de précision (malgré ibid., 33 et n. 41).

Topic and Comment in the Amarna Texts from Canaan

Anson F. Rainey
Tel Aviv University

One of the cardinal features of the EA (El Amarna) texts from Canaan that impressed scholars very early on is the marked difference in word order compared to the word order of more standard Akkadian.[1] However, apart from noting the differences, subsequent studies practically ignored the semantic implications of WS (West Semitic) word order in the texts from Canaan. In recent times,[2] T. J. Finley made an important statistical study of the Levantine EA texts and a selection of documents from Ugarit. Though his emphasis was on verbal clauses, he did not distinguish between various types of clauses, for example, indicative, injunctive, or interrogative. Word order in the native texts from Ugarit was studied by Huehnergard in comparison with the word order of texts sent to Ugarit from Carchemish.[3] He later updated his work on the native texts in somewhat more detail.[4]

Author's note: During our student days at Brandeis University, Baruch Levine and I often had time to discuss grammatical problems, especially in the many hours we spent together preparing some text for the next day's seminar. Although neither of us has lost his interest in the fundamentals of language, the intervening years have seldom permitted us such pleasures. This essay is a sort of attempt to fill that gap.

1. F. M. T. Böhl, *Die Sprache der Amarnabriefe mit besonderer Berücksichtigung der Kanaanismen* (Leipziger Semitische Studien 5/2; Leipzig, 1909; reprinted, Leipzig: Zentral Antiquariat der DDR, 1968) 78, §36c; D. H. Müller, *Die Gesetze Hammurabis und die mosäische Gesetzgebung: Text in Umschrift, deutsche und hebräische Übersetzung. Erläuterung und vergleichende Analyse* (Vienna, 1903) 245–46, 262–64.

2. T. J. Finley, *Word Order in the Clause Structure of Syrian Akkadian* (Ph.D. dissertation, University of California, Los Angeles, 1979).

3. J. Huehnergard, *The Akkadian Dialects of Carchemish and Ugarit* (Ph.D. dissertation, Harvard University, 1979) 93–98, 288–303.

4. J. Huehnergard, *The Akkadian of Ugarit* (HSS 34; Atlanta: Scholars Press, 1989) 211–24.

Meanwhile, van Soldt had also made a detailed study of the Akkadian texts from Ugarit.[5]

Word order variation in the Byblos EA texts was taken up by A. Gianto[6] in an exemplary study that dealt with the main types of clauses employed (fixed introductory formulas, etc., are part of the Western Peripheral repertoire and therefore not useful in determining the local Byblos dialectical syntax). Although his analysis was restricted to the Byblos texts plus a few others sent by the ruler of Byblos while he was in exile in Beirut, Gianto also realized that the entire collection of letters written from other places in Canaan share the peculiar dialectical features of the Byblos texts (with a few regional peculiarities). In a detailed review of Gianto's monograph,[7] it was suggested that Gianto's study be expanded to cover all of those other letters. Furthermore, it was shown that there are some categories of sentences/clauses that Gianto failed to include. The present study deals with the principal categories of clauses not only from Byblos but also from elsewhere in Canaan.

Terminology and Rationale

Throughout his book, Gianto is searching for the rationale behind the various word orders for different types of clauses. One should note in passing that the present discussion will adopt the usage proposed in the abovementioned review, namely, that the term *sentence* be applied to a complete, independent syntagma. For dependent or subordinate syntagmas, the term used herein will be *clause*. A sentence, then, may be comprised of one or more clauses. Two or more independent clauses may be joined syndetically to form a compound sentence. A main clause may have subordinate clauses as components. What Gianto[8] sometimes refers to as the "predicative structure" can thus simply be called a clause.

Within the clause, Gianto defines the subject (S), the verb (V), the object (O), and the complement (C). These symbols will be adopted here as well. In verbal clauses, Gianto generally considers the verb form to be the *predicate*. In nonverbal clauses, the predicate is recognized as the component being stated, that is, predicated, concerning the subject. It is obvious that Gianto speaks only of the grammatical subject and the grammatical predicate. A more useful approach, which would pertain to every category of clause discussed, would be to speak in terms of the *logical subject* and the *logi-*

5. W. H. van Soldt, *Studies in the Akkadian of Ugarit: Dating and Grammar* (Ph.D. dissertation; University of Leiden, 1986) 476–528; idem, *Studies in the Akkadian of Ugarit: Dating and Grammar* (AOAT 40; Neukirchen-Vluyn: Neukirchener Verlag, 1991) 476–518.

6. A. Gianto, *Word Order Variation in the Akkadian of Byblos* (Studia Pohl 15; Rome: Pontifical Biblical Institute, 1990).

7. A. F. Rainey, "Topic and Comment in Byblos Akkadian," *BO* 49 (1992) 329–58.

8. Gianto, *Word Order Variation*, 1, 174.

cal predicate. The former is the known datum, recognized already by the speaker/writer and the auditor/reader. The latter is the new information being provided about the *logical subject*. In the ensuing discussion, the *logical subject* will be called the *topic*, while the *logical predicate* will be referred to as the *comment*. The application of this distinction will facilitate the proper understanding of the clauses under consideration.

Gianto's success in highlighting the various syntagmas in which a particular component in the clause/sentence is fronted shows that he has a feel for the approach to which we are alluding. Often enough, he talks about some component or other as being *emphasized*. Frequently, an emphasized component is such because it is fronted, and sometimes it is accompanied by specific modifiers or particles. The need to express *emphasis* often requires a departure from the normal VSO word order in verbal clauses.[9] This *emphasis* is in fact the raising of a particular component in the clause to the status of the *comment*. While the grammatical subject normally corresponds to the logical subject and the grammatical predicate equals the logical predicate in nonverbal clauses, there are some exceptions. But the situation is especially complex with regard to verbal clauses. The verb, the grammatical predicate, is often not the logical predicate! Many syntagmas in which some other element in a verbal clause is fronted or otherwise emphasized will be discussed below.[10] One means in Akkadian by which the comment, or logical predicate, may be indicated is by the addition of the enclitic *-ma*.[11]

Gianto mentions some words that have a fixed position regardless of the ensuing syntagma. These *function words*[12] include presentation particles, conditional particles, conjunctions, and other adverbials. He observes that the function words are often followed by clauses that normally have V-S-O-C word order. However, the function words do not actually seem to determine the order of the ensuing clause.

Alongside the function words, Gianto ranks the interrogatives as words that must come at the head of their clause, whether the clause be verbal or nonverbal.[13] Here Gianto has evidently missed the point. In a question, the interrogative component is normally the logical predicate, that is, the comment. The interrogative may be a pronoun, "who?" "which?" "what?" or an adverbial, "when?" "where?" "why?" "how?" and so on. As the comment, the interrogative component is fronted. In verbal clauses of this nature, the verb may be the grammatical predicate, but it is not the logical predicate (comment) unless, of course, the sentence is a reply to a question such as "What

9. Ibid., 4, citing Finley, *Word Order in the Clause Structure*, 64–69.

10. For Biblical Hebrew, cf. T. Muraoka, *Emphatic Words and Structures in Biblical Hebrew* (Jerusalem: Magnes/Leiden: Brill, 1985).

11. A. F. Rainey, "Enclitic *-ma* and the Logical Predicate in Old Babylonian," *IOS* 6 (1976) 51–58.

12. Gianto, *Word Order Variation*, 16.

13. Ibid., 16–17.

did he do?" In nonverbal clauses, the interrogative may be S or P, but it is most often the comment. By the same token, in clauses that are responses to a question, the component that corresponds to the interrogative element in the original question is now the comment, whether it is S, V, O, or C. Understanding this simple principle will help to analyze other syntagmas. Furthermore, it should be noted that every clause is, in a sense, the response to a question, whether the question is articulated or merely implicit between the speaker/writer and the auditor/reader. The component in the clause that answers this question is thus the comment of the clause; the comment is not always the P/V component. In fact, adverbs, which are natural responses to interrogatives, are frequently the comment of their clause contexts.

Nonverbal Clauses

Equational Clauses

Gianto describes the tendencies governing the position of S and P in nonverbal clauses where the predicate is a modified noun phrase in the nominative case.[14] Huehnergard's definition of the personal pronoun in such constructions as the grammatical subject[15] will generally be seen to apply here. The grammatical subject is the topic.

Two word orders are known for clauses of this type, namely, SP and PS. Gianto gives contrasting examples of each.[16] For SP note:

a-na-ku ÌR *ki-ti-ka*
I am your loyal servant. (EA 108:22, 116:56)

a-mur / a-na-ku ÌR *ki-ti a-na šàr-ri* [*ù*] / *ia-nu ki-ma ia-ti-ia* ÌR *a-na / šàr-ri*
Look, I am the loyal servant of the king [and] there is none like me, a servant of the king. (EA 109:41–44)[17]

For PS examples, all in subordinate clauses, note:

ti-i-de pa-ar-ṣa-ia . . . i-nu-ma / ÌR [*k*]*i-it-ti-ka a-na-ku*
You know my conduct . . . that I am your loyal servant. (EA 73:39–42)

ù yi-de šàr-ru i-nu-ma / ⸢ÌR⸣ *ki-ti a-na-ku a-na ša-šu*
that the king may know that a loyal servant am I to him.
(EA 119:24–25)[18]

One may also note similar contexts from elsewhere in Canaan—for example, the following selection of independent clauses with SP order:

14. Ibid., 23–36.
15. J. Huehnergard, "On Verbless Clauses in Akkadian," ZA 76 (1986) 246–47.
16. Gianto, *Word Order Variation*, 22.
17. Ibid., 29.
18. Ibid., 25.

a-mur-mi a-na-ku ⌜ÌR⌝-⌜*di*⌝ / *ša ki-it-*[*t*]*i* / ⌜*šàr-ri* EN-*ia*
Behold, I am the loyal servant of the king, my lord. (EA 228:10–12; also EA 295:8; 296:9–10; 298:18)[19]

a-mur a-na-ku ÌR LUGAL *ù* / UR.GI$_7$ *ša* É-*šu*
Behold, I am the servant of the king and the (watch)dog of his house. (EA 60:6–7)

a-nu-um-ma a-na-ku ÌR *ša* LUGAL EN⟨-*ia*⟩ / *ù* GIŠ.GIR.GUB *ša* GÌR.MEŠ-*šu*
Now, I am the servant of the king, ⟨my⟩ lord, and the footstool of his feet. (EA 141:39–40;[20] cf. EA 147:4; 151:4; 185:74; 187:9; 198:10, 13, 16; 209:9; 211:8–9, 14; 212:11; 228:10; 241:9, 19; 254:10–11; 257:7; 264:5; 288:66; 296:9)

There are also subordinate clauses with PS word order, providing the ideogram stands for an adjective and not a stative:

i-nu-ma TUR *a-na-ku ù* / *šu-ri-ba-ni a-na* KUR *Mi-iṣ-ri*
When I was young, then he brought me to Egypt. (EA 296:25–26)

li-iš-al-mi / *šàr-ri* LÚ.MAŠKÍM.MEŠ *e-nu-ma* KAL.GA É *ma-gal*
May my king ask the commissioners whether the house is very strong. (EA 287:33–34)[21]

However, there are clear indications that even in independent equational clauses the order may be PS, probably to stress the comment:

ÌR LUGAL *a-na-ku* / *u* [*e*]*p-ri ša* 2 GÌR.MEŠ-*ka*
A servant of the king am I, and the dirt under your two feet. (EA 298:18–19)

ÌR-*ka a-na-ku*
your servant am I. (EA 289:51)

In the following Jerusalem passages, independent equational clauses with SP are paralleled by others with PS:

a-mur a-na-ku la-a ^{LÚ}*ḫa-zi-a-nu* / ^{LÚ}*ú-e-ú* ⟨*a-na-ku*⟩ *a-na šàr-ri* EN-*ia*
Behold, I am not just a city ruler; a soldier am ⟨I⟩ of the king, my lord. (EA 288:9–10 = 285:5–6)[22]

19. S. Izre'el, "The Gezer Letters of the Amarna Archive: Linguistic Analysis," *IOS* 8 (1978) 47, §6.1.2.

20. W. L. Moran, *Les lettres d'el Amarna: Correspondance diplomatique du pharaon* (with collaboration by V. Haas and G. Wilhelm; trans. D. Collon and H. Cazelles; Paris; du Cerf, 1987) 370–71; idem, *The Amarna Letters* (Baltimore: Johns Hopkins University Press, 1992) 227.

21. S. Nitzán, *The Jerusalem Letters from the el-ʿAmarna Archive: Linguistic Aspects* (M.A. thesis, Tel Aviv University, 1973) 68 [Heb.].

22. M. Liverani, "Contraste e confluenze di concezioni politiche nell'età di El-Amarna," *RA* 61 (1967) 15 n. 4; Moran, *Les lettres d'el Amarna*, 516 n. 1; idem, *The*

a-mur a-na-ku LÚ*ru-ʾì šàr-ri* / *ù ú-bi-il* GUN *šàr-ri a-na-ku*
Look, I am a companion of the king and a bringer of the king's tribute am I. (EA 288:9–12)

Gianto[23] seems confused with regard to interrogative nonverbal clauses. He says, "the order, which is expected to be PS, is inverted." Further on he says, "Thus the fronting of P [in interrogative passages EA 76:11–16 and EA 116:67–71] is not conditioned by emphasis, but by the question." Here are the relevant contexts:

[. . . *š*]*a-ni-tam mi-nu šu-ut* / Iì[R-]A-*ši*[-*ir-*]*ta* UR.GI$_7$ *ù yu-ba-ú* / [*la*]-*qa ka-li* URU.MEŠ *šàr-ru*(sic!) dUTU / [*a-n*]*a ša-a-šu šàr* KUR *Mi-ta-na* / *ù šàr* KUR *Ka-aš-ši*$_x$(ŠE) *šu-ut i-nu-ma* / ⌜*yu*⌝*-ba-ú la-qa* KUR LUGAL *a-na ša-a-šu*
[Fur]thermore, who is he? (this) ʿAbdi-Ashirta, the dog, that he seeks [to ta]ke all the cities of the king, the sungod, for himself? Is he the king of Mitanni land or the king of Cassite land, that he seeks to take the land of the king for himself?
(EA 76:11–16; cf. also EA 71:16–22; 88:9–11; 123:38–40; 125:40–43)

mi-ia-mi šu-n[*u*] / DUMU.MEŠ IÌR-*A-ši-ir-ta ù* ⌜*la*⌝*-qú* KUR LUGAL *a-na ša-šu-nu* / *šàr* KUR *Mi-ta-na šu-nu ù šàr* / [K]UR *Ka-ši ù šàr* KUR *Ḫa-ta*
Who are they? (these) sons of ʿAbdi-Ashirta, that they have taken the land of the king for themselves? Are they the king of Mitanni land or the king of Cassite land or the king of Ḫatti land?
(EA 84:16–17; 85:63–64; 108:25–26; 116:67–71; cf. EA 104:17–21; 117:35–36; 138:21)

The order, as these two passages show, is PS. The reason for this is that, as stated above, the interrogative component in a question is always the logical predicate because it is asking for the new information.

The following example shows fronting of a numeral, or rather of a substantive modified by a numeral:

ù 4(?) ŠEŠ *ni-nu-u*$_{16}$ *ù aš-t*[*ap-p*]*ár* / *a-na ša-šu-nu a-na re-ṣí-ia*
And four(?) colleagues are we, so I wrote to them for help.
(EA 92:44–45)[24]

It has been observed that, in Old Babylonian, numerals are often fronted in nonverbal clauses.[25] Such a format was probably determined by the function of bookkeeping entries in inventory texts. This might be the explana-

---

Amarna Letters, 331 n. 1; contra W. F. Albright, G. Mendenhall, and W. L. Moran, "The Amarna Letters," in *ANET*, 488b.

23. Gianto, *Word Order Variation*, 34.

24. Ibid.; R. F. Youngblood, *The Amarna Correspondence of Rib-Haddi, Prince of Byblos (EA 68–96)* (Ph.D. dissertation, Dropsie College, 1961) 371.

25. Huehnergard, "On Verbless Clauses in Akkadian," 221–22 n. 13, 234 n. 62.

tion in the present passage as well. However, it is more likely that here the predicate is fronted for emphasis. Note that the numeral, normally read 'three', has traces in Schroeder's copy of another wedge, albeit horizontal; the context requires 'four' to make proper sense (three rival kings and Rib-Ḫaddi himself).[26]

By contrast, the PS order in dependent clauses seems more firmly fixed. There is one example of a dependent clause where Gianto seems not to have grasped the key element.[27] The context contains a nonverbal, subordinate clause followed by a parallel verbal clause (also subordinate):

> *ù qí-ba-mi / a-wa-ta$_5$ an-ni-ta a-na pa-ni / šàr-ri* EN-*ka i-nu-ma / a-bu ù be-lu at-ta-ma / a-na ia-ši ù a-na ka-ta$_5$ / pa-ni-ia na-ad-na-ti*
> So speak this message before the king, your lord, because you are father and master to me and it is to you that I have turned my face.
> (EA 73:33–38)

The verbal clause, with fronting of *ana kâta*, makes it clear that the emphasis in both clauses is on Amanappa's being the official responsible for the welfare of Rib-Ḫaddi. He is "father and master" to him. But in the subordinate non-verbal clause, the consistent order is PS. So the P should be *abu u belu*. Note, however, that the enclitic attached to the personal pronoun, *attama*, is for emphasis. What needs to be recognized here is that enclitic *-ma* in verbal and nonverbal clauses can raise a component to the status of comment (logical predicate) even though it is not the grammatical predicate of the syntagma. This is what has happened here. The scribe felt constrained to follow the order PS in which S is an independent pronoun, even though he intended that the pronoun should be the comment. He overcomes his constraint by affixing the enclitic and thus drawing the intonation to the pronoun. The fronting of *ana kâta* was felt to be sufficient to make that complement the comment, without recourse to another enclitic.[28]

The choice of SP or PS is not "entirely dictated by the status"[29] of the clause. On occasion, there are logical predicates that receive fronting or other syntactic means of emphasis contrary to the word order customary for the type of clause (independent or dependent).

Clauses with Adverbial Component

This section deals with some verbless clauses consisting of a nominal expression and a prepositional phrase. The two categories into which Gianto[30] has divided them, locative and existential, are useful and instructive. In the

26. Youngblood, *The Amarna Correspondence*, 371.
27. Gianto, *Word Order Variation*, 25, 27, 155.
28. Rainey, "Topic and Comment," 333.
29. Gianto, *Word Order Variation*, 36.
30. Ibid., 37–39, §3.1.

locative, the prepositional phrase is the predicate (P), explaining something about the nominal (S). Since the prepositional phrase may express something other than location (e.g., the clauses of comparison with *kīma* phrases),[31] they can more appropriately be called clauses with adverbial predicate. In the existential clause, it is the nominal component that is the predicate, the prepositional phrase being a secondary modifier. Gianto points out that the subject of the clause with adverbial predicate is "determinate, given, or recoverable from the preceding context."[32] This is exactly what is expected from the topic (logical subject). The topic is something already known. The new information is the whereabouts, and so forth, of the topic. Thus the prepositional phrase is the comment, the logical predicate. These naturally correspond in a verbless clause to the grammatical subject and predicate, respectively. Subordinate clauses with prepositional phrases as predicate do not seem to switch to PS word order as do the equational clauses treated above. Note, for example, the following:

i-nu-ma a-na-ku a-na URU-*li*^{KI} *a-na-ṣa-ar-ši* / *a-na be-li-ia*
When I was in (sic!) the city, I guarded it for my lord.
(EA 137:53–54; Gianto, *Word Order Variation*, 41)

ù / *ti-mu-ru* URU.⸢KI⸣ ⸢*i*⸣*-nu-*⸢*ma*⸣ ⸢ERÍN⸣.MEŠ *sa-nu* \ *a-ša-bu* / *a-na* URU.KI *ù* ⸢*ti*⸣-⸢*ma*⸣*-ga-*⸢*ru*⸣ / *i-re-bi a-na* ⸢URU⸣.KI
but the city saw that other troops were located in the city, and they were agreeable to my entering the city.
(EA 138:60–63; Gianto, *Word Order Variation*, 43–44; Rainey, Review of Moran, 63a)

i-nu-ma ^{LÚ}MAŠKÍM L[UGAL] / [*it-t*]*i-nu ù a-na* [*š*]*a-*[*šu*] / [*nu-uš-pu-*]*ru* ⸢*ú*⸣*-ul nu-*⸢*uš*⸣*-pu-ru a-na* [*ka-*]*ta*$_5$
Inasmuch as the k[ing's] commissioner was with us and to ⸢him⸣ [we are writ]ing, we do not write to [yo]u. (EA 85:82–84)[33]

One may note that the verbless clause in the following example is in fact the comment of a clause with extraposition which is itself the protasis of a conditional sentence:

i-nu-ma 1 *ḫa-za-nu* / *lìb-bu-šu it-ti lìb-bi-ia* / *ù ú-da-bi-ra* ^{I}ÌR-A*-ši-ir-ta* / *iš-tu* KUR A*-mur-ri*
If there were one city ruler whose heart is with my heart, then I would expel ʿAbdi-Ashirta from the land of Amurru. (EA 85:86–89)[34]

31. Ibid., 41.
32. Ibid., 39.
33. Ibid., 44; A. F. Rainey, Review of Moran, *Les lettres d'el Amarna: Correspondance diplomatique du pharaon*, in AfO 36/37 (1989–90) 59a.
34. Gianto, *Word Order Variation*, 42 no. 16.

The next passage is not simply a determinate subject with an adverbial phrase as predicate. The enclitic *-ma* converts the ostensible subject into the predicate, that is to say, the comment:

> *yi-du* LUGAL *ma-ni* UD.KAM.MEŠ / *yi-pu-šu du-um-qa* / *a-na ia-ši i-nu-ma* / *ia-nu lìb-bi ša-na a-*⌜*na*⌝ *ia-ši* / *pa-nu-ia-ma a-na a-ra-ad* / *šàr-ri* EN-*ia*
> The king knows how many days he has treated me well because I have no other mind; it is my intention to serve the king, my lord.
> (EA 119:39–44;[35] also EA 118:39–40)

The emphasized noun, *pānūyama*, is evidently meant to begin an independent clause. The application of the *-ma* makes it the comment of its clause, even if it might be construed as the grammatical subject.

The following example is typical of the "possessive" force of the preposition *ana:*[36]

> *a-na ša-šu* / URU*Ṣu-mu-ra a-na ša-šu* / URU.MEŠ *šàr-ri* 1-*en* URU*Gub-la* / *is-sí-la-at sàr-ri*
> To him belongs Ṣumur, to him belong the towns of the king; alone, Byblos remains(?) to the king. (EA 140:14–17)[37]

Geography may help to explain the locative prepositional phrase in the following passage. The town in question, probably to be read *Yaʿliya*, was evidently somewhere north of Byblos but south of Sumur, probably south of Nahr el-Kebîr. In EA 104:6–13 it is associated with Ullasa, Ardata, Ampi, and Shigata, all towns in the vicinity of modern Tripoli. In EA 114, Rib-Ḫaddi is stressing the fact that he is virtually isolated from the sea lanes. He had to send an Egyptian messenger to Egypt via Alashia (EA 114:51–53). The phrase *ina Yaʿliya* most certainly belongs at the end of the sentence about the capture of Rib-Ḫaddi's men (lines 9–12), the point being that the men sent to Sumur were apprehended by Aziru at a place along the way northward. Furthermore, the ships of the neighboring rulers were all in Amurru. They were at peace (or: safe) while Rib-Ḫaddi was at war. Thus read:

> *ù* / LÚ.MEŠ *ša-a* ⌜*uš*⌝*-ši-ir-ti a-na* / URU*Ṣu-mu-ra ṣa-*‹*ab*›*-bat i-na* / ⌜URU⌝*Ya-á*ʾ*-li-ia* GIŠ.MÁ.MEŠ LÚ.MEŠ / URU*Ṣur-ri* URU*Be-ru-ta* URU*Ṣí-du-na* / *gáb-bu i-na* KUR*A-mur-ri šal-mu šu-nu* / *a-na-ku-mi* ⌜NU⌝.KÚR
> And the men whom I sent to Sumur he (Aziru) captured in Yaʿliya; as

35. Ibid., 42; Rainey, "Topic and Comment," 335.

36. A. F. Rainey, "Genitive *ana* in the Canaanite El-Amarna Tablets," in *Bar-Ilan Studies in Assyriology Dedicated to Pinḥas Artzi* (ed. J. Klein and A. Skaist; Ramat Gan: Bar-Ilan University Press, 1990) 171–76.

37. Gianto, *Word Order Variation*, 48, no. 7; Rainey, "Review of Moran," 64a; idem, "Topic and Comment," 336.

for the ships of the rulers of Tyre, Beirut and Sidon, all are in Amurru; they are safe but as for me, I am at war. (EA 114:9–15)[38]

The scribe resorts to two sentences with extraposition (Huehnergard's "suspended noun").[39] He wants to contrast the situation of the ships of the neighboring towns with his own situation. The locative, nonverbal clause is *gáb-bu i-na* ^{KUR}A-*mur-ri* 'all are in Amurru'.

There are instances when the prepositional phrase is fronted for further emphasis upon it as the comment.[40] Compare the following:

^{URU}*Ṣu-mu-ra a-na ša-šu*
Ṣumur belongs to him. (EA 140:15)

a-na ša-šu-nu ^{URU}*Ar-da-ta* / ^{URU}*Ya-aḫ-li-ia* ^{URU}*Am-bi* / ^{URU}*Ši-ga-ta ka-li* / URU.MEŠ *a-na ša-šu-nu*
They have Ardata, Yaʿlia, Ambi, Shigata, all the cities are theirs. (EA 104:10–13)

The latter example is an interesting contrast between two clauses, the first with the fronted adverbial comment to stress to whom the cities now belong and the second with fronted noun phrase containing the quantifier as comment to emphasize that it is all those towns that have fallen into the adversary's hands.

Extraposition

A frequent syntactic and rhetorical device in these texts is extraposition. This is a special means of prediction concerning a particular topic. The extrapolated noun or pronoun is truly the "suspended subject." That it is the topic of the sentence is obvious by the fact that it is always the known datum. The ensuing clause, whether verbal or nonverbal, is the comment, the new information predicated for the extrapolated topic. Since the extrapolated item is the subject of the sentence, there is no way that the suspended subject could be identical with the predicate of the clause that is being predicated about it. The resumptive pronoun or other similar component can, of course, be in the genitive:

a-mur a-⸢na⸣-ku pa-nu-ia-ma / a-⸢na⸣ a-ra-ad LUGAL
Behold, (as for) myself, it is *my* face that is set to serve the king. (EA 118:39–40)

accusative:

38. Contra Gianto, *Word Order Variation*, 49, no. 8; cf. Rainey, "Topic and Comment," 336–37.

39. Huehnergard, "On Verbless Clauses," 237; F. I. Andersen, *The Hebrew Verbless Clause in the Pentateuch* (JBL Monograph Series 14; Nashville: Abingdon, 1970) 36, 42, 45; Muraoka, *Emphatic Words*, 93–99.

40. Gianto, *Word Order Variation*, 46–50, §3.4.

a-mur a-na-ku la-a ^{LÚ}*a-bi-ia* \ *ša-ak-na-ni* / *ù la-a* ^{MÍ}*ú-mi-ia* / *i-na aš-ri an-ni-e*
Behold, as for myself, it was not my father that placed *me*, and not my mother, in this place. (EA 286:9–11)[41]

dative:

an-nu-ú a-na-ku ú-ul / *ma-ṣa-ar-tu ù ú-ul* / *ba-la-aṭ* LUGAL *a-na* /*ia-ši*
Behold, as for me, *I have* no garrison and no royal sustenance. (EA 122:28–31)

or other oblique position:

a-mur a-na-ku / *nu-kúr-tu*$_4$ UGU-*ia* 5 MU.MEŠ
Behold, (as for) myself, there has been hostility against *me* five years. (EA 106:16–17)

a-nu-ma ^{URU}*Ṣu-mu-ur nu-kùr-tu*$_4$^{MEŠ} *ma-gal* / KAL.GA UGU-*ši*
Now, as for Ṣumur, hostilities are very strong against her. (EA 106:8–9)

a-mur a-na-ku ia-nu / *ḫa-za-na i-na ar-ki-ti-ia*
Behold, (as for) myself, there is no city-ruler behind *me*. (EA 117:9–10)

It can also be the topic of the clause:

[*a*]-*mur a-na-ku* GIŠ.GÌR.GUB *ša* GÌR-*pe* / LUGAL BE-*ia a-na-ku ù* ÌR *ki-it-ti-šu*
[Be]hold, as for myself, the footstool of the king, my lord, am I, and his loyal servant. (EA 106:6–7)

On the rhetorical level, a contrast may be made between the respective situations of two topics. But within each sentence, the extrapolated element is the topic, not the comment. Note Rib-Ḫaddi's familiar compliant:

LÚ.MEŠ *ḫa-za-nu-tu* URU.MEŠ-*šu-nu* / *a-na ša-šu-nu* LÚ.MEŠ / *ḫu*!-〈*up*〉-*šu-šu-nu i-na* / *šap-li-šu-nu ù* / *a-na-ku* URU.MEŠ-*ia a-na* ^{I}*A-zi-ri*
As for the city rulers, they have their towns, their yeo〈man far〉mers are subservient to them; but as for me, my towns belong to Aziru. (EA 125:33–37; also EA 121:11–16; 122:26–31)

Verbal Clauses

Readers of classical Akkadian are familiar with the standard word order of most epistolary and legal documents, in which the verb comes at the end of

41. Nitzán, *The Jerusalem Letters*, 68, §5.22.

the clause.[42] The fact that this is not always so in the EA texts from Canaan became clearer after the discovery and analysis of the Codex Ḫammurapi and other related literature.[43] In the Canaanite EA letters, there are various syntagmas for verbal clauses, the word order of which is determined by the relative importance of the components, namely, subject (S), verb (V), and compliment(s) (C). As mentioned above, Finley[44] made statistical studies of the clauses in the EA letters from Canaan with regard to word order, especially VSO versus SVO, but he did not attempt to sort out the clauses according to mode, that is, indicative versus injunctive. The ensuing discussion will emphasize the distinction between different kinds of discourse and their respective modal expressions. There is considerable similarity to Biblical Hebrew.[45]

Narrative Discourse (Indicative)

Verb-Subject. Frequently the writer of an epistle recounts an event or series of events. Some typical examples of this category of narration will show that while SV may be used when a specific subject is being introduced, VS characterizes the progress of the action. The ruler of Acco reported on the movements of a certain Zirdamyashda (numbers denote sentences, not lines):

(1) *[^{I}Zi-ir]-dam-ia[-a]š-da / p[a-]ṭá-ar iš-t[u] / [^{I}B]ir$_5$-ia-wa-za* SVC
[Zir]damyashda des[er]ted from [B]iryawaza.

(2) *i[-ba-ši] / it-ti ^{I}Su-ta* ì[R] / *šàr-ri i-na* URU ⌜UN⌝.[*-ti*] VC$_1$C$_2$
He w[as] with Shuta, the ser[vant] of the king in
the garrison town.

(3) ⌜*la*⌝*-a yi-qa-bi mi-im-*⌜*mi*⌝ / *[a-n]a ša-šu* Neg. + VOC
He didn't say anything [t]o him.

(4) *tu-uṣ-ṣa* / ERÍN.MEŠ LUGAL EN-*ia* VS
The army of the king, my lord, came forth.

(5) *i-ba[-ši] / it-ti-ši i-na* ^{URU}*Ma-gíd-d[a*^{KI}*]* VC
He wa[s] with it in Megiddo.

42. GAG 183, §130c.

43. A. Ungnad, "Zur Syntax der Gesetze Hammurabis," ZA 17 (1903) 353–78; 18 (1904) 1–67; Müller, *Die Gesetze Hammurabis*, 245–46, 262–64.

44. Finley, *Word Order in the Clause Structure*.

45. For the contrast between narrative discourse and injunctive discourse in Biblical Hebrew, cf. R. E. Longacre, "Discourse Perspective on the Hebrew Verb: Affirmation and Restatement," in *Linguistics and Biblical Hebrew* (ed. W. R. Bodine; Winona Lake, Ind.: Eisenbrauns, 1992) 177–89.

(6) *la-a qa-bi mi-mu a-na ša-š[u]* Neg. + VSC
Nothing was said to hi[m].

(7) *ù yi-ip-ṭú-ra a-na mu-ḫi-ia* Conj. + VC
Then he deserted to me.

(8) *ù a-nu-ma / ia-aš-pu-ra* [I]*Šu-ta / a-na ia-ši* . . . VSC[O]
And now Shuta has written to me. . . .

(9) *ù la-a i-ma-gur na-da-an-šu* Neg. + VO
But I did not agree to hand him over. (EA 234:11–27)

At the beginning, Satatna introduced the person under discussion (1), so Zirdamyashda comes first in the clause, followed by the verb. Next, (2) the subject is understood as still being Zirdamyashda, so he is not mentioned; the predication (stative *ibašši*) heads the clause; a new person is introduced, Shuta, who will be the subject of the next clause. Since the negative always precedes its verb, it begins (3) but Shuta is not mentioned by name. It is the fact of the army's coming forth (arrival from Egypt) that is important to the next clause (4), so the ventive verb, *tuṣṣâ*, heads the clause followed by the subject. Even though there is a change of subject back to Zirdamyashda (5), the stative (harking back to [2]) is sufficient to carry forward the story. The form of (6) corresponds to (3), but the verb is passive and the subject expressed. Since (6) ends in "to him (= Zirdamyashda)," it was logical to begin (7) without naming the clearly understood subject. The new stage in the narrative (8) starts with the function word, *anumma*, and since the actor, Shuta, is already identified in (2), he does not come at the head of the clause. It is the act of his writing to Satatna that is important. The direct quotation with its imperative is the direct object of the verb *yašpura* and is omitted here. The final clause in the story (9) begins with a negated verb; its 1st common singular form is sufficient to identify the subject. An independent pronoun is not needed because the emphasis is on the action of refusing. It is clear that the explicit subject is only fronted in (1) because it is important to introduce him. One is inclined to see here an extraposition à la Huehnergard, that is, "As for Zirdamyashda, he deserted from Biryawaza." This suggests that Zirdamyashda had been the subject of a letter sent to Satatna, who was obliged to explain what had happened to him.

In passages like the above, portrayal of the progression of actions is the main intention. Except for the first clause, the verb precedes any explicit subject even when a new one is introduced, for example, "the army" in (4). The verbal predicate is therefore the comment.

When the infinitive is used as a finite verb,[46] it invariably comes at the head of its clause and is usually marked by an enclitic *-ma* or *-mi*. Obviously,

46. Cf. E. Ebeling, "Glossar," in J. A. Knudtzon, *Die El-Amarna-Tafeln* (VAB 2; Leipzig, 1915; reprinted, Aalen: Zeller, 1964) 1491; W. L. Moran, *A Syntactical Study*

the emphasis is on the verbal action; it is the comment of the clause.

a-ṣé-mi ERÍN.MEŠ / *pí-ṭá-ti*
The army has come forth. (EA 73:12–13; Rainey, Review of Moran, 58)

ù [a]-la-ak-mi a-na-⟨ku⟩ a-na URUA.PÚ[KI] / *a-na da[-ba-b]i a-na ma-ḫar* I*Ḫa-mu-ni[-ri]*
So ⌜I⌝! [w]ent to Beirut in order to plead before ʿAmmuni[ra]. (EA 138:51–52)

a-ṣé-mi ERÍN.MEŠ *pí-ṭá-tu ù ša-mu / a-na ú-mi ka-ša-di-ši ù ta-ra-at* URU.KI *a-na* LUGAL *be-li-ia*
As soon as the army comes forth and they hear about the day of its arrival, then the city will return to the king, my lord. (EA 137:49–51)[47]

al-lu / pa-ṭá-ri-ma LÚ.MEŠ *ḫu-up-ši ù / ṣa-ab-tu* LÚ.MEŠ GAZ.MEŠ / URU
Behold, if the yeomen farmers desert, then the *ʿapîru* men will seize the city. (EA 118:37–39)[48]

ṣa-bat-mi / ni-nu-u$_{16}$ URU.MEŠ *Gub*^{ub}*-li / ù da-na-nu-u*$_{16}$
And they are saying, "If we capture the town(s) of Byblos, then we will be strong." (EA 362:25–27)

Subject-Verb. It was seen in (1) above that the subject may precede the verb when the context requires it. Although the PN is not the comment of that clause, it is fronted and may very well be in a sort of extraposition. Thus, it is the topic. On the other hand, there are instances when the grammatical subject is the comment of the clause. Fronting is the usual device for achieving this emphasis, but the addition of an augment such as enclitic *-ma* (also *-mi* in these texts) or a modifier, for example, "me myself," is a frequent practice.

a-nu-ma a-na-ku-ma / er-ri-šu \ *aḫ-ri-šu*
Now, it is I who am cultivating. (EA 365:10–11)

of the Dialect of Byblos as Reflected in the Amarna Tablets (Ph.D. dissertation; Johns Hopkins University, 1950) 57–59; idem, "The Use of Canaanite Infinitives Absolute as a Finite Verb in the Amarna Letters from Byblos," *JCS* 4 (1950) 169–72; idem, "Does Amarna Bear on Karatepe?—An Answer," *JCS* 6 (1952) 76–80; idem, "The Hebrew Language in Its Northwest Semitic Background," in *The Bible and the Ancient Near East*, (ed. G. E. Wright; New York, 1961) 61–62 (reprinted, Anchor Book Edition; Garden City, N.Y.: Doubleday, 1965) 69–70.

47. Cf. Moran, "The Use of the Canaanite Infinitive Absolute as a Finite Verb in the Amarna Letters," *JCS* 4 (1950) 170; idem, *Les lettres d'el Amarna*, 358 and 360 n. 9; idem, *The Amarna Letters*, 218 and 220 n. 9.

48. Moran, *A Syntactical Study of the Dialect of Byblos as Reflected in the Amarna Tablets*, 57; idem, "Use of the Canaanite Infinitive Absolute," 169–70; contra CAD A/1 358b.

u a-na-ku-ma / ub-ba-lu LÚ.MEŠ *ma-as-sà*M[EŠ]
And it is I who am bringing corvée workers. (EA 365:13–14)

a-na-ku-ma \ ya-ḫu-du-un-ni / ub-ba-lu LÚ.MEŠ *ma-as-sà*MEŠ
It is I, by myself, who am bringing corvée workers. (EA 365:24–25)

ù / a-na-ku-ma ù ÌR-*ḫe-ba / nu-kúr-tu₄ i-na* LÚ.⌜SA⌝.GAZ
But it is I and ʿAbdi-Ḫeba who are fighting the *ʿapîrû*. (EA 366:19–21)

šu-ni-ma in₄-né-ri-ru
It was they (two) who hastened to help. (EA 366:24)[49]

On the other hand, note that the following example has an independent 1st common singular pronoun emphasized by enclitic *-mì* (it is hardly a marker of direct speech here).

a-na-ku-mi ep-ša-ti / i-mu-t[a] a-n[a] URU*Ṣur-ri / i-ba-šu i-na pa-ni-ia*
It was I who made a marriage contract with Tyre; they were on good terms with me. (EA 89:17–19)[50]

Contrary to Gianto's interpretation,[51] the contrast in the following is not between Rib-Ḫaddi and his host, ʿAmmunira, but between Rib-Ḫaddi and his own younger brother.

šá-ni-tam a-na-ku-mi-i₁₅ / al-ka-ti a-na ma-ḫar-ri I*Ḫa-mu-ni-ri / ù* ŠEŠ-*ia* TUR *iš-tu- ia-ti / i-na-kar₅-mi* URU*Gub-la*KI */ a-na na-da-ni* URU.KI-*li / a-na* DUMU.MEŠ ÌR-I*A-ši-ir-ti*
Furthermore, when I myself had gone to ʿAmmunira, my brother who is younger than I, alienated Byblos in order to give my city to the sons of ʿAbdi-Ashirta. (EA 137:14–19)

Object-Verb. Gianto demonstrates that OV is a means of emphasizing the object. There are very few instances of the use of other markers of emphasis. One can only concur with Gianto[52] when he says, "object fronting itself is a strong emphatic device." It is not certain that every fronted object can be taken as the comment of its clause, but this analysis seems to fit many or most of the contexts. Although the following passage may be construed as argumentative, it is still a sample of narration:

ù a-wa-ta ša-a i-de / ù ša-a eš-te-me aš-pu-⌜ru⌝ / a-na šàr-ri EN-*ia*
And it is the word that I know and that I have heard, that I write to the king, my lord. (EA 108:23–25; also EA 116:15–16)

49. W. L. Moran, "The Dual Personal Pronouns in Western Peripheral Akkadian," *BASOR* 211 (1973) 51.
50. W. F. Albright and W. L. Moran, "Rib-Adda of Byblos and the Affairs of Tyre (EA 89)," *JCS* 4 (1950) 164–66; Gianto, *Word Order Variation*, 83, no. 10.
51. Ibid., 84, no. 12.
52. Ibid., 136.

Rib-Ḫaddi is stressing that his reports to the king are based on factual knowledge, not on lies or figments of his imagination.

> *ù* ERÍN.MEŠ SA.GAZ.MEŠ *ù* GIŠ.GIGIR.MEŠ / *ša-ki-in*$_4$ *i-na lìb-bi-*⟨*ši*⟩(?)
> And it is both *ʿapîrû* troops and chariots that he (ʿAbdi-Ashirta) has stationed within ⟨it⟩. (EA 87:21–22)

Here Rib-Ḫaddi wants to emphasize the strength of the enemy's forces posted so close to his own city, both foot troops *and* chariots.

For emphasis, the infinitive standing in the accusative as the object of a governing verb may be placed at the head of the clause:

> *ša-ḫa-at-ši i-le-ú ù ṣa-bat-ši* / *la i-le-ú*
> To besiege it they are able but to capture it they are not able. (EA 106:12–13)

> ⌜*ù*⌝ *uš-šar-šu-nu a-na* URU*Ṣu-mu-ra* / [*l*]*a-a i-le-*[*ú aš-š*]*um* ⌜GIŠ⌝MÁ.[MEŠ] ⌜URU⌝*Ar-wa-da*
> But to send them to Ṣumur I am unab[le bec]ause of the ships of Arvad. (EA 105:86–87)

For further emphasis, the object of the governed infinitive may precede the finite verb:

> *šá-ni-tam šum-*[*ma*] / ⌜URU⌝*Gub-la ú-ba-ú ṣa-ba-ta*
> Furthermore, if it is Byblos that he seeks to take. (EA 88:21–22)

This must be compared with a unique instance in which the object begins the clause but the governed infinitive of which it is the object is expressed by an adverbial compliment of purpose, which itself appears at the end of the clause:

> URU*Ṣur-ri* / *la-a i-lé-ú-ni*$_7$ *a-na ṣa-bat*
> Tyre they are unable to capture. (EA 149:65–66)

One must note, nevertheless, that other means were sometimes employed to emphasize the object, in addition to fronting. In the following passage, the enclitic *-ma* is attached to the direct object, which is also fronted and repeated. The passage must be interpreted as follows:

> *ù* / [TI.LA] ⌜ZI⌝-⌜*ia*⌝ *ka-li* DINGIR.MEŠ-*nu* / ⌜*ù*⌝ [dNIN *š*]*a* URU*Gub-la*KI / ⌜TI⌝.LA ⌜*ù*⌝?[*šu-u*]*t* LÚ *ša-a yu-ba-ú* / ⌜*lum*⌝*-na a-n*[*a* EN-*š*]*u šum-ma du-na du-na-ma* / [*ú*]*-ba-ú a-na-ku* [*a-n*]*a* EN-*ia*
> And [as] my soul [lives], as all the gods ⌜and⌝ [the lady o]f Byblos live, ⌜then⌝ [h]e is the man who seeks evil for [hi]s [lord], while it is only power, power that I seek [fo]r my lord. (EA 109:53–55)[53]

53. Cf. Moran, *Les lettres d'el Amarna*, 310 n. 14; idem, *The Amarna Letters*, 184 n. 14; Gianto, *Word Order Variation*, 89, §5.4; 133, §7.5.

The contrast is between the evil that the other person (Aziru) seeks for pharaoh and the effective power and influence that Rib-Ḫaddi wants him to have. In the first clause the subject is fronted, "He is the man . . . ," and the object follows the verb, but in the second, the order is reversed, that is, OVS. This may be a kind of *chiasmus*; in any case, the comment of the latter clause is the object.

Position of the Complement. The most useful chapter in Gianto's book is his study of the adverbial complements to verbal clauses.[54] We would propose a slightly different nomenclature for his six categories of complements:[55] (a) dative, (b) locative, (c) comitative, (d) modal, (e) causal, and (f) temporal. By complements, Gianto means prepositional phrases, with the exception of temporal expressions, which are often noun phrases in the adverbial accusative (but note also *ina ūm*[*i*]). It turns out that there is usually a sequential preference for the various categories, namely, a + b + c + d + e + f.[56] There are, of course, many other adverbs that can be fronted if they are the comment of the clause. Temporal complements are usually fronted; if that is not possible, then they take the last position on the right.

The complement of time is usually fronted in narration or in noninjunctive dialogue.

> *a-mur iš-tu da-*⸢*ri*⸣*-*[*ti*] / *la-a i-te*$_9$*-li-*⸢*yu*⸣(?) / *i-na* ᵁᴿᵁ*Gub-la* DINGIR.MEŠ
> Behold, from of old, the gods have never gone away from Byblos. (EA 134:4–6)[57]

In cases where two temporal complements are employed, the second comes at the end of the clause:

> *ù a-nu-um-ma i-na-ṣa-*⸢*ru*⸣ / ᵁᴿᵁ*Ma-gi*$_5$*-da*ᴷᴵ / . . . UD.KÁM *ù* GI$_6$*-ša*
> and now I am guarding Megiddo . . . day and night. (EA 243:10–13)[58]

Especially worthy of note is the syntax of the following example:

> *a-mur-mi a-na ú-mi tu-ṣú* / *ù i-né-pu-ša-at gáb-bi* / KUR.MEŠ *a-na* LUGAL *be-li-ia*
> Behold, on the day you come forth, then all the territories will go over to the king, my lord. (EA 362:62–64)[59]

54. Gianto, *Word Order Variation*, 137–58.

55. Ibid., 137–38.

56. Ibid., 139.

57. Cf. Moran, *Dialect of Byblos*, 177; note the Gt separative with a verb of motion, for which see Rainey, "Verbal Forms with Infixed *-t-* in the West Semitic el-Amarna Letters," *IOS* 1 (1971) 87–89.

58. A. F. Rainey, "Morphology and the Prefix-Tenses of West Semitized El-ʿAmarna Tablets," *UF* 7 (1975) 404; cf. Moran, *Les lettres d'el Amarna*, 467 n. 1; idem, *The Amarna Letters*, 297 n. 1.

59. Gianto, *Word Order Variation*, 146, no. 20; Rainey, "Topic and Comment," 346.

This is a verbal clause, *tūṣû*, dependent upon a construct noun (cf. *awat iqbû*). The entire syntagma thus comprises the temporal complement. Nevertheless, the main clause is introduced by the conjunction; this is a variation of the "as soon as" formula (cf. EA 82:16–17). Though the passage is a departure from narration, it does describe a situation prevailing in the region.

Gianto gives seven apparent examples of variation from the normal sequence of complements (EA 105:29–31; 139:11–12, also EA 88:10–11; 82:17–20; 103:25–29, 44–47; 105:20–21; 107:21–24),[60] and in each case there is some special explanation or mitigating factor. This serves to illustrate the fact that the "normal sequence" is not a hard and fast rule.

Inasmuch as complements are adverbials and adverbs basically are answers to questions (how? when? where? why?), it should not be surprising that they are often the comment—the new information—supplied by the clause. Thus, the following example can be rendered in English by a cleft sentence:

is-tu KUR*Ia-ri-im-mu-ta* / *nu-bal-li-iṭ*
It was from Yarimuta that we had to get supplies. (EA 68:27–28)[61]

Injunctive Discourse

Gianto notes that injunctives—that is, imperatives, jussives, and volitives[62]—come at the head of their clauses.[63] This, of course, is diametrically opposed to classic Akkadian practice, where a whole series of injunctions in a letter may come at the end of their respective clauses. Among Gianto's examples, he includes (rightly) the secondary injunctives that come in purpose or result clauses.

An important corollary observed by Gianto[64] is that injunctives (imperatives, jussives, volitives, and precatives) do not normally tolerate fronting of some other component to their left. The reason for this is that the injunctive is usually the comment of its clause. But note exceptional cases such as this clause with an imperative:

ù i-na UD.KÁM.MEŠ / [*an-nu*]-*ti uš-ši-ra* ERÍN.MEŠ [GAL]
So at [thi]s very time send a [large] army. (EA 85:79–80)[65]

60. Gianto, *Word Order Variation*, 141–43.

61. Ibid., 151, no. 1; Rainey, "Topic and Comment," 346.

62. For this terminology, cf. A. F. Rainey, "The Prefix Conjugation Patterns of Early Northwest Semitic," in *Lingering over Words: Studies in Ancient Near Eastern Literature in Honor of William L. Moran* (ed. T. Abusch, J. Huehnergard, and P. Steinkeller; Atlanta: Scholars Press, 1990) 407–20.

63. Gianto, *Word Order Variation*, 18–19.

64. Ibid., 143.

65. Youngblood, *The Amarna Correspondence*, 281; Moran, *Les lettres d'el Amarna*, 271 n. 10; idem, *The Amarna Letters*, 158 n. 12; Gianto, *Word Order Variation*, 149, no. 30.

Gianto cites three problematic constructions in which an injunctive appears to be preceded by a complement.[66] The first one (EA 74:31) is perhaps best explained with Youngblood[67] to the effect that ʿAbdi-Ashirta wrote to the troops that were in Bīt-NINURTA; he did not say, "assemble in Bīt-NINURTA." On the other hand, Gianto is right to note that a command to assemble without designating the place of assembly is awkward. Therefore, one could still render:

> AŠ É NIN.IB *pu-ḫu-ru-nim-mi ù / ni-ma-qú-ut!*(WA) UGU URUGub-la
> In Bīt Ḥoron(?) assemble so that we may fall on Byblos.
> (EA 74:31–32)

In the second example (EA 95:31–32), the *ana yâši* preceding the volitive verb most likely belongs with the previous clause. In the third passage, the passive volitive *yu-da-na* is preceded by the locative complement,

> *iš-tu* KUR *Y[a-ri-mu-ta] / yu-da-na* [š]E-[*IM*.ḪÁ] / [*a-n*]*a a-ka-li*[*-nu*]
> From the land of Y[arimuta] may gr[ain] be given for [us] to eat.
> (EA 86:46–47)

With regard to Gianto's examples of VS clauses having an independent pronoun as subject,[68] he has correctly discerned that all of the clauses are in modal congruence.[69] Congruence is required by the relationship between the verbs of result clauses and the verb of the clause upon which they are dependent. The verbs happen to be all injunctives (volitive or jussive) that are normally the logical as well as the grammatical predicate of their clauses; hence, they are fronted. The use of an independent pronoun in such clauses is not to serve as the comment but rather to signal a change in subject. Someone does something in the first clause and as a result something has to be done by someone else in the ensuing clause. One illustration will suffice:

> *li-it-ri-[iṣ] / i-na pa-ni* LU[GAL E]N-*ia yu-wa-ši-ra* / [L]Ú-*šu ù yi-zi-iz i-na-an-na ù ak-šu-*⸢*ud*⸣ / *a-na*[*-k*]*u a-na ma-ḫar šàr-ri* EN-⟨*ia*⟩
> May it seem rig[ht] in the sight of the king, my lord, that he send his [m]an that he may take up the post now, and that I may reach the presence of the king, ⟨my⟩ lord. (EA 74:59–62)

Interrogative Clauses

There are many interrogative clauses in the EA texts from Canaan. Some of the most common types will be touched on here along with some rarer examples of special interest. The interrogative component in question is

66. Ibid., 156–57, nos. 1–3.
67. Youngblood, *The Amarna Correspondence*, 141–42.
68. Gianto, *Word Order Variation*, 89–90, nos. 23–25.
69. W. L. Moran, "Early Canaanite *yaqtula*," *Or* n.s. 29 (1960) 9–11.

normally the comment. This holds true for both verbal and nonverbal clauses.

Verbal Clauses. As mentioned earlier, the parallelism between a declarative clause and an interrogative clause may serve to identify the comment in the former. Note the following conditional sentence:

[ù šum-m]a ⸢*šàr*⸣*-ru la-a* / *[yi-n]a-ṣa-ru-ni mi-nu* /*yi-na-ṣá-ru-ni*
[But i]f the king does not protect me, who [wil]l protect me? (EA 112:16–18)

The fronted subject in the protasis is the comment because it corresponds to the interrogative in the apodosis, "If it isn't the king, who will protect me. . . ?"

In verbal clauses the interrogative pronoun, adverb or particle usually is fronted. Note these examples with the nominative personal pronoun; the word order is naturally SV or SVC and the subject is the comment:

ù ma-an-nu ìl-te$_9$*-qa-*⸢*ni*⸣ / *ì[š-]tu qa-ti-šu*
Then who will rescue m[e] from his hand? (EA 82:24–25)[70]

ma-an-nu / *yi-na-ṣí-ra-ni*
Who will protect me? (EA 130:19–20)

mi-ia-mi yi-ma-lik i-zi-za [i]-na pa-ni / ERÍN.MES *pí-ṭá-at* LUGAL *be-lí-ia*
Who would advise to resist the regular troops of the king, my lord? (EA 94:12–13)[71]

The interrogative pronoun may also be in the accusative:

ù mi-n[a-a]m / *a-qa-bi a[-na-k]u*
And what could I say? (EA 92:29–30)

mi-na-⸢*am*⸣ *id-*⸢*din*⸣ *a-na ša[-š]u-nu*
What has he given to t[he]m? (EA 92:43)

ša-ni-tam mi-na-am-mi ep-ša-ku-mì / *a-na šàr-ri* EN*-ia*
Furthermore, what have I done to the king, my lord? (EA 245:36–37)

mi-na ip-ša-ti a-[na] / [I]*Ia-pa-*[d]IŠKUR
What have I done to Yapaʿ-Ḫaddi? (EA 113:11–12)

mi-na ip-ša-ti$_7$ *a-na* [I]Mi-il-ki-lí
What have I done to Milkilu? (EA 249:6)

70. Moran, *The Amarna Letters*, 152; W. F. Albright and W. L. Moran, "A Reinterpretation of an Amarna Letter from Byblos (EA 82)," *JCS* 2 (1948) 246 n. 19; Youngblood, *The Amarna Correspondence*, 232.

71. Contra Moran, *Les lettres d'el Amarna*, 285; idem, *The Amarna Letters*, 169.

ù mi-na yi-pu-šu a-na ia-ší-nu
And what will he do to us? (EA 74:41)

Adverbial interrogative nuances may be expressed by the interrogative impersonal pronoun with adverbial suffix *-u*(*m*) instead of a prepositional phrase (*ana mīni*[*m*]):

ša-ni-tam mi-nu-um ya-di-nu / *mi-im-ma ù ba-la-ta*$_5$ / LUGAL *a-na* LÚ.MEŠ *ḫa-za-nu-ti ib-ri-ia* / *ù a-na ia-ši la-a-mi* / *ia-di-nu mi-im-ma*
Furthermore, why does the king give goods and sustenance to the city rulers, my colleagues, but to me he does not give anything? (EA 126:14–18)

mi-nu-mi la-a yu-da-n[*u*] / *iš-tu* É.⌜GAL⌝ *mi-im*[*-m*]*u* / *a-na ia-ši*
Why are goods not issued to me from the palace? (EA 126:49–51)

The adverbial *-ī* is also a sufficient marker, especially for some adverbial interrogatives, such as the following:

a-di ni-na-ṣa-ru-š[*u*!]
We are still guarding him. (EA 100:30; Rainey, "Morphology and the Prefix Tenses," 408 n. 11)

ki-i in$_4$*-né-bi-tu* / *šàr* URU*Pí-ḫi-li iš-tu* / *pa-ni* LÚ.MEŠ *ra-bi-ṣí* \ *šú-ki-ni* / *šàr-ri* EN*-šu*
How would the king of Piḫilu flee from the presence of the commissioners of the king, his lord? (EA 256:7–10, for lines 4–5)

ma-ti-mi i-mur / *pa-ni* LUGAL *be-li-ia*
When will I see the face of the king, my lord? (EA 147:59–60)[72]

An adverbial particle may also be in the accusative:

⌜*a*⌝*-ya-mi ti-ìl-qú* LÚ.MEŠ *a-na a-ša-bi* / *i-na* ⌜URU⌝.KI
(From) where will you take people to dwell in the city? (EA 138:41–42)

The most commonplace syntagma for adverbial interrogatives is the prepositional phrase. Such phrases in verbal clauses are normally fronted. Sometimes they are also augmented by an enclitic (*-ma* or *-mi*).

a-di ma-ti ti$_7$*-du-* / *ku-nu*
How long will you smite us? (EA 138:40)

a-na mi-ni$_7$ / *qa-la-ta ù la-a* / *ti-iq-bu a-na šàr-ri*
Why are you silent and do not speak to the king? (EA 71:10–12; 73:6–8; cf. also EA 83:7–8; 114:35–37; 126:14–18, 49–50; 289:10)

72. CAD M/1 407b.

am-mi-ni-mi qa-la-ta / iš-tu URU*Ṣu-mu-ra*
Why is it that you ignore Ṣumur? (EA 98:3–4)

am-mi-nim-mi a-na-⟨ku⟩ e-pu-uš / \ ar-na a-na LUGAL EN-*ri*(sic!)
For what reason would I commit a crime against the king, my lord? (EA 286:14–15)

iš-tu ma-an-ni i-na-ṣa-ru-na
By what means shall I protect myself? (EA 112:10; cf. also EA 119:10)[73]

The following passage, dealt with by Gianto,[74] is not a case of modal congruence in the EA sense because the sentence is interrogative. The verb in the first clause is broken. An injunctive is not expected in a question; it may very well have been a ventive. Nor is an injunctive called for in the ensuing clause, which in this case is not a result but a parallel circumstance. The verb evidently has a lexical ventive, not a *yaqtula* volitive ending.[75] The independent pronoun in this second clause is also mainly restored but the restorations seem certain and there is not only room on the tablet but also logic in restoring the enclitic *-ma*:

ù a-na mi-ni ya-[di-na?] / šar-ru 30 *ta-pal* [ANŠE.KUR.RA.MEŠ] */ ù ti-ìl-qa at[-ta-ma] /* 10 *ta-pal*
And why should the king give thirty pairs of [horses] while you, yourself, have taken ten pair? (EA 86:41–44)[76]

The contrast in this compound sentence is between giving (by the king) and taking away (by the official). Thus the sequence within the verbal clauses, both of which are made interrogative by the adverbial *ana mīni*, is VS, that is to say, CVS followed by (C)VS.

Rhetorical questions also tend to have the comment fronted:

ú-ul ta-qa-al-mi a-na ÌR-*ka*
Have you not ignored your servant? (EA 74:13)[77]

ú-ul la-qí / IÌR-*A-si-ir-ta*
Was not ʿAbdi-Ashirta captured? (EA 117:27; 108:32–33; 132:16–17)[78]

73. Moran, *A Syntactical Study*, 169; idem, *Les lettres d'el Amarna*, 313 n. 1; idem, *The Amarna Letters*, 186–87 n. 1.

74. Gianto, *Word Order Variation*, 90, no. 26.

75. Rainey, "Is There Really a *yaqtula* Conjugation Pattern in the Canaanite Amarna Tablets?" *JCS* 43–45 (1991–93) 108–12.

76. Rainey, "Topic and Comment," 342–43.

77. Knudtzon, *Die El-Amarna-Tafeln*, 373; Youngblood, *The Amarna Correspondence*, 127.

78. Cf. Moran, *A Syntactical Study*, 167, 171.

The answer to each of these questions is "Yes." The fronted negative particle emphasizes the rhetorical nature of the question: "Is it not that you have ignored your servant?" or "It is not that ʿAbdi-Ashirta was captured?" In other words, the negative particle is the comment.

In the following rhetorical question, the independent pronoun is practically in extraposition. This is an especially pertinent observation, since the verb, *tīde*, is one of the prefix statives:

> *at-ta ú-ul / ti-de* KUR *A-mur-ri i-nu-ma / a-šar da-an-ni ti-la-ku-na*
> As for you, don't you know Amurru, that they follow the stronger party? (EA 73:14–16)[79]

The negative particle *ul* in this rhetorical question is certainly the logical predicate, since it is the interrogative component. Rib-Ḫaddi is writing to an official who had served in Amurru and who knew very well the nature of the leadership there: "As for you (of all people), is it not that you are well acquainted with Amurru?"

The following Alashia passage has a nominative independent pronoun in extraposition. This may explain the choice of negative particle (*la* instead of *ul*). Not only is the object in extraposition (taken up by the subsequent accusative pronominal suffix), the explicit subject of the verb is also fronted within the predicate clause:

> *šu-ú* ŠEŠ*-ia / la-a i-de*$_4$*-šu*
> That very thing, did my brother not know it? (EA 38:8–9)

The verb is the prefix stative, *īde*. It is not surprising, therefore, that the nominal subject precedes it. It is as if the *šū* is in extraposition and *aḫuya* is in extraposition within the predicate clause.

Nonverbal Clauses. There are interrogative nonverbal clauses with PS and SP order. The interrogative element is naturally the predicate—that is, it corresponds to the comment. The subject (S) is some known element about which some unknown fact is being requested.

When the interrogative is a pronoun, whether personal or impersonal, the normal order is PS. The subject may either be a noun:

> *ma-an-nu* LÚ*-lu*$_4$ */ ù ša-pár* LUGAL / EN*-šu a-na ša-[šu] / ù la-a yi-iš-⸢mu⸣-mi*
> Who is the man to whom the king his lord has written that would not listen? (EA 232:12–15)

> *u ma-an-nu* LÚ *kal-bu / ša la-a yi-⸢iš⸣-mu / a-na* ^{LÚ}MAŠKÍM LUGAL
> but who is the man, the dog, who would not listen to the commissioner of the king? (EA 322:17–19; also EA 319:19–21)

79. Cf. Gianto, *Word Order Variation*, 82–83; Rainey, "Topic and Comment," 340.

ma-an-nu mu[-ta]-nu / UGU-*ḫi* ANŠE.MEŠ [*i*]-*nu-m*[*a*] / *la-a ta-la-ku-*[*na*] / ANŠE.MEŠ
What pes[tile]nce affects the asses ⌜so that⌝ the asses cannot wa[lk]? (EA 96:14–17)[80]

or an independent personal pronoun:

[*mi*]-*ia šu-nu* UR.GI$_7$.[MEŠ] *k*[*a-al-bu*] (EA 129:7)
mi-ia šu-nu UR.GI$_7$.MEŠ
Who are they, the dogs? (EA 129:81)

mi-ia šu-nu / *i-nu-ma i-pu-šu ar-na ù da-a-ku* LÚMAŠKÍM *sú-ki-na* I*Pí-wu-*⌜*ri*⌝
Who are they that they should commit a crime and kill the commissioner Piwuru? (EA 362:68–69)

In the following passage, there is a reply to the second interrogative in which the answer is fronted, because it is the comment:

mi-nu / IÌR-A-*ši-ir-ta* ÌR / UR.GI$_7$ *ù* ⌜*yi*⌝-*ìl-qú* / KUR LUGAL *a-na ša-a-šu* / *mi-nu ta-la-at-šu* / *ù* KAL.GA *i-na* LÚGAZ GA.KAL / *til-la-at-šu*
Who is ʿAbdi-Ashirta, the slave, the dog, that he takes the land of the king for himself? Who are his support troops that he is strong? It is because of the *ʿapîru* that his support troops are strong.
(EA 71:16–22; also EA 76:11–16; 88:9–11; 123:38–40; 125:40–43)

Conversely, the interrogative locative adverb generally comes after its subject; thus SP (topic-comment) is the resultant word order:

i-nu-ma yi-qa-bu a-na [*pa-ni*] / LUGAL *ia-nu-mi* ŠE.MEŠ NINDA.MEŠ / *a-ka-al* ERÍN.MEŠ *pí-ṭá-ti a-ia-mi*
If they say be[fore] the king, "There is no grain for bread," where is the food for the army? (EA 131:41–43)

mi-im-mu / *ša yi-iš-ši-ru a-ya-ti Ṣu-mu-\ru* / *ù mi-im* I*ḫa-za-ni* LUGAL / *š*[*a d*]*a-ak yi-iš-ši-ru* / *a-na ka-ta*
The property that he is sending, from where (does it come)? (It is from) Ṣumur! And it is the property of the king's city ruler wh[om he has s]lain that he is sending to you! (EA 139:35–39)

yi-il-te-qú šàr-ru / *mim-mi-ia ù mim-me* / I*Mil-ki-li-lì a-ia-ka-am*
The king is always taking my property, but where is the property of Milkili? (EA 254:25–27)

One exception is in a text from Beirut where the interrogative is repeated:

80. Moran, *Les lettres d'el Amarna*, 289 n. 2; idem, *The Amarna Letters*, 170 n. 2.

a-ya-mi i-nu-ma ia-aš-pu-ru / LUGAL *be-èl-ka* [*a*]⌜*na*⌝ MAḪ-ka / *a-ya-mi* ERÍN.MEŠ [*i*]-⌜*nu*⌝-*ma uš-ši-ra-at* / *a-na ka-a-ta*$_5$
Where (are they), if the king, your lord, is corresponding with you? Where are the troops, if they have been sent to you?
(EA 138:122–26)

Compound Sentences

There are some combinations of clauses in which one is the topic and the other(s) is/are the comment. Such a combination is the conditional sentence.[81] The protasis acts as the topic, the particular condition assumed to be potentially possible of realization. The apodosis is the comment, the suggested result or implication of the realization of the condition posed in the protasis.

šum-ma i-ba-aš-ši LÚ.ERÍN.MEŠ *pi-ṭa-ti* / *i-na* MU *an-ni-ti i-ba-aš-ši* KUR.ḪÁ LUGAL EN⟨-*ia*⟩ *ù šum-ma ia-a-nu-mi* LÚ.ERÍN *pi-ṭa-ti* / ⌜*ḫal*⌝-*qa-at* KUR.ḪÁ LUGAL EN-*ia*
If there are regular troops this year, (then) the lands of the king, ⟨my⟩ lord, will still be; but if there are no regular troops, (then) the lands of the king, my lord, are lost. (EA 286:57–60)

The topic is whether troops will be sent. The comments, positive and negative, are the maintenance of control over the king's territory.

The second clause combination contains a "that" clause as topic, with the main clause as comment.[82]

i-nu-ma yi-iš-tap-pa-ra / *šàr-ru a-na ia-ši a-nu-ma* ᴵ*I-ri-ma-ia-aš-ša* / *ia-ak-šu-du-na a-na* / *mu-ḫi-ka ù-ul ka-ši-id* / *a-na mu-ḫi-ia*
Although the king has written to me, "Now ʾIrimayassa is surely coming to you," he has not come to me. (EA 130:9–14)

The "that" clause usually refers to a known communication and the comment is a response to it.

81. Cf. H. J. Polotsky, "Amharic Minutiae," in *Ethiopian Studies Dedicated to Wolf Leslau on the Occasion of His Seventy-Fifth Birthday* (ed. S. Segert and A. J. E. Bodrogligeti; Wiesbaden: Harrassowitz, 1983) 302–6.

82. A. F. Rainey, "*Inūma* Clauses in the Amarna Letters from Canaan," *IOS* 12 (1992) 186–89.

Non–Word Divider Use of the Small Vertical Wedge in *Yariḫ and Nikkal* and in an Akkadian Text Written in Alphabetic Cuneiform

Anne F. Robertson
New York, NY

There are three kinds of organizational systems generally required to produce a written text: a primary sign system, consisting of the signs that convey the words (for example, pictographs, syllabaries, alphabets); a secondary sign system, consisting of graphic devices that organize the words (for example, spaces between words, commas, periods); and a tertiary system, consisting of the various ways of laying out larger groups of words (paragraphs, titles, indexes, footnotes).

The secondary sign systems used in the ancient Near East employed various and different graphic devices. For example, Ugaritic and Old Assyrian texts written in cuneiform employed the vertical wedge, while Egyptian texts written in hieratic employed the small red ink dot, usually referred to as a point. When discussing more than one kind of use of such a graphic device, it is helpful to be able to refer to all such uses by a single short term. I will employ the term *mark* for all uses of a graphic device in a secondary sign system. Hence the small vertical wedge in Ugaritic, or the long vertical wedge in Old Assyrian, or the red ink point in Egyptian hieratic will all be termed *marks*.

In the ancient Near East, there were two basic types of uses of a mark in written texts: unit markers and spot markers.[1] Unit markers define the significant segment of text as that which lies between two marks. There are

Author's note: In honor of my teacher, adviser, and friend, Dr. Baruch Levine, I offer an examination of non–word divider use of the small vertical wedge in two texts found at Ugarit. The use of the small vertical wedge, or other graphic device, as a word divider is one aspect of that cuneiform written tradition which was to survive through the mediation of such Western sources as Ugarit to influence Israelite culture and tradition.

1. For further explanation of the kinds of marking systems found in ancient Near Eastern texts, cf. my *Word Dividers, Spot Markers and Clause Markers in Old Assyrian*,

two kinds of unit marker systems: (1) word dividers, which mark a word or word group as a single unit (found in Old Assyrian and Ugaritic texts);[2] and (2) clause markers, which mark a clause as a single unit (found only in Egyptian hieratic texts).[3] Spot markers define the significant location within a text as that place at which the mark occurs; they do not mark units. Spot markers have been identified so far only in Old Assyrian texts, where there are a wide variety of different uses for them.[4]

* * *

The marking system employed on almost all marked texts found at Ugarit is the word divider marking system.[5] In this paper, I will examine two texts found at Ugarit that are marked but are not marked with word dividers. This

Ugaritic, and Egyptian Texts: Sources for Understanding the Use of the Red Ink Points in the Two Akkadian Literary Texts, "Adapa" and "Ereshkigal," Found in Egypt (Ph.D. Dissertation, New York University, 1994) 7–10; hereafter, *Word Dividers*.

2. Most modern word divider systems employ a space as the graphic device and mark even very small units, such as prepositions or conjunctions, as single units. Most ancient Near Eastern word divider systems marked a number of combinations of words as single units. Among the words that were usually marked in combination with some other word(s) are negations, determinative-relative pronouns, some prepositions, and some conjunctions. Ugaritic also employed a second, variant word divider system, used only for some nonliterary texts, which marked such words as negations, determinative-relative pronouns, some prepositions, and some conjunctions as single units, just as modern word divider systems do. For a partial list of word divider rules in Akkadian and Ugaritic, cf. my *Word Dividers*, Appendix I, 395–406. For Ugaritic, cf. also W. Horowitz, *Graphemic Representation of Word Boundary: The Small Vertical Wedge in Ugaritic* (Ph.D. Dissertation, Yale University, 1971); hereafter Horowitz, *Graphemic Representation*.

3. Clause markers in Egyptian hieratic are generally termed *verse points*. For the most important studies of these, cf. J. Foster, "Thought Couplets in Khety's 'Hymn to the Inundation,'" *JNES* 34 (1975) 1–29; idem, *Thought Couplets and Clause Sequence in a Literary Text: The Maxims of Ptah-hotep* (Society for the Study of Egyptian Antiquities Publications 5; Toronto: Society for the Study of Egyptian Antiquities, 1977); idem, "Sinuhe: The Ancient Egyptian Genre of Narrative Verse," *JNES* 39 (1980) 89–117; and idem, *Thought Couplets in The Tale of Sinuhe* (Münchner Ägyptologisches Unterschungen 3; Frankfurt am Main: von Zabern, 1993). For the theory of verse points as indicators of metrical units, cf. G. Fecht, "Die Wiedergewinnung der altägyptische Verskunst," *MDAIK* 19 (1961) 54–96. For bibliography of theories of verse points in Egyptian, cf. B. Mathieu, "Études de métrique égyptienne, I: Le Distique heptamétrique dans les chants d'amour," *RdÉ* 39 (1988) 63.

4. For the different kinds of spot markers so far identified in Old Assyrian texts, cf. my *Word Dividers*, 180–208, 214–21.

5. I have attempted to survey Ugaritic literary texts to determine whether there are any other examples of non–word divider marking. I have also briefly checked for

paper will identify the marking system on these two texts as a combination marking system employing both clause markers and spot markers. The method will be a comparison to the Egyptian clause-marking system and to the Old Assyrian spot-marking system.[6] In the conclusion, I will discuss further the sources for this combination marking system and its significance for the development of marking systems.

The longest, best preserved, and most important of the two texts for study here is the Ugaritic literary text *Yariḫ and Nikkal* (KTU 1.24 = CTA 24 = RS 5.194 = UT 77 = AO 19.995). It was obvious at first glance that the text was marked but not with normal Ugaritic word divider marking.[7] However, exactly what sort of marking it is has remained unknown.

The other text for study here is KTU 1.69 (= RS 5.213 = UT 104). It is one of the four Akkadian literary texts written in alphabetic cuneiform found at Ugarit.[8] These four texts have almost exactly the same provenance as *Yariḫ and Nikkal*,[9] and they too display unknown marking systems.[10]

---

any marked Akkadian texts. However, I have made no attempt to check Ugaritic nonliterary texts for examples of non–word divider marking.

I doubt there are other examples of major Ugaritic literary texts marked with a non–word divider marking system. There may be some small sections in which the marking is actually of a phrase or a clause rather than true word division. For example, UT 2 Aqht II:34–36: *snnt* . *ṯlṯ rbʿym* . *yšl* (35) *ḥm kṯrt w yššq* (36) *bnt hll snnt* . has both a clausal type marking and a split word. However, it is an isolated instance, not the marking system used throughout the text or even on one side of a tablet. It is interesting to note that this example also involves the *kṯrt*, who figure prominently in *Yariḫ and Nikkal*, one of the three texts with non–word divider marking studied here. There are also texts with very sloppy marking, such as KTU 1.100.

6. For discussion of the dating criteria of the texts used for comparison, cf. my *Word Dividers*, 30–43.

7. By normal Ugaritic word divider marking, I refer to the system used on both literary and some nonliterary texts and to the variant system employed only on some nonliterary texts. For more on the differences between the two variants of the Ugaritic word divider system, cf. my *Word Dividers*, 264–80. There are, of course, also texts that are completely unmarked.

8. The four Akkadian texts written in alphabetic cuneiform and found at Ugarit are KTU 1.67 (= RS 5.199 = UT 105), KTU 1.69 (= RS 5.213 = UT 104), KTU 1.70 (= RS 5.156 = UT 103), KTU 1.73 (= RS 5.303 = UT 102). KTU 1.73 is actually half Akkadian and half Ugaritic, with a horizontal line separating the two parts.

9. P. Bordreuil and D. Pardee, *La trouvaille épigraphique de l'Ougarit* (Paris: Editions recherche sur les civilisations, 1989) 1.36–38. They were excavated in the fifth campaign at Ras Shamra. The provenance "Acropole 'Tr. + IV p.t. 67 à 0,95' (= p.t. 484,486)" is given for RS 5.194 (= KTU 1.24 *Yariḫ and Nikkal*), RS 5.211 and 214 (part of the same text as RS 5.156 = KTU 1.70, RS 5.199 = KTU 1.67, and RS 5.213 = KTU 1.69, RS 5.156 = KTU 1.70) is given as "(= p.t. 480)." There is no exact information available for RS 5.303 (= KTU 1.73). It evidently was noted only as a number in the original inventory. [footnote continues on next page]

My analysis of *Yariḫ and Nikkal* and KTU 1.69 will focus solely on determining what sort of non–word divider marking systems were used. Consequently, I have not commented on any of the numerous difficulties of these texts that are not directly and immediately essential to the effort of determining what the marking system is. Further, in my analysis of the marking, I relied on the scribe to mark correctly, even though of course, any scribe could make a mistake. I consider it essential in determining an unknown marking system to begin from the premise that the scribe knew what he was doing and that the marking is essentially correct. Unless one does so, either one risks identifying only a partial marking system, that is, one that includes only some marks but not all, or one risks identifying a marking system that has more errors than correct marking. Neither of these alternatives really qualifies as identifying a marking system. The identification of errors in a marking system requires that first one have identified the marking system. Errors can be determined only after there is knowledge of what the correct marking should be.

* * *

The Ugaritic literary text *Yariḫ and Nikkal* (KTU 1.24) is well known for its difficult and unusual qualities,[11] one of which is the use of the mark. Generally speaking, marking in Ugaritic texts is occasionally noted or discussed within the context of some other matter but seldom if ever made the focus of a study.[12] Even in the case of *Yariḫ and Nikkal*, where the use of the mark

---

There are also a number of other alphabetic cuneiform texts with exactly the same provenance, whose marking systems, if any, I have not yet studied. They are RS 5.195 = KTU 7.51, RS 5.196 = KTU 7.52, RS 5.197 = KTU 4.31, RS 5.198 = KTU 1.7 13–44, RS 5.200 = KTU 1.68, RS 5.212 = KTU 4.31, RS 5.215, RS 5.216 = KTU 5.2, RS 5.217 = KTU 4.32, RS 5.218 = KTU 7.55, RS 5.219, RS 5.220 = KTU 7.20, RS 5.221, RS 5.222, and RS 5.223.

10. There are several reasons I do not include the other three texts in this study. The limitation of space obviously is one reason. KTU 1.67 is extremely fragmentary, although perhaps relevant to this study in a minor way. KTU 1.70 and 1.73 may actually employ some unusual form of word dividers and hence not be useful for comparison to *Yariḫ and Nikkal*.

11. For the original publication of *Yariḫ and Nikkal* (KTU 1.24 = CTA 24 = RS 5.194 = UT 77 = AO 19.995), cf. C. Virolleaud, "Fragments alphabétiques divers de Ras-Shamra," *Syria* 20 (1939) 114–33. For further publications, transliterations, translations, and commentaries, cf. J. Cunchillos, *La trouvaille épigraphique de l'Ougarit* (Paris: Editions recherche sur les civilisations, 1989) vol. 2.

12. To the best of my knowledge, Horowitz is the only scholar to study the use of the mark in Ugaritic; cf. *Graphemic Representation*; idem, "Some Possible Results of Rudimentary Scribal Training," *UF* 6 (1974) 75–83; and idem, "Our Ugaritic Mythological Texts: Copied or Dictated?" *UF* 9 (1977) 123–30.

is itself problematic, there has been relatively little attention to what its use may be. The idea that the mark indicates a verse unit has been proposed. Probably the first to suggest this was Goetze, who in 1941 proposed that the mark "serves to mark sense units rather than words" and that the marking "facilitates recognizing the metrical units of the text which normally will represent syntactical units."[13] However, he made no analysis of the marks as verse-unit indicators. In fact, to my knowledge, only one study focuses on the marks as verse-unit indicators. In 1977, Horowitz proposed that the mark in our copy of *Yariḫ and Nikkal* represents the end of the line in an earlier completely unmarked copy of the text, from which our text was presumably copied.[14] He believes that Ugaritic mythological texts were originally written to indicate a line of verse by a line of text. In the case of *Yariḫ and Nikkal*, the copyist was evidently unable to accommodate this scheme and instead used the mark to indicate where the lines of verse and, originally, the lines of text were to be identified. I will not specifically address the question of whether or not the marks are verse-unit indicators. My intention is to try to understand at the simplest level what they indicate. However, I will briefly indicate how my conclusions would correlate with the idea that they are verse indicators and with Horowitz's idea that they indicate verses by indicating lines.

I will begin with a brief review of split words. Next, I will consider the marks best understood as clause markers, and the comparison will be to clause markers in Egyptian hieratic. Then, I will consider the marks best understood as spot markers, and the comparison will be to spot markers in Old Assyrian. For the purposes of this study, only lines 16–46 will be considered, since lines 1–15 are too badly damaged to be usable, and lines 47–50 are entirely unmarked.[15]

In the Ugaritic word divider marking system, all ends of lines functioned as marks. Hence no actual mark was necessary at the end of a line, nor is one

13. A. Goetze, "The Nikkal Poem from Ras Shamra," *JBL* 60 (1941) 354.

14. Horowitz, "Our Ugaritic Mythological Texts," 127–30.

15. One might wonder whether the fact that the last four lines are unmarked is merely an oversight or has some purpose. The last few lines of a text being unmarked in order to save space is not unusual in Old Assyrian texts marked with word dividers. For an example, cf. I. Spar (ed.), *Cuneiform Texts in the Metropolitan Museum of Art* (New York: Metropolitan Museum of Art, 1988) vol. 1, nos. 74, pls. 68–69 (hereafter Spar, *Cuneiform Texts* MMA *1*). Certainly in Egyptian clause marking, a text only partially marked is quite common in a later period. For any number of such examples, cf. A. Gardiner, *Late Egyptian Miscellanies* (Bibliotheca Aegyptiaca 7; Brussels: Fondation Égyptologique Reine Élisabeth, 1937). On the other hand, Horowitz believes that the unmarked last four lines of *Yariḫ and Nikkal* corresponded to the last four lines on the original unmarked text from which the scribe copied. His theory is that this was not the case for the rest of the text, and that this is the reason for the clause marking; cf. "Our Ugaritic Mythological Texts."

usually present.[16] All lines can be assumed to end words or the equivalent thereof as determined by the rules of word dividers.[17] Hence splitting a word between two lines is the equivalent of placing a mark within a word.[18] This would be highly unusual in a word divider marking system and, in fact, words split between two lines are rare in the corpus of Ugaritic texts.[19] Consequently, numerous split words in a single text would be one possible indicator that the marking system may not be a word divider marking system.[20]

In *Yariḫ and Nikkal*, there are at least 13 words that can definitely be classified as split words in the 31 lines from line 16 through line 46.[21] There may have been more. This is an extremely large number of split words, far more than can be attributed simply to error or lack of space. Thus I think they must be intentional, and I think the purpose they serve is like that of a flag.

16. The same is true of the Old Assyrian word divider system.

17. For a partial list of rules of word dividers in Ugaritic, cf. my *Word Dividers*, Appendix I, 395–406.

18. There are a few marks within words in Ugaritic. C. Gordon notes six examples: cf. *Ugaritic Textbook* (Rome: Pontifical Biblical Institute, 1967) 24. In the conclusion to his study of word dividers in Ugaritic, Horowitz mentions marks within words as one of the four types of irregular cases (cf. *Graphemic Representation*, 130). However, I have not been able to locate his discussion of these within the body of that work. Marks within words in Old Assyrian texts are extremely rare. For a possible example, cf. Spar, *Cuneiform Texts* MMA 1, 78a, line 15. To my knowledge, the only marks within words that are definitely not errors but part of an intended marking system are the marks in the Amarna recension of the Akkadian literary text *Ereshkigal and Nergal*; cf. my *Word Dividers*, 128–34.

19. For a recent study of all examples of split words, cf. S. Segert, "Words Spread over Two Lines," *UF* 19 (1987) 283–88. For another list of all examples of split words and also all examples of lines ending with a mark, cf. Horowitz, "Our Ugaritic Mythological Texts," 126 n. 17.

20. Generally, in Ugaritic there is no difficulty in discerning whether a text is marked with word dividers, since usually the only other alternative would be not to mark the text at all. This is not always the case for Old Assyrian texts. There were two basic marking systems: word dividers and spot markers. It is not always immediately apparent, especially in the case of short texts with short lines, whether a text is marked with word dividers or spot markers. I do not know of any split words in Old Assyrian texts. They were certainly not employed to indicate spot marker texts.

21. The split words are between the following lines: 17/18, 18/19, 19/20, 20/21, 21/22, 25/26, 36/37, 38/39, 40/41, 41/42, 44/45, 45/46, 46/47. There are ten lines with no split word: 16/17, 30/31, 31/32, 32/33, 33/34, 34/35, 35/36, 37/38, 39/40, 42/43. There are two lines that end in elements that would not be marked alone in the Ugaritic word divider system for literary texts: (23) *w*(24)*yʿn* and 24 *l* (25)*nʿmn*. The rules of word dividers would not permit either *w* or *l* to be at the end of a line in a literary text; cf. my *Word Dividers*, 277–79. There are five ends of lines with damage, making it difficult to be sure whether there might be a split word or not: 22/23, 24/25, 26/27, 27/28, 29/30. There are two ends of lines that can be classed as questionable: 28/29 and 43/44.

They help to alert the reader to the fact that in this text the mark is not being used as a word divider.

Only lines 16–23 and 30–39 of the text will be presented for the discussion of clause markers below. I omit lines 23–30 and lines 40–46, because they have difficulties that make clause recognition more problematic. However, I will include the examples from the omitted sections that may be spot markers in the discussion of spot markers below.

Clause Marking in Yariḫ and Nikkal

The transliteration below is my transcription from C. Virolleaud's hand drawing.[22] I have noted in the footnotes all the instances in which KTU presents a different reading of the marks.

The first section is from line 16 to line 23.

---

(16) *ylak yrḫ nyr šmm . ʿm* (17) *ḫr[ḫ]b mlk qẓ .*	1 clause—1 spot marker
. tn nkl y(18)*rḫ ytrḫ . ib tʿrbm bbh*(19)*th .*	3 clauses—1 spot marker
. watn mhrh la(20)*bh . alp*[23] *ksp . wrbt*[24] *ḫ*(21)*rṣ .*	1 clause—2 spot markers
. išlḥ ẓhrm iq(22)*nim .*	1 clause
. atn ḫdh krmm (23) *ḫd ddh ḥrnqm .* [25]	1 clause

Yariḫ, the heavenly lamp, sends (a message) to Hrhb, king of Qz: "Give away Nikkal; (for) Yariḫ seeks to wed Ib that she may enter into his house. And I will pay her bride-price to her father: 100 silver and a lot of gold. I will send lapis-lazuli. I will give field, vineyard, field . . (?) orchard."

The second section is from line 30 to line 39.

. wyʿn (31) *yrḫ nyr šmm .*	1 clause
. wnʿn (32) *ʿmn nkl ḫtny .*	1 clause
. aḫr (33) *nkl yrḫ ytrḫ .*	1 clause
. adnh (34) *yšt mṣb . mẓnm .*	1 clause—1 spot marker
. umh (35) *kp mẓnm .*	1 clause
. iḫh yṯʿr (36) *mšrrm .*	1 clause
. aḫtth[26] *la*(37)*bn mẓnm .*	1 clause
. nkl w ib (38) *dašr .*	1 clause
. ar yrḫ .	1 clause
. wy(39)*rḫ yark .*	1 clause

22. Virolleaud, "Fragments alphabétiques," 114–33.
23. KTU shows a mark here.
24. KTU shows a mark here.
25. KTU shows *ḥrnq[m.] w*(24)*yʿn*, etc.
26. KTU shows a mark here.

And Yariḫ, the heavenly lamp, answered: "The answer is that it is with Nikkal that my marriage shall be!"

Afterward, Yariḫ paid the bride-price for Nikkal. Her father set the stand of the balances, (and) her mother the pan of the scales. Her brothers set up the beams, (and) her sisters are the balance weights.

"It is to Nikkal-w-Ib that I sing. Bright is Yariḫ, (and) Yariḫ shall shine upon you!"

In the text as presented above, there are eleven clauses marked as a single unit with no spot markers, two clauses marked as a single unit with one spot marker, one clause marked as a single unit with two spot markers, and one three-clause unit with one spot marker. In the same text as presented in KTU, there are nine clauses marked as a single unit with no spot markers, three clauses marked as a single unit with one spot marker, one clause marked as a single unit with four spot markers, a three-clause unit with one spot marker, and one clause not marked as a single unit due to damage. By either reading, most of the clauses in these two sections are marked as single units. However, the first clause (lines 16–17) actually has no mark at the beginning and therefore strictly speaking should not be counted. There is one example in which the marked unit is unusual. It is the three-clause unit, lines 17–19, which has no mark at the end of the first clause, no marks at the beginning or end of the second clause, and no mark at the beginning of the third clause.

There is only one clause marker system presently identified in use in the ancient Near East, and that is the clause marker system used in Egyptian hieratic. Egyptologists commonly refer to this as "verse pointing," since the basic unit, the clause, is equivalent to a single line of verse. In a number of studies, J. Foster has shown that the basic unit of verse in Egyptian is the couplet and that a single marked unit equals one line of that two-line unit.[27] He has identified a number of cases in which a single line of verse is made up of two clauses, which are thus marked as a single unit. My own study of the *Sesostris I Building Inscription* and some portions of *Ptahhotep* suggests the possibility that there could in some circumstances be three clauses in a single marked unit and hence presumably in a single line of verse.[28] Since the Egyptian clause-marking system almost certainly existed prior to the marking of *Yariḫ and Nikkal*,[29] I think it is likely that the Egyptian clause-marking system is the probable source for the idea of clause marking in *Yariḫ and Nikkal*, even though the actual identification of the Ugarit marking as clause marking really requires little if any reliance on the specifics of Egyptian clause marking. Indeed, there is little more that can be said about the com-

27. For primary references, cf. Foster, "Thought Couplets."

28. Robertson, *Word Dividers*, 312–14.

29. For the question of dating in regard to Egyptian texts, cf. ibid., 35–42.

parison between Egyptian clause marking and the clause marking in *Yariḫ and Nikkal* without first examining the case for whether the clause marking in *Yariḫ and Nikkal* is indeed intended as verse marking, since that is definitely the purpose of the Egyptian clause marking.

Spot Marking in Yariḫ and Nikkal

In the sections lines 16–23 and 30–39 presented above, there are 5 spot markers. KTU shows 8 spot markers in the same two sections. I will discuss all of these spot markers as well as the spot markers in lines 23–30 and 40–46, which were not presented above. However, it should be noted that most of the examples of spot marking in *Yariḫ and Nikkal* occur within the clause-marked sections presented above.

I will discuss spot markers in comparison to the kinds of spot markers found in Old Assyrian in the following order: (1) spot markers separating two or more nominal elements in a list, including nominal elements joined by a conjunction, (2) spot markers separating two or more nominal elements in apposition, (3) spot markers separating the two elements of a nominal clause, and (4) spot markers separating the verb from the remainder of the clause, effectively nominalizing the clause for the purpose of emphasizing a nonverbal element.[30] There are two spot markers in *Yariḫ and Nikkal* that cannot be compared to any Old Assyrian spot marker. These two spot markers separate the construct and its genitive. One is within the body of text for analysis in this study. It is *mṣb . mznm* (line 34). The other example is in text not for analysis in this study. It is *mlk . qz .* (line 2).[31] I will not discuss these further.[32]

(1) There is one example of a spot marker that can be compared to the Old Assyrian spot markers separating two or more nominal elements in a list

30. As far as I know, mine is the only study of Old Assyrian spot markers; cf. ibid., 180–209. I studied twenty-two of the twenty-four Old Assyrian texts owned by the Metropolitan Museum of Art in New York City; cf. Spar, *Cuneiform Texts MMA 1*, 92–143, nos. 71–98, pls. 66–99, 134, 137, 138, and 156. Fourteen texts were marked with spot markers. Six texts were marked with word dividers. Two texts could not be classified. Although there were more spot marker texts than word divider texts, the sheer number of examples was far larger in the case of word divider texts. Some kinds of spot markers can be considered well established, even if there were only a few examples available. Other spot markers cannot be considered so well established due to lack of evidence.

31. The identical words have no spot marker in line 23. This was common in Old Assyrian spot marking, where there was no need to mark all examples; cf. my *Word Dividers*, 180–81.

32. These two spot markers are mentioned again below (p. 107). They may have some similarity to the confused marking of some compound prepositions in the two marked Akkadian texts, *Adapa* and *Ereshkigal*, found at Tell el Amarna in Egypt; cf. ibid., 99–101, 116–19. The marking on *Adapa* and *Ereshkigal* is discussed briefly in the conclusion to this paper (pp. 108–109).

including nominal elements joined by a conjunction.[33] This example is from a section of text presented above in the analysis of clause marking.

(20) . *alp ksp . wrbt ḫ*(21)*rṣ* .	100 silver and a lot of gold[34]

(2) There are three examples of spot markers that can be compared to the Old Assyrian spot markers separating two or more nominal elements in apposition.[35] These all come from sections of the text not presented above in the analysis of clause marking.

(27) *abh . bʿl* [36]	her father, Baal
(29) *ybrdmy . bt* [*a*](30)*bh*	Ybrdmy, daughter of her father
(40) *bn*(41)*t hll . snnt . bnt h*(42)*ll*	daughters of Hll, the swallows, daughters of Hll

There are two more nominal elements in apposition immediately preceding the examples in lines 40–41, which are not marked: (40) [*ilh*]*t kṯrt bn*(41)*t hll*.[37] However, since in Old Assyrian spot marking there was no requirement for all examples to be marked,[38] this would not be a problem for identifying this example as similar to Old Assyrian examples of this kind of spot marker.

(3) There is one example of a spot marker that can be compared to the Old Assyrian spot markers separating the two elements of a nominal clause.[39]

(36) *aḫtth . la*(37)*bn mẕnm*	her sisters are the balance weights

This example is problematic. There are only a few examples of such spot markers in Old Assyrian texts, and those have the purpose of insuring that the nominal clause is not misread, for example, as a noun and its adjective.

33. For spot markers in Old Assyrian separating two or more nominal elements in a list including nominal elements joined by a conjunction, cf. ibid., 182.

34. KTU shows this marking as (20)*bh . alp . ksp . wrbt. ḫ*(21)*rṣ* . If this is the correct marking, then this would not be an example comparable to any use of spot markers in Old Assyrian. Instead, it would be the only line in the text marked with word dividers. There is one possible example of word dividers in KTU 1.69 (line 4: . *mʿnh*. Cf. p. 104 below).

35. For spot markers in Old Assyrian separating two or more nominal elements in apposition, cf. my *Word Dividers*, 182–83.

36. This mark is shown in KTU.

37. There is another example of two nominal elements in apposition separated by a spot marker in the first section of the text, (2) *ḫrḫb . mlk*, which is repeated with no spot marker in lines 2–3.

38. In Old Assyrian spot marking, there was no need to mark all examples; cf. my *Word Dividers*, 180–81.

39. For spot markers in Old Assyrian separating the two elements of a nominal clause, cf. ibid., 184–85.

That could be the purpose in this example in *Yariḫ and Nikkal*. On the other hand, it could also be that the verb of the previous clause applies to this one, and hence the translation should be 'the sisters place the balance weights'. In that case, this would not be an example comparable to an Old Assyrian spot marker and would simply be unexplained. At this point, I think it more useful to try to explain marks whenever possible rather than to leave them unexplained, and so I have included this example as a spot marker.

(4) There are two examples of spot markers that can be compared to the Old Assyrian spot markers separating a verb from the remainder of the clause, effectively nominalizing the clause for the purpose of emphasizing a nonverbal element.[40] These both occur in a section of the text presented above in the analysis for clause marking.

(16) *ylak yrḫ nyr šmm .ʿm* (17) *ḫr[ḫ]b mlk qz .*
Yariḫ, the heavenly lamp, sends (a message) to Hrhb, king of Qz

(17) *tn nkl y*(18)*rḫ ytrḫ . ib tʿrbm bbh*(19)*th .*
Give away Nikkal; (for) Yariḫ seeks to wed Ib that she may enter into his house

In the first example, the mark is before the prepositional phrase, separating subject, verb, and direct object from the prepositional phrase that functions as the indirect object. In the second example, the mark is placed before the direct object, separating subject and verb from the direct object. In the Old Assyrian examples, marks of this type are placed before the verb that is the last element in the clause. Thus the mark separates the verb from the remainder of the clause.[41] In these Ugaritic examples, obviously, that would not be possible, because the verb is not regularly placed at the end of the clause, as it is in Old Assyrian.

This type of spot marker is far more complex than the other types of spot markers discussed above. This kind of spot marker supplies not simply the equivalent of a common punctuation mark, such as the examples in (1) and (2) in which the mark is being used much like the modern comma; nor does it supply mere reading assistance, such as the examples in (3) in which the mark flags a nominal clause to help prevent its being missed. Instead, spot markers of this type change the kind of clause from verbal to nominal, and they do so for the purpose of emphasizing a nonverbal element. To establish the existence of such spot markers, there must be a reason from context why such emphasis is needed. There are some examples in Old Assyrian texts for which such reasons can be provided, but there are also examples for which

40. For spot markers in Old Assyrian separating the verb from the remainder of the clause, cf. ibid., 186–97.

41. In the majority of the Old Assyrian examples, there was only one other element besides the verb, though there were a few examples with two elements; cf. ibid., 194–96.

too little information about the context is contained in the text for reasons to be provided. Consequently, I regard this kind of spot marker as less well established even though it is certainly far more interesting than the uses of spot markers, for example, simply to separate two or more nominal elements in a list.

I shall now present the examples again, and this time translate them with the element intended for emphasis underlined.[42]

(16) *ylak yrḫ nyr šmm .ʿm* (17) *ḫr[ḫ]b mlk qẓ .*
It is to Hrhb, king of Qz, that Yariḫ, the heavenly lamp, sends (a message)'

This example emphasizes the name of the person to whom the message is addressed. There is a similar example in Old Assyrian,[43] but in neither case can I propose any reason for a need to emphasize the name of the person to whom the message is addressed.

(17) *tn nkl y*(18)*rḫ ytrḫ . ib tʿrbm bbh*(19)*th .*
Give away Nikkal; (for) it is Ib that Yariḫ seeks to wed that she may enter into his house

This example emphasizes the direct object. There are two similar examples in Old Assyrian, and in both there is evidence from the context for emphasis.[44] The reason for the emphasis in the example above, however, is not clear. There does seem to be a suggestion of another possible bride, Pdry, in the more problematic section in lines 24–30. Thus it may be that there is reason for wishing to emphasize that it is Ib and not someone else that Yariḫ wishes to wed.

There is another reason, besides the apparent similarity, to think that the Old Assyrian spot markers of this kind were the inspiration behind this marking. For large sections of the text (lines 19–23 and 30–39), a clause-marking system is used. The examples of spot markers that occur within these sections are not only unlike Old Assyrian spot marking in this regard, but also unlike Egyptian clause marking in this regard. Old Assyrian spot markers occur in texts or sections of texts with no other marking system. Egyptian clause marking also occurs in texts with no other marking system. These two examples of spot markers in *Yariḫ and Nikkal*, used to nominalize a verbal clause, are spot markers that occur in a context that could be construed as a disruption

42. I have translated them as cleft sentences, following the practice of Egyptologists translating clauses in which an apparently verbal clause is understood to be functioning as a nominal clause with an emphasized element.

43. For this example, cf. Spar, *Cuneiform Texts* MMA 1, no. 81, line 1; also cf. my *Word Dividers*, 193.

44. For the Old Assyrian spot markers separating a verb from the remainder of the clause, effectively nominalizing the clause for the purpose of emphasizing the direct object, cf. ibid., 187–89.

of clause marking. The first example (lines 16–17) has no mark at the beginning of the clause. The second example actually occurs within a clause that is unmarked at both ends. It is part of a three-clause unit. It could be that the failure to mark the beginning of the clause in lines 16–17 and the creation of a three-clause unit in lines 17–19 were both intentional omissions of marks intended to make this marking more like its Old Assyrian counterpart. Of course, it could also be that the marks omitted for clause marking were simply oversights or were even allowed within the clausal marking system. Too little is known or likely to be known about the clause-marking system in *Yariḫ and Nikkal* to say for certain.

There are three conclusions that I think can be drawn from the above analysis of spot markers in *Yariḫ and Nikkal* and in Old Assyrian. First, there are two kinds of very simple spot markers, quite similar to modern uses of the comma, which can be considered well established for Old Assyrian spot marking and clearly identifiable in *Yariḫ and Nikkal*. Second, there are two kinds of spot markers of considerably greater complexity that are less well established for Old Assyrian spot marking and thus less clearly identifiable in *Yariḫ and Nikkal*. Third, I think it is fair to say that these marks in *Yariḫ and Nikkal* can be understood and identified as spot markers on the basis of comparison with the spot markers in Old Assyrian texts.

* * *

My purpose in this study was to see whether non–word divider marking on texts from Ugarit can be adequately understood by comparison to non–word divider marking known elsewhere in the ancient Near East. In the case of *Yariḫ and Nikkal*, I think it is clear that the non–word divider marking can be understood and in fact can be identified by comparison with other non–word divider marking.

If one compares the clause-marking system to the clause-marking system of Egyptian hieratic, there are two important things to notice. First, the comparison is largely of a surface nature. I have not attempted to analyze *Yariḫ and Nikkal* to see whether its clause marking is intended to show verse units such as couplets, which is the real purpose of Egyptian clause marking. Second, the hypothesis that marking in *Yariḫ and Nikkal* is intended to show verse units does find support from the fact that it is clause marking and can be compared to another system of clause marking that does show verse units.

If one compares the spot marking in *Yariḫ and Nikkal* to the spot marking of Old Assyrian, one notices that the comparison is much closer than is the comparison to Egyptian clause marking. Specific kinds of spot markers can be compared in *Yariḫ and Nikkal* and Old Assyrian. There is no such correlation to specifics of the Egyptian clause-marking system.

When one considers the marking of *Yariḫ and Nikkal* as a whole, the similarity both to Egyptian clause marking and to Old Assyrian spot marking begins to break down. Both of these marking systems were used as single marking systems. There is no spot marking or any other marking in Egyptian texts with clause markers.[45] There is no clause marking or any other marking system used in Old Assyrian texts with spot markers.[46] Likewise, there are no examples of any other marking system used in Ugaritic texts or in Old Assyrian texts marked with word dividers. Thus the marking on *Yariḫ and Nikkal* would seem to be unique, because its marking system is actually made up of two different marking systems, one a clause-marking system and the other a spot-marking system. Thus it may be said to have one combination marking system, since these two marking systems are used simultaneously, rather than alternately. I will consider this subject further at the end of the paper. For the present, I will only comment briefly on what light these findings may shed on the two previous theories about the marking in *Yariḫ and Nikkal.*

The identification of the marking system of *Yariḫ and Nikkal* as a clause-marking system and a spot-marking system does have some bearing both on the theory that the purpose of the marking is to indicate verse units and on Horowitz's theory that the purpose of the marking is to denote the line breaks of the original, unmarked text. In both cases the spot markers have been ignored or dismissed as errors.[47] Neither theory could include the spot markers. The fact that there is so much specific similarity to kinds of spot markers in Old Assyrian texts makes it impossible simply to dismiss these marks in *Yariḫ and Nikkal* as errors. They are spot markers, and they are part of what must be explained in order to understand the marking system used in *Yariḫ and Nikkal.* On the other hand, I do not think the fact that both theories ignore the spot markers is necessarily proof that either theory is simply wrong. It merely shows that both theories actually apply only to the clause-marking system in *Yariḫ and Nikkal.*

The comparison of the clause-marking system to the Egyptian clause-marking system strengthens the case for the theory that these marks do also indicate verse units, since this was true of Egyptian clause marking. Horowitz's theory, that the tablet of *Yariḫ and Nikkal* that we have was actually

45. This refers solely to Egyptian texts that can be reasonably well dated to a period prior to the period in which *Yariḫ and Nikkal* was likely to have been marked. For more on such Egyptian texts and their dating, cf. ibid., 35–42.

46. Spot markers in Old Assyrian texts are usually confined to texts using no other marking system. However, there are some letters that are marked with word dividers throughout the body of the text but that are best understood as marked with spot markers in the opening formula; cf. ibid., 164–70, 206–9.

47. I have not detailed exactly which marks are not used as verse unit marks, for instance, by Goetze, or as end of line marks by Horowitz. They are not necessarily exactly the same as the marks that I have designated spot markers, since there can be differences of viewpoint concerning where clauses should be broken or where lines would be likely to end. For the exact marks omitted, cf. Goetze, "Nikkal Poem," 353–74; and Horowitz, "Our Ugaritic Mythological Texts," 123–30.

copied from an unmarked original, could help to explain how spot markers came to be on a Ugaritic text marked with a clause-marking system. If the original text was unmarked, then perhaps the spot markers as originally envisioned would have been like Old Assyrian spot markers—that is, in a text with no other marking system. However, if the scribe of our tablet discovered that he could not keep the ends of lines the same as in his original and if he then decided to use marks as indicators of original line lengths rather than as word dividers, the unusual phenomenon of a tablet with two marking systems could have occurred.[48]

* * *

KTU 1.69 was first published by Virolleaud,[49] first recognized as Akkadian by Dhorme,[50] and subsequently briefly studied by Astour[51] and van Soldt.[52] The text is fifteen lines long, twelve lines on the obverse and three lines on the reverse. There are seven marks in the text. The transliteration below on the left is my transcription from Virolleaud's hand drawing. The Akkadian on the right is from Dhorme's transcription, though Astour's rendering is virtually the same. I have given the differences in marking evident in KTU and in van Soldt in the footnotes here. The translation below is Astour's for lines 1–12 and Dhorme's for line 15.

Obverse

(1) *d̠mrk bltn il*[	*zamraku beletni il*[*at*[53]
(2) *mṯmṯty klt mk*[	*muši mušiti kallati muk*[*katimti*[54]

48. Horowitz's intent was to address a larger question: whether the mythological texts were copied or dictated; cf. "Our Ugaritic Mythological Texts." Since my study deals solely with marking, I have not dealt with this larger aspect of his theory. I would say, however, that I am dubious about applying the findings about the marking system of *Yariḫ and Nikkal* to the great body of Ugaritic mythological texts, since *Yariḫ and Nikkal* is so clearly an unusual case.

49. Virolleaud, "Fragments alphabétiques," 114–33.

50. É. Dhorme, "Textes accadiens transcrits en écriture alphabétique de Ras Shamra," *RA* 37 (1940–41) 83–96.

51. M. Astour, *Hellenosemitica* (Leiden: Brill, 1965) 133–34. Astour considers this a hymn, rather than a magic spell. I am inclined to wonder if this might instead be a sort of set of instructions for the order in which to sing a set of songs, and thus only the titles or first lines of the songs are given.

52. W. van Soldt, *Studies in the Akkadian of Ugarit: Dating and Grammar* (AOAT 40; Neukirchen-Vluyn: Neukirchener Verlag, 1991) 296–99; hereafter van Soldt, *Studies*.

53. Van Soldt reads *belti* + *ina* (?) *ilati*. He also transcribes the line with a mark, *d̠mrk bltn . i* [*lt*; cf. ibid. If a mark is present, then his rendition of the Akkadian is unlikely. Not only are there no similar spot markers known from Old Akkadian, but if there were, they would violate the rules of word dividers. I know of no example from

<table>
<tr><td>(3) n ll irbt ryb . l[</td><td>ina lili erbeti riba l[[55]</td></tr>
<tr><td>(4) t aḏmr . mʿnh . w[</td><td>. . . azamur . mʿnh . w[[56]</td></tr>
<tr><td>(5) km ṯtmr . mṯt klt[</td><td>kima ša tammiri mušiti kallatu[[57]</td></tr>
<tr><td>(6) mṯty klt mkktm[</td><td>muši kallati mukkatim[ti -----er][58]</td></tr>
<tr><td>(7) bt ryb lḏmrk y[</td><td>-beti riba luzmurki[[59]</td></tr>
<tr><td>(8) ušsk utllt . x[</td><td>ušassuki utullat . [[60]</td></tr>
<tr><td>(9) [---]d u umam(?)[</td><td>. . . u umam . . .[61]</td></tr>
<tr><td>(10) [--]l . im | mṯ[</td><td>. . . ema la maše. . .</td></tr>
<tr><td>(11) [---]nu bly[</td><td>[-- A]nu bel i[lani</td></tr>
<tr><td>(12) [---]nmq p(?)</td><td>[-bel]nemeqi . . .[62]</td></tr>
<tr><td>Reverse</td><td></td></tr>
<tr><td>(13) [----]n [</td><td></td></tr>
<tr><td>(14) [----]w an[</td><td></td></tr>
<tr><td>(15) [--]sh . ill aẖ(?)[</td><td>. . . ellil aẖ(?)</td></tr>
</table>

Astour's translation of lines 1–12:

(1) I sing our Lady, the god[dess]
(2) of the night, of the night, the vei[led] bride,
(3) In the evening thou enterst [*sic*] into the sunset [ ]

---

the Old Assyrian spot markers in which the spot marker would be in violation of word divider rules. Virolleaud's transliteration showed two marks in this line: *ḏmrk . bltn . i* [*lt*; cf. "Fragments alphabétiques," 114–33. However, his hand drawing did not show either of these marks. I am inclined to believe that the hand drawing is the better source, and hence I have relied on it. Neither Dhorme nor Astour showed these marks; cf. Dhorme, "Textes accadiens," 83–96; and Astour, *Hellenosemitica*, 133–34. However, if Virolleaud's transliteration is correct, then this line may belong with lines that employ word dividers. If only the mark after *bltn.* is correct (as van Soldt reads the line; cf. *Studies*, 296–97; contra Dhorme and Astour, who read no mark after *beletni*), then this is a spot marker like the Old Assyrian spot markers separating two nouns in apposition; cf. my *Word Dividers*, 182–83. KTU reads the line *ḏmrk bltn i* . [. This would presumably place a mark within a word, which would be highly unusual both in Ugaritic and in Old Assyrian. For discussion of split words, cf. discussion above for *Yariẖ and Nikkal.*

54. Van Soldt omits the first word in the line and reads after *kallati*: . . [*kuttumti*; cf. *Studies*, 296–99.

55. Van Soldt does not present this line; cf. ibid.

56. Van Soldt reads only *azammur.*

57. Van Soldt reads *tammaru/tammari.*

58. Van Soldt reads after *kallati*: . . *kuttum*[*ti*.

59. Van Soldt reads only *luzmurki.*

60. Van Soldt reads *ušassiki u telilta*(??). . . . This is the last line he presents.

61. KTU shows line 9: [ ]*rd u.uman**[. Presumably this would be some kind of spot marker, but I think there is too little evidence to discuss it further.

62. This is the last line Astour presents; cf. *Hellenosemitica*, 133–34.

(4) . . . I sing. His answer is . . . [ ]
(5) When thou has [*sic*] shined, O Night, bride [ ]
(6) of the night, veiled bride [thou en-]
(7) terst [*sic*] into the sunset. May I sing thee [ ]
(8) They invoke thee, the herds of . . . [ ]
(9) [ ] . . . and the cattle of . . . [ ]
(10) [ ] . . . not to forget [ ]
(11) [A]nu, the Lord of the g[ods]
(12) [. . Lord] of wisdom . . . [ ]

Dhorme's translation of line 15:

(15) son [auteur]: Ellil-aham-[idinnam]

The fact that there are only seven marks in fifteen lines makes it highly unlikely that this could be even a fairly poorly marked word divider text. Furthermore, one can easily discern a great many errors in marking, if this were a word divider text. I will not discuss the negative examples, because I think it is reasonably obvious that this text is not marked with a word divider marking system.

In KTU 1.69, there are two split words identified by Dhorme. Since there are no complete ends of lines for the text, all examples are dependent on restoration of the text. The first is between lines 3 and 4, and Dhorme makes no restoration for this example. The second example is (6)](7)*bt*, which Dhorme restores *er*]-*beti*. Split words in *Yariḫ and Nikkal* were an indication that the text was not marked with word dividers. However, in this case, where the two split words both rely on restoration, I am not inclined to regard them as particularly significant. I think it is obvious that this is not a word divider text, but it is not clear whether split words were used to help alert the reader to this fact.

It is thus surprising to note that there are, in fact, two marks that appear to be used as word dividers. These occur before and after the Ugaritic word *mʿnh* 'His answer is' (line 4). This word, similarly marked, occurs in all three of the other Akkadian texts in alphabetic cuneiform found at Ugarit. Word dividers are, of course, the normal marking system in Ugaritic. Thus one could regard these marks around *mʿnh* as simply having come along with the word. I do not know whether importing such a foreign word with its marking into an Akkadian text is unusual or not. If it is unusual, then possibly these marks are an indication of clause-marking or even of a special "unit marker" type of spot marker. Whatever they are, they are not part of a word divider marking system used in this text, because word dividers are not employed sporadically. They may stop at some point before the end of the text, but they do not occur simply to mark a single word in a text.

I will attempt to determine what sort of non–word divider marking system is used in this text by considering (1) clause markers and (2) spot markers.

Clause Markers

I will consider only the positive evidence for possible clause marking. I will not consider in detail the negative evidence, which can be either failure to mark the beginning or end of a clause or inclusion of a mark that is not correct for clause marking. I do not do so because damage to the text makes it impossible. Both of the examples below are marked only at one end of the clause, and so neither is certain as a clause marker. There are other marks that are not immediately apparent as clause markers, but since they may be spot markers, they are not necessarily to be considered incorrect for clause marking. They may merely not be part of the clause-marking system, just as the spot marking in *Yariḫ and Nikkal* is not part of the clause-marking system.

There are five examples of clause marking in this text. The first is *n ll irbt ryb* . (line 3). The Akkadian transcription given above is *ina lili erbeti riba*, and the translation given above is 'In the evening thou enterst [*sic*] into the sunset'. This certainly can qualify as a clause, and it has a mark at the end. The end of the previous line is lost, so there is no way to know whether there was a mark at the end of the line or whether there were words included in this clause at the end of the line. However, this is best explained as a clause marker. I do not know of a kind of spot marker in Old Assyrian texts or *Yariḫ and Nikkal* that presents any obvious and direct similarities to this kind of marking. This example can be said to be accepted as a probable clause marker.

The second example of possible clause marking is *km ṯtmr . mṯt klt*[(line 5). As given above, the Akkadian transcription is *kima ša tammiri mušiti kallatu*[, and the translation is 'When thou has shined, O Night, bride'. This example also rests on the assumption that there was a mark either at the end of the previous line or prior, showing that more was included in this clause. As for the example in line 3, so for this example, I do not know of a kind of spot marker in Old Assyrian texts or *Yariḫ and Nikkal* that presents any obvious and direct similarities to this kind of marking. This example can be accepted as a probable clause marker.

It could also be said that the marks around the Ugaritic word *mʿnh* serve as beginning and ending marks for clauses, in addition to serving as word dividers for the Ugaritic word. Thus one might count a total of four examples of probable clause marking in this text.

There is one final example that may be considered an example of possible clause marking. It is [--]*l* . *im l mṯ* (line 10). As given above, the Akkadian transcription is *ema la maše*, and the translation is 'not to forget'. I do not consider this an example of probable clause marking because there is too little text available. This might be a clause, but it might as easily not be a clause. It is not just a mark that is missing; there is no reasonable degree of certainty that this could be a complete clause. Consequently, I do not think this example can be said to be a probable clause marker. Furthermore, since I also cannot identify this as a spot marker, it must remain simply unexplained.

Spot Markers

There are two examples of possible spot markers. The first example is *ušsk utllt* . x[(line 8). As given above, the Akkadian transcription is *ušassuki utullat*, and the translation is 'They invoke thee, the herds of . . .'. If *utllt* is a construct, then it can be presumed to be followed by its genitive, from which this mark separates it. There is no similar kind of spot marker known in Old Assyrian texts. However, there are two such examples in *Yariḫ and Nikkal* (line 2 and line 34; cf. p. 97 above). I think this example can be said to be a probable spot marker.

The second example is [--]*sh*. *ill aḫ*(?)[(line 15). The Akkadian transcription is . . . *ellil aḫ*(?), and the translation is 'son [auteur]: Ellil-aham-[idinnam]'. This could qualify as similar to the Old Assyrian spot markers separating two or more nominal elements in apposition. There are no examples presently available of such a mark before the scribe's name in Old Assyrian texts because there are no scribes named in the Old Assyrian texts analyzed for the presence of spot markers.[63] I think this example can be said to be a probable spot marker.

There are two conclusions that can be drawn about the marking system on KTU 1.69. First, this text may include both clause marking and spot marking; therefore, second, it may exhibit a combination marking system similar to the one on *Yariḫ and Nikkal*. Damage to KTU 1.69 makes it unlikely that any certainty about the marking system can ever be attained. However, since a well-established example of a text with such a marking system exists, namely *Yariḫ and Nikkal*, I do not think it too farfetched to identify the marking system on KTU 1.69 as likely to be a similar combination system. The comparison to Egyptian clause marking and to Old Assyrian spot marking is far less significant for identifying the marking system in the case of KTU 1.69 than in the case of *Yariḫ and Nikkal*. Without the example of the *Yariḫ and Nikkal* combination marking system, I think it would be unlikely that any guess could be made about the marking system on KTU 1.69.

* * *

My purpose in this study was to identify the non–word divider marking on two texts found at Ugarit by comparison to non–word divider marking known elsewhere in the ancient Near East. The two elements of the marking system on *Yariḫ and Nikkal* can be understood and identified by comparison to clause marking in Egyptian and to spot marking in Old Assyrian. The same can be said for KTU 1.69, although in practice, the comparison to *Yariḫ and Nikkal* is far more important for the identification of this marking system.

63. Witnesses and judges were recorded but no scribes. For the Old Assyrian texts in my study, cf. Spar, *Cuneiform Texts* MMA 1, 92–143, nos. 71–98, pls. 66–99, 134, 137, 138, and 156.

In conclusion, I will briefly consider the significance and possible sources of the marking system found on these two texts. *Yariḫ and Nikkal* and KTU 1.69 employ a combination of clause marking and spot marking. This combination marking system is unique to marking in the ancient Near East up to this period, insofar as is presently known. There are no other combination marking systems appearing in any body of texts from any site. However, there are two other individual texts with combination marking systems, the Akkadian literary texts *Adapa* (EA 356) and *Ereshkigal* (EA 357), which were found at Tell el Amarna, site of Akhetaten, the short-lived capital of Egypt built by Akhenaten.[64] The reverse of *Adapa* is marked with a combination clause-marking and spot-marking system very similar to *Yariḫ and Nikkal* and KTU 1.69.[65] *Ereshkigal* is also marked with a combination marking system, but it is a quite different one, employing word dividers and marks within words.[66]

These four texts, *Adapa*, *Ereshkigal*, *Yariḫ and Nikkal*, and KTU 1.69 constitute unique examples of combination marking systems. Since they are not representatives of any marking system used in a body of texts, one might well ask if they are significant to the development of marking systems? The answer is yes. The reason is that these texts are the first clues we have of the attempt to create useful combination marking systems. Combination marking systems of any kind constitute a great advance over single marking systems

64. For the publication of *Adapa* and *Ereshkigal* in cuneiform print font, hand drawing, and transliteration, cf. C. Bezold and E. A. W. Budge, *The Tell Amarna Tablets in the British Museum* (London: British Museum, 1892) no. 82; O. Schroeder, *Die Tontafeln von el-Amarna* (Voderasiatische Schriftdenkmäler der königlichen Museen zu Berlin 12; Leipzig: Hinrichs, 1914–15) nos. 194 and 195; J. Knudtzon, *Die El-Amarna Tafeln mit Einleitung und Erläuterungen* (Leipzig: Hinrichs, 1915; reprint 1964) vol. 2, nos. 356 and 357. For the complete publication history, cf. A. Rainey, *El Amarna Tablets 359–379* (2d ed.; AOAT 8; Neukirchen-Vluyn: Neukirchener Verlag, 1978). For a brief history of the discovery of what came to be known as the Amarna Archive, cf. W. Albright, "The Amarna Letters from Palestine," in *Cambridge Ancient History*, vol. 2/2: *The Middle East and the Aegean Region c. 1380–1000* B.C. (3d ed.; Cambridge: Cambridge University Press, 1980) 98–116; and for the bibliography, pp. 927–29.

65. For more on the combination clause marker and spot marker system used on *Adapa* (EA 356) reverse, cf. my *Word Dividers*, 124–28 and 135–36.

The obverse of *Adapa* is marked with a word divider marking system that is not exactly like either the Ugaritic or the Old Assyrian word divider marking systems. For more on this word divider marking system, cf. ibid., 43–123.

The combination clause marker and spot marker system on *Adapa* reverse actually seems to alternate with word divider marking. Thus there may be some comparison possible with the other two Akkadian texts written in alphabetic cuneiform (KTU 1.70 and 73) that appear to employ some kind of word divider marking at least for parts of the text.

66. For more on the marking system of *Ereshkigal* combining word dividers and spot markers within words, cf. my *Word Dividers*, 78–123 and 128–36.

such as word dividers because they provide many more possibilities for different kinds of marking in a single text. Such combination marking systems are steps in the development of complex secondary sign systems and hence of true punctuation systems.[67]

The basic sources of the combination clause-marking and spot-marking system found on *Yariḫ and Nikkal*, KTU 1.69, and *Adapa* are fairly simple. The origin of the idea of a clause-marking system almost certainly comes from Egyptian clause marking. There are no other clause-marking systems known. Egyptian clause marking in its broad sense could easily have been known both in the school of Akkadian at Akhetaten and at Ugarit, since there is considerable evidence of connection between the schools of Akkadian at these two sites.[68]

The origin of the idea of spot marking is somewhat more complex. Certainly the connection between the types of spot marking in *Yariḫ and Nikkal*, KTU 1.69, and *Adapa*, and the types of spot marking in Old Assyrian texts is quite close. These three texts display not just an adaptation of the broad idea of spot marking, but the specific types of spot marking found in Old Assyrian texts. The knowledge of such marking certainly originated at Ugarit, not in Egypt.[69] But how did the knowledge of spot marking come to Ugarit? By what route, and from what site or sites was the knowledge of spot marking, evident in Old Assyrian texts, transmitted to Ugarit? Or is there some source of spot marking, perhaps earlier than the spot marking in Old Assyrian texts, that served as a common origin? At present, no answers to such questions are available. Further study may change this.

Obviously, the search for the origins of the spot marking in these texts with combination marking systems leads one into the far broader question of the origins of marking[70] and thus of secondary sign systems generally in the ancient Near East.

67. Our modern punctuation systems employ a great many graphic devices (periods, commas, etc.), and many of these can be used for more than one purpose.

68. For more on the connections between the school of Akkadian at Aketaten and Ugarit, cf. P. Artzi, "Studies in the Library of the Amarna Archive," in *Bar-Ilan Studies in Assyriology Dedicated to Pinhas Artzi* (ed. J. Klein and A. Skaist; Ramat Gan: Bar-Ilan University Press, 1990) 139–56.

69. The spot marking in *Ereshkigal* does not display any of the specific types of spot marking found in Old Assyrian texts. The spot markers all occur within words, which is unlike anything else in any other known marking system. They appear to have been created specifically to help Egyptian students learn to read Akkadian; cf. my *Word Dividers*, 126–34. Hence, this type of spot marking undoubtedly did originate in Egypt in its school of Akkadian.

70. To my knowledge, no one has addressed this question. However, Horowitz did give a brief summary of his estimation of the three basic possibilities for the origins of the mark in Ugaritic ("Our Ugaritic Mythological Texts," 128 n. 26).

Livraisons et dépenses royales durant la Troisième Dynastie d'Ur

Marcel Sigrist
École Biblique et Archéologique Française de Jérusalem

Grâce à une abondante documentation épigraphique provenant principalement de cinq tells du sud de la Mésopotamie dont Drehem, Lagaš, Nippur, Umma et Ur, la période de la Troisième Dynastie d'Ur est relativement bien connue. Cependant l'essentiel de l'information ne vient que de la seconde partie du règne de Šulgi, de celui de ses deux successeurs, Amar-Sîn et Šu-Sîn et du début du règne d'Ibbi-Sîn, dernier roi de la dynastie. En somme, seule la seconde moitié du temps d'activité de cette dynastie est bien documentée. Néanmoins les archives provenant de ces différentes villes et trouvées la plupart par des fouilleurs clandestins permettent de bien connaître le fonctionnement de l'administration du pays et celle des ses grands centres urbains.

Ainsi l'étude des archives de Drehem, le centre comptable du bétail du pays, permet de reconstruire le système d'imposition qui avait cours ainsi que celui de la redistribution de ces mêmes animaux pour les besoins du culte, du palais royal et de certains membres de la famille royale. Mais l'étude de son fonctionnement permet de dégager les principes mêmes de l'organisation de ce centre comptable ainsi que leur modification et adaptation à travers les règnes successifs des différents rois de cette dynastie. Entre autres, on citera l'introduction de l'usage du sceau au début du règne de Šu-Sîn, pratique déjà courante dans l'administration des autres villes du royaume.

La ville de Lagaš a livré des milliers de tablettes relatives au travail des champs et à la production de l'orge. Les énormes troupeaux de cette ville requéraient une comptabilité spécifique, sans oublier celle de la laine provenant de ses moutons et travaillée par les fileuses pour en faire des habits de toutes sortes.

Les tablettes d'Umma traitent également du travail des champs; mais à la culture de l'orge s'ajoute la plantation des palmiers-dattiers et d'autres produits végétaux pour la consommation ou le culte. L'élevage du bétail est source de laine travaillée dans d'importantes filatures ainsi que de peaux dont le tannage donnera du cuir et d'innombrables objets faits en cuir. S'y ajoute l'administration et la gestion des ouvriers, guruš, géme et des jeunes travaillant aux champs et dans les filatures.

La ville d'Ur, capitale du royaume dont l'archive a continué jusqu'à la chute du royaume, est riche en information sur le travail de la laine et du métal ainsi que sur les besoins du culte.

Enfin Nippur, capitale religieuse durant toutes les périodes de l'histoire, a livré à ce jour des documents surtout privés, fort intéressants pour la connaissance de la vie domestique durant une période où l'état apparemment gérait l'ensemble des biens.

Le site de Drehem, qui n'a pas encore été régulièrement fouillé, a pourtant déjà livré aux fouilleurs clandestins près de 8000 tablettes dont on peut dire que la plupart ont été publiées ou, du moins, sont connues des spécialistes. Cette énorme masse de matériel a permis de reconstruire de manière relativement sûre le fonctionnement administratif de ce centre depuis sa fondation[1] jusqu'au dernier jour de la seconde année de règne du roi Ibbi-Sîn, date de sa fermeture.

Par delà les diverses archives de Drehem, dont celle qui enregistre les impôts en bétail, il en est encore une, mal connue à ce jour, qui porte sur la gestion des troupeaux d'animaux amenés à Drehem et qui devaient y demeurer quelque temps dans l'attente de leur consommation. Les tablettes de cette archive proviennent des bergers et des engraisseurs travaillant en relation avec le centre de Drehem. Il serait bon de pouvoir en savoir davantage sur leur organisation. Disposaient-ils de pâturages pour leurs troupeaux? Si oui, dans quelles limites du terrain de la ville? Pendant la période de l'été quand il n'y avait pas d'herbe à brouter pour le bétail pouvait-on assurer sa subsistance avec de l'orge ou même continuer son engraissement? La fermeture du centre de Drehem est-elle uniquement due au danger d'invasion ou au fait que les lignes de communication étant coupées avec le nord du pays les livraisons de bétail et de grain ne pouvaient plus atteindre le centre? Quelle fut la solution de rechange adoptée pour garantir l'approvisionnement de Nippur malgré la fermeture de Nippur? Toutes ces questions relatives à la vie de Drehem attendent encore des études complémentaires qui pourront faire fonds sur les inédits encore enfouis dans le tell.

Mon propos se limite à mettre en lumière un aspect particulier du fonctionnement de l'administration de Drehem, notamment celui des livraisons et dépenses relevant directement de la cour, les mu-túm lugal et zi-ga lugal.

Durant les 9 années du règne du roi Amar-Sîn, qui pourraient constituer l'époque classique du fonctionnement de ce centre, les opérations comptables se déroulaient comme suit: les livraisons de bétail étaient toute prises

1. Šulgi 39: mu é *puzur-iš-*[d]*Da-gan* ba-dù. Cf. mon étude d'ensemble: M. Sigrist, *Drehem* (Bethesda, Md.: CDL, 1992).

en compte par un seul responsable Abbašaga ou par quelqu'un de son bureau. Dans la terminologie bureaucratique cette opération est dite: mu-túm, c'est-à-dire 'il a apporté, livré.' Souvent on se contente de traduire par le mot 'livraison.' Cette opération de prise en compte conclue, à savoir l'enregistrement de ce bétail dans la comptabilité de Drehem achevé, Abbašaga avait trois options pour disposer des animaux confiés à son contrôle:

1. Il envoyait à l'engraisseur le bétail qui lui avait été livré en attendant que le moment de son utilisation arrive;
2. Les animaux n'ayant que transité par son bureau étaient immédiatement confiés à l'un des pourvoyeurs des temples de Nippur, du palais royal ou même d'autres centres de culte comme ceux d'Uruk ou d'Ur, par exemple. Ces opérations ne constituaient pour l'administration que des transferts de comptabilité puisque les animaux restaient toujours dans les comptes de Drehem. Dans ces deux cas, la phraséologie est: ki Ab-ba-ša$_6$-ga-ta NP i-dab$_5$, de Abbašaga NP a pris;
3. Mais dans quelques cas, Abbašaga dépense directement certains des animaux qui lui sont envoyés. Ces dépenses sont enregistrées sous la rubrique 'zi-ga lugal,' à savoir 'dépenses pour le roi'. On ne trouve jamais dans l'archive d'Abbašaga l'expression courte zi-ga ou ba-zi, par contre toujours zi-ga lugal.[2] Cette bizarrerie apparente s'explique par la position de ce fonctionnaire dans l'organigramme de Drehem. Il contrôlait les livraisons et ne faisait que les transmettre à d'autres responsables pour engraissement ou dépense. Ce n'est que dans le cas particulier des livraisons royales qu'il assurait lui-même directement la dépense. Mais si donc il y a des dépenses propres au roi, il doit aussi y avoir des entrées spécifiques, à savoir des mu-túm lugal.

Ainsi donc aux mu-túm lugal répondent bien les zi-ga lugal car les dépenses royales ne sont rendues possibles que par les livraisons préalables pour le roi. En d'autres termes, ce qui a été réceptionné au titre du dû pour le roi sera aussi dépensé sous la même rubrique.

Les fonctions d'Abbašaga dans l'organigramme de Drehem sont donc doubles:[3]

1. Abbašaga supervisait un bureau d'enregistrement du bétail; l'opération de prise en compte accomplie, il transférait ce bétail à d'autres, bergers ou pourvoyeurs pour le culte.
2. Abbašaga gérait directement et totalement le service des obligations royales, tant les prises en compte que les dépenses. Schématiquement:

2. Dans presque tous les cas, quand on trouve seulement zi-ga, on peut prouver qu'il s'agit en fait de 'zi-ga lugal'; cela invite toujours à quelque précaution dans l'interprétation des formulaires.

3. Ce qui est en italique relève des activités du bureau d'Abbašaga.

prise en compte de mu-túm → dépense = zi-ga
par Abbašaga
prise en compte de mu-túm lugal → zi-ga lugal
par Abbašaga   Abbašaga

Toutes ces informations sont déjà connues par différentes tablettes. Mais seules les tablettes récapitulatives permettent de prouver parfaitement ce qui ne peut être qu'inféré par les tablettes écrites au jour le jour.

Par chance, en cataloguant la collection YBC de Yale,[4] j'ai trouvé deux grandes tablettes récapitulatives de chacune de ces deux opérations, qui permettent donc d'établir sans l'ombre de doute le fonctionnement des livraisons particulières pour le roi ou pour la couronne (mu-túm lugal) et leur emploi (zi-ga lugal).

Les tablettes récapitulatives sont établies a posteriori, à la fin du mois, reprenant chacune des tablettes écrites au jour le jour pour chaque livraison d'animal et chaque dépense.[5]

Les 2 tablettes mu-túm lugal et zi-ga lugal analysées dans ce travail ne se répondent pas quant à la date. Mais même si on trouvait par chance deux tablettes de ce type datées du même mois, il n'y aurait cependant pas exacte correspondance car la composition des tablettes enregistrant les recettes et les dépenses pour le roi sont plus complexes qu'il ne semble. En effet les dépenses, les zi-ga lugal, pourvoyaient aux dépenses de la famille royale mais aussi à l'alimentation des hommes de service, les àga-uš qui avaient diverses responsabilités de garde dans le royaume. Leur nourriture venait des bergers, donc d'un autre système de comptabilité auquel il a été fait allusion plus haut. Aussi ces deux tablettes ne font pas connaître l'ensemble du fonctionnement du système des contributions pour le roi car l'archive des bergers n'est encore que peu connue si ce n'est par les tablettes šà-bi-ta.

mu-túm lugal ↘
                          prise en compte → *zi-ga lugal*
animaux šu-gíd ↗

4. Je remercie vivement le professeur W. W. Hallo, conservateur de la Yale Babylonian Collection, pour m'avoir permis de publier les deux grandes tablettes YBC 3635 et YBC 4190, et pour m'avoir donné sa transcription de YBC 3635, faite il y a plusieurs années.

5. Il faut présumer que des ordres étaient envoyés à tous les contribuables, probablement pour l'année ou la mi-année, lesquels sur la base des quantités nécessaires au culte ou au palais leur intimaient les quantités de bétail à livrer. Ce genre de budget des prévisions n'a jamais été trouvé alors que l'administration n'aurait jamais pu fonctionner sans un tel outil de travail. C'est pourquoi il est parfois tentant de penser que les grandes tablettes que nous croyons être récapitulatives sont en fait selon prévisionnelles. Mais il n'y a pas vraiment d'argument dans un sens ou dans l'autre, pour considérer ces documents comme des récapitulatifs ou des prévisions pour le mois.

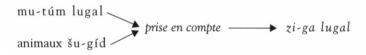

Analyse de la tablette YBC 3635

Grande tablette de 6 colonnes, YBC 3635 récapitule les livraisons mu-túm lugal enregistrées par Abbašaga. Elle est datée du 11ème mois de la seconde année d'Amar-Sîn, l'année de la prise de la ville d'Arbèles (Urbilum).

face
(colonne 1)
[xx PN]
[xx PN]
[xx PN]
[u_4 1-kam]
1 $sila_4$ Nir-ì-da-gál
2 $sila_4$ Ṣe-lu-uš-^{d}Da-gan
1 $sila_4$ gukkal Ur-^{d}Ištaran
2 $sila_4$ Nu-ì-da
1 $sila_4$
1 máš
en ^{d}Inanna
1 $sila_4$ énsi Nibru^{ki}
9
u_4 2-kam
1 gu_4 niga
9 udu
1 $sila_4$
Hu-un-hu-ub-še
1 gu_4 gùn-a
Lú-É-a Mar-tu
1 $sila_4$
Ur-mu
1 $sila_4$
Šu-^{d}Da-gan
14
u_4 3-kam
1 máš Nir-ì-da-gál
1 máš Ṣe-lu-uš-^{d}Da-gan
1 máš Gìr-ir
3
u_4 4-kam
1 gu_4
1 áb
Ma-li-a
4 gukkal
Da-na-bí-id
4 udu A-na-na
1 udu
2 gukkal
Lú-re-e-ù
Mar-tu-me
[1 $sila_4$] Id-da-a
1 $sila_4$ I-pi_4-iq-na-ni
[1 $sila_4$] ^{d}Šu-^{d}Šul-gi
[1 $sila_4$] ^{d}Nin-gal-du
[1 $sila_4$] [ ]-tum

(colonne 2)
1 $sila_4$ énsi Gír-su^{ki}
1 $sila_4$ énsi Šuruppak^{ki}
1 $sila_4$ Bur-Ma-ma
1 máš Ṣe-lu-uš-^{d}Da-gan
1 $sila_4$ Ur-^{d}EN.ZU
2 $sila_4$ Ša-at-ra-at
1 $sila_4$ niga Lú-^{d}Nin-šubur
1 $sila_4$ niga Lú-^{d}Nanna
1 $sila_4$ niga Šeš-zi-mu
1 máš Da-da
29 **u_4 5-kam**
1 $sila_4$ Ur-ni_9
2 $sila_4$ Ur-^{d}Tilla (U.AN) sanga
1 $sila_4$ Ša-lim-ku-na
1 $sila_4$ Šu-^{d}Šamaš
2 $sila_4$ Ur-sukkal
1 $sila_4$ Šu-^{d}EN.ZU
8
u_4 6-kam
1 $sila_4$ A-mur-É-a
1 máš Da-da dumu Ur-Ma-ma
2
u_4 7-kam
1 $sila_4$ Sag-^{d}Nanna-zu

1 máš Igi-an-na-ke$_4$-zu
1 máš Ba-za-mu
1 sila$_4$ Šu-ru-uš-ki-in
1 sila$_4$ Ur-mes
1 máš I-din-^{d}EN.ZU
18 gu$_4$ niga 2 gu$_4$
35 udu niga 1 sila$_4$ niga
4 máš-gal niga 1,40 udu
2 sila$_4$ 1,0 máš-gal gùn-a
kaš-dé-a Eš$_4$-tár-ìl-šu
3,48
u$_4$ 8-kam
4 udu niga
4 gukkal niga
8 sila$_4$
Ur-mes

(colonne 3)
1 sila$_4$ Má-li-li
1 máš I-li-iš-ti-kal
3 udu 1 sila$_4$
A-a-ì-lí-šu
2 máš-gal a-dara$_4$
1 máš Kur-gìr-ni-šè
1 sila$_4$ I-zu-a
1 sila$_4$ Á-píl-la-lum
3 udu niga
1 máš-gal niga
1 lulim níta niga
1 u$_8$ sila$_4$ nu-a
1 ùz máš nu-a
2 sila$_4$
Šu-^{d}EN.ZU
1 sila$_4$ Ur-^{d}Nanna
1 sila$_4$ Ip-hur kuš$_7$
1 sila$_4$ nu/PAP Ki-na-na
39
u$_4$ 9-kam
1 gu$_4$ 5 udu niga
1 sila$_4$ Ur-ni$_9$-gar
2 gu$_4$ 7 udu
3 sila$_4$ Ì-lí-dan
4 udu niga
2 sila$_4$ Ur-mes

1 sila$_4$ Eš$_4$-tár-ìl-šu
2 udu 1 sila$_4$
Amar-gi$_7$
1 sila$_4$ A-hu-ni
1 sila$_4$
Lugal-má-gur$_8$-re
1 sila$_4$ énsi Adab^{ki}
31
u$_4$ 10-kam
1 sila$_4$ Za-la-a
1 sila$_4$ 1 máš
en ^{d}Inanna
1 sila$_4$ I-din-^{d}EN.ZU dumu
Hu-un-ha-ab-ur
1 sila$_4$ Nam-ha-ni um-mi-a
4 udu niga 2 sila$_4$
En-úr-kù-sig$_{17}$

(colonne 4)
(1 ou 2 lignes perdues)
1 sila$_4$ [ ]
1 sila$_4$ [ ]
1 sila$_4$ [ ]
1 máš Ab-[ ]
15
u$_4$ 11-kam
4 gu$_4$ niga
1 gu$_4$
40 udu 10 máš
I-ri-ib-um
4 gu$_4$ 30 udu
10 máš
érin A-bí-ba-na^{ki}
4 gu$_4$ 20 udu
20 máš
érin Kak-ku$_8$-la-tum^{ki}
1 gu$_4$ 8 udu
2 máš
I-gi$_4$ nu-bànda
5 udu 1 máš
Lú-ša-lim nu-bànda
5 udu 1 máš
Suhuš-ki-in nu-bànda
ugula I-ri-bu-um

4 gu_4 niga 2 gu_4
2 $šeg_7$-bar níta
1,0 lá 1 udu
1 $sila_4$
Šeš-$ša_6$-ga
4 $sila_4$ Ur-^{d}Tìlla sanga
2 $sila_4$ énsi Nibru^{ki}
1 $sila_4$ Suhuš-ki-in
1 $sila_4$ U-li-be-lu-uk
1 $sila_4$ Hu-ba-a
1 amar-az níta mu-[ ]
2 $sila_4$ Nu-ì-da
1 $sila_4$ $Eš_4$-tár-ìl-šu
1 máš Id-da-a
1 $sila_4$ Wa-at!-ra-at
4,9
u_4 12-kam
1 $sila_4$ Ma-na-a
1 $sila_4$ Šu-ra-nu-um
1 $sila_4$ I-za-nu-um
1 $sila_4$ Lu-lu-ba-ni

(colonne 5)
(9 lignes cassées)
[ ]
u_4 13-kam
10 gu_4 niga
1,38 udu
2 máš
Zi-kur-ì-lí
1 gu_4 10 udu
Ša-lim-ku-na
1 gu_4 9 udu
1 máš
Bur-^{d}Adad
1 gu_4 10 udu
$Puzur_4$-^{d}Ha-ìa
1 gu_4 8 udu
2 máš
Šar-ru-um-ì-lí
1 gu_4 10 udu
Da-hi-iš-še-en
1 gu_4 7 udu
3 máš Ša-lim-be-lí
1 gu_4 8 udu
2 máš Ir-íb-ìl-šu
1 gu_4 10 udu
A-ki-a nu-bànda-me
15 gu_4 2,12 udu
18 máš
érin Zi-mu-dar^{ki}
ugula Zi-kur-ì-lí
1 $sila_4$ Ur-mes
1 $sila_4$ ^{d}Nin-é-gal-igi-du
1 $sila_4$ Be-lí-dan
1 $sila_4$ $Puzur_4$-^{d}Adad
1 $sila_4$ Šeš-kal-la
1 $sila_4$ Ilum-ba-ni
1 $sila_4$ [ ]

(colonne 6)
(premier tiers cassé, 12 lignes)
ugula [ ]
1 máš [ ]
1 $sila_4$ Be-lí-[ì-lí]
1 $sila_4$ Ba-za-[ ]
1 $sila_4$ Igi-an-na-ke_4-zu
18 $šeg_7$-bar níta
22 $šeg_7$-bar mí
1 anše
Šar-ru-um-ba-ni
7,8
u_4 14-kam
3 udu niga
$Eš_4$-tár-ìl-šu
1 $sila_4$ Da-la-a
mu-túm lugal
1 $šeg_7$-bar níta
4 $šeg_7$-bar mí
Šar-ru-um-ba-ni
mu-túm A-bí-sí-im-ti
9
u_4 15-kam
1 $sila_4$ 1 máš
en ^{d}Inanna
2 $sila_4$ ^{d}Nin-e-ma-an-ág
2 $sila_4$ Wa-at-ra-at
2 $sila_4$ Ur-^{d}Tìlla sanga

2 amar az
Šu-^{d}EN.ZU
10
u_4 16-kam
1 $sila_4$ niga
Zi-kur-ì-lí
1 $sila_4$ 1 máš
en ^{d}Inanna
1 $sila_4$ Šar-ru-um-ì-lí
1 $sila_4$ énsi Gír-su^{ki}
1 máš Ur-^{d}Nin-[ ]

rev
(colonne 7)
1 máš Nu-úr-^{d}EN.ZU
7
u_4 17-kam
6 udu
4 máš-gal
1 máš
Be-lí-a-rí-ik
1 gu_4 niga
5 udu
4 máš
1 $sila_4$
I-din-É-a
1 $sila_4$ Wa-tá-ru-um
1 $sila_4$
Ni-in-mu nu-bànda
1 $sila_4$ 1 máš
Ama-mu
1 $sila_4$ Šeš-$ša_6$-ga
1 $sila_4$ A-at-tum
1 $sila_4$ Za-la-a
1 $sila_4$ Lugal-á-zi-da
1 máš Ur-sukkal
1 amar-az Šu-^{d}EN.ZU
1 $sila_4$ Ur-mes
33
u_4 18-kam
1 máš I-ṭur-ì-lí
1 máš Ilum-ba-ni
1 máš Šu-^{d}Adad
1 máš [x]

1 $sila_4$ [x]
(12 lignes cassées)

(colonne 8)
1 máš Lugal-má-gur_8-re
1 máš Ik-šu-tum
1 amar-az Šu-^{d}EN.ZU
1 máš Na-ra-am-É-a
13
u_4 21-kam
18 mašda Ku-ù
2 amar-az Šu-^{d}EN.ZU
2 $sila_4$ Nu-ì-da
1 máš-gal niga a-$dara_4$
1 $sila_4$ A-mur-É-a
1 ^{mí}ašgar niga Ì-la-lum
25
u_4 22-kam
1 $sila_4$
3 amar-az Šu-^{d}EN.ZU
1 $sila_4$ Lugal-má-gur_8-re
1 $sila_4$ Šeš-kal-la
1 $sila_4$ U-li-be-lí-uk
7
u_4 23-kam
1 $sila_4$ énsi Már-da^{ki}
1 $sila_4$ $Eš_4$-tár-ìl-šu
1 amar-az Šu-^{d}EN.ZU
1 máš Še-li-bu-um
1 $sila_4$ énsi Nibru^{ki}
5
u_4 26-kam
1 [ ]
(10 lignes manquantes)

(colonne 9)
1 máš Lú-bala-$ša_6$-ga
1 $sila_4$ Lú-kal-la
4 udu niga 2 $sila_4$
énsi Gír-su^{ki}
1 $sila_4$ énsi Gir_{13}-giš^{ki}
1 $sila_4$ Ur-mes
3 amar-az Šu-^{d}EN.ZU
1 máš Ir_{11}-da-ni

1 sila$_4$ Lú-dingir-ra
17
u$_4$ 30-kam

(colonne 10)
šu-nígin 38 gu$_4$ niga
šu-nígin 41 gu$_4$
šu-nígin 1 gu$_4$ gùn-a
šu-nígin 1 áb
šu-nígin 1 lulim níta niga
šu-nígin 21 šeg$_7$-bar níta
šu-nígin 26 šeg$_7$-bar mí
šu-nígin 1,6 udu niga
šu-nígin 4 gukkal niga
šu-nígin 1 udu Šimaški niga
šu-nígin 5 sila$_4$ niga
šu-nígin 5 máš-gal niga
šu-nígin 1 máš-gal Šimaški niga
šu-nígin 1 máš-gal a-dara$_4$ niga
šu-nígin 1 ^{mí}ašgar niga
šu-nígin 10,8 udu
šu-nígin 6 gukkal
šu-nígin 3,0 lá 1 sila$_4$
šu-nígin 1 sila$_4$-gukkal
šu-nígin 1 u$_8$ sila$_4$ nu-a
šu-nígin 4 máš-gal
šu-nígin 1,0 máš-gal gùn-a
šu-nígin 2 máš-gal a-dara$_4$
šu-nígin 1,48 máš
šu-nígin 1 ùz máš nu-a
šu-nígin 23 mašda
šu-nígin 17 az

(colonne 11)
šu-nígin [3]8 gu$_4$ niga
šu-nígin 42 gu$_4$
šu-nígin 1 áb
šu-nígin 1 lulim nita niga
šu-nígin 21 šeg$_7$-bar níta
šu-nígin 26 šeg$_7$-bar mí
šu-nígin 1,16 udu niga
šu-nígin 6 máš niga
šu-nígin 1 máš a-dara$_4$ niga
šu-nígin 1 ùz niga
šu-nígin 1 u$_8$
šu-nígin 2,52 máš
šu-nígin 2 máš a-dara$_4$
šu-nígin 1 ùz
šu-nígin 23 mašda
šu-nígin 17 az
lagab-ba 1,20 gu$_4$
lagab-ba 1 áb
lagab-ba 1 lulim níta
lagab-ba 21 šeg$_7$-bar níta
lagab-ba 26 šeg$_7$-bar mí
labag-ba 14,40 udu
lagab-ba 1 u$_8$
lagab-ba 3,1 máš
lagab-ba 2 ùz
lagab-ba 23 mašda
lagab-ba 17 az

(colonne 12)
šu-nígin 40+x gu$_4$-áb hi-a
šu-nígin 1 lulim
šu-nígin 47 šeg$_7$-bar
šu-nígin 17,34 udu-máš hi-a
šu-nígin 23 mašda
šu-nígin 17 az
20,23 (= 1223)
mu-túm lugal
Ab-ba-ša$_6$-ga ì-dab$_5$
iti ezem-Me-ki-gál
mu ^{d}Amar-^{d}EN.ZU lugal-e
Ur-bí-lum^{ki} mu-hul

Structure de la tablette

Vers la fin de l'époque babylonienne ancienne et surtout pendant l'époque cassite les scribes quadrillent leurs tablettes pour créer des colonnes et y inscrire les produits comptabilisés. A l'époque d'Ur III le scribe écrit encore, l'un à la suite de l'autre, les produits reçus ou dépensés durant une période de temps donné.

Récapitulant les tablettes de livraison, le scribe néanmoins n'enregistre pas les animaux pêle-mêle mais toujours dans un ordre donné, du plus grand au plus petit. De la sorte on commence avec les bovins: boeuf et vache, gu$_4$ et áb, pour passer aux ovins: udu et sila$_4$. Ces derniers sont suivis par des animaux plus différenciés, plus rares et ne rentrant pas dans les catégories usuelles. Ce sont les ours (az), un type de cervidé (šeg$_7$-bar) et les ânes (anše).

Tel est l'ordre suivi dans les deux sections récapitulatives:

bovins: engraissés ou non-engraissés

gu$_4$ niga	boeufs gras
gu$_4$	boeufs nourris à l'herbe
gu$_4$ gùn-a	boeufs à la peau colorée
áb	vache

cervidés

lulim níta niga	lulim gras mâle
šeg$_7$-bar níta	cervidé mâle
šeg$_7$-bar mí	cervidé femelle

ovins engraissés

udu niga	mouton gras
gukkal niga	mouton gras à grosse queue
udu Šimaški niga	mouton gras de Šimaški
sila$_4$ niga	agneau gras
máš-gal niga	bouc gras mâle
máš-gal Šimaški niga	bouc gras mâle de Šimaški
máš-gal a-dara$_4$ niga	bouc gras mâle de race hybride
^{mí}ašgar niga	chevrette grasse

ovins non engraissés

udu	mouton
gukkal	mouton à grosse queue
sila$_4$	agneau
sila$_4$-gukkal	agneau à grosse queue
u$_8$ sila$_4$ nu-a	moutonne ayant eu un agneau
máš-gal	bouc de reproduction
máš-gal gùn-a	bouc de reproduction avec des tâches de couleur sur la peau
máš-gal a-dara$_4$	bouc de reproduction de race hybride
máš	bouc
ùz máš nu-a	chèvre ayant eu un petit

divers

mašda	gazelle
az	ours

La seconde section récapitulative de la tablette se contente de réduire les catégories

bovins		
	engraissés	gu_4 niga
	non-engraissés	gu_4
		áb
cervidés		
	lulim engraissés	lulim níta niga
	$šeg_7$-bar mâle et femelle	$šeg_7$-bar níta / mí
ovins		
	engraissés	udu niga
		máš niga
		máš a-$dara_4$ niga
		ùz niga
	non-engraissés	udu
		u_8
		máš
		máš a-$dara_4$
		ùz
divers		
	gazelle	mašda
	ours	az

Les catégories de classement des animaux sont relativement simples dans ce deux textes. On distingue ceux à la couleur de peau uniforme d'avec ceux à la peau bigarrée, moins prisés que les premiers. Les animaux à la peau blanche sont rares. Les ovins à grosse queue[6] et les moutons de Šimaški constituent une race particulière. Les catégories de classification sont souvent beaucoup plus marquées dans d'autres livraisons pour Drehem. Mais dans le cas présent il s'agit en fait surtout d'animaux apportés par des individus qui ne disposaient que d'espèces communes. Et sans doute cela était-il suffisant car ces animaux étaient tous destinés à la consommation.

6. La grosse queue des moutons représente en fait une importante poche de graisse de ces animaux.

Il n'est pas fait mention de l'état de la toison des ovins. Enfin l'appréciation de l'engraissement du bétail est très superficielle; on est loin des catégories niga-sig$_5$ subdivisés en 5 groupes. D'ailleurs ces catégories ne sont pleinement employées qu'à l'époque de Šu-Sîn.

Cette tablette YBC 3635 est récapitulative des livraisons journalières. Et en dépit des quelques dommages dont souffre la tablette il est possible de prouver qu'il n'y avait pas eu de livraisons tous les jours du mois; d'ailleurs le scribe devait pour ces jours 'sans livraison' trouver dans la corbeille à tablettes une tablette 'mu-túm nu-ub-tuk' qui notait qu'une livraison n'a pas eu lieu. Les livraisons faites le premier jour du mois n'ont pu être retrouvées, suite à la cassure de la tablette. Ont été sans livraisons les jours 3, 8, 19, 24, 25, 27, 28, 29 de ce mois. Une erreur est possible pour les 3 derniers jours du mois à cause de la cassure de la tablette.

Suite à ces remarques d'ordre général, il s'agit de prendre en considération les contribuables des mu-túm lugal, l'imposition qui leur est faite, sans considérer la part des bergers qui apparaîtra indirectement dans la seconde tablette avec les animaux šu-gíd.

Quantités

En général le nombre d'animaux livrés est réduit, souvent un agneau, un mouton ou une chèvre. Mais on retrouve cependant ce qui est régulier pour les livraisons ordinaires (mu-túm): le rapport de 1 bovin (boeuf ou vache) pour 10 têtes d'ovins; tel est le cas, par exemple, de Hunhubše, le 4ème jour.

Comme cette tablette est réservée exclusivement aux livraisons mu-túm lugal, livraisons particulières pour le roi, le scribe s'est permis pour le 15ème jour d'insérer une autre livraison de type analogue au mu-túm lugal, le mu-túm *Abisimti*, livraisons pour Abisimti. On lit:

1 šeg$_7$-bar nita
4 šeg$_7$-bar mí
Šar-ru-um-ba-ni
mu-túm A-bí-sí-im-ti
u$_4$ 15-kam

cinq cervidés livrés par Šarrum-bani pour le fonds Abisimti.

Ce genre de rapprochement dans le texte prouve que mu-túm lugal et mu-túm *Abisimti* doivent s'entendre dans même sens, livraison pour le roi et pour la reine Abisimti. Mais surtout il s'agit du même type de livraisons, à savoir non les livraisons pour les services réguliers des temples et du palais, mais pour la cour, dont le roi, la reine et certaines princesses constituent le noyau le plus important.

Périodicité des livraisons pour un mois

Certaines personnes sont à devoir faire des livraisons plus d'une fois par mois; ainsi

A-mur-É-a	u_4 7-kam	1 $sila_4$
A-mur-É-a	u_4 22-kam	1 $sila_4$, 1 máš-gal niga $a\text{-}dara_4$
en dInanna	u_4 2-kam	1 máš, 1 $sila_4$
en dInanna	u_4 11-kam	1 máš, 1 $sila_4$
en dInanna	u_4 16-kam	1 máš, 1 $sila_4$
en dInanna	u_4 17-kam	1 máš, 1 $sila_4$
Nu-ì-da	u_4 2-kam	2 $sila_4$
Nu-ì-da	u_4 12-kam	1 amar az níta mu [ ], 2 $sila_4$
Nu-ì-da	u_4 22-kam	2 $sila_4$
Ṣe-lu-uš-dDa-gan	u_4 2-kam	2 $sila_4$
Ṣe-lu-uš-dDa-gan	u_4 4-kam	1 máš
Ṣe-lu-uš-dDa-gan	u_4 5-kam	[ ] máš
Šar-ru-um-ba-ni	u_4 14-kam	5 $šeg_7$-bar
Šar-ru-um-ba-ni	u_4 17-kam	1 $sila_4$
Šeš-$ša_6$-ga	u_4 12-kam	1 $sila_4$, 1,0 lá 1 udu, 2 $šeg_7$-bar níta
Šeš-$ša_6$-ga	u_4 12-kam	2 gu_4, 4 gu_4 niga
Šeš-$ša_6$-ga	u_4 18-kam	1 $sila_4$

Pour pouvoir chiffrer avec exactitude les quantités imposées aux contribuables de Drehem, tant leurs obligations pour les mu-túm, les mu-túm lugal et d'autres services, il faudrait disposer de l'archive complète d'une année. Cela est encore loin d'être le cas. Aussi suffit-il de constater que les rhythmes de livraison sont plus compliqués qu'on pourrait le croire.

Les énsi, les gouverneurs de ville du royaume, doivent contribuer aux mu-túm lugal. Bien que l'essentiel de leurs apports fut pour les bala, la contribution faite dans le cadre de l'amphictyonie, ils devaient également participer aux contributions régulières et de plus n'étaient pas exempts de la contribution pour la couronne, même si l'apport est mince. Pour ce 11ème mois il y a la participation des:

énsi Adabki	u_4 10-kam	1 $sila_4$
énsi Gir_{13}-giški	u_4 30-kam	1 $sila_4$
énsi Gír-suki	u_4 5-kam	[1] $sila_4$
énsi Gír-suki	u_4 17-kam	1 $sila_4$
énsi Gír-suki	u_4 30-kam	2 $sila_4$, 4 udu niga
énsi Már-daki	u_4 26-kam	1 $sila_4$
énsi Nibruki	u_4 2-kam	1 $sila_4$
énsi Nibruki	u_4 12-kam	2 $sila_4$
énsi Nibruki	u_4 26-kam	1 máš
énsi Šuruppakki	u_4 5-kam	[1] $sila_4$

Durant ce 11ème mois 6 ensis apportent des contributions; cette fréquence est nettement plus importante que celle observée pour les bala; l'ensi de

Girsu, par exemple, est responsable des livraisons bala pour la durée de tout un mois. Ici les contributions sont minces. Il n'est guère possible de dire s'il s'agit de livraisons programmées ou d'appoints exigés au dernier moment.

Durant ce même mois, un seul prêtre-en apporte une faible contribution, toujours la même de 1 máš et un $sila_4$. Un sanga Ur-Tilla, responsable religieux d'un temple, apporte à 3 reprises une contribution:

en ^{d}Inanna	u_4 2-kam	1 máš, 1 $sila_4$
en ^{d}Inanna	u_4 11-kam	1 máš, 1 $sila_4$
en ^{d}Inanna	u_4 16-kam	1 máš, 1 $sila_4$
en ^{d}Inanna	u_4 17-kam	1 máš, 1 $sila_4$
Ur-^{d}Tìlla (U.AN) sanga	u_4 6-kam	2 $sila_4$
Ur-^{d}Tìlla sanga	u_4 12-kam	4 $sila_4$
Ur-^{d}Tìlla sanga	u_4 16-kam	2 $sila_4$

Les amorites sont souvent les récipiendaires de livraisons faites par Drehem. Mais en cette circonstance, probablement en fonction de leur position et de leur degré d'insertion dans la vie du royaume, quelques uns doivent payer leur dû. La liste est sans doute plus importante, mais certaines cassures empêchent d'en indiquer davantage avec certitude.

Lú-É-a	u_4 3-kam	1 gu_4 gùn-a		
Ma-li-a	u_4 5-kam	1 gu_4	1 áb	
Da-na-bi-id	u_4 5-kam			4 gukkal
A-na-na	u_4 5-kam		4 udu	
Lú-re-e-ù	u_4 5-kam		1 udu	2 gukkal

Certaines livraisons sont aussi importantes que celles des érin ou nubànda. Pour d'autres ce sont d'humbles contributions. D'autres noms d'étrangers se retrouvent dans le texte pour lesquels il est difficile de savoir s'il s'agit d'amorite, d'élamite, de hourrite ou de tout autre groupe ethnique du royaume.

Parmi ces étrangers on relève

Be-lí-a-ri-ik	u_4 18-kam		6 udu, 4 máš-gal 1 máš
Hu-un-hu-ub-še	u_4 3-kam	1 gu_4 niga	1 $sila_4$, 9 udu
I-din-Sîn dumu Hu-un-ha-ab-ur		u_4 11-kam	1 $sila_4$
Ša-lim-ku-na	u_4 6-kam		1 $sila_4$
Ša-lim-ku-na	u_4 14-kam	1 gu_4	10 udu
U-li-be-lí-uk	u_4 23-kam		1 $sila_4$
U-li-be-lu-uk	u_4 12-kam		1 $sila_4$

On notera le nom parfaitément akkadien, Iddin-Sîn de quelqu'un né d'un père étranger du nom de Hunhabur. Le scribe a aussi hésité entre l'écriture U-li-be-lu-uk et U-li-be-lí-uk.

Les livraisons des **érin**, les soldats de garnison qui sont dans 3 villes des frontières A-bí-ba-na^{ki}, Kak-ku$_8$-la-tum^{ki} et Zi-mu-dar^{ki} sont des plus importantes. De telles livraisons bien connues par d'autres textes sont toujours faites sous la supervision d'un ugula, un responsable en quelque sorte qui accompagne le convoi. Souvent même cet ugula apporte sa contribution propre. On notera qu'on respecte bien le rapport de 1 bovin pour 10 ovins: Les érin de Zimudar apportent 15 boeufs et 132 moutons et 18 chèvres (máš), soit bien 150 ovins.

Pour le 12ème jour la séquence est la suivante:

5 boeufs gras	40 moutons	10 chèvres	- Iribum
4 boeufs	30 moutons	10 chèvres	- érin Abibana
4 boeufs	20 moutons	20 chèvres	- érin Kakkulatum
1 boeuf	8 moutons	2 chèvres	- Igi nu-bànda
	5 moutons	1 chèvre	- Lú-šalim nu-bànda
	5 moutons	1 chèvre	- Suhuškin nu-bànda ugula Iribum
6 boeufs gras	59 moutons	1 chèvre	- Šeš-ša$_6$-ga-ga
+ 2 gazelles			

On doit remarquer que les livraisons des érin sont accompagnées de celle de leur capitaine. La faible contribution faite par ces derniers fait penser à des livraisons personnelles et non ex officio. Il faut présumer que Iribum de la première livraison est un nu-bànda qui fait une livraison officielle donc importante et qu'il est en même l'ugula, le responsable, du l'envoi ou même du convoi.

Donc l'organisation de l'envoi est le suivant: les colons-érin envoient leur dû augmenté de la participation personnelle de leurs capitaines. Le convoi est sous la responsabilité, peut-être même l'accompagnement personnel d'un des capitaines de ces colons. Mais par ailleurs le capitaine est astreint par son office de responsable militaire à un impôt spécifique relativement important comportant bovins et ovins. Ces érin figurent parmi les gros contributeurs des mu-túm lugal.

Les livraisons ex-officio des **nu-bànda**, des capitaines, sont très importantes, le 14ème jour par exemple. Leur contribution est dans la proportion de 1 bovin pour 10 ovins:[7]

7.

Da-hi-iš-e-en, nu-bànda	u$_4$ 14-kam	1 gu$_4$	10 udu	
I-gi$_4$ nu-bànda	u$_4$ 12-kam	1 gu$_4$	8 udu, 2 máš	
Ir-íb-ìl-šu, nu-bànda	u$_4$ 14-kam	1 gu$_4$	8 udu, 2 máš	
Lú-ša-lim nu-bànda	u$_4$ 12-kam		5 udu, 1 máš	
Me-^{d}Iškur, nu-bànda	u$_4$ 14-kam	1 gu$_4$	9 udu, 1 máš	
Ni-in-mu nu-bànda	u$_4$ 18-kam			1 sila$_4$
Puzur$_4$-Ha-ìa, nu-bànda	u$_4$ 14-kam	1 gu$_4$	10 udu	
Suhuš-ki-in nu-bànda	u$_4$ 12-kam		5 udu, 1 máš	1 sila$_4$
Ša-lim-be-lí, nu-bànda	u$_4$ 14-kam	1 gu$_4$	7 udu, 3 máš	
Ša-lim-ku-na, nu-bànda	u$_4$ 14-kam	1 gu$_4$	10 udu	
Šar-ru-um-ì-lí, nu-bànda	u$_4$ 14-kam	1 gu$_4$	8 udu, 2 máš	
Zi-kur-ì-lí, nu-bànda	u$_4$ 14-kam	10 gu$_4$-niga	1,38 udu, 2 máš	

10 boeufs gras	98 moutons	2 chèvres	Zikur-ili	nu-bànda
1 boeuf	10 moutons		Šalim-kuna	nu-bànda
1 boeuf	9 moutons	1 chèvre	Me-Iškur	nu-bànda
1 boeuf	10 moutons		Puzur-Haia	nu-bànda
1 boeuf	8 moutons	2 chèvres	Šarrum-ili	nu-bànda
1 boeuf	10 moutons		Dahiš-šeen	nu-bànda
1 boeuf	7 moutons	3 chèvres	Šalim-beli	nu-bànda
1 boeuf	8 moutons	2 chèvres	Irib-ilšu	nu-bànda
1 boeuf	10 moutons		Akia	nu-bànda

Ces nu-bànda, capitaines, sont aussi des responsables des érin, des colons vivant aux marches du royaume. D'ailleurs la liste est suivie immédiatement par des livraisons des érin de Zimudar. Ce sont

15 boeufs	132 moutons	18 chévres	érin Zimudar	ugula Zikur-ili

Il est vraisemblable que Zikur-ili dans cette ligne est le même que le nu-bànda mentionné plus haut. Il en resort donc qu'il est capitaine.

Il faut encore mentionner l'importante contribution du kaš-dé-a de Eštar-ilšu le 8ème jour; il comporte

18 boeufs gras	2 boeufs		20
35 moutons gras	1 agneau gras	4 boucs gras	100 moutons
	2 agneaux	60 boucs à la toison bigarrée	202

kašdea Eštar-ilšu.

Les deux troupeaux, de bovins et d'ovins, sont importants. Les proportions sont respectées: 20 et 202. Doit-on s'étonner du léger dépassement des ovins? Sans doute point, car il y a souvent de subtiles équivalences entre les animaux bigarrés dont la valeur paraît inférieure aux animaux à pelage normal. Bien qu'on s'attende à ce que le kaš-dé-a soit une libation de bière pour une divinité donnée ou dans un temple donné il est clair par ce texte que le kaš-dé-a entre directement dans les comptes speciaux des livraisons pour le roi qui en disposera. Ce kaš-dé-a vient de Eštar-ilšu, un fils du roi. Par ailleurs, il contribue encore 4 fois aux livraisons pour Drehem durant le même mois.

Eš$_4$-tár-ìl-šu kaš-dé-a	u$_4$ 8-kam	18 gu$_4$ niga
		2 gu$_4$
		35 udu niga
		100 udu
		1 sila$_4$ niga
		2 sila$_4$
		60 máš-gal gùn-a
		4 máš-gal niga
Eš$_4$-tár-ìl-šu	u$_4$ 10-kam	1 sila$_4$
Eš$_4$-tár-ìl-šu	u$_4$ 12-kam	1 sila$_4$

Eš$_4$-tár-ìl-šu	u$_4$ 15-kam	3 udu niga
Eš$_4$-tár-ìl-šu	u$_4$ 26-kam	1 sila$_4$

Un autre grand contributeur est Šu-Sîn; il participe 9 fois durant le mois, presque pour 1/3 des jours du mois. Il paraît difficile de penser que ce soit le futur successeur d'Amar-Sîn.

Šu-^{d}EN.ZU	u$_4$ 6-kam	1 sila$_4$
Šu-^{d}EN.ZU	u$_4$ 9-kam	1 lulim níta niga, 1 máš-gal niga, 1 u$_8$ sila$_4$ nu-a, 1 ùz máš nu-a, 2 sila$_4$, 3 udu niga
Šu-^{d}EN.ZU	u$_4$ 16-kam	2 amar az
Šu-^{d}EN.ZU	u$_4$ 18-kam	1 amar az
Šu-^{d}EN.ZU	u$_4$ 21-kam	1 amar az
Šu-^{d}EN.ZU	u$_4$ 22-kam	2 amar az
Šu-^{d}EN.ZU	u$_4$ 23-kam	3 amar az, 1 sila$_4$
Šu-^{d}EN.ZU	u$_4$ 26-kam	1 amar az
Šu-^{d}EN.ZU	u$_4$ 30-kam	3 amar az

Du tableau de ses contributions il est manifeste que Šu-Sîn s'occupe avant tout des animaux classés comme divers notamment les jeunes ours (13) et les lulim (cervidés au statut pas nettement défini). Des textes présentent le roi luttant avec les ours. Cela expliquerait la nécessité de livraisons fréquentes si l'animal disparaissait dans les jeux de cour.

Il suffit de donner les noms des autres contribuables en note. Leur participation est mince et de peu d'intérêt pour cette recherche.

A-a-ì-lí-šu	u$_4$ 9-kam	1 sila$_4$
A-a-ì-lí-šu	u$_4$ 9-kam	3 udu
A-at-tum	u$_4$ 18-kam	1 sila$_4$
A-hu-ni	u$_4$ 10-kam	1 sila$_4$
A-ki-a, nu-bànda	u$_4$ 14-kam	1 gu$_4$
A-ki-a, nu-bànda	u$_4$ 14-kam	10 udu
A-mur-É-a	u$_4$ 7-kam	1 sila$_4$
A-mur-É-a	u$_4$ 22-kam	1 máš-gal-niga a-da
A-mur-É-a	u$_4$ 22-kam	1 sila$_4$
A-na-na, Mar-tu	u$_4$ 5-kam	4 udu
Á-píl-la-lum	u$_4$ 9-kam	1 sila$_4$
Ab-[ ]	u$_4$ 11-kam	1 máš
Ab-[ ]	u$_4$ 11-kam	1 sila$_4$ [ ]
Ab-[ ]	u$_4$ 11-kam	1 sila$_4$ [ ]
Ab-[ ]	u$_4$ 11-kam	1 sila$_4$ [ ]
Ama-mu	u$_4$ 18-kam	1 máš
Ama-mu	u$_4$ 18-kam	1 sila$_4$
Amar-šè	u$_4$ 10-kam	1 sila$_4$
Amar-šè	u$_4$ 10-kam	2 udu

Ba-za-mu	u_4 8-kam	1 máš
Ba-za-[ ]	u_4 14-kam	1 $sila_4$
Be-lí [ ]	u_4 14-kam	1 $sila_4$
Be-lí-a-rí-ik	u_4 18-kam	1 máš
Be-lí-a-rí-ik	u_4 18-kam	4 máš-gal
Be-lí-a-rí-ik	u_4 18-kam	6 udu
Be-lí-dan	u_4 14-kam	1 $sila_4$
Bur-Ma-ma	u_4 5-kam	1 $sila_4$
^{d}Nin-e-ma-an-ág	u_4 16-kam	2 $sila_4$
^{d}Nin-gal-du-du	u_4 5-kam	
^{d}Šu-^{d}Šul-gi	u_4 5-kam	
Da-da dumu Ur-Ma-ma	u_4 7-kam	1 máš
Da-da	u_4 5-kam	1 máš
Da-hi-iš-e-en, nu-bànda	u_4 14-kam	1 gu_4
Da-hi-iš-e-en, nu-bànda	u_4 14-kam	10 udu
Da-la-a	u_4 15-kam	1 $sila_4$
Da-na-bi-id, Mar-tu	u_4 5-kam	4 gukkal
$Eš_4$-tár-ìl-šu kaš-dé-a	u_4 8-kam	1 $sila_4$-niga
$Eš_4$-tár-ìl-šu kaš-dé-a	u_4 8-kam	1,0 máš-gal gùn-a
$Eš_4$-tár-ìl-šu kaš-dé-a	u_4 8-kam	1,40 udu
$Eš_4$-tár-ìl-šu kaš-dé-a	u_4 8-kam	2 gu_4
$Eš_4$-tár-ìl-šu kaš-dé-a	u_4 8-kam	2 $sila_4$
$Eš_4$-tár-ìl-šu kaš-dé-a	u_4 8-kam	4 máš-gal-niga
$Eš_4$-tár-ìl-šu kaš-dé-a	u_4 8-kam	18 gu_4-niga
$Eš_4$-tár-ìl-šu kaš-dé-a	u_4 8-kam	35 udu-niga
$Eš_4$-tár-ìl-šu	u_4 10-kam	1 $sila_4$
$Eš_4$-tár-ìl-šu	u_4 12-kam	1 $sila_4$
$Eš_4$-tár-ìl-šu	u_4 15-kam	3 udu-niga
$Eš_4$-tár-ìl-šu	u_4 26-kam	1 $sila_4$
en ^{d}Inanna	u_4 2-kam	1 máš
en ^{d}Inanna	u_4 2-kam	1 $sila_4$
en ^{d}Inanna	u_4 11-kam	1 máš
en ^{d}Inanna	u_4 11-kam	1 $sila_4$
en ^{d}Inanna	u_4 16-kam	1 máš
en ^{d}Inanna	u_4 16-kam	1 $sila_4$
en ^{d}Inanna	u_4 17-kam	1 máš
en ^{d}Inanna	u_4 17-kam	1 $sila_4$
En-úr-kù-sig_{17}	u_4 11-kam	2 $sila_4$
En-úr-kù-sig_{17}	u_4 11-kam	4 udu-niga
énsi $Adab^{ki}$	u_4 10-kam	1 $sila_4$
énsi Gir_{13}-$giš^{ki}$	u_4 30-kam	1 $sila_4$
énsi Gír-su^{ki}	u_4 5-kam	x $sila_4$
énsi Gír-su^{ki}	u_4 30-kam	2 $sila_4$
énsi Gír-su^{ki}	u_4 30-kam	4 udu-niga
énsi Már-da^{ki}	u_4 26-kam	1 $sila_4$
énsi $Nibru^{ki}$	u_4 2-kam	1 $sila_4$
énsi $Nibru^{ki}$	u_4 12-kam	2 $sila_4$
énsi $Nibru^{ki}$	u_4 26-kam	1 máš
énsi Šuruppak	u_4 17-kam	1 $sila_4$
énsi $Šuruppak^{ki}$	u_4 5-kam	x $sila_4$
érin A-bí-ba-na^{ki}	u_4 12-kam	4 gu_4
érin A-bí-ba-na^{ki}	u_4 12-kam	10 máš

érin A-bí-ba-na^{ki}	u$_4$ 12-kam	30 udu
érin Kak-ku$_8$-la-tum^{ki}	u$_4$ 12-kam	4 gu$_4$
érin Kak-ku$_8$-la-tum^{ki}	u$_4$ 12-kam	20 máš
érin Kak-ku$_8$-la-tum^{ki}	u$_4$ 12-kam	20 udu
érin Zi-mu-dar^{ki}	u$_4$ 14-kam	2,12 udu
érin Zi-mu-dar^{ki}	u$_4$ 14-kam	15 gu$_4$
érin Zi-mu-dar^{ki}	u$_4$ 14-kam	18 máš
Gìr-ir	u$_4$ 4-kam	1 máš
Hu-ba-a	u$_4$ 12-kam	1 sila$_4$
Hu-un-hu-ub-še	u$_4$ 3-kam	1 gu$_4$-niga
Hu-un-hu-ub-še	u$_4$ 3-kam	1 gu$_4$-niga
Hu-un-hu-ub-še	u$_4$ 3-kam	1 sila$_4$
Hu-un-hu-ub-še	u$_4$ 3-kam	1 sila$_4$
Hu-un-hu-ub-še	u$_4$ 3-kam	9 udu
Hu-un-hu-ub-še	u$_4$ 3-kam	9 udu
I-din-^{d}EN.ZU dumu Hu-un-ha-ab-ur	u$_4$ 11-kam	1 sila$_4$
I-din-^{d}EN.ZU	u$_4$ 8-kam	1 máš
I-din-É-a	u$_4$ 18-kam	1 gu$_4$-niga
I-din-É-a	u$_4$ 18-kam	1 sila$_4$
I-din-É-a	u$_4$ 18-kam	4 máš
I-din-É-a	u$_4$ 18-kam	5 udu
I-gi$_4$ nu-bànda	u$_4$ 12-kam	1 gu$_4$
I-gi$_4$ nu-bànda	u$_4$ 12-kam	2 máš
I-gi$_4$ nu-bànda	u$_4$ 12-kam	8 udu
I-li-iš-ti-kál	u$_4$ 9-kam	1 máš
I-pi$_4$-iq-na-ni	u$_4$ 5-kam	x sila$_4$
I-ri-ib-um	u$_4$ 12-kam	1 gu$_4$
I-ri-ib-um	u$_4$ 12-kam	4 gu$_4$-niga
I-ri-ib-um	u$_4$ 12-kam	10 máš
I-ri-ib-um	u$_4$ 12-kam	40 udu
I-za-nu-um	u$_4$ 13-kam	1 sila$_4$
I-zu-a	u$_4$ 9-kam	1 sila$_4$
I-dur-ì-lí	u$_4$ 21-kam	1 máš
Ì-la-lum	u$_4$ 22-kam	1 mí-ašgar-niga
Ì-lí-dan	u$_4$ 10-kam	1 gu$_4$
Ì-lí-dan	u$_4$ 10-kam	3 sila$_4$
Ì-lí-dan	u$_4$ 10-kam	7 udu
Id-da-a	u$_4$ 5-kam	
Id-da-a	u$_4$ 12-kam	1 máš
Igi-an-na-ke$_4$-zu	u$_4$ 8-kam	1 máš
Igi-an-na-ke$_4$-zu	u$_4$ 14-kam	1 sila$_4$
Ik-šu-tum	u$_4$ 21-kam	1 máš
Ilum-ba-ni	u$_4$ 14-kam	1 sila$_4$
Ilum-ba-ni	u$_4$ 21-kam	1 máš
Ip-hur kuš$_7$	u$_4$ 9-kam	1 sila$_4$
Ir-íb-ìl-šu, nu-bànda	u$_4$ 14-kam	1 gu$_4$
Ir-íb-ìl-šu, nu-bànda	u$_4$ 14-kam	2 máš
Ir-íb-ìl-šu, nu-bànda	u$_4$ 14-kam	8 udu
Ir$_{11}$-da-ni	u$_4$ 30-kam	1 máš
Ki-na-na	u$_4$ 9-kam	1 sila$_4$ nu
Ku-ù	u$_4$ 22-kam	18 mašda

Kur-gìr-ni-šè	u_4 9-kam	1 máš
Lu-lu-ba-ni	u_4 13-kam	1 $sila_4$
Lú-ša-lim nu-bànda	u_4 12-kam	1 máš
Lú-ša-lim nu-bànda	u_4 12-kam	5 udu
Lú-bala-$ša_6$-ga	u_4 30-kam	1 máš
Lú-^{d}Nanna	u_4 5-kam	1 $sila_4$-niga
Lú-^{d}Nin-šubur	u_4 5-kam	1 $sila_4$-niga
Lú-dingir-ra	u_4 30-kam	1 $sila_4$
Lú-É-a Mar-tu	u_4 3-kam	1 gu_4 gùn-a
Lú-É-a Mar-tu	u_4 3-kam	1 gu_4 gùn-a
Lú-kal-la	u_4 30-kam	1 $sila_4$
Lú-re-e-ù, Mar-tu	u_4 5-kam	1 udu
Lú-re-e-ù, Mar-tu	u_4 5-kam	2 gukkal
Lugal-á-zi-da	u_4 18-kam	1 $sila_4$
Lugal-má-gur_8-re	u_4 10-kam	1 $sila_4$
Lugal-má-gur_8-re	u_4 21-kam	1 máš
Lugal-má-gur_8-re	u_4 23-kam	1 $sila_4$
Ma-li-a, Mar-tu	u_4 5-kam	1 áb
Ma-li-a, Mar-tu	u_4 5-kam	1 gu_4
Ma-na-a	u_4 13-kam	
Má-li-li	u_4 9-kam	1 $sila_4$
Me-^{d}Iškur, nu-bànda	u_4 14-kam	1 gu_4
Me-^{d}Iškur, nu-bànda	u_4 14-kam	1 máš
Me-^{d}Iškur, nu-bànda	u_4 14-kam	9 udu
Na-ra-am-É-a	u_4 21-kam	1 máš
Nam-ha-ni dub-sar	u_4 11-kam	1 $sila_4$
Ni-in-mu nu-bànda	u_4 18-kam	1 $sila_4$
Nin-é-gal-igi-du	u_4 14-kam	1 $sila_4$
Nir-ì-da-gál	u_4 2-kam	1 $sila_4$
Nir-ì-da-gál	u_4 4-kam	1 máš
Nu-ì-da	u_4 2-kam	2 $sila_4$
Nu-ì-da	u_4 12-kam	1 amar az níta mu
Nu-ì-da	u_4 12-kam	2 $sila_4$
Nu-ì-da	u_4 22-kam	2 $sila_4$
Nu-úr-^{d}EN.ZU	u_4 17-kam	1 máš
$Puzur_4$-^{d}Adad	u_4 14-kam	1 $sila_4$
$Puzur_4$-Ha-ià, nu-bànda	u_4 14-kam	1 gu_4
$Puzur_4$-Ha-ià, nu-bànda	u_4 14-kam	10 udu
Sag-^{d}Nanna-zu	u_4 8-kam	1 $sila_4$
Suhuš-ki-in nu-bànda	u_4 12-kam	1 máš
Suhuš-ki-in nu-bànda	u_4 12-kam	5 udu
Suhuš-ki-in	u_4 12-kam	1 $sila_4$
Ṣe-lu-uš-^{d}Da-gan	u_4 2-kam	2 $sila_4$
Ṣe-lu-uš-^{d}Da-gan	u_4 4-kam	1 máš
Ṣe-lu-uš-^{d}Da-gan	u_4 5-kam	x máš
Ša-at-ra-at	u_4 5-kam	2 $sila_4$
Ša-lim-be-lí, nu-bànda	u_4 14-kam	1 gu_4
Ša-lim-be-lí, nu-bànda	u_4 14-kam	3 máš
Ša-lim-be-lí, nu-bànda	u_4 14-kam	7 udu
Ša-lim-ku-na	u_4 6-kam	1 $sila_4$
Ša-lim-ku-na, nu-bànda	u_4 14-kam	1 gu_4

Ša-lim-ku-na, nu-bànda	u_4 14-kam	10 udu
Šar-ru-um-ba-ni	u_4 14-kam	1 anše
Šar-ru-um-ba-ni	u_4 14-kam	18 $šeg_7$-bar níta
Šar-ru-um-ba-ni	u_4 14-kam	22 $šeg_7$-bar mí
Šar-ru-um-ba-ni	u_4 17-kam	1 $sila_4$
Šar-ru-um-ì-lí, nu-bànda	u_4 14-kam	1 gu_4
Šar-ru-um-ì-lí, nu-bànda	u_4 14-kam	2 máš
Šar-ru-um-ì-lí, nu-bànda	u_4 14-kam	8 udu
Šeš-$ša_6$-ga	u_4 12-kam	1 $sila_4$
Šeš-$ša_6$-ga	u_4 12-kam	1,0 lá 1 udu
Šeš-$ša_6$-ga	u_4 12-kam	2 $šeg_7$-bar níta
Šeš-$ša_6$-ga	u_4 12-kam	2 gu_4
Šeš-$ša_6$-ga	u_4 12-kam	4 gu_4-niga
Šeš-$ša_6$-ga	u_4 18-kam	1 $sila_4$
Šeš-kal-la	u_4 14-kam	1 $sila_4$
Šeš-kal-la	u_4 23-kam	1 $sila_4$
Šeš-zi-mu	u_4 5-kam	1 $sila_4$-niga
Še-li-bu-um	u_4 26-kam	1 máš
Šu-^{d}Šamaš	u_4 6-kam	1 $sila_4$
Šu-^{d}Adad	u_4 21-kam	1 máš
Šu-^{d}Da-gan	u_4 3-kam	1 $sila_4$
Šu-^{d}Da-gan	u_4 3-kam	1 $sila_4$
Šu-^{d}EN.ZU	u_4 6-kam	1 $sila_4$
Šu-^{d}EN.ZU	u_4 9-kam	1 lulim níta niga
Šu-^{d}EN.ZU	u_4 9-kam	1 máš-gal-niga
Šu-^{d}EN.ZU	u_4 9-kam	1 u_8 $sila_4$ nu-a
Šu-^{d}EN.ZU	u_4 9-kam	1 ùz máš nu-a
Šu-^{d}EN.ZU	u_4 9-kam	2 $sila_4$
Šu-^{d}EN.ZU	u_4 9-kam	3 udu-niga
Šu-^{d}EN.ZU	u_4 16-kam	2 amar az
Šu-^{d}EN.ZU	u_4 18-kam	1 amar az
Šu-^{d}EN.ZU	u_4 21-kam	1 amar az
Šu-^{d}EN.ZU	u_4 22-kam	2 amar az
Šu-^{d}EN.ZU	u_4 23-kam	1 $sila_4$
Šu-^{d}EN.ZU	u_4 23-kam	3 amar az
Šu-^{d}EN.ZU	u_4 26-kam	1 amar az
Šu-^{d}EN.ZU	u_4 30-kam	3 amar az
Šu-ra-nu-um	u_4 13-kam	1 $sila_4$
Šu-ru-uš-ki-in	u_4 8-kam	1 $sila_4$
U-li-be-lí-uk	u_4 23-kam	1 $sila_4$
U-li-be-lu-uk	u_4 12-kam	1 $sila_4$
	u_4 21-kam	1 máš x
	u_4 21-kam	1 $sila_4$ x
ugula I-ri-pu-um		
Ur-^{d}EN.ZU	u_4 5-kam	1 $sila_4$
Ur-^{d}Ištaran	u_4 2-kam	1 $sila_4$
Ur-^{d}Ištaran	u_4 2-kam	4 gukkal
Ur-^{d}Nanna	u_4 9-kam	1 $sila_4$
Ur-^{d}Nin-[ ]	u_4 17-kam	1 máš
Ur-^{d}Tílla (U.AN) sanga	u_4 6-kam	2 $sila_4$
Ur-^{d}Tílla sanga	u_4 12-kam	4 $sila_4$
Ur-^{d}Tílla sanga	u_4 16-kam	2 $sila_4$
Ur-mes	u_4 8-kam	1 $sila_4$

Ur-mes	u$_4$ 9-kam	4 gukkal-niga
Ur-mes	u$_4$ 9-kam	4 udu-niga
Ur-mes	u$_4$ 9-kam	8 sila$_4$
Ur-mes	u$_4$ 10-kam	2 sila$_4$
Ur-mes	u$_4$ 10-kam	4 udu-niga
Ur-mes	u$_4$ 14-kam	1 sila$_4$
Ur-mes	u$_4$ 18-kam	1 sila$_4$
Ur-mes	u$_4$ 30-kam	1 sila$_4$
Ur-mu	u$_4$ 3-kam	1 sila$_4$
Ur-mu	u$_4$ 3-kam	1 sila$_4$
Ur-ni$_9$	u$_4$ 6-kam	
Ur-ni$_9$	u$_4$ 6-kam	1 sila$_4$
Ur-ni$_9$-gar	u$_4$ 10-kam	1 gu$_4$
Ur-ni$_9$-gar	u$_4$ 10-kam	1 sila$_4$
Ur-ni$_9$-gar	u$_4$ 10-kam	5 udu-niga
Ur-sukkal	u$_4$ 6-kam	2 sila$_4$
Ur-sukkal	u$_4$ 18-kam	1 máš
Wa-at | (-□I)-ra-at	u$_4$ 12-kam	1 sila$_4$
Wa-at-ra-at	u$_4$ 16-kam	2 sila$_4$
Wa-tá-ru-um	u$_4$ 18-kam	1 sila$_4$
Za-la-a	u$_4$ 11-kam	1 sila$_4$
Za-la-a	u$_4$ 18-kam	1 sila$_4$
Zi-kur-ì-lí	u$_4$ 17-kam	1 sila$_4$-niga
Zi-kur-ì-lí, nu-bànda	u$_4$ 14-kam	1,38 udu
Zi-kur-ì-lí, nu-bànda	u$_4$ 14-kam	2 máš
Zi-kur-ì-lí, nu-bànda	u$_4$ 14-kam	10 gu$_4$-niga
[ ]	u$_4$ 14-kam	
[ ]	u$_4$ 14-kam	1 sila$_4$
[ ]-tum	u$_4$ 5-kam	

Bien qu'identique, quant à son fonctionnement, aux autres systèmes de livraison, les mu-túm lugal font resortir l'importante contribution des érin pour la couronne et une fréquence de livraison beaucoup plus élevée que celle relevée pour les mu-túm réguliers. Ce système des livraisons royales, moins connu, mérite encore des études complémentaires pour mieux l'identifier et le distinguer des livraisons mu-túm ordinaires.

La tablette YBC 4190, tablette de dépenses, zi-ga lugal, met en lumière l'utilisation faite des animaux donnés au titre du mu-túm lugal. Cette tablette est plus endommagée que la précédente.

face
(colonne 1)
[1 gu$_4$-ú]
[5 udu-ú]
[mu] kaš$_4$-ke$_4$-ne-šè
[1] gu$_4$-ú
[5] udu-ú
[mu] àga-ús-e-ne-šè
[šu-gíd] é-muhaldim
Ir$_{11}$-mu maškim
2 ⟨gu$_4$⟩10 ⟨udu⟩ a-rá 1-kam
[2] gu$_4$-ú
[10] udu-ú
u$_4$ 1-kam

[ ] gu$_4$-ú
[ ] udu-ú
[mu] kaš$_4$-e-ne-šè
[ ] u$_8$ ú
[ ] udu-ú
[mu] àga-ús-e-ne-šè
[ù lú]-šúkur-ra-ke$_4$-ne-šè
[šu-gíd é-muhaldim]
[Ir$_{11}$]-mu [maškim]
[x] + 1 gu$_4$
[x] + 16 udu
u$_4$ 2-kam
[ ] udu-ú
[mu] dumu ^{d}En-líl-lá-šè
[ ] A-bí-sí-im-ti
[x] gu$_4$-ú
[ ]

(colonne 2)
[ ]
17 u$_8$-ú
alan didli
šà é ^{d}En-líl-lá
17 u$_8$-ú
alan didli
šà é ^{d}Nin-líl-lá
uzu a-bal
sískur gu-la
[1] udu kur udu
lugal ku$_4$-ra
[30] + 5 udu
u$_4$ [7]-kam

10 udu-ú
10 sila$_4$
11 máš
šu-gíd é-muhaldim
mu àga-ús ù [lú šúkur-ra-ke$_4$]-ne-šè
[Ir$_{11}$-mu maškim]
[31 udu]
[u$_4$ 8-kam]

[udu-ú]
[-ú]
[šu-gíd é-muhaldim]
[mu àga-ús ù lú šúkur-ra-ke$_4$-ne-šè]
Ir$_{11}$-mu maškim
18 udu
u$_4$ 9-kam

20 udu-ú
12 máš-gal-ú
[šu-gíd é-muhaldim]
[mu àga-ús ù lú šúkur-ra-ke$_4$-ne-šè]
[Ir$_{11}$-mu maškim]
[32 udu]
[u$_4$ 10-kam]

[udu-ú]
[ ]

(colonne 3)
[ ] máš-gal-ú
šu-gíd é-muhaldim
mu àga-úš-e-ne-šè
Ir$_{11}$-mu maškim
18 udu
u$_4$ 11-kam

2 gu$_4$-ú
1 gu$_4$ mu 1
15 udu-ú
4 ùz-ú
šu-gíd é-muhaldim
mu àga-úš-e-ne-šè
Ir$_{11}$-mu maškim
3 gu$_4$ 19 udu
u$_4$ 15-kam

1 anše bar-an níta šu-gíd
10 dusú mí šu-gíd
ur-gi$_7$-re ba-ab-kú
ki Šeš-kal-la
gìr Hu-na-zi nu-bànda
Ir$_{11}$-mu maškim
1 anše bar-an
10 dusú
u$_4$ 16-kam

1 udu-ú
sískur rá-gaba-e-ne-šè
gìr ^{d}Šu-^{d}EN.ZU-ba-ni a-zu
Ba-ba-ti maškim
10 udu-ú
šu-gíd é-muhaldim

(colonne 4)
mu kaš$_4$-ke$_4$-ne-šè
Ir$_{11}$-mu maškim
11 udu
u$_4$ 19-kam

1 gu$_4$-ú
10 udu-ú
2 máš-gal-ú
šu-gíd é-muhaldim
mu kaš$_4$-ke$_4$-ne-šè
Ir$_{11}$-mu maškim
1 gu$_4$
12 udu
u$_4$ 20-kam

3 áb-ú
10 udu-ú
5 máš-gal-ú
mu àga-úš-e-ne-šè
10 ùz-ú
mu kaš$_4$-ke$_4$-ne-šè
šu-gíd é-muhaldim
Ir$_{11}$-mu maškim
3 gu$_4$
25 udu
u$_4$ 21-kam

10 udu-ú
20 máš-gal-ú
šu-gíd é-muhaldim
mu àga-úš ù lú šúkur-ra-ke$_4$-ne-šè
Ir$_{11}$-mu maškim
30 udu
u$_4$ 22-kam

30 udu-ú
mu àga-úš ù lú šúkur-ra-ke$_4$-ne-šè
3 gu$_4$-ú
10 udu-ú
5 máš-gal-ú

(colonne 5)
mu kaš$_4$-ke$_4$-ne-šè
šu-gíd é-muhaldim
Ir$_{11}$-mu maškim
3 gu$_4$
45 udu
u$_4$ 23-kam

3 áb-ú
15 udu-ú
10 ùz-ú
šu-gíd é-muhaldim
mu àga-úš ù lú šúkur-ra-ke$_4$-ne-šè
Ir$_{11}$-mu maškim
3 gu$_4$
25 udu
u$_4$ 24-kam

2 áb-ú
1 gu$_4$ mu 3
10 u$_8$-ú
15 ùz-ú
šu-gíd é-muhaldim
mu àga-úš ù lú šúkur-ra-ke$_4$-ne-šè
Ir$_{11}$-mu maškim
3 gu$_4$
25 udu
u$_4$ 25-kam

10 udu-ú
mu kaš$_4$-ke$_4$-ne-šè
1 gu$_4$-ú
5 máš-gal-ú
mu àga-úš a-tu$_5$-a-ka égal-la
ku$_4$-ra-ne-šè
1 áb-ú
10 udu-ú
15 ùz-ú

(colonne 6)
mu àga-úš ù lú šúkur-ra-ke_4-ne-šè
šu-gíd é-muhaldim
Ir_{11}-mu maškim
2 gu_4
40 udu
u_4 26-kam

20 u_8-ú
alam didli
šà é ^{d}En-líl-lá
17 ùz-ú
alam didli
šà é ^{d}Nin-líl-lá
uzu a-bal
sískur gu-la
nì-dab_5 ezem gan-gan-è
^{d}En-líl-a-bu-šu sagi maškim
1 máš é-uz-ga
ki Uri_5^{ki}-ki-du_{10} muhaldim
A-mur-ilum rá-gaba maškim
1 áb-ú
5 udu-ú
mu $kaš_4$-ke_4-ne-šè
20 máš-gal-ú
mu dumu-mí Lugal-má-gur_8-re-šè
3 áb-ú
12 udu-ú
15 máš-gal-ú
mu àga-úš ù lú šúkur-ra-ke_4-ne-šè
šu-gíd é-muhaldim
Ir_{11}-mu maškim
[4 gu_4]
[1.30 = 90 udu]
u_4 27-kam]

(colonne 7)
1 gu_4-ú
[ ] udu-ú
[máš-gal-ú]
mu àga-úš ù lú šúkur-ra-ke_4-ne-šè
šu-gíd é-muhaldim
Ir_{11}-mu maškim
1 gu_4
15 udu
u_4 28-kam

7 gu_4-ú
1,43 udu-ú
42 máš-gal-ú
ugula Šà-kù-ge
7 gu_4-ú
5 áb-ú
1,2 udu-ú
18 máš-gal-ú
ugula É-a-ba-ni
30 udu-ú
18 máš-gal-ú
ugula Lugal-kù-zu
1 gu_4-ú
7 udu-ú
ugula ^{d}Nin-líl-zi-mu
2 udu-ú
ugula A-mur-ilum
25 udu-ú
ugula $Puzur_4$-[ ]
25 udu-ú
ugula ^{d}Šul-gi-[ ]
16 udu-ú
ugula Nu-úr-^{d}[ ]
šu-gíd
u_4 Géme-[^{d}En-líl-lá]
Tum-ma-al
ti-a-ba [ ]

rev
(colonne 8)
[anše baran]
1 dúsu
ur-gi_7-re ba-ab-kú
gìr A-x
Ir_{11}-mu maškim
[21+ gu_4]
[5.28 + udu]
3 + [anše bar-an]
u_4 29-kam

50 + x gu_4

3 + x anše bar-an
10 + x dusú
14,42 udu
zi-ga lugal
gìr ^{d}Nanna-ma-ba
ù Lú-ša-lim

1 máš šùr-ra KA-x-x-du_8-a
á-gi_6-ba-a
u_4 15-kam
1 máš gú-šùr-ra-ke_4
ki-tag-ga
šà Uri_5^{ki}-ma
1 udu
1 $sila_4$
^{d}Nin-a-zu
1 udu ^{d}Ereš-ki-gal
1 udu
1 $sila_4$
^{d}Nin-šubur
šà EN.DÍM.GIG^{ki}
1 udu
1 $sila_4$
^{d}Nin-gis-zi-da
šà GIŠ-bàn-da^{ki}
1 $sila_4$ má-a du_8-x
1 $sila_4$ ama-[ ]
1 máš [ ]
1 $sila_4$ [ ]
1 $sila_4$ [ ]

(colonne 9)
1 $sila_4$ ká gu-la
^{d}Amar-^{d}EN.ZU
kar-re lugal
é ^{giš}gu-za
1 máš ^{giš}giš-a-nag
gidim šul-[ ]
1 $sila_4$ ^{giš}giš-a-nag
gidim gín-bar-ra
á-gi_6-ba-a
1 máš balag ^{d}Nanna
1 máš balag ^{d}Nin-sún
1 máš ^{d}Utu-gú-sùr-ra
1 $sila_4$
1 máš
sùr-ra šu bar-ra
giš-a-nag gidim tu-ru-na
á-u_4-te-na
šà Uri_5^{ki}-ma
u_4 16-kam

1 udu šakirá (ki-^{d}Utu) giš-a-nag gidim
1 udu giš-a-nag gidim è-è
1 udu abul gu-za
1 udu ^{d}Nin-giš-te-te
1 udu ^{d}Ama-abzu-kár
1 udu ^{d}Ne-ti / Pe_5-ti
1 udu ^{d}Lugal-engar-du-du
1 udu ^{d}Nin-pú-mun-na
1 udu ki búr-búr
1 udu ^{d}Nin-šubur
1 máš érim
^{d}[ ]
[ ]
[ ]
alan

(colonne 10)
[šà] é Ur-^{d}Nammu
1 udu ^{d}Ba-ba_6
1 udu 1 $sila_4$
^{d}Nì-érim-nu-dab
1 $sila_4$ ^{d}Ha-ìa
1 máš ^{d}Inanna ^{giš}tukul
1 máš ^{d}Be-la-at-suh-nir
1 udu
1 máš
kar-a kar-ra
1 máš
suh á-ki-ti
1 udu ^{d}Nin-a-a-mu
1 udu ^{d}Utu
1 udu ^{d}Mes-lam-ta-è-a ha-zi
1 udu gùn ^{d}Amar-^{d}EN.ZU
1 $sila_4$ ^{d}Geštin-an-na
1 máš ^{d}Al-la-tum

1 $sila_4$ ká giš-kin-ti gu-la
1 máš abul lugal
1 máš ká ^{d}Gu-la
1 $sila_4$ é-gi-na-ab-tum
šà-ge-pàd-da
^{d}Nanna
1 $sila_4$ ^{d}Bìl-ga-mes
1 udu gán udu
^{d}Nin-kù-nun-na
1 máš ^{d}Nin-é-an-na šà uru
1 $sila_4$
dúr ^{giš}ha-lu-úb
1 $sila_4$ ér-e ki tag-ga
šà $^{giš}kiri_6$

(colonne 11)
^{d}Nin-[ ]-si_4
1 máš gùn ^{d}Dumu-zi-da
1 $sila_4$ ^{giš}gu-za
(cassure de plusieurs lignes)
[ ]-ra
1 $sila_4$
ká sùr-ra
1 udu 1 máš
du_6 giš-gan-na
nì-siskúr-ra a kar-ra-a
3 áb 3 gu_4 mu-2 ga
4 áb mu-2 gìš nu-zu
7 u_8
7 $sila_4$ ga
7 ùz
7 máš
14 udu níta
14 máš níta
sùr-ra ba-an-si
1 udu 1 máš
kùn
1 máš
balag ^{d}Nin-sún
nì-dab ki kùn-na
á-gi_6-ba-a
u_4 17-kam

Lugal-á-zi-da maškim

1 $sila_4$ ^{giš}gu-za Ur-^{d}Nammu
gìr Nam-ha-ni sagi
Ri-mi-èl rá-gaba maškim

(colonne 12)
(2 ou 3 lignes perdues)
[^{giš}]gu-za ^{d}Šul-gi-ra
1 máš ^{giš}gu-za ^{d}Amar-^{d}EN.ZU
á-gi_6-ba-a
u_4 20+[ ] kam

1 udu giš-dù abul lugal
1 udu giš-dù suh [ ]-du-du
1 udu giš-dù
abul ^{d}Nin-gal
ga kú-šè
gìr Nam-ha-ni sagi
Ú-la-i-nì-iš šu-i maškim
kislah (ki-u_4) 9
u_4 25-kam

2 máš-gal
ù (=HUL) šim šà é-gal
gìr Lú-sukkal-an-ka lú mu_{13}-mu_{13}
Ri-mi-èl rá-gaba maškim
u_4 28-kam

2 udu 5 máš-gal-ú
é dingir-re-ne gá-gá-dè
gìr Sal-li $gudu_4$
Ri-mi-èl rá-gaba maškim
u_4 29-kam

10 gu_4
2,22 udu
^{giš}giš-a-nag gidim ^{d}Šu-^{d}EN.ZU ba-ak

(colonne 13)
(début cassé, 10 lignes)
šu-nígin [ ] gu_4 X
šu-nígin 3 gu_4 mu-3
šu-nígin 1 gu_4 mu-1
šu-nígin 22 áb-ú
šu-nígin 4 áb mu-2

šu-nígin 3 anše bar-an níta
šu-nígin 10 dusú mí
šu-nígin 9,51 udu-ú
šu-nígin 1,4 u_8-ú
šu-nígin 3,22 máš-gal-ú
šu-nígin 1,18 ùz-ú
šu-nígin 22 + x $sila_4$
šu-nígin x máš
(reste de la colonne cassé)

(colonne 14)
šu-nigin 1.0 gu_4-áb[hi-a]
šu-nigin 3 anše bar-an
šu-nigin 10 dusú
šu-nigin x+17,5 udu-máš[hi-a]

le reste est perdu, avec la date

Cette tablette est extraordinaire pour son contenu et sa structure. Son état général de préservation n'est que moyen avec beaucoup de cassures aux 4 angles. Toutefois beaucoup de restaurations sont possibles grâce à la régularité de la structure de composition adoptée et suivie par le scribe.

L'originalité de la tablette tient au fait qu'elle presente l'une à la suite de l'autre 2 séquences chronologiques concomittantes. La première partie présente les jours successifs d'un mois donné (probablement gan-gan-è, 9ème mois du calendrier de Nippur) pendant lesquels ont pris place des zi-ga lugal, des dépenses royales. Cette section est suivie par d'autres dépenses pour un certain nombre de jours du même mois. Toutefois on ne devrait pas y voir un désordre quelconque. La première partie traite avant tout des livraisons d'animaux šu-gíd pour les cuisines et pour les gens-d'armes. La seconde série traite de livraisons pour des circonstances particulières. Il est à présumer que la tablette date de la dernière année de Šu-Sîn.

La première partie est résumée ainsi:

50 gu_4	50 bovins
3 anše bar-an	3 ânes baran
10 dusú	10 ânes
14,42 udu	882 ovins
zi-ga lugal	dépense royale
gìr ^{d}Nanna-ma-ba ù Lú-ša-lim	

En règle générale, la section d'un jour donné se présente de la manière suivante:

x bovins nourris à l'herbe	gu_4 ú
x ovins nourris à l'herbe	udu ú
reçus au titre de l'impôt payé par les bergers	šu-gíd
destinés aux cuisines	é muhaldim
pour les àga-uš et les rationnaires	mu àga-úš ù šúkur-ra-ke_4-ne-šè
Irmu est le responsable	Ir_{11}-mu maškim
total des bovins dépensés	x gu_4
total des ovins dépensés	x udu
$n^{ième}$ jour du mois	**u_4 X-kam**

Pour composer sa tablette le scribe a repris les tablettes de dépenses quotidiennes pour les cuisines qui représentent en fait les livraisons de bétail provenant des bergers et engraisseurs. C'est pourquoi il précise toujours šu-gíd. Ces animaux de qualité médiocre vont aux cuisines du palais pour les gens-d'armes, sous le contrôle de Irmu. A la fin de l'énumération de la quantité de chaque type de bétail, le scribe fait des totaux. Ce procédé est des plus utiles pour se retrouver dans les comptes et aussi pour savoir où finit une section.

La première section consiste en dépenses à la charge du roi et devrait donc constituer l'exact pendant des mu-túm lugal, des livraisons pour le roi. En fait on voit bien que les apports de bétail enregistrés sur la première tablette analysée dans ce travail ne sont pas pour les cuisines. Il n'y est jamais fait mention d'animaux šu-gíd. Par contre les cuisines sont ravitaillées par un autre circuit, celui des bergers, différent de celui qui pourvoit aux besoins de la cour ou de certains membres de la famille royale.

Un berger voit son troupeau augmenter chaque année par des naissances. Tous les animaux du troupeau ne peuvent être gardés ou être engraissés par manque de fourrage; ils doivent donc en être retirés. Mais loin de nourrir les bergers, ces animaux dits šu-gíd, retirés du troupeau, constituent l'impôt royal qu'ils doivent payer sur leur troupeau. En général ces animaux nourris seulement à l'herbe, donnent une viande de qualité très moyenne et sont destinés en fin de compte à la cuisine du palais. Etant entrés dans les comptes comme impôt pour le roi, mu-túm lugal, il est donc aussi naturel de les voir fonctionnés comme dépense pour le roi, zi-ga lugal. Cette seconde tablette permet donc de découvrir le double circuit de livraisons qui couvre les dépenses royales. Cette tablette a l'avantage de montrer les deux circuits, l'un après l'autre, prouvant par là que les scribes ne mélangeaient ou ne les confondaient pas, celui des bergers pour les cuisines et celui des érin et autres pour le roi, la famille royale et le culte.

Ce bétail, livré par Drehem, est destiné à Nippur, la capitale religieuse du royaume et notamment aux temples d'Enlil et de Ninlil. Ces animaux doivent aussi nourrir les gens-d'armes dont la fonction n'est pas encore bien définie et les rationnaires les lú-šúkur-ra-ke_4-ne. Il est fort vraisemblable que ces àga-uš sont eux aussi à Nippur.

Déroulement des dépenses

Il est impossible dans la première colonne de la tablette de retrouver les livraisons du premier au 6ème jour. On notera tout juste qu'il y a eu le même jour des livraisons qui ont dû être réitérées. Cela est marqué par l'expression: a-rá x-kam.

Le septième jour est marqué par une entrée royale dans le temple: lugal-ku_4-ra. A cette occasion les statues qui sont dans les temples d'Enlil et de Ninlil reçoivent des offrandes. Les viandes de ces animaux ne sont pas particulièrement bien apprêtées puisqu'elles sont cuites à l'eau (uzu a-bal) par contraste avec une rôtissage ou un braissage sous les cendres dans d'autres circonstances.[8] L'occasion spécifique est une grande cérémonie: sískur gu-la qui pourrait bien devoir être mise en relation avec le premier quart de la lune.[9]

Pour le lendemain il n'y a qu'une simple livraison de bovins destinés aux cuisines. Il en va de même pour les jours suivants.

La livraison du 16ème jour sert à nourrir les chiens. On leur donne des ânes šú-gíd, donc ceux qui avaient été livrés au titre de l'impôt par les âniers. Irmu est également responsable de ces transferts. La tablette situe cette transaction chez Šeškalla. On notera donc à cette occasion que les livraisons pour le roi servent au fonctionnement général de toutes les instances du palais: le culte, la famille royale, le service de garde, les chiens. Les chiens[10] pourraient avoir été des chiens de garde, mais aussi les chiens de Gula.[11]

Le 19ème jour Šu-Sîn-bani, le médecin, assure l'envoi d'un mouton aux messagers, sískur rá-gaba-e-ne-šè. L'inspecteur Babati contrôle cette opération quelque peu exceptionnelle.

Le 26ème jour, à part les livraisons coutumières pour les coureurs, les gens d'armes et les rationnaires, il y a celle d'un boeuf et de 5 boucs à l'occasion de l'entrée des àga-uš dans le palais. Cette entrée est circonstanciée par une lustration.[12] S'agit-il des gens-d'armes aidant aux lustrations ou eux-mêmes devant être purifiés? Les livraisons pour cette purification ont lieu avant la nouvelle lune. Mais le jour de la purification lui-même n'est pas connu.

Le 27ème jour commencent des livraisons particulières pour des fêtes dont le festival du mois gan-gan-è (9ème mois). A cette occasion des livraisons vont comme le 7ème jour aux statues dans les temples d'Enlil et de Ninlil. D'autres vont à la demeure appelée é-uz-ga.[13] Les autres livraisons sont pour les gens d'armes. On notera dans le cadre de ces livraisons un apport

8. M. Sigrist, *Textes du Princeton Theological Seminary*, vol. 1 (Philadelphia, 1990) 87, BIN 3 369, *'Atiqot* 4 55.

9. Il y a de fait d'autres attestations de sískur gu-la avec livraisons de viandes cuites à l'eau et offrandes pour Enlil et Ninlil, comme: SET 72, TRU 341, AnOr 7 108.

10. Les références sont nombreuses concernant les ânes servis en patûre aux chiens: TRU 257, PDT 467, MVN 8 118, Or 47–49 126, TLB 3 45. Dans ces textes relatifs aux chiens on donne souvent le nom de l'ânier, mais Irmu n'y apparaît jamais. Ce fait s'explique par le fonctionnement du système administratif. La tablette YBC 4190 se situe à la fin de la chaîne des transferts et l'on se contente d'indiquer le responsable de l'alimentation des cuisines. Les autres tablettes saisissent l'opération au début, le passage de l'animal de son troupeau à la comptabilité de Drehem.

11. PDT 584, MVN 11 184.

12. Cette lustration est attestée de ŠS 3 à IS 2: PDT 11, 169, AnOr 7 108, BIN 3 255, 397, 460, etc.

13. Je pense que l'é-uz-ga dont l'étymologie pourrait être é-uzug-ga est une maison réservée à des grands personnages de l'état. Les plats qui y sont servis sont toujours spécialement apprêtés.

important pour le fille de Lugal-má-gur$_8$-re, personnage important du royaume.

Enfin le 29ème jour enregistre une quantité invraisemblable de bovins et d'ovins le jour où Geme-Enlila, la femme de Ibbi-Sîn (entre?) dans le Tummal. Malheureusement on ne connaît pas la circonstance précise de cette visite.

Cette section s'arrête par le résumé des livraisons déjà donné plus haut. Ce sont tous des zi-ga lugal, donc livraisons pour les institutions du royaume.

S'y attache une autre section qui débute dans la 9ème colonne. Ce sont des dépenses cultuelles relèvant du même système des dépenses royales. Le scribe les a en quelque sorte accrochées à cette place parce qu'elles jouissent du même statut administratif que les précédentes, bien que ces dépenses n'aient pas été prévues dans le régime ordinaire des dépenses du mois. Elles sont en effet imprévues car elles traitent des dépenses faites à l'occasion du deuil pour Šu-Sîn.[14] La grande variété et surtout le caractère presque unique d'un certain nombre d'entr'elles invite à les étudier plus en détail.

Le 16ème jour du mois ont lieu des livraisons de petit bétail pour des services cultuels se déroulant dans la capitale du pays Ur. En fait il s'agit de services funéraires. On peut penser que Šu-Sîn était mort ce jour-là ou la veille:

1 máš		
1 sila$_4$	ká gu-la ^{d}Amar-^{d}EN.ZU-kar-re lugal é-^{giš}gu-za	
1 máš	^{giš}giš-a-nag gidim im-a-x	
1 sila$_4$	^{giš}giš-a-nag gidim gín bar-ra	
		á-gi$_6$-ba-a
1 máš	balag ^{d}Nanna	
1 máš	balag ^{d}Nin-sun$_2$	
1 máš	^{d}Utu-gú-sùr-ra	
1 sila$_4$		
1 máš		
	sùr-ra šu bar-ra	
	giš-a-nag gidim tu-ru-na	
		á-u$_4$-te-na
šà Uri$_5$^{ki}-ma		
u$_4$ **16-kam**		

Il s'agit de livraisons pour des cultes se déroulant le soir et durant la nuit à Ur. Au service de vêpres un agneau va à la grande porte du roi Amar-Sîn-du-quai[15] dans la salle du trône.

14. Cf. M. Sigrist, "Le deuil pour Šu-Sin," in *DUMU-E$_2$-DUB-BA-A: Sudies in Honor of Åke W. Sjöberg* (ed. H. Behrens, D. Loding, and M. T. Roth; Philadelphia: University Museum, 1989) 499–505.

15. 1 sila$_4$ ká gu-la ^{d}Amar-^{d}EN.ZU-kar-re lugal é-^{giš}gu-za. La formule ^{d}Amar-^{d}EN.ZU-kar-re lugal est neuve pour moi et je ne vois pas à quoi elle correspond.

Les deux autres ovins sont pour deux tables en bois utilisées pour les offrandes aux esprits: les ^{giš}giš-a-nag gidim. Un autre texte[16] mentionne cette table en relation avec l'esprit de Šu-Sîn. Il y a deux précisions[17] qu'il m'est difficile de clarifier. La première fait-elle une mention d'argile? La seconde semble mentionner quelque chose d'extérieur.

Durant la nuit il y a des offrandes pour les harpes qui sont près de Nanna et de Ninsun.[18]

^{d}Utu-gú-sùr-ra, Utu de la berge du cours d'eau, est inconnu à ce jour. Toutefois y aurait-il un lien avec le dieu de la justice près de la rivière ordalie. Enfin deux ovins sont pour la table des offrandes pour les esprits; il est ajouté tu-ru-na. Faut-il penser au fourneau? Il est encore précisé à propos des deux ovins: sùr-ra šu bar-ra. S'agit-il de ces deux ovins libérés sur la berge de la rivière? Un tel rituel ne m'est pas connu par ailleurs. Mais l'ensemble de la cérémonie semble porter sur la libération des esprits au bord de la rivière. Il s'agit bien sûr de l'esprit du roi Šu-Sîn. Enfin ces livraisons sont faites le 16 du mois, lendemain de la disparition du roi.

D'importantes livraisons sont prévues pour les cérémonies du lendemain, le 17 du mois. Si apparemment plus de divinités sont connues par leur nom, il n'est reste pas moins que l'ensemble de cette liturgie demeure obscure.

1 udu šakirá giš-a-nag gidim
1 udu giš-a-nag gidim è-è
1 udu abul gu-za
1 udu ^{d}Nin-giš-te-te
1 udu ^{d}Ama-abzu-kár
1 udu ^{d}Ne-ti
1 udu ^{d}Lugal-dar-du-du
1 udu ^{d}Nin-pú-mun-na
1 udu ki búr-búr
1 udu ^{d}Nin-šubur
1 máš érim
[ ]

(colonne 10)
[šà?] é Ur-^{d}Nammu
1 udu ^{d}Ba-ba$_6$
1 udu
1 sila$_4$
^{d}Nì-érim-nu-dab

1 sila$_4$ ^{d}Ha-ìa
1 máš ^{d}Inanna ^{giš}tukul
1 máš ^{d}Be-la-at-suh-nir
1 udu
1 máš
kar-kar-ra
1 máš
suh á-ki-ti
1 udu ^{d}Nin-a-a-mu
1 udu ^{d}Utu
1 udu ^{d}Mes-lam-ta-è-a-ha-zi
1 udu gùn ^{d}Amar-^{d}EN.ZU
1 sila$_4$ ^{d}Geštin-an-na
1 máš ^{d}Al-la-tum
1 sila$_4$ ká giš-kin-ti gu-la
1 máš abul lugal
1 máš ká ^{d}Gu-la
1 sila$_4$
é-gi-na-ab-tum šà gi-pàd-da ^{d}Nanna

16. MVN 10 172.

17. 1 máš ^{giš}giš-a-nag gidim im-a-x voir MVN 10 172, la même expression avec giš?-gal; 1 sila$_4$ ^{giš}giš-a-nag gidim gín bar-ra.

18. Ninsun est la mère des rois de la Troisième Dynastie d'Ur.

1 $sila_4$ ᵈBìl-ga-mes
1 udu gán udu ᵈNin-kù-nun-na
1 máš ᵈNin-é-an-na šà uru
1 $sila_4$
dúr ᵍⁱšha-lu-úb
1 $sila_4$ ér-e ki tag-ga
šà ᵍⁱškiri₆

(colonne 11)
ᵈNin-[ ]-si4 ᵈDumu-zi-da
1 $sila_4$ ᵍⁱšgu-za
(plusieurs lignes cassées)
1 $sila_4$ 4 túg sùr-ra
1 udu
1 máš
du_6 giš-gan-na
nì-sískur-ra
a kar-ra-a
3 áb 3 gu_4 mu-2 ga
4 áb mu-2 giš nu-zu
7 u_8
7 $sila_4$ ga
7 ùz
7 máš
14 udu níta
14 máš níta
sùr-ra ba-an-si
1 udu 1 máš
kùn
1 máš
balag ᵈNin-sún
nì-dab ki kùn-na
á-gi_6-ba-a
u_4 17-kam

Les activités liturgiques de ce jour sont très élaborées et aussi fort difficiles à interpréter par leur nouveauté. Un mouton est donné pour le vase (šakir) qui doit servir près de la table d'offrandes aux esprits. Les livraisons de bétail sont pour les giš-a-nag gidim, les tables d'offrande aux esprits. La seconde pourrait être pour les esprits qui se lèvent: gidim è-è. Un autre mouton est pour la grande porte du trône.[19] Puis suit une longue liste de divinités d'Ur dont beaucoup sont pour ainsi dire inconnues. Ce sont Nin-giš-TE-TE, Ama-abzu-kár (la mère de l'abzu-. . .), la divinité NE-ti, Lugal-engar-du-du et Nin-PÚ-mun-na. Inséré parmi ces divinités est le lieu de la libération, le ki-búr-búr,[20] suivi de Nin-šubur qui est une divinité de Nippur. Toutes ces offrandes semblent avoir pris place dans le temple de Ur-Nammu.

Les offrandes suivantes sont dit nì-sískur-ra a-kar-ra-a: les choses pour les cérémoines faites près ou sur l'eau du quai.

La première divinité dans cette liste est Baba, divinité du palais, puis ᵈNì-érim-nu-dab, le dieu qui n'a pas fait de mal(?), suivi de Haia divinité de Ku'ara, Inanna-de-l'arme, et de la divinité de la Diyala, Belat-suhnir. Du bétail va à juste titre aux quais, aux fondations du bâtiment á-ki-ti et à nouveau à des divinités dont certaines peu connues: Nin-a-a-mu, Utu, Meslamtaea ḪA.ZI,[21] Geštin-anna du palais, la soeur de Dumuzi, Allatum,[22]

19. On peut s'étonner de l'absence du giš pour spécifier le trône. Mais surtout ne s'agirait-il pas en raccourci de la grande porte de la salle du trône, donc en fait de nouveau de la porte d'Amar-Sîn le roi?

20. À l'image du nam-búr-bi.

21. Une expression identique HA.ZI se trouve en StudOr 9/1 27.

22. Divinité du monde inférieur, originaire de Zimudar dans le Diyala. Les uns voudraient y reconnaître une divinité hourrite.

la porte du grand atelier, la grande porte royale, la porte de Gula et l'entrepôt favori de Nanna. La cohérence du choix de ces divinités n'est sûrement pas très facile à dégager.

La suite des livraisons est pour Bilgames,[23] Ninkununna (une forme d'Inanna d'Ur), Nineanna dans la ville, le siège fait en bois de chêne[24] (*haluppu*). Un agneau est tué durant la lamentation se déroulant dans la palmeraie de Nin-[ ]-si$_4$.

Dumuzi, puis est offert 1 agneau pour le trône et pour la porte sur le bord de la rivière.[25] Un agneau va au du$_6$ ^{giš}gan-na, c'est-à-dire à la colline du cordeau à mesurer. Tout cette cérémonies se passe près de l'eau du quai de Ur. S'ajoute un ensemble impressionnant de livraisons d'animaux aux catégories très distinctes: ainsi

3 vaches et 3 boeufs âgés de 2 ans, encore nourrais au lait
4 vaches de 2 ans, n'ayant pas encore été saillies et 56 ovins

sùr-ra ba-an-si, qui se tiennent près du cours d'eau. On notera que le petit bétail va par groupe de 7 ou de 14.

Enfin 2 moutons dits kùn (*hašlu*) écrasés et un autre sans caractéristique précise, les trois pour la harpe de Ninsun, importante divinité d'Ur et de la dynastie fondée par Ur-Nammu.

Toute cette cérémonie se déroule la nuit au ki-kùn-na, le lieu de la destruction. Il faut, de suite, préciser qu'une telle cérémonie est tout à fait inconnue à ce jour, c'est-à-dire qu'aucun parallèle n'est attesté; pour le moins elle est le témoin d'un culte multiforme et inattendu par rapport à ce que les tablettes classiques de Drehem auraient permis de déduire. Même s'il faut rester très discret sur cette cérémonie, il faut pour le moins soupçonner une importante cérémonie concernant la vie après la mort: une grande fête des morts de la dynastie, unique à ce jour dans les archives de Drehem.

Lugal-á-zi-da maškim

Cette ligne est anormalement située dans la construction de la tablette. Probablement faut-il la rattacher aux activités du 17e jour. De toutes les livraisons mentionnées pour ce jour Lugal-á-zi-da en est le pourvoyeur.

Pour le 20e jour il y a, la nuit, des livraisons pour les 3 trônes des rois défunts, Ur-Nammu, Šulgi et Amar-Sîn. Il n'y en a pas pour le trône de Šu-Sîn car il n'est pas encore édifié puisqu'il s'agit de faire passer son esprit dans l'autre monde:

23. Déjà mentionné sous cette forme dans les listes de dieux de Fara; cf. M. Krebernik, "Die Götterlisten aus Fāra," ZA 76 (1986) 161–204.

24. S'agirait-il du siège de Gilgames tombé en enfer?

25. Parmi les articles traitant de la mort en Mésopotamie il est peu d'aide pour interpréter ce texte; tels W. G. Lambert, "The Theology of Death," in *Death in Mesopotamia* (CRRAI 26; ed. B. Alster; Mesopotamia 8; Copenhagen: Akademisk, 1980) 53–66.

1 $sila_4$ ^giš^gu-za Ur-^d^Nammu
gìr Nam-ha-ni sagi
Ri-mi-èl rá-gaba maškim
(colonne 12)
[^giš^]gu-za ^d^šul-gi-ra
1 máš ^giš^gu-za ^d^Amar-^d^EN.ZU
[Ri-mi-èl rá-gaba maškim]
á-gi_6-ba-a
u_4 20-kam

Les livraisons des 3 autres jours les 25, 29 et peut-être 30 sont plus simples.

1 udu giš-dù abul lugal
1 udu giš-dù suh du-du
1 udu giš-dù
abul ^d^Nin-gal
ga kú-šè
gìr Nam-ha-ni sagi
Ú-la-i-nì-iš šu-i maškim
kizlah 9
u_4 25-kam

2 máš-gal
ù šim šà é-gal
gìr Lú-sukkal-an-ka lú mu_{13}-mu_{13}
Ri-mi-èl rá-gaba maškim
u_4 28-kam

2 udu 5 máš-gal-ú
é dingir-re-ne gá-gá-dè
gìr Sal-li $gudu_4$
Ri-mi-èl rá-gaba maškim
u_4 29-kam

10 gu_4
2,22 udu
^giš^giš-a-nag gidim ^d^Šu-^d^EN.ZU ba-ak

[u_4 30-kam]

Les livraisons du 25 sont un peu spéciales. Livraison de 3 moutons, udu giš.dù, 3 moutons qui étaient sexuellement actifs, un pour la grande porte du roi, un pour la fondation DU-DU[26] et le troisième pour la grande porte du

26. Je n'ai pas d'explication pour DU-DU.

roi. Il est ajouté ga-kú-šè, pour être mangés avec du lait.[27] Cela est confirmé par la présence du sagi. Ulanuiš le šu-i est celui qui est en charge de la livraison. La présence d'un sagi et d'un šu-i, à défaut de plus de clarté, est cependant le signe de l'importance de cette cérémonie aux portes du roi et de Ningal. L'indication de la dernière ligne kislah (ki-ud) 9 ne livre aucun sens.

La livraison du 28 jours: 2 boucs pour un cérémonie dans le palais: ù-šim. Cette cérémonie requiert la présence d'un exorciste: lú-mu_{13}-mu_{13}.

L'avant-dernier jour du mois 7 ovins nourris à l'herbe sont placés dans le temple des dieux. Un prêtre-$gudu_4$ est responsable de cette livraison. C'est le prêtre qui fait des onction d'huile.

Enfin le dernier jour une énorme livraison constituée de 10 boeufs et 142 moutons pour construire l'autel de l'esprit de Šu-Sîn.

Cette tablette dans sa seconde partie enregistre à partir du 17 du mois gan-gan-è des offrandes fort complexes pour le deuil du roi. Le mois suivant sera tout entier un mois de deuil avec la présence active du nouveau roi parcourant le pays pour se rendre dans différents sanctuaires.[28]

Conclusion

L'analyse de ces deux tablettes de la Yale Babylonian Collection a permis de mieux dégager différents systèmes comptables, celui des livraisons et dépenses régulières de Drehem ainsi que celui des livraisons et dépenses pour le roi. Dans ce dernier genre se trouve de multiples renseignements concernant les activités de la cour d'Ur. Par chance une tablette de ce type ajoute aux activités normales les dépenses encourues exceptionnement par le deuil du roi Šu-Sîn dont la mort peut maintenant être fixée au 16 du mois gan-gan-è de la 9ème année de son règne.

Postscript by William W. Hallo

With the kind permission of Marcel Sigrist, I am taking this opportunity to add some further remarks on YBC 3635 and the related text NBC 2456 (= BIN 3:44).

The totals of YBC 3635 actually come in five separate formulations, each larger and more inclusive than the preceding. They throw considerable light on native conceptions of animal taxonomy, a subject to be taken up elsewhere. Here they are charted in the two-dimensional format devised for representing archival texts—both cuneiform and biblical—by Baruch Levine and myself; see Levine and Hallo, "Offerings to the Temple Gates at Ur,"

27. W. Sallaberger, *Der Kultische Kalender der Ur III-Zeit*, Teil 1 (Berlin: de Gruyter, 1993) 300.

28. Sigrist, "Le deuil pour Šu-Sin," 499–505.

HUCA 38 (1967) 17–58, esp. p. 20 and n. 16, with previous literature (see table 1, p. 148).

Note that the translations of the more exotic species remain debatable. I translate šeg$_7$-bar or šeg$_9$-bar by 'wild sheep' (cf. CAD, *s.v. sappāru*) based on its association with the šeg$_9$, the 'wild ram' in literary contexts (CAD, *s.v. atūdu*). Piotr Steinkeller prefers to regard it as a kind of deer, since it is grouped with deer and gazelles in archival texts, and suggests that it may represent the Mesopotamian fallow deer ("Sheep and Goat Terminology in Ur III Sources from Drehem," *Bulletin on Sumerian Agriculture* 8 [1995] 50). I translate máš-gal a-dara$_4$ by 'adult goat with ibex horns', based on the assumption of a syllabic spelling for á-dara$_4$ (cf. CAD, *s.v. adrû*). Landsberger had suggested 'Schraubenhornziege' (screw-horned goat; cf. *Fauna* [1934] 95; MSL 8/2 [1960] 56). Steinkeller regards it as a hybrid of the domestic goat with the bezoar ("Sheep and Goat Terminology," 54).

Note also that "ditto" stands (for convenience) for the corresponding entry in the previous column.

YBC 3635 represents a summary of one month's activities in regard to royal deliveries at Puzrish-Dagan. Another text housed at Yale (NBC 2456) and published in 1971 as BIN 3:44, bears on the same deliveries. They had all been taken in charge by Abba-shaga, who now in his turn transferred most of the domesticated sheep and goats among them to Ur-kununna. There are thus numerous overlaps between the two texts. In detail, note the correspondences (see table 2, p. 149).

As can be seen from the table, YBC 3635 includes many animals not entered in NBC 2456 even when confining the comparison to sheep, lambs, and goats. But there are also many days on which the entries for these categories of animals agree in whole or in part in the two texts. Complete agreement occurs notably on days 3, 6, 7, 16, and 26 (as restored). It should also be noted that days 24, 25, and 29 are blank in both ledgers, though for 24 there is a separate entry at the end of NBC 2456. When allowance is made for the several days that are broken on one or both of the texts (1, 8, 13, 19–23, 27, 28, 30), the remaining discrepancies do not loom so large. Identification of additional parallel texts may throw further light on the royal role at Drehem.

Table 1. YBC 3635 in two-dimensional format (totals only)

Sums of individual entries	*Sums*	*Subtotals*	*Totals*	*Grand Total*
(1) 38 grain-fed oxen	[3]8 ditto		81 large cattle (assorted oxen and cows)	
(2) 41 oxen	42 oxen	80 oxen		
(3) 1 spotted ox				
(4) 1 cow	1 ditto	1 ditto		
(5) 1 grain-fed male stag	1 ditto	1 male stag	1 stag	
(6) 21 male wild sheep	21 ditto	21 ditto	47 wild sheep	
(7) 26 female wild sheep	26 ditto	26 ditto		
(8) 66 grain-fed sheep				1223 royal delivery month and year
(9) 4 grain-fed fat-tailed sheep	76 grain-fed sheep			
(10) 1 grain-fed Shimashkian sheep				
(11) 5 grain-fed lambs				
(12) 5 grain-fed adult goats	6 grain-fed goats			
(13) 1 grain-fed Shimashkian adult goat		870 sheep (76+794)		
(14) 1 grain-fed adult goat with ibex horns	1 grain-fed goat with ibex horns			
(15) 1 grain-fed female kid	1 grain-fed nannygoat		1,054 small cattle (assorted sheep and goats)	
(16) 608 sheep				
(17) 6 fat-tailed sheep	794 sheep			
(18) 179 lambs				
(19) 1 fat-tailed lamb				
(20) 1 pregnant ewe	1 ewe	1 ditto		
(21) 4 adult goats				
(22) 1 spotted adult goat (misread as 60)	172 goats	181 goats (6+1+172+2)		
(23) 2 adult goats with ibex horns	2 goats with ibex horns			
(24) 108 goats				
(25) 1 pregnant nannygoat	1 nannygoat	2 ditto (1+1)		
(26) 23 gazelles	23 ditto	23 ditto	23 ditto	
(27) 17 bear (cubs)	17 ditto	17 ditto	17 ditto	

Table 2. Correspondences between YBC 3635 and NBC 2456

Day	*YBC 3635*			*NBC 2456*		
	sheep	*lambs*	*goats*	*sheep*	*lambs*	*goats*
1		[lost]			4	
2		7	1		6	1
3	9		3	9		3
4			3		1	
5	11	11	2		10	2
6		8			8	
7		1	1		1	1
8	135	6	67	15	5	3
9	15	17	6	3	17	2
10	18	11		9	11	
11	4	9	[2]		9	2
12	167	14	45	27	12	45
13		4+			10	
14	302	10	28	201	24	18
15	3	1			1	
16		7	1		7	1
17		4	3		3	3
18	11	9	11	3	8	6
19	[ ]	1+	4+		3	3
20	[		]		6	
21	[		] 3+	[2	3	2]*
22		4	1		8	
23		4		[		]
24				[97		36]**
25						
26		3	1		[3]	1
27	[		]		2	
28	[		]	2	1	
29						
30	4+	5+	2		8	2

*Delivery for Shulgi in Ur.
**Property of Giri-ki-ir.

Part II

Bible

Preliminary Remarks for the Sociological Study of Israelite "Official Religion"

Jacques Berlinerblau
Hofstra University

The term *official,* whether employed as an adjective, an adverb, or a part of a construct phrase, is often encountered in studies of Israelite religion. In *The Religion of Ancient Israel,* T. C. Vriezen discusses "official prohibitions" and the "official cult."[1] In a monograph devoted to the study of the goddess Asherah, Saul Olyan examines this deity's role within "official Israelite religion."[2] Phyllis Bird, contributing to the important collection *Ancient Israelite Religion,* refers to "officially sanctioned" elements of the Israelite cultus.[3] Within the same volume, Jeffrey Tigay makes passing mention of "unofficial religion."[4]

Similar references may also be found among archaeologically-oriented studies of the Old Testament world. John S. Holladay, Jr. writes about "official shrines and sanctuaries" during the era of David and Solomon.[5] Elizabeth Bloch-Smith, investigating Judahite practices and beliefs regarding the

1. T. C. Vriezen, *The Religion of Ancient Israel* (Philadelphia: Westminster, 1967) 101, 199.

2. S. Olyan, *Asherah and the Cult of Yahweh in Israel* (SBLMS 34; Atlanta: Scholars Press, 1988) 37; also see J. Alberto Soggin, "The Davidic-Solomonic Kingdom," in *Israelite and Judaean History* (ed. J. Hayes and J. Miller; Philadelphia: Westminster, 1977) 361.

3. Phyllis Bird, "The Place of Women in the Israelite Cultus," *Ancient Israelite Religion: Essays in Honor of Frank Moore Cross* (ed. P. D. Miller Jr., P. Hanson, and S. McBride; Philadelphia: Fortress, 1987) 399.

4. Jeffrey Tigay, "Israelite Religion: The Onomastic and Epigraphic Evidence," in *Ancient Israelite Religion,* 162.

5. John Holladay, Jr., "Religion in Israel and Judah under the Monarchy: An Explicitly Archaeological Approach," in *Ancient Israelite Religion,* 281.

deceased, concludes that it was "'official' policy" in the late 8th century to "discredit the dead and those who attained their knowledge from the dead."[6] William Dever, in his groundbreaking article "Archaeology Reconstructs the Lost Background of the Israelite Cult," speaks of "the official version of Israelite religion enshrined in the Hebrew Bible."[7]

Yet although this term appears quite frequently throughout the massive corpus of literature devoted to the study of Israelite religion, very little analysis has been devoted to the question of what *official*, in any of its grammatical incarnations, might actually mean. In most cases the scholar who mentions the word *official* refrains from offering any definition or substantive discussion of this construct. Occasionally, one might come across a brief statement equating "official" with "orthodoxy" or "established religion"[8] or "normative religion"[9] or "state religion" or the religion of an elite or the concerns of the community as opposed to the individual.[10] What emerges then, are several distinct assumptions regarding the meaning of one very ambiguous term.

The first objective of this contribution consists of forwarding some basic criteria by which we may be able to define *official religion*. In so doing, we will need to make a somewhat prolonged detour through various fields of nonbiblical scholarship. By drawing upon the work of sociologists, anthropologists and historians, we will undertake to erect a provisional "ideal-type" of the "official religion" construct.

In the second part of this study we will attempt to view Israelite "official religion" through the optic of these normative criteria. This application of our ideal-type will afford us ample opportunity to delineate the (often unnoted) theoretical and methodological complexities inherent in the study of this subject. Further, it will assist us in identifying and then interrogating one of the prevailing axioms of Old Testament scholarship: the belief that

6. Elizabeth Bloch-Smith, *Judahite Burial Practices and Beliefs about the Dead* (JSOTSup 123; Sheffield: JSOT Press, 1992) 150.

7. William Dever, "Archaeology Reconstructs the Lost Background of the Israelite Cult," *Recent Archaeological Discoveries and Biblical Research* (Seattle: University of Washington Press, 1990) 166.

8. See, for example, J. B. Segal, who in an article on "popular religion," speaks of "the established cult with its fixed calendar, its set ritual and its priestly orders" ("Popular Religion in Ancient Israel," *JJS* 27 [1976] 11).

9. For references to "normative" Yahwism, see Patrick Miller, "Israelite Religion," in *The Hebrew Bible and Its Modern Interpreters* (ed. D. Knight and G. Tucker; Chico, Calif.: Scholars Press, 1985) 215. Also see William Dever, "The Contribution of Archaeology to the Study of Canaanite and Early Israelite Religion," in *Ancient Israelite Religion: Essays in Honor of Frank Moore Cross* (ed. P. D. Miller Jr., P. Hanson, and S. McBride; Philadelphia: Fortress, 1987) 220; and Dever, "Archaeology Reconstructs," 127.

10. See, for example, Segal, "Popular Religion," 2.

the "official" Yahwism preserved in the Old Testament and the actual "official religion" of ancient Israel were one and the same thing.

What is "Official Religion"?

Class-Based Analysis

Materialist or class-based readings provide one possible theoretical avenue of approach to the question of "official religion." In orthodox Marxist thought, religion is viewed as a component of the superstructure. Hence, when Marx opined in *Capital: A Critique of Political Economy* that "the religious world is but the reflex of the real world," he was maintaining that the form and content of any given religion are conditioned by material circumstances.[11] Engels' remark, "each of the different classes uses its own appropriate religion: the landowning class—Catholic Jesuitism or Protestant orthodoxy; the liberal and radical Bourgeoisie—rationalism; and it makes little difference whether these gentleman themselves believe in their respective religions or not," reiterates this position.[12] In this approach it is asserted that religion is merely an ideological "banner" through which particular class interests are expressed.[13]

The interests of various classes, of course, do not peacefully coexist. As Otto Maduro notes: "In a class society every religious activity is an activity carried out within class conflicts, and as such is an activity permeated, limited, and orientated by these conflicts."[14] From this we may deduce that within a class society a structure of stratification emerges whereby one class, and the particular religion to which it adheres, attempts to dominate others.[15]

11. Karl Marx, *Capital: A Critique of Political Economy, Vol. 1: Marx/Engels: On Religion* (Moscow: Progress, 1985) 117.

12. Frederick Engels, *Ludwig Feuerbach and the Outcome of Classical German Philosophy* (New York: International, 1974) 59.

13. Also see Frederick Engels, *The Peasant War in Germany* (Moscow: Progress, 1969) 41.

14. Otto Maduro, *Religion and Social Conflicts* (Maryknoll, N.Y.: Orbis, 1982) 67.

15. The issue of economic class figures prominently in discussions of *popular religion* as well. Many authors—whether explicitly or implicitly—construe "popular religion" as the religion practiced by economically nonprivileged groups. As Enzo Pace notes, many Italian social scientists view "popular religion" as "a class phenomenon which most especially involves subaltern classes and most predominantly, though not exclusively, agricultural classes" ("The Debate on Popular Religion in Italy," *Sociological Analysis* 40 [1979] 73). Also see Daniel Levine, "Religion, the Poor and Politics in Latin America Today," in *Religion and Political Conflict in Latin America* (ed. D. Levine; Chapel Hill: University of North Carolina Press, 1986) 4; Michael Carroll, *Madonnas That Maim: Popular Catholicism in Italy since the Fifteenth Century* (Baltimore: Johns Hopkins University Press, 1992) 7. Reference to *popular religion* is made here since *popular* and *official* religion are *relational* terms that must be studied together.

A materialist approach to the question of "official religion" would identify the latter as the religion of the economically-dominant class within a society (e.g., the owners of the means of production). It would concentrate upon the role that this religion plays in giving "ideological form" to a particular system of material production and class domination. Insofar as Marx and Engels maintained that the "ideas of the ruling class are in every epoch the ruling ideas," we could say that "official religion" is that matrix of metaphysical beliefs and practices used by an economically-privileged class as a means of promulgating and defending its interests.[16]

Rationalization/Intellectuals

A rather different approach emphasizes the tendency of "official religion" to display characteristics consonant with the broad sociological process referred to by Max Weber as "rationalization."[17] While many interpretations of this term can be found, for now we shall employ Wolfgang Schluchter's definition of "metaphysical-ethical rationalism" as

> the systematization of meaning patterns. This involves the intellectual elaboration and deliberate sublimation of ultimate ends. In this sense rationalism is a consequence of a cultured man's 'inner compulsion' not only to understand the world as a 'meaningful cosmos' but also to take a consistent and unified stance to it.[18]

Stanley Brandes suggests that the ideas of an "official religion" are "systematized and codified into some internally consistent, all-encompassing cosmol-

---

For a theoretical elaboration of this point, see my *Vow and the "Popular Religious Groups" of Ancient Israel: A Philological and Sociological Inquiry* (JSOTSup; Sheffield: Sheffield Academic Press, 1996).

16. Karl Marx and Frederick Engels, *The German Ideology, Part One* (New York: International, 1991) 64.

17. As Anthony Giddens notes, even though the notion of rationalization occupied a central place in Weber's thought, he seems to take its meaning for granted; *Capitalism and Modern Social Theory: An Analysis of the Writings of Marx, Durkheim and Weber* (Cambridge: Cambridge University Press, 1992) 36.

18. Wolfgang Schluchter, "The Paradox of Rationalization: On the Relation of Ethics and the World," *Max Weber's Vision of History: Ethics and Methods* (with G. Roth; Berkeley: University of California Press, 1984) 15. Let us not neglect to mention that another major part of Weber's concept of rationalization addresses "the negation or overcoming of *simple* magic and ritual forms as the major modes by which man related to the 'other' world" (S. N. Eisenstadt, "The Format of Jewish History: Some Reflections on Weber's Ancient Judaism," *Modern Judaism* 1 [1981] 55). For Weber this overcoming of magic was a salient feature of ancient Judaism (*Ancient Judaism* [New York: Free Press, 1967]); also see Freddy Raphaël, "Max Weber and Ancient Judaism," *Yearbook Leo Baeck* 18 (1973) 51, and Wolfgang Schluchter, *Rationalism, Religion and Domination: A Weberian Perspective* (Berkeley: University of California Press, 1989) 166.

ogy, such as clerics, philosophers, and other intellectual specialists might have the time and inclination to develop."[19] Thomas Luckmann writes: "The 'official' model is, of course, formulated and elaborated by the experts and the various dimensions of the 'official' model eventually become the subject of specialized knowledge, such as doctrine, liturgy 'social ethics' and so forth."[20]

In this scenario, "official" religion is distinct from other varieties insofar as it consciously aspires to elaborate, systematize, codify, and clarify the particular metaphysical beliefs upon which it is predicated. Such an endeavor necessitates a group of specialists who are trained to perform the tasks mentioned above. For purposes of analysis we shall refer to such a group as the intellectuals.[21]

Male Domination

Other researchers have called attention to a particular gendered division of labor that characterizes religion in general. In a discussion of Somali pastoralists, I. M. Lewis observes:

19. Stanley Brandes, "Conclusion: Reflections on the Study of Religious Orthodoxy and Popular Faith in Europe," in *Religious Orthodoxy and Popular Faith in European Society* (ed. E. Badone; Princeton: Princeton University Press, 1990) 185.

20. Thomas Luckmann, *The Invisible Religion: The Problem of Religion in Modern Society* (New York: Macmillan, 1972) 74; also see A. J. Wichers, "Some Reflections on the Position of the Christian Religion in a Situation of Affluence: The Welfare State," in *Official and Popular Religion: Analysis of a Theme for Religious Studies* (ed. P. H. Vrijhof and J. Waardenburg; The Hague: Mouton, 1979) 200. Of course, we must be cautious in positing rationality, coherence, systematization, etc., as unique attributes of "official religion," for implicit in this view lies the assumption that "popular religion" has either less rationality or—as many earlier generations of scholars suggested—no rationality at all (on this point see Brandes, "Conclusion," 186; Aron Gurevich, *Medieval Popular Culture: Problems of Belief and Perception* [Cambridge Studies in Oral and Literate Culture 14; Cambridge: Cambridge University Press, 1990] xiv; Jane Schneider, "Spirits and the Spirit of Capitalism," 24). Yet studies such as Carlo Ginzburg's *The Cheese and the Worms: The Cosmos of a Sixteenth-Century Miller* (New York: Penguin, 1982) or Jane Schneider's impressive study of peasant ethics show how reflective and complex the world views of nonofficial religious groups can actually be (also see Brandes, "Conclusion," 197). As such, the question of the superior "rationality" of "official religion" is still open to debate.

21. On the subject of intellectuals, Weber remarked: "It is the intellectual who conceives of the 'world' as a problem of meaning. . . . As a consequence, there is a growing demand that the world and the total pattern of life be subject to an order that is significant and meaningful" (*Economy and Society: An Outline of Interpretive Sociology* [ed. G. Roth and C. Wittich; Berkeley: University of California Press, 1978] 506); also see Ahmad Sadri, *Max Weber's Sociology of Intellectuals* (New York: Oxford University Press, 1992) 61, 71,.

this public cult is almost exclusively dominated by men, who hold all the major positions of religious authority and prestige. Women are in fact excluded from the mosques in which men worship and their role in religion tends to be little more than that of passive spectators.[22]

In her study of Mexican-American women's devotion to The Lady of Guadalupe, Jeanette Rodriguez remarks: "The very nature of the hierarchy of the Roman Catholic church and of its traditional teachings has called for women to be subordinate to men, but this system has not precluded them from playing an active role in the practice of popular religiosity."[23]

Thus, we could maintain that another characteristic of an "official religion" is its tendency to be administered by men, while relegating women to secondary status. As such, the latter are typically excluded from positions of authority and prestige.

(Coercive) Power

Perhaps the most important analytical tool for the study of "official religion"—and social phenomena in general—is a discussion of the subject of power.[24] Since there are many sophisticated and distinct sociological approaches to the question of power, we will limit ourselves to one particular treatment of this issue.[25]

In his well-known definition, Max Weber refers to power as "the probability that one actor within a social relationship will be in a position to carry out his own will despite resistance, regardless of the basis on which this probability rests."[26] As Habermas notes, for Weber power is the "possibility of forcing one's own will, whatever it may be, on the conduct of others."[27] In order to sharpen this definition further we might add C. Wright Mills's observation that the means of power accrue to "those who occupy the command posts" within a given social order.[28] Mills's study of the United States,

22. I. M. Lewis, *Ecstatic Religion: A Study of Shamanism and Spirit Possession* (London: Routledge, 1989) 65, 69.

23. Jeanette Rodriguez, *Our Lady of Guadalupe: Faith and Empowerment among Mexican-American Women* (Austin: University of Texas Press, 1994) 59.

24. Anthony Giddens, *The Constitution of Society: Outline of the Theory of Structuration* (Berkeley: University of California Press, 1986) 283.

25. For more detailed treatments of the question of power, see Dennis Wrong, *Power: Its Forms, Bases and Uses* (Chicago: University of Chicago Press, 1988); and Thomas Wartenberg (ed.), *Rethinking Power* (Albany: State University of New York Press, 1992).

26. Max Weber, *The Theory of Social and Economic Organization* (New York: Free Press, 1964) 152.

27. Jürgen Habermas, "Hannah Arendt: On the Concept of Power," *Philosophical-Political Profiles* (Cambridge: Massachusetts Institute of Technology Press, 1990) 173.

28. C. Wright Mills, *The Power Elite* (New York: Oxford University Press, 1959) 23.

The Power Elite, proffers a modern case study of how the type of power discussed above functions.[29] It is concentrated in the hands of distinct groups situated at key institutional points. Here, power has a definitive locus, it radiates out from some particular place, and its effects are felt by others in the power relationship. As Dennis Wrong notes: "for Mills the power of a group in a stratified society is necessarily exercised over and at the expense of a subordinate group."[30]

By extrapolating from these remarks, we could claim that an "official religion" retains the capacity to force its will upon others. As such, it is that religion that possesses the requisite power to make its doctrines, beliefs, practices, and so on, stand as those that *must* be followed and accepted by all members of a society. As Berger and Luckmann note: "Those who occupy the decisive power positions are ready to use their power to impose the traditional definitions of reality on the population under their authority."[31] The use of various institutions of coercion (e.g., armies, police, courts, fiscal organizations, etc.) is one means by which an "official religion" exercises its power. But not the only means.

Coercion and Consent: The Gramscian Perspective

It would be a mistake to maintain that "official religions" wield power *solely* through coercion. The exclusive use of force, punitive sanctions, repressive measures, and so forth, as many have noted, results in a very precarious form of social domination.[32] This insight was not lost upon Pope Gregory, who once observed, "by force one does not achieve anything."[33]

It was the opinion of the Italian political philosopher Antonio Gramsci that a successful ruling apparatus may wield power by *combining* coercion and consent. In "The Modern Prince," Gramsci observes: "The 'normal' exercise of hegemony on the now classical terrain of the parliamentary régime is characterised by the combination of force and consent, which balance each other reciprocally, without force predominating excessively over consent."[34]

29. However, I do not mean to imply that "power elite" theories are identical with Weberian approaches to power.

30. Wrong, *Power*, 238.

31. Peter Berger and Thomas Luckmann, *The Social Construction of Reality: A Treatise in the Sociology of Knowledge* (New York: Doubleday, 1967) 121.

32. Benedetto Fontana, *Hegemony and Power: On the Relation between Gramsci and Machiavelli* (Minneapolis: University of Minnesota Press, 1993) 144; Carl Boggs, *The Two Revolutions: Antonio Gramsci and the Dilemmas of Western Marxism* (Boston: South End, 1984) 159; also see Maduro, *Religion*, 72–73.

33. Quoted in J. A. Huisman, "Christianity and Germanic Religion," in *Official and Popular Religion: Analysis of a Theme for Religious Studies* (ed. P. H. Vrijhof and J. Waardenburg; The Hague: Mouton, 1979) 66.

34. Antonio Gramsci, *Selections from the Prison Notebooks* (ed. Q. Hoare and G. N. Smith; New York: International, 1975) 80 n. 49; also see Fontana, *Hegemony*,

For Gramsci, social institutions such as schools, churches, media, art, and so on, are also used by the hegemonic group in order to secure the *consensus*, the voluntary obedience, of the populace.[35] A ruling group may thus effectively achieve and maintain its power by manipulating various *cultural* arteries as opposed to relying solely upon coercive institutions. By using the former to inculcate certain values, beliefs, and attitudes among other groups, the hegemonic apparatus effectively limits its dependence on the always unstable use of coercion.

These considerations are quite germane to the study of "official religion." For the latter typically has at its disposal an entire apparatus of socialization through which it imparts its views upon other members of society. Towler observes: "The teachings of official religion are formally propagated as part of a person's socialization in the home, at school and at church."[36] Similarly, Luckmann writes: "The individual is brought up in a situation in which religion constitutes a coherent system of meaning which refers to a symbolic reality that is recognized by everybody as religious and which is represented in society by men, buildings, procedures and so forth whose religious quality is clearly marked."[37]

We could say that an "official religion" controls and manipulates the cultural command posts of a society. Situated as such, it retains the capacity to teach others the difference between "orthodoxy" and "heterodoxy."[38] Thus, in any given society one group has access to the means by which they can make known the "truth" of their position and the "falsity" of all others. These means range from techniques such as physical force, to other, more efficient, mechanisms that rest on bringing the agent internally to accept and voluntarily to acquiesce to the teachings of the "official religion." For now, what must be stressed is that there cannot be "official religion" without the type of coercive and consensual power discussed above.

141, 145. Elsewhere, in an apparent reference to hegemony, Gramsci indicates that force must be "ingeniously combined" with consent and persuasion (p. 310).

35. Antonio Gramsci, *Selections from Cultural Writings* (ed. D. Forgacs and G. N. Smith; Cambridge: Harvard University Press, 1991) 389; also see James Scott, "Hegemony and the Peasantry," *Politics and Society* 7 (1977) 273; Renate Holub, *Antonio Gramsci: Beyond Marxism and Post-Modernism* (London: Routledge, 1992) 6; Joseph Femia, *Gramsci's Political Thought: Hegemony, Consciousness, and the Revolutionary Process* (Oxford: Oxford University Press, 1981) 26.

36. Robert Towler, *Homo Religiosus: Sociological Problems in the Study of Religion* (New York: St. Martin's, 1974) 154.

37. Luckmann, *The Invisible Religion*, 72.

38. W. T. M. Frijhoff, "Official and Popular Religion in Christianity: The Late Middle-Ages and Early Modern Times (13th–18th Centuries)," in *Official and Popular Religion: Analysis of a Theme for Religious Studies* (ed. P. H. Vrijhof and J. Waardenburg; The Hague: Mouton, 1979) 90; also see J. C. Schmitt, "'Religion populaire' et culture folklorique," *Annales Économies, Sociétés, Civilisations* 31 (1976) 947.

Israelite "Official Religion"

"Official Religion" in Biblical Scholarship

In the preceding section we examined various analytical strategies that social-scientists and historians have forwarded for the study of "official religion." The reader should not assume that these approaches exhaust all of those employed by researchers who engage this issue. Nor do I wish to convey the impression that my analysis of each individual criterion is by any means definitive. On the contrary, the study of this construct is currently in its inchoate stages, and each approach will need to be refined through further investigation.

For purposes of analysis, however, let us combine these criteria—or perhaps "mix and match" is a more apt description—in an effort to construct a makeshift "ideal type." As we proceed, let us bear in mind the words of Stephen Kalberg: "Rather than being endowed with the capability to 'replicate' the external world or define any particular phenomenon, ideal types are constructed 'utopias' that alone aim to facilitate empirical inquiry."[39] The criteria to be forwarded below are thus submitted not with the intention of describing empirical reality, but in hopes of providing some "hypothesis-forming models" for the study of Israelite religion.[40]

For now, we will claim that there are five basic qualities of an "official religion":

a. The leaders of this religion either own the means of production themselves or are closely associated with those who do.
b. This religious group exerts great effort to: (1) articulate, (2) systematize, and (3) render internally consistent its belief system. In order to accomplish this feat it establishes and supports a group of intellectuals (e.g., scribes, poets, historians, theologians, and so on.)
c. Positions of authority, power, and prestige within this religion are delegated almost exclusively to men.
d. This religious group retains the capacity to "force its will" upon others. This is accomplished through social institutions of coercion (e.g., an apparatus of violence such as an army, a "morals" squad, a tax-collecting apparatus, legal organisms, etc.).
e. This religious group controls the institutions that serve to synthesize consent among the populace. It is via these institutions of socialization that it succeeds in imprinting its particular metaphysical world view

39. Stephen Kalberg, *Max Weber's Comparative-Historical Sociology* (Chicago: University of Chicago Press, 1994) 85; also see Giddens, *Capitalism*, 141.

40. Ibid., 92.

> upon others. In this manner, other members of society come to view this religion as the "natural" and "correct" alternative.[41]

Some biblical scholars who have employed the term *official* make use of it in one or more of the senses discussed above. The view of ancient Israel's "official religion" as being dominated by males appears with increasing frequency in Old Testament research. Phyllis Bird offers an excellent illustration of the disparity between men's and women's roles in the Israelite cultus:

> Leadership of the cultus appears at all times to have been in the hands of males. . . . Males occupy the positions of greatest authority, sanctity, and honor and perform tasks requiring technical skill and training. They preside over the presentation of sacrifices and offerings, have charge of the sacred lots, interpret the sacred law and instruct the congregation, pronounce blessing and curse, declare absolution and pardon, and guard the purity of the sanctuary and the worshipers.[42]

Attempts to link Israel's "official religion" with power also surface, albeit without much attention to issues of coercion and consent. This approach may be detected in the work of the scholars who draw an association between the religion of the monarchy/state (i.e., the prevailing locus of power in ancient Israel) and the "official religion" of ancient Israel. Helmer Ringgren observes: "There existed side by side, for example, the so-to-speak official religion of the Temple and monarchy (in the Southern Kingdom), a popular syncretistic religion, the religion of the great literary prophets, and the religion of the Deuteronomistic circle."[43] Elsewhere, William Dever refers to "the 'official' religion of the Jerusalem temple and the royal cultus in the Monarchy."[44]

41. It must be recalled that these variables cannot in reality be analytically separated from one another. One is likely to find that coercive and consensual power are both a cause *and* an effect of privileged economic status. As such, we must see these five characteristics not as individual qualities, but as codetermining qualities of an "official religion." They have been separated solely for analytical purposes.

42. Phyllis Bird, "The Place," 403, 405. Also see Phyllis Bird, "Israelite Religion and the Faith of Israel's Daughters: Reflections on Gender and Religious Definition," in *The Bible and the Politics of Exegesis: Essays in Honor of Norman K. Gottwald on His Sixty-Fifth Birthday* (ed. D. Jobling, P. Day, and G. Sheppard; Cleveland: Pilgrim, 1991) 108; Carol Meyers, *Discovering Eve: Ancient Israelite Women in Context* (New York: Oxford University Press, 1988) 11–12. David Sperling, "Israel's Religion in the Ancient Near East," in *Jewish Spirituality: From the Bible through the Middle Ages* (ed. A. Green; New York: Crossroad, 1986) 28–29.

43. Helmer Ringgren, *Israelite Religion* (Philadelphia: Fortress, 1980) 58.

44. Dever, "Archaeology Reconstructs," 123; also see Vriezen, *The Religion of Ancient Israel*, 183; J. Alberto Soggin, "Der offiziell geförderte Synkretismus in Israel während des 10. Jahrhunderts," *ZAW* 78 (1966) 179–204; idem, "The Davidic-Solomonic Kingdom," 370; Gerhard von Rad, *Old Testament Theology, Volume One: The Theology of Israel's Historical Traditions* (New York: Harper & Row, 1962) 44; Marvin

Keith Whitelam has taken some of the first steps in demonstrating the use of consensus-generating institutions in ancient Israel. He writes:

> The use of force was too costly and on the whole inefficient in maintaining royal power, giving rise to the heavy investment in means to propagate the royal symbolic universe. States could only survive if they attained legitimacy, often through the manipulation of religious symbols. . . . Royal ideology provided a justification for the control of power and strategic resources.[45]

Materialist readings of ancient Israel's "official religion," while not ubiquitous, also surface in biblical research. Soft versions of this approach may be detected among those authors who, while eschewing orthodox Marxism, evince a healthy awareness of the relationship between "official religion" and class.[46] Harder versions, based more rigorously on the Marxist program, have also surfaced in recent years.[47]

Conceptualizations of Israel's "official religion" in terms of "metaphysical-ethical rationalization" are encountered less frequently. One does, however, come across references to the existence of a monarchy/state–sponsored intellectual elite responsible for the production of religious literature. As Sweet observes in his article "The Sage in Mesopotamian Palaces and Royal Courts": "The palace was thus a natural center for experts—the wise—of every kind."[48] As regards ancient Israel, R. N. Whybray posits the existence of scribes working under the auspices of the monarchy:

Chaney, "Systemic Study of the Israelite Monarchy," *Semeia* 37 (*Social-Scientific Criticism of the Hebrew Bible and Its Social World: The Israelite Monarch*; ed. N. K. Gottwald; 1986) 68. For a similar association in the Akkadian context, see Aage Westenholz, "The Earliest Akkadian Religion," *Or* 45 (1976) 214–16.

45. Keith Whitelam, "Israelite Kingship: The Royal Ideology and Its Opponents," *The World of Ancient Israel: Sociological, Anthropological and Political Perspectives* (ed. R. E. Clements; Cambridge: Cambridge University Press, 1989) 121.

46. E.g., Chaney, "Systemic Study," 61; Morton Smith, *Palestinian Parties and Politics That Shaped the Old Testament* (London: SCM, 1987) 76; Max Weber, *The Agrarian Sociology of Ancient Civilizations* (London: Verso, 1988) 146; Max Weber, *Ancient Judaism*.

47. Norman Gottwald, *The Tribes of Yahweh: A Sociology of the Religion of Liberated Israel, 1250–1050 B.C.E.* (Maryknoll, N.Y.: Orbis, 1985); Norman Gottwald, *The Hebrew Bible in Its Social World and in Ours* (Atlanta: Scholars Press, 1993). A pure Marxist reading of ancient Israel would hinge on the question of the problematic "Asiatic Mode of Production." For an excellent treatment of this issue, see Gottwald's article "A Hypothesis about Social Class in Monarchic Israel in the Light of Contemporary Studies of Social Class and Social Stratification," *The Hebrew Bible*; also see Diakonoff and others, "Introduction," in *Early Antiquity* (ed. I. M. Diakonoff; Chicago: University of Chicago Press, 1991) 6–14.

48. Ronald F. G. Sweet, "The Sage in Mesopotamian Palaces and Royal Courts," in *The Sage in Israel and the Ancient Near East* (ed. J. G. Gammie and L. G. Perdue; Winona Lake, Ind.: Eisenbrauns, 1990) 101, 107.

> In Israel as elsewhere in the ancient Near East the courts were the intellectual centers of the two kingdoms. . . . There can be little doubt that much of the literature composed during the period of the Monarchy was the work of either the royal or the priestly scribes. The main types of literature that may safely be attributed to this period are annals and historical narratives, poetry (especially psalms), laws and cultic material such as the description of the Temple in 1 Kings 6, and wisdom literature such as is now extant in the Book of Proverbs.[49]

In Moshe Greenberg's important work *Biblical Prose Prayer as a Window to the Popular Religion of Ancient Israel*, it is suggested that certain parts of the Hebrew Bible originate from—and thus reflect the world view of—this educated elite: "The two most prominent and ample sources of information about the religious practice of ancient Israel—the temple rituals and the psalms—are thus deficient as mirrors of the commoners' religion; both are prescriptions of the schooled; they belong to a class of experts."[50]

"Official Religion" and the Old Testament

Two important observations emerge from our brief review of biblical scholarship's treatment of the "official religion" construct. First, many maintain—rightly, I believe—that some sort of association must have existed between the monarchy/state and the "official religion" of preexilic ancient Israel. Given the fact that the monarchy/state typically retains access to institutions of coercive and consensual power, it is certainly not implausible to assume that a monarchic regime would be able to establish its preferred religion as an orthodoxy.

Second, it was noted that in Israel, like most ancient Near Eastern societies, the monarchy/state often sponsored the production of religious literature. Accordingly, it is likely that the Judahite and Israelite monarchies retained cadres of intellectuals whose task it was to rationalize, in the sense discussed above, their state religions. The work that they produced provided the intellectual foundations for the promulgation of an "official religion" of Judah and/or Israel.

Implicit in the writings of many biblical scholars is the assumption that components of this "official religion" are preserved on the pages of the Old

49. R. N. Whybray, "The Sage in the Israelite Royal Court," in *The Sage in Israel and the Ancient Near East*, 137; also see Meyers, *Discovering Eve*, 11; Dever, "Archaeology Reconstructs," 123; for a discussion of the characteristics of intellectuals in antiquity, see Bernhard Lang, *Monotheism and the Prophetic Minority* (SWBA 1; Sheffield: Almond, 1983) 154.

50. Moshe Greenberg, *Biblical Prose Prayer as a Window to the Popular Religion of Ancient Israel* (Berkeley: University of California Press, 1983) 6. For a discussion and critique of Greenberg's important work, see my "Some Sociological Observations on Moshe Greenberg's *Biblical Prose Prayer as a Window to the Popular Religion of Ancient Israel*," *JNSL* 21 (1995) 1–14.

Testament. The methodological corollary of this view consists of the strategy of using the words of the sacred text as a means of elucidating "official" policy, religion, practices, and so on, at some particular time and place in Israelite history. As such, most discussions of these subjects are based on information gleaned from *particular biblical verses*.

It will not be necessary to point to specific examples of this practice insofar as it surfaces, in some form or another, in nearly all works of biblical scholarship that make passing mention of the term *official*. Of greater interest are the arguments that seek to delineate some of the difficulties inherent in this view. In recent years some elementary doubts have been expressed as to the validity of using the Old Testament as a means of studying "official religion."[51] In what remains of this paper, we will further develop this line of critique by calling attention to some of the salient sociological issues raised by the aforementioned approach.

Antimonarchism and Its Implications

It has been my view that "official religion" cannot be understood without reference to power. The group that wields power over other groups within a society, I argued, typically has at its disposal a core of intellectuals entrusted with the task of articulating its "ruling ideas." Now if the Yahwism adumbrated on the pages of the Hebrew Bible reflects the prerogatives of an "official religion," then we must assume the existence of a link between the literary Yahwists who produced this document (i.e., intellectuals) and the institutions of power discussed above.

This assumption is rendered problematic when we take the following fact into consideration: the text in question, the one allegedly composed on behalf of an "official religion," often evinces a patently critical stance toward institutions of monarchial/state power. In commenting on Deut 17:14, Albrecht Alt notes,

> the monarchy is not presented there as an essential in the life of the nation as Yahweh described it. It is seen as an additional feature which was optional, which could only be adopted if all kinds of precautions were taken to see that it did no damage, and which was unlikely to be accorded any function which was indispensable for the well-being of the nation. It must never be thought that the monarchy had the power in any way to alter or supersede the ancient law of God by its own legislation.[52]

An even more piercing critique can be detected in the first book of Samuel. In 1 Samuel 8 the elders of Israel beseech Samuel to appoint a king over Israel. In his response the prophet enumerates a veritable litany of

51. See Miller, "Israelite Religion," 217–18.

52. Albrecht Alt, *Essays on Old Testament History and Religion* (New York: Anchor, 1968) 313; J. Pedersen, *Israel: Its Life and Culture*, vols. 3–4 (London: Oxford University Press, 1947) 95– 101.

antimonarchic complaints. These include: excessive taxation, corvée labor,[53] conscription, and the imposition of arbitrary fiscal burdens (1 Sam 8:10–18). A few chapters later, the authors point out that the God of Israel is not satisfied with this institution or with His people, who will be punished for having chosen this alternative (12:12–17).

Nor are criticisms and unflattering portraits of individual kings lacking in the Old Testament.[54] The names of Joram (2 Kgs 8:16–18), Ahaz (2 Kgs 16:1–4), Manasseh (2 Kgs 21:1–17), Amon (2 Kgs 21:19–22), and Abijam (1 Kgs 15:1–4), to name but a few, attest to the fact that the Old Testament authors rarely hesitated in reproaching monarchs with whom they disagreed.

This unambiguously critical approach to institutions of power makes the Old Testament unique among contemporary documents. As Morton Smith notes: "There is nothing comparable to this in any other religious literature from the ancient Mediterranean or Mesopotamian worlds."[55] For here we have a body of documents that do not restrict themselves to hagiographic depictions of monarchs and adjacent institutions of power. On the contrary, the authors of the Old Testament exhibit little compunction in excoriating kings, even revered kings (e.g., 2 Samuel 12; 1 Kgs 3:2–3, 11:5–13, 15:5), and calling into question the very legitimacy of the monarchy. The impression one receives is that those who wrote certain sections of the Old Testament, far from being loyal devotees of the monarchy, actually lived in a state of high tension with this institution.[56] As P. Kyle McCarter, Jr. notes: "the biblical writers themselves indicate that the branch of preexilic religion they are embracing was a dissenting viewpoint during much of the Israelite monarchy."[57]

These considerations force us to pose questions to people who use the Hebrew Bible as a resource for the study of Israelite "official religion": if the literature found on the pages of the Old Testament was indeed authored by a monarchy/state–sponsored intelligentsia, then how can we explain its often critical approach toward the monarchy/state? If the Old Testament reflects

53. See I. Mendelsohn, "On Corvée Labor in Ancient Canaan and Israel," *BASOR* 167 (1962) 31–35.

54. See Weber, *Ancient Judaism*, 195

55. Smith, *Palestinian Parties*, 35.

56. As Peter Berger notes in discussing Israelite prophets, we find a group of intellectuals "essentially in opposition to the official institutional structure of Israel as represented by monarchy and priesthood" ("Charisma and Religious Innovation: The Social Location of Israelite Prophecy," *American Sociological Review* 82 [1963] 941); also see David Petersen, "Max Weber and the Sociological Study of Ancient Israel," *Social Inquiry* 49 (1979) 127.

57. P. Kyle McCarter, Jr., "Aspects of the Religion of the Israelite Monarchy: Biblical and Epigraphic Data," *Ancient Israelite Religion: Essays in Honor of Frank Moore Cross* (ed. P. D. Miller Jr., P. Hanson, and S. McBride; Philadelphia: Fortress, 1987) 137.

the "official religion" of ancient Israel, then how may we account for the fact that its authors are often critical of the very institutions of power that typically buttress an "official religion"?

Five Hypotheses

One possible answer, and an unlikely one at that, is to assume that the kings of ancient Israel willingly permitted and cultivated expressions of dissent among the intellectuals of their court. Following this line of reasoning we would have to assume that the former presaged something of the Enlightenment spirit of critique—*Sapere aude* in the words of Immanuel Kant. Accordingly, Yahwistic intellectuals who were critical of the monarchy were nevertheless supported and sponsored by this very institution.

Second, we could adopt a type of Church/State model well known to modern sociologists of religion. We could speculate that in ancient Israel there existed two entities whose particular relation to one another oscillated in time: the State with its seat in the monarchy and the Church comprised of devout Yahwists who dedicated themselves to maintaining the cult of their deity.[58]

Let us consider three modes of interaction between Church and State: theocracy, caesaropapism, and antagonism. At some points in Israelite history we could identify a theocracy that refers to "union of church and state, with emphasis . . . on church autonomy."[59] Here, we could attribute the antimonarchial tone of the Old Testament to the displeasure that an independent and powerful Yahwist party felt towards individual monarchs.

Caesaropapism, as Robertson notes, refers to a "union of church and state, with a low degree of church autonomy."[60] In this type of Church/State relation, Yahwism would still be an "official religion," albeit one closely regulated by the state/monarchy. It would be difficult to account for the critical impulses found in the Old Testament under such circumstances.

Last, we may also envision moments of full-blown antagonism between Church and State. A particular king may have wished to establish his own idiosyncratic brand of Yahwism, to combine it with the worship of other deities or to reject it altogether. Perhaps, it was the existence of such a rupture between the monarchy and a Yahwist party that provided the impetus for the critical reports we find in the Hebrew Bible. We will have more to say about the antagonistic model momentarily.

58. For a discussion regarding the concept of state in ancient Israel, see Whitelam, "Israelite Kingship," 120.

59. Roland Robertson, "Church-State Relations in Comparative Perspective," *Church-State Relations: Tensions and Transitions* (ed. T. Robbins and R. Robertson; New Brunswick: Transaction, 1987) 157.

60. Ibid.

As useful as a Church/State approach might be, we should not lose sight of the possibility that there may have been periods in Israelite history when no "official" church existed.[61] Accordingly, there was a state/monarchy but no corresponding religious *orthodoxy*. Groups critical of the former were free to express their opinions due to the unwillingness, or perhaps the inability, of the crown to challenge them. Following this third hypothesis, the antimonarchial sentiments described in the Hebrew Bible could have been formulated and circulated by Yahwistic intellectuals without fear of interference or retribution. In this case, we would imagine the Yahwist party as neither an "official" nor a "popular" religion," but one religion among many.[62]

A fourth explanation would maintain that there exists a fundamental difference between the "official religion" of ancient Israel and the "official" Yahwism preserved on the pages of the Old Testament. In this scenario we posit the existence of two contemporaneous, albeit distinct, religious groups. The first, the "official religion" of ancient Israel was backed by the coercive and consensual power of the state/monarchy. It employed its own intellectuals, whose job it was to articulate the tenets of an "official religion" whose contents we presently know almost nothing about. The second group, the Yahwists, retained little or no access to these institutions of coercive and consensual power. They may be envisioned as an opposition party, a "popular religion," a persecuted minority, and so on.[63] Accordingly, the Yahwistic intellectuals produced texts that expressed their disdain of the monarchy and the non-Yahwistic "official religion" that it advocated.[64]

These concerns are directly related to a fifth and final possibility, one that calls attention to issues of periodization and text redaction. The antimonarchic impulses of the Old Testament could be explained as a consequence of textual editing that took place at another period in time. Thus, the critique found in the Old Testament was leveled from a period far removed from the events described—from a "critical distance," so to speak.[65] At some later

61. Such a state of affairs is not unprecedented (see W. E. A. van Beek, "Traditional Religion as a Locus of Change," in *Official and Popular Religion: Analysis of a Theme for Religious Studies* (ed. P. H. Vrijhof and J. Waardenburg; The Hague: Mouton, 1979) 539; Huisman, "Christianity and Germanic Religion," 57; P. H. Vrijhof, "Conclusion," in *Official and Popular Religion*, 678. P. Staples makes the important point that "there may also be other styles of religion which are neither *official* nor *popular*" ("Official and Popular Religion in an Ecumenical Perspective," in *Official and Popular Religion*, 250).

62. For a discussion of *popular religion*, see my "'Popular Religion' Paradigm in Old Testament Research: A Sociological Critique," *JSOT* 60 (1993) 3–26; and idem, *The Vow and the "Popular Religious Groups."*

63. Here, we are coming quite close to the antagonistic model discussed under the church/state paradigm.

64. See McCarter, "Aspects of the Religion," 137.

65. For a discussion of some of the issues involved in the dating of the "antimonarchic source," see Whitelam, "Israelite Kingship," 122–28.

period, when Yahwism actually might have been something resembling an "official religion" as described above (e.g., in the Persian province of Yahud or Judah in the age of the Ptolemies and Seleucids or during the Hasmonaean monarchy), its intellectuals composed texts harshly critical of non-Yahwistic "official religions" past.[66]

If the fourth and fifth possibilities were to be true then we would seriously have to reassess the method of using biblical texts as a means of learning about "official religion," for a particular verse from the book of Kings would not necessarily elucidate some aspect of Israelite "official religion" as practiced in that day. This verse (according to the fourth hypothesis) could have been composed contemporaneously with the events it describes, but since its authors were Yahwists (i.e., not the "official religion" of the period), their testimony would reflect what they believed *should have been* the "official religion" of the land.

In line with our fifth theory, we could propose that these verses in the book of Kings were not authored contemporaneously with the events they describe. Instead, they reflect the opinions of Yahwists of a much later age. We could imagine that postexilic Yahwists—whose beliefs and practices might actually have been, at some points, an "official religion" of sorts—retrojected the precepts of their religion into the hoary, preexilic past.

Conclusion

At the beginning of this article it was noted that students of Israelite religion who employ the term *official* rarely offer any definition or analysis regarding what it means. Accordingly, we turned to sociological, anthropological, and historical research in an attempt to erect some theoretical foundations for the study of Israelite "official religion." An ideal-typical schema was forwarded in which it was suggested that: (1) privileged economic class position, (2) tendencies toward rationalization via intellectuals, (3) male dominance and, in particular, access to (4) coercive, and (5) consensual institutions of power stood as normative criteria for the investigation of this subject.[67]

In my analysis of ancient Israel, I chose to concentrate on the relation between power and "metaphysical ethical rationalization" as carried out by the

66. We must take seriously the possibility that, when written, these texts constituted not an "official religion" but, in Smith's very apt phrase, "a cult collection" (*Palestinian Parties*, 14). For a discussion of "official religion" in the Second Temple Period, see J. W. Doeve, "Official and Popular Religion in Judaism," in *Official and Popular Religion: Analysis of a Theme for Religious Studies* (ed. P. H. Vrijhof and J. Waardenburg; The Hague: Mouton, 1979) 325–39.

67. Such a view, I would add, is very different from the brief descriptions that biblical scholars have given of "official religion." To refer to "official religion" as "normative," "established," or "orthodox" is to ignore the crucial role that power plays in making religious ideas achieve this status within a society.

intellectuals. An ideal-typical "official religion," I speculated, would employ a group of intellectuals to give cultural shape to its metaphysical beliefs; power underwrites the creation and dissemination of "ruling ideas." That some of the ideas expressed in the Hebrew Bible should be so blatantly inimical to the central locus of Israelite power is a state of affairs that challenges some of the core assumptions of Old Testament scholarship.

By using the words of the Hebrew Bible as a means of learning about "official religion," many biblical scholars implicitly associate power, the state-sponsored intelligentsia, and the devotees of Yahwism. In this contribution, I sought to call this equation into question. Can the Yahwists responsible for the contents of the Old Testament, with their often pronounced hostility to the state/monarchy, really be equated with institutions of Israelite power? It was in light of these considerations that I forwarded the possibility that Israelite "official religion" and the "official" Yahwism described in the Bible may not be synonyms. If this is the case, then scholars need to exert greater caution in using biblical verses as a means of gaining insight into "official religion."

While the preceding analysis was confined to the preexilic era, this does not mean that our ideal-type cannot be applied to other periods of (Israelite) history. The essential methodological task lies in identifying the prevailing locus of institutional power in the period under study, be it the monarchy, the office of the high priest, or the appointed governor, or someone else. Once identified, we must proceed to investigate the relation between these institutions and the people responsible for the authorship and redaction of the Old Testament or other texts in question. Only in this manner we will be able to claim that a specific passage in the Hebrew Bible apprises us of ancient Israelite "official religion."

Kings and Prophets: Cyrus and Servant

Reading Isaiah 40–55

Robert G. Boling†
McCormick Theological Seminary

Why revisit the question of a "Second" and "Third" Isaiah, that is, chaps. 40–55 and 56–66, respectively, of the great Isaiah-book? Recent scholarship has increasingly focused instead on the challenge of reading the finally redacted collection as one "book" in its own right.[1] Two reasons, mainly, have motivated this study. First, the separate structural integrity of large exilic and postexilic segments of the book has been greatly clarified in recent years. Second, I have become more and more preoccupied with biblical responses to the enduring enigma of meaningless suffering, responses represented most poignantly and dramatically by the book of Job, on one hand, and the poems of "Second" Isaiah, on the other. Why do bad things happen to good people? It is no merely academic question. If the book of Job is designed to help the *solitary* sufferer to cope yet without providing a satisfactory rationalization of Job's suffering, it is the burden of Isaiah 40–55 to counter in other ways the despair of *corporate* suffering. In our day the question of meaningless suffering intrudes itself with ever greater poignancy, as the march of warfare and the pace of tragedy continue to escalate. In this "postmodern" world, the celebrated "songs of a suffering servant" continue to exert their existential magnetism.

Thus the primary focus in these pages is the Second Isaiah. I am trying to understand chaps. 40–55 in their own right, as well as in relation to what precedes and what follows. How does the implied reader make the abrupt

Author's note: It is a special privilege to submit this essay for a collection honoring Baruch Levine. I have benefited from his critical response to an earlier version of the paper, presented in a meeting of The Biblical Colloquium.

1. See especially E. W. Conrad, *Reading Isaiah* (OBT; Minneapolis: Fortress, 1991).

transitions between major segments of the long Isaiah-book?[2] There are many questions that this middle segment continues to evoke. According to the poet and/or redactor in exile, what will be the relationship between Israel and the nations? On the way to the feast with which the section culminates in chap. 55, what, if any, is to be the relationship between Cyrus and the evocative figure who flutters in and out of focus in these chapters as "servant" of YHWH? Is there in fact a story line that runs from the call and commissioning of the prophet-poet in chap. 40 to the invitation to a feast in chap. 55?

Ever since the work by James Muilenburg in *The Interpreter's Bible*, which divided the chapters into 21 poems,[3] many scholars have suspected that there is indeed an intentional dramatic arrangement of compositions in Isaiah 40–55. Unlike other prophetic books which present more or less miscellaneous collections of oracles, these chapters show signs of a somewhat more elaborate plan. See now, especially, Richard Clifford, *Fair Spoken and Persuading*.[4] Clifford argues for recognition of these chapters as prophetic *speech*: for all such writing in antiquity was produced for hearing. Clifford finds chaps. 40 to 55 to be comprised of a total of 17 speeches, in which the prophet functions as interpreter of the national story. That national story is found in two forms or "types" in scripture. There was a historical or folk-memory type, according to which YHWH through Moses rescues the people from state slavery in Egypt and brings them to serve him in his land, Canaan. There was also a cosmogonic or "world-making" type, according to which YHWH at the creation of "Israel" overcomes the power of sea, desert, and river (all personified or representative of chaos in Canaanite myth) that keeps his people from his land. YHWH removes the hostile power by making a path on which the people Israel may walk safely through to YHWH's place. Both the historic and cosmogonic types are important in Second Isaiah, in which "the prophet has fused the Exodus-Conquest and the cosmogonic version of Israel's origins,"[5] so that the new Exodus-Conquest will be at the same time New Creation!

In this reading Cyrus is not merely the legitimate bearer of international power, he is also presented as the powerful wind of the storm-god YHWH.[6] Israel in exile must once again engage in the very act whereby it first came into being: the Exodus-Conquest, trusting YHWH to emerge victorious from

2. Throughout this paper, *First Isaiah* refers to material that stems mainly from the 8th-century prophet, preserved in chaps. 1–39 together with some materials in those chapters from later periods. The later periods, however, are most clearly represented in two major segments (chaps. 40–55 and 56–66), each of which displays an elaborate macrostructure (described below).

3. J. Muilenburg, "Isaiah 40–66: Introduction and Exegesis," *IB* 5.381–776.

4. R. J. Clifford, *Fair Spoken and Persuading* (New York: Paulist Press, 1984).

5. Ibid., 21.

6. Ibid., 10.

the struggle of conquest/creation, so that the people may once again march in procession to God's shrine. The "new thing" that YHWH is about to accomplish is simultaneously Exodus-Conquest and New Creation.

Clifford's approach via the phenomenology of a foundation myth has the advantage of recognizing high structural significance to the feast in 55:1–5. For Clifford this is a feast that can only take place in Jerusalem because Zion is the Temple site. "Seek YHWH while he may be found / Call upon him while he is near" (55:6). Clifford rather forcibly retranslates this ultimate exhortation to read "*where* he may be encountered / *where* he is present" (italics mine) in direct reference to the sanctuary on Zion. But if it is only at the Temple site that YHWH's presence may be experienced, what is the exiled poet's reason to hope for the attention of other exiles to the poet's exhortation? I think it is more likely that the feast in chap. 55 is intended as hortatory preparation for the new wilderness journey. In any case, we may assume that once we start reading in chap. 40, we are not supposed to stop until we have arrived at the end of chap. 55.

Background in Classical Prophecy

A major impetus to this study stems from an article published by G. Ernest Wright in 1965.[7] Building upon George Mendenhall's discussion[8] of the Roman *imperium* (that is, the right or power of command, mastery), Wright argued that the classical or preexilic prophets were "internationalists in viewpoint, who took the question of international treaties and world order very seriously."[9] The prophets were representatives of YHWH's *imperium*.

Drawing upon the work of his colleague Frank M. Cross and their student Waldemar Janzen, Wright understood many of the oracles against foreign nations as serving a purpose very different from that of imprecation or curse. Cross, for example, had proposed, in an unpublished paper, to understand the series of oracles at the outset of the book of Amos against the collapse of a treaty network stemming from the Davidic empire ("For three transgressions of X, and for four, I will not revoke the punishment," etc.).[10] At the same time, Janzen's work had shown that the oracle against a foreign nation, introduced by the particle *hoy*, was generally to be read as an ironic (if not sarcastic) lament evoked by the bad things that the nation-states in question were doing to other peoples or nations.[11] Not "Woe to the bloody city . . ." but "Alas. . . ." It is a picture of YHWH and/or the prophet lamenting the

7. G. E. Wright, "The Nations in Hebrew Prophecy," *Encounter* 26 (1965) 225–37.

8. An unpublished address at Harvard University. See now G. E. Mendenhall, *The Tenth Generation* (Baltimore: Johns Hopkins University Press, 1973).

9. Wright, "The Nations," 237.

10. Ibid., 236.

11. W. Janzen, "*ʾAŠRE* in the Old Testament," *HTR* 58 (1965) 215–26.

inevitable. In the prophetic view there would be consequences of certain behaviors that were as predictable as what we used to mean when we could still say, within the parameters of Newtonian physics, that "what goes up must come down."

The Dramatic Vision

One ruling idea in this essay, therefore, is that what holds together some three or more "Isaiahs" in one "book" is precisely the notion of the prophet of YHWH functioning parallel with—but not subordinate to—the legitimate political authority. The prophet is representative of a cosmic imperium, one that is international in scope, encompassing the known world, not limited to the territorial state and population legitimately governed by the Israelite or Judahite king. While the occupant of the Jerusalem throne was heir to a dynastic promise regarding a limited territory and populace, the prophet was the freely recruited and enlisted emissary for the CEO of the universe—direct spokesperson for the Sovereign of all the world.

It is significant that the prophetic indictment was addressed first, in the 10th and 9th centuries, to the king and those close to the seat of power—a small political and priestly elite. They are faulted precisely for their misuse of political and economic power together with ecclesiastical exploitation of social status. Eighth-century prophets thus alternate between denouncing and lamenting an unholy interdependence of sacral and political clout, with concomitant exploitation and impoverishment of the bulk of the population.

Then comes a major development in diplomacy and prophecy. In the 8th and 7th centuries the prophetic indictment is broadened to include the general populace for its participation and/or acquiescence in the misuse of political and ecclesiastical power. The "covenant lawsuit" becomes a dominant form in prophecy from the 8th century on. It is scarcely coincidental that this shift came close on the heels of a similar development in conduct of international diplomacy, in which the emissary of the suzerain made appeal not only to the vassal but to the vassal's subjects.[12]

In the prophetic books from the 8th century on, and into the exile and later, the frequency of forms and vocabulary drawn from the realm of international relations and the conduct of diplomacy is indeed striking.[13] It strongly suggests that the role of YHWH's *ambassador* was central to the self-understanding of prophets in the premonarchy era. The idea of careers modeled to some significant extent upon the role of ambassador will speak directly to understandings of prophetic behavior and the societal response,

12. J. S. Holladay, Jr., "Assyrian Statecraft and the Prophets of Israel," *HTR* 63 (1970) 29–51.

13. J. Harvey, "Le 'rîb-pattern': Réquisitor prophétique sur la rupture de l'alliance," *Bib* 43 (1962) 172–96.

from the consolidation of the monarchy in the 10th century to the terrible disasters of 598 and 587 B.C.E.

The ambassador in the ancient world had the weighty responsibility of being more than a messenger, bearing the sovereign's indictment into the presence of the accused vassal. The ambassador's role then as today was to negotiate on behalf of the Sovereign. The prophet's task was to maneuver in such a way as to evoke the appropriate response—confession (if guilty) and requisite change of behavior. Otherwise, it was to be expected that the Suzerain's army would soon follow the indictment. For there were no international courts, apart from the realm of the gods, who were therefore invoked as witnesses to both the treaty and any subsequent proceedings. Thus the diplomatic indictment in the ancient world was in effect a declaration of war.[14]

It was, I submit, the history of kingship and prophecy interacting on such a model over nearly half a millennium *before* the Babylonian exile that evoked the parallel literary appearance of Emperor Cyrus and YHWH's servant *during* exile, as the promise of a future for Israel *beyond* exile unfolds in Isaiah 40–55.

In other words, Isaiah 40–55 sets forth a scenario for the implementation and recognition of YHWH's governance among the nations, beginning with the restoration of Jewish exiles to their homeland. Current usage has broadened the sense of "scenario," originally referring to an outline or synopsis of a play, to any "imagined or projected sequence of events, especially any of several detailed plans or possibilities."[15] I suggest that what we have in Isaiah 40–55 may be understood as a scenario for the existential drama. It is a drama in which the hearers/readers of these chapters are invited, by virtue of poetic form, to participate: restoration of the exiles to their homeland, to be followed by YHWH's nonviolent world-conquest, and acknowledgment of YHWH's transnational governance.

In a close reading of the introductory poem in Second Isaiah (40:1–11), D. N. Freedman discerns a complex chiastic (that is, X-like) arrangement, centering on vv. 5–6a. Chiastic patterns are being discovered throughout Hebrew prose and poetry in material ranging in scope from the brief poetic line to large, book-length symmetries. In such a literary structure the key to meaning lies at the center, while the beginning and end of the composition form a sort of envelope around the body of the unit. Concerning this introductory poem, Freedman comments:

> The coming of Yahweh with his exiled people back to his land and his city, to be welcomed by the inhabitants left behind during the Babylonian Captivity, is the fulfillment of the message transmitted through the poem. The final act in

14. Harvey, "Le 'rîb-pattern.'"

15. *Random House Dictionary of the English Language* (2d ed.; New York: Random, 1987) 1712.

the drama, which occurs at the same time, is the manifestation of the glory of the God of Israel to the whole world, which is announced in v. 5:

> And the glory of Yahweh shall be revealed
> And all flesh shall see it together
> For the mouth of Yahweh has spoken.[16]

The poetic scenario begins with a realistic assessment of life in exile. It sets forth, admittedly in hyperbolic imagery, what I suggest was intended to be a realizable eschatology. Along the way the spotlight shifts from the disappointing record of a disloyal servant Israel *in the past*[17] to a loyal servant Israel *newly introduced*,[18] who has been commissioned to lead the people back to Yhwh in the second exodus. The second exodus in turn will set the stage for worldwide acknowledgment of Yhwh's sovereignty. The loyal servant, like Cyrus, clearly occupies an office that functions both for the homecoming of exiles and the salvation of the nations.

This important distinction between two "servants" (one past, the other present/future) has been independently recognized and persuasively argued by A. Laato. In core materials of "servant passages" which he reads as intimately connected with the royal ideology (e.g., in 41:8–13, 42:1–4, 45:1–7, 49:1–6), Laato finds traces of "an exilic messianic program" reflected.[19] If correct, such passages could bespeak, at one and the same time, an ideal Israel and a messianic individual. One way of understanding the relation between Cyrus and servant, then, would follow from the unanticipated demise of Babylon and subsequent revision of expectations: "Cyrus and the ideal Israel each take on aspects of the role of the messiah."[20] However, I think that this last assertion muddies the waters. While the contrast between loyal and disloyal servants (both identified with Jacob/Israel) is very significant, attention to the macrostructure of chaps. 40–55 (see below) will indicate that probably none of the servant passages is in any sense "messianic."

Cyrus is one of two key individuals introduced to the assembly of the nations and/or their representatives (the kings, their idol gods). It is a downright shocking claim: if the exiles desire to see the worldwide acknowledgment of Yhwh's governance, one of the first things to be learned is that the most powerful Gentile of the day bears for as long as Yhwh wills it two favorite titles of the former Jerusalem kings (Yhwh's "shepherd" and

16. D. N. Freedman, "The Structure of Isaiah 40:1–11," in *Perspectives on Language and Text: Essays and Poems in Honor of Francis I. Andersen's Sixtieth Birthday, July 28, 1985* (ed. E. W. Conrad and E. G. Newring; Winona Lake, Ind.: Eisenbrauns, 1987) 174.

17. Isa 41:8–13; 42:18–25; 43:1–7, 8–13.

18. Isa 42:1–9, 49:1–13, 50:4–11(?), 51:4–8, 52:13–53:12.

19. A. Laato, *The Servant of Yahweh and Cyrus* (ConBOT 35; Stockholm: Almqvist & Wiksell, 1992).

20. Ibid., 282.

"anointed"). Cyrus's power is, to be sure, only temporary—a stage on the way to YHWH's direct governance of all the world.

How is the reader to understand the fact that in Second Isaiah's vision, Cyrus has wide-ranging political power, divinely legitimated? The fact that Cyrus is singled out as YHWH's "anointed" was written off by G. von Rad as merely "rousing rhetorical exaggeration inspired by the actual situation."[21] Another doubtful solution has been to dismiss the references to Cyrus as secondary additions to the exilic poet's work.[22]

The other pivotally important individual in this scenario is clearly recognizable and has developing identity—YHWH's servant. I say "developing identity" because the direct address by YHWH, or references by YHWH, to Israel/Jacob as "my servant" (41:8; 42:19; 43:10; 44:1, 2, 21 bis) cease abruptly once that identification of Israel as servant is made clear to Cyrus (45:4). In the meantime, in contrast to the failures for which the servant Israel/Jacob is faulted and has received just punishment, according to chaps. 40–48, a servant has been introduced to the assembled nations (42:1–4) who will in truth succeed, who will bring in his person and display in his faithfulness the strategy for YHWH's enlightenment of the world. "*Here* is my servant . . ." (42:1). The emphasis in Hebrew word order is clear.

This servant is introduced to the nations, for their edification and future well-being, in the first Servant Song (42:1–4). This same servant then speaks of his call in the second Servant Song (49:1–6). He had heard YHWH saying "*Thou* art the Israel in whom I glorify myself." Martin Buber read it as paradoxical: "the servant succeeds and replaces Israel."[23] Finally, it is this same servant who has *conveyed* and has *lived out* the *policy* for the guidance of Israel and conversion of the nations—the final Servant Song (52:13–53:12)—in this most creative exercise of prophetic imagination. In other words, in the battle plan for the Divine Warrior's world conquest, Cyrus exercises legitimately expanding imperial government for as long as YHWH wills it, while the *faithful servant* brings and models the essentially nonviolent strategy.

The parallelism between king and Cyrus, prophet and servant, is not total. The servant par excellence, as depicted in these poems, does not speak directly to Cyrus. But neither are the exiles in any position to exercise influence on the formation of imperial policy. The exiles are accountable to YHWH, not to Cyrus.

If 61:1 comes ultimately from the same source, then it appears that Deutero-Isaiah could also speak of a servant as "anointed."[24] It is doubtful,

21. G. von Rad, *The Message of the Prophets* (trans. D. M. G. Stalker; New York: Harper & Row, 1992) 211 n. 9.

22. J. D. Smart, *History and Theology in Second Isaiah* (Philadelphia: Westminster, 1965), esp. 10 and 33.

23. M. Buber, *The Prophetic Faith* (New York: Harper, 1960) 220.

24. Ibid., 219.

however, that this servant has acquired kingly traits or status. There is a broad consensus of scholars who have concluded that it was first of all Moses and the great prophets of the monarchy era (perhaps especially Hosea and Jeremiah) who originally sat for the portrait of this *servant par excellence*. Yet it does not suffice to say merely that the servant is "the idea or typical" prophet.[25] The servant who is introduced in 42:1–4, who speaks autobiographically in 49:1–6, and whose faithfulness unto death is vindicated in poetic imagination by restoration to fullness of life in 52:13–53:12—this servant surely fulfills the old Deuteronomic promise of a prophet like Moses.[26] The story of this servant is, in any case, the vindication of the faithfulness of the "classical" (i.e., preexilic) prophets.

The scenario unfolds within a framework provided by a prologue and epilogue. The prologue has two parts: 40:1–8 corresponding to chaps. 41–48, and 40:9–11 corresponding to chaps. 49–55. The prologue, in turn, has its concluding counterpart in 55:6–13. References to the eternally established word of YHWH (40:8) and the self-enacting word of YHWH (55:11) form a strong inclusio around the Second Exodus–New Covenant scenario.

The drama begins in chap. 40 with a vision of YHWH's imminent arrival in Jerusalem, which only awaits a feast of covenant renewal (55:1–5) as prelude to a second exodus and new wilderness trek. It is a curious fact that, with all of Deutero-Isaiah's use of the Exodus imagery, there is simply no indication of interest in events of Sinai (theophany/covenant/law-giving); no interest, that is, unless the feast in Isaiah 55 is intended as counterpart to the mountaintop feast in Exod 24:1–11. There are, to be sure, no new covenant stipulations. Chapter 40 had underscored the old stipulations as more than adequate ("double for all their sins," 40:2b). Commentators are frequently diverted from Sinai by the reference to the *ḥasdê dāwid* (NRSV 'steadfast sure love for David') in 55:3. It is worth noting, however, that the form is plural. It might therefore be better translated 'evidences of steadfast love'. The old *ḥasdê dāwid* are henceforth to be enjoyed by anyone and everyone who accepts this invitation and comes to this feast. Scholars generally interpret the verse as promising a "democratization" of the promises to David. It may also be taken as a democratizing of the old "J-source" version of the Sinai feast (Exod 24:1–2, 9–11). In that elitist version, only Moses, Aaron, Nadab, Abihu, and seventy elders enjoy the covenant meal. In contrast, the more egalitarian tradition of the "E-source" involved all "the people" in the culmination of negotiations at the Holy mountain (Exod 24:3–8).

The movement in Deutero-Isaiah is, in other words, from fulfillment (40:2) to promise (55:13)—one long, enticing invitation to be lifted out of the despair of exile. It was time to make a new beginning as YHWH's model commonwealth and peculiar army of salvation, with YHWH as Commander-

25. W. M. W. Roth, *Isaiah* (Knox Preaching Guides; Atlanta: John Knox, 1988).
26. Deut 18:15.

in-chief and without any human king in Israel/Judah. Deutero-Isaiah does not have to mention Sinai, because the vindication of the prophet's suffering is also ratification of the ethic and faithfulness that are already grounded in Mosaic tradition. In the poet's understanding, it was massive disregard of that teaching that had brought on the suffering. The promise of these chapters is indeed unconditional, but it is not made, as formerly, to the power elite, centering in a royal family.

The further we go in such analysis, the more radically antiestablishment (or better, "transestablishment") these chapters appear. In this case, it would appear that the "establishment" was comprised of those "bad figs," who according to Jeremiah[27] had been left behind in Jerusalem in 598 and 587. They were thus to be found firmly in control of the Temple institutions two generations later, when Third Isaiah and the disciples returned, with the master's poetry ringing in their ears. It appears that the returnees were mistaking the exilic poet's metaphors as the literal description of a program.[28]

And so, outmaneuvered by an entrenched opposition in control of the Jerusalem Temple precincts, the poetry of Third Isaiah tends more and more to sound the apocalyptic note.

Deutero-Isaiah's scenario shows a major transition between chaps. 48 and 49. This has been frequently noted by critics, but with next to no agreement on the significance of the shift. It is in fact the midpoint of the work. After chap. 48 there is no more mockery of idols and no more talk of Cyrus (or clear allusion to him). There are no more full-blown courtroom scenes, no more rebukes of Jacob/Israel. In chaps. 40–48, YHWH and the poet plead with Jacob/Israel (rarely Zion), whereas in chaps. 49–55, it is just the reverse. The shift might be compared to the major pause or caesura in a poetic line, were it not for the isolated prose statement that concludes the first half of the work: "'There is no peace,' says the Lord, 'for the wicked.'"[29] Thus concludes the first half of the work, wherein the only explicit criticism of Jacob/Israel and Jerusalem/Zion is found. It is therefore not merely "curious," as remarked by William L. Holladay,[30] but structurally important. Commenting on the transition, D. N. Freedman wrote: "The first act of the drama is concluded: the redemption of Israel through the intervention of Cyrus the anointed of the Lord."[31] The audience/readership is therefore prepared for

27. Jer 24:8–10, 29:17. For Jeremiah the "good figs" were precisely the exiles, some of whom had become the congregation of the Second and Third Isaiah.

28. The process is well described as follows: ". . . when metaphor is denied its semantic integrity and is misshaped into a literal referent, when similarity becomes identity, metaphor loses its dynamic, tensive power and dies" (L. G. Perdue, *Wisdom in Revolt* [Sheffield: Almond, 1991] 26).

29. Isa 48:22; cf. 57:20–21.

30. W. L. Holladay, *Isaiah: Scroll of a Prophetic Heritage* (Grand Rapids, Mich.: Eerdmans, 1978) 147.

31. D. N. Freedman, "The Slave of Yahweh," *Western Watch* 10 (1959) 14.

the next act of the drama, where YHWH's servant occupies the center of the stage. It is the work of the servant that "will result in the deliverance of the world."[32]

In what sense, "deliverance"? Deliverance from what? The answer may be found in what the bystanders (presumably the kings) say when they see the resuscitation/resurrection of the servant in the scene portrayed by the final Servant Song:

> Surely he has borne our infirmities
> and carried our diseases;
> yet we accounted him stricken,
> struck down by God, and afflicted.

It was recognition of the arrogant equation of royal justice and divine justice that had evoked the confession of misplaced guilt:

> But he was wounded for our transgressions,
> crushed for our iniquities;
> upon him was the punishment that made us whole,
> and by his bruises we are healed.
> All we like sheep have gone astray
> we have all turned to our own way,
> and the Lord has laid on him
> the iniquity of us all. (53:5–6)

Thus say the convicted bystanders. They are speaking, surely, for the "nations," who will respond to the invitation and enticement of Israel, following the covenant renewal feast:

> See, you shall call nations that you do not know
> and nations that do not know you shall run to you,
> because of the Lord your God, the Holy one of Israel,
> for he has glorified you. (55:5)

Curtain down. The eschatological scenario now complete, there remains only to renew the plea (55:6–9) and restate the promise (55:12–13) in poems that frame the last words on the self-enacting reliability of YHWH's own word (55:10–11)!

Excursus on Macrostructure of "Third Isaiah" (Chapters 56–66)

The final segment of the long Isaiah-book is as distinctive as the first two segments. Yet nothing like a continuous story line unites chaps. 56–66 in any way comparable to the roles of principal characters in the drama of chaps. 40–55. It is widely recognized that the poetry in chaps. 56–66 is, for the most part, decidedly different. Moreover, the historical setting and social location of poet and audience have changed. Unlike the contents of the Second

32. Ibid.

Isaiah, which may be read as addressed to exiles, most of chaps. 56–66 clearly presuppose the period of the restoration. It is addressed to a struggling community in and around Jerusalem/Zion. The challenge confronting Second Isaiah in exile was to penetrate and counter a solidarity of despair. But there are clear signs of a polarized community of believers in this third and final section of the Isaiah-book. The followers of Third Isaiah represent one of the factions. Unlike Second Isaiah, prophetic rebuke and reproach are much more frequent here, sharing more characteristics with the indictment speeches in chaps. 1–39. In contrast to Second Isaiah, laments and indictments in Third Isaiah are evoked by an exclusionary temple establishment. The poet's opponents are most ardent in maintaining the performance of religious functions at the salvaged Temple site. At the same time they are accused of socioeconomic oppression, indeed outright bloodshed, to the extent that the poet's followers are driven to the brink of despair.[33] The opposition's stranglehold on the cultus marginalizes and excludes the poet's faction.[34]

Most striking is the fact that these chapters are produced by a poet or poets who do not once use a singular form of the word for "servant"! And yet they never tire of referring to their own audience as YHWH's "servants."[35] In these chapters the word "servants" has none of the evocative ambiguity that characterizes Second Isaiah's usage.

The status of foreigners in this third segment of the Isaiah-book is also especially significant, in view of a chiastic arrangement to chaps. 56–66 that is increasingly acknowledged by scholars. It is schematically presented (fig. 1) by Norman Gottwald.[36] At the center of the pattern are three chapters (60–62) setting forth a visionary restoration scenario. Around this center are balanced roughly matching panels to produce the chiasm.

> The symmetrically balanced panels that create a widening "ripple" effect from the center toward the outer limits are as follows: core proclamation of restoration + theophany of judgment + lament + indictment of corrupt worship + promise of salvation to Jerusalem/Judah + indictment of evil leaders + promise of salvation to foreigners. . . . By opening and closing chaps. 56–66 with words of salvation and by awarding the fullest scope to salvation at the center, the redactor clearly gives priority to the authorial voice of salvation. In the middle panels of this ring arrangement, however, indictments and laments

33. See especially Isa 63:11ff., 15, 19b–64:3, 8–12.

34. This is the reading persuasively presented by P. D. Hanson in *The Dawn of Apocalyptic* (Philadelphia: Fortress, 1975).

35. Isa 56:6; 61:6; 63:17; 65:8, 9, 13, 14, 15, 17; 66:14.

36. Here adapted from N. K. Gottwald, *The Hebrew Bible* (Philadelphia: Fortress, 1985) 508. The pattern was first recognized by R. Lack, *La Symbolique du Livre d'Isaïe: Essai sur l'image littéraire comme élément de structuration* (AnBib 59; Rome: Pontifical Biblical Institute, 1973) 142. See also R. Rendtorff, *The Old Testament: An Introduction* (trans. J. Bowden; Philadelphia: Fortress, 1991) 197.

Chiastic Arrangement of Isaiah 56–66 with Terminal Intensification of "Message" Content

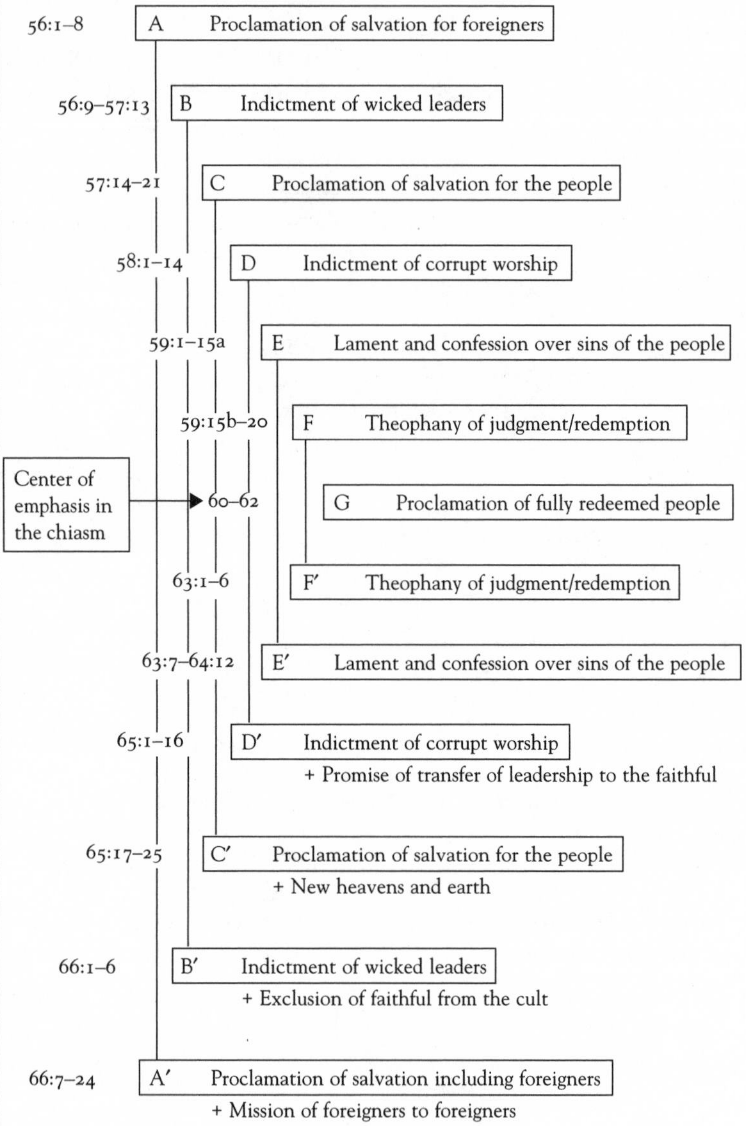

Figure 1. See N. K. Gottwald, *The Hebrew Bible: A Socio-literary Introduction* (Philadelphia: Fortress, 1985) 508.

> underscore the dire impediments to communal salvation which call for the severest judgment.[37]

The impression given by these chapters is that some group has consolidated its hold on priestly office and has pushed other claimants and their prophetic partisans out of the cult altogether.

At the heart of the chiastic arrangement in chaps. 60–62 is the material in "Third" Isaiah that has always, in fact, sounded most like the "Second" one. It is the promise of full redemption of Zion's people, forming a model community as prelude to the conversion of the nations. This was the promise first articulated by the prophet in exile, who in turn considered himself a disciple (*limmud*) of the 8th-century prophet, as asserted in 50:4 ("The Lord God has given me the tongue of those who are taught").[38] The promise was still in effect in the postexilic generation, despite the sharp contrast between the glowing descriptions of the future in the exilic poetry and the harsh realities of life in the restoration community.

Isaiah 40–55: Macrostructure

The published recognition of chiastic arrangement in chaps. 56–66 has emboldened me to seek further sense in a similar pattern that I have long suspected lies before the reader in chaps. 40–55 (fig. 2). A very different and more elaborate schema (fig. 3) has been proposed by A. Laato,[39] which treats the final Servant Song (52:13–53:12) as a lengthy epilogue, opposite a very brief prologue (40:1–2). Apart from the imbalance represented by the proposed prologue and epilogue, Laato's analysis leaves chaps. 54 and 55 entirely outside the macrostructure. Yet another schema proposed by Webster (fig. 4), embracing all of chaps. 40–55, which finds chiastic and parallel structures both in smaller literary units and in the macrostructure of the whole corpus, has been published and critiqued by Laato.[40]

Proceeding independently of other proposals, the chiastic pattern represented in my analysis (fig. 2) seemed to emerge, while working one's way inward from the outer limits formed by the word-of-Yahweh inclusio (40:1–11 and 55:6–13), to see what might lie at the center. The pivotal poem, as it turned out, without excessive disagreement with the form-critical division of units, is precisely the abrupt New Exodus departure command:

> Go out from Babylon, flee from Chaldea,
>   declare this with a shout of joy, proclaim it,
> send it forth to the end of the earth;

37. Gottwald, *The Hebrew Bible*, 506–7.

38. Rendering with RSV et al. against the NRSV's emendation, 'tongue of a teacher'.

39. A. Laato, "The Composition of Isaiah 40–55," *JBL* 109 (1992) 207–28; and idem, *The Servant of Yahweh and Cyrus*.

40. See ibid., 13–16.

Symmetry in Second Isaiah

A Good news, Jerusalem! (40:1–11)
- B Yahweh the incomparable, Holy One of Israel (40:12–31)
  - C Meaning of Cyrus, and servant-people status for Israel (41:1–29)
    - D Introduction to a SERVANT par excellence and new things; versus the idols (42:1–9)
      - E New Song time; Divine Warrior to clear way for return (42:10–43:8)
        - F Liberated witnesses, restored to be a servant (43:9–44:23)
          - G Legitimation of Cyrus (44:24–45:25)
            - H Versus Bel and Nebo and daughter Babylon (46:1–47:15)
              - I Final word about Cyrus, and final reproach (48:1–19)
                - • NEW EXODUS exhortation (48:20–21)
              - I′ The SERVANT speaks, as ambassador, to the nations (49:1–6)
            - H′ Zion's children to be brought home (49:7–13)
          - G′ Yahweh will signal to the nations (49:14–26)
        - F′ Poet's testimony (50:1–10) confirmed by YHWH as that of a servant (50:11–51:8)
      - E′ Prayer to Divine Warrior/Creator and exhortation to Zion (51:9–52:12)
    - D′ Vindication and future of the SERVANT (52:13–53:12)
  - C′ A future for mother Zion: heritage of the "servants" (54:1–17)
- B′ Feasted by YHWH, the Holy One of Israel (55:1–5)

A′ Homeward bound! (55:6–13)

Figure 2. Laato's Structural Analysis

say, "The Lord has redeemed his servant Jacob!"
They did not thirst when he led them through the deserts;
he made water flow for them from the rock;
he split open the rock and the water gushed out.[41]

In fig. 2, it will be observed that these pivotal verses are flanked by panels that concern the leading characters in the drama. Here is the last word about Cyrus together with a final reproach of Jacob/Israel (I), balanced by the self-presentation of the loyal servant (I′).

41. Isa 48:20–21, NRSV.

Laato's Structural Analysis

40:1–2	Q	Prologue to the cycles
40:3–8	a	
9–11	b	
12–26	c	Cycle I
27–31	d	
41:1–7	e	
8–20	F	Return to Jerusalem
21–29	e′	
42:1–4	d′	
5–9	c′	
10–13	b′	
14–17	a′	
42:14–17	a	
18–25	b	
43:1–7	c	Cycle II
8–13	d	
14–15	E	Babylon's fall (predicted)
16–21	a′	
22–28	b′	
44:1–5	c′	
6–8	d′	
44:9–20	*	
21–22	a	Cycle III
23	b	
24–28	c	Cyrus conquers Babylon and makes the return to Jerusalem possible
45:1–7	c′	
8	b′	
9–13	a′	
45:14–46:2	*	
46:3–7	a	
8–11	b	Cycle IV
12–13	c	
47:1–15	D	Babylon's fall (realized)
48:1–11	a′	
12–16	b′	
17–21	c′	
48:20–21	a	
49:1–13	b	
14–21	c	
22–26	d	Cycle V
50:1–3	e	
4–11	f	
51:1–3	G	The rebuilding of Jerusalem
4–8	f′	
9–16	e′	
17–23	d′	
52:1–6	c′	
7–10	b′	
11–12	a′	
52:13–53:12		Epilogue to the cycles

Figure 3. See A. Laato, *The Servant of Yahweh and Cyrus* (ConBOT 35; Stockholm: Almqvist & Wiksell, 1992).

In this pattern, the introduction of special status for Israel as a servant people (C) is balanced by the climactic reference to the heritage of "the servants" (C′).[42]

A panel presenting liberated witnesses as a collective servant (F) is balanced by YHWH's confirmation of the poet's testimony (F′). Here we may agree with Buber and others, reading 50:4–9 as prophetic autobiography and not another Servant Song.

Introduction to the servant par excellence in the first Servant Song (D) is balanced by the lengthy poem of vindication in the final Servant Song (D′).

The introductory poem celebrating the incomparability of the Holy One of Israel (B) is balanced by description of the feast that is to be hosted by the Holy One of Israel (B′).

Good news for Jerusalem, first and last, is securely grounded in YHWH's word (A and A′). It was time to go home.

Final Isaiah

We have seen that at the heart of the chiastic structure in chaps. 56–66 is the material in the "Third" Isaiah that has always in fact sounded most like the "Second" Isaiah—the promise of full redemption of Zion's people, forming a model community as prelude to the conversion of the nations. If the poem in 50:4–9 is rightly understood as prophetic autobiography, Second Isaiah has understood himself as a 6th-century disciple (Heb. *limmud*) of the great 8th-century Isaiah. The earlier prophet had spoken words of both threat and promise to Israel/Judah and had lamented the prospects for foreign nations in his day, while proclaiming Assyria as agent of YHWH's administrative discipline (thus the larger part of chaps. 1–39). The familiar "swords and plowshares" oracle, anticipating Zion's international peace-making role, attributed to both Isaiah and Micah,[43] may well be older than either of those 8th-century prophets. Isaiah of Jerusalem had also promised that YHWH would preserve a "remnant" of the nation. At one point the 8th-century prophet withdrew from public life into the circle of his disciples (*limmudim*), who most likely represented that remnant.

In the view of both First Isaiah and Second Isaiah, foreign nations had sometimes served YHWH unknowingly (Assyria, Babylonia, Persia). And now, according to the poetry of the Third Isaiah, YHWH is going to work such a wonder (salvation of the marginalized faithful), that every knee will bow. The poetic imagination foresees at last that among the Gentile recruits who will speak for YHWH throughout the nations of the word, there will be some whom YHWH will take "as priests and as Levites" (66:21).

42. This is the sole occurrence of the plural, "servants," in chaps. 40–55, the last word preceding the climactic invitation to a covenantal feast (54:17).

43. Isa 2:1–4 // Mic 4:1–4.

Webster's Structural Analysis

					Periods
		Prelude	40:1–26		43
A		Israel, the chosen	40:27–42:9		73
		Introduction		40:27–41:7	
	a	The servant: the people Israel		41:8–16	
	b	The Preparer of the way		41:17–29	
	a	The servant: the faithful one		42:1–9	
B		Hope for the blind: Israel called	42:10–43:28		72
	a	The Lord acts (exodus)		42:10–17	
	b	The blind and the deaf, a despoiled people		42:18–25	
	a	The Lord's love (exodus)		43:1–7	
	b	The blind and deaf chosen		43:8–13	
	a	The Redeemer's way (exodus)		43:14–21	
	b	Israel's guilt: flagrant but forgiven		43:22–28	
A		Israel, formed from the womb	44:1–44:28 + 35:1–10		72
	a	The servant: the revived people		44:1–5	
	b	The Preparer of the way		35:1–10 + 44:6–10	
	a	Israel and the servant's word		44:21–28	
B		Redemption prepared: Babylon's fall	45:1–48:22		74 + 73 = 147
	a	Cyrus called for Jacob's sake		45:1–13	
	b	Israel saved and nations called by the Creator		45:14–25	
	c	Fall of the idols		46:1–13	74
	d	Babylon in the dust		47:1–7	
	c	No succor for the city		47:8–17	
	b	Former things declared; new things created		48:1–11	
	a	Cyrus and Jacob, guided by the Lord		48:12–22	
A		Israel and the prophet	49:1–50:11		76
	a	The servant: personified in the prophet		49:1–7	
	b	The Preparer of the way		49:8–26	
	a	The servant: the obedient sufferer		50:1–11	
B		Zion's deliverance	51:1–52:15		74
	a	To the exiles: salvation comes		51:1–8	
	a′	To the exiles: the Creator comes		51:9–16	
	b	To Jerusalem: the Restorer comes		51:17–23	
	b′	To Jerusalem: the Liberator comes		52:1–6	
	c	The Lord's return to Zion: salvation announced		52:7–10	
	c′	The servant exalted		52:11–15	
A		Restoration	53:1–55:13		74
	a	The servant: the righteous sufferer		53:1–12	
	b	The Redeemer		54:1–10	
	a	The heritage of the Lord's servant		54:11–17	
		Conclusion		55:1–13	

Figure 4. See A. Laato, *The Servant of Yahweh and Cyrus*, 13–16.

Conclusion

It appears that those who comprise the intimates of "Third" Isaiah had misread hyperbole in poems of the "Second" Isaiah. They had mistaken evocative poetry for a literal program and had been outmaneuvered. Jerusalem and the temple environs in the restoration period were but extremely poor copies of the originals, in no way fulfilling poetic expectations as set forth by the poet in exile.[44] And yet the transnational sweep of Second Isaiah's scenario was not lost on the final redactor, who arranged poetic units in a chiasm, placing salvation of foreigners first and last in the chiastic structure that centers precisely in the proclamation of a fully redeemed people. Universalism as well as YHWH's commitment to a particular people are here both powerfully affirmed. All Jerusalem's children would become disciples (Heb. *limmudîm*) of YHWH (54:13). That in turn would bring about the salvation of all the nations.

44. Isa 54:11–12.

Kippēr and Atonement in the Book of Isaiah

Michael L. Brown
Brownsville Revival School of Ministry

The root *k-p-r* has been the subject of considerable scholarly attention in the past two decades, dating back in particular to B. A. Levine's seminal study of cultic terminology published in 1974.[1] Of special note is the

Author's note: It is both an honor and a pleasure to dedicate this study to Prof. Levine, my principal mentor in Semitics and Bible from 1977 to 1983. I have been guided by the principle he articulated twenty years ago, namely, that "one whose ultimate goal it is to reconstruct biblical civilization will have to transcend philology, in the last analysis, but he cannot bypass it as the proper, first step in solving problems of biblical interpretation" (B. A. Levine, *In the Presence of the Lord: A Study of Cult and Some Cultic Terms in Ancient Israel* [Leiden: Brill, 1974] ix).

1. Levine, *In the Presence of the Lord*; cf. also idem, "*Kippûrîm*," *ErIsr* 9 (Albright Volume; 1969) 88–95 [Heb.]; other recent studies include B. Lang, "*kippēr*," *TWAT* 4.303–18; F. Maas, "*kpr*; pi, sühnen," *THAT* 1.842–57; H. C. Brichto, "On Slaughter and Sacrifice, Blood and Atonement," *HUCA* 47 (1976) 19–55; D. Kidner, "Sacrifice: Metaphors and Meaning," *TynBul* 33 (1982) 119–36; M. V. Kuzhivelil, "Reconciliation in the Old Testament," *Biblebhashyam* 9 (1983) 168–78 (*kpr* and *šlm*); D. McC. L. Judisch, "Propitiation in the Language and Typology of the Old Testament," *Concordia Theological Quarterly* 48 (1984) 221–43; F.-L. Hossfeld, "Versöhnung und Sünde," *BK* 41 (1986) 54–60; R. E. Averbeck, "*kpr*," in *New International Dictionary of Old Testament Theology and Exegesis* (5 vols.; ed W. Van Gemeren; Grand Rapids, Mich.: Zondervan, 1997) 2.689–710. The most comprehensive study of *kippēr* to date, with an exhaustive bibliography, is B. Janowski, *Sühne als Heilsgeschehen: Studien zur Sühnetheologie der Priesterschrift und zur Wurzel KPR im Alten Orient und im Alten Testament* (Neukirchen-Vluyn: Neukirchener Verlag, 1982); cf. further idem, "Auslösung des verwirkten Lebens," *ZTK* 79 (1982) 25–54; a review of recent literature dealing with *kpr* is included in M. A. Klopfenstein, "Alttestamenliche Themen in der neueren Forschung," *Theologische Rundschau* 53 (1988) 332–53; relevant themes are also treated in N. Kiuchi, *The Purification Offering in the Priestly Literature* (JSOTSup 56; Sheffield: Sheffield Academic Press, 1987); for the most recent treatment by J. Milgrom, see *Leviticus 1–16* (AB 3; New York: Doubleday, 1991) 1079–84. Other pertinent studies will be referred to in the balance of this paper.

emphasis that has been placed on etymology and comparative lexicography in treating the meaning and usage of *kippēr* in the Hebrew Bible, especially when one considers that the last twenty years have also witnessed a decided shift away from diachronic study in favor of the synchronic approach, which, in the broadest possible terms, can be characterized as a move away from philology and toward linguistics.[2] Thus, Levine's premise has been borne out that "in studying the verb *kippēr* the importance of etymology and comparative lexicography cannot be overemphasized."[3] It will be the purpose of this study to demonstrate how mistaken philological presuppositions concerning the root meaning of Heb. *kippēr* have led to and continue to lead to exegetical and theological inaccuracies, seen with particular clarity in the book of Isaiah, carrying implications for later Jewish and Christian thought.

With respect to Jewish law and theology, Isa 22:14 (with *kpr* in the *Pual*) became the locus classicus in the discussion of the ultimate atoning power of one's own death (this is treated in greater length at the conclusion of this study). Implications relating to Christian theology include: (1) the common teaching that in the Old Testament, sins were only 'covered' (based especially on the traditional understanding of *kpr*) as opposed to being 'wiped away' (although such teaching, for the most part, is limited to popular, nonscholarly circles); and (2) the strong emphasis placed on the necessity of blood for atonement (cf. Heb 9:22; and see Rashi to *b. Yoma* 5a; Tosafot to *b. Zebaḥ*. 6a, sub *wĕhălôʾ*; note also the Maimonidean reference to the Temple altar as the *mizbaḥ kapparâ* in *Mishneh Torah, Hilkhot Teshuvah* 1:3, and cf. *b. Sukk.* 55b). This presents exegetical problems when *kippēr* (automatically associated with 'expiation' and 'atonement') occurs in bloodless contexts (as in, e.g., Isa 27:9, for which see below).[4] First, however, it will be useful to review the two main approaches to the etymology and semantic development of *kpr*.[5]

2. There is, of course, considerable overlap in the sciences, not to mention a certain fluidity of use in the terms themselves. The articles published in *ZAH* 6 (1993) 3–123, are, by and large, germane to these issues; and note especially J. Greenfield, "Etymological Semantics," ibid., 26–37; cf. further my paper, "Etymology and Semantics: A Positive Assessment for Semitic Studies," delivered at the North American Conference of Afroasiatic Linguistics (1992), and forthcoming.

3. Levine, *In the Presence*, 56. Some, however, view the spate of etymological discussions of *kpr* as ultimately adding little or nothing of real substance to our understanding of the biblical usage; cf., e.g., the remarks of S. Herrmann, below.

4. For a critique of some of these historic Christian interpretations, cf. M. Anderson and P. Culbertson, "The Inadequacy of the Christian Doctrine of Atonement in Light of Levitical Sin Offering" (*ATR* [1986] 303–28), incorporating also recent philological advances in the understanding of *kippēr* (though, in my judgment, it goes too far in "correcting" the perceived problems).

5. Cf. J. A. Fitzmyer ("The Targum of Leviticus from Qumran Cave 4," *Maarav* 1 [1978] 15), who notes that the etymological debate surrounding *kpr* "has shifted

The classic (and by no means obsolete) understanding of *kpr* devolves from the concept of 'covering' and is based on both cognate evidence, in particular Arab. *kafara/kaffara*, as well as apparent biblical usage, which (outside of Gen 6:14) includes a comparison of Jer 18:23 with Neh 3:37, where the latter has *tĕkas* ('cover up') in place of Jeremiah's *tĕkappēr*.[6] Thus one achieves atonement by means of covering one's sins from the deity's sight. The nominal Hebrew form *kōper* then means 'ransom, bribe' because it covers the offense in the eyes of God or the judge (or, because it covers their eyes so as not to see the offense), while the cultic *kappōret* is the 'lid' or 'covering' of the ark. Relevant to this is the observation by J. A. Fitzmyer that *kappōret* in Lev 16:14 is rendered by the Qumran Targum with *kĕsāyāʾ*, indicating that it "was understood by at least one group of pre-Christian Palestinian Jews as the 'cover' or 'lid' over the ark of the testimony in the Holy of Holies."[7] The other approach sees the fundamental meaning of *kpr* as 'wiping away'. It was first articulated by Rashi (see immediately below), considered last century by W. R. Smith, who based himself on Aram. usage, and championed in this century by Levine (although anticipated by G. B. Gray and G. R. Driver), who relied in particular on Akk. usage (*kapāru/kuppuru*) and apparent biblical evidence as well.[8] Thus, the original cultic concept

---

ground" from KB to *HALAT*, with the former presupposing a *Grundbedeutung* of 'cover' for usage in the Hebrew Bible (see KB, 451–52), while the latter (see *HALAT* 2.470) "begins the whole discussion with meanings like 'überstreichen' (smear over), 'abwischen' (wipe away), or 'sühnen' (expiate)." Fitzmyer, however, does not mention KB's closing etymological remarks, which set forth both views as possible (p. 452b).

6. Cf., e.g., S. P. Tregelles (ed.), *Gesenius' Hebrew and Chaldee Lexicon* (repr. Grand Rapids: Eerdmans, 1949) 411; BDB 497–98 (although W. R. Smith's suggestion to begin with definitions such as 'wash away, rub off' is cited; see below, n. 8, and cf. also nn. 15, 19); R. B. Girdlestone, *Synonyms of the Old Testament* (repr. Grand Rapids: Eerdmans, 1974) 127–31; for a recent study, cf. E. Beaucamp, "Aux origines du mot 'rédemption': Le 'rachat' dans l'Ancien Testament" (*Laval théologique et philosophique* 34 [1978] 49–56), where it is argued that the LXX's rendering of *kōper* with *lutrō* (five times out of thirteen total occurrences) is not correct, since the fundamental meaning of the Hebrew root is 'cover'. Similar views will be cited as relevant, below. For a different reading of the biblical material, see Levine, *In the Presence*, 56–58.

7. Fitzmyer, "The Targum of Leviticus," 15. See also K. Beyer, *Die aramäischen Texte vom Toten Meer* (Göttingen: Vandenhoeck & Ruprecht, 1983) 279. Cf. further P. W. Coxon ("*šyqw*['*šmy*'] in 11QtgJob XXXI,7," *IEJ* 27 [1977] 207–8), who follows the initial editors' reconstruction of Aram. *šyqw*['*šmy*'] in Job 38:29, corresponding to Hebrew *kĕpōr šāmayim* ('hoarfrost of the sky') but misunderstood by the Targum as meaning 'covering of the sky' and thus serving as another indication that some early translators equated *kpr* with 'cover'; for a very different reading, cf., e.g., Beyer, *Die aramäischen Texte*, 295 (*šyqy*[*h*] *m*[*n yld*]*h*, rendered with '[*wer hat* sein] Schmelzen [*hervorgebracht*]?').

8. Cf. F. Buhl, *Wilhelm Gesenius' Hebräisches und Aramäisches Handwörterbuch über das Alte Testament* (repr. Berlin: Springer, 1962) 359 ('sühnen'), with reference to both

was that sin was expiated by means of its being wiped away or removed, and *kōper*, in Levine's words, was a "payment made for the purpose of erasing or 'wiping away' guilt incurred by the offense,"[9] while the *kappōret* was the 'propitiatory' or 'place/means of expiation'. This is the classic rendering of the LXX (*hilastērion*); see also the Vulgate's *propitiatorium* (6×) and the Peshiṭta's *ḥūsāyāʾ* (from *ḥsy* 'to pity, spare').

Interestingly, as pointed out by Fitzmyer, the first occurrence of *kappōret* (Exod 25:17) is rendered in the LXX with *hilastērion epithema* (the latter meaning 'lid'), but thereafter—beginning with the very next verse!—it is simply *hilastērion.*[10] One might also compare here the practice of some modern versions that, unable to decide between the meanings of 'cover' and 'means of expiation', choose to *combine* both meanings (cf., e.g., the NIV's 'atonement cover'), something, however, which the Hebrew almost certainly did *not* convey (see further BDB 498, where it is claimed that the term 'propitiatory' is to be derived from the concept of covering over sin, whereas the rendering 'covering' or 'lid' has "no justification in usage").[11] In any case, because there is at least one definite example of a Hebrew *k-p-r* with the sense of 'cover' (namely, Gen 6:14b, which is also the only occurrence of *kpr* in the *Qal*) and because this sense is also evidenced in other Semitic languages, the verbal usage of the Hebrew root has often been subdivided into *kpr* I and *kpr* II.[12] Others, most notably B. Landsberger, followed by J. Milgrom, de-

---

W. R. Smith, *The Old Testament in the Jewish Church* (cf. the 2d ed.; London: Black, 1908) and Rashi on Gen 32:21 (see immediately below), along with Jewish Aram. and Syr. *kĕpar* and Akk. *kuppuru*, although he compares other Semitic roots that mean both 'cover' and 'forgive' (e.g., Arab. *ǵfr* and *'q'*), as possible explanations for the Hebrew usage; see also G. B. Gray, *Sacrifice in the Old Testament* (repr. New York: Ktav, 1968) 67–73; G. R. Driver, "Studies in the Vocabulary of the Old Testament," *JTS* 34 (1933) 33–44 (specifically, 34–38; see also below, n. 23).

9. Levine, *In the Presence*, 61.

10. Fitzmyer, "The Targum of Leviticus," 15; cf. p. 16 for discussion of the Vulgate and Peshiṭta as well; the only exception to the LXX's rendering with *hilastērion* is 1 Chr 28:11. See also J. Lust, E. Eynikel, and K. Hauspie, A *Greek-English Lexicon of the Septuagint* (Stuttgart: Deutsche Bibelgesellschaft, 1992), part I/A-I, p. 214.

11. For further philological discussion, cf. J.-M. de Tarragon ("La *kappōret* est-elle une fiction ou un élément du culte tardif?" *RB* 88 [1981] 5–12), who regards the *kappōret* as the pedestal for the cherubim. For etymological explanations of *kappōret* based on alleged Egyptian borrowings, cf. Y. M. Grintz, "Archaic Terms in the Priestly Code," *Leš* 39 (1974–75) 163–81 (especially 163–68); M. Görg, "Eine neue Deutung für *kappōret*," *ZAW* 89 (1977) 115–18; idem, "Nachtrag zu *kappōret*," *Biblische Notizen* 5 (1978) 12. These proposals, however, have gained little support.

12. In contrast to BDB, Gesenius-Buhl, *Handwörterbuch*, and *HALAT*, all of which subdivide verbal *kpr* into I and II, KB makes no such distinction. For discussion of the proposed division of Akk. *kapāru* into I ('trim, strip, clip off'), II ('wipe off'), and III ('smear with bitumen', denominative from *kupru*), see concisely H. R.

rived both the meanings of 'cover' and 'wipe off' from one and the same root, suggesting a proto-meaning 'to rub' (hence, 'to rub off' → 'to efface, wipe away'; 'to rub on' → 'to cover').[13]

Naturally, it is impossible to *prove* the correctness of any of the positions just set forth, especially when seeking to reconstruct the prehistoric *Grundbedeutung* of a proto-Semitic root.[14] Furthermore, S. Herrmann argued years ago that "the various Semitic analogies do not permit us to make a definitive distinction between 'to cover' and 'to wash away'," stating that "There are Semitic analogies for regarding forgiveness of sins both in terms of covering and in terms of washing away."[15] This is similar to the verdict of B. Janowski (*Sühne*) who, after treating the Semitic data in depth, views the cognate evidence as inconclusive. Nonetheless, it seems clear that recent studies have sufficiently demonstrated that Biblical Hebrew *kippēr* includes the semantic range of 'wipe away' and, consequently, the failure to recognize this can lead to unnecessary exegetical difficulties.

A good example of wrong philological presuppositions leading to interpretive confusion is found in Gen 32:21, where an anxious Jacob sends gifts to his estranged brother, Esau, saying, *ʾăkappĕrâ pānāyw bamminḥâ hahōleket lĕpānāy*, rendered by E. A. Speiser 'If I first propitiate him with advance presents', with the comment that 'propitiate' is literally 'screen the face'.[16] According to G. von Rad, "Jacob speaks quite frankly about 'reconciliation' with Esau, more precisely about covering his face,"[17] and C. Westermann claims that "the consequence of covering the face is that he no longer sees the guilt."[18] Rashi, however, explains that Jacob's intent was to appease Esau's anger (*ʾăbaṭṭēl rûgzāyw*), noting that in his opinion, "every time *kappārâ* occurs with the words 'guilt' and 'sin' or with the word 'face,' it is to be interpreted as an expression of wiping off (*qinnûaḥ*) or removal (*haʿăbārâ*)." Thus, as suggested by Levine (with no reference to Rashi), the expression *ʾăkappĕrâ pānāyw* is to be interpreted as an abbreviated idiom meaning 'that

(C.) Cohen, *Biblical Hapax Legomena in the Light of Akkadian and Ugaritic* (SBLDS 37; Missoula, Mont.: Scholars Press, 1978) 53–54 n. 8, with reference to B. Landsberger, Levine, AHw and CAD (see also n. 13, immediately below).

13. Cf. B. Landsberger, *The Date Palm and Its By-Products according to the Cuneiform Sources* (AfO Beiheft 17; 1967) 32; Milgrom, *Leviticus 1–16*, 1080.

14. For reflections on the value of such endeavors, in addition to the works cited above in n. 2, cf. my *Israel's Divine Healer* (Studies in Old Testament Biblical Theology; Grand Rapids: Zondervan, 1995) 28–30 (with notes on pp. 255–60).

15. S. Herrmann, "*kpr*" (sub "*hileos*"), *TDNT* 3.302, citing W. R. Smith for support.

16. E. A. Speiser, *Genesis* (AB 1; Garden City, N.Y.: Doubleday, 1964) 253, 255.

17. G. von Rad, Genesis (OTL; trans. J. H. Marks; rev. ed., Philadelphia: Westminster, 1976) 319.

18. C. Westermann, *Genesis 12–36* (trans. J. J. Scullion; Minneapolis: Augsburg, 1985) 510; cf. also R. A. Soloff, "Yom Kippur: Cover Up or Plea for Probation?" *Jewish Bible Quarterly* 25 (1997) 86–89.

I may wipe off (the wrath) from his countenance'.[19] This understanding is more suitable contextually and is also psychologically appropriate, since Jacob offers Esau gifts with the hope of appeasing his anger, not covering over his previous shameful actions (although one could argue that Jacob's gifts were a kind of *kōper* to appease Esau's anger *by means* of covering Esau's face to his brother's previous deceitful deeds).[20]

Now, when Rashi sought to demonstrate the appropriateness of his interpretation of Gen 32:21, he not only cited examples of similar usages of Talmudic Aramaic *kpr*, but he also provided two clear instances of parallel usage from the book of Isaiah, namely Isa 28:18 and 47:11. And, while some might still argue for the traditional understanding of Gen 32:21, it appears certain that Isa 28:18, Rashi's first example, can only be explained with reference to the etymological understanding of 'wiping away' or 'removing'.

We read in Isa 28:18 *wĕkūppār bĕrîtĕkem ʾet-māwet wĕḥāzûtĕkem ʾet-šĕʾôl lōʾ tāqûm*, translated in the NJPSV 'Your covenant with Death shall be annulled, your pact with Sheol shall not endure'. (Note also the graphic references in v. 17 to the hail that "shall *sweep away* the refuge of falsehood" and the flood-waters that shall "*carry off* your shelter" [my emphasis], as well as to the "sweeping flood" of v. 18 that will pass through.) Now all this makes perfect sense in light of the meaning of *kūppār* suggested by Rashi and others. It is also in harmony with the LXX's rendering of *kūppār* with *aphēlē* (from *aphaireō* 'to take away, remove') and *Tg. J.*'s *wîbaṭṭēl*. Those seeking to derive *kūppār* from a root meaning 'to cover' generally emend to *tūpār* with no textual justification and with only a scant parallel in Isa 8:10. In contrast, the pre-Assyriological attempt of J. A. Alexander to exegete this passage in terms of *kpr* = "*covering*, or perhaps more specifically *smearing over*,"[21] actually comes very close to the proper sense, indicating the degree of semantic overlap that can occur between 'smearing over' and 'smearing off'. Those emending to *tūpār* often point to the Targum's *b-ṭ-l* for support (sometimes with reference to the LXX's *aphaireō* as well),[22] but the Targumic rendering may well reflect an accurate understanding of *kūppār*. See, for example,

19. Levine, *In the Presence*, 60; cf. already BDB 497, which cites Smith: "'wipe clean the face,' blackened by displeasure, as the Arabs say, 'whiten the face'" (from *The Old Testament in the Jewish Church*, 381).

20. For a more thorough treatment, cf. A. Schenker ("*kōper* et expiation," *Bib* 63 [1982] 32–46; repr. in idem, *Text und Sinn im Alten Testament: Textgeschichtliche und bibeltheologische Studien* [OBO 103; Freiburg: Universitätsverlag / Göttingen: Vandenhoeck & Ruprecht, 1991] 120–34), who compares Gen 32:21 with Prov 16:14 and concludes that a translation such as 'mollify, placate', based on such nominal meanings for *kōper*, is appropriate.

21. J. A. Alexander, *Commentary on the Prophecies of Isaiah* (orig. ed., 1846; repr. Grand Rapids: Zondervan, 1974) 455–56.

22. Cf. the typical statement of Maas, "Der Text wird von den meisten nach dem Targum in *wᵉtūfār* 'wird zerbrochen' (*prr* ho.) geändert," "*kpr*," 852.

Rashi's comment on Gen 32:21 above, in which he used the Hebrew verb *bṭl* to explain *kpr* there, and see further David Qimḥi (Radaq) to Isa 28:18, where he explains *wĕkūppār* "and it will be abolished [*wĕyitbaṭṭēl*; so also Rashi] and removed [*wĕyûsār*]," comparing Prov 16:14b, *wĕʾîš ḥākām yĕkappărenāh*. This last verse is cited here as well by Ibn Ezra, who adds, "in the sense of destruction [*hašḥātâ*] and removal [*hasārâ*]"; see also Ibn Ezra to Isa 27:9, cited below. Note further that the LXX renders *kippēr* in Isa 27:9 with *aphaireō*, where few, if any, would seek to emend *kpr*.[23]

Modern English versions, which almost always place *kippēr* within the semantic domain of atonement and forgiveness (e.g., the RSV, NKJV, NIV, TEV, old JPSV), here render with 'annul, disannul' or the like, some with a marginal note reflecting a proposed emendation to *tūpār* and others without such a reference, apparently on the strength of the ancient versions.[24] It should be pointed out, however, that the LXX renders *kippēr* with *aphaireō* in both Isa 27:9a and 28:18a, also rendering *sar* in 27:9b with *aphaireō*. (For a similar phenomenon, in which two distinct Hebrew roots in parallel clauses are rendered with one and the same lexeme, see for example *Tg. Onq.* to Exod 32:13, where *šûb* and *nḥm* are both rendered with forms of *tûb*, due, no doubt, to the philological equation between *šûb* and *tûb*, on the one hand, and to the ideological connection between *nḥm* and *tûb*, on the other hand.) The LXX also renders *sār* with *aphaireō* in Isa 6:7b (in parallelism again with *kpr* in the *Pual*, which this time is translated with *perikatharizō*) and often elsewhere, clearly underscoring the meaning of 'remove' in the LXX's rendering of *kippēr* in both Isa 27:9a and 28:18a.

More interesting from a religious and theological viewpoint is Isa 6:7, where the prophet, having had the burning coal from God's altar touch his sinful lips, hears the words *hinnēh nāgaʿ zeh ʿal-śĕpātêkā* 'now, this has touched your lips', *wĕsār ʿăwōnekā wĕḥaṭṭaʾtĕkā tĕkūppār* 'and your iniquity has departed and your sin been purged away'. In light of our previous observations, as well as the parallelism between *sār* and *kūppār*, there seems to be no compelling reason to read this verse in terms of expiation. Yet, with a fundamentally different notion of the root meaning of *kippēr*, Franz Delitzsch launches into an eloquent discussion of the expiatory powers of the flames of

23. See further G. R. Driver, "'Another Little Drink': Isaiah 28:1–22," in *Words and Meanings: Essays Presented to David Winton Thomas* (ed. P. R. Ackroyd and B. Lindars; Cambridge; Cambridge University Press, 1968) 47–67 (specifically, 60–61), who also cites the rendering of Symmachus (*exaleiphthēsetai* 'it shall be blotted out') and counters the objection that the grammatically masculine *kūppār* cannot be used with the feminine subject *bĕrît*, for which cf. further P. Joüon and T. Muraoka, A *Grammar of Biblical Hebrew* (Rome: Pontifical Biblical Institute, 1991) 554–55, §150j.

24. Commenting on the AV's rendering here with 'disannul', Girdlestone (*Synonyms*, 129) explains: "This use of the Caphar is interesting. To be disannulled is to be treated as nonexistent; and this is the way in which God covers sin; to use the vivid language of the Bible, He casts it behind His back."

divine love, stating that "the fire, which revealed itself in the smoke and consumed the incense-offering, and which must necessarily have been divine because of its expiatory power, was in effect the love of God with which He reciprocated the offerings of the seraphim."[25] Similarly, albeit with less poetic flair, O. Kaiser notes that, "Isaiah, cleansed from sin and blessed against every expectation, can now hear the voice of God and answer it in the right way," observing that, "because the coal comes from the consecrated altar, it possesses in itself an atoning and purifying force for the congregation (Num. 16:46f.)."[26] H. Wildberger suprisingly renders 'your sin is covered' but then explains that "The verb *kpr* (cover over) belongs to the vocabulary of the cult [with reference to J. J. Stamm and G. R. Driver] . . . and it is used in this special sense for an act of expiation to remove bloodguilt . . . ," adding, "It is naturally not just by chance that Isaiah uses this exact verb in this place, since he is relating this to details of a well-known cultic rite."[27]

Now, while there is truth to Wildberger's insistence on the cultic background to this cleansing event,[28] and while Kaiser is correct in terms of his emphasis on the expiatory powers of the altar and that which comes from it, one wonders whether discussions such as these—which could easily be multiplied—would occur if a wider semantic range for *kippēr* were more fully considered. (The words "more fully considered"—as opposed to "recognized"—are carefully chosen here since virtually all the 20th-century scholars cited are doubtless cognizant of the argument that *kpr* can mean 'wipe away'.) Note, however, that Milgrom, who certainly *has* fully considered the meaning of *kpr*, writes: "Here we have an amalgam of both the early and the late stages of *kippēr*. Isaiah is purged by contact with a sacred detergent (the altar coal), and at the same time his sins are *expiated*" (his emphasis).[29] But should the last meaning really be included here?[30] Certainly, there is no reason to think that Isaiah did not experience a real sense of forgiveness and internal cleansing in his visionary experience, yet the wider context and specific language speak rather of the *removal* of the stain of sin from the prophet's lips. It would seem unjustifiable therefore to follow translations similar to the ones found in, for example, the RSV, NASB, TEV ('for-

25. F. Delitzsch and C. F. Keil, *Isaiah* (trans. James Martin; Commentary on the Old Testament 5/1; repr. Grand Rapids: Eerdmans, 1973) 197.

26. O. Kaiser, *Isaiah 13–39* (trans. R. A. Wilson; OTL; Philadelphia: Westminster, 1974) 81.

27. H. Wildberger, *Isaiah 1–12* (trans. T. H. Trapp; Minneapolis: Fortress, 1991) 248–70.

28. Many scholars point to analogous purification rituals in Egypt and Mesopotamia; cf., e.g., ibid., 270; J. H. Hayes and S. A. Irvine, *Isaiah the Eighth-Century Prophet: His Times and His Preaching* (Nashville: Abingdon, 1987) 111.

29. Milgrom, *Leviticus 1–16*, 1084.

30. Cf. also, more broadly, Brichto, "On Slaughter and Sacrifice, Blood and Atonement."

given'), NIV ('atoned for'; see old JPSV's 'expiated'), and modern commentaries.[31] See also the recent commentary of J. A. Motyer, wherein it is claimed that *kpr* here (and frequently elsewhere) means 'atone' in the sense of 'to effect a *kōper*' or 'ransom price', thus pointing to "the death of the substitute sacrifice on the altar" as the payment that "divine justice sees as sufficient to cover the sinner's debt."[32] However, while it is widely recognized that *kippēr* is often used in the sense of 'to effect a *kōper*', Motyer's treatment is not appropriate with regard to Isa 6:7.

Turning to Isa 27:9, we are confronted with a theological dilemma caused by a narrow understanding of *kippēr*. For in contrast to Isa 6:7, where notions of atonement can at least be supported by the reference to the coal taken from the altar, 27:9 leaves no such way of escape. Surprisingly, J. N. Oswalt actually deduces relevant truths concerning the Christian doctrine of atonement from the usage of *kippēr* in this verse. This is in spite of the fact that Oswalt, who provides his own translation of a section of Sargon's letter to the god Ashur, is quite aware that *kippēr* might mean 'wipe away', citing G. R. Driver in reference to Isa 28:18, although he states that, "*kpr* normally means 'cover up' and not 'annul' as here [i.e., Isa 28:18]. . . ."[33] More appropriately, the NJPSV translates this verse: "Assuredly, by this alone shall Jacob's sin be purged away; this is the only price for removing his guilt: that he make all the altar-stones like shattered blocks of chalk—with no sacred post left standing, nor any incense altar" (the text again exhibits parallelism between *kippēr* in the *Pual* and *sār*, this time in the *Hiphil*, as well as once more joining together the nouns *ʿāwōn* and *ḥaṭṭāʾt*, reading *lākēn bĕzōʾt yĕkūppār ʿăwōn-yaʿăqōb wĕzeh kol-pĕrî hasir ḥaṭṭaʾtô*). Of course, the presence of words such as "iniquity" and "sin" immediately leads most interpreters to think in terms of *expiation*. (Among the works previously cited, those of Janowski and Hossfeld in particular make reference to the usage of *kippēr* in the context of human guilt.) Moreover, the division between "cultic" and "noncultic" life contexts may not have been as strict as modern literary critics might imagine (cf. also the comments of Milgrom on Isa 6:7, cited above). Nonetheless, in a study such as this, where the primary question deals with issues of interpretation, exegesis, and theology, distinctions between the varied senses of *kippēr* are important.

31. Cf., among many, J. N. Oswalt, *The Book of Isaiah 1–39* (NICOT; Grand Rapids: Eerdmans, 1986) 171 ('atoned for') 184–85; and note J. D. W. Watts (*Isaiah 1–33* [WBC; Waco, Tex.: Word, 1985] 67), who renders, 'Your sin has been atoned!' although his translation of the Hebrew passive form results in rather infelicitious English, since the verb 'atone' in English requires an indirect object (i.e., instead of sin being "atoned," English usage requires "atoned for").

32. J. A. Motyer, *The Prophecy of Isaiah: An Introduction and Commentary* (Downers Grove, Ill.: InterVarsity, 1993) 78.

33. G. R. Driver, *Isaiah 1–39*, 515 n. 9; cf. pp. 496, 498 for Driver's treatment of Isa 27:9; for his rendering of the Sargon text, cf. pp. 704–5.

In the specific text at hand, the prophet is not speaking of atonement but rather of the removal and wiping out of shameful idolatrous practices. This understanding is also reflected in the LXX with its rendering of *kūppār* with *aphaireō* (as in 28:18, discussed above, but contrast here *Tg. J.*'s 'forgiven'), and it is concisely expressed by Abraham Ibn Ezra who states: "the meaning (of the words) is that the decree (of judgment) will be abolished if they abolish (their) idolatrous worship." (Note that 'abolish' in this quotation both times renders Hebrew *bṭl*, which, as pointed out above, is used several times by the classical rabbinic commentaries and once by *Tg. J.* to explain or translate the meaning of *kippēr*.) Yet even G. B. Gray, in spite of his fairly accurate exegesis of this verse, found it appropriate to translate 'Therefore on this condition shall the iniquity of Jacob be expiated', although there is no hint of expiation to be found.[34] See similarly RSV, NRSV, NAB, NIV, TEV, and the old JPSV. The NASB goes one step further, rendering *kūppār* with 'forgiven' and then *hāsir* with 'pardoning'(!). Thus, the association of *kippēr* with 'atone, forgive' was so strong in the minds of the translators that it actually controlled their rendering of *sûr*, the meaning of which is clearly *not* 'pardon' but rather 'remove'. J. D. W. Watts also rendered *kūppār* with 'be expiated', although in his comments he referred to the *removal* of the "accumulated guilt of Israel's sins."[35] However, for the conservative evangelical scholar E. J. Young, again translating with 'be expiated', one can read between the lines and sense that this verse presented a theological difficulty: How can sin be atoned for without a blood sacrifice? Thus he explains: "the prophet is not stating that the exile provided an atonement for the iniquity of Israel, but merely that by means of exile, there was purification."[36]

Yet the text here does not speak of atonement; rather this concept has been read into the verse by a misinterpretation of the meaning of *kippēr*. A more fruitful line of discussion might have been to begin with the concept of 'removing" and 'wiping away' iniquity and sin, then moving to the issue of how sin was dealt with cultically in Israel, that is, how was sin removed → expiated?[37] This also opens up the broad questions of the historical development of the phenomenology of Israelite religion, in particular the question of how abstract, religious concepts and rites developed out of more "earthly" concepts and rites. And it is right to ask just how greatly the "average Israelite" separated such concepts; in other words, how great a distance was per-

34. G. B. Gray, *The Book of Isaiah* (ICC; Edinburgh: T. & T. Clark, 1912) 456, 458.

35. Watts, *Isaiah 1–33*, 350.

36. E. J. Young, *The Book of Isaiah* (3 vols.; Grand Rapids: Eerdmans, 1970) 2.242; cf. Alexander (*Isaiah*, 440), "*yĕkūppār*, though it strictly means *shall be atoned for*, is here metonymically used to denote the effect and not the cause, purification and not expiation." The NKJV renders 'covered' here.

37. Cf. more broadly D. P. Wright, *The Disposal of Impurity* (SBLDS 101; Atlanta: Scholars Press, 1987); and see also idem, "Day of Atonement," *ABD* 2.72–76.

ceived between the concepts of 'wipe away', 'expiate', and 'forgive'? And from a cultic perspective, how distinct were the concepts of 'expiation' and 'propitiation'? However, this discussion, in spite of its perennial interest, takes us too far afield for now.

Before turning to the last theologically significant usage of *kippēr* in Isaiah, we should cite the other two occurrences of the root in this prophetic book for the sake of completeness. First, in Isa 43:3, the exiles are told that God gave Egypt as a *ransom* (*kōper*) for His people, Ethiopia and Saba in exchange (*taḥat*) for them. Quite clearly, *kōper* simply means 'ransom', with no possible nuance of expiation to be found, which, of course, is unexceptional for the noun. Similarly, Isa 47:11 contains no reference to atonement, although the translation of the whole verse is not entirely clear. As rendered in the NJPSV, 'Evil is coming upon you which you will not know how to charm away,[38] disaster is falling upon you which you which you will not be able to appease' (*lōʾ tûkĕlî kappĕrāh*). Obviously, one does not make atonement for 'disaster' (*hōwâ*); one wards it off or appeases the divine anger that has determined the punishment. Thus C. R. North, also translating with 'appease', correctly notes that "'Expiate' (RSV), the more usual sense of the verb, is surely wrong here."[39] Rather, the usage here may well be similar to the usage discussed above in Gen 32:21 (cf. again Prov 16:14), or *kappĕrāh* may simply mean 'wipe it out' in the sense of 'make it go away'.

Of the modern English versions consulted, only the NIV actually tried to combine the context with a usage of *kippēr* clearly related to *kōper*, rendering *lōʾ tûkĕlî kappĕrāh* with 'ward off with a ransom', explained by Motyer[40] as meaning, 'it cannot be bought off'. As previously noted, the view that some instances of biblical *kippēr* are to be explained as denominative/semantic developments from *kōper* is common. Similar to the NASB's extremely forced rendering of *hāsir* with 'pardon' at Isa 27:9 (cf. the discussion to this verse, above) is the RSV's rendering of *šaḥrāh* here with 'expiate'(!), dictated once again by the rendering of *kippēr* with 'atone'. This is corrected in the NRSV, which renders 'charm away' and 'ward off'. See also the NKJV, which renders 'put it off' in the text but adds in the marginal note, 'cover it; atone for it'; and note the LXX's *katharos genēsthai*.

38. The footnote points out that the meaning of Hebrew *šaḥrāh* (NJPSV's 'charm away') is unclear, and the common emendation to read 'bribe', that is, *šaḥdāh*, is suggested.

39. C. R. North, *The Second Isaiah* (Oxford: Oxford University Press, 1964) 72. This verse is also noteworthy in that it contains the only instance of *kpr* in the *Piel* in Isaiah, and still its usage seems to fall outside of the semantic range of 'expiate, atone'. Regardless of questions of authorship, this could be another instance of the language of the book of Isaiah evidencing notable stylistic and linguistic similarities throughout.

40. Motyer, *Isaiah*, 374.

In any case, Isa 47:11 has not served as a proof text in support of a major theological position. The same, however, cannot be said of Isa 22:14, a text that plays a "supporting" role in traditional Jewish theological discussion of atonement.[41] The context for this important passage is well known. The prophet, having announced one last divine call for his people to repent with weeping, mourning, rending of clothes and girding of sackcloth, is shocked by what he sees and hears: joy and gladness, killing of cattle and slaughtering of sheep, eating of meat and drinking of wine, "Eat and drink, for tomorrow we die!" Thus he receives the terrible divine oath *ʾim-yĕkūppār heʿāwōn hazzeh lākem ʿad-tĕmūtûn* 'Surely this iniquity shall not be purged from you until you die'.

Now at this point it must be confessed that almost all ancient and modern translations—the Vulgate (rendering here *dimittetur* 'send away', exactly as in Isa 27:9), the AV, and the NEB/REB being notable exceptions[42]—return to the traditional sense of 'forgive, expiate' or the like. See the renderings of 'be forgiven' in the LXX (*aphethēsetai*); *Tg. J.* (*yištĕbaq*); as well as, for example, in the RSV, NRSV, NASB, TEV, and NJPSV; see also the NAB ('pardoned'); the old JPSV ('expiated'); and the NIV ('atoned for'; cf. the NKJV's 'atonement'). *Tg. J.* even adds the interpretive gloss that the death spoken of here is "the second death," which Rashi quotes referring to the world to come. As stated, this verse became the biblical underpinning for the later Talmudic discussion of the atoning power of one's death, a discussion that may be briefly reviewed here.

The specific debate before the sages had to do with the subject of the various levels of transgression (specifically, three or four classes) and the necessary means of atoning for them (*b. Yoma* 85b–86a; *t. Yoma* 5(4).6–9; and see *m. Yoma* 8:8). Thus if one violates a positive commandment and repents, he is immediately forgiven (with reference to Jer 3:22), but if he violates a negative commandment and repents, his forgiveness is suspended until the Day of

41. For a traditional Jewish discussion of the different functions of *asmakta* (lit. 'support', in the sense of 'supporting text, proof text'), cf. "*ʾasmaktāʾ*, I," *Talmudic Encylopedia* (rev. ed.; Jerusalem: Talmudic Encyclopedia Institute, 1986) 105–8 [Heb.]; see more broadly D. W. Halivni, *Peshat and Derash* (New York and Oxford: Oxford University Press, 1991), especially 13–16.

42. Cf. also Hayes and Irvine, *Isaiah*, 283 ('purged', with reference to their treatment of Isa 27:9, on pp. 317–18). It is extremely interesting to note that, although the AV renders *kippēr* 'atone' or the like about 80 times, it renders *kippēr* in Isa 6:7, 22:14, and 27:9 with 'purge' (likewise Prov 16:6), 28:18 with 'disannul', and 47:11 with 'put it off'; cf. Girdlestone, *Synonyms*, 128–29. Thus, none of the verbal occurrences of *kippēr* in Isaiah are rendered as 'atone' by the AV. Among modern versions, only the NEB and REB boast a similar phenomenon, due, no doubt, to the influence of Driver (see "Studies in the Vocabulary of the Old Testament" and "Another Little Drink"). If one does not accept the theory of influence by rabbinic commentaries on the translators, then an explanation for the AV translation is that the bloodless context of the Isaianic passages was a prime factor in the translators' thinking.

Atonement (this is supported by Lev 16:30).[43] If he transgresses a commandment punishable by *kārēt*[44] or liable to capital punishment by the Court and then repents, both his repentance and the effects of the Day of Atonement are held in abeyance, and he achieves atonement by means of suffering (*yissûrîn*; citing Ps 89:33). In the event, however, that he is guilty of profaning the divine Name, the merits of his repentance, the Day of Atonement, and his chastisements are all suspended (or, provide partial atonement), and it is only death that cleanses (*mîtâ měmāreqet*) and procures complete atonement, as it is said, ". . . surely this iniquity shall not be forgiven you until you die" (Isa 22:14). All this is repeated virtually verbatim by Maimonides in his code (*Hilkhot Teshuvah* 1:4), with Isa 22:14 being cited again as the final proof text.[45] In this context, it should also be noted that the rabbinic usage of *mrq* ('polish, scourge', here in the sense of 'cleanse, purge') is quite appropriate in conjunction with *kpr*, and both roots exhibit a similar semantic development from physical purging (or scouring; wiping away) to spiritual purging (or wiping away; cleansing).[46]

In any case, putting halakhic midrash aside, does Isa 22:14 relate to atonement at or through death? First, it is better to understand the Hebrew oath clause as expressing the fact that this terrible sin will not be removed (or, according to others, expiated; more on this immediately below) as long as the guilty parties lived.[47] In other words, it would never be remedied, as opposed to remedied at or by death. This is reflected in versions that render along the lines of: 'this iniquity will never be forgiven you'. See also S. D. Luzatto (Shadal), who makes the interesting observation that the prophet knew that the people would *not* die (i.e., "tomorrow," as they supposed),

43. In the new translation of Rabbi E. Touger, *Maimonides, Mishneh Torah: Hilchot Teshuvah, Laws of Repentance* (Brooklyn: Maznaim, 1987) 16 (with brief commentary), the Hebrew phrase *tešûbâ tôlâ* is rendered 'Teshuvah has a tentative effect' (cf. also p. 18).

44. For recent discussion, cf. and contrast B. A. Levine, *Leviticus* (JPS Torah Commentary; Philadelphia: Jewish Publication Society, 1989), excursus 1: "That Person Shall be Cut Off," 241–42; J. Milgrom, *Numbers* (JPS Torah Commentary; Philadelphia: Jewish Publication Society, 1990), excursus 36: "The Penalty of 'Karet,'" 405–8, with reference to D. J. Wold, *The Biblical Penalty of Kareth* (Ph.D. dissertation, University of California, 1978).

45. For further treatment of the rabbinic background, cf. R. Avraham di Boton's *Leḥem Mishneh* to *Hilkhot Teshuvah* 1:4; and see concisely in English, Touger, *Laws of Repentance*, 14–19.

46. Such developments, of course, are common in many languages; cf., e.g., the varied meanings of Greek *katharizō*, for which see LSJ 850. For related rabbinic usage of *mrq*, cf., e.g., *b. Šeb.* 13a (again with *mîtâ*); *b. Ber.* 5a (with *yissûrîn*).

47. For a similar use of *ʿad* with *môt*, cf., e.g., 2 Sam 6:23: "and Michal, the daughter of Saul, had no children until the day of her death" (*ʿad yôm môtāh*), which, of course, does not mean, "she had no children until the day of her death—at which time she bore a child!"

since the (Assyrian) enemy would not come to Jerusalem. Rather, God is saying to them, "Know that even though you will not die, your iniquity will be stored up [*šāmôr*] for you, and in the day of My visitation I will visit you, for you will not be pardoned [*perdonata* in the translation] for ever."[48]

Second, and more importantly, it is noteworthy that there are only seven biblical attestations of the *Pual* of *kippēr*, yet four of them occur in Isaiah 6–28 (for the other verses, see Exod 29:33, Num 35:33, both cultic/priestly, and Prov 16:6—*bĕḥesed weʾĕmet yĕkūppār ʿāwôn*—which is rendered in the modern versions along similar lines as are the Isaianic occurrences. Thus the RSV, NRSV, NKJV, NAB, old JPSV, and NIV translate with 'atone' or 'expiate', while the NEB, REB, NJPSV, and AV render 'wipe out' or 'purge'). It has also been argued above that in two of these occurrences, namely, Isa 28:18 and 27:9, the concept of 'atonement' is not found, while in the third, Isa 6:7, such a nuance for *kippēr* is by no means demanded. The context of Isa 22:14 is also similar to the context of 27:9 and 28:18 in that it is a primarily religious/political context, as opposed to being priestly/cultic. It is better therefore to render 'surely this iniquity will not be purged away, to your dying day'—meaning that the stain of guilt would never be removed.

Certainly, the concepts of atonement and expiation are critically important to the Hebrew Scriptures, the New Testament, and later Jewish and Christian literature,[49] and no doubt, such themes are not foreign to the book of Isaiah itself. However, those seeking to build a theology of reconciliation, propitiation, and atonement from the passages considered here in Isaiah will be disappointed. On the other hand, they will gain insight into the meaning and usage of *kippēr*, which in turn leads to a clearer understanding of the semantic and ideological development of the process of removing, wiping away, and expiating sin. And so, properly undergirded with sound philology, exegesis and theology can build soundly. Without it, however, the foundations will be faulty.

48. S. D. Luzatto, *Il Profeta Isaia* (Padua: Antonio Bianchi, 1867) 261 [Italian translation of Isaiah with Hebrew commentary]. For a very different view, note that Touger (*Laws of Repentance*, 19) states that, "the texts of *Mussar* are filled with descriptions of the punishments undergone by the soul [i.e., after death] to gain atonement."

49. With regard to the Hebrew Scriptures, one can now observe that the ever-increasing scholarly interest in Israel's cult is at last becoming proportionate to the emphasis placed on such matters by the biblical authors and editors themselves. As for the NT, a foundational truth of Christianity is that final atonement *has been made* (for a classic expression of this, in which the death of Jesus is described as a *hilastērion*, cf. Rom 3:25; and see C. E. B. Cranfield, *The Epistle to the Romans*, *Vol. 1* [ICC; Edinburgh: T. & T. Clark, 1974] 208–18; J. D. G. Dunn, *Romans 1–8* [WBC; Dallas: Word, 1988] 161–83, for in-depth treatment and full bibliography). For a study of important *kippēr* texts in the Dead Sea Scrolls (with reference also to key verses in Daniel and Zechariah), cf. A. Laato, "The Eschatological Act of *Kippēr* in the *Damascus Document*," in *Intertestamental Essays in Honour of Józef Tadeusz Milik* (ed. Z. J. Kapera; Cracow: Enigma, 1992) 91–107, treating CD IV 9–10, XIV 18–19, and XX 34.

The Goddess Wisdom—"Where Can She Be Found?"

Literary Reflexes of Popular Religion

Michael D. Coogan
Stonehill College

There is a scholarly consensus, despite considerable disagreement about the origins and interpretation of the language used, that Wisdom is depicted as a goddess in such texts as Proverbs 1–9, Wisdom of Solomon 7–9, Ben Sira 24, Baruch 3:9–4:4, and *Enoch* 42. In these texts, the goddess Wisdom is described as more beautiful than the sun or any constellation (Wis 7:29). She is Yahweh's partner in creation (Prov 8:22–30; Wis 8:4, 9:9) and as such has primary responsibility for maintaining cosmic order (Prov 8:15–16, Wis 8:1). She is a member of the divine council (Sir 24:2) and, as befits a deity of her status, has built herself a temple (*bayit*, Prov 9:1; cf. 7:6). She is Yahweh's sexual partner as well—his lover (Wis 8:3), his wife (Philo *De cherubim* 14.49), his delight (Prov 8:30). Like other goddesses in the eastern Mediterranean, from Ishtar to Venus,[1] she looks down from the window of her "house" (Prov 7:6), enticing the young man to a life of personal—and erotic—fulfillment (Sir 51:13–19 [11QPs^a]) as his "sister" (Prov 7:4), lover (Prov 8:17; Wis 6:12, 8:2; Sir 4:12), and wife (Wis 7:28, 8:2, 17; Sir 15:2). She is the teacher of her initiate (Prov 8:6–14) and is also for him a tree of life (Prov 3:18).

The texts in which these characterizations occur are of course literary, and scholars have traced their connections to other ancient Near Eastern depictions of goddesses such as Ishtar, Anat, Aphrodite, and, though in my

1. See W. Fauth, *Aphrodite Parakyptusa: Untersuchungen zum Erscheinungsbild der vorderasiatischen Dea Prospiciens* (Abhandlungen der Geistes- und Sozialwissenschaftlichen Klasse 6; Wiesbaden: Akademie der Wissenschaften und der Literatur in Mainz, 1966); O. Eissfeldt, "Aphrodite Parakyptusa," *Göttingische Gelehrte Anzeigen* 22 (1968) 302–9 = *Kleine Schriften* 5.106–12.

view more remotely, Maat and Isis as well.[2] Richard Clifford's explications of the links between the biblical presentation of Wisdom and Canaanite tradition have been especially insightful.[3] But contrary to the views of some, the primary source of this mythological portrait of Wisdom is not just literary invention, as though this were simply an antiquarian trope; neither is it simply the "borrowing" of the language and mythological depiction of non-Israelite goddesses, as though the religion of Israel were a static, fully formed reality subject only to tangential and heterodox modification; nor is Wisdom a mere hypostatization or an apotheosis, the personification of an abstract quality and its subsequent elevation to divine or quasi-divine status, like Nike, Justice, or Marianne.[4] Rather, I suggest, the authors of Proverbs drew on a living religious tradition in ancient Israel itself for which we have sporadic but continuous epigraphic and iconographic data (more and more, as new texts are discovered) as well as the polemics of the prophets. To put it simply, we have in Proverbs 1–9 and related texts more evidence for the ongoing worship of a goddess as consort of Yahweh,[5] evidence that should be taken into account as examination of "popular religion" continues.[6]

2. See recently T. Frymer-Kensky, *In the Wake of the Goddess: Women, Culture, and the Biblical Transformation of Pagan Myth* (New York: Fawcett Columbine, 1993) 179–83.

3. R. J. Clifford, "Proverbs ix: A Suggested Ugaritic Parallel," *VT* 25 (1975) 298–306; idem, "Woman Wisdom in the Book of Proverbs," *Biblische Theologie und gesellschaftlicher Wandel* (Norbert Lohfink Festschrift; ed. G. Braulik et al.; Freiburg: Herder, 1993) 61–72.

4. Nike is, however, given an appropriate genealogy by Hesiod (*Theogony* 383). The personification of abstract qualities does occur in biblical literature; see Ps 85:11–14 and cf. Ps 43:3, Isa 59:14.

5. Both epigraphic and biblical evidence suggests that at different periods and in different settings the primary goddess in ancient Israel could be Asherah (as at Khirbet el-Qom and Kuntillet Ajrud; see, among others, S. M. Olyan, *Asherah and the Cult of Yahweh in Israel* [SBLMS 34; Atlanta: Scholars Press, 1988]; S. Ackerman, "The Queen Mother and the Cult in Ancient Israel," *JBL* 112 [1993] 385–401); Astarte (see Susan Ackerman, "'And the Women Knead Dough': The Worship of the Queen of Heaven in Sixth-Century Judah," *Gender and Difference in Ancient Israel* [ed. P. L. Day; Minneapolis: Fortress, 1989] 109–24); and even Anat (note her occurrence in personal and place names in the premonarchic period as well as Anatyahu at Elephantine). Among the titles used for this goddess was "queen of heaven" (Jer 7:18, 44:17–19; Elephantine [Hermopolis 4.1]); see Ackerman, "And the Women Knead Dough."

6. The term *popular religion* is somewhat misleading and is used here to include all forms of Israelite belief and practice that fall outside the orthodoxies of the prophetic, Deuteronomic, and priestly traditions; it can include officially sanctioned as well as local and private forms, both elite and nonelite, urban and rural. See further S. Ackerman, *Under Every Green Tree: Popular Religion in Sixth-Century Judah* (HSM 46; Atlanta: Scholars Press, 1992); and W. G. Dever, "The Silence of the Text: An

A kind of negative evidence to support this understanding of the intrinsic relationship of the goddess Wisdom to a continuous tradition in Israelite religion is the recurring and systematic effort to correct the mythological features of Wisdom, to demythologize her, as it were. Examples include the disingenuous and facile equation of Wisdom with the Torah (Sir 24:23, Bar 4:1), discussed further below, and the cliché that with (his) wisdom Yahweh founded the earth, established the world, and made all things (Ps 104:24; Prov 3:19; Jer 10:12, 51:15), an affirmation that is unremarkable only when the background of the goddess Wisdom is bracketed from consideration.

For a more detailed example of this correcting orthodoxy, consider first the change made in the Septuagint of Prov 7:6. In the Masoretic Text, it is Wisdom herself who as a divine seducer looks down from her window on the young man below, whereas in the Greek, with a change of pronouns, it is the foreign woman, the notorious *ʾiššâ zārâ*. Likewise, in Sir 51:13–19 the highly suggestive and erotic language of the original Hebrew as preserved in 11QPs[a] is softened to bland abstractions by the Greek translator.[7]

Against this background, I wish to look more closely at Job 28. Let me remark at the outset that in my view the poem is not a part of the earliest Job book, and I remain unconvinced by the efforts of Habel, Janzen, Hartley, Andersen, and others to see in it an integral part of the final Masoretic form of that work. Chapter 28 is altogether anomalous. Without a separate introduction of its own, it appears to belong to the sequence of Job's speeches. But how different from his earlier views it is in tone. The poem, for all its beauty, is out of place and should be viewed as an independent work that attempts to answer the perennial question "Where is wisdom?" inserted at a late date into the book of Job because of some tenuous verbal links with it (e.g., Job 1:1).[8] Moreover, the present conclusion of the poem (v. 28) is moralistic: "And he said to human beings: 'Fear of the Lord: that is Wisdom' "—a sentiment familiar from wisdom literature (e.g., Prov 1:7, 9:10; Ps 111:10).[9] Only here in the poem is *ḥokmâ* used without the definite article, and the circumlocution *ʾădōnāy* for the divine name is another indication of secondary origin. Thus, it is best to treat v. 28 as a later addition disturbing the symmetrical balance of the poem's three stanzas (12/8/8 bicola) and as contrary to the implied isolation of Wisdom as God's companion.

Archaeological Commentary on 2 Kings 23," in *Scripture and Other Artifacts: Essays on the Bible and Archaeology in Honor of Philip J. King* (ed. M. D. Coogan et al.; Louisville: Westminster John Knox, 1994) 143–68.

7. See conveniently J. A. Sanders, *The Dead Sea Psalms Scroll* (Ithaca, N.Y.: Cornell University Press, 1967) 114–15.

8. See S. A. Geller, "'Where Is Wisdom?': A Literary Study of Job 28 in Its Settings," *Judaic Perspectives on Ancient Israel* (ed. J. Neusner et al.; Philadelphia: Fortress, 1987) 178.

9. Note the analogous tag in Qoh 12:13.

The poem as a whole has three stanzas, with their divisions clearly marked by the refrain *wĕhaḥokmâ mē'ayin timmāṣē'/tābô' wĕ'ê zeh mĕqôm bînâ* in vv. 12 and 20. The first stanza of the poem (vv. 1–11) describes in remarkable detail human efforts to extract ores and precious stones from the ground. One of the most elaborate descriptions of prospecting and mining technology from the ancient Near East, this passage has as its point the successful completion by human beings of a quest beyond the abilities of any other creature, whether the far-seeing falcon or the lion (or perhaps more appropriately, as some have argued, the serpent [*šaḥal*][10]). Humans, then, have extraordinary abilities to bring what is hidden to light, as their uncovering of gold, iron, copper, and sapphires shows.

Wisdom, however, as the second stanza (vv. 12–19) elaborates, is much more valuable than gold and precious minerals, and, more importantly, is beyond human attainment. This is an explicit contradiction of the piety of the wisdom literature, which while often comparing wisdom favorably with precious metals and stones (Prov 8:10–11; cf. 31:10), also stresses her availability; Prov 3:13–18 is representative:

> Happy is anyone who finds wisdom,
> anyone who acquires understanding.
> Trading in her is better than trading in silver,
> she is more profitable than gold,
> She is more precious than rubies,
> she is incomparable . . .
> A tree of life to all who hold on to her.

Job 28:13, by contrast, while accepting the superior value of Wisdom, asserts that she is inaccessible:

> Humans do not know her path;[11]
> and she cannot be found in the land of the living.

The third stanza (vv. 20–27) repeats the interrogative refrain and answers it: only God (*'ĕlōhîm*[12]) (and the omniscient narrator) knows where wisdom is to be found—"she is hidden from the eyes of all" others (v. 21)—for wisdom originates before creation.

Little attention has been paid to this remarkable hymn in discussions of the figure of Wisdom, in part because most translations understand *haḥokmâ* as an 'it' rather than as a 'she'.[13] Notable exceptions are the translations of

10. See most recently Geller, "Where Is Wisdom?" 179 n. 14, following Mowinckel and Pope.

11. Reading *darkāh* with the LXX, rather than the MT's *'erkāh* ('value'?).

12. Another indication of the chapter's independent origin; see S. R. Driver and G. B. Gray, *A Critical and Exegetical Commentary on the Book of Job* (ICC; Edinburgh: T. & T. Clark, 1921) xxxv–xxxvi.

13. Even M. H. Pope made Wisdom an object in his commentary (*Job* [AB 15; 3d ed.; Garden City, N.Y.: Doubleday, 1973]).

Robert Gordis, E. M. Good,[14] and the Jerusalem Bible, all of which render the appropriate verbal and pronominal forms into English as feminine rather than as neuter. (The Septuagint is ambiguous, like the Hebrew.)

Yet the poem as a whole is replete with mythological language. In the parallelism of v. 14, Deep (*tĕhôm*) and Sea (*yām*) speak:

Tehom says, "She is not in me";
and Yam says, "Not with me."

In other ancient Near Eastern texts, as not infrequently in the Bible, Deep and Sea are divine beings, and outside the Bible they and their cognates have a great deal to say. But nowhere else in the Bible is a direct speech of Tehom or Yam quoted.[15] Likewise, in v. 22, Abaddon and Death speak: "With our ears we have heard a report of her." Death (Mot/Mawet) is a well-attested deity in the Ugaritic texts and is occasionally personified in the Bible as well.[16] Abaddon is, as far as we know, an exclusively Israelite epithet for the underworld, often paired with Sheol, and personified in Prov 27:20 as well as in Rev 9:11 (as "the angel of the bottomless pit"). Again, there are no other biblical examples of either Death or Abaddon speaking as they do here. Job 28 thus exhibits a very high mythology.

In this context, then, as well as in the light of other occurrences of the goddess Wisdom in the Bible summarized earlier, Wisdom (*haḥokmâ*) in Job 28 is best understood as personal rather than abstract, and as divine. The third stanza connects this presentation of Wisdom to other traditions: not only is God the only power, human or divine, who knows how to find Wisdom, but she also apparently preexisted creation. At that time, when he "weighed the wind, measured the waters, made a channel for the rain, a path for the thunderstorms" (vv. 25–26; cf. Job 38, esp. vv. 10 and 25), then—at that time—he saw her, appraised her, and searched her out. God here is presented as a miner superior to humans—note the echoes of vv. 3 and 10: God found Wisdom, as humans find gold, but this should not lead to the

14. R. Gordis, *The Book of God and Man: A Study of Job* (Chicago: University of Chicago Press, 1965); E. M. Good, *In Turns of Tempest: A Reading of Job with a Translation* (Stanford, Calif.: Stanford University Press, 1990).

15. In Hab 3:10, Deep utters its voice (*nātan tĕhôm qôlô*), and in Ps 42:8, deep calls to deep (*tĕhôm ʾel tĕhôm qōrēʾ*), but in neither case are actual words cited. The only possible exception is Isa 23:4, but the sense of the passage is not clear and in any case one exception is not significant.

16. See conveniently T. J. Lewis, "Mot," *ABD* 4.922–24, and note especially Job 18:13, as well as Isa 28:15, 38:18; Jer 9:20; Hos 13:14; Hab 2:5; Pss 18:5, 49:15, 116:3; Prov 13:14; Cant 8:6. Note also the names Ahimoth, Azmaweth, and Hazarmaweth; the evidence of the Israelite onomasticon is generally neglected in discussions of popular religion; a notable exception is J. H. Tigay, *You Shall Have No Other Gods: Israelite Religion in the Light of Hebrew Inscriptions* (HSS 31; Atlanta: Scholars Press, 1986); and see also Olyan, *Asherah and the Cult of Yahweh in Israel*, 35–37.

conclusion that Wisdom is simply an object; she is, rather, supremely inaccessible, except to God.

And here is my major difficulty in understanding this text. What function does a *dea abscondita* serve? The description of Wisdom in Job 28 is clearly related to the description in Proverbs: as in Prov 3:14–15 and 8:13, Wisdom is more precious than silver, gold, or precious stones; as in Prov 3:19–20 and 8:22–31, she existed before creation. But in Proverbs, as well as in later texts that can in some senses be viewed as orthodox corrections of Proverbs' presentation of Wisdom as a goddess, she is always accessible, even a seducer, enticing the young man into her dwelling to become her sexual partner. In Job 28, on the other hand, she is supremely remote; she is God's partner, and his alone, and humans cannot reach her.

It is difficult to know where to place this view in the history of biblical and postbiblical traditions. A somewhat similar sentiment is found in *Enoch* 42:2, where Wisdom, having failed (at least for the present) to find a dwelling among humans, has returned to the heavens and sits among the angels. There is a closer relationship with the transcendence of Yahweh as revealed in his speeches in Job 38–41; I would argue that there is a literary dependence here, with Job 28 being a variation by another author on the theme of those divine addresses to Job, God's vast and qualitative superiority to human beings. Perhaps closest of all is the pessimism of Qoheleth, for whom to try to "know" wisdom is to chase the wind (1:17), and who, when he said, "I would be wise," discovered that she (it?) "is far from me—deep, so deep—who can find her" (7:23; see also 3:11, 8:17, 11:5, 9:11, 11:5).

Where, then, is the goddess Wisdom to be found? In Israelite literary tradition she is the consort of Yahweh, supplying the *anima* lacking in a patriarchal monotheism. In portraying her, biblical writers, especially of the wisdom schools, drew on continuous religious traditions, which often included the worship of a goddess; Wisdom is, in a sense, an orthodox legitimation of the worship of the goddesses, and served many of the same functions. As time went on, however, orthodoxy recognized that this daring use of popular polytheism was at least a source of confusion if not an outright threat[17] and so took pains to demythologize the goddess Wisdom, to make her an abstraction. Thus, in Sir 24:23 she simply becomes identified with the Torah. This is elaborated in Bar 3:15–4:4: who has found Wisdom? Not the rulers of the nations; not the Canaanites or those from Teman, Hagar's offspring; not the ancient storytellers. Only God knows her—the creator, who called

17. An analogy of sorts is the attitude toward Baal-language in Yahwistic tradition. The exuberant use of Baal-language in early Israelite poetry, together with the continuing worship of Baal himself within Israel, testified to by both biblical and nonbiblical texts, must have been troubling to prophetic and Deuteronomic Yahwism, and corrections had to be made: Yahweh is not in the storm (1 Kgs 19:11–12); Yahweh is not to be called *baʿal* (Hos 2:18).

the stars and they said, "Here we are!"—he found Wisdom and gave her to Israel. "She is the book of the commandments of God, the eternal Torah."[18] But popular religion could not be denied, and so in different periods and in different contexts she reappears, with the language used of her continuing to be derived from such deities as Isis (see, for example, the Nag Hammadi tractate "The Thunder, Perfect Mind").

The case of wisdom is functionally reminiscent of that of the mother of Jesus in Christian tradition, and not surprisingly, literarily as well, for the vocabulary of Wisdom is used in what scholastic theologians with careful precision call the veneration (but which phenomenologically must be considered worship) of Mary. The first reading in the traditional Roman liturgy for the feast of the Immaculate Conception (December 8) is Prov 8:22–35 (which, in the suggestive phrasing of the Vulgate, begins, *Dominus possedit me in initio viarum suarum*).[19] Mary's union with God in the Incarnation (which makes the virgin also a mother) and her reunion with him by the Assumption into heaven is the logical conclusion of the relationship between God and Wisdom, as Jung correctly observed.[20] And, in the litany of popular devotion (*lex orandi lex credendi*), with unconscious echoes of Israelite popular religion, heterodox by prophetic standards, she is called not just queen of heaven (*regina caeli*)[21] and thus queen of the angels, queen of the patriarchs, queen of the prophets, and queen of the apostles, but also 'seat of wisdom' (*sedes sapientiae*).

18. This passage is a reworking of Job 28, with help from Job 38. Note the similar alteration in the traditional *Tg. Job* 28:22: "The house of Abaddon and the angel of death say: 'We have heard a rumor with our hearing of its being given to Israel'" (C. Morgan [trans.], *The Targum of Job* [The Aramaic Bible 15; Collegeville, Minn.: Liturgical Press, 1991] 66). Wis 7:25, in an even higher abstraction, calls Wisdom "a pure emanation of the power of the Almighty" (NRSV).

19. The same text is also used for the feasts of the Nativity of the Virgin Mary (September 8) and the Holy Rosary (October 7). Note also the use of Ben Sira 24 (*Transite ad me, omnes qui concupiscitis me* [v. 19]) in the feasts of Mary, Queen of All Saints (May 31), the vigil of the Assumption (August 14), and the Immaculate Heart (August 22), as well as that of Cant 2:8–14 for the feast of the Visitation (July 2).

20. C. G. Jung, *Antwort auf Hiob* (1952), translated as "Answer to Job," in *The Collected Works of C. G. Jung*, vol. 11: *Psychology and Religion: West and East* (2d ed.; Bollingen Series 20; Princeton: Princeton University Press, 1969) 355–470.

21. Cf. *Ave, regina caelorum, ave domina angelorum* 'Hail holy queen enthroned above'.

The Seven-Day Siege of Jericho in Holy War

DANIEL E. FLEMING
New York University

The recitation of Jericho's fall in Joshua 6 remains compelling by the very fact that it is no dry report of human military success. Israel's conquest of the promised land is initiated by a blow from heaven, and Yahweh himself seizes the first Canaanite stronghold in the path of his people. Such warfare needs no siege engines and is engaged rather by ritual procession. Priests, not the hero Joshua, stand at center stage once battle begins. Above all, the wall falls as if pushed over by the hand of God.

Ritual procession with the ark of Yahweh and its attendant priests resembles Israel's entry into the land across the dried-up Jordan River (Joshua 3–4), which leaves the gathered host at Gilgal (Josh 4:19–20). Gilgal is known as a cult center. For example, 1 Sam 11:14–15 has Saul installed as king there, after Samuel had presented sacrifices there (10:8; cf. 13:8), and Amos and Hosea denounce it as an active cult place (Amos 4:4, 5:5; Hos 4:15, 9:15, 12:12). After encampment at Gilgal, the seven days of marching around Jericho easily suggest a festival like the annual events of Maṣṣot (Unleavened Bread, Exod 23:15; Lev 23:6, 8; Deut 16:3–4) and Sukkot (Booths, Lev 23:39–42, Deut 16:13), each of which comes to be framed by a seven-day interval. Calendrical celebration of Yahweh's gift of the land could include a collective visit from nearby Gilgal for circumambulation of the Jericho

Author's note: Baruch Levine has devoted much of his career to examination of biblical texts and traditions in light of comparative evidence. His interests have consistently returned to the fascinating and problematic juncture of ritual and literature against the backdrop of the larger culture. The paper offered here attempts to reevaluate one well-known biblical tradition in the same spirit, in appreciation of Baruch and the privilege of working with him at New York University. I would like to thank Dr. Raymond Hobbs for his helpful response to an early draft of this paper.

mound.[1] Some scholars have hesitated to approve such precise definition of a cultic setting as the original inspiration for Joshua 6 and instead attribute evidently ritual ingredients such as the ark, its priests and procession, and the trumpets to later revisions.[2] In a narrative core, Yahweh gives victory when the people shout, perhaps by supernatural power but not by ritual.[3]

Interpreters handle the seven days of the Jericho siege no more uniformly than the rest of the text, but to my knowledge none treats the period as a natural expression of divine activity in war, at home in narrative without cultic function. Unlike Gilgal, however, Jericho displays no direct record of function as a cult site, a considerable barrier to association with any specific ritual incorporated into Israelite life. Joshua 6 never associates the siege with the sabbatical week, a separate biblical tradition. On the other hand, the Ugaritic tale of King Keret displays a more general application of the seven-day interval for describing war under divine plan, without any directly ritual aspect.[4] The Ugaritic text is no myth or liturgy for sacred drama but a nar-

1. Early proponents include J. Dus, "Die Analyse zweier Ladeerzählungen des Josuabuches (Jos 3–4 und 6)," *ZAW* 72 (1960) 119; J. A. Wilcoxen, "Narrative Structure and Cult Legend: A Study of Joshua 1–6," *Transitions in Biblical Scholarship* (ed. J. C. Rylaarsdam; Chicago: University of Chicago Press, 1968) 46–47, 53–54, 70; and E. Otto, *Das Mazzotfest in Gilgal* (Stuttgart: Kohlhammer, 1975) 191–92. R. G. Boling advocates an alternative cultic explanation as "protective ritual exercises" after plague (*Joshua* [AB 6; Garden City, N.Y.: Doubleday, 1982] 206, 213–15), based on E. V. Hulse, "Joshua's Curse and the Abandonment of Ancient Jericho: Schistosomiasis as a Possible Medical Explanation," *Medical History* 15 (1971) 376–86.

2. J. M. Miller and G. M. Tucker observe the lack of concrete evidence for any specific celebration and point to holy war conceptions (*The Book of Joshua* [Cambridge: Cambridge University Press, 1974] 54–55). G. W. Coats objects that the ritual character of Joshua 3–4 does not guarantee that the audience is not simply more broadly popular ("The Book of Joshua: Heroic Saga or Conquest Theme?" *JSOT* 38 [1987] 28).

3. An extremely attenuated version is offered by B. Peckham, who attributes only Josh 6:2, 16b, and 20aα and bβ to the core, designated Dtr[1] ("The Composition of Joshua 3–4," *CBQ* 46 [1984] 427 and n. 23). L. Schwienhorst allows a larger *Grundschicht*, which already included a separate command and fulfillment, for a silent siege with battle cry that brings down the city walls (*Die Eroberung Jerichos: Exegetische Untersuchung zu Josua 6* [Stuttgart: Katholisches Bibelwerk, 1986] 40–43). Again, any ritual capable of repeated observance is assigned to stages of revision. Compare also Miller and Tucker, *Joshua*, 54; J. Gray, *Joshua, Judges and Ruth* (The Century Bible; London: Nelson, 1967) 75–76. Only Miller and Tucker connect the form with holy war explicitly.

4. G. del Olmo Lete has already observed the similarity of siege narratives, including the seven-day attack, but with the assumption that a primitive tale is transformed into cult-drama for a Jericho sanctuary ("La conquista de Jerico y la leyenda Ugaritica de Krt," *Sefarad* 25 [1965] 3–15, especially 14). Jericho displays no record of such use as a cult place, as stated above. A more general comparison with seven-day

rative exploration of kingship dependent on religious powers, based on a legendary figure not otherwise known to us. Seven-day intervals belong to the sacred time of a military campaign undertaken by divine command. Similar assumptions may underlie references to seven days in military contexts in 1 Sam 11:3, 13:8; 1 Kgs 20:29; and 2 Kgs 3:9, though I have not found these compared to Joshua 6.

Joshua's seven-day siege belongs to the imagery for sacred warfare in storytelling convention. Biblical description of holy war joins elements surely practiced in fact, such as the battle cry, to a religious interpretive matrix that leaves ambiguous the distinction between doing and telling. Ritual was incorporated into warfare as into every other aspect of ancient life, though the seven-day siege seems to present an unlikely prospect for practical execution. In spite of any logistical obstacles to attack within a preconceived duration, Mari letters document two sieges that last seven days. No detail demonstrates a religious motivation, but in a collection with very rare references to this unit of time, the Mari evidence merits examination. It is possible that even these reports reflect at least a similar convention for sacred warfare (see below, on Letters from Mari).

Given the present lack of consensus regarding the general nature of the Deuteronomistic History and its sources, this study is not undertaken in hope of settling the literary history of Joshua 6. It focuses instead on the seven-day period, which in the Jericho tale belongs to narration of a popular heritage infused with Yahweh's mighty acts, not to narrowly defined cultic practice. Once even the seven days are identified with holy war narrative, much of the division between cultic and supposedly nonritual elements for separate redactional stages seems arbitrary. The literary history of Joshua 6 might then be simplified toward either a coherent Deuteronomistic creativity or an older Jericho tale joined early to the Jordan crossing. The narrative envisioned here does not exclude the creative work proposed by Peckham for the postexilic Dtr^2, for instance. Joshua 6 does not contain the most widely acknowledged Deuteronomistic language, however, and Noth attributed only the priests who carry the ark to Dtr in this chapter, by relation to the "Levite-priests" of Josh 3:3.[5] This "Levite" tag stands alone among frequent references to the priests who carry the ark and does not identify the whole tradition of priestly bearers as Deuteronomistic. Neither the capture of Jericho nor the Jordan River crossing refers to known postexilic cultic or religious traditions, so that the postexilic date remains unproven.

---

intervals in Ugaritic texts is drawn by S. E. Loewenstamm, "The Seven-Day Unit in Ugaritic Epic Literature," *IEJ* 15 (1965) 131.

5. M. Noth, *The Deuteronomistic History* (JSOTSup 15; Sheffield: JSOT Press, 1981) 37, 93. The ark is attended in the ark narrative of 1 Sam 4:4 (cf. vv. 11, 17) by priests, whom Noth does not attribute to Dtr.

Ritual in the Jericho Siege

Interpretation of the Jericho siege narrative in Joshua 6 grapples with interwoven problems of history, religion, and literature. Repeated excavations at Jericho have supplied no accepted hook for an Israelite capture of the city. Garstang's identification of a Late Bronze double wall was corrected to Early Bronze (3d millennium B.C.E.) by Kenyon, who placed its destruction at the end of the Middle Bronze (mid–16th century).[6] Late Bronze occupation would then cover only a small part of the tell, until disappearance in the early 13th century (1425/1400–1275).[7] Iron Age pottery only begins to appear for the 11th century, with first building in the 10th.[8] Wood argues that local Late Bronze I pottery should move the destruction of the last walled city to ca. 1400 B.C.E., but even this adjustment leaves a long gap before the generally acknowledged 12th-century bloom of likely Israelite settlements in the hill country.[9]

Doubt about the historical content of the biblical stories actually originates in the texts themselves as much as in the archaeological record. Some have salvaged a less supernaturally tinted victory in the spies' mission and their contact with an inside agent (Rahab) in Joshua 2,[10] but narration of the attack itself in chap. 6 is completely dominated by the religious framework of holy war by divine command and an act of God ritually prepared. This is no battle report, and even the victorious general Joshua serves only as mediator of divine instructions.[11] Regardless of the debated date of the various contents, emphasis on the miraculous fall of Jericho's wall and participation of ark and priests displays not a siege but a celebration of Yahweh, seemingly with more interest in cultic procedure than warfare in any mundane terms.[12]

6. J. Garstang, *The Story of Jericho* (London: Marshall, Morgan, and Scott, 1948) 135–40; K. Kenyon, *Digging up Jericho* (London: Ernest Benn, 1957) 170–71.

7. P. Bienkowski, *Jericho in the Late Bronze Age* (Warminster: Aris and Philips, 1986) 120, 136.

8. H. and M. Weippert, "Jericho in der Eisenzeit," *ZDPV* 92 (1975) 145.

9. B. G. Wood, "Did the Israelites Conquer Jericho? A New Look at the Archaeological Evidence," *BARev* 16/2 (1990) 50–52; I. Finkelstein, *The Archaeology of the Israelite Settlement* (Jerusalem: Israel Exploration Society, 1988) 324–30, etc.

10. On the alternative version of capture, see: Gray, *Joshua, Judges and Ruth*, 53; J. A. Soggin, *Joshua* (OTL; Philadelphia: Westminster, 1972) 38; M. D. Coogan, "Archaeology and Biblical Studies: The Book of Joshua," *The Hebrew Bible and Its Interpreters* (ed. W. H. Propp, B. Halpern, and D. N. Freedman; Biblical and Judaic Studies from The University of California, San Diego 1; Winona Lake, Ind.: Eisenbrauns, 1990) 20.

11. G. Mitchell makes this point, though the form-critical choices need not be reduced to "cultic description" and "battle report" (*Together in the Land: A Reading of the Book of Joshua* [JSOTSup 134; Sheffield: JSOT Press, 1993] 51–52).

12. Soggin declares that the elements of holy war described in Joshua 6 are so stylized as to "have nothing warlike about them except the name" (*Joshua*, 86). Note that

The siege of Jericho is described in Josh 6:1–16, and v. 20. A layered effect is created by the tiers of instruction and execution, and the accumulation of detail through these recapitulations leaves considerable uncertainty about the history of transmission.[13] One widely observed distinction separates a silent siege culminating in the war cry from the whole notion of procession, with its ark, priests, and horns.[14] The narration gives the greatest space to the final siege:

- v. 1, the stage set
- vv. 2–5, Yahweh instructs Joshua
- vv. 6–7, Joshua instructs the priests and the people
- vv. 8–16, 20, executed siege
  - vv. 8–11, day one: initiation of procession (vv. 8–9), command of silence (v. 10), culmination in circumambulation (v. 11)
  - vv. 12–14, day two, as model for six days: initiation of procession (vv. 12–13), culmination in circumambulation (v. 15)
  - vv. 15–16, 20, day seven: initiation of seven circuits (v. 15), shout, penetration of city at seventh circuit (vv. 16, 20)

This outline addresses only the siege of Jericho, which does not represent a separate narrative unit. Conquest of Jericho is recounted in two interwoven tales now located in Joshua 2 and 6: Rahab and the Israelite spies (chap. 2; 6:22–23, 25), and the capture of the city, which is introduced by Joshua's encounter with the general of Yahweh's army (5:13–15).[15] The capture of

---

more and more of Joshua 6 and nearby chapters is being attributed to the exile and later. For instance, Peckham adds only 3:5, 10b, and 16b to 6:2, 16b, and 20aα + bβ to represent a preexilic Deuteronomistic historian Dtr[1] in the ark material of chaps. 3–4 and 6 ("Composition of Joshua 3–4," 427). The rest belongs to an exilic Dtr[2].

13. Consider for example the eight levels of Schwienhorst, three of Deuteronomistic type (*Josua* 6, 23); J. Maier, six levels with the last one Deuteronomistic (*Das altisraelitische Ladeheiligtum* [Berlin: Alfred Töpelmann, 1965] 37); similar to H. Seidel, five levels ending with the Deuteronomist ("Der Untergang Jerichos [Jos 6]: Exegese ohne Kerygma?" *Theologische Versuche* 8 [1977] 11–20). Many commentators decline to produce a detailed scheme.

14. This division is advocated by Gray (*Joshua, Judges and Ruth,* 75–76), and Miller and Tucker (*Joshua,* 54). Schwienhorst's *Grundschicht* is defined by the same early stage (*Josua* 6, 40), though he correctly recognizes even the shout as part of warfare under divine power and leaves in Yahweh's instruction to Joshua (6:2), in contrast to an idea of a secular core narrative (Gray, p. 75).

15. This confrontation is generally regarded as independent of the Jericho siege narrative, though it does place the meeting at Jericho. Soggin observes the argument that an independent validation of Joshua's leadership, comparable to Moses on Sinai, is originally placed *in* the city itself, not merely nearby (*Joshua,* 76–77). Although one can conceive of such a meeting in the city after it is taken, the divine approbation is most needed before the conquest begins, just as Moses met God on Sinai before

Jericho in Joshua 6 does seem to have been recounted originally without reference to the concerns that are woven into the conclusion at chapter's end. Regardless of the relative date attributed to an original Rahab story, in the narrative as it now stands, both the spies' visit (chap. 2) and the failure at Ai (chaps. 7–8) serve a theme now contingent on the capture itself. Contrasting insistence on universal observance of the חרם ban and the possibility of exception are explored in these two commentaries on initiation of divine warfare in the promised land at Jericho.[16] In chap. 6 itself, both the חרם demand (vv. 17–19, 21, 24; cf. the curse of v. 26) and the exception of Rahab for her advocacy of Yahweh's cause (vv. 22–23, 25) are appended to the core narration and depend on it at least in some essential form, rather than the reverse. Verses 17–19 thus intrude at the climax of the attack in order to prepare for the discussion of the ban that follows, and the shout of v. 20 is separated from the command of v. 16.

Yahweh's guarantee to Joshua in 6:2 that he has "delivered Jericho and its king into your hand" echoes the report of the spies in 2:24 that "Yahweh has delivered the whole land into our hand." Both the idiom for handing over enemies and the reference to Jericho's king anticipate the account of the regional victories in chaps. 10 and 11, which also pay great attention to the execution of the חרם ban (see especially 10:29–30, with reference to Jericho). Coogan uses this connection and interest in the king (cf. Josh 24:11) to reconstruct a separate tradition for conquest of Jericho without the whole scheme of 6:3–21, which perhaps assumes a betrayal from within the city by Rahab.[17] If such a capture by betrayal ever was conceived, it is not preserved in any biblical narrative, nor would it offer a more secular account, since 6:2 attributes the victory to Yahweh in language of divine warfare (נתן ביד). The scarlet rope of 2:18, 21 in no way assists in the defeat of Jericho, but only serves Rahab's escape. Furthermore, the fall of Jericho's wall need not have been conceived as collapse of the full circumference, but only breach, so that Rahab's signal stands in no particular conflict with Joshua 6, even if the two stories indeed derive from originally separate Jericho traditions.[18] Akkadian "collapse" of a city wall describes victorious siege (see CAD, s.v. *maqātu* 1a), and Išme-Dagan elaborates on the process required in ARM 1 135:8–10, where he announces that he made the wall (*dūrum*) of Qirḫadat fall (*maqā-*

---

undertaking his mission. Surely the interchange assumes Jericho was not yet taken, as concluded by whoever set it in its current position.

16. L. D. Hawk proposes that the Rahab story presents an implicit disobedience to the command (*Every Promise Fulfilled: Contesting Plots in Joshua* [Louisville: Westminster/John Knox, 1991] 73), but the book of Joshua never indicates any divine disapproval, and Rahab's good fortune is only portrayed as the fruit of her surprising adherence to Yahweh's cause, against her own people.

17. Coogan, "The Book of Joshua," 19–21.

18. Contrast Soggin, *Joshua*, 83.

tum, Š) 'by breaches' (*ina pilšī*), which the CAD interprets as "mine tunnels" (s.v. *maqātu* 8c).

Beyond this introduction in Josh 6:2, the siege account shows no association with the conquest and חרם ban of Joshua 2 and 7–11. The siege as told here is more intimately related to chaps. 3 and 4, which present Israel's first entry into the promised land as a replay of the divine intervention in the escape from Egypt at the Reed Sea (Yam Suph; see 4:23). In this rendition of entry into the promised land, Yahweh himself leads the mustered people through the waters that bar the path, and Yahweh himself dooms the city that guards the entry. Both are accomplished by the presence of his ark (3:3, 6, 8, etc.; 6:4, 6, 7, 8, 9, 11, 12, 13). Movement of the ark as such sets up a ritual situation with the procession of the deity in sacred array. Sacred personnel are essential to any movement of Yahweh's cultic presence, as they would be for transportation of divine statues in the wider ancient Near East.[19] Priests and ark in a parade are inseparable, so priests must carry the ark into the Jordan River (3:3, 6, 8, etc.) and around Jericho (6:4, 6, 12, 13).[20] The blowing of horns, on the other hand, pertains more narrowly to attack in battle, as at Midian (Judg 6:16–22, passim) and is not incorporated into the Jordan River narrative.

The ritual presence of Yahweh certainly dominates both Joshua 3–4 and chap. 6, and these stories are incorporated into an introduction to the conquest, which identifies Gilgal as the first camp. Nevertheless, Joshua 6 makes no mention of Gilgal, and neither the ark nor its attendant priests in the river crossing are associated directly with the Gilgal holy site or its immediate traditions, which are recorded in 4:20–5:12. In the initial account of crossing with the ark, the stones that the Israelites remove from the river for a monument to Yahweh's great act are simply placed "where you spend the night" (4:3; cf. v. 8). These stones are only said to be set up at Gilgal in 4:20–24. There, the new generation of Israelite men is circumcised en masse (5:2–8), an event that attracts an accompanying explanation of the name Gilgal (v. 9). Manna then ceases when they observe the first Passover in the promised land (vv. 10–12). None of these Gilgal ritual traditions involves priests or ark. While the Jordan River crossing and the capture of Jericho are described in terms strongly colored by ritual language associated with the movement of Yahweh, the movement is not primarily connected with Gilgal in any of the texts at hand. This separation of the Gilgal material from the ark texts should caution against automatic attribution of the crossing and

19. The *wābil ilā'ī* of the Emar cult in 13th-century Syria is perhaps best explained as 'bearer of gods'; see my *Installation of Baal's High Priestess at Emar* (Atlanta: Scholars Press, 1992) 85 and n. 56, after D. Arnaud in the original publication.

20. If the word "priests" was added to "who carry the ark" by the Deuteronomist in 3:14, 17, etc. (e.g., Soggin, *Joshua*, 44–47), it still would not change the basic ritual requirement.

capture narratives in their current processional form to specific cult festivities at Gilgal, never mind Jericho or the Jordan.[21]

The siege of Jericho is made a ritual procession first of all by the presence of the ark. This transformation is then expressed with a play on the common idea of siege as encirclement, where fixed encirclement becomes circumambulation (verbs סבב and נקף).[22] When Jericho is encircled with the ark, the city is enclosed in a ring of Yahweh's power and doomed to fall before it. In the story as it now stands, the seven days and seven circuits on the seventh day only define further a procession already introduced by the ark. One could propose that the ark and procession revise an older tale that included the seven-day siege without circumambulation, but given the fact that both the seven days and the ark communicate notions of divine warfare, the rationale for a distinction between a cultic and a noncultic version is surely weakened.

The ritual portrayed in Joshua 6 does not focus on the participants, as might be expected of a regular festive procession around ruined fortifications.[23] On the contrary, every detail is visible or audible to those inside Jericho. No part of the procession takes place in private, away from the city; none serves the army, the ritual personnel, or even Yahweh himself separate from Jericho. Although the blowing of horns appears to derive from the cultic domain dominated by the ark, and the silence of the people serves a separate ritual logic that culminates in the climactic battle cry, both are calculated to inspire fear in the inhabitants of Jericho. The silence is not for secrecy, when the enemy has already barred its gates against the Israelite intruders (6:1, and assumed throughout), but rather it highlights the coming shout. Horns proclaim the presence of Yahweh for battle, as the attacking force moves with their deity at center. Placement of the phrase הלוך ותקוע בשופרים 'going along blowing the horns' at the end of vv. 9 and 13 is somewhat awkward,[24] but it is much easier to associate trumpets with the ark and its bearers in a summary than to suppose an underlying trumpet guard at the rear. If this music were separated from the immediate company of the ark, it would more likely lead than follow. In Emar processions, for instance, the

21. Miller and Tucker express similar reservations about evidence for connecting Joshua 6 with any particular ceremony (*Joshua*, 54–55).

22. Siege is denoted in Akkadian by the verb *lawû*(*m*), a semantic equivalent (see below, for Mari). See Ps 48:13 for the Hebrew verbs with this rare meaning (cf. Isa 15:8 for נקף). One might compare the circumambulation preserved in the famous Islamic rites at the Kaʿba of Mecca; the description of J. Wellhausen is still useful (*Reste arabischen Heidentums* [Berlin: de Gruyter, 1961] 68–70, etc.). There, however, the worshipers walk around the cult center, whereas in Joshua 6 the marker of the divine presence is itself carried around a site not otherwise identified with that marker, the ark.

23. See, for example Gray, *Joshua, Judges and Ruth*, 75–76.

24. See Soggin, *Joshua*, 82; Miller and Tucker, *Joshua*, 54.

musicians (*zammārū* 'singers') always walk in front.[25] Repetition of the whole procedure through seven days and seven times on the seventh day on one hand stages a perfect sacred time for operation of divine power and on the other hand builds the expectation that the horns and the silence presage an attack at a moment that the defenders are intended to comprehend. Siege is by nature the mode of warfare least oriented toward surprise.[26]

Although the inhabitants of Jericho never become explicit players in the drama of chap. 6 as they do in chap. 2, the siege account in Joshua 6 envisions a sentient target that will have to admit and even fear attack by Yahweh himself. This feature represents one more facet of the narrative reality in Joshua 6, that in spite of the religious elements this is not liturgy for any known festival but story-telling with a divine centerpiece. The crossing of the Reed Sea in Exodus 14 offers a useful comparison, the more relevant by its relation to the Jordan River crossing of Joshua 3–4. There, the divine intervention is described both by the sea driven back (*Hiphil*, הלך) with an east wind (v. 21) and even more impressively as walls of water (v. 22). In either case, the narrative surely never existed without divine intervention, an act of God that was always essential to the plot. Even the Song of the Sea proclaims that Yahweh himself cast Pharaoh's army into the sea (Exod 15:3–4). Just as the act of Yahweh at the escape from Egypt identified the source and character of the rescue, so Israel crosses the Jordan and captures the first Canaanite fortification in its path by the same divine power.

Other biblical tales of Yahweh at war place an act of God at the essential center that cannot be reduced to exclude it except in speculation about natural events that inspired the telling. Gideon defeats Midian with a surprise burst of light and sound that is presented not as promising military strategy but as the device used for supernatural intervention (Judg 7:16–22, especially). The ark of Yahweh is carried into battle by priests in the unusual narrative of 1 Samuel 4–6, where not victory but defeat is explained against the backdrop of Yahweh's presence in battle. After arrival of the ark and its priests, the sons of Eli (4:4), the people prepare attack by a great shout (4:6–7; cf. Josh 6:5, 10, 16, 20). The presence of Yahweh, celebrated by the battle cry, does provoke fear in the Philistine opposition, which they manage to overcome (1 Sam 4:8–10). Display of Yahweh's power arrives only with his sojourn in Philistia, after the initial defeat, but the story as a whole is no less suffused with the miraculous.

25. Fleming, *Installation*, 93 and n. 81.

26. Y. Yadin suggests by Roman comparison that the repeated encirclement of Jericho might be calculated to lower the enemy's guard (*The Art of Warfare in Biblical Lands* [New York: McGraw-Hill, 1963] 1.99–100); cf. A. Malamat, "Israelite Conduct of War in the Conquest of Canaan," *Symposia Celebrating the Seventy-Fifth Anniversary of the Founding of the American Schools of Oriental Research (1900–1975)* (ed. F. M. Cross; Cambridge, Mass.: American Schools of Oriental Research, 1979) 47–48. The seven-day interval, however, indicates certainty rather than surprise.

None of these tales of holy war is identified with any sacred site that permits reconstruction of a supposed liturgical occasion. In Joshua, proximity to the Gilgal sanctuary, the stone memorial for the Jordan crossing, and the seven-day siege at Jericho understandably have raised the possibility of cultic reenactment, but in fact no further evidence demonstrates such practice at these sites. Indeed the Joshua stories are infused with a religious cast, and the ark introduces specific ritual traits. Such narrative may well have been preserved in a cult institution, though the association of the ritual elements with the ark might as easily indicate a Jerusalem tradition, without substantial connection to the Gilgal sanctuary. This religious color may more fruitfully be defined within the domain identified since von Rad under the rubric "holy war."[27]

As a biblical subject, holy war is first of all not a repertoire of military techniques but an ancient way of thinking and talking about war. Thus, the characteristics gathered by von Rad are dominated by assurances that Yahweh makes the cause his own, goes in front, hands the enemy over to his people, fills the enemy with confusion and fear, which his own people may put aside.[28] Narration of divine warfare is not restricted to a purely cultic setting, though no doubt tales of Yahweh's victories entered liturgy before a completed collection of the biblical texts. At the same time, the language of holy war is adapted to events also conceived as battle between human adversaries, and it partakes of both the military setting generally and probably specific practices as well. For instance, the description of "the people of Yahweh" being mustered to fight (e.g., Judg 5:11, 13) plausibly reflects a situation that preceded the standing armies of later monarchies, while preparation for battle by sacrifice (e.g., 1 Sam 7:9) and the battle cry itself (Josh 6:5, etc.) should also be viewed as more than narrative fictions. The annals for Sargon's eighth campaign boast, 'I made the roar of my army as frightful as that of the thunder (Adad)' (*rigim ummānīya galtu kīma Adad ušašgim*).[29] Even the divine command that initiates the Jericho siege is rooted in the ritual practice of oracular instruction before battle. The consultation of Micaiah in 1 Kgs 22:5ff. provides a detailed account that should reflect actual practice. David's royal campaigns against the Philistines are portrayed as successful by divine oracle, consulted in advance (see 2 Sam 5:19–20, 22–25; cf. 1 Sam 23:1–5). Sometimes a prophet will deliver an oracle without the initiative of the commander or king, as in the case of Ahab in 1 Kgs 20:13–14.[30] Other details are more difficult to judge. Whether or not 1 Samuel 4–6 recalls

27. Gerhard von Rad, *Der heilige Krieg im alten Israel* (Zürich: Zwingli, 1951).

28. Ibid., 6–13, on "theory of holy war."

29. CAD, s.v. *galtu*; cf. AHw, s.v. *rigmu(m)* 4a.

30. On the war oracle in prophetic writings, see D. L. Christensen, *Transformations of the War Oracle in Old Testament Prophecy: Studies in the Oracles against the Nations* (Missoula, Mont.: Scholars Press, 1975).

actual loss of Yahweh's ark, its portrayal of the ark in defeat does not serve an immediate liturgical setting and is founded on the idea that capture was once possible.

While interpretation of Joshua 6 varies widely, the seven days that give the siege its frame are consistently identified with the duration of festivals, and they represent one narrative element that is seen as demanding a cultic context. Examination of the biblical text alone casts doubt on this conclusion, and now I shall consider comparisons from Ugarit and Mari that help sketch an alternative.

Seven Days in Keret and the Mari Letters

Keret, KTU 1.14 iii 2–20 (cf. iv 44–v 15)

As already observed by del Olmo Lete, the Ugaritic Keret legend includes a seven-day siege that provides a unique comparison for the Jericho story.[31] The Keret tale represents one of the major literary finds from Late Bronze Age Ugarit, along with the Baal and Aqhat myths. Bereft of any heir, a king from days of old laments the loss of his family. King Keret is addressed in a dream by El, the divine father of all, who supplies him with a plan that will bring a fruitful marriage. Keret must set out in full military array toward a city called Udm in a seven-day march (iii 2–10). Although the Ugaritic setting builds from a base of professional troops, the divinely ordered campaign is to muster every able-bodied male and even the bed-ridden and the blind, so that they descend on their object like a locust plague (ii 51–iii 1), a veritable act of God. When Keret reaches Udm, women working in the fields and at the threshing floors flee into the city, but instead of initiating attack, the army must remain silent (*dm* 'be still') for six days (iii 11–13). They will not bombard the city with arrows and stones, in apparent contrast to normal siege procedure (lines 14–15).

By the seventh day, Pbl, the king of Udm, will be unable to sleep, awakened by every lowing ox, braying ass, and barking dog (lines 16–20). Six days of siege should not be sufficient to deplete greatly the stores of a city so that human or animal inhabitants go hungry.[32] On the contrary, sleeplessness is a common biblical expression of anxiety: in Ps 6:7 the one facing death spends the night in grief and prayer; Nebuchadnezzar cannot sleep when he has troubling dreams (Dan 2:1) and when he is concerned about Daniel in the lion's den (6:18). Akkadian *diliptu* refers equally to sleeplessness (verb

31. Del Olmo Lete, "La conquista de Jerico," 3–15.

32. S. B. Parker interprets Pbl's sleeplessness as the effect of hungry animals (*The Pre-Biblical Narrative Tradition: Essays on the Ugaritic Poems Keret and Aqhat* [Atlanta: Scholars Press, 1989] 152). A. Caquot, however, understands Pbl's initiation of negotiations to be inspired by fear (*Textes ougaritiques* [ed. Caquot et al.; Paris: du Cerf, 1974] 1.485).

dalāpu) and worry. Seven days of waiting have not worn out Pbl by their length, but the operation of divine power has reduced the besieged king to neurotic insomnia, causing him to jump awake at every bump in the night. Elaboration of the noises that prevent Pbl's sleep suggests that the stillness of Keret's army is truly silence (root *dmm*), by contrast. Context does not demonstrate whether the seven days are consciously understood by the king to communicate a coming attack on the last day or whether his anxiety is caused only by the power of El working subconsciously in sacred time. His urgent parley before the onset of intense suffering suggests the first.

Whereas in the Jericho siege there is one seven-day period, the Keret story presents two complementary seven-day intervals in the divine plan. The repetition in Keret involves a seven-day period announced at the time of instruction between the time of departure and the reaching of the target, a seven-day period that Joshua 6 lacks. El orders two seven-day periods, one to transport Keret and his army to Udm and a second for the siege. Both serve the same purpose, to immerse Keret's mission in sacred time. By operating in seven-day intervals, Keret moves in synchronicity with El in heaven, and success is guaranteed when the driving force comes from above.

Although the number seven has wide use at Ugarit and elsewhere, the seven-day period in Ugaritic literary texts applies more specifically to activity touching the divine sphere.[33] The temple–palace that is the focus of tablets 3 and 4 of the Baal myth is created in seven days of fire (KTU 1.4 vi 24–33). Danʾel brings offerings to the gods for seven days with resulting response from Baal (KTU 1.17 i 2–16) and then does the same for the birth-goddesses who will oversee birth of his son Aqhat (ii 30–40). KTU 1.22 i 21–26 describes a seven-day feast for the Rapiʾūma with overtones of affairs beyond earthly domains. All of these seven-day intervals indeed produce a literary effect, but choice of the number seven cannot be separated from a religious, though not narrowly cultic, interest.[34] Repetition of the period in the Keret episode shows that the seven days ultimately belong not to siege as such but to intervals of activity under divine supervision and power. Because Keret bears a personal burden in loss of his family, it is possible to miss the underlying concern for kingship and the city under the dynasty's care. Not simply Keret but also his dominion require an heir for a successful future, and the military campaign reflects identification of the king's need with the good of the populace.

33. Loewenstamm addressed the seven-day unit at Ugarit as a symbol of completeness borrowed from Mesopotamia for general literary use ("The Seven Day-Unit," 121–33).

34. K. T. Aitken addresses the literary effect of these and other instances of counted time, without pursuing any special associations of seven-day or seven-year intervals ("Formulaic Patterns for the Passing of Time in Ugaritic Narrative," *UF* 19 [1987] 1–10).

In both Joshua 6 and the Keret story, the god initiates a military campaign, and there is no reason to assume in either context a hypothetical festival. The seven days indeed have religious import, but this sacred character pertains to divine initiation and oversight of conflict, with some people appearing outside the immediate sphere of divine care. In both situations the conflict is not incidental but stands at the focus of what El and Yahweh intend to do. In both cases the divine plans entail advocacy of a favored group in a conflict that is by nature military, so that the seven days belong to narration of military encounters under heavenly imperatives. Keret and Joshua 6 inject a sacred interval into a holy-war narrative that has ritual overtones in both societies but need be confined to a narrow cultic setting in neither.

The Udm and Jericho sieges share more than the seven days. Both require the silence of the attackers throughout the waiting period. Emphasis on the divine plan is expressed in explicit communication between the leaders and their gods. When the schemes are repeated in the description of their execution, the narratives underline the benefit of rigorous obedience.[35] In its two-part attack, Keret incorporates a processional element in the divine attack by its separate seven-day march against Udm, where Joshua 6 instead marches the army around Jericho. The Jericho campaign takes on an explicitly ritual aspect not present in Keret when Yahweh is introduced into battle by the ark, though divine power underlies both assaults. More important than any single similarity is the fact that the whole comparison derives from an Ugaritic tale with strong religious interest but no evident liturgical purpose. In light of Keret, the seven days of the Jericho siege need not be attributed to a reenacted festival drama but naturally belong to a narration about warfare by divine plan.

Letters from Mari

It has been observed above in discussion of the biblical traditions for holy war that the conventions of the telling, with their dominant religious interpretation, should not be isolated absolutely from plausible practice. This holds true not merely for the muster and the battle cry, which some may improperly reduce to secular procedure, but for the preparatory sacrifice as well.[36] The religious aspects of ancient war were not restricted to interpretation after the fact but touched the battlefield itself. Mesopotamian diviners (Akkadian *bārû*) not only joined military campaigns to provide up-to-date divine guidance and encouragement, but they went to battle, sometimes at the head of an army.[37]

35. See del Olmo Lete on these similarities ("La conquista de Jerico," 3, 9–12).

36. On rites preparing for battle in Mari texts, see Jack M. Sasson, *The Military Establishments at Mari* (Rome: Pontifical Biblical Institute, 1969) 36–37.

37. See CAD s.v. *bārû* b1′: position and status, connected with the army; c′: AKA 351 iii 20, *ālik pān ummānātīšunu* 'who marches in front of their army'. Sasson observes the same phenomenon at Mari (*Military Establishments*, 37 and n. 218).

While there is no reason to exclude out of hand the sacred seven-day interval from actual conduct of war, it is true that such a ritual interval would have affected the large movements of armies much more concretely than preparatory sacrifice or good-luck diviners. It is much easier to imagine the seven-day siege being left to the weavers of tales than to conceive such interference in battle procedure. Nevertheless, among the occasional references to duration of siege in ancient Near Eastern literature, the letters found at Mari offer a peculiar point of contact that deserves examination in this context.

To my knowledge, only three published Mari letters mention the duration of a siege, and two of those sieges are conceived to last seven days (ARM 1 131:14–16 and 26 405:3).[38] The third instance places capture on the eighth day of siege (ARM 1 135:11–13). These descriptions could conceivably reflect estimated time or coincidental periods in a range of actual conduct of war, but they certainly represent real battles recounted for ultimately pragmatic purposes by players in Mari foreign affairs. No overt religious interest is associated with narration of these military affairs. The Mari intervals stand out from most reported assaults against cities, which generally are divided between immediate capture and prolonged siege. Assyria's royal annals mention only one- and two-day battles to take specific cities or strongholds in successful campaigns: Assur-naṣir-pal (9th century) against Pitura in two days of constant attack and against Suru with two days of combat in the city; Šamši-Adad V (9th century) against the Mesai in a one-day battle against their mountain retreat; Sargon II (8th century) against Dur Atḫara and the king of Babylon in one day.[39] The Babylonian Chronicles describe a similar one-day success against Raḫilu.[40] Mesha claims in his Moabite stela to have taken the Israelite town of Nebo in a battle from night to noon (line 15). First-millennium Assyrian campaigns were oriented toward seasonal invasion and decisive battle, though the intervals cited may refer to attack after initial preparation. They do not show a uniformity that would indicate a

38. These data are based on examination of counted time in Old Babylonian Mari letters, presented in my "Counting Time at Mari and in Early Second-Millennium Mesopotamia," *MARI* 8 (1997) 675–92. The letter ARM 1 138:7–11 offers an interesting contrast by describing capture (verb *ṣabātum*) of the town of Ḫatka *without* siege 'in a single day' (*ūmakkal*). The verb used for the manner of victory is unusual in this context, *saḫāpum* 'to cover' (so, overwhelm). Sieges are mentioned fairly frequently without reference to duration (verb *lawûm*): see ARM 1 4:6, 14–16; 90:18–21 (unique verb *kapāpum* 'to trace a circle'); 2 39:4; 42:6, 8; 44:27; 4 87:6; 5 2:5; 6 54:18; 65:6; 14 92:10; 120:14; 26 405:16′; 406:5; cf. 407:5; *RA* 42 36 rev. 7′; 38:18; 41:28; A.2730:27–28 (unpublished; see *AEM* I/2, 33).

39. See D. D. Luckenbill, *Ancient Records of Assyria and Babylonia* [hereafter *ARAB*] (Chicago: University of Chicago Press, 1926–27) 1.156 §463, 160 §470, 256 §718; 2.15 §31.

40. See *ANET*, 304; *ARAB* 2.419 §1175.

wholly stylized reckoning of time. Long blockades represent an entirely different undertaking, not a simple extension of the direct assault. Sieges stretching across the turn of seasons occur occasionally in other Mesopotamian sources and were pursued against a well-defended opponent who needed to be subdued for long-term stratetic goals.[41]

The three Mari examples fall in the category of direct assault under shorter time horizon, but the durations are unusual. ARM 1 131 is a letter to Yasmaḫ-Addu, king of Mari, from his older brother Išme-Dagan, king of Ekallatum. Išme-Dagan outlines a campaign that began with the successful capture of Tarram, Ḫatka, and Sunḫam, before he describes in more detail the siege of Ḫurarâ. This attack is engaged in distinct steps: approach (*sanāqum* 'to arrive at a locality', line 9), encirclement for siege (*lawûm* 'to surround', line 10), construction of tower and ram (Š *izuzzum* 'to stand', line 13), and capture (*ṣabātum* 'to seize', line 16).[42] No chronology is offered for the stages of siege, and only final capture of the city is designated 'on the seventh day' (*i-na* U_4.7.KAM), without specification of when the count began.

King Zimri-Lim of Mari receives ARM 26 405 from a senior diplomat named Yasīm-El who works at the northern frontiers of the realm, in the region south of the Djebel Sinjar dominated by the kingdoms of Andarig, Kurdâ, and Karanâ.[43] Atamrum, king of Andarig, is trying to expand his influence by siege of a town called Ašiḫum, while Yasīm-El holds his Mari troops nearby and refuses engagement on behalf of Atamrum without royal instructions. In this letter, Yasīm-El is more concerned to account for his own decisions than to describe the siege itself, perhaps because the attack may have failed, and the siege appears to result in a stand-off with a negotiated solution.[44]

This failure to defeat Ašiḫum outright is evidently reflected in the only direct mention of the siege, at the head of the letter (line 3). Capture of the

41. CAD L (s.v. *lamû* 4a to besiege a city, 3′ other occs.) lists the following: nine years (Balkan Letter 31, to Kaniš); three years (Laessoe Shemshāra Tablets 77 SH 812:59; Thompson Gilg. pl. 59 K.3200:15, of Uruk). For further examples, including Nebuchadnezzar of Babylon against Tyre and Jerusalem, Shalmaneser V of Assyria against Tyre, and Ashurbanipal of Assyria against Babylon, see I. Ephʿal, "On Warfare and Military Control in the Ancient Near Eastern Empires: A Research Outline," in *History, Historiography and Interpretation* (ed. H. Tadmor and M. Weinfeld; Jerusalem: Magnes, 1983) 94. Legal documents drawn up to acquire food because of famine in prolonged siege reflect the same horizon (A. L. Oppenheim, "'Siege-Documents' from Nippur," *Iraq* 17 [1955] 69–89).

42. See n. 38 for encirclement; for "standing" siege towers, ARM 1 135:6–7 (below); 26 407:7; for seizure of cities, ARM 1 4:8, 5:33, 69:6′, passim at Mari.

43. Francis Joannès, "Correspondance de Yasîm-El," in *AEM* I/2, 235–36.

44. The bottom of the tablet is broken, so that the transition from obverse to reverse is obscured, together with the outcome of the siege.

city is never indicated by the verb *ṣabātum*, and the seven days refer to the duration of encirclement (verb *lawûm*) rather than the moment of victory.

> *a-lam A-ši-ḫa-am*[ki] *A-tam-ru-um* U$_4$.7.KAM *il-wi-ma*
> Atamrum besieged the city of Ašiḫum for seven days . . .

One other letter from Išme-Dagan to his brother Yasmaḫ-Addu describes a siege in terms that include a length of time. ARM 1 135 celebrates the capture of Qirḫadat by a procedure similar to the siege sketched in ARM 1 131. Išme-Dagan approaches Qirḫadat (verb *sanāqum*, line 5) and sets up a siege tower (verb *izuzzum*, line 7, read as Š).[45] Actual penetration of the city naturally depends on the "fall" of the wall (verb *maqātum*, Š), so that he captures the city on the eighth day (verb *ṣabātum*, line 13):

> [8]BÀD-*šu* [9]*i-na pí-il-ši* [10]*ú-ša-am-qí-i*[*t-ma*]
> I caused its wall to fall by breaches,[46] and

> [11]*i-na* U$_4$.8.[KAM] [12]*a-lam Qí-ir-ḫa-*[*da-at*[ki]] [13]*aṣ-ṣa-ba-*[*at*]
> on the eighth day I captured the city of Qirhadat.

This third reference to siege duration indeed does not match the seven days of the other two, but it evidences a noticeable pattern nevertheless.[47] Israel's festival system ends up with an eight-day definition of the feast of Sukkot (Lev 23:36, 39), but this is constructed from a seven-day base (vv. 36, 41, 42), like the feast of Maṣṣot. The one letter that describes the interval itself (ARM 26 405) refers to siege 'for seven days' (verb *lawûm*), while the two letters from Išme-Dagan designate instead the day of capture (verb *ṣabātum*). Capture might easily be delayed a day within the same seven-day scheme.

This speculation is only worthwhile because the seven- and eight-day cluster stands apart so visibly from other ancient Near Eastern siege evidence. Seven or eight days do not declare the quick success boasted in the Assyrian annals, nor do they represent sufficient time to starve an enemy into submission.[48] Why then such consistency among the three attested durations for siege in the Mari letters? Whether or not the counts are intended to be precise, these letters suggest the possibility that seven days were regarded in early second-millennium northern Mesopotamia as a conventional term for siege.

In light of this possibility it is important to realize that seven days are not part of the normal framework of time estimation evident in letters found at

45. See also AHw, s.v. *izuzzu*(*m*) Š II 2.

46. CAD, s.v. *maqātu* 8c, conceives these as 'mine tunnels' (above, p. 217).

47. Collation of the ARM 1 tablets would offer a useful check on the apparent difference.

48. Ephʿal ("On Warfare," 93) observes that sieges of months and years were necessary to overcome an enemy by famine, and ancient Near Eastern texts as a whole show that this was rare, and sieges were generally completed by breaching the city walls.

Mari. Conventional estimation of time is seen most often with future intervals, which are rendered consistently by the pattern of three, five, and ten days. Temporal expressions with *ina* 'on' focus on conclusion of an interval and show remarkably distinct patterns for precise counts of past time and estimated future:

Past time:	
2 days	ARM 26 369:12–13; 511:43; 526:32–33
3	26 127:13–17; 369:15–16; 434:12–13
4	2 39:16–18; 26 411:16; 458:13–22
6	26 494:29–31
7	1 131:14–16 (siege text)
8	26 313:31; 405:11–13 (siege text)
Future time:	
3	3 29:18–19
5	2 13:19–20; 44:19–20; 140:12–14; 3 3:25–26
5 (and) 6	26 13:17–19
10	3 79:5′–6′; 14 14:31; 24:4′[49]

Numbers outside the common pattern either intend greater precision or serve some other norms.

Seven-day intervals are not common in the Mari letters, and they do not appear to be estimated when they occur. ARM 3 4:8–9 refers to six days of work on a canal already completed and water to begin flow tomorrow, on the seventh. Another letter mentions seven days that have passed since a certain person was sent (ARM 6 43:25–27), so also past. Besides these instances of precise past counts, seven-day periods appear only with ritual associations. Two of these speak of seven-day residence in the *unqātum* or 'rings' of a sacred place, once by the king in the temple of Dagan (ARM 26 5:7) and once with some reference to Addu of Maḫānum (A.861 [*AEM* II]:3–4; see *AEM* I/1, p. 84). A prophetic and divinatory inquiry on behalf of Zimri-Lim asks about the king's safety when he embarks on a seven-day residence in some location (Durand: *ka-*[*wa-tim*], outside city walls) for performance of rites, perhaps ablutions (Durand: *ra-ma-*[*ak-šu*]).[50]

If the accounts of siege length in letters to Mari indeed reflect a convention built around the seven-day interval, the context is most likely religious. It is impossible to know whether a convention for battle under divine oversight in sacred time that influenced reports in letters might have matched practice in the field. Remembering that the calculations in the Assyrian annals appear to begin with the actual attack and may omit time devoted to

49. This pattern also appears among others in examples with *adi* 'until', which include more with three days: ARM 2 37:23–24, 48:13; 3 30:9; 26 127:11.

50. ARM 26 216:11; for discussion of this text, see my "*Nābû* and *munabbiātu*: Two New Syrian Religious Personnel," *JAOS* 113 (1993) 179–81.

preparation, seven days need not be counted from first arrival at an enemy city. The seven-day circumambulation at Jericho itself is set for sometime after the city has already shut itself against attack (Josh 6:1). None of the Mari texts, however, answers the question of ritual practice by mention of anything but military affairs. It should be noted that the Mari sieges represent a more sustained focus than involved in a passing raid, though they do not envision a settled blockade that lasts through the turn of seasons.

Joshua 6 and the Seven-Day Siege

Both in the Bible and in wider ancient Near Eastern literature, accounts of warfare under divine oversight build the details of battle onto a framework rooted in religious thought. Such stories may invoke divine power at a distance or let the gods walk directly onto the stage of human affairs, but all share a theoretical foundation that expects the supernatural to invade and infuse nature. The language of divine warfare constantly touches ritual but need not envision any concrete cultic setting, while practice of war may involve ritual defined by the occasion rather than the calendar. The seven-day intervals in both Joshua 6 and the Keret tale should derive from such battle narrative.

In fact, the Bible does mention other seven-day periods in military situations that plausibly reflect the same narrative convention. The elders of Jabesh Gilead ask for seven days under siege to send for help, with surrender to follow on the last day (1 Sam 11:3). If the day of surrender in v. 10 is the original seventh day, Saul's divinely empowered deliverance arrives on that same seventh day (v. 11). Saul begins his failure when a seven-day wait at Gilgal before battle exhausts the courage of his troops (1 Sam 13:8). Samuel does finally arrive late on the crucial seventh day for the sacrifices that invite and acknowledge divine intervention. Israel and Aram are said to remain encamped against each other for seven days after a prophet proclaims Yahweh's victory (1 Kgs 20:29), at the end of which, battle is engaged successfully. Finally, Israel, Judah, and Edom march for seven days in the desert against Moab (2 Kgs 3:9), before divine provision for victory is introduced by the prophet Elisha. If "the next morning" in v. 20 falls after the seven-day period, actual victory would occur on the eighth day in this account. However Joshua 6 may have been shaped in revision, the seven days of Jericho's siege are entirely at home in a tale told without festival or shrine, in celebration of Yahweh's victory.

Quantitative Measurement in Biblical Hebrew Poetry

David Noel Freedman and Jeffrey C. Geoghegan
University of California, San Diego

While many leading scholars in our field deride the idea that there is meter in Hebrew poetry and dismiss the evidence in support of such a notion, the method of counting syllables continues to be useful in analyzing the poetry of the Bible, since the data repeatedly point to a quantitative factor in the construction of Hebrew poems.

In what follows we will present examples of poems in the Hebrew Bible in which the overall structures are the same, the line and stanza boundaries are easily fixed, and their lengths readily determined by counting words or syllables. This is true whether we count all syllables or only accented ones. We will focus our study on alphabetic acrostic poems, most of which are to be found in the book of Psalms, but other examples turn up in Proverbs (chap. 31) and Lamentations (chaps. 1–4). Many other poems closely resemble this corpus in structural features but do not include the alphabetic factor (e.g., Lamentations 5, Proverbs 2, etc.).

But first things first. Before proceeding we should address a more basic question that has been raised in recent books and articles on the subject of the literature of the Hebrew Bible. Is the traditional distinction between poetry and prose a valid one for the Hebrew Bible? Are the two genres really distinct and are they properly separable? Scholars like Kugel and Alter argue that features considered diagnostic of poetry, on the one hand, or prose, on the other, are actually found present in both categories.[1] Instead of separate blocks of literature, there is a single continuum where elements of both kinds are found mixed together. Without denying a measure of truth in such analyses and while agreeing that there is much in the Hebrew Bible that

1. J. L. Kugel, *The Idea of Biblical Poetry: Parallelism and Its History* (New Haven: Yale University Press, 1981); and R. Alter, *The Art of Biblical Poetry* (New York: Basic Books, 1985).

reflects the mixture of prosaic and poetic elements, we may define the spectrum somewhat differently. At one end is a category of real poetry—poetry that is rhythmic, exhibits good parallelism, and was surely meant to be sung, if not also marched or danced to. At the other end is plain prose, without any of the features we normally associate with poetry. In between is a great deal of material that reflects an admixture of some kind or other, in which prosaic elements are combined with poetic ones to produce either a prosaic poetry or a poetic prose.

That the composers or editors of the Hebrew Bible thought in at least two categories and deliberately divided the Bible into what we may call prose and poetry is shown abundantly by an almost unbroken tradition extending backward from the major medieval MSS like codices Aleppo and Leningrad all the way to the Qumran documents. As is well known, the books of the Torah and Prophets are written as prose in the ordinary manner that we use to this day—in lines and paragraphs forming blocks of material. At the same time, certain pieces such as those in Exodus 15, Deuteronomy 32, Judges 5, 2 Samuel 22, and so on, are written differently, in a way that is very much the way poetry or verse is traditionally written in English or other modern (and ancient) languages. In addition, while most of the parts of the books of the Hebrew Bible are written as prose, three books—Psalms, Proverbs and Job—are singled out for special treatment, for these are written differently, as poetry, corresponding to but not identical with the way the poems in the Primary History are written. The patterns and layout of the books of Psalms, Proverbs, and Job demonstrate that the biblical authors and editors were clearly conscious of the difference between poetry and prose. In a book like Job, where we have a mixture of prose and poetry that are separable from each other, the opening and closing are written as prose, while the dialogue in chaps. 3–42 is written as poetry. We can conclude that everything in the Bible that is written in one of the distinctive visual ways identified as poetry actually is a poem. At the same time, what all would agree is prose is written as such. Given the self-imposed limitations of their method and use of means, this is a considerable accomplishment and shows beyond doubt that they were conscious of an important difference between prose and poetry and wanted to express this difference visually so that the reader would be immediately aware of the distinction and adjust accordingly as he/she read the text.

The major difference between those who wrote the Hebrew Bible as we find it and modern scholarship has to do with the Latter Prophets. These books are all written as straight prose in the old manuscripts, but modern scholarship, agreeing with Robert Lowth, has recognized that many prophetic oracles are poetry or at least more poetic than prosaic.[2] Some pieces

2. R. Lowth, *Lectures on the Sacred Poetry of the Hebrews* (repr., New York: Garland, 1971).

are indistinguishable from the poems in the three poetic books already mentioned so far as structure and texture are concerned. Others, however, fall somewhere between standard prose and lyric poetry and belong to or constitute a middle category: oracular prophecy or elevated discourse, perhaps comparable to the blank verse of Shakespearean plays or possibly the free verse of more recent English writers.

A convenient (although not necessarily precise) system for classifying prose and poetry and the degrees between has been worked out by Andersen and Forbes, which involves the simple calculation of the relative paucity or frequency of so-called prose particles in given texts.[3] It has long been recognized that particles such as *ʾēt* and *ʾăšer* are characteristic of prose writing, while they do not occur very much in poetry. The same is true of the definite article *ha-*, but the distinction in this case is not as neat or sharp. By combining the counts for all three particles and testing their frequency throughout the whole Hebrew Bible, Andersen and Forbes discovered and demonstrated that the previous supposition is indeed supported and confirmed by the actual data preserved in the MT. Broadly speaking, any substantial composition in the range from 0 to 5% (of prose particles as a percentage of the total number of words) is bound to be pure poetry or as pure as Hebrew poetry is likely to be. At the other end, anything above 15% is going to be prose. There may be, and probably are, marginal exceptions, but the correspondence is close to 100%, certainly at the low end and probably at the high end as well. A few Psalms have relatively high percentages and these may reflect a secondary tendency in poetry. Later poets, especially in the postexilic period, tended to use more prose particles than earlier poets, so a few late poems may land at the higher end of the scale.

Similarly, literature in the middle range (from 5% to 15%) may be classified as poetry with prosaic elements (5% to 10%) prose with some poetic elements (10% and 15%). It is significant that much of oracular prophecy falls in the middle range, with the preponderance in the 5%–10% bracket rather than in the 10%–15% category.

In a more detailed study of a more limited sample, we examined all of the set poems in the Primary History, including not only those written as poetry (Exodus 15, Deuteronomy 32, Judges 5, 1 Samuel 2, and 2 Samuel 22), but also those that are written as prose (Genesis 49, Numbers 23–24, Deuteronomy 33, etc.). The results showed that the range was entirely within the primary poetic category, 0–5%, while the average was about 2%. (There was no detectable difference in percentage between the first group of poems,

3. F. I. Andersen and A. D. Forbes, "'Prose Particle' Counts of the Hebrew Bible," in *The Word of the Lord Shall Go Forth: Essays in Honor of David Noel Freedman in Celebration of His Sixtieth Birthday* (ed. C. L. Meyers and M. O'Connor; Winona Lake, Ind.: Eisenbrauns, 1983) 165–83. Cf. also F. I. Andersen, *Spelling in the Hebrew Bible: Dahood Memorial Lecture* (Rome: Pontifical Biblical Institute, 1986).

written as poetry, and the second group of poems, written as prose.) This result was in marked contrast with the surrounding parallel prose accounts (e.g., Exodus 14 // Exodus 15 and Judges 4 // Judges 5), which were all at the high end of the scale and averaged out at 8 times the percentage of prose articles.[4]

The classic example of parallel structures and convergent data is the first three chapters of Lamentations. These poems, and they clearly are poems, although written as prose in the Hebrew Bible, also reflect the appropriate prose particle count criterion mentioned above.

	# of Words	אשר	את	ה	Total	% of Total
Lamentations 1	377	5	2	4	11	2.9
Lamentations 2	382	3	2	5	10	2.6
Lamentations 3	381	0	1	9	10	2.6
Overall Total	1140	8	5	18	31	2.7

In spite of the relatively late date of these poems (6th century B.C.E. or possibly later), they have all of the characteristic features of classic Hebrew poetry.[5] As can be seen from the chart, the poems are almost identical in length, having approximately the same number of words (a maximum variation of slightly more than 1%). In format they all belong to the category of alphabetic acrostic poems, consisting of 22 stanzas of three lines each (with some modifications). Chapter 3 is the most rigorously constructed, with each line of each stanza beginning with the same letter as the other two. Thus the three lines of the first stanza begin with *ʾalep* while the three lines of the second stanza begin with *bet*, and so on. In the other chapters only the first line of each stanza begins with the proper alphabetic marker, thus allowing more freedom to the composer.

At the same time, an important variation in each of the first two chapters is to be noted: each of them contains one four-line stanza along with the other 21 three-line stanzas, whereas chap. 3 is restricted to 22 stanzas of 3 lines each. While many, if not most, scholars emend away the excessive

4. It may be noted that of all of the poems, Exod 15:1–18, 21, the Israelite national anthem, turned out to have no prose particles at all. Cf. D. N. Freedman, "Prose Particles in the Poetry of the Primary History," *Biblical and Related Studies Presented to Samuel Iwry* (ed. A. Kort and S. Morschauser; Winona Lake, Ind.: Eisenbrauns, 1985) 49–62.

5. Of the three particles, overall the most prosaic is *ʾēt*, which occurs the fewest times, while *ha-*, the least prosaic, is the most frequent, and *ʾăšer* comes in between, as it should.

fourth line in chaps. 1 (v. 7) and 2 (v. 19), we think this is a mistake in view of the fact that the same phenomenon occurs in two poems rather than only one. If a supposed mistake is repeated, it is less likely to be a mistake and more likely to be part of a deviational pattern.[6] Furthermore, if we take overall length into consideration, then it is clear that in their present form the three poems are of equal length in spite of the fact that two of them have 67 lines and one has only 66. If we remove one line from each of the first two poems, the important feature of equal totals would be undercut. This symmetry is even more clearly shown in the table of syllable counts.[7]

Lamentations 1	67 lines	874 syllables	377 words
Lamentations 2	67 lines	869 syllables	382 words
Lamentations 3	66 lines	873 syllables	381 words

The syllable counts show that the three poems in their present form are almost exactly equal in overall length, the margin of difference being about 1/2 of one percent. Given the fact that our texts are hardly in pristine condition and that we do not know exactly how Hebrew words were pronounced, much less how Hebrew poets may have squeezed or expanded them depending upon rhythmic or musical considerations, the close correspondence remains remarkable and can hardly be accounted for without reference to deliberate and purposeful counting, that is, the quantitative factor.[8] In these cases they might have counted words or they might have counted syllables. As the appended charts show, it is less likely that they counted

6. Freedman, "Deliberate Deviation from an Established Pattern of Repetition in Hebrew Poetry as a Rhetorical Device," *Proceedings of the Ninth World Congress of Jewish Studies*, Division A: *The Period of the Bible* (Jerusalem: World Union of Jewish Studies, 1986) 45–52; idem, "Patterns in Psalms 25 and 34," in *Priests, Prophets and Scribes: Essays on the Formation and Heritage of Second Temple Judaism in Honour of Joseph Blenkinsopp* (JSOTSup 149; Sheffield: JSOT Press, 1992) 125–38.

7. There are a few minor corrections in the new tables as compared to my earlier counts ("Acrostics and Metrics in Hebrew Poetry," *HTR* 65 [1972] 367–92). In general we recognize on the basis of historical grammar and transcriptions in Greek and Latin that single-letter prepositions normally add a syllable to the word, in spite of regular contractions in the MT vocalization, and that masculine construct plural forms also retained an original second vowel, rather than losing it as in the MT (e.g., **dabarê* → MT *dibrê*).

8. Cf. F. M. Cross's discussion of the many minor variant readings in 4QLam ("Studies in the Structure of Hebrew Verse: The Prosody of Lamentations 1:1–22," *The Word of the Lord Shall Go Forth: Essays in Honor of David Noel Freedman in Celebration of His Sixtieth Birthday* [ed. C. L. Meyers and M. O'Connor; Winona Lake, Ind.: Eisenbrauns, 1983] 129–55).

only accented syllables. If they did, we are in a difficult position because of the notable variations in the way accents are used or withheld in the MT.

Further comment may be in order. For these three poems, the primary consideration is overall length. What is curious and of special interest here is that while the number of lines varies, the totals do not, or not in a way to reflect the difference in the number of lines. The average line length is going to be 13 syllables, with chap. 1 slightly over and chap. 2 slightly under the precise number "871" (67 × 13 = 871).[9] We might have expected chap. 3 to be shorter than the other chapters overall, because it has only 66 lines, but apparently symmetry and equality were larger considerations. The required total was filled out by adding a word and its syllables here and there rather than a whole line, as in the earlier chapters.

Other conclusions also may be drawn about the nature of this poetry and its quantitative aspects. As a cursory glance at our appended tables will show, there is little or no consistency in line length or stanza length. While the norm would be 13 syllables per line and 39 per stanza (except for the 4-line stanzas), the actual numbers vary widely on both sides of the norm. At the same time a significant plurality of lines and stanzas are close to those norms. While some lines and stanzas may be imperfect and are not now what the poet composed or wrote, it would require so much extensive emendation to make the poetry fit any kind of regular meter, such as we find in Greco-Roman poetry or in any other system, as to be totally unconvincing and self-defeating. That would be an act of creation not restoration. So in the sense of formal mathematical patterns, there is no visible or determinable meter in Hebrew poetry. But metrical analysis does not account for the very visible quantitative component in these poems: they are for all practical purposes identical in overall lengths. It is very difficult to see how the poet could have arrived at such a result if nothing was being counted (intentionally) and the poet put together lines and stanzas of widely varying lengths.[10] Given the subject matter and the interchangeability of ideas expressed, it would not be at all difficult to put together two or three poems out of the same materials varying as widely and proportionately in overall length as is the case here with the lines and stanzas. Some third form of quantitative control has been at work to produce the end results we have obtained.

We will make brief comments on the changes in the tables and then attempt to draw some conclusions about quantity in at least one kind of Hebrew poetry. We will explain the figures in the tables and the changes under three headings:

9. Chapter 3 reaches the presumably required total differently, by having a slightly higher average line length rather than by adding a 67th line somewhere or by having a lower total (66 lines at 13 syllables would come to 858).

10. There is greater variation in length between the shortest and longest lines of the poems than between the poems as a whole, and the discrepancy is much greater in regard to stanzas.

1. *Kethiv-Qere*, where the choice affects the syllable count.
2. Counting the so-called inseparable prepositions and masculine plural construct forms.
3. Other elements including
   a. the interchange of *yhwh* and *ʾdny* in the MT and other sources
   b. a few heterogeneous cases.

Before proceeding, let us state that the general counting is based on the most reliable information we have about the actual pronunciation of Hebrew in biblical times. While the MT is certainly the best source for this information, in a certain number of cases the Masoretic vocalization is secondary and diverges from a more original pronunciation, as in the case of segholate formations, secondary very short vowels attached to laryngeals, and certain other cases.

Kethiv-Qere

There are four cases in the three poems involving a change in the syllable count. In every case we have adopted the *Qere* as the better reading, but a case can be made for the *Kethiv* as the more difficult or unusual reading.

1. *Lam 1:18.* The *Kethiv* has *kl-ʿmym* for *kol-ʿammîm*, while the *Qere* has *kol-hāʿammîm*. The meaning would be the same. A case could be made that in Lamentations the poet has used the archaic form of the expression without the article, but if so, it is unique in the Bible, since the form with the article is used extensively and indiscriminately in prose and poetry. Since Lamentations is relatively late, we think the original no doubt read *kol-hāʿammîm* and the loss of the *heʾ* for the article was simply an accident. The true poetical equivalent of the ordinary prose expression would be *ʿammîm kullām*, which occurs in several passages. If we adopted the *Kethiv*, the total for the poem would be 873 instead of 874.

2. *Lam 2:2 and 19.*

a. In v. 2, the *Kethiv* has *lʾ ḥml* for *lōʾ ḥāmal*, while the *Qere* has *wĕlōʾ* for *lōʾ*. The difference is slight and the *Kethiv* may be more original.[11] A firm decision is not easy.

b. In v. 19, the *Kethiv* has *blyl*, while the *Qere* has *ballayĕlâ* (for which we read *ballaylā* with three syllables), which is the more usual expression. The only other occurrence of *ballaylā* is in Prov 31:18 (another alphabetic acrostic poem) and a *Qere* occurs at that point also. Apparently the Masoretes felt that the shorter form was an error or at least not up to the formal standard.

3. *Lam 3:32.* In v. 32, the *Kethiv* has *ḥsdw*, perhaps for *ḥasdô*, while the *Qere* has *ḥăsādāyw*, the plural form. It is possible that the *Kethiv* also reflects the plural form written defectively (with *-w* rather than the *-yw* ending). We could adopt the *Kethiv* but read it vocalizing according to the *Qere*, that is,

11. Cf. 2:21, where we have *lōʾ ḥāmaltā*, but many Hebrew MSS have *wĕlōʾ* for *lōʾ*. Note also, in v. 17 *wĕlōʾ ḥāmal* in a very similar context.

the plural form of the noun with the 3d-masculine-singular suffix. The Masoretes may not have properly understood the defective spelling of the *Kethiv* or they may have wished to call attention to the correct reading of the ambiguous spelling. There are only three cases of this expression. It is clearly plural in Isa 63:7 (from the context), and this is likely in the other two cases (Ps 106:45 and Lam 3:32).

The differences in these cases of *Kethiv/Qere* would show up as follows:

	Kethiv	*Qere*
Lamentations 1	873	874
Lamentations 2	867	869
Lamentations 3	872	873

Inseparable Prepositions and Masculine Construct Plural Forms

Turning to the second category, we find a number of expressions in which a syllable has been elided or contracted in the MT, whereas earlier transcriptional evidence suggests that the older, more original pronunciation was longer by a syllable. Thus, we add a syllable to the readings in the MT in which a preposition precedes a noun:

Lamentations 1	5c	*lpny*	3 syllables
	6c	*lpny*	3 syllables
	7b	*mymy*	3 syllables
	7c	*bnpl*	3 syllables
	14c	*bydy*	3 syllables
	15b	*lšbr*	3 syllables
	15c	*lbtwlt*	4 syllables
Lamentations 2	11c	*brḥbwt*	4 syllables
	12b	*brḥbwt*	4 syllables
	17b	*mymy*	3 syllables
Lamentations 3	26	*ltšwʿt*	4 syllables
	27	*bnʿwryw*	4 syllables

In the MT, masculine construct plural nouns are often contracted, but earlier transcriptional evidence indicates that these masculine plural construct forms had the same number of syllables as the absolute nouns.

Lamentations 1	4a	*drky*	3 syllables

Lamentations 2	10a	*zkny*	3 syllables

Lamentations 3	22	*ḥsdy*	3 syllables
	48	*plgy*	3 syllables
	62	*śpty*	3 syllables

Suffixed Forms including Third-Feminine-Singular and Second-Masculine-Singular Pronominal Elements

The problem of these suffixed forms is not easily resolved, since Masoretic vocalization does not always agree with the underlying spelling with consonants and vowel letters. Thus we have the anomaly of vowels inserted after the final letter of the word: for example, *tā* and *kā*, also *hā*. Because there is considerable evidence to show that both short and long forms existed simultaneously in the language (*-t* and *-th*, *k* and *-kh*, *-h* and *-hh*) and the vocalization of the MT reflects this phenomenon, the simplest procedure is to follow the MT and accept its vocalization throughout.[12]

Regarding the substitution of *ʾădōnāy* for *yhwh*, in the MT, as compared with the readings in the Qumran Scroll of Lamentations 1, it is quite possible that an original *yhwh* has been replaced here and there by *ʾădōnāy* in the received text. In view of the fact that the occurrences of *ʾdny* are sporadic, and they make it clear that the effort was not systematic, and in view of the likelihood that in some cases at least the word *ʾdny* was the original reading, it seems best to follow the MT in this respect as well.[13]

The slight changes introduced in the new set of tables do not affect the principal thesis suggested some years ago, namely, that the remarkable equivalence in overall length among these three alphabetic acrostic poems is not the result of happenstance or coincidence but, rather, the outcome of an intentional effort to make each one equal to the others in length, whether we measure the length by words or syllables.

12. P. Bordreuil, F. Israel, and D. Pardee, "Deux Ostraca Paleo-Hebrew de la Collection Sh. Moussaieff," *Sem* 46 (1996) 49–76; H. Shanks, "Three Shekels for the Lord: Ancient Inscription Records Gift to Solomon's Temple," *BARev* 23/6 (1997) 28–32.

13. Cross, "Studies in the Structure of Hebrew Verse," 129–55.

Further Observations

This revisit to Lamentations 1–3 and review of the metrical structure of the three poems have prompted a reexamination of the hypothesis of Karl Budde concerning the so-called Qina meter or falling rhythm commonly described or demonstrated in accentual terms as 3:2, in contrast with balanced patterns, for example 3:3 or 2:2. Since Budde himself used an accentual system, one that continues to be followed by a majority of scholars who work in this area, we have prepared one set of tables in the same way; in deciding line divisions, especially in chaps. 1 and 2, we follow the indications in the Masoretic punctuation and accentuation, and also in counting and tabulating the accented syllables themselves. While questions can be raised about some of the Masoretic choices in areas both of line division and accentual practice, on the whole and in view of the size of the samples, we are reasonably confident that the MT reflects actual practice belonging to an authentic and realistic tradition. It is better on the whole and in most particulars to adhere to a thoroughly documented tradition rather than to undertake an independent journey into this perilous country of deciding where lines begin and end and which words should be accented and when and where.

The results of the investigation are given in the following table for each of the three chapters separately, and then the findings are consolidated for the group as a whole. In general, the Budde thesis is confirmed or supported by the data, although surprisingly only a little over half of the identifiable lines conform to the falling rhythm: 103 lines out of 200. Nevertheless, this is the largest single pattern, more than any other or the rest put together. Within this group the familiar 3:2 pattern clearly dominates with a number of variations (e.g., 4:2, 4:3, 3:1), but none of these is sufficiently numerous to constitute a realistic alternative: they are simply variants belonging to the same overall picture.

Along with the falling rhythm, we have a number of lines with the reverse pattern, a rising rhythm. Not many of these occur, but they are sufficiently numerous to make it unlikely that they are all mistakes requiring revision and recalibration, and therefore it is a very dubious enterprise to emend them out of the text and out of existence. Of the total of 200 lines, 20, or 10%, are of this kind and reflect the same tendency toward deliberate deviation that we have noted in different places and under other circumstances, in Hebrew biblical literature. The ratio of 10:1 shows that the dominant pattern is a falling rhythm, but there is, contrary or counter to this pattern, a rising rhythm as well. The prevailing accentual pattern in this group is 2:3, the exact converse of the predominant 3:2 of the other group. (Whether in practice the Hebrew composers or reciters of this poetry overrode the grammatical and syntactical groupings to conform to the presumed 3:2 meter is a question that can be raised but can hardly be addressed, much less answered.)

The major surprise is the large remaining group of lines: balanced lines, mostly 3:3, but with a large group in the 2:2 bracket. (Cross attempts to dispose entirely of this group as incompatible with the nature of Qina poetry in Lamentations and elsewhere, but the great profusion in Lamentations 1–3, especially chap. 1, makes such a procedure logically questionable and dangerous in the extreme.) Out of the 200 lines, 77 belong to this category and in chap. 1 they constitute a substantial plurality of the cases.

The net effect is to show a significant tendency toward the Qina or falling rhythm, although hardly with the sharpness or clarity that we might have expected. However, two factors militate against a simple judgment about the correlation between Qina content and falling rhythm:

1. The effect of examples of rising rhythm in these same poems is to cancel out an equal number of lines with falling rhythms in the statistics. If we separate out the exceptional lines as mirror images of the regular lines, we get a clearer picture of what is actually the case.
2. The large number of balanced lines dilutes the effect of the falling rhythm and we think must be recognized as a deliberate decision of the poet to produce poems of a mixed meter. The result is an alloy with notable aspects of the falling rhythm, but mixed with numerous lines of the balanced-meter type.

Two more observations may be in order:

1. Qina content and falling rhythm should not be tied together too closely. This mixed pattern occurs in poems having little or nothing to do with formal laments (e.g., Deuteronomy 32), and on the other hand formal laments may have a very different meter, for example, Lamentations 5, which conforms to the standard 3:3 pattern for the most part, while sharing content, attitude, sentiment, and vocabulary with all of the preceding chapters.
2. It may well be that the major difficulty with the results lies in the premises and methods used to describe the meter of the poems: the accentual system may not work very well either in detail or overall to identify the phenomena involved, and hence the real pattern may not be revealed.

To test the last of these issues, we turn to the syllable-counting system and compare the results with results obtained by the accentual method. If instead of accents we count all of the syllables, the general picture presented by the former is not only strengthened and sharpened but confirmed for each individual poem and the group as a whole. Each poem exhibits the same tendencies and presents the same profile overall, while the details vary from poem to poem, stanza to stanza, and line to line.

Summary

	Lamentations 1	2	3	Total
Falling Rhythm (FR)	46	51	54	151
Balanced Rhythm (BR)	11	7	5	23
Rising Rhythm (RR)	10	9	7	26
	67	67	66	200

When we count syllables, the tables show a vast preponderance of lines with a falling rhythm in all three poems. In fact, the proportions among the three categories are approximately the same throughout, with a gradual increase in the number of lines in falling rhythms and a corresponding slight diminution in the other categories. The numbers thus confirm the impression given by the accent-counting method but at the same time strengthen the conviction considerably. Slightly more than 75% (3/4) of all the lines exhibit a falling rhythm, while around 1/8 is balanced and the remaining 1/8 exhibits the contrarian trait of a rising rhythm. Thus more than 7/8 of all the lines show an unbalanced character, which is distinctive for this kind of prosody.

If we provide the actual syllable counts for the three poems in the different rhythmic categories, we come up with the following table:

	Lamentations 1		2		3		Total	
	Syllables	Average	Syllables	Average	Syllables	Average	Syllables	Average
FR A	357	7.8	398	7.8	431	8.0	1186	7.9
FR B	245	5.3	263	5.2	293	5.4	801	5.3
Subtotal	602	13.1	661	13.0	724	13.4	1987	13.2
BR A	73	6.7	49	7.0	31	6.2	153	6.7
BR B	73	6.7	49	7.0	31	6.2	153	6.7
Subtotal	146	*13.3	98	14.0	62	12.4	306	*13.3
RR A	54	5.4	41	4.6	29	4.1	124	4.7
RR B	72	7.2	69	7.7	58	8.3	199	7.7
Subtotal	126	12.6	110	*12.2	87	12.4	323	12.4
Total	874	13.0	869	13.0	873	13.2	2616	13.1

* Discrepancies due to rounding of decimals.

Next on our agenda are the numbers for each poem according to cola A and B, and the poems as a group.

	Lamentations							
	1		2		3		Total	
	Syllables	Average	Syllables	Average	Syllables	Average	Syllables	Average
Colon A	484	7.2	488	7.3	491	7.3	1463	7.3
Colon B	390	5.8	381	5.7	382	5.7	1153	5.7
Subtotal	874	13.0	869	13.0	873	13.0	2616	13.0

Overall the poems exhibit almost identical structural features. The lines have the same average length, and they divide into cola of the same uneven lengths. The average line length is 13 syllables, while the cola divide between A = 7.2 or 7.3 and B = 5.7 or 5.8. This is sufficient to demonstrate the falling rhythm of each entire composition, but the numbers are skewed somewhat by the conflicting internal arrangements. Thus, when we break the poems down according to the three types of lines in their rhythmic patterns, we note important differences. While overall line lengths average out pretty much the same, the lines with the dominant falling rhythm come out with A cola of nearly 8 syllables (7.9 to be exact), and the corresponding B cola have slightly over 5 syllables (5.3). Similarly, these lines with the contrary rising meter come out nearly as mirror images, with A cola of nearly 5 syllables (4.8) and corresponding B cola much closer to 8 syllables (7.7).

The remaining lines belong to balanced cola, thereby splitting the 13 available syllables in half (6.7 syllables per colon, 13.3 per line). We can therefore substantiate the original impression about these poems, namely that they are constructed on a model that called for lines of 13 syllables each divided into unequal cola, so as to produce a falling rhythm with roughly 8 syllables and 3 accents in the first colon and 5 syllables and 2 accents in the second. In a limited number of cases, the poet deliberately reversed the procedure with lines of approximately the same length, but divided with an A colon of 5 syllables and 2 accents and a B colon of 8 syllables and 3 accents. In addition, other lines, approximately equal in number to those with a rising rhythm, are balanced with either 2 or 3 accents in each colon matched by the same number of accents in the other colon and with the same number of syllables likewise.

The three poems are so similar in all these respects that we are compelled to conclude that they were all constructed in this unusual way from the same model. This evidence shows that a quantitative element or control is present and plays an important role in the composition of Hebrew poetry. As such, it should be acknowledged and dealt with in any serious study of Biblical Hebrew poems.

Table 1. Lamentations—Syllable Counts

Chapters

	1				2				3		
	A	B	Total		A	B	Total		A	B	Total
(1)	7	6	13	(1)	7	7	14	(1)	8	5	13
	7	6	13		6	5	11	(2)	7	4	11
	7	5	12		8	4	12	(3)	4	7	11
Total	21	17	38	Total	21	16	37	Total	19	16	35
(2)	A	B	Total	(2)	A	B	Total		A	B	Total
	7	7	14		9	6	15	(4)	8	5	13
	5	6	11		6	7	13	(5)	7	5	12
	8	7	15		4	9	13	(6)	8	5	13
Total	20	20	40	Total	19	22	41	Total	23	15	38
(3)	A	B	Total	(3)	A	B	Total		A	B	Total
	9	6	15		6	5	11	(7)	8	5	13
	7	6	13		7	5	12	(8)	8	6	14
	9	5	14		11	5	16	(9)	8	6	14
Total	25	17	42	Total	24	15	39	Total	24	17	41
(4)	A	B	Total	(4)	A	B	Total		A	B	Total
	8	7	15		7	7	14	(10)	5	6	11
	8	7	15		3	5	8	(11)	11	5	16
	7	4	11		5	7	12	(12)	9	6	15
Total	23	18	41	Total	15	19	34	Total	25	17	42
(5)	A	B	Total	(5)	A	B	Total		A	B	Total
	7	6	13		8	5	13	(13)	6	5	11
	5	6	11		8	5	13	(14)	9	7	16
	9	4	13		7	7	14	(15)	8	5	13
Total	21	16	37	Total	23	17	40	Total	23	17	40
(6)	A	B	Total	(6)	A	B	Total		A	B	Total
	7	4	11		7	5	12	(16)	8	6	14
	9	6	15		7	5	12	(17)	8	5	13
	7	5	12		7	4	11	(18)	7	7	14
Total	23	15	38	Total	21	14	35	Total	23	18	41
(7)	A	B	Total	(7)	A	B	Total		A	B	Total
	7	9	16		8	5	13	(19)	8	4	12
	5	8	13		6	7	13	(20)	4	7	11
	8	5	13		8	4	12	(21)	6	4	10
	5	8	13								
Total	25	30	55	Total	22	16	38	Total	18	15	33

Table 1. Lamentations—Syllable Counts

Chapters

	1				2				3		
(8)	A	B	Total	(8)	A	B	Total		A	B	Total
	8	8	16		7	5	12	(22)	10	7	17
	10	6	16		3	8	11	(23)	7	7	14
	5	5	10		7	5	12	(24)	9	5	14
Total	23	19	42	Total	17	18	35	Total	26	19	45
(9)	A	B	Total	(9)	A	B	Total		A	B	Total
	7	7	14		9	9	18	(25)	6	6	12
	6	5	11		9	3	12	(26)	7	6	13
	7	5	12		5	9	14	(27)	3	8	11
Total	20	17	37	Total	23	21	44	Total	16	20	36
(10)	A	B	Total	(10)	A	B	Total		A	B	Total
	5	6	11		5	9	14	(28)	7	5	12
	6	5	11		7	5	12	(29)	4	8	12
	5	8	13		7	7	14	(30)	8	5	13
Total	16	19	35	Total	19	21	40	Total	19	18	37
(11)	A	B	Total	(11)	A	B	Total		A	B	Total
	6	5	11		8	6	14	(31)	7	3	10
	9	4	13		7	5	12	(32)	4	8	12
	8	7	15		8	6	14	(33)	7	6	13
Total	23	16	39	Total	23	17	40	Total	18	17	35
(12)	A	B	Total	(12)	A	B	Total		A	B	Total
	9	6	15		7	6	13	(34)	6	5	11
	8	5	13		8	5	13	(35)	6	5	11
	6	6	12		6	5	11	(36)	8	6	14
Total	23	17	40	Total	21	16	37	Total	20	16	36
(13)	A	B	Total	(13)	A	B	Total		A	B	Total
	11	4	15		9	6	15	(37)	7	6	13
	6	6	12		9	6	15	(38)	7	6	13
	7	5	12		7	4	11	(39)	7	5	12
Total	24	15	39	Total	25	16	41	Total	21	17	38
(14)	A	B	Total	(14)	A	B	Total		A	B	Total
	6	7	13		6	4	10	(40)	11	7	18
	6	4	10		8	6	14	(41)	9	5	14
	7	7	14		4	8	12	(42)	9	6	15
Total	19	18	37	Total	18	18	36	Total	29	18	47

Table 1. Lamentations—Syllable Counts

Chapters

	1				2				3		
(15)	A	B	Total	(15)	A	B	Total		A	B	Total
	6	6	12		7	5	12	(43)	10	7	17
	6	6	12		9	6	15	(44)	7	6	13
	6	8	14		13	6	19	(45)	9	5	14
Total	18	20	38	Total	29	17	46	Total	26	18	44
(16)	A	B	Total	(16)	A	B	Total		A	B	Total
	8	8	16		6	4	10	(46)	7	5	12
	9	4	13		8	6	14	(47)	7	5	12
	7	5	12		9	6	15	(48)	8	5	13
Total	24	17	41	Total	23	16	39	Total	22	15	37
(17)	A	B	Total	(17)	A	B	Total		A	B	Total
	9	5	14		8	5	13	(49)	9	5	14
	7	5	12		8	6	14	(50)	5	5	10
	7	6	13		8	5	13	(51)	8	6	14
Total	23	16	39	Total	24	16	40	Total	22	16	38
(18)	A	B	Total	(18)	A	B	Total		A	B	Total
	5	6	11		8	5	13	(52)	7	5	12
	7	6	13		7	5	12	(53)	7	5	12
	8	6	14		7	6	13	(54)	6	6	12
Total	20	18	38	Total	22	16	38	Total	20	16	36
(19)	A	B	Total	(19)	A	B	Total		A	B	Total
	8	5	13		7	5	12	(55)	8	5	13
	7	5	12		6	6	12	(56)	5	14	19
	7	7	14		6	5	11	(57)	9	6	15
					7	5	12				
Total	22	17	39	Total	26	21	47	Total	22	25	47
(20)	A	B	Total	(20)	A	B	Total		A	B	Total
	7	6	13		8	6	14	(58)	9	5	14
	7	6	13		8	6	14	(59)	9	5	14
	6	4	10		10	5	15	(60)	7	6	13
Total	20	16	36	Total	26	17	43	Total	25	16	41
(21)	A	B	Total	(21)	A	B	Total		A	B	Total
	9	5	14		7	4	11	(61)	8	7	15
	12	6	18		8	5	13	(62)	9	5	14
	7	6	13		8	7	15	(63)	9	6	15
Total	28	17	45	Total	23	16	39	Total	26	18	44

Table 1. Lamentations—Syllable Counts

Chapters

1				2				3			
(22)	A	B	Total	(22)	A	B	Total		A	B	Total
	10	5	15		6	6	12	(64)	8	6	14
	7	5	12		9	5	14	(65)	8	6	14
	6	5	11		9	5	14	(66)	8	6	14
Total	23	15	38	Total	24	16	40	Total	24	18	42
Overall totals:											
	A	B	Total		A	B	Total		A	B	Total
	484	390	874		488	381	869		491	382	873

Table 2. Lamentations—Accent Counts

Chapters

1

	A		B		Total	
(1)	3		3		6	
	2		2		4	
	2		2		4	
Total	7		7		14	
(2)	A		B		Total	
	3		3		6	
	2	(1)	1		3	(1)
	3		3		6	
Total	8	(1)	7		15	(1)
(3)	A		B		Total	
	3		2		5	
	3		3		6	
	2		2		4	
Total	8		7		15	
(4)	A		B		Total	
	3		3		6	
	2		2		4	
	2		2		4	
Total	7		7		14	
(5)	A		B		Total	
	3		2		5	
	2	(1)	2		4	(1)
	3		1		4	
Total	8	(1)	5		13	(1)
(6)	A		B		Total	
	2		1		3	
	3		2		5	
	2		2		4	
Total	7		5		12	
(7)	A		B		Total	
	2		3		5	
	2		4		6	
	3		3		6	
	2		2	(1)	4	(1)
Total	9		12	(1)	21	(1)

2

	A		B		Total	
(1)	3		2		5	
	3		2		5	
	2		2		4	
Total	8		6		14	
(2)	A		B		Total	
	4		3		7	
	2		2		4	
	2		3		5	
Total	8		8		16	
(3)	A		B		Total	
	2	(1)	3		5	(1)
	3		2		5	
	4		2		6	
Total	9	(1)	7		16	(1)
(4)	A		B		Total	
	3		3		6	
	1		2		3	
	2		3		5	
Total	6		8		14	
(5)	A		B		Total	
	3		2		5	
	2		2		4	
	2		2		4	
Total	7		6		13	
(6)	A		B		Total	
	3		2		5	
	3		2		5	
	2	(1)	2		4	(1)
Total	8	(1)	6		14	(1)
(7)	A		B		Total	
	3		2		5	
	2		2		4	
	3		2		5	
Total	8		6		14	

3

	A	B	Total
(1)	4	2	6
(2)	3	2	5
(3)	3	3	6
Total	10	7	17
	A	B	Total
(4)	3	2	5
(5)	3	2	5
(6)	2	2	4
Total	8	6	14
	A	B	Total
(7)	4	2	6
(8)	4	2	6
(9)	3	2	5
Total	11	6	17
	A	B	Total
(10)	4	2	6
(11)	3	2	5
(12)	3	2	5
Total	10	6	16
	A	B	Total
(13)	2	2	4
(14)	3	2	5
(15)	2	2	4
Total	7	6	13
	A	B	Total
(16)	3	2	5
(17)	3	2	5
(18)	3	2	5
Total	9	6	15
	A	B	Total
(19)	2	2	4
(20)	2	3	5
(21)	3	2	5
Total	7	7	14

Table 2. Lamentations—Accent Counts

Chapters

	1						2						3				
8)	A		B	Total		(8)	A		B	Total			A	B		Total	
	3		3	6			3		2	5		(22)	4	3		7	
	2	(1)	2	4	(1)		2		3	5		(23)	2	2		4	
	2		2	4			2	(1)	2	4	(1)	(24)	4	3		7	
otal	7	(1)	7	14	(1)	Total	7	(1)	7	14	(1)	Total	10	8		18	
9)	A		B	Total		(9)	A		B	Total			A	B		Total	
	2		3	5			3		3	6		(25)	3	2		5	
	2		3	5			3		2	5		(26)	3	2		5	
	3		3	6			1		3	4		(27)	2	3	(1)	5	(1)
otal	7		9	16		Total	7		8	15		Total	8	7	(1)	15	(1)
10)	A		B	Total		(10)	A		B	Total			A	B		Total	
	3		2	5			2		3	5		(28)	3	3		6	
	2	(1)	2	4	(1)		3		2	5		(29)	3	3		6	
	3		3	6			3		2	5		(30)	3	2		5	
otal	8	(1)	7	15	(1)	Total	8		7	15		Total	9	8		17	
11)	A		B	Total		(11)	A		B	Total			A	B		Total	
	2		2	4			3		2	5		(31)	4	1		5	
	3		2	5			3		2	5		(32)	2	3		5	
	3		3	6			3		2	5		(33)	4	2		6	
otal	8		7	15		Total	9		6	15		Total	10	6		16	
12)	A		B	Total		(12)	A		B	Total			A	B		Total	
	4		2	6			2		3	5		(34)	3	3		6	
	3		3	6			2		2	4		(35)	2	3		5	
	3		3	6			2		2	4		(36)	3	3		6	
otal	10		8	18		Total	6		7	13		Total	8	9		17	
13)	A		B	Total		(13)	A		B	Total			A	B		Total	
	3	(1)	1	4	(1)		3	(1)	2	5	(1)	(37)	4	3		7	
	3		2	5			3		2	5		(38)	4	2		6	
	2		2	4			3	(1)	2	5	(1)	(39)	3	2		5	
otal	8	(1)	5	13	(1)	Total	9	(2)	6	15	(2)	Total	11	7		18	
14)	A		B	Total		(14)	A		B	Total			A	B		Total	
	3		2	5			3		2	5		(40)	3	2		5	
	2		2	4			2	(1)	2	4	(1)	(41)	3	2		5	
	2		3	5			2		3	5		(42)	3	3		6	
otal	7		7	14		Total	7	(1)	7	14	(1)	Total	9	7		16	

Table 2. Lamentations—Accent Counts

Chapters

	1				2				3		
(15)	A	B	Total	(15)	A	B	Total		A	B	Total
	2	2	4		3	2	5	(43)	3	3	6
	3	2	5		3	2	5	(44)	3	2	5
	3	2	5		5	2	7	(45)	3	2	5
Total	8	6	14	Total	11	6	17	Total	9	7	16
(16)	A	B	Total	(16)	A	B	Total		A	B	Total
	3	4	7		3	1	4	(46)	3	1	4
	3 (1)	2	5 (1)		2 (1)	2	4 (1)	(47)	4	2	6
	3	3	6		4	2	6	(48)	3	2	5
Total	9 (1)	9	18 (1)	Total	9 (1)	5	14 (1)	Total	10	5	15
(17)	A	B	Total	(17)	A	B	Total		A	B	Total
	3	3	6		4	2	6	(49)	4	2	6
	3	2	5		3 (1)	3	6 (1)	(50)	2	2	4
	2	2	4		3	3	6	(51)	3	3	6
Total	8	7	15	Total	10 (1)	8	18 (1)	Total	9	7	16
(18)	A	B	Total	(18)	A	B	Total		A	B	Total
	3	3	6		3	2	5	(52)	3	2	5
	2	2	4		3	2	5	(53)	3	2	5
	2	2	4		3 (1)	2	5 (1)	(54)	2 (1)	2	4 (1
Total	7	7	14	Total	9 (1)	6	15 (1)	Total	8 (1)	6	14 (
(19)	A	B	Total	(19)	A	B	Total		A	B	Total
	2	2	4		3	2	5	(55)	3	2	5
	2	2	4		3	3	6	(56)	2	4	6
	3 (1)	2	5 (1)		3	2	5	(57)	3	2	5
					2	2	4				
Total	7 (1)	6	13 (1)	Total	11	9	20	Total	8	8	16
(20)	A	B	Total	(20)	A	B	Total		A	B	Total
	3 (1)	2	5 (1)		3	3	6	(58)	4	2	6
	3	3	6		3	2	5	(59)	3	2	5
	2	2	4		3	2	5	(60)	2	2	4
Total	8 (1)	7	15 (1)	Total	9	7	16	Total	9	6	15
(21)	A	B	Total	(21)	A	B	Total		A	B	Total
	4	3	7		3	2	5	(61)	3	2	5
	4	3	7		2	2	4	(62)	3	2	5
	2	2	4		3	3	6	(63)	3	2	5
Total	10	8	18	Total	8	7	15	Total	9	6	15

Table 2. Lamentations—Accent Counts

Chapters

	1				2				3		
2)	A	B	Total	(22)	A	B	Total		A	B	Total
	3	2	5		3	2	5	(64)	4	2	6
	3	2	5		4	2	6	(65)	3	2	5
	2 (1)	2	4 (1)		2	2	4	(66)	3	3	6
tal	8 (1)	6	14 (1)	Total	9	6	15	Total	10	7	17
verall totals:											
	A	B	Total		A	B	Total		A	B	Total
	174 (9)	156 (1)	330 (10)		183 (9)	149 (0)	332 (9)		199 (1)	148 (1)	347 (2)

* Parenthetical numbers reflect the presence of a *metheg*, a possible secondary accent in the MT.

The Terms נפל and הפיל in the Context of Inheritance

Moshe Greenberg
The Hebrew University of Jerusalem

After listing the lands that remained unconquered by Joshua, Josh 13:6b has God commanding Joshua: רק הַפִּלֶהָ לישראל בנחלה. The NJPSV renders: 'apportion their lands by lot among Israel'. A footnote referring to "their lands" says, "lit.: 'it'." Similarly, M. Noth translates the verb by *verlose* 'dispose by lot';[1] other English translations use 'allot', a more general expression that retains the allusion to lots. Modern lexicons reflect the common opinion that הפיל in this context means 'assign, apportion, by lot' (BDB, GB, KB), deriving its meaning from the expression הפיל גורל 'cast lot' (e.g., Isa 34:17, Jonah 1:7) because the land was in fact divided among the tribes by lot (חלק בגורל, e.g., Num 26:55–56). In Josh 13:6b–7a (הפיל(ה . . . בנחלה) and (חלק (את הארץ הזאת בנחלה are, to be sure, equivalent syntactically, but that does not establish their semantic equivalence. The expression *הפיל (הארץ) בגורל *'assign (the land) by lot' does not exist. Moreover, in the book of Joshua the casting of lots is expressed by the verbs ירה (18:6) and השליך (18:8, 10) but never by הפיל.[2] To my knowledge, no one has explained the process of condensation that resulted in the alleged sense. G. A. Cooke, for example, is content with the vague remark that, in ובהפילכם את

Author's note: Baruch Levine has made a signal contribution to the understanding of the cults and cultic terminology of the ancient Near East, with particular attention to biblical Israel. The following study of two related terms from the realm of inheritance (never far from religion), tendered to him in appreciation, will I hope engage his interest both as a seasoned philologist and as a commentator on the book of Numbers, in which these terms first occur.

1. M. Noth, *Das Buch Josua* (2d ed.; HAT; Tübingen: Mohr, 1953).

2. The three verbs express different aspects of the technique: השליך 'throw' is the general term; ירה 'shoot' refers to the forceful ejection and rapid emergence of the lot from hand or container; הפיל 'cause to fall' refers to the groundward direction of the throw. See the brief but illuminating description by M. Lichtenstein, "Lots, Biblical Data," *EncJud* 11.510–11. For further details, see below, n. 8.

הארץ בנחלה (Ezek 45:1) and similar constructions in 47:22 and 48:29, גורל is "omitted."[3] Y. Kaufmann follows the prevalent view that הפיל בנחלה = חלק בגורל, but he acknowledges that

> sometimes הפיל בנחלה does not mean allot portions but rather convey ownership [of a tract of land] in general; designate as a possession and a patrimony. This is doubtless the meaning in Num 34:2; Ezek 47:14.[4]

I shall argue that the expression in question and its congeners have no reference to (division by) lots but to allocation and appropriation of a tract of (undivided) territory.

(a) In Num 34:2 the verb appears in the *Qal* form, with הארץ as subject: The boundaries of the promised land are introduced by the clause זאת הארץ אשר תפול לכם בנחלה 'this is the land that shall fall to you for an inheritance' (RSV; 'as your portion', NJPSV).[5] BDB 657a classifies this usage with נפל said

3. G. A. Cooke, *Ezekiel* (ICC; New York: Scribner's, 1937) 505. W. Zimmerli (*Ezechiel* [BKAT; Neukirchen-Vluyn: Neukirchener Verlag, 1968] 1206) comments on תפילו אותה בנחלה in 47:22b: "Originally תפילו was to be complemented by גורל. So G[reek] *baleite* [*autēn*] *en klērō* throughout [actually only here and 48:29, M.G.], in accordance with the sense." This is not clear. הפיל גורל 'cast a lot' is rendered, literally, *ballein klēron* (e.g., Prov 1:14)—the verbal complement being a direct object (accusative in Greek). But the verbal complement in Ezek 47:22 and 48:29 is adverbial *en klērō*, which phrase renders both בגורל and בנחלה. Since *הפיל בגורל never occurs, *ballein en klērō* must render הפיל בנחלה, and so it is not an attestation of Greek's retention of an "original" idiom that somehow (but how?) included גורל. Indeed *ballein* + accusative + *en klērō* 'cast [land] by/in inheritance' is so slavish a rendering of our Hebrew that one wonders what a Greek speaker could have made of it. Comparable is the LXX at Josh 23:4, *eperripha humin ta ethnē . . . en tois klērois* 'I have cast at/upon you the . . . nations by/in inheritances'. Liddell and Scott record no meaning for *ballein* and *epirriptein* that fits here. The LXX's variety of renderings of הפיל in property contexts (add to the foregoing examples: *diadidonai* 'give over, assign', Josh 13:6; *katametreisthai* 'measure', Ezek 45:1) suggests that the translators were guessing when they were not slavishly literal.

4. Y. Kaufmann, *Commentary to the Book of Joshua* (Jerusalem: Kiryat-Sepher, 1960) 162–63 [Heb.].

5. For recent discussion of the untranslatable term נחלה, see A. Malamat, *Mari and the Early Israelite Experience* (Schweich Lectures 1984; Oxford: Oxford University Press, 1989) 48–52 ("hereditary share, inheritance portion, or, simply, patrimony," p. 48).

The ב of בנחלה—*beth essentiae* in grammarese (P. Joüon and T. Muraoka, *A Grammar of Biblical Hebrew* [Rome: Pontifical Biblical Institute, 1991] §133c) appears in similar construction in ועשיתם . . . עולה או זבח . . . בנדבה 'you make a whole or "peace"-offering as a freewill offering' (Num 15:3); בקודש קדשים תאכלנו 'you shall eat it as [in the category of] holiest things' (Num 18:10; see A. B. Ehrlich, *Randglossen zur Hebräischen Bibel* [Leipzig: Hinrichs, 1909] 2.179–80). Examples in Mishnaic Hebrew: והוא חתום עליו בעד 'and his signature is on it as a witness' (*m. Ketub.* 13:6); ניתן במתנה 'given as a gift' in passage (e) below.

of lots (as Ezek 24:6, Jonah 1:7) and defines the verb in Num 34:2 as 'fall, be allotted to'; GB 512a more explicitly: *jem. zufallen* (*bei einer Teilung*) ('to fall to someone [in a dividing-up]'). But here it is not a question of division or allotment by lot; the whole land of Israel delimited by its boundaries is allocated by divine fiat to the people.

(b) Similarly, Ezek 47:14, ונפלה הארץ הזאת לכם בנחלה makes no allusion to division by lot but refers to the whole land as 'falling to (= coming into the possession of)' the Israelites as a patrimony. The semantic parallel with English 'fall', the verb used in the translations, suggests that in Hebrew as in English we are dealing with a direct evolution from the basic sense of נפל 'fall' to the extended senses 'come (by chance, by succession, as duty), devolve' ('the estate fell to his brother').

(c) The suggestion is supported by the Aramaic usage in Ezra 7:20: 'any other needs of the House of your God די יפל לך למנתן, that it falls to you to supply' (NJPSV). The duty to supply needs of the Temple did not come about by the fall of lots.

(d) Even the unique usage in Ruth 3:18, איך יפול דבר has its exact English parallel 'how the matter will fall' (AV, RV; NJPSV: 'turn out'). GB notes in connection with the sense of the Ruth passage that Latin *cadere* and *accidere*—both basically 'fall'—have comparable extensions of usage (as has Greek *piptein*, German *fallen*). Closer to home, Syriac נפל, Akkadian *maqātu*, and Arabic *waqaʿa*, all basically 'fall', develop into 'happen, fall to', as in Hebrew.

Mishnaic Hebrew exhibits this usage with greater variety of subjects and constructions. The following examples are taken from Ben-Yehudah's *Thesaurus of the Hebrew Language*, 3725–26.

(e) פירות שביעית שנפלו לו בירושה או שניתנו לו במתנה 'produce of the seventh (= fallow) year that fell to him as an inheritance or was given to him as a gift' (*m. Šeb.* 9:9). The syntax is identical with that of Biblical Hebrew; בירושה here = biblical בנחלה, an adverb.

(f) האשה שנפלו לה נכסים . . . כספים . . . עבדים ושפחות זקנים 'a woman to whom goods . . . money . . . old male and female servants fell (as an inheritance)' (*m. Ketub.* 8:1, 3, 5). Here the qualifying adverb is omitted without change of meaning; (דבר) נפל ל(פלוני) by itself means 'something fell to someone by inheritance'. This construction (I shall argue) appears in Josh 17:5 ((h) below) and Ps 16:6 ((i) below).

(g) שמא תפול לה ירושה ממקום אחר 'perhaps an inheritance may fall to her from elsewhere' (*m. Ketub.* 5:7). Here ירושה has been taken out of the adverb (בירושה, see (e) above) and made the subject of the verb; such a conversion of the biblical equivalent בנחלה does not appear in Biblical Hebrew (on its reflection in the LXX of Judg 18:1, see (j) and n. 9 below). The identical usage occurs in Palestinian Jewish Aramaic.[6]

6. See S. Lieberman, *Tosefta Ki-Feshuta* (New York: Jewish Theological Seminary, 1962) 3.348 n. 28.

(h) This usage established, Josh 17:5 ויפלו חבלי מנשה עשרה may be rendered 'there fell ten portions to Manasseh' (AV; similarly RSV, NJPSV). חבל 'rope → measuring line → measured tract, portion of land' (BDB 286b) contains no allusion to lots.[7]

(i) Ps 16:6, חבלים נפלו לי בנעימים '(land-)portions have fallen to me in pleasant places', is related in meaning to the foregoing example, though grammatically different (see n. 7). In context it appears to be a metaphor, meaning: I have been favored with good fortune.

Despite the similar idiom in Josh 17:5 ((h) above), where the consensual rendition of חבלים is 'portions', here many hold to the traditional 'the lines have fallen for me, etc.' (RSV; similarly AV, NEB), referring to the use of lines to measure and divide plots of land; for example, Amos 7:17 'your land shall be divided up with a measuring-line' (בחבל תחלק). KB equates this expression with our חבלים נפלו, supplying the occasion for both as 'at the casting of lots for a field'. But parceling a tract of land by measuring-line and casting lots for the parcels are separate acts; the two are kept clearly apart in Isa 34:17: והוא הפיל להן גורל וידו חלקתה להם בקו 'He cast lots for them, and his hand divided it for them by the line'.[8] The main cause of confusion is the

7. The NEB must insinuate an echo of the phantom lot: "There fell to Manasseh's lot ten shares." The construct חבלי מנשה is a nice instance of "the dative . . . expressed by the genitive" (Joüon-Muraoka, *Grammar*, §129h); it is equivalent to (ויפלו) חבלים למנשה (עשרה) '(there fell) portions to Manasseh (ten)'. (The standard dative construction -חבלים נפלו ל occurs in Ps 16:6; see (i) below.) Other examples of the dative expressed by the genitive are found in Exod 3:21, ונתתי את חן העם הזה בעיני מצרים = 'I will grant favor to this people (= חן לעם הזה) in the eyes of the Egyptians' (= I will dispose the Egyptians favorably toward this people). As Joüon-Muraoka note, most examples are with the genitive (possessive) pronoun suffix; e.g., Exod 2:9, אתן את שכרך 'I will pay you a wage' (= שכר לך; so LXX). This pronominal usage has been exhaustively treated by S. Kogut, "Alternative Usages of Independent and Suffixed Personal Pronouns to Express Possession in Biblical Hebrew," in *Studies in Bible and Exegesis* 3 (Goshen-Gottstein Memorial Volume; ed. M. Bar-Asher et al.; Ramat Gan: Bar-Ilan University Press, 1993) 401–11 [Heb.].

8. The natural order of the acts seems to be reversed, for we expect that the tract to be parceled would first be divided into portions by measure and then the portions would be assigned to each claimant by lot. There is no clear biblical evidence for this procedure, but both GB and KB lexicons refer to the following description of periodic land apportionment by Arab farmers given by Alois Musil in his *Arabia Petraea* (Vienna: Holder, 1908) 3.293–94 (my translation from German):

> among the ʿAmârîn [a tribe of the ʿAraba] in mid-March every year the fields are divided into equal plots by rope, *ḥabel* [חבל]. The individual plots are thus-and-so long, thus-and-so wide, get boundary markers and are disposed of by lot to the individual families. The representative of each family takes a token—a little stone, a string, a little piece of wood, or the like—and puts it into a covered vessel appointed therefor, which is held by a boy. The sheikh takes up the parcels one by one, and at each the boy draws an object, *es-sihme*, out of the vessel. The parcel in question falls to whom the object belongs.

tenacious prejudice that every נפל connected with real estate is colored by the phrase נפל הגורל 'the lot fell'. Removing the lots from the scene leaves us with "lines" falling. Now a measuring-line may extend, stretch, run, or lie along the ground (only נטה קו 'stretch a line' [Job 38:5] actually appears); but why should it "fall"? (On Mic 2:5, משליך חבל בגורל, see (s) below.) The similarity of our חבלים נפלו לי to ויפלו חבלי מנשה in Josh 17:5, where 'lines' is obviously inept, militates against 'lines' and speaks for '(land-)portions' in Ps 16:6. The literal sense is: pleasant are the tracts that have come into my possession––whether by lot, inheritance, gift, or other happenstance is not to the point.

(j) In Judg 18:1 we read that the Danite tribe was seeking an inheritance כי לא נפלה לו עד היום ההוא בתוך שבטי ישראל בנחלה 'for (such)[9] had not fallen to it till that day among the tribes of Israel as an inheritance'. NJPSV "no territory had fallen to their lot" or NEB "they had not come into possession of the territory allotted to them" reveals the prejudice that נפל connotes the casting of lots. All that is said is that the Danites had not yet come into a patrimony.

We return to our starting-point. If נפל (מקום) ל(פלוני) בנחלה means 'place X fell to person Y as an inheritance'—the verb being in *Qal*—then if the verb is in *Hiphil*, הפיל (פלוני) (מקום) ל(אלמוני) בנחלה must mean 'person X

Among the Ḥanâjre [a tribe located south of Wadi Ghazza] the whole territory is divided by ropes into sections for each individual clan. Then the representatives of each clan take tokens—a small stone, a piece of dung, or the like—which a disinterested party collects and hands over to a boy, who holds them in his hand.

When they come to a parcel they say: "Cast our lot, *irmi qurʿatna!*"

The boy takes out an object and displays it, saying: "Here is your lot, *hâkû qurʿatku.*" The field belongs to the clan of the person whose lot it is.

The members of the clan then divide the parcels, *aḥbâl*, among themselves in the same manner, and plant *bâṣûl* [a type of onion] along the borders of the individual plots.

For a more varied and fuller collection of evidence on land distribution by lot in Palestine early and late, see G. Dalman, *Arbeit und Sitte in Palästina* (Gütersloh: Bertelsmann, 1932) 2.36–46. Caution: in his account of the procedure of the Ḥanâjre—taken from Musil according to n. 2 on p. 41—after the boy cries, "Here is your lot," Dalman writes: "whereupon he probably casts it on the plot." This detail, affecting the definition of "casting lots" (see Lichtenstein, "Lots, Biblical Data") is absent in Musil's account. Perhaps Dalman imported it from inheritance and partnership procedures from es-Salt, which he goes on to describe on p. 41.

9. The verb נפלה here has no evident subject; possibly נחלה in the previous clause was carried over (I have indicated this by inserting "such"); then the fixed phrase נפל בנחלה influenced the wording of the rest of the sentence. The LXX reads 'for there had not fallen (*enepesen*, from *em-piptein*) to it . . . an inheritance', as though the last word was נחלה and was the subject of the verb. This is certainly an easier text, but elsewhere in Biblical Hebrew the sequence is נפל\הפיל בנחלה—the noun in adverbial construction. The conversion of נחלה into the subject of the verb by dropping the ב smacks of postbiblical treatment of the synonym ירושה; see (g) above.

caused place Y to fall to person Z as an inheritance', or, in other words: X allocated or appropriated place Y to Z as an inheritance (Z could be X himself). The pertinent passages are the following:

(k) Josh 13:6: רק הפילה לישראל בנחלה 'only allocate it [הארץ הנשארת 'the remaining land', v. 2] to Israel as an inheritance'; and

(l) Josh 23:4: הפלתי לכם את הגוים הנשארים האלה בנחלה לשבטיכם 'I have allocated to you these remaining nations as an inheritance for your tribes'. Reference is made to lands of the nations that Israel had not dispossessed in Joshua's time but that Joshua must/did allocate to Israel as an inheritance. We are not told how such allocation was to be effected; Kaufmann conjectures:

> Presumably the reference here [Josh 13:6] is not to allotment into portions but to a solemn ceremony of granting possession, of giving the people title to the whole land in God's name by means of some symbolic act or solemn proclamation.[10]

However we judge this conjecture (and it is not clear why Kaufmann supposes that the ceremony gives title to more than "the remaining land"), Kaufmann rightly points out that at least part of this territory was never apportioned by lot among the tribes (from Baal Gad in the valley of Lebanon to Lebo Hamath). Hence there must be a difference between tribal allotment and allocation/appropriation to the tribal collective of a territory in bulk—the present case.

(m) Ezek 45:1: ובהפילכם את הארץ בנחלה 'and when you appropriate the land as an inheritance'. Ezekiel knows nothing about dividing the land by casting lots; in chap. 48 he fixes the boundaries and location of each tribe, leaving nothing to lots. This simple fact is decisive for the rest of the Ezekiel instances. The translation in the NEB, 'when you divide the land by lot among the tribes for their possession', is altogether misleading.

(n) Ezek 47:22: v. 21 follows the definition of the boundaries of the future land with the injunction: "You shall divide (וחלקתם) this land among the tribes of Israel." Then comes an important annex (v. 22): והיה תפילו אותה בנחלה לכם ולהגרים הגרים בתוככם 'and this shall be: you shall appropriate it as an inheritance to yourselves and to the aliens who reside among you'. The division of the land among the tribes (in v. 21) is clearly distinguished from its falling—as a whole—to both Israelites and resident aliens as a common heritage (v. 22).

On אתכם יפלו בנחלה in v. 22b, see (r) below.

(o) Ezek 48:29: זאת הארץ אשר תפילו מנחלה לשבטי ישראל ואלה מחלקותם 'This is the land that you will appropriate as an inheritance[11] to the tribes

10. Kaufmann, *Commentary to the Book of Joshua*, at 13:6.

11. The word מנחלה is probably an error for בנחלה, as all the ancient versions render it. L. C. Allen (*Ezekiel 20–48* [WBC; Dallas: Word, 1990] 276) suggests that it may be a misplaced gloss to נחלה in the preceding verse.

of Israel, and these are their divisions'. Again, there is a clear distinction between the land as a whole that "you will cause to fall" to the collectivity of the tribes as their common patrimony, and the discrete divisions of each tribe.

(p) Ps 78:55, ויגרש מפניהם גוים ויפילם בחבל נחלה 'He drove out nations before them, and allocated them (= the nations' lands) as a hereditary portion'. The cryptic second clause has been variously analyzed:

- AV: 'divided them an inheritance by the line'. The suffix on the verb is taken, unusually, as a dative ('for them'—for Israel). The word בחבל is isolated and taken as 'measuring-line'. The word נחלה is the direct object of the verb, which is understood as 'divide (by line)'. The NJPSV 'allotting them (= to them, to Israel) their portion by the line', seems to reflect a similar analysis.
- Kissane: 'allotted them by line as an inheritance'.[12] The verbal suffix is the direct object ('them' = the nations); 'by line', as AV; נחלה = בנחלה.
- RSV: 'he apportioned them for a possession'. The measuring-line is gone; the noun in בחבל appears in the "portion" of "apportioned," and its preposition is attached to נחלה 'for a possession' = בנחלה.
- NEB: 'he allotted their lands to Israel as a possession'. This reading is essentially the same as the RSV, with the ghost of "line" = "lot" hidden in "allotted."

My guide in interpreting this verset is its relation to elements in Josh 13:6 + 23:4:

Josh 13:6: כל יושבי [הארץ הנשארת] אנכי אורישם מפני בני ישראל רק הפילה [את הארץ] לבני ישראל בנחלה.

Josh 23:4: הפלתי לכם את הגוים הנשארים האלה בנחלה. Just as the direct object of הפיל in these passages is the remaining lands of the nations, so in the second verset of Ps 78:55 the verbal suffix in ויפילם is of a direct object and refers to the (lands of the) גוים mentioned in the preceding verset. And just as the verb of the Joshua passages is qualified by adverbial בנחלה, so the verb in the Psalms verset is qualified by בחבל נחלה. The separation of the words of this pair (as in AV, etc.) ignores their fusion into a single concept—"hereditary portion"—and their consequent treatment as a grammatical unit; cf. Deut 32:9, חבל נחלתו 'his hereditary portion' (not 'the portion of his inheritance'). Hence I translate the second verset of Ps 78:55: 'and he allocated them (= their lands) as a hereditary portion'. To whom? To the referent of the preceding pronominal suffix—מפניהם 'before them'—namely, the Israelites.

(q) In later Hebrew הפיל 'cause to fall (to someone, by succession, etc.)' appears in מפילים נחלות '(courts) assign estates / allocate inheritances' (*b. B.*

12. E. J. Kissane, *The Book of Psalms* (Dublin: Browne and Nolan, 1964) 356.

Bat. 113b). This is not an importation from Biblical Hebrew in which this idiom does not exist. The noun, in what was in Biblical Hebrew the adverbial element (בנחלה), drops its ב and is converted into the direct object of the verb (cf. (g) above, which shows an analogous conversion in the Mishnaic *Qal* construction).

Paralleling this usage, Akkadian *šumqutu*, the causative of *maqatu* 'fall', has 'assign' as one of its extended meanings.

Two peculiar skewings of Hebrew idiomatic usage remain to be considered.

(r) Ezek 47:22b: אתכם [הגרים] יפלו בנחלה must mean, according to its context: the aliens shall join with you in appropriating the land as an inheritance. Just how it comes to mean this is obscure (but note English 'fall in with' = join). The widely accepted emendation יפילו requires problematic supplementation; e.g., אתכם יפילו [אותה להם? לכם?] בנחלה. Maybe that is why tradition avoided it.

(s) Mic 2:5 is invoked by some to defend the image of 'lines falling' in Ps 61:6. The pertinent sequence reads משליך חבל בגורל, which D. Hillers, remarking its uniqueness, translates 'one to cast the cord over your allotted land'.[13] The Semitic versions felt something was elided here and filled out the sequence: Targum Jonathan: מתח חוט משח בעדבא 'who stretches out a line, who measures by lot'; Peshiṭta: דמשח בשויתא דמפלג בפצא 'who measures with a cord, who divides by lot'. On the other hand, moderns have regarded the text as conflated: "'Measuring-line' and 'lot' will likewise be variants, of which the second is probably to be preferred (cf. Josh 18:8, 10 [השליך גורל])."[14]

The beginning of wisdom in this case is to admit that משליך goes with חבל (in the sense of 'cord') only by giving it an unattested value—as did the Targum ('stretch') and Peshiṭta ('measure with'). The NJPSV keeps to the regular sense of השליך in its rendering: 'cast a lot cord' (as though the text read חבל גורל?), which is glossed in its note c: "On a piece of land, thus acquiring title to it; cf. Josh 18:6; Ps 16:6." I have not been able to verify the alleged symbolic act; the references do not attest to it.[15] Yet it is undeniable that all three words belong to the terminology of land-acquisition. I suggest, with diffidence, that each word is being used in a sense borrowed from its synonym (also part of the vocabulary of land-acquisition); thus:

משליך = מפיל	'one who appropriates
חבל = חלק	a (land-) portion
בגורל = בנחלה	as an inheritance'.

13. D. Hillers, *Micah* (Hermeneia; Philadelphia: Fortress, 1984) 31–32.

14. A. Alt, *Kleine Schriften* (Munich: Beck, 1959) 3.377 n. 3.

15. Cords cast as lots onto parcels as a sign of ownership do not appear in the evidence presented in n. 8.

The word מפיל is a synonym of משליך in the phrase מפיל\משליך גורל; here משליך takes from מפיל the specialized sense of appropriation of property. The word בנחלה is a synonym of בגורל in such passages as Judg 1:2. The synonymy of חלק and חבל is evident in Deut 32:9. This obliquity is perhaps not too much of a strain on the poetry of Micah.

The phrase נפל ל- with property as subject means 'fall to, come into the possession of (by undefined means)'; הפיל ל- with property as direct object means literally 'cause to fall to', or idiomatically, 'allocate / appropriate to (by undefined means)'. The property in question 'falls' as a whole to the receiver. This extended meaning is paralleled in many languages. The assumption of an "omitted" or hidden or implicit גורל in this usage is unwarranted.

Jeremiah of Anathoth: A Prophet for All Israel

Herbert B. Huffmon
Drew University

Introduction

Jeremiah is the most accessible of the prophets; Jeremiah is the most hidden of the prophets. The portrait of Jeremiah in biblical scholarship varies considerably, and this variation continues even with the spate of recent publications. Since 1986, three major, large-scale commentaries on Jeremiah, by W. L. Holladay, R. P. Carroll, and W. McKane, have appeared. There is also, since 1986, the collaborative commentary begun by P. C. Craigie and completed by P. H. Kelley and J. F. Drinkard Jr., together with G. L. Keown, P. J. Scalise, and T. G. Smothers, as well as the modestly briefer commentaries by W. Brueggemann and D. R. Jones, the first two fascicles of S. Herrmann's major commentary, and the brief commentary by R. E. Clements.[1] The book of Jeremiah presents an unusual range of problems, and there is no present

1. W. L. Holladay, *Jeremiah* (Hermeneia; 2 vols.; Philadelphia; Fortress, 1986–89); R. P. Carroll, *Jeremiah* (OTL; Philadelphia: Westminster, 1986); W. McKane, *A Critical and Exegetical Commentary on Jeremiah* (ICC; 2 vols. Edinburgh: T. & T. Clark, 1986–96); P. C. Craigie, P. H. Kelley, and J. F. Drinkard Jr., *Jeremiah 1–25* (WBC 26; Dallas: Word, 1991), and G. L. Keown, P. J. Scalise, and T. G. Smothers, *Jeremiah 26–52* (WBC 27; Dallas: Word, 1995); W. Brueggemann, *To Pluck Up, To Tear Down: A Commentary on the Book of Jeremiah 1–25* (International Theological Commentary; Grand Rapids, Mich.; Eerdmans, 1988); and idem, *To Build, To Plant: A Commentary on Jeremiah 26–52* (International Theological Commentary; Grand Rapids, Mich.: Eerdmans, 1991); D. R. Jones, *Jeremiah* (NCB; London: Marshall Pickering / Grand Rapids, Mich.: Eerdmans, 1992); S. Herrmann, *Jeremia* (BKAT 12/1–2; Neukirchen-Vluyn; Neukirchener Verlag, 1986–90), reaching almost to the end of Jeremiah 2; and R. E. Clements, *Jeremiah* (Interpretation; Atlanta; John Knox, 1988).

prospect of any general consensus as to the mission and character of the "historical Jeremiah."[2] But these quite genuine difficulties do not prohibit an examination of the question of the associations of Jeremiah, whose native city—better, village—is within three or four miles of Jerusalem. In particular, one should examine the suggestion that Jeremiah is to be classified as an Ephraimite rather than a Judean prophet. In other words, was his message in continuity with prophetic traditions of the Northern Kingdom as distinct from the prophetic traditions of the Southern Kingdom?

That there is a close relationship between the book of Jeremiah and the Deuteronomic tradition is not in dispute. That Jeremiah is to be identified with traditions and interests of the Northern Kingdom as opposed to those of the Southern realm is herein disputed.

Status of the Question

A review of the literature shows that there seem to be four basic perspectives on Jeremiah with reference to the above issue:

1. Many commentators are noncommittal, in the sense that they do not stress particularities in the background of Jeremiah, though noting the relationship with the Deuteronomic tradition and Hosea. Others are suggestive of a general derivation from Israelite prophecy, at times stressing the individual personality of Jeremiah.
2. Some commentators stress Jeremiah's identity as a Judean. For example, Henri Cazelles declares that "Jeremiah remains a Judean speaking to Judeans, even if he has taken part in a reform based on Deuteronomy."[3]
3. Some scholars, for example Karl Elliger, see Jeremiah as representing "a conflict of the countryside with the capital city, as in the case of Micah (6:1; not, as many presume, the older N–S conflict!)."[4]
4. A long-held interpretation of Jeremiah emphasizes his being a Benjaminite from the priestly village of Anathoth and associates him with Northern traditions, especially with the prophet Hosea. For example, Adam Welch says that Jeremiah "belonged by sympathy as well as by

2. Note the range of opinion represented in P.-M. Bogaert (ed.), *Le livre de Jérémie—Le prophète et son milieu: Les oracles et leur transmission* (Louvain: Louvain University Press / Peeters, 1981); and L. G. Perdue and B. W. Kovacs (eds.), *A Prophet to the Nations: Essays in Jeremiah Studies* (Winona Lake, Ind.: Eisenbrauns, 1984); as well as the survey by S. Herrmann, *Jeremia: Der Prophet und das Buch* (Erträge der Forschung 271; Darmstadt: Wissenschaftliche Buchgesellschaft, 1990).

3. H. Cazelles, "Jeremiah and Deuteronomy," in *A Prophet to the Nations: Essays in Jeremiah Studies* (ed. L. Perdue and B. Kovacs; Winona Lake, Ind.: Eisenbrauns, 1984) 97.

4. K. Elliger, "Benjamin," *IDB* 1.384.

> descent to the northern kingdom."[5] Emphasizing Jeremiah's derivation from Anathoth and his dependency on Hosea, G. von Rad suggests that "the traditions cherished both in Benjamin and in Ephraim were those specific to Israel, those of the Exodus and the covenant at Sinai, which we have to differentiate from the traditions of Judah," so that although Jeremiah makes use of the David traditions, he represents a "different theological world" from that of Isaiah and the Zion tradition.[6] J. A. Thompson agrees with some other scholars in the assumption that "Jeremiah's family was probably descended from Eli, the priest of Shiloh," so that Jeremiah had "both family and geographical links to the north."[7] J. Muilenburg refers to "the northern traditions of the Elohist, Elijah, Deuteronomy, and Jeremiah."[8] Especially in recent years, several commentators have promoted the understanding of Jeremiah as reflective of Northern or Ephraimite traditions, specifically as an Ephraimite prophet in contrast to Judean prophets.[9]

All of these perspectives have a degree of plausibility. Obviously, the data allow a variety of opinions and do not dictate any one view. Nevertheless, the Ephraimite assignment of Jeremiah, an interpretation that entices many, encounters some serious objections.

The Ephraimite Jeremiah

Apart from the general affiliation of the book of Jeremiah with the Deuteronomic tradition (a tradition widely assigned to the Northern Kingdom but, if only through the reforms of Josiah, clearly incorporated into Judean circles by the time of Jeremiah), the following points have been advanced for viewing Jeremiah as an Ephraimite prophet as opposed to being a Judean prophet:

5. A. C. Welch, *Jeremiah: His Time and His Work* (Oxford: Oxford University Press, 1928) 33. A similar emphasis on the Northern traditions preserved in Anathoth is found in Clements, *Jeremiah*, 17. See also below.

6. G. von Rad, *Old Testament Theology* (2 vols.; New York: Harper & Row, 1962–65) 2.192. Note that von Rad also stresses the distinctiveness of Jeremiah from other prophets.

7. J. A. Thompson, *Jeremiah* (NICOT; Grand Rapids, Mich.: Eerdmans, 1980) 81.

8. J. Muilenburg, "The 'Office' of Prophet in Ancient Israel," in *The Bible in Modern Scholarship* (ed. J. P. Hyatt; Nashville: Abingdon, 1965) 91. In a longer list, he includes "to a degree, Second Isaiah" (p. 91), and he also notes that "the southern prophets not infrequently avail themselves of the same traditions, notably Amos and Micah" (p. 95).

9. For the basic argument, see the very important book by R. R. Wilson, *Prophecy and Society in Ancient Israel* (Philadelphia: Fortress, 1980) 233–41; complemented by D. Petersen, *The Roles of Israel's Prophets* (JSOTSup 17; Sheffield: JSOT Press, 1981) 83–87.

1. Jeremiah comes from the priests of Anathoth, in Benjamin, who may themselves be descended from the Shiloh priesthood through Abiathar, whose grandfather, Ahitub, in turn may be identified with the Ahitub who is a grandson of Eli (1 Sam 14:3, 22:20; 1 Kgs 2:26–27). As already indicated, it is therefore argued that Jeremiah has an Ephraimite perspective by descent and by geography.
2. As also cited above, many argue that Jeremiah reflects Ephraimite theology, namely, the Exodus and the Sinai covenant traditions viewed as specific to the Northern Kingdom, and avoids the Zion theology of Judah. This Northern affiliation is also inferred from Jeremiah's use of Hosea.
3. Some scholars argue that Jeremiah uses a somewhat peculiarly Ephraimite literary form, namely, "the judgment speech to individuals" (or, "the announcement of disaster to individuals").[10]
4. It is also argued that Jeremiah is given the Ephraimite designation *nābîʾ*, as opposed to the Judean designation *ḥōzeh*, which may correspond to the prophet as characterized by "spirit possession" and connection with the covenant (Ephraim) as opposed to visions and connection with the divine council (Judah).[11]
5. Intercession is listed as an Ephraimite characteristic.[12]

Anathoth of Benjamin

Anathoth is one of the Levitical cities in Benjamin (Josh 21:18, 1 Chr 6:45[60]), located, on the authority of Josephus and Eusebius, about three or four miles north of Jerusalem. The modern village of Anata, less than three miles directly northeast of Jerusalem, remains the most likely site for Anathoth, although the town name may have migrated somewhat over the centuries.[13] Anata is clearly within the orbit of Jerusalem, a city also assigned to Benjamin (Josh 18:28). For that matter, Anathoth surely was under the jurisdiction of the government in Jerusalem from the time of the capture of the city by David through the entire duration of the kingdom of Judah,[14]

10. Wilson, *Prophecy and Society*, 142–43; following the analysis of C. Westermann, *Basic Forms of Prophetic Speech* (Philadelphia: Westminster, 1967) 137–68.

11. Ibid., 136–38, 254–56; Petersen, *The Roles of Israel's Prophets*, esp. 51–88. A possible geographical separation of related terminology, suggested by 1 Kings 13, is explored but rejected by R. Rendtorff, who notes that "one might be inclined to regard *ʾîš ʾĕlōhîm* as the [prophetic] title in Judah and *nābîʾ* as that in Northern Israel, but 1 K. 13 and 2 K. 23:16–18 are undoubtedly late and the other instances do not support this distinction" ("*Prophētēs*," *TDNT* 6.809).

12. Wilson, *Prophecy and Society*, 228–29, 238–41.

13. See Y. Nadelman, "The Identification of Anathoth and the Soundings at Khirbet Deir es-Sidd," *IEJ* 44 (1994) 62–74, favoring Anata.

14. Cf. J. R. Lundbom, who argues that "by tradition, and earlier by virtue of its location within the territory of Benjamin, Anathoth belonged to northern Israel,

though of course the southern border of the Northern Kingdom was also close—Bethel is within eight airline miles of Anathoth, but with no direct route. Those who are associated with Anathoth also indicate a bond with the Southern Kingdom. Abiathar, a survivor of the massacre at Nob, and David's priest, is subsequently sent by Solomon to his fields in Anathoth, apparently his home city. Though not a supporter of Solomon, Abiathar was a staunch supporter of David and his house. And although Abiathar is regarded as a descendent of Eli (1 Kgs 2:26–27) and therefore is linked with Shiloh, Abiathar is also firmly tied to David. Jeremiah is also tied to Abiathar as part of the lore of his native Anathoth, for which bond ultimate family descent of Jeremiah from Abiathar is not necessary. (Such descent is not even statistically likely. As a Levitical city, Anathoth must have had several more priestly families than Abiathar's.)

The problem of speculative descent or identification is illustrated further by Jeremiah's father, Hilkiah, of Anathoth. Hilkiah is a common name, especially among priests and Levites—there are at least three other priestly Hilkiahs. Yet some scholars choose to identify Jeremiah's father with the high priest Hilkiah (2 Kgs 22:8) who is associated with Josiah and the finding of "the book of the law." Wilson, who sees the identification as possible, suggests that such an identification would lend support to the Ephraimite associations of Jeremiah,[15] a rather curious understanding of a Jerusalemite high priest!

The tradition identifies two other figures from the earlier history as being from Anathoth, namely, Abiezer, one of David's mighty men (2 Sam 23:27 [cf. 1 Chr 11:28], 1 Chr 27:12), and Jehu, another prominent supporter of David (1 Chr 12:3–7). Indeed, special mention is made of Benjaminites, kinsmen of Saul, who supported David (1 Chr 12:3–7, 29). These persons seem poor material for Ephraimite associations in contrast to Judean-Davidic associations.

Anathoth, with its geographical, historical, and political associations, does not provide any particular support for the identification of Jeremiah as Ephraimite. For that matter, whatever character Anathoth imprinted on its residents, the opposition to Jeremiah by "the men of Anathoth" (Jer 11:21–

---

though *now* [emphasis mine] it was nothing more than a satellite community to Judah's capital city" (*The Early Career of the Prophet Jeremiah* [Lewiston, N.Y.: Mellen, 1993] 81). This satellite status had been more than 300 years in duration. Yet Lundbom, who paints a detailed picture of Jeremiah growing up listening to Northern traditions, for which Anathoth was a "storehouse," while also affirming that he listened to traditions in Jerusalem, even in the Jerusalem Temple (pp. 82–83), does not argue for Jeremiah as an Ephraimite prophet. Lundbom even suggests that Jeremiah may have attended a scribal school in Jerusalem presided over by Shaphan (p. 85) and that he "was an active participant in temple worship and led people, at various times, in temple liturgies" (p. 91).

15. Wilson, *Prophecy and Society*, 234.

23), not to mention the "generous" offer of Hanamel, Jeremiah's cousin, to sell him a field in Anathoth during a time of siege (Jeremiah 32), indicates that the village did not imprint an ideological consensus.

With reference to the orientation of people from Benjaminite cities during the last days of Judean independence, note also that the prophet Hananiah, son of Azzur, is from Gibeon (Jer 28:1), a city in Benjamin. Even though Gibeon has a distinctive history, nonetheless Gibeon, like Anathoth, is listed as a Levitical city (Josh 21:17). Hananiah, the prophet from Gibeon, is in direct opposition to Jeremiah and certainly presents a "non-Ephraimite" message. Contrariwise, the prophet described in the tradition in Jer 26:20–23 as having prophesied "against this city and against this land according to all the words of Jeremiah," and as having been put to death by Jehoiakim, is a Judean, Uriah son of Shemaiah, described as being from Kiriath-jearim. Geography is not the key to understanding Jeremiah.

All of this argumentation takes the Anathoth references in Jeremiah quite seriously, a course that not everyone would grant.[16] Taking the Anathoth references seriously, however, does not provide any particular support for viewing Jeremiah as an Ephraimite.

Jeremiah's Theology

Before discussing the character of Jeremiah's theology, we need to take note of at least two important characteristics of his historical setting. First, whether or not Jeremiah's active career overlapped with part of the reign of Josiah, Josiah helped to shape the period. Josiah (ca. 640–609) was uniquely different from his predecessors in his successful expansion of Jerusalem's control, especially into much of the former Davidic territory. He carried out cultic reform in Samaria and even in Galilee, apparently extending some form of dominance into Gilead and Philistia, although the exact boundaries are speculative. Although this expansion proved to be quite temporary, the people at that time were obviously unaware of just what the future held. There must have been a tremendous appreciation of Josiah's accomplishment and a sense of the reestablishment of the days of Israel's glory during the United Monarchy. Such a sense might prove to be an illusion of grandeur, but there was some cause for rejoicing at the time. In light of Josiah's success we can better understand the strong urging by various circles for the political independence of the kingdom of Judah. Second, Jeremiah's lifetime was a period of rapidly shifting power not only among the great powers but also within the various political parties striving for dominance in the kingdom of Judah. There were at least three major parties, whose "membership" must have continually fluctuated and changed. Some strove for indepen-

16. Concerning the Anathoth references, Carroll judges that they are "a marginal element in the book and may be regarded as part of the later additions to the developing traditions, typified by 1.1" (*Jeremiah*, 91; see also pp. 280–82).

dence, others favored alliance with Egypt or alliance with Babylon. Many may well have concurred with Jehoiakim who, in spite of his relatively brief reign, managed to adopt all three positions. These divisions reached into the royal family as well, as illustrated by Jehoahaz's succeeding his father, Josiah, aided by the "people of the land," in preference to his elder brother Jehoiakim, who was quickly installed as his replacement by the Egyptians. The various political affiliations were intermixed with differing reactions to the religious policies of Josiah (Jehoiakim and his son Jehoiachin are condemned in 2 Kings 24, as is Jehoiachin's uncle Zedekiah, but details are lacking).

Jeremiah's clear affinities with Hosea and, especially, Deuteronomy, help to show the path taken by the prophet from Anathoth. Deuteronomy, widely regarded as deriving either from the kingdom of Israel or from refugees from the North, whether before or after the fall of Samaria, illustrates the theological complexity. Deuteronomy, whatever its origins—and there are those who view it as a Judean production—is generally seen as the basis for the reforms of Josiah, himself very much a Davidic king ruling from Jerusalem of Judah. But even apart from those who regard Deuteronomy as more of a Judean document, one must admit that Deuteronomy was taken up in Judah by Judeans and cannot, for the time of Jeremiah, be viewed as evidence of a Northern, Ephraimite location for the prophet. E. W. Nicholson has emphasized that the compilers of Deuteronomy, even though in his view refugees from the North, saw the future of Israel (i.e., of the whole people of God) as lying in Judah and made important concessions to the Jerusalem cult tradition as part of their revival vision.[17]

In a similar way, though with different emphases, Jeremiah represents a theology dominated by the question of the possible future of the people. Jeremiah is not to be characterized as pro-Babylonian, though many of his contemporaries so viewed him, but as pro-Israel. This stance did not demand political independence. The survival of God's people Israel at that time meant, for Jeremiah, submission to God theologically and submission to Babylonia politically. This is not an Ephraimite stance but a prophetic stance. Jeremiah sought the continuation and revival of God's people. The policies of the Davidic kings and the Jerusalemite cult were, for Jeremiah, incapable of sustaining a future for the people. As well expressed by W. Brueggemann, for Jeremiah, "God is at work to *create a new alternative community.*"[18]

My conclusion is that the last years of Davidic kingship in Judah were a time that called forth a distinctive prophetic response in the person of Jeremiah. This was not the time for a "theology of glory," such as the Zion theology. The theological perspectives of Hosea (who surely was known in the South as well as in the North; note the Judean redaction of Hosea), relating

17. E. W. Nicholson, *Deuteronomy and Tradition* (Philadelphia: Fortress, 1967) 94, 98, 102.

18. Brueggemann, *To Pluck Up, To Tear Down*, 16.

as they do to the last days of the kingdom of Israel, should have had special appeal to a prophet at that time. And the traditions of the Exodus and the covenant upon which Jeremiah draws can hardly have been restricted to the Northern Kingdom. (This ambiguity is clear in Muilenburg's observation that the "Northern" stream of tradition is also found with, "to a degree, Second Isaiah."[19] Second Isaiah surely was a Judean in background as, for this paper, was Jeremiah.) Jeremiah, also like Second Isaiah, was disengaging from power politics. He was not an advocate of any of the shifting royal policies. His policy was not rebellion or alliance but submission. God's people were now making their way in a new international order and needed a unifying theology not linked to political independence, a theology, as with the Josianic reform in its widely accepted foundation in at least part of Deuteronomy, that helped to bring together all that was left of Israel. As in the advice to the community in exile, the time after 609 was a time to "seek the well-being of the city to which I have exiled you" (Jer 29:7), to seek one's well-being within the structures of the international power of Babylon, at least for the present. Nebuchadnezzar, therefore, may even be God's "servant" (Jer 27:6, where it is perhaps original; cf. Jer 25:9 and 43:10, MT).

Use of Literary Forms

Jeremiah uses a didactic question and answer form (Jer 5:19, 9:11–15, 16:10–13, 22:8–9) that has Deuteronomic parallels (Deut 29:21–27, 1 Kgs 9:8–9) and might be considered an Ephraimite pattern.[20] An even more prominent feature in Jeremiah is "the judgment speech to individuals," with ten or so examples, a form found especially in the Deuteronomic History with reference to various prophets. But these prophets include Isaiah (2 Kgs 20:14–19) and other Judean prophets (2 Kgs 21:10–15).[21] As presented by Westermann, the same form also occurs in Amos 7:14–17, Isa 22:15–25, 37:22–30, and perhaps also Isa 7:10–16 and Ezek 17:11–21, examples illustrating that this form is not unknown to Judean prophets.[22] Furthermore, the usage in Jeremiah is distinctive, in that these judgment speeches are predominantly addressed to kings (as in Jer 22:10–12, 13–19, 24–27, 30; 36:29–30; 37:17; and perhaps 22:28), and uniquely in Jeremiah some judgment speeches are addressed to "false" prophets (Jer 28:12–16, 29:24–32, possibly 29:21–23). Note also that "the announcement of judgment against Israel" is presented by Westermann "as a further development of the announcement of judgment against the individual," citing numerous examples from Amos, Hosea, 1 Isaiah, Micah, and Jeremiah.[23] These literary usages in Jeremiah do not offer very strong support for the notion that Jeremiah is Ephraimite.

19. See n. 8, above.
20. Wilson, *Prophecy and Society*, 236.
21. Ibid., 143.
22. Westermann, *Basic Forms of Prophetic Speech*, 137–68.
23. Ibid., 169–98, esp. 169–76.

Prophetic Titles

With reference to the common title *nābîʾ* 'prophet' and the comparatively infrequent title *ḥōzeh* 'visionary', usage of these titles does not seem to reflect geographic variation.[24] Amaziah, the priest of Bethel in the Northern Kingdom, uses the title *ḥōzeh* in regard to Amos, who is from Tekoa in Judah, and then tells Amos to no longer prophesy (*hinnābēʾ*) in Bethel. In his response, Amos—as the text stands—first denies that he is a *nābîʾ* or a *ben nābîʾ* but then adds that God took him from his work in following after the flock and said to him, "Go, prophesy (*hinnābēʾ*) to my people Israel" (Amos 7:12–14). Amos, from the standpoint of Amaziah, is associated with both titles and seemingly disavows somewhat the "Judean" title, *nābîʾ*.

In Mic 3:5–7, the oracle first condemns "the *nebîʾîm* who lead my people astray," who will lack a night vision (*ḥāzôn*) and will be unable to divine (*qesōm*). After referring again to the darkness connected with the *nebîʾîm*, it continues with reference to the *ḥōzîm* and the *qōsemîm*. The variation seems stylistic, not geographic.

Gad, of unknown origin but associated with David from the time of David's flight from Saul, has the title *ḥōzeh* most frequently (2 Sam 24:11; 1 Chr 21:9, 29:29; 2 Chr 29:25). Yet Gad is also identified as a *nābîʾ* (1 Sam 22:5) and is once described as *hannābîʾ ḥōzeh hammelek* (2 Sam 24:11). And although textual variations occur with Gad's titles, wherein he is generally distinguished from Nathan the *nābîʾ*, a firm supporter of David and Solomon, the different title most likely reflects a functional difference rather than a geographical difference. Note that in Chronicles *ḥōzeh* also identifies Iddo, who, however, has both titles and is associated with the records of King Rehoboam and his son Abijah (2 Chr 12:15, 13:22; cf. *yʿdy*, 2 Chr 9:29, who has visions concerning/against Jeroboam I). Likewise, Jehu son of Hanani is identified as a *ḥōzeh* associated with Jehoshaphat (2 Chr 19:2) and also as a *nābîʾ* who prophesied a bit earlier against Baasha (1 Kgs 16:7, 12). The titles are not geographically specific.

Isa 29:10 uses the two titles in parallelism, and the two titles are likewise associated in 2 Kgs 17:13. In Isa 30:10, in the context of hearing the torah of the Lord, there is synonymous parallelism of *rōʾîm* and *ḥōzîm* and

24. A. Jepsen concluded that the terms are linked for "Nebiismus," which he distinguished from the writing prophets, who challenge nebiism, [and] renounce . . . the use of this word [*ḥzh*] (*Nabi: Soziologische Studien zur alttestamentlichen Literatur und Religionsgeschichte* [Münich: Beck, 1934] 55–56), a view he subsequently modified slightly ("*chāzāh*," *TDOT* 4.280–290, with bibliography). A. R. Johnson (*The Cultic Prophet in Ancient Israel* [2d ed.; Cardiff: University of Wales Press, 1962] 9–29) doubts that "any distinction was observed in practice" for *rōʾeh* and *ḥōzeh* (p. 15) and argues that differentiation from *nābîʾ* has to do with visual/auditory experiences as opposed to divination. A. S. van der Woude also suggests historical or functional variation, not geographical ("*ḥzh* schauen," in *THAT* 1.535, with bibliography).

of verbal forms of *dbr* and *ḥzh*, for which it is difficult to posit regional or derogatory usage.

Although *ḥzh* may represent a vocabulary substratum (some suggest a borrowing from Aramaic[25]), the fact that *ḥōzeh* relates to functional or behavioral characteristics of the manner of revelation (judged inferior by some, such as Ezekiel) rather than geography is also suggested by the Chronicler's use of this title for the Temple musicians Asaph, Heman, and Yeduthun (1 Chr 25:5; 2 Chr 29:30, 35:15). The interplay between prophecy and music is also noted by usage of *nibbāʾ* in connection with these same Temple musicians (1 Chr 25:1–3).

Complications for the geographical separation of the terms also arise from the usage of *ḥazôn* to refer to the oracles of such Judean prophets as Isaiah (1:1; cf. 2:1, 13:1), Obadiah (1), Habakkuk (2:2–3; cf. 1:1), and Nahum (1:1), and similar verbal usage with Amos (1:1) and Micah (1:1).[26] Furthermore, Judean prophets are commonly given the title *nābîʾ*, contrary to the suggested Ephraimite/Judean separation. That Jeremiah is consistently referred to as a *nābîʾ* does not identify him as an Ephraimite.

Role as Intercessor

Moses is the model of an intercessor, and the "concept of the Mosaic prophet who serves as an intermediary between God and the people" may well be granted, especially if we may label this concept as characteristically Deuteronomic and not specifically "Ephraimite."[27] But to argue that an intercessory role for Jeremiah assigns him to the Ephraimite realm creates two different problems. First, aside from Moses and Samuel and apart from the issue with Jeremiah, Amos and Ezekiel are intercessors who are not Ephraimites.[28] Second, in regard to Jeremiah who admittedly is at times an intercessor, one Ephraimite advocate notes that "it is striking that there is little

25. A. Jepsen suggests that "at about the same time the ecstatic prophecy of the nabis was borrowed from the Canaanite realm, the practices of the 'seers' were borrowed from the Arameans" ("*chāzāh*," *TDOT* 4.285, 290), finding both linguistic and functional variation. See also M. Wagner, *Die lexikalischen und grammatikalischen Aramäismen in alttestamentlichen Hebräisch* (BZAW 96; Berlin: Alfred Töpelmann, 1966) 53–54.

26. Jepsen concludes that "a *chāzôn* is . . . an event through which Yahweh speaks to a nabi, who therefore is also called *chōzeh*" ("*chāzāh*," *TDOT* 4.286), so that the redactors do not hesitate to use this language with the "literary" prophets (*TDOT* 4.287).

27. Wilson, *Prophecy and Society*, 228.

28. See Y. Muffs, *Love and Joy: Law, Language and Religion in Ancient Israel* (New York: Jewish Theological Seminary, 1992) 9–48 ("Who Will Stand in the Breach? A Study of Prophetic Intercession").

evidence of intercessory activity in the prophet's oracles."[29] The intercessory role does not provide a basis for regarding Jeremiah as Ephraimite.

Conclusion

Jeremiah, rather than being an Ephraimite as opposed to being a Judean, is an independent voice. His theology and practice cannot be characterized as Ephraimite as opposed to Judean. Jeremiah of Anathoth is not to be set aside from the context of Jerusalem and the Judean realm within which he lived and worked, yet he stands in the prophetic tradition of connectedness with all Israel. Indebted as he is to Hosea, he is a worthy successor of Amos, the prophet from Judah who proclaimed the word in Ephraim, and of the Judeans Isaiah of Jerusalem, and Micah, who addressed words to both Ephraim and Judah. Jeremiah is not an Ephraimite prophet; he is a prophet of the Lord. He cannot be adjusted to a regional theology. His focus is not Ephraimite as opposed to Judean but Israelite in the broad sense. The people needed a theological understanding for the present despair and the future hope, not the sense that "this can't be happening."

The intent of this paper is not to deny that there might be a separate Ephraimite prophetic tradition, but to argue that Jeremiah of Anathoth, a prophet during the last days of Judah, cannot be properly understood in such regional terms.[30] Jeremiah is a prophet of the Lord who draws upon various traditions and insights to advocate a theology for all Israel.

29. Wilson, *Prophecy and Society*, 238.

30. Note J. Blenkinsopp, *A History of Prophecy in Israel* (Philadelphia: Westminster, 1983) 15–16, 133 n. 78, modified by p. 167; Holladay, *Jeremiah*, 2.72.

Textual "Information Gaps" and "Dissonances" in the Interpretation of the Book of Jonah

George M. Landes
Davenport Professor Emeritus of Hebrew and Cognate Languages
Union Theological Seminary

As most students of the Hebrew Bible know, the Hebrew text has been relatively stable since a century or so after the inception of the Common Era, but interpretations of a verse or context that remain largely fixed can nonetheless be quite different. When this is not due to a text-critical issue, as is usually the case with the book of Jonah, whose text is largely free of variants, it is striking how often these differences in interpretation can be attributed to places in the text where either sufficient information was not offered on how a word, phrase, clause, or verse was to be precisely interpreted, or certain breaks had been created in the coherence of the narrative development without obvious clues being provided as to why they occur. These phenomena, which may be labeled "information gaps" and "dissonances" (the latter a special subtype of the former), are familiar to all biblical exegetes, though commentators do not always explicitly acknowledge them as such or address them as clearly as desirable.

On first reading, the story and plot-line of the book of Jonah seem easy to follow and understand. It is only when one scrutinizes the text much more closely that the extent of the information the author has *not* communicated becomes evident, without which the meaning is more or less problematic. In undertaking a meticulous, close rereading of Jonah's 48 verses, I have noted

Author's note: I would like to express my thanks to Profs. Lilian Klein and Jack Sasson for their helpful critical comments on an earlier version of this paper and to the members of the Columbia University Seminar for the Study of the Hebrew Bible (including Prof. Baruch Levine, to whom this paper is dedicated), who responded to a revised form of it at their meeting in March 1992. Obviously, I take full responsibility for any errors or infelicities that may still remain in it.

no fewer than 63 places in the text where the author's deliberate or inadvertent withholding of information poses at least some interpretive issue for the reader and, in addition, 13 places where narrative features create a dissonance in the logic or coherence of the story.

In his *Poetics of Biblical Narrative*, Meir Sternberg devotes two of his thirteen chapters[1] to describing and analyzing the literary phenomenon of textual informational omissions and discordances. He focuses attention on the important question of how the interpreter is to find closure for the various gaps encountered, closure based most fruitfully upon either direct or more subtle clues provided by the biblical writer. In my own work with the text of Jonah, I have found it helpful to classify the numerous gaps cropping up in Jonah's story line by arranging them in accordance with the degree of closure each seems to offer, and in this process I have tentatively come up with the following five general categories:[2]

1. First, the places in the text where the biblical author simply did not supply information, presumably because it was deemed irrelevant, superfluous, or unnecessary for understanding the meaning of what was being conveyed. Sternberg labels these lacunae "blanks,"[3] because either no or hardly any data are provided to fill the gaps that seem to be relatively important for the modern reader if not the ancient writer. Examples in the book of Jonah include the lack of any concrete temporal or geographical information in the opening verse to suggest the time and place of the prophet's call or any clear hint in 2:1 why the author had Jonah reside for three days and three nights within the belly of the great fish.
2. Places where a narrative feature is left unexplained, either because the author assumed that the readers had sufficient explanatory information at their disposal, or the author, whether deliberately or unintentionally, left an ambiguity in the text. In Jonah one wonders why the sailors use בַּאֲשֶׁר instead of בְּשֶׁלְּמִי in addressing their initial request to Jonah (1:8) or why Jonah proceeds to go obediently to Nineveh without a moment's hesitation or murmur of dissent (3:1).
3. Points at which some information is supplied toward closing a gap but not enough to avoid leaving some ambiguity that is never resolved (at

1. M. Sternberg, *The Poetics of Biblical Narrative: Ideological Literature and the Drama of Reading* (Bloomington: Indiana University Press, 1985) chaps. 6–7. For the phenomenon of gapping more related to the book of Jonah, see now Phyllis Trible's monograph, *Rhetorical Criticism: Context, Method, and the Book of Jonah* (Guides to Biblical Scholarship, Old Testament Series; Minneapolis: Fortress, 1994) index (under "gap," p. 262).

2. As will become evident, it did not seem possible to define the categories in such a way as to make them wholly mutually exclusive, and thus to which category a particular "gap" may best be assigned is sometimes arguable.

3. Sternberg, *Poetics of Biblical Narrative*, 236.

least from the standpoint of the reader). In this category, one example would be at the beginning of the book regarding the implied divine intention behind the commission to send Jonah to Nineveh: was it an announcement of judgment or of deliverance or something of both? Another example would be how the intensity of Jonah's reaction to the divine failure to overthrow Nineveh (4:1) is to be explained: was it because Jonah's prophecy was canceled or because God did not stand behind the divine word or because Jonah did not like it when the divine mercy apparently superseded justice?

4. Places where at first glance the rationale for, or situation of, an event are left unclear or unexplained, though after a more careful consideration of the immediate or larger narrative context it does appear that a hint of explanation is being provided. Here one is reminded of Jonah 1:5, where most interpreters have thought that the text means the sailors threw the ship's cargo overboard to lighten the vessel מֵעֲלֵהֶם 'from upon them'. However, on the basis of 1:11, the author may have understood that it was the sea—not the cargo—which was being lightened 'from upon them'.[4] Also, in the opening verse of the psalm in chap. 2, the context of the psalm itself (vv. 3B–7B) suggests that it is not Jonah's situation in the belly of the fish that is motivating his cry of distress, indicated in v. 3, but his previous plight of nearly drowning in the sea.
5. Finally, and closely related to the fourth category just mentioned, are the places where the text does provide relatively clear explanatory information, but its presentation is not at the point where the gap occurs; it is delayed until a later point in the narrative. In Jonah 1:3 the author leaves the definition of the "evil" of the Ninevites unexplained, but in 3:8 its nature is made much clearer. Again in 1:3, Jonah is not made to tell us why he decides to flee to Tarshish, but in 4:2, in his prayer to Yahweh, he reveals the rationale for his flight.

As already indicated, textual dissonances and discontinuities are probably best cataloged under the rubric of information gaps, specifically because they tend to arise from an insufficiency of explanation that might help the reader understand how the author perceived these features to fit within the overall narrative logic. Among the categories of gaps outlined above, the dissonances are perhaps best subsumed under numbers (2) and (3), since rarely, if ever, would a writer consider them "blanks," that is, irrelevancies (category 1), and they tend to be accompanied by less explicit information in the text (than would be the case with categories 4 and 5), thus making it more difficult for

4. While it is true that nowhere else do we find the root קלל with הים as its subject either explicitly or implicitly, and in 1:11 a different verbal root is used with הים, nonetheless the context of 1:5 and the presence of both הים and מעליהם in 1:5, and הים and מעליהם in 1:11 suggest the author may have been construing הים as a possible subject for the verb קלל in 1:5, as it is for ישתק in 1:11.

interpreters to achieve consensus regarding how these dissonances are to be understood within the narrative as a whole.

Space considerations force me to be very selective in giving detailed attention to some examples from the gap categories I have described, but I will endeavor to focus on several (including some dissonances) that still engender interpretive disagreement over Jonah. Some of these I have already alluded to above; others I have not. Because of the general obviousness of examples from category 5, I shall not treat any of them.

The Historical Setting of Jonah as an "Information Gap"

I begin with an instance belonging to the first category, namely, an information gap seemingly of no interest at all to the ancient writer but of greater import to the modern interpreter. I refer to the topic of the historical setting out of which the book of Jonah was written and the audience for which it was composed.[5] As is well known, Jonah's author contributed very few useful data to this issue, though this has not deterred scholars from constructing hypotheses about the book's date and setting based on the character of Jonah's language, implications from some of the book's words and themes, and the application of certain extrabiblical materials deemed relevant.

While in his Anchor Bible commentary on Jonah, Sasson is appropriately very cautious about any attempt to date the book closely,[6] in their monograph on Jonah, André and Pierre-Emmanuel Lacocque are much more assured about its setting.[7] Indeed, it would seem that a major reason they have rewritten their 1981 study entitled *The Jonah Complex*[8] is a new conviction about the book's provenance. Lacocque and Lacocque think that the author

5. As Jack Sasson has suggested to me (in a personal communication), such information may have been omitted simply because it was not germane to the genre chosen for the work, whether one considers the genre prophetic legend, midrash, or *mashal*.

6. J. Sasson, *Jonah: A New Translation with Introduction, Commentary, and Interpretations* (AB 24B; Doubleday: New York, 1990). His discussion ("Dating the Composition of Jonah," 20–28) provides an excellent summary of contemporary thinking on the issue of Jonah's date. While he concludes (p. 27) that the evidence he has assembled under the rubric "Literary and Linguistic Features" "suggests that a final editing or composing of Jonah took place during the exile, but more likely during the postexilic period," I am inclined to think the earlier phase of that spectrum more likely than the later, though I would now have to admit that my own arguments for that judgment fall short of convincing demonstration, which in any event is probably not possible. See my studies, "Linguistic Criteria and the Date of the Book of Jonah," *ErIsr* 16 (Orlinsky Volume; 1982) 147*–170*; and "A Case for the Sixth Century BCE Dating for the Book of Jonah," in the *Festschrift for Edward F. Campbell* (ed. by T. Hiebert and P. H. Williams; forthcoming).

7. A. Lacocque and P.-E. Lacocque, *Jonah: A Psycho-Religious Approach to the Prophet* (Columbia: University of South Carolina Press, 1990).

8. Lacocque and Lacocque, *The Jonah Complex* (Atlanta: John Knox, 1981).

of Jonah was heavily influenced by the satires of Menippus, a Palestinian from Gadara who initially wrote in the first half of the 3rd century B.C.E.[9] But the case they make for this thesis is seriously weakened by their failure to present sufficient evidence to support it. Thus, for example, they do not show whether Menippus actually composed his satires in Palestine or at his later domicile in Thebes. Moreover, since all of Menippus's works are now lost except for their titles, some brief quotes, and a more lengthy paraphrase in much later classical writings, no evidence is presented to indicate that any of them circulated in Palestine as early as the 3d century B.C.E. From what can be gleaned about their content and formal features, some analogues with the book of Jonah are evident; however, there are also some striking differences. In light of what meager early data we have, it would seem just as cogent to posit Jonah as a precursor influencing Menippus than as one of the latter's literary descendants. On such a fragile basis, it seems hazardous to interpret the book of Jonah as a response to a 3d-century B.C.E. milieu, as the Lacocques proceed to do. The effort is not convincing. So while I would not discount the scholarly legitimacy of pursuing closure on issues of no apparent concern to biblical authors or their audience, it must be done with full acknowledgement of the limitations burdening such a task and with a definite circumspectness about imposing one's conclusions upon a text whose setting has not been adequately demonstrated.

Some Examples of "Gaps" in Jonah Posing Interpretive Problems

I would now like to examine five texts from Jonah where either a smaller or a greater amount of information is lacking, thus posing a significant interpretive problem. The first two examples I classify as a category-4 gap. That is to say, the immediate context provides various clues for closure: in the first instance by the content and structure of the verses in which a gap emerges; in the second by the verses that follow the gap.

Jonah 1:8–9

In v. 8, the sailors' initial question to Jonah seems puzzling. What is it they want to know when they ask Jonah, בַּאֲשֶׁר לְמִי־הָרָעָה הַזֹּאת לָנוּ? Actually, their query seems unnecessary, since they appear to have already learned the

9. See their discussion in Lacocque and Lacocque, *Jonah*, 26–48. That the Jonah story represents a close parallel to a Menippean satire has also been suggested by J. S. Ackerman, "Satire and Symbolism in the Song of Jonah," in *Traditions in Transformation: Turning Points in Biblical Faith* (F. M. Cross festschrift; ed. B. Halpern and J. D. Levenson; Winona Lake, Ind.: Eisenbrauns, 1981) 227. For important studies of Menippean satire, see E. P. Kirk, *Menippean Satire: An Annotated Catalogue of Texts and Criticism* (Garland Reference Library of the Humanities 5; New York: Garland, 1980) and J. C. Relihan, *Ancient Menippean Satire* (Baltimore: Johns Hopkins University Press, 1993).

answer to it through the casting of the lots in 1:7. It is Jonah "on whose account this great evil [i.e., the storm] is to them." Sasson[10] therefore construes the בַּאֲשֶׁר-clause in 1:8 as a relative clause referring to Jonah, which he renders: "Tell us, *you who are bringing this calamity upon us*. . . ." This cleverly explains why בַּאֲשֶׁר לְמִי has replaced בְּשֶׁלְּמִי of 1:7; the two words have different sentence functions. The first serves as a prepositional phrase introducing a noun clause as direct object after the verb 'to know', while the second functions as a conjunction introducing a relative clause in apposition to the subject of the imperative הַגִּידָה 'tell us'.

Though this interpretation of the grammar appears possible, it nonetheless seems somewhat forced and awkward for בַּאֲשֶׁר לְמִי. Since בְּשֶׁלְּמִי and בַּאֲשֶׁר לְמִי are morphologically equivalent compound words (composed of preposition + relative pronoun + preposition + objective pronoun) used in similar contexts, it is not obvious that they must serve different sentence functions. The two forms differ only in the identity of their relative pronouns, the former employing the more North Israelite dialectal בְּשֶׁל,[11] the latter the more classical Hebrew בַּאֲשֶׁר. By introducing the shift from בְּשֶׁלְּמִי to בַּאֲשֶׁר לְמִי, the narrator may possibly have been adding a realistic touch by indicating a difference in the linguistic character of the speech of the sailors and Jonah, respectively. The story makes this plausible even prior to Jonah's explicit assertion of his ethnic identity to the sailors in 1:9, when in 1:3 he is said to have hired the ship to go to Tarshish, inferring negotiations that would doubtless have made the sailors conscious of his linguistic identity. In any event, by substituting בַּאֲשֶׁר for בְּשֶׁל the narrator portrays the sailors as showing a certain awareness of Jonah's more familiar linguistic idiom. Indeed, Jonah appears to return the compliment in 1:12, when in responding to the sailors' question of 1:11 he employs their term, בְּשֶׁלִּי, instead of a presumably more customary Hebrew of בַּאֲשֶׁר לִי (which, admittedly, is not attested elsewhere in the Hebrew Bible in this precise construction).

But there is obviously more to understanding the meaning of Jonah 1:7–8 than attempting to explain why בְּשֶׁלְּמִי is used in one verse and בַּאֲשֶׁר לְמִי in the other. The exact repetition immediately following each of these words in vv. 7 and 8, respectively, has led many critics to label the בַּאֲשֶׁר לְמִי-clause in v. 8A a gloss and counsel its deletion,[12] but without any weighty manuscript support for its omission, this is surely a counsel of desperation. Sasson

10. Sasson, *Jonah*, 112–13.

11. Cf. my discussion in "Linguistic Criteria and the Date of the Book of Jonah," 153*–54*. Also note the comments of R. Polzin in his *Late Biblical Hebrew: Toward an Historical Typology of Biblical Hebrew Prose* (HSM 12; Missoula, Mont.: Scholars Press, 1976) 39–40.

12. See the note in BHS to Jonah 1:8; and cf. J. A. Bewer, "A Critical and Exegetical Commentary on Jonah," *A Critical and Exegetical Commentary on Haggai, Zechariah, Malachi, and Jonah* (ICC; Edinburgh: T. & T. Clark, 1912) 37; J. D. Smart,

is certainly correct that the change in words (בַּאֲשֶׁר לְמִי for בְּשֶׁלְּמִי) signals a change in situations, but the question is whether the new situation in v. 8A is best explained in terms of grammar or semantics.

I return to my original question: what is it the sailors want to know when they ask Jonah, "On account of whom is this great evil to us?" While it is conceivable that they only want Jonah to confirm the result of their lot-casting,[13] it is more likely they are after something else. When they prayed to their gods at the onset of the storm in 1:5, one assumes that its magnitude and severity not only motivated them to attribute it to some divine source, but also to seek their deliverance from it through divine action. But which deity (or deities) was responsible? None whom they addressed responded. When the lot fell on Jonah, they would presumably realize it was not enough to have identified the human factor provoking the storm's threat; they would also want to know the divine cause, specifically the identity of Jonah's god.[14] The plausibility of this is suggested by the narrative structure of vv. 8–9.

Verse 8 contains the sailors' questions to Jonah, while v. 9 offers Jonah's response. The sailors have five questions for Jonah, but the queries are divided into two parts, corresponding to the two major divisions of v. 8. The first part is the single question seeking information about the identity of the one who has caused the calamity of the storm (v. 8A); the second part is made up of four questions, all seeking information about Jonah (v. 8B). Jonah's response is also made up of two parts: the first tersely affirms his identity (v. 9A); the second reveals the name of the god he venerates (v. 9B). A close examination of these verses suggests that Jonah is responding to the sailors' questions but in a chiastic order:

		ויאמרו אליו
A	(v. 8A)	הגידה־נא לנו באשר למי־הרעה הזאת לנו
B	(v. 8B)	מה־מלאכתך ומאין תבוא מה ארצך ואי־מזה עם אתה
	(v. 9A)	ויאמר אליהם
B′		עברי אנכי
A′	(v. 9B)	ואת־יהוה אלהי השמים אני ירא אשר־עשה את־הים ואת־היבשה

"The Book of Jonah: Introduction and Exegesis," *IB* 6.882; W. Rudolph, *Joel-Amos-Obadja-Jona* (KAT 13/2; Gütersloh: Mohn, 1971) 340; H. W. Wolff, *Obadiah and Jonah: A Commentary* (Continental Commentary; Minneapolis: Augsburg, 1986) 107.

13. So L. C. Allen, *The Books of Joel, Obadiah, Jonah, and Micah* (NICOT; Grand Rapids, Mich.: Eerdmans, 1976) 209.

14. Contrast D. Stuart (*Hosea–Jonah* [WBC 31; Waco, Tex.: Word, 1987] 460), who thinks that even the initial question of the sailors in v. 8 is aimed at learning more about Jonah's identity, in addition to what the lots have told them.

While Jonah's laconic answer in v. 9A seems most directly to answer only the fourth of the sailors' questions in v. 8B, the narrator may well have thought that the predication of a Hebrew identity also implied something about Jonah's mission, purpose, land, and ethnic affiliation. If, then, vv. 8B and 9A are appropriately linked as corresponding question and answer, one is tempted to see the same relationship intended in vv. 8A and 9B. Thus, in 9B Jonah is responding to the sailors' initial question in 8A,[15] indicating that he is interpreting their question to elicit the identity of his god. Otherwise, why would he even mention Yahweh in this context? While it is conceivable that Jonah is moved to volunteer information that the sailors had not asked for,[16] it makes better sense to see a meaningful correspondence between vv. 8A and 9B. Hence, when the sailors ask for the one responsible for the disastrous storm against them, Jonah discerns that what they really want to know is the name of his god and not simply for him to confirm the lot that pointed to him as culprit.

Jonah 1:12

Jonah's request of the sailors to cast him overboard is another good illustration of a category-4 type of gap, only now the information providing at least some resolution to the gap comes not from v. 12 itself, but from the immediately following verses.

What the reader would like to know here is what intention may be imputed to Jonah in asking the sailors to throw him into the sea. The Lacocques follow a fairly widespread interpretation, namely, Jonah is making an oblative act of generosity, a magnanimous, altruistic gesture of self-sacrifice so that the sailors will be saved.[17] Sasson, on the other hand, correctly sees that Jonah's invitation to the sailors is intended to force them to make an unpalatable decision, on the basis of which they would have to bear full responsibility for what must happen,[18] though he also thinks that Jonah's offer of himself had the effect of reassuring the sailors that they would incur no penalty if they did what Jonah asked.[19] What does the context tell us?

First, Jonah's words to the sailors do indicate what will actually take place: when they cast him overboard, "the sea will quiet down from upon them" (see v. 15). But does this mean that even though he rightly shoul-

15. I would therefore disagree with Wolff (*Obadiah and Jonah*, 114) and others who aver that Jonah here is answering only the fourth of the sailors' questions.

16. So Smart ("Book of Jonah," 882) and J. Limburg (*Jonah: A Commentary* [OTL; Louisville, Ky.: Westminster/John Knox, 1993] 54).

17. Lacocque and Lacocque, *Jonah*, 89. For others who have interpreted 1:12 in this vein, see Smart, "Book of Jonah," 883–84; Rudolph, *Joel-Amos-Obadja-Jona*, 344; T. E. Fretheim, *The Message of Jonah: A Theological Commentary* (Minneapolis: Augsburg, 1977) 88; Stuart, *Hosea–Jonah*, 462.

18. Sasson, *Jonah*, 124.

19. Ibid., 125.

dered the onus for the sailors' endangerment, he also saw the offering of his life as a sacrifice primarily intended to save their lives? While Jonah has not been earlier portrayed as treating the sailors in an unkind or hostile manner, neither has he been overly friendly. Upon boarding the ship, he does not fraternize with them; instead he rather quickly descends into the ship's hold, where he remains in isolation through the early part of the storm until the captain comes to fetch him. He thus does not join the crew in helping to throw the cargo overboard, nor does he add his own prayers for divine assistance to the others, even when the captain explicitly invites him to do so. And at the crucial moment, he does not see it as his option to change his mind and go to Nineveh after all, requesting the sailors not to kill him but to turn the ship back to shore so he can do what Yahweh wants him to do—an action that, presumably, would also have caused the storm to abate.

But what is most important here is what the narrator records as the sailors' response to Jonah's request for death. Their first move (1:13) is to try to bring Jonah back to dry land, possibly sensing from their somewhat limited perspective that this is more in keeping with what Yahweh wants for Jonah than throwing him into the sea.[20] Next (1:14) they pray to Jonah's god, not to thank Yahweh for Jonah's gracious proposal as a way of saving them, but to beg for their lives and implore that no blood guilt be imputed to them for taking Jonah's life. This suggests that they view Jonah's offer as no *modus operandi* whereby they will surely be saved, but more than likely just the opposite! If they throw Jonah overboard, the storm could well cease, but they could still be held accountable for disposing of a messenger whose god seems to want him more alive than dead. Thus it would seem that the sailors' prayer does not lend support to that part of Sasson's interpretation of Jonah's invitation to the sailors to cast him overboard, with the suggestion that they will have nothing to fear if only they do what Jonah requests. If that were the intention the narrator assigns to Jonah, it fails completely from the sailors' perspective. Their prayer indicates that they are not reassured they will escape culpability if they do what Jonah wants them to do.

That the narrator, nonetheless, has the sailors ultimately carrying out Jonah's request to be cast overboard leaves the reader to conclude that

20. Of course, from the perspective given Jonah through the psalm in chap. 2, his being cast into the sea is not simply in accordance with Yahweh's will; it is even Yahweh's deed (2:4)! To the reader (like myself) who would not see 1:15A and 2:4A in a contradictory relationship, the sailors function as *Yahweh's* agents in throwing Jonah overboard (so also H. C. Brichto, *Toward a Grammar of Biblical Poetics: Tales of the Prophets* [New York: Oxford University Press, 1992] 72). Though one can plausibly imagine that they also saw themselves as his agents when they confessed the divine sovereignty in the closing words of their prayer to Yahweh (1:14B) and then immediately experienced the sudden cessation of the storm after they had hurled Jonah into the sea (1:15B), this might not have been their conclusion had they successfully been able to return Jonah to dry land.

Jonah's offer of himself is designed more to benefit himself than the sailors:[21] that is, he proposes it in hopes of removing any possibility that he might ever have to go to Nineveh. Moreover, Jonah does not volunteer to jump overboard—which would apparently accomplish the same purpose—but insists on involving the sailors in his demise, which suggests that he may not really be interested in their survival or even in shielding them from a continuing threat.[22] So while what Jonah tells the sailors is correct (the sea will become calm if they throw the prophet into it), it is not due to any sacrificial gesture on Jonah's part, but both to Yahweh's gracious response to the sailors' prayer and to Jonah's recalcitrance, which ultimately forces them to do what Jonah has asked, after which they learn that this is in keeping with the divine pleasure, for which they have prayed.

Jonah 2

My next example I would classify as a category-3 type, wherein the author does supply some information to close a gap but not enough to make a full interpretation fairly certain. I have in mind Jonah 2 and the role of the great fish in conjunction with Jonah's prayer from within the fish.

What is the function of the fish in the story according to Jonah 2? Actually, the text presents not one but two possibilities, the first an inference from 2:1, the second from the psalm in vv. 3–10. Here I assume that the psalm is not only original and genuine to the book[23] but also that it could have been composed for the story by its narrator/author.[24] While it is true

21. Cf. J. C. Holbert's comments ("'Deliverance Belongs to Yahweh!': Satire in the Book of Jonah," *JSOT* 21 [1981] 68): "Jonah's request to be thrown into the sea is hardly an offer of self-sacrifice. His escape from Yahweh is being foiled; death, the final descent, is the only option now. Thus his request to the sailors is Jonah's final self-serving act, a grand finale to a life of disobedience."

22. Thus I do not find A. J. Hauser's interpretation convincing, which sees Jonah's attitude toward the Gentiles here as having "grown to be essentially positive and constructive. . . ." See his article, "Jonah: In Pursuit of the Dove," *JBL* 104 (1985) 26.

23. I defended this thesis in my article ("The Kerygma of the Book of Jonah: The Contextual Interpretation of the Jonah Psalm," *Int* 21 [1967] 3–31) against the predominant scholarly consensus at the time. More recently, an increasing number of the commentators on Jonah tend to agree that the psalm is probably not a secondary interpolation to the book. See, e.g., the commentaries by Allen, *The Books of Joel, Obadiah, Jonah, and Micah*, 183; Stuart, *Hosea-Jonah*, 438–39; Sasson, *Jonah* (somewhat cautiously), 16–18; and Limburg, *Jonah*, 31–33. See also the study of Ackerman, "Satire and Symbolism in the Song of Jonah," 214 n. 1, 215. For the older view, see J. Watts, *Psalm and Story: Insert Hymns in Hebrew Narrative* (JSOTSup 139; Sheffield: Sheffield Academic Press, 1992).

24. So now also Jonathan Magonet, *Form and Meaning: Studies in Literary Techniques in the Book of Jonah* (BBET; Bern: Herbert Lang / Frankfurt/M.: Peter Lang, 1976) 54. Brichto (*Toward a Grammar of Biblical Poetics*, 268 n.14) takes me to task for

that the psalm does create some dissonances with narrative features set forth in Jonah 1, I do not deem this an adequate basis for either deleting it or treating it as a secondary insertion, as other scholars have done. In reality, the psalm is only one of a number of dissonances that occur within the story, so it would seem appropriate to view its presence as an intentional literary creation of the author that the reader should attempt to interpret in context.

The first perspective on the function of the fish is God's: the deity "appoints" the fish "to swallow" Jonah (2:1). As Ackerman has astutely pointed out,[25] the verb בלע in the Hebrew Bible regularly carries only a pejorative connotation. Hence, in the divine view, it would appear that the fish was an instrument to punish Jonah, presumably for his persistence in rebelling against and trying to escape the divine command to go to Nineveh.

But Jonah is also made to have his own perspective on this, and it is quite different from God's. From what he says in his prayer, it seems clear that the prophet has no sense of being punished by the fish. Rather he apparently sees it as the vehicle Yahweh has sent to save him from drowning in the sea. The imagery of the psalm (esp. vv. 4–7) does not suggest that the distress Jonah is complaining about comes from his experience within the fish[26] but from what he encountered in the sea after the sailors had tossed him overboard. Indeed, in 2:4, Jonah's words to Yahweh indicate that it is his near-death-by-drowning in the sea that Yahweh has punitively instigated, not his current situation in the fish. This of course does create an obvious dissonance with 1:12, where, as we have seen, it is Jonah himself who invites the sailors to cast him overboard, and it is they—not Yahweh—who carry it out. The total context does not obviously resolve this dissonance, but perhaps because in 1:12–15 Yahweh does nothing to stop the sailors from disposing of Jonah and in their prayer to Yahweh they ask that what they do to Jonah may be in accord with the divine pleasure, the reader may be allowed to infer a certain plausibility to Jonah's conclusion in the psalm that Yahweh bore some responsibility for the prophet's winding up in the sea.

While the two perspectives on the fish's function are juxtaposed, Jonah's is the one that ultimately prevails, since nowhere is it indicated that he suffers anything from simply being within the fish. Actually, he seems to be quite happy inside the fish, not only for the shelter it offers him from the

---

not entertaining the possibility in my 1967 article that the author of Jonah was also the composer of the psalm, but at the time I was not as convinced of this judgment as I am now. In her recent rhetorical analysis of Jonah (*Rhetorical Criticism*, 161), Phyllis Trible acknowledges that the psalm needs to be interpreted within the structure of Jonah, though she sees it as predominantly more dissonant than harmonious within that structure.

25. Ackerman, "Satire and Symbolism in the Song of Jonah," 220.

26. As a number of Jonah interpreters have thought; cf. more recently Wolff, *Obadiah and Jonah*, 133; Rudolph, *Joel-Amos-Obadja-Jona*, 352; Lacocque and Lacocque, *Jonah*, 101–2 (where they attribute a quotation to me that I never wrote!).

threatening sea, but also perhaps because he may see his sojourn there as more attractive than a trip to Nineveh! But if that perspective is hinted at (and the text's ambiguity leaves it uncertain) Yahweh counters it by forcibly expelling Jonah from the fish's interior (2:11)[27] back onto dry land, where the prophet can once again receive the command to head to Nineveh (3:1).

Thus, the information the author provides in Jonah 2 shows at least two perspectives on the fish's function. Though they are in tension with each other, it is Jonah's perspective that is allowed to dominate. Other perspectives remain ambiguous. Dissonances created with the surrounding context (only one of which I have dealt with here) are left with only elusive hints at resolution.

Jonah 4:5

This verse in Jonah is an example of one whose function is left unexplained, either because it was the narrator's purpose to leave a deliberate ambiguity in the text, or it was thought the readers knew enough to figure out its meaning on their own (category 2).

The initial problem here is how 4:5 can be seen to fit into the chronological sequence of the narrative. *When* did Jonah decide to leave Nineveh, and what prompted him to leave?

Given the story line up to this verse, one solution has been to conclude that 4:5 does not refer to what Jonah did after Yahweh's question in 4:4 (הַהֵיטֵב חָרָה לָךְ) but to his action immediately after he had delivered his prophecy in 3:4. Since he had predicted that the city would be destroyed within 40 days and, like the Ninevites, believed that this oracle would come true, it is understandable why he would leave as quickly as possible, not wanting to run the risk of being caught in the impending destruction. But if 4:5 was meant to refer to Jonah's situation sequent to the delivery of his prophetic oracle, why did the author delay mentioning this until the context of 4:5?

Resorting to the hypothesis that 4:5 was originally placed after 3:4 must be rejected, not only because there are no ancient textual witnesses supporting it, but also because there is no satisfactory explanation for moving a verse from its original logical chronological sequence to a place where its narrative coherence comes seriously into question.[28] Moreover, if 4:5 was

27. Cf. the apt comments on 2:11 by Holbert, "Deliverance Belongs to Yahweh!" 74; and E. M. Good, *Irony in the Old Testament* (Bible and Literature Series 3; 2d ed.; Sheffield: Almond, 1981) 46–47.

28. For a brief survey of the critical disputation over the appropriate position of 4:5, see Allen, *The Books of Joel, Obadiah, Jonah, and Micah*, 231 n. 16; and Sasson, *Jonah*, 287–90. Among modern scholars still favoring the transposition of 4:5 to the context of 3:4, John Day stands almost alone. See his essay, "Problems in the Interpretation of the Book of Jonah," *OTS* 26 (*In Quest of the Past: Studies on Israelite Religion, Literature and Prophetism*; 1990) 32–47, esp. 42–43. In her monograph on

intended to refer to the context of 3:4, its *waw* consecutive imperfect verbs must be construed with pluperfect tense meaning, something whose permissibility a number of Hebraists question.[29] If Hebrew *waw* consecutive imperfects should not be assigned pluperfect meaning (and I am not of a fixed mind about this but not prepared to argue the point here), then 4:5 must be interpreted in its present narrative context following 4:4. But this raises some equally formidable problems.

First, it assumes that after delivering his prophecy Jonah remained in Nineveh, despite the threat, and witnessed both the universal contrition of the Ninevites as well as Yahweh's apparent unwillingness to make good on the promised judgment. This belies Jonah's tendency—in chap. 1 and then again in chap. 4—to remain aloof and isolated from foreigners whenever possible.

Second, it presumes that Jonah's decision to leave Nineveh was prompted by Yahweh's question and was, indeed, a misinterpretation of that question. The question, of course is rhetorical, anticipating either a "yes" or "no" answer, with "no" most likely what Yahweh hoped for. From the deity's standpoint, Jonah's disaffection at the seeming divine revocation of Nineveh's punishment was unjustified, presumably because of the impressive quality of the Ninevites' repentance (not to mention its quantity, embracing everyone!). From Jonah's perspective, the appropriate answer would also seem to be "no," but for a different reason. He can hear Yahweh's question as prompting the thought that the decision to cancel Nineveh's judgment day was not final. After all, how long could Ninevites be thought to maintain their repentant ways? Eventually—and probably sooner rather than later—they would revert to their former conduct and thus merit the destruction that God had promised them through Jonah. Hence, the prophet opted to leave the city, and settle comfortably east of it to see if indeed that would happen. But this interpretive scenario is highly problematic, for it reads a great deal into the thought processes of both God and Jonah without any clear promptings from the text.

Where, then, does that leave us with this troubling verse? I find very suggestive Sasson's observation[30] that 4:5 be interpreted primarily as serving a purely literary function, namely, to emphasize a paronomasia in chap. 4 on

---

rhetorical criticism and the book of Jonah, Phyllis Trible presents a strong case for the rhetorical analysis and external design of Jonah supporting the location of 4:5 next to 3:4, but she also acknowledges the force of the arguments against such a textual move and does not recommend it (see *Rhetorical Criticism*, 118 n. 33, 205–6).

29. See Sasson's discussion in relation to 4:5 (*Jonah*, 288), as well as his earlier comments on this issue in connection with the interpretation of 1:5 (p. 99) and 3:6 (p. 247). Note also the general discussion of the issue (with some pertinent bibliography) in B. K. Waltke and M. O'Connor, *An Introduction to Biblical Hebrew Syntax* (Winona Lake, Ind.: Eisenbrauns, 1990) 552, §33.2.3.

30. Sasson, *Jonah*, 289.

the root קדם. Thus מִקֶּדֶם in v. 5 plays especially on the adjective קָדִים in v. 8, for the purpose of placing Jonah east of Nineveh so that he is appropriately situated to feel the blast of the easterly wind and the heat of the sun when it rises. If this is so, it leads to a further observation: the narrator may have had no interest at all in the chronological question that 4:5 seems to raise for modern interpreters. The opening clause of the verse should then perhaps be rendered temporally, which is certainly permissible, even though the grammar conveys the typical paratactic style of a series of *waw* consecutive imperfect clauses.[31] Verse 5 would then begin, "When Jonah went out of the city . . . ,"[32] indicating that at some point Jonah did leave the city, but precisely when is not being specified. Furthermore, although through 4:5 the narrator may have been most interested in placing Jonah for the concluding scene of the story, the purpose is possibly more complex than this.

First, 4:5 also makes clear Jonah's isolation and solitude, except for Yahweh's presence, in keeping with other places in the story where Jonah is alone when interacting with the deity (e.g., when receiving his divine commission in 1:1–2; in the sea [2:1]; inside the fish [2:3–10]; expelled from the fish [2:11]; receiving a second divine commission [3:1–2]).

Second, 4:5 provides a basis for understanding why Jonah asks his נֶפֶשׁ to die in v. 8, since, unlike in the roughly parallel scene in 1:12 where the mariners are present to assist in his death wish, there are now no Ninevites available to get involved.

Third, 4:5 introduces Jonah's סֻכָּה so that it can implicitly be contrasted with Yahweh's קִיקָיוֹן, setting up a comparison between Jonah's own and Yahweh's provision for his comfort.[33]

Finally, and most intriguingly, 4:5 does make it clear that Jonah actually passed across the entire city of Nineveh to emerge on its east side, implying in the light of 3:3 that he must have spent at least three days within the city.[34] This suggests not only a fascinating parallelism with his three-day and

31. For temporal clauses introduced by the *waw* consecutive + the imperfect, see R. J. Williams, *Hebrew Syntax: An Outline* (Toronto: University of Toronto Press, 1967) §495.

32. Brichto (*Toward a Grammar of Biblical Poetics*, 77) also employs this rendering.

33. Sasson (*Jonah*, 298) also interprets the קִיקָיוֹן as a "sign of a new equilibrium between [Jonah] and God, of a renewed understanding between the two."

34. Alan Cooper (in his article, "In Praise of Divine Caprice: The Significance of the Book of Jonah," in *Among the Prophets: Language, Image and Structure in the Prophetic Writings* [ed. P. R. Davies and D. J. A. Clines; JSOTSup 144; Sheffield: JSOT Press, 1993] 153) sees a correspondence between the one-day lifespan of the קִיקָיוֹן in 4:10b and Jonah's one-day sojourn in Nineveh. But 3:4 says that Jonah "began (ויחל) to enter the city, a journey of one day," not that he traversed the whole city within the confines of a single day. The larger context, keeping in mind the end of 3:3 and 4:5, suggests that Jonah spent at least three days within the great metropolis.

three-night sojourn within the fish but also that he was within Nineveh long enough to have witnessed the penitent response of the Ninevites to his prophecy.[35] This could mean that there actually is a textual clue that Jonah's departure from Nineveh was not immediately after he delivered his prophecy but sometime later.

From all of this it seems we can conclude that 4:5 is in exactly the place the narrator intended it to be and for more than a single purpose. Whether or not any precise chronological significance was attached to it, however, remains open and unclear.

Jonah 4:6–11

The concluding example is the most difficult and perplexing—the verses that make up the final episode of the book—for here it would appear that the author does not provide enough information to allow several features in these verses to be understood (a category-2 type). This ambiguity undermines some facet of every interpretation of what the ending of the book might mean and the point of the work as a whole.

First, the ending presents the problem of how the parable of the קִיקָיוֹן-plant is to be interpreted. In v. 6 we are told that God "appointed" the קִיקָיוֹן "to be a shade over [Jonah's] head" and "to deliver him from his evil" (without this "evil" being further defined, though perhaps 4:1 was thought to take care of that). Does Jonah's joyous response mean that the divine purpose for the קִיקָיוֹן has succeeded? If so, that success is extremely short-lived, for within a day (cf. 4:10B) the קִיקָיוֹן is destroyed through the divinely dispatched worm, explicitly removing the first purpose the plant was intended to serve (that is, giving shade to Jonah's head) and implicitly its second purpose, removing Jonah's evil, if that refers to his anger.[36] There is an obvious dissonance between the stated purpose of the קִיקָיוֹן in v. 6 and the countering of that purpose in v. 7. Why does God suddenly want to destroy the plant? Is Jonah's request in v. 3 that Yahweh take his life now about to be honored? Some of the content in v. 8 lends plausibility to this, for after shifting to a destructive mode with regard to the plant (reason not given), God follows the same strategy with Jonah, mortally threatening the exposed

35. Against Brichto (*Toward a Grammar of Biblical Poetics*, 78), who interprets the concluding portion of v. 5 to mean "that we are now in an earlier time frame; Jonah does not yet know that the city has taken the track of penance."

36. While I recognize that the idiom חָרָה לְ (with אַף omitted) may convey more specific nuances than 'to be angry' (cf. Sasson's discussion, *Jonah*, 273–74), a rendering with 'dejected' or 'depressed' or 'grieved' does not seem as suitable a description of Jonah's response to the turning away of the divine wrath in 3:9 as the rendering 'he was angry'. In other words, God's anger toward Nineveh has been superseded by Jonah's anger toward God. See also S. H. Blank, "Doest Thou Well to Be Angry? A Study in Self-Pity," *HUCA* 26 (1955) 29–41.

prophet with the broiling sun accompanied by a hot[37] east wind. But if God is now acceding to Jonah's earlier request for death, one would expect the prophet more explicitly to acknowledge this at the end of v. 8 by simply reiterating the words of v. 3A. Instead, he asks for his נֶפֶשׁ to die, not for God to take it. Has the heat so gotten to Jonah that he doesn't grasp what God is doing? Or is God's appointing the worm to destroy the קִיקָיוֹן in the interest of teaching Jonah a lesson?[38] The text is not wholly clear.

The dissonances continue in v. 9, where God offers the divine interpretation of Jonah's anger. This is another shift, since the only textually stated response of Jonah previously to the קִיקָיוֹן has been one of great joy (v. 6).[39] The clear implication is that Jonah's anger has returned. Indeed, Jonah acknowledges this, for when God asks him if he is angry over the קִיקָיוֹן, he readily admits it: angry even to the point of death, he says. It is quite understandable, of course, that the sudden demise of the plant followed by the onset of a deadly heat wave would bring back the prophet's anger, if for no other reason than that it was a blatant contradiction to the beneficent purposes of the קִיקָיוֹן, which the prophet originally experienced and enjoyed. But why should God want to afflict Jonah in such a threatening way? The narrator simply does not tell us.

With v. 10, the text presents another dissonant shift. Abruptly, Yahweh abandons all mention of Jonah's anger over the קִיקָיוֹן plant and introduces an entirely new term to describe the prophet's reaction to it, the verb חוס, meaning something like 'to pity, have compassion for, spare'.[40] What is Yah-

37. If that is indeed what the *hapax* חֲרִישִׁית means. Sasson (*Jonah*, 304) thinks it may be a synonym for גְּדוֹלָה 'big' or עַזָּה 'strong, powerful'.

38. This is the most common interpretation among the commentators, though there is not always agreement as to exactly what the lesson is.

39. But as Phyllis Trible has clearly shown in her analysis of the structure of Jonah 4:6–8 (*Rhetorical Criticism*, 221), v. 10Aab fills the gap at the end of v. 7, where no response from the prophet to the demise of the קִיקָיוֹן is stated, breaking the pattern in vv. 6 and 8, where Jonah's reaction to what God does is explicitly indicated. In other words, the narrator has God inform the reader that Jonah did react to the plant's withering by expressing his "pity" for it.

40. Sasson's effort (*Jonah*, 309–10), inspired by Jerome's translation, to soften the dissonance by rendering the root to mean 'to fret' in v. 10 is resourceful, but ultimately unsatisfactory, since it not only undermines the obviously intended parallelism with the same verb in v. 11, where a translation 'to fret' seems out of the question, but also is based on the premise that because the object of חוס is nonhuman in v. 10 but human in v. 11, the rendering of the verb should be different in each verse. I do not find this argument persuasive. See also Trible's comments, *Rhetorical Criticism*, 218–19. For the meaning of חוס in the Hebrew Bible, see the excellent word-study by S. Wagner in *TDOT* 4.271–77; and for a very insightful analysis of its sense here in Jonah 4:10–11, cf. T. E. Fretheim, "Jonah and Theodicy," *ZAW* 90 (1978) 227–37, esp. 232–33, 236.

weh saying here? Apparently, at least in the divine view, Jonah has two reactions to the plant's destruction: anger and then a compassionate desire to spare the קִיקָיוֹן. While neither receives the divine approval, it is only the latter one that Yahweh now addresses. The concluding relative clauses of v. 10 reveal what purport to be the divine reasons why Jonah's "pity" for the plant is unsuitable. In expressing an emotion that should devolve into a saving action, Jonah has done absolutely nothing to see that the plant is spared: he has not cultivated it, promoted its growth, or done anything to protect it against a quick demise. Why this is so is not stated, but perhaps, in light of the usage of חוס elsewhere, it is understood that he has no sovereign control over the plant.[41] Both its origin and destiny are out of his hands. Thus the emotion expressed by חוס is simply inappropriate.

This provides the basis for the concluding analogy that v. 11 sets up. But what really is being analogued, and what is the point being scored? What is to be made of the formal structural parallelism with v. 10, but the lack of semantic parallelism between the concluding relative clauses? Should v. 11 be rendered a question (as most scholars contend) or a statement? The text provokes all of these questions but offers little by way of answering them.

The initial units of vv. 10 and 11, respectively, show the most coherence, both at the formal and semantic levels, indicating that an analogy is being drawn between Jonah's reaction to the קִיקָיוֹן and Yahweh's to the Ninevites:

v. 10Aab	ויאמר יהוה
	אתה חסת על הקיקיון
v. 11A	ואני לא אחוס על נינוה

Both reactions are characterized by the verb חוס, though when Yahweh is the subject, it is accompanied by the adversative negative particle. The implication would seem to be that while Jonah's response to the plant's disappearance is misplaced, Yahweh's to the Ninevites is altogether apropos. The point at stake is that Jonah is being asked to acknowledge the deity's right to exercise divine, delivering compassion,[42] especially when it is people—any people, including those who are or have been morally obtuse—who are involved.

But is this a viable interpretation given the dissonance in the parallelism between the concluding clauses in vv. 10 and 11? While v. 10AcdB seems to be giving an explanation about why Jonah's compassion for the קִיקָיוֹן is not legitimate, v. 11B hardly seems to be explaining why Yahweh should exercise compassion for the Ninevites:

41. Ibid., 236.

42. J. H. Walton makes essentially the same point in his study, "The Object Lesson of Jonah 4:5–7 and the Purpose of the Book of Jonah," *BBR* 2 (1992) 47–57, esp. 51–52, 55.

v. 10AcdB
אשר לא עמלת בו
ולא גדלתו
שבן לילה היה
ובן לילה אבד
v. 11B
אשר יש בה הרבה משתים עשרה רבו אדם
אשר לא ידע בין ימינו לשמאלו ובהמה רבה

The clauses in 11B describe the immensity of the human and animal population of Nineveh, along with the lack of moral discrimination among the humans (and perhaps also the animals). But it seems absurd that these descriptions might be intended to indicate why Yahweh was moved to show pity to Nineveh. It would be as if to say: it is not any action on the part of the Ninevites, not even their repentance, but the mere fact that they (and their animals) are numerous and ignorant that can finally be counted upon to elicit the divine delivering compassion. Further complicating the issue is the fact that the description of the Ninevite's lack of discriminating knowledge is in tension with what is said about them in chap. 3, where obviously they are insightful enough to change their conduct so that Yahweh is moved to relent from the promised divine punishment. How, then, does this incongruous description at the end function in relation to Yahweh's compassion for Nineveh, and how does it relate to the conduct of the Ninevites described earlier? The text does not offer any clear answers.[43]

43. Trible (*Rhetorical Criticism*, 216–17) presents some new suggestions regarding the semantic connections between the clauses in v. 10AcdB and v. 11Bab. Pairing 10Acd (in which Yahweh reminds Jonah that he did not labor for the קִיקָיוֹן or make it grow) with 11Ba (describing the large population of Nineveh), she sees the meaningful connection between these two units focusing on the large size both of the plant and the city. But it is questionable whether the use of גדלתו in 10Ad was intended to stress the size of the plant rather than a human effort to nurture its growth (supported by the linkage with עמלת in 10Ac). While as plants go, the קִיקָיוֹן may have been thought to be larger than most, no special point of this is made in the narrative (except to indicate in v. 6 that it was tall enough to provide a shade over Jonah's head). Somewhat more problematical is the corresponding meaning Trible derives from the pairing of 10B (describing the plant's short life span) and 11Bb (referring to the ignorance of the Ninevites). She arrives at this principally through her literal rendering of the phrase בן־לילה as 'child of the night', implying that the immaturity of the plant (like that of a child) corresponds to the immaturity of the Ninevites, who do not know their right hand from their left (a description often thought by commentators to refer to a child's mentality). But in Hebrew understanding it is doubtful that בן־לילה was primarily construed as referring to immaturity in contrast to age (even though, admittedly, the two are not unrelated), that is, the קִיקָיוֹן became one-night-old and perished one-night-old. The stress is on the brief temporality of the plant, as Trible acknowledges in another context. More convincingly, she points out semantic

Finally, is v. 11 to be read as a question or a statement? While the usual understanding of it as a question does not resolve any of the problems already mentioned, reading it as a statement (that is, "But as for me, I will not [in the future] spare the great city Nineveh . . .") does offer some intriguing though not ultimately satisfying possibilities.[44]

Opting for a declarative reading of 4:11 suggests that in the end God will not spare[45] Nineveh, confirming what everyone reading the book of Jonah in the postexilic period knows, namely, that Nineveh was destroyed with no signs of revival. It also explains the parable of the קִיקָיוֹן somewhat differently, the plant's ultimate purpose being its destruction, thus foreshadowing the final demise of Nineveh and informing the prophet why his anger at what God had done earlier to Nineveh was misplaced. Finally, it reassures Jonah (and the readers of the book) that the old Israelite theology still holds true: though God might forgive in the face of sincere human repentance, the deserved divine penalty for human sin could only be delayed, never canceled. The point of the book, then, is not that God is capricious and unpredictable[46] but on the contrary, that the deity is always faithful to the divine word, and the word is reliable. Adherents must only be patient and trustful.

This interpretive tack, however, does not explain why in addition to the plant God should want grievously to afflict Jonah at the end or why there is

---

cross connections. On the one hand, there is a connection between 10Acd and 11Bb, where Jonah's lack of power over the plant is compared with the Ninevites' lack of knowledge. And on the other, there is a connection between 10B and 11Ba, where "the singularity and ephemerality of the plant" is paired with "the plurality and gravity of the Ninevites." Nonetheless, as insightful as these rhetorical observations are, in themselves they do not contribute as much as one would like toward clarifying the meaning of Yahweh's final words to Jonah.

44. Almost alone among modern scholars, Cooper ("In Praise of Divine Caprice," 158) vigorously defends the rendering of 4:11 as a statement rather than a question, averring that the interrogative reading "flies in the face of the parallelism with 4.10." But parallelism does not have to be synonymous, and since antithetical parallelism is rather clearly signaled here, a shift from the indicative to the interrogative mood is not contextually precluded. In fact, Cooper admits that "the Book of Jonah itself gives no grounds for choosing between the interrogative and declarative renderings of 4.11, since it simply ends here," adding "my preference for the latter is based on reading Jonah in the light of Nahum." While such a reading is quite legitimate, one needs to adjudicate between a reading in agreement with, or as an alternative to, Nahum's perspective and then defend that reading much more convincingly than Cooper does. In this connection, note the comments of Trible, *Rhetorical Criticism*, 215 n. 48.

45. A better rendering of לא אחוס על than 'I do not care about' (Cooper, "In Praise of Divine Caprice"). The whole thrust of the book of Jonah is that God *does* care about Nineveh, as well as about Jonah, but the caring is to some degree, at least, contingent upon human conduct.

46. Against Cooper, ibid., 150, 162–63.

dissonance between the concluding clauses in vv. 10 and 11 and between 11B and earlier portions of the book. It is possible, of course, that the author of Jonah has deliberately created this dissonance at the end to emphasize that while Jonah's pity for the plant was inappropriate for clearly statable reasons, God's compassion for the mighty but flawed Nineveh has no basis in anything that its inhabitants can do. As David Noel Freedman has put it,[47] the whole repentance business in Jonah 3 was simply a charade to lead Jonah to see that human repentance is not always and ultimately a prerequisite upon which divine compassion depends. The divine will to spare a people is not triggered by any prescribed human conduct but simply out of God's concern for people. One can grant a certain plausibility to this understanding of the ending of Jonah, but it too falls short of being wholly convincing. This is because it would seem to undermine the major theological theme in the book of Jonah, namely, human repentance is a necessary if not always sufficient action motivating the divine will to deliver.[48] Thus the interpretive intractability of Jonah 4:6–11 generates a variety of interpretations of the meaning of the ending of the book, none of them wholly assured.[49]

Some Concluding Observations

What conclusions may be drawn from this study? I would cite the following:

1. The phenomenon of literary gapping, including textual dissonance, requires a response that aims to elicit an acceptable and satisfactory understanding of the text, even though the achievement of that understanding may be beset with a number of problems, some of which may be irresolvable.
2. When the gaps highlight concerns especially of the modern interpreter, care must be taken that the information brought to the text from outside it does not generate a reading that forces or shapes that text's meaning primarily in conformity with the external data, not allowing the internal clues to be given their due weight.

47. D. N. Freedman, "Did God Play a Dirty Trick on Jonah at the End?" *Bible Review* 6/4 (1990) 26–31, esp. 31.

48. Cf. the comment of Walton ("The Object Lesson of Jonah 4:5–7," 65): "What is communicated then about repentance is that though it is insufficient to provide deliverance by its own virtue, it has the ability like nothing else to stimulate God's graciously bestowed compassion."

49. Near the end of her rhetorical analysis of Jonah, P. Trible posits two theologies for the book: "the theology of repentance and the theology of pity" (*Rhetorical Criticism*, 222–23), the former emerging most clearly in chap. 3 (esp. vv. 9–10), the latter in chap. 4 (esp. vv. 10–11). Since the book itself does not offer much guidance on how these two theologies are to be held together, the narrator leaves it to the reader to ponder that for her/himself.

3. When the lack of information arises mainly from the final shape of the text, careful atttention needs to be paid to both the narrower and larger context for guidance regarding the most likely closure.
4. When the internal clues are only partial or virtually nonexistent, the search for closure should not diminish. However, hypotheses developed without some kind of firm textual support should be honestly acknowledged for what they are and not presented as categorical understandings without exception.

The book of Jonah, as well as the rest of the Bible, is replete with informational lacunae and incongruities, and commentators need to be more explicit in dealing with them. Moreover, we should be grateful for these phenomena, for they provide a prime impetus to interpretive endeavors. Indeed, without them, biblical exegetes might not have much to do! As we have seen, some of the interpretive problems in the book of Jonah that its gaps and dissonances have created are not easy to resolve, and they will never all be resolved. But that does not stop us from trying, and failing, and trying again.[50]

50. For a different reading, see M. Orth, "Genre in Jonah: The Effects of Parody in the Book of Jonah," in *The Bible in the Light of Cuneiform Literature: Scripture in Context III*(ed W. W. Hallo et al.; ANETS 8; Lewiston, N.Y.: Edwin Mellen, 1990) 257–81.

History and Time

Brian Peckham
University of Toronto

They say that you would have to have a lot of time on your hands to spend it on chronology. The biblical historians could spend theirs on better things. They did not measure time against an absolute scale but used time to mark the relative significance of the events they recorded. Time was critical for the biblical historians, not as a fact, not as a part of their data, but as a basic principle of their interpretation.[1]

History, analogously, was not a mass of facts from the past, but an interpretation of the past in the light of the present and the future. The dates and sequences that are explicit or implicit in the biblical histories, consequently, can be correlated with a true system of absolute or relative dating by first understanding the meaning they originally were meant to convey.

The Uses of Time

The confluence of history and time in the interpretations of the biblical histories can be illustrated by the historians' intrusion into their works, by their understanding of authorship, and by their feeling for historical context. History supposes the continuity of past, present, and future, and the biblical historians' interpretations were a matter of letting the words and the times coincide.

The distant past, for instance, is measured by the distance that the text puts between the narrator and the story, either explicitly as: "In those days

1. On time as an option rather than a constraint, cf. B. Halpern, "A Historiographic Commentary on Ezra 1–6: Achronological Narrative and Dual Chronology in Israelite Historiography," in *The Hebrew Bible and Its Interpreters* (ed. W. H. Propp, B. Halpern, and D. N. Freedman; Biblical and Judaic Studies from the University of California, San Diego 1; Winona Lake, Ind.: Eisenbrauns, 1990) 81–142.

there was no king in Israel";[2] or implicitly as: "This too was considered Rephaim country: Rephaim lived in it previously and the Ammonites called them Zamzummim";[3] and in either absolute or relative terms as: "he and his sons were priests to the tribe of the Danites until the day of the exile of the land," or, "Hebron had been built seven years before Zoan in Egypt."[4] The present, similarly, can be insinuated by including information pertaining to the time of the author rather than to the time of the story, as "Ur of the Chaldaeans" situates the ancient city with reference to its modern occupants to give the story of Abram a subtle contemporary significance.[5] The future, likewise, gives meaning to the past and the present, as when Abraham, who has just survived a proleptic sojourn in Egypt, surveys Israel's future oppression and exodus from Egypt, or, in another version becomes, with Sarah, the ancestor of the Northern and Southern Kingdoms.[6]

Authorship is critical in prophecy, but it also plays a part in historical writing. The historians often emphasize that their works, or their sources, were written,[7] and it is not unusual for an account to end in the historians' own time. The first version of the Deuteronomistic History, for instance, stops in the reigns of Hezekiah and Sennacherib, but also includes a reference to the kings of Assyria and Egypt who were ruling in the writer's days.[8] The second version, similarly, was designed to explain the fate of Judah and Jerusalem, but exceeds its scope by extending to the author's time with the news of Jehoiachin's release from prison.[9] History and time went hand in

2. Judg 17:6, 18:1, 19:1, 21:25.

3. Deut 2:20. Authorial distance, without specific reference to its temporal significance, is discussed by R. Polzin, *Moses and the Deuteronomist, A Literary Study of the Deuteronomic History, Part One: Deuteronomy, Joshua, Judges* (New York: Seabury, 1980) 29–33.

4. Judg 18:30, Num 13:22.

5. Gen 11:28, 31; 15:7. Biblical time is not univocal and cannot be transposed unambiguously into an unrelated absolute system of chronology: cf. G. W. Ahlström, *The History of Ancient Palestine* (Minneapolis: Fortress, 1993) 30–31, 181–82. The Chaldeans are known, apart from the Priestly writer, only from 7th- and 6th-century texts (Hab 1:6; Ezekiel, the Deuteronomist, and the book of Jeremiah).

6. Gen 15:12–16; 17:6, 16; cf. Gen 35:11.

7. Exod 31:18, 32:15–16, 34:27–28; Deut 6:4–9; 31:9, 24.

8. Evidence for the Hezekian version is discussed in B. Halpern and D. S. Vanderhooft, "The Editions of Kings in the 7th–6th Centuries B.C.E.," *HUCA* 62 (1991) 179–244. This version omits the accession of Manasseh and notes the accession of Esarhaddon but uses for it the Judean accession formula (*wayyimlok . . . bĕnô taḥtāyw*, 2 Kgs 19:37; cf. 2 Kgs 15:38, 16:20, etc.). Inclusion of Tirhakah (2 Kgs 19:9), similarly, collapses absolute and relative time and reveals the historian's temporal perspective.

9. M. Noth, *The Deuteronomistic History* (JSOTSup 15; Sheffield: JSOT Press, 1981) 12, 74, 98. The effect of this concluding live reportage and its relation to the general thrust of the Deuteronomistic history have been explored by J. D. Levenson, "The Last Four Verses in Kings," *JBL* 103 (1984) 353–61.

hand for a biblical historian and, as these instances suggest, the past was understood as everything that pertained to the present.

The prophets were less reticent. They gave their names to their works and tended to include themselves among the actors in their prophetic dramas.[10] It is not surprising, then, that the writers who redid their texts regularly assigned them to the time of the events that they purportedly described. Isaiah could be assigned to the reign of Hezekiah, because he seemed to dwell on the invasion of Sennacherib, or to the time of Ahaz, because his summons to the Assyrians seemed to refer to the intervention of Tiglathpileser in the Syro-Ephraimite war.[11] Amos's references to Bethel and the house of Jeroboam I allowed the Deuteronomist to include the unflattering legend of a fallible Judean prophet who went to Bethel to berate Jeroboam I for establishing the cult at Bethel. This legend was incorporated into the prophet's biography when his work was revised and he was assigned to the time of Jeroboam II who, his editor supposed, was the king to whom the prophet had referred.[12] Micah's reference to Omri and Ahab was the reason the Deuteronomist included him among the prophets at the court of Ahab, but a quotation from Isaiah suggested to his editor that he was a younger contemporary of this prophet.[13]

10. In the superscriptions to their works the prophets identified themselves by name (and patronymic), sometimes by their hometown, if they they did not live in Jerusalem. Their intrusions into the text are autobiographical (first person) or biographical (second or third person). Isaiah was subtle (Isa 5:1, 30:8), Amos quite explicit (Amos 7:1–9, 8:1–3), Hosea fully present (Hosea 1; 9:7–8, 14, 17), and Micah's personal confrontation with the people of Jerusalem became the substance of his prophecy (Mic 2:1–11, 3:8, 6:9, 7:1–7). The biographical strain reached a climax in Ezekiel, and the autobiographical tendency was so pervasive in Jeremiah that the identity of the first-person speaker became an issue for his biographer.

11. Isa 1:7–8 describes the results of Sennacherib's invasion (2 Kgs 18:13), and the Deuteronomist brought Isaiah into the debate (2 Kings 19–20; cf. Isaiah 36–39). In the revision of Isaiah, the Song of the Vineyard was understood to refer to the crushing of the Northern Kingdom (Isa 5:7), the summoning of the Assyrians (Isa 10:5–7) was linked to the appeal to Assyria in the time of Ahaz (Isa 7:1; cf. 2 Kgs 16:5, 7), and the words of the prophet were expanded to deal with the perennial conflict between Judah and Ephraim (Isaiah 7–11 passim), and so Isaiah was assigned to the time of Ahaz son of Uzziah and of his corregent Jotham (Isa 1:1; cf. 2 Kgs 14:5).

12. Amos refers to Jeroboam I (7:7–9) as the founder of the cult at Bethel (4:4–5, 5:4–7). The legend (1 Kings 13) was retold in defense of the prophet (Amos 7:10–17) and Amos was redated by his editor to the reign of Jeroboam II (Amos 1:1). The Deuteronomist had recorded the similarity between these two kings but also had alluded to prophetic intervention in the time of Jeroboam II, and the editor confirmed this date by alluding to the Deuteronomistic text (Amos 6:14; cf. 2 Kgs 14:24–27). The mention of Uzziah (Amos 1:1) reflects the Deuteronomistic synchronism (2 Kgs 15:1).

13. Mic 6:16, 1 Kgs 22:1–28. Micaiah and Micah are identified by a quotation (1 Kgs 22:28b = Mic 1:2a) and by a reference to Ahab in Micaiah's speech (1 Kgs

In this scheme of things, it was not just that individuals and their words could be assigned to the time they interpreted but, conversely, that individuals and words could be interpreted by assigning them to particular times. Abram's claim to the land of Canaan could be vindicated simply by associating him with the aboriginal inhabitants of the land.[14] A later reinterpretation of Ezekiel consisted in redating his vision and assigning his prophetic career, which apparently had no effect, to the time after the fall of Jerusalem when it was too late to be of any practical prophetic use.[15] In the same way, a later writer could deal with the predictions of repentance and restoration made by Jeremiah just by changing his vague autobiographical manner into a biography, by fitting the biography into a history with precise dates, and by stringing his words over his lifetime and over the lives of the kings to coincide with the time of their fulfillment.[16] This is fiction at its best, a creative understanding of the past and its prior interpretations in an imaginary time where all the pieces could fit. Time was critical, but without substance apart from the words and interpretations it sustained.

22:20) even though the context, for historical reasons, refers only to "the king of Israel." Micah's explicit quotation of Isaiah (Mic 2:10 *lōʾ zōʾt hammĕnûḥâ*; Isa 28:12 *zōʾt hammĕnûḥâ*) and redoing of Isaiah's themes suggested, if events and their interpretations were supposed to coincide, that the two were close contemporaries (cf. Mic 1:1 and Isa 1:1).

14. Abraham's claim to the land is narrated (Gen 12:1, 5; 13:12) and affirmed (Gen 15:20, 17:8). The people who fought with the Mesopotamian invaders (Gen 14:5–7) eventually turn out to be the original inhabitants of the land (Deut 2:11, 12, 20, 22, 24).

15. The vision that Ezekiel says occurred in the thirtieth year was redated to the fifth year of Jehoiachin (Ezek 1:1–3). It was then possible to add biographical details on his dumbness and, since this prevented him from exercising a normal prophetic role, to make him a symbolic prophet (Ezek 4:3; 12:6, 11; 24:24, 27) or a priest (1:3, 4:12–15) whose public career began after Jerusalem had fallen (33:21–22).

16. Jeremiah's words, in the book attributed to him, have been spread out over time. This literary fiction usually is projected into real time where the words lose their literary and historical significance and become datable things: so, in W. L. Holladay's exegesis, the words are related to political events and assigned to successive dates in Jeremiah's lifetime (cf. *Jeremiah: A Commentary on the Book of the Prophet Jeremiah Chapters 26–52* [Hermeneia; Minneapolis: Fortress, 1989] 11–35); in W. McKane's view the words can be imagined as accumulating casually over the years that it took to finish the book (cf. *Jeremiah I: Introduction and Commentary on Jeremiah I–XXV* [Edinburgh: T. & T. Clark, 1986] l–lxxxiii). However, the distribution of the words over time, in keeping with historiographic practice, allowed the writer of the book of Jeremiah to understand the immediate past by matching the facts, as the Deuteronomist interpreted them in Kings, with their prophetic and authoritative meaning.

The Earlier Historians

The various historians[17] had different conceptions of time, but all of them were constrained by the chronological perceptions of their predecessors. In the case of Jeremiah, for instance, the Deuteronomistic Historian could assign him to the time of Josiah and, in the guise of Huldah the prophet, make him out to be a liar who misled the king and the people and did nothing to avert the fate incurred by the crimes of Manasseh.[18] In salvaging his words, the historian who redid his prophecies dealt with the constraints of time by extending Jeremiah's career past the reign of Josiah into the reigns of the kings who, by ignoring his words, actually were to blame for the fall of Judah and Jerusalem. Each history was an interpretation, and each had a peculiar use of temporal schemes.

The Yahwist Epic

The Yahwist was not concerned with chronology, but had an interesting sense of time. Dates are not noted, but the passage of time, measured in days, seasons, and years, is intrinsic to the epic's purpose. Since the Yahwist's rendition was the source of subsequent versions of the history of Israel, the epic's timing was critical and destined for constant manipulation.

The first episode alludes to the past as a time before the invention of rain and the seasons. The story of Adam occupies a full day (*bĕyôm*) and ends in the evening with God's walking in the garden, conversing with Adam and Eve, and musing on the future. In relation to this day in the garden, the future is conceived as another day (*bĕyôm*), or as undefined following time (*lĕʿôlām*). In the second episode, the flood is situated with reference to an indefinite time in a singular (*mēʿôlām*) or repeated past (*kol hayyôm*), and the story is told in stately sequences of seven, forty, and seven days. The third episode fills just one day—the visitors meet Abraham at midday in Hebron, arrive in Sodom in the evening, and Abraham views the smoking ruins in

17. The relative order of the biblical historians and the texts that can be assigned to each have been described in my *History and Prophecy: The Development of Late Judean Literary Traditions* (New York: Doubleday, 1993).

18. Huldah's oracle to Josiah repeats the gist of Jeremiah's oracle to Judah and Jerusalem (2 Kgs 22:16a; Jer 4:6, 6:19). The reason she gives, conversely, is quoted in Jeremiah as the reason that evil is about to overtake Jerusalem and the inhabitants of the land (Jer 1:16 = 2 Kgs 22:17a). Her promise that Josiah would die in peace, when in fact he died a violent death, is countered in the book of Jeremiah by insisting that it was not Jeremiah but the lying prophets who expected peace (2 Kgs 22:20; cf. Jer 4:10, 6:14, etc.). The Chronicler (2 Chr 35:20–25) tried to resolve the conflict by fulfilling Huldah's prophecy (although Josiah was wounded at Megiddo, he died in Jerusalem and was buried with his ancestors), by making Necho a prophet and by assigning Jeremiah a positive role in the narrative.

the morning—and then without further delay skips to the following spring (*kāʿēt ḥayyâ*) when Isaac was born. In the fourth episode, days meld into years. Jacob is supposed to spend a few days (*yāmîm ʾăḥādîm*) in Harran but actually spends a month (*ḥodeš yāmîm*) before anything happens. He works periods of seven years for his wives, but the seven he spent working for Rachel seemed to him a few days (*yāmîm ʾăḥādîm*)—a day lasting from evening to morning—although in fact they were more like a week (*šĕbuaʿ*). His negotiations with Laban take place on a given day (*hayyôm, bayyôm hahûʾ*), but the rest of the story follows in narrative sequence without reference to the passage of time. The story of Joseph in the fifth episode is told without any mention of days or years or any kind of time, except for the three days that the brothers spent in prison, a formulaic time symbolizing, as the text explains, the passage from death to life.[19] In the story of Moses in the last episode, time is the transition from night to morning in a single day, a delay of three days followed by forty days and nights at Mount Sinai, a three-day journey from Sinai and then forty days spent reconnoitring the land,[20] or a rough calculation of the days of oppression in Egypt.[21] The passage of time is inherent in the narrative sequence, but most of the story is atemporal, and all of it is without chronological precision. The sabbath and the seasons mark time, but the most precise date in the epic is the day of Israel's arrival at Mount Sinai (*bayyôm hazzeh*) which is exactly the same day that Yahweh saved them at the Sea (*bayyôm hahûʾ*),[22] but it too is entirely relative.

The episodes are linked in linear time and encroach on the time of writing. The flood is separated from the story of Adam by the time it took for his daughters to give birth to the demi-gods and heroes. Abraham traveled to Canaan in the migrations of the sons of Adam when the whole world was populated. His son Isaac settled among the Philistines as a farmer and herdsman. His son Jacob was a contemporary of the Arameans.[23] His son Joseph was next, but in a typical and indeterminate time, when Israel trafficked with Egypt, as it did in the time of the kings.[24] The foci of the story of Moses and Israel are the covenant on Sinai, like the treaties that Judah made with

19. Gen 42:17, 18a. After three days in prison Joseph commands his brothers, "Do this and live." The three-day interval between calamity and survival is associated with rising and restoration to life in Hos 6:1–2.

20. Exod 19:11, 16; 34:28; Num 10:33, 14:25.

21. Exod 2:11 ('in those days' [*bayyāmîm hāhēm*]); Num 20:15 ('we lived in Egypt for many days' [*yāmîm rabbîm*] . . .).

22. Exod 14:30 and 19:1b, 2b. In 19:1b–2a the Priestly writer interposes a three-month delay between the Exodus and arrival at Sinai.

23. Cf. *bĕnê qedem* (Gen 29:1) and *harerê qedem // ʾărām* (Num 23:7). The Elohist and Priestly writers, in commenting on the Jacob cycle, associated him with the Arameans in Mesopotamia or Gilead (Gen 28:1–5, 31:4–54).

24. Cf. Isa 30:1–5, Hos 9:6, Jer 2:18.

Aramean and Assyrian kings,[25] and the oracles of Balaam, nearly contemporary with the epic,[26] which envision the people separated from the nations and living under a monarchical system.[27] The lifespans of the epic protagonists are not computed, and none of them dies, but at the end Moses has disappeared from the scene, and Israel is assured of victory over formidable but unspecified enemies.[28] The first episode does not take place at the beginning of time, and the end of the story is separated from it only by the lifetimes of a few remarkable people.

This linear chronology, clearly, is an epic artifice that the author does not attempt to conceal. The artificiality of the genealogical links is revealed clearly in the identification of Jacob and Israel. The episodes share similar features which make them alternatives rather than sequential: Abraham is among those who migrated from the East (*miqqedem*) and left the land of his birth and the house of his father to travel to Canaan, and Jacob migrates from the East (the *bĕnê qedem*) to return to the land of his fathers and the place of his birth;[29] Isaac migrates to Gerar during a famine, and Israel migrates to Egypt during a famine; Jacob and Israel, with Yahweh their God among them, settle in a garden that resembles the Garden of Eden, but now the affinity of Adam and God is resolved by affirming that God is not a man or a son of Adam. The compression of time, most obvious in collapsing the interval between the defeat of the Egyptians and encampment at Sinai, is not a chronology, but a way of organizing material in order to understand it, and it has no substance other than the intelligibility it conveys. The episodes, in effect, are not in chronological order but are synchronic presentations of the history of Israel aligned in time to establish a single coherent interpretation.

Different interpretations required different conceptions of time. The Priestly and Elohist writers, in particular, had other uses for time, but they were bound by the interlocking serial and synchronic schemes in the history they inherited.

25. 1 Kgs 15:19, 2 Kgs 16:7–8; cf. 2 Sam 7:14.

26. The literary features of the biblical and Transjordanian Balaam tradition have been described by B. A. Levine, "The Deir ʿAlla Inscriptions," *JAOS* 101 (1981) 195–205; "The Balaam Inscriptions: Historical Aspects," in *Biblical Archaeology Today* (ed. J. Amitai; Jerusalem: Israel Exploration Society, 1985) 326–39; "The Plaster Inscriptions from Deir ʿAlla: General Interpretation," in *The Balaam Text from Deir ʿAlla Re-evaluated* (ed. J. Hoftijzer and G. van der Kooij; Leiden: Brill, 1991) 58–72.

27. Num 23:21, 24:7. Additions to Balaam's oracles (Num 24:14–24) extend them to include Assyrian deportations and the destruction of the Assyrian empire.

28. In Num 20:14 Moses sends a message to the king of Edom, but Israel sends messengers to the king of the Amorites (Num 21:21), and Moses plays no part in the Balaam incident.

29. Gen 11:2a, 12:1, 29:1, 31:3.

The Priestly writer adds commentary to emphasize that the episodes are discontinuous but mainly unravels the time that the epic condensed. Creation is the beginning of time and takes not a day but a week. It is separated from the flood by the hundreds of years that the antediluvians lived. The flood is not over in a matter of days but lasts a little more than a year. The migration that brought Abraham to Canaan did not follow right on the flood, but three centuries later, and more than two centuries intervened between his migration and Israel's settlement in Egypt. The epic says that Israel was in Egypt a considerable time (*yāmîm rabbîm*), but the Priestly writer says that it was exactly 430 years. The time at Sinai was symbolic for the Yahwist, but it was real time lasting more than a year in the Priestly version.[30] In the epic it was a matter of days before Israel was settled, but for the Priestly writer settlement in the land was postponed for forty years in the wilderness. Holy days, such as sabbath and Passover, are dated in relation to particular past events, and do not coincide with the seasons as they do in the epic. In stringing out the Yahwist's condensed chronology, the Priestly writer had literary precedents, mathematical models, and a sense that Israel dated from the distant past, but the extension of epic time from creation to the death of Moses also reflected the distance the Priestly writer meant to put between the history of the world and the holiness of a transcendent God.

The Elohist, next in the sequence of historians, does not follow the calendar or the careful computations of the Priestly writer but continues the easy temporal rhythm instituted by the Yahwist. As in the epic, time is measured in days; days are a succession of evenings and early mornings when heroic activity begins, and days easily meld into seasons, years, and individual lifetimes.[31] When accurate measurements of time occur they have a liturgical or legal significance: the fact that Jacob worked six years for Laban's flock, in addition to the fourteen the Yahwist said he worked for his wives, proved that he had acquired it in payment for his services and not by stealth and substantiated his right to manumission in the seventh;[32] Joseph's age is noted, and the passage of time is measured, to reflect the mythical and cultic

30. The coincidence of Yahweh's victory at the Sea and Israel's arrival at Sinai described in the epic becomes, in the Priestly writer's estimation, the coincidence of Exodus and Passover (Exod 12:41 *bĕʿeṣem hayyôm hazzeh*).

31. For instance: the protagonist rises early in the morning when a crisis is at hand (Gen 20:8, 21:14, 22:3, 28:18, 32:1); things happen "at that time" (Gen 21:22), or "after these things" (Gen 22:1, 39:7, 40:1); children grow up (Gen 21:8, 20); Abraham stays in the land of the Philistines for many days (*yāmîm rabbîm*, Gen 21:34); Jacob becomes rich in the mating season (Gen 31:10), and the days and nights that he worked for Laban (Gen 31:39–40) add up to twenty years (31:41).

32. Gen 31:41–42. Six years' slavery, manumission in the seventh along with the wives and children he acquired before becoming a slave, and the right of appeal to God are included in the Elohist legislation (Exod 21:2–6, 22:8).

significance of his sojourn in Egypt;[33] criminal law and liturgical ordinances always include specific numbers of days and years.[34] Elohist time, when it is not narrative, has deliberately practical use.

The Elohist, however, differs from the Yahwist in redating individual episodes by narrative implication. Abraham rather than Isaac is a client of the Philistines and, by narrative allusion to the law of centralization narrated in the sequel to the epic, Isaac is redated to the period of the monarchy when this law was enforced. Isaac lived in Beersheba and Jacob worshiped at Bethel, as Amos and Hosea noted when explaining the reasons for the ruin of the kingdoms.[35] Jacob's dealings with his Aramean relatives are redated to include the confrontations with Aram in Gilead.[36] Joseph is representative of the Northern Kingdom, the exile and restoration of which Hosea described in terms of death and resurrection.[37] The law that God wrote on tablets and gave to Moses preempts the covenant that an earlier historian claimed had been effectual in the time of Hezekiah:[38] it is also the law that was rewritten in Deuteronomy, and the book of the law that, according to a later historian, was operative in the time of Josiah.[39] The Elohist, in this manner, continues the contemporizing of the past begun by the Yahwist by including in the interpreted past recent events that had significance for the author's understanding of history.

33. Joseph is 17 at the beginning of the story (Gen 37:2), 30 when he enters Pharaoh's service (41:46), and 110 when he dies (50:22). Three days mark the difference between life and death (40:13, 19, 20), embalming takes 40 days, 70 days are spent in mourning (50:3) and the famine lasts 7 years. His brothers refer to Joseph as Baal (*baʿal haḥălōmôt*, 37:19), he refers to himself in his glory as Adonis (*ʾādôn*, 45:8–9, 13) and as a source of life to his brothers (45:5, 6; 50:20), and they treat him like a God (50:19). The ritual mood is maintained by keeping his bones in a casket which, at the time of divine visitation, is carried up to the land in solemn procession (Gen 50:25, Exod 13:19). Cf. J. Isaac, "'Here Comes This Dreamer': Joseph the *baʿal haḥălōmôt*" (paper presented at the annual meeting of the Canadian Society for Biblical Studies, Calgary, Alberta, June 1994).

34. Exod 21:2, 22:29, 23:10–16.

35. Amos 4:4–5; 5:4–7; 7:7–9; Hos 10:5, 8; 12:3.

36. Gen 31:23, 25, 51–54; cf. 31:46–48; 1 Kings 22; 2 Kings 8–9.

37. Hos 6:1–7; 13:1, 14.

38. 2 Kgs 18:12; cf. Deut 5:2–3, 27; 12:13–14.

39. 2 Kings 22–23. The precise dates that the Elohist lists in the Joseph story do not enter into any other computation of Israel's sojourn (430 years, Exod 12:40) or slavery (400 years, Gen 15:13) in Egypt. The mention of the survival of a remnant (Gen 45:7) and an insistence on the promise that Joseph's brothers would return to the land after his death, or after the three generations that preceded his death (Gen 45:7; 50:20, 22–26; cf. Gen 15:16, Exod 1:6), may reflect speculation on the date of return of the exiles from the Northern Kingdom (cf. Jeremiah 30–31).

The Judean Sequel to the Epic

The Judean sequel to the epic is the skeleton and basic plot of the Deuteronomistic History. It begins by repeating, almost verbatim, the text of the epic covenant and it proves, through the vagaries of political and military machinations, that the covenant was operative throughout the history of Judah, most amazingly in the reign of Hezekiah. Its conception of time was instrumental in this proof and, apart from the compression that it borrowed from the epic, bore very little resemblance to prior or subsequent chronologies. It was revised, contradicted, or narratively suppressed in the Deuteronomistic History, and its most egregious interpretations were anticipated in the Priestly and Elohist redoing of the corresponding episodes in the epic.

In Deuteronomy, the past and the present are contemporary and integral, while the future stands out as measurable in days, months, and years. The future includes the festivals, celebrated annually or, in the case of Passover, from night to morning in the month Abib, as well as the conquest, which will follow the measured years of Moses' lifetime. The rest is present, occurring "here" and "today" and includes primarily the covenant, with the law of centralization, and the crossing of the Jordan conceived as a contemporary event. The present time of the covenant exceeds all measure to include not only those who are present but those who are absent.[40] Although this is compatible with rhetorical license, it reflects a nearly perfect compression of time, which makes the covenant an omnipresent and hidden force in history. The covenant is never mentioned explicitly in the rest of the sequel, but it underlies and guides the course of events until it is finally implemented in the historian's time.

There is a progression in the book of Joshua from "today" of Deuteronomy to the rapid succession of a limited number of days occupied in conquering the land. Night can mark a pause in the action, miracles begin early in the morning, and any variation is significant. The spies spend the night in Jericho and three days in the mountains. Jericho is captured after Israel marched around it once a day for six days, and then rose early the seventh day to march around it seven times. Although an ambush was sent out at night, the battle of Ai began early in the morning, at the appointed time, and the speed of the combatants brought it to a hasty conclusion. The distance the Gibeonites traveled is not measured in days but, cunningly, by the state of their provisions and the wear and tear on their garments and shoes. Jerusalem and its allies were thrown into confusion because Joshua and his troops came upon them suddenly, having marched all night from the camp at Gilgal. The battle with the king of Hazor also happened suddenly, and victory took no

40. Deut 5:2–3; 29:9a, 11, 13–14. In the same vein, the "hewers of wood and drawers of water" are included proleptically (29:10b) in the covenant to sustain the Deuteronomist's notion that Joshua was justified in making a covenant with the Gibeonites (Joshua 9).

time at all. In the book of Joshua, time is not static and omnipresent, as it is in Deuteronomy, but synthetic and simultaneous: the cities of Judah were captured the day Jerusalem was conquered and also the next day, which counts as "at one time" in the sequel's estimation.[41]

In the books of Samuel, time may be measured in days but is mostly coincidence or happenstance. The festivals at Shiloh are celebrated on certain days every year (*miyyāmîm yāmîmâ, litqūpôt hayyāmîm*), and Samuel offers sacrifice at the high place the very day that Saul arrives.[42] Important events, journeys, and battles begin in the morning, usually last one day, and are separated by intervals of three or seven days.[43] Things happen by accident or coincidence, at exactly or nearly the same time: Saul chances on Samuel; David happens to be at the scene of the battle with the Philistines and, fortunately, Saul notices him and takes him that very day into his service; Saul, his three sons, his armor-bearer, and all his men died together on the same day; David captured Zion, and that same night he was assured by Nathan's oracle that his sons would succeed him on the throne; Uriah the Hittite was killed in the battle of Rabbah, as luck and the machinations of David would have it; Absalom came by accident on David's servants and was killed. It is only when David is anointed king that time begins to be measured in years, and the time that counts pertains to the dynastic succession—David's age at accession, the length of his reign, the timing of Absalom's rebellion.[44]

In Kings, by contrast, time passes solemnly and with great deliberation. The focus remains dynastic succession—the length of a king's reign, his age at accession, his legitimacy, and his imitation of David—but interest shifts to the Temple and to the competing high places in Israel and Judah.[45] The Judean shrines are mentioned explicitly, but the fact that Israel worshiped at Bethel and Dan rather than in Jerusalem is noted at the beginning and merely insinuated thereafter by synchronisms with the kings of Israel. The goal of this partial chronology is the synchronism between Hoshea of Israel and Hezekiah of Judah, and the contrast between Samaria, which went into exile for not obeying the law of centralization, and Jerusalem, which was

41. Josh 10:28–43, without the references to the ban (*ḥrm*) and the absence of survivors (*šʾr, śrd*). The capture of the land "on that day" (10:28), "on the second day" (10:32), or 'at one time' (10:42 *paʿam ʾeḥāt*) contrasts with the Deuteronomist's statement that the wars lasted a long time (Josh 11:18 *yāmîm rabbîm*).

42. 1 Sam 1:3, 4, 20; 9:12, 19, 24.

43. 1 Sam 1:19; 9:19, 20, 26; 11:3, 9–11; 17:20; 2 Sam 11:14; 18:8, 19; 19:1–8.

44. 2 Sam 5:4, 13:23, 15:7. Time before David's accession is an indeterminate past (2 Sam 5:2a), and time after his death is an uncalculated future (2 Sam 7:12).

45. The arguments for including references to the high places and to David as exemplar of the kings in the pre-Deuteronomistic book of Kings are developed in I. W. Provan, *Hezekiah and the Books of Kings: A Contribution to the Debate about the Composition of the Deuteronomistic History* (BZAW 172; Berlin: de Gruyter, 1988) 57–131.

saved from the Assyrians because Hezekiah removed the high places and centralized worship in the Temple.[46]

The chronology begins, after repeating that David reigned for forty years, with the building of the Temple in the fourth year of Solomon's reign, 480 years after the people of Israel had come out of Egypt.[47] The Temple is dated, by this calculation, with reference to the promulgation of the law of centralization in Deuteronomy which, according to the sequel's conceit, was addressed to those who had come out of Egypt and witnessed the covenant at Horeb.[48] The total number of years far exceeds the time that elapsed in the stories of Joshua, Samuel, Saul, and David, but retrieves the actual years which were compressed in them to fit the sequel's interpretation, and which are the basis of the real synchronic time of the kingdoms. These synchronisms are suited to the reigns of individual Judean kings who warred or made peace with Israel and who managed to ward off threats to Jerusalem. They end with a flurry in the reign of Hezekiah: he acceded to the throne in the third year of Hoshea; in his fourth year, Hoshea's seventh year, Shalmaneser besieged Samaria; in his sixth year, Hoshea's ninth year, Samaria was captured.[49] The synchronisms cease at the end of the history, but a sense of real historical time is maintained by mentioning the Egyptian and the Assyrian kings who were contemporary with Hezekiah's anticlimactic and unnamed successor.

A theory of time made the building of the Temple the turning point in the sequel's history of Israel. The steady sequence of Judean kings, whose ages at accessions and regnal years were known, gave substance to the line of David. Maintenance of the high places implicitly kept attention on the Mosaic covenant they contravened. Comparison with David as the exemplar

46. The synchronisms between Judean kings and kings of Israel may be ascribed to the author of the sequel; those between kings of Israel and Judean kings, however, seem to be the work of the Deuteronomistic Historian. The texts and literature are discussed in W. H. Barnes, *Studies in the Chronology of the Divided Monarchy of Israel* (HSM 48; Atlanta: Scholars Press, 1991) 137–49.

47. 1 Kgs 6:1, 38a. The building of the Temple is followed by Jeroboam's insurrection (11:26, 40), Solomon's death (11:41–43), the division of the kingdom, and Jeroboam's inauguration of the cult of the Golden Calf at Bethel and Dan. The description of the Temple was inserted into the sequel's bare chronological facts by repeating bits of the original text at the beginning and end of the new material: 6:2 ("the house which King Solomon built for the Lord") = 6:1 ("in the fourth year in the month Ziv . . . of Solomon's reign, he built the house for the Lord") and 6:37 ("in the fourth year . . . in the month Ziv") = 6:1.

48. The dating of the Temple (1 Kgs 6:1, 38a) usually is assigned to the Deuteronomistic system, even though these 480 years do not match the total number of years (564) that the History gives for the period from the Exodus to the building of the Temple; cf. Noth, *The Deuteronomistic History*, 18–25.

49. 2 Kgs 18:1, 9–10.

of the kings was a constant allusion to the dynastic promise. Synchronisms with the kings of Israel demonstrated repeatedly that the North lacked a similar dynastic succession and did not share in the promise. The incomparable Hezekiah was the climax of the royal line, and the implementation of the law in his reign was the culmination of history and time. The theory was farfetched but allowed the author of the sequel to gather a selective array of historical data under the light of an overriding interpretation.

The Deuteronomistic Historian

The Deuteronomist is the historian who rewrote the earlier histories—Yahwist, Priestly, Elohist, and Judean—from the perspective of law and prophecy. The History imitates their ideas of time but also adds competing systems running concurrently and attempts to correct their chronology. The result, especially as history rushes to a close in the Deuteronomist's own days, is an intricate weave of times and interpretations.

The Yahwist, Priestly, and Elohist histories were changed by inclusion of past, present, and future time. Dating is by days or vague reckoning, and an exact number of years is recorded only when repeating items from the Priestly and Elohist timetables or in imitating the annals of the kings.[50] The present is suggested in etiological and liturgical time.[51] The future is intimated in promises and predictions and in measurements of ritual time. The past is an indefinite antecedent time[52] or measured time between a command and its fulfillment or literary time computed by quoting or alluding to a preceding narrative.[53] Time varies from era to era and different kinds

50. Noah was 600 when the flood began (Gen 7:6 = P in 7:11); Jacob was 130 when he arrived in Egypt (Gen 47:9 = P in 47:28); Isaac was 40 when he married (Gen 26:34 = P in 25:20); Israel spent 40 years in the wilderness (Deut 8:2 = P in Deut 1:3); and the Exodus occurred "on that very day" (Exod 12:51 = P in 12:41). The dating of the Exodus to the fourth generation (Gen 15:16 and Exod 6:16–20) was prompted by the Elohist (Gen 50:23), but the equivalent 400 years of oppression (Gen 15:13) was calculated by subtracting the 17 years Jacob spent in Egypt (Gen 47:28) and the years of Joseph's sojourn in Egypt from the 430 years mentioned by the Priestly writer (Exod 12:40). The war that pitted Sodom and Gomorrah and their allies against the king of Shinar and his allies includes an annalistic account of its twelfth-fourteenth years (Gen 14:4–5).

51. For example: "until today", Gen 19:38, 47:26; "today", Exod 13:3–4, 14:13.

52. For example: "after these things" (Gen 15:1, 22:20); "before a king ruled over the people of Israel" (Gen 36:31); "at that time" (Gen 38:1); "time went by" (Gen 38:12); "not since Egypt became a nation" (Exod 9:24); "had not been before . . . and will not be afterward" (Exod 10:14, 11:6).

53. For example: the famine in the time of Isaac is related to the story of the famine in the time of Abraham (Gen 26:1; cf. 12:10–20); Isaac again dug the wells that Abraham had dug in an earlier version (Gen 26:18; cf. 20:30); Jacob's prayer includes the promises God made in the past, as recounted in the Yahwist and Elohist stories

predominate during the patriarchal age, before and after the Exodus, and while the people are in the wilderness. None of the Deuteronomistic changes reflects a serious interest in chronology but rather a concern for the uses of time in historical interpretation.

The sequel to the epic was redone to make it less parochial and doctrinaire. The age-old rifts between Israel and Judah were bridged by subsuming the nations and kingdoms in a tribal system. The sequel's partial interpretation of history, its focus on the covenant, and its preoccupation with the affairs of Judah and Jerusalem, were corrected by undermining its fantastic notion of time.

In Deuteronomy, the sequel's concentration on the present is furthered by similar references to "today," but the Deuteronomist diminishes its rhetorical force by contrasting it with a recorded past or a predictable future. The Priestly observation that Moses spoke to the people in the fortieth year had already undermined the sequel's notion that he addressed the people who came out of Egypt. The Deuteronomist, aware that two of these years had been spent at Sinai, left thirty-eight years for the Exodus generation to die in the wilderness, and filled them by retelling the story told in Numbers.[54] Before the sequel's version of the covenant on Horeb can begin, the Deuteronomist situates it in a past (*bāʿēt hahîʾ*) that the Elohist had described[55] and preempts it with another version in which Moses refers to "today" but contrasts it with the original day at Horeb and situates it with reference to the beginning (*yāmîm riʾšônîm*) and the end of time (*bĕʾaḥărît hayyāmîm*).[56] After the sequel's version is finished, the "today" of the covenant is contrasted with the "tomorrow" when they will be asked by their children to explain, not the covenant, but the statutes and ordinances. Further doubt is cast on the covenant by recounting, on the basis of earlier texts, how the covenant had been rejected in the past, the past of the earlier texts, by the people who originally witnessed it.[57] When the sequel refers to annual tithes

(Gen 32:10–13; cf. 22:17, 31:3); Jacob also recalls important events in his life, as told by the Elohist and the Priestly writer (Gen 48:3–7; cf. 28, 35, and 41); Moses and Jethro praise God for the events of the Exodus as narrated by the Priestly writer (Exod 18:6–12).

54. Deut 1:3 (40 years), 1:46 (*yāmîm rabbîm*), 2:14 (38 years); Exod 40:17 and Num 1:1 (2d year).

55. Deut 1:9–18. The story conflates the Elohist account of the institution of the courts at Horeb (Exodus 18) and themes from the Deuteronomistic story in Numbers 11.

56. Deut 4:4, 8, 26, 38–40 ("today"); 4:10, 15 (the day at Horeb; cf. 4:14 "at that time"); 4:30 (the latter days; cf. 4:9 "all the days of your life"); 4:32 ("the days that are past"). All these "days" become historical time in descriptions, adapted from other texts, of the events that distinguish them.

57. Deut 9:1–10:12. The account is situated in an uninterrupted series of past rebellions and is punctuated by references to past ("at that time," 9:20; 10:1, 8; "on that occasion," 9:19, 10:10) or prior time (9:18 *kāriʾšōnâ*; 10:10 *yāmîm hāriʾšōnîm*).

and festivals, the Deuteronomist adds the triennial tithes, the septennial year of release, and a sequential calendar of the festivals omitted by the sequel. At the end of the book, the Deuteronomist reverts to the sequel's "today" but contrasts it with a future time of blessing or curse and with a past that extends into the Historian's lifetime.[58]

In Joshua, the Deuteronomist corrects the sequel, continues the dating begun in Deuteronomy, and introduces competing systems of chronological reckoning. The 3 days that the sequel gives the spies to get to and from Jericho become the 3 days that Joshua allows in preparation for the crossing of the Jordan. This takes place in ritual time, on the 10th day of the first month, and is followed by the celebration of Passover on the 14th day of the first month, in the 41st year after the Exodus from Egypt.[59] The conquest, which in the sequel's theory required only a few days, took a long time in the Deuteronomist's opinion, and the partitioning of the land—which in the Deuteronomist's version is the point of the crossing—became instantaneous in its place. The Historian did not believe in the conquest and diminished the force of the sequel's account by giving it a ritual and symbolic significance and by changing the few days it took into 5 years while assigning no time at all to the tribal allottments.[60] At the end of the book, Joshua and Eleazar, who represent the second generation after the Exodus, are dead, and only a few of the elders will outlive them to usher in the period of the judges.

The book of Judges, where the Historian's theory of partial and insecure possession of the land replaces the sequel's theory of the conquest, has a similar overlay of chronological systems. There is a kind of biographical time according to which Joshua and his generation die at the beginning of the book, and the next generation, represented by Jonathan the grandson or great-grandson of Moses, and by Phinehas the grandson of Aaron, is still alive at the end of the book.[61] This generation encloses but does not mesh with the passage of historical time, totally 413 years, that is characterized by alternating periods of war and peace. These periods, in turn, are listed but do not actually occur and are reduced in the telling to the few days, rarely

58. In Deut 34:10 (*wĕlōʾ qām nābîʾ ʿôd bĕyiśrāʾēl kĕmōšeh*) 'never again' expresses absolute time, relative to the writer's point of view. It contrasts with the relative time that is expressed in the evaluations of Hezekiah and Josiah (2 Kgs 18:5, 23:25 "before him . . . after him").

59. Josh 1:11 and 3:2; compare 2:22. In the sequel, the crossing takes place on the 4th day (Josh 3:5), but in this version it takes place on the 14th day of the first month (4:19). The people of Israel ate the manna for 40 years (Exod 16:35), and it ceased the day after Passover in the first month (Josh 5:10, 12) of the 41st year.

60. Josh 11:18 (*yāmîm rabbîm*). The 5 years are mentioned only incidentally (Josh 14:7, 10). The distribution of the land, like the instantaneous conquest, is the product of historical theory: it takes place between identical references to Joshua's advanced age rather than in measurable time (Josh 13:1 and 23:2).

61. Judg 2:8–10, 18:30, 20:28.

months, spent in the wars and intrigues of the protagonists. The systems are not compatible but conform to the historical interpretations imposed on otherwise neutral and unconnected stories: the succession of generations defines the structure of the book, and the theory it implies is articulated in the imputations of sin and punishment that are injected incoherently into each of the episodes;[62] the artificial periods of oppression and peace do not coincide with the exploits of the heroes but belong to the Deuteronomistic calculation, which will correct the 480 years that the sequel counted between the Exodus and the building of the Temple.[63] Chronology, as the clash of systems suggests, is optional. The historical system pretends that the book is in chronological order, but the system of generations reveals that it is not. One views the era of the judges from the perspective of the monarchy and the decline of the kingdoms, while the other antecedently implicates the people of Israel as a whole in the sins that the book of Kings imputes to their leaders.[64]

In the books of Samuel, the sequel's chance occurrences are related to plans made by God and revealed in advance or become a manipulation of events by shrewd and unscrupulous agents. The narratively irrelevant accumulation of years continues, while the length of individual reigns is noted and their actual duration is conveyed by counting the days. Eli judged Israel

62. The book of Judges is arranged in concentric order: the first and last parts match (Judges 1–5 and 17–21), the second and fourth correspond (Judges 6–9 and 13–16), and the middle part (Judges 10–12) surrounds the story of Jephthah with lists of judges to create a miniature of the same arrangement. In the first, the generation of Joshua is applauded, but the following generation is singled out for its ignorance of Yahweh and the things he did for Israel (Judg 2:10). In the last, this generation includes descendants of Moses and Aaron who supervised the cult of the heterodox shrines at Bethel and Dan (18:30, 20:27–28). It is only in the climactic middle part, and then only in cliches, that the guilt imputed to the people is substantiated, and it is only in the much-different final part, where the cliches are omitted, that guilt creeps into the narrative structure.

63. A notable instance of the disjunction between narrative and chronological time is Jephthah's calculation of the years since Israel had settled in Transjordan (Judg 11:26): the 300 years he mentions do not accord with the 319 years that have been counted up to this point but might add up if this middle section is not in chronological order, so that the Ammonite war and the embassy to the Ammonites can be conceived as prior or unrelated to the 18 years of Ammonite oppression (Judg 10:8). The Deuteronomist seems to assume that readers of the History can keep track of the years (e.g., that 40 + 45 = 85, Josh 14:7, 10).

64. The stories at the end of Judges (17–21) are told from the explicit perspective of a later time (e.g., "in those days," 20:27–28). This is the time of the monarchy ("in those days there was no king in Israel," 17:6, 18:1, 19:1, 21:25) and sometime after the exile of the land (18:30). The stories revolve around Bethel and Dan and also include all the places that are important later in describing the inauguration of kingship.

for 40 years that left no trace in the narrative, and the ark of the covenant was stored at Kiriath-jearim for 20 years that merely mark a lull in the story. The story of Samuel, conversely, begins before his birth, watches him grow to maturity, describes him in his prime putting the Philistines to rout, lingers over the inauguration of the kingdom in his declining years, and records his death without ever counting the years or mentioning a specific time. Then Saul is said to have reigned for 2 years, and the narrative follows him from night to morning, day after day, in the early months of his reign, but fills up the rest of the time by counting the days that David spent in the service of Achish of Gath.[65] The reign of Ishbosheth, similarly, lasted 2 years, and the passage of time is noted by recording events on specific days and interspersing them with reference to elapsed time and to temporal events in the concurrent reign of David in Hebron.[66] The years of David's reign are noted, but the passing days are not narrated and nothing is dated. Instead the Deuteronomist breaks up the quick succession in which the sequel drew the connection between unrelated events. In the sequel, Saul's wars with the Philistines and the anointing of David seemed to follow on one another without interval, but in the Deuteronomist's version they are separated by the 4 years of Saul's and Ishbosheth's reigns; Nathan announced the dynastic oracle the night that David captured Zion, but in this version it is delayed by

65. 1 Sam 13:1, 27:7. The passage of time is noted in various ways in each of the separate incidents. In recounting Jonathan's exploits, for instance, there are references to "one day" and "that day" (14:1, 23, 24, 31, 37) and "today" (14:30, 41, 45) to punctuate his victory and his father's humiliation. In the next incident, in which Saul is deposed by Samuel, time is ominous, marked by the transition from night to morning and by reference to the day of his death (15:11–12, 35), but in the next in which David is anointed time is measured 'from that day forward' (16:13 *mēhayyôm hahûʾ wamaʿlāh*). When David enters into Saul's service, repeated time is marked by reference to that particular day, the following day, a typical day, the succession of days, and every day (1 Sam 18:2, 9, 10, 29), with pauses either when time is up or when it is not (18:19, 26). The days that David spent among the Philistines amounted to a year and 4 months (27:7, 29:3), during which the wars with Israel, recounted next, occurred (28:1 "in those days"). In the flow of the Deuteronomist's narrative Saul died in one of these battles, after David had left the service of Achish, and so the total of 2 years assigned to Saul is sustained by the narrative sequence: cf. P. K. McCarter, Jr., *I Samuel* (AB 8; New York: Doubleday, 1980) 222–23.

66. 2 Sam 2:10. The fight between Joab and Abner begins on one day and ends at dawn the next (2 Sam 2:17, 24, 29, 32). Time passes in the protracted war between the house of Saul and the house of David (3:1), and particular days during this time are described in the stories leading up to the anointing of David. Ishboseth's reign is preceded by David's anointing in Hebron, and its duration is suggested by noting the length of David's reign and listing the children born to him in Hebron during this time (2 Sam 2:1–4, 11; 3:2–5). The passage of time is also indicated by looking back to the report of Saul's death when Mephibosheth, who soon will have children of his own (2 Samuel 9), was only 5 years old.

messengers from Hiram of Tyre, the birth of sons and daughters in Jerusalem, wars with the Philistines, and 3 months' waiting for the ark to be brought to the city; the oracle is followed by the wooing of Bathsheba the following spring, but in the Deuteronomist's narrative, the conquest of the whole land and the defeat of all of Israel's enemies intervenes; it appears, from the sequel's narrative sequence, that the revolt of Absalom took place in the years of Solomon's minority, but this edition extends the time with another revolt in Israel, a famine lasting 3 years, wars with the Philistines, and a census that took the better part of a year.

In the book of Kings time continues to be manipulated in any one of the established ways. The duration of Solomon's reign is emphasized by keeping track of the days, months, and years: at the start he is promised length of days, and scattered references to "all the days of his life"[67] keep attention on the promise; time is measured by his monthly provisions and by the monthly relays of his laborers in Lebanon;[68] years seem to elapse in Solomon's annual sacrifices, in the 3-year voyages to Tarshish, in the 7 years that it took to build the Temple, the 13 spent in building the palace, and in the total of 20 years before construction was completed.[69] Other reigns are filled out with an assortment of legends of the prophets. All of these comment on an interpretation in the Judean sequel, and at least two of them correct its chronology: the story of the prophets in the time of Ahab and Jehoshaphat redates the Aramean wars in Ramoth-gilead, which the sequel put in the time of Joram and Ahaziah of Judah, to the reigns of Jehoshaphat of Judah and Joram of Israel;[70] the role of Isaiah in the time of Hezekiah's wars with Assyria cor-

67. 1 Kgs 3:14; 5:1, 5; 11:25. The expression is a cliche, but in one instance (5:1), where it is followed by a list of provisions consumed in one day (5:2), it has a literal calendrical meaning.

68. 1 Kgs 4:7; 5:7, 28.

69. 1 Kgs 6:38b; 7:1; 9:20, 25; 10:22. The Deuteronomist's interest in measuring elapsed time is evident in the redundant addition "and he built it seven years" (1 Kgs 6:38b), calculated from the numbers in the sequel's version (1 Kgs 6:1, 38a). The addition is also an editorial link with the following story of the construction of the palace which begins by repeating its key terms (7:1).

70. The correction is made gradually: by transferring the fate that Elijah predicted for Ahab to the time of Joram (1 Kgs 21:29, 2 Kgs 9:25–26); by recounting under the rubric of Ahab's reign a duplicate of the sequel's battle at Ramoth-gilead (1 Kgs 22:1–38) in which—the kings of Israel and Judah being disguised (1 Kgs 22:30)—it is Jehoshaphat rather than Ahaziah (2 Kings 9) who is the ally of the king of Israel; by having this king of Israel die both as Elijah predicted (1 Kgs 21:19, 22:38) and as Joram of Israel died in the sequel's account (1 Kgs 22:29–36, 2 Kgs 9:21–26); and, generally, by retelling about Elisha in the time of Jehoram and Ahaziah the stories that were told about Elijah in the time of Ahab. The basic mistake was the sequel's synchronism between Ahab and Jehoshaphat (1 Kgs 22:41), but it was compounded by confusion in the reigns and relative dating of the Ahaziahs and J(eh)orams of Israel and Judah. The fundamental correction consisted in inserting Jehoshaphat into the

rected the synchronisms that the sequel had devised for his reign.[71] However, the most disturbing correction of the sequel's chronology consisted in juxtaposing with it another completely incompatible system: the sequel's synchronisms between kings of Judah and Israel were not susceptible to piecemeal revision; the Deuteronomist's solution was to include the opposite synchronisms between Israelite and Judean kings.[72] The Deuteronomist, in this way, could incorporate the Judean sequel and its chronology but could also register disagreement with the sequel's interpretation by including another chronology and another idea of time.

Conclusion

Chronology is a form of historiography and does not exist apart from historical texts. In biblical times, each historian had a different conception of

---

sequel's synchronism between Joram of Israel and Jehoram of Judah (2 Kgs 8:16 "In the fifth year of Joram son of Ahab king of Israel—*when Jehoshaphat was king of Judah*—Jehoram son of Jehoshaphat king of Judah came to the throne"). The Deuteronomist has already established that Jehoshaphat and J(eh)oram were contemporaries (2 Kgs 3:1) and, despite the sequel's synchronism (2 Kgs 8:25 "In the 12th year of Joram the son of Ahab king of Israel, Ahaziah the son of Jehoram, king of Judah came to the throne"), has insinuated that Jehoram the son of Jehoshaphat did not become a king of Judah but became the king of Israel (2 Kgs 1:17): the sequel calls Joram, the king of Israel, "the son of Ahab" (2 Kgs 8:28–29), but the History calls him simply "Joram" in commenting on the sequel's text (2 Kgs 9:14–17), and "Joram son of Ahab" only in order to refer to and correct the sequel's synchronism (2 Kgs 9:29 = 2 Kgs 8:25). The discrepancy in Ahaziah's accession year (in the 11th [2 Kgs 9:29, DTR] or 12th year of Jehoram [2 Kgs 8:25, sequel]) may be due to the fact that Jehoram, who came to the throne in the 2d year of Jehoram son of Jehoshaphat (2 Kgs 1:17), had been co-regent while Ahaziah was king of Israel. This duplication of the sequel's text in order to correct it produces a dense and confused account which is open to many interpretations: É. Puech, for instance, reconstructs the House-of-David stele from Tel Dan by making Ahab and Jehoshaphat allies in the Aramean wars ("La stèle araméenne de Dan: Bar Hadad II et la coalition des Omrides et de la maison de David," *RB* 101 [1994] 215–41).

71. Both the sequel and the Deuteronomist date the siege and the capture of Samaria in the 7th and 9th years of Hoshea of Israel (2 Kgs 17:1–6, 18:9–12). But, in the Deuteronomist's opinion, the synchronism proposed in the sequel between these dates and the 4th and 6th years of Hezekiah was wrong. In order to reduce the discrepancy, the Historian introduced Isaiah into the narrative to add 15 years to Hezekiah's reign (2 Kgs 20:6; cf. the 15 years in 2 Kgs 14:17).

72. The distinctive origins and formulations of the Judean and Israelite synchronisms were noted by S. R. Bin-Nun, "Formulas from Royal Records of Israel and of Judah," *VT* 18 (1968) 414–32. Their distribution in different editions of the History is consistent with the Judean sequel's exclusive interest in Judah and Jerusalem and with the Deuteronomist's inclusive concern for the North.

time, but each was constrained by preceding interpretations of history. It was the biblical manner, as well, to let interpretations and systems of time accumulate, without excising any or trying to subsume them in a harmonic and consistent chronology. Chronology, therefore, remains what it was for these writers, a matter of understanding and interpreting the past.

It is not unusual to read the Bible from the start as if it were in chronological order or as if history was an accumulation of facts fixed in objective time. This does not do justice to the sophistication of its authors whose narratives anticipate the future or revise the sequence of the past from the perspective of their own time. Time, for these biblical historians, was not when things happened but when the past, with its antecedents and consequences, became intelligible and open to interpretation.

No Entry: The Limits of the Sacred in Near Eastern Monotheism

F. E. Peters
New York University

Holiness and piety are central notions in the Pentateuch, particularly in those parts of it attributed to Priestly sources. How stringently the early regulations of these matters were observed generally is not always discernible from the later books of the Bible, but if we confine our attention to the Temple in Jerusalem, we are left in no doubt that not only was ritual purity defined; the means of its observance were extended and refined. It matters not for our purposes whether Exodus's desert Tabernacle was a retrojection of Solomon's Temple or whether the latter was modeled on the former: the fact is that the Israelites of David's and Solomon's day, and likely earlier ones as well, regarded the Tabernacle/Temple as a holy and purified place and attempted to preserve this quality both through ritual, as Baruch Levine long ago persuaded us,[1] and through limiting profane physical access to its holiest parts. Tabernacle and Temple were surrounded by what Menahem Haran aptly described as a "graduated taboo."[2] Only the ritually pure, that is, the priests, might touch, see, or approach the holy areas of the sanctuary;[3] all the others

Author's note: For Baruch Levine—in matters of the letter, a colleague; in matters of the spirit, a teacher; in all things, a friend.

1. B. A. Levine, *In the Presence of the Lord: A Study of Cult and Some Critical Terms in Ancient Israel* (Leiden: Brill, 1974) 55–114, on *kippêr* and its associated rituals; see, in particular, pp. 72–79.

2. M. Haran, *Temples and Temple-Service in Ancient Israel* (Oxford: Clarendon, 1978; reprinted, Winona Lake, Ind.: Eisenbrauns, 1985) 175–88.

3. Even the king was banned from the interior of the Temple (2 Chr 26:16–21), and Nehemiah was convinced that if he, a layman entered the Temple, he would surely die (Neh 6:11).

("the others" in its earliest definition included only the Levites and "the Israelites") were kept at a distance (2 Chr 29:16). In architectural terms, this limitation of access was expressed by the discrimination between the sacred building and its surrounding court.

The distinction between Temple and court seems to have been the only distinction in Solomon's Temple: the priests alone were permitted access to the interior of the Temple; all others (apparently without further discrimination[4]) could enter its courtyard. Solomon's Temple appears to have had but a single surrounding temple courtyard; a second "greater" courtyard also enclosed not only the Temple but the king's throne room and his very secular palaces (1 Kgs 7:9, 12). Later a second *temple* court appears (2 Kgs 1:5, 23:12), though we cannot say whether the alteration was purely architectural or represented further distinctions in access. In any event, the protection of the sacred from the profane appears to have been enforced with severity. The biblical tradition emphasized that God Himself might strike the interloper dead: witness the frequent invocation of the phrase "lest he [that is, the ritual trespasser] meet death"[5] and, in a phrase that strongly suggests that the Levitical guards enforced the ban on the Lord's behalf, "he [i.e., the trespasser] shall be put to death."[6]

In Ezekiel's visionary temple, a new distinction is introduced, in imagination, if not in fact. There are now *two* exterior courtyards surrounding the temple, an inner court reserved for the priests and an outer one where access was permitted to Levites and others.[7] Thus by Ezekiel's time the notion of an inner "court of the priests" had emerged, and likely the exclusion of nonpriests from that inner court was operative in the Second Temple. By the Herodian era, however, perhaps due to the Pharisaic ascendancy in Hasmonean times, the Temple's taboo zones had been further extended. The "Israelites" who had shared Ezekiel's outer court with the Levites were now further distinguished: Israelite women were segregated into a zone one degree more remote from the high sanctity of the Holy of Holies. Beyond them, however, we encounter an apparent anomaly, the "Court of the Gentiles," an invitation to, it would seem, or at least an accommodation to, the unclean, though accompanied by a grave warning. In Ezekiel's program, uncircumcised foreigners were banned from the sanctuary altogether, and,

4. Though it seems likely that there were no restrictions on access to this courtyard, some modern scholars want to keep all nonpriests away from the vicinity of the altar; so Haran, *Temples and Temple-Service*, 184–86.

5. Occurrences are listed in J. Milgrom, *Studies in Levitical Terminology* (Berkeley: University of California Press, 1970) 7 (table B); cf. Levine, *Presence*, 72.

6. Milgrom, *Studies*, part 2, pp. 5–59.

7. Ezek 44:15–19, 27; cf. 40:44–46. The Levites and ordinary Israelites have access only to the outer court: 44:10–14; cf. 40:38–43; cf. Haran, *Temples and Temple-Service*, 187.

according to Isaiah and Joel, they would not even have been permitted inside Jerusalem.[8]

Herod, as we know, was fastidious about his version of the Jerusalem Temple, if about little else. The Temple precincts were patrolled by guards both day and night, and other wardens were stationed at the gates. They kept the unfit out of the areas inappropriate to them,[9] a delicate task, and we are not at all sure how it was accomplished. But the king also appears to have accepted the inevitable magnetism of this, the largest sacred edifice in the ancient world, to the Gentiles (it was generally an era of growing Gentile interest in matters Jewish) and to have attempted to regulate their access to Israel's sacrosanct shrine. Signs posted on the balustrade of the outer court in Herod's Temple expressly forbade the unclean—in this instance non-Jews[10]—to come closer under the explicit threat of death.[11]

The banishment of the unfit *pro fano*, the process of limiting access to a place, what we may call "haramization," is a telltale sign that we are in the presence of the holy. A boundary was set about Mount Sinai, where the presence of God was made manifest, and those who violated it were subject to death (Exod 19:12–13). Touching or even seeing holy objects—how much more the face of God (Exod 33:20)—was forbidden, and Moses, who spent a great deal of time in the presence of the Lord, had to veil his shining face after each dangerous encounter (Exod 34:33–35).

Moses had experienced a recurring theophany, and attention has often been drawn to the role of the theophany in the consecration of a place. Some of the earliest biblical theophanies are associated with specific places (Abraham's meeting with the three strangers at Mamre, Moses' encounter with the Lord on Sinai, and Jacob's at Bethel), but somewhat oddly, the locus of Israel's most important theophany was not site-tied in the ordinary sense. The God of premonarchical Israel had signaled His unmistakable presence through cloud and fire, either at the mobile "Tent of Meeting," where Moses and others encountered Him in scenes reminiscent of Sinai[12] (though now institutionalized in format) or at the mobile Tabernacle of the Ark,

8. Ezek 44:9, Isa 52:1, Joel 4:17.

9. Philo *Leg. Spec.* 1.156; cf. Josephus *Ag. Ap.* 2.106; and E. P. Sanders, *Judaism: Practice and Belief* (Philadelphia: Trinity, 1992) 81–82.

10. See ibid., "Gentiles, Purity and the Temple, " 72–76.

11. Josephus *J.W.* 5.193; on the carrying out of this penalty, see P. Segal, "The Penalty of the Warning Inscription from the Temple of Jerusalem," *IEJ* 39 (1989) 79–84. The Gentiles may now apparently do as they please; the Chief Rabbinate's posted warning against entering the contemporary Temple Mount precincts because of "the holiness of the place" is directed only to Jews.

12. The texts are analyzed in Haran, *Temple and Temple-Service*, 262–69; see, for example, Num 7:89 and B. A. Levine, *Numbers 1–20: A New Translation with Introduction and Commentary* (AB 4; New York: Doubleday, 1993) 258.

whose progress He guided across the wilderness (Exod 40:36–38).[13] But once the Lord became permanently housed, when the *miškān* became truly His *dwelling*, first at Shiloh, and then, in its final *bayît* form, in Jerusalem, those visible theophanies ceased,[14] though not the conviction that the Glory of the Lord dwelled within. It was enthroned atop the circle of the cherubim's enormous outstretched wings above the Ark now resting within the inner, cube-shaped chamber (*dĕbîr*) that was the holiest place in Israel.[15]

Solomon's Temple was explicitly built and furnished to house the deity. In an "epic passage" in 1 Kings, Solomon cries out, "O Lord, who has set the sun in the heaven but has chosen to dwell in thick darkness, here have I built You a lofty house, a habitation for you to occupy forever."[16] The holiness of Solomon's edifice is unmistakable in its nomenclature, which imitated (or was imitated by) the appellations—*miqdāš*, *miqdaš haqqōdeš*, and so forth—used of the Tabernacle in the Pentateuch. It was a holiness that proceeded from within, from that of "the resident deity,"[17] Yahweh, who alone was holy, and was protected by a series of curtains, gates, or baffles, and what we have seen was a "graduated taboo." Both the architecture and the taboos had as their objective keeping impurity at a safe physical distance from the abode of the deity, just as the various rites of expiation served as a spiritual prophylaxis or inoculation against the approach of impurity.[18]

Jerusalem was not, however, the original or even the primary Jewish holy place, in terms of a theophany. The city possessed no intrinsic sanctity of its own; its holiness began at a rather precisely marked point: when David had the Ark of the Covenant carried to the city and housed in a tent he had constructed (2 Sam 6:1–17), a temporary shelter later exchanged for the more permanent grandeur of Solomon's Temple, at which point "the cloud was filling the house . . . for the glory of the LORD filled his house" (1 Kgs 8:11). But

13. We are not yet certain whether the two Israelite structures were distinct buildings or part of a single complex (Haran, *Temple and Temple-Service*, 189–91; cf. Levine, *Numbers*, 129–30), but the Priestly source at least seems to point to the "Tent of Meeting" as the place of theophany, where the God of the desert-bound Israelites manifested himself to Moses and others, while the "Tabernacle" more properly housed the Ark of the Covenant.

14. The last theophany is recorded in 1 Kgs 8:10–11, shortly after the installation of the Ark: "The priests came out of the Holy Place since the cloud was filling the House of the Lord, and they could not continue to minister because of it, for the Glory of the Lord filled His house." Thenceforward it was believed that God resided within, though all the earlier outward signs were no longer present.

15. On the dimensions of the *dĕbîr* (20 × 20 × 20 cubits or ca. 35 × 35 × 35 feet), see 1 Kgs 6:20. The external dimensions of the present Kaʿba are ca. 30 × 30 × 30 ft. On Yahweh's enthronement above the cherubim: 2 Kgs 15:19.

16. 1 Kgs 8:12–13; cf. Levine, *Presence*, 75.

17. Ibid., 72, 75.

18. Ibid., 55–114, on *kippêr* and its associated rituals; see, in particular, pp. 72–79.

God was no longer leading, as He had in the desert (Exod 40:36–37), but following: the cloud signaled the Lord's continuing (or following) presence, His assent, so to speak, to the political judgment made by David and ratified and translated into architectural terms by Solomon.[19]

Throughout the Bible, the purity or holiness of persons consists in part in moral behavior, but in part it is, like the purity of places and objects, affected by contact. As for the purity of objects, the Torah goes to some lengths, and the rabbinic writings to even greater ones, to explain holiness, or rather, its absence, in objects; but neither the rabbis nor the Bible have a great deal to say about holy places.[20] The common connection of a holy place with a theophany comfortably fits a biblical holy place, and more specifically, an Israelite one. When we turn, however, to the other Near Eastern monotheistic community in the Near East with a parallel temple cult, the community of the Muslims, we are faced with comforting similarities to and baffling differences from what had once been in Jerusalem.

In the midst of Mecca stands a large cubical building made of gray-black mortared stone. It is the still-living example of the type of building that has, in some of its textually attested forms, attracted the attention of Baruch Levine over a long and distinguished career. For this is assuredly a holy place: in addition to its purely descriptive name of *al-Kaʿba* 'the Cube', it is also *Bayt Allâh* 'God's House', and it dominates a large but delimited open space called, after alleged Qurʾānic practice, *al-Masjid al-Ḥarâm* 'the Sacred Shrine'. The Meccan building, its cults, and their attendant analogues among the Arabs have all been well known to biblical scholars since the publication of Julius Wellhausen's *Reste arabischen Heidentums* and W. Robertson Smith's *Lectures on the Religion of the Semites*,[21] and they have worked their way deep into Old Testament scholarship. Solutions to the riddles

19. An appropriate theophany was devised later, however, and is found in 1 Chr 22:1 and 2 Chr 3:1; cf. J. Z. Smith, *To Take Place: Toward Theory in Ritual* (Chicago: University of Chicago Press 1987) 164 n. 46.

20. The common biblical usage is *māqôm* (cf. Exod 20:24; Jer 7:12, 14), which Levine argues ("The Next Phase in Jewish Religion: The Land of Israel as Sacred Space," *Tehillah le-Moshe: Biblical and Judaic Studies in Honor of Moshe Greenberg* [ed. M. Cogan, B. L. Eichler, and J. H. Tigay; Winona Lake, Ind.: Eisenbrauns, 1997] 245–57) should be understood as 'cult place', a place rendered notable by reason of the *ritual* practiced there.

21. Smith had read Wellhausen's *Reste* in its first (1887) edition, and Wellhausen's second edition of 1897 in turn reflects a careful reading of the 1894 edition of Smith's *Semites*. Both Wellhausen and Smith were working exclusively with Arab literary sources and their imperfect recollections of a vanished pre-Islamic paganism, but since then the excavations of Arab Palmyra in the Syrian steppe and of the Nabatean Arab domains in southern Jordan and the northern Hijaz have added both epigraphic and iconographic evidence to bolster and illuminate further the Israelite-Arab parallels.

posed by the various, and often contradictory, notions of the biblical 'Tent of Meeting' (*ʾôhel môʿēd*) and the 'tabernacle' (*miškān*), for example, have often included references to Arab parallels, both pre- and post-Islamic.[22] The Meccan Kaʿba shows signs of being just another such tent or tabernacle, as we shall see, but Solomon's grandiose and glittering successor to the Israelite tents and booths of the desert passage seems, like the present-day mortared and roofed Kaʿba, to belong to another, more sedentary, more urban world.

We cannot speak uniquely of the Kaʿba, however; there are three religiously defined and connected areas in Mecca and environs. First is the just-noted *Bayt Allâh*, the *naos* or *templum* that still stands at the center of the modern city: cubical in shape, windowless, with access through a door that in historical times was, and is, six feet above the ground and could only be approached by means of a mobile stairway rolled up to it for that purpose. The second is the area immediately surrounding the *naos*. It was not properly a *temenos*, in that originally it was not *defined* in any sense other than that it was open: the walls of the surrounding dwellings provided its only definition. Under Islamic auspices it was enlarged and later enclosed by a columned and gated arcade, which effectively converted it from an open into a constructed space.[23] Finally, there is the larger district of Mecca. In this instance there *were* markers, sacred stones (*anṣâb*) which, like the Greek Hermes, were both boundary signs and objects of veneration; from very early times they defined the sacred territory of Mecca.[24]

As for the matter of access, it is perhaps more illuminating to proceed in the opposite direction, from the periphery to the center. The city-territory of Mecca, today marked by large signs in Arabic and English on the Saudi thruways banned to all non-Muslims,[25] shows no signs of having been so restricted in late paganism or early Islam. But there are other indications that it did in fact constitute a *ḥaram*, the 'secure sanctuary' of Sura 28:57 of the Qurʾān. The sacred stones at its limits have already been remarked; and

22. See, for example, J. R. Porter, "Ark," *HBD* 63; J. L. Castelot and A. Cody, "Religious Institutions of Israel," *NJBC* 1260; *et alii multi*.

23. F. E. Peters, *Mecca: A Literary History of the Muslim Holy Land* (Princeton: Princeton University Press, 1994) 92–94.

24. J. Wellhausen, *Reste arabischen Heidentums* (2d ed.; Berlin: Georg Reimer, 1897) 105.

25. Efforts were made as early as the second Caliph, Umar (reigned 634–44 C.E.) to extend the *ḥaram* to all of Arabia. In the 19th century the principle yielded to commercial concerns—Jidda had become an important international port—and in the early 20th to military ones. Today entry to the Kingdom of Saudi Arabia is strictly controlled, but it is by no means prohibited to non-Muslims, save of course the two *ḥaramayn* of Mecca and Medina; M. Gaudefroy-Demombynes, *Le Pélerinage, à la Mekke* (Paris: Geuthner, 1923) 25 n. 2; W. Heffening, *Das islamische Fremdenrecht bis zu den islamisch-fränkischen Staatsverträgen* (Hannover, 1925; reprinted, Osnabruck: Biblio, 1975); Peters, *Mecca*, 107.

within it no trees or shrubs were to be cut down and no wild animals hunted,[26] no blood spilled in violence;[27] indeed, no profane (*ḥill*) soil should be mixed with that of the *ḥaram*.

These are all familiar traits, and particularly so in Arabia where the *ḥimâ*, or sacred territory thought to belong to the god, is a well-known phenomenon both before and after Islam,[28] though the restrictions connected with it had more to do with use rather than simple access. Significantly, the Quraysh had their houses within it, which strongly suggests that they were religiously significant sense "people of the god,"[29] a "holy family," as they have been called, and thus, in the case of Mecca, the people of Allah.[30] Finally, it was at the limits of the same territory that pilgrims to Mecca (in pre-Islamic days, outsiders intending to participate in the seasonal rites of the city[31]) had to enter the "haramized" or taboo state (*iḥrâm*),[32] putting on fresh clothing and henceforward refraining from certain proscribed acts such as felling trees and killing wild animals or even cutting the hair or nails, as well

26. For the later and more juridically sophisticated Muslim reading of these primitive prohibitions, see Gaudefroy-Demombynes, *Pélerinage*, 6–15.

27. Wellhausen, *Reste*, 106ff. The right of asylum, however, also characteristic of such sanctuaries, was limited to the Kaʿba itself, or rather, those who took hold of the Kaʿba; Sura 3:97; Azraqi, *Die Chroniken der Stadt Mekka*, vol. 1: *Akhbâr Makka* (ed. F. Wüstenfeld; Leipzig, 1858; reprinted, Beirut: Khayats, 1964) 96, 111; and cf. Gaudefroy-Demombynes, *Pélerinage*, 3–4.

28. W. Robertson Smith, *The Religion of the Semites: The Fundamental Institutions* (2d ed.; London, 1894; reprinted, New York: Meridian, 1972) 142; Wellhausen, *Reste*, 105–9; H. Lammens, *Le Berceau de l'Islam: l'Arabie occidentale à la veille de l'Hégire* (Rome: Pontifical Biblical Institute, 1914) 60–64; R. B. Serjeant, "Haram and Hawtah: The Sacred Enclosures in Arabia," in *Mélanges Taha Husain* (ed. A. Badawi; Cairo: Dar al-Maʿarif, 1962) 52–54.

29. Or perhaps, simply 'people of the house' (*ahl al-bayt*), where 'the house' is, of course, the Kaʿba; cf. Serjeant, "Haram and Hawta," 54–55; M. Sharon, "Ahl al-bayt: People of the House," *Jerusalem Studies in Arabic and Islam* 8 (1986) 169–84.

30. The suggestion supported by the very early Sura 106, which adjures the Quraysh to "worship the Lord of this House [pointing?], who has fed them against hunger and made them safe from fear."

31. Muhammad's later abolition of intercalation destroyed forever the seasonal ties of the Muslim festivals; Qurʾān 9:37; and see F. E. Peters, *Muhammad and the Origins of Islam* (Albany: State University of New York Press, 1994) 252; idem, *The Hajj: The Muslim Pilgrimage to Mecca and the Holy Places* (Princeton: Princeton University Press, 1994) 368 n. 142 and the literature cited there.

32. Muslim pilgrims enter the *iḥrâm* state at the *mawâqît* 'stations'. These are generally located two (though in one case ten) "stages" distant from Mecca (Gaudefroy-Demombynes, *Pélerinage*, 19–25) and were allegedly determined by the Prophet himself. They are not, however, the limits of the original Meccan territorial *ḥaram*, which was a more narrowly circumscribed area; it embraced, according to one Muslim legend, the area grazed by Abraham's flocks (Azraqi, *Akhbâr Makka*, 358).

as all sexual contact.[33] But in this instance the prohibition is time- as well as place-tied. No such restrictions are imposed on the Muslim entering the sacred territory at other times or for other purposes.

What originally distinguished the area immediately around the Kaʿba was that it was *open*; in other words, the Quraysh had not built there. In Islamic times this locality was known as *al-masjid al-ḥarâm*, the 'sacred shrine',[34] though when the Qurʾān uses that expression, it appears to refer to Mecca generally (2:196, 217; 8:34) or to the Kaʿba (9:7).[35] The locus classicus for the identification of *al-masjid al-ḥarâm* with the area surrounding the Kaʿba is Sura 17:1, where God's "servant," likely Muhammad, is carried at night from the 'sacred shrine' (*al-masjid al-ḥarâm*) to the 'distant shrine' (*al-masjid al-aqṣâ*). The verse as it stands, however, is absolutely opaque in regard to locality, as it is in the other thirty-odd instances where a *masjid* is mentioned,[36] and this despite the later exegetes' confident localization of the first "shrine" as the vicinity of the Kaʿba and the latter as the Temple Mount in Jerusalem.

Was the space surrounding the Kaʿba in fact a *ḥaram*? The Muslim theologians debated the question,[37] and in Muhammad's own day the area seems in fact to have displayed none of the characteristic signs of a sanctuary. Rather, it appears to have been the Quraysh's "common," land belonging to no one and open to the use of all. That usage was still remembered in Islamic times as the pasturage and watering of flocks[38]—this was the area surround-

33. Compare the prescribed behavior for the Israelites at the foot of the Sinai *ḥaram*: they had, among other things, to "wash their clothes" (Exod 19:10) and "not go near a woman" (Exod 19:15).

34. *Masjid* literally means 'a place of prostration', hence, a 'place of worship'. The term eventually came to be applied to the Muslim worship hall, the mosque—the English word and its romance analogues derive in fact from *masjid*—along with another term equally descriptive of the original function of the mosque, *jâmiʿ* 'place of assembly'. The *masjid al-ḥarâm* at Mecca is not, of course a mosque, the prototype of which was laid out in Medina by the Prophet himself; Peters, *Muhammad*, 194–97.

35. H. Lammens, in "Les sanctuaires pré-islamites dans l'Arabie occidentale" (*Mélanges de l'Université Saint-Joseph* [1926] 39–173), writes on p. 42: "Of these thirty-odd Quranic references (to *masjid*), half slavishly reproduce the expression *masjid al-ḥarâm*. But—let us merely note it for the present—in the lexicon of the Book of Allah this complex *masjid al-ḥarâm* can designate either the isolated building of the Kaʿba, or the Kaʿba and its immediate surroundings, with its *fanâʿ* or esplanade, or town or the territory of Mecca (as in 22:25, 26), or even all of these at the same time, to wit, the entirety of *Mecca sacra* of Arab paganism."

36. Lammens, "Sanctuaires."

37. Gaudefroy-Demombynes, *Pélerinage*, 114 n. 4.

38. Uri Rubin, "The Kaʿba: Aspects of Its Ritual, Functions, and Position in Pre-Islamic and Early Islamic Times" (*Jerusalem Studies in Arabic and Islam* 8 [1986] 98 and 106), where it is suggested that the *ḥijr*, the area immediately adjacent to the northwest face of the Kaʿba and partially enclosed by a low, semicircular wall, was originally a pen for the animals consecrated to the god(s).

ing the settlement's only source of water, the well called the Zamzam. Whatever the case, there is no indication that Muhammad banned pagan Meccans or others from the area even after he prohibited them from participating in the now Islamicized pilgrimage;[39] indeed, Qur'ān 22:25 suggests quite the opposite. It is, as usual, God who is speaking: "Those who are unbelievers, and would keep (men) back from the path of God and from *al-masjid al-ḥarâm*, which We have made for all men—equal is the dweller there and the foreigner—and those whose purpose there is profanity or impiety, those We will cause to taste a grievous punishment."

Finally, we return to the *Bayt Allâh*. Not a great deal can be concluded from the present Kaʿba, which substantially dates from a ground-up rebuilding in 1629.[40] From the many literary descriptions we possess, the 17th-century reconstruction seems to have differed little from the building that stood there all through the medieval era and back to the late 7th century. In 683 C.E., however, the Kaʿba had been rebuilt on *ideological* grounds. The rebel Ibn al-Zubayr, who then held Mecca against the caliphal government, reconstructed it, we are told, as it was in Abraham's day. The original building was joined to the *ḥijr* wall at the northwest face—how or to what purpose we are not told—and had two ground-level doors, "one toward the east for people to enter and one toward the west for people to exit."[41] This tradition goes back to Muhammad, on the authority of his wife, Aisha. The Prophet was recalling the rebuilding of the Kaʿba in his own day, sometime about 605 C.E., a project in which he cooperated but did not approve, since it distorted Abraham's original building.[42] The reason that the Quraysh closed one door and lifted the other well above ground level was, according to the same tradition from Muhammad, "to make sure that no one but whom they [that is, the Quraysh] wished would enter it." The clear implication was that the Kaʿba was intended to be open to all but that access was, in Muhammad's day, controlled, not by any notions of purity or holiness, but by the will of the Quraysh, who had guardianship (*ḥijâba*) of the building.[43]

Though it may contain a kernel of truth, this entire story raises doubts. When the caliphal armies finally retook Mecca from Ibn al-Zubayr, they promptly rebuilt the Kaʿba the way it had been before, in the shape and form allegedly disapproved of by Muhammad and essentially the one we see today. Second, none of the accounts we have of the Kaʿba prior to its reconstruction

39. Peters, *Hajj*, 58–59.

40. Peters, *Mecca*, 289–90.

41. Peters, *Hajj*, 63–64.

42. *The Life of Muhammad: A Translation of Ishaq's Sirat Rasûl Allâh*, with introduction and notes by A. Guillaume (Oxford: Oxford University Press, 1955) 84–85; cf. my *Muhammad*, 138–41.

43. This was one of the two offices—the other was the *siqâya* or the water-distribution rights—that survived into the Islamic era and are, in fact mentioned in the Qur'ān (9:19).

by the Quraysh in 605 C.E. points to anything remotely resembling the edifice put up by Ibn al-Zubayr in 683. In pre-Muhammad days the Kaʿba was reportedly a rather haphazardly assembled stone enclosure without a roof. Then, apparently, it was called an *ʿarîsh*, a 'tabernacle', the same word used by the Arabs to describe the Mosaic tabernacle,[44] and it was in fact draped with cloth hangings, as it still is today. All indications are that the Kaʿba was originally thought of as a tent, though perhaps differently shaped from the tents around it.[45] We do not know when the name Kaʿba became current, but it was scarcely the shape of the original construction that suggested Kaʿba 'cube' or 'cubical'. It is possible that the word, or its Greek analogue, *kubos*, had taken on the more generic meaning of 'temple' or 'sacred building'.[46]

In historical times there were objects within the Kaʿba, various idols, notably that of Hubal, and in a pit or well a mixed bag of items that constituted the "treasure" of the building and were at various times and under various circumstances buried and then "rediscovered."[47] The pit inside the Kaʿba has suggested to some the trenches dug before altars in various other Semitic sanctuaries, into which sacrificial blood and other offerings were collected.[48]

44. See Rubin ("Kaʿba," 98–99) on early traditions about the Kaʿba, and cf. M. Kister ("'A Booth like the Booth of Moses . . .': A Study of an Early Hadith," *BSOAS* 25 [1962] 150, 154) for the Mosaic 'tabernacle'.

45. Wellhausen, *Reste*, 73; Toufic Fahd, *Le Panthéon d'Arabie centrale à la veille de l'hégire* (Paris: Geuthner, 1968) 204–5.

46. Possibly by way of *qubba* 'dome, domed'? Note that in that same century Sophronius, the Greek Patriarch of Jerusalem, writing in Greek, refers to the building of the Holy Sepulcher, which is no more cube-like than the pre-Muhammad Kaʿba, as a *kubos*; H. Donner, *Die anakreontische Gedichte Nr. 18 und Nr. 20 des Patriarchen Sophronius* (Heidelberg, 1981) 12, 23, 36–37; cf. J. Wilkinson, *Jerusalem Pilgrims before the Crusades* (Jerusalem: Ariel, 1977) 91 n. 2; and, in a wider context, Fahd, *Panthéon*, 204.

47. Azraqi, *Akhbâr Makka*, 31: "Abraham dug a pit inside the House, to the right of its entrance as a treasury for the House, where the gifts to the Kaʿba were kept. This was the pit by which Amr ibn Luhayy set up Hubal, the idol worshiped by the Quraysh, and before which they used to do divination by the shaking of arrows, after Amr brought it from Hit (in Mesopotamia) to the lands of Arabia." And again (p. 73), now specifically citing the authority of Ibn Iṣḥaq, the classical biographer of the Prophet: "Muhammad ibn Iṣḥaq said that the well which was inside the Kaba to the right of its entry, and which is three cubits deep, is said to have been dug by Abraham and Ismael so as to keep in it the gifts offered to the Kaʿba. It continued to be so used until the time of (the Khuzaʿi) Amr ibn Luhayy . . ."; cf. Wellhausen, *Reste*, 75; G. R. Hawting, "The Disappearance and Rediscovery of Zamazam and the 'Well of the Kaʿba,'" *BSOAS* 43 (1980) 51; and Rubin, "Kaʿba," 117–18. Amr ibn Luhayy, if he was a historical character, lived many centuries before Muhammad.

48. Wellhausen, *Reste*, 103; Smith, *Semites*, 197–98; Fahd, *Panthéon*, 38–41. This is, in fact, one of the suggestions offered to explain the hole/cavern cut into the rock beneath the Muslim shrine-dome on the Temple Mount, that it was a collection pit

Muhammad cleared out the place—sparing only some paintings of Jesus and Mary—together with the rest of the Haram when Mecca came under his control in 630 C.E.[49]

Why was the Kaʿba built? The answer is not immediately apparent, since all of the Arab foundation myths, like pre-Islamic Arab mythology generally, have disappeared. They were replaced, at what we surmise was some time before Muhammad began to preach, by an Abraham-myth, a body of stories that placed the biblical patriarch in Mecca and environs.[50] This was taken over and expanded by Muhammad, notably in the Medina *sûras* of the Qurʾān, where the effects of the presence of a Jewish community in the oasis are readily notable.[51] The Meccan biblical calque and its Medinan enlargement eventually provided Muslims with their standard etiology—and justification—for many of the Meccan cult practices taken over into Islam, but they are of little help to us in determining their real origins. To house a god is the most obvious answer to the question of why the Kaʿba was built. But despite its name, *Bayt Allâh*, it housed no one or no thing at the time it

for the blood flowing from the altar that both the Muslim and the Jewish tradition connected with the rock; see Z. Vilnay, *The Legends of the Sacred Land*, vol. 1: *Jerusalem* (Philadelphia: Jewish Publication Society, 1973) 5–36.

49. Ibn Iṣḥaq, *Life*, 550–53; cf. my *Mecca*, 82–83. The paintings were either done or installed there by the Christian craftsman who supervised the reconstruction of 605 C.E.: Ibn Iṣḥaq, *Life*, 84; cf. my *Mecca*, 48.

50. Our surmise is based on Muhammad's use of the Abraham and related material. We know they antedated the Prophet's preaching from the Qurʾān's extremely allusive and elliptical use of biblical material, a presentation that would render most of his preaching unintelligible without some prior knowledge of the stories being referred to. In the early Meccan Sura 85, Muhammad is instructing the pagan Meccans that "the punishment of the Lord is stern." To illustrate this he says (vv. 17–18) "You've heard the story of the hosts of the Pharaoh and the Thamud, haven't you?" In our sequence of the *sûras* he has in fact told, in bare outline form, the story of the disbelieving Arab tribe of the Thamud (91:10–14) but nowhere has there been any reference to the Pharaoh. We have only two options: either we must so rearrange the *sûras* that a passing reference, like this one to the Pharaoh story, occurs only after a more complete and intelligible version of the referent, or else we must accept the fact that Muhammad's audience was indeed acquainted with the story of the Pharaoh and his hosts and could draw the appropriate moral from it. As it turns out, we do not have the first option at all. There are far too many Qurʾānic stories that are simply allusive, which to all appearances require the audience to know more than is being told.

51. This represents the second enlargement of the biblical material. A third and more massive reworking of what had been transformed by Muhammad from "biblical" to "Qurʾānic" stories of the patriarch occurred in the next generation of Muslims after the Prophet, when the major contributors were Jewish converts to Islam, particularly in the Yemen; see R. Firestone, *Journeys into Holy Lands: The Evolution of the Abraham-Ishmael Legends in Islamic Exegesis* (Albany: State University of New York Press, 1990).

comes into our view, neither a domestic idol nor even the *sakîna*, or sacred presence of a god,[52] as in the Jewish tradition. As has been noted, there once may have been a statue of the god Hubal inside, but all signs indicate that he was not at home there. The Arab tradition marks Hubal as an import, as does his anthropomorphic statue redolent of northern Hellenism.[53] Finally, the building was called the "House of Allah," and though the Qurʾān is much concerned with Meccan paganism, Hubal does not find a single mention there.

There is one obvious clue as to the true nature of the Kaʿba. There was and is no prohibition against entering the Kaʿba and no particular merit—or danger—in praying within it.[54] Quite to the contrary, the most primitive cult traditions associated with the building have the Meccans and their pilgrim guests behaving much like the perfidious Ephraimites who "mumbled their prayers" and kissed their calf-idols, as other idolaters kissed the image of Baʿal.[55] Before Islam, and even after, the devotees at Mecca were not kept away from the Kaʿba, as the Israelites were from Sinai or the inner Temple precincts, but rather attempted to establish as close contact as possible with it: they clung to the drapes of the building, pressed themselves against its walls, and touched and kissed the Black Stone embedded in one of its corners.[56] The Israelites feared impurity by contagion; the pre-Islamic Arabs of Mecca, like many others early and late, were more interested in the contagion of holiness.

There was, then, nothing *ḥaram* about "Allah's House" in Mecca. Even after Muhammad had effected his "high-god" revolution there and created an analogy whereby the Kaʿba should have exactly corresponded to the Holy of Holies in the Temple in Jerusalem—an analogy strongly urged by Muhammad's changing his direction of prayer from Jerusalem to the Meccan Kaʿba during his early days at Medina[57]—the old rituals continued to be followed. Muhammad's close associate, and the second caliph of Islam, Umar ibn al-Khattab, apparently had a more perfectly formed Muslim conscience than

52. The Muslims had a notion of the *sakîna* (*shekinah*)—the word occurs six times in the Qurʾān—but not always a clear understanding of what this obvious loanword meant; I. Goldziher, "La notion de la sakina chez les mohametans," *RHR* 28 (1893); reprinted in Joseph Desomogyi (ed.), *Gesammelte Schriften* (Hildesheim: Olms, 1967) 3.296–308.

53. Nabi Faris, *The Book of Idols of Ibn al-Kalbi* (Princeton: Princeton University Press, 1952) 23–24; cf. Fahd, *Panthéon*, 101; Peters, *Muhammad*, 108–10.

54. Gerald R. Hawting, "We Were Not Ordered with Entering It but Only with Circumambulating It: *Ḥadîth* and *Fiqh* on Entering the Kaʿba," *BSOAS* 47 (1984) 228–42.

55. Hos 13:2, 1 Kgs 19:18; cf. the Qurʾān's patronizing description of the pagan cult at Mecca as little more than "whistling and clapping of hands" (Qurʾān 8:35).

56. Wellhausen, *Reste*, 109.

57. Peters, *Muhammad*, 207–9.

Muhammad himself when he remarked, "If I had not seen the Prophet kissing it [that is, the Black Stone], I would never have kissed it again."[58] The Islamic revolution was one of concept, not of cult.

Nor does the Kaᶜba have any notable association with Muhammad's communication with Allah. If the principal Mosaic theophanies took place in circumstantially described places, that is, Mount Sinai or at the 'tent of meeting' (*'ôhel môᶜêd*), those that were granted to Muhammad occurred, according to his own words, in no particular place. The few topographical details supplied in the early Meccan Sura 53—"in the highest part of the horizon" (v. 7) and "near the lote-tree beyond which none may pass" (v. 14)—strongly suggest that these apparitions occurred somewhere outside the town and had nothing to do with the Meccan Kaᶜba or its surrounding Haram. Even the biographical attempts to imagine Muhammad's earliest revelations place them in a cave on a nearby mountainside and nowhere near the Kaᶜba.[59]

It was this kind of evidence that prompted Wellhausen to suggest that the Kaᶜba was not a *bayt* at all but the very idol that was being worshiped, an extension of the Black Stone lodged in its side.[60] Arab "litholatry" is well attested.[61] Sacred stones, both housed and unhoused, were common in Arabia, and the Black Stone was but one, albeit the most famous, of the betyls lodged in various parts of the Kaᶜba structure.[62] On this view, the Kaᶜba was merely a setting, a type of frame, without a proper "interior," and the holiness of the stone(s) it held spread to the entire construct so that to touch a part was to touch the whole. All the *functional* evidence we possess on the Kaᶜba points in the direction of Wellhausen's suggestion. There is no sign of a tabooed priesthood in Mecca or elsewhere in ancient western Arabia—the Arab *kâhin* was, despite the suggestive Hebrew parallel, a *vates* pure and simple, without any marked sacerdotal functions—and pre-Islamic lay sacrifice, indeed all cultic activity connected with the Kaᶜba, was conducted on altars or sacred stones *outside* of the building, though precisely where we cannot now say.[63]

58. Bukhari, *Ṣaḥîḥ*, 1.211.

59. Peters, *Muhammad*, 128–30.

60. Wellhausen, *Reste*, 74.

61. J. Henninger, "Pre-Islamic Bedouin Religion"; translated in *Studies on Islam* (ed. M. L. Swartz; New York: Oxford University Press, 1981) 8; H. Lammens, "Le culte des bétyles et les processions religieuses chez les Arabes préislamites," *L'Arabie Occidentale avant l'Hégire* (Beirut: Imprimerie Catholique, 1928) 100–180; Fahd, *Panthéon*, 24–31.

62. Lammens, "Culte des bétyles," 142–47; G. R. Hawting, "The Origins of the Islamic Sanctuary at Mecca," in *Studies on the First Century of Islam* (ed. G. H. A. Juynboll; Carbondale: University of Southern Illinois Press, 1982) 38–40.

63. Peters, *Hajj*, 29–30. Islam abolished all sacrifices in the vicinity of the Kaᶜba; the sole surviving sacrifice—imitated but not prescribed in the Islamic diaspora—is the sacrifice performed (by laymen) at Mina, well outside of Mecca, toward the end of the Hajj; ibid., 254–55, 307–10

The appellation *Bayt Allâh* aside, everything we know about the Kaʿba makes it clear that, in historical times at least, it shared none of the religious characteristics of either of the Mosaic desert tabernacles or of the Jerusalem Temple. The Kaʿba generated no taboos; it required no protection from surrounding impurity; it was the site of no theophanies either in *jâhili* or in Islamic times. Rather, it speaks of another type of sanctity altogether. It has been argued that we misunderstand ancient Arab litholatry, that "it is not to the stone itself that the worshiper gives his adoration, but to the god which it contains."[64] Perhaps so, but the Arabs could distinguish perfectly well between spirits, like the *jinn*, which *were* dangerous and needed cautious treatment,[65] and *holy objects*, which had a transferable power but were not dangerous.[66] The Kaʿba and its betyls fall into the latter category: the worshiper in Mecca had nothing to fear from drawing near to the structure or what it enshrined, nor did the Kaʿba from the worshipers' approach. A different order of sanctity was at work here.

64. René Dussaud, *La pénétration des Arabes en Syrie avant l'Islam* (Paris: Geuthner, 1955) 41 and n. 3.

65. Wellhausen, *Reste*, 148–49, 213.

66. Cf. the almost casual approach to sacred stones in the story transmitted by Ibn Saʿd (*Ṭabaqât* 4/1: 159):

> When a part of the tribe which had no god of its own was camping in a place, one man went out and looked for four stones, of which he set up three for his cooking pot and chose the most beautiful as the god he adored. If later he found a more beautiful one, he exchanged it for the first. At the next encampment he found another such.

The Pleiades, the Flood, and the Jewish New Year

Ellen Robbins
Johns Hopkins University

The interrelation of biblical text and Israelite festival is well known and ranges from liturgical psalms to the historical and quasi-historical events of biblical narrative commemorated at fixed dates in the liturgical calendar. Among the events the memory of which was evoked and honored in Israelite cultic practice, the Flood does not seem to appear, yet there is mounting evidence that the Flood not only remained a subject of speculation but also had an impact on specific cultic practices, in particular on the festivals that took place in the seventh month of the year. Two aspects of the biblical story of the Flood have attracted attention in recent years: its "mythological" prologue and the chronology within the narrative. The earliest extant interpretations in the Babylonian Talmud and later midrash indicate that these aspects were viewed together; the motif uniting them was the constellation of the Pleiades. Exploring pre- and postbiblical traditions of the Flood allows us to view some of the conceptual developments that led to the growing prominence of seventh-month festivals in later biblical and early Jewish calendars.

Before the Israelites adopted the month names of the Babylonian calendar during the exile or shortly thereafter, they referred to months by numerical designations, beginning with the first month in the spring. During this period, we have no evidence for a New Year celebration independent of the several annual festivals connected with the agricultural cycle. There is not a single biblical reference to a New Year festival; rather, the annual cultic calendar is consistently presented as beginning with the celebration of the *maṣṣôt*/*pesaḥ* festival in the spring.[1] The month in which the latter festival took place was emphatically the first month of the year: 'This month is for

Author's note: This essay is dedicated to Baruch Levine, on the occasion of his 65th birthday.

1. Exod 34:18–23, Leviticus 23, Numbers 28–29, Deut 16:1–16.

you the beginning (lit., head) of months; for you it is the first of the months of the year' (החדש הזה לכם ראש חדשים ראשון הוא לכם לחדשי השנה);[2] and the extraordinary sanctity of this month is reflected in and legitimated by its multiple connections with the Exodus narratives.

For purposes of time-reckoning, the biblical calendar employed lunar months, and the months in which sowing and harvest took place tended to be dense with ritual activity. These rituals, in addition to their seasonal character, acted as a magnet to attract and integrate myths and events of historical significance into the annual cultic calendar; *Jubilees* and rabbinic literature demonstrate that the process of providing dates for events in the distant past continued and intensified in the postbiblical period. The fact that in biblical tradition no primordial or preexilic historical event is associated with Tishri 1 is further evidence for the late development of a New Year festival on that date. Although the return from exile was said to have taken place in Tishri,[3] and the first gathering of the exiles and public reading of Torah were dated Tishri 1,[4] these events were never exploited as a pretext for the celebration of Rosh Hashanah or recalled specifically in the New Year liturgy, the thematic content of which focuses on divine sovereignty and judgment.[5]

Throughout its history, the calendar of ancient Israel was an adjusted lunar calendar in which an extra intercalary month was added ad hoc whenever the twelve-month lunar calendar fell too far behind the solar year on which taxation and agricultural offerings depended. The spring festival was based on the first stages in the ripening of the barley crop, and by early spring a judgment was made on whether it would be necessary to intercalate an extra month in order to delay the beginning of the festival cycle until the barley crop was more mature.[6]

In the Babylonian calendar, intercalation involved doubling the sixth or twelfth month, with an earlier predilection for the sixth month shifting to the twelfth month in the Neo-Babylonian period.[7] It was not until the fourth century that a fixed cycle of intercalary months was adopted. It is not

2. Exod 12:2; cf. y. *Roš Haš.* 1:1 (56d) on this verse: "Just as elsewhere the use of 'the months of' is counted only from Nisan, so 'the months of' here is counted only from Nisan."

3. Ezra 3:1, Neh 7:73.

4. Neh 8:2.

5. For the New Year liturgy, see N. H. Snaith, *The Jewish New Year Festival: Its Origins and Development* (London: Society for Promoting Christian Knowledge, 1947) 165–203; R. J. Adler, "The Rabbinic Development of Rosh Hashanah," *Conservative Judaism* 41 (1988–89) 34–41.

6. B. A. Levine, *Leviticus* (JPS Torah Commentary; Philadelphia: Jewish Publication Society, 1989) 265.

7. R. A. Parker and W. H. Dubberstein, *Babylonian Chronology 626 B.C.–A.D. 75* (Providence: Brown University Press, 1956).

known on what basis prior decisions to intercalate were made; several theoretical schemes have been identified, although these were apparently never implemented.[8] In a study of actual intercalations in the Neo-Babylonian period,[9] Neugebauer observed that the effective timing kept the autumn equinox closely correlated with the lunar calendar, which in cultic practice would have resulted in a seasonal adjustment for the fall *akītu* festival; in Exod 34:22 the fall festival Sukkôt is dated to *tĕqūpat haššānâ*, using what would become the rabbinic technical term for equinox and solstice.[10] This makes sense for a calendar tied to the agricultural cycle, since the first festival of the agricultural year was defined by the *approach* of the barley harvest and did not actually require ripe produce. In practical terms, the only biblical festival in which availability of ripe produce was highly problematic was Sukkôt, earlier known as חג האסיף 'the festival of ingathering'.[11]

The timing of the Sukkôt festival must have been a source of contention between Israel and Judah because crops mature a full month or more later in Galilee than in Judah.[12] It is likely that this factor was the basis for the calendar change effected by Jeroboam I who, perhaps by means of an intercalation, celebrated the fall harvest festival a month later than had been the practice during the period of the United Kingdom. In 1 Kings 12 the story of this change is told from the Judean point of view, with the result that the Northern Kingdom observed Sukkôt in what appeared to the Judeans to be the eighth month but was undoubtedly the seventh month of the Northern calendar.[13]

By the postexilic period, the biblical festival calendar had become weighted in favor of the autumn celebration of Sukkôt, which was reflected in the relative numbers of sacrificial animals for the various festivals in the

8. A. Sachs, "Sirius Dates in Babylonian Astronomical Texts of the Seleucid Period," *JCS* 6 (1952) 105–14; J. Schaumberger, *Sternkunde und Sterndienst in Babel: Ergänzungen* (Münster: Aschendorffschen, 1935) 337–44; H. Hunger and E. Reiner, "A Scheme for Intercalary Months from Babylonia," *WZKM* 67 (1975) 21–28.

9. O. Neugebauer, "The 'Metonic Cycle' in Babylonian Astronomy," in *Studies and Essays in the History of Science and Learning Offered in Homage to George Sarton* (ed. M. F. A. Montagu; New York: Schuman, 1944) 443–44.

10. *B. Sanh.* 13a.

11. Exod 23:16, 34:22.

12. M. *Šeb.* 9:2–3, *b. Sanh.* 11b, *y. Sanh.* 1.2 (18d), *t. Sanh.* 2.3. There seems to be substantial disagreement on this easily verifiable point; compare S. Talmon, "The Reform of Jeroboam I" (*King, Cult, and Calendar in Ancient Israel: Collected Studies* [Jerusalem: Magnes, 1986] 120); with J. B. Segal, "Intercalation and the Hebrew Calendar" (*VT* 7 [1957] 257–59, and references there cited).

13. This discrepancy of one month between the two calendars also appears in the story of Hezekiah's gesture toward the Israelite populations of the recently fallen Northern Kingdom in the form of an invitation to "all Israel" to celebrate Passover in Jerusalem in the second month, that is, the second month of the Judean calendar (2 Chronicles 30).

later calendar (Numbers 28–29). At the same time additional festivals became part of the cultic calendar of the seventh month.[14] The first day of the seventh month, later known as Rosh Hashanah, is variously described as *šabbatôn, zikrôn* 'commemoration', (*yôm*) *tĕrûʿâ* '(day of) sounding (the shofar)', and *miqrāʾ qōdeš* 'holy convocation'. This abbreviated list of characteristics of the Tishri 1 festival in Leviticus 23 is supplemented in Numbers 29 by the specification of a substantial sacrificial offering in addition to the usual daily and new moon offerings.

We should regard the development of a fall New Year festival in terms of the matrix of events to which it is proximate as an introduction to the series of seventh-month festivals with common concerns in terms of both myth and ritual.[15] The prescribed ritual for Tishri 1 included sounding the shofar; this instrument had particular associations with festivals of the seventh month, especially the first day of the month,[16] even representing autumn in early synagogue decoration.[17] The shofar seems to be intimately linked to the seventh month as the prelude to the period of winter rains. Making deafening sounds is based on sympathetic magic, according to which imitating the sound of thunder should bring rain. In a literal application of this principle, a shofar was occasionally sounded into a cistern or pot, apparently a symbolic act to direct the anticipated rainfall straight into its container.[18] In a converse statement of the magical association with rainfall, the shofar could be sounded in all cases of danger to the community except excessive rains.[19] Sounding the shofar also characterized the Sukkôt festival,[20] which in mishnaic Judaism was explicitly connected with the coming rainy season, in both myth (divine judgment expressed in the amount of rainfall allotted for the coming year)[21] and ritual (water libations).[22] Like the sound of the shofar, water libations were thought to produce rain by sympathetic magic:

14. Lev 23:23–25, Num 29:1–6.

15. Levine, *Leviticus*, 160; A. Michel, "Nouvel an," *DBSup* 6.620.

16. Num 29:1; cf. Ps 81:4; *m. Roš Haš.* 3:7; *b. Roš Haš.* 16b, 34a; *y. Roš Haš.* 4.1 (59b). See also J. Heinemann, "The Ancient 'Orders of Benedictions' for New Year and Fasts," *Tarbiz* 45 (1976) 16–26 [Heb.]; T. H. Gaster, *Festivals of the Jewish Year* (New York: Morrow, 1978) 116–18.

17. On the mosaic floor of the 6th-century Naʿaran synagogue, where the corresponding term for autumn is *tĕqūpat* Tishri, see R. Hachlili, "The Zodiac in Ancient Jewish Art: Representation and Significance," *BASOR* 228 (1977) 66, fig. 5; p. 71.

18. *B. Roš Haš.* 27b–28a.

19. M. *Taʿan.* 3:1–3, 8.

20. M. *Sukk.* 4:9, 5:4.

21. M. *Roš Haš.* 1:2, *y. Roš Haš.* 1.3 (57b), *b. Taʿan.* 2b; cf. *Jub.* 12:16, where Abraham observed the sky on the night of the new moon of the seventh month to ascertain the expected rainfall for the coming year.

22. M. *Sukk.* 4:1, 9; 5:5; *b. Roš Haš.* 16a; *t. Roš Haš.* 1.12–13. On this ritual, see *b. Sukk.* 53a; R. Patai, *Man and Temple* (New York: Ktav, 1967) 24–53; and idem, "The 'Control of Rain' in Ancient Palestine," *HUCA* 14 (1939) 281 n. 152.

R. Eliezer said: When the water libations are carried out on the Festival [of Sukkôt], Tehôm says to his fellow, "Let your waters come forth; I hear the voice of two friends."[23]

When a New Year festival began to be celebrated in the autumn, the Jewish calendar acquired the peculiar characteristic of celebrating its New Year in what had been since time immemorial the seventh month of the calendar year. This peculiarity did not go unremarked. Because the seventh month had assumed such importance in the cultic calendar in terms of judgment of the individual and of the community (with respect to necessary rainfall), the rabbis were faced with a complex of ideas in search of a biblical prooftext, one that ideally would relate divine judgment to a specific time of year. In the relevant passage in tractate *Roš Haššana*, the discussion focuses on Gen 7:11, which not only marks the beginning of the most devastating act of divine judgment reported in the Bible, but also fortuitously contains the first calendar date in a sequential reading:

In the 600th year of Noah's life, in the 2d month, on the 17th day of the month. . . .

Since the biblical use of numerical month names beginning with the spring was indisputable, R. Joshua opts for the plain meaning of Gen 7:11:

R. Joshua said: That day was the 17th day of Iyyar [second month in numbered-month calendar], a day when the constellation of the Pleiades (מזל כימה) sets during the day (ביום) and the water sources (מעיינות) decrease, and because they changed their behavior (שינו מעשיהן), the Holy One, blessed be He, changed (שינה) for them the behavior of the created world (מעשה בראשית) and made the constellation of the Pleiades rise during the day and took two (שני) stars from the Pleiades and brought a flood on the world.

And R. Eliezer, who frequently opposed the opinions of R. Joshua, responded:

That day was the 17th of Marḥeshwan [eighth month in numbered-month calendar], a day when the constellation of the Pleiades rises during the day and the water sources increase; and because they changed their behavior, the Holy One, blessed be He, changed for them the behavior of the created world, and caused the constellation of the Pleiades to rise during the day, and took away two stars and brought a flood on the world. (*b. Roš Haš.* 11b–12a)

The period when the Pleiades set during the day corresponds to the dry season, while the period in which they rise during the day corresponds to the rainy season. Taking ביום to mean 'during the day' resolves the logical and astronomical difficulties raised by the usual translation 'at daybreak',[24] which is more commonly בשחר or שחרית, and eliminates the need to emend

23. *B. Taʿan.* 25b.
24. Similarly ליומא in an astronomical passage in *b. Roš Haš.* 21a refers to the visibility of the moon in the morning sky. This period bears no relation to the visibility of rising constellations which only occurs before daybreak when the sky is still dark.

the text, since both statements now agree with astronomical fact (see chart, p. 339).

Thanks to the quotation of these statements in a discussion about the priority of the spring- or autumn-epoch year, reflections on the physical mechanism by which the Flood was produced were preserved. Both rabbis were well versed in the scientific thinking of the day. Both spoke Greek and represented the Jewish people in meetings with Roman officials, while R. Joshua had devised a system for determining the beginning of the lunar month, one of the thorniest problems in ancient astronomy.[25] For these sages it was insufficient to appeal to divine omnipotence to explain the Flood; God brought the deluge, as people pray for rain, in the rainy season.[26] Just as one needed to know which actions provoked such a divine response, so one wanted to know precisely how the trick was done.

In Israel, there are two rainy seasons, the heavier 'early rains' (מורה, יורה) in the fall and winter that prepare the ground for ploughing and sowing and nourish the grain crops through the winter months, and the rains of spring and early summer (רביבים, מלקוש) that were lighter and more occasional, although equally necessary to see the crops through to maturation.[27] R. Joshua, often a literalist, follows the plain meaning of "second month" in Gen 7:11 as an ordinary date in the numbered-month calendar. However, he is aware of the difficulty that this interpretation raises: if he is correct in asserting that the "second month" in the Flood story corresponds to a month in late spring, he must explain how it came about that the Flood occurred at the start of the dry season. He turns to the apparently well-known connection between the Pleiades and the rainy season, basing his reasoning on an assumed change in the very structure of the universe. He further conditions this interpretation by reading the divine promise made at the conclusion of the Flood to keep the order of the seasons (Gen 8:22) to imply that the seasons were disturbed during the period of the Flood. R. Eliezer claims that even during the Flood the seasonal structure of the year was maintained, consistent with his position in *b. Roš Haš.* 11b–12a.[28]

This text asserts that the positions taken by R. Joshua and R. Eliezer agree with their arguments elsewhere, which is to say that their thinking was understood to be systematic and rigorous. R. Eliezer figures as a prominent proponent of the autumn-epoch year, even associating it with patriarchal birthdays and a miscellany of biblical events.[29] His statement that the Flood

25. M. *Roš Haš.* 2:8–9, *b. Roš Haš.* 24a–25b.

26. M. *Ta'an.* 1:2; cf. M. Douglas, *Purity and Danger* (London: Routledge and Kegan Paul, 1966) 58.

27. R. B. Y. Scott, "Meteorological Phenomena and Terminology in the Old Testament," ZAW 64 (1952) 22–23.

28. *Gen. Rab.* 22:4, 25:2, 34:11; note the addition of "not change their order" to "shall not cease" (Gen 8:22) in *Jub.* 6:4.

29. *B. Roš Haš.* 10b–11a, 27a; cf. *Lev. Rab.* 29:1.

occurred in Marḥeshwan, the eighth month in the numerically-designated calendar, although going against the plain sense of the biblical text, is found in other postbiblical traditions. According to one midrash, rains fell annually for 40 days in the month of Marḥeshwan until the building of the Temple the construction of which was completed in the month בול, equivalent to the eighth month (i.e., Marḥeshwan);[30] furthermore, by a fanciful etymology, the month name בול is derived from מבול 'flood' by removing the letter *mem*, whose numerical equivalent is 40, the 40 days of rain during the Flood.[31] In fact, R. Eliezer seems to represent the more generally accepted view. According to the Palestinian Talmud, "everyone admits that it [17 Marḥeshwan] is the time of the setting of the Pleiades (כימה לשקע), for on it the Flood came in the world,"[32] and the passage from *b. Roš Haš.* 11b–12a concludes with the statement that "the scholars of Israel reckon the flood according to R. Eliezer and the *tĕqûpâ* according to R. Joshua; the scholars of the nations of the world also reckon the flood according to R. Joshua." This date commanded not only intellectual assent. According to *m. Ta'an.* 1:4, a series of 3 fast-days was observed when no rain had fallen by the 17th of Marḥeswan.

Both sages agree that the Flood involved a change in the structure of the universe. R. Eliezer's position requires only a minor change, removing two stars from the Pleiades. By making more sense in terms of celestial patterns and seasons, R. Eliezer necessarily lessens the drama and weakens the argument with respect to the basic assumption of substantial change. His purpose is clearly to make a point about the beginning of the year, to retroject the autumn-epoch year into antediluvian time.

The one point of agreement is that the rising of the Pleiades during the day was essential to the timing of the Flood. For other sages, with less astronomical sophistication, the Flood was occasioned by a variety of changes in the structure of the universe; the assumption of change functions as an a priori without fixed content. Some argued that the Flood involved a change in the movement or effects of the planets during the year-long duration of the Flood,[33] while according to *'Abot R. Nat.* 32.1.3, God 'changed the order of the universe' (שינה עליהם הקב"ה סידורו של עולם) by causing the sun to rise in the west and set in the east.

Enoch traditions agree with the biblical text that the Flood was brought on as a divine judgment on human actions, extrapolating on Gen 6:1–4 in a detailed portrayal of בני האלהים as fallen angels who bear a greater share of responsibility. Nevertheless, in the midst of a description of the teachings

30. 1 Kgs 6:38. *Bul* is a well-attested Phoenician month-name; see E. Koffmahn, "Sind die altisraelitischen Monatsbezeichnungen mit den kanaanäischen identisch?" *BZ* n.s. 10 (1966) 201–2.

31. *Tanḥ.* Noah 17 (ed. S. Buber).

32. *Y. Ta'an.* 1.3 (64a); cf. *Gen. Rab.* 33:7; *Tg. Esth* II 3:7.

33. *Gen. Rab.* 25:2, 34:11.

transmitted to mortals by the angels, *1 Enoch* 8:1 has the enigmatic intrusion: "and the world was changed."[34] We also find phraseology similar to *b. Roš. Haš.* 11b–12a in an Aramaic *Enoch* fragment from Qumran:[35]

שנה [ושנה לא ישניון עבדהן ו]כלהן עבדין ממרה ואנתן שניתן עבדכן.

> 'Year [after year they (the seasons) do not change their works, but] all of them do His Word; but you, you have changed your work'. . . .

The *idée fixe* underlying these texts is that the Flood was brought about by a substantial change in the structure of the universe and was justified by a prior change in the terrestrial realm, the defiling of the created order that in the *Enoch* (and biblical) traditions resulted from an incursion of divine beings. These traditions elaborate on what is missing in *b. Roš Haš.* 11b–12a, the unstated subject of the verb **שינו**: "*they* changed (*their* behavior)." In 11b–12a, the language of corresponding changes in the earthly and terrestrial realms functions as an argument for the appropriateness of the divine act; the precision of divine justice is indicated by a word-play on **שנה** 'change' and **שני**, the number of stars removed. The text purports to represent a dispute about the antiquity of the autumn-epoch year, and on the surface that is why it appears in this particular place in the Talmud. But in fact there is another level in the argument that points to reflections on the Flood in terms of its physical and moral causes that antedate the biblical account itself.

The Physical Causes of the Flood

R. Joshua's argument, taken in its entirety, is concerned with what he perceived as an inconsistency in the account in Genesis. The problem he faced was this: the plain interpretation of 'second month' means that the Flood took place in the late spring/early summer, after the end of the rainy season in Palestine. In order to maintain the plain meaning of the text and at the same time provide a realistic account of the Flood, he is forced to explain how such a rainstorm could have occurred in the wrong season. On the other hand, R. Eliezer, through a radical reinterpretation of "second month" in Genesis 7, was able to make several points: first, he located the Flood realistically during the rainy season; he established the hoary antiquity of the autumn-epoch year; and he implicitly connected the judgment that brought on the Flood with the rabbinic characterization of the autumn New Year festival as introducing the annual period of divine judgment.

The questions for both R. Joshua and R. Eliezer were: how exactly did the Flood take place? What is the cause of seasonal rain, and how is normal rain-

34. See discussion in M. A. Knibb, *The Ethiopic Book of Enoch* (Oxford: Oxford University Press, 1978) 2.81.

35. 4QEnoch[a] 1 ii 11–12; J. T. Milik, *The Books of Enoch: Aramaic Fragments of Qumrân Cave 4* (Oxford: Oxford University Press, 1976) 146–47.

fall connected with the excessive rains that brought on the Flood? It should be noted that both were searching for a naturalistic explanation, a description of the mechanism that actually causes rain; neither was interested in an argument that appealed to an omnipotent god, who can bring rain by some indeterminate process at any time.

Their answer to these questions was not meteorological but cosmological: it rains because the cosmos is structured in such a way that at certain times of the year rains fall. They then had to provide an explanation for the extraordinary rainfall that continued without cease for 40 days. Their conclusion was that something structural happened to the universe so that the Flood could occur; this was expressed as a change in "the behavior of the created world." The point of agreement in their arguments is that this change had something to do with the Pleiades. Their agreement indicates a traditional association of the Pleiades with winter rains that made the rest of the argument plausible.

In order to understand this association we must look at the Pleiades and their place in the ancient world. All stars at a sufficient distance from the polestar disappear from the night sky for some part of the year. After a period of invisibility, when a particular star or constellation rises and sets during the daytime, it again comes into view on the eastern horizon just before sunrise. This appearance is referred to as its heliacal or visible morning rising. Because the earth is moving slowly around the sun, completing its motion in a solar year, and the earth is simultaneously rotating on its axis each 24 hours, at the end of each day the earth is in a slightly different position with respect to the fixed stars. The day after its heliacal rising, a constellation will rise four minutes earlier and be visible in the night sky slightly longer before it fades away at sunrise. As the months pass, the constellation is visible for a longer period of time until its setting is visible for the first time just before sunrise, referred to as its cosmical or visible morning setting. After its cosmical setting, the constellation rises during the day and sets earlier and earlier in the night sky until it sets at sunset, ushering in a period of invisibility. In the case of the Pleiades, this period lasts approximately 40 days.[36] Since the heliacal risings and cosmical settings of stars like the Pleiades that are located near the path of the sun and planets (the ecliptic) recur at the same time each solar year, they can be taken as reliable predictors of concurrent seasonal phenomena. It is but a short mental step to endow this predictability with causative significance.

To the naked eye, the Pleiades are seen as a cluster of stars resembling a small ball of dust enclosing 6 or 7 small stars. In Japanese the constellation is called Subaru, and the logo of the automobile of that name represents the Pleiades compressed into an oval. The Pleiades are part of Taurus, a constellation of the zodiac lying slightly northeast of Orion, which rises after the

36. G. Dalman, *Arbeit und Sitte in Palästina* (Gütersloh: Bertelsmann, 1928) 1/2.284–85.

Pleiades and follows it through the night sky. The chart (see p. 339) shows the visibility of the Pleiades throughout the year. The periods after their heliacal rising and cosmical setting are those referred to in the argument in *b. Roš Haš.* 11b–12a with which we began. Five thousand years ago, the heliacal rising of the Pleiades coincided with the vernal equinox. Because of a wobble in the earth's axis, the equinox shifts slowly backward through the zodiacal constellations, the constellations located near the ecliptic, so that by the 5th century B.C.E., this took place somewhat later, approximately May 19. In Palestine it is the winter rains that begin in November that fill the cisterns and rivers, and the end of the winter rains occurs in striking proximity to the heliacal rising of the Pleiades.[37] Thus, in antiquity, the months following the heliacal rising, when the Pleiades rose above the horizon earlier and earlier each night, corresponded to the dry season. The months following their cosmical setting in the autumn, during which they set earlier and earlier in the night sky, corresponded to the period of heavy rains essential for the agricultural cycle.

An analogous connection between the Pleiades and the seasons is found in the traditions of ancient Greece. Hesiod associates the heliacal rising of the Pleiades with the beginning of the harvest season in the spring and their cosmical setting with ploughing and sowing in the fall.[38] For Hesiod, as for R. Joshua and R. Eliezer almost a thousand years later, the cosmical setting of the Pleiades was associated with the beginning of the rainy season, and their rising signaled the beginning of the dry season. In Greece, where maritime considerations were on a par with agricultural concerns, the most common reference was to the period following the cosmical setting of the Pleiades at the onset of winter, a time of danger to sailors: "When the Pleiades plunge into the misty sea [i.e., set visibly during the night] to escape Orion's powerful strength, then truly gales of all kinds rage. Keep ships no longer on the sparkling sea. . . ."[39]

The Pleiades constitute one of many constellations surrounding the ecliptic, of which the zodiacal constellations became the most prominent. Throughout the ancient world, the cycle of seasons was correlated with constellations visible in the night sky at different times of the year. In order to fix these patterns in memory, proximate stars were grouped together, and,

37. Ibid., 1/2.294–96. In Dalman's opinion, the connection with the Pleiades was already present in the Genesis account, since the 364-day period seems to indicate an interest in a sidereal year, the time in which a particular configuration of sun and constellations recurs.

38. Hesiod *Works and Days* 383–84; compare a similar rule based on the Pleiades in *b. B. Meṣ.* 106b; *Midr. Tad.* 6. At the time of Hesiod, ca. 700 B.C.E., the heliacal rising of the Pleiades occurred around mid-May, their cosmical setting toward the end of October.

39. Hesiod *Works and Days* 619–22; cf. Quintus Smyrnaeus 7.308–11; Aratus *Phaenomena* 1082–87.

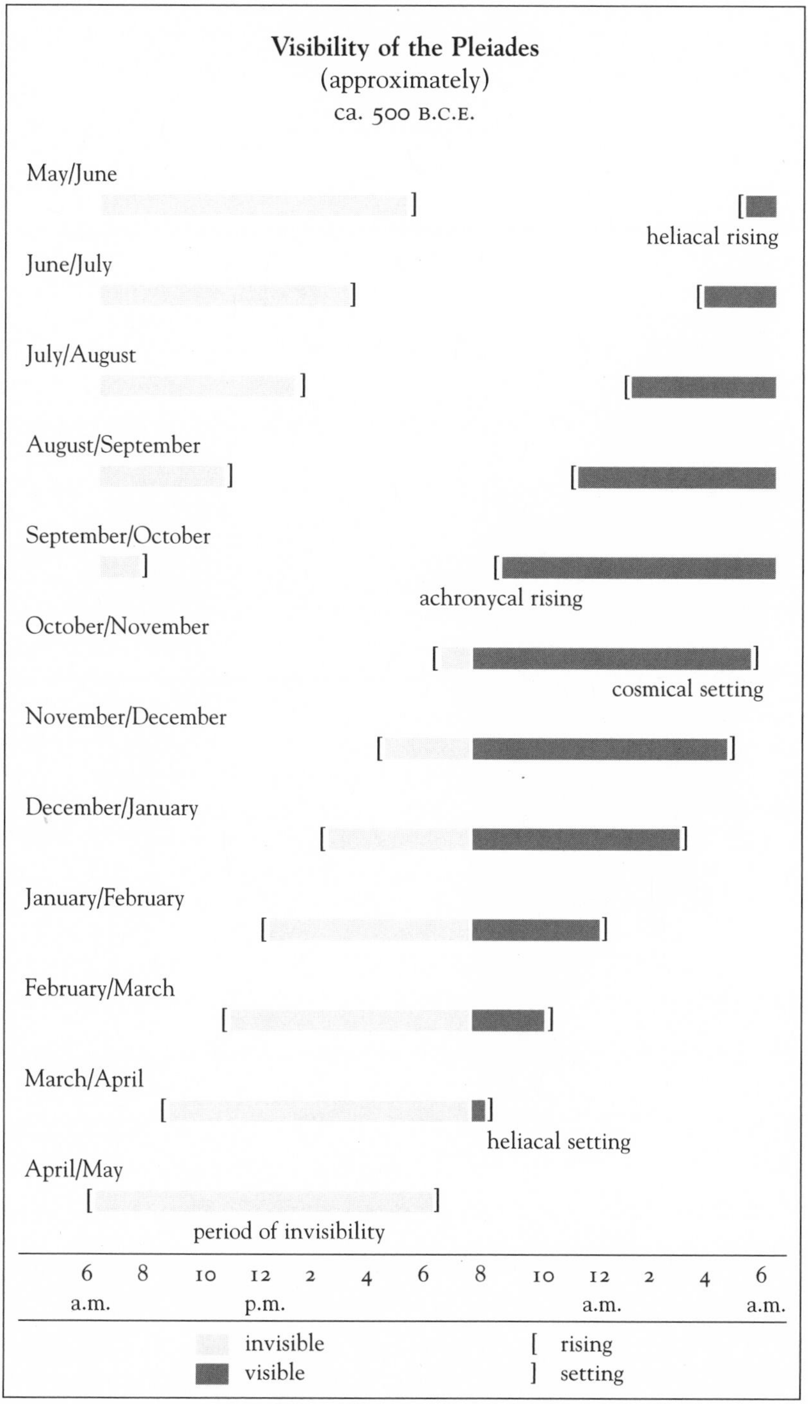
Visibility of the Pleiades
(approximately)
ca. 500 B.C.E.
May/June
heliacal rising
June/July
July/August
August/September
September/October
achronycal rising
October/November
cosmical setting
November/December
December/January
January/February
February/March
March/April
heliacal setting
April/May
period of invisibility
6 a.m.
8
10
12 p.m.
2
4
6
8
10
12 a.m.
2
4
6 a.m.
invisible
visible
[rising
] setting

like the game of finding animal shapes in cloud formations, these constellations were identified and named and stories told about their relationship to one another, so that, for example, constellations that followed one another were described in terms of a pursuit. Such a description is found in *b. Ber.* 58b–59a, which, in agreement with the Qumran Targum, renders Job 38:32 "*ʿAyish* will be comforted for her children":

> This shows that it lacks something, and in fact it looks like a piece torn off, and the reason why she follows her is because she is saying to her: "Give me my children." For at the time when the Holy One, blessed be He, wanted to bring a flood upon the world, "He took two stars from *Kimah* and brought a flood on the world" (*b. Roš Haš.* 11b–12a). And when he wanted to stop it, He took two stars from *ʿAyish* and stopped it.

Here the explanation of the physical mechanism of the Flood is completed: the Flood ended when the stars taken from the Pleiades were replaced by two stars from the constellation *ʿAyish*, frequently identified with Ursa Major, but more likely Aldebaran and the minor Hyades that closely follow the Pleiades through the night sky.[40]

In rabbinic literature the name for the Pleiades is *kîmâ*, assumed no doubt correctly to be the meaning of biblical *kîmâ*. In Amos 5:8 and Job 9:9, Yahweh is described as the maker of *kîmâ* and *kĕsîl* (Orion). Current translations of the third passage, Job 38:31, are based on emending a presumed metathesis, yielding 'bands'.[41] The medieval astrological interpretation of Naḥmanides and Gersonides led to the KJV translation as 'sweet influences of the Pleiades', based on a presumed causative connection to the heliacal rising of the constellation and the appearance of spring flowers. The binding and unbinding of constellations in the Job pericope points to an underlying story involving the Pleiades and Orion and may contain an oblique reference to the explanation of the Flood as a physical change in the configuration of the Pleiades. This interpretation occurs as early as the Qumran *Targum of Job*, where *tĕhôm* in Job 38:30 is rendered *mbl*[ʾ] 'flood'. Another indication that the targumist had the Flood story in mind is his use of נפילא 'the fallen one' for Heb. כסיל 'Orion'. This unusual name for Orion occurs only in the *Targum of Job*[42] and is apparently based on associations of the constellations, the Flood prologue, and catasterism à la Greek myth: in one version of the origin of the Pleiades, seven mortal women, pursued by the divine hunter Orion,

40. Proposed by G. Schiaparelli, *Astronomy in the Old Testament* (Oxford: Oxford University Press, 1905) 54–60, 161–68; followed by G. R. Driver, "Two Astronomical Passages in the Old Testament," *JTS* n.s. 7 (1956) 1–11

41. For the history of interpretation, see M. H. Pope, *Job* (AB 15; 3d ed.; New York: Doubleday, 1965) 300.

42. Thanks to Jerome Lund of the *Comprehensive Aramaic Lexicon* project for information on the various Aramaic renderings of Orion.

were saved by Zeus, who transformed them into doves[43] and then placed them in the sky as stars, forever fleeing but safe, just beyond Orion's grasp.

The Moral Causes of the Flood

The passage from *b. Roš Haš.* 11b–12a is concerned with the physical changes in the universe that brought about the Flood. Other Flood traditions were not limited to the question of natural causation but rightly inquired about its moral causes, what could have gone so wrong as to warrant such a cataclysmic divine response. The rationale for the Flood elaborates on the mythological prologue to the Flood narrative (Gen 6:1–4), which indicates succinctly the events that provoked God to bring on the Flood: the sexual mingling of "sons of God" with mortal women and the presence of *Nephilim*, whom the author of Genesis identifies in euhemeristic fashion with legendary heroes, and later traditions with fallen angels, based on the etymology of *Nephilim.*[44]

The prologue in Gen 6:1–4 is only tenuously connected to the story of the rescue of humankind through the righteous Noah. In ancient Greece, a myth of destruction as punishment for similar sexual transgression was associated with a historical event, the fall of Troy. Hendel[45] has suggested a connection between the Genesis Flood story and Hesiod's account of the cause of the Trojan War as an attempt by Zeus to destroy life on earth in order to keep the sons of the gods (*tekna theôn*) from mating with mortal women, to ensure the separation of gods and mortals.[46] The biblical and Greek versions trace back to a story in which a Flood brings to an end a breakdown in the barrier between gods and mortals, a tale that Hesiod connects to the Trojan War and biblical tradition to the story of Noah.

The biblical account begins with a concise statement of sexual transgression, which remains the dominant motif in later interpretation. This motif is present in the continuation of the passage from *b. Roš Haš.* 12a:

43. A word-play based on assonance of Pleiades with *peleiades* 'doves', the false etymology becoming part of the story; M. L. West (ed.), *Hesiod: Works and Days* (Oxford: Oxford University Press, 1978) 254–55.

44. *Tg. Ps.-J.* 6:4: "Šemḥazai and ʿAzaʾel had fallen from heaven and were on the earth in those days." Cf. J. Morgenstern, "The Mythological Background of Ps 82," *HUCA* 14 (1939) 83–114.

45. R. S. Hendel, "Of Demigods and the Deluge: Toward an Interpretation of Genesis 6:1–4," *JBL* 106 (1987) 13–26; cf. R. Scodel, "The Achaean Wall and the Myth of Destruction," *Harvard Studies in Classical Philology* 86 (1982) 33–50; R. S. Fisher and A. M. Lewis, "Agamemnon, Troy and the Pleiades," *Revue belge de philologie et d'histoire* 62 (1984) 5–15.

46. Hesiod *Catalogue of Women and Eoiae* 68.2.2–50; published in H. G. Evelyn-White (ed.), *Hesiod: The Homeric Hymns and Homerica* (LCL; Cambridge: Harvard University Press, 1967) 198–203.

> Again, in R. Joshua's view we see what change there was in the work of creation, but in R. Eliezer's view what change was there? The answer is found in the dictum of R. Ḥisda; for R. Ḥisda said: With hot liquid (רותחין) they sinned and with hot liquid they were punished. "With hot liquid they sinned," i.e., with sexual transgression (עבירה).

The *Enoch* traditions in their Aramaic, Ethiopic, and Greek versions develop the identification of the בני האלהים and *Nephilim* as fallen or rebellious angels whose miscegenation with mortal women was but one of their transgressions. In *1 Enoch*, 200 angels led by Šemîḥazâ/Šahmîzâd/Semiaza descend to earth, where their sexual unions with mortal women result in a race of giants.[47] According to Milik, this *Enoch* tradition antedated and was abridged in the biblical account,[48] a suggestion that becomes more plausible as the length of time separating the *Enoch* and later biblical traditions narrows.[49]

There was a tendency, already present in *Targum Pseudo-Jonathan*, to limit the number of fallen angels to 2, Šemiḥazai and ʿAzaʾel, the latter name appearing with variants ʿAzazʾel/ʿAzaʾzel. Even in the *Enoch* traditions in which ʿAzaʾel is a minor figure, he is responsible for introducing the arts of metallurgy and cosmetics, the very arts by which women entice men to sexual transgression,[50] and he alone is held accountable and suffers the punishment for the sins of the following generation of giants.[51]

In *b. Yoma* 67b, the behavior of the angel ʿAzaʾel is used to explain the scapegoat ritual of the Day of Atonement, another seventh-month festival the thematic content of which concerns expiation and judgment: "R. Ishmael: ʿAzaʾzel who atones for the behavior of ʿÛza and ʿAzaʾel."[52] If Milik is correct that ʿAzazʾel is the earlier form of biblical ʿAzaʾzel, mentioned in the atonement ritual described in Leviticus 16, we would have another indication of the antiquity of the mythological fragment in Gen 6:1–4, as well as

47. Accounting for LXX rendering of נפלים as *gigantes* 'giants'. The sense of 'giants' was also given to the translation גברים found in various targums; *Gen. Rab.* 26:7 "R. Abba said in the name of R. Joḥanan: the marrow of each one's thigh bone was 18 cubits long."

48. J. T. Milik, "Problèmes de la littérature hénochique à la lumière des fragments araméens de Qumrân," *HTR* 64 (1971) 349; Milik, *Enoch*, 31–32; followed by M. Black, *The Book of Enoch or I Enoch* (Leiden: Brill, 1985) 14–15. Barker finds reference to this Enochic tradition in Psalms 58 and 82; M. Barker, "Some Reflections upon the Enoch Myth," *JSOT* 15 (1980) 19–24.

49. M. E. Stone, "The Book of Enoch and Judaism in the Third Century B.C.E.," *CBQ* 40 (1978) 483–86; P. R. Davies, "Sons of Cain," in *A Word in Season: Essays in Honour of William McKane* (JSOTSup 42; Sheffield: Sheffield Academic Press, 1986) 46–48.

50. *1 Enoch* 6–9.

51. *1 Enoch* 10:2–8, 13:1–2, 86:1; see Black, *Book of Enoch*, 258 n.1.

52. *B. Roš Haš.* 16a; 4Q180, *181*; 4QEnGiants[a] 7; see Milik, *Enoch*, 250–52, 312–14.

an insight into the background of the atonement ritual itself: as Davies remarks, "the reason for sending the sins to Azazel is that Azazel is responsible for bringing them into the world."[53] In *1 Enoch* 10:4, his place of punishment is called Dudael, a name that Black connects to בית חדודי,[54] identified in *Tg. Ps.-J.* Lev 16:21–22 as the wilderness to which the scapegoat was sent.[55]

The interweaving of Enochic, biblical, and astronomical motifs continued to develop within medieval Judaism. Among later midrashim, we find another expansion of this complex of traditions:

> R. Joseph was asked what was the story of Šemḥazai and ʿAzaʾel, and he replied: "When the generation of Enosh arose and practiced idolatry and when the generation of the flood arose and corrupted their actions (וקילקלו את מעשיהם), the Holy One, blessed be He, was grieved that He had created man, as it is said, 'And God repented that He created man, and He was grieved at heart.' Then two angels rose, whose names were Šemḥazai and ʿAzaʾel, and said before Him: 'O Lord of the Universe, did we not say to You when You created the world, "Do not create man"?', as it is said, 'What is man that You should remember him?' The Holy One, blessed be He, said to them: 'Then what shall become of the world?' They said before Him: 'We will attend to it.' He said: 'It is revealed and known to me that if you had lived in that world, the evil inclination would have ruled you just as much as it rules over the sons of man, but you would be more stubborn than they.' They said before Him: 'Give us your sanction and let us descend among the creatures and then You will see how we shall sanctify Your name.' He said to them: 'Descend and dwell among them.' Then the Holy One allowed the evil inclination to rule over them as soon as they descended. When they saw the daughters of men that they were beautiful, they began to corrupt themselves with them, as it is said, 'When the sons of God saw the daughters of man,' they could not restrain their inclination. Then Šemḥazai saw one young girl whose name was ʾEsṭêrah; fixing his eyes at her he said: 'Listen to my (request).' But she said to him: 'I will not listen to you until you teach me the Name by which you ascend to the firmament as soon as you mention it.' He taught her the Ineffable Name. What did she do? She mentioned It and thereby ascended to the firmament. The Holy One said: 'Since she has departed from sexual transgression [מן העבירה], go and set her among the stars.' It is she who shines so brightly in the midst of the seven stars of the Pleiades; so that she may always be remembered, the Holy One then fixed her among the Pleiades. . . ."[56]

As the story proceeds, Šemḥazai and ʿAzaʾel find other mortal women and beget children who are identified with the *Nephilim*. This story differs substantially from the traditions incorporated in the Ethiopic *Book of Enoch*: in

53. Davies, "Sons of Cain," 48.

54. Black, *Book of Enoch*, 134; cf. Morgenstern, "Mythological Background," 88 n. 103.

55. See *m. Yoma* 6:8, *b. Yoma* 68b.

56. For this text, see Milik, *Enoch*, 322–28; cf. *1 Enoch* 8:1–2 = 4QEnoch^{b} 1 ii 26–29.

the story there is no rebellion of angels. The list of angels is replaced by two already known from *Targum Pseudo-Jonathan*, who are bungling but seemingly well intentioned, and there is the catasterized Esṭêrah, whose name appears to be a Semiticized feminine of Greek *astêr* 'star' and whose fate seemingly derives from Greek mythology, where the Pleiades had been described as catasterized women pursued by the giant hunter Orion. In this late midrash, the Pleiades become a gendered celestial reminder of the corruption that preceded the Flood, parallel to the rainbow that memorializes its end. The midrash concludes with the fate of ʿAzaʾel, employing allusions to *Enoch* traditions to explain the scapegoat ritual:

> ʿAzaʾel did not repent. And he is appointed chief over all the dyes which entice men to commit sexual transgression (עבירה) and he still continues to corrupt them. Therefore, when the Israelites used to bring sacrifices on the Day of Atonement, they cast one lot for the Lord that it might atone for the iniquities of the Israelites, and one lot for ʿAzazʾel/ʿAzaʾzel that he might bear the burden of Israel's iniquity. This is the ʿAzaʾzel mentioned in the Torah.

Before concluding, I am tempted to comment on the substratum of mythic thought that underlay the biblical, Enochic, and rabbinic traditions on the breach between the divine and human realms. The rains that fall from above were thought to be male, like the divine beings who came to earth, while the waters below were female, like the humans with whom the divine beings mated. The mixing of the waters was viewed as a kind of cohabitation resulting in fecundity.[57] The copulation of celestial male water and terrestrial female water is homologous to the sexual union of the בני האלהים and mortal women, and represents a violation of the original separation of waters at the time of creation. After appropriate punishment is meted out, homeostasis is reestablished and marked by the rainbow that signals the end of a rainstorm (Gen 9:13–17); "the rainbow re-establishes the disjunction of heaven and earth previously united by the intermediation of rain."[58] By the time we meet an elaborated and peopled version of this myth, it had become the basis for the scapegoat ritual on the Day of Atonement. Its status as part of the Flood story, the sin-and-expiation tale par excellence, ensured the preservation of the myth, while the calendric association with winter rains gave it a place in the developing liturgy of seventh-month festivals.

57. Isa 55:10; references in Patai, "Control of Rain," 260–64.
58. C. Lévi-Strauss, *Le cru et le cuit* (Paris: Plon, 1964) 252.

Elisha at Dothan (2 Kings 6:8–23): Historico-literary Criticism Sustained by the Midrash

Alexander Rofé
The Hebrew University of Jerusalem

Taking my cue from the episode of Elisha at Dothan, I propose to reexamine the accepted method of historico-literary criticism, in particular its procedures for detecting interruptions in biblical texts and, consequently, for identifying distinct layers of composition.[1] Anticipating what will be claimed further on, let me state my opinion that, although this kind of criticism starts out on the right track, perceiving real difficulties in the composition of biblical literary units, its course is later vitiated by rather arbitrary reasoning, so that the conclusions are often questionable. To my mind, this is due to the lack of pointers that may lead criticism in the direction it should follow. This defect could be corrected, I believe, if we had at hand a criterion that would allow us to determine the motives and tendencies of the late biblical authors, those who by means of interpolations, commented on the ancient texts that had come into their possession. Assisted by such a tool, the critical argumentation would certainly be validated. Indeed, we do possess such a means: it lies in the postbiblical Jewish tradition, which, since it carries on the work of the last biblical scribes, may lead us to a better understanding of these authors.[2] The story of Elisha at Dothan offers a clear instance of the approach I have in mind.

1. An earlier effort in this direction was made in my *Book of Balaam: A Study in Methods of Criticism and the History of Biblical Literature and Religion* (Jerusalem: Simor, 1979) [Heb.].

2. I have recently tried to illustrate this kind of research in two articles: "Ruth 4:11 LXX: A Midrashic Dramatization," in *Texts, Temples, and Traditions: A Tribute to Menahem Haran* (ed. M. V. Fox et al.; Winona Lake, Ind.: Eisenbrauns, 1996) 119*–124* [Heb.]; "The Methods of Late Biblical Scribes as Evidenced by the Septuagint

* * *

While the prophet Elisha sojourned at Dothan, the king of Aram decided to capture him (2 Kgs 6:13). Thus the king sent a strong contingent strengthened by chariots and horses against the prophet; the force reached Dothan at night and surrounded the city (v. 14). Then we read (vv. 15–20):[3]

> (15) The next day,[4] the man of God rose early and went outside and lo, a force surrounded the town, with horses and chariots. Thus his servant asked him: "Alas master, what shall we do?" (16) "Have no fear," he replied. "There are more on our side than on theirs." (17) Then Elisha prayed, saying, "Lord please open his eyes and let him see!" And the Lord opened the servant's eyes and he saw, lo the hill was covered with horses and chariots of fire, all about Elisha. (18) And they came down to him.[5] Then Elisha prayed to the Lord saying, "Strike, please this people with a blinding light!"[6] And He struck them with a blinding light as by the word of Elisha. (19) Elisha said to them, "This is not the road and that is not the town, follow me and I will lead you to the man you want." And he led them to Samaria. (20) When they entered Samaria, Elisha said, "Oh Lord, open the eyes of these ones, so that they see." The Lord opened their eyes and they saw, lo they were inside Samaria.

Elisha had them freed, saving them from the vengeance of the Israelite king, so that the Arameans returned safely to their master. Thereafter, no more Aramean bands invaded the land of Israel (vv. 21–23).

The reader, coming to the end of v. 17, having learned that Elisha is defended by fiery horses and chariots that encircle him unseen, expects an inevitable clash between the two cavalries, the terrestrial Aramean force and the celestial one that has descended to succor the man of God. However, nothing of the kind happens. The heavenly expedition does not intervene; rather, Elisha applies directly to the Lord, asking him to hit the Arameans with a blinding light (v. 18a). The Lord complies (v. 18b), and thus Elisha misleads the Arameans, capturing them inside Samaria (v. 20). Naturally, the question arises: what was the purpose of the fiery cavalry around Elisha?

The question is not a new one; it was already posed by the medieval commentators. Commenting on v. 17, Rabbi Levi ben Gerson (Gersonides,

---

Compared with the Other Textual Witnesses," in *Tehillah le-Moshe: Biblical and Judaic Studies in Honor of Moshe Greenberg* (ed. M. Cogan, B. L. Eichler, and J. H. Tigay; Winona Lake, Ind.: Eisenbrauns, 1997) 259–70.

3. The English translation is adapted from the NJPSV.

4. Here I accept the conjectural emendation *mimmoḥŏrāt* instead of *mĕšārēt*; cf. the critical commentaries.

5. The subject is the "horses and chariots of fire" mentioned in the preceding verse; cf. below.

6. For this translation, see R. La Barbera, "The Man of War and the Man of God: Social Satire in 2 Kings 6:8–7:20," *CBQ* 46 (1984) 643, with reference to A. Jirku. For the etymology of *sanwērîm*, cf. M. Cogan and H. Tadmor, *II Kings* (AB 11; New York: Doubleday, 1988) ad loc.

1288–1344), to be followed by Abravanel (1437–1508) and Altschuler (Mĕṣudat David, 18th century),[7] solves the problem as follows:

> Even though Elisha was not assisted by them, he had to show them to his servant, to stem his fear, lest he cry out, which could cause the city dwellers to panic; that would have helped [the Arameans] to obtain their desire, because thus they would know that Elisha was in their midst.

The comment is ingenious indeed but rather forced. Did Elisha need heavenly intervention to calm down his servant? Too much for too little! The charismatic authority of the prophet alone could have mastered the crisis.

More sophisticated than Gersonides' solution is that of Radaq (Rabbi David Qimḥi), who preceded him (1160–1235).[8] Radaq addressed v. 17 as follows:

> But Elisha was inside the city while the fiery horses and chariots were outside the city, on the hill! However, the Lord showed them to the servant in this way, to lend him courage, that he should not be afraid.

Apparently Radaq introduces a distinction: the heavenly cavalry was on the hill outside the city, having descended there as the Lord's chariot. The servant, however, was shown the celestial force as surrounding his master, in order to reassure him. This solution does away with our query regarding the view of Gersonides; the problem is that it lacks all support in the text.

In my opinion, other harmonistic solutions, such as the one that takes the Arameans to be blinded by the blaze of the celestial cavalry, fare no better.[9] Suffice it to say that such a reconstruction of the miraculous events is certainly plausible, but it is not the one described by our author. The text does not say that the Arameans were blinded by the fiery chariots; nor does it say that anybody, besides Elisha and his servant, ever saw the heavenly vision. Rather, it asserts that the blinding of the enemies happened through the direct intervention of the Lord, following the second prayer of Elisha.

Another way out is to limit the scope of the servant's vision. According to this interpretation, the Lord showed the boy an illusive vision in order to reassure him, but actually there were no fiery horses and chariots, which, consequently, did not participate in any rescue of Elisha.[10] But even this rationalistic interpretation has no basis in the text: the prayer of Elisha in v. 17 presupposes the presence of a fiery cavalry; he sees it; his attendant,

7. For Gersonides and Altschuler, see the rabbinic Bibles; the commentary of Abravanel was reprinted in Jerusalem in 1955.

8. Radaq has also been included in the rabbinic Bibles.

9. R. R. Wilson, *Prophecy and Society in Ancient Israel* (Philadelphia: Fortress, 1980) 205: "When the Syrians attempt to surround the prophet and cut off the flow of information, he is protected by a heavenly army that blinds the would-be captors."

10. Cf. E. S. Artom, *The Book of Kings, Explained* (Tel Aviv: Yavneh, 1956; 4th ed., 1959) ad loc. [Heb.]; M. Rehm, *Das Zweite Buch der Könige: Ein Kommentar* (Würzburg: Echter, 1982) 70.

however, being a common mortal, does not; he needs special divine grace, impetrated by the prophet, to "open his eyes."

Finally, there is the commentator who makes an appeal to the artistic faculties of our author, attributing to him the gift of sarcasm: the Lord, opening the eyes of the servant, would have shown him that the Aramean chariots (*sic*!) were fiery ones. The divine intervention was thus counterproductive. In this way, the miracle defied its perpetrator—a token of the author's sarcasm.[11] Such unlimited fantasy puts us, the readers, at risk of being blinded, because, if the Aramean chariots are fiery ones, the scene is a different one altogether: either it belongs to a mythical theomachy or it is now taking place not at Dothan but in the underworld. Both cases are, to say the least, highly unlikely.

The fact remains that the appearance of the fiery cavalry around Elisha, no doubt in order to protect him, is an element that has no follow-up in the story; in the itinerary the plot makes us go through, this is a kind of dead end, which once entered can only be left by going all the way back. Therefore, according to the method of historico-literary criticism, we may suspect the presence of an interpolation, a secondary augmentation of the text introduced by a later hand. The introduction of an extraneous element disturbed the coherence of the original story.[12]

In addition, there is an external sign that reveals an interpolation: It is the resumptive repetition of v. 17 by v. 18:

> v. 17: Then Elisha prayed, saying: "Lord . . ."
> v. 18: Then Elisha prayed to the Lord, saying, ". . ."

This phenomenon, well known by its German name *Wiederaufnahme*, occurs rather often in the Hebrew Bible. Various scholars have noted that it frequently indicates the intervention of a second hand in the text. Scribes, when interpolating texts, sought to integrate their contributions by making them begin or end with the same words as the existing text. Thus, they believed, they would lead the reader back to the point from which they had taken him.[13]

If we rely on the indicator of *resumptive repetition*, we can more exactly delimit the interpolated passage: it comprises the first two words of v. 18: *wayyērĕdû ʾēlāyw* 'they came down toward him'. Therefore, the subject of this phrase is not the Arameans mentioned in the original story in v. 15, but the celestial protectors of Elisha, introduced by the interpolation in v. 17. The second author apparently asserted that whenever Elisha faced danger, he was encircled by fiery horses and chariots which, at the right moment, came to his rescue.

11. Cf. T. R. Hobbs, *2 Kings* (WBC; Waco, Tex.: Word, 1985) 78.

12. I took this position in my volume *The Prophetical Stories* (Jerusalem: Magnes, 1988) 62–63 [trans. from Heb.].

13. Cf. M. Anbar, "La 'réprise,'" *VT* 38 (1988) 385–98.

In order to be plausible, the detection of an interpolation should rely not only on the analysis of the coherence of a literary work and on formal signs of sequence interruption; it should offer a satisfactory explanation of the motives of the interpolator, distinguishing his message from that of the first author. This argument will be developed below, after comparing the present analysis with the results obtained by other critics, specifically by some of the German scholars who excel, as is well known, in the art of biblical stratigraphy.

* * *

Contemporary criticism also sets out by noting that v. 17 diverts the advance of the plot rather than carrying it forward, which would indicate that this verse is secondary. The analysis, however, does not stop there: there is wide agreement that the entire episode mentioning the prophet's attendant, vv. 15b–17, should be deleted as secondary.[14] Some critics go even further and excise vv. 18 and 20 as well, on the basis of their affinity with v. 17, since vv. 18 and 20 also deal with the Lord's giving or denying the gift of vision.[15]

Let us first examine the latter hypothesis, which has been embraced by some outstanding critics. The argument developed is that of analogy. In v. 17 Elisha prays, and the Lord "opens" the eyes of the servant. In v. 20 the same happens to the Arameans (disparate kinds of vision are dealt with here, but let us not be pedantic); in v. 18 again, Elisha prays in order to obtain the opposite effect: striking the Arameans with a blinding light. Do these affinities prove that all three verses derive from the same hand? Not at all, in my opinion. The interpolators, since they are epigones, imitate or reproduce elements of the source on which they are working. Well known is the instance of the oracle to Judah in Amos 2:4–5, secondary within the frame of Amos's oracles to the nations (1:3–2:16): it makes use of expressions contained in Amos's *ipsissima verba* in that collection. Therefore, questioning the originality of vv. 18 and 20 because of their affinity to v. 17 is a sheer nonsequitur. On the contrary, guided by the instance of Amos, one should infer that v. 17, secondary in this composition, has probably been modeled on the original expressions found in vv. 18 and 20.

14. This is the position of K. Galling, "Der Ehrenname Elisas und die Entrückung Elias," *ZTK* 53 (1956) 129–48; H. Schweizer, *Elischa in den Kriegen* (Studien zum Alten und Neuen Testament 37; Munich: Kösel, 1974) 211–66. In addition, see the critics mentioned in n. 15.

15. H. C. Schmitt, *Elisa: Traditionsgeschichtliche Untersuchungen zur vorklassischen nordisraelitischen Prophetie* (Gütersloh: Gütersloher Verlag, 1972) 91–93; E. Würthwein, *Die Bücher der Könige: 1 Kön 17–2 Kön 25, übersetzt und erklärt* (ATD 11/2; Göttingen: Vandenhoeck & Ruprecht, 1984) 304–7; G. Hentschell, *2 Könige* (EB; Würzburg: Echter, 1985) ad loc.

Indeed, the arguments for excising vv. 18 and 20 from this story are rather tenuous. One cannot understand the logic of this operation if one does not pay careful attention to its results: in the remainder (vv. 19, 21–23), Elisha no longer asks for the Lord's intervention, and the Lord plays no role in the story. It is Elisha who by means of his own faculties (rhetoric?) misleads the Arameans, making them prisoners. This is what criticism has been after: a hypothetical original tale without divine participation. I beg to differ concerning the correctness of this approach. Certainly there are legends in the Elisha cycle in which everything depends on the prophet's action: such are the tales about the miracles of the oil (2 Kgs 4:1–7), the stew (4:38–41), and the axe that floated (6:1–7). In other cases, it seems plausible that prayer to the Lord or His word has been secondarily introduced into the plot (2 Kgs 2:21, 4:33b, 4:43–44). But the existence of these cases does not allow us to trim all of the Elisha legends according to one model. On the contrary, we should expect to find a certain variety. Some legends no doubt originated in a plebeian milieu, but others were composed by more sophisticated authors. The former expressed vulgar amazement vis-à-vis acts of magic; the latter insisted on the divine presence escorting the prophet. Thus, the attempt at reducing all of the Elisha narratives to an alleged primordial shape is nothing but a futile illusion.

Let us now consider the other direction of the critical "surgery," that is, the excision of vv. 15b–16 along with v. 17. In this way, the presence of Elisha's servant is eliminated, and the plot runs smoothly from the moment the prophet sees the Arameans (v. 15a as corrected) up to their being blinded by the Lord (v. 18) or to their being misled by Elisha (v. 19). Is this analytical procedure more justified?

We note, in the first place, that this course lacks any stylistic support. In attributing v. 17 to a second hand, we relied on the resumptive repetition, "Then Elisha prayed . . . ," at the beginning of v. 18; such an indicator is absent for vv. 15b–16. Besides, the bold excision of vv. 15b–16 eliminates an important element in the development of the plot: it is the desperate cry of the dismayed servant and, against it, the serene reassurance uttered by the man of God. Both elements, the expression of doubt and of confidence are most characteristic of the Elisha *legenda*, because they repeatedly occur therein: 2 Kgs 4:2a, 15b, 31b, 43a; 5:7, etc., for the former, 5:8, 6:32, etc., for the latter. They belong, indeed, to this literary genre;[16] as such they can hardly be attributed to a second hand!

The crucial point in the critical analysis of v. 16 lies in Elisha's declaration: ". . . there are more on our side than on theirs." If the prophet hinted thereby at a confrontation between heavenly and human cavalries, v. 16 (along with v. 15b) goes with v. 17 and is likewise interpolated. But if Elisha

16. Concerning the character and history of the *legenda* about Elisha, I refer the reader to my book *The Prophetical Stories*.

merely expressed his confidence that the Lord's strength is greater than the strength of the Arameans, vv. 15b–16 are original, and only v. 17 should be circumscribed as secondary. For the reasons already stated, I prefer the latter alternative. One should explain, however, the nexus that obtains between the bold affirmation, "there are more . . ." and the appearance of the celestial army. It is here that we turn for assistance to Jewish midrash.

* * *

A salient characteristic of Jewish midrash, which started to develop in Second Temple times, is the literal and concrete interpretation of expressions that originally were figurative or abstract.[17] In this way midrash often furnishes scripture with dramatic and hyperbolic episodes that gratify listeners and readers. Some instances are adduced here to illustrate this point.

"Do I lack madmen?" asks Achish, disgusted at the sight of David's exhibitions (1 Sam 21:16). The midrash however, takes the "madmen" literally and supplies the information that Achish already had two madwomen at home, his wife and daughter.[18]

"The God of my father . . . delivered me from the sword of Pharaoh," says Moses (Exod 18:4). "When was this?" inquires the midrash and relates that before his flight to Midian, Moses had been arrested and condemned to death; a sword was already at his throat, an actual sword, when an angel coming down from heaven confused the executioner; thus the Egyptians "seized the angel and let Moses go."[19]

The most famous literal interpretation is the one we Jews recite every year in reading the Passover *Haggadah*: "It is the finger of God," remarked the Egyptian magicians concerning (one of) the ten plagues (Exod 8:15), while after the Egyptian army had been drowned in the Red Sea the author commented: "And Israel saw the great feat (lit., the great hand) the Lord had performed against the Egyptians . . ." (Exod 14:31). Thus, comments the midrash, if with one finger the Lord had inflicted on his enemies in Egypt ten plagues, when he hit with His hand, on the sea, He smote them with fifty plagues.[20]

This midrashic quality is not a late Jewish creation: it already obtains in the biblical book of Chronicles, originating in the mid–4th century B.C.E. Concerning Oved Edom it had been said in the book of Samuel that "the

17. Cf. I. Heinemann, *The Methods of the Aggadah* (Jerusalem: Magnes / Tel-Aviv: Massada, 1954) 118–19 [Heb.]; J. Fraenkel, *The Methods of the Aggadah and Midrash* (Givataim: Massada, 1991) 1.96–97 [Heb.].

18. *Midrash Tĕhillim* (*Shoḥer Ṭov*) (ed. S. Buber; Vilna, 1891; repr. Jerusalem: Wagschall, 1976–77) 246.

19. *Mĕkhiltah dĕRabbi Ishmael* (ed. H. S. Horovitz and I. A. Rabin; repr. Jerusalem: Wahrmann, 1959–60) 192.

20. The Haggadah borrowed this homily from the Mekhilta᾿ot; cf. E. D. Goldschmidt, *The Passover Haggadah* (Jerusalem: Bialik, 1960) 47–48 [Heb.].

Lord blessed him and his house" (2 Sam 6:11). Chronicles repeats this (1 Chr 13:14) but then comments on it with a midrashic concretization, asserting that Oved Edom had 8 sons and 62 descendants (70 in all?), because the Lord had "blessed him" (1 Chr 26:4–8, esp. v. 5b).[21]

Coming back now to the episode of Elisha at Dothan, we find this midrashic quality in the relation of v. 17 vis-à-vis 16. Elisha had said: "There are more on our side than on theirs," vaguely meaning that divine assistance was stronger than the Aramean force. The midrashic exposition, however, takes him literally: who are these "more," these *rabbîm*? They are the divine cavalry that came down to rescue the prophet (v. 17). Consequently, the interpolation should be circumscribed to v. 17, and the first two words of v. 18, which attribute a literal, concrete sense to the preceding verse. Verse 16 is scripture, while v. 17 and the beginning of v. 18 are its midrash!

This does not exhaust the midrashic function of the apparition of the fiery cavalry around Elisha. One should ask what relation exists between this vision and 2 Kgs 13:14, where Joash, King of Israel, addresses the dying Elisha with the epithet, "Father, father, Israel's chariots and horses!" To my mind, in this passage the appellation reflects the original meaning, that is, Elisha as deliverer of his people in war.[22] In the course of the Aramean crisis (839–802 B.C.E.), Elisha had been left as Israel's sole defense; he replaced the whole corps of cavalry now extinct. As against this, in 2 Kgs 6:17 the display of heavenly chariotry around Elisha is only a literal interpretation of the original metaphorical epithet. According to this method of exposition, why was Elisha called "the chariots and horses of Israel"? Because he was surrounded, especially when menaced, by an invisible celestial cavalry, which protected him. This is also consistent with the literal interpretation typical of the midrash.

Finally, let us try to elucidate the nature of the relationship that exists between the vision of 2 Kgs 6:17 and the story of Elijah's ascension to heaven, when fiery chariots and horses separated Elijah from his disciple Elisha (2 Kgs 2:11). The ascension narrative assumes that only once, when he was taken to heaven, was Elijah encircled by a fiery cavalry—an exceptional event indeed, which stands out even among the many portents of the Elisha cycle.[23] On the other hand, here in v. 17 it is presumed that the fiery chariotry was always at the disposal of the prophet: always present, invisible, but ready to intervene. What had been a singular event has become routine; it

21. Cf. I. L. Seeligmann, "The Beginnings of *Midrash* in the Books of Chronicles," *Tarbiz* 49 (1979–80) 15 [Heb.] = *Studies in Biblical Literature* (Jerusalem: Magnes, 1992) 455 [Heb.].

22. Galling's hypothesis ("Ehrenname Elisas," 129–48), suggesting a mythical origin of the title of Elisha in 2 Kgs 13:14 (later transferred to Elijah), is implausible. Galling himself was one of the first to consider 2 Kgs 6:17 to be interpolated.

23. That 2 Kgs 2:1–18 originates from within the Elisha cycle has been repeatedly demonstrated; cf., e.g., my *Prophetical Stories*, 44–45.

has become a constant trait of the man of God. This too is a process typical of epigonic writers, one we encounter in the midrash. I have had the opportunity of illustrating it in dealing with the passage in 4QSam[a] that describes Nahash, the Ammonite king, as the cruel conqueror who customarily gouged out the right eye of the people he subjugated.[24] In the case of Nahash as well, the midrash penetrated a biblical manuscript, exactly as I propose to be the case in 2 Kgs 6:17.

The conclusion, which, I submit, is unequivocal: in the story of Elisha at Dothan, the addition by a second hand should be circumscribed to v. 17 and the first two words of v. 18 only.[25] In more comprehensive terms, I would like to invite the community of scholars to use criticism with more circumspection. In order to declare a passage interpolated, one needs a number of indicators: interruption of contents, external signs of secondary intervention, and last but not least, affinity with conceptions and qualities of late biblical literature and of the Jewish creativity that carried on in its wake.[26]

24. Cf. A. Rofé, "The Acts of Nahash according to 4QSam[a]," *IEJ* 32 (1982) 129–33.

25. Therefore, I do not subscribe to the scepticism of Long, who renounces critical analysis, in face of the divergences between critics; cf. B. O. Long, *2 Kings* (FOTL; Grand Rapids, Mich.: Eerdmans, 1991) 83. I believe we do possess criteria to distinguish between founded and unfounded hypotheses.

26. Zakovitch maintains "that there is a clear continuation in the process of interpretation . . . which started in the Bible itself and was carried on into post-biblical literature" (Y. Zakovitch, *An Introduction to Inner-Biblical Interpretation* [Even-Yehuda: Reches, 1992] 134 [Heb.]). By my method, one should emphasize that comments made by the midrash enable us to identify younger elements within biblical literature.

"I Will Be Your God and You Will Be My People": The Origin and Background of the Covenant Formula

SEOCK-TAE SOHN
Reformed Theological Seminary, Seoul

The phrase 'I will be your God and you will be my people' והייתי לכם לאלהים ואתם תהיו־לי לעם (Gen 17:7; Exod 6:7; Lev 26:12; Deut 29:13; Jer

Author's note: Abbreviations used in this article, in addition to those in the volume's abbreviation list, are as follows:

ARN	M. Çiğ, H. Kizilyay, and F. R. Kraus. *Altbabylonische Rechtsurkunden aus Nippur*. Istanbul: Turk Tarih Kurumu Basimevi, 1952.
BAP	B. Maiguer. *Beiträge zum altbabylonischen Privatrecht*. Leipzig: Hinrichs, 1893.
BE	The Babylonian Expedition of the University Pennsylvania, Series A: Cuneiform Texts. Philadelphia, 1893–1911; Munich, 1913–14.
BIN	*Babylonian Inscriptions in the Collection of J. B. Nies* (8 volumes). Volume 2 = J. B. Nies and C. E. Keiser. *Historical, Religious and Economic Texts and Antiquities*. New Haven: Yale University Press, 1920. Volume 7 = J. B. Alexander. *Early Babylonian Letters and Economic Texts*. New Haven: Yale University Press, 1943.
BMAP	E. G. Kraeling. *Brooklyn Museum Aramaic Papyri*. New Haven: Yale University Press, 1953.
KAV	Keilschrifttexte aus Assur verschiedenen Inhalts. Leipzig: Hinrichs, 1920.
Nbk	J. N. Strassmaier. *Inschriften von Nabuchodnosor*. Leipzig: E. Pfeiffer, 1889.
Nrg	*Inscriptions of the Reign of Neriglissar*. Leipzig: E. Pfeiffer, 1892.
PBS	Publications of the Babylonian Section. Volume 8/2 = Edward Chiera. *Old Babylonian Contracts*. Philadelphia: University Museum, University of Pennsylvania, 1922.
TIM	*Texts in the Iraq Museum*. Baghdad: Directorate General of Antiquities, 1964–.
VS	*Vorderasiatische Schriftdenkmäler* (7 volumes). Leipzig: Hinrichs, 1907–16.
YOS	Yale Oriental Series (12 volumes). Volume 2 = H. F. Lutz. *Early Babylonian Letters from Larsa*. New Haven: Yale University Press, 1917. Volume 8 = D. E. Faust. *Contracts from Larsa Dated in the Reign of Rim-Sin*. New Haven: Yale University Press, 1941.

7:23; 11:4; 30:22; 31:1, 33; 32:38; Ezek 11:20; 14:11; 36:28; 37:23) is widely recognized as a covenant formula.[1] Along with this the formula, 'I will take you as my own people and I will be your God' ולקחתי אתכם לי לעם והייתי לכם לאלהים (Exod 6:7) can also be regarded as a covenant formula. What is the setting in life from which this formula originated? What is its background as the Israelites used it? The answer to these questions will be a considerable help in understanding the concept of the biblical covenant.

Good proposed that this formula originated from the client formula used in Arabic culture to adopt a client into a tribe.[2] In his view, the phrase 'tent rope touching tent rope' (*aṭ-ṭunub biṭ-ṭunub*) was used among ancient nomadic peoples to establish the client relationship. One poet named Al-muthallam proclaimed concerning *ʾAshjaʿ* as follows:

> *lafafnā lbuyūta bilbuyūti faʾ aṣbaḥū*
> *banī ʿamminā man yarmihim yarminā maʿā*[3]

> We enclose their tents with ours so that they became our cousins,
> whoever shoots at them shoots at us as well.

According to Good, the concept of establishing a client relationship by touching the ropes of tents is found in the proposal Jacob's sons made in response to Shechem, who had asked for Dinah as his wife after his sexual violation of her. The sons of Jacob then agreed to give their sister on the condition of circumcision:

> We will give our consent to you on one condition only: that you become like us by circumcising your males. Then we will give you our daughters and take your daughters for ourselves. We will settle among you and become one people with you. (Gen 34:15–16)

Good also notes that the covenant formula is well preserved in biblical literature, particularly in the book of Ruth. When Ruth was asked by Naomi, her mother-in-law, to go back to her mother's house, she replied:

> Do not urge me to leave you or to turn back from you. Where you go I will go, and where you stay I will stay. Your people will be my people and your God my God. Where you die I will die, and there I will be buried. May the Lord deal with me, be it ever so severely, if anything but death separates you and me. (Ruth 1:16–17)

1. R. Smend identifies it as 'Bundesformel', E. Kutsch as 'Zugehörigkeitsformel', G. Fohrer as 'Zusammengehörigkeitsformel', and P. Kalluveettil as 'Declaration Formula' (P. Kalluveettil, *Declaration and Covenant: A Comprehensive Review of Covenant Formula from the Old Testament and Ancient Near East* [Rome: Pontifical Biblical Institute, 1982] 1).

2. R. M. Good, *The Sheep of His Pasture: A Study of the Hebrew Noun ʿAm(m) and Its Semitic Cognates* (HSM 29; Chico, Calif.: Scholars Press, 1983) 83.

3. *Ḥamāsa* (Freytag) 187; quoted by Good, *Sheep of His Pasture*, 83.

Here the phrase "Your people will be my people and your God my God" is a kind of client formula, and the situation of traveling and spending the night together fits well with the formula.

Good goes further and relates the movement of nomadic peoples to Israel's journey through the wilderness. Just as a nomadic people establishes a client relationship by touching the tent ropes and moves as a group, so the Israelites pitched their tents around the tabernacle and followed it in their covenant relationship with Yahweh. He regards Exod 29:45, "I will dwell among the Israelites and be their God," as having originated in the client formula. Thus he asserts that the covenant formula developed from the custom of establishing client relationships in the ancient nomadic world.

However, it must be said that both Jacob's proposal and Ruth's plea were spoken in the context of marriage. In view of this, I propose that the formula of marriage and adoption used both in ancient Israel and in Mesopotamia provides the origin and background of covenant formulas, rather than the client formula itself. Of course, Good knows that the covenant formula has the formal character of an adoption. However, he points out that "this formal insight has not been successfully exploited in seeking the formula's life setting."[4] And he argues that the limitations imposed by the analogy of marriage and father-son adoption brought about this failure. After all, the covenant formula records neither the taking of a bride nor the adoption of a son. It also lacks the terms of reference *husband* and *wife*, *father* and *son*.[5]

Therefore, we are required to investigate the soundness of Good's proposal and to identify the real background and origin of the covenant formula. In order to do so, we will analyze the structure and meaning of the marriage covenant as well as the adoption covenant, comparing them with the covenant between YHWH and Israel.

The Marriage Formula and the Covenant Formula

In Jer 31:31–33, the prophet proclaims the new covenant as follows:

4. Good, *Sheep of His Pasture*, 81.

5. "The structure of the covenant formula seems nevertheless to be that of an adoption. The failure of researchers to account adequately for this stems from the limitations imposed by the analogy of marriage and father-son adoption. It should be immediately evident that the covenant formula records neither the taking of a bride nor the adoption of a son. It lacks the words 'husband' and 'wife,' 'father' and 'son.' The terms it offers are *ʿam*(*m*) and 'god,' as though to portray the adoption of a tribe by a deity. But the formula for such an occasion hardly existed for routine use in the ancient Near East. At least it is fair to say that such a formula must be patterned after a more useful formula, the adoption of a tribe by an individual, a 'client' formula" (ibid., 82).

"The time is coming," declares YHWH,
  "when I will make a new covenant
with the house of Israel
  and with the house of Judah.
It will not be like the covenant
  I made with their forefathers
when I took them by the hand
  to lead them out of Egypt,
my covenant which they broke,
  then I was a husband to them" (ואנכי בעלתי בם), declares YHWH.
"This is the covenant I will make with the house of Israel
  after that time," declares YHWH.
"I will put my law in their minds
  and write it on their hearts.
I will be their God
  and they will be my people." (Jer 31:31–33)

It is noticeable that the formula "I will be their God and they will be my people" is used in the covenant context. The covenant that YHWH made with Israel on the day of leading them out of Egypt is an obvious reference to the covenant of Sinai. On the day he made this covenant with Israel,[6] YHWH declares that he was the husband of Israel (בעלתי בם).[7] Then Israel, his covenant partner, is assumed to be his bride. Jeremiah understands the Sinaitic covenant as a marriage between YHWH and Israel.[8] In human society a wedding is the ceremony that proclaims the legality of marriage and through this ceremony a couple enters into the legal relationship of marriage, which involves responsibilities and obligations. Furthermore, only a legal marriage is protected by law. In the ancient Near East a marriage was also a type of contract that carried legal force, and a marriage document was

6. Most translators and commentators render the conjunction *waw* (ו) in ואנכי as 'although' (E. W. Nicholson), 'though' (J. Bright, D. R. Jones), or 'while' (W. Holladay). However, syntactically as well as contextually these translations are not proper. The conjunction *waw* (ו) should be translated simply as 'and' or 'at that time', since there is the time indicator 'when I took them by the hand' (ביום).

7. Here we have textual variants in the reading of בעלתי. The LXX reads it as ἠμέλησα ('I disregard'), Syriac reads *bsjt* = געלתי ('I abhorred'), and the NJPSV takes בעלתי as equivalent to בחלתי ('I rejected'). However, most versions follow the MT and read בעלתי. Translators fall into two groups in rendering בעלתי. One group is modern Bible translators who translate it 'husband', and the other group is commentators, such as W. L. Holladay, S. B. Freehof, and J. Bright, who gloss it as 'lord' or 'master'. Since a husband was a master of his wife in the ancient Near East, superficially there seems to be no difference. However, if we take into account that Jeremiah viewed the relationship between YHWH and Israel as husband and wife (3:1–10), 'husband' is more convincing.

8. S.-T. Sohn, *The Divine Election of Israel* (Grand Rapids, Mich.: Eerdmans, 1991) 184–89.

to be drawn up by both partners. The Code of Eshnunna required a formal marriage contract if a man and woman were to obtain full social and legal recognition for their marriage.[9] The Code of Hammurabi acknowledged only those marriages for which contracts had been drawn up.[10] In Egypt it was common practice to write a marriage contract.[11] This concept of marriage as covenant is also found among the Israelites in Gen 31:50 and Mal 2:14.[12] Tobit 7:12 shows that the covenant documents in marriage were drawn up even after the biblical period.[13] In the Mishnah the marriage document was known as Ketubbah.

Just as the ancient Near Eastern peoples, including the Hebrews, regarded the husband-wife relationship, one of the most intimate of human relationships, as a covenant, the people of Israel viewed their relationship with YHWH in terms of a covenant. In particular, Jeremiah sees the covenantal relationship between YHWH and his people from the perspective of marriage. In Jer 3:8, YHWH says that he sent Israel away and gave her 'a writ of divorce' (ספר כריתתיה) because of her adulteries (נאפה). This obviously refers to Israel's apostasy and deportation to Assyria. For Jeremiah, the marriage relationship between YHWH and Israel was legally initiated in the covenant at Mount Sinai and dissolved at the fall of Samaria.

Based on the above observation, we are warranted in locating the basic setting of covenant in the context of marriage. We can now proceed to examine the marriage formula in order to trace the origin of the covenant formula.

In the ancient Near East, symbolic rites and proclamation formulas were used in various legal transactions. According to Greengus, symbolic rites were used in divorce, manumission, sale, service contracts, surety, and treaty

9. Code of Eshnunna, §27: "If a man took another man's daughter without asking her father and mother and did not arrange for a libation and marriage contract with her father and mother and though she live in his house for a year, she is not a wife." §28: "If ... he arranged for a marriage contract and libation with her father and mother and took her, she is wife; the day she is caught with (another) man she shall die; she shall not live" (quoted from S. Greengus, "The Old Babylonian Marriage Contract," *JAOS* 89 [1969] 505).

10. "If a seignor acquired a wife, but did not draw up the contract for her, that woman is no wife" (CH §128; *ANET*, 171).

11. N. Reich, "Marriage and Divorce in Ancient Egypt: Papyrus Documents Discovered at Thebes by the Eckly B. Coxe Jr. Expedition to Egypt," *The Museum Journal* (Philadelphia: University of Pennsylvania Press, 1924) 50–57.

12. The thorough research of G. P. Hugenberger on Mal 2:14 shows that in the Bible marriage was regarded as covenant (*Marriage as Covenant: A Study of Biblical Law and Ethic Covering Marriage, Developed from the Perspective of Malachi* [Leiden: Brill, 1994]).

13. On marriage in Tobit, see P. Grelot, "The Institution of Marriage: Its Evolution in the Old Testament," *Concilium* 55 (1970) 39–50.

formation, while proclamation formulas are found in connection with adoption, divorce, and service contracts.[14] The proclamation of marriage was an important element in the covenant-ratifying oath for marriage. It was proclaimed or recited in the solemnization of marriage by either one of the partners or someone else such as the father of the bride.[15] Two kinds of formula in the marriage proclamation seem to have existed from the Old Babylonian period. One is a proclamation formula, which is generally known as a *verba solemnia* or a verbal oath,[16] and the other is a descriptive formula.

The Proclamation Formula

Three types of proclamation formula in marriage are observed in the ancient Near Eastern texts. First of all, it may be reciprocal or mutual. The groom and bride declare to each other their relationship established through the marriage. The phrase 'you are my wife' or 'you are my husband' belongs to this category. According to Greengus, 'You are my husband' *mutī atta* from one of the OB legal documents found in Ishchali is not strictly a marriage formula, but her words could be patterned after the marriage formulas: *lū mutī atta* or *attā lū mutīma*.[17] However, the text from MAL §41(KAV 1 vi 1–5) clearly shows this category of marriage formula. In the text a man who desires to make his concubine (*esirtu*) his wife convenes six or seven of his peers and, after covering her head, declares *aššīt šit* ('she is my wife').[18] The more convincing evidence for this formula can be traced in the divorce formulas, such as 'you are not my wife' (*ul aššati atta*), 'you are not my husband' (*ul muti atta*), 'she (^{f}PN) is not my wife', 'he is not my husband', 'I will not be your wife',[19] and 'you are not my wife, you are not my husband' (*ul aššatī attī, ul mutī attā*).[20] A cuneiform text from Nippur of ancient Babylonia records the marriage contract as follows:

ukun-bi ^{l}a-wi-li-ya na-ra-am-tum dam-a-ni-ra
dam-mu nu-me-en ba-na-an-du$_{11}$ 1/2 ma-na kù-babbar ì-lá-e
tukun-bi ^{l}na-am-tum a-wi-li-ya dam-a-ni-ra
dam-mu nu-me-en ba-na-an-du$_{11}$ umbin al-ku$_{5}$ ru-dè kù-šè-bí-ib-sum-mu-uš

14. Greengus, "The Old Babylonian Marriage Contract," 515.
15. Ibid., 522.
16. Kalluveettil, *Declaration and Covenant*, 1.
17. Greengus, "Old Babylonian Marriage Contract," 517 n. 57.
18. Ibid., 515–16 n. 48. Greengus introduces the similar formulas recorded in the Neo-Babylonian sources as well. Cf. *VS* 6 95:6; Strassmaier VI Congrès 1883 no. 8:6, 'may she be my wife' (*lu-ú áš-šá-ti ši-i*); Nbk 101:4; Nrg 13:5 (*lu-ú* dam *ši-i*); *VS* 6 6:3f., 'may she be my wife' (*lu-ú* dam-a *ši-i*), etc.
19. Hugenberger, *Marriage*, 219 nn. 13–17.
20. BAP 89:20–23, 36–38; 90:11–12; BIN 7 173:16–29; Böhl Leiden Collection 772:6–10; CT 2 44:6–16; 8 7b:13–16; Kich 1 B17:10′–17′ ; PBS 8/2 252:18–26; *TIM* 4 46:5′–17′, 47:16–25, 48:8ff., 49: rev 1′–4′ (beginning broken); YOS 12 371:6–15. Cf. Greengus, "Old Babylonian Marriage Contract," 517 n. 58.

> If Awiliya says to Naramtum his wife, "You are not my wife," he will pay 1/2 mina of silver. If Naramtum says to Awiliya her husband, "You are not my husband," he will shave her and place a slave mark on her and give her for silver.[21]

It is obvious that the negative statement of divorce presupposes the positive proclamation formula in marriage. Since marriage carried legal force, divorce was also regulated by the law. A similar type of formula is also found in the Egyptian marriage contracts.[22]

The second type is unilateral. In this case only the groom or bride declares the formula toward his or her counterpart. One of the well-known proclamation formulas of this type in the Old Babylonian period is from the Gilgamesh Epic, where Ištar proposes to Gilgamesh,

> Come Gilgamesh, be thou my (var. an) espouser (var. groom);
> give me thy charms for a gift;
> be thou my husband, I will be thy wife
>
> *alkamma Gilgameš lū ḫāʾir* (var. *ḫāmir, ḫutanī*) *attā;*
> *inbīka iâši qâšu qîšamma;*
> *attā lū mutīma anāku lū aššatka.* (vi 7–9)

A similar passage appears in the myth of Nergal and Ereshkigal; the queen of the netherworld, threatened by Nergal, pleads for her and says:

> You be my husband, I will be thy wife . . .
> Be thou master, I will be mistress

21. BE 6/2 = A. Poebel, *Babylonian Legal and Business Documents from the Time of the First Dynasty of Babylon, Chiefly from Nippur* (1902) 6/2.48, cited in E. C. Stone and D. I. Owen, *Adoption in Old Babylon Nippur and the Archive of Mannum-mešu-liṣṣur* (Mesopotamian Civilizations 3; Winona Lake, Ind.: Eisenbrauns, 1991) 51–52. The following is found among the Late Sumerian Marriage Contracts:

> If Enlil-izzu ever says to Ama-sukkal, his wife, "You are no longer my wife," he shall return the 19 shekels of silver and he shall also weigh out 1/2 mina as her divorce settlement. On the other hand, if Ama-sukkal ever says to Enil-izzu, her husband, "You are no longer my husband," she shall forfeit the 19 shekels of silver and she shall also weigh out 1/2 mina of silver. In mutual agreement they have sworn together by king. (The names of eight men, two women, the scribe, and the notary as witness, each preceded by the witness sign.) (Sealed with two seals, twice each.)

Published and translated in A. Poebel, *Babylonian Business and Legal Documents*, no. 40; cited in *ANET*, 219.

22. "The woman has said to the man: 'You have made me your wife.' The man has said to the woman, 'I have made you my wife.' " Cf. P. W. Pestman, *Marriage and Matrimonial Property in Ancient Egypt* (Leiden: Brill, 1961) diagram A, §12–5; diagram B, §§11–12, quoted in Hugenberger, *Marriage*, 217 n. 2. According to E. M. Yamauchi's observation, the Egyptian marriage contract typically began with the phrase, "I have made you my wife"; see "Cultural Aspects of Marriage in the Ancient World," *Bibliotheca Sacra* 135 (1978) 245; quoted by Hugenberger, *Marriage*, 226.

attā lū mutīma anāku lū aššatka . . .
attā lū bēlu anāku lū bēltu. (EA 375:82–85)

As some scholars have suggested, these texts record a proposal for mythological marriage rather than an actual marriage event. However, if we remember that ancient mythology is a reflection of human life,[23] the proposals for marriage can be regarded as an actual practice in ancient Near Eastern society. The clearest example of this formula is from the "*eṭlu* tablet," a bilingual magical text from the Old Babylobian period.

6. *māri rubí anāku iqbiš*
7. *kaspa ḫurāṣa sūnka umallu*
8. *attā lū aššatu anāku lū mutka iqbiši*
6. '"I am of princely descent," he said to her;
7. "thy lap I will fill with silver and gold;
8. you be my(!) wife, I will be thy husband," he said to her'.[24]

According to Hugenberger, this text describes an exorcism rite, through a symbolic "marriage" between a piglet and a sickness-figurine, in which the god Šamaš acts as witness. Deliverance from the demon is accomplished by tricking the demon to leave its victim in order to marry the figurine instead.[25] The parallel text is found in the *ardat lili* tablet reconstructed by Lackenbacher (rev. col. II, lines 1–6).[26] This one-sided proclamation formula in marriage is also found in the well-known Elephantine papyrus. In the papyrus, the groom usually proclaims: 'She is my wife and I am her husband from this day and forever' (הי אנתתי ואנה בעלה מן יומא זנה עד עלם).[27] Similarly, in a contract of the second century C.E. found in the Judean Desert, the formula is 'Thou shall be my wife'.[28]

The third type of formula is an indirect one. A third person pronounces the proclamation formula. *TIM* 4 45:1–9, a Middle Assyrian document, is a good example.

ū ^{f}PN *ina migratīšunu mutūtu ū aššutūta idbubū* PN *mussa*
ū ^{f}PN *aššassu ina eqli ū libbi ā[lim] palāḫa aḫu a[ḫa] ippušū*

23. Greengus, "Old Babylonian Marriage Contract," 517; Hugenberger, *Marriage*, 218–19.

24. Greengus, "Old Babylonian Marriage Contract," 516.

25. Hugenberger, *Marriage*, 224.

26. 'I [be your husband, be y]ou [(my) wife, these are] his [wor]ds(?), . . . [si]lver and gold [he t]ied [in] her [h]em' (ibid., 225).

27. B. Porten and A. Yardeni, *Textbook of Aramaic Documents from Ancient Egypt, Volume 2: Contracts* (The Hebrew University Department of the History of the Jewish People: Texts and Studies for Students; Jerusalem: Hebrew University, 1989) B2.6, 4. Cf. B3.3, 3f.; B3.8, 4; B6.1, 3f. Cf. A. E. Cowley, *Aramaic Papyri of the Fifth Century* B.C. (Oxford: Clarendon, 1923) 15:3f.; *BMAP* 2:3f., 7:4, 14:4f.

28. R. de Vaux, *Ancient Israel* (New York: McGraw-Hill, 1961) 1.33.

> PN and ᶠPN of their own accord agreed to marriage; PN is her husband; ᶠPN is his wife. They shall show respect to one another at home and abroad.[29]

This text shows that a third person other than the couple pronounces the marriage proclamation formula. We are not sure who proclaimed the formula in this case, but either the father of the bride or the head of the tribe may have done so.

According to Greengus, the marriage contract that was required in the Code of Eshnunna and the Code of Hammurabi was not necessarily a written document. He asserts that "the term *riksātum* can be translated as 'binding agreement, pact, covenant', or in a broad sense 'contract'; but *prima facie* there is nothing in the terms *riksātum* or *rakāsum* to indicate a written document."[30] If this is correct, the proclamation formula itself can be said to have carried the same legal force as a written document. The proclamation formula in marriage also can be regarded as the covenant. The oral proclamation effected the bond and defined the nature of the relationship. In order to carry legal force, this proclamation was always made in the presence of an official assembly as its witness.[31] A Middle Assyrian Law, KAV 1 vi 1–5 (*ANET*, 183), stipulates that a groom must bring five or six of his neighbors as witnesses in order to veil his concubine and say "she is my wife" in their presence. This means that the marriage proclamation was to be made before the public in order to ratify the marriage union. One observation to be noted here is that all of these proclamation formulas consist of nominal clauses, that is, verbless sentences.

Now we can return to the Bible and see how these proclamation formulas are related to biblical marriage formulas and covenant formulas. In Hos 2:4[2:2], YHWH asked the children of Gomer to contend with their mother and said, 'for she is not my wife, and I am not her husband' כי־היא לא אשתי ואנכי לא אישה. This is apparently modeled on a marriage formula similar to the one used in Elephantine: 'She is my wife and I am her husband from this day and forever' (הי אנתתי ואנה בעלה מן יומא זנה עד עלם).[32] Along with this understanding, the rejection formula in Hos 1:9 requires our attention: 'And YHWH said, "Name him Loammi, for you are not my people and I am not your God"'[33] קרא שמו לא עמי כי אתם לא עמי ואנכי לא־אהיה לכם. This is exactly the same divorce formula that was used in Old Babylonian: 'you are not my wife, I am not you husband' *ul aššatī attī, ul mutī attā*. The rejection

29. Greengus, "Old Babylonian Marriage Contract," 521 n. 75. Cf. Hugenberger, *Marriage*, 223.

30. Greengus, "Old Babylonian Marriage Contract," 506.

31. Kalluveettil, *Declaration and Covenant*, 110.

32. Cf. M. A. Friedman, "Israel's Response in Hosea 2:17b: 'You Are My Husband,'" *JBL* 99 (1980) 199–204; Greengus, "Old Babylonian Marriage Contract," 522 n. 82; Hugenberger, *Marriage*, 231.

33. BHS proposes to add אלהיכם.

formula in Hos 2:1[1:10], 'You are not my people' לא עמי אתה, is also a modification of the proclamation formula of divorce 'you are not my husband' *ul mutī attā*, used in the ancient Near East. YHWH's rejection of his people is described in terms of a husband's denouncement of his wife. The conformity of the rejection formula in the Bible to the divorce formula in the ancient Near East allows us to see the conformity of the marriage formula with the covenant formula. The terms "You are my people" and "Thou art my God" in Hos 2:23 are modified from the reciprocal proclamation formula in marriage. YHWH's proposal for marriage to Israel in Hos 2:19–20 clearly supports this understanding. And the covenant formula "I will be your God and you will be my people" is also modified from the proclamation formula of marriage, "You will be my wife and I will be thy husband."

One point to be noted in this parallelism is that the covenant formula is not a nominal clause, as is the proclamation formula in marriage. The verb היה plays a key role in the covenant formula. The word היה simply means 'to be, to become'. According to G. S. Ogden's research, היה is mainly used (1) to connect words as a copula, (2) to indicate the existence of a subject, and (3) to indicate the transition from one sphere of existence to another.[34] According to his classification, the use of היה in this case is both connecting and transitional in describing the concept of covenant. As a connecting word, it establishes a relationship, and by taking the preposition ל twice, it specifies the direction of transition (לו) and the relationship between the subject and the predicate (לאשה). Therefore, I do not find any syntactical difference between the marriage formula and the covenant formula. This means that "You are my people" and "Thou art my God" are basically covenant-ratifying formulas like "I will be your God and You will be my people," and these covenant formulas between YHWH and Israel originated in the marriage formulas. In particular, Deut 26:17–19 ("You have declared YHWH, this day, to be your God . . . and YHWH has declared you, this day, to be his treasured people") seems to be the most convincing evidence that the covenant formula is a reflection of the mutual declaration in marriage.[35]

The Descriptive Formula

Along with the proclamation formula in marriage, a descriptive marriage formula was used in the ancient Near East. The descriptive formula of marriage is distinguished from the proclamation formula by its form and usage. The descriptive formula of marriage is mostly used in a written document. Unlike the proclamation formula, the groom or the third person describes or explains that the marriage relationship has been established between the partners and they have entered into the bond by law.

34. G. S. Ogden, "Time, and the Verb היה in O.T. Prose," *VT* 21 (1971) 451.
35. Friedman, "Israel's Response in Hosea 2:17b," 199–204.

Among the descriptive formulas of marriage in the Hebrew Bible, 'X (man) took Y (woman) for his wife' (לקח X את־Y ל/X לאשה) and 'X took Y and she became X's wife' (לקח X את־Y ותהי־ל/X לאשה) are most frequently used.[36] One of the best examples for the first formula is found in Exod 6:20.

ויקח עמרם את־יוכבד דודתו לו לאשה׃

Amram married his father's sister Jochebed. (NIV)[37]

Here we can see the verb לקח takes the preposition ל twice. The first ל denotes the direction of transference, while the second one denotes the use of the taking. Thus Amram takes Jochebed to himself for the purpose of wife. However, two sentences are joined in the second formula, and the double ל is led by the verb היה.[38]

ויקח בעז את־רות ותהי־לו לאשה׃

Boaz took Ruth and she became his wife. (Ruth 4:13)[39]

As a modification of this formula, ותהי is replaced with להיות, the infinitive form of היה. Then the formula is לקח X את־Y להיות ל/X לאשה (X took Y to be his wife).

ועתה לא־תסור חרב מביתך עד־עולם עקב כי בזתני ותקח את־אשת אוריה החתי
להיות לך לאשה׃

Now therefore, the sword shall never depart from your house, because you have despised me, and have taken the wife of Uriah the Hittite to be your wife. (2 Sam 12:10)[40]

It is important for our understanding of marriage in the Bible that the formulas descriptive of marriage are expressed with the Hebrew verb לקח and the double ל. The word לקח is a marriage term, like בעל, נשׂא, הושיב, בוא, קנה, and ארשׂ, and so on.[41] The Semitic root *lqḥ* is extensively used as a marriage term in the ancient Near East. *Leqû*, the Akkadian cognate of לקח, is a marriage term used alongside *aḫāzum*. *Lqḥ*, the Ugaritic cognate, also carries the same meaning. However, these cognates are not syntactically identical to the Hebrew verb לקח in taking double ל.[42] The Hebrew descriptive formula for

36. Sohn, *The Divine Election of Israel*, 31–32.

37. Cf. Gen 25:20; 34:4, 21; Exod 6:20, 23, 25; Deut 21:11; 25:5; Judg 3:6; 1 Sam 25:39, 40; 2 Sam 5:9; Ezek 44:22.

38. See Good (*Sheep of His Pasture*, 65–68) for an extensive discussion about the life setting of this formula: היה ל־ . . . ל־ . . . .

39. Cf. Gen 24:67, 1 Sam 25:43.

40. See also Deut 24:4.

41. Sohn, *The Divine Election of Israel*, 10–29.

42. The Akkadian literature describes it in a simple sentence, RN *mārat* RN_2 *ana* DAM-*ut-ti-šu il-te-qè* 'Ammistamru took the daughter of Bentešima as his wife' (MRS 9 126 = RS 17.159:6, quoted from CAD L 137).

marriage is a unique one. Basically, לקח carries the concept of possession by either agreement or capture. The subject (X) of the verb possesses (לקח) the object (Y) for the purpose of being X's wife (אשה). A wife was the special property of her husband.[43] Wedding was a kind of proclamation ceremony at which the groom demonstrated ownership of his bride.

Surprisingly enough, this descriptive formula of marriage is used for the relationship between YHWH and his people. The people of Israel employed the imagery of marriage to describe their intimate relationship with YHWH. They use the marriage term לקח as a term of election and modified the marriage formula for the election formula.[44] As an election formula, "I will take you for my people and I will be your God" or "YHWH has taken you to be a people for his own possession" is frequently found in the Hebrew Bible.

> ולקחתי אתכם לי לעם והייתי לכם לאלהים וידעתם כי אני יהוה אלהיכם המוציא אתכם מתחת סבלות מצרים:
>
> Then I will take you for my people, and I will be your God; and you shall know that I am YHWH your God, who brought you out from under the burdens of the Egyptians. (Exod 6:7)

The wording of the election formula, ולקחתי אתכם לי לעם והייתי לכם לאלהים 'I will take you for my people and I will be your God', is in accord with the marriage formula "לקח X את־Y ותהי־ל/X לאשה," except for the substitution of the pronoun, עם 'people', and אלהים 'God'. The modified formula "לקח את־Y להיות ל/X לאשה (X)" is found in Deut 4:20:

> ואתכם לקח יהוה ויוצא אתכם מכור הברזל ממצרים להיות לו לעם נחלה כיום הזה:
>
> But YHWH has taken you and brought out of the iron furnace, from Egypt, to be a people for his own possession, as today.

The formula ואתכם לקח יהוה . . . להיות לו לעם נחלה 'YHWH has taken you . . . to be a people for his own possession' also accords with the descriptive formula of marriage: 'YHWH has taken you to be his people' or 'I will take you for my people and I will be your God'. As the marriage was a proclamation of the groom's ownership of his bride, YHWH also proclaims the ownership of Israel as a special possession. Israel is described as עם סגלה (Deut 7:6, 14:2, 26:18; cf. Exod 19:5, Mal 3:17, Ps 13:4) and עם נחלה (Deut 4:20, 1 Kgs 8:35). The word נחלה is derived from the verb נחל, which means 'to possess'. Most English versions render it 'inheritance'. However, the Ugaritic cognate *nḥlt* has the concept of possession. The realm of Mot is called *arṣ nḥlt* (the land of his possession),[45] and Ṣapan, the holy mountain of Baal's sanctuary, is *ǵr nḥlt* 'the mountain of my possession'.[46] In view of these usages, the rendering

43. Sohn, *The Divine Election of Israel*, 18–19.
44. Ibid., 33–37.
45. CTA 4 VIII 13–14.
46. CTA 3 III 27.

of עם נחלה as 'the people of possession' is preferable to 'the people of inheritance'. The word סגלה, carrying the meaning of 'valued property', is essentially the same as נחלה. According to Rogers, the term סגלה is always used to refer to an elected group in Biblical Hebrew, whereas נחלה is not.[47] The Akkadian cognate *sug/kullu* carries the meaning 'herd'.[48] In ancient Near Eastern nomadic societies, the herd or flock would be counted as valued property. Therefore, עם נחלה and עם סגלה carry the concept of possession. Just as לאשה carries the concept of property or possession in the marriage formula לקח X את־Y ל/X לאשה, so לעם carries the concept of possession in the election formula. The election formula seems to add נחלה and סגלה to עם in order to clarify the concept of possession.

Based on this analogy, the concept and formulas of covenant expressing the intimate relationship between Yahweh and Israel are essentially the same as those of marriage. Many commentators regard Exod 6:7 as a covenant formula, since the later parts of the formula ("I will be your God") echo the covenant formula ("You will be my people and I will be your God").[49] But the election formula does not always conform to the covenant formula. YHWH elected Israel in the land of Egypt and made the covenant with them at Mount Sinai; thus he became the God of Israel and Israel became the people of YHWH. YHWH and Israel entered into a mutual relationship through election and into a legal bond through a covenant. As a result, the covenant carried legal force along with mutual responsibilities and obligations. Election necessarily entails a covenant in order to carry legal, binding force. Election and covenant always go together. Without election, there is no covenant, and if there is election, covenant naturally follows. Therefore, the election formula and covenant formula are used interchangeably throughout the Bible. This leaves us unable to make a clear distinction between the election and covenant formulas. However, the significant point here is that the YHWH-Israel relationship, whether it is election or covenant, is described with marriage terminology and marriage formulas.

Returning to Good, we find that he does not ignore the similarity between the nomad's custom of adoption into the tribe by attaching his tent rope and the Israelite practice of pitching their tents around YHWH's tabernacle. In view of this similarity, he proposes that the covenant formula was

47. R. G. Rogers, *The Doctrine of Election in the Chronicler's Work and the Dead Sea Scrolls* (Ph.D. Diss., Boston University, 1969) 108.

48. AHw 2.1053f.; CAD S 345. See also E. Klein, A *Comprehensive Etymological Dictionary of the Hebrew Language for Readers of English* (New York: Macmillan, 1987) 434.

49. J. I. Durham regards this as 'covenant promise' (*Exodus* [WBC 3; Waco, Tex.: Word, 1987] 78). J. P. Hyatt believes that "the fundamental idea of covenant relationship is expressed here" (*Commentary on Exodus* [NCC; London: Oliphants, 1971] 94). Cf. A. Cole, *Exodus* (London: Tyndale, 1973) 86. M. Noth calls it 'covenant formula' (*Exodus: A Commentary* [OTL; London: SCM, 1962] 60).

derived from the client formula. But Israel's pitching their tents around YHWH's tabernacle should be understood in a different perspective. YHWH says in Exod 29:45–46, "Then I will dwell among the Israelites and be their God. They will know that I am YHWH their God, who brought them out of Egypt so that I might dwell among them. I am YHWH their God." Since YHWH's deliverance of Israel and making the covenant on Mount Sinai are explained in terms of the marriage metaphor shown above, YHWH's dwelling among the Israelites can be compared to that of a newly wedded couple in their new home. YHWH's dwelling in the midst of Israel reinforces the analogy of a marriage relationship with them. The visible symbol of his residence among the Israelites was his tabernacle placed in the midst of their tents, and the people of Israel believed in the presence of YHWH because the tabernacle was with them. The YHWH-Israel relationship is far more intimate and binding in nature than the tribal relationship of the client formula that Good proposed.[50]

In sum, the terms and formula of a covenant accord with the terms and formula of marriage. Even the ideas implied in marriage and covenant parallel each other. This leads us to conclude that the origin and background of the covenant were the marriage practices of the people of Israel. The people of Israel employed marriage terms and imagery to describe their intimate and dynamic relationship with YHWH.

The Adoption Formula and the Covenant Formula

It is widely acknowledged that there are similarities between the covenant formula and adoption formula in their respective terms, formulas, and concepts. The proclamation formulas in adoption found in the Hebrew Bible are 'I will be his father and he shall be my son' אני אהיה־לו לאב והוא יהיה־לי לבן[51] and 'Israel is my firstborn' בני בכרי ישׂראל. As for the descriptive formula, 'A became a son to B' (A היה ל/B לבן) is used. And in a rare case, 'A took B as his son (daughter)' (לקח A את־B ל/A לבן[ת]) is also found.[52] However, we are not sure that adoption was practiced in biblical

50. Z. W. Falk and M. A. Friedman think that the covenant formula "you will be my people and I will be your God" is closely associated with the marriage formula "you are my wife; you are my husband" (Z. W. Falk, *Hebrew Law in Biblical Times* [Jerusalem: Wahrmann, 1964] 135; Friedman, "Israel's Response in Hosea 2:17b," 199–204); Sohn, *The Divine Election of Israel*, 188–89; R. Smend, *Die Bundesformel* (Zurich: EVZ, 1963); idem, *Die Mitte des Alten Testaments* (Zurich: EVZ, 1970) 49–54; N. Lohfink, "Dt. 26:17–19 und die Bundesformel," *Zeitschrift für katholische Theologie* 91 (1969) 517–53; Hugenberger, *Marriage*, 180 n. 58.

51. Cf. 2 Chr 17:13, 22:10.

52. Esth 2:7, 15.

society because an actual example of it is not found in the Bible.[53] Although the cases of Moses and Esther may be the best illustrations in the Bible, the two events took place outside of biblical society. A strong tribal consciousness, the practice of polygamy, and even levirate marriage seem to have obviated the necessity for adoption. Nevertheless, the custom of adoption seems to have been well known to the people of Israel, since the concept and formula of adoption are utilized to express the theological concept in the Bible.

Proclamation Formula

In 2 Sam 7:14, YHWH promised David that he would raise up a descendant after him, who would build a temple, and he added: 'I will be a father to him and he shall be a son to me' אני אהיה־לו לאב והוא יהיה־לי לבן. YHWH announces his promise to adopt one of David's sons as his. This announcement is a part of the covenant between YHWH and David.[54] A similar example is found in 2 Kgs 16:7, when Ahaz, king of Judah, sent messengers to Tiglath-Pileser, king of Assyria, for military aid at the time of the attack by the allied forces of Rezin of Aram and Pekah of Samaria. Ahaz made the following request: 'I am your servant and I am your son. Come up and save me . . .' עבדך ובנך אני עלה והושעני. Ahaz identifies the suzerain-vassal relationship with father-son relationship. By offering himself to be the son of Tiglath-pileser, Ahaz became his vassal. This reflects the ancient Near Eastern practice of a suzerain's adopting his vassal as son. This kind of adoption was established by treaty, and such international treaties obviously reflected the contemporary custom of adoption in ancient society.[55]

The regulations applicable to the withdrawal of sonship are frequently found in the adoption texts of Old Babylonian Nippur.

> If Enlil-nišu his father and Aḫtum his mother [say] to Ninurta-abi their son, "You are not our son," they will pay 1/2 mina of silver. And if Ninurta-abi says to Enlil-nišu his father and to Aḫtum his mother, "You are not my father, you

53. Therefore, H. Donner asserts that Israel did not have the institution of adoption ("Adoption oder Legitimation? Erwägungen zur Adoption im Alten Testament auf dem Hintergrund der altorientalischen Rechte," *OrAnt* 8 [1969] 87–119).

54. Even though the term for covenant, ברית, is not used in 2 Sam 7:12, this announcement is regarded as the covenant between YHWH and David. Cf. 2 Sam 23:5; Ps 89:3–4, 34–35; 132:11.

55. A similar example can be traced to the Hittite treaty between Šuppiluliuma the suzerain and his vassal Šattiwazza: "The great king grasped me with his hand and said: When I conquer the land of Mitanni I shall not reject you, I shall make you my son. I will stand [to help you in war] and will make you sit on the throne of your father . . . the word which comes out of his mouth will not turn back" (E. Weidner, *Politische Dokumente aus Kleinasien: Staatsverträge in akkadischer Sprache aus dem Archiv von Boghazköi* [Boghazköi Studien 89; Leipzig: Hinrichs, 1923] 29–30, 40ff.), cited from *IDBSup*, 190.

> are not my [mother]," [they will] shave him [and place a slave mark on him and give him for silver]. Aḫtum annually (two lines missing) [Thus have they sworn in the name of the king].[56]

"You are not our son" and "you are not my father, you are not my mother" obviously convey the dissolution of the father-son relationship. Since this proclamation was conducted in the name of the king, it must have carried legal force. Thus, adoption was established through a legal process similar to the enactment of a covenant.

A formula of dissolution in adoption such as "You are not our son" or "You are not my father" implies the existence of a proclamation formula in adoption as part of the legal process, just as we observed in marriage. In fact, we can find such a proclamation formula in adoption in ancient Near Eastern texts. Examples are: 'you are my son' (*māru*^{meš}-*ú-a*);[57] 'he is your son' (*lú-u māru-ki*);[58] 'I, the king, called him my son' (LUGAL-*ru* [*al*]-*si-šu-ma* DUMU(?)-*am*);[59] and 'behold, Muršiliš is now my son'.[60] A much later example of such a proclamation is found in an Aramaic papyrus, 'My son he shall be' ברי יהוה.[61]

The people of Israel seem to borrow this idea of adoption to describe their covenant relationship with YHWH. The statement in Jer 31:9, 'I am Israel's father, and Ephraim is my firstborn son' כי־הייתי לישׂראל לאב ואפרים בכרי הוא, can be regarded as the adoption proclamation formula similar to the proclamation formula of marriage. The characteristic covenant formula, ...ל־ היה ...ל־, is used here. YHWH commanded Moses to say to Pharaoh, 'This is what YHWH says: Israel is my firstborn son' ואמרת אל־פרעה כה אמר יהוה בני בכרי ישׂראל (Exod 4:22). Israel was the slave of Pharaoh at the time of this instruction. But YHWH proclaims to Pharaoh his fatherhood over the Israelites through Moses. If we remember that adoptees were chosen from among slaves in the ancient Near East, YHWH's choosing of his son from the slaves echoes this custom. "Israel is my firstborn son" obviously parallels the proclamation formula of adoption in the ancient Near East.

56. E. C. Stone, *Nippur Neighborhoods* (Studies in Ancient Oriental Civilization 44; Chicago: Oriental Institute, 1987) 30; cited in Stone and Owen, *Adoption in Old Babylonian Nippur*, 48.

57. CH §170.

58. *VS* 7 10–11 (HG 3,32 = Schorr, *Urkunden*, 78), cited in S. M. Paul, "Adoption Formulae: A Study of Cuneiform and Biblical Legal Clauses," MAARAV 2/2 (1979–80) 179.

59. F. Sommer and A. Falkenstein, *Die hethitisch-akkadische Biligue des Hattušili I* (Labarna II) (Abhandlungen der Bayerischen Akademie der Wissenschaften, Phil.-hist. Abt. n.s. 16; Munich: Bayerischen Akademie der Wissenschaften, 1938) 1:2–4; cited in Paul, "Adoption Formulae," 179 n. 13.

60. Ibid., line 1:37.

61. *BMAP* 8:5 (p. 226); cited in Paul, "Adoption Formulae," 180.

The Descriptive Formula

The following is one of the adoption contracts from Old Babylonian Nippur:

> Ilabrat-tayyar has adopted Patiya as his son ([Id]nin-šubur-*ta-a-a-ar*-ke$_4$ [I]*pa-ti ya-ra* [nam]-dumu-ni-šè ba-da-an-ri-ke$_4$). House, field, orchard, all that there is, Ilabrat-tayyar has given to Patiya his son. If Patiya says to Ilabrat-tayyar his father, "You are not my father," he will pay 1/3 mina of silver, and if Ilabrat-tayyar says to Patiya his son, "You are not my son," he will pay [1/3+(?)] mina of silver and he will forfeit his house and all his property. Patiya will provide to Ilabrat-tayyar, paid monthly, an annual ration of 1 gur 1 pi if barley, [ ] mina of wool, and 6 sila of oil. (PBS 8/2 153)[62]

The formula "A adopted B as his son," as in "Ilabrat-tayyar has adopted Patiya as his son," is the typical wording that begins the adoption contracts found in Old Babylonian Nippur.[63] This formula describes the relationship between the contract partners. There is a possibility that a third person other than the contract partners, such as a scribe or tribal leader, may have announced it. This differs from the proclamation formula in adoption. However, this formula of adoption is parallel with the descriptive formula in marriage. The basic meaning of Sumerian, nam.dumu.ni.šè.ba.da.an.ri is 'to adopt' and its Akkadian cognate *ana mārūti leqû* 'to take into the status of sonship' also carries the same meaning.[64] In Hebrew the verb לקח is used for the adoption term. Therefore, לקח A את־B לו לבן exactly corresponds to the descriptive formula in the Old Babylonian adoption formula. And this formula is applied to YHWH's adoption of Israel as his son and to the covenant relationship: "YHWH took Israel for his people."

Jer 3:19 describes YHWH's adoption of Israel as his son in terms of the typical Akkadian idiom.

ואנכי אמרתי איך אשיתך בבנים
ואתן־לך ארץ חמדה נחלת צבי צבאות גוים
ואמר אבי תקראו־לי ומאחרי לא תשובו:

> Then I said, "How I would set you among my sons,
> and give you a pleasant land,
> the most beautiful inheritance of the nations!"
> And I said, "You shall call me 'my father'
> and not turn away from following me."

According to S. M. Paul, Hebrew שים בבנים is the semantic equivalent of Akkadian *ana mārūti šakānu* (Sumerian, nam.dumu.ni.šù.in.gar), the meaning of which is 'to establish sonship relations, i.e., to adopt'.[65] The

62. Stone and Owen, *Adoption in Old Babylonian Nippur*, 42.

63. Cf. *TIM* 4:14; BE 6/2, 28; *ARN* 45; *ARN* 65; BE 6/2, 24; BE 6/2, 57.

64. For a similar Sumerian expression, nam.dumu.ni.šè.šu.ba.an.ti.eš, see Paul, "Adoption Formulae," 181.

65. Ibid., 180, 182. Paul translates this verse 'I will surely adopt you as my child'.

characteristic expression for adoption is relevant to the discussion of the origin of the covenant formula. Usually adoption entails changing the name of the adoptee to the name of his adopter and bestowing the status of heir on the adoptee. First of all, YHWH asks Israel to call him *father* here. Along with this, YHWH's special designation for Israel, 'my people who are called by my name' עמי אשר נקרא־שמי עליהם,[66] is worth mentioning. Israel's being called by the name of YHWH is a modification of the adoption custom in which the adoptee is called by the name of his adopter, the new father. Through adoption by YHWH, Israel became a name-bearer of YHWH. Second, YHWH's giving of the land to Israel is a typical concept connected with adoption. Further, the appellation 'the people of inheritance' עם נחלה and the promise of 'the land that YHWH your God is giving you as an inheritance to possess' ארץ אשר יהוה אלהיך נתן־לך נחלה לרשתה also have to do with the idea of adoption.[67] The word נחלה is used in the context of marriage as well as adoption. Whereas נחלה in marriage carries the concept of possession, נחלה in adoption bears the concept of a grant to an adopted son, who will retain the נחלה as his inheritance after the death of his adoptive father. The estate becomes an inheritance only in the course of time. Just as an adoptee became the heir of an adopter, Israel became the heir of YHWH, the owner of the earth (Ps 24:1), and was given "a desirable land, the most beautiful inheritance of any nation" (Jer 3:19).[68] This is the reason that YHWH called Israel 'the people of inheritance' עם נחלה.

From the above discussion, we can see that there are many similarities between the covenant formulas and adoption formulas in terminology, formulation, and implied ideas. This suggests that the covenant formula does not originate from the client formula used among the nomads in the ancient Arabic world, as Good has proposed. Rather, it derived from the marriage formula and adoption formula of the Israelite and Mesopotamian world. Marriage and adoption must have acquired legal force as the society organized and developed. This led to marriage and adoption carrying the concept of a covenant. The Israelites borrowed the concepts of marriage and adoption to describe their relationship with YHWH, since these covenants represented the most intimate and personal relationships between partners.

66. 2 Chr 7:14; Isa 43:7, 63:19; Jer 14:9, 15:16; Dan 9:19.

67. Sohn, *The Divine Election of Israel*, 69–72.

68. Most likely one should understand צבאות as the plural construct form of צבי. The literal rendering would then be 'a heritage of the beauty of beauties of the nations'. 'The beauty of beauties' expresses the superlative in Hebrew, as we see in 'song of songs' and 'Lord of lords'. However, the LXX reads 'the patrimony of the Lord of hosts' צְבָאוֹת. See J. A. Thompson, *The Book of Jeremiah* (NICOT; Grand Rapids, Mich.: Eerdmans, 1980) 207; P. C. Craigie, P. H. Kelley, and J. F. Drinkard Jr., *Jeremiah 1–25* (WBC 26; Dallas: Word, 1991) 63. J. Bright, *Jeremiah* (AB 21; Garden City, N.Y.: Doubleday, 1984) 23.

Pants, Persians, and the Priestly Source

S. David Sperling
Hebrew Union College

The first significant critical[1] attempts to overturn the consensus established by Wellhausen that the Priestly source (P) is later than the Deuteronomic source (D) were made by Y. Kaufmann. As observed by Menahem Haran,[2] in order to show that P was preexilic, Kaufmann analyzed biblical cultic institutions in a manner that did not differ methodologically from Wellhausen.[3] More recent advocates of a preexilic P, notably Avi Hurvitz,

Author's note: To Baruch I extend the blessing of Darius: *Utā taya kunavāhi*, *avatai̯ Aurmazdā ucāram kunau̯tu*. In other words, *mimma mala teppušu Uramazda ina qātēka lusteššer*.

My friend and colleague Baruch Levine has long been in the forefront of the modern critical study of Torah-literature. The Priestly source (P) in particular has occupied much of his scholarly attention. This paper, which approaches the problem of the dating of P from the perspective of realia, is offered in tribute to our honoree. An earlier version of this paper was presented to the international meeting of the Society of Biblical Literature in Leuven, Belgium, in August 1994.

1. Unlike Kaufmann, the Orthodox Jewish scholar David Z. Hoffmann was doctrinally committed to the Mosaic authorship of the Pentateuch. Nonetheless, Hoffmann's work engaged the Wellhausen thesis seriously and made contributions that remain significant from a critical standpoint. See B. Levine apud S. D. Sperling, *Students of the Covenant: A History of Jewish Biblical Scholarship in North America* (Atlanta: Scholars Press, 1992) 20.

2. M. Haran, "The Character of the Priestly Source," in *Proceedings of the Eighth World Congress of Jewish Studies*, Panel Sessions, A: *Bible Studies and Hebrew Language* [hereafter *P8WCJS*] (Jerusalem: Magnes, 1983) 131–38, esp. 131–32.

3. Kaufmann's thesis is elaborately articulated in his four-volume *History of Israelite Religion* (2d ed.; Jerusalem: Bialik, 1967) [Heb.]. The first edition was abridged and translated by M. Greenberg as Y. Kaufmann, *The Religion of Israel* (Chicago: University of Chicago Press, 1960). The Kaufmann school continues to influence Israeli scholars in particular. See, e.g., M. Weinfeld, "Social and Cultic Institutions in the

Ziony Zevit, Gary Rendsburg, Robert Polzin,[4] and others have based their conclusions on reconstructions of the history of the Hebrew language. Naturally, the adherents of an exilic or postexilic date for P have countered with linguistic arguments of their own. Among these, the studies of Baruch Levine have been especially compelling.[5]

Art historical evidence has played a less significant role in determining the date of P, although material of great potential value is found in studies of

---

Priestly Source against Their Ancient Near Eastern Background," *P8WCJS*, 95–129; idem, "Julius Wellhausen's Understanding of the Law of Ancient Israel and Its Fallacies," *Shnaton* 4 (1989) 62–93 [Heb.]; idem, *Deuteronomy 1–11* (AB 5; New York: Doubleday, 1991) 25–37; M. Haran, *Temples and Temple-Service in Ancient Israel* (Oxford: Oxford University Press, 1978; repr. Winona Lake, Ind.: Eisenbrauns, 1985); idem, "Judaism and the Bible in the Thinking of Yehezkel Kaufmann," *Madaʿe Ha-Yahadut* 31 (1991) 69–80 [Heb.]; I. Knohl, *The Sanctuary of Silence: The Priestly Torah of the Holiness School* (Minneapolis: Fortress, 1995). Among Americans, Kaufmann's procedures and essential conclusions have found their continuators in such scholars as Richard Friedman, *The Exile and Biblical Narrative: The Formation of the Deuteronomistic and Priestly Works* (Chico, Calif.: Scholars Press, 1982); and J. Milgrom, "Priestly ('P') Source," *ABD* 3.453–62 (with references to his previous work). It is noteworthy that in his later publications, the great American biblicist H. L. Ginsberg, who had supported Kaufmann's theories about preexilic P for decades, concluded from his studies of the pentateuchal cultic calendars that Wellhausen's dating of P was more likely. See H. L. Ginsberg, *The Israelian Heritage of Judaism* (New York: Jewish Theological Seminary, 1982); cf. the review by B. A. Levine in *AJS Review* 12 (1987) 143–57.

4. See, e.g., A. Hurvitz, *A Linguistic Study of the Relationship between the Priestly Source and the Book of Ezekiel* (Paris; Gabalda, 1982); idem, "The Language of the Priestly Source and Its Historical Setting: The Case for an Early Date," in *P8WCJS*, 83–94; idem, "Dating the Priestly Source in Light of the Historical Study of Biblical Hebrew a Century after Wellhausen," *ZAW* 100 (1988) Supplement 88–100.

Z. Zevit, "Converging Lines of Evidence Bearing on the Date of P," *ZAW* 94 (1982) 481–511.

G. Rendsburg, "Late Biblical Hebrew and the Date of 'P,'" *JANES* 12 (1980) 65–80.

R. Polzin, *Late Biblical Hebrew: Toward an Historical Typology of Biblical Hebrew Prose* (Missoula, Mont.: Scholars Press, 1976). Polzin takes an intermediate position in which P's language is transitional between Early Biblical Hebrew and Late Biblical Hebrew.

5. See, e.g., B. A. Levine, "Research in the Priestly Source: The Linguistic Factor," *ErIsr* 16 (Orlinsky volume; 1982) 124–31 [Heb.]; idem, "Late Language in the Priestly Source: Some Literary and Historical Observations," *P8WCJS*, 69–82; idem, *Leviticus* (JPS Torah Commentary; Philadelphia: Jewish Publication Society, 1989); idem, *Numbers 1–20* (AB 4; New York: Doubleday, 1993) 101–8; idem, "On the Semantics of Land Tenure in Biblical Literature: The Term *ʾaḥuzzāh*," in *The Tablet and the Scroll: Near Eastern Studies in Honor of William W. Hallo* (ed. M. Cohen et al.; Bethesda, Md.: CDL, 1993) 134–39.

cultic appurtenances, such as the work of Carol Meyers on the menorah.[6] One such detail that has apparently been overlooked in the debate over the dating of P comes from the history of clothing.[7]

The Hebrew of Exod 20:23 reads as follows:

ולא תעלה במעלות[8] על מזבחי אשׁר לא תגלה ערותך עליו

This relatively early[9] passage concludes a larger pericope, which describes what constitutes a proper altar:

> Make for me an altar of earth[10] and sacrifice on it your burnt offerings and your sacrifices of well-being, your sheep and your oxen; in every place where I cause my name to be mentioned I will come to you and bless you. But if you make for me an altar of stones, do not fashion them hewn, for by wielding your blade upon it you have profaned it. Do not ascend my altar by steps, that your nakedness may not be exposed upon it.

The prohibition against ascent by steps to an altar is linked grammatically (ולא . . . אשׁר לא) and thematically with the exposure of nakedness. That is, one may not ascend to an altar by steps because that ascent might lead to an exposure of nakedness (Heb. ערוה).[11] In other words, it is prohibited to build a stepped altar such as attested at some ancient Palestinian sites.[12] A simpler

6. See C. Meyers, *The Tabernacle Menorah* (Missoula, Mont.: Scholars Press, 1976); idem, "Lampstand," *ABD* 4.141–43.

7. In his article "Dress and Ornaments" (*IDB* 1.869–71), J. M. Myers collected much of the data cited in the present article without indicating their significance for dating. He observed (p. 870) that "breeches or drawers are mentioned only in connection with priestly vestments." He notes further that Josephus "calls these breeches ἀναξυρίδες (*Ant.* 3 §152), a term used by Herodotus" (see below). Worth quoting in full is the entry "Beinkleider," by R. Smend in *Biblisch-historisches Handwörterbuch* (ed. B. Reicke and L. Rost; Göttingen: Vandenhoeck & Ruprecht, 1962) 1.214: "aus Leinwand, Bestandteil der nach-exil (?) isr. Priesterkleidung (Exod 28: 42 u.ö.). Sonst wurden B. nicht getragen." The most recent author to overlook the full chronological significance of his observations about clothing is Nahum Sarna, *Exodus* (JPS Torah Commentary; Philadelphia: Jewish Publication Society, 1991) 117. Sarna notes the verses in which priests are instructed to wear "linen breeches to cover their nakedness." He then remarks that "breeches are otherwise unknown in the Bible and Near East in preexilic times. The dress of the ordinary person included a shirtlike garb but not breeches." By "otherwise unknown," Sarna means: archaeologically unknown and attested only in the exilic Ezekiel and the Priestly source, which most scholars do not consider preexilic.

8. The vocable is attested in the early text Amos 9:6.

9. See Levine, *AJS Review* 12, 144–45.

10. For opinions on what is meant by an "altar of earth," see R. Haak, "Altar," *ABD* 1.163.

11. This seems to be directed against inadvertent exposure rather than ritual nudity. Contrast Sarna, *Exodus*, 117.

12. On altars in the biblical period, see Haak, *ABD* 1.162–67. On stepped altars in Canaan, see p. 163. "Steps" are mentioned in the description of the altar in Ezek 43:17.

solution, or at least an option to the prohibition of steps, might have been a
requirement for officiants to wear trousers. [13] Indeed, that is the solution offered by God to Moses in Exod 28:42–43. Exod 28:42 reads:

ועשׂה להם מכנסי בד[15] לכסות בשׂר ערוה ממתנים ועד ירכים יהיו[14]

You shall also make for them linen[16] trousers to cover their nakedness; they
shall extend from the hips to the thighs.

The text continues:

They shall be worn by Aaron and his sons when they enter the tent of meeting
or whey they approach the altar to officiate in the sanctuary, so that they do
not incur punishment and die. It shall be a law for all time for him and for his
offspring to come.

There is no question that Exod 28:42 addresses the problem of Exod 20:23
and probably that text itself. The phrase מכנסי בד לכסות ערוה in 28:42 seems
to respond to לא תגלה ערותך in 20:23. It will be recalled that כסה ערוה and
גלה ערוה are antonymous phrases.[17] Second, the conclusion of the pericope,
"It shall be a law for all time (חקת עולם) for him and his offspring to come,"
has the appearance of an innovation meant to be permanent.[18]

---

13. See *Mekilta D'Rabbi Ismael* (ed. H. Horovitz and I. Rabin; Jerusalem: Bam-
berger and Wahrman, 1960) 245; cf. Rashi, ad. loc.: שעל ידי המעלות אתה צריך
להרחיב פסיעותיך ואף על פי שׁאינו גילוי ערוה ממשׁ שׁהרי כתיב עשׂה לך מכנסי בד.
14. The LXX reads: καὶ ποιήσεις αὐτοῖς περισκελῆ λινᾶ καλύψαι ἀσχημοσύνην
χρωτὸς αὐτῶν· ἀπὸ ὀσφύος ἕως μηρῶν (thigh) ἔσται. For Heb. מכנסים the Greek employs περισκελῆ, literally 'round the leg', hence 'drawers'. See LSJ 1386. Gk. σκέλος
refers to the leg from the hip downward. See LSJ 1606; Philo follows the LXX in his
account of priestly garb in *Life of Moses* 2.143. See R. Dunbar, *The Account of the Israelite Tabernacle and the First Priesthood in the "Jewish Antiquities" of Flavius Josephus*
(Ph.D. dissertation; Annenberg Research Institute: Philadelphia, 1991) 206; The
Peshiṭta to Exod 28:42 reads: ועבד להון פרזומא דבוצא למכסיו בסרא דערטליותהון מן
חציהון ועדמא לעטמתהון נהוון. Syriac פרזומא is a loan from Gk. περίζωμα, a girdle
around the loins worn by athletes, smiths, and priests. See LSJ 1374. It is this term
that Philo employs in his account of priestly clothing in *Special Laws* 1.83. See Dunbar, *Account of the Israelite Tabernacle*, 206; both *Tgs.* Onqelos and *Neofiti* translate by
מכנסין, cognate to the Hebrew vocable; Saadia employs Arabic סראויל (= *sarāwīl*) for
the Pentateuch's מכנסים. See *Version arabe du Pentateuque de R. Saadia Ben Iosef Al-
Fayyoûmî* (ed. J. Derenbourg; Paris: Leroux, 1893) 123, 140, 149. The Arabic is borrowed from Persian. See below.
15. The term בד refers to the cloth made from the flax = פשׁתן plant. The words
שׁשׁ/בוץ refer to the linen thread. See A. Hakam, *The Book of Exodus* (Jerusalem: Mosad Harav Kook, 1991) 2.213 [Heb.].
16. On flax (linen = *linum usitatissimum*), see I. and W. Jacob, "Flora," *ABD* 2.815.
17. Cf. Gen 9:23 with Lev 18:7, and Ezek 16:8 with 16:37.
18. Cf. the similar phraseology in Exod 12:17 (a new festival) and Lev 3:17. The
innovative significance of the phrase is particularly clear in Lev 17:7 and Num 18:21–

We may ask when the innovation of trousers was likely to have been made and why the use of trousers was not suggested by the legislator of Exodus 20.[19] Let us first observe that the Hebrew word for 'trousers' or 'breeches' is attested biblically three more times in the Pentateuch. First, in Exod 39:28 we have the phrase ואת מכנסי הבד שׁשׁ משׁזר 'and the linen trousers of fine twisted linen'. The next attestation is in Lev 6:3, which reads in part ומכנסי בד ילבשׁ על בשׂרו 'and linen trousers he shall wear on his flesh'.[20] Finally, Lev 16:4 has ומכנסי בד יהיו על בשרו 'and linen trousers shall be on his flesh'.[21]

All of the above passages[22] describe priestly clothing and occur in what are universally agreed to be selections from the Priestly source. The sole other biblical occurrence of the term likewise describes priestly clothing and, not surprisingly, is in Ezek 44:18:

פארי פשתים יהיו על ראשם ומכנסי פשתים יהיו על מתניהם לא יחגרו ביזע

They shall have linen turbans on their heads and linen breeches on their loins; they shall not gird themselves with anything that causes sweat.

Of the five occurrences of the term for 'trousers', the attestation in Ezekiel has never been taken to be preexilic. Of course, advocates of a preexilic date for P may reply that Ezek 44:18 is simply a case of the dependence of Ezekiel on the Priestly Code. What is decisive then is the whole question of when trousers or breeches came to be worn in the Near East and who introduced them. According to the late Edith Porada, one of the leading ancient Near Eastern art historians, the answer is clear.[23]

24, where the audience is instructed 'no longer' (עוד) to practice what they had been doing. All of the above passages are from P. See further Levine, *Leviticus*, 17.

19. J. Milgrom understands Exod 20:23 as referring to "private altars attended by breechless laity," which were forbidden to have steps (idem, *Leviticus 1–16* (AB 3; New York: Doubleday, 1991) 385. If he is correct, then Exod 20:23 would not necessarily be older than Exod 39:28; Lev 6:3, 16:4; and Ezek 44:18.

20. 'Flesh' בשׂר is elliptical for בשׂר ערוה 'genitals' in Exod 28:42. See D. Hoffmann, *Sefer Vayyikra* (Jerusalem: Mosad Harav Kook, 1953) 1.159.

21. In these passages the LXX has περισκελὲς.

22. For מכנסים in later Hebrew, see the description of Aaron in Sir 45:8, in A. Hartom, *HaSefarim HaHiṣonim: Ben Sira* (Tel-Aviv: Yavneh, 1963) 169; P. Skehan and A. Di Lella, *The Wisdom of Ben Sira* (AB 39; New York: Doubleday, 1987) 507. The Greek has περισκελῆ; J. Charlesworth, A *Graphic Concordance to the Dead Sea Scrolls* (Louisville: John Knox, 1991) has no listing for מכנסים; the term מכנסים is attested four times in the Mishnah: *m. Yoma* 7:5; *m. Sukk.* 5:3; *m. Tamid* 5:3; *m. Kelim* 27:6. In the Tosepta the vocable is found in *t. Ned.* 4.3; *t. Menaḥ.* 1.8; the Mekilta (Yitro 2:11 [ed. Horovitz and Rabin, 244–45]) attests the vocable solely in a quotation from Exod 20:23.

23. See E. Porada, "Classic Achaemenian Architecture and Sculpture," in *Cambridge History of Iran* [hereafter *CHI*] (ed. I. Gershevitch; Cambridge: Cambridge University Press, 1985) 2.793–827. The quotation is from p. 822.

> In Near Eastern art in general, differentiation among peoples was mostly made on the basis of dress. Here the trousers, which appeared for the first time in the Persian reliefs,[24] were an important feature documenting the inclusion of new peoples in the population of the Persian Empire in the north-west, the north and the north-east. The Medes wore tight trousers, shoes, a long coat with false sleeves, called κάνδυς, which was laid over the shoulders like a cloak, and a bulbous hat with a short tail-like appendage. Many other peoples in the reliefs wore trousers, some tight, like the Armenians and Cappadocians, some loose, like the Arians, Bactrians, Arachosians, and Drangianians. The Scythian peoples, as well as the Sogdians, Chorasmians and Skudrians, all wore trousers, they had a distinctive kind of headdress with earflaps fastened under the chin, they also wore a long-sleeved belted jacket.

The peoples mentioned in the list are all non-Semites within the sphere of Iranian culture. In a note to her text,[25] Porada approvingly cites Calmeyer's suggestion that trousers appeared somewhat earlier,[26] but in Fars, still in Iran. We may compare Porada's statement with one by Mary Boyce:

> There are representations from the Achaemenian period of men who appear to be magi, in that they are engaged in solemnizing ritual acts; and these men are shown wearing what used to be called "Median" garb,[27] that is, the trousers and close-fitting tunic of a horseman, sometimes with a sleeved mantle (called,

24. Cf. P. Calmeyer, "Hose," *RlA* 4.472: "Fast bis zum Ende der altorientalischen Kultur ist die Hose ganz unbekannt geblieben; sie taucht erst in deren letzter Periode, der achaemenidischen, plötzlich und in vielerlei Varianten auf, und zwar *ausschließlich* [emphasis mine] bei Völkern der nordwestlichen, nördlichen und nordöstlichen Randgebiete, die zum Teil erst jetzt in die Sphäre dieser Kultur geraten waren."

25. Porada, "Achaemenian Architecture," 822 n. 4.

26. I. Seibert (*Woman in Ancient Near East* [Leipzig: Edition Leipzig, 1974] 45) cites Diodorus Siculus, the historian who lived in the first century B.C.E. (*Library of History* 2.6) as evidence that the invention of trousers was a military strategm of Queen Semiramis (Akkadian: Sammuramat), wife of Shamshi Adad V of Assyria (824–810 B.C.E.). Diodorus reports that Semiramis "devised for herself a garment that made it impossible to determine if the wearer was a man or a woman." This same garment "allowed her to do whatever she wished . . . and was altogether so convenient to her that later the Medes . . . wore the dress of Semiramis, as did afterwards the Persians." But Diodorus's statement is unsubstantiated by literary or art-historical evidence. There are no extant depictions of trousered Assyrian women or men from the 9th century or later. The fact that Diodorus himself specifically associates trousers with Iranians is in agreement with the art-historical evidence that we do have. Diodorus's primary aim was to account for the peculiarities of Iranian dress. See E. Murphy, *The Antiquities of Asia: A Translation with Notes of Book II of the Library of History of Diodorus Siculus* (New Brunswick: Transaction, 1989) 9.

27. A document from the Nippur Murashû archive refers to TÚG *Ma-du-ʾ-i-tu* 'Median garb'. See R. Zadok, "Iranians and Individuals Bearing Iranian Names in Achaemenian Babylonia," *IOS* 7 (1977) 113; idem, "Iranian and Babylonian Notes," *AfO* 28 (1981–82) 138. (I thank Eva von Dassow for bringing these references to my attention.)

in Greek rendering, the "kandys"). It has now been established . . . that this type of dress, with only minor variations, was in fact worn generally by Iranians of east and west in the sixth century (and presumably earlier) and that the Persians themselves kept it as their military garb, wearing the Elamite robe probably only at home and in court.[28]

In the same work, Boyce refers to

the general Iranian garb, which was a horseman's wear and consisted essentially of trousers[29] and a short, close-fitting tunic.[30]

That the trousers of the Priestly code have a Persian connection is highlighted by the following passage from Josephus:[31]

Moreover vestments (στολαὶ) were made for the priests, both for the general body, whom they call χααναίας (כהניא) and in particular for the high priest whom they entitle ἀναραβάχην (כהנא רבא), signifying "high priest." Now the vestments of the high priest are as follows. When the priest is proceeding to perform his sacred ministrations, after undergoing the purification which the law provides, first of all what he puts on is called the μαχανάσην.[32] The word denotes a binder (συνακτῆρα) in other words drawers (διάζωμα) covering the loins (αἰδοῖα = private parts), stitched of fine spun linen (βύσσου) into which the legs are inserted (ἐμβαινόντων) as breeches (ἀναξυρίδας). This garment is cut short above the waist and terminates at the thighs, around which it is drawn tight.

As observed by J. R. Meyers, the Greek word translated 'breeches',[33] ἀναξυρίδας,[34] is the same term used by Herodotus in his description of the troops of Xerxes:

28. M. M. Boyce, *A History of Zoroastrianism* [hereafter *HZ*] (Leiden: Brill, 1982) 2.20.

29. "The Persians thought it indecorous to leave any part of the body uncovered, and they viewed the Greeks as seminaked savages; whereas the Greeks equated trousers, which the Persians wore beneath all their other clothes, with the barbarism of the Scythian nomads" (Murphy, *Diodorus*, 9 n. 26).

30. Ibid., 10. For a detailed study of the depictions of the different ethnic groups on the Persepolis reliefs, see G. Walser, *Die Völkerschaften auf den Reliefs von Persepolis* (Berlin: Deutsches Archäologischen Institut, Abteilung Tehran Bd. 2, 1966). (Persepolis was founded by Darius I [522–486 B.C.E.] and continued by Xerxes [486–465 B.C.E.].) For an accessible treatment of the reliefs, accompanied by very clear photographs, see R. Ghirshman, *The Arts of Ancient Iran from Its Origins to the Time of Alexander the Great* (New York: Golden, 1964) 147–223; see also *ANEP*, pls. 28 and 29 and the comments on p. 253.

31. *Ant.* 3 §§150–52. The quotation is cited from LCL 4 (Cambridge: Harvard University Press, 1938) 386–87. For a detailed study of the passage, see Dunbar, "Account of the Israelite Tabernacle," 202–14.

32. For the different spellings in the MSS and a grammatical analysis, see ibid., 204.

33. In contemporary American English, the word *breeches* survives as a regionalism.

34. According to Dunbar ("Account of the Israelite Tabernacle," 206), this is "the most common word that would have been most instructive to his readers."

> Firstly, the Persians; for their equipment they wore on their head loose caps called tiaras (τιάρας), and on their bodies sleeved tunics (κιθῶνας) of diverse colours, with scales of iron like in appearance to the scales of fish,[35] and breeches on their legs (περὶ δὲ τὰ σκέλεα ἀναξυρίδας).[36]

In all likelihood, it was the importance of horsemanship in the Iranian cultural sphere that prompted the invention of trousers.[37] Be that as it may, the Iranian advance westward brought trousers to the attention of other peoples. The fact that, among others, magi wore trousers may have influenced the P legislator to consider them appropriate priestly garb. Short trousers such as dictated by P were more efficient in performing priestly duties[38] than were longer robes and more modest than kilts, which had the potential to expose one's nakedness.

The implications of trousers for dating the final form[39] of the Priestly source are obvious. No biblical writer would have seen Iranian garb before the 6th century B.C.E. The occurrence of an Iranian article of clothing[40] in

35. Cf. the description of Goliath's armor in 1 Sam 17:5. See A. Rofé, "The Battle of David and Goliath," in *Judaic Perspectives on Ancient Israel* (ed. J. Neusner et al.; Philadelphia: Fortress, 1987) 132; K. Galling, "Goliath und seine Rüstung," in *Volume du Congrès International pour l'étude de l'Ancien Testament: Genève, 1965* (VTSup 15; Leiden: Brill, 1966) 150–69.

36. Herodotus *Hist.* 61. Cited from LCL (Cambridge: Harvard University Press, 1928) 375–77.

37. For an illustration of a 5th-century B.C.E. Persian horseman wearing trousers, see O. Dalton, *The Treasures of the Oxus with Other Examples of Early Oriental Metal Work* (3d ed.; London: British Museum, 1964) following pl. 40 (catalog number 124098). Cf. also p. 15, pls. 18, 30. (I thank Professor James R. Russell of Harvard University for bringing this book to my attention.)

38. If Mishnaic tradition is reliable, priests often had to run. See *m. Yoma* 2:1–2; *m. Tamid* 5:6.

39. Given the conservatism of religious rites, it is hard to disagree with the scholarly consensus that P contains ancient material. As a parallel, compare the rituals published by F. Thureau-Dangin, *Rituels accadiens* (Paris: Leroux, 1921; cf. *ANET*, 331–45). The colophons date the texts to the Seleucid period, and the Akkadian is certainly postclassical. Nonetheless, archaic elements, including the use of Sumerian, are remnants of earlier times.

40. In the book of Daniel (3:21, 27), reference is made to an article of clothing termed סרבל in Aramaic. The term is also attested in 1QDan[b] [3:27] as well as in Babylonian Talmudic sources (see K. Beyer, *Die aramäischen Texte vom Toten Meer* [Göttingen: Vandenhoeck & Ruprecht, 1984] 648; B. Kasowski, *Thesaurus Talmudis* [Jerusalem: Jewish Theological Seminary, 1971] 27.343–44). The סרבל in Daniel refers to an article of clothing that might burn quickly and visibly. Context and etymology have justifiably led scholars to the Persian word for 'trousers' that appears in Middle Persian as *šalwār* (written *šlwʾl*; see D. MacKenzie, *A Concise Pahlavi Dictionary* [Cambridge: Cambridge University Press, 1971] 79; the Middle Persian reflects an Old Persian **salavāra*; see J. Montgomery, *A Critical and Exegetical Commentary on*

Hebrew texts leads to the inescapable conclusion that the Hebrew texts in question must be no earlier than the 6th century B.C.E. If the Northerners who were exiled to the cities of Media in the 8th century B.C.E. (2 Kgs 17:6, 18:11) saw breeches or trousers there, their records of such sightings have not reached us.

The etymology of מכנסים[41] is by no means clear. Josephus who, as we have

---

the Book of Daniel [ICC; Edinburgh: T. & T. Clark, 1927] 213; see F. Rosenthal, *Aramaic Grammar* [Wiesbaden: Harrassowitz, 1963] §189), which survives in Modern Persian *šalvar*, the common word for 'trousers'. Further support for סרבל in Daniel in the meaning 'trousers' comes from Syriac שׁרבלא 'wide trousers', which translates Aram. סרבל in Peshiṭta to Dan 3:21, 27 (for other references see R. Payne Smith, *Thesaurus Syriacus* [Oxford: Clarendon, 1901] 2.4325]). In addition, in several talmudic passages סרבל is found in contexts where baggy trousers would be appropriate. See, e.g., *b. B. Qam.* 99a; *b. B. Meṣ.* 81b; cf. E. Z. Melamed, *Talmud Babli Maseket Baba Qamma* (Jerusalem: Razal, 1952) 165; idem (ed.), *Talmud Babli Maseket Baba Mezia* (Jerusalem: Razal, 1960) 150; idem, *Dictionnaire Araméen-Hebreu* (Jerusalem: Feldheim, 1992) 325. In the Daniel 3 passages, סרבל probably refers to the wide trousers known as early as the 2d century B.C.E. from bronze Parthian sculptures (see illustrations in R. Ghirshman, *Persian Art 249 B.C.–A.D. 651* [New York: Golden, 1962] 89). Chronologically later, the talmudic passages presumably refer to the baggy trousers of the Sasanian period (see, e.g., ibid., pls. 165, 196, 205, 212, 218). These סרבלין would differ from the מכנסים of P and Ezekiel, which are short and might be construed as 'undergarments'. Cf. Josephus above.

The complete philological and sartorial picture of סרבל is far from clear. Among the problems: (1) Not all of the talmudic attestations refer to 'trousers'. See Kasowski, *Thesaurus Talmudis* 27.343–44; cf. J. Levy, *Wörterbuch über die Talmudim und Midraschim* (Berlin: Harz, 1924) 3.585. (2) In some cases at least, talmudic סרבל appears to be synonymous with טלית, the general term for 'garment' (see, e.g., *b. B. Meṣ.* 112a [ed. Melamed, 219]; 2). Is the Aramaic/Late Hebrew verb סרבל 'was thick, fattened, swelled up, covered with fat' relevant to the discussion? See Levy, *Wörterbuch*, 584–85; M. Moreshet, *A Lexicon of the New Verbs in Tannaitic Hebrew* (Ramat-Gan: Bar-Ilan University Press, 1980) 255 [Heb.]; cf. M. Sokoloff, *A Dictionary of Palestinian Jewish Aramaic of the Byzantine Period* (Ramat-Gan: Bar-Ilan University Press, 1990) 388. (3) What is the connection between סרבל and the Mishnaic hapax legomenon (*m. Kelim* 26:3) שרוול ('sleeve' in Modern Hebrew), whose precise meaning is uncertain? See E. Kutscher, *Words and Their History* (Jerusalem: Kiryath Sefer, 1961) 109–14. (4) What is the relevance of the Arabic data? Saadia's use of *sarāwīl* (plural of *sirwāl*) has been noted above (see n. 14). Complete discussion of סרבל must also take into account Arabic *sirbāl* 'shirt, coat of mail, garment' and its associated verb *sarbala* 'to clothe with a *sirbāl*' (much more specific in meaning than *labisa* 'wear, dress', etc.). See Payne Smith, *Thesaurus*, 2.4325; E. Lane, *Arabic-English Lexicon* (Edinburgh: Williams and Norgate, 1872) book 1/part 4, p. 1343.

41. Dillmann's suggestion cited in BDB 488a, to derive מכנסים from a root כנס, distinct from כנס 'gather, collect' and allegedly an alloform of the (Mishnaic Hebrew) verb גנז, which is derived from the Persian noun **ganz* (→ Middle Persian *ganǰ* 'treasure, treasury'; see *HALAT*, 191; Moreshet, *Lexicon*, 125), must be rejected as fanciful.

seen above, provides the earliest extant explanation, appears to waver.[42] His translation συνακτῆρα[43] points to BH and Mishnaic כנס 'assemble, gather'. But his use of the verb ἐμβαινόντων,[44] which includes the senses 'step into, insert', might support a connection with Mishnaic נכנס 'enter'.[45] A satisfactory solution, which would require disentangling the various senses of כנס in Hebrew[46] and Aramaic and כנס/כנש in the different dialects of Aramaic, is beyond the scope of this paper.[47]

Despite the general consensus to date P and thus the bulk of the Pentateuch in the Achaemenid period, biblicists have expended relatively little effort in exploring Iranian influences on Torah-literature.[48] Given that the consensus date would now appear to be supported by realia, it behooves us to call attention to other elements in the P source that invite further study against an Iranian backdrop,[49] although a full investigation is likewise beyond the scope of this paper.

First, P and Zoroastrian sources call for the avoidance of defilement and an emphasis on purity that extends to all members of the community and is not confined to periods of public ritual. For example, defilement caused by menstruating women[50] is very much of concern to P[51] and very significant

42. Contrast Thackeray in LCL, ad. loc., 387.

43. See LSJ 1694.

44. Ibid., 538. The LXX employs ἔμβηθι to translate Heb. בואי in Nah 3:14.

45. See, for example, S. Mandelkern, *Hekal Haqqodesh* (Leipzig, 1896) 588. Note that the *Hiphil* and *Niphal* forms of the verb(s), which are extremely common in Postbiblical Hebrew, are unattested in Biblical Hebrew.

46. For a good selection of references, see E. Ben Yehuda, *A Complete Dictionary of Ancient and Modern Hebrew* (Berlin: Langenscheidt, 1915) 5.2442–50.

47. Thus, *HALAT*, 461 relates BH and Mishnaic כנס; in contrast, C. Kasovsky (*Thesaurus Mishnae* [Jerusalem: Massada, 1958] 3.974) separates Mishnaic כנס itself into three verbal roots.

48. Cf. the statement of James Barr: "It is . . . striking that, on the whole, biblical . . . studies have remained very much aloof from the study of Iranian language and literature. . . . Comparatively few Old Testament scholars seriously study Iranian materials" ("The Question of Religious Influence: The Case of Zoroastrianism, Judaism and Christianity," *JAAR* 53 [1985] 201–2). The Iranologists have proved more eager comparatists. See, e.g., Boyce's chapter, "The Priestly Code and Zoroastrian Influences," in *HZ* 2.191–95.

49. We follow Boyce (*HZ* 2.40–48), who argues that both branches of the Achaemenian royal house had accepted Zoroastrianism by the early 6th century B.C.E.

50. Referred to in Pahlavi sources as *zan ī daštān*, the menstruating woman is under strict prohibitions. The penalty for intercourse with her (*daštān-marz*) is as high as the penalty for killing a human being. See F. Vahman, *Arda Wiraz Namag* (London: Curzon, 1986) 252.

51. E.g., Lev 12:5, 15:19–24, 18:19; cf. Ezek 18:6, 22:10. This is not to say that the impurity of menstruation originated with P (commentators regularly cite 2 Sam 11:4 as evidence of the notion in earlier Israel). Note, however, that P's term for menstruation, נדה, is apparently derived by Rashi and Saadia (see Num 19:10) from

in Zoroastrianism.[52] As for corpse-defilement, Levine has observed that Ezek 43:7–9 contains, "for the first time outside of Torah-literature, the doctrine that corpses and bones of the dead and their flesh are potent contaminators."[53] Such a doctrine would be incompatible with earlier Near Eastern cults of the dead known to have been practiced, among other places, in Israel[54] but is chronologically compatible with the prominence of corpse-defilement in Zoroastrianism.[55] Boyce observes that, if Nehemiah served as cup-bearer to Artaxerxes as claimed (Neh 2:1), he would have had to keep Zoroastrian purity laws, so as not to bring pollution on his royal master.[56]

Second, immediately following on the instruction to wear linen trousers in Lev 6:3 we find in vv. 5 and 6 the command that "a fire shall always be burning on the altar; it shall not go out."[57] Because Hebrew **תמיד** may merely mean 'regular' rather than 'continuous', the writer found it necessary to stipulate that the fire must burn continuously and never be extinguished.[58] It is

---

Aramaic **נדי** 'to sprinkle', a vocable whose native Hebrew reflex is **נזה** (with *zayin*). (That a menstruating woman is a "sprinkling woman" is semantically much sounder than derivations from **נדד** 'to wander' [according to Gen 31:35, it was credible that a menstruant couldn't move] or Akkadian *nadû* 'throw, etc.' [CAD N/1 68–100 has no references to a menstruant {Akkadian: *ḫarištu*} in its 30-page article, s.v. *nadû*, verb]. Contrast, e.g., Milgrom, *Leviticus 1–16*, 745.) If the derivation offered by Rashi and Saadia is correct, then BH **נדה** was borrowed into Hebrew from Aramaic after the inner-Aramaic shift of [ḏ] → [d], that is, not before the 6th–5th century B.C.E., thus furnishing another indication of P's date (for the date of the phonemic shift, see S. Kaufman, *ABD* 4.176–77).

52. See Boyce, *HZ* 1.307–8.

53. Levine, *Numbers 1–20*, 105.

54. See T. Lewis, *Cults of the Dead in Ancient Israel and Ugarit* (Atlanta: Scholars Press, 1989); idem, "Ancestor Worship," *ABD* 1.240–42; idem, "Dead, Abode of the," *ABD* 2.101–5; C. Kennedy, "Dead, Cult of the," *ABD* 2.105–8.

55. See Boyce, *HZ* 1.300–306.

56. Boyce, *HZ* 2.189; Barr ("Question of Religious Influence," 228) is less certain. In a general caveat against overdone comparatism, Barr observes (p. 218) that the Jews, in contrast to the Greeks, lacked "any indication of curiosity about the distinctive character of Persian religion." But the lack of an articulated curiosity is no bar to religious influence. The book of Daniel shows no overt interest in Persian religion, but some of its central teachings are otherwise unintelligible (see, e.g., L. Hartman and A. Di Lella, *The Book of Daniel* [AB 23; New York: Doubleday, 1978] 31–33). To cite a contemporary example, many Jews who have evinced an interest in the "spirituality" that has become popular in Judaism in the past 20 years would be surprised (and perhaps upset) to learn that the notion of "spirituality" has reached them indirectly through St. Paul and Alcoholics Anonymous (this is not to demean either the saint or the organization).

57. Or as later in Pahlavi, *ātaxš* ⟨*ī*⟩ *hamēšag-sōz* 'the ever-burning fire'. See Vahman, *Arda-Wiraz* 6:1, 86–87, 238.

58. See Levine, *Leviticus JPS*, 96.

difficult to avoid seeing here the influence of Zoroastrianism, because "the cult of fire is at the very heart of Zoroastrian devotional life."[59] Zoroaster associated fire with Asha 'Righteousness' and enjoined his followers always to pray in its presence. It was long assumed that the temple cult of fire belonged to primitive Zoroastrianism. Even if this assumption were correct, it would have been unlikely to come to the attention of Hebrews before the rise of the Persian Empire. More recently, however, the researches of S. Wikander, of Boyce, and of K. Schippmann have led them to the conclusion that the temple cult of fire was a late outgrowth of the older veneration of the hearth fire. Specifically, the temple fire may have originated as the fire that had burned in the royal palace transferred to a public place. On Boyce's analysis, the temple cult fire arose in the 4th century B.C.E. in reaction to the image cult.[60] If so, then we would seek a date in the 4th century for Leviticus 6. It must be noted, however, that there is evidence for a special category of fire-stoking priests—Elamite *haturmakša* = Old Persian **ātrvaš*,[61] from the Persepolis fortification tablets (509–494 B.C.E.)[62]—which would be relevant to our discussion.[63]

One brief final remark is in order. Over the years, the supposed parallels between Genesis 1 and Mesopotamian creation accounts have proved unconvincing.[64] Boyce and other Iranologists have noted similarities between Genesis 1 and the admittedly late Bundahishn.[65] Boyce did not, however, comment on a particularly significant feature of the creation account in Genesis 1, to which James Barr has called attention:

> Why is there emphasis, so evident in Genesis 1, on the fact that the creation was *good* [emphasis in original]—an element for which, so far as I know, no close Mesopotamian parallel has been found, and which is so strongly emphasized nowhere else in the Old Testament?[66]

59. M. Boyce, "On the Zoroastrian Temple Cult of Fire," *JAOS* 95 (1975) 454–65.

60. For the research of Wikander, Boyce, and Schippmann mentioned above, see ibid., 454–65; idem, *HZ* 2.221–22; G. Gnoli, in *Encyclopedia of Religion* (New York: Macmillan, 1986) 1.477–78.

61. See Schwartz, *CHI* 2.688; for detailed discussion, see H. Koch, "Götter und ihre Verehrung im achämenidischen Persien," *ZA* 77 (1987) 239–78, esp. 254 n. 88.

62. For the date, see Boyce, *HZ* 2.133.

63. Boyce does not accept the suggested Old Persian equivalence of the *haturmakša* nor does she agree that the official in question was a priest (*HZ* 2.135–36).

64. See M. Weinfeld, "The Creator God in Genesis 1 and in the Prophecy of Deutero-Isaiah," *Tarbiz* 37 (1968) 112 [Heb.].

65. The Bundahishn is a commentary on a lost Avestan text and preserves extremely ancient material. See J. R. Russell, "Yamauchi, *Persia and the Bible*," *JQR* 82 (1992) 258.

66. Barr, "Religious Influence," 208.

To some extent Barr was anticipated by Moshe Weinfeld, who observed that the notion of Genesis 1 that creation is "good" was opposed by Deutero-Isaiah (Isa 45:7).[67] Of Gen 1:2, Weinfeld writes:

> The darkness and the primordial water symbolize . . . negativity and evil. It is these that the good god has come to remove and repel. This viewpoint conforms to the priestly notion of the existence of a demonic sphere that constitutes an opposition to the divine sphere, which embodies the good.[68]

If we keep in mind the historical circumstances of P's composition, the answer to Barr's question is adumbrated in Weinfeld's observation. The "good creation" of Ahura Mazda is fundamental to the Zoroastrian dualistic world view in which Angra Mainyu (Ahreman) is characterized as "having an evil creation."[69] In Genesis 1, the Priestly writer provides a Hebrew adaptation of the Iranian notion that creation is all good. As shown by Weinfeld, Deutero-Isaiah (Isa 45:7) opposed this notion by attributing the creation of both good and evil to the Hebrew creator-god.[70]

67. Weinfeld, "Creator God," 123.

68. Ibid., 121–22 [my translation from Hebrew]. Weinfeld was apparently aware that his reading of Genesis 1 undermined his own advocacy of a preexilic P (see nn. 1 above and 70 below.) He asserts (ibid., n. 89) that "It should not be concluded from this [interpretation] that the [creator] god [in Genesis 1] is doing battle with a primeval demonic-Ahremanic [Heb: דימוני-אהורמני] force."

69. See Schwartz, in *CHI* 2.681.

70. Weinfeld, "Creator God," 123. In no way does this support Weinfeld's claims (pp. 105–32; cf. more recently idem, *Deuteronomy 1–11*, 25–37) that P is preexilic. On the contrary, Genesis 1 and Deutero-Isaiah were both strongly influenced by Iranian culture (for Deutero-Isaiah, see M. Smith, "II Isaiah and the Persians," *JAOS* 83 [1963] 415–20) but differed over which elements in that culture to accept.

Isaiah 34, Chaos, and the Ban

PHILIP D. STERN
White Plains, NY

In my doctoral dissertation on the biblical ban,[1] I operated under the insightful guidance and thoughtful humanity of Baruch A. Levine. His training enabled me to analyze the appropriate texts from a comparative and innerbiblical perspective. I reached the novel conclusion that the ban represented, through the means of "sanctification through destruction," a triumph over chaos as personified by a deadly enemy. The ban is therefore to be analyzed as a method of creating a world order (or *Weltordnung*) for Israel.[2] Isaiah 34 more than any other biblical source gives substance to this claim. Images of chaos appear in this chapter far more than anywhere else in the Bible, although many commentators seem not to have noticed this.[3]

As G. W. Ahlström put it in an Egyptian context, "The idea is that the enemies represented the chaos powers and thus had to be completely defeated."[4] Significantly, he adds, "This ideology and literary style is also well known from the Bible."[5] If one looks for this ideology in the Hebrew Bible, it is most strongly marked and most developed at length in the ban, most particularly in Isaiah 34, as will be the burden of this paper to demonstrate.

1. Referred to here in revised form is P. D. Stern, *The Biblical HEREM: A Window on Israel's Religious Experience* (BJS 211; Atlanta: Scholars Press, 1991).

2. By *world order* I mean the conglomeration of things essential to the proper functioning and well-being of a people. Primary is safety from enemies. The biblical obsession with obtaining a particular land promised by God and dwelling there flowed from an ideologically religious view of what constituted world order.

3. E.g., the commentary of H. Wildberger, *Jesaia* (BKAT: Neukirchen-Vluyn: Neukirchener Verlag, 1982) 3.1326–33. O. Kaiser mentions chaos in passing (in *Isaiah 13–39: A Commentary* [OTL; London: SCM, 1974] 359) but only because the word "chaos" is in the text.

4. G. W. Ahlström, *The History of Ancient Palestine* (Minneapolis: Fortress, 1994) 298.

5. Ibid., 298 n. 1.

The chapter itself is unique, and it behooves us to begin to understand it from the beginning.[6] The opening, an appeal to all the earth and its fullness to give heed, makes the point that the message to follow is one of cosmic dimensions. The second verse introduces the first of two mentions of the ban:

> For the Lord is furious against the nations, and wrathful against all their host.
> He has put them to the ban; he has given them to slaughter.[7]

Three representative translations from different times, the RSV, the NEB, and the NRSV, translate ban as 'doom' or 'destruction'. The question is, granted that Isaiah 34 is a late text,[8] do the sacral connotations of the word exist in this passage? If one compares the verse to the Mesha Inscription, one finds in the latter a reference to slaughter (*hrg*) in conjunction with the ban. Yet no one questions that *ban* there is in its full force as consecration through/to destruction. In KTU 1.3, the earliest ban text involving the same root as the Hebrew for 'ban', the three verbs involved are *ḫrm*, *š*[*k*]*ll*,[9] and *hrg* 'ban, destroy, slay'. In the Bible, de Moor pointed out, 'ban' and *hrg* are found in parallel contexts in Josh 8:24 and 26.[10] Thus the poetically embellished references to slaughter in Isaiah 34 fit directly and precisely into the older tradition of the depiction of the ban. Another point: usually the sacral ban is executed under the direction of a divinely designated agent, such as Joshua, Moses, or Mesha. The attribution of the ban directly to God, without an agent, actually strengthens the likelihood that what is spoken of is no mere secular destruction or doom but rather the sacral "consecration through destruction" that characterized the earlier ban. Or we may ask, does God engage in secular acts?

M. Pope has shown through a study of the vocabulary and other components of Isaiah 34 that the chapter is part of the corpus of Isaiah 40–66.[11] In Isa 43:27, we read that YHWH has given Israel to the ban. In that verse, חרם 'ban' is used in conjunction with קדש 'holiness, sanctuary', showing that the prophet is playing on the sacral connotations of the root חרם and strengthening the likelihood that in Isaiah 34 the ban has not been desacralized.

6. G. von Rad, *Holy War in Ancient Israel* (Grand Rapids, Mich.: Eerdmans, 1991) has an interesting chapter on "Holy War in the Prophets," but unfortunately von Rad does not deal with Isaiah 34.

7. In more than one prophecy against Edom, the nations are cited as objects of divine wrath; by subsequently focusing on Edom, the prophet further emphasizes the degree of God's wrath against Edom.

8. Such is the scholarly consensus: see M. H. Pope, "Isaiah 34 in Relation to Isaiah 35, 40–66," *JBL* 71 (1952) 235–43.

9. Reconstructed in light of the text given in J. C. de Moor and K. Spronk, *A Cuneiform Anthology of Religious Texts from Ugarit* (Leiden: Brill, 1987) 58–59.

10. Ibid., 58–59.

11. Pope, "Isaiah 34," 235–43. So W. Caspari long before, in "Jesaja 34 und 35," *ZAW* 49 (1931) 86.

Further, just as the Ugaritic text KTU 1.13 makes the goddess Anat the executor of the ban, so in Isaiah 34 YHWH may be seen as the subject carrying out the sacral ban. As the parallels with KTU 1.13 make clear, Isaiah 34 actually preserves extremely ancient threads of tradition in which the sacral ban is utilized directly by the deity. The situation of Isaiah 34 is one in which no Israelite army is available to execute the war ban, no agent of God like Joshua positioned to take God's instructions. The prophet considers the concept of ban appropriate to God, because God can surely execute the war ban without a human agent. The war ban is in any event a special case of the triumph of the Divine Warrior[12] in battle. Another factor in favor of reading the ban in Isaiah 34 as the sacral war ban of old is its affinities to old ban texts in the Bible, as has been pointed out by J. Lust.[13] It uses even more of the language of the Mesha Inscription.[14] Further affinities with KTU 1.13 are especially interesting. J. Muilenburg points out that

> the poet was fully aware of the power of the figure of the stars falling from heaven as leaves from trees. . . .[15]

KTU 1.13,[16] which has a Ugaritic verb 'to ban' (*ḫrm*)[17] and which deals with a question essential to world order, the assurance of giving birth to children, has a verse similar to this figure; line 13 reads *[k]b!kbm ṯm. tpl. klbnt* 'there the stars fall like Storax(?)-trees'.[18] One of the figures leading to the falling of the leaves in Isa 34:4 is the rotting of the "host of heaven," which has a parallel in the figure previous to the Ugaritic figure just given: KTU 1.13, line 12: *lk prẓ pt* 'go and cut the sky to pieces'. Here and in Isaiah 34, a breakdown of order and the reestablishment of primordial-type chaos are being described.[19] The word *pt* is unlikely to be, as some have thought, a

12. On divine war, see the treatment of Sa-Moon Kang, *Divine War in the Old Testament and in the Ancient Near East* (BZAW 177; Berlin: de Gruyter, 1989), esp. the introduction, pp. 1–7. Scholars such as F. M. Cross, P. D. Miller, and M. Weinfeld, among others, have all made well-known contributions in this field.

13. J. Lust, "Isaiah 34 and the Ḥerem," in *The Book of Isaiah: Le Livre d'Isaïe* (ed. J. Vermeylen; BETL 81; Leuven: Leuven University Press, 1989) 285.

14. Stern, *The Biblical HEREM*, 189–90.

15. J. Muilenburg, "The Literary Character of Isaiah 34," *JBL* 59 (1940) 346.

16. Neal H. Walls (*The Goddess Anat in Ugaritic Myth* [SBLDS 135; Atlanta: Scholars Press, 1992] 139–44), in a recent review of the research, gives KTU 1.13 a minimalist reading and does not discuss the ban. His argument against Anat's being equated with a cow runs against the text, which twice clearly labels Anat a cow (lines 22, 29).

17. First correctly understood as such by J. C. de Moor, "An Incantation against Infertility," *UF* 12 (1980) 305–10. See further my *Biblical HEREM*, 5–8, 79–80.

18. *HALAT* 492 cites Arabic *lubnā*; cf. UT 51 V 73, *bt arẓm* // *bt lbnt*. Another possible support is Akk. *bit labbuni*, which according to CAD L 25b was a part of the Aššur temple and made of wood. Others: bricks, white petals (the latter would give an even closer parallel). The particular tree does not matter.

19. Muilenburg, "Literary Character," 345.

Ugaritic verb, for following two verbs it is much more likely to be the object of the verbs, as is also suggested by its biliteral character. Instead it should be construed as a loanword from the Egyptian *pet* = 'sky'. Its presence in this text may be attributable to direct Egyptian influence on this text, which is measurable in its adoption of a technique prominent in Egyptian incantations, the "mythical antecedent." By portraying a myth in which the desired outcome occurs, the sufferer hopes to participate magically in the good outcome portrayed in the incantation. The use of an Egyptian word here should not be too surprising since, as is well known, there are Egyptian names and words in the Hebrew Bible[20] even though biblical Israel did not have the same close mercantile and religious connections that Ugarit had with Egypt. The usage of *pt* here is a reflex of the incantation's device of identifying the sky-and-cow-goddess Hathor with Cow Anat, whose dwelling is in the "vault of heaven."[21] For Ugarit there is sufficient evidence of Egyptian influence, from an Egyptianized style of art to objects with hieroglyphics. One find from Ugarit, written in hieroglyphs, reports the marriage of Niqmad, king of Ugarit, to an Egyptian princess.[22] There are further indications of Egyptian influence on Ugarit in the portrayal of Anat in Ugarit.[23] In the case of the proposed loanword *pt*, the context favors Egyptian 'sky', for the words 'the stars fall like Storax-trees' follow it directly. This shows that both Isaiah 34 and KTU 1.13 project similar images of the dissolution of the cosmic order by means of the dissolution of stars and sky. KTU 1.13 deals with the ban, world order, and chaos in language surprisingly close though not identical to the language of Isaiah 34.[24]

These affinities with everything from KTU 1.13 and old biblical ban texts to the Mesha Inscription are highly significant indicators that the writer of Isaiah 34 was not using the term *ban* in a late, desacralized sense. The ancients used the term freely, without usually commenting directly on its underlying ideology. But in Isaiah 34 the connection between the sacral war

20. D. Redford, *Egypt, Canaan, and Israel in Ancient Times* (Princeton: Princeton University Press, 1992) 417–19. In addition to personal names, there are place-names, such as חרנפר 'Horus is good' (*HALAT* 1 355a), and other loanwords, such as חשמן, from an Egyptian word for a red dye (ibid., 362b), חרטם 'magician' (ibid., 353a), and many others.

21. See N. Wyatt, "The ʿAnat Stela from Ugarit and Its Ramifications," *UF* 16 (1984) 328–37, for more information on the "Egyptianization" of Anat at Ugarit.

22. See C. F. A. Schaeffer et al., "Matériaux pour l'étude des relations entre Ugarit et l'Égypte," in *Mission de Ras Shamra* (Ugaritica 3; Paris: Imprimerie Nationale, 1956) 7.164–226; A. Caquot and M. Sznycer, *Ugaritic Religion* (Leiden: Brill, 1980) plates 9d, 12, 17b, 23e.

23. See N. Wyatt, "The Stela of the Sealed God from Ugarit," *UF* 15 (1983) 271–77, esp. p. 272.

24. This result, which can hardly be accidental, vindicates de Moor's, Spronk's, and my readings against the readings of Walls and others.

ban and the ancient Near Eastern idea (stemming from Egypt) of the enemy as the forces of chaos is made explicit, as will be seen below. It should be noted that this view, which I propounded in my previous work on the ban, has profound implications for understanding the ethical substructure—or lack of it—of the ban. By assigning the enemy (internal or external) the role of chaos, the depersonalization of the enemy was complete, and the slaughter of men, women, and children could follow, as it did in Egypt, without the ban even being regarded as an ethical question. Obviously, the theory of the thing was not always carried out in practice. In 1 Samuel 15, for instance, Saul was unable to detach himself from his fellow monarch Agag, but the prophet Samuel dispatched the Amalekite king himself before YHWH.[25] Samuel was extremely concerned with the question of obeying YHWH, and to the ancients the idea that the ban was God's command was a powerful one that also inhibited ethical calculations of a modern sort. Of course such "modern" ethical considerations have not prevented the people of this century from repeatedly levying mass destruction on each other on a scale inconceivable to the people of biblical times, a destructiveness accomplished without any incentives derived from religious ideology. Saul's own reason for sparing Agag was not ethical rebellion against YHWH's edict as delivered by Samuel. It seems that he rather innocently considered that he had so sufficiently obeyed YHWH in his attack on Amalek, that sparing the life of one man, Agag, was an act of no consequence. He underestimated the rigor of the ban and hence misunderstood what the ban entailed. But the chapter illustrates that he was far from alone in that misunderstanding.

In her recent study of biblical warfare, S. Niditch in her twofold understanding of the ban places great emphasis on understanding the ban as sacrifice.[26] Oddly enough, she scarcely enters into the domain of Isaiah 34's connection with the ban, even though a superficial reading of part of the chapter might suggest that the author regarded the ban as a sacrifice. It is clear, however, that the use here of זבח is simply the product of a prophet's rhetoric, occasioned in the first instance by the word's assonance with the word for slaughter, טבח. That the word זבח, a sacrifice which, according to Baruch Levine, involved a "shared sacred meal,"[27] is a figure of speech is certain, for such a shared meal was the opposite of what transpired under the ban. However, even if the word is used figuratively, does not that in itself

25. S. Niditch (*War in the Hebrew Bible: A Study in the Ethics of Violence* [New York: Oxford University Press, 1993]) sees the language of the execution of Agag as pointing toward the ban as sacrifice. However, the chapter regards the people's attempt to sacrifice animals as wrongheaded (cf. 1 Sam 15:20–22). Actually, the chapter condemns the notion of ban as sacrifice (with relation to the cattle) and then utilizes the comparison with the ban as part of the book's sacrifice polemic against Saul.

26. Ibid., 28–37, 49–54, passim.

27. B. A. Levine, *Leviticus* (JPS Torah Commentary; Philadelphia: Jewish Publication Society, 1989) 6.

indicate that there was some basis in ideology or fact for interpreting the ban as a sacrifice? Both the ban and sacrifice shared the unusual property or quality of being sacralizations of death, so that even though the differences between the two in scale, circumstance, function, and underlying ideology were great, biblical writers were, quite naturally, sometimes drawn into making analogies between the two based on the degree of similarity that did exist. If we begin with the practical side, we can start with the obvious fact that the word זבח 'communal sacrifice'[28] is a part of the terminology of the sacrificial cult. It is also clear that the ban is not part of the sacrificial cult. It is treated apart from the sacrifices, and the lists or enumerations of sacrifices both within the Torah and without never mention the ban among the sacrifices. In addition, the ban is an act of war; a sacrifice is not.

Superficially, one might label the war ban a kind of sacrifice because of the necessity to devote people and plunder to God. But Num 21:1–3 illustrates how wrong this labeling is. In the sacrificial cult, it is one's own property that one is sacrificing. Using someone else's property would vitiate the act entirely. (Gen 22:13, where Abraham's sacrificial victim appears from nowhere, is hardly typical of institutionalized sacrifice.) Nor is there any guarantee that YHWH will immediately respond to a sacrifice in order to act on behalf of the bringer of sacrifice. Otherwise the God-concept would be reduced to a mechanistic farce and God's freedom of action would be abridged. The situation is totally different in the case of the war ban. There the Israelites are not giving up anything that is their own. Indeed, left to their own devices, as the Israelites in Num 21:1–3 clearly recognize, they would have no chance at conquering the cities and seizing the booty. Instead, the Israelites plead with God that if the deity will see fit to grant them success in battle, they will sanctify God by devoting to God the city (or cities) and their associated treasures. Israel did not sacrifice anything of its own, but instead gained something infinitely more precious than the physical objects they were devoting to destruction, namely, victory and continued survival in the face of their enemies. Indeed, in the ban there is no sacrifice of an individual's own property, for the whole essence of it is to render to God what has never been Israel's but has always been God's—the lives and property of the enemy.

The war ban is also an exchange in a way a sacrifice normally is not, and an uneven exchange, since what YHWH has to offer is immensely more valuable than what God receives in return (what God receives is the right to have God's property treated as sacrosanct; what God gives is victory and life). In contrast to sacrifice, in which nothing is guaranteed in return, in the war ban, God always assures the victory! There is no instance of the use of ban terminology when Israel (or Moab in the Mesha Inscription) lost to the foe, in contrast to the sacrifice in which the outcome was uncertain or in

28. *HALAT* 1 262.

which the sacrifice was simply an act of piety. Another aspect is raised by Lev 19:5, in which a category of sacrifice is to be performed "at a propitious time for you."[29] This terminology is never applied to the ban.

Another difference between the ban and sacrifice is that while sacrifice in biblical Israel and in most of the ancient Near East was a regular feature of the cultic life of the people, performed at particular sacred times, the war ban was an exceptional practice, irregularly performed, and only in extreme circumstances. Sacrifice could be and was regularized; the ban by its nature could not be regularized (the closest attempt to do so, in Joshua 10–11, fell completely flat and lacks any historical credibility). A still more crucial distinction between sacrifice and the ban is that sacrifice in Israel was an essential part of the celebration of sacred occasions. The ban, on the other hand, never ranked as a celebration. Even more significantly, in ancient Israel's conception of sacrifice, a miscarried offering (e.g., one offered at the wrong time according to Lev 19:5–8) is never treated as a matter of life and death for the perpetrator. In stark contrast, doom does impend with the ban not only for the perpetrator but for the community at large, as happened in the story of Achan's infringement of the ban in Joshua 7. This major distinction demonstrates that the ban possessed an entirely different dimension from sacrifice.

At a relatively early juncture, accounts of execution of the war ban cease altogether. From the biblical evidence, it is likely that Israel voluntarily ceased to employ the ban. Mesha's ban is not reported to have been returned in kind (see 2 Kings 3).[30] The laws of Deut 20:15–18 may have been designed with that end in mind. It took many more centuries for sacrifice to come to a halt in Judaism, and there is no question that it came to a halt only as a result of coercion. Jews have been praying for thousands of years for a return of the sacrifices, but they have yet to pray for a restoration of the ban. This reflects a genuine and ancient perception that the ban is of a different nature from sacrifice. The difference is marked. The prophets inveighed against the sacrificial cult (e.g., Amos 5:21–23, Jer 7:21–23) but not against the ban. The prophets perpetuated the ban in their imagery even when it had ceased to be.

By using the term *war ban* (pace Brekelmans), I emphasize that the ban in instances such as 1 Samuel 15 or Joshua 6 is manifestly an act of war. Sacrifice in the ancient Near East might take place at the start of wars or during wars, but in itself sacrifice was considered an act of religious devotion, not an act of war. Applying the term *sacrifice* to the war ban blurs a distinction that should be upheld. It is true that the tricky part for Israel came after the

29. For the translation, see the following verses. It is close to but perhaps slightly preferable to NJPSV 'so that it may be accepted on your behalf'.

30. On 2 Kings 3, see my "Of Kings and Moabites: History and Theology in 2 Kings 3 and the Moabite Inscription," *HUCA* 64 (1993) 1–14.

victory, when the spoils lay close at hand. The demand of ban certainly required discipline and renunciation at that point. But renunciation of something not Israel's but already God's (in other words, a renunciation of stealing from the divine as illustrated by Joshua 7) was not sacrifice but common sense for those who feared God. Indeed, for those who fear God, what is YHWH's should have little allure. YHWH displayed awesome power on behalf of Israel by wreaking havoc on the enemy, as at Jericho. But in return for this display of power, God made conditions: the city itself and its booty must be consecrated to God. The proponents of the ideology of the war ban saw a danger to the whole community if all Israel did not live up to its share of the bargain. Achan impinged on YHWH's sanctity by stealing certain items belonging to God, a dangerous thing to do. If one compares Achan to Uzzah (2 Sam 6:6–7), whom God struck dead for trying to right the Ark, one sees that Achan's offense was far more serious. The biblical conception of collective responsibility illustrated by Num 16:20–22 also came into play. Achan's family as well became included with Achan's fate. The family of a malpracticing sacrificer was never punished.

Joshua 7 has a good parallel in a letter from ancient Mari.[31] In good English it reads:

> *Obv.* At the time of the defeat of Larimnuma, whom the king slew and to A. . . . I spoke harshly to the "section chief" and his officers saying, "Whoever takes of the booty shall have eaten the *asakku*[32] of ^{d}Addu and ^{d}Shamash. He, two bronze containers . . . silver and gold. Outside correc[tness] (*ki-it*)-[*tim*]?[33] from the booty he has taken.
> *Rev.* Let them kill. . . . Have perished. This man according to the sacrilege of Addu and of Shamshi-Addu and of Yasmaḫ-Addu, my lord, the . . . of this man Ten shekels in silver or 15 gold grains.

31. See ARM 5 72 (treated in my *Biblical HEREM*, 149–50) for notes to the translation.

32. One of the pioneers in the study of the ban//*asakku* is A. Malamat, most recently in his book, *Mari and the Early Israelite Experience* (Oxford: Oxford University Press, 1989) 70–79. My critique of Malamat's approach in an earlier but similar formulation is found in *The Biblical HEREM*, 150–53. A more recent critique is found in M. Greenberg, "Is There a Parallel in the Mari Texts to the Biblical Banning of the (Spoils) of the Enemy?" *ErIsr* 24 (Malamat Volume; 1993) 49–53. One of his animadversions is that in the Mari text there is no banning of a city, with which the banning of booty is indissolubly connected in the Bible. We do not know what was done in this defeat, but the idea that the king was slain is promising. I think ARM 5 72, with its various differences from the biblical text, still reflects something of the same dynamic as Joshua 7, so that Malamat has rendered a service in presenting this text.

33. *Kittum seems* to be the logical restoration; I previously rendered it 'justice', but 'correctness' may fit the context better.

Looking at Joshua 7 in the context of this tantalizing Mari letter, we see that the concept of sacrifice is not in the picture.

For all these reasons, it should be clear that to apply the term *sacrifice* to the war ban is to mischaracterize it profoundly. To apply it is to say that Israel in its war ideology advocated or practiced mass human sacrifice. But mass killing in battle was never viewed as sacrifice in the ancient Near East—not in Egypt, not in Assyria, not among the Hittites.[34] Nor is there evidence that Israel looked at the ban as a mass-killing sacrifice that is not based on a misunderstanding. Some might try to use Deut 13:17, where the term כליל appears, as evidence. Israelite cities that go over to idolatry are treated as enemies dwelling in the heartland—and hence by a determination parallel to the laws of Deuteronomy 20, liable to the war ban. However, כליל appears not because the ban is a sacrifice but because the writer wished to use a graphic and powerful figure of speech, playing on the degree of similarity that did exist (see above) between the two disparate items. This is also true of זבח in Isa 34:5 and of the death of Agag in 1 Samuel 15.

The second of the two understandings that Susan Niditch applies to the ban is divine justice.[35] If her understanding were correct, one would expect plentiful examples of this readily accessible concept to be found in connection with the ban. Yet the term משפט 'justice, judgment' is found only once in a ban context (Isa 34:5), and here the meaning is clearly 'judgment', not 'justice'. This suggests that in this one instance, a biblical writer saw the application of the concept of judgment under the special circumstances of Isaiah 34, with God's acting as direct agent of the ban in an oracle against Edom. So the one usage of משפט scarcely begins to imply that divine justice is the overarching explanation for much of the usage of the ban. The verb שפט 'to judge' never arises in connection with the ban, as one would expect if this were the correct explanation of the ban. We would also expect to see many phrases such as "the ban of My justice" or "My just ban" or an idiom "the ban I judged," but instead there is silence. It is not true that the argument from silence is always weak. Sometimes, as here, silence speaks volumes. The fertile and copious use of the substantive משפט in the Bible suggests that its use in connection with the ban would hardly be lacking if justice were a fundamental conceptual underpinning of the ban. Verbs intimately associated with the ban in both the Mesha Inscription and biblical texts form the semantic field from which it is possible to draw basic conclusions about the meaning of the ban in ancient Israel (according to accepted linguistic practice). By this measure, the ban, in both the Mesha

34. On Hittite warfare, see among others, J. G. MacQueen, *The Hittites and Their Contemporaries in Asia Minor* (Boulder, Colo.: Westview, 1975) 92–111; S. Lloyd, *Early Highland Peoples of Anatolia* (New York: McGraw-Hill, 1967) 68–69.

35. Niditch, *War in the Hebrew Bible*, 56–77 et passim. This second understanding is not independent but is interconnected with the first.

Inscription[36] and biblical texts, is most intimately associated with a group of verbs dealing with battle, conquest, and possession of land.[37] The sacred dimension of the ban (which is of course etymological), the bringing into holiness, is married to the focus on killing the enemy and acquiring land. This leads one to the conclusion that the ban is an attempt to create world order for Israel—a sacred space—out of the forces that oppose it, which are of a chaotic character by definition. The enemies, if they have their way, will not allow Israel to function in its natural order. If the ban were explicable in such basic and accessible biblical concepts as sacrifice and justice, one must wonder why confusion about the ban ever arose (1 Samuel 15 and, to some extent, Joshua 7), or why D and Dtr had to go to such lengths to define it. The only novel ingredient in the Deuteronomic conquest message is the ban. We can illustrate this with Deut 7:1–11, which is basically a recapitulation of Exod 33:5–16. Both expound similar religious ideologies using, at times, identical language; only Deuteronomy 7 throws in the ban (cf. Numbers 21 versus Deuteronomy 2–3). This seems to indicate that, rather late in the day, Israel was still making an ideological adjustment to the ban.

The confusion regarding correct practice of the ban in some of the earliest ban texts and its in-and-out role in Torah texts are perhaps marks of imperfect assimilation of an originally foreign practice. The extra-Israelite origin of the ban is assured by the combination of three texts: the text of Iddi(n)-Sin of Simurrum,[38] an early text that already has the ban concept fully fleshed out; even more so, by Ugaritic text KTU 1.13, in which, as we have seen, the goddess Anat is beseeched to execute the ban;[39] and of course the Mesha Inscription,[40] which in its ban to Ashtar- or Ishtar-Kemosh by itself

36. It was study of the Mesha Inscription that first led me to the idea of the ban as bringing world order out of chaos. The treatment of the enemy and the enemy god is similar to the way of the Egyptians, who, as is well known, saw the enemy as the forces of chaos—as did the Assyrians according to J. J. Glassner, "Sargon, 'roi de combat,'" *RA* 79 (1985) 125–26. Mesha's building activities were thus bringing order out of chaos, and this jibes with ancient Near Eastern mythic conceptualizations, such as the building of Baal's house (see my *Biblical HEREM*, 41–42). This receives additional support from Niditch (*War in the Hebrew Bible*, 38), when she says, "After . . . the battle, and the victory, comes a procession, often a palace or house-building, which in ancient Near Eastern creation texts is synonymous with the defeat of chaos and the creation of the world. . . ."

37. Stern, *The Biblical HEREM*, 226.

38. Ibid., 39–40, 78–79.

39. See J. C. de Moor, "An Incantation against Infertility (KTU 1.13)," *UF* 12 (1980) 305–10; Stern, *The Biblical HEREM*, 5–8, 79–80.

40. Niditch (*War and the Hebrew Bible*, 47) implies that my belief in the foreign origin of the ban is the result of my preconceptions about the nature of Israel's God. This is not so. The extrabiblical evidence is massive. C. H. W. Brekelmans was also of the opinion that the ban's origins were pre-Israelite. See him on origins in *De ḥerem in het Oude Testament* (Nijmegen: Centrale Drukkerij, 1959) 149–52.

is powerfully suggestive. To this we may add massive comparative evidence of ban-like practices in various places and times.[41]

We turn now to the second instance of the ban:

> My sword has drunk (blood) unto heaven. See, it will descend on Edom,[42] on the people of my ban, for judgment. (Isa 34:5)[43]

The use of the verb *rwh* in close proximity to the ban corresponds to a similar situation in the Mesha Inscription, a similarity the importance of which is hard to overstate, since the application of the ban in the Mesha Inscription is preceded by something called *ryt*. C. H. W. Brekelmans was the first to connect Moabite *ryt* with the *rwh* of Isa 34:5.[44] This co-incidence is not likely to be a coincidence and argues once more against the late secular use of the ban in Isaiah 34. Indeed, it is no more likely to be secular than 1 Kgs 20:42, which employs the expression "man of my ban," meaning "the man I set apart," that is, "consecrated for destruction." The most powerful argument for the translation "people of my ban" is that the ban here is followed by the extended exposition of chaos. Of the theories of ban that have been advanced, this fits only one: only my theory makes the connection between the ban and chaos. Further, the arguments that have been made above showing that the verb form of the ban is the sacral war ban also apply to Isa 34:5. The effect of משפט 'justice' or 'judgment' is to emphasize the unique character of Edom—that, because it was regarded a special case among the nations by many of the prophets, it was subject to the ban as a special, and extremely dire, form of judgment. Not even Amalek was described in these terms. One of the interesting things about the prophet's dual use of the ban is that it is so true to the earliest understandings of the war ban, yet it is essentially a late, figurative expression of the rage of a prophet at Edom. One may infer from the ban language of the chapter and the use of משפט, both of which really require a concrete object and not a symbolic one, that the prophet is expressing anger—or rather fury—at the concrete behavior of a concrete

41. Niditch, *War in the Hebrew Bible*, 5–17, 67–88.

42. As others have observed, enemy peoples were considered to embody the forces of chaos, not only in ancient Egypt. The kingdom of the Nile had its own individual concept of chaos, which has been thoroughly documented by E. Hornung, *Conceptions of God in Ancient Egypt: The One and the Many* (Ithaca, N.Y.: Cornell University Press, 1982), in the chapter on the "Non-existent." For Israel see, among others, P. Bordreuil, "Michée 4:11–13 et ses parallèles ougaritiques," *Sem* 21 (1971) 25: "Mot, personnification des forces du chaos; dans l'A.T. ces dernières figurent souvent les ennemis du peuple." J. J. M. Roberts, *Nahum, Habakkuk, and Zephaniah: A Commentary* (OTL; Louisville: Westminster, 1991) 81. Speaking of Hab 3:3–15, Robert says, "This vision of Yahweh's coming intervention against the powers of chaos, embodied at the moment in the Babylonians. . . ."

43. Some translate 'his *ḥérem*', but this is not necessary.

44. Brekelmans, *De ḥerem*, 31.

Edom. It is not a symbolic usage of the word *Edom*, as Y. Hoffman concludes in a thoughtful analysis of prophetic oracles against Edom.[45]

In the end it is the imagery that Isaiah 34 employs that makes it a key text for understanding the biblical view of the ban. Certainly, the fact that the author of Isaiah 34 chose to make explicit the connection of chaos with the ban is fortunate for those interested in understanding what the Israelite ban was. The use of language to depict chaos is varied and in some instances unique.[46]

It should not be thought that the language of chaos is not found in other oracles against the nations. One finds, for example, the language of chaos creeping into the oracles of Ezekiel in some places.[47] In the oracle against Tyre in Ezek 26:2b–5, there are repeated references to disorder or chaos:

> Aha, the gates of the people are broken,
> They have opened to me;
> I will take my fill of the devastation.

This verse refers to chaos in the form of war, for the ban reflects the fact that war is a human brand of chaos. The shattered city gates allude to the fact that the cities referred to have lost the ability to preserve order. Chaos in the form of the enemy is about to enter, bringing devastation, an extreme form of chaos. In Ezek 26:3, 5, Ezekiel refers repeatedly to the sea as a destructive force; the sea is an image of chaos in the ancient Near East. In v. 4, the text uses the image of a "bare rock"—an image in which all order has been wiped out by the forces of chaos (the sea), and chaos is therefore regnant. Examples in Ezekiel's oracles against the nations could be multiplied. In comparison to Isaiah 34, however, the imagery of disorder/chaos is muted in Ezekiel, and it is thus no coincidence that Ezekiel never invokes the ban in his oracles against the nations.

In Isaiah 34 the language of chaos is anything but muted. We have already analyzed the imagery of the vanishing stars, which emblemize the order of the gods or of God. Beginning with v. 9, the text launches into a full-scale description of the chaos inflicted on Edom through the destruction unleashed against Edom by God's ban. It begins with a description of general ruination, although we can see that the established order of nature is being turned on its head:

45. Y. Hoffman, "Edom as the Symbol of Wickedness in the Prophetic Literature," in *Bible and Jewish History* (ed. B. Uffenheimer; Tel Aviv: Tel Aviv University, Faculty of Humanities, 1971) [Heb.]. See her rationale and its applications, pp. 76–79.

46. D. G. Johnson, *From Chaos to Restoration: An Integrative Reading of Isaiah 24–27* (JSOTSup 61; Sheffield: Sheffield Academic Press, 1988) 118. Johnson points out that *nbl* in *Qal* is used nine times in the book of Isaiah and twice in other prophets but that in its application to the stars in Isaiah 34, it is unique.

47. On these prophecies, see B. Gosse, "Ezéchiel 35–6, 1–15 et Ezéchiel 6: La désolation de la montagne de Seir et le renouveau des montagnes d'Israël," *RB* 96 (1989) 511–17.

Her wadis will be turned to pitch, her dirt [will be turned] to brimstone, and her earth will become burning pitch. Day and night it will not be extinguished. Its smoke will go up forever—from generation to generation. It will be a perpetual ruin, with none to pass [it] by. (Isa 34:9–10)

Now the full-scale description of chaos erupts, replete with wonderful images of disorder. Each verse has one or two images of chaos. Although in some cases the images employed would not by themselves be explicable as images of chaos, in the context of the chapter this is how they must be interpreted, whether we take the image of night birds hovering over ruination, thistles growing where the king, the principal of order, once resided, or the image of the "Non-Kingdom," it is clear that a prophet is using all of his inventiveness to depict chaos:

The owl[48] and the jackdaw shall take possession of it, the night hawk and the raven shall dwell in it. He shall stretch upon it a measuring line of chaos, and weights of emptiness. Satyrs shall dwell there and its nobles shall cease to exist.[49] They will call it a Non-Kingdom that isn't there; its leaders will be void. Thistles will sprout in its massive kingly residences, weeds and thorn bushes. It shall become a habitation of jackals, and a settlement for unclean birds (ostriches). Demons shall meet with goblins, and a goat demon shall call to his fellow; even there Lilith shall find repose, and procure a resting-place for herself. There the small serpent shall make her nest and escape [her enemies] and hatch [eggs] and brood in the shadows. Also there birds of prey will be gathered each to its fellow. (Isa 34:11–15)

This is an ingenious evocation of chaos-imageries, all to fall on Edom with YHWH's ban. The fomenters of chaos in Israel are to have it fall on themselves, all by the will of YHWH and the order YHWH promulgates for Israel (Isa 34:16–17). The picture of chaos for Edom is part of the order YHWH fosters for Israel. In Isa 34:16 there is a reaching out, an ordering. The phrase "not one of them is missing" may be a reference to Isa 40:26, in which the prophet uses much the same wording with the stars to punctuate his vision of God's order. This connection is strengthened by the fact that the prophet of Isaiah 34 begins with the destruction of the stars to portray the collapse of order. The "measuring line of chaos" found in v. 11 is contrasted with the "eternal line of YHWH" (v. 17), which, in spelling eternal doom for Edom also implies that the world order of Israel is brought about by acts of the Divine Warrior against Edom.

The last words of the chapter are ironic. Speaking of the demons and other creatures of chaos that have gathered, YHWH says that they shall possess [the land] and dwell in it. This is a part of the semantic domain, the

48. The identity of some of the birds mentioned here is dubious. But they are birds of the night, birds that haunt ruins. For convenience, I follow J. L. McKenzie's nomenclature in *Second Isaiah* (AB 20; Garden City, N.Y.: Doubleday, 1968) 4. The image of the nightbirds in possession is one of reverting to chaos.

49. Following McKenzie (ibid., 4), as he restores the MT from the LXX.

language associated with the ban to which I referred above—the language dealing with battle, conquest, and possession of land that provides the context through which any understanding of the ban must be filtered. Its presence at the end of the chapter binds the ban with the depiction of chaos and confirms that the parts of the chapter are purposefully linked. The ban and chaos are in tandem for a reason.

Chapter 35, by either authorial intent or redaction, begins with a ringing affirmation of Israel's world order. The result: the enemy's chaos is Israel's order. In Isaiah 35, Israel takes advantage of the chaos YHWH inflicts on Edom to recover from its own exposure to chaos and to celebrate the order that was endangered by the encroachment of Edom. The two chapters, however they were put together, reflect an understanding of the ban. The understanding of the ban in relation to chaos and order has a strong footing in other texts, such as the Mesha Inscription, Joshua 6,[50] 1 Samuel 15, and KTU 1.13, but in Isaiah 34 we have it in its most fully realized and fleshed-out form.

Postscript. One of the more intriguing open questions concerning the ban is: why did Assyria never adopt some version of it, seeing that so many of the characteristics of its holy war were held in common with Israel?[51] One answer may be that Assyria was not generally in the precarious position of the small states of ancient Canaan. Another is that the character of the god Aššur was not strong enough for the likes of the ban. Moreover, the Assyrian divinely-commanded practice of deportation was, in effect, a mild version of the ban. Alongside these considerations is the one raised by W. G. Lambert, who once wrote an interesting essay on the contrast between Mesopotamian civilization and Israel. He concludes his essay, "the gods had taught all the arts of civilization at the beginning, and nothing further was to be expected."[52]

Since the ban was not the norm of ancient Mesopotamian history, it was not to be expected that the gods would suddenly "fix the fates" in that direction, and the Assyrians would suddenly adopt it either on their own or from the west. This may sound too simple, but it reflects a difference, of which the ban is only one facet, in the fundamental fabric of the Mesopotamian and Israelite cultures.

50. This is why Jericho is depicted as containing all the Canaanite nations. They represent the chaos that Joshua is to dispel with the ban.

51. See for example B. Oded, "'The Command of the God' as a Reason for Going to War in the Assyrian Royal Inscriptions," *Ah, Assyria . . . : Studies in Assyrian History and Ancient Near Eastern Historiography Presented to Hayim Tadmor* (ed. M. Cogan and I. Ephʿal; ScrHier 33; Jerusalem: Magnes, 1991) 223–30, esp. p. 225.

52. W. G. Lambert, "Destiny and Divine Intervention in Babylon and Israel," in *The Witness of Tradition* (ed. M. A. Beek et al.; Leiden: Brill, 1972) 72.

"The Appointed Time Has Not Yet Arrived": The Historical Background of Haggai 1:2

Hayim Tadmor
The Hebrew University of Jerusalem

Why was the restoration of the Second Temple not carried out as sanctioned by Cyrus in his Edict to the Jews but delayed until the early years of Darius I? This problem already concerned the ancient chronicler in Ezra 4, who compiled his account well over a century after the events. He attributed the delay to the enmity of the "adversaries of Judah and Benjamin" (vv. 1–5), usually taken as an archaistic reference to those who would later be known as the Samaritans.[1]

Modern scholars rightly stress the dismal economic conditions in Judah, which had been hit by a prolonged drought (Hag 1:6, 10–11), as the main reason for the failure to build the Temple during the reigns of Cyrus and Cambyses.[2] Another possible reason, of an entirely different nature, was suggested by E. J. Bickerman:[3] the Jews, or some of them, were unwilling to

Author's note: This study was prepared during my stay in Philadelphia as a Fellow of the Annenberg Research Institute in the spring of 1993. It is a pleasure to dedicate it to Baruch Levine as a token of long-standing friendship.

1. A. Alt, "Die Rolle Samarias bei der Entstehung des Judentums," *Kleine Schriften zur Geschichte des Volkes Israel* (Munich: Beck, 1953) 2.321–22; P. R. Ackroyd, *Exile and Restoration* (London: SCM, 1968) 149–51; H. G. M. Williamson, *Ezra, Nehemiah* (WBC 16; Waco, Tex.: Word, 1985) 49–50.

2. E.g., M. Noth, *The History of Israel* (London: Black, 1958) 309; and recently Sara Japhet, "The Restoration of the Temple," in *Ah, Assyria . . . : Studies in Assyrian History and Ancient Near Eastern Historiography Presented to Hayim Tadmor* (ed. M. Cogan and I. Ephʿal; ScrHier 33; Jerusalem: Magnes, 1991) 178–79.

3. E. J. Bickerman, "The Edict of Cyrus," *JBL* 65 (1946) 267; updated and revised in *Studies in Jewish and Christian History* (Leiden: Brill, 1976) 1.101–3. Bickerman's analysis of the Hebrew text of the Edict of Cyrus should be supplemented by the critical

acknowledge a Gentile king as the restorer of the Temple. Only a descendant of David would be worthy of that honor. The compromise eventually reached, under Darius I, was that the rebuilding of the Temple was entrusted to Zerubbabel, governor of Judea, who was a Davidide prince. However, another source pertaining to our problem has not been properly evaluated. It is the popular slogan quoted at the outset of Haggai's prophetic mission, one of the few instances in the Bible where the *vox populi* is quoted verbatim.[4] The following inquiry seeks to examine the message of this slogan and its historical context.[5]

In the second year of Darius I, king of Persia, on the first day of the month of Elul, the prophet Haggai passionately called upon the people of Judah to begin rebuilding the Temple of Yahweh in Jerusalem, which—as he claimed—at the time still lay in ruins. Addressing the leadership, Zerubbabel the governor of Judah and Joshua the high priest, he began by quoting a popular slogan, which he proceeded vigorously to contest (Hag 1:2): "These people say, 'The appointed time has not (yet) arrived'" (*lō᾽ ʿet-bō᾽*).

In the next clause, the ancient author explains: the people's slogan refers to "the appointed time—for the rebuilding of the house of the Lord."[6] The message encoded in the slogan is quite clear: the (appointed) time has not

---

remarks of Baruch Levine, "Comparative Perspective of Jewish and Christian History," *JAOS* 99 (1979) 84.

4. For similar slogans see M. Greenberg, "The Citations in the Book of Ezekiel as a Background to the Prophecies," *Beth Miqra* 50 (1972) 273–78 [Heb.]. See also H. Tadmor, "The Origins of Israel as Seen in the Exilic and Post-Exilic Ages," in *Le origine di Israele* (Rome: Academia Nazionale dei Lincei, 1987) 15–17.

5. See, in brief, H. Tadmor, in *Cambridge Ancient History*, vol. 6: *Macedon 401–301 B.C.* (2d ed.; ed. D. M. Lewis et al.; Cambridge: Cambridge University Press, 1994) 266–69.

6. Modern translations and commentaries take this explanatory clause as part of the people's slogan, thus arriving at a text that seems redundant and in need of emendation. The ICC on Haggai (H. G. Mitchell, *A Critical and Exegetical Commentary on Haggai and Zechariah* [ICC; Edinburgh: T. & T. Clark, 1912] 51) suggests three possibilities: in one, the consonants of the text are retained, but the vocalization is changed, yielding *bā᾽* instead of *bō᾽* (thus the KJV); or *ʿet bō᾽* is changed to *ʿattâ bā᾽*, producing 'not now is the time come'. Another possible emendation involves consonantal changes, reading: *lō᾽ ʿôd bā᾽ ʿet* or *lō᾽ ʿattâ bā᾽ ʿet*. The third possibility is to delete the first *ʿet* and substitute *bā᾽* for *bō᾽*. This method essentially follows the ancient versions: the Septuagint has *ouk heiken ho kairos*, which, when retroverted to Hebrew, would be *lô᾽ bā᾽ ʿēt*, and the Vulgate too has *nondum venit tempus domus domini aedificandae*. On the other hand, if the Masoretic reading, *lō᾽ ʿet bō᾽*, is retained, *bō᾽* can be taken either as an infinitive construct, like *ʿēt sĕpôd* or *ʿēt rĕkôd* in Qoh 3:4, or as an infinitive absolute, a form used here just a few verses later: *᾽ākôl . . . lābôš . . . šātô* . . . (Hag 1:6). In their recent commentary, C. L. Meyers and E. M. Meyers do not emend the text but view the repetition of *ʿēt* as a rhetorical device: *Haggai, Zechariah 1–8* (AB 25B; Garden City, N.Y.: Doubleday, 1987) 19–20.

yet arrived for the Temple to be rebuilt. From the formal-communicative point of view, the slogan consists of three monosyllabic words, each possessing one long vowel (ō, ē, ō). The staccato of the monosyllabic structure is compensated by the elongation of the vowel, thus conveying an effect of continuity (compare the modern slogan, "Nó móre wár"). It is, indeed, characteristic of populist slogans to be as short and catchy as possible. They usually are composed metrically and sometimes include rhyme, alliteration, or verbal play. One could even argue that the staccato form and rhythm may explain the irregular use of the verb *bōʾ* in the infinitive.

Turning our attention to the message itself, we find that the very same words, *ʿet* and *bōʾ*, are used in a prose oracle of Jeremiah in reference to Nebuchadnezzar, king of Babylon (Jer 27:6–7):

> I herewith deliver all these lands to my servant King Nebuchadnezzar of Babylon. . . . all nations shall serve him, his son and his grandson—until the appointed time of his own land comes (*ʿad bōʾ ʿēt ʾarṣô gam hûʾ*).[7]

Another oracle of Jeremiah makes it explicit that "the appointed time" is seventy years (Jer 25:11–12):

> And those nations shall serve the king of Babylon for seventy years. When the seventy years are over, I will punish the king of Babylon and that nation and the land for their sins . . . and I will make it a desolation for all time.[8]

The period of seventy years as a fixed time-span for a "period of divine wrath," frequently discussed in scholarly literature,[9] seems to represent the ideal life-span of a person: "The span of our life is seventy years or, 'given the strength', eighty years" (Ps 90:10).

Taking Jer 27:6–7 and 25:11–12 together, "seventy years" would also be the equivalent of three generations: ". . . him, his son, and his grandson." The same time-span is also mentioned in Isa 23:15, in reference to Tyre: "Tyre shall remain forgotten for seventy years," here explicitly qualified as "the lifetime of one king."[10]

7. This verse, among others, is missing in the LXX. The longer and explanatory MT version of this oracle was probably compiled before 560, when Neriglissar seized the throne from Nebuchadnezzar's son (J. Bright, *Jeremiah* [AB 25; Garden City, N.Y.: Doubleday, 1965] 200). For a different opinion, cf. E. Tov, "Exegetical Notes on the Hebrew Vorlage of the LXX of Jeremiah 27(34)," *ZAW* 91 (1979) 85; and most recently, W. McKane, *Jeremiah* (ICC; Edinburgh: T. & T. Clark, 1996) 2.689–92.

8. Bright, *Jeremiah*, 160–63, 208–9; M. Weinfeld, *Deuteronomy and the Deuteronomic School* (Oxford: Clarendon, 1972; repr., Winona Lake, Ind.: Eisenbrauns, 1992) 143–46.

9. E.g., P. R. Ackroyd, "Two Old Testament Historical Problems of the Early Persian Period," *JNES* 17 (1958) 23–27; M. Fishbane, "Revelation and Tradition: Aspects of Inner-Biblical Exegesis," *JBL* 99 (1980) 355–58; V. A. Hurowitz, *I Have Built You an Exalted House* (JSOTSup 115; Sheffield: Sheffield Academic Press, 1992) 140–43.

10. Cf. Weinfeld, *Deuteronomy*, 144.

It was noted long ago that the best parallel to the pattern of seventy years of divine wrath appears in the inscriptions of the Assyrian king Esarhaddon, describing the restoration of Babylon, which had been destroyed by his father, Sennacherib.[11] The text relates that Marduk, the god of Babylon, had become so enraged by the social and cultic misdeeds committed by the Babylonians that he resolved to punish his people and destroy his city and his temple, Esagila. He decreed seventy years of desolation for Babylon, but then, out of compassion for the city, regretted this decision and renounced the decree by reversing the order of the signs, thereby turning the seventy (𒁹𒌋) into eleven (𒌋𒁹) years.[12]

On another occasion in Assyro-Babylonian history, Marduk is said to have abandoned Babylon and moved his abode to Assyria, where he stayed for twenty-one years. When the predestined time of reconciliation[13] arrived, he became appeased and gladly returned to his sacred city. This tradition, appearing in the autobiographical inscription of Nabonidus,[14] refers to Marduk's exile in Assyria from 689, when Babylon was destroyed by Sennacherib, to 668, when Marduk's statue was restored to Esagila, in the first year of Sennacherib's grandson Shamash-shum-ukin.[15]

In Jeremiah's prophecy of seventy years, the divine reconciliation also presupposes the destruction of Babylon, once the period of affliction is terminated. Yahweh will turn against Nebuchadnezzar, Babylon will be ruined,

11. D. D. Luckenbill, "The Black Stone of Esarhaddon," *AJSL* 41 (1924–25) 166–67; R. Borger, "An Additional Remark on P. R. Ackroyd *JNES* XVII, 23–27," *JNES* 18 (1959) 74.

12. R. Borger, *Die Inschriften Asarhaddons Königs von Assyrien* (AfO Beiheft 9; Graz, 1956) 15, episode 10; H. Hirsch, "*Eliš ana šapliš ušbalkit*," *AfO* 21 (1966) 34. On the reversal of the numerals, see P.-A. Beaulieu, "An Excerpt from a Menology with Reverse Writing," *Acta Sumerologica* 17 (1995) 5. Babylon fell in the winter of 689, and the destruction followed immediately. The eleventh year of desolation (by inclusive counting) was 679—Esarhaddon's second regnal year. The restoration work in Babylon must have started that year. The earliest economic document of Esarhaddon from Babylon is dated 14–X–2 (G. Frame, *Babylonia 689–627* B.C. [Leiden: Nederlands Historisch-Archaeologisch Instituut, 1992] 68 n. 25). The colophon in the Babylon Inscriptions of Esarhaddon (Borger, *Die Inschriften Asarhaddons* 25), phrased in the Babylonian manner, "Accession Year of Esarhaddon King of Assyria," cannot be taken literally; see M. Cogan, "Omens and Ideology in the Babylon Inscriptions of Esarhaddon," in *History, Historiography and Interpretation* (ed. H. Tadmor and M. Weinfeld; Jerusalem: Magnes, 1983) 85–87; Frame, *Babylonia*, 67 and n. 18.

13. See the lexical evidence in CAD A/1 99, s.v. *adannu kašādu*, which corresponds semantically to *ʿēt bōʾ*, and CAD S 103, s.v. *salīmu rašû*: 'to have mercy, to grant reconciliation'.

14. S. Langdon, *Die neubabylonischen Königsinschriften* (Vorderasiatische Bibliothek 4; Leipzig: Hinrichs, 1912) 270, col. I 23–34 (= A. L. Oppenheim, "Babylonian and Assyrian Historical Texts," in *ANET*, 309).

15. Frame, *Babylonia*, 104–5.

and it will become desolate foreover (Jer 25:12–13). The same idea, formulated somewhat differently, recurs in Jeremiah's letter to the exiles after the deportation of King Jehoiachin (Jer 29:10):

> When Babylon's seventy years are over, I will take note of you, and I will fulfill to you any promise of favor to bring you back to this place.

But from what point in the history of Judah was the period of seventy years understood to begin? If the starting point, as indicated in Jer 25:1, was the fourth year of Jehoiakim, when Judah fell under the dominion of Nebuchadnezzar (604),[16] the seventy years would have terminated in 534, several years after the conquest of Babylon by Cyrus (539). This understanding of Jeremiah's prophecy is echoed in Ezra 1:1, the editorial introduction of Cyrus's edict.[17]

In the second year of Darius I, at the time when Haggai contested the popular slogan *lōʾ ʿet bōʾ*, the notion of seventy years of divine wrath acquired a new dimension. It was now perceived as relating not to the duration of Babylonian dominion but rather to the duration of the Judeans' exile: the latter could have been counted either from Jehoiachin's deportation to Babylon (598) or, more likely, from the destruction of the Temple (586). This understanding seems to be implicit in the cry of the Angel of the Lord in the first vision of Zechariah (1:12):

> O Lord of Hosts! How long will You withhold mercy from Jerusalem and the towns of Judah, with which You have been angry these seventy years?

The plea "how long" presupposes that the period of seventy years has already been completed.

Haggai does not mention the period of divine wrath, but its binding force is implicit in the popular slogan. This slogan reflected the "orthodox" interpretation. Its adherents, sons and grandsons of those who had witnessed the destruction, in accordance with Jeremiah's prophecies of doom, insisted on taking literally Jeremiah's other prophecy: only when the seventy years, beginning with the destruction of 586, have come to a close should the rebuilding of the Temple begin. Zerubbabel, the governor, must have sided with Haggai, who insisted that the work of rebuilding should start immediately. It would seem that a compromise was reached between the two conflicting views. Though the inaugural ceremony,[18] with Zerubbabel laying the foundations (Zech 4:7–10), took place in Kislev of the second year of Darius

16. H. Tadmor, "Chronology of the Last Kings of Judah," *JNES* 15 (1956) 228; see recently N. Naʾaman, "Nebuchadnezzar's Campaign in Year 603 B.C.E.," *Biblische Notizen* 62 (1992) 41–44, with bibliography.

17. On this verse, see the comments of Levine, "Comparative Perspectives," 84.

18. On this ceremony and its Mesopotamian parallels, see B. Halpern, "The Ritual Background of Zechariah's Temple Song," *CBQ* 40 (1978) 167–81; and Meyers and Meyers, *Haggai, Zechariah 1–8*, 246–48, 253–55.

(Hag 2:18), the work was completed, according to Ezra 6:15, only in Adar of the sixth year, March 515 according to the Babylonian reckoning—that is, six months after the termination of the seventy-year period. One is tempted, therefore, to suggest that the builders paced the progress of construction so as to complete their work just when the seventy years had elapsed, thereby staving off the risk involved in completing the work before the appointed time.[19]

In referring to Zerubbabel, the Persian governor and also a Davidide prince, as the man appointed to restore the Temple, Haggai and Zechariah were also envisaging the restoration of the Davidic monarchy. Zech 6:12–13 speaks of "a man called the Shoot (*ṣemaḥ*),"[20] who "shall build the Temple of the Lord," "shall assume majesty (*hōd*), and shall sit on his throne and rule." Haggai's message is even more extreme. In an oracle addressed to Zerubbabel dated to 24 Kislev, in the second year of Darius, he speaks of the election of the Davidide prince together with the fall of "the kingdoms of the nations"—that is, of the Persian Empire (2:21–23):

> I am going to shake the heavens and the earth. And I will overthrow the thrones of kingdoms and destroy the might of the kingdoms of the nations. I will overturn chariots and their drivers. Horses and their riders shall fall, each

19. Hurowitz, *Exalted House*, 142. The next stage in the transformation of the notion "seventy years of wrath" comes in 2 Chr 36:21. According to this late midrash, the king of Babylon destroyed the Temple and exiled the people of Judah "in fulfillment of the word of the Lord spoken by Jeremiah, until the land has made up for its sabbaths; as long as it lay desolate it kept sabbath, till seventy years were completed." Here, two passages of different origin have been combined: Jer 25:11–12, and Lev 26:34–35 (see S. Japhet, *I and II Chronicles* [OTL; Louisville: Westminster/John Knox, 1993] 1075–76). Two lexical comments on v. 21 are in order: (a) B. Levine noted that "in certain contexts, the verb *rṣh* means 'to expiate, make up'." According to Levine, the passive form *nirṣāh* reflects this meaning in Isa 40:2: "that her iniquity is expiated" (*Leviticus* [JPS Torah Commentary; Philadelphia: Jewish Publication Society, 1989] 189). (b) There is a striking similarity between the phrase *kol yĕmê hoššammâ* 'throughout the time that it lay desolate' in Chronicles and Leviticus and the Akkadian phrase: *minūt nidūtiša* in Esarhaddon's text referring to Babylon, above, n. 11: "(Marduk had written '70 years') as the number (of years) for it to lie desolate/uninhabited" (cf. CAD N/2 212).

20. See S. Mowinckel, *He That Cometh* (Oxford: Blackwell, 1956) 160–64; J. Liver, *The House of David from the Fall of the Kingdom of Judah to the Fall of the Second Commonwealth* (Jerusalem: Magnes, 1959) 97–103 [Heb.]; Meyers and Meyers, *Haggai, Zechariah 1–8*, 202–3, 355. *Ṣemaḥ* harks back to the *ṣemaḥ ṣaddîq/ṣemaḥ ṣĕdāqâ* of Jer 23:5 and 33:15, and also to the *ḥōṭer* ('shoot' of Jesse) of Isa 11:1. It may also allude to Zerubbabel's name, *Zer-Bābilî* 'the seed of Babylon'. Compare similar epithets of Assyrian and Babylonian kings: "precious scion (*pirʾû*) of Baltil (= Ashur)"; "seed (*zĕru*) of kingship": M.-J. Seux, *Épithètes royales akkadiennes et sumériennes* (Paris: Letouzey et Ané, 1967) 225–26; 375–76. See also W. G. Lambert, "The Seed of Kingship," in *La Palais et la Royauté* (ed. P. Garelli; Paris: Geuthner, 1974) 427–40.

> by the sword of his fellow. On that day—declares the Lord of Hosts—I will take you, O my servant Zerubbabel son of Shealtiel—declares the Lord—and make you as a signet, for I have chosen you.

The hope for the restoration of the Davidic dynasty is understandable when seen against the background of the shock waves that spread throughout the Persian Empire following Darius's accession to the throne. In several major provinces that did not accept Darius's legitimacy as the sovereign, the insurgents called for the restoration of the local dynasties: Nebuchadnezzar's in Babylonia, Hshathrita's in Media, and Cyrus's in Persia.[21] Judah and the entire satrapy of Trans-Euphrates seem not to have participated in these uprisings, remaining loyal to Darius.

These events bring us to our last point: the question of chronology. The oracles of Haggai and Zechariah concerning the restoration of the Temple are dated the second year of Darius. It has generally been accepted[22] that these dates reflect the Babylonian system of reckoning, used by the Persian administration throughout the western provinces. Year 2 of Darius, according to this reckoning, was counted from Spring 520 to Spring 519.[23] However, by that time, the rebellions had been quelled mercilessly. A year after peace had already been restored throughout the empire, it seems unlikely that the Judean prophets would have encouraged Zerubbabel in hopes that, if they were to materialize, would only mean a belated uprising doomed from its inception to fail.[24]

21. A. T. Olmstead, *History of the Persian Empire* (Chicago: University of Chicago Press, 1948) 107–10; M. A. Dandamayev, *Persien unter den ersten Achämeniden* (Wiesbaden: Reichert, 1976) 108–35; idem, *A Political History of the Achaemenid Empire* (Leiden: Brill, 1989) 114–31, with a critical reappraisal of the sources.

22. E.g., D. L. Petersen, *Haggai and Zechariah 1–8* (OTL; Philadelphia: Westminster, 1984) 43–44; Meyers and Meyers, *Haggai, Zechariah 1–8*, xlvi; T. C. Mitchell, "The Babylonian Exile and the Restoration of the Jews to Palestine (586–c. 500 B.C.)," *Cambridge Ancient History* vol. 3/2: *The Assyrian and Babylonian Empires and Other States of the Near East, from the Eighth to the Sixth Centuries* B.C. (2d ed.; Cambridge: Cambridge University Press, 1991) 436.

23. R. A. Parker and W. H. Dubberstein, *Babylonian Chronology 626* B.C.–A.D. *75* (Providence: Brown University Press, 1956) 18, 30.

24. To resolve this problem, it has been suggested that Haggai and Zechariah reckoned the regnal years of Darius according to the Judean practice current before 586, i.e., using the Autumn (*Tishri*) Calendar and the nonaccession (*antedating*) system. Thus Darius's "Year 2" would correspond to his "Year 1" counted in the Babylonian manner. See L. Waterman, "The Camouflaged Purge of the Three Messianic Conspirators," *JNES* 13 (1954) 76–78; followed by B. Uffenheimer, *The Visions of Zechariah: From Prophecy to Apocalyptic* (Jerusalem: Kiryat Sepher, 1961) 43–46. Uffenheimer's impressive argument, modified in response to Bickerman's posthumous study (below, n. 25), appears in his contribution to *The World History of the Jewish People*, vol. 5: *Restoration—The Persian Period* (ed. H. Tadmor and I. Ephʿal; Jerusalem: Pelʾi/

An alternative solution therefore should seriously be considered. Elias Bickerman, in a paper published posthumously,[25] proposed that the year in question was not 520 but rather 521, at the height of the rebellion. Darius's regnal years, according to this proposal, conform with what must have been the Persian reckoning in the royal court, in which the beginning of the regnal year was counted, not in the Babylonian style, from Nisan following the accession, but rather from the death of the royal predecessor. In the case of Darius, there was an additional complication. Though his predecessor, Cambyses, died between April and July 522, the throne had been seized in March of that year by Bardia-Gaumata, a usurper, who held it for six months. Darius, viewing Gaumata's reign as illegitimate,[26] must have counted his own reign retroactively from the accession of Gaumata, or rather from the death of Cambyses. According to this proposal, Haggai's sermons and Zechariah's visions concerning the restoration of the Temple and the selection of Zerubbabel for the task would be dated to that fateful earlier year of 521, the "second year" of Darius by his own reckoning system, current at his court.

Whatever the actual date was, the cataclysmic events that shook the Persian Empire at the beginning of Darius's reign fell very close to the end of the predetermined seventy years of affliction. Hence the persuasive force of Zechariah's cry, "how long will You withhold pardon from Jerusalem . . ."—and Haggai's firm belief that time for rebuilding the Temple had indeeed come.

ʿAm ʿOved, 1983) 158–59, 290–91 [Heb.]. However, there are ample reasons to believe that the practice in Judah toward its fall was entirely different: both the Spring (*Nisan*) Calendar and the accession-year system (*postdating*) were in use. See my "Chronology," *EncBib* 4, cols. 263–68 [Heb.]; "The Chronology of the First Temple Period," in *The World History of the Jewish People*, vol. 4/1: *The Age of the Monarchies: Political History* (ed. A. Malamat; Jerusalem: Massada, 1978) 44–51; G. Galil, "The Babylonian Calendar and the Chronology of the Last Kings of Judah," *Bib* 72 (1991) 367–78; M. Cogan, "Chronology," *ABD* 1.1006.

25. E. J. Bickerman, "En marge de l'Écriture," *RB* 88 (1981) 11–23 (= *Studies in Jewish and Christian History* [Leiden: Brill, 1986] 3.327–36).

26. E. J. Bickerman and H. Tadmor, "Darius I: Pseudo-Smerdis and the Magi," *Athenaeum* n.s. 56 (1978) 239–47.

Some More Delocutives in Hebrew

Jeffrey H. Tigay
University of Pennsylvania

In 1967, D. R. Hillers called attention to the phenomenon of delocutive verbs in Biblical Hebrew.[1] Delocutives are similar to denominatives but, instead of being derived from nouns, they are derived from locutions or formulas used in discourse. Thus English "to hail" and "to welcome" are derived from the greetings "Hail!" and "Welcome!" Similarly, Latin *salutare* is derived not from the vocable *salus* 'well' but from the wish *salus/salutem* 'Hail!' with which one greets another; and Arabic has such verbs as *kabbara* 'to say *ʾallah ʾakbar*'; *sallama* 'to say *ʾas-salam ʿalaykum*'; and *basmala* 'to utter the invocation *bismillahi ʾar-raḥman ʾar-raḥim* ('In the name of God, the Beneficent, the Merciful')'.[2]

Author's note: I am grateful to W. Randall Garr and Michael Sokoloff, who helped me clarify the issues discussed here, though they are not responsible for my formulation or conclusions.

1. D. R. Hillers, "Delocutive Verbs in Biblical Hebrew," *JBL* 86 (1967) 320–24. Hillers borrowed the term from the linguist E. Benveniste. Medieval Hebrew grammarians were aware of the possibility of delocutive verbs; several of them consider ותהינו in Deut 1:41 to be derived from הננו in Num 14:40 or from הן 'yes!'; see Rashi, Rashbam, Ibn Ezra, and Bekhor Shor at Deut 1:41; Radaq, ספר השרשים (*Rabbi Davidis Kimchi Radicum Liber*) (ed. J. H. R. Biesenthal and F. Lebrecht; Berlin, 1847) 79, s.v. הין; and H. Filipowski, מחברת מנחם (*Antiquissimum Linguae Hebraicae et Chaldaicae Lexicon . . . a Menahem Ben Saruck Hispaniensi*) (London and Edinburgh: self-published, 1854) 72, s.v. הן; cf. Aquila, cited by M. Weinfeld, *Deuteronomy 1–11* (AB 5; New York: Doubleday, 1991) at Deut 1:41. In modern times, it has been suggested that the Christian Palestinian Aramaic verb שענן is derived from הושע-נא 'O deliver!' though this derivation is debated (F. Schwally, *Idioticon des christlich palästinischen Aramäisch* [Giessen: Ricker, 1893] 97; F. Schulthess, *Grammatik des christlich-palästinischen Aramäisch* [Tübingen: Mohr, Siebeck, 1924] 146).

2. Hillers, "Delocutive Verbs." Cf. also Latin *benedīcere* 'bless', which according to E. Partridge means 'say *bene*, well': *Origins: A Short Etymological Dictionary of Modern English* (New York: Macmillan, 1959) 153.

Hillers argued that several *Hiphil* and *Piel* verbs in Biblical Hebrew are best explained as delocutives and not simply declaratives. The most impressive example, in my opinion, is אשר (*Piel*) 'to say אשרי ("how fortunate") to/of someone'.[3] Hillers' list can be supplemented by the Talmudic Hebrew verb קלס (*Piel*) 'praise', which Saul Lieberman explained as meaning literally 'say *kalos* ("beautiful!")', a Greek loanword.[4]

Some verbs that are not derived in the first place from locutions have specific nuances that are. For example, the *Piels* of חזק and אמץ, which both normally mean 'strengthen' (Isa 35:3, Job 4:4), also have a delocutive sense, 'say the formula חזק or חזק ואמץ "be strong" or "be strong and resolute" to someone'.[5] In English, we could translate the idiom as 'to *ḥazaq* (or *ḥazaq ve'emaṣ*) someone'. This sense is found in such passages as Deut 1:38 and 3:28, where God commands Moses, with reference to Joshua, אותו חזק, and חזקהו ואמצהו. That these commands mean 'say (ואמץ) חזק ("be strong [and resolute]!") to him', not 'imbue him with strength (and courage)' (NJPSV), is clear from Deut 31:7, where Moses carries out this instruction by saying to Joshua, חזק ואמץ (cf. 31:23 and Josh 1:6–9, 18).

The *Piel* and *Hiphil* forms of קדש seem to have delocutive nuances in Jewish liturgy. The Kedushah, the angelic declaration of Isa 6:3, is regularly introduced by passages declaring the worshipers' intent or the angels' preparations to recite it, expressed by נקדש and נקדיש. The introduction to the קדושת יוצר, the Kedushah before the Shema in the morning service, describes the angels preparing "להקדיש their Creator" and then reciting the Kedushah. Similarly, in the Kedushah of the Shaḥarit ʿAmidah, the worshipers' declaration "נקדש Your name on earth . . ." is followed by their reciting the same passage. In these contexts, the verbs probably do not mean 'sanctify' or 'declare holy', but "recite קדוש קדוש קדוש ה׳ צבאות, מלא כל הארץ כבודו" 'Holy, holy, holy! The Lord of Hosts! His presence fills all the earth!'—in short, "to *qadoš* God."[6]

3. Gen 30:13; Mal 3:12; Ps 41:3, 72:17; Prov 31:28; Job 29:11; Cant 6:9.

4. S. Lieberman, קלס קילוסין, in עלי עי״ן (Salman Schocken Festschrift; Jerusalem, 1951–52) 75–81. The Talmudic verb should not be confused with biblical קלס 'scorn, mock'.

5. The formula is common; see, for example, 2 Sam 10:12, Isa 41:6, Hag 2:4, Ps 27:14, Ezra 10:4.

6. Note the paraphrases in the commentary of Y. Weingarten, הסדור המפורש השלם, Sephardic version (Jerusalem: Gefen, 5751/1991): לומר קדושה = להקדיש ליוצרם ליוצרם(p. 128); נקדישך (in the Sephardic text of the Shaḥarit ʿAmidah) = נאמר לפניך קדושה (p. 148). This meaning is confirmed for the Shaḥarit ʿAmidah by the *Seder Rav Amram*, where the wording is: יחד כולם קדושה לך ישלשו. The introduction to the Kedushah in the Musaf service, נעריצך ונקדישך, based on *Sop.* 16:12 and the Siddur of Saadia Gaon, might suggest that נקדישך here has a declarative meaning, since נעריצך must mean something like 'declare Your awesomeness'. However, this wording is an

However, the picture is complicated by passages in which the *Hiphil* of קדש appears in a string of verbs that refer to praising God, not to reciting a specific formula. For example, shortly before the קדושת יוצר, the text reads that all the angels open their mouths and מברכים ומשבחים ומפארים ומעריצים ומקדישים וממליכים 'bless, praise, glorify, declare awesome, sanctify, מקדישים, and declare sovereign God's name'. Since none of the other verbs in this string refers to a specific formula, it is difficult to insist that here מקדישים means 'recite קדוש קדוש קדוש'. This leaves us uncertain that worshipers would understand the verb to have that meaning a few lines further on.

Similar possibilities and problems arise in connection with the use of ברך (*Piel*). Often, it seems possible to understand the verb as meaning 'to recite ... ברוך (or: 'יברכך ה)'—in other words 'to *baruk̲*, or to *yeb̲arek̲ek̲a*, so-and-so'—rather than 'to bless'. When a person blesses (מברך) another, the blessing frequently says 'ברוך פלוני לה or 'יברכך ה 'may so-and-so be blessed by the Lord' or 'may the Lord bless you'. Two examples are: ויברכהו ויאמר ברוך אברם לאל עליון ... 'he ברך-ed him, saying: "May Abram be ברוך by God Most High"' (Gen 14:19); and ... 'ואברך את ה, 'I ברך-ed the Lord' (Gen 24:48), referring to v. 27, ... 'ויאמר ברוך ה 'he said, ... 'ברוך ה'. In Deut 10:8 and 21:5, לברך means 'recite the priestly benediction, יברכך ה' וישמרך ... "may the Lord bless you and protect you ..."' (Num 6:23–26). The fact that Hebrew, Phoenician, and Aramaic employ two alternative blessing formulas, one using the *Piel* of ברך and the other its passive participle ברוך, also implies that the *Piel* (with human subject) is delocutive, based on the passive participle. In Ps 118:26, 'ברוך הבא בשם ה 'may he who enters be blessed in the name of the Lord'[7] is paralleled by 'ברכנוכם מבית ה 'we ברך you from the house of the Lord' (cf. Ps 129:8, 'ברכת ה' עליכם // ברכנו אתכם בשם ה 'the blessing of the Lord be upon you // we bless you in the name of the Lord'; ברכת ה' עליכם is yet another blessing formula).[8] In the Arad letters and the pithoi from Kuntillet Ajrud, we find 'ברכתך/ברכת אתכם לה, 'I ברך you to the Lord', while votive inscriptions from Ajrud and elsewhere use the formula 'בר(ו)ך פלוני לה 'may so-and-so be blessed by the Lord'.[9] These equivalences

allusion to Isa 29:23, and it probably represents a secondary expansion of נקדישך, based on the biblical verse.

7. For this translation, cf. Sheldon H. Blank, "Some Observations concerning Biblical Prayer," *HUCA* 32 (1961) 75–79; idem, *Prophetic Thought: Essays and Addresses* (Cincinnati: Hebrew Union College Press, 1977) 77–80.

8. See also 2 Sam 6:18; 1 Chr 23:13; 1 Kgs 8:14–15, 55–56; cf. Isa 19:25. Deut 24:13b presumably refers to a prayer or wish like those in 1 Sam 23:21, 25:32–33; 2 Sam 2:5; Ruth 2:20, 3:10. 2 Kgs 4:29 probably refers to greetings like those in 1 Sam 15:13a and Ruth 2:4b (but see also Ruth 2:4a).

9. See Arad letters 16:2–3, 21:2, 40:3, and the inscriptions from Kuntillet Ajrud and elsewhere cited in S. Aḥituv, *Handbook of Ancient Hebrew Inscriptions* (The Biblical Encyclopaedia Library 7; Jerusalem: Bialik, 1992) 70, 76, 88, 111, 116, 153, 157, 202.

imply that the verb ברך was understood as meaning 'to recite . . . ברוך (or: יברכך ה׳)'. In rabbinic literature and liturgy, the finite verb often means to recite a specific blessing beginning with ברוך אתה ה׳ 'may you be blessed, O Lord' (in the sense of 'may you be praised', 'thank you'),[10] such as the blessing over wine or the blessing after meals.

Here, too, however, the picture is complicated by the fact that there are also blessings introduced by the verb ברך that do not include ברוך or יברכך. For example, in Gen 24:60, ויברכו את רבקה ויאמרו לה אחותנו את היי לאלפי רבבה ויירש זרעך את שער שנאיו 'and they blessed Rebekah and said to her, "O sister! May you grow into thousands of myriads; may your offspring seize the gates of their foes"'.[11] There are also passages in which we find the cognate accusative phrase ברך ברכה 'to recite (lit., "bless") a blessing'.[12] In such cases, the verb must mean simply 'bless', 'recite a blessing', and we therefore cannot rule out the possibility that it was understood that way in all cases.

Whatever the precise nuance of קדש and ברך in such cases, I am happy to join in this expression of blessing to ברוך Levine, who has done so much to clarify the history and meaning of blessing and worship in the Bible.

10. See M. Greenberg, *Biblical Prose Prayer as a Window to the Popular Religion of Ancient Israel* (Berkeley: University of California Press, 1983) 34–36; A. B. Ehrlich, *Mikrâ Ki-pheshutô* (reprinted New York: Ktav, 1969), at Deut 8:10.

11. See also Gen 27:27–30, 32:27, 35:9–12, 48:2–3; Deut 33:1; 1 Sam 2:20.

12. For example, Gen 27:41; *m. Pesaḥ.* 10:9; *m. Tamid* 5:1. As Hillers notes, "the situation is complicated by the presence of the noun *berakhah*, which may have figured in the derivation, and by the state of affairs with respect to this verb in other Semitic languages, where it also exhibits peculiarities" (Hillers, "Delocutive Verbs," 324). B. A. Levine notes that "No satisfactory etymology for the verb *bērēk* has been proposed. It is possible that the verb and the participial forms . . . are all denominative of *berākāh*, 'gift, blessing'"; *Numbers 1–20* (AB 4A; New York: Doubleday, 1993) 227.

Poetry and Prose in the Book of Jeremiah

Robert R. Wilson
Yale University

From the standpoint of literary analysis, the book of Jeremiah presents some of the most frustrating problems to be found anywhere in the Hebrew Bible. On the one hand, the basic varieties of prophetic literature contained in the book are relatively obvious, even to the casual reader. Scholars thus have long agreed that Jeremiah contains three basic types of prophetic material: first, there are poetic oracles of doom and salvation; second, there are biographical prose narratives treating the life of the prophet Jeremiah; and third, there is additional prose material that does not seem to be primarily biographical in character.[1] On the other hand, while scholars have basically agreed on the distinction to be drawn between the poetic and prose passages in the book, they have been unable to reach a consensus on the literary origins of the two different types of prose. Furthermore, the relationship of the prose materials to each other is highly controverted, as is the relationship between either type of prose and the poetic oracles.

This scholarly debate has been particularly sharp in the case of the non-biographical prose, and the study that follows will concentrate on this particular component of Jeremiah. However, it must be remembered that, while this material can be isolated for the purpose of analysis, it remains intimately related to the rest of the book, and for this reason a full discussion of the poetry-prose problem in Jeremiah must eventually involve a treatment of the poetic oracles and the biographical prose as well.

1. This characterization of the contents of Jeremiah is accepted not only by scholars interested in reconstructing the book's compositional history but also by critics seeking to deal with the text solely in literary terms. See, for example, J. Rosenberg, "Jeremiah and Ezekiel," *The Literary Guide to the Bible* (ed. R. Alter and F. Kermode; Cambridge: Harvard University Press, 1987) 184–90.

A History of Research

The critical literary analysis of the book of Jeremiah is usually said to have begun with Bernhard Duhm, who was the first in modern times to call attention to the problem of the nonbiographical prose in the book. In his Jeremiah commentary of 1901, Duhm sounded two important notes that would reverberate strongly in much of the subsequent discussion. First, like many scholars of his era, he assumed that prophetic inspiration and poetic inspiration were closely related, and he therefore located the authentic words of Jeremiah within the relatively brief, lyrical poetic oracles now found in chaps. 1–25. Second, he divided the book's prose material into two categories. The first of these, consisting of about 220 verses identified primarily on the basis of content, he saw as the scribe Baruch's biographical accounts of the prophet's activities in the years just before the second deportation in 586. In the present book, these biographical narratives appear as a collection in chaps. 26–45. In the second category, Duhm placed about 850 verses of nonbiographical prose, which he attributed to later editors. Duhm considered these materials to be more amorphous than the biographical narratives, but he noted that much of the prose was rhetorical and sermonic in style. In Duhm's opinion, this material showed little originality and was heavily dependent on earlier biblical texts, particularly the Deuteronomistic History, Ezekiel, and Second and Third Isaiah. These didactic prose editorial additions are scattered throughout the whole book according to no obvious rationale, and for Duhm they were the antithesis of the original Jeremiah poetry. In contrast to the divinely inspired poetic oracles, the nonbiographical prose was stereotypical, unoriginal, and wholly derived from earlier literary sources. It reflected the religious concerns of the postexilic community and was therefore of little use in interpreting the prophet's life or message.[2]

Duhm's observations were further elaborated by Sigmund Mowinckel, whose famous literary analysis of 1914 set the terms for much of the later scholarly debate. Like Duhm, Mowinckel recognized within the book a core of original poetic oracles created by the prophet and now found primarily in chaps. 1–25. This poetic collection Mowinckel labeled "A." In addition to isolating the poetry, Mowinckel followed Duhm in identifying prose narratives dealing with the life of Jeremiah, and this material, labeled "B," Mowinckel assigned to Baruch. The second type of prose, which Mowinckel called "C," was rhetorical and monotonous in style and had strong linguistic and thematic links with Deuteronomistic literature. Many of the C passages were introduced with a variant of the formula "the word which was to Jeremiah from the Lord" (7:1) and contained mostly collections of stereotypical Deuteronomic words and phrases. On the basis of this Deuteronomistic vocabulary and contents, and with the help of the introductory formulas,

2. B. Duhm, *Das Buch Jeremiah* (KHAT; Tübingen and Leipzig: Mohr, 1901) xii–xxii.

Mowinckel identified the following passages as C: 7:1–8:3; 11:1–5, 9–14; 18:1–12; 21:1–10; 25:1–11a; 32:1–2, 6–16, 24–44; 34:1–7, 8–22; 35:1–19; 44:1–14. He also assigned to C certain passages thought to have Deuteronomistic background, even though they lacked the customary introductory formula. The basic collection of C material was thus expanded to include 3:6–13, 22:1–5, 27:1–22, 29:1–23, 39:15–18, and 45:1–5. Like Duhm, Mowinckel had a low opinion of the worth of the C prose and thought that it simply obscured the creative originality of the prophet.[3]

Following the work of Mowinckel, the history of scholarship has until recently focused primarily on clarifying the relationship between C and the prophet's original words, on the one side, and on clarifying the relationship between C and the Deuteronomist on the other. Representative of this sort of research is the work of J. Philip Hyatt, who argued, primarily on linguistic grounds, that the prophet Jeremiah knew an early edition of Deuteronomy but consciously formulated some of his articles in order to oppose some Deuteronomic positions. Later, the book underwent a thorough Deuteronomic editing in order to make the prophet appear to be a supporter of the Deuteronomic point of view. This editing was much more extensive than anything envisioned by Mowinckel and touched most chapters of the book.[4] Hyatt's observations on the pervasiveness of Deuteronomic vocabulary in Jeremiah was also noticed by John Bright, who explored the matter a bit further, eventually coming to the conclusion that some of the so-called Deuteronomic material was in fact distinctive to Jeremiah. Bright therefore concluded that the prophet was simply using a vocabulary and perhaps even occasionally writing a kind of prose that reflected the same sort of seventh-/sixth-century rhetoric employed by the Deuteronomists. Although Bright did not claim that all of the C prose was in fact the work of the prophet, he did hold out the possibility that some of it did reflect Jeremiah's original oracles as they were remembered by later tradition. In any case, Bright was unwilling, on linguistic grounds, to date the C material much later than the exile.[5]

3. S. Mowinckel, *Zur Komposition des Buches Jeremia* (Kristiania: Dybwad, 1914) 20–45. Following scholarly convention, this study will use Mowinckel's designations for the various types of literature in Jeremiah, even though it may be that the book actually contains more varieties of literature than he realized. The material that is the main concern of this study will thus be called "C prose" or "didactic prose," although the latter designation is not intended to imply anything about its authorship or any function that it might have had before it was added to the present book. Another common designation for this material, "prose sermon," will be avoided because it implies too much about the material's original setting and function.

4. J. P. Hyatt, "Jeremiah and Deuteronomy," *JNES* 1 (1942) 156–73; "The Deuteronomic Edition of Jeremiah," *Vanderbilt Studies in the Humanities* (Nashville: Vanderbilt University Press, 1951) 1.71–95.

5. J. Bright, "The Date of the Prose Sermons of Jeremiah," *JBL* 70 (1951) 15–35; *Jeremiah* (AB 21; Garden City, N.Y.: Doubleday, 1965) lxvii–lxxiii.

With the work of Hyatt and Bright, the sharp distinctions between A, B, and C that Mowinckel drew began to break down. In spite of Enno Janssen's attempt to show on form-critical grounds the relation between C and the Deuteronomistic history, more recent research has tended to further complicate the literary analysis of Duhm and Mowinckel.[6] E. W. Nicholson, for example, maintains that the C prose stems from the work of exilic preachers in Babylon, who, during the exile, developed the implications of Jeremiah's oracles for a new situation. For Nicholson the so-called prose sermons do reflect thematic links with Deuteronomic tradition, but he believes that many of the prose passages grew out of genuine sayings of the prophet.[7] Winfried Thiel, in a detailed two-volume analysis of the language of Jeremiah, revives the earlier thesis of Hyatt and argues for massive Deuteronomic editing throughout the book. The hand of the Deuteronomists is thus not confined to the C material but is much more pervasive.[8] Again on linguistic grounds, Helga Weippert reaches conclusions diametrically opposed to those of Thiel. Weippert argues that the alleged similarities between C and the prose of the Deuteronomistic History are more apparent than real and that much of the C prose is peculiar to Jeremiah. Furthermore, some of Jeremiah's poetic vocabulary is also found in the book's prose, a fact that suggests to Weippert that the historical Jeremiah was responsible both for the poetry and much of the C prose.[9] Links between the poetic oracles and the C prose are also maintained by William L. Holladay, although he sees a less direct connection between the two than does Weippert. Holladay speaks of the poetry as generating the prose sermons, so that the C prose is best understood as a reflection of the prophet's voice rather than as an independent literary source.[10]

Thus, the current state of scholarship on the C material reflects a good bit of frustration and confusion. On the one hand, most scholars, at least at a descriptive level, maintain Mowinckel's distinctions between the A, B, and C materials in the book, although there is a general recognition that Jeremiah contains other types of materials as well (particularly non-B, non-C prose). On the other hand, the relationship among these basic types of materials is seen to be increasingly complex, and there is a growing reluctance to solve the problem in strictly literary terms. Typical of this trend is the recent com-

6. E. Janssen, *Juda in der Exilszeit* (Göttingen: Vandenhoeck & Ruprecht, 1956).

7. E. W. Nicholson, *Preaching to the Exiles* (New York: Schocken, 1970).

8. W. Thiel, *Die deuteronomistische Redaktion von Jeremia 1–25* (Neukirchen-Vluyn: Neukirchener Verlag, 1973); *Die deuteronomistische Redaktion von Jeremia 26–45* (Neukirchen-Vluyn: Neukirchener Verlag, 1981).

9. H. Weippert, *Die Prosareden des Jeremiabuches* (Berlin: de Gruyter, 1973).

10. W. L. Holladay, "Prototype and Copies: A New Approach to the Poetry-Prose Problem in the Book of Jeremiah," *JBL* 79 (1960) 351–67; "A Fresh Look at 'Source B' and 'Source C' in Jeremiah," *VT* 25 (1975) 394–412; *Jeremiah 2* (Hermeneia; Minneapolis: Fortress, 1989) 11–15.

mentary by William McKane, who argues that the sort of detailed literary analysis provided by Thiel and Weippert has reached the point of diminishing returns. While acknowledging that there are somewhat vague similarities between Jeremiah and the Deuteronomistic History, he nevertheless maintains that the book of Jeremiah grew into its present form over a long period of time and represents a complex history of development and not just a three- or four-stage growth process (A + B + C + random late additions). Following the lead of Weippert, McKane suggests that the most fruitful approach to the book is to concentrate on the internal relationships among its various components. This approach seems to presuppose a written text from the very beginning of the book's development and to point to a literary process something akin to midrash, although McKane does not use the term.[11] McKane's notion of describing the book as a "rolling corpus" is viewed positively by Robert P. Carroll, who acknowledges the complexity of the C material but offers no comprehensive account of its origin and development. Like Thiel, Carroll sees much Deuteronomistic editing in the book, but he also argues in a general way for the presence of some post-Deuteronomic material that was influenced by the Deuteronomic movement but was not from Deuteronomistic circles.[12]

McKane's focus on the internal dynamics of the book of Jeremiah is shared by Christopher R. Seitz, who accepts the general distinction between the types of literature usually labeled A, B, and C, but who also recognizes a certain amount of shared discourse among the types. However, rather than concentrating on the purely literary dimensions of the problem, Seitz sees the two different types of prose as resulting from different reactions to the complex theological problems posed by the exile. Seen in this light, the book of Jeremiah begins to resemble a literary record of the debates that took place among the various groups bearing the Jeremiah traditions.[13] The highly dynamic character of this process is also suggested by the work of Louis Stulman, who makes a careful comparison of the MT of Jeremiah and the shorter Old Greek text. This comparison shows that, while Deuteronomic thought is fully represented in the Old Greek version of the C prose, the additional material found in the MT more often than not adds characteristic Deuteronomistic vocabulary without changing the fundamental meaning found in the shorter text. This suggests that in some circles the trend toward "Deuteronomizing" the C material continued longer than it did in other circles.[14]

11. W. McKane, *A Critical and Exegetical Commentary on Jeremiah* (ICC; 2 vols.; Edinburgh: T. & T. Clark, 1986) 1.xli–lxi.

12. R. P. Carroll, *Jeremiah* (OTL; Philadelphia: Westminster, 1986) 42.

13. C. R. Seitz, *Theology in Conflict* (Berlin: de Gruyter, 1989) 229–32.

14. L. Stulman, *The Prose Sermons of the Book of Jeremiah* (Atlanta: Scholars Press, 1986).

A New Approach

This review of research on the Jeremiah C material suggests that the discussion has reached an impasse. While most scholars still recognize the distinctive character of the didactic prose, there is no agreement on its origins or development and no consensus on its relationship to other biblical material. While McKane's focus on internal literary connections in the book is suggestive, his own analysis is still somewhat atomistic, and holistic interpretations of the sort pioneered by Moshe Greenberg and Robert Alter have not yielded satisfactory results in Jeremiah.[15] Therefore, rather than pursuing traditional linguistic and thematic approaches any further or abandoning entirely the notion of different types of literature within the book and attempting a "simple" literary reading, it might be more fruitful to explore a different approach to the problem of the C material. In order to do so, it is necessary to consider two interrelated questions, which have not yet been adequately treated. First, if, as most scholars claim, the C material is an editorial addition to the A and B material, why was this additional material cast in prose rather than poetry? Second, why was the C material scattered throughout the book rather than being gathered together in one place as the B material was? In the end both of these questions may be unanswerable, but exploring them may at least suggest some additional aspects of the problem that are worth considering.

The first question, the issue of poetry versus prose, is one that has not been asked, but it is one that is potentially important, for in fact it is not at all obvious why the editor or author chose to cast the C material in prose. A quick glance at other prophetic books will dramatize the unusual nature of the choice. In books such as Amos and Hosea, editorial additions are usually, although not always, made in a way designed to blend in with the texts to which they are added. Poetry is added to poetry and occasionally prose to prose in such a way as to obscure the marks of editorial activity. The same is generally true in Isaiah and Ezekiel, with the result that in most prophetic books there is little scholarly agreement about what is an addition and what is not. Against this background, the case of the C material in Jeremiah forms a sharp contrast, at least in the first twenty-five chapters of the book, where most of the poetic oracles are found. Here the shift from poetry to prose is absolutely clear and unambiguous, and no attempt has been made by the editor or author to hide the literary seams. The case is somewhat different in the last half of the book, which is predominantly prose, although differences in genre are still marked. Most of the B prose is narrative, while the occasional C material tends to be didactic or exhortatory.

15. Joel Rosenberg, for example, makes many useful comments about the literary structure of Jeremiah, but his literary characterization of the book as a whole moves the discussion very little beyond the point where Mowinckel left it (Rosenberg, "Jeremiah and Ezekiel," 184–94).

The few scholars who have worried about the question of why C is in prose have rarely given direct answers to it, but answers can sometimes be inferred. Critics around the turn of the century, such as Duhm and Mowinckel, would probably have located the explanation in a theory of a gradual decline in poetic/prophetic inspiration. Because in their estimation the C material was late and certainly not from the prophet himself, it was lacking in inspiration and therefore had to have been in prose form. Such explanations, of course, make romantic assumptions about literature and creativity that most modern scholars would not accept. Another suggestion has been that the didactic prose already existed in this form in a separate literary source and was simply incorporated in its original form without making any attempt to blend it into its new setting. However, if this were in fact the case, one might expect more continuity within the C material itself, and one might also expect the didactic prose to appear in a single block or in a limited number of blocks rather than to be scattered throughout the book. The inadequacy of these explanations prompts a third explanation: namely, that the prose form was chosen deliberately for some reason.

Any exploration of what that reason might be, however, is hampered by a relative lack of theoretical studies on the uses of prose. Much has been written in recent years on the nature of poetry, and there has been considerable attention to narrative prose, but to date little attention has been paid to nonnarrative prose. Usually prose, if discussed generally at all, is defined only in contrast to poetry. Typically, an attempt is made to define the features of poetry, and then prose is said to be the antithesis of poetry. Often the image of a continuum is employed, with "pure" poetry at one end and "pure" prose at the other, and mixed forms appearing somewhere in the middle. This approach to the problem of prose has some limitations, but for an understanding of the nature of the C material it may be adequate. Although there is still much disagreement about what constitutes Hebrew poetry, most would agree that it consists of a collection of phenomena that would include constraint on line length, terseness, various types of parallelism (whatever one understands parallelism to be), and a high density of evocative imagery and figurative language. Poetry is thus by its nature likely to be imprecise and for this reason to be an ideal medium for expressing ambiguity. Poetry invites interpretation and requires a rather high degree of reader involvement.[16] If one were then to define prose as the antithesis of poetry, then one might suggest that prose lines are not normally constrained; terseness need not be present; parallelism, if it exists at all, is less marked; and there tends to be a relatively low density of evocative imagery and figurative language. This means that

16. T. Longman, III, *Literary Approaches to Biblical Interpretation* (Grand Rapids: Zondervan, 1987) 121–32; J. L. Kugel, *The Idea of Biblical Poetry* (New Haven: Yale University Press, 1981) 59–95; N. Frye, *The Great Code* (New York: Harcourt Brace Jovanovich, 1982) 207–13.

prose is better suited than poetry to express precision and to resolve ambiguity. It also allows for less reader involvement and more clarity of expression, although it is not always crafted in such a way as to realize this potential.

This rough description of prose suggests the possibility that the C material in Jeremiah has been cast in prose in order to take advantage of the particular strengths of that literary medium. In short, the didactic passages may be in prose in order to maximize their explanatory potential. In order to explore this theory more fully, it is necessary to turn now to the second question listed above, the question of why the didactic prose units are located where they are rather than somewhere else. Of course, there is no way to uncover the original intentions of the authors or editors, but it is at least possible to examine the way in which the C prose functions in its present literary contexts. In this brief study it is impossible to explore all of the C material, but it is possible to look at representative samples of C editorial work. Accordingly, the discussion that follows will treat one didactic prose unit appearing in the context of poetic judgment oracles (7:1–8:3), one didactic prose unit appearing in the context of poetic promise oracles (32:1–34), and finally a selection of didactic prose units interwoven with B biographical narratives (27:1–22, 29:1–32, 44:1–14). Most critics understand these didactic passages to be clear examples of C prose, although they do so for various reasons, and there is no scholarly argument about the identification of the C material.

Jeremiah 7:1–8:3

Probably the most famous of the C prose passages is the so-called Temple Sermon now found in 7:1–8:3. In its present position, it appears after a large block of A poetry containing a complex collection of oracles. It is of course impossible in this brief space to analyze all of this poetic material in detail, but it is sufficient here to note two of its major characteristics. First, with respect to literary genre, the oracles are highly diverse. A number of different genres are represented, although there are relatively few introductory and concluding formulas, and the connections between oracles are not clearly marked. Thus, for example, between 3:13 (the end of the first block of C material in the book) and 7:1 (the beginning of the second block of C material), there are examples of the following genres: (1) calls to repent, either with or without the technical term *šûb* (3:22a; 4:3–4, 14; 6:16); (2) confessions of guilt by the people (3:22b–25); (3) announcements of disaster (4:5–13, 15–17, 23–31; 6:19–23); (4) statements of the reasons for the disaster (4:18 and brief allusions elsewhere); (5) conditional promises contingent on repentance (4:1–2); (6) laments (4:19–21); and (7) private addresses to the prophet (5:1?; 6:27–30).

The second characteristic of this poetic material is that it is highly evocative and ambiguous. The ambiguity embraces all of the major aspects of the oracles. For example, it is not always clear who the addressee is intended to be, and several different addressees are mentioned from time to time throughout the collection. There are addresses to the people of Judah and Jerusalem (4:3, 5, 10, 20); to Israel (although it is not always clear what is meant by this designation [4:1]); to the house of Jacob (5:20); and to the people of Benjamin (6:1). The references to the Northern Kingdom are particularly puzzling, given Jeremiah's dates, and some scholars have suggested that the prophet began to prophecy first in the North as part of Josiah's attempt to regain control over this piece of the old Davidic empire. The oracles to Judah and Jerusalem could have come from any time during the prophet's career, but the biographical narratives suggest that he was particularly active during the crucial years between the two deportations (597–586).

If the addressee in the oracles is not clear, neither is the crime that the prophet is attributing to the addressee. Sometimes Jeremiah speaks simply of general evil (4:18, 22), while at other times he mentions a variety of more specific offenses. Thus the people are said not to have acted justly (5:1, 28); to have sworn falsely (5:2); to have sworn by other gods (5:7); to have committed adultery (5:7–8); to have refused to hear the word of God (5:21, 6:10); or to have rejected the prophets whom God has sent to warn them (6:17). The people are accused of not worshiping God (5:23–24), and particular officials, especially prophets and rulers, are singled out as contributing to the problem (5:31, 6:13–15).

Similarly, the oracles express various opinions about what is to be the result of the people's crimes. Sometimes Jeremiah simply speaks in highly evocative terms of a general disaster (5:6), but more normally he alludes to some sort of military invasion (5:15–17, 6:1–8). However, in the latter case, the enemy is rarely identified specifically and when referred to at all is usually identified only as the traditional "enemy from the north."

In addition, it is not clear what the prophet wants from his hearers. Sometimes the point of the oracles seems to be simply to announce the coming disaster. However, it is important to note that calls for repentance are scattered throughout the collection (3:22a; 4:3–4, 14; 6:16), and in at least one case (3:22b–25) a confession of guilt is actually put on the lips of the people, perhaps as an example of what is required.

Finally, throughout the collection, the speaker is not always clearly identified. Jeremiah often speaks the word of God, but the prophet also occasionally speaks in his own voice. God seems to speak directly to the people at times but also speaks privately to the prophet, and in one remarkable passage (4:19–21), the reader may overhear a divine soliloquy in the form of a lament.[17] Then, too, the people are sometimes quoted, either talking to each other or talking to God (or perhaps talking to God through the prophet).

17. For this interpretation of the passage, see most recently J. J. M. Roberts, "The Motif of the Weeping God in Jeremiah and Its Background in the Lament Tradition of the Ancient near East," *Old Testament Essays: Journal of the Old Testament Society of South Africa* 5 (1992) 361–74.

This profusion of voices in the oracles sometimes even reaches the point where the present arrangement of the units implies a kind of dialogue going on between God, Israel, and the prophet (chaps. 5–6).

Against the background of this sort of literary ambiguity and dialogic exposition, the contrast with the didactic prose unit in 7:1–8:3 is striking. Suddenly all of the ambiguities are removed and certain implications of the preceding poetic oracles are amplified, modified, or reversed.

The C material in 7:1–8:3 is set in a specific location, the temple gate (at least in the MT; contrast the Old Greek) and is addressed to a particular audience, the people of Judah. God is the speaker throughout the whole passage, a fact underlined by the introduction, the frequent use of the messenger formula (7:3, 11, 21; 8:3), and the consistent use of the first person. There is no attempt to reproduce the dialogic style of the preceding chapters. The passage opens with an exhortation to the people to improve their behavior (7:3), an exhortation that elaborates the repentance motif from the preceding chapters and that is motivated by a conditional promise of the sort often associated with Deuteronomistic exhortation: if the people truly improve their behavior by executing justice, not oppressing the stranger, orphan, and widow, by not shedding innocent blood, and by not worshiping other gods, then God will allow them to remain where they are (or God will continue to dwell with them, depending on how one reads v. 7). However, like all conditional promises, this one also carries with it an implied threat: if the people do not reform, then they will not be allowed to remain. It is this motif of threat and ultimately of judgment that is developed in the remainder of the passage. The threat is underlined by reference to the fate of Shiloh, the sanctuary that God had earlier destroyed (v. 12). The reader expects the Shiloh reference to serve as a warning and to function as the basis for further appeals for reform, but instead the passage takes a surprising turn. God outlines the people's past history of refusing to listen to the divine word (a divine word presumably delivered by prophets, another motif from the poetic oracles), and this becomes the grounds for an announcement of disaster: "I will do to the house which bears my name . . . just what I did to Shiloh, and I will cast you out of my presence as I cast out your brothers, the whole brood of Ephraim" (7:14–15). The announcement of disaster is unqualified and seems to override the earlier conditional promise. The conditional promise in retrospect now seems to function more as a statement of the "rules of the game" than as an actual possibility, a point that is underscored by the passage's next unit, a private oracle to Jeremiah forbidding him to intercede with God on behalf of the people (7:16–20). Because people have worshiped other gods, God is determined to destroy them and is unwilling to be persuaded otherwise. The background of this notion of the prophetic intercessor is to be found in the Deuteronomistic understanding of prophecy. From the Deuteronomistic perspective, communication with God is to take place only through the prophet, who delivers God's word to the people, but who also serves as a conduit for the people's petitions to God. By forbidding intercession, God effectively blocks future communications from the people and makes it impossible for them to repent and avoid the coming judgment. The termination of intercession also marks an end to the sort of dialogue implied in the arrangement of the poetic oracles and makes repentance apparently irrelevant to Israel's future.

The motif of inevitable judgment is reinforced by the remainder of the passage. The people in the past have refused to listen to God or to reform their behavior. Now they must pay the price (7:21–8:3). Even Jeremiah's efforts in this exhortation, the prophet is told (7:27), will not change the situation. The time for repentance has passed, and the judgment is now inevitable.

In its context, then, the C prose unit summarizes and simplifies the preceding poetic material, underscoring some of it but eliminating much content in the process. The various themes of the earlier oracles are now reduced to a simple, unambiguous message having to do with the inevitability of judgment.

Jeremiah 32:1–44

Turning now to a C prose unit embedded in the matrix of poetic promise oracles, 32:1–44, we can see a situation rather similar to the one in the passage that has just been examined. The immediate context of this particular block of C material is the so-called Book of Consolation, a small collection of promise oracles now found in chaps. 30–31. Although earlier scholars such as Duhm and Mowinckel tended to view these oracles as post-Jeremianic, more recent research usually assigns them to the prophet and considers them part of Mowinckel's A material. It is not possible to examine these oracles in detail, but it is sufficient to note that they have many of the same features exhibited by the judgment oracles in chaps. 3–6. There is much ambiguity in the promise oracles, but two points in particular should be underlined. First, it is clear that many of the promises seem to have been addressed originally to the Northern Kingdom, although various prose additions, including the introduction to the collection (30:1–4), broaden the scope to include Judah along with Israel. Thus there are frequent references to Jacob/Israel (30:10, 18; 31:4, 7, 21) and to Ephraim (31:6, 18, 20), along with the famous address to Rachel, the eponymous ancestor of the Northern tribes (31:15–17). Although some of these references are ambiguous, there is considerably less uncertainty about the addressee than is the case in the judgment oracles that open the book.

A second point to underscore is the understanding of return that these oracles reflect. In line with Jeremiah's insistence on repentance as a way of avoiding threatened judgment, the return of the people to the land also seems to be contingent on repentance in exile.[18] This notion is most clearly displayed in the Rachel oracle, in which the return of her children is related to their lament confessing their past sins and begging for forgiveness (31:18–19). This admission of guilt apparently motivates God to bring the people back (31:20–22).

As in the case of chap. 7, the insertion of the C prose material in chap. 32 removes a number of ambiguities in the preceding poetic oracles and dramatically reinforces certain motifs at the expense of others. The didactic prose passage is interwoven with a biographical narrative, the specificity of which reminds the reader of the B material and suggests some effort to integrate the exhortatory material into the larger block of B prose now found in the last half of the book. The biographical narrative unambiguously places the incident in Jerusalem, and the recipients of the promise of return are specifically the people who have been exiled from Jerusalem, and perhaps by implication, from Judah. There is no reference to the Northern Kingdom, and the poetic notion that Ephraim and Judah are to be restored together is apparently rejected. Much of the C passage is in fact taken up with a long explanation for the impending judgment, and in this sense the unit is quite similar to the one in 7:1–8:3. The people have exhibited a long history of sin, and now they must accept the inevitable punishment (32:26–35). The promise of return, when it is finally elaborated, turns out to be conceived in a way that contrasts markedly with the ideology of the promise oracles. The promise is now absolute rather than conditional. The didactic prose makes no reference to repentance as a necessary precondition for the return, as do the promise oracles. Just as the judgment is inevitable, so also God's election of the people is absolute and eternal, and God's fidelity will result in the promised return (32:36–44).

Jeremiah 27:1–22, 29:1–32, 44:1–14

The above two examples of C material in poetic contexts appear to support the suggestion made earlier about the choice of prose as the medium of expression in C and about the function of the didactic prose units in their poetic contexts. These units seem designed to elaborate and clarify the poetic oracles and are strategically placed for that purpose, sometimes even showing evidence of being linked literarily and thematically to a particular context.

Unfortunately, this conclusion concerning the purpose of the didactic prose appears premature when the C material in the context of B narratives is brought into the picture. To examine adequately the relationship between B and C would require more discussion than is possible here, but it will nevertheless be helpful to make some general remarks about three representative passages.

18. On this point, see J. Unterman, *From Repentance to Redemption* (JSOTSup 54; Sheffield: JSOT Press, 1987).

The C material in 27:1–22 immediately follows a biographical narrative often thought to be B's version of C's "Temple Sermon" in 7:1–8:3. However, the peculiarities of B's account in 26:1–24 need to be noted. In contrast to chap. 7, which turned quickly into an announcement of inevitable judgment, B characteristically sees Jeremiah's appearance in the temple court as an opportunity for genuine repentance and thus for the avoidance of judgment, a point of view that B shares with the A oracles. Thus Jeremiah's message in 26:4–6 is conditional, but it is a conditional judgment rather than a conditional promise. If the people do not obey, then God will make the Jerusalem temple like the temple at Shiloh. B also characteristically personalizes Israel's strengths and weaknesses by focusing on the reactions of particular historical individuals to Jeremiah's words. While C typically rehearses a long history of disobedience, B graphically portrays some people who obey and some who do not. Thus the reactions to Jeremiah's temple oracle vary. Some people hear the oracle as one of unconditional judgment (almost as if they were hearing 7:13–15), and they want to kill Jeremiah. Others recognize the role of the prophet as one that can lead to repentance and thus to an avoidance of judgment, and they are apparently willing to listen. In this instance, the issue is left unresolved, and Jeremiah is helped to escape.

Coming after B's version of the "Temple Sermon," the C prose in chap. 27 focuses again on the topic of inevitable judgment. It is interesting to note, however, that this C material is cast in biographical form, almost as if it were being consciously blended into the preceding B material. The C material of chap. 27 supplies a summary of Jeremiah's message by focusing on the incident of the yoke. According to C, judgment is inevitable, and the king should simply accept that fact and submit peacefully to the Babylonians. Missing from the chapter is B's notion that repentance might forestall the judgment. At most, capitulation might preserve the city, but it cannot prevent the exile (27:17–18).

Jer 29:1–32 is a block of C material that immediately follows B's story of prophetic conflict in chap. 28. As in the earlier B passage examined above, B here simply poses two alternatives and then resolves them only at the very end of the story. Either Hananiah is correct in predicting that the exile is almost over, or Jeremiah is correct in predicting a long exile. The C material in chap. 29 returns to these themes and reinforces the correctness of Jeremiah's position. The exile will last for seventy years, after which the people will be brought back. As in chap. 32, there is no reference to repentance as a precondition for return, but the restoration seems to occur according to a divinely established timetable. In addition to reinforcing motifs from B's narrative in chap. 28, C also includes in chap. 29 the sorts of specific historical references that are normally associated with B and thus seems to be making a conscious attempt to blend the two chapters.

Finally, Jer 44:1–14 provides C's perspective on the portion of the population that migrated to Egypt after the fall of Jerusalem. The material follows a B passage dealing with the same subject (chap. 43). For B, the true Israel appears to be limited to the community resident in Babylon, so it is not surprising that chap. 43 views the migration to Egypt as an act of disobedience that deserves severe divine punishment.[19] The focus of the C material, however, is entirely different. There is no implication that the Egyptian community is in any way illegitimate but, rather, the interest of the chapter is the community's religious behavior. The people in Egypt are judged for the worship of other gods in the same way that the preexilic community in the land was judged, and for the same reasons.

Conclusion

In order to draw firm conclusions concerning the functions of the C material, it would of course be necessary to examine all of the examples of such material. However, even the small bit of it that has been examined here suggests some preliminary observations. First, some of the C material is more consciously integrated into its immediate context than is sometimes thought to be the case. This integration is particularly visible in prose contexts, where scholars sometimes have difficulty distinguishing B and C. The C prose material in poetic contexts is more obviously visible, but even here there are sometimes linguistic and thematic links with the context. Second, while the C prose sometimes disambiguates the surrounding poetic oracles, this is not its only function. Sometimes C elaborates its context, as in chap. 29, or supplies a completely different perspective, as in chap. 44. Third, there is some continuity in perspective and even in vocabulary within the C material but possibly less than scholars have usually thought.

The above observations have two major implications for future research on the Jeremiah C prose. First, the apparent lack of consistency in function and theme in the C material and the variations in the way in which it is integrated into its context suggest that C editorial activity may not have all taken place at one time. If it did not, then perhaps McKane's notion of a "rolling corpus" provides the best model for understanding the way in which C came into the present text. Second, the variations in content and function that have been observed above raise questions about the utility of continuing to use the designation C as if it referred to a unified body of literature created by a single individual or group. It is also possible that what has traditionally been called C in fact represents a number of different editorial acts spread over a relatively long period of time. This notion seems to be supported by recent work on the textual history of Jeremiah, which suggests that the Hebrew text represents editorial activity that took place after the shorter Greek text was already fixed. If in fact C represents a somewhat lengthy his-

19. For a thorough discussion of the importance of the Babylonian exilic community in the later portions of Jeremiah, see K.-F. Pohlmann, *Studien zum Jeremiabuch* (Göttingen: Vandenhoeck & Ruprecht, 1978); and Seitz, *Theology in Conflict*.

tory of editorial activity, then thematic and linguistic continuity within the C material may have to be explained by assuming the existence of a relatively long-lived group responsible for the continuing work on the book. Who this group might have been would be the next obvious question, but that question will have to be a subject for future research.

The Exodus from Ur of the Chaldeans: A Chapter in Literary Archaeology

Yair Zakovitch
Hebrew University

The book of Genesis gives three reasons for Abraham's leaving his father's home for the land of Canaan:

(a) According to "the line (תולדות) of Terah" (Gen 11:27–32), it was Terah, Abraham's father, who initiated the exodus from Ur:

> Terah took his son Abram, his grandson Lot, the son of Haran, and his daughter-in-law Sarai, the wife of his son Abram, and they set out together from Ur of the Chaldeans for the land of Canaan; when they had come as far as Haran they settled there. The days of Terah came to 205 years; and Terah died in Haran. (vv. 31–32)

This literary element is continued in 12:4b–5:

> Abram was 75 years old when he left Haran. Abram took his wife Sarai and his brother's son Lot, and all the wealth that they had amassed, and the persons that they had acquired in Haran; and they set out for the land of Canaan.

The chronological data supplied by the author is important: In 11:26 we read: "When Terah had lived 70 years, he begot Abram, Nahor and Haran." Since Abram was 75 years old when he left Haran (12:7), his father was 145 years old at that time. According to this chronological system, Terah lived for 60 years after Abram left Haran, until he died at the age of 205 (11:32). The reader finds no answer to the inevitable question why Terah gave up his intention of reaching the land of Canaan and why his son Abram carried into reality his father's ambition. The Samaritan Pentateuch offers a different age for Terah at his death: 145 years. According to this figure, Terah died soon after reaching Haran—this explains why he could not continue his journey to Canaan and why Abram's journey to Canaan was the fulfilment of his father's will.

The Samaritan chronology is also reflected in Acts 7:4: "Then came [Abram] out of the land of the Chaldeans, and dwelt in Haran, and from thence, when his father was dead, [God] removed him into this land, wherein ye now dwell." The Samaritan Pentateuch (and, then, the New Testament), I propose, has preserved the original reading, which was then altered by the Masoretic Text (for reasons to be explained later).

The "line of Terah," along with other 'line' (תולדות) elements in Genesis, is attributed to the Priestly document. Critical scholars tend to uproot vv. 28–30 from P and to attribute them to J,[1] despite the absence of typical J characteristics. However, vv. 28–30 are required by the context (see below), if for no other reason than for mentioning the death of Haran: "Haran died in the lifetime of his father Terah, in his native land, Ur of the Chaldeans" (v. 28). Haran's death explains why Lot, Haran's son, leaves Ur without his father but with his grandfather, Terah, and with Abram, his uncle.

(b) A different tradition presents Abram's journey to Canaan as Abraham's own response to the divine test: "The Lord said to Abram, 'Go forth from your native land and from your father's house to the land that I will show you . . .' " (12:1–4a). This tradition is presently located in chap. 12, immediately after the tradition of the "line of Terah," and thus after Terah has died in Haran. God's command to Abraham is then given only when Abraham is already in Haran. According to this view, God does not even reveal his destination to Abram: Abram's positive response to God's command is the act that elevates him and illuminates the character of the patriarch—an aspect missing entirely from the first explanation. In this view, Abraham's setting out for Canaan represents his passing the "test" of God's command. Echoes of the "Go forth" motif can be found throughout biblical literature.[2]

(c) The third concept, like the first, sees Ur of the Chaldeans as the point of departure for the journey. In the story of the Covenant between the Pieces, God says to Abraham: "I am the Lord who brought you out from Ur of the Chaldeans to assign this land to you as a possession" (Gen 15:7). Another expression of this view can be found in Neh 9:7: "You are the Lord God, who chose Abram, who brought him out of Ur of the Chaldeans and changed his name to Abraham." It is well known that the formulation of God's words to Abraham carry the imprint of the first commandment: "I the Lord am your God who brought you out of the land of Egypt" (Exod 20:2, Deut 5:6), while the story of the Covenant between the Pieces indeed foretells the servitude of Israel in Egypt and the liberation from bondage (vv. 13–14, 16) and forms the scene of the covenant in a way that hints at both the enslavement and the redemption.[3] The words "I am the Lord who brought

1. See, e.g., J. Skinner, *Genesis* (ICC; 2d ed.; Edinburgh: T. & T. Clark, 1930) 235; E. A. Speiser, *Genesis* (AB 1; Garden City, N.Y.: Doubleday, 1964) 77.

2. See my "Through the Looking Glass: Reflections/Inversions of Genesis Stories in the Bible," *Biblical Interpretation* 1 (1993) 143–47.

3. See my *"And You Shall Tell Your Son": The Concept of the Exodus in the Bible* (Jerusalem: Magnes, 1991) 60.

you out from Ur of the Chaldeans" express divine grace, as becomes clear from the analogy to the Exodus from Egypt—a view that does not agree with the "test" concept of "Go forth. . . ." The analogy to the Exodus raises the question of the meaning of God's redemption of Abraham from Ur. For the time being I will leave this question open.

The strongest disagreement in the three different views described above is between the first two: the one that presents Terah as initiating the journey from Ur to Canaan, and the one that views the journey as Abraham's response to God's testing him. Already within the first tradition, one can distinguish certain adjustments that were made in order to make it more compatible with the second:

1. The Samaritan Pentateuch preserves the original reading concerning Terah's age at death as being 145. By lengthening his life, the MT created the impression that Terah had second thoughts about continuing the journey to Canaan and that his son, Abraham, then responded to the divine command to "Go forth . . ." in Haran, when he left his father (who was still alive) and his house behind him.
2. The words 'and they set out with them' (ויצאו אִתָּם) in 11:31 are difficult. It seems that other major textual witnesses (the Samaritan Pentateuch, LXX, and Vulgate) preserve the original reading: 'and he brought them out' (ויֹּצֵא אֹתָם).[4] The change was made by a reader who already knew the "Go forth . . ." tradition, which conflicted with a depiction of the departure for Canaan as resulting from Terah's initiative, not God's; this reader tried to diminish Terah's role by making his act a collective one: 'and they set out' (ויצאו). A further possibility is that the word 'them' (אֹתָם) was omitted first, but when reintroduced into the text, it was vocalized as אִתָּם ('with them') instead of אֹתָם ('them').

More courageous efforts to harmonize the contradicting traditions were made beyond the borders of the Hebrew Bible. One example is from the New Testament:

> The God of glory appeared unto our father Abraham, *when he was in Mesopotamia, before he dwelt in Haran.* And said unto him, Get thee out of thy country, and from thy kindred, and come into the land which I shall show thee. Then came he out of the land of the Chaldeans, and dwelt in Haran: and from thence, *when his father was dead*, he removed him into this land, wherein ye now dwell. (Acts 7:2–4, emphasis mine)

This paraphrase of Genesis firmly places the divine command in Ur, before Abraham and Terah's exodus from there. It also omits from the divine command the words "and from your father's house," since, according to its interpretation, Abraham left Ur with his father and his house. And, as we have

4. See, e.g., Skinner, *Genesis*, 238.

already seen, this tradition follows the chronology of the Samaritan Bible: Abraham continues to Canaan after his father's death.

The tradition in Acts, according to which God's command to Abraham to "Go forth" was delivered in Ur, is also found in the midrash: "While Terah was still in Ur of the Chaldeans the word was to Abraham 'Go forth,' and yet Terah left with him and died in Haran after some time" (*Lekaḥ Tob* on Genesis, 28b). Ibn Ezra writes: "It seems to me that God's command to Abraham, 'Go forth,' has preceded this verse, 'Terah took . . .' " (on Gen 11:31; see also his commentary to Gen 12:1). In Ibn Ezra's comments to Gen 15:7, he even tries to bring the third tradition into agreement with the first two: " 'who brought you out of Ur of the Chaldeans,' [this is] evidence that the command 'Go forth' was given there and not in Haran" (cf. Qimḥi on Gen 11:31, 12:1).

Another attempt to reconcile the contradicting traditions was made by Josephus Flavius:

> Terah, having come to hate Chaldea because of the loss of his lamented Haran, they all migrated to Haran in Mesopotamia, where Terah also died and was buried, after a life of 205 years . . . and at the age of 75 he [Abraham] left Chaldea, God having bidden him to remove to Canaan, and there he settled. (*Ant.* 1.6.5–1.7.1, §§151–54)

Josephus has omitted any reference to Terah's initiative to leave for Canaan, thereby causing the ominous schisms between the two neighboring traditions in chaps. 11–12 to magically disappear.

The messages of the different traditions vary. That of the "Go forth" tradition is obvious: with the words "Go forth . . . ," the series of tests set for Abraham both begins and ends, as one finds later in Gen 22:2: "Take your son, your favored one, Isaac, whom you love, and go forth to the land of Moriah." The midrash discusses this connection: "The Holy One, blessed be He, said to Abraham: 'The first test and the last test I try you with "go forth": "Go forth from your native land," and "Go forth to the land of Moriah" ' " (*Tanḥ*. Buber, Lech 4). The third tradition, that of "I am the Lord who brought you out from Ur . . ." (Gen 15:7), on the other hand, presents the patriarch's exodus as an expression of divine grace. The motive for the grace, however, whether there was a threat to Terah's family or they were suffering some sort of hardships, remains unclear. Regarding the first tradition we are left even more in the dark: how can we explain Terah's sudden decision to leave Ur for Canaan? I would like to focus now on this problem, that of uncovering the catalyst for Terah's leaving Ur in Gen 11:27–32. Finding the answer will also help solve the problem of the tradition in Gen 15:7.

The answer begins with a better understanding of Gen 11:28–30:

> Haran died in the lifetime of his father Terah, in his native land, Ur of the Chaldeans. Abram and Nahor took to themselves wives, the name of Abram's wife being Sarai and that of Nahor's wife Milcah, the daughter of Haran, the father of Milcah and Iscah. Now Sarai was barren, she had no child.

As I mentioned above, scholars have tended to argue that these verses are not intrinsic to their present P context. In fact, these verses supply information necessary for understanding a number of elements later on in the Abraham cycle. Already in the next verse, the information provided by these verses is vital, since they explain why Lot leaves Ur with his grandfather, Terah, but without his father, Haran:

> Terah took his son Abram, his grandson Lot the son of Haran, and his daughter-in-law Sarai, the wife of his son Abram, and they set out together from Ur of the Chaldeans for the land of Canaan; but when they had come as far as Haran, they settled there. (Gen 11:31)

The information is vital for other stories as well.

1. Terah's leaving for Haran will explain the settling of one of the family branches there (Gen 27:43, 28:10, 29:4), this despite the fact that Nahor and his family are not listed with the people who depart from Ur in v. 31. The narrative focuses instead on the characters who will continue on to Canaan.[5] The Samaritan Pentateuch deals with the absence of Nahor and his house from the list of those who leave Ur by adding them to the list in v. 31, though it creates some confusion: "Terah took his son Abram, his grandson Lot the son of Haran, and Sarai and Milcah his daughters-in-law, the wife of Abram and Nahor his sons. . . ." Certain Greek manuscripts read: "Abram and Nahor his sons" instead of "Abram his son."
2. The family line of Milcah is reported in v. 30, thus setting the scene for when she will bear children to Nahor (22:20–23).[6]
3. There is a curious absence of any reference concerning the identity of Sarah's father, while the identity of Milcah's father is revealed. This seeming omission, however, is important, for it will enable Abraham to half explain–half apologize concerning Sarah's identity in chap. 20: ". . . she is in truth my sister, my father's daughter though not my mother's; and she became my wife" (v. 12).[7]
4. The final verse of chap. 11 describes Sarah as barren (v. 30). This serves to introduce tension early on in the narrative, since it appears to contradict the recurrent promises for seed.

5. The biblical narrative always drops the secondary characters when they cease to be functional in the plot. See U. Simon, "Secondary Characters in the Biblical Narrative," in *Proceedings of the Fifth World Congress of Jewish Studies* (Jerusalem: Magnes, 1969) 1.31–36 [Heb.].

6. It seems that the words "the father of Iscah" are just an alternative reading to "the father of Milcah"; pay attention to the partial graphic identity of the two names. The verse thus preserves both readings, the wrong one, "the father of Iscah," and its emendation, "the father of Milcah."

7. See N. Sarna, "The Anticipatory Use of Information as a Literary Feature of the Genesis Narratives," in *The Creation of Sacred Literature* (ed. R. E. Friedman; Berkeley and Los Angeles: University of California Press, 1981) 79.

The elements embedded in the report about Terah's journey from Ur to Haran will thus help us to understand important matters in the course of the Abraham cycle, but they also add another difficulty to the difficulties we already face in this short tradition: why has Haran died during the lifetime of his father Terah? Is there any connection between his death and the departure of Terah from Ur, as claimed by Josephus Flavius (quoted above)?

The short tradition is expanded and interpreted in postbiblical literature. There, a story of Abraham's destroying the idols is linked to Haran's death in a fire—a name derivation of Ur (אור) from אוּר 'furnace'. The oldest known version of this story is found in the book of *Jubilees*:

> Abram arose by night, and burned the house of the idols, and he burned all that was in the house, and no man knew it. And they arose in the night and sought to save their Gods from the midst of the fire. And Haran hastened to save [the idols] but the fire flamed over him and he was burnt in the fire, and he died in Ur of the Chaldeans before Terah his father, and they buried him in Ur of the Chaldeans. And Terah went forth from Ur of the Chaldeans, he and his sons, to go into the land of Lebanon and into the land of Canaan. (*Jub.* 12:12–15)[8]

The fire/Ur tradition is very similar to the story of Hananiah, Mishael, and Azariah in the fiery furnace in Daniel 3. The question must be asked, therefore, whether the gaps that were left in the biblical story regarding Haran's death and Terah's departure were filled by borrowing from the story in Daniel. This addition may have been triggered by the association between the name *Ur* and the fiery furnace in Daniel.[9] On the other hand, perhaps the opposite is correct: an ancient story about Abraham and Haran, which for certain reasons was rejected by the writers of Genesis, left its imprint instead in Daniel 3, where its storyline was "recycled," but later found its way into the pseudepigrapha and rabbinic literature.

Cassuto was aware of the possibility that the later, extrabiblical literature preserved an older tradition, but he excused himself from addressing the

8. A development of the tradition of Abraham's being saved from the fire is found in Pseudo-Philo, *Bib. Ant.*, chap. 6; rabbinic literature knows many expressions of the story about Haran's death in the fire and Abraham's escaping it: see L. Ginzberg, *Legends of the Jews* (Philadelphia: Jewish Publication Society, 1904–38) 1.198–203, and esp. the comments, 5.212–14.

9. A similar process happens in Pseudo-Philo, *Bib. Ant.* 38, in the story about the death of the wicked judge Yair in the fiery furnace as a punishment for his command to worship the Baal. The story covertly derives the name Yair (יאיר) from אוּר 'furnace', and the name of the place where Yair was buried, Kāmôn (Judg 10:5), from the word קמין (*kamin*) in Postbiblical Hebrew. See my "Story of Yair and the Fiery Furnace," in *The Bible in the Light of Its Interpreters* (ed. S. Japhet; Jerusalem: Magnes, 1994) 141–56 [Heb.]. I now disagree with what I wrote there (p. 143), that the story of Abraham and Haran in Ur of the Chaldeans was modeled after the pattern of Daniel 3.

question: "It may be that the midrashic tales about Haran and his death preserve some vestiges of the ancient tradition, but obviously we are not in a position to come to any detailed conclusions."[10] I would like to continue from the point at which Cassuto stopped and to demonstrate that the tradition of Haran's death in the fire and Abraham's rescue from it was known to the writer of the Priestly document, who nonetheless decided to reject it from his document. This tradition also left its imprint on Daniel 3 and on postbiblical literature. In order to make my point, I must address two issues. First, I must provide evidence for the antiquity of the rejected tradition; and second, I must explain why the Priestly writer would have rejected it.

Before I turn to this task, it is worth mentioning that the phenomenon of an older, rejected tradition that influences the formation of other traditions is not unknown to us. Let me briefly discuss two examples. Loewenstamm, in his article "The Death of Moses,"[11] shows that Deuteronomy 34, which reports the death of Moses, is a case of covert polemics: by telling of the death of Moses and of his unknown burial place, Deuteronomy 34 rejects another tradition, that Moses did not actually die but instead ascended to heaven. The rejected tradition made its way into postbiblical literature and finds expression in Josephus's *Antiquities* (4.8.48, §326) and in the Babylonian Talmud (*b. Soṭa* 5a, 13b). It was also used in the formation of another biblical story: the story of Elijah's ascension in 2 Kgs 2:1–18 (as also other elements of Elijah's story follow the life-story of Moses[12]). The tradition about Moses' ascension was rejected because of the danger that he would become an object of worship—the reason also that Elijah's story was equally restrained: 2 Kgs 2:1–18 is a story whose hero is not Elijah but Elisha (the story of Elijah's spirit settling on Elisha), and Elijah's ascension is mentioned only incidentally (2 Kgs 2:1, 11).[13]

A second example is the birth story of the twins Perez and Zerah in Gen 38:27–30. This story, in which Perez overpowers Zerah and is thereby awarded his brother's firstborn birthright, was modeled after the birth story of the other twins who preceded them: Jacob and Esau. In both stories we find the sentence והנה ת(א)ומים בבטנה ('there were twins in her womb', Gen 25:24, 38:27). The story of Genesis 38 does not borrow directly from Gen 25:22–25, according to which Jacob emerges second from his mother's womb, but from the original tradition about Jacob and Esau, which was rejected from Genesis 25 but which nonetheless survived in one verse in the Bible, in the prophet Hosea's words about Jacob: 'in the womb he supplanted his brother' (בבטן עקב את אחיו, 12:4)—according to the tradition known to

10. U. Cassuto, *A Commentary on the Book of Genesis* (Jerusalem: Magnes, 1964) 2.271.

11. S. E. Loewenstamm, "The Death of Moses," in *Studies on the Testament of Abraham* (ed. G. W. E. Nickelsburg, Jr.; Missoula, Mont.: Scholars Press, 1976) 185–217.

12. See, e.g., my "Still Small Voice," *Tarbiẓ* 51 (1982) 329–46 [Heb.].

13. See A. Rofé, *The Prophetical Stories* (Jerusalem: Magnes, 1988) 44–46.

Hosea, already in the womb Jacob cheated his brother in order to emerge first! The author of Genesis 25 rejected this tradition because it cast a negative light on Jacob, but he left a vague echo of it in v. 26: readers so inclined may still claim that in the womb Jacob was already holding his brother back, since we are told that the two brothers struggled in their mother's womb (v. 22) and that Jacob "emerged, holding on to the heel of Esau" (v. 26). In fact, the author has cunningly transformed the original tradition: Jacob (יעקב) does not earn his name for cheating his brother (עָקֹב) but for merely holding on to his heel (עָקֵב, 25:26).[14]

Let me now return to our own problem and provide the evidence for the antiquity of the tradition regarding the fire in Ur.

(1) The words noting Haran's death, 'Haran died in the lifetime of his father' (וימת הרן על פני תרח אביו, Gen 11:28), are similar to the words referring to the death of the sons of Aaron in Num 3:4. There, "Nadab and Abihu died before the Lord (לפני יהוה) when they offered alien fire before the Lord in the wilderness of Sinai; and they left no sons. So it was Eleazar and Ithamar who served as priests in the lifetime of their father Aaron" (על פני אהרן אביהם). This verse has apparently become corrupted; originally it read: 'But Nadab and Abihu *died in the lifetime of their father* Aaron when they offered alien fire before the Lord . . .' (וימתו נדב ואביהוא על פני אהרן אביהם בהקריבם אש זרה לפני יהוה). This reading finds support in the version of 1 Chr 24:2: 'Nadab and Abihu died before their father' (וימת נדב ואביהוא לפני אביהם; and not 'before the Lord'!). We may compare also the comment of Naḥmanides: "'in the lifetime (על פני)' returns to the [first part of the verse]: but Nadab and Abihu 'died before the Lord in the lifetime of their father when they offered alien fire'; so reads Chronicles. . . ."

A reference to a son's death in the lifetime of his father is not found in this language anywhere else in the Bible. Another common element is fire: Nadab's and Abihu's death by fire, "And fire came forth from the Lord and consumed them; thus they died before the Lord" (Lev 10:2), may have been influenced by the story of Haran's death by fire, from which was also taken the expression למות על פני אביהם.

The connection between the two stories is made in the midrash:

> "So Eleazar and Ithamar served as priests in the presence of their father" (Num 3:4); R. Isaac said it was when he was alive. R. Ḥiyya b. R. Abba said: It was after he died. In conformity with the view of R. Isaac, who said that it was while he was yet alive, here the word "presence" is written and elsewhere it says, "And Haran died in the presence of Terah his father" (Gen 11:28).[15]

14. See my "Jacob's Deceit," in *B. Ben-Yehuda Jubilee Volume* (Tel Aviv: The Israel Society of Biblical Literature, 1981) 125–28 [Heb.]; Y. Zakovitch and A. Shinan, *The Story of Judah and Tamar* (Jerusalem: Institute of Jewish Studies, Hebrew University, 1992) 223–24 [Heb.].

15. *Lev. Rab.* 20:11; trans. J. Neusner (Chicago and London, 1986) 389.

(2) Daniel 3 (which I believe was written under the influence of the story of Abram in Ur of the Chaldeans) takes place in the plain of Dura (בקעת דורא, v. 1). Menahem Ibn Saruk (in his Maḥberet, under אור 4) explains the meaning of אור as a 'plain' (בקעה),[16] finding support in Neh 9:7, Isa 24:15, and other verses: "Ur of the Chaldeans is the plain of Chaldean." He identifies the plain with the one mentioned in Gen 11:2: "A plain (בקעה) in the land of Shinar."[17]

The word Dura (דורא), a place-name in Daniel, is translated in *Codex Venetus* of the Septuagint as 'bonfire' (πρήσεως); compare וְדוּר העצמים תחתיה 'also pile the wood [read עצים for עצמים] under it' (Ezek 24:5) and also המדורה 'blaze' (v. 9). Rashi and Qimḥi on Ezekiel, as well as the Septuagint, reflect similar understandings of the meaning of the word.[18]

This evidence suggests that the name בקעת דורא 'plain of Dura' was intended to carry a double meaning: אור 'Ur', with the meaning of 'plain' but also with the meaning of 'fire', derived from the story of Abraham in Ur.

(3) Some imprints of the lost tradition can be traced in the life story of Haran's son, Lot, in the book of Genesis: Haran was burned in the fire (as a punishment for his sin), but his son, Lot, did not sin and so escaped death in the burning city of Sodom when he was rescued by God: ". . . and brought him out (ויצאהו) and left him outside the city" (19:16; cf. 11:31).

(4) The word הוצאה 'bringing out', which we find in relation to Lot, reopens the question regarding the nature of the divine grace to which God refers in his words to Abraham in Gen 15:7: "I am the Lord who brought you out from Ur of the Chaldeans." It seems that the author of this tradition had in mind the story of Haran's death in the fire and Abraham's rescue from it; the word "Ur" in Gen 15:7 hints at the name derivation of Ur in the lost tradition. If I am correct, then Gen 15:7 is not a third, independent tradition about circumstances of the departure to Canaan, but a reference to the story that hides behind the vague traditions about Ur in Genesis 11.

It is interesting that the chapter that mentions God's favor to Abraham by bringing him out of Ur also mentions תנור 'oven' in the picture of the covenant: ". . . there appeared a smoking oven, and a flaming torch which passed between those pieces" (v. 17)[19] —אור and תנור are synonymous, as we find in Isa 31:9: ". . . who has a fire (אור) in Zion, who has an oven (תנור) in Jerusalem."

A reader who accepts my claim that an ancient story about Haran's death in Ur and Abraham's rescue from the fire was rejected by the Priestly writer will still wonder about the motive behind silencing this tradition. The Bible

16. Ibn Saruk, *The First Hebrew and Chaldaic Lexicon to the Old Testament by Menaḥem Ben Saruk* (trans. H. Filipowski; London, 1854) 32.

17. See also Rashi on Gen 11:10; Isa 11:8, 24:15.

18. See J. A. Montgomery, *Daniel* (ICC; Edinburgh: T. & T. Clark, 1927) 199.

19. Zakovitch, "*And You Shall Tell Your Son,*" 60.

does hint at a tradition according to which Israel's ancestors were idol-worshipers before their arrival in Canaan: "Beyond the Euphrates lived your forefathers in olden times, Terah father of Abraham and Nahor, and worshiped other gods" (Josh 24:2).[20] The book of Genesis, however, does its best to minimize the impression of idol-worship in order to remove any possible association with idol-worship from the nation's ancestors and from the ancestors' ancestors.[21] A similar phenomenon can be found in a Christian apocryphal work, the *Protevangelium of James*, which portrays even the birth of Mary, the mother of Jesus, as a miraculous birth, in order to more fully dis-associate Jesus from any suggestion of physical passion in his origins.[22]

The Priestly document prefers to begin the presentation of the relationship between God and Abraham in the land of Canaan, in a covenant between them (chap. 17). This represents the second of four covenants made in this document. With each one the human partner in the covenant becomes smaller: with the renewed humanity following the flood (Gen 9:8–17); with all of Abraham's descendants (Genesis 17); with the children of Israel (Exod 31:12–17); and with the priesthood, the climax of the process (Num 25:10–13).[23]

It seems, then, that the Priestly document indeed hides from us a tradition according to which Terah wanted to leave Ur of the Chaldeans and to go to Canaan following the death of Haran in the fire and the rescue of Abraham. But Terah managed only to reach Haran (where some members of the family settled), where he died. In this way Terah, the idol-worshiper, is prevented from entering Canaan, whereas Abraham, the one who challenged idol-worship, is allowed to enter the promised land.

The pre-Priestly tradition was rejected but continued to be told orally. Daniel 3 was created in its image. In postbiblical literature, the lost tradition made its way to the surface, both in apocryphal works and in rabbinic literature. In the book of Genesis we can still find a few traditions concerning the motive for leaving the old world: the one about Terah who wishes to go to Canaan (Gen 11:27–32) and, in contrast to it, the tradition about Abraham who is commanded by his God to go there (12:1–4a). Efforts to bring the two

20. The words "Terah, father of Abraham and father of Nahor" are an addition; they were added in order to prevent any thought about Abraham's being one of the idol-worshipers. See ibid., 122.

21. Exceptional are the story about Rachel's theft of the Teraphim (Genesis 31; but the Teraphim may be understood there as mantic objects and not as gods) and the story about the burial of alien gods by Jacob in Shechem (Gen 35:2bα, 4), a secondary polemical element, the intent of which is to present Shechem as a site of idolatry defiled forever; see my "Through the Looking Glass," 126 and 141.

22. For an English translation of the text, see E. Hennecke, *New Testament Apocrypha* (Philadelphia: Westminster, 1963) 375–88.

23. For the four covenants of the Priestly document and their mutual relationship, see my *For Three . . . and for Four* (Jerusalem: Makor, 1979) 141–43 [Heb.].

into agreement are already reflected in Genesis 11 (and the textual witnesses even strengthen the evidence for this process). The third tradition, the one about divine grace which brings Abraham out of Ur (15:7), is but a continuation of the lost tradition, a reference to it that hangs in the air and cannot find a foothold in the book.

This short paper is an exercise in literary archaeology: an attempt to penetrate the surface of the written traditions into the depths of more ancient layers with the assistance of some reflections of the missing tradition in later parallels and in its own phases that found their way into later literary strata.

Part III

Judaica

Signs of Ambivalence in Islamic Spain: Arabic Representations of Samuel the Nagid

Ross Brann
Cornell University

שְׁמוֹ בָּרוּךְ וְהוּא כִּשְׁמוֹ מְבֹרָךְ
וְהַמִּתְבָּרְכִים בִּשְׁמוֹ בְּרוּכִים:
—Judah ha-Levi

Despite its reputation as a highly tolerant society and its romanticized popular image as an interfaith utopia, Muslim Spain of the High Middle Ages was repeatedly torn by tribal and ethnic social cleavages, and socio-economic struggles and factional rivalries among Andalusian-Arabs, Berbers, the *ṣaqāliba*, and Mozarabic Christians. For their part the Jews prospered materially under Muslim rule and apparently ranked among the most acculturated and politically complacent groups in the society. They readily accepted Muslim political and cultural hegemony and, until the rivalries between the *taifa* kingdoms of the 11th century, seem to have had no stake in the various internecine disputes among Muslims. Associations between Muslims and Jews in al-Andalus nevertheless seem to have been charged on occasion and, it appears, marked by contradiction. On the one hand were extended periods of calm and tolerance; on the other were sporadic outbreaks of tension, reaction, and deteriorating relations between the two communities.

Research on this complex relationship has primarily relied on the "direct testimony" of historical chronicles, *adab* and travel literature, legal codes and

Author's note: Research for this essay was made possible by fellowships from the National Endowment for the Humanities and the John Simon Guggenheim Memorial Foundation. The author wishes to thank both institutions for their generous support.

responsa, literary polemics, documentary materials pertaining to Spain preserved in the Cairo Genizah,[1] and to a lesser extent upon information culled from imaginative narratives and poetry. Have these various documentary and literary sources been exhausted or, if we ask different questions of them, can they legitimately be read in new ways? Apart from their significance as primary materials for the political, social, and cultural history of al-Andalus, the texts that have come down to us are insufficiently utilized as sources for exploring the nuances of how the Muslims and Jews of al-Andalus thought of and lived with one another during the High Middle Ages. In the words of Brian Stock:

> Accounting for what actually happened is now recognized to be only part of the story; the other part is the record of what individuals thought was happening, and the ways in which their feelings, perceptions, and narratives of events either influenced or were influenced by the realities they faced.[2]

If we apply to medieval texts poststructuralist methods and insights critical to literary study, we are likely to generate new readings of the sources—readings that emphasize the *construction of social meaning* and the reciprocal way in which texts both reflect and shape the attitudes of the society in which they are produced. Issues of power relations among social groups, for example, are frequently played out in textual representations of individuals and events, crisscrossing the imaginary textual boundary between the supposedly objective and the allegedly subjective, the "real" and the "imaginary."[3] Again, to cite Stock's keen formulation of the two orders of the textual experience:

> The historical is not isolated from the literary as fact and representation. The two aspects of the textual experience are multidimensional, and the objectivity of the alleged events spills over into the alleged subjectivity of the records, perceptions, feelings and observations.[4]

1. On the extent of *genizah* materials pertaining to Spain, see S. D. Goitein, *A Mediterranean Society: The Jewish Communities of the Arab World As Portrayed in the Documents of the Cairo Genizah* (6 vols.; Berkeley: University of California Press, 1967–93) 1.70. On business partnerships among Jews and Muslims in Spain, ibid., 428.
2. Brian Stock, "History, Literature, and Medieval Textuality," *Yale French Studies* 70 (1986) 7.
3. As explained by the critic W. J. T. Mitchell, "Representation," *Critical Terms for Literary Study* (ed. Frank Lenticchia and Thomas McLaughlin; Chicago: University of Chicago Press, 1990) 15:

> representation . . . can never be completely divorced from political and ideological questions; one might argue, in fact, that representation is precisely the point where these questions are most likely to enter a (literary) work. If literature is a "representation of life" then representation is exactly the place where "life," in all its social and subjective complexity, gets into the literary work.

4. Stock, "History, Literature and Medieval Textuality," 16.

Whereas the fabulous aspects of Latin and Arabic accounts of the Muslim conquest of Spain have been recognized,[5] the literary construction of the Jew and Muslim in Hispano-Arabic and Hispano-Hebrew historiography, *adab* literature, narratives, and poetry have yet to be studied. We may thus re-read Arabic (and Hebrew) annalistic and literary sources *as texts*, reconsidering what they choose to report (and not to report) and examining *how* they relate, that is, their discursive language, narrative and rhetorical strategies, and their historically contingent relationship to other forms of cultural discourse.

How then did Muslim and Jewish literary intellectuals represent members of one another's community? The slavishly fawning lyrics of the Hispano-Arabic poet al-Munfatil in praise of Samuel ibn Naghrīla,[6] for example, or the positive representation of Jewish courtiers and intellectuals such as Ḥasdai ibn Shapruṭ or Abū al-Faḍl ibn Ḥasdai in Ṣāʿid al-Andalusī's (b. 1029) *Ṭabaqāt al-umam* seem completely at odds with the notorious attacks on the Jews produced by ʿAlī ibn Ḥazm (d. 1064) and Abū Isḥāq of Elvira (d. 1067), devised during nearly the same time and in the same place. For their part, Hebrew and Judeo-Arabic texts from the period oscillate between a willingness to represent trenchant Muslim foes in a negative light, as in Ibn Naghrīla's (993–1056) poetic portrayal of the ʿAbbādids of Seville, and a deep-seated reluctance to portray Muslims in any light, almost to the point of silence.

For purposes of this paper, part of a larger project devoted to mapping literary reflections of power relations among Jews and Muslims in al-Andalus, I would like to concentrate on the figure of Samuel the Nagid, known in Arabic historiography as (Abū Ibrāhīm) Ismāʿīl ibn Naghrīla. Rabbinic scholar, Hebrew poet and grammarian, and arguably the most significant Jewish cultural mediator of the 11th century, Ibn Naghrīla was also a highly skilled *kātib* who began a gradual rise through the ranks of the state chancery around 1020 to prominence at the court of Zirid Granada. As a consequence of the unique range of his literary and scholarly activities and his political savvy and opportunism, Samuel's stature grew along parallel tracks in two distinct domains, the Muslim civic sphere and the specifically Jewish social and cultural milieu. In the latter, Ibn Naghrīla came to assume the eminent role of Nagid, the unofficial head of the Jews of al-Andalus,[7] whereas in the former he functioned as the highest fiscal (*jibāyat al-māl*; revenue collection)

5. See Roger Collins, *The Arab Conquest of Spain, 710–797* (Oxford: Basil Blackwell, 1989) 17–18, 23–36; and ʿAbdulwāḥid Dhanun Ṭāha, *The Muslim Conquest and Settlement of North Africa and Spain* (London and New York: Routledge, 1989) 84–93.

6. Ibn Bassām al-Shantarīnī, *al-Dhakhīra fī maḥāsin ahl al-jazīra* (8 vols.; ed. Iḥsān ʿAbbās; Beirut: Dār al-Thaqāfa, 1979) part 1/vol. 2.761–65. This text and the tradition transmitted in Ibn Bassām's own name are analyzed in my work in progress, *Power in the Portrayal: Representations of Muslims and Jews in Islamic Spain.*

7. According to Abraham ibn Daud (*Sefer ha-Qabbalah / Book of Tradition* [ed. and trans. Gerson D. Cohen; Philadelphia: Jewish Publication Society, 1967] Heb. text, p. 56; Eng. trans., p. 74), the title was apparently conferred upon him around 1027.

and administrative official of the Banū Zīrī from 1038 until his death in 1056. Ibn Naghrīla may have served Granada in some military capacity as well. According to the 41 so-called "war poems" and their Arabic superscriptions preserved in his *dīwān*, the poet accompanied the army of Granada on some 20 expeditions, although the nature and extent of his involvement, unattested in any Arabic source, are open to question.[8]

Ismāʿīl ibn Naghrīla, the Nagid, is thus an ideal subject for a study of Arabic representations of Jews in Muslim Spain on account of his singular importance as a protean figure to the Jews of that land during the 11th century, the influence he achieved and political power he wielded within al-Andalus, and the variety of Arabic (and Hebrew) texts in which he is mentioned. If (as noted above) these texts have been handled as direct historical testimony on Ibn Naghrīla's role in the affairs of Muslims and Jews respectively,[9] how has the attitude of the texts toward Ibn Naghrīla been assessed by modern readers? Conventional wisdom is divided on this question. Several scholars emphasize that Ibn Naghrīla was highly regarded by the Arab chroniclers of Spain especially for his "modesty, prudence, and munificence"[10] and that "Muslim writers . . . speak of Samuel with great respect."[11] Reading the same sources, others conclude that Muslim writers (with the notable exception of Ṣāʿid al-Andalusī) speak of Ibn Naghrīla with enmity and contempt.[12] Clearly, the construction of Ibn Naghrīla in Hispano-Arabic literature can

8. The texts and superscriptions may be found in Dov Yarden (ed.), *Dīwān shᵉmuʾel ha-nagid*, vol. 1: *Ben Tᵉhillim* (Jerusalem: Hebrew Union College Press, 1966) 3–145. See Ḥayyim Schirmann, "The Wars of Samuel the Nagid," reprinted in *Studies in the History of Hebrew Poetry and Drama* (2 vols.; Jerusalem: Bialik, 1979) 1.149–89 [Heb.]; and Angel Sáenz-Badillos and Judit Targarona Borras, *Šĕmuʾel ha-Nagid, Poemas I: Desde el Campo de Batalla Granada 1038–1056* (Cordoba: El Almendro, 1988).

9. David J. Wasserstein ("Samuel ibn Naghrīla ha-Nagid and Islamic Historiography in al-Andalus," *al-Qanṭara* 14 [1993] 109–25) recently showed how investigation of the historical Ibn Naghrīla has proceeded along strictly divided linguistic and cultural lines. Wasserstein insightfully calls for a new inclusive approach to Ibn Naghrīla that would utilize all the available sources.

10. See Amin T. Tibi (trans.), *The Tibyān: Memoirs of ʿAbd Allāh b. Buluggīn Last Zirid Amir of Granada* (Leiden: Brill, 1986) 206. In this respect Ismāʿīl is typically contrasted with his son Yūsuf, who is portrayed as conceited and arrogant. See Henri Pérès, *La poésie andalouse en arab classique au xiᵉ siècle* (2d ed.; Paris: Adrien-Maisonneuve, 1953) 270.

11. Sarah Stroumsa, "From Muslim Heresy to Jewish-Muslim Polemics: Ibn al-Rāwandī's *Kitāb al-Dāmigh*," *JAOS* 107 (1987) 769. So too Arie Schippers (*Spanish Hebrew Poetry and the Arabic Literary Tradition: Arabic Themes in Hebrew Andalusian Poetry* [Leiden: Brill, 1994] 54), who writes: "Muslim sources speak favourably of Samuel han-Nagid."

12. For example, see S. M. Stern, "Two New Data about Ḥasdai B. Shapruṭ," *Zion* 11 (1946) 143 n. 6 [Heb.]; and Neḥemya Allony, "Songs of Zion in the Poetic Works of R. Shmuel Hanagid," *Sinai* 68 (1971) 212–15 [Heb.].

be seen as unstable and complex rather than as determined and unambiguous.[13] The problem lies in the texts as much as between the readers.

Ṣāʿid al-Andalusī—Ṭabaqāt al-umam

Let us now turn to the representative texts—first a brief passage found at the close of the final chapter (chap. 14 devoted to the Banū Isrāʾīl and their descendants the Jews) of Ṣāʿid b. Aḥmad al-Andalusī's universal history of science and culture, *Ṭabaqāt al-umam*. Ṣāʿid al-Andalusī, it should be noted, was a *qāḍī* in Toledo and according to the testimony of *Ṭabaqāt al-umam*, a historian of science committed to the transconfessional search for truth.[14]

The seemingly insignificant and laconic passage in *Ṭabaqāt al-umam* presents Ibn Naghrīla in a completely positive light. He is introduced by his *kunya* Abū Ibrāhīm, a sign of respect:[15]

> Of those (experts in Jewish law) who lived in al-Andalus, we have Abū Ibrāhīm Ismāʿīl ibn Yūsuf al-Kātib, known by the name of al-Ghazal, who worked in the service of al-ʾAmīr Bādīs ibn Ḥabbūsh al-Ṣanhājī, the king of Granada and its provinces. *He was the director* [*mudabbir*] *of the state. He knew the Jewish laws and how to defend and protect them more than any other Jewish scholar of al-Andalus.*[16] [emphasis mine]

The text notes Ibn Naghrīla's preeminent administrative (i.e., political) position within Islamic Granada, passing over it without protest. More revealing is the observation of Samuel's distinctive role within Jewish society: he is identified as one who not only possesses expert knowledge of religious law but also as one who strives successfully to "protect and defend" its application and observance. The text thus projects a uniquely important value of

13. See the various lines of verse concerning Ibn Naghrīla assembled by Pérès, *La poésie andalouse en arab classique*, 268–73.

14. On this attitude as manifested in Baghdad during the High Middle Ages and the inclusion of non-Muslim minorities in the intellectual and cultural life of the age, see Joel L. Kramer, *Humanism in the Renaissance of Islam: The Cultural Revival during the Buyid Age* (Leiden: Brill, 1986) 75–86.

15. See Ignaz Goldziher, *Muslim Studies* (2 vols.; ed. S. M. Stern; trans. C. R. Barber and S. M. Stern; London: Allen & Unwin, 1967) 1.242.

16. Ṣāʿid ibn Aḥmad al-Andalusī, *Ṭabaqāt al-umam* (ed. Louis Cheiko; Beirut: al-Maṭbaʿa al-Kāthūlīkiyya li-l-Ābāʾ al-Yaṣuʿiyyīn, 1912) 90; idem, *Science in the Medieval World* (trans. Semaʿan I. Salem and Alok Kumar; Austin: University of Texas Press, 1991) 82. Compare the translations of Joshua Finkel ("An Eleventh Century Source for the History of Jewish Scientists in Mohammedan Land [Ibn Ṣāʿid]," *JQR* 18 [1927] 54): "Abū Ibrāhīm's mastery of the Talmud and his skill for its vindication were such that none of his predecessors in Spain ever displayed"; and Moshe Perlmann ("Eleventh-Century Andalusian Authors on the Jews of Granada," *PAAJR* 18 [1948–49] 271): "he was learned in the law of the Jews and understood how to prevail in disputes on its behalf and to rebut its opponents."

Islamic behavior onto a Jewish communal leader and religious scholar operating within the context of his own religious community: Ibn Naghrīla corresponds to the image of a just Muslim ruler whose obligation to uphold Islamic law defines his legitimacy in the eyes of God and Muslim society![17]

Is it a coincidence that such an image turns up in an 11th-century Hispano-Arabic text even though the subject in question is a non-Muslim? The record of the various *mulūk al-ṭawā'if* in observing and maintaining Islamic law was continuously called into question by Muslim jurists, scholars, and literati. Many writers go so far as to accuse the party kings of breaking faith with Islam, particularly for their excessive materialism, their association with *dhimmīs*, and habit of elevating non-Muslims to positions of authority.[18] Such charges were by no means unique to 11th-century al-Andalus. Similar criticism was sounded in the Muslim East regarding the ruler's betrayal of Islamic values in showing preferences to Jews and Christians.[19] Because appointment of non-Muslims to high government office was a persistent source of complaint,[20] the image of Ibn Naghrīla as upholder of [Jewish] holy law

17. On the ruler's obligation to uphold the *sharīʿa* and the nomenclature used to describe various types of rulers in Islam, see Bernard Lewis, "Usurpers and Tyrants: Notes on Some Islamic Political Terms," in *Logos Islamikos: Studia Islamica in Honorem Georgii Michaelis Wickens* (ed. Roger M. Savory and Dionisius A. Agius; Toronto: Pontifical Institute of Mediaeval Studies, 1984) 259ff.

18. Several prooftexts for this pious complaint are discussed in David Wasserstein, *The Rise and Fall of the Party Kings: Politics and Society in Islamic Spain, 1002–1086* (Princeton: Princeton University Press, 1985) 280. So too ʿAlī ibn Ḥazm, "*al-Radd ʿalā ibn al-naghrīla al-yahūdī*," in *Rasā'il ibn ḥazm al-Andalusī* (4 vols.; ed. Iḥsān ʿAbbās; Beirut: al-Mu'assasa al-ʿarabiyya li-l-dirāsāt wa-l-nashr, 1980–83) 3.41; 67, on which see below. For a faint echo of a complaint about Ḥasdai ibn Shapruṭ who served as a physician and diplomat at the court of ʿAbd al-Raḥmān III, see the line of verse preserved in Ibn Rushd's (d. 1198) *Talkhīṣ kitāb arisṭūṭālīs fī-l-shiʿr* (Averroes' Middle Commentary on Aristotle's Poetics) (trans. Charles E. Butterworth; Princeton: Princeton University Press, 1980) 115; and Stern, "Two New Data about Ḥasdai B. Shapruṭ," 141.

19. See the account of the Caliph al-Ma'mūn's experience with an influential but brazen Jew and similar stories transmitted by Ghāzī ibn al-Wāsiṭī (13th century), "*Radd ʿala ahl al-dhimma wa-man tabaʿahum*" (ed. and trans. by Richard Gottheil) "An Answer to the Dhimmīs," *JAOS* 41 (1927) text, 396; trans., 429–30. On public opposition to Jewish officials in Fatimid Egypt, see Walter Y. Fischel, *Jews in the Economic and Political Life of Mediaeval Islam* (London: The Royal Asiatic Society, 1937) 88–89; and Goitein, *A Mediterranean Society*, 2:374ff. On *dhimmi* public service in general, see Arthur S. Tritton, *The Caliphs and Their Non-Muslim Subjects: A Critical Study of the Covenant of ʿUmar* (London: Oxford University Press, 1930; reprinted London: Frank Cass, 1970) 18–36; and now Mark R. Cohen, *Under Crescent and Cross: The Jews in the Middle Ages* (Princeton: Princeton University Press, 1994) 65–68.

20. Bernard Lewis, *The Jews of Islam* (Princeton: Princeton University Press, 1984) 28ff.

and "director of the [Islamic] state" serves as a doubly ironic comment on the Islamic scene.

Ibn Ḥayyān—al-Iḥāṭa fī akhbār gharnāṭa (Ibn al-Khaṭīb)

A more fully drawn portrait of Ibn Naghrīla emerges in a tradition reported by the great Hispano-Arabic historian Abū Marwān Ibn Ḥayyān al-Qurṭubī (987/988–1076). It is transmitted in *al-Iḥāṭa fī akhbār gharnāṭa*, a chronicle of Granada compiled by the 14th-century Andalusī scholar Ibn al-Khaṭīb (1313–75):

> This cursed man was a superior man, although God did not inform him of the right religion. He possessed extensive knowledge and tolerated insolent behavior with patience. He combined a solid and wise character with a lucid spirit and polite and friendly manners. Endowed with refined courtesy, he was able to utilize any circumstances to flatter his enemies or to disarm their hatred with his kind conduct. He was an extraordinary man. He wrote in both languages: Arabic and Hebrew. He knew the literatures of both peoples. He went deeply into the principles of the Arabic language and was familiar with the works of the most subtle grammarians. He spoke and wrote classical Arabic with the greatest ease, using this language in the letters which he wrote on behalf of his king. He used the usual Islamic formulas, the eulogies of God and Muḥammad, our Prophet, and recommended to the addressee to live according to Islam. In brief, one would believe that his letters were written by a pious Muslim. He was excellent in the sciences of the ancients, in mathematics as well as astronomy. Also in the field of logic he possessed ample knowledge. In dialectics he even prevailed over his adversaries. Despite his lively spirit he spoke little and reflected much. He assembled a beautiful library. He died on the 10th of Muḥarram, 459 A.H. The Jews decorated his coffin and bowed in deference (as it passed by). They held fast to him in their anguish and mourned him publicly.[21]

Apart from its perfunctory reference to Samuel's "accursed" religious identity, the *Iḥāṭa*, like *Ṭabaqāt al-umam*, casts Ibn Naghrīla in an uncommonly favorable light. The text attributes to him every conceivable trait of a noble and aristocratic character: refined manners, disarming resourcefulness in dealing with associates and enemies, linguistic skill and eloquence, and literary and scientific knowledge and learning such as were valued in al-Andalus and all of medieval Islam.

Ibn Ḥayyān's depiction of Ismāʿīl is at least as significant for what it neglects to report as for what it relates. The tradition transmitted in his name by Ibn al-Khaṭīb alludes to but makes no explicit mention of Ibn Naghrīla's pivotal role in the political and financial administration of Zirid Granada. In

21. Ibn Ḥayyān quoted by Lisān al-Dīn ibn al-Khaṭīb, *al-Iḥāṭa fī akhbār gharnāṭa* (2 vols.; ed. Muḥammad ʿAbd Allāh ʿInān; Cairo: al-Khanjī, 1973) 1.438–39; partial trans. Schippers, *Spanish Hebrew Poetry and the Arabic Literary Tradition*, 54–55.

this respect the text can be said to portray Ibn Naghrīla as a "mere" court secretary, a singularly gifted and important one to be sure, but certainly not as a central actor in the exercise of the power of the Islamic state. This striking omission is rectified and balanced by the previous source reported by Ibn al-Khaṭīb, a brief citation from *al-Bayān al-mughrib* by Ibn ʿIdhārī al-Marrākushī. Ibn ʿIdhārī identifies Ibn Naghrīla as an essential figure in the exercise of power in Zirid Granada. As though it were a case in point of the harm that comes to Islam when a non-Muslim attains such a position, the text reports that Ibn Naghrīla and the lower-level Jewish functionaries who accompanied his designation as *wazīr* amassed wealth and displayed arrogant behavior toward the Muslims.[22]

ʿAbd Allāh b. Buluggīn, the last *amīr* of Zirid Granada (r. 1073–90), takes a completely different approach to portraying Ibn Naghrīla in *al-Tibyān*. In sharp contrast to Ibn ʿIdhārī's renegade Jewish *wazīr*, ʿAbd Allāh's revisionist historical memoir makes Ismāʿīl out to be a perspicacious political operator who conducts his affairs responsibly in the interests of the ruler and the state. Moreover, Ibn Naghrīla accepts working in accordance with the sensibilities of Muslims and within the limits circumscribed for *dhimmī* subjects by Islamic law. ʿAbd Allāh asserts with complete assurance that

> Abū Ibrāhīm was a Jewish *dhimmi* who would not lust after power. . . . Abū Ibrāhīm, however, was not accorded any power over Muslims in any issue whether right or wrong.[23]

Based on the poetic account of the Nagid's military exploits in his *dīwān* and the extent of his political and financial functions described in other Arabic sources, it appears that the *Tibyān* aims to minimize Ibn Naghrīla's role in the affairs of state in order to salvage Bādīs' (ʿAbd Allāh's grandfather) sullied reputation as a pious Muslim.[24]

To return to Ibn Ḥayyān: the *Iḥāṭa* presents Ibn Naghrīla as the veritable embodiment of courtly virtues and secretarial skills. Most significantly, Ibn

22. Ibn al-Khaṭīb, *al-Iḥāṭa*, 1.438; and Ibn ʿIdhārī al-Marrākushī, *al-Bayān al-mughrib fī akhbār al-maghrib* (ed. E. Lévi-Provençal; Beirut: Dār al-Thaqāfa, 1930; reprinted, 1967) 3.264. When Yaddayr schemed to depose his cousin Bādīs (1038), Ibn Naghrīla came to the aid of the new *amīr*. He foiled the plot, bringing down the (Muslim) conspirators as a result. The Nagid describes his and Granada's final reckoning with Yaddayr (1041) in two very long poems, "*Sheʿeh mini ʿamiti we-ḥaveri*," in Yarden (ed.), *Dīwān shemuʾel ha-nagid*, 1.31–34 [#7] and "*Levavi ḥam be-qirbi*," in ibid., 1.35–38 [#9]. These lyrics are noteworthy for the way in which they establish a correspondence between the poet's personal adversaries and the enemies of Israel, that is, the Jews. The literary construction of Muslims in the Nagid's poetry will be studied in my monograph-in-progress on representations of Muslims and Jews in Islamic Spain.

23. *The Tibyān*, 55–56.

24. *The Tibyān*, 211; Lisān al-Dīn ibn al-Khaṭīb, *Aʿmāl al-aʿlām fī man būyiʿa qabl al-iḥtilām min mulūk al-islām* (ed. E. Lévi-Provençal; Beirut: Dār al-Makshūf, 1956) 232. The *Tibyān*'s portrayal of Yūsuf ibn Naghrīla is another matter.

Naghrīla is lauded for his exquisite use of the appropriate formulas of Islamic piety in his correspondence on behalf of the Zirids.[25] What with the words of the inimitable Qurʾān flowing from his stylus if not literally from his lips, Samuel's Jewishness is something of a marvel to behold, nearly more apparent than real. Signs of Ibn Naghrīla's cultural otherness are limited to his knowledge of Hebrew language and literature. Reference to any form of behavior contrary to Islam and abhorrent or incomprehensible to Muslims is suppressed. Much like the image of the noble Moor in the *Poema de Mio Cid* (ca. 1207),[26] the figure of Ibn Naghrīla in *al-Iḥāṭa* is less a Jew than a Jew inscribed in the text, an emblem of an idealized *dhimmī* who is a Muslim in all but name.[27]

ʿAli Ibn Ḥazm—al-Fiṣal fī-l-milal; al-Radd ʿala ibn al-naghrīla al-yahūdī

The figure of Samuel ibn Naghrīla is also a subject in a text, possibly two texts, by ʿAlī ibn Ḥazm [994–1064], the outstanding Hispano-Arabic literary intellectual of the 11th century. The texts present a fundamentally different portrait of Ibn Naghrīla than either Ṣāʿid b. Aḥmad al-Andalusī or Ibn

25. The legendary vignette (preserved by Abraham ibn Daud, *Sefer ha-Qabbalah*, 54–55 [Eng. trans., pp. 72–73], and for which S. M. Stern, "The Life of Samuel the Nagid," *Zion* 15 [1950] 135–38 [Heb.], identified a Hispano-Arabic parallel in a tale of how al-Manṣūr's eloquence and stylistic gifts hastened his ascent to power) concerning Samuel's accidental "discovery" in a Malagan spice shop is a significant illustration of the ecumenical importance of the rhetorical ideal of life and of the Andalusi Jews' expert knowledge of Arabic. Saʿadya ibn Danān (15th century), "*Ha-maʾamar ʿal seder ha-dorot*," in Zvi Hirsch Edelmann (ed.), *Ḥemdah g^enuzah* (Königsberg: Gruber and Guphrat, 1856) 29a = Judit Targarona ("*Ha-maʾamar ʿal seder ha-dorot* de Seʿadyah ibn Danān: Edición, Traducción y Notas," *Miscelanea de Estudios Arabes y Hebraicos* 35 [1986] 96) furthermore relates that the Nagid composed a seven-line panegyric in seven languages ("each verse in a different language") for the *amīr* Ḥabbūs. So too the famous "ethical will" of Judah ibn Tibbon to his son: "You know that the great men of our people attained their greatness and many virtues only because of their ability in writing Arabic. You have already seen what the Nagid, of blessed memory, said about the greatness he achieved through it. . . . The achievement of his son as well was due to it"; trans. Israel Abrahams, *Hebrew Ethical Wills* (2 vols.; Philadelphia: Jewish Publication Society, 1926) 1.59.

26. Here I have benefited from reading Israel Burshatin, "The Moor in the Text: Metaphor, Emblem, and Silence," in Henry Louis Gates, Jr. (ed.), *"Race," Writing, and Difference* (Chicago: University of Chicago Press, 1986) 117–39.

27. It should also be noted that the date given by Ibn Ḥayyān for Ibn Naghrīla's death is none other than the tenth of Muḥarram, a Muslim holy day (*ʿĀshūrāʾ*) and the most sacred day in the Shīʿī liturgical calendar. Ibn Ḥayyān's tradition may belong among the (Sunnī) texts linking the Shīʿa with the Jews. See Steven M. Wasserstrom, "'The Shīʿis Are the Jews of Our Community': An Interreligious Comparison within Sunnī Thought," *IOS* 14 (1994) 297–324 .

Ḥayyān al-Qurṭubī. They are of interest not only because of their extensive treatment of Samuel but also on account of Ibn Ḥazm's personal acquaintance with the subject of his remarks.[28]

Shortly after the collapse of the unified Islamic state in Spain (1013), during a period of profound social and political unrest, Ibn Ḥazm and Ibn Naghrīla were forced to flee Cordoba on account of the Berber riots that sacked the city. Ibn Ḥazm made his way to Almeria; Ibn Naghrīla sought refuge in Malaga. As had been his practice in Cordoba, Ibn Ḥazm consulted and often debated other religious scholars and literary intellectuals, including Jews and Christians. In this way he came into contact with Samuel in 1013, probably in Almeria. Although no mention of it is made in any Jewish source, a report of their meeting and debate is preserved in Ibn Ḥazm's monumental heresiography, *al-Fiṣal fī-l-milal wa-l-ahwā' wa-l-niḥal* (Book of Opinions on Religions, Sects, and Heresies), written between 1027 and 1030 but incorporating material from another, now lost work refuting Judaism and Christianity entitled *Iẓhār tabdīl al-yahūd wa-l-naṣārā li-l-tawrāt wa-l-injīl* (Exposure of Jewish and Christian Falsifications in the Torah and Gospels).[29]

Al-Fiṣal introduces Ibn Naghrīla as "the most knowledgeable and the most accomplished debater among the Jews."[30] It is scarcely surprising that Ibn Ḥazm would acknowledge Samuel's merits in the context of this report, if only because so excellent a disputant as ʿAlī surely deserved to be matched against an intellectually worthy, although religiously misguided opponent. Ibn Naghrīla's forensic talent aside, *al-Fiṣal* expresses contempt for Judaism and antipathy toward its adherents.[31] The text's disdain for the Jews proceeds primarily from familiar Islamic theological objections with Judaism, chiefly the 'unreliable transmission' (*tawātur*) of the corrupted Hebrew Bible

28. As noted above, my primary interest lies in examining the figure of the Nagid represented in the texts—not in utilizing the sources for rehearsing details of Samuel's biography. Thus in addressing the early encounter between Ibn Ḥazm and Ibn Naghrīla, I am not concerned with the specific views of Judaism set forth by Muslim heresiographers except insofar as their ideas are reflected in the literary construction of the Jew and might inform the attitude and behavior of Muslims toward Jews in 11th-century al-Andalus. The subject of religious polemics between Jews and Muslims including Ibn Ḥazm has now been capably and dispassionately studied by Steven M. Wasserstrom, *Species of Misbelief: A History of Muslim Heresiography of the Jews* (Ph.D. diss., University of Toronto, 1985); and Camilla Adang, *Muslim Writers on Judaism and the Hebrew Bible from Ibn Rabban to Ibn Ḥazm* (Leiden: Brill, 1996).

29. On the incorporation of the earlier into the later work, see Perlmann, "Eleventh-Century Andalusian Authors," 270.

30. *Al-Fiṣal fī-l-milal wa-l-ahwā' wa-l-niḥal* (5 vols. in 2; Baghdad, 1964 [photocopy of Cairo ed., 1899–1903]) 1.152.

31. Perlmann ("Andalusian Authors," 271) refers to the sections in *al-Fiṣal* as "the only extensive work written by a Muslim author on the subject; it is the only work of anti-Jewish polemics written by one of the great minds of Islam."

(*taḥrīf*) and the counterfeit Jewish tradition of the rabbis. Nevertheless, readers of *al-Fiṣal* have long been struck by the abrasive manner with which it transfers rejection of the belief onto the believers themselves:

> They, both the ancient and the contemporary, are altogether the worst liars. Though I have encountered many of them, I have never seen among them a truth seeker, except two men only.[32]

For a heresiographical text to take issue with doctrinal claims put forward by a rival monotheism and reject the validity of its tradition is perfectly understandable. That, after all, is the purpose of such a text. Yet to our rhetorical sensibility as readers, only a degree of *al-Fiṣal*'s caustic argumentation against Judaism and the Jews can reasonably be attributed to the requirements of the genre and its style. Ibn Ḥazm's vitriolic treatment of Christianity and Christians in *al-Fiṣal* is in fact characterized by similar rhetorical excesses. Many readers have also noted ʿAlī's stylistic trademark—his tendency to engage various opponents, including Muslims not belonging to the Ẓāhirī *madhhab*, with hyperbolic and venomous language. Ibn Ḥazm's blanket condemnation of the national character of the Jews, while perhaps deeply felt and drawing upon the Qurʾānic topos of the deceitfulness of the Jews, appears to be a function of the discursive style established by al-Jāḥiẓ (d. 869) in the 9th century.[33]

The text of *al-Fiṣal* (noted above) spares Samuel as the central target of its spirited barbs. But labeling all (but two) Jews, ancient and modern, mendacious in effect renders their written and spoken discourse undeserving of serious attention. It thus serves to dismiss and *silence them* and to marginalize Ibn Naghrīla as unrepresentative of his religious and textual community. An even more blunt articulation of this polemical and rhetorical strategy is *Ifḥām al-yahūd* (Silencing the Jews), a tract by Samauʾal al-Maghribī, a 12th-century Jewish convert to Islam residing in the Muslim East.[34] Moses Maimonides, a refugee from Almohad persecution in Spain and North Africa, further testifies to the diffusion of this topos and the apparent effectiveness of its message at some times and in some places in the famous "Epistle to Yemen," which characterizes the Jews as a people required "to bear its suffering [under Islam] *in silence*."[35]

32. *Al-Fiṣal*, 1.156 (trans. Perlmann, "Andalusian Authors," 279) and elsewhere follows the Qurʾānic prooftext (5:41–45) on the Jews' innately mendacious nature.

33. See J. Sadan, "Some Literary Problems concerning Judaism and Jewry in Medieval Arabic Sources," in *Studies in Islamic History and Civilization in Honour of David Ayalon* (ed. M. Sharon; Jerusalem: Cana, 1986) 353ff.; and Joshua Finkel, "A Risāla of al-Jāḥiẓ," *JAOS* 47 (1927) 311–34.

34. Samauʾal al-Maghribī, *Ifḥām al-yahūd* (ed. and trans. Moshe Perlmann), *PAAJR* 32 (1964).

35. *Iggeret teiman le-rabbenu moshe ben maimon* (ed. Abraham S. Halkin; New York: American Academy for Jewish Research, 1952) 96; trans. in Abraham Halkin,

The political subtext as opposed to strictly religious text of *al-Fiṣal*'s discourse emerges in one of the crucial points of engagement in Ibn Ḥazm's report of the debate with Ibn Naghrīla, namely, the famous discussion regarding the historical significance of Gen 49:10 ("The scepter shall not depart from Judah, nor the ruler's staff from between his feet till Shiloh (i.e., 'tribute') come [to him]").[36] Ibn Ḥazm's account emphasizes the Jews' loss of sovereignty:

> This verse is untrue because the scepter departed from Judah and leaders from his offspring,[37] but the One sent, whom they await, did not come. The kingdom of Judah found its end in the time of Nebuchadnezzar more than one thousand five hundred years ago. . . . I have repeated this passage to one of the Jews' most learned polemicists, namely Ishmūʾāl b. Yūsuf al-Lāwī, the famous author known as Ibn al-Naghrāl, in the year 1013. And he said to me: "The Exilarchs are the offspring of David and from the sons of Judah and they have leadership and kingdom and authority in our days." But I told him: "This is a mistake, because the Exilarch cannot exert power on the Jews or on anybody else and it is therefore a title only, but no reality."[38]

For the Jews of al-Andalus, as elsewhere, belief in the uninterrupted continuity of the "House of David" was a necessary and certain article of faith. Seemingly relegated to the margins of a history dominated by Islam and Christendom, at least they could look to the figure of the Exilarch or "Head of the Exile" (Heb. *roʾsh ha-golah*; Aram. *reʾsh galutaʾ*; Arab. *raʾs jālūt*) for a sign of hope in the messianic promises of their eventual political restoration

---

Crisis and Leadership: Epistles of Maimonides (Philadelphia: Jewish Publication Society, 1985) 127. As the historian S. D. Goitein observed (*A Mediterranean Society*, 2.284): "Worship of the non-Muslim denominations under Islam had to be inconspicuous. . . ." While strictly addressing Christians, the so-called "Pact of ʿUmar" also applied to the Jews. This document states: "We shall not display our crosses or our books in the roads or markets of Muslims. We shall only use our clappers in our churches very softly. We shall not raise our voices in our church services or in the presence of Muslims, nor shall we raise our voices when following our dead" (trans. Bernard Lewis, *Islam*, vol. 2: *Religion and Society* (New York: Oxford University Press, 1987) 218.

36. *Al-Fiṣal*, 1.152–53.

37. Although this passage avers that leadership of the Jews ("leaders from his offspring") departed from the House of David, in *Jamharat ansāb al-ʿarab* ([ed. ʿAbd al-Salām Muḥammad Hārūn; Cairo: Dār al-Maʿārif, 1982] 506), Ibn Ḥazm asserts that the leaders of the Jews down to his day do indeed descend from David.

38. Trans. Hava Lazarus-Yafeh, *Intertwined Worlds: Medieval Islam and Bible Criticism* (Princeton: Princeton University Press, 1992) 98–99. Lazarus-Yafeh notes Samauʾal al-Maghribī's contrasting treatment of the biblical passage in Perlmann (ed.), *Ifḥām al-yahūd*, text, 23; trans., 41–42. Ironically, Samuel the Nagid seems to have been partly responsible for moving the Jews of Spain away from complete dependence upon (if not allegiance to) the Eastern rabbinical authorities.

(recorded in the Hebrew Bible).[39] Consider, for example, Benjamin of Tudela's (12th-century) account of his visit to Baghdad. In this blend of realia and fantasy, we find a vivid depiction of the dignity of the *roʾsh ha-golah*. The Muslims of Baghdad, for whom the biblical David is a prophet, pay tribute to the Exilarch, referring to him as *sayyidnā bin dāwūd*.[40] According to Benjamin's imaginative reconstruction, the ceremonious recognition of the Exilarch as a genuine sovereign and equal at the Caliph's court represents the literal realization of the prophecy voided by Ibn Ḥazm. Here are his words of encouragement for the disempowered Jews of his age:

> And the Head of the Captivity is seated on his throne opposite the Caliph, in compliance with the command of Muḥammad, to give effect to what is written in the Law—"The scepter shall not depart from Judah. . . ."[41]

Benjamin of Tudela's message of comfort notwithstanding, Ibn Ḥazm was correct in assessing the actual authority of the Exilarch during the 11th century. As the historian S. D. Goitein has shown, the Exilarch's power, like the caliph's, had long since declined. The *roʾsh ha-golah* was reduced to little more than an ecumenical figurehead and limited to dispensing honorific titles.[42] Real communal authority rested in the hands of the talmudic academies and their heads, the *g^eonim*. Ibn Ḥazm's rejoinder to Samuel concerning the Exilarch goes further still, stripping the Jews of even the appearance of temporal power and wresting from them the semblance of hope for the future.[43] Perhaps the reader can sense in Ibn Ḥazm's rejection of the chain of symbolic Jewish political authority a sign of the Andalusī Muslim's dismay

39. On the history of this office during the High Middle Ages, see Avraham Grossman, *The Babylonian Exilarchate in the Gaonic Period* (Jerusalem: Zalman Shazar, 1984) [Heb.].

40. Benjamin of Tudela, *Sefer massaʿot / The Itinerary of Benjamin of Tudela* (ed. and trans. Marcus Adler; reprinted New York: Feldheim, 1960) Heb. text, pp. 61–63; Eng. trans., 39–41.

41. Benjamin of Tudela, *Sefer massaʿot*, 62; Adler, *The Itinerary*, 40. For a discussion of Benjamin's world and his message of consolation, see the introduction by Michael A. Signer, *The Itinerary of Benjamin of Tudela* [*Travels in the Middle Ages*] (Malibu: Joseph Simon Pangloss, 1983) 13–33.

42. Goitein, *A Mediterranean Society*, 2.17ff. On Muslim attitudes toward the Exilarch, see Ignaz Goldziher, "Renseignements de source musulmane sur la dignité de *Resch-Galuta*," *REJ* 8 (1884) 121–25, reprinted in *Gesammelte Schriften* (ed. Joseph Desomogyi; Hildesheim: Olms, 1967–68) 2.132–36; Walter Y. Fischel, "The *Resh Galuta* in Arabic Literature," in *The Magnes Anniversary Book* (ed. F. I. Baer et al.; Jerusalem: Hebrew University Press, 1938) 181–87 [Heb.]; and now on the specifically Shīʿī interest in this figure, Wasserstrom, "The Shīʿīs Are the Jews of Our Community."

43. There are good reasons why Jewish messianism might appear seditious even if its prospects for realization were beyond reason. See my "Power in the Portrayal: Representations of Muslims and Jews in Judah al-Ḥarizi's *Taḥkemoni*," *Princeton Papers in Near Eastern Studies* 1 (1992) 1–22.

over the demise of the Umayyad caliphate in 11th-century al-Andalus and his disgust at the succession of Umayyad pretenders to that dignified office.[44]

What of the second and chronologically later text, in which Ibn Ḥazm mounts a frontal assault on Judaism, the Jews, and an unnamed opponent bearing a resemblance to Ismāʿīl ibn Naghrīla? A comparison of the representation of Ibn Naghrīla in *al-Fiṣal* and Ibn Ḥazm's literary adversary in the so-called *Radd ʿalā ibn al-naghrīla al-yahūdī* (The Refutation of Ibn Naghrīla, the Jew = "The Refutation") is instructive, for the intellectually resourceful (although greatly mistaken) Ibn Naghrīla in the former is replaced by a variously obtuse, base, and diabolical figure in the later work. That figure has been identified with Ismāʿīl ibn Naghrīla or alternately with his son and successor Yūsuf.[45] Embracing traditional elements from *tafsīr* and *ḥadīth* literature in its defense of Islam and polemic against Judaism, employing Qurʾānic prooftexts cautioning Muslims to avoid fraternizing with *ahl al-dhimma* (e.g., 3:118, 5:51–56), and incorporating arguments already employed in *al-Fiṣal*, "The Refutation" is a piece of political propaganda as well as a religious polemic.[46] It nevertheless sets a new standard for vilification of a religious group.[47] As is well known, Ibn Ḥazm supposedly undertook writing "The Refutation" when he learned a Jew had written a book exposing alleged inconsistencies and logical contradictions in the Qurʾān.[48] Unable to obtain a copy of the text, Ibn Ḥazm reports that he had to rely on the work of another Muslim scholar, who had already come to the defense of Islam in refuting the arguments put forward by the Jew.[49] Without identifying the offending party, Ibn Ḥazm signals his familiarity with him in the following cryptic remark:

44. On which see David J. Wasserstein, *The Caliphate in the West: An Islamic Political Institution in the Iberian Peninsula* (Oxford: Oxford University Press, 1993) 192–93.

45. In his introduction to "*al-Radd*" (*Rasāʾil ibn ḥazm*, 3.17), Iḥsān ʿAbbās reasons that the pamphlet's author was not Ismāʿīl but Yūsuf ibn Naghrīla, with whom such an impudent effort would supposedly have been more in character. ʿAbbās thus attempts to solve the problems associated with ascribing the work to the first Ibn Naghrīla. Arabic historiography does indeed paint a more crass and insolent picture of the son than the father, making Yūsuf a more likely candidate for authorship in ʿAbbās's thinking. Yet no mention is made of Yūsuf as the author in any other source. See also Eliyahu Ashtor, *Qorot ha-yᵉhudim bi-sᵉfarad ha-muslemit* (2 vols.; Jerusalem: Kiryat-Sefer, 1960–66) 2.354 n. 116; Paul B. Fenton, "Jewish Attitudes to Islam: Israel Heeds Ishmael," *Jerusalem Quarterly* 29 (1983) 91; and the other sources cited by Stroumsa, "From Muslim Heresy to Jewish-Muslim Polemic," 770 n. 28.

46. Wasserstein, *Rise and Fall*, 205.

47. See the comments of E. Garcia Gomez, "Polémica Religiosa entre Ibn Ḥazm e Ibn al-Naghrīla," *al-Andalus* 4 (1936) 3–5.

48. Ibn Ḥazm, "*al-Radd*," 42.

49. Ibid. Following Stroumsa, Maribel Fierro ("Ibn Ḥazm et le *zindīq* juif," *Revue du monde musulman et de la Méditerranée* 63–64 [1992] 85) posits that al-Jubbāʾī served as Ibn Ḥazm's Muslim source for refuting the anti-Qurʾānic arguments.

> By my life, the argument he makes demonstrates how limited is the extent of his knowledge and how scant the scope of his understanding, *about which I already know something*. . . . [emphasis mine][50]

Ibn Ḥazm's account and enigmatic comment notwithstanding, there is much to suggest that "The Refutation" may have been undertaken as a politically motivated literary exercise rather than as a response to a contemporary anti-Qurʾānic work.

"The Refutation" may be outlined as follows: the introduction assails the Jewish culprit and the party-kings who permit such and other offenses against Islam and Muslims (pp. 41–43); part one in the form of eight chapters represents the body of the work as defined in the introduction (pp. 43–60). This is where the text undertakes a point-by-point defense of the problematic Qurʾānic passage, followed by a counterattack on passages in the Torah more objectionable than the one questioned in the Qurʾān. Part Two, an epilogue (pp. 60–67), mounts a full-blown assault on the theological absurdities in the Hebrew Bible and rabbinic tradition. The conclusion (pp. 67–70) restates the reasons for which the treatise was composed and reiterates the shrill diatribe against the Jewish author, the Jews in general, and the party-kings who grant the Jews license. The puzzling structure of "The Refutation" thus appears to offer a means of grappling with the contradictions of the text and provides a key to its significance.[51]

Here is how Ibn Ḥazm acquaints the reader with his adversary and introduces the subject of the treatise:

> Now then, a man whose heart seethes with malice toward Islam and its community of believers and whose liver is molten with hostility for the Messenger, may God bless him and grant him peace, a man who belongs to the "materialist" (*al-mutadahhira*) heretics who conceal themselves among the most abject of religions and most destestable of religious doctrines, namely Judaism, upon whose adherents God's curse falls constantly and upon whose followers God's wrath, may He be exalted and magnified, resides permanently. Insolence has loosened this man's tongue and hubris has released his reins. His contemptuous soul has become arrogant because of his abounding wealth, and the abundance of gold and silver in his posessesion has inflated his detestable ambition, such that he composed a book in which he expressly intended to expose alleged contradictions in the Word of God, may He be exalted and magnified, in the Qurʾān . . . , treating men of religion with disdain on the one hand and the political leadership with impudence on the other.[52]

50. Ibn Ḥazm, "*al-Radd*," 43.

51. Perlmann ("Andalusian Authors on the Jews of Granada," 281) already noted the difference between the tone of the introduction and conclusion and the so-called "body" of the work. This difference is also noted by Stroumsa, Fierro, and others.

52. Ibn Ḥazm, "*al-Radd*," 42–43.

The manifestly political discourse of the introduction is grounded entirely in the social and political scene of 11th-century al-Andalus. It makes no pretense of contributing to the world of religious ideas but instead excoriates the depraved ruler in whose realm the Jew resides, assails the wealth and influence of the Jews, and decries the insolence, baseness, and idiocy of the unnamed author. By contrast, part one deals with theological differences between Judaism and Islam such as those explored at length in *al-Fiṣal* and in other heresiographical works such as *al-Milal wa-l-niḥal* by al-Shahrastānī (d. 1153). The conclusion of "The Refutation" returns to the universe of political discourse, issuing an ominous warning to the party-kings and passing the sternest of judgments upon the responsible Jew:

> It is my firm hope that God will treat those who befriend the Jews and take them into their confidence as He treated the Jews themselves. . . . For whosoever amongst Muslim princes has listened to all this and still continues to befriend the Jews, holding intercourse with them, well deserves to be overtaken by the same humiliation and to suffer in this world the same griefs meted out to the Jews. . . .[53]

Anticipating the rhetorical strategy and political goal of Abū Isḥāq al-Ilbīrī's famous poetic diatribe against Yūsuf ibn Naghrīla and the Jews of Granada,[54] the text neither marginalizes nor robs the Jew of cultural otherness but demonizes him for violating the essential regulations of the social contract stipulated by Islam going back to the so-called "Pact of ʿUmar":

> giving him the punishment mandated by law: the shedding of his blood, the confiscation of his property, and captivity of his women and children. [He deserves this punishment] because he promoted himself, cast off the mark of submission from his neck, and disavowed the contract of protection.[55]

Setting aside the social-psychological factors that are thought to have shaped Ibn Ḥazm's attitude toward the Jews in general and Ibn Naghrīla in

53. Ibn Ḥazm, "*al-Radd*," 67 (trans. Perlmann, "Andalusian Authors on the Jews of Granada," 281–83). Ironically, Ibn Ḥazm ("*al-Radd*," 68–69) envisions for the culpable Andalusian elite the wretched and accursed fate reserved for the Jews (i.e., Israelites) in the ultimate *biblical* prooftext (Deuteronomy 28). Ibn Ḥazm's critique of the authenticity of the Hebrew Bible to the contrary, Lazarus-Yafeh observes that Muslim writers sometimes found it useful to employ biblical prophetic passages rebuking the Israelites (*Intertwined Worlds*, 43–44 n. 66).

54. Text in James T. Monroe, *Hispano-Arabic Poetry: A Student Anthology* (Berkeley: University of California Press, 1974) 206–13. For a detailed study of this poem in its historical context, see Bernard Lewis, "An Ode against the Jews," in *Islam in History: Ideas, People and Events in the Middle East* (rev. and expanded ed.; Chicago: Open Court, 1993) 167–74.

55. Ibn Ḥazm, "*al-Radd*," 47 (trans. Stroumsa, "From Muslim Heresy to Jewish-Muslim Polemics," 772). For the circumstances under which the protection guaranteed to non-Muslims must be withdrawn, see Lewis, *The Jews of Islam*, 39–40.

particular, what historical factors (between the original encounter of 1013, the drafting of *al-Fiṣal fī-l-milal* [1027–30], its incorporation of materials from the *Iẓhār*, and the appearance of "The Refutation" around 1056) might have contributed to a deepening of the anti-Jewish rhetoric in the later text?[56] From the standpoint of a pious and ideologically-minded Muslim intellectual, the events of the 11th century were altogether lamentable. Dispirited scholars such as Ibn Ḥazm were all too aware of the progressive social and political disintegration of al-Andalus and the resultant evaporation of its influence as a Mediterranean power.[57] Troublesome rumblings of revitalized Castile under Ferdinand I (1035–1065) certainly reached al-Andalus, further contributing to an abiding sense of unease. Consider the following remarkable passage transmitted by the North African historian Ibn ʿIdhārī (13–14th centuries). It preserves remarks attributed to King Ferdinand I of Castile (1035–65), addressed to a delegation of Muslims from Toledo:

56. Although set aside for purposes of this paper, an interpersonal dimension may well inform some of the anti-Jewish animus and rhetoric of "The Refutation." By 1027–30, when the literary account of Ibn Ḥazm's encounter with Ibn Naghrīla was drafted, the issue of the exercise of Jewish temporal power within the *Dār al-Islām* had unexpectedly become entangled in the *personal* histories of Samuel and ʿAlī. Both lives were profoundly touched by social and political upheaval, but while Samuel's fortunes rose as a result of changes in the administration of al-Andalus and the opportunities presented to ambitious and talented Jews, Ibn Ḥazm's once promising prospects for following in his father's political footsteps were effectively scuttled. Ibn Naghrīla was already entrenched in the fiscal bureaucracy of the Zirid regime, a position from which he would eventually enter the confidences of the next *amīr* Bādīs. He had also acquired the title and attained prestige as the Nagid of the Jews of al-Andalus (ca. 1027). By contrast Ibn Ḥazm's political fortunes precipitously declined. The privileged son of a once-influential *wazīr* of the Umayyad caliph was set to flight, repeatedly elevated (including a very brief stint as *wazīr* of the ill-fated Caliph al-Mustaẓhir [ca. 1024]) and incarcerated (his imprisonment in Granada by Ḥabbūs [Bādīs's father] is related in Ibn Bassām, *al-Dhakhīra*, ed. ʿAbbās; part 1/vol. 2.660), largely on account of his unswerving loyalty to the Umayyad cause and Umayyad claimants, and finally owing to his aggressive advocacy of the *Ẓāhiriyya*. When attempts at reviving his political career at provincial centers failed, Ibn Ḥazm's ambition and boundless intellectual energy turned exclusively to research. Accordingly, some students of Ibn Ḥazm have imagined an embittered and disillusioned ʿAlī reflecting upon the ascent and position of Ibn Naghrīla, the Jewish interlocutor of his youth. Ismāʿīl's success supposedly reminded Ibn Ḥazm of his own failures as much as of the collapse of an orthodox Islamic polity in al-Andalus and its replacement by the party-kings. See Adang, *Muslim Writers on Judaism*, 43–44; Stroumsa, "From Muslim Heresy to Jewish-Muslim Polemics," 769.

57. For Ibn Ḥazm's highly vocative comments on the state of Cordoba after the *fitna*, see *Ṭawq al-ḥamāma fī-l-ulfa wa-l-ullāf* (ed. Ṣalāḥ al-Dīn al-Qāsimī; Baghdad: Dār al-Shuʾūn al-Thaqāfiyya al-ʿĀmma, 1986) 182–83.

> We seek only our lands which you have conquered from us in times past at the beginning of your history. Now you have dwelled in them for the time allotted to you and we have become victorious over you as a result of your own wickedness. So go to your own side of the straits [of Gibraltar] and leave our lands to us, for no good will come to you from dwelling here with us after today. For we shall not hold back from you till God decides between us.[58]

This address captures a sense of the shifting political fortunes of Islam and Christendom in 11th-century Iberia, ostensibly from the perspective of a Christian Spanish monarch. But the discourse must have struck a chord among Muslim scholars in the *maghrib* who preserved and transmitted it, on account of its particular reading of the Andalusians' failure and collapse.

Besides the disintegration of the unified state and the resultant civil strife over conflicting claims to political authority, a visible sign of internal weakness directly related to the proliferation of competing principalities in Muslim Spain was the elevation of Jewish (and to a lesser extent Christian) officials to positions of power by the *mulūk al-ṭawāʾif*. This practice was naturally seen by resentful Muslim intellectuals as violating the Islamic character of al-Andalus and experienced by them as undermining the social and political conditions necessary for the perfect practice of Islam. Influential Jews could already be found at the Umayyad and ʿĀmirid courts of the 10th century—a development that apparently did not go uncriticized in some quarters[59]—yet Muslim anxiety over Jewish empowerment surfaced more sharply and openly during the 11th century as a direct consequence of the loss of unified Muslim authority. Heightened concern about the proper place of non-Muslims in Andalusī society articulated in the introduction and conclusion of "The Refutation" found an echo in an admonitory and programmatic document by Muḥammad ibn ʿAbdūn (11th–12th century) prescribing among other things strict regulations on the behavior of Jews and Christians.[60] Indeed, in drawing a typology of the persecution of minorities in premodern Islam, Bernard Lewis identifies *dhimmī* arrogance and high public rank as primary causes in moving Islam to strike an aggressively defensive posture vis-à-vis its "protected peoples."[61] As evidenced by Ibn Ḥazm's habit of conferring with Jewish scholars, neither the presence of Jews in Andalusī

58. Ibn ʿIdhārī, *al-Bayān al-mughrib*, 3.282 (trans. Wasserstein, *Rise and Fall of the Party Kings*, 250).

59. Although the evidence seems scant, Stern ("Two New Data about Ḥasdai ibn Shapruṭ," 141–43) and Allony ("Songs of Zion," 212–15) contend that popular anti-Jewish sentiment already emerged in the 10th century. In their view, the vilification of Samuel and Yūsuf ibn Naghrīla in the 11th century was simply a continuation of a predominant anti-Jewish vein in Andalusī society.

60. Ibn ʿAbdūn, "Un document sur la vie urbane et le corps de la métiers a Seville au debut du XIIième siècle: Le traité d'Ibn ʿAbdūn" (ed. E. Lévi-Provençal), in *JA* 224 (1934) 238–48.

61. Lewis, *Jews of Islam*, 53.

Muslim society nor even their relative prosperity was cause for concern. Rather, the Jews' visible trespass into the affairs of state seemed threatening, never more so than while Islam was in retreat.

Recent research on "The Refutation" has focused on source-critical exposition of Ibn Ḥazm's polemic and on determining the identity of his literary adversary.[62] For our purposes, we may set aside a definitive solution to the problem of whether or not Samuel the Nagid actually composed a treatise against the Qur'ān.[63] Suffice it to say that Sarah Stroumsa argues that the *al-Radd ʿalā ibn al-naghrīla al-yahūdī* actually refutes a 9th-century heterodox Muslim source rather than an 11th-century Jewish polemical text. In her view, Ibn Ḥazm hoped to pin a capital offense on Ibn Naghrīla by ascribing to him the anti-Qur'ānic arguments.[64] Maribel Fierro, by contrast, identifies two free-thinking Jewish physicians living in Almeria with whom Ibn Ḥazm was acquainted and who could have written such a work in the intellectual and social climate of 11th-century al-Andalus, perhaps by drawing upon existing heterodox Muslim texts such as Ibn al-Rāwandī's *Kitāb al-Dāmigh* discussed by Stroumsa.[65] Either Ibn Ḥazm found it useful to ascribe an offensive anti-Qur'ānic tract to a highly conspicuous Jew such as Ibn Naghrīla or he genuinely believed the author of the unavailable text to be a Jewish contemporary in Muslim Spain.

To read "The Refutation" as an artifact of Hispano-Arabic culture in a moment of crisis we need not feel obliged (in the absence of compelling textual evidence) to identify the particular Jew who meets all of the various conditions set forth in the text: a free-thinking member of the *dahriyya*; a dignitary known to Ibn Ḥazm; a Jew of such substantial means and influence that he was unafraid to openly voice criticism of the Qur'ān and Islam in the form of a religious polemical text written in Arabic.[66] Since "The Refutation" itself is silent on the identity of the alleged Jewish polemicist, we may wonder why the editors (or editor) responsible for supplying the title of the treatise and later literary historians such as Ibn Bassām al-Shantarīnī and Ibn Saʿīd al-Maghribī (d. 1286) all take it for granted that Ibn Naghrīla was the

62. See Moshe Perlmann, "The Medieval Polemics between Islam and Judaism," in *Religion in a Religious Age* (ed. S. D. Goitein; New York: Ktav Publishing, 1974) 108ff.

63. The rationale for and against the existence of such a pamphlet is carefully discussed by Wasserstein, *Rise and Fall*, 199–205. Ibn Bassām (*al-Dhakhīra*, part 1/vol. 2.766) claims that Ibn Naghrīla composed a book in response to something Ibn Ḥazm had written, perhaps *al-Fiṣal*'s critique of the Hebrew Bible.

64. Stroumsa, "From Muslim Heresy to Jewish Muslim Polemics."

65. The two men are Ismāʿīl b. Yūnus al-Aʿwar (also mentioned in *Ṭawq al-ḥamāma*, 67) and Ismāʿīl b. al-Qarrād. See Fierro, "Ibn Ḥazm et le *zindīq* juif," 82. Fierro notes Ibn Ḥazm's reference already in *al-Fiṣal* to his acquaintance of two Jewish physicians who were adherents of the *dahriyya* (materialists and agnostics).

66. "Free-thinking materialism" could not reasonably be attributed to Samuel.

object of the "The Refutation's" invective.[67] Other high-ranking Jews could be found during the 11th century in Saragossa (Abū al-Faḍl ibn Ḥasdai; Yequtiel ibn Ḥasan), Almeria, Seville (Abraham ibn Muhājir), and Toledo.[68] The answer I believe is that Samuel was the most visible and important member of this group and the only one to attain ecumenical status among the Jews of al-Andalus. Imagine what Muslim scholars might have thought had they access to the Nagid's Hebrew poetry produced for Jewish consumption or if a hint of the Jewish hubris he expresses in that verse was evident in his public demeanor.[69]

If Ismāʿīl appears to his Muslim counterparts as the incarnation of Jewish empowerment and arrogance, the city-state of Granada under the administration of successive Ibn Naghrīlas, sometimes referred to in Arabic texts as *gharnāṭat al-yahūd* ('Jewish Granada'),[70] is a perfect locus for various grievances against Jewish power and influence within the Islamic polity.[71] Indeed, Ibn ʿIdhārī charges that Yūsuf ibn Naghrīla sought to establish an independent Jewish kingdom (in Almeria), giving the impression that under successive Ibn Naghrīlas the Jewish community appeared to function as a quasi-independent polity and aspired to complete independence.[72] With respect

67. Ibn Bassām, *al-Dhakhīra*, part 1/vol. 2.766; Ibn Saʿīd al-Maghribī, *al-Mughrib fī ḥulā al-maghrib* (ed. Shawqī Ḍayf; 2 vols.; Cairo: Dār al-Maʿārif bi-Miṣr, 1955) 2.114.

68. See Eliyahu Ashtor, *The Jews of Moslem Spain* (trans. Aaron Klein and Jenny Machlowitz Klein; 3 vols.; Philadelphia: Jewish Publication Society, 1973–84) 2.197, 217–21, 225, 238, 253–64; and Wasserstein, *Rise and Fall*, 190–222.

69. I am thinking specifically of the Nagid's preoccupation with his aristocratic (Levitic) lineage, his concerted effort to bring his public image into line with the typology of King David, and his pretensions to higher authority. See Ross Brann, *The Compunctious Poet: Cultural Ambiguity and Hebrew Poetry in Muslim Spain* (Baltimore: Johns Hopkins University Press, 1991) 47–58. As Gerson Cohen noted: "the hope for the fulfillment of the messianic dream in Andalus, through the class of Jewish courtiers, was not a secret of the Jewish underground. The Jewish pride, which the Muslims construed as Hubris and defiance of Islam, drew its nourishment from the assumption that the age of the Bible was again come to life and that the exiles of Judea in Sefarad would soon assume their rightful station" (Cohen, *The Book of Tradition*, 277). Open, public defiance toward Islam is another matter, even if the Nagid never uttered an Arabic word on the subject.

70. *The Tibyān*, 206–7, citing al-Ḥimyarī, *Kitāb al-Rawḍ al-Miʿṭār* (ed. and trans. E. Lévi-Provençal; Leiden: Brill, 1938) 23.

71. During the Zirid era, the Jews of Granada represented a significant, perhaps even predominant, segment of the town's population. Appointment of two successive *dhimmis* to high office appears to have been part of a system of checks and balances specific to Berber rule in 11th-century Granada. See Andrew Handler, *The Zirids of Granada* (Coral Gables, Fla.: University of Miami Press, 1974) 26, 45. For an estimate of the Jewish population in al-Andalus, see Eliyahu Ashtor, "The Number of Jews in Moslem Spain," *Zion* 28 (1963) 34–56 [Heb.].

72. Ibn ʿIdhārī, *al-Bayān al-mughrib*, 3.266; and Ibn Bassām, *al-Dhakhīra*, part 1/vol. 2.766.

to the unusual powers of Ismāʿīl and his son as well as to the number of ranking Jewish officials serving at the courts of other party-kings, the Andalusian situation did not exist elsewhere in Islam, including Fatimid Egypt, where Jews (and Jewish converts) served in positions of government.

Ibn Ḥazm, subsequent Muslim literary intellectuals, or the medieval editor of "The Refutation" might have identified Ibn Naghrīla as the source of the subversive discourse or thought it natural to cast him in this menacing role on account of his singularly conspicuous position, prominence, and political agency, all of which can be identified as contributing to *fitna*.[73] Later sources such as Ibn ʿIdhārī and Ibn al-Khaṭīb, it will be recalled, cite the Jews of 11th-century Granada in general and the Ibn Naghrīlas in particular for their accumulation of wealth.[74] Yūsuf is further singled out for his partiality toward Jewish secretaries in filling lower-level administrative and financial offices.[75] The episode involving Ibn Naghrīla and Aḥmad ibn ʿAbbās, *wazīr* of neighboring Almeria, is also indicative of Ismāʿīl's notorious standing among some Andalusī Muslims (and instructive as a failed rehearsal of what eventually befell Yūsuf ibn Naghrīla in 1066). Unremittingly hostile to the Zirid's Jewish *wazīr,* Ibn ʿAbbās is said to have circulated letters among influential Muslims of Granada and petitioned Ḥabbūs and Bādīs successively in a concerted effort to depose Samuel from office. For good measure he also enlisted Ibn Abī Mūsā, the Ḥammūdid prince of Malaga, and Zuhayr, the Slav prince of Almeria, in a plan to isolate Granada, intervene in its administration, and bring down the Jew and his supporters.[76] Ibn Ḥazm himself must have been aware of the opposition to Ibn Naghrīla because these events coincided with his term of service in Almeria's army as reported by Ibn ʿIdhārī.[77]

In accordance with "The Refutation's" fuzzy testimony on the identity of the Jewish polemicist and the traditional identification of the treatise with Ibn Naghrīla, it seems preferable to think of Ibn Ḥazm's alleged literary adversary as a composite Andalusian Jewish notable, courtier, and intellectual suggestive of Samuel—a construct of the social imagination of an 11th-century Muslim intellectual. The Jew in the text, uniformly assumed by subsequent Islamic tradition to be Ibn Naghrīla, is thus a *typological figure* comparable in function to Almanzor (i.e., al-Manṣūr) in Latin and Romance texts.[78] He embodies a spectrum of offensive beliefs, attitudes, and conduct

73. According to L. Gardet ("Fitna," *EI*² 2.930), the idea of *fitna* came to be understood as "'revolt', 'disturbances', 'civil war', but a civil war that breeds schism and in which the believers' purity of faith is in grave danger."

74. Ibn ʿIdhārī, *al-Bayān al-mughrib*, 3.264–65.

75. Ibid., 3.265.

76. Ashtor, *Jews of Moslem Spain*, 2.71–79.

77. Ibn ʿIdhārī, *al-Bayān al-mughrib*, 3.171.

78. For example, see the Latin account (preserved as an appendix to the *Historia Turpini*) of al-Manṣūr's affliction with dysentery in Colin Smith (ed. and trans.),

considered dangerous to Islam and threatening to the well-being of Muslims in al-Andalus.[79] A typological approach to the cast of characters presented in "The Refutation" explains why Ibn Bassām and Ibn Saʿīd al-Maghribī rely on Ibn Ḥazm but confuse and conflate Ismāʿīl and Yūsuf ibn Naghrīla, apparently unwittingly. Whatever Ibn Ḥazm's intention in drafting "The Refutation" (and whoever his target), the text took on a life of its own in subsequent Hispano-Arabic tradition.[80]

Hispano-Arabic discourse on Ismāʿīl ibn Naghrīla presents the reader with seemingly contradictory figures at whose poles are an intelligent, skilled, and noble Jew deserving of homage, and a vile, stupid, and fiendish enemy of God and Islam. Despite differences in tone and approach that can be attributed to genre (e.g., history of science, historical chronicle, heresiography, religious polemic), each of the textual representations of Ibn Naghrīla discussed in this paper is directly or indirectly concerned with issues of sovereignty and the exercise of power and reflective of concerns and paradigms internal to Islam for which the Jew serves as a mirror. The discourse variously depicts Ibn Naghrīla as a wise and skilled reader whose own texts are valid for him and his textual community (Ṣāʿid al-Andalusī, *Ṭabaqāt al-umam*); strips Ismāʿīl of his cultural otherness by embracing him as (almost) one of its own (Ibn Ḥayyān, *al-Iḥāṭa*); and depicts him as belonging to a community of liars, asserting the absolute discursive authority of the Muslim textual community over others and depriving the Jew of speech (Ibn Ḥazm, *al-Fiṣal*). At its most extreme ("*al-Radd*"), the discourse indicts the Jew for violating the essential conditions of the contract between Islam and *ahl al-*

Christians and Moors in Spain, Volume I: AD *711–1150* (Warminster: Aris & Phillips, 1988) 76–79.

79. Maribel Fierro ("Religious Beliefs and Practices in al-Andalus in the Third/Ninth Century," *RSO* 66 [1992] 21–22) cites an Andalusian anecdote related in *Kitāb al-ʿāqiba*, an unpublished treatise on eschatology by Ibn al-Kharrāṭ (d. 1186), in which a person is described as a Jew so as to disqualify him. Fierro writes: "It is worth noting that the anonymous person who liked to discuss God and the Qurʾān is described as a Jew by Abū Marwān. . . . As he tried to introduce young Muḥammad to certain theological doctrines considered suspect, he resembled more a Jew than a Muslim, in the same way that his doctrines were not Islamic."

80. John Dagenais's recent study, *The Ethics of Reading in Manuscript Culture: Glossing the Libro de buen amor* (Princeton: Princeton University Press, 1994), argues that scholars frequently place too much emphasis on the establishment of a single authoritative text in order to recover the "author's intention." In so doing they commit themselves to a process that deprives us of the possible readings supplied by variant traditions, that is, the scribal notations found on the margins of the manuscripts. This instructive argument can be extended to the dialectical relationship between the author's text, in this case Ibn Ḥazm, and the place of the text within the broader literary and cultural tradition.

dhimma and consequently divests him of his property and his life in accordance with Islamic law.

In this study we have seen that divergent textual strategies for making sense of or objectifying the historical Ibn Naghrīla signify an unstable construction of the Jew in 11th-century al-Andalus. To re-read the conflicting literary representations of Ismāʿīl ibn Naghrīla in their textual environment further illuminates some of the subtleties of the paradoxical relations between Muslims and Jews in Islamic Spain, in which extended periods of tolerance were punctuated by outbreaks of reaction and hostility.[81] Accordingly, the representations of the critical historical figure of Ibn Naghrīla suggest that the Hispano-Arabic sources can be read as a textualization of the shifting, fluctuating, and ambivalent relations between the Muslims and Jews of al-Andalus, at least on the level of elites.

81. See Bernard Lewis, *The Jews of Islam*, 87.

The Hebrew First-Crusade Narratives and Their Intertextual Messages

Robert Chazan
New York University

The Hebrew First-Crusade narratives continue to perplex and fascinate historians of the medieval Jewish experience more than a century after their scientific publication by Adolf Neubauer and Moritz Stern.[1] Early on,

Author's note: My colleague and friend Baruch Levine has argued the centrality of the Bible for the field of Judaic studies throughout his illustrious academic career. While acknowledging—indeed insisting upon—the significance of the Bible for a variety of other academic and intellectual contexts, he has indefatigably championed the cause of the Bible within the web of disciplinary and area interests that constitute Judaic studies. His case has been a relatively simple one: So much subsequent Jewish thinking and literary expression have been shaped by the biblical legacy that students of all periods of the Jewish past must perforce have some sense of the Bible in order to appreciate properly the materials with which they find themselves engaged. With respect and in friendship, I have decided to present this intertextual reading of a portion of the Hebrew First-Crusade narratives on the occasion of this festschrift in his honor.

1. The three Hebrew First-Crusade narratives were published in a critical edition by A. Neubauer and M. Stern, *Hebräische Berichte über die Judenverfolgungen während der Kreuzzüge* (Berlin: Leonhard Simion, 1892), which will be cited in this study as N & S; the same texts were republished, with notes referring to subsequent suggested readings, by A. Habermann, *Sefer Gezerot Ashkenaz ve-Ẓarfat* (Jerusalem: Sifre Tarshish, 1945), which will be cited in this study as Habermann. All three narratives are available in English translation by Shlomo Eidelberg, *The Jews and the Crusaders* (Madison: University of Wisconsin Press, 1977), which will be cited as Eidelberg. The two original narratives are also available in my own translation, *European Jewry and the First Crusade* (Berkeley: University of California Press, 1987), which will be cited as Chazan. I have regularly retranslated the texts utilized in this study. Because I do not believe that the lengthiest of the narratives was composed by a Jew named Solomon ben Simson and because I do not see much meaning in designating the shortest of the three as the Mainz Anonymous, I shall continue to use the letter L to refer to the lengthiest of the narratives, the letter S to refer to the shortest of the three narratives, and the letter P̣ to refer to the epitome of L embellished with poetic insertions.

scholars were concerned primarily with technical questions of composition, complicated by the problem of passages shared among the three extant narratives.[2] Of late, there has been considerable attention accorded to the related issues of the historicity of these narratives and the objectives and techniques of the authors in composing their accounts.[3] Recently, Jeremy Cohen essayed an intertextual reading of three of the fullest and literarily richest passages from the lengthiest of the Hebrew narratives. The field of intertexts upon which he drew was an extended one, including biblical citations, rabbinic texts, and 12th-century Christian thought and practice.[4] While Cohen himself acknowledges the difficulty associated with such intertextual interpretations and notes that the specific readings that he proposes are surely open to debate, his approach makes excellent sense to me.[5] In this paper, I offer an intertextual reading of a different section of this lengthiest of the narratives.[6] I shall focus on the opening paragraphs of this narrative, in which the editor introduces the villains of the piece, the crusaders, and presents its heroes, the Jewish martyrs.

Whereas Cohen chose three sections that are extraordinarily rich in literary themes, with a focus on dramatic and bloody acts of martyrdom, I have chosen the rather prosaic opening segments of L upon which to focus. I have done so for two reasons. First, the opening portions of the extant three narratives are quite different from one another, at least in the case of the two

2. For a review of the views held concerning the relationships among the three narratives, see A. S. Abulafia, "The Interrelationship between the Hebrew Chronicles of the First Crusade," *JSS* 27 (1982) 221–39. Much rethinking is in order with respect to this issue. I have become increasingly convinced that each text must first be examined in its own right before fruitful discussion of the texts' interrelationships can be essayed. I am currently completing a study of S, which will appear in the festschrift in honor of Yosef Haim Yerushalmi, and a study of the Trier unit of L, which will appear in the festschrift in honor of Isaac E. Barzilay.

3. I dealt with these related issues in *European Jewry and the First Crusade*, chaps. 2 and 5. They were addressed by I. G. Marcus in his review of that book in *Speculum* 64 (1989) 685–88; and in "History, Story and Collective Memory: Narrativity in Early Ashkenazic Culture," *Prooftexts* 10 (1990) 1–23. My response to the Marcus views can be found in "The Facticity of Medieval Narrative," *AJS Review* 16 (1991) 31–57. J. Cohen has recently dealt with some of the same issues in "The 'Persecutions of 1096'—From Martyrdom to Martyrology: The Sociocultural Context of the Hebrew Crusade Chronicles," *Zion* 59 (1994) 169–208.

4. While I disagree with Cohen's utilization of his intertexual analysis to shed light on the historicity of the Hebrew narratives, I find his notion of intertextual reading of these important compositions very suggestive.

5. See Cohen, "The 'Persecutions of 1096'—From Martyrdom to Martyrology," 205–8.

6. It is worth noting that, in general, S is considerably poorer than L in intertextual references.

original narratives, S and L.[7] Of all the elements in these narratives, the opening sections give us the clearest sense of the specific author/editors, their interests, and their attitudes.[8] Second, precisely the prosaic quality of the narrative makes the intertextual message all the more striking, as I hope to show. I have also decided to restrict somewhat the range of intertexts, focusing specifically on biblical citations and the fuller passages that they echo. Again, there are a number of reasons for this decision, reflecting in part the interests of the honoree for this volume and partly my sense that biblical language and intertexts would have been the most immediate for both the authors of our texts and those who heard or read them.[9]

The opening paragraphs of L constitute an introduction to the narrative that follows.[10] It breaks down into three obvious parts: (1) a broad statement on the persecution; (2) arousal of the crusaders and their anti-Jewish animus; (3) the failed efforts of the Jewish objects of crusader wrath to elicit divine favor and the reasons for that failure. At the conclusion of this introductory statement, the narrative proper commences with brief reference to the abortive assault on Speyer Jewry and then proceeds to the far more devastating attacks on the Jewish communities of Worms and Mainz.

Let us begin with a look at the crusaders, more precisely the editor's overt portrait of them:

> There rose up initially the ruthless, the barbaric, a fierce and impetuous people, both French and German. They committed themselves to journeying to the Holy City, which had been defiled by a ruffian people, in order to seek there the sepulcher of the crucified bastard and to drive out the Muslims who dwell in the land and to conquer the land. They put on their insignia and placed an idolatrous sign on their clothing—the cross—all the men and women whose spirits moved them to undertake the pilgrimage to the sepulcher of their messiah, to the point where they exceeded the locusts on the land—men, women, and children. With regard to them, it is said: "The locusts have no king. . . ."[11] It came to pass that, when they traversed towns where there were Jews, they said to one another: "Behold we journey a long way to seek the

7. Again, as noted already, I see P as an abridgement of L, with poetic embellishment.

8. I shall refer to the composer of L as an editor, while referring to the composer of S as an author. This distinction will be substantiated in the two forthcoming studies mentioned above, n. 2.

9. For some broad reflections on the problems associated with intertextual readings, see the closing paragraph of this study.

10. The opening section of S is quite different. There are no broad introductory observations, such as those in L; rather, the author embarks immediately on a close reconstruction of the opening phases of the crusade and its anti-Jewish spin-offs.

11. The Hebrew text includes the word *we-gômēr*, which can be readily translated as 'etc.'.

idolatrous shrine and to take vengeance upon the Muslims. But here are the Jews dwelling among us, whose ancestors killed him and crucified him groundlessly. Let us take vengeance first upon them. Let us wipe them out as a nation; Israel's name will be mentioned no more. Or else let them be like us and acknowledge the son born of menstruation."[12]

The overt message here is fairly constricted and relatively obvious. The crusaders are portrayed as powerful, at least in their numbers. On the other hand, they are depicted as totally in error, undertaking a religious mission based on pure vanity. This is rather clearly the central message in the Jewish depiction of the crusaders. While the original target of crusader hatred was the Muslims, upon whom they were bent on taking vengeance, the passion for revenge was soon turned against the Jews, with the argument that the Jews were actually a more heinous enemy than the Muslims. The alternatives to be offered to the Jewish enemy were death or baptism. This seems a fairly accurate, if cursory depiction of the emergence of anti-Jewish animus in certain sectors of the crusading campaign.[13] Careful attention to the specific language of the text and to its intertextual implications fleshes out this portrait and complicates it to an extent.

Curiously, there are two lexical usages that seem somewhat favorable to the crusaders. In chaps. 35–39 of Exodus, there is extensive description of the tabernacle. Early on in this extensive description, there is a focus on the generosity of the Israelites, who bring so much out of their own free will that Moses must eventually order cessation of these thoroughly voluntary offerings. The Hebrew phrase that appears in this regard is *kol ʾîš ʾăšer nĕśāʾô libbô* 'every man whose spirit moved him' (Exod 35:21).[14] There is an interesting reflection of this phrase in L's depiction of the crusaders as "all those men and women whose spirit moved them to undertake the pilgrimage to the sepulcher of their messiah."[15] Amidst all of the Jewish denigration of the crusaders and their enterprise, this laudatory phrase, suggesting genuine religious enthusiasm, is striking.

There is a second interesting reference to the crusading hordes that seems to betray once more grudging admiration. Immediately following the reference to "men and women whose spirit moved them to undertake the pilgrim-

12. N & S, 1; Habermann, 24; Eidelberg, 21; Chazan, 243–44.

13. Again, S is far fuller and more accurate in its depiction of the evocation of anti-Jewish animus.

14. Cf. Exod 35:26 and 36:2. The NJPSV, which I generally use throughout this study, has 'everyone who excelled in ability'. I find the translation 'who excelled in ability' problematic and have thus altered it. I have also eschewed the 'everyone' in favor of 'every man', because of the medieval narrative's specification of men and women, which notes explicitly the involvement of women in the crusading enterprise.

15. As noted just now, the specific reference to both men and women is striking. In the Hebrew narratives, Jewish women play a remarkable role in resistance and martyrdom.

age to the sepulcher of their messiah," the editor of L indicates that the numbers so moved were extensive, "exceeding the locusts on the land," with an attendant citation from Proverbs: "The locusts have no king" (Prov 30:27). Now, this combination of depiction and citation is a bit ambiguous. At the overt level, it is surely negative: The crusaders are compared to locusts, and the chaotic nature of the enterprise is highlighted by its lack of leadership. At the same time, the text alluded to transforms the meaning of the simile. Proverbs 30 includes a section that is headed: "Four are among the tiniest on earth, yet they are the wisest of the wise" (v. 24). The third of the four are the locusts: "The locusts have no king, yet they all march forth in formation" (v. 27). This seems to reflect covert respect for the crusader capacity for organization, despite the well-known lack of centralized leadership. In this instance, there is an interesting discepancy between the overt meaning of the depiction and its intertextual referent.

These positive reflections on the crusaders are more than counterbalanced by a series of references that are wholly negative, identifying them with Israel's historic enemies. The anti-Jewish slogan of the crusaders includes the following: "Let us take vengeance first upon them. Let us wipe them out as a nation; Israel's name will be mentioned no more." This extended phrase is a quotation from Ps 83:5, the setting of which is a plea for divine punishment of Israel's historic enemies. Let us note the opening verses of this plea:

> O God, do not be silent;
>   do not hold aloof;
>   do not be quiet, O God!
> For your enemies rage,
>   your foes assert themselves.
> They plot craftily against your people,
>   take counsel against your treasured ones.
> They say, "Let us wipe them out as a nation;
>   Israel's name will be mentioned no more."
> Unanimous in their counsel,
>   they have made an alliance against you—
>   the clans of Edom and the Ishmaelites,
>   Moab and the Hagrites,
>   Gebal, Ammon, and Amalek,
>   Philistia with the inhabitants of Tyre;
>   Assyria too joins forces with them;
>   they give support to the sons of Lot.

The crusaders thus take their place in a long line of persecutors of the Jewish people, with obvious implications for the ultimate fate of the seemingly powerful crusader forces.[16]

16. For further observations on the implications of the depiction of both crusaders and Jews for future developments, see the end of this study.

The specific language used with respect to the crusaders echoes yet another passage from Psalms, a passage that once again beseeches divine retribution against the enemies of the Jewish people. In the depiction of the crusaders that I have cited, there is a curious expression—*wĕ-śāmû ʾôtōtām ʾōtôt*, which I have translated simply as 'they put on their insignia'.[17] This unusual usage is a direct quotation from Ps 74:4, a description of the enemies who pillaged the Temple. In terms reminiscent of Psalm 83, the psalmist laments the arrogance and audacity of this enemy:

> They made your sanctuary go up in flames;
> they brought low in dishonor the dwelling place of your presence.
> They resolved, "Let us destroy them altogether!"
> They burned all of God's tabernacles to the ground.

Once again, through the specific terminology utilized by the author, imagery of the crusaders as synonymous with the historic enemies of the Jewish people is created.

To cite a third and last reference to Israel's traditional enemies based on Psalms, the crusaders are designated early on as *ʿam lōʿēz*, which I have chosen to translate as a barbarian people. The reference conjured up from Ps 114:1 is that of the Egyptian enemy: "When Israel went forth from Egypt, the house of Jacob from a people of strange speech [*mēʿam lōʿēz*]." Thus, for a third time, the specific usage in L echoes the language of Psalms and reinforces the sense of the crusaders as yet one more link in the historic chain of enemy peoples. Just as the earlier enemies of Israel have met their doom, so too shall the crusaders.

This sense of a chain of enemy peoples is reinforced from the utterances of the prophets, specifically Habbakuk. The book of Habbakuk opens with a Psalm-like plea to God to undo the injustice of Israel's suffering at the hands of its enemies, with a focus in this case—as in Psalm 74—on the Babylonian destroyers of the Temple. This Babylonian enemy is designated *hagôy hammar wĕhannimhār*, which I have translated 'a fierce and impetuous people' (Hab 1:6). Utilization of this phrase in the early depiction of the crusaders conjures up once more the sense of a historic chain of persecutors.

The very first descriptors used by the editor of L to designate the crusaders portrays them as *ʿazey pānîm* 'the ruthless'. This is a particularly evocative term, because it sends the auditor/reader back to one of the most striking warnings in the Pentateuch. In chap. 28 of Deuteronomy, there is a contrasting set of predictions, a set of positive outcomes that were to eventuate from observance of the laws transmitted by Moses, followed by a chilling set of catastrophes that would flow from failure to observe those laws. The latter predictions open with natural calamity, which is then succeeded by the ap-

17. The phrase involves a curious combination of words in the Hebrew, a combination that is not amenable to literal translation.

pearance of powerful and merciless enemies. A few verses from this section of the Mosaic prediction are worth noting for our purposes:

> The Lord will bring a nation against you from afar, from the end of the earth, which will swoop down like an eagle—a nation whose language you do not understand, a ruthless nation, that will show the old no regard and the young no mercy. (Deut 28:49–50)[18]

The expression *ʿazey pānîm* thus serves as a striking evocation of this Deuteronomic prophecy, affording the sense that the crusaders are precisely the ruthless people that the Lord had threatened to bring upon Israel. Given the emphasis throughout the latter sections of L upon the utter lack of pity that the crusaders in fact showed to the young and the old, this evocation of the imagery of the ruthless enemy rings very true for the actual behavior of the crusading hordes.

In a natural way, this last intertextual reference provides a transition from the imagery of the persecutors to the imagery of the persecuted. Given the introduction of Deuteronomy 28 through the term *ʿazey pānîm* for the persecutors of the Jews, we are justified in extending the imagery of that harsh prediction and concluding that the Jews of 1096 are portrayed as falling victim to terrible persecutors precisely because of their failure to follow the laws of the Lord as laid out before them by Moses. Such a conclusion, however, flies in the face of the overt portrayal of the martyrs of 1096 provided in the introductory section of L. Let us cite a bit of this third section of L's opening observations. After depicting the Jews' frantic reactions to the news of crusader anti-Jewish wrath, the author speaks of the results of their entreaties:

> But their Father did not answer them. He shut out their prayer and screened himself off with a cloud, that no prayer might pass through. Their tent was rejected, and he banished them from his presence. For a decree had been enacted before him from [the time when God had spoken] of a day of accounting, and this generation had been chosen as his portion, for they had the strength and valor to stand in his sanctuary and to fulfill his commandments and to sanctify his great Name in his world. Concerning them, David said: "Bless the Lord, O his messengers, mighty ones who do his bidding, ever obedient to his bidding" (Ps 103:20).[19]

This is obviously a complex passage, but the overwhelming impression created by its conclusion is that the martyrs of 1096 were a unique group, singled out for suffering because of their greatness—by no means because of their religious inadequacy. That is surely the overt message of the introduction to

18. With respect to the notion of 'a nation whose language you do not understand', recall the *ʿam lōʿēz* already noted; with respect to the enemy swooping down "like an eagle," it is interesting to note that S speaks early on of the crusaders as "rising like eagles."

19. N & S, 1–2; Habermann, 25; Eidelberg, 22; Chazan, 244.

L, a message that is powerfully buttressed through intertextual reference as we shall see. The message provided by the editor of L—on both the overt and intertextual level—is, however, ambiguous. While proclaiming the greatness of the martyrs, the introductory section also speaks of the Lord as rejecting the Rhineland Jews in their prayer and banishing them from his presence. Clearly, the innovative theodicy proclaimed in the wake of the catastrophe of 1096, the assertion that God brought suffering upon his people as a means of testing them and thus—ultimately—of rewarding them, could not efface thoroughly the older tradition of suffering as the outcome of sin. Thus, the overt message of L's introductory section includes both the innovative and the more traditional views, and both are buttressed by the intertextual references of this introductory passage.[20]

Because we have, in a sense, begun our discussion of the intertextual references to the persecuted by highlighting the notion of their shortcomings through the introduction of Deuteronomy 28, let us stay with this aspect of the intertextuality of the introduction to L. The depiction of divine indifference to the prayers of the endangered Rhineland Jews includes three obvious references to Lamentations. In the description of Jewish appeals to God, which has not been quoted, the Jews of the Rhineland are portrayed as fasting intensely, to the point that "their skin shriveled on their bones and became dry as wood," a direct citation from Lam 4:8.[21] Similarly, the striking images of God shutting out the prayers of the Jews and screening himself off with a cloud, that no prayer might pass through, are both taken from Lamentations 3.[22] Now, it is most natural that, when Jews came to depict tragedy, the language of Lamentations should be introduced.[23] The complication is, however, that the stance of this critical biblical book involves the traditional sin-punishment paradigm for the explanation of suffering. Thus, while it is almost second nature for the editor of L to introduce some of the dramatic language of Lamentations into his account, in so doing he inescapably reinforced the older paradigm, as opposed to the more innovative explanation of the 1096 events that he seemingly wished to highlight.

Since I have adduced a number of instances of the use of Psalms in the depiction of the enemies of the Jews, let us note a striking instance of its utilization in the portrayal of the Jews themselves. In the passage cited above, there is an image of God as rejecting the tent of the Jews. This image is based on Ps 78:67, which depicts God as rejecting the tent of Joseph[24] and not

20. The ambiguity of L's stance toward the Jewish martyrs is a central theme in Cohen, "The 'Persecutions of 1096'—From Martyrdom to Martyrology."

21. N & S, 2; Habermann, 25; Eidelberg, 22; Chazan, 244.

22. Lam 3:8 and 3:44.

23. Note the centrality of Lamentations in the important study by Alan Mintz, *Ḥurban: Responses to Catastrophe in Hebrew Literature* (New York: Columbia University Press, 1984).

24. The NJPSV has 'the clan of Joseph'.

choosing the tribe of Ephraim. Once again, it is important to have a sense of the larger biblical context in which this phrase occurs. Psalm 78 is a lengthy recital of the historic shortcomings of the Israelite people. These shortcomings are chronicled from Egypt onward, with the Israelites indicted for their faithlessness all through the liberation from Egypt and the subsequent wandering in the wilderness. The proclivity to sinfulness continued to manifest itself among the peoples of the Northern Kingdom, for whom God designed appropriate punishment. Thus, in alluding to this lengthy indictment, the editor of L once again reinforces powerfully the notion of Jewish sinfulness as lying at the root of the disaster associated with the First Crusade.

Precisely the same set of events—the destruction of the Northern Kingdom—is conjured up by the phrase that immediately follows the image of rejection of the tent of the Rhineland Jews. In this phrase, God is portrayed as banishing these Jews from his presence. The language of this phrase serves as an unmistakable allusion to 2 Kgs 17:23. Chapter 17 of 2 Kings contains an extremely terse description of the rebellion of King Hoshea of Israel against his overlord, the king of Assyria, the reprisal of the Assyrian king, and the deportation of the Israelites of the north into Assyrian territory. All of this is told in six verses. The author of 2 Kings then proceeds to devote seventeen verses to an explanation of these events, an explanation that is simply an indictment of the Israelite kingdom for its sinfulness. This indictment concludes on the following note, which includes the phrase that I have isolated from the introductory section of L: "In the end, the Lord banished Israel from his presence, as he had warned them through all his servants the prophets." Again, then, the rhetoric of rejection ineluctably conjures up a sense of Jewish sinfulness.

Since the 2 Kings narrative makes reference to the warnings of the prophets, let us note that these prophetic warnings also make their appearance in our section of L. In L's depiction of the reaction of the Jews to the news of the crusader forces and their anti-Jewish bent, a pair of phrases from Ezekiel 21 are highlighted. The Jews are portrayed in the following terms: "The hands of the holy people hung nerveless, and their hearts sank."[25] The central prophecy of Ezekiel 21, to which these phrases direct us, is horrendous, a chilling prediction of terrible destruction.

> And you, O mortal, sigh; with tottering limbs and bitter grief, sigh before their eyes. And when they ask you, "Why do you sigh?" answer, "Because of the tidings that have come." Every heart shall sink and all hands hang nerveless; every spirit shall grow faint and all knees turn to water because of the tidings that have come. It is approaching, it shall come to pass—declares the Lord God.
>
> The word of the Lord came to me: O mortal, prophesy and say: Thus said the Lord God: A sword! A sword has been whetted and polished. It has been

25. N & S, 2; Habermann, 25; Eidelberg, 22; Chazan, 244.

whetted to wreak slaughter; [therefore] it has been ground to a brilliant polish. (Ezek 21:11–15)

What follows is a frightening prediction of destruction, grounded once more in the traditional notion of divine punishment visited upon a sinning people.

There is yet one more reference to Jewish sinfulness. It is the reference with which L concludes its description of divine rejection of the Rhineland Jews, their prayers, and their self-affliction. After detailing the Jewish efforts and the divine rebuff of these efforts, L finishes with the following note of explanation: "For a decree had been enacted before him from [the time when God had spoken of] a day of accounting." The reference here is to Exodus 32, the chapter that recounts the sin of the golden calf and the extreme actions of Moses in the face of the breathtaking sin of the people.[26] On the morrow, Moses addresses the Lord, acknowledges the sinfulness of the people, and asks for either divine forgiveness or for total destruction, himself included. The divine response is as follows: "He who has sinned against me, him only will I erase from my record. Go now, lead the people where I told you. See, my angel will go before you. But when I make an accounting, I will bring them to account for their sins" (Exod 32:33–34). This seems, then, to presage a temporary delay for any retribution beyond what was enacted immediately by Moses. The sin remains in force, but retribution will be exacted at a later time. Once again, Jewish sinfulness would seem to lie at the heart of L's portrayal of the events of 1096.

Yet, at precisely this point, L pushes our thinking in an alternative direction. Surely, the sin of the golden calf could hardly be laid at the doorstep of the Rhineland Jews. Indeed, L itself suggests that a somehat curious divine decision took place. While in Exodus 32 God had told Moses of his intention to deal eventually with the people who bore direct guilt for making the golden calf, the author of L suggests that the Rhineland Jews were chosen for vicarious expiation of that terrible misstep by the biblical Israelites. The reason that the Rhineland Jews were singled out to bear the onus of the sin of the golden calf was in fact precisely the opposite of their sinfulness. They were chosen to suffer the divinely promised punishment because "they had the strength and valor to stand in his sanctuary and to fulfill his command and to sanctify his great Name in his world." It is religious strength, not religious weakness, that led God to single out this particular group for the punishment that had been held in abeyance for so long.[27]

Once alerted to this alternative view of the Rhineland Jews, we can identify a number of intertextual references that mitigate the portrait of sinfulness painted earlier. Thus, the powerful passage from Ezekiel can be used to introduce the other side of the picture, the effort to diminish the sense of

26. Note the killing of some 3000 Israelites. This is, in a sense, a portent of what was to happen in the Rhineland.

27. The Christological parallels are, of course, striking.

Jewish guilt and to ground the suffering of the Rhineland Jews in an alternative theory. While the prediction of slaughter in Ezekiel 21 is rooted in the traditional sin-punishment paradigm, there is an interesting complication introduced. Not all those slaughtered will themselves be personally culpable.

> Then the word of the Lord came to me: O mortal, set your face toward Jerusalem and proclaim against her sanctuaries and prophesy against the land of Israel. Say to the land of Israel: Thus said the Lord: I am going to deal with you! I will draw my sword from its sheath, and I will wipe out from you both the righteous and the wicked. (Ezek 21:6–8)

Punishment yes, but not necessarily culpability on the part of all those punished.

Intertextual suggestions of alternatives to the traditional sin-punishment paradigm are available elsewhere in L's introductory section. In describing the Jewish reaction to the news of the crusading venture and its anti-Jewish implications, L describes the following actions: "They afflicted themselves with fasting and thirst for three consecutive days—night and day in addition to fasting daily."[28] Embedded here are a number of interesting intertextual allusions. In the first place, the notion of fasting three consecutive nights and days takes us back to the biblical book of Esther, specifically the fourth chapter, where Esther, willing to endanger herself on behalf of her fellow-Jews, enjoins them to fast—along with her—in this unusual way (4:15–16). Now, the entire thrust of the Esther story involves the utter innocence of the threatened Jews, thus mitigating the presentation of Jewish culpability earlier noted.

Included in this picture of Jewish fasting is reference to similar behavior on the part of another group of innocent Jews. In depicting the daily fasting, above and beyond the extreme three-consecutive-day total fast, the term used is *hitʿanû*, a somewhat unusual usage that takes us back to the biblical book of Ezra. There, chaps. 7 and 8 depict the return of a group of Babylonian Jews to Jerusalem under the leadership of Ezra. After listing the constituents of his camp, Ezra proceeds to describe the following: "I proclaimed a fast there by the Ahava River, to afflict ourselves [*lĕhitʿanôt*] before our God to beseech him for a smooth journey for us and for our children and for all our possessions" (8:21). There is an interesting irony here, in the appeal to an image of Jews making their way—peacefully—to the Holy City. Important for our purposes, however, is the evocation of fasting on the part of Jews who were the opposite of sinful, Jews who were engaged in acts of high piety involving, in fact, return to the Holy Land.

The same sentence in L upon which we have been focused includes yet another highly evocative term—*ʿinû napšām* 'they afflicted themselves'. This important expression recurs repeatedly in the descriptions of the Day of

28. N & S, 2; Habermann, 25; Eidelberg, 22; Chazan, 244. The daily fasts are to be understood as sunrise-to-sundown fasts.

Atonement ritual in Leviticus and Numbers.[29] Now, this ritual of affliction is a critical element in a process of purification and atonement. While it may be argued that such atonement presupposes prior guilt, in fact the focus is upon the atonement and not the guilt. In this sense, the intertextual implication of this term dovetails perfectly with the overt argument that the events of 1096 represent an atonement for the unpunished guilt associated with the sin of the golden calf. As already noted, for L, the Rhineland Jews had been singled out for slaughter because "they had the strength and valor to stand in his sanctuary and to fulfill his command and to sanctify his great Name in his world." Thus the self-affliction alludes to the atonement ritual, and the innovative twist imposed in L is that the atonement ritual goes far beyond fasting, that the remarkable behavior of the martyrs of 1096 constitutes in and of itself a new-style atonement ritual.

This brings us to the concluding imagery of L's introduction, the imagery of Psalm 103. This psalm begins and ends with calls for praise of the Lord. That which is praiseworthy constitutes the centerpiece of the psalm, and it is the infinite mercy extended by the Lord to the puny creatures he has fashioned. Thus, in concluding his introduction with reference to this particular psalm, the author of L mitigates yet further the sense of Jewish guilt which he has, to be sure, introduced. Jews are guilt-ridden, but simply because, after all, that is the nature of humanity. More important is the fact that the God who created guilt-ridden humanity is the source of never-ending mercy in relating to frail humanity.

> The Lord is compassionate and gracious,
> slow to anger, abounding in steadfast love.
> He will not contend forever,
> or nurse his anger for all time.
> He has not dealt with us according to our sins,
> nor has he requited us according to our iniquities.
> For as the heavens are high above the earth,
> so great is his steadfast love toward those who fear him.
> As east is far from west,
> so far has he removed our sins from us.
> As a father has compassion for his children,
> so the Lord has compassion for those who fear him.
> For he knows how we are formed;
> he is mindful that we are dust. (Ps 103:9–14)

This central message of Psalm 103 forms a useful counterbalance to the broad notion of Jewish culpability that has been previously discerned. Here the emphasis is placed on divine mercy, as opposed to human shortcoming.

29. Lev 16:31; 23:27, 32; Num 29:7.

The author of L concludes his introduction with v. 20 of Psalm 103. As noted, the psalm begins and ends with a call in a variety of directions to praise the Lord, of whose goodness the psalmist speaks. Just as the central segment of the psalm is built around the contrast between the human and the divine, so too the call to praise covers the entire spectrum of creation. The opening addressee of the call is the human soul—"Bless the Lord, O my soul, all my being, his holy Name. Bless the Lord, O my soul and do not forget all his bounties" (vv. 1–2). The closing call to praise the Lord is addressed to the heavenly hosts and then to the totality of creation, uniting all levels, from the human through the celestial. The call to the heavenly hosts to praise the Lord is interpreted by the author of L as a reference to the Rhineland martyrs: "Bless the Lord, O his angels, mighty creatures who do his bidding, ever obedient to his bidding" (v. 20). Here the innovative theodicy is expressed sharply. The Rhineland martyrs did not, in fact, suffer for their inadequacies; they were singled out for their superhuman—taken literally—devotion to God: They are "ever obedient to his bidding." In referring Ps 103:20 to these Rhineland martyrs, the author of L ends his introductory remarks by reawakening once more the imagery of Exodus 32. The tangible sign of God's reconciliation to the Israelites after the sin of the golden calf was to be the angel that would lead them. Now, as the Jews of the Rhineland prepare to shoulder the burden of that sin—because of their unique ability to do so—they are compared by the author to angelic figures. They are the symbol, as it were, of divine reacceptance of the people of Israel.

Thus, the author of L simultaneously presents at both the overt level and the intertextual level a complex and ambiguous picture of Jewish sinfulness and Jewish strength, of inadequacy and stunning capacities. What does all of this mean in terms of ultimate outcomes? We have already seen that the presentation of the crusaders as simply another link in the chain of historic enemies of the Jewish people implies unmistakably that the fate of the new antagonist will ultimately be the fate of prior foes. Viewing the same issue from the perspective of the Jewish victims, the implications of both the negative and positive portraits coincide. Whether one prefers to highlight the sinfulness of the Rhineland Jews or their remarkable loyalty to the God of Israel, the end result will surely be the same. If the shortcomings of the Rhineland Jews are highlighted, then in any case the compassionate God who is devoted to his people will, of course, eventually be reconciled to them. Even the horrific predictions of Deuteronomy 28 are eventually softened by the promise of an unbreakable convenant provided in Deuteronomy 30. However harsh the punishment might be, upon genuine contrition, "then the Lord your God will restore your fortunes and take you back in love" (30:3). If, on the other hand, the innovative explanation for the catastrophe and the alternative portrait of a blameless and heroic set of Jews is highlighted, then the reward that awaits such merit is even less open to doubt.

Thus, whichever direction is taken, the ultimate outcome of the catastrophe of 1096 will be positive. Christian claims of permanent divine rejection of the Jews, alluded to throughout the Hebrew narratives, are fatuous.[30]

Some closing comments. Reading the intertextual allusions in L is a somewhat risky enterprise, attended by serious dangers of misinterpretation and misguided conclusions.[31] Let us try to identify a pair of potential pitfalls. The first problem with intertextual reading lies in the possibility that the phrases isolated and analyzed might simply be common usages, introduced by the author/editor because they are widely utilized expressions and not for their intertextual resonance.[32] While this is a genuine pitfall in intertextual analysis, it hardly constitutes a serious danger in this study. What must be recalled is that L is a carefully crafted narrative in Hebrew that transforms the vernacular context in which the events originally took place. Thus, the editor of L was hardly likely to cite Hebraic biblical phrases as a reflection of the common usages of the figures whom he depicts. Rather, we are justified in assuming that there is a significant level of contrivance reflected in L and that biblical references were indeed intended to draw the attention of the auditor/reader to the sacred text. Indeed, in many of the instances cited above, the editor of L introduces an entire phrase or clause, allowing no question about his allusion to the biblical referent.[33] In other cases, the lexical forms are so unusual that they obviate any likelihood of casual word usage.[34]

30. Throughout the Hebrew narratives, Christians—sometimes hostile and sometimes quite sympathetic—argue that the catastrophe itself serves as tangible evidence of God's abandonment of the Jewish people. In the face of this abandonment, there is obviously no reasonable alternative for these Jews but to convert.

31. Recall my earlier indication of J. Cohen's recognition of the perilous nature of intertextual readings, above, n. 5.

32. As I was writing this paper, I was involved in reading the interesting book by J. Appleby, L. Hunt, and M. Jacob, *Telling the Truth about History* (New York: Norton, 1994). After detailing in the first part of their study the modern development of an ostensibly objective and scientific history and the thoroughness with which it replaced the prior Judeo-Christian vision of history, the authors proceed to depict the assault on this vision during the middle decades of the 20th century. The second chapter of this second part of their book is entitled "Discovering the Clay Feet of History." Fully immersed in issues of intertextuality at the time, I was convinced that a reference to the imagery of the biblical book of Daniel was the furthest thing from the authors' mind in their use of the phrase "clay feet."

33. Note, inter alia, L's citation of significant segments of verses from Psalm 83, from Exodus 32, and from Psalm 103. Intentional reference to these verses is obvious.

34. Phrases like *kol ʾîš ʾăšer nĕśāʾô libbô, wĕśāmû ʾôtōtām ʾōtôt, ʿam lōʿēz, hagôy hammar wĕhannimhār*, to cite but a few, can likewise hardly be accidental. To be sure, the reference to Prov 30:27, "The locusts have no king," is somewhat troubling. Given the context in which this reference is embedded, which is derogatory to the crusaders, the positive implication of the biblical referent is problematic. The editor of L may simply have introduced the phrase without attending to or intending the positive implication that full attention to the biblical context conveys.

Far more problematic is the relationship of biblical language or imagery, its context, and the meaning intended by the author/editor. Can we be certain, for example, that by alluding to Lamentations the editor of L intended to introduce to the thinking of his auditor/reader the theodicy that lies at the heart of that biblical book? Alternatively, is it not possible that the editor of L was attracted to the language of Lamentations, without in any way intending to conjure up a sense of sinning Israel? The answer to this question is not easy to establish. I would, at this juncture, simply wish to propose diverse levels of certainty/uncertainty in this regard. When the editor of L has the crusaders using precisely the language of Psalm 85, I would be inclined to conclude that he did indeed intend to establish a connection between the crusaders and the earlier enemies of Israel. When the same editor falls back on phraseology from Lamentations, I would suggest a good deal more tentatively that he is implying the traditional notion of catastrophe as rooted in the sin-punishment paradigm. Given the fact that the editor of L introduces ambiguity in his overt depiction of the Jewish victims of crusader violence, we are justified in accepting such ambiguity at the intertextual level as well. Were the references to Lamentations utterly at variance with the overt message of L, I would be considerably more reluctant to suggest conscious arousal of the Lamentations paradigm of sin and suffering.[35] Thus, I remain comfortable with the suggestions advanced above, while urging in a general way that intertextual readings must always be proposed with a considerable measure of caution.

35. The dissonance between the overt and the intertextual message cited in the previous note provides an example of the possibility of careless citation of biblical phraseology, without requisite attention to its implications.

Hebrew Nationalism and Biblical Criticism: The Attitude of Perez Smolenskin

David Engel
New York University

In 1913 Max Soloweitschik, a young educator and Jewish activist from Lithuania,[1] published a series of articles in the *Bulletin of the Society for the Promotion of Enlightenment among the Jews in Russia* outlining some of the findings of recent Western European historical-critical scholarship on the Bible—

1. Soloweitschik (1883–1957) published a number of general works on the Bible, including: *Ocherki po yevreiskoi istorii i kulture: Bibleiskii period* (Essays on Jewish History and Culture: The Biblical Period) (St. Petersburg: Jewish Historic and Ethnographic Society, 1912); *Yesoydes fun der Eltster Yudisher Kultur-Geshikhte* (Foundations of Jewish Cultural History in Ancient Times) (Wilno: Kletzkin, 1922); *Seḥiyot haMiqra* (Berlin: Dvir-Mikra, 1925) (English: *The World of the Bible* [London: Shapiro, Vallentine, 1926]); and *Leqsiqon Miqra'i* (Lexicon Biblicum) (Tel Aviv: Dvir, 1965). The last of these books was published posthumously under the Hebraized name Menahem Solieli, which he adopted after the establishment of the State of Israel. An ardent Jewish nationalist, he was among the founders of the Russian-language Zionist newspapers *Yevreiskaya Zhizn* and *Razsvet* and served as a member of the Zionist Executive. In 1919 he was elected to the Lithuanian parliament and served as minister of Jewish affairs in the Lithuanian government. He left Lithuania in 1922 in order to devote himself to Zionist work on a full-time basis, but a clash with the president of the World Zionist Organization, Chaim Weizmann, forced his withdrawal from the Zionist arena. Thereafter he served on the editorial board of *Jüdisches Lexikon* (1927–30) and as editor of the Bible section of the German-language *Encyclopedia Judaica* (1928–34). After settling in Palestine in 1933, he became a director of the Anglo-Palestine Bank and head of the Education Department of the General Council of the Palestine Jewish Community (1944–48). In 1948 he was named the first director of the Voice of Israel radio service. See Y. Grünbaum, *Pene ha-Dor: Morim, Ḥaverim, Yerivim* (The Face of the Generation: Teachers, Friends, Rivals) (Jerusalem: HaSifriyah haṢiyonit, 1958) 1.306–11; Y. Slutsky, *Ha'Itonut haYehudit-Rusit beReshit haMe'ah ha'Esrim* (The Russian-Language Jewish Press in the Early Twentieth Century) (Tel Aviv: Bialik, 1978) passim.

that manner of investigation that posed as its primary object not the biblical text as presently constituted but the historical process by which the text assumed its present form—and discussing the adjustments that Jews would need to make, in his opinion, in understanding their sacred book as a result of this research. For Soloweitschik there was no doubt that "the conclusions of *Bibelwissenschaft* . . . are not simply an academic matter; rather they have made us change and consider afresh the way we look at the development of the spirit and religious life of Israel in ancient times."[2] Jews ought to regard this development positively, he argued: only "the evolutionary understanding of the essence of the Biblical world" that non-Jewish scholars had been expounding for decades was capable, to his mind, of "introducing a clear light into the dark recesses of the ancient history of Israelite culture, of fleshing out the blurry figures of the people who created our own peculiar spiritual character."[3]

To be sure, Soloweitschik appears to have appreciated the difficulties that stood in the way of effecting such a reorientation: he acknowledged that for generations Jews had looked upon the Bible first and foremost as a repository of divinely-ordained behavioral norms, whose origins and operation over the centuries were not subject to question and thus could never be made subjects of critical investigation.[4] On the other hand, he observed, even "those Jews who have joined European culture and left the spiritual environment of the Middle Ages behind them" tended to view the Bible as "material . . . for demonstrating the force of the unique Hebrew genius and for proving that the [Jewish] people might create such gems once again in the future if only they could live in . . . more favorable conditions." Such people, he feared, would not take kindly to the suggestion, generated by critical historical study, that the common Jewish apologetic argument according to which the Hebrew prophets were the first to preach social justice—"as if Solon were not of the same generation as Jeremiah and the laws of Amraphel did not precede the laws of the Torah by at least six or seven hundred years"—might be false.[5] Hence he predicted that the critical study of the Bible would make significant inroads among Jews only following an internal Jewish *Kulturkampf*. Such a struggle, he believed, would of necessity be most bitterly

2. M. Soloweitschik, *Rashei-Peraqim beMada'e haMiqra* (Outline of Academic Biblical Scholarship) (Odessa: Moriah, 1915) 83. This volume included Hebrew translations of the entire article series, which had originally appeared in Russian.

3. Ibid., 6.

4. Ibid., 26.

5. Ibid., 5. In a bibliographical note, he did acknowledge "the scientific efforts made during the *Haskalah* period, especially by the *Wissenschaft des Judentums* scholars in Western Europe." However, he claimed that such efforts had created "neither a method nor a[n academic] school; therefore the works [of the *Wissenschaft* scholars], for all their importance, cannot be regarded as [showing] the correct way to study the Bible scientifically" (p. 89).

fought, "for many in Israel cannot see in [the critical approach to the Bible] anything except an attack upon the foundations of Judaism and a danger to its very existence."[6]

There was, however, at least one group of Jews whom Soloweitschik had thought would join the battle on the side of critical biblical scholarship. "The [Hebrew] national movement of recent decades," he wrote, "ought to have shown particular affection for the fountain from which Hebrew culture flows and to have afforded it special treatment; it should have directed our recently awakened historical consciousness toward clarifying the content of the Bible's spiritual world." After all, he asserted, "every national movement among each and every one of the peoples of the world has . . . created a living sense of an immediate connection with the classical period of that nation's history and with the finest creations of its independent life."[7] Nonetheless, he had to confess that so far his expectation had not been fulfilled. "The [Jewish national] movement," he complained, "has not brought about any change in the manner in which thoughtful people among us look upon the Biblical literature."[8] Still, however, he counted upon Jewish nationalists eventually to begin thinking about the Bible according to Western critical models, for only in this fashion, he believed, would "the creative thought of Israel grow to recognize itself, finding in the holy scriptures . . . a reliable basis for future national cultural creativity."[9]

Twelve years later Soloweitschik returned to the same subject, together with his collaborator Zalman Rubashov, who had earlier translated Soloweitschik's 1913 articles into Hebrew.[10] In the interval he does not appear to have noticed much movement in the desired direction. As before, he was able to speak only of "the first buds, expressing the need" for a new orientation toward the Bible, "harbingers of change" yet to come, as he renewed his call to "bring down the barrier that separates the [people that] created [the Bible] from its creation and from the scientific labor that serves to place [the

6. Ibid., 6.
7. Ibid., 5.
8. Ibid., 5.
9. Ibid., 7.
10. Rubashov (1889–1974), like Soloweitschik, was an educator and political activist as well as a scholar. Born in Belorussia, he was close to the leadership of the Labor Zionist movement in Russia. During World War I he studied history under Friedrich Meinecke at the University of Berlin and biblical criticism with Wilhelm Nowack at the University of Strassburg, while at the same time organizing Labor Zionist circles throughout Germany. After settling in Palestine in 1924, he became an editor of the leading Hebrew daily newspaper, *Davar*. Following the establishment of the State of Israel, Rubashov (who had since Hebraized his name to Shazar) served as Minister of Education (1949–51) and head of the Department of Education and Culture in the Diaspora of the Jewish Agency (1954–60). In 1963, he became Israel's third president, serving two full terms (until 1973).

Bible] in context."[11] Rubashov, too, though he tried to put as optimistic a face on the situation as possible, had to acknowledge, for example, that Abraham Kahana's "scientific commentary" on the Bible[12]—which the great Hebrew writer and nationalist thinker Micha Josef Berdyczewski termed the first significant step on the road to "planting [the seed of] Biblical criticism in Hebrew"[13]—had been greeted favorably by only a few isolated (if nonetheless prominent) voices.[14] In the end he too could speak only of the tentative appearance of "fresh buds" that might perhaps lead to a new approach to biblical study: "With great hesitation, with measured steps, and with delay, scientific thought in Hebrew is claiming its due; and who is to say that gates that have remained locked until now may not open in the future . . . ?"[15]

As it happened, in the same year that Rubashov's rhetorical question appeared in print it received a tacit reply from the institution that was supposed to constitute the intellectual center of the Hebrew national movement. In their search for someone to direct the Institute of Jewish Studies at the newly-opened Hebrew University of Jerusalem, several of the university's founders, including the preeminent Hebrew poet and man of letters Hayyim Nahman Bialik, had proposed the name of Hirsch Perez Chajes, a noted biblicist, ardent Zionist, and chief rabbi of Vienna. Chajes's appointment, however, was not approved, nor was he invited to serve as the university's first lecturer in Bible—largely, it seems, because of his vocal support for the critical approach to biblical study.[16] In fact, biblical scholarship in any form did

11. M. Soloweitschik and Z. Rubashov, *Toledot Biqoret haMiqra* (A History of Biblical Criticism) (Berlin: Dvir-Mikra, 1925) 2.

12. A. Kahana (ed.), *Torah Nevi'im Ketuvim im Peruš Mada'i beHištatfut Lamdanim Mumḥim* (Torah, Prophets, and Writings with a Scientific Commentary, with the Participation of Expert Scholars) (Zhitomir, Kiev, and Warsaw: Kahana, 1903–).

13. M. J. Berdyczewski, "*LeMi?*" (For Whom?), *Kitvei M. J. Berdyczewski (Bin Gorion): Ma'amarim* (Tel Aviv: Dvir, 1960) 246.

14. Soloweitschik and Rubashov, *Toledot Biqoret haMiqra*, 160. Rubashov was listed in the introduction to the volume as responsible for the chapter on biblical criticism in modern Hebrew literature in which this statement appeared (ibid., 6). Berdyczewski, who was one of the few favorable voices Rubashov had mentioned, noted that Kahana had had to publish and distribute his work on his own, at his own expense, and that the appearance of his commentary had attracted virtually no attention in Hebrew nationalist circles (Berdyczewski, "*LeMi?*" 245–46).

15. Soloweitschik and Rubashov, *Toledot Biqoret haMiqra*, 161.

16. On this episode, see A. Marx, "*Tsvi Perets Chajes: ʿAl Qivro*" (On the Grave of Hirsch Perez Chajes), *Hadoar*, 23 December 1927, 114; M. Goshen-Gottstein, "*Šišim Šanah beHora'at haMiqra ba'Universitah haʿIvrit: Kivunim, Migbalot veTaṣpiyot*" (Sixty Years of Teaching the Bible at the Hebrew University: Directions, Limitations, and Prospects), in *Meḥqarim beMada'ei haYahadut: Asupat haHarṣa'ot vehaDiyunim šeNiś'u beKenes haYovel haŠišim šel haMakon [leMadaʿe haYahadut]* (ed. M. Bar-Asher; Jerusalem: Akademon, 1986) 41–42. On Chajes in general, see S. W. Baron, "*Tsvi*

not become institutionalized at the Hebrew University until the early 1930s, and the university's first two professors of biblical studies, M. Z. Segal and Umberto Cassuto, though not opposed ideologically to historical-critical analysis of the Bible in any form,[17] were widely known as opponents not only of the prevailing documentary hypothesis but even of the notion that exploring the process by which Torah literature was composed was of central importance for elucidating the biblical text.[18] The attitudes of these two scholars toward biblical criticism were to extend far beyond their own era; indeed, even in the final decades of the 20th century, rejection of the fundamental object (let alone the findings) of historical-critical biblical

---

Perets Chajes: LiDemuto" (The Character of Hirsch Perez Chajes), *HaDo'ar*, 23 December 1927, 114–16; N. Sokolow, "*Tsvi Perets Chajes*," in *HaṢofeh leVet Yiśra'el* (The Observer of the House of Israel) (ed. G. Kressel; Jerusalem: HaSifriyah haṢiyonit, 1961) 515–19.

17. Segal had contributed notes on the books of Samuel to Abraham Kahana's scientific commentary (*Torah Nevi'im Ketuvim im Peruš Mada'i*), while Cassuto had actually studied with Chajes at the University of Florence around 1904. See also the following note.

18. Goshen-Gottstein, "*Šišim Šanah*," 42–43. For a concise statement of Segal's attitude toward these issues, see M. Z. Segal, *Mevo haMiqra* (Introduction to the Bible) (8th ed.; Jerusalem, Kiryat-Sefer, 1973) 1.147:

> The stylistic rule in storytelling is that the storyteller generally varies his style by using first and last names interchangeably, according to his inclination and personal feelings. As far as we are concerned, this rule explains the alternation in the use of divine names in the Book of Genesis. Thus the primary foundation upon which the assumption that the Torah is made up of multiple documents was based is undermined. When the foundation falls the entire assumption falls, and with it the whole grand edifice of the evolutionary method in the study of the Bible and the history of Israelite religion.

Cassuto was a bit more moderate in his approach:

> Most of the commentaries on one or another of the books of the Torah that have been written in our generation are devoted mainly to exploring and determining the process by which the sources were joined together; they interpret the fragments of the sources that they discern in the book more than they interpret the book itself. The great importance that commentators are attaching to the issue of the sources distracts them from looking into the [literary] work that was created out of those sources. They hold the study of the sources to be of paramount significance and the study of the book itself to be trivial. My opinion is the exact opposite. . . . To be sure, [the investigation of the sources] is an important means [for understanding and appreciating the book] . . . , and I have given it a not insignificant place in my commentaries . . . ; but in the final analysis . . . only the existence of [the book] is an actual fact rather than an imaginary creation that has no foundation except mere speculation. (M. D. Cassuto, *Peruš 'al Sefer Šemot* [Commentary on the Book of Exodus] [5th ed.; Jerusalem: Magnes, 1969] 7)

See also idem, *Torat haTe'udot veSiduram šel Sifre haTorah* (The Documentary Hypothesis and the Arrangement of the Books of the Torah) (Jerusalem: Hebrew University Press, 1941).

scholarship remains a notable though by no means preponderant feature of academic writing on the Bible in Hebrew.[19]

Several hypotheses have been advanced to explain why the hopes of Soloweitschik and Rubashov materialized only so slowly and partially, why the Hebrew national movement was so hesitant to embrace the historical-critical study of the Hebrew Bible. Soloweitschik and Rubashov themselves suggested three reasons. In the first place, they argued, early nationalists, filled with affection and admiration for the Bible as the principal repository of the Jewish people's romantic heritage, feared that any academization of biblical study was liable to "darken the splendor of the Book of Books." Second, they observed that the intentions of German Protestant biblical critics were often perceived by Eastern European Jews with suspicions: "Wellhausen and his followers . . . were regarded as destroyers of the vineyard of Israel, and who in Israel would lend them an ear?" Finally, they noted that Jewish nationalism had its origins in a dialectical rejection of the Western European *Haskalah* (Enlightenment) movement, which had come to posit an exclusively religious basis for Jewish identity and to deny the Jews any national character whatsoever. Because many adherents of this movement (which had inspired the German *Wissenschaft des Judentums* school of Leopold Zunz and Abraham Geiger, among others) had been inclined toward the critical study of the Bible, they reasoned, Hebrew nationalists had felt themselves duty-bound ideologically to abjure any such approach, whose implications they perceived as entirely antinational.[20] Many later writers who have com-

19. See, for example, M. Greenberg, "*Ḥeqer haMiqra vehaMeṣi'ut ha'Artsiyiśre'elit*" (Biblical Scholarship and the Israeli Reality), in *haMiqra ve'Anaḥnu* (ed. U. Simon; Tel Aviv: Dvir, 1979) 71–72: "The task of Biblical scholarship in Israel . . . is to transfer the focus of study from the surroundings of the text (its background, its stages of formation, its relation to parallel texts, etc.) to the text itself." For Greenberg, any prior versions or component parts that biblical scholarship might identify of the biblical text as presently constituted must of necessity remain hypothetical constructs, in contrast to the tangible reality of the books of the Bible in their present form. For an elaboration of this theme, see idem, *Understanding Exodus* (New York: Behrman, 1969) 1–8. For an example of a contemporary Hebrew-language affirmation of the centrality of "the problem of composition" in Bible study and an acceptance of the reality of the Bible's component documents as identified by modern critical scholarship, see M. Haran, *Tequfot uMosdot baMiqra* (Periods and Institutions in the Bible) (Tel Aviv: Am Oved, 1972) ix–xiv. On the tension between these two approaches, see Goshen-Gottstein, "*Šišim Šanah*," 46–47. On the lack of agreement on the basic assumptions of biblical criticism among biblical scholars writing in Hebrew, see M. Haran, *Biblical Research in Hebrew: A Discussion of Its Character and Trends* (Jerusalem: Hebrew University Press, 1970) 26–27.

20. Soloweitschik and Rubashov, *Toledot Biqoret haMiqra*, 158. In the event, critical biblical scholarship played only a minor role in the investigations of the *Wissenschaft* school, as Soloweitschik and Rubashov acknowledged elsewhere (pp. 128–29). For a discussion of *Wissenschaft* and Bible study, see, among others, B. Levine, "The

mented on the problem have posited an even more blatantly ideological basis for the observed phenomenon, seeing in Hebrew-language biblical scholarship a clear design "to become free of Western influence and to return to the original sources"[21] or "a polemical response to Protestant scholarship."[22]

In virtually all cases, though, such hypotheses appear to have been offered *en passant*, as incidental addenda to studies concerned more with *describing* the relationship of Hebrew nationalism to biblical criticism than with *explaining* the relationship. Proving any of them, on the other hand, requires detailed, systematic investigation not only of the positions taken by the leading figures of the Hebrew national movement but of the arguments advanced in support of those positions. However, such comprehensive research has not been undertaken to date; in fact, even exhaustive studies of the attitudes of individual nationalist thinkers, writers, and educators toward biblical criticism—and even more of the justifications given for those attitudes—are lacking.

What follows is offered as an initial step toward filling this lacuna.

* * *

By virtually any measure, one of the most influential of the immediate intellectual progenitors of the Hebrew national movement was Perez ben Moshe Smolenskin (1842–85). A prolific Hebrew novelist and short-story writer hailed in his time, with considerable hyperbole, as a literary artist of the first order,[23] Smolenskin founded and edited the monthly *HaShaḥar* (The Dawn), the preeminent Hebrew periodical of the 1870s and early 1880s.[24] In the pages of this journal, Smolenskin limned an approach to the

---

European Background," in *Students of the Covenant: A History of Jewish Biblical Scholarship in North America* (ed. S. D. Sperling; Atlanta: Scholars Press, 1992) 15–32.

21. H. Sheli, *Meḥqar haMiqra beSifrut haHaśkalah* (Biblical Scholarship in *Haśkalah* Literature) (Jerusalem: Reuven, 1942) 115. See also M. Haran (Diman), "*Ḥaqirat haMiqra beʿIvrit biTequfat haTeḥiyah haLeʾumit*" (Bible Study in Hebrew during the Period of National Revival), *Bitzaron* 23 (1951) 193.

22. B. Uffenheimer, "Some Reflections on Modern Jewish Biblical Research," *Creative Biblical Exegesis: Christian and Jewish Hermeneutics* (ed. B. Uffenheimer and H. G. Reventlow; Sheffield: JSOT Press, 1988) 165. Of course, those who continue to maintain a skeptical attitude toward the premises of biblical criticism would argue for a sound evidentiary rather than an ideological basis for its rejection. See, for example, Greenberg, "*Ḥeqer haMiqra*," 71–74.

23. See the introduction to P. Smolenskin, *Qevurat Ḥamor* (A Donkey's Burial) (Jerusalem: Bialik, 1968) 7, annotated and with an introduction by David Weinfeld.

24. For a testimony to the influence of *HaShaḥar*, see S. L. Citron, "A Pilgrimage to Peretz Smolenskin," in *The Golden Tradition: Jewish Life and Thought in Eastern Europe* (ed. L. S. Dawidowicz; Boston: Beacon, 1967) 140–41:

> *HaShachar*, the monthly which Smolenskin began to publish in the late sixties, was an extraordinary happening in the life of that Jewish intelligentsia which resisted the

fundamental cultural problem facing European Jewry in his day—determining the proper relationship for Jews between behavioral norms and values derived from traditional rabbinic Judaism and those derived from extra-traditional, non-Jewish sources—that assumed a middle ground between two seemingly mutually antagonistic positions that had crystallized during the previous century. On the one hand Smolenskin rejected the claim of tradition, as interpreted by rabbis, to exclusive authority over Jewish behavior. Religious law, he argued, must change over time, in accordance with reason and logic, as the external conditions of Jewish life changed, whereas the traditional course of study for rabbis, being rooted not in reason and logic but in the false belief that the totality of religious law commanded to previous generations remained an essential guarantor of religious faith in the present, could not be counted upon to generate changes as they became necessary.[25] Instead Smolenskin posited a sort of Jewish *volonté générale* as the ultimate arbiter of Jewish conduct: "We shall not wait for [the rabbis] to begin the process of reducing our burden," he declared, "but the people will be charged with correcting and annulling [outmoded laws]," which, "if they are indeed harmful, will fall by themselves, because the people will ignore them."[26] At the same time, however, he inveighed vigorously against those who had claimed since the 1780s to represent the general will against rabbinic rule—the spiritual descendants of Moses Mendelssohn, who had begotten the Berlin-centered movement known as *Haskalah*. These so-called enlighteners,

> assimilatory currents and heeded the Hebrew word. For the Orthodox youth educated in the yeshivas and prayer houses, *HaShachar* was practically a revolutionary upheaval. Every copy in the hands of these young people was like a match put to a powder keg. *HaShachar* revolutionized their minds, undermined old ideas infested with traditional moldiness, stimulated them to new ideas. . . . There was not one yeshiva in all the Russian Pale to which Smolenskin's *HaShachar* had not found its way.

25. P. Smolenskin, "*ʿAm ʿOlam*" (The Eternal People), *Maʾamarim* (Jerusalem: Keren Smolensky, 1925) 1.26–27 (originally published in *HaShaḥar* 3 [1872]). Smolenskin maintained that "[religious] faith is the air we breathe, for at this time it is what provides us our existence as a people, whereas [religious] laws are articles of clothing to be changed according to the temperature." Hence, he postulated,

> whenever the heat of faith decreases in temperature, new laws are given us to warm our hearts, and we can accept them; but just as wearing many articles of clothing raises our temperature and makes us want to remove them, so too wearing many laws becomes a burden upon the people, keeping them from pursuing their livelihood and their interests . . . , and the heart of the people stirs itself to remove the burden from their shoulders, that it may not become a stumbling block in their life's way.

However, he claimed, because "the rabbis . . . sit secluded in their homes and have nothing in common with those who work for a living," they "can neither know nor understand the distress that the multiplicity of laws causes." For additional comments by Smolenskin on the education of rabbis, see idem, "*Bate Sefer leRabanim beAustriya*" (Rabbinical Schools in Austria), in *Maʾamarim*, 2.291–97.

26. Idem, "*ʿAm ʿOlam*," 28.

he charged, had capriciously despaired of all possibility that the Jewish people could, through the operation of normal social processes, adapt their traditional norms to contemporary needs, contending instead (erroneously, he thought) that "throughout all the generations our ancestors felt their way blindly in the darkness."[27] He complained that such despair had impelled them to inscribe upon their banner the slogan of imitation of the ways of the Gentiles and to proclaim that Jews ought to be distinguished from their non-Jewish neighbors by nothing more than a few basic ceremonial practices.[28] He thus characterized their attitude as one that "declares war upon all that Israel has ever possessed, war upon the Torah, war upon love of the people, war upon the hope of being reunited again." "A new spirit has gone forth from Berlin," he wrote, "determined to overturn the House of Israel at its roots, burying alive those who remain behind under mounds of dust. . . ."[29]

Against these two poles Smolenskin proposed to view Jews as representing neither a clerically-governed religious community nor a minor denominational variant within the Western European cultural mainstream but a culturally distinct 'nation of the spirit' (*ʿAm haRuaḥ*), united not by a common territory, a common set of laws, or even a common language but in the final analysis by nothing more than an ongoing subjective sense of belonging to a single unified people.[30] Smolenskin regarded this sense of national identity, along with its concomitant feelings of love for the national group and pride in its historic accomplishments, as positive values, not merely for Jews but for all peoples. Although humanism and universal altruism—"the idea that one should love only humanity as a whole and not specific individuals, such as the members of one's own household, his family, or his countrymen"[31]—were noble ideals, to his mind they were unlikely to lead to the

27. P. Smolenskin, "*ʿEt Laṭaʿat*" (Time to Plant), part 3, in *Maʾamarim* (Jerusalem: Keren Smolenky, 1925) 2.216 (originally published in *HaShaḥar* 9 [1878]). For Smolenskin's view of the social processes that make periodic reform a natural phenomenon, see "*ʿAm ʿOlam*," 5–24.

28. Idem, "*ʿEt Laṭaʿat*," part 1, *Maʾamarim*, 2.62ff. (originally published in *HaShaḥar* 6 [1875]).

29. Idem, "*ʿEt Laṭaʿat*", part 3, 216. For a brief selection in English revealing Smolenskin's attitude toward the Berlin *Haskalah*, see idem, "The Haskalah of Berlin," in *The Zionist Idea* (ed. A. Hertzberg; New York: Meridian, 1959) 154–57. See also Ts. Nardi, "*Temurot biTenuʿat haHaśkalah beRusiyah biŠenot haŠišim vehaŠivʿim šel haMeʾah ha-19*" (Changes in the *Haskalah* Movement in Russia during the 1860s and 1870s), in *HaDat vehaḤayim: Tenuʿat haHaśkalah haYehudit beMizraḥ Eiropah* (Religion and Life: The Jewish *Haskalah* Movement in Eastern Europe) (ed. E. Etkes; Jerusalem: Merkaz Zalman Shazar, 1993) 318–19.

30. Smolenskin, "*ʿEt Laṭaʿat*," 19ff., 145ff. On Smolenskin's claim to represent a middle ground between religious orthodoxy and religious denominationalism, see Y. Salmon, "The Emergence of a Jewish Nationalist Consciousness in Europe during the 1860s and 1870s," *AJS Review* 16 (1991) 127–30.

31. Smolenskin, "*ʿAm ʿOlam*," 14.

more peaceful, more perfect world they were intended to advance; on the contrary, only a person who loved himself and his more immediate social spheres was capable of ever developing a broader love of humanity.[32] Hence the strengthening of the Jews' regard for their essential unity as a people, their awareness of and commitment to the ties that bound them to one another across political and linguistic borders, constituted for Smolenskin a primary task for Jewish leaders, not only for the Jews' own sake but for the sake of all mankind.[33]

In his preface to the first volume of *HaShaḥar*, Smolenskin declared his intention to use the periodical as a vehicle for "bringing together the hearts of all Israel to become [again] a single people."[34] This goal was to be accomplished through a twofold struggle, both against obscurantist clerics who sought to keep the fruits of reason and logic far from the popular consciousness, and against misguided enlighteners "who despise the entire nation . . . , betraying their people and their faith with a false universalism."[35] Against the latter he spoke out with particular animation:

> They say to us, "Let us be like all the nations!" And I, too, say with them: let us indeed be like all the nations, pursuing knowledge and attaining it, leaving behind the ways of wickedness and foolishness, becoming loyal residents of the countries of our dispersion. But let us also be like all the nations in displaying no shame toward the source from which we have been hewn. Let us be like all the nations in valuing our language and our people's honor! . . . Let all be aware in advance: just as I have set my hand against those obsequious false pietists who wrap themselves in holy garments and bring catastrophe upon us by keeping knowledge and wisdom away from the House of Jacob, so too shall I raise my hand against those hypocritical prophets of wisdom who banish the Children of Israel from the heritage of their fathers. . . . I shall continue

32. Ibid., 15, 136ff. Smolenskin regarded the British people as the most outstanding example of the beneficial consequences of national egoism:

> Britain . . . has not sought to embrace and caress all human beings . . . , [but] has understood that a person's first task is to look out for himself, then for his people and only later for human beings [in general]. In their love for themselves and for their people the British have sought freedom in their country; they have removed the burden of taxes wherever they have been able and have labored mightily to improve the state of commerce in order to generate wealth . . . ; they have refrained from going to war even when it was within their power to do so. . . . If only all of the nations had done as they have done, then wars would by now have ceased and peace reigned throughout the earth. The British love their people, and by loving their people they do good for all mankind, whereas the Germans and the French profess to love all mankind, but not only have they done nothing to the benefit of humanity but they have done harm to their own peoples." (Ibid., 138–39)

33. Ibid., 42.
34. Idem, "*Petaḥ Davar*," *HaShaḥar* 1 (1869) v.
35. Ibid., iv, vi.

along this path and shall not tire. . . . May love of our people be a lamp unto our feet.[36]

Evidently such a statement of mission accorded with a hostile attitude toward biblical criticism. Indeed, from early in its history *HaShaḥar* became a leading forum for attacks on biblical studies conducted in a historical-critical spirit. Smolenskin himself set the tone for the journal's anticritical orientation in its third volume with a withering review of Heinrich Graetz's commentary on the Song of Songs, which he castigated as the work of a man "craving renown as a scholarly innovator" but showing little regard for the truth.[37] In this excoriation of the German Jewish scholar's treatise, Smolenskin likened criticism of the biblical text to pre-Socratic sophistry and to the now discredited casuistic approach to the study of traditional Jewish texts (*pilpul*), both of which were built, he charged, on a foundation of unprovable conjecture. "*Pilpul*," he wrote, "has left . . . the study houses of Poland and migrated to Germany, where . . . it now appears in [the guise of] biblical criticism, but it has not changed its method in the slightest; now as then its way is to build fanciful castles in the air, joining north and east by force and turning words of truth and charm into tasteless falsehood."[38] His most extensive programmatic essay, "*ʿAm ʿOlam*" (The Eternal People), published in the same volume, contained a similar condemnation of those who, by "subjecting the Holy Scriptures to criticism, have set about making a confusion of what is written."[39] Smolenskin returned to this theme in later volumes of the journal as well, lambasting those who "arrogate to themselves [the title of] biblical scholars" as having "inverted everything, making chaos of the words of the seers, turning them into a pile of nothingness onto which they have heaped more piles of nothingness *ad infinitum*."[40] He also offered *HaShaḥar* as a platform for essays and scholarly studies on the Bible by opponents of the critical approach—foremost among them the Odessa-based Judaicist David Kahana, whose vigorous and extensive defense on empirical grounds of the authenticity of the Masoretic Text and of the validity of the rabbinic tradition concerning the dating and authorship of the biblical books, *Masoret Seyag laMiqra*, was serialized in two successive volumes of Smolenskin's periodical before being released in book form by a publishing

36. Ibid., vi.

37. Idem, "*Mišpaṭ Ḥaruṣ*" (A Decisive Judgment), *Ḥamišah Maʾamare Biqoret* (Wilno: Katzenellenhosen, 1914) 112 (originally published in *HaShaḥar* 3 [1872]). In a later reference to the same work, Smolenskin called Graetz "a haughty and self-aggrandizing man who wishes with all his heart to gain the respect of scholars, no matter whether he does so justly and honestly or not" (*HaShaḥar* 11 [1883] 186).

38. Idem, "*Mišpaṭ Ḥaruṣ*," 67.

39. Idem, "*ʿAm ʿOlam*," 139.

40. Idem, *HaShaḥar* 10 (1880) 508. Cf. *HaShaḥar* 10 (1880) 206; 11 (1883) 588.

house that Smolenskin himself managed.[41] Small wonder, then, that Soloweitschik and Rubashov considered Smolenskin to have been the ringleader of a circle dedicated to preventing even "the slightest echo of the impressive accomplishments of the scientific work [on the Bible] being pursued abroad at the time from penetrating into Hebrew literature."[42]

Soloweitschik and Rubashov attributed *HaShaḥar*'s imputed tendency—in accordance with their general assumptions regarding the sources of Hebrew nationalist attitudes toward biblical criticism—primarily to "the haughty and arrogant attitude toward the West" that allegedly characterized the journal's editor and contributors, as well as to a fear that the critical approach would reduce respect, among Jews and non-Jews alike, for the national treasure of the Jewish people.[43] Such an assessment, however, does not appear to chime with Smolenskin's own statements of the reasons for his position. In a summary comment on the subject, Smolenskin denied emphatically that he repudiated the historico-critical approach because its findings threatened to undermine a source of Jewish national pride: "In speaking out against the biblical critics," he wrote, "I am concerned not only with the national honor, for in reality the national honor will not be harmed if it turns out that the books [of the Bible] were written a thousand years after the time that the earliest commentators assigned them or if they incorporated material from other peoples as well."[44] He also consistently urged against the automatic dismissal of the opinion of a Western biblical critic solely on the grounds of origin; in fact, on one occasion he even took David Kahana to task for failing to acknowledge that some of the interpretations of those against whom he wrote might be true.[45] Rather he professed to base his rejection on considerations that were essentially academic and empirical: "I have spoken against the Biblical critics," he wrote, "solely because for the most part their criticism is built upon empty foundations, upon lack of knowledge of the [Hebrew] language."[46]

41. D. Kahana, *Masoret Seyag laMiqra* (Tradition is a Fence around the Bible) (Vienna: George Bragg, 1882) (originally published in *HaShaḥar*, vols. 9–10). The title was evidently taken from an early 13th-century work by Meir Abulafia, entitled *Masoret Seyag laTorah*, which discussed the Masoretic Text of the Pentateuch and set forth rules for its copying. On Kahana, see Sheli, *Meḥqar haMiqra*, 137–42. Another opponent of biblical criticism who published in *HaShaḥar* was the historian Ze'ev Jawitz; see his work in *HaShaḥar* 11 (1883) 41–48. On Jawitz, see Haran (Diman), "*Ḥaqirat haMiqra*," 39–40.

42. Soloweitschik and Rubashov, *Toledot Biqoret haMiqra*, 158.

43. Ibid., 158–59. See also above, at n. 20.

44. Smolenskin, *HaShaḥar* 11 (1883) 153.

45. See his criticism of Kahana's commentary on Ecclesiastes in *HaShaḥar* 10 (1880) 509. See also Smolenskin, "*Mišpaṭ Ḥaruṣ*," 102–3.

46. See Soloweitschik and Rubashov, *Toledot Biqoret haMiqra*, 158–59.

Was Smolenskin's campaign against biblical criticism motivated in fact primarily by considerations of a purely scholarly nature? On the surface there appear to be several reasons to take him at his word. To begin with, it was a general feature of Smolenskin's teaching that uncensored objective empirical investigation according to the Western scientific model was an essential therapeutic instrument for correcting what he called the "confusions [that] have multiplied in the present era"—confusions that to his mind had split the Jewish people into warring camps, threatening the people's basic sense of national unity.[47] In fact, he professed to have founded *HaShaḥar* largely for the purpose of fostering such objective study of the Jewish past, convinced that it would provide an effective counterweight to what he viewed as the dogmatism of both traditionalists and radical Westernizers.[48] He regularly referred his readers both to the classics of Western literature and to important works of recent Western scholarship, and he himself appears to have founded his discussions of the dynamics of ideological division among Jews and the problem of religious reforms (two of the primary foci of his essays) largely on recent German, French, and English historical and social scientific works.[49] Even in the specific field of Bible study, he was not averse to recommending certain works of Western scholarship whose conclusions appeared to him valid and valuable.[50]

Nor does Smolenskin appear to have rejected automatically the scholarly products of Western Jewish *Haskalah* and *Wissenschaft*. On the contrary, although he clearly had little regard in general for the work of the *Wissenschaftler* Zunz, Geiger, I. M. Jost, and others,[51] and even less for Graetz's (his historical studies as well as his biblical commentaries),[52] he drew upon certain specific findings of all of these researchers in buttressing his ideological

47. P. Smolenskin, "*ʿEt Ledaber*" (Time to Talk), *Ḥamišah Maʾamare Biqoret*, 55–57 (originally published in *HaShaḥar* 2 [1871]).

48. Ibid., 51–52.

49. See, int. al., ibid., 56–61; idem, "*ʿAm ʿOlam*," 11–24; idem, "*ʾEven Yiśraʾel*" (The Rock of Israel), *Ḥamišah Maʾamare Biqoret*, passim (originally published in *HaShaḥar* 1 [1869]).

50. See, for example, *HaShaḥar* 5 (1874) 79–80, in which Smolenskin praised a recently published treatise on Psalms by G. Phillips of Queens College, Cambridge, for "the diligence and industry the author has shown in his commentary and especially in his wonderful introduction . . . despite the fact that his opinion about [the text's foretelling of the coming of Jesus] is not ours." Smolenskin concluded that "not only Christians but also the enlightened among our own people will find quite a few useful and honest items in this commentary."

51. See, for example, his comments in Smolenskin, "*ʿEt Laṭaʿat*," part 3, 272.

52. Cf. his observations on Graetz's monumental history of the Jews in "*ʿEt Laṭaʿat*": "We shall not be judging Graetz too severely if we conclude that he has not written the history of Israel at all but rather a fictional story with historical foundations; he has written only what his own spirit values, not the history of Israel as it *actually happened*" [italics his]. See also ibid., 236.

positions.[53] There were even certain *Maskilim* whose scientific studies he tended regularly to laud, including most notably—and most strangely—the Russian-educated, Berlin-based philologist Leon Mandelstamm. Mandelstamm had once served as an adviser to the government of Tsar Nikolai I on the education of Russian Jewry, and Smolenskin might have perceived him with good reason as standing ideologically rather close to those extreme Westernizers that he had vowed in his initial statement in *HaShaḥar* to fight.[54] The ideological opposition between the two, however, did not prevent Smolenskin from labeling Mandelstamm's 1862 German-language series of critical biblical studies a "superior work" written by a "great scholar."[55]

53. See, for example, idem, "*ʿAm ʿOlam*," 50, 56, 61, 97–100, 107, 111, 133, 136.

54. Idem, "*Even Yiśra'el*," 41; idem, "*ʿAm ʿOlam*," 39; idem, "*Mišpaṭ Ḥaruṣ*," 79. Mandelstamm (1819–89), the first Jew to graduate from a Russian university, was known as one of the most radical Russian *Maskilim* of his generation. During the 1840s, he helped to organize a system of government-sponsored schools for Russian Jews in which German was a primary language of instruction and Bible was studied according to Moses Mendelssohn's German translation and commentary. He also sought to use the schools as instruments for the inculcation of Russian patriotism. These positions ran sharply counter to Smolenskin's ideological predilections. On Mandelstamm see, int. al., M. Stanislawski, *Tsar Nicholas I and the Jews: The Transformation of Jewish Society in Russia, 1825–1855* (Philadelphia: Jewish Publication Society, 1983) 101–3, 112–13, 120; J. Shatzky, *Kultur-Geshikhte fun der Haskole in Lite* (Cultural History of the *Haskalah* in Lithuania) (Buenos Aires: Tsentral farband fun Poylishe Yidn in Argentine, 1950) 114–17; E. Etkes, "*Parašat Ha'Haśkalah Miṭaʿam' vehaTemurot beMaʿamad Tenuʿat haHaśkalah beRusiyah*" (The Episode of 'Compulsory Enlightenment' and the Changes in the Status of the *Haskalah* Movement in Russia), *Zion* 43 (1978) 311–12.

55. Smolenskin, "*ʿAm ʿOlam*," 39. Mandelstamm's work consisted of a number of detailed studies in biblical philology, chronology, and history, as well as an extensive analysis of developments in the field of source criticism from Spinoza to his own time—that is, before the appearance of the works of Graf and Wellhausen. Regarding this matter he represented his position as that of an objective scientist largely unconvinced by the work of most source critics, often finding himself preferring the Masoretic Text and traditional Jewish exegesis on purely academic grounds. M. Mandelstamm, *Biblische Studien* (2 vols.; Berlin: Friedlander, 1862); see especially 2/1.4–6:

> Unser Standpunkt wird die Bibel selbst seyn, ganz wie die Natur für den Naturforscher. . . . Gegen die alten Ueberlieferungen über die Namen der Verfasser und die Zeit der Abfassung der verschiedenen Bücher des alten Testaments, hat die Kritik Behauptungen aufgestellt, aus denen sie zu folgern versuchte, daß die ganze Bibel wahrscheinlich ein Werk späterer Zeiten und unzähliger unbekannter Verfasser sey, daß ihr Inhalt in sich gar viele Widersprüche enthalte u.s.w. Alles, was diesen Kritikern in der Bibel dunkel vorkam, galt ihnen für sinnlos; was sie mit ihrem Verstand nicht zu fassen vermochten, für unverständlich, und was ihren persönlichen Ansichten zuwider war, für irrig und falsch. Wir wollen hier einstweilen nicht darüber sprechen, wie sehr die neuen kritischen Versuche den einfachen alten Ueberlieferungen an Tiefe, Wahrheit und Wahrscheinlichkeit nachstehen,—nur das müssen wir von vorn herein erklären, daß wir die Kritik, so viel davon zu unserer Kenntniß gelangt ist, nicht scheuen. . . . Wir werden nur von unserm guten Rechte Gebrauch machen und, mehr vertrauend auf die Autorität

Finally, Smolenskin's most extended statement in opposition to a position that he identified with the historical-critical school (his rejoinder to Graetz's commentary on the Song of Songs) was indeed based largely on contentions of a purely academic nature. Much of Smolenskin's explication of his objections to this work consisted of linguistic arguments, challenging not only Graetz's overall command of the Hebrew language but also his rendering of specific words from the Hebrew text into German, his dating of certain Hebrew forms, and his ascription of Greek origin to words that, in Smolenskin's view, had already been shown by previous scholars (including Ewald and Delitzsch) to stem from Semitic roots.[56] Smolenskin also raised objections of a historical nature. He devoted much space to a detailed refutation of Graetz's complex discussion of what the latter took to be the Greek origins of several customs mentioned in the biblical text, arguing, for example, that the lack of any description in the historical books of the Bible of opulent canopied palanquins like the one depicted in Cant 3:9–10 did not necessarily prove that such conveyances were unknown in Solomonic times and that the novelty of a bridegroom in Israel wearing flowers at his wedding could be established only by a willful and arbitrary correction of the Masoretic Text of Isa 61:10.[57] He questioned, too, how Graetz could be certain that the existence

der heiligen Schrift, als auf die der leichtfertigen Zweifler, ihrem Zweifel Kritik entgegenstellen; aber auch dann noch, wenn unsere Bemühungen von dem glücklichen Erfolge—die Autorität der heiligen Schrift durch Vernunft wieder hergestellt zu haben—gekrönt seyn werden, haben wir dadurch selbst der Vernunft das höchste Richteramt im Reiche menschlicher Gedanken eingeräumt, ohne die ja jede selbstständige Ueberzeugung der Menschen unmöglich wäre.

This position was quite similar to the one Smolenskin professed to occupy; this affinity was undoubtedly the source of Smolenskin's praise. Nevertheless, Smolenskin did not hesitate to criticize Mandelstamm when he felt that he was in error; see, for example, Smolenskin, "*Mišpaṭ Ḥaruṣ*," 108.

56. Ibid., 73ff., 80–81, 82ff. Interestingly, these challenges often distorted Graetz's arguments. For example, whereas Smolenskin took Graetz to task for rendering the word ברה in Cant 6:9 as 'keusch' and suggested that Graetz had mistakenly interpreted the book as a polemic in favor of chastity on the basis of this erroneous reading, Graetz in fact rendered the word in question (more accurately) as 'lauter' and viewed the book not as a polemic in favor of chastity but as one against superficial sensual love (among other things). See Graetz, *Schir ha-Schirim oder das Salomonische Hohelied übersetzt und kritisch erläutert von Dr. H. Graetz* (Vienna: Wilhelm Braumüller, 1871) 31, 37–39, 184–85. In similar fashion, where Smolenskin had taken Graetz to task for ignoring the findings of previous research in his discussion of the origins of the word אפריון, Graetz had actually offered an extended discussion of the treatment of the word in earlier scholarly literature, citing philological studies that supported its derivation from the Greek φορεῖον and discussing the shortcomings of various attempts to adduce a Semitic origin, specifically including the attempts of Ewald and Delitzsch (see ibid., 54–55).

57. Smolenskin, "*Mišpaṭ Ḥaruṣ*," 88–91; cf. Graetz, *Schir ha-Schirim*, 60–62.

of parallels between the biblical text and the poems of the Greek Theokrit, a contemporary of Ptolemy Philadelphus, proved that the Hebrew writer had borrowed from the Greek rather than the Greek from the Hebrew.[58] It was on the basis of these objections that Smolenskin dismissed the central thesis of Graetz's essay, that the Song of Songs was composed during the Macedonian period, specifically in the days when Joseph the Tobiad farmed the taxes of Judea for the Ptolemaic rulers (around the end of the third century B.C.E.), as a polemic against the excessive materialism and moral laxity of the times.[59] Graetz, he argued, had in the final analysis failed to advance any compelling philological, historical, or literary reason for preferring a later dating of the book to an earlier one; on the contrary, he asserted, a linguistically accurate and historically sensitive reading of the text made a preexilic dating (perhaps even to the time of Solomon himself) more probable.[60] Nor to his mind had Graetz sufficiently established the book's essentially polemical nature and intent; after reading Graetz's discussion, he still found no basis for believing that the Song of Songs was not simply what it purported to be on its surface—a love poem, pure and simple.[61]

It was Smolenskin's analysis of Graetz's proposition that the Song of Songs had been written for essentially polemical purposes that appears to have catalyzed a broader consideration of the premises of biblical criticism as a whole. For Smolenskin, Graetz's attempt to ascribe a hidden intention to the author of the biblical book was actually a symptom of a fundamental gulf of mentality between modern Western man and the spirit of ancient Israel as manifested in the Hebrew Bible. Ancient Hebrew literature, he claimed, was unique and could not be understood according to standard European analytical categories derived in the main from Greek modes of thought. Whereas in his view the Greeks, a polytheistic people, acknowledged the legitimate existence of various alternative sources of knowledge and created a literature expressing through its various forms the diverse paths taken by individuals in pursuit of truth, the monotheistic forebears of the Jews, whose voice is heard in the Bible, made the one God who created the universe the ultimate subject of all that they wrote.[62] As a result, he maintained, the choice of literary

58. Smolenskin, "*Mišpaṭ Ḥaruṣ*," 92–93; cf. Graetz, *Schir ha-Schirim*, 67–73.

59. Smolenskin, "*Mišpaṭ Ḥaruṣ*," 79; cf. Graetz, *Schir ha-Schirim*, 81–88.

60. Smolenskin, "*Mišpaṭ Ḥaruṣ*," 79, 107. Smolenskin did not insist on Solomonic authorship, merely on authorship during Solomon's time or shortly thereafter.

61. Ibid., 107.

62. Ibid., 106:

> The spirit of the Greeks, who worshipped many gods, was divided among various ideas, with each individual thinking according to his own lights. . . . Hence they went to great pains to establish separate paths for each individual, so that all could be explored. Not so the Jews, for whom one God was the source of all their thought and faith; they did not seek to separate but to unite all together and to base everything upon a single cornerstone, a single God. The poet who wrote songs of praise praised the one God; the elegist

form for the Hebrew writer, unlike for the Greek, bore no essential connection to his subject; it was nothing more than a reflection of the writer's emotional state at the time of writing, and a particular form was employed entirely for its own sake. "What point is there in inquiring about a [Hebrew] poet's aim?" he asked rhetorically; "his aim was *to sing*, just as the elegist's aim was to express mourning."[63] The composer of the Song of Songs, then, according to Smolenskin, sought nothing more than to write beautiful poetry; his creation was the result of a fundamental emotional impulse, not a conscious criticism of the society in which he lived. He chose to write love poetry, in Smolenskin's view, not because of any clearly-defined intention but simply because love, as an integral part of divine creation, was a most appropriate subject—albeit an unusual one—for a Hebrew poet.[64] Nevertheless, modern biblical critics appeared to Smolenskin unable to contemplate such a possibility: "in recent generations most people . . . cannot understand something done with no particular end in mind."[65] As a result, he objected, they insisted on forcing the biblical text into familiar intellectual categories rather than attempting to confront the text on its own terms:

> Those hundreds of people who have written commentaries on the Song of Songs have not sought out the plain meaning of the text; rather they have gone chasing after absurdities. They have piled question upon question: What is the formal structure of the Song of Songs? Should it be called a drama? An epic poem? A pastoral song? An idyll? Bucolic poetry? In this fashion they go looking for bears where there is not even a forest. What formal structure shall we ascribe to the Song of Songs? The formal structure of the Song of Songs itself is what we ought to ascribe to it. How are we to expect a Hebrew poet who lived before any of these terms for different kinds of poems had been invented, in a country where European systems of categorization were foreign, to proceed according to the dictates of the Greeks and Romans and to arrange his thoughts the way they did?

In Smolenskin's opinion, such insistence on the part of biblical critics led them—ironically—to flights of fancy not very different in their essence from the homiletical exegesis of the rabbis. The attribution of a polemical motivation to the author of Song of Songs, for example, might fit certain preconceived Western notions of the impulses that gave rise to much of the biblical

---

> mourned the city of God and the one people that was the people of God; the poet of love sang in honor of a love that came from God. The entire universe, the whole of creation were as one to them; everything came from the one God.

63. Ibid. (emphasis his).

64. Ibid.:

> Why should a Hebrew poet not sing a song of love? Does love not enter man's heart because of God? . . . Why should he not sing if his heart is full of joy and gladness, if he has not yet seen travail and sorrow? Have the Jews been created solely to mourn and to wail? Are all other emotions foreign to them?

65. Ibid.

literature; but in the end it was to his mind merely an unfounded piece of speculation, and as such it could claim no greater validity than the classical rabbinic reading of the book as an allegory of the love between God and Israel.[66] To be sure, he acknowledged that modern scholars supported their interpretations with an array of putative linguistic evidence; but, he claimed, when that evidence was carefully reviewed it generally revealed those who offered it to possess a most imperfect command of the Hebrew language.[67] In fact, he suspected that much of this ostensible evidence was often deliberately concocted in order to fit hypotheses formulated a priori; passages from the Masoretic Text that appeared unintelligible to critics (more often than not because of those critics' deficiencies in Hebrew) were corrected, as it were, in order to provide artificial prooftexts for their readings.[68]

Evidently Smolenskin saw nothing over the next decade to improve his assessment of the critical enterprise. When Graetz published his commentary on Psalms in 1883 (twelve years after his work on Song of Songs had appeared in print and eleven years after Smolenskin had dissected it in sections and ground it to dust), the editor of *HaShaḥar* dismissed it and all other works of its type with a single phrase of contempt: "The judgment most appropriate to books of this sort is to pass over them in silence."[69]

* * *

Why, then, did he not simply ignore works of biblical criticism in his journal altogether, instead of turning *HaShaḥar* into a bastion of resistance to the new approach? After all, for all of his impressive familiarity with the fruits of Western scholarship, Smolenskin was himself not a scholar but a novelist and journalist, committed to exploring not problems of a purely academic nature but pressing issues of contemporary public import.[70] Hence it seems curious that he would have embarked on an extended hostile confrontation with the entire historical-critical enterprise in biblical studies unless he

66. Ibid., 104. Smolenskin believed that biblical criticism originated to a significant degree in the discipline of theology, whose method, he claimed, is "to grope in the dark, building propositions upon assumptions alone, drawing definite inferences from things that are opaque." This approach, he charged, had been carried over into the study of the Bible, with the result that "assumptions became fruitful, and increased abundantly, and multiplied [פרו רבו וישרצו], to the point where most of today's scholars have returned to the ways of earlier generations, substituting *homily* for *clear explication of meaning*" (ibid. [emphasis his]).

67. Ibid., 68.

68. Ibid., 86–88, 97–101.

69. Idem, *HaShaḥar* 11 (1883) 186. With regard to Graetz's new work, he wrote, "not only did reading this book make me nauseous, but writing about it [has made me nauseous as well]" (ibid.).

70. See Weinfeld's introduction to Smolenskin, *Qevurat Ḥamor*, 12–13; Haran (Diman), "*Ḥaqirat haMiqra*," 38.

sensed that certain of this school's fundamental propositions carried significant implications for debate within the Jewish public arena. Viewed from this perspective it appears that, his own protestations notwithstanding, Smolenskin's interest in the findings of contemporary biblical research might not have been an academic one alone. And indeed, in a long ideological essay published in the same year as his review of Graetz's work on the Song of Songs, Smolenskin indicated clearly that to his mind biblical criticism led not merely to falsehood but incidentally to a set of ideas that endangered the very existence of the Jewish people altogether.

In this essay, "*ʿAm ʿOlam*," Smolenskin represented biblical criticism as a symptom of the antinational humanist cosmopolitanism that he regarded as essentially regressive.[71] The object of biblical critics, he asserted, was to promote a world view in which "no one would pay attention to nationality or religion, but all would belong to the same nation and share a single religion"; hence it was no accident that the critics' stronghold was Germany, which Smolenskin regarded as the fountainhead of the cosmopolitan spirit.[72] Similarly, he declared, it was no accident that, among Jews, the Jews of Germany and not some other community had displayed the greatest affinity for the critical approach; "if we observe the actions of the Jews in various countries we shall find that their beliefs and love of their people are expressed in precisely the same fashion as are those of the territorial peoples in whose midst they reside."[73] Hence, Smolenskin explained, British Jews, who lived in the country least affected by the cosmopolitan fallacy,[74] had no use for biblical criticism; they were not ashamed of their religious law and were thus content simply to observe it instead of subjecting it to analysis. German Jews, on the other hand, were convinced, in Smolenskin's opinion, of the need to break down, in the name of cosmopolitanism, all barriers between themselves and their surrounding society; as a result,

> when critics arose to analyze the Holy Scriptures and set their hand to making a confusion of them (because they did not understand them), so too did the Jewish critics hasten to compete with them and to imitate them; and the work of making a confusion of Scripture became a labor of honor and glory, the greater the confusion the more praiseworthy, for this is the way of the gentile scholars.[75]

Unfortunately, Smolenskin explained, the spirit of cosmopolitanism prevailed only in German intellectual circles, not among broad segments of the German people, let alone among the masses of the remaining nations of the

71. See above, at nn. 31–33.
72. Smolenskin, "*ʿAm ʿOlam*," 136, 139–40.
73. Ibid., 139.
74. See above, n. 32.
75. Smolenskin, "*ʿAm ʿOlam*," 139–40.

world.[76] "There are other powerful nations and faiths in the world," he warned, "who did not wish to place their necks into the yoke of the new, single religion of all mankind that [the cosmopolitans] have offered them"; on the contrary, these nations "continue to magnify and exalt [their faiths] with all their might and with all the resources at their disposal."[77] In such a situation, he admonished, the spread of the cosmopolitan ideal among Jews was liable to leave them more vulnerable to conversionist pressure than they had ever been before:

> When [the Jews] rise up against their [particular] religion and faith and national aspirations, those who adhere to another faith will take encouragement; they will spread money around like dust and send their emissaries to the far corners of the earth in order to cleanse the children of Israel of their faith—not for the purpose of creating a single faith all over the earth but to bring them to the faith [of the Gentiles].[78]

Biblical criticism, as a manifestation of the cosmopolitan spirit that promoted a universalist, rational understanding of the biblical text rather than one rooted in traditional Jewish loyalties and folk beliefs, could only serve, to Smolenskin's mind, to foster this unwelcome eventuality. "Not all people are sufficiently strong, courageous, and secure in their opinions to live entirely according to the dictates of reason," he wrote; "the masses need the sight of the eyes more than the wandering of the desire,[79] and if we take from them the superstition in which they have believed since their youth they will not forsake it for the benefit of wisdom but will seek an alternative superstition to replace it."[80] In other words, the historical-critical approach to the Bible was not likely, in Smolenskin's view, to promote a more sophisticated reading of the biblical text among most Jews but merely to weaken their regard for the principal historical creation of the Jewish people, thereby leaving them with a spiritual void more likely to be filled by the dominant religion of the surrounding society than by rational philosophy or even by plain common sense.[81]

76. Ibid., 140. According to Smolenskin, German intellectuals had failed to translate cosmopolitan ideals into practice:

> This great idea was born in Germany . . . , but [the Germans] have shown that they are capable only of giving birth to it, not of raising it. . . . Just as the Chinese knew about printing and gunpowder for thousands of years but did not know how to turn them to their advantage, so too did the Germans give birth to this idea but did not know how to apply it in straightforward fashion, for this people is great in theoretical matters but weak in practical applications. . . . The Germans love all mankind in the same way that Don Quixote loved Dulcinea—in their imaginations alone. (ibid., 136–37)

77. Ibid., 140.
78. Ibid.
79. Cf. Qoh 6:9.
80. Smolenskin, "*ʿAm ʿOlam,*" 140–41.
81. Ibid., 141–42.

In this essay Smolenskin did not explain precisely what he believed the subversive message of the biblical critics to be or whether he could identify anything specific in the findings of critical biblical scholarship that, aside from being empirically false, was liable to separate masses of Jews from their spiritual moorings. Indeed, he does not appear ever to have addressed this question directly in any of his writings. It does seem significant in this context, however, that alongside his objective refutations of certain findings of critical scholarship (as in his review of Graetz) Smolenskin also railed at length against what he took to be the esthetic consequences of the critics' labors. One of his oft-stated objections to biblical criticism in general was that it tended "to make the straight crooked and to turn that which is beautiful into something with neither form nor comeliness."[82] Graetz, in his opinion, exemplified this general tendency; he had endeavored to establish that "the Song of Songs is chock full of errors and confusion, and so he cut and severed and chopped and shattered its verses as he saw fit."[83] What remained following Graetz's surgery, Smolenskin complained, was an ugly, repulsive mess:

> To me he [Graetz] looks like a person who has acquired such knowledge of nature and its mysteries that he is capable in a mere moment, whenever his wisdom so moves him, of changing gold into stone and a young cedar into rotten wood.[84] Here he comes into a garden of delights, calling the many onlookers to witness the marvels he is about to perform. He stretches forth his hand, picks a lovely rose from a furrow, and loudly declares, "Ladies and gentlemen, observe! For years this rose has been an object of love. All who have seen it have looked upon it with joy; poets have sung praises to its charms, making it the symbol of beauty and purity. Seekers of pleasure have smelled its pleasing odor, pretty young maids have bedecked their heads with it. . . . But all of them together have been fooled and led astray, for they have not understood what it is in reality. . . . " And as he speaks he plucks away one of its petals, which turns immediately in his hand into a frog. A second petal becomes a mouse, a third a bat, and in but a moment all of its petals are changed into every creature that creeps and crawls upon the earth, its beautiful fragrance into putrescent stench and the splendor of the rose into a thing of loathing and disgust.[85]

According to Smolenskin, such esthetic ruin of the foremost creation of the Jewish national spirit was inherent in the very nature of the critical enterprise; it was the inevitable result of the attempt to analyze the biblical text according to categories not its own. "The Hebrew sense of order prefers disorder," he asserted, "and because this is its way, only this way becomes it."[86] Hence in his view "the poet who wrote the Song of Songs sought to present his listeners and readers neither with a drama nor with an epic poem,

82. Smolenskin, "*Mišpaṭ Ḥaruṣ*," 67. Cf. Isa 40:4, 53:2.
83. Ibid., 69.
84. Cf. Job 41:19.
85. Smolenskin, "*Mišpaṭ Ḥaruṣ*," 69.
86. Ibid., 105.

nor even with a love poem written according to the canons of Greek poetry, but with a Jewish love poem written according to the jumbled rules and canons [of Jewish poetry], without any definite structure; and precisely therein lies its beauty."[87] However, he alleged, the analytical presuppositions of biblical criticism blinded the critics to its esthetic merits.

The esthetic implications of the critical method appear to have been especially frightening to Smolenskin because they echoed an earlier attempt to present to Jews an essentially Westernized version of the biblical text—an undertaking that, to Smolenskin's mind, had brought disastrous consequences upon the Jewish people largely because it too had made the Bible appear ugly in Jewish eyes. This endeavor was the publication of Moses Mendelssohn's translation of the Pentateuch into German. Smolenskin discussed Mendelssohn's work at length in his essay "*ʿEt Laṭaʿat*" (Time to Plant), published serially in *HaShaḥar* between 1875 and 1878. In this long, discursive polemic he charged that Mendelssohn had not embarked on his translation for the legitimate purpose of making the Bible intelligible to persons (Jews or non-Jews) who could not comprehend the text in the Hebrew original; rather, he had intended it to serve as a vehicle for introducing Jews to the German language and to German modes of thought.[88] In order to fulfill this purpose, Smolenskin suggested, the translator had employed German idioms and concepts that distorted the spirit of the Hebrew original and in so doing had rendered the text not merely unattractive but even repulsive in the eyes of masses of Jews. "Let us give an account of what he [Mendelssohn] did," Smolenskin wrote; "he took the Holy Scriptures, which had been the delight and glory of all Israel . . . , the storehouse of its faith, its history, and its beauty for thousands of years, and turned them into perfumers and cooks[89] in the service of the German language."[90]

Smolenskin implied that Mendelssohn had felt entitled to skew the sense of the Hebrew text because of his (in Smolenskin's eyes false) belief that Jews were united merely by a set of laws, which could be studied in isolation from the literary and linguistic context in which they had initially been presented, rather than by a unique national spirit and subjective sense of com-

87. Ibid., 105–6.

88. Idem, "*ʿEt Laṭaʿat*," part 1, 73. In support of his contention regarding the purpose of the translation, Smolenskin called Mendelssohn's biographer, Meyer Kayserling, to witness, quoting him as saying that Mendelssohn had intended "to educate [his co-religionists] in German speech and German thought" (p. 72). Smolenskin argued that most German Jews at the time understood Hebrew better than German and thus had no need for a translation to make the biblical text more intelligible to them. This view has been strongly disputed on the basis of considerable documentary evidence by Mendelssohn's most recent biographer; see A. Altmann, *Moses Mendelssohn: A Biographical Study* (Philadelphia: Jewish Publication Society, 1973) 368–75.

89. Cf. 1 Sam 8:13.

90. Smolenskin, "*ʿEt Laṭaʿat*," part 1, 72; see also p. 74.

mon destiny made manifest in large measure precisely in the Hebrew Bible and the Hebrew language.[91] In Smolenskin's opinion, this notion and its esthetic consequences had driven a wedge between Jews and the basis of their national identity. Few Jews, he suggested, could find any positive reason for continuing to explore what had been the undisputed fountainhead of Jewishness now that Mendelssohn's translation had rendered the Bible both ugly and superfluous:

> What was the result of his [Mendelssohn's] actions? Did he bring the hearts of his brethren closer to their Holy Scriptures and the language of their fathers? Not at all! He drove them away from them by force. From the time that the Holy Scriptures were translated [by Mendelssohn] the dignity [formerly] attached to them declined; they came to be looked upon as nothing more than a passageway to the German language for those aspiring to learn it. . . . When [these people] achieved their goal, they discarded [the Holy Scriptures and the Hebrew language] like an unwanted vessel;[92] and once these are no longer looked upon as valued vessels, what will remain of the heritage of Israel? . . . Is this why their fathers and their fathers' fathers suffered killing and burning, why they walked through fire and water for thousands of years—so that in the end of days the Holy Scriptures would be turned into the slave of the German language?[93]

Smolenskin predicted that the abandonment of the study of the Hebrew Bible by Jews would eventually bring about nothing less than the destruction of the Jewish people. Mendelssohn's foundation of Jewish identity upon observance of a common set of laws was in his view not merely false but also misguided; for there had always been Jews who disregarded or disobeyed Jewish law, and since Mendelssohn's time their number had grown mightily.[94] If these Jews were not presented with a positive incentive to identify with the Jewish nation, he warned, they were liable simply to discard all pretense of Jewishness; in fact, many had already done so:

> They neither wish nor are able to observe the laws, and they have discarded the Torah, so is there yet any portion or inheritance for them in the House of Israel?[95] All that remained for them was the name, and it was not long before they began to think: What unparalleled nonsense it is to suffer a cruel fate for

91. Ibid., 14–17, 26–28, 32–33, 38–42, 83–86. Here, too, Smolenskin's reading of Mendelssohn is subject to challenge. See, for example, Y. Kaufmann, *Golah veNekar: Meḥqar Histori-Soṣiyologi biŠeʾelat Goralo šel ʿAm Yiśraʾel miYeme Qedem veʿad haZeman haZeh* (Exile and Foreign Soil: A Historical-Sociological Investigation into the Question of the Fate of the Jewish People from Earliest Times until the Present Day) (Tel Aviv: Dvir, 1928) 2.294–95.

92. Cf. Jer 48:38.

93. Smolenskin, "*ʿEt Laṭaʿat*," part 1, 73, 72.

94. Ibid., 27, 137–38, 146–48.

95. Cf. Gen 31:14.

> the sake of the name of Israel! Let my name be something else, so that I may enjoy life like any other human being. And indeed, they have done so.[96]

To Smolenskin's mind, the necessary positive incentive could be found in what he called "the glory of the Torah and the Hebrew language"—the uniquely Jewish mentality through which alone, he claimed, the Hebrew Bible could be perceived as a source of great beauty and great truth.[97] Hence, he reasoned, the education of Jews needed first and foremost to inculcate this mentality, and the Hebrew Bible itself constituted the principal vehicle for accomplishing this goal.[98] The employment of Mendelssohn's translation of the Pentateuch in teaching young Jews, however, negated the possibility that a true sense of Jewish uniqueness could be conveyed. As proof of the detrimental consequences of the translation, Smolenskin cited the case of Mendelssohn's own children, four of whom converted to Christianity following their father's death. Although Mendelssohn had begun to prepare the translation largely for his children's benefit, he observed, "he was snared in the work of his own hands":[99]

> The effect [of Mendelssohn's work] was this; the road that he paved for them [his children] brought them to this end. They saw that he studied only foreign disciplines and also that he had made the brightness of the Holy Scriptures cease,[100] so what else could they have done? . . . This is why all his disciples and the members of his household have left the House of Israel never to return, and even those few who remained behind were not of much greater value to Israel than they were.[101]

Making the brightness of the Holy Scriptures cease through the study of foreign disciplines was also what Smolenskin regarded as the essential outcome of the historical-critical approach to the study of the Bible. Evidently, then, biblical criticism seemed to him to be little more than an extension of the work Mendelssohn had begun a century earlier, and its effects were bound to be similar.[102] Its reconstructions and explications of the biblical text obliterated, in Smolenskin's view, the beauty of the Hebrew original and hid from the sight of Jewish readers any hint of the unique Jewish spirit that had created it. As a result, he believed, it could serve ultimately only to weaken the sense of belonging to a distinct people that made the Jews a

96. "*ʿEt Laṭaʿat,*" part 1, p. 73.

97. The quoted phrase is employed in ibid., 90. The concept is elaborated on in part 2, 204–7 (originally published in *HaShaḥar* 8 [1877]).

98. "*ʿEt Laṭaʿat,*" part 1, 26.

99. Ibid., 73. Cf. Ps 9:17.

100. Cf. Ps 89:45.

101. "*ʿEt Laṭaʿat,*" part 1, 73.

102. In this connection it appears significant that the example of the fate of Mendelssohn's children was also raised during one of his direct discussions of biblical criticism. See Smolenskin, "*ʿAm ʿOlam,*" 141.

nation of the spirit in the first place. For this reason he could not ignore it, despite his advice to pass over works of biblical criticism in silence; in the final analysis biblical critics (even Jewish ones) were enemies of the Jewish people. As he explained to the readers of *HaShaḥar* in his short notice on Graetz's commentary on Psalms, written in the wake of the Russian pogroms of 1881 and the subsequent enactment of anti-Jewish discriminatory legislation by the government of Tsar Alexander III,

> At this time, when Israel's honor has been trampled underfoot by evil men on all sides . . . , if we see a Jew . . . among those who can find nothing better or more sensible with which to torture his soul than to stand like a woodchopper with an axe, cutting down branch after branch and stem after stem in the garden of Israel, making them objects of derision and mockery, then we must protest not merely against his false conclusions and his lack of knowledge of the Bible and the Hebrew language . . . but also against the lack of feeling and empathy that he has demonstrated in his book by using it to rob us of our ancient treasures—and this at a time when we are drinking from the poisoned cup, and all that the many unfortunate among us have to refresh and heal them is the memory of bygone days.[103]

103. Smolenskin, *HaShaḥar* 11 (1883).

Ruḥamah's Daughter: From Hysteria to Her-Story in Ruth Almog's *Shorshei 'Avir*

YAEL S. FELDMAN
New York University

The publication in 1987 of Ruth Almog's ambitious novel, *Shorshei 'Avir* (Dangling Roots) constituted a bold departure from the feminist romance in Israeli literature.[1] A prolific writer of short stories (1969, 1976, 1986, 1993) and novels (1970, 1980, 1982),[2] Almog (b. 1936) justifiably won the hearts of both critics and readers with this complex, prize-winning narrative. Structured in two dissimilar parts, ranging from late 19th-century Palestine to Europe of the 1960s, this novel offers a critique not only of her Israeli predecessors' optimistic liberatory feminism but perhaps also of some of the master narratives of Enlightenment-based feminism in general.

Author's note: Ruth Almog, *Shorshei 'Avir* (Jerusalem: Keter, 1987). All translations from Hebrew are mine.

1. I introduced the term *feminist romance* in a number of lectures between March 1991 (at Yale University) and May 1993 (at Brandeis University). For a fuller exposition of the history of this modality in Israeli literature, see my "From Feminist Romance to an Anatomy of Freedom," *The Boom in Contemporary Israeli Fiction* (ed. A. Mintz; Hanover, N.H.: University Press of New England, 1997) 71–113. See also my book *Beyond Feminist Romance: Gender, Nation and Subjectivity in Israeli Women's Fiction* (New York: Columbia University Press, forthcoming).

2. Almog's only novel to be published in English is *Mavet bageshem* (Jerusalem: Keter, 1982), in English, *Death in the Rain* (trans. D. Bilu; Santa Fe: Red Crane, 1993). For a commentary, see R. Domb, *Home Thoughts from Abroad: Distant Visions of Israel in Contemporary Hebrew Fiction* (London: Vallentine Mitchell, 1995) 62–78. Almog's preoccupation with European culture, central to *Death in the Rain* as well as to her earlier *Be'eretz Gezera* (The Exile) (Tel Aviv: 'Am 'Oved, 1970), is crucial for *Dangling Roots* as well. Also available in English is her feminist critique of Israeli culture; see "On Being a Writer," *Gender and Text in Modern Hebrew and Yiddish Literature* (ed. N. B. Sokoloff, A. L. Lerner, and A. Norich; New York: Jewish Theological Seminary Press, 1992) 227–34.

Interestingly, this critique is implicit rather than explicit, for on the surface, *Dangling Roots* is a typically "masculine [virile], political novel," as the author herself suggested in an interview: "I was trying to engage large, important themes. . . . I was inspired by a woman who impressed me with her courage—a feisty woman, diametrically opposed to the passive women I have treated so far."[3] This "transition" rings a familiar tone—a few years earlier, Israel's foremost feminist writer, Amalia Kahana-Carmon, declared a similar turning away from passive characters to active ones.[4] Following in her footsteps, Almog was determined to counteract what she saw as the Israeli marginalization of women's experience: "In Israel, if you do not write about national issues and you do not have a socio-political message—you (f.) do not exist!"[5] But here the resemblance ends. For unlike her predecessors, Almog has woven together two novelistic modalities hitherto employed mostly by Israeli *male* writers: the fictional autobiography and the historical novel.[6] Book I of the novel, "Madness Is the Wisdom of the Individuum" (pp. 7–160), is a dialogic narrative in which the two modalities alternate antiphonally, chapter by chapter. In one, Mira Gutman, a conventionally autobiographic narrator, recounts her atypical life story in a typical *moshavah* in the early years of the state. (Notice the here and now of this strand of the story line.) In the other, she attempts to piece together, in what may at first seem a somewhat frantic and chaotic manner, the life story of her maternal great-grandfather, *Lavdovi* (or perhaps *Levadovi* 'Mr. Alonely'?), an eccentric Zionist of the first *ʿAliya*. Her involvement with this father-figure is not historical in the strict sense of the word. It is psychological and ideological, displacing contemporary concerns that reached their peak in the wake of the 1982 Lebanon War (Jewish-Arab relations and general attitudes towards power) to the historical events. Yet it is this strand of the narrative that contains the seeds of the "politically masculine" novel that will come to fruition in book II of the novel, "Anatomy of Freedom" (pp. 161–359).

Almog therefore allowed her heroine both the closed intimacy of stereotypic female *Bildung* and the ostensibly open horizons of the male hero's quest. Furthermore, more than any Israeli woman writer before her, she fully developed both the psychological and the sociopolitical matrices of her protagonist, making her the first Israeli heroine to narrate a complete lifespan—

3. L. Fuchs, "An Interview with Ruth Almog," *HaDoar*, Jan. 13, 1989, 14–15. In other interviews Almog revealed the identity of her model: the late Livia Rokah, the daughter of the mayor of Tel Aviv, who in the 1960s was a left-wing activist in Italy, married there, and stayed in exile until her premature death by her own hand.

4. For more about this point, see my "From Feminist Romance to an Anatomy of Freedom."

5. Fuchs, "Interview."

6. On fictional autobiography in Israel, see my "Gender / Difference in Contemporary Hebrew Fictional Autobiography," *Biography* 11/3 (1988) 189–209.

from childhood in a small town (modeled on *Zichron Yaʿakov*) through urban adolescence in Jerusalem (the least developed of the three) to an allegedly autonomous adulthood abroad. Thematically and generically, *Dangling Roots* comes as close as possible to the "malestream" of the Hebrew literary canon, a fact that has no doubt contributed to the warm reception it received from the literary establishment and the reading public alike.

At the same time, however, the novel sports some highly "feminine" features. Most significantly, Mira is the first Israeli female protagonist to be endowed with a mother who cuts an impressive figure, crucial to the shaping of her daughter's life. In this she is indeed fundamentally different from Almog's earlier (and later!) heroines, who as a rule suffer from a "father fixation," without the benefit of a viable maternal role-model (most notoriously, the heroines in the collection *Nashim* [Women], which appeared shortly before the novel, in 1986). This shift to mother-daughter relations deserves our attention not only because of its novelty (it has subsequently been discovered by younger Israeli writers[7]), but because it makes Almog's "take" on feminism so complex and, in the final analysis, also subversive. If we recall that it was precisely this psychological nexus that was unearthed from Freudian unknownability by feminists on both sides of the Atlantic (to different ends, to be sure[8]), the significance of its belated entry into the discourse of Hebrew feminism may surface.[9]

7. Most notoriously, Gur's *Lo kach teʾarti li* (Afterbirth) (Jerusalem: Keter, 1994); but see also D. Zilberman, *Woman inside Woman* (Tel Aviv: ʿAm ʿOved, 1991); I. Bernstein, *Provision* (Tel Aviv: ʿAm ʿOved, 1991); and some short stories by S. Liebrecht, H. Bat-Shahar, S. Gilboa, and O. Ofer. Recently, a new anthology, *ʾImahot u-Banot* (Mothers and Daughters) (ed. S. Modan and M. Devash; Tel Aviv: Modan, 1997) has made its appearance.

8. I develop this contrast in my "Otherness and Difference as Strategies of Gender Subjectivity," forthcoming in *The Other as Threat: Demonization and Antisemitism* (ed. R. Wiestrich; Reading, England: Harwood, 1998).

9. The general shift from the Oedipal to the pre-Oedipal in psychoanalytic theory, typical of the object relations school, foregrounds the role of mothering in general and "corrects" Freud's untested theories about female psychology in particular. The psychosociological implications of this shift were argued by N. Chodorow, *The Reproduction of Mothering: Psychoanalysis and the Sociology of Gender* (Berkeley: University of California Press, 1979), who claims that the symbiotic identification of a daughter with her [same-sex] mother is one of the reasons for the female's capacity for empathy and hence for the *difference* of the female ego—its less firm boundaries and its more relational attitude to the external world. Similarly, the French theorists Hélène Cixous and Luce Irigaray attribute the fluidity of the female psyche to the fact that the girl retains much of her initial bonding with the mother. Unlike Chodorow, however, they use this "sexual difference" for a deconstruction of the heterosexual paradigm. In this they resemble feminist Adrienne Rich on this side of the Atlantic, who moved from an emphasis on motherhood and daughtering, in *Of Woman Born*

Curiously, however, none of the reviews of *Dangling Roots* even mention its feminist connection.[10] Apparently, Almog succeeded in her ploy: her novel was perused for all of the "serious," namely, politically relevant, issues it explored, as well as for the psychological implications of the symbiotic co-dependency of its two heroines, but not, as far as I know, for the potential questioning of feminism that it harbors. That she does this by means of a bi-cultural "pun" on the biblically-derived name *Ruḥamah* passed totally unnoticed. In what follows, we will reverse this procedure: relegating to another occasion the rich stylistic and ideational tapestry that comprises the novel, we will focus on the semantic distance traveled by Ruḥamah's daughter from the Greek to the Hebraic connotations of her mother's name and on the implications for feminist ideology that this transformation harbors.

Ruḥamah, Mira's mother, is portrayed as a stereotypically feminine charmer, exemplifying almost every possible cliché: she is attractive, sensuous, artistic, imaginative, in tune with nature (and with her own sexuality), communicative when she feels like it and enigmatically distant when she does not, and, most importantly, an expert inventor of stories. At the same time, however, she is a woman alone, an outsider living on the outskirts of the small town. Independent by default—she was left by her estranged husband to run the estate by herself—she is hopelessly self-centered and capricious, hysterical and suicidal, as her name may unobtrusively imply.

For the Hebrew reader, the first connotation of this name is, of course, one of compassion and mercy, *raḥamim*. A more semantically inclined reader may recall that it is etymologically related to *reḥem* 'womb'. A biblically oriented reader would no doubt conjure up the full matrix of its appearance in the Bible: Hos 1:6, where *lo'-Ruḥamah*, the allegorical daughter of the prophet's wanton wife, is promised redemption by being renamed *Ruḥamah* (2:2). A feminist reader, however, cannot help recalling the significant (should we say "pregnant"?) divergence between the semantic fields associated with the female womb in the Hebraic and Greek traditions: between compassion (even love) and malady or pathology ('hysteria', from the Greek

---

(New York: Norton, 1976), to a "lesbian continuuum" in "Compulsary Heterosexuality and Lesbian Existence," *Signs* 5 (1980) 631–60.

For scholarship on the literary representation of this paradigm, see *The Lost Tradition: Mothers and Daughters in Literature* (ed. C. N. Davidson and E. M. Broner; New York: Ungar, 1980); M. Hirsch, *The Mother/Daughter Plot: Narrative, Psychoanalysis, Feminism* (Bloomington: Indiana University Press, 1989). Recent reevaluations include M. M. Johnson, *Strong Mothers, Weak Wives* (Berkeley: California University Press, 1988); idem, *Daughtering and Mothering: Female Subjectivity Reanalysed* (ed. J. van Mens-Verhulst et al.; London: Routledge, 1993).

10. The literature on Almog consists mainly of short book reviews and interviews, but no extensive study has been written about her work yet.

hystéra 'womb').[11] In Ruḥamah's life and personality we may discern a curious conflation of the semantic associations of two divergent cultures: having a life of *lo'-Ruḥamah,* she in actuality lives up to the Greek/European connotations of the Hebrew etymology of her name.

Living in a fantasy world and always on the brink of emotional breakdown, [*lo'*] Ruḥamah is heavily dependent on Mira, who, in a reversal of roles, loyally "mothers" her with all the ambivalence that such family dynamics of necessity entail. This unhappy woman, in short, could have readily been another "Madwoman in the Attic,"[12] had this not been a 1980s novel whose first part carries the enigmatic title "Madness is *the Wisdom* of the Individuum" (emphasis mine).

That the "exoneration" of madness is at least one of the psychological questions with which this book grapples is no doubt clear. The title of book I and several of its major themes clearly smack of R. D. Laing's idealization of schizophrenic "madness," from *The Divided Self* (1960) through *The Politics of Experience* (1967). We may recall that these theories enjoyed quite a vogue among left-wing ideologues of the 1960s—precisely the time frame of book II of our novel and the ostensible "moment of writing" of its autobiographic narrator.[13] If we add to this Almog's general fascination (both textual and extratextual) with the "thin line" between sanity and insanity,

11. And see on this point P. Trible, *God and the Rehtoric of Sexuality* (Philadelphia: Fortress, 1978).

12. The reference is to S. M. Gilbert and S. Gubar, *The Madwoman in the Attic: The Woman Writer and the Nineteenth-Century Literary Imagination* (New Haven: Yale University Press, 1979).

Feminist scholarship on the heavily loaded issue of *Women and Madness* ranges from Phyllis Chesler's book by this name (New York: Doubleday, 1972) to Shoshana Felman's 1975 essay by the same name (in *Diacritics* [Winter, 1975] 2–10) to Marilyn Yalon's *Maternity, Mortality and the Literature of Madness* (University Park, Penn.: Pennsylvania State University Press, 1993). Within this general theme, hysteria has held a special position ever since its "discovery" by the 19th-century medical establishment. Its Freudian career and its post-Freudian reevalution by Foucault, Lacan, and French feminism (esp. H. Cixous and C. Clément, *The Newly Born Woman* [trans. B. Wing; Minneapolis: University of Minnesota Press, 1986]) is well known. A most useful summary is *Hysteria beyond Freud,* by S. Gilman et al. (Berkeley: University of California Press, 1993). See there especially E. Showalter's "Hysteria, Feminism and Gender" (pp. 268–344) for a different position on this issue (esp. pp. 327, 333, 334).

However, the theory of madness most relevant to our text is, as we shall see, R. D. Laing's. Romantically interpreting madness as existential freedom, his approach, developed in the stormy 1960s, was absorbed into the revolutionary discourse of that period and left its marks on Ruth Almog's narrative world.

13. Laing's name is mentioned briefly in book II, p. 326, as expecting to cause a scandal in a meeting of psychiatrists in Bonn, which Mira is to cover for her journal.

particularly her equivocation over the question whether or not an escape into madness is a matter of free *choice*, a conscious rebellion against the social order,[14] the deep structure of the novel begins to emerge. The legacy of madness, woven together by the two narrative strands of book I (both Mira's mother and her great-grandfather), may have been inspired by R. D. Laing and A. Esterson's *Families of Schizophrenics.*[15] Although not schizophrenic in the clinical sense, Mira's family bears some features typical of Laing's case-histories: the centrality of the mother-daughter relations (accompanied by an "absent father"), as well as "the feminine predicament" of "leaving home and letting go."[16] Yet Almog's treatment of this paradigm takes another route. While book I both foregrounds and problematizes a Laingian-like idealization of individual madness (namely, the "wisdom" of this ostensible personal freedom), book II offers a merciless analysis of the other side of the coin—the use and (aggressive) misuse, both personal and political, of the philosophies of freedom and of existential choice.

Bearing in mind this nexus of madness and freedom under question, we may better understand the significance of Lavdovi's act of self-mutilation or Ruḥamah's symbolic castration of her daughter (her furious cutting of Mira's beautifully long hair). On another level, it may explain Mira's "tolerance" of her mother's other deviances, the playful as well as the grievous (her attempted suicides). Still, one is hard put to accept Mira's total acceptance of her mother's rationalization for her symptomatic flights into fantasy:

> Mom told me once, and I have never forgotten it: "What did God give humans imagination for, if not to invent things. I am telling you, to invent stories is the most marvelous thing there is. Fantasy knows no limit. One can even invent a life for oneself."
>
> [. . .] And when Dr. Shapira would reprimand her for fibbing, she would say: "This is no fib. It is fanciful and amusing. After all, life is so gray. Nothing interesting ever happens here. Ever. So I tell stories and make life more exciting. And you know what? Sometimes such a story even becomes true." (p. 75)

"Nothing interesting ever happens here"—could this be a description out of an Israeli novel? Is this a valid assessment of life in a country as volatile as

14. Plato's praise of madness as 'the gift of God' (*phaedrus*), is used as the epigraph of her book *'Et hazar veha'oyev* (The Stranger and the Foe) (Tel Aviv: Sifriyat Po'alim, 1980). To the question of whether or not one can choose insanity, Almog answers: "I don't know. I once thought it was possible, but today I do not know. I once even thought one can consciously choose insanity. But new scientific findings undermine this supposition." See an interview with Ora Zarnitzky, "*Sheḥikah*" (Erosion), *Devar hashavu'a*, Dec. 4, 1987.

15. R. D. Laing and A. Esterson, *Families of Schizophrenics* (London: Tavistock, 1964).

16. For an exposition of the evolution of Laing's theories and a critique of their implication for female psychology and feminist ideology, see J. Mitchell, *Psychoanalysis and Feminism* (New York: Vintage, 1974) 227–73.

Israel? Wouldn't it require a greater measure of the "suspension of disbelief" normally expected of the reader? I suspect it would, particularly if the reader is preconditioned by the androcentric canon of Hebrew literature, notorious for its preoccupation with the always-urgent issues of the public arena. But this is, of course, precisely Almog's point. In order to have her younger protagonist experience both the pleasure and the pain of the "real" world, she must make her break away from the "private sphere"—the prison-house of female experience—in which, presumably, "life is so gray."[17] For although her mother's strategy of self-invention, the age-old Sheherezade foible of spinning stories, is approved by the protagonist as an act of personal freedom ("I did not care. Like Mom, I believed that anyone had the privilege to invent his or her life any way they wished"), it will not serve as her role-model. Mira is not going to stay home and amuse the neighbors with potentially self-fulfilling stories; she will actively make one of these stories come true.

That the model she chooses is typically androcentric should come as no surprise: this may be one more link in a tradition, both within and without Hebrew literature, of the Enlightenment-based, masculine-modeled strategy of self-invention, inspired mostly by Simone de Beauvoir's existential feminism. What is less predictable is Mira's attitude toward this model. For although Mira fashions her life in the image of several father-figures (Lavdovi, her half-imagined great-grandfather; Alexandroni, her mother's life-long admirer;[18] her own father, David Gutman; and later also her lover/husband, Jacques Berliavsky), she does not do this out of blind admiration. If her penetrating critique of her own father is any measure, she is fully cognizant of the true dimensions of his ("masculinist") world. Indeed, it is this insight that makes Mira's evolution so psychologically interesting.

On the face of it, Almog seems to offer a "feminist" corrective to the Laingian predicament, reinscribing the absent father into Mira's life. This psychoanalytic "missing third term"[19] is supposed to help her get over the hurdle of the claustrophobic (if not schizophrenic) feminine symbiosis with her mother and move her into the world of political action and masculinist freedom. And so it does. But at what price?

17. Almog herself reacted in a similar vein to the question "Why don't you write about your daily experience?" in an interview conducted after the publication of her earlier novel, *Death in the Rain*, in 1982: "To write about this? Never. This is what I want to escape from. My real life takes place elsewhere . . . when I begin to travel, in my imagination" (interview with Avraham Balaban, *Yediot ʾAḥaronot*, n.d. [1982]).

18. Mira's later attempt to consummate Alexandroni's attachment to her mother through his devotion to her resonates with shades of Agnon's *Bidmi yameha* (At the Prime of Her Life). In both cases, the older lover is the bearer of knowledge, of the Symbolic Order (signified here by his name, evoking Alexandria, the ancient site of wisdom). Similarly, Berliavsky also belongs to her parents' generation, an incestual choice that exacerbates her jealousy of her mother.

19. Mitchell, *Psychoanalysis and Feminism*, 285ff.

> [Mira] told herself that her father was a man who looked into a small mirror all his life, but there was nothing one could do about this, because he was unable to be any different, he was simply not capable of looking into a bigger mirror, because such a mirror did not exist for him, at least not in his reality. There, in his world, only two options existed: either a tiny mirror, or a magnified picture, namely: national concerns. . . . But this was not all. . . . Not only was his mirror small, it was also always positioned in the same right angle and it would never dawn on him that it was possible, really possible, and sometimes even greatly needed, to position the mirror diagonally, for example, perhaps in a 45 degree angle, or 135 degree or even 180. . . . True, the portrait reflected in the mirror might be slightly cut off, at the chin or the forehead, but instead some other views might be reflected in the free areas along it. Yes, yes, Mira told herself, Mira's Dad is an onlooker, merely an onlooker, not an insightful observer. This is how his eyes are built, that's all. This is why, Mira thought, his opinions are so predetermined and unequivocal, and this is why he is preoccupied only with issues external to him. (pp. 133–34)

The apologetic tone of this inner monologue is unmistakable. Mira is clearly caught between an oedipal idealization of her father and a ruthless adolescent observation of his dogmatism and self-centeredness.[20] She therefore uses the mirror metaphor defensively, protecting herself from fully comprehending the brunt of her own accusation. Moreover, this is the first time that the "autobiographic" narrative voice splits itself into first and third persons, being itself conscious of the defensive function of this specific technique:[21]

> Yes, with all this turbulence of fear, rage and insult, also came elucidation. And I told myself that at times I stopped being me and that Mira particularly stopped being me when she was thinking about her father, that father of Mira. . . . Mira wanted to protect him for me, she wanted to protect him from me, because it was important to keep him away, safe from my harsh disappointment, from my hurt. It was important to keep him for herself in some way, because she did not want to lose him completely and she was afraid of me, because I exposed and befouled him. (p. 133)

Fettered by one of the oldest psychological taboos, Mira is unable to integrate her father's betrayal—his refusal to help her get rid of an unwanted pregnancy. Her solution to the conflict is ingenious: instead of splitting off the "bad" father, she externalizes her own forgiving, rationalizing self, while

20. Seriously motivated as this passage may be, one cannot avoid its tragicomic effect on a reader versed in contemporary psychoanalytic discourse: this paternal figure seems to be stuck forever in an unfinished, infantile mirror-stage, a travesty of Lacan's great symbol of the birth of the human "split" ego.

21. The self-consciousness of the protagonists, here and elsewhere in the novel, is in fact one of the weaknesses of this novel. Whether in dialogues or inner monologues, the characters are often (particularly in book II) too transparent to themselves and to the reader, as if the author had very little trust in her readers' ability to infer and generalize.

"internally regressing into her 'deviant' thinking," which she uses as "a dam against the rage he would arouse in me" (p. 134). It is here, in this crucial event, that the protagonist of *Dangling Roots* emerges as a postmodernist (Lacanian) split subject. Yet this split is doubly motivated because it bears the unmistakable stamp of the modern *female* condition. For Mira, an integrated self is unrealizable, not only because of the universally endemic gulf between one's authentic perceptions and the perceptions about self that are approved by the Symbolic Order (or the social contract), but also because of her very personal impossible choice between the Scylla of Mom's rich but totally vicarious fantasy life and the Charybdis of Dad's active but narrow-minded public life.

Indeed, it is this tragic conflict that is dramatized by the break in the hitherto smooth flow of Mira's first-person retrospection: from now until the end of book I, her narration shuttles between first and third persons, indecisively moving from the ostensibly authentic but private "I" to the "other," more public "Mira," who is perhaps better socialized but also more repressed and alienated from her "true" self. That this splitting originates in the mock mirror-stage scene attributed to the father is of course part of an inescapable irony—trying to avoid one kind of vicarious life, Mira unwittingly undertakes another. And although the last word is given to the narrating "I," its actual actions speak louder than its discourse:

> I then crossed the street. There, on the other side, Dad was already waiting for me. Together we entered the port and boarded the ship. (p. 160)

The choice is made; the Rubicon crossed. The protagonist has left behind mother, home, hometown, and homeland. Now she is on her way to join the sound and fury of her father's world, that other world of which she used to be so critical. Unlike her mother, she is going to invent a life, not a story of a life. But will she escape the typical female lot, shared by her mother as well, of living vicariously? Will she emerge as the first "New Hebrew Woman"[22] to sidestep the trap of the feminist romance? Will she, in short, live up to the "work and love" agenda of feminist expectations?

Ruth Almog's answer seems ambiguous. Yes, she allows her protagonist the freedom of choice (book II is entitled "Anatomy of Freedom") and sends her off to Italy to study medicine. True, she releases her from the prison-house of the female private sphere, where "nothing interesting ever happens" and plunges her into the "colorful" world of international journalism and left-wing politics (this is Europe of the 1960s, the students' revolts, and the Russian invasion of Prague). At the same time, she immerses her in the discourse on freedom, both personal and political, of that generation (behaviorism versus existentialism, Freudianism versus Marxism, Marcuse versus Fromm,

22. For the history of this concept and its fictional representation, see my "From Feminist Romance."

possessiveness versus ego boundaries, authenticity versus power relations), only to find out their blind alleys (pp. 176, 182, 190–96ff., 237ff.). She also involves her in one of the most intriguing love-affairs of Hebrew literature, enabling her to conduct a dialogic discourse on love and female desire, while testing first hand the practical in/validity of the rhetoric of freedom. The eccentric, unpredictable, and finally also unreliable Prof. Jacques Berliavsky is one of the most exasperating, finely drawn character portraits in Israeli fiction. Yet one should not miss the irony implied by the title of part A of book II, "Freedom according to Jacques" (pp. 163–266).[23]

This version of the "New Hebrew Woman" definitely has a fair share of work and love. But they do not dwell happily together. Nor do the protagonists. In a twist that is quite predicable for the sober realism of this novel, Mira's "total, absolute love" (pp. 189ff.) founders on the rocks of marriage (pp. 218ff.). And although the reason for its foundering is overdetermined (her dependency, the vacuousness of his "freedom"), it clearly takes Mira one step further in the deconstruction—which began with her critique of her father—of the masculine ideal. The hard lesson of her exercise in "freedom according to Jacques" is that "love and work" elude not only an aspiring young female, they are rare in the male world as well. Other differences notwithstanding, Jacques' "balance sheet" turns out to be just as warped as her father's. From this perspective, it is not Mira who has failed the test of the "masculine, political" plot; it is the ideal that has failed her.

Nevertheless, she is denied a continuous voice, an uninterrupted line of discourse. Although Mira remains the central consciousness through which book II is focalized, she loses her own voice. As we meet her again in book II, she is presented to us mostly through third-person narration, with several exceptions: her brief homecomings (for her wedding and for her mother's funeral, pp. 207–22, 298–317); her traumatic fantasy, evoking the "primary neurosis" of her childhood—her jealousy of her beautiful mother (pp. 258–59); and her final, long letter to her father (pp. 333ff.).

It is on the pages of this letter that the autobiographic quest for self-knowledge finally materializes. And it is here that the protagonist discovers the paradoxical truth about the "otherness" of her self. For although successfully disengaged from her mother's vicarious life, Mira has not really come into her own. To her surprise and perhaps horror she learns that in all her love ("object") choices she has unconsciously recapitulated the structure of her relationship with her father, thereby "ensuring" their failure. Furthermore, her ideological positions are constantly referred to as "borrowed," "re-

23. In addition to reverberations of John Irving's *The World according to Garp* (New York: Pocket Books, 1976), *Jacques* evokes the name of Jean Jacques Rousseau, the father of the romantic philosophies of freedom, the source of "liberté, egalité," etc. Mutatis mutandis, it also brings to mind the other two *Jacques* of the rebellious 1960s, Lacan and Derridá.

cited," "cheap recipe," and so on. In the final analysis, it is not her own life that Mira has invented. Although in a different fashion, her self turns out to be no less vicarious than her mother's, and her "freedom"—both political and psychological—seems nothing more than spurious. The road to freedom, Mira finds out, leads through a history of masculine violence and aggression, terror and rape (which she experiences first hand). Fraternity is taken over by fratricide, equality by oppression. It is therefore not surprising that the charming autobiographic "I" of book I has almost no place in the harsh world of book II. By the inner logic of this novel, autobiographic introspection and political or other "malestream" activism are mutually exclusive.

Dangling Roots both continues and transcends two novelistic trends recently developed by Israeli women: the "feminist romance" and the "masked autobiography."[24] Without these antecedents, the specific features of this novel in their particular combination would have been unthinkable. At the same time, however, Almog deserves credit for the steps she took to transform these models both structurally and thematically. Unlike her predecessors, she is far from idealizing the masculinist construction of the female self, ostensibly inspired by de Beauvoir's existential feminism; neither does she trust compromises of either Virginia Wolff's "androgyny" or Julia Kristeva's "third-generation" women, to which some of her peers subscribe; nor does she find consolation in the apotheosis of sexual difference argued by French feminisms and ambivalently practiced by some of her contemporaries.

Hers is the sober observation of the specific, intensely personal, psychological matrix of a female subject (filtered in this novel through the prism of various psychoanalytic models), and the no-less intense and painful political contingencies imposed upon it. Her protagonist stands alone in Israeli fiction in her endeavor to actually carry out, here and now, "classical" feminist expectations. But at the same time, the outcome of Mira's "education" undoes or deconstructs the very ideal it has set out to achieve. Almog's venture, the inscription of a female protagonist into "a masculine, political novel" (her own wording) has turned out to be its own best refutation. That this endeavor takes place in exile, outside of the borders of Israel, is of course part of the critique implied in the structure of this novel. Yet the critique is double-pronged, for this "portrait of the feminist as a young woman" crashes against the unyielding realities of both the protagonist's internal (psychological) and external (sociopolitical) worlds. In the final analysis, the source of discontent of this novel is not easily determined (or perhaps it is overdetermined?). Is the inhospitality of Israeli culture to blame for the exile, if not disappearance, of the New Hebrew Woman, as repeatedly argued (extratextually) by Ruth Almog herself (as by Amalia Kahana-Carmon before

24. On the latter, see my "Feminism under Siege in Israeli Literature," *Prooftexts* 10 (1990) 493–514.

her)?[25] Or is Western feminism itself under scrutiny here, exposing the naïveté and risky optimism of some of its basic propositions?

Almog's answer to these questions is imbedded in her narrative, by means of plot, discourse and . . . closure. Although at the end of her sad story Mira is still in exile, smarting from her psychological and ideological wounds, her final actions harbor a glimpse of hope: lifting the lid of repression from her childhood traumas, she is finally ready to embrace the "madness" of her maternal heritage, which she has attempted to suppress throughout book II (pp. 335ff.). Replacing Ruḥamah's oral story-telling by the autobiographer's pen, she is about to find her authenticity in (creative?) writing, not in political action. Given the limitations of our condition, Almog seems to be saying, creativity is the only true freedom, one that transcends gender, class and national divisions. "Artistic imagination fashions the unconscious memory of failed emancipation, of a betrayed promise," Mira finds in one of Jacques' books. It is followed by a quotation from Adorno, that "Messiah" so "often quoted by her German friends": " 'In the absence of freedom art can preserve the spirit of freedom only by negating non-freedom.' Mira grimaces and closes the book. The words sound hollow. She, at least, does not understand them" (pp. 355ff.).

Mira may not understand, but her imagination does. "Jacques hates disorder, she thinks, for him everything has to be in place. Only within order he feels free . . . only within order . . . only within order. . . . How? How? . . ." (p. 356). Needless to say, she does not find out how. Rather than decoding the secret of the obsessional scientist's "Symbolic Order," she gives in to the rhythms, sounds and fragrances of her near and distant memories. In a tapestry of free associations, her imagination shuttles back and forth between past and present, the real and the imaginary, finally replicating the very language that was earlier used to represent her mother's unique bond with nature. With this, Ruḥamah's madness is not only internalized, it is also redeemed. The Freudian (Greek) connotation of her name (*reḥem* 'womb', *hystéra*) gives way to its biblical (Hebrew) meaning (*raḥamim* 'compassion, love'). Exhibiting the cadences of Freudian primary processes, of Lacanian pre-oedipal Imaginary, or of Kristeva's maternal Semiotic, these final pages hold the promise for artistic sublimation. We are not sure whether Mira will return from her exile ("I do not want to walk in the footsteps of my maternal great-grandfather . . . and be called a madwoman," p. 358) or whether she will fare better in her future love choices, but we feel confident that she may be able to "befriend" her legacy of madness and contain it within the "chaos" of artistic creativity.[26]

25. See their essays in *Gender and Text.*

26. It is hard to determine whether Almog sides with Juliet Mitchell, who claims (pace Hélène Cixous) that "the woman novelist must be an hysteric, for hysteria is simultaneously what a woman can do to be feminine and refuse femininity, within practical discourses" (*Woman: The Longest Revolution* [London: Virago, 1984] 288ff.), or

Indeed, Almog's latest book (1993) is entitled *Tikun ʾomanuti* (Invisible [lit. Artistic] Mending). In it she artistically "mends" the life stories of a variety of characters who are socially marginal without necessarily being hysteric and/or female. Feminist anger seems to have given way to a generalized empathy for the outcast of any kind; hysteria has been finally sublimated into creativity.[27]

---

with Elaine Showalter's counterargument that "female hysteria seemed to be on the wane, as feminism was on the rise" and that "the despised hysterics of yesteryear have been replaced by the feminist radicals of today" ("Hysteria, Feminism, and Gender," 327, 334).

27. A more elaborated version of this essay forms a chapter in my forthcoming book, *Beyond the Feminist Romance*.

Jewish Studies and Medieval Jewish Philosophy: The Odd Couple

Alfred L. Ivry
New York University

From its inception in this country, Jewish studies as a field has encompassed many disciplines, their number ever increasing. Each discipline exerts a centrifugal force upon the field as a whole, often forcing a reassessment of that whole. Certain areas of scholarship, such as Talmud and Rabbinics, were traditionally considered to represent the heart, if not the significant entirety, of Jewish "learning," and some scholars in these areas appear to have equated this Jewish learning with the field of Jewish studies, being reluctant to subsume their intellectual *cum* religious enterprise within a larger academic framework. In other cases, the discipline itself, be it philology or archaeology, history or literature, has forced the scholar into purely disciplinary pursuits that sometimes leave the "Jewish" dimension of the subject peripheral.

Training in the disciplines themselves does not require any particular Jewish education or skill, at least not until the discipline is qualified with the word "Jewish." Though this adjective modifies the discipline, it does not change it, or should not. The significance of the qualification lies in the nexus that it establishes to other similarly qualified disciplines. Jewish history is related to Jewish literature and other Jewish subjects not because they are Jewish disciplines but because each is part of the field of Jewish studies, each a partial expression of the totality of the Jewish experience that the field attempts to encompass.

The disciplines within Jewish studies are thus engaged in a dialectical relationship with each other and with their common field, a whole that is more than the sum of its parts. Thus, though the scholar in each discipline must be professionally responsible to that discipline, the Jewish aspect of the study necessarily relates it to wider concerns.

Author's note: This article is dedicated with affection to Baruch Levine, the model for me of the biblical scholar discussed in these pages.

In good part, this is the case in all academic pursuits, the narrow disciplinary road theoretically leading to broader cross-disciplinary pursuits and vistas. Jewish studies is thus a subfield of the Humaniites as a whole, a particular prism in which to view the human comedy—and tragedy.

Of course, Jewish studies purports to study the divine comedy too, though many would object to applying this term to the religious texts of Judaism. The seriousness with which the Bible was taken by the rabbinic tradition, much more seriously often than the Bible took itself,[1] and the orthopractic zeal of the rabbis[2] combine to place an extra burden upon the scholar of traditional religious texts. Here the weight of communal pressure can also be felt, inhibiting scholarship.

"Religious studies" may be the most problematic discipline for Jewish studies, since it claims to study comparatively a phenomenon that many in the Jewish tradition regard as inappropriate to their own unique faith. Interestingly, others object to treating Jewish studies as "religious studies" because in their opinion it reduces the entire Jewish experience to a single category.

The discipline of religious studies is not the only or even the primary discipline that is looked at askance by many in the Jewish community; many also have had strong reservations about such diverse fields as biblical studies and Jewish philosophy. Whereas the biblical scholar is often regarded as secularizing the sacred word of God, the philosophical scholar is seen as hallowing the secular teachings of Plato and Aristotle, finding them echoed in Scripture. Perhaps in response to these charges, and also to assure themselves, some scholars in these disciplines present what amounts to apologia for traditional views.

Biblical studies are particularly vulnerable to tendentious interpretations, since the traditional approach of Jews has been to study the text together with its commentaries. Disassociating the one from the other is often seen as practising a non-Jewish methodology, unrepresentative of the "Jewish" Bible. Here the contemporary biblical scholar has to acknowledge the historical truth of this position, while rejecting its perpetuation as the sole valid methodology for Jewish scholars. There is obvious justification, within a Jewish studies program, for the study of rabbinic biblical commentaries and for appreciating them as the traditional Jewish understanding of Scripture, but this approach should be distinguished from the study of the Bible itself.[3] Both text and commentary should be taught, not necessarily separately, but

1. Witness the many sibling (and, for Abraham, pseudosibling) stories of the Patriarchal period, in which infractions of tradition, guile, and deception openly prevail and are sanctioned with a minimum of protest, versus the later rabbinic attempts to justify these actions.

2. A zeal which has, however, ample biblical precedent (God even being described as *ʾēl qānāʾ*) and is central to the halakhic structure of Judaism.

3. Current literary and even philosophical fashion might argue that there is no Bible "itself," no text independent of interpretation. The contemporary biblical

as separate entities. The scholar of this discipline must be aware of the cultural and societal characteristics of diverse periods and know the various ancient cognate languages that can illuminate the Hebrew text.

The scholar of medieval Jewish philosophy faces similar demands, in terms of diverse language requirements (ideally, the Hebrew of the philosophers, Arabic and Judaeo-Arabic, Greek and Latin) and knowledge of both ancient and modern philosophy, besides the three sister philosophies of the Middle Ages, Jewish, Muslim, and Scholastic. Yet a question here intrudes: is the very subject still significant to the field today?

As with its modern counterpart, medieval Jewish philosophy has never attracted large numbers of students. The discipline of philosophy itself remains abstruse to most university students. Few are interested in more than an introduction to classical philosophy and fewer still interested in the philosophers of late antiquity and the Middle Ages, let alone Jewish or Muslim medieval philosophers.

Most students in Jewish studies are not prepared to study Arabic or Islamic culture, the necessary background for reading and appreciating most medieval Jewish philosophical texts. Even more, the specific curriculum and issues that attracted all philosophers historically, be they Greek, Jew, Christian, or Muslim, are mostly not issues that draw students interested in Jewish studies. The physics, metaphysics, and science of the Middle Ages are judged irrelevant today, the political philosophy undemocratic, conservative at best.

Jewish studies students are interested in studying political and historical issues, and/or in becoming familiar with Judaism as a religion, or rather as a spiritual phenomenon. Thus it is that the Bible and Buber are found attractive, as is the study of the Holocaust and Zionism, and particularly the Israel-Arab conflict. Lately, there has been increasing interest in Jewish mysticism as well, owing to a number of factors: the relative novelty of the subject and its exotic and bold character. Nowhere else within the sphere of religious Jewish texts is comparable license taken with seemingly pagan, demonic, and erotic imagery. The mystic's path is generally very removed from the path of the philosopher, with the latter's denial, mostly, of divine attributes and images of a personal and corporeal God.

There is, of course, some affinity between mystical teachings and medieval Jewish philosophy, and it is also true that medieval philosophy contains a degree of polemical and theological writing. Medieval Jewish philosophers lived in either a Muslim or Christian milieu, and their work reflects this. The Muslim philosophers, who themselves conceded little philosophically to their faith, were generally embraced by the Jewish philosophers; the Muslim theologians, the *mutakallimun*, were imitated by some and rejected by others.

---

scholar may well consider this view, among others, but in every instance will have to resort to a working Scriptural Ur-text from which to argue a particular interpretation.

Christianity posed a greater theological challenge to Judaism than did Islam, but not a greater philosophical threat. The doctrines of the Trinity and of the Incarnation seemed so illogical to the philosophers' understanding of the oneness of God that they dismissed them from serious philosophical investigation; witness Judah Halevi's remarks in the opening of the *Kuzari.*[4] Similarly, the messianic claims of Christianity were seen as counterhistorical, reading history from a Jewish standpoint. The rabbis and scholars who did confront Christianity frontally, such as Saadia Gaon and Abraham ibn Daud,[5] did so from within a theological or politically polemical framework that is largely outside of normal philosophical study.

Within Christianity itself there is a division between theologians and philosophers or between theological and philosophical types of discourse engaged in by the same person, as for example Thomas Aquinas. A parallel phenomenon is to be found in the division between philosophical and legal writing in the Rambam, where different principles are at play. There is of course overlapping between Scholastic philosophy and theology, as between rabbinic and philosophical teachings, but the main body of discourse is different in its assumptions and concerns. It is only when the lines of investigation between philosophy and theology in Judaism become really blurred, particularly in our century, that such a division is no longer tenable.

Who then comes into a class in Jewish philosophy voluntarily? Are they only those students who are interested in the history of ideas or in the ideas themselves, in philosophy as a discipline? It would seem that, with rare exceptions, this is not the case; even the philosophically oriented student does not study Jewish philosophy *lishmah*, for its own sake, but rather because of its connection with "Judaism" or with the Jewish people. For these students the uniqueness of Jewish philosophy is less its body of ideas than the fact that these ideas were expressed by Jewish people, that Jewish philosophy is part of the history of Jewish culture and creativity. Students interested in these broader themes are occasionally prepared to study Jewish philosophy, particularly when these students are inclined to philosophy in general.

We find, accordingly, that involvement in Jewish philosophy is usually tempered and conditioned by a student's interest in Jewish history and religion. Jewish philosophy is thus regarded as ancillary to other disciplines and concerns even by most of the students interested in it.

These students are not alone in their perception of the field; many a teacher also subsumes the subject matter of Jewish philosophy under a larger

4. Cf. *Kuzari* I:5, in the critical edition of D. Baneth and H. Ben Shammai, *Kitâb al-Radd wa-'l-Dalîl fi al-Din al-Dhalîl* (Jerusalem: Magnes, 1977) 8.

5. Cf. Saadia's "Book of Doctrines and Beliefs," II:5; in the edition and translation of J. Kafih, *Sefer hanivḥar be'emunot uvedeʿot* (Jerusalem: Sura, 5730/1969) 90. See also G. D. Cohen's introduction to his edition and translation of Ibn Daud's *Sefer Ha-Qabbalah* (The Book of Tradition) (Philadelphia: Jewish Publication Society, 5728/1967) xxxiii.

category: ultimately, Jewish survival, religious and/or national. The subject is often taught as a way to defend the faith intellectually, to provide a rationale for allegiance to one's tradition and people. Along with the rest of Jewish studies, Jewish philosophy thus takes its place, explicitly or implicitly, as one more expression of political ethnicity. More than other disciplines within the field, however, medieval Jewish philosophy and Jewish studies appear to many to be an odd couple, the demands of the discipline out of all proportion to the benefits gleaned by the field.

What, then, given the above circumstances, is the rationale for studying medieval Jewish philosophy today?

First, the very historic and political dimensions of Jewish philosophy need not be underestimated. Similarly, the theological/religious concerns of Jewish philosophy, which render most of it authentic religious philosophy, deserve recognition. Jewish philosophy is part and parcel of the Jewish experience, and appreciating its social and historical significance is no worse than situating Greek philosophy within the context of classical Greek culture, or German philosophy within the experience of German history. Ideas do not have a life of their own, at least not on earth.

It is another thing, however, to consider the theological/religious aspects of a people's or of a culture's philosophy as the essential elements of their philosophy. The historical and political, and even religious (as popularly understood) components of philosophy are not its essential core. They may help set the stage for the ideas themselves, they may locate the ideas on that stage, and even provide an incentive for appreciating the ideas, viewing them as the philosophical analogue to parallel intellectual and social currents of a period. Sooner or later, however, history, politics, and conventional religious considerations have to yield to the disciplinary subject matter of philosophy, which is philosophy, whether Jewish, Greek, or German.

Philosophers have long prided themselves on being in effect cosmopolitan in outlook, despite national and religious biases. They have given full credit to the ideas of their predecessors, believing that truth is universal and not the possession of any one group. Maimonides is notable for his explicit endorsement of the teachings of Alfarabi,[6] while Aristotle was acknowledged as the "first master" by all medieval philosophers. Even Judah Halevi, the most partisan and historically minded Jewish philosopher of the Middle Ages, required a theory of supposed universal scope to support his claims for the superiority and uniqueness of the Jewish people.

It is not coincidental that Halevi's theory found little resonance among medieval Jewish philosophers. Their metaphysical schemes apparently provided no justification, in their opinion, for such a particularistic reading of the universe. The Agent Intellect, that universal force commonly recognized

6. This endorsement is found in his famous letter to Samuel ibn Tibbon, for which cf. A. Marx, "Texts by and about Maimonides," *JQR* n.s. 25 (1934–35) 374–81.

as endowing the sublunar world with its forms, was not considered partial to any one place, group, or faith community. It emanated potential forms upon all peoples, and then left the individuals—of all nations—to realize their potential. Halevi's introduction of an analogous emanative force with particularizing effects, his "Divine Command" (or "Thing," that is, a reified Will, the *ʾamr ʾilahi* or *ʿinyan ʾelohi*),[7] was tacitly rejected by the philosophers, clearly regarded as outside the bounds of accepted scientific doctrine.

Halevi's philosophy is thus an excellent source for noting the opposition to philosophy as expressed already in the medieval heyday of the discipline and for observing the differences in the approaches of its adherents and detractors. Halevi had a philosophy of Judaism that was much more congruent with traditional Jewish views of the chosen people; however, his attitude, though couched in philosophical terms, was basically dogmatic and patently circular.[8]

Halevi exposes, nevertheless, the dogmatic and arbitrary assumptions of the philosophers, particularly in the field of physics and epistemology.[9] He shows that the foundations of classical and medieval philosophy and science are not proven, in effect they are no more reliable than his own special set of assumptions. In doing this, Halevi renders philosophy a service and makes his own book worthy of philosophical study.

Thus, Halevi is both different from and the same as other philosophers, and much of the *Kuzari* is a philosophical book. Halevi adopts the manners of the philosophers even when arguing against them, using the logic and science of the philosophers for his own purposes.

Halevi parts company with other philosophers in the particular twist he gives to the Divine Will and in his reliance upon history for confirmation of his theory. It was in the latter sphere that Halevi disassociated himself definitively from philosophical discipline as commonly understood until then, confusing historiography and history. Granted, medieval thinkers were not particularly aware of the difference between the two, yet they obviously sensed that appeals to history were philosophically suspect. Each people had a history and national pride that could be adduced to support whatever claims it chose to make, and there was no means of verifying the historicity

7. Cf. the *Kuzari* I:27, 42; II:36. See also H. A. Davidson, "The Active Intellect in the Cuzari and Hallevi's Theory of Causality," *REJ* 131 (1972) 381–95.

8. Halevi's tendentiousness is rendered even more apparent in light of evidence indicating that he borrowed critical elements of his philosophy from Ismaili sources. Cf. S. Pines, "Shiʿite Terms and Conceptions in Judah Halevi's *Kuzari*," *Jerusalem Studies in Arabic and Islam* 2 (1980) 167–210; A. Ivry, "The Philosophical and Religious Arguments in Rabbi Yehuda Halevy's Thought," in *Thought and Action: Essays in Memory of Simon Rawidowicz* (*Hagut umaḥshavah*) (ed. A. Greenbaum and A. Ivry; Tel Aviv: Tcherikover, 1983) 23–33 [Heb.].

9. Cf. the initial paragraphs of part V of the *Kuzari*, particularly §14.

of the argument. The circularity of Halevi's arguments, using the Bible to prove the truth of the Bible, is all too obvious.

Halevi's reliance on the Bible for his image of God is as philosophically naive as the specious logic employed in his historical argument. It is a personal deity with the sorts of human attributes attested to in Scripture; a God who enters into personal communication with the patriachs and then with the people Israel, the God who vouchsafes them ultimate vindication and return to their land. In short, Halevi's God is the Jewish God, as traditionally understood from biblical times on. The *Kuzari*, as its real title indicates,[10] is a defense of this faith, a philosophical apologia for an essentially unphilosophical tradition.

What makes this tradition unphilosophical is that the claims made for such a deity fly in the face of the philosopher's understanding of the requirements of divine unity and uniqueness. It is not just that the philosophers had a tradition of denying the deity attributes and hence personal characteristics in order to preserve His unity, but that the philosophers were convinced that such a denial was logically necessary. The theologians of Islam had struggled with this dilemma and were unable to resolve it logically, but at least they recognized the extrarational recourse to which they were drawn in affirming that God's attributes are and are not identical with His essence. Halevi's bold affirmations in this area had to be regarded by all as philosophically irresponsible.

Halevi's work is thus a clear hybrid of philosophy and theology, philosophical in its critique of the philosophers, theological in its affirmations. There is a consistency to his argument and an internal logic but a peculiarly indifferent evasion of the philosophers' notion of divine necessity. If Halevi felt that the philosophers had not established their image of God adequately, he had no further reason to believe he had done any better. Simply believing in the Bible and its facticity is not the same as arguing definitively for that view.

Halevi thus exemplifies the limits of classical and medieval philosophical discourse, illustrating what falls within those limits and what falls outside of them, and why. The ultimate lesson to be learned is that the most partisan of medieval Jewish philosophers is the most suspect of philosophers. Of course, those who are bent on treating Jewish philosophy as an expression of Jewish creativity will not recognize the alleged limitations as limitations, and they will not be bothered by the philosophical dilemmas Halevi creates; they will see them, rather, as brave affirmations of Jewish identity. Moreover, those who force modern or contemporary philosophical attitudes onto Halevi's teachings may well feel justified in teaching him as a precursor of Rav Kook or of Franz Rosenzweig. No matter if the conceptual schemes are basically

10. Translated by its editors, D. Baneth and H. Ben Shammai, as "The Book of Refutation and Proof on the Despised Faith," in *Kitâb al-Radd*.

different, sufficient points of commonality exist to draw parallels, show influences, and emphasize Halevi's historical and ideational significance.

Halevi here becomes the source of, or an important link in, a theological *cum* mystical tradition of itself, yet one no more philosophical for the company it keeps than Halevi is in himself. In all these instances, philosophy has become ancillary to theology or to national pride.

Jewish philosophy thus seems to be in the unenviable position of opposing popular notions and beliefs, its God austerely indifferent to the fate of individuals and nations, even the fate of His own chosen people. The voluntarism that distinguishes Halevi's deity is markedly subdued when other writers describe him. They may claim that God knows and wills all that occurs, but upon close examination, many—including the most distinguished writers—clearly mean something much more remote than a personal providence as commonly understood. Other notions, like free will, creation, and personal immortality also frequently emerge as something other than what would be assumed for Jewish thinkers.

Herein lies the uniqueness of Jewish philosophy: it does not yield to religious sentiment; its practitioners are not essentially apologists and propagandists for the faith as commonly understood. They are not detractors or naysayers either, secretly wishing to overthrow popular belief and establish a kingdom of the elite. They are certainly not assimilationists or secularists. Jewish philosophers in the Middle Ages represented a viewpoint that distinguishes them from all other members of the community, presenting their understanding of the deity and its relation to the world in a way that attempted to integrate the scientific knowledge of the day with Jewish beliefs. In the process, these beliefs were often radically transformed, and a new religious understanding, new to the Jewish community, was born.

This new understanding cloaked itself in the language and proof texts of tradition, so that to the unpractised eye—and all too often to the practised eye as well—the boldness of the philosophers' vision is not apparent, their subtleties lost on the uninitiated. This approach is typical, however, of all innovative religious thought in the Jewish community, particularly in the Middle Ages, in that it disclaims its originality and purports to find legitimation within the biblical and rabbinic tradition. The Jewish philosophers may be thought to have believed as firmly as all others that their particular understanding of Scripture and midrash was indeed the understanding originally intended, the original presentations being regarded as deliberately simplified by their forebears.

Medieval philosophy encompasses a sophisticated political philosophy, one that assesses the relation between philosophy and popular religion very carefully. The philosophers appreciate the need for the type of discourse and argument—dialectical and rhetorical—that traditional societies require and for the law by which they are governed. Political theory and ethics constitute the practical side of the philosophers' concerns. They follow Plato by and large in adopting a prudential approach to politics and, with Aristotle, adopt a moderate ethical stance on most issues.

The *halakhah* is included in this broad scheme as an ideal expression of political and moral guidance. The paradigmatic feature of Jewish law is assumed with the thinnest of convincing arguments, the reasons adduced being persuasive only to readers already persuaded. Presumably the philosophers knew that there are no really demonstrable proofs for political and ethical claims and that the rhetoric required for religious discourse of this sort must mask its limitations. As responsible members of their community, the philosophers endorsed its laws. Moreover, they undoubtedly believed in the efficacy of the *halakhah*, that it did serve to protect society and prepare those inclined to study philosophy to do so. No more could be asked of any legal system.

The philosophers did not believe that the practical sphere of life was where ultimate meaning lay. For them the theoretical sciences, physics and metaphysics in particular, held the greatest attraction. To know these principles of the universe was to approach God, to be part of the divine and eternal scheme. This way led to immortality, however construed, identifying through cognition with eternal and therefore divine truths.

Medieval philosophy shared with classical Platonic and Neoplatonic thought the belief in the divine origin of truth and being, endowing science with a religious aura. Scientific investigation thus became a sacred pursuit, and the philosopher, the man who understood scientific theory and discourse, a religious person.

It is in this light that we must see Maimonides' description of the course of instruction that he wished to have the addressee of his *Guide of the Perplexed* undergo: to have him learn mathematics, astronomy, and logic before embarking upon physics and metaphysics.[11] And it is in this light that the *Guide* itself needs to be read, assuming familiarity on the part of the reader with the various political, physical, metaphysical and astronomical theories of the day.

Of course the reader/addressee of the *Guide* is "perplexed" and not just about the problem of resolving apparent discrepancies between the claims of science and faith. Such discrepancies are regularly resolved on behalf of science, now regarded as sacred. However, as Maimonides progresses through the book, it becomes clear that science itself is being held up to scrutiny, that it too has its share of problems and unresolved dilemmas. Foremost among these is the conflict between creation and eternity: whether the laws of logic and physics necessitate acceptance of an eternal universe, as philosophers had long since believed, or whether a creationist view can be defended philosophically.[12]

11. Cf. the "Epistle Dedicatory" preface to the *Guide*, in the translation of S. Pines (Chicago: University of Chicago Press, 1963) 3.

12. Cf. *Guide* II:13–24.

This question is part of a broader problem, the problem of determining the limits of logical discourse: whether our notions of possible and impossible actions need to be guided by and restricted to present physical and cosmic realities or whether the imagination may be allowed to construct any view it wishes, barring patently self-contradictory statements.[13]

Maimonides explores this issue fully in his exposition of Kalam Occasionalism. He concludes, with what amounts to an admission of defeat, that he cannot theoretically resolve the issue of the limits of logic and hence the limits that may be placed on theoretical constructs of the universe.[14] It is clear that he rejects Occasionalism, signifying that in practice he believes in the necessary limitation of our logical discourse to the hylomorphic world of necessary causal relations that Aristotle has laid out. It would appear that he realizes that our very language assumes the hylomorphic world, so that we lack the vocabulary to understand what we mean in claiming otherwise.

Yet in his discussion of the possibility of creation and the nonnecessity of believing in an eternal universe, Maimonides entertains a creationist hypothesis and appears to favor it.[15] He does not, however, elaborate on the possible nature of that creation, perhaps all too conscious of the impossibility of saying much about what is professedly outside of physical existence as we know it.

Maimonides' deviations from Aristotelian physics and the logic of scientific discourse are accordingly strongly circumscribed. Like Halevi, he argues philosophically against certain philosophical tenets. Unlike Halevi, however, Maimonides does not proffer an alternative metaphysics. Creation aside, the laws of the physical universe are regarded as necessary and eternal, with God not any the more personal for having (possibly) exercised the role of Creator. Maimonides thus does not critique the science of his day in order to develop an extrascientific theology, one more compatible with the full range of popular religious belief. He is not prepared to abandon philosophical models of reality for models based on dogma and tradition.

For the student of Jewish philosophy, Maimonides is thus a wonderful source for exploring the philosophy of language and of logic and the relation between logic and physics, that is, the philosophy of science. It is his awareness of the issues involved in these areas that constitute Maimonides' own perplexities, which he is willing to share—partially—with his readers. Thus, behind the perplexities of the average reader of the *Guide*, who is grappling

13. Ibid., I:73, the tenth premise. See Ivry, "Maimonides on Possibility," in *Mystics, Philosophers, and Politicians: Essays in Jewish Intellectual History in Honor of Alexander Altmann* (ed. J. Reinharz et al.; Durham, N.C.: Duke University Press, 1982) 67–84.

14. *Guide*, p. 211, and see III:15.

15. Ibid., II:13. The literature analyzing Maimonides' allegedly esoteric position on this point is considerable. Cf. recently Ivry, "Maimonides on Creation," in *Shlomo Pines Jubilee Volume* (ed. M. Idel, W. Z. Harvey, and E. Schweid; 2 vols.; Jerusalem Studies in Jewish Thought 9; Jerusalem: Magnes, 1990) 2.115–37 [Heb.].

with the divergent presentations of theological and philosophical discourse, lay the perplexities of the author of the work, who is searching for reliable if not absolute scientific guidelines.

Maimonides' quest is the high point of medieval Jewish philosophy, but it is not unique. All the philosophers share with him a commitment to rational, logical discourse based upon models of the universe then construed as scientific. The two major competing models of medieval philosophy are the Aristotelian and Neoplatonic schemes, part of the heritage of the history of philosophy, which in their particulars are no longer believed scientifically valid. Yet the principles of reason that informed these views remain operative: the distinction between induction and deduction, empirical and hypothetical reasoning, certainty and probability. Moreover, the very reliance upon reason and a natural world view (however mediated by Aristotle's canon) have striking parallels with contemporary critical thought.

Maimonides and his medieval colleagues do require a considerable investment in exploring issues that are not usually considered Jewish. Likewise, the solutions often arrived at fall outside the parameters of traditional Jewish teaching. The particularities of Jewish history and of national survival are scarcely addressed, and the traditional mainstay of Jewish society and religion, the *halakhah*, is largely ignored in the philosophical compositions. When the laws are examined and praised there, they are done so within a political framework of marked philosophical weakness.

Medieval Jewish philosophy is oriented more toward theoretical concerns than practical issues, more toward universal than particular questions. In this, most philosophers see themselves as imitating the Almighty. However, where the midrash has God studying the Torah primarily if not exclusively, our philosophers have accepted the primacy, or at least equal status, of philosophical and scientific texts.

This is the revolutionary stance of medieval Jewish philosophy: it acknowledges the significance of nature and of a physical world that is largely outside the four cubits of Talmudic study. Instead of the self-referential and essentially self-contained world of *talmud torah*, the philosophers concentrate upon the world laid out in the scientific treatises of their Greek and Muslim predecessors. This is supposedly a world of objective and undogmatic fact, a world with its own set of authorities, rendered such solely by their intellectual prowess.

Medieval Jewish philosophy can thus teach one a great deal about that moment in their history when Jews felt they could take on the scientific world and be part of it intellectually, when they bought into the credo of Western science and reason, viewed as instruments towards impartial and universal truth. Medieval Jewish philosophy is therefore a moment of encounter between the traditionally exclusivist stance of Jewish learning that focuses on the Talmud and a newer, essentially positive, attitude toward Western thought.

It is nevertheless true that much of medieval Jewish philosophy is troubled over this encounter and wishes desperately to minimize any possible conflict between traditional beliefs and philosophical views. The philosophers are not abandoning the faith of their fathers, or their practices, including *talmud torah*. Among some philosophers, a clear apologetic line is taken in defense of the faith. However, it minimizes their significance to portray the philosophers as essentially guardians of the law, concerned primarily with defeating challenges to it. The philosophers were concerned with the tenets of their faith in light of the teachings of science and reason, and it was their involvement in the tenets of their faith that dictated their responses to the teachings of science and reason.

This may be the main historical lesson that medieval Jewish philosophy has to offer its readers, that there was a time before our own when Jews who saw themselves as full members of their community, felt it legitimate, even necessary, to become citizens of the intellectual world as well. True, it was only the Western world, but that was the only non-Jewish world to which they had real access. Medieval Jewish philosophy represents the expansion of Jewish existence to include a physical and scientific world formerly regarded as having little intrinsic religious significance. The religion of the philosophers is if anything broader in scope than the religion of the rest of the community, but it is less insulated and less insular.[16]

From a Jewish studies perspective, the main point of medieval Jewish philosophy is the very synthesis between reason and faith that was sought by our philosophers. They showed that one could be Jewish and Western, heirs to both civilizations, and that one need not be forced to choose betweeen them. If Athens dictated the terms of the discourse essentially, Jerusalem often dictated its contents.[17] And furthermore, one's allegiance did not need to be torn politically.

There is relevance here to the contemporary condition of Jewish students both in Israel and the Diaspora, and this view helps give medieval Jewish philosophy a firm purchase within Jewish studies. However, it does not begin to address the nuts and bolts of the subject; it only establishes a perspective within which to study it. The discipline itself is concerned, as stated, with

16. There is a certain parallel, it seems to me, between the attitude toward the scientific and philosophical heritage of the Western world here expressed as characteristic of medieval Jewish philosophers and the attitudes of the idealogues of Zionism. The latter also had a positive attitude toward the achievements of the Western world in the fields of science and a desire to expand their intellectual horizons beyond what was to be found in traditional religious texts. However, most Zionists were animated by an antagonistic attitude toward traditional religious beliefs and by a political program that required physical separation from the world that they wished to inhabit intellectually.

17. Pace the views of Leo Strauss and others who see an irremediable split between the mentalities of Athens and Jerusalem.

issues quite remote from Jewish studies as usually understood, and is of interest per se to relatively few. However, it is only by being prepared to engage the often recondite issues of medieval philosophy in a disciplined way that real justice can be done to the philosophers and their subject matter and that the relation between the philosopher and his community can be fully appreciated. Moreover, difficult as it is, the study of medieval Jewish philosophy balances other disciplines within the field of Jewish studies, guarding it from excessive parochialism and inclining it toward integration with the more profound and universal elements of Western culture.

Karaite Perspectives on *Yôm Tĕrûʿâ*

Philip E. Miller

Hebrew Union College-Jewish Institute of Religion

The Torah refers to the first day of the seventh month, Tishri, by two names. In Num 29:1, it is called *yôm tĕrûʿâ* (יום תרועה) 'a day of *tĕrûʿâ*', and in Lev 23:24, *zikrôn tĕrûʿâ* (זכרון תרועה) 'remembrance of *tĕrûʿâ*'. The Torah gives no further indication of this holy day's purpose or how it is to be celebrated, other than to state that it is a day of solemn assembly (מקרא קדש) and of rest.

According to Aaron ben Elijah of Nicomedia (14th-century Byzantium), the early Karaite sages minutely examined the word *tĕrûʿâ* and words related to it in their efforts to understand the words of the Torah. They pointed out that the lexical root upon which the word *tĕrûʿâ* was based meant 'to shout' and 'to make a joyous sound', as in Ps 66:1, הריעו לה׳ כל הארץ 'Shout to Adonai, all the earth', and Ps 95:1, לכו נרננה לה׳ נריעה לצור ישענו 'Oh, come! Let us sing to Adonai; let us shout for joy to the Rock of our salvation!' Thus, according to the Karaite sages, it was incumbent to pray on *yôm tĕrûʿâ* with great joy, singing, and celebration.

The Rabbanites, however, found a different thrust, maintaining that the key symbol of the holy day was the sounding of the *šôpār* (שופר), the ram's horn. Karaite tradition rejected this, and Karaite sages wrote a great deal about the *šôpār* and associated Rabbanite interpretations in order to demonstrate their incorrectness.

Before going further, let us recall that in ancient times music was performed in the Temple at Jerusalem while the sacrifices were being offered, with the Levites providing both choruses of singers and orchestras of musicians, and priests (כהנים) sounding horns at critical moments during the ritual. Two kinds of horns were used in the Temple: the *ḥăṣōṣĕrâ* (חצצרה), which was fabricated out of metal (and is generally translated 'trumpet'), and the *šôpār*, which was crafted out of an animal's horn. The metal horns were blown daily during the sacrifices, while the animal horns were blown only at the new moon (*rōš ḥōdeš* = ראש חדש) sacrifices and to proclaim the jubilee year.

Since *yôm tĕrûʿâ* was also *rōš ḥōdeš*, it was entirely appropriate to sound the *šôpār*. Karaite sages never objected to the sounding of the *šôpār* on *yôm tĕrûʿâ*, since it was also *rōš ḥōdeš*; but they did take strong exception to making the *šôpār* the key symbol of the holy day. They pointed out that תקיעה (*tĕqîʿâ*) was the word in Scripture associated with sounding the *šôpār*, as in Ps 81:4, תקעו בחדש שופר 'sound the ram's horn at the new moon', but *tĕrûʿâ* was the word associated with sounding the trumpet. They insisted, therefore, that *yôm tĕrûʿâ* was a day on which it was more important to blow trumpets, in addition to the animal horns of the new-moon offering. However, with the destruction of the Temple, the Sages, according to Aaron ben Elijah, replaced the clamor *tĕrûʿâ* of the trumpets with the joyful noise *tĕrûʿâ* of people's voices.[1]

There was also an attempt to reconcile the distinction in the formulation between *yôm tĕrûʿâ* and *zikrôn tĕrûʿâ*. Judah Hadassi (13th-century Byzantium) wrote that *zikrôn tĕrûʿâ* referred to the celebration "in our Exile," that is, outside the Land of Israel, and *yôm tĕrûʿâ* referred to the celebration within "our land," that is, in the Land of Israel, where one could go to Jerusalem and hear the trumpets sounding. He went on to add that *zikrôn tĕrûʿâ* referred to the joyous singing in praise of God.[2]

There was another aspect relating to *yôm tĕrûʿâ* that Karaite tradition also rejected, namely, calling the first of Tishri *rōš haššānâ* (ראש השנה) 'New Year's Day'. The earliest Karaite sages condemned this, reasoning that Tishri was the seventh month. How, they asked, could a year begin in the seventh month? Moreover, they pointed out, Scripture stated explicitly that the first day of Nisan was the first day of the new year: "This month shall be unto you the beginning of months; it shall be the first month of the year for you" (Exod 12:2). Moreover, the Karaites rejected the Rabbanites' contention that Tishri was the anniversary of Creation, *hărat ʿôlām* (הרת עולם) 'the birthday of the world'.

In rabbinic literature (*b. Roš Haš.* 11a), there is a debate whether the world was created in Nisan or Tishri. Rabbanite tradition followed the tradition that the world was created in Tishri; hence *yôm tĕrûʿâ* became *rōš haššānâ*, New Year's Day. The Karaites, perhaps not unexpectedly, accepted the first of Nisan as New Year's Day. But to the Karaites, what was unfortunate was that when *yôm tĕrûʿâ* became Rabbanite New Year's Day, the nature of this holy day changed totally, with its biblical name *yôm tĕrûʿâ* becoming almost totally neglected in Rabbanite tradition and practice.

1. *Gan ʿEden* (Eupatoria, 1864) 58d: ומהם אמרו כי אין זאת התרועה בכלים אלא על ידי שיר והלל כאשר יריעו האנשים בקדשה כמו שאמר וירע העם תרועה גדולה.

2. *ʾEshkol ha-Kofer* (Eupatoria, 1836) §265 (86b): תוכן קדושת זכרון תרועה בגלותנו ויום תרועה בארצנו: זכרון תרועה להזכיר שבחות . . . ושירות להריע ולהלל ולשבח ולפאר שם ה׳.

While earlier Karaite sages condemned referring to the first of Tishri as *rōš haššānâ*, it became a practice popular among the Karaite masses that later Karaite sages came to tolerate. Aaron ben Elijah of Nicomedia, for example, spoke out against the practice, yet within the same chapter of his work, *Gan ʿEden*, where he condemned the practice, he also explicitly referred to the day as *rōš haššānâ*.[3]

Indeed, today, in the calendar issued annually by the Karaite Religious Council in the State of Israel, which is an official publication of the Council, Tishri is the first month listed in the calendar, with the first of Tishri being called both *yôm tĕrûʿâ* and *rōš haššānâ*. As for the first of Nisan, these calendars simply list it as Roš Ḥodeš Nisan, but above it or below it is the citation from Exod 12:2, an implicit nod to Karaite tradition.

As mentioned above, *yôm tĕrûʿâ* was in the Karaite tradition a joyful, happy time. They emphasized this against what they saw among the Rabbanites, where observance of the holy day was marked by subdued solemnity. The solemnity of Rabbanite practice can perhaps be traced back to *Targum Onqelos*, in which the Hebrew word *tĕrûʿâ* was translated *yabābāʾ* (יבבא), which means 'mournful wail'. Hence, Karaite sages alleged, the Karaite observance of *yôm tĕrûʿâ* stressed a merry and joyful aspect, while the Rabbanite did not. Not only did the Rabbanite interpretation of this holy day lead to a loss of the holy day's joyful nature, it also became a kind of "Judgment Day," anticipating *yōm hakkippûrīm*, which occurred ten days later.

The Karaite sages pointed out that such solemnity was entirely inappropriate to both the letter and the spirit of Scripture. Citing Nehemiah 11, they recalled how the people assembled to hear Ezra read the Torah. According to v. 7, there were people present "who caused the people to understand the Torah," that is, they repeated the text of the Torah in an Aramaic translation so that the people would understand what was being read to them. The people wept, however, over their inability to understand the original Hebrew. Then they are told, "This day is holy to Adonai your God; do not mourn or weep. Go your way, eat the fat and drink the sweet, and send portions to those for whom nothing is prepared" (vv. 9–10). Consequently, solemnity and weeping were inappropriate to the occasion.

But Karaism, like Rabbanism, did admit that *yôm tĕrûʿâ* began a ten-day period of introspection and repentance that culminated in *yôm hakkippûrīm*. But since this seemed not to be explicitly stated in Scripture, how could it be

3. *Gan ʿEden* 58d: ... ונהגו כל ישראל מראש השנה ועד יום הכפורים שהם עשרה ימים. There is the possibility of a scribal error in the manuscript transmission, except that the introduction to the printed edition, prepared by Isaac Savuskan, indicated the unusual history and provenance of the four manuscripts that were used in the preparation of this printed edition. Moreover, one suspects that the Crimean Karaites, in their desire to distance themselves from Rabbanite Jews and their practices, would have avoided calling the holy day *rōš haššānâ* unless it was already a regular and accepted practice among them.

justified in the Karaite tradition? Judah Hadassi provided the earliest known textual proof, citing Job 33:26: וירא פניו בתרועה 'he shall see His face with *tĕrûʿâ*'.[4]

The theme of this chapter in Job was God's love and concern for the sinner. By repenting, the sinner would "see" God's face reflecting *tĕrûʿâ*, the word in this context generally translated as 'joy', a joy that signified forgiveness. Here, the word *tĕrûʿâ* was to be derived from the root ר-ע-ה 'to be friendly, close, familiar', whereas *tĕrûʿâ* in other contexts was derived from the root ר-ו-ע 'to clamor', or 'to make a joyous sound'. The use of this biblical verse from Job captured both themes of the holiday, joy as well as repentance and judgment. By use of *heqqēš* 'analogy', the hermeneutic so favored by the Karaites, Hadassi found a way through the biblical text of justifying the practice of repentance, which was not explicitly stated in the Pentateuch. What is especially extraordinary is that this verse that Hadassi used, Job 33:26, appears not have been used anywhere in rabbinic literature as a proof text applied to *rōš haššānâ*.

Within the same paragraph, Hadassi shifted his focus from the penitential aspect of *yôm tĕrûʿâ* to the motif of divine judgment. He invoked an image of God as a shepherd who reviews his herd in order to determine which animal will live and which will die.[5] It is interesting that Hadassi adduced no biblical text to support this image. Moreover, the introductory word in the paragraph, ורועיך, in addition to having no previous textual antecedent, raises a philological problem, for there is an implied relationship between the *tĕrûʿâ* of *yôm tĕrûʿâ* and the act of herding animals. Perhaps we have here another bit of false or folk etymology, where the grammatical roots ר-ו-ע 'to clamor' is confounded, intentionally or otherwise, with ר-ע-ה, another, and homophonous root meaning 'to tend animals'.

Another point of interest has to be the unmistakable resemblance between Hadassi's language and imagery and the Rabbanite liturgical poem *Ûnĕtānnê tōqep*. Hadassi's text is also unusual in that one can see both a military motif like that found in the Mishnah and Tosepta, which is one rabbinic Urtext for the poem, and an agricultural motif like the one in *Unetaneh toqep* as it appears. Elsewhere I have written that what has apparently come down to us is a conflation of these two authentic motifs, the military and the agricultural, and I conjecture that these motifs existed side by side in Judaism long before a schism between Rabbanism and Karaism occurred.[6]

4. *Eshkol ha-Kofer* §265 (86b).

5. *Eshkol ha-Kofer* §265 (86b): ורועיך פירושו ביום תרועה יושב הקב"ה על כסא הדין ועוברים לפניו כל העולם כבני מרון. פירושו כבני מרון מעשרותיהם וגדודיהם. בני הצאן וכל עזים וטלאים וגוזר עליהם ביום אי זה לחרב ואי זה לרעב אי זה לשובע ואי זה לשלום ממות ובריות כלל היצורים בו יפקדו לחיים ולמות בימיהם.

6. See my article "Was There Karaite Aggadah?" in "*Open Thou Mine Eyes . . .*": *Essays on Aggadah and Judaica Presented to Rabbi William G. Braude* (Hoboken, N.J.: Ktav, 1992) 209-18, especially pp. 210–12.

Judah Gibbor, a Karaite sage who lived in Constantinople in the late 15th and early 16th centuries and is best remembered for his poetic work *Minḥat Yĕhûdâ*, employed another verse that included the word *tĕrû‘â*, meaning 'to be friendly, close, familiar'. In his *Sēper hammô‘ădîm* (which remains unpublished), Gibbor understood לא הביט עון ביעקב ולא ראה עמל בישראל, ה׳ אלהיו עמו ותרועת המלך בו (Num 23:21) as 'None has seen iniquity in Jacob or perverseness in Israel; Adonai his God is with him, and the Presence of the King is in him'. Here, following *Targum Onqelos*, Gibbor understood the word *tĕrû‘â* as meaning the Shekhinah, God's Presence.[7] As with Hadassi, the word *tĕrû‘â* in this context was derived from ר-ו-ע, another lexical root, which means 'affection' and 'love', rather than the one meaning 'clamor'. Thus, for Judah Gibbor, the paramount meaning of *yôm tĕrû‘â* was a holy day that celebrated God's eternal love for Israel through the presence of the Shekhinah. Again, as in the case of the verse from Job given above, this verse from Numbers appears not have been used anywhere in rabbinic literature as a proof text applied to *rōš haššānâ*.

There is an impression that Karaism is a grim and dreary version of the Mosaic faith. Perhaps this impression has been predicated on stereotypes. The Karaite approach to the Scriptures is regularly portrayed as literalistic, and this is frequently exemplified by an image of their sitting in unlighted and unheated houses and eating cold food on the Sabbath. Another impression is that because Karaites traditionally eschewed mysticism or mystical speculation, their *Weltanschauung* was rationalistic and therefore "cold." As is frequently the case with stereotypes, there may be a kernel of truth within this one, but the examples adduced above concerning one word, *tĕrû‘â*, should demonstrate that the Karaite tradition possessed a creative spirituality capable of revealing rich *pānîm*, facets of Torah, that more than a millennium of dynamic rabbinic culture did not.

7. Where early Karaite sages rejected Targum out of hand as a legitimate authority, later sages, Gibbor among them, did accept it, albeit selectively.

Those Cantankerous Sepphoreans Revisited

STUART S. MILLER
University of Connecticut at Storrs

There have been few attempts to describe the social realities of individual urban centers of ancient *ʾEreṣ Yisraʾel* since 1909, when A. Büchler published his groundbreaking work, *The Political and Social Leaders of the Jewish Community of Sepphoris in the Second and Third Centuries.*[1] Unfortunately, Büchler took great liberty with the sources and tended to utilize information that in no way is certain to have applied to Sepphoris.[2] The result is a colorful description of life at Sepphoris that portrays the Jewish residents of that city in rather negative terms, but that, as I will attempt to show using an alternative approach, rests upon shaky foundations.

Author's note: The inclusion of this study in a volume dedicated to Professor Baruch A. Levine is for me an immense honor. Prof. Levine's research and insights into the ancient world have been a constant source of inspiration to me since my undergraduate and graduate days at New York University. His classes and seminars provided my earliest exposure to the tools and methodologies for the critical study of the classical sources of Judaism. There too, I began to wrestle with the possible ways in which the texts of Jewish tradition reflect the societies and peoples that produced them. Prof. Levine's influence also extends beyond the classroom, because I have always found his profound (and numerous!) perspectives on the life of the scholar—and much else—most illuminating. And to all, he brings his usual encouragement and good cheer! Truly, he embodies the spirit of one through whom נהנין ממנו עצה ותושיה בינה וגבורה ('people benefit from counsel and wisdom, insight and strength', *m. ʾAbot* 6:1). An earlier version of this inquiry was presented at the annual meeting of the Association for Jewish Studies (1994), an organization that Prof. Levine played an instrumental role in founding. It is, therefore, a fitting, if insufficient, thank you.

1. A. Büchler, *The Political and Social Leaders of the Jewish Community of Sepphoris in the Second and Third Centuries* (London: Jew's College, 1909).

2. See below.

Büchler opens with an assessment of the *gedole Ṣippori* ('the great ones of Sepphoris'), whom he regards as the wealthy, mostly lay, leaders of Sepphoris who served on the town council (*boulē*), were responsible for tax collection, and represented the Jews before the Romans.[3] The rabbis, says Büchler, attacked these leaders for all sorts of abuse of power, especially for shifting the tax burden to the people and for serving as corrupt judges.[4] They further charged the wealthy and the "land-owning middle class" with lewdness and violence and with failing to pay their promised charitable contributions.[5] In response, the affluent would refuse to support the students and rabbis who, Büchler asserts, were subject to poverty. Even when the affluent did provide for the scholars, the rabbis claimed they were insincere.[6] Wealthy women in particular hated the sages![7] The sages' frequent ridicule of the wealthy enabled them to gain the support of the lower classes, who mostly suffered at the hands of their haughty (*gasse ha-ruaḥ*) leaders.[8]

At the same time, the general population of Sepphoris was not immune to the criticism of the sages. The people at large were also guilty of licentiousness and generally only appealed to the rabbis in their time of need.[9] According to Büchler, they were indifferent to the news of the death of scholars and would slight the rabbis who lived among them.[10] Students of the rabbis were also blameworthy, because they studied Torah but failed to observe it, seeking instead to infiltrate the ranks of the sages.[11] Of course, the wealthy and the priests also showed little interest in study.[12]

From the sound of it, Sepphoris was hardly the place for a genuine *talmid ḥakham* ('scholar') to live! Yet rabbinic literature testifies to the fact that this was hardly the case, since the city was home to many sages, including the 2d-century *tanna* R. Yose ben Ḥalafta and the pivotal 3d-century sage R. Ḥa-

3. Büchler, *Political and Social Leaders*, 7–17.
4. Ibid., 25–33, 41–42.
5. Ibid., 34–49.
6. Ibid., 66–77.
7. Büchler (ibid., 75) alludes to *b. B. Bat.* 75a, where the wives of the *ʿammei ha-ʾareṣ* are said to hate scholars even more than their husbands do.
8. Büchler, *Political and Social Leaders*, 17–20, 32–33. For a recent discussion of *gassut ha-ruaḥ* in rabbinic sources, see R. G. Marks, *The Image of Bar Kokhba in Traditional Jewish Literature: False Messiah and National Hero* (University Park: Pennsylvania State University Press, 1994) 34. Marks explains that people guilty of *gassut ha-ruaḥ* indulge in self-magnification to the point that no place is left for God. Such arrogance, therefore, implies denial of God. M. Kadushin (*Organic Thinking: A Study in Rabbinic Thought* [New York: Bloch, 1938] 147–48, 305) refers to *S. ʾEliyahu Rab.*, chaps. 18 and 31, where *gassut ruaḥ* is a form of defiance of God and, like idolatry, is regarded as an 'abomination' (*toʿevah*) that brings about all sorts of misfortunes.
9. Büchler, *Political and Social Leaders*, 50–54.
10. Ibid., 54–57.
11. Ibid., 61–65.
12. Ibid., 67–70.

nina bar Ḥama.[13] In addition, R. Judah Ha-Nasi is said to have spent the last 17 years of his life at Sepphoris,[14] and both he and Ḥanina taught many important sages there. Most noteworthy among Ḥanina's disciples were R. Yoḥanan and Resh Laqish, who later became leading figures at Tiberias.[15] Furthermore, as S. J. D. Cohen has shown, more cases were brought before the rabbis of Yavneh and Usha by lay residents of Sepphoris than by residents of other large towns, with the exception of Lod.[16] Reports from both the tannaitic and amoraic periods have the Sepphoreans consult with rabbis at Sepphoris and allude to the many decisions and discourses of the town's sages before the people.[17]

Even Büchler's assertion that Sepphoreans were not likely to attend the funerals of the sages is patently false. In fact, the attendance of the Sepphoreans at the funerals of both patriarchs and sages is specifically highlighted in the sources. Thus we hear of the trepidation of the *Ṣippora'e* when they expected the news of the death of Judah Ha-Nasi and the great number of people who flocked to the funeral.[18] The passing of other members of the

13. *Mekilta de Rabbi Shimeon ben Yoḥai* (ed. Hoffman, p. 98) has Yose ben Ḥalafta refer to his hometown, without naming it, as a "large city of sages and scribes," which he would not desert for the sake of material wealth. The same thought is attributed to R. Yose ben Qisma in *pereq Qinyan Torah* (*m. 'Abot* 6:9), but the attribution to Yose ben Ḥalafta may be more accurate since Yose ben Qisma was from Caesarea Phillipi (see *b. 'Abod. Zar.* 18a), which was not particularly known as a center of rabbinic activity. See also *Midrash Ha-Gadol* to Exod 19:14. Contrast *S. Eliyahu Rab.* 18 and *S. Eliyahu Zuṭa'* 1, which have a similar story involving the narrator Elijah, with Yavneh (according to *Codex Vaticanus* 31) as the place or city "of sages and rabbis" that he would not desert. On Ḥanina, whose life bridged the tannaitic and amoraic periods, see my "R. Ḥanina bar Ḥama at Sepphoris," in *The Galilee in Late Antiquity* (ed. L. I. Levine; New York: Jewish Theological Seminary, 1992)175–200.

14. See *y. Kil.* 9.32b, *y. Ketub.* 12.35a.

15. See *y. Nid.* 2.50b, where Ḥanina himself appears as a disciple of Rabbi. Cf. *y. Roš Haš.* 2.58b and *y. Sanh.* 1.18c. Also, see my "R. Ḥanina bar Ḥama at Sepphoris," 176.

16. S. J. D. Cohen, "The Place of the Rabbi in Jewish Society of the Second Century," in *The Galilee in Late Antiquity* (ed. L. I. Levine; New York: Jewish Theological Seminary, 1992) 160.

17. See, for example, the *taqqanot* of R. Yose at *b. Sanh.* 19a and cf. *y. Ber.* 3.6b. For other halakhic decisions of Yose at Sepphoris, see *t. Mak.* 1.3 (cf. *b. B. Bat.* 171a) and *b. Šabb.* 38a. For Rabbi's decisions at Sepphoris, see *y. Šeb.* 6.37a; *y. Šeqal.* 7.50c; and *b. Ḥul.* 50b (cf. *b. Ḥul.* 58b). For the amoraic period, see my "R. Ḥanina bar Ḥama at Sepphoris," 181–85; and idem, *Studies in the History and Traditions of Sepphoris* (Leiden: Brill, 1984) 43.

18. *Y. Kil.* 9.32b; *y. Ketub.* 12.35a; and *Qoh. Rab.* 7:11 and 9:10. On the identification of the *Ṣippora'ei*, see my "*Ẓippora'ei, Tibera'ei* and *Deroma'ei*: Their Origins, Interests, and Relationship," *Proceedings of the Tenth World Congress of Jewish Studies (1989)*, Division B / Volume 2: *The History of the Jewish People* (Jerusalem: Magnes, 1989) 15–22.

patriarchal house at Sepphoris is also noted in contexts that discuss whether a *kohen* could become impure by attending the funeral of a *Nasi*, or for that matter, of a member of his family.[19] The death of Ḥanina bar Ḥama was recalled as an occasion upon which "all the people (of Sepphoris) came running."[20] Finally, in the 4th century, the death of R. Mana at Sepphoris is used as an example of how all of Israel paid their respects when a sage passed away.[21]

Moreover, the *gedole Ṣippori* only appear in contexts that accentuate their importance and their positive relations with the rabbis. Thus we are informed of R. Yose's visit to "one of the *gedole Ṣippori*" when his son passed away.[22] R. Simeon ben Ḥalafta, an important 3d-century sage who lived in nearby Ein Teʾenah, reportedly attended the circumcision of the son of one of these *gedole Ṣippori*.[23] The occasion actually highlights the worthiness of scholars, since the child's life is said to have been prolonged because of the blessing of Simeon and his colleagues. Other *gedolim* of Sepphoris reportedly received threatening letters from the government (*malkhut*) and inquired of the early 2d-century *tanna* R. Eleazar ben Parta whether they should flee on the Sabbath.[24] These *gedolim* sought the advice of a noted sage. So the rabbbis of Sepphoris and environs honored the families of the *gedole Ṣippori* by attending their life-cycle commemorations. At the same time, the *gedolim* were dependent on the merit and advice of the learned, or so rabbinic circles wished to convey.

Büchler went even further in his lesser-known "Familienreinheit und Sittlichkeit in Sepphoris im zweiten Jahrhundert," which appeared a quarter of a century after *Political and Social Leaders*.[25] Referring to a *baraitaʾ* at *b. Qidd.* 28a, which he attributes to the 2d-century Sepphorean *tanna* R. Yose ben Ḥalafta, Büchler argued that the terms *ʿeved* ('slave') and *mamzer*[26] were commonly used as invectives at Sepphoris.[27] Jews of the city, he claims, in-

19. See *y. Ber.* 3.6a; and my *Studies*, 116–20.

20. *Y. B. Meṣ.* 2.8d.

21. *Qoh. Rab.* 11:3. The sadness attending the death of R. Yose ben Ḥalafta appears to be alluded to at *b. Moʿed Qaṭ.* 25b. Contrast the reading at *y. ʿAbod. Zar.* 3.42c and *b. B. Meṣ.* 84a.

22. *Gen. Rab.* 14:7, on which, see my "*Minim* of Sepphoris Reconsidered," *HTR* 86 (1993) 386–92; and idem, "Further Thoughts on the *Minim* of Sepphoris," *Proceedings of the Eleventh World Congress of Jewish Studies (1994)*, Division B / Volume 1: *The History of the Jewish People* (Jerusalem: Magnes, 1994) 2.

23. *Qoh. Rab.* 3:2. Cf. *Deut. Rab.* 9:1.

24. *Num. Rab.* 23:1.

25. Büchler, "Familienreinheit und Sittlichkeit in Sepphoris im zweiten Jahrhundert," MGWJ 78 (1934) 126–64.

26. The usual translation of *mamzer* as 'bastard' is misleading because the term is used in rabbinic parlance to refer to the offspring of certain prohibited liaisons, not to someone born out of wedlock.

27. The Vilna edition reads:

דתניא הקורא לחבירו עבד יהא בנידוי ממזר סופג את הארבעים רשע יורד עמו לחייו

dulged in adultery and other sexual liaisons with individuals of forbidden degrees of consanguinity. Furthermore, it was common for slaves of priests to pass themselves off as priests to collect the dues at the threshing floor; these slaves would eventually insinuate themselves into the priestly line, thereby casting doubt on the status of their descendants. Similarly, Büchler maintains, Jews at Sepphoris had sexual relations with their maidservants. Fathers of offspring of these unions would naturally have taken exception to references to their children as "slaves." Once he moved on to Sepphoris, R. Judah Ha-Nasi himself, says Büchler, took a harsher view of the offspring of a woman who cohabited with either an *ʿeved* or a *nokhri* ('non-Jew'); now such offspring were to be characterized as *mamzerim*, whereas earlier they were merely tainted (*mezoham, mequlqal*).[28]

Büchler further asserts that the moral life, particularly among the lower classes at Sepphoris, left much to be desired. Büchler points to R. Yose's decree at Sepphoris that a child should always walk before its mother, apparently because of some sexual attack that had once occurred.[29] Here at least the Babylonian Talmud alludes to Sepphoris. In another passage, *y. Ber.* 3.6c, Yose tells a donkey driver (*ḥamar*) who was determined to undergo a ritual ablution at night in a dangerous place that he need not do so. The *ḥamar* appears to have had adulterous relations with a menstruating woman. Except for the mention of R. Yose, in this case there is no obvious connection with Sepphoris.[30] Büchler uses R. Ḥanina bar Ḥama's rebuke of the *Ṣipporaʾe* at

---

> It was taught: One who calls his fellow a servant should be banned, [one who calls him] a *mamzer* receives forty (lashes), [one who calls him] a wicked person descends with him to his [station in] life.

Büchler ("Familienreinheit," 127) connects the *baraitaʾ* with Yose because the words "descends with him to his [station in] life" are attributed to Yose at *t. B. Meṣ.* 6.17 and at *b. Yoma* 75a.

28. See *b. Yebam.* 45a and the anonymous view at *m. Yebam.* 7:5, which Büchler ("Familienreinheit," 147–48) takes to be the later view of Rabbi, who lived at Sepphoris the last 17 years of his life (see above).

29. *B. Sanh.* 19a. Cf. Rashi. R. Yose reports the rape of a young girl in the vicinity of Sepphoris at *b. Ketub.* 15a and *y. Ketub.* 1.25d. Büchler ("Familienreinheit," 154–55) takes R. Yoḥanan ben Nuri's gloss to Yose's statement at *m. Ketub.* 1:10 to be an indication that Yoḥanan was aware of the presence of halakhically blemished persons at Sepphoris. On Yoḥanan ben Nuri and Sepphoris, see below, n. 105.

30. The same is true of *b. B. Meṣ.* 83b, which Büchler ("Familienreinheit," 138) also uses as proof of the immorality of the Sepphoreans. The donkey driver in our passage refuses to listen to Yose and loses his life, apparently by drowning. The commentators are hard-pressed to explain the donkey driver's determination, since he seems more concerned about having suffered a seminal emission, thereby requiring ablution, than about his violation of the more serious transgressions of adultery and relations with a menstruant. L. Ginzberg (*Perushim Ve-Ḥiddushim Ba-Yerushalmi* [4 vols.; New York: Jewish Theological Seminary / Ktav, 1941–61] 2.255–56) argues that the *ḥamar* was protesting to Yose that he was merely fulfilling an ablution decreed by the sages

y. Taʿan. 3.66c, where the sage states that rain does not fall because the present generation is replete with "Zimris" (Numbers 25), as further evidence of the wanting moral fibre of the Sepphoreans. [31]

Whether the terms 'slave' and *mamzer* were commonly heard on the streets of Sepphoris any more than elsewhere as invectives aimed at individuals of dubious lineage is questionable. The attribution of the *baraitaʾ* at *b. Qidd.* 28a to R. Yose is hardly certain and, in any event, it does not specifically allude to Sepphoris. As in *Political and Social Leaders*, very few of Büchler's prooftexts mention the city. Much of his evidence merely points to the rabbis' general concern about sexual liaisons that would result in halakhically tainted offspring. Büchler is undoubtedly right that the rabbis wished to persuade others not to engage in these relationships, but there is absolutely no reason to assume that the problem they were addressing was especially acute in Sepphoris.

Still, the general view of the Sepphoreans offered by Büchler is practically a commonplace among later scholars. S. Lieberman in particular speaks of the *Ṣipporaʾe* who contested the ordination of Ḥanina bar Ḥama at *y. Taʿan.* 4.68a as a "mob" of "famous Sepphoreans who would naturally begrudge him the exemption" from taxes that was one of the benefits of appointment.[32] "Sepphoris," says Lieberman elsewhere, "was notorious in the age of the Palestinian Talmud for its boisterous and rebellious spirit and for its many criminals."[33] Indeed, the reputation of the Sepphoreans was much like that of the residents of Alexandria and Antioch, who are singled out in ancient literature for their vociferous and arrogant nature.[34] Finally, in his discussion of *t. Soṭa* 13.8, Lieberman notes that the people of Sepphoris were known for their stinginess toward the *ḥakhamim* and labels them *merive kohen* (Hos 4:4) because of their supposed treatment of local priests.[35]

---

and that he was not guilty of adultery or relations with a menstruating woman, to which he alludes *with irony*. The donkey driver's point was that he had nothing to fear since he was *not* a sinner; he merely wanted to fulfill the *taqanah* requiring ablution of one suffering a seminal impurity (*baʿal qeri*).

31. Büchler, "Familienreinheit," 156. See discussion below.

32. S. Lieberman, "Palestine in the Third and Fourth Centuries," in *Texts and Studies* (New York: Ktav, 1974) 146. See my discussion in "R. Ḥanina bar Ḥama at Sepphoris," 196, and below.

33. Lieberman, "Jewish Life in *Eretz Yisrael* as Reflected in the Palestinian Talmud," in *Texts and Studies*, 186.

34. See idem, "Palestine," 124; and idem, "*Kakh Hayah Ve-Kakh Yihyeh: Yehudei ʾEreṣ Yisraʾel Ve-Yahadut Ha-ʿOlam Bi-Tequfat Ha-Mishnah Ve-Ha-Talmud*," reprinted in S. Lieberman, *Meḥqarim Be-Torat ʾEreṣ Yisraʾel* (ed. D. Rosenthal; Jerusalem: Magnes, 1991) 332, 337 [Heb.]. On the Alexandrians and Antiochians, see below.

35. S. Lieberman, *Toseptaʾ Ki-Peshutah*, vol. 8: *Nashim* (10 vols.; New York: Jewish Theological Seminary, 1955–88) 745 n. 31, and discussion of the attitude toward priests below.

M. Beer finds hints of criticism of the leaders of 3d-century Sepphoris in *Gen. Rab.* 60:3, in which Phineas, son of Eleazar, and Jephthah are faulted for the death of Jephthah's daughter (Judg 11:30–31).[36] The passage, he claims, promotes the idea that leaders, whether great or small, need to consult with one another or great tragedy will ensue. Since this view is elsewhere attributed to R. Yonatan,[37] a 3d-century sage who is thought to have lived at one time at Sepphoris, Beer believes that the criticism is leveled at the leadership of Sepphoris, in this case the well-born sages exemplified by Phineas and the political rulers, represented by Jephthah.[38] Even if we accept the attribution to Yonatan, there is no reason to associate the comment with the situation in Sepphoris, since the length of Yonatan's stay in Sepphoris is uncertain,[39] and, in any event, the sentiment expressed could have been meant in general terms. Indeed, it is unlikely that Beer would have connected the midrash with Sepphoris had it not been for Büchler's "pioneering work," and he, in fact, cautiously concludes that regardless of whether he is correct about the attribution to Yonatan (and, therefore, the Sitz im Leben), the criticism is clearly aimed at "certain leaders *in ʾEreṣ Yisraʾel*" (emphasis mine).[40]

Beer's circumspection gets to the heart of the methodological problem first posed by Büchler's work. Büchler provides useful insights, but because he relies so heavily on attributions to Sepphorean scholars, regardless of whether the city is mentioned specifically in the relevant tradition, his portrayal of matters *in Sepphoris* is unreliable. This is particularly true because a large number of rabbis whom Büchler places at Sepphoris had tenuous connections

36. M. Beer, "*ʿAl Manhigim shel Yehude Ṣippori Ba-Meʾah Ha-Shelishit*," *Sinai* 74 (1974) 133–38 [Heb.].

37. *B. Taʿan.* 4a.

38. R. Kimelman ("*Ha-ʾOligaʾrkiyah Ha-Kohanit Ve-Talmidei Ha-Ḥakhamim Bi-Tequfat Ha-Talmud*," *Zion* 48 [1983] 141 n. 40 [Heb.]) suggests that the allusion to Phineas really points to criticism of the priests of Sepphoris, whom he sees as a major focus of opposition among the sages in 3d-century Sepphoris. See the discussion below.

39. S. Klein ("*Ṣippori*," *Maʾamarim Šonim Le-Haqirat ʾEreṣ Yisraʾel* [Vienna: Menorah, 1924] 75–76 [Heb.]) follows W. Bacher (*ʾAggadot ʾAmoraʾe ʾEreṣ Yisraʾel* [Tel Aviv: Dvir, 1926] 1.1:58 [Heb.]) in placing Yonatan ben Eleazar at Sepphoris. Klein further identifies him with a Yonatan who appears at times with the titles *śar ha-birah* or *ʾiš ha-birah* and contends that these designations suggest that he was a descendant of priests who once held a prominent position at the Second Temple. Unfortunately, it is not at all clear that Yonatan was at Sepphoris, since it is only through association with Sepphorean scholars that he is thought to have been there. In fact, A. Hyman (*Toledot Tannaʾim Ve-ʾAmoraʾim* [3 vols.; Jerusalem: Boys Town, 1964]) places him in Tiberias; and I. S. Zuri (*Toledot Ha-Mishpaṭ Ha-Ṣibburi Ha-ʿIvri: Šilton Ha-Nesiʾut Ve-Ha-Vaʿad, Tequfat Rabbi Yehudah Ha-Nasiʾ* [Paris: Reuben Mass, 1931] 122 [Heb.]) regards him as a Southerner. Zuri especially takes Büchler to task for relying on statements attributed to Yonatan for information about Sepphoris.

40. See M. Beer, "*Manhigim*," 133 (where Büchler's work is regarded as an *ʿavodah ḥaluṣit*) and 138.

with the city at best.[41] Moreover, Büchler assumes that since Sepphoris was the capital of Galilee for much of its history, statements that refer to life in general in that region certainly reflect the situation in Sepphoris. This is precisely the point—the societal conflicts at Sepphoris may not have been any better or worse than anywhere else, and the people of the city may not have deserved the ill repute that Büchler believes the sources assign to them.[42]

This is not to say that of the rabbinic traditions that specifically mention Sepphoris there are no negative appraisals of the city's residents. On the contrary, there are passages that seem to hint at class conflict and others that accuse priests, rabbis, and other Sepphoreans of blameworthy behavior. By limiting our inquiry to these Sepphoris-specific traditions, all of which occur in Palestinian sources,[43] we can further assess the image of life at Sepphoris that has come down to us and perhaps appreciate better the actual situation in the city. We turn now to these traditions.

Tensions between the Ruling Class and the Commoners

Y. Hor. 3.48c (= *y. Šabb.* 12.13c) suggests that families (*zarʿiyan*) of commoners (*pagani*[44]) once attempted to usurp the right of the councilmen, the *bouleutai*, to appear first before the *Nasi* during the daily *salutatio* at Sepphoris.[45] When the *pagani* acquired knowledge of Torah, R. Yoḥanan, the 3d-

41. See in particular Zuri's critique, *Toledot*, 122–23.

42. It is interesting that E. E. Urbach ("Class-Status and Leadership in the World of the Palestinian Sages," *Proceedings of the Israel Academy of Sciences and Humanities* 2/4 [1966] 30–32) alludes to many of the same tensions that Büchler discusses but assigns them to Galilean society *as a whole*. Urbach's treatment is also somewhat more balanced. Note, for example, his examples of sages ingratiating themselves with the wealthy and of rabbinic appreciation for kindness on the part of ordinary folk.

43. There are occasional parallels in the Babylonian Talmud, which will also be discussed.

44. On the meaning of *pagani*, see Kimelman, "*Ha-ʾOligaʾrkiyah Ha-Kohanit*," 137; and J. F. Gilliam, "Paganus in *B. G. U.*, 696," *AJP* 73 (1952) 75–78.

45. The *Nasi* intended here is probably R. Judah II. For other occasions of *salutatio* before the *Nasi* see *y. Taʿan.* 2.68a where Samuel and the house of Shila appear before the patriarch daily. Here "*Nasi*" may refer to the Babylonian exilarch. See D. Goodblatt, *The Monarchic Principle: Studies in Jewish Self-Government in Antiquity* (Tübingen: Mohr, 1994) 295. *Lev. Rab.* 18:2 has R. Simeon ben Ḥalafta appear before the *Nasi* at the start of each month. The practice seems to have been especially associated with the patriarchate of the 3d century, when the *nesiʾut* apparently grew in prestige. See L. I. Levine, "The Jewish Patriarch (Nasi) in Third Century Palestine," ANRW II:19.2 (Berlin: de Gruyter, 1979) 661–63. It should be noted that none of these texts, including those under discussion, actually uses the term *salutatio*, but it is evident that the formal greeting of the *Nasi* resembled that of Roman dignitaries. On the *salutatio* at the imperial court of Rome, see R. J. A. Talbert, *The Senate of Imperial Rome* (Princeton: Princeton University Press, 1984) 68–70. On *salutatio* in general, see T. Reekmans, "Juvenal's Views on Social Change," *Ancient Society* 2 (1971) 153.

century sage, was asked whether they were now entitled to greet the *Nasi* first. Yoḥanan ruled in their favor, seemingly invoking *m. Hor.* 3:8: "Even when a *mamzer* is a scholar and a high priest is an ignorant person (*ʿam ha-ʾareṣ*), the scholarly *mamzer* precedes the ignorant high priest."[46]

R. Kimelman has suggested that the reference to the 'holy council' (IEPAC BOYΛHC) on coins of Caracalla minted at Diocaesarea (Sepphoris) provides insight into the identity of the Sepphorean *bouleutai*. The use of the term 'holy' (ἱεράς), he contends, suggests that the council at Sepphoris was largely composed of priests, who were a significant part of the population of Sepphoris, where the priestly course of *Yedaʿyah* had settled.[47] According to Kimelman, Yoḥanan's quotation from the Mishnah, with its mention of the high priest, would now be even more apt, since our passage would be alluding to local tensions between the sages and an "oligarchy" of priests who served on the *boulē*. As far as R. Yoḥanan, an erstwhile resident of Sepphoris, is concerned, those with knowledge of Torah, that is, the sages, deserved greater honor.[48]

46. *Y. Hor.* 3.48c, MS Leiden:

תרתין זרעין בציפרין בלווטייא ופגנייא הוון עלין ושאלין בשלמיה דנשייא בכל יום והוון
בלווטייא עלין קדמאי ונפקין קדמאי אזלון פגנייא וזכון לאורייתא אתון בען מיעול
קדמאי אישתאלת לר׳ שמעון בן לקיש שאלה ר׳ שמעון בן לקיש לר׳ יוחנן עאל ר׳ יוחנן
ודרשה בבית מדרשא דר׳ בנייה אפי׳ ממזר תלמ׳ חכם וכהן גדול עם הארץ ממזר תלמ׳
חכם קודם לכהן גדול עם הארץ

There were two families [*zarʿiyan*] in Sepphoris, [one belonging to] the councilmen [*bulevatayya'* = Greek: *bouleutai*] and [the other to] the commoners [*paganayya'* = Latin: *pagani*]. Every day they would enter to inquire concerning the welfare of the patriarch [*Nasi*]. And the councilmen would enter [before the patriarch] first and emerge first. The commoners went and acquired Torah [knowledge]. [Now] they came desiring to enter first. R. Simeon ben Laqish was asked [who had priority]. R. Simeon ben Laqish [thereupon] asked R. Yoḥanan. R. Yoḥanan entered and declared [*derash*] in the *bet midrash* of R. Benayah, "Even when a *mamzer* is a scholar [*talmid ḥakham*] and a high priest is an ignorant person [*ʿam ha-ʾareṣ*], the scholarly *mamzer* precedes the ignorant high priest."

47. Kimelman, "*Ha-ʾOligaʾrkiyah Ha-Kohanit*," 141–43. In *Studies in the History and Traditions of Sepphoris* (pp. 62–132), I have shown that the settlement of priests at Sepphoris appears to have been gradual and that the *mishmar* of *Yedaʿyah* is not likely to have settled there before the 3d century at the earliest. See below. The relevant coins, which include an issue of Elagabalus, are discussed by Y. Meshorer, "Sepphoris and Rome," in *Greek Numismatics and Archaeology: Essays in Honor of Margaret Thompson* (Wetteren: NR, 1979) 168–69; idem, "*Matbeʿot Ṣippori Ke-Maqor Histori*," *Zion* 43 (1978) 194–97 [Heb.]; and idem, *Matbeʿot ʿAre ʾEreṣ Yisraʾel Ve-ʿEver Ha-Yarden Ba-Tequfah Ha-Romit* (Jerusalem: Israel Museum, 1984) 37 [Heb.]. Meshorer suggests that the 'holy council' (IEPAC BOYΛHC) actually alludes to the Sanhedrin under R. Judah Ha-Nasi at Sepphoris. See, however, my "Intercity Relations in Roman Palestine: The Case of Sepphoris and Tiberias," *AJSReview* 12 (1987) 7; and below, n. 58. On the nature of the Sanhedrin and the likelihood of its existence at this time, see L. I. Levine, *The Rabbinic Class of Roman Palestine in Late Antiquity* (Jerusalem: Yad Izhak Ben-Zvi / New York: Jewish Theological Seminary, 1989) 76–83; and Goodblatt, *Monarchic Principle*, 232–76.

48. Kimelman, "*Ha-ʾOligaʾrkiyah Ha-Kohanit*," 146.

The priests of Sepphoris were not, however, the focus of Yoḥanan's view. Although *m. Hor.* 3:8 refers to the high priest, the point of departure *in the gemara* is the more complete formulation found in the Tosepta (*Hor.* 2.8–10), where a sage precedes a *king*, a king takes precedence over a high priest, a high priest over a prophet, and so on.[49] The *gemara* even repeats the argument of the Tosepta (2.8) that there is no one who can replace a sage who dies, whereas in the case of the *king*, anyone in Israel can rule.[50] The discussion that follows emphasizes the different levels and types of Torah knowledge and culminates in a consideration of whether the Southerners or the Tiberians deserve to be appointed *zeqenim* ('elders') first. Once again, the contrast is made between political leaders and those who have acquired Torah. The Southerners, we hear, "go up first" in war (see Judg 1:2) but are not appointed as (learned) elders before the Tiberians receive this honor.[51] Finally, a brief discussion concerning those "suitable for divine inspiration" (*ru'aḥ ha-qodesh*), that is, the elite among the scholars, appears before the *gemara* considers the matter of *salutatio* at the court of the *Nasi*.

Thus the *sugia'* so far emphasizes that those who are learned in Torah deserve greater honor than all others and are most entitled to rule. At this point, directly preceding our passage concerning the contention between the *bouleutai* and the *pagani* of Sepphoris, the *gemara* introduces a similar rivalry between the houses of bar Pazi and bar Hoshaya.[52] When members of the

49. The Tosepta's order of priority continues with various priestly officials—Levites, Israelites, *mamzerim*, *netinim*, proselytes, and slaves. Cf. *Num. Rab.* 6:1. This is followed by the identical statement of *m. Hor.* 3:8, "But if a *mamzer* is a scholar and a high priest is an ignorant person (*ʿam ha-'areṣ*), the scholarly *mamzer* precedes the ignorant high priest," which is quoted by R. Yoḥanan in our passage. Indeed, the whole *sugia'* seems to be constructed around the comments of the Tosepta. See nn. 52 and 57.

50. To prove the point, the *gemara* provides an exegesis attributed to R. Hili (Ila, late 3d–early 4th century), who takes Job 28:1–2, "For there is a mine for silver. . . . Iron is taken out of the earth," as an allusion to lay rulers, and Job 28:12, "But where can wisdom be found?" as a reference to scholars. The death of R. Simon bar Zevid is the occasion for R. Ila's exegesis. Cf. *y. Ber.* 2.5c. For a discussion of the appointment of kings who were not of the house of David or of the tribe of Judah, see the comments of Naḥmanides to Gen 49:10, where he maintains that *y. Hor.* 3.48c has in mind rulers who were not annointed and who served in emergency situations (*kefi ṣorekh ha-šaʿah*). Cf. D. R. Schwartz, *Studies in the Jewish Background of Christianity* (Tübingen: Mohr/Siebeck, 1992) 49–50. Biblical verses are rendered throughout in accordance with the NJPSV.

51. According to R. Mana, the Tiberians who "had access to the royal presence" (Esth 1:14), that is, to the patriarch (see below, n. 54), were more worthy. R. Simon (who appears as R. Simon "of the South" in *Esth. Rab.* 4:4) invokes Judg 1:2 but fails to convince Mana otherwise. See below, nn. 53 and 55.

52. Both episodes are framed by a discussion of *minnuy* (on which, see below, n. 84), leading some scholars to conclude that actual appointments at the court of the patriarch were at stake. See, for example, Levine, *Rabbinic Class*, 93–94, 161. Cf.

house of bar Pazi married into the patriarchal line, they thought they were entitled to inquire after the welfare of the *Nasi* ahead of the bar Hoshaya family, who until then greeted the patriarch first.[53] In this instance, however, R. Immi (Ammi), the late-3d-century *amora*, decided that the order of

---

S. Lieberman, *Ha-Yerushalmi Ki-Feshuṭo* (Jerusalem: Darom, 1934) 175. This is certainly implied in the presentation of the bar Hoshaya/bar Pazi episode at *Esth. Rab.* 4:4, but this may be a later reading and understanding of the talmudic versions. (For further discussion of *Esth. Rab.* 4:4, see below, nn. 53 and 55.) At *y. Hor.* 3.48c, the bar Hoshaya/bar Pazi story is preceded by a discussion of who deserved to be appointed elders first, the Southerners or the Tiberians. However, there is no obvious connection of that theme with our passage, and this discussion is almost parenthetical, embedded as it is within a larger one devoted, once again, to the benefits of attaining different levels of Torah knowledge. True, the bar Hoshaya/bar Pazi and *bouleutai/pagani* accounts are followed by a discussion of whether a learned *talmid ḥakham* also deserves to take precedence over a high priest when it comes to *yeshivah* ('session'), obviously the honored ranking according to appointment in the court. But this discussion grows naturally out of the comment attributed to R. Yoḥanan, which in turn is merely a quote from *m. Hor.* 3:8/*t. Hor.* 2.10. Thus it may have no bearing on the earlier two episodes. On *yeshivah*, see most recently, Goodblatt, *Monarchic Principle*, 252–53. Our passage also appears at *y. Šabb.* 12.13c, where it is introduced because Exod 26:30 (see next note) is relevant to the preceding discussion there. The passage seems to be original to *y. Horayot*, where it evolves out of the discussion of *m./t. Horayot*. R. Yoḥanan's view, after all, closes the *sugia*ʾ and is a direct quote from the Mishnah/Tosepta. Moreover, as shown above, the *sugia*ʾ follows closely the thematic order of *t. Horayot*, where *minnuy* is certainly not the issue.

53. *Y. Hor.* 3.48c, MS Leiden:

> אילין דבר פזי ודבר הושעיה הוו עלין ושאלין בשלמיה דנשייא בכל יום והוון אילין דר׳
> הושעיה עלין קדמאי אזלון אילין דבר פזי ואיתחתנון בנשיאותא אתון בעון מיעול קדמאי
> אתון ושאלון לר׳ אימי והקמות את המשכן כמשפטו וכי יש משפט לעצים אלא אי זה קרש
> זכה לינתן בצפון יינתן בצפון בדרום יינתן בדרום

> Those of the [house] of bar Pazi and of bar Hoshaya used to go to inquire concerning the welfare of the *Nasi* every day. And those of the [the house] of R. Hoshaya would enter first. Those of the [house] of bar Pazi went and married into the [family of] the Patriarchate. [Cosequently] they came desiring to enter first. They came and asked R. Immi [Ammi] [who alluded to Exod 26:30:] "'They set it up according to the manner of it (*mishpaṭo*) [that you were shown on the mountain].' And is there a 'manner' (*mishpaṭ*) for trees? Rather, the plank which aquired (*zakhah*) a place on the north (side of the Tabernacle) should be placed in the north. [That which belonged] to the south [side of the Tabernacle] should be placed in the south."

Here, the *Nasi* intended is probably Judah III. See Levine, "The Jewish Patriarch," 661. Judah III may have moved on to Tiberias but reportedly was eulogized at Sepphoris. See *y. Ber.* 3.6a. Cf. Y. Cohen, "*Ha-ʿIm U-Matai ʿAvrah Ha-Nesiʾut Li-Teveryah*," *Zion* 39 (1974) 117–18 [Heb.]; and my *Studies*, 117–18. The relative chronology of the second episode is irrelevant to the point made here. However, the parallel at *Esth. Rab.* 4:4 has some curious differences that warrant attention. First, the text has R. Yehudah ben Pazi (not "those of the house of bar Pazi"), who is generally thought to have lived

the *salutatio* was not to be changed. Evidently, marriage into the *nesi'ut*, which was regarded as royalty,[54] was of no consequence; the family of bar Hoshaya, apparently because of its greater knowledge of Torah,[55] would continue to take precedence. On the other hand, the *pagani* who acquired Torah at Sepphoris deserved greater honor than members of the *boulē*. The point is,

---

in the early 4th century (see H. Albeck, *Mavo' La-Talmudim* [Tel Aviv: Dvir, 1969] 329–30 [Heb.]), marry into the family of *Rabbi*. This, of course, would be impossible unless *Rabbi* is taken as a loose designation for the patriarchal house or for a later *Nasi*. Cf. J. Schwartz, *Ha-Yishuv Ha-Yehudi Bi-Yehudah Mi-Le-'Aḥar Milḥemet Bar Kokhba' Ve-ʿAd Le-Kibbush Ha-ʿAravi, 135–640 La-Sefirah* (Jerusalem: Magnes, 1986) 238 n. 42 [Heb.]. (Schwartz, however, assumes it is the son of Yehudah ben Pazi who marries into the patriarchal family, but *Esther Rabbah* says it was Yehudah.) In addition, MS Pesaro to *Esther Rabbah* has *Rabbi*, not R. Ammi, also prevent the house of Pazi from entering first after the marriage. While a scribal error is possible considering the likely confusion between רבי אמי and רבי אמר, there are still other points to consider. The neat attachment of the remark/exegesis of R. Simon Daroma, presumably R. Simeon ben Pazi, father of Yehudah, who contends that Southerners are appointed first, and the response/exegesis of Mana indicating that Tiberians deserve that honor, appears to change the subject, as now the issue is appointment to rabbinic office. This entire discussion appears earlier in the *sugia'* at *y. Hor.* 3.48c, where it does not seem connected to the bar Hoshaya/bar Pazi episode. See previous note. In addition, the bar Hoshaya/bar Pazi episode at *Esth. Rab.* 4:4 is in Hebrew as opposed to the Aramaic rendering in *y. Horayot* (and *y. Šabbat*, where the comments of R. Simon and R. Mana do not appear). Note how *Esther Rabbah* switches to Aramaic when it introduces the opinions of Simon and Mana immediately after the bar Hoshaya/bar Pazi account. The composite nature of the whole is clear. Although Lieberman (*Ha-Yerushalmi Ki-Peshutah*, 175) maintains that the passage in *Esther Rabbah* has priority and that the parallels in the Jerusalem Talmud are confused, it should be recalled that *Esther Rabbah* was edited considerably later than the Jerusalem Talmud. See M. D. Herr, "Esther Rabbah," *EncJud* 6.915–16.

54. On the *nesi'ut* as royalty, see *y. Sanh.* 2, 6.20c–d; *Gen. Rab.* 80:1 (p. 950–52); and the use of Esth 1:14 at *Esth. Rab.* 4:4 (but note that the connection of Esth 1:14 with the *nesi'ut* is not as evident in our *sugia'* in *y. Horayot*. See preceding note). The *Nasi* was also thought to have been a descendant of the House of David. Origen *Epistle to Africanus* 14 (PG XI, 81, 84) compares the "ethnarch" of the Jews to a king. See especially Goodblatt, *Monarchic Principle*, 130–75. Cf. R. Kimelman, "The Conflict of R. Yoḥanan and Resh Laqish on the Supremacy of the Patriarchate," *Proceedings of the Seventh World Congress of Jewish Studies (1977)*, vol. 3: *Studies in the Talmud, Halacha and Midrash* (Jerusalem: Magnes, 1981) 12, 15–16.

55. It is possible that here too we have a continuation of the North–South tension evoked earlier in the discussion of the primacy of the Tiberians over the Southerners. Accordingly, the family of bar Hoshaya probably represented the academies of Caesarea and the family of bar Pazi, those of Lud. See Schwartz, *Ha-Yishuv*, 238 n. 43; and cf. idem, *Lod (Lydda), Israel: From Its Origins through the Byzantine Period, 5600 B.C.E.–640 C.E.* ([Oxford: British Archaeological Reports, Tempus Reparatum, 1991] 112), where Schwartz argues that the Galileans managed to derail the attempt of the

therefore, clear throughout: Torah knowledge empowers those who attain it to even surpass *political* rulers.[56]

Thus, despite R. Yoḥanan's allusion to *m. Hor.* 3:8/*t. Hor.* 2.10 with its reference to a *kohen gadol*, the thrust of the *sugia'* hardly supports the contention that the *bouleutai* of Sepphoris should be seen as priests.[57] Nor is support for priestly domination of the *boulē* to be found in the "holy council" of the Sepphorean coins. This designation more likely alludes to the Senate of

---

sages of Lod (that is, the South) to change the established protocol for appearances at the court of the patriarch. He apparently relies on the difference of opinion between R. Simon and R. Mana (see n. 53) who seem to represent the interests of the Southerners (and the bar Pazi family) and the Tiberians/Galileans respectively. The direct connection between the opinions of Simon and Mana and the bar Hoshaya/bar Pazi account is only made in *Esth. Rab.* 4:4, which, as maintained above (nn. 52 and 53), may be a later, more stylized version of themes that were originally only tenuously connected. To be sure, overtones of a North–South tension are otherwise apparent in our *sugia'*. The main thrust of the passage at *y. Hor.* 3.48c, however, is that knowledge of Torah empowers, and the more evident tension is that between the learned and the less learned or ignorant. Interestingly, a member of the House of Pazi refuses to marry into the patriarchal family at *y. 'Abod. Zar.* 3.42c and *y. Soṭa* 9.24c because he feels unworthy. Note that in this passage it is the patriarchal house that seeks the union with the house of Pazi, but here too the context emphasizes the worthiness of the sages. Especially interesting is the reference to Jehoshaphat that follows and the view at *b. Ketub.* 103b and *b. Mak.* 24a that he would rise from his throne before a sage, embrace and kiss him, and then address him as *rabbi, rabbi, mari, mari* ('My master, my master, my lord, my lord')! Curiously, the notice concerning those who deserve to be endowed with *ruaḥ ha-qodesh* found before our accounts at *y. Horayot* and *y. Šabbat* also appears in the *sugi'ot* at *y. 'Aboda Zara* and *y. Soṭa*, where it also drives home the primary motif, that is, the value of Torah knowledge.

56. See the earlier discussion in the *sugia'* of the relationship of Moses and of Joshua to the *zeqenim* ('elders') and *ra'shim* ('heads') of their time. In the address of Moses in Deut 29:9, the heads are situated before the elders because, the *gemara* explains, they were his students and because of their attainment of knowledge of Torah. Joshua, in contrast, stationed the *ziqne Yisra'el* before the heads not only because he had greater need of them during the Conquest but also because the elders of his time expended more of an effort than the *ra'shim* to acquire Torah wisdom. Cf. *Pene Moshe* to *'al yede shelo' nityaga' ba-Torah*. For other passages in the Jerusalem Talmud that suggest competition between the rabbis and the patriarchs for authority, see J. Neusner, *Judaism in Society: The Evidence of the Yerushalmi* (Chicago: University of Chicago Press, 1983) 177–97.

57. This is true even though the *sugia'* (and *t. Hor.* 2.10) closes with an understanding of Prov 3:15: "She is more precious than rubies (*mi-peninim*)" as an allusion to the high priest who enters within (*peninim*, that is, the Holy of Holies). The verse merely supports R. Yoḥanan's view, which comes at the end of the entire *sugia'* in which the honor due to priests as opposed to scholars is not at stake.

Rome, since the term ἱερά was often applied to this and other Roman institutions that were believed to be under "divine protection."[58]

To be sure, Yoḥanan may very well be referring to tensions between the councillors and the commoners at Sepphoris, but there is no reason to assume that these were more pronounced at Sepphoris. The entire *sugia'* testifies to the belief of the sages that the acquisition of Torah knowledge entitled *whoever* acquired it to greater honor. Apparently, the Tiberian editors of the Jerusalem Talmud thought that Northerners, or more specifically the Tiberians, had done a better job at becoming well versed in Torah than the Southerners. By the same token, R. Yoḥanan[59] may have believed that the *pagani* were more likely than the council members to do so. The *boulē* of Sepphoris was probably no different than that of Tiberias or any other town in which

58. See H. G. Liddel and R. Scott, *A Greek-English Lexicon* (Oxford: Clarendon, 1976) 822. Accordingly, the complete legend would read: "Diocaesarea, Holy, Refuge, Autonomous, Loyal, Friend [and] Ally of the Holy Senate and of the People of Rome." Contrast the rendering of Meshorer ("Sepphoris and Rome," 168–69), who assumes that a treaty between the *boulē* at Sepphoris and the Roman Senate is intended: "Diocaearea, the Holy, City of Shelter, Autonomous, Loyal (a treaty of) friendship and alliance between the Holy Council (IEP[AC] B[OYΛHC]) and the Senate (C[YΓKΛHTOY]) of the people of Rome." C. M. Kraay ("Jewish Friends and Allies of Rome," *American Numismatic Society Museum Notes* 25 [1980] 57) regards the C of CYΓKΛHTOY as the final letter of BOYΛHC and rejects Meshorer's understanding of the legend. Cf. K. Strobel, "Aspecte des politischen und sozialen Scheinbildes der rabbinischen Tradition: Das spatere 2. und das 3. Jh. n. Chr., Mit einem Anhang: Zur Munzpragung von Diocaesarea-Sepphoris in severischer Zeit," *Klio* 72 (1990) 496; and K. Harl, *Civic Coins and Civic Politics in the Roman Near East, A.D. 180–275* (Berkeley: University of California Press, 1987) 81. Even if σύγκλητος does appear in the legend, documents of the Empire frequently use the term together with Βουλή to refer to the Roman Senate. Imperial documents also use these terms in combination with ἱερά to invoke the 'sacred Senate'. See ibid., 74–75; Talbert, *The Senate of Imperial Rome*, 495; and H. J. Mason, *Greek Terms for Roman Institutions: A Lexicon and Analysis* (Toronto: Hakkert, 1974) 121–23. Meshorer ("Sepphoris and Rome," 170) takes ἱερά to be an allusion to the prestige of the city council or possibly the Sanhedrin (see above, n. 47) at Sepphoris, "the spiritual and political center" of the Jews. Kimelman ("*Ha-'Oliga'rkiyah Ha-Kohanit*," 143 n. 56) argues that the term must have had greater significance; otherwise we would expect to find it on coins of Tiberias. Thus he suggests that the word hints at the preponderance of priests on the city council. In either case, the use of the term earlier in the legend to refer to Diocaesarea itself should not color our understanding of IEPAC BOYΛHC. On the application of ἱερα to cities of Palestine, see J. Geiger, "Local Patriotism in the Hellenistic Cities of Palestine," in *Greece and Rome in Eretz Israel: Collected Essays* (ed. A. Kasher, U. Rappaport, and G. Fuks; Jerusalem: Yad Izhak ben-Zvi, 1990) 142–43, 150.

59. Or, at the very least, the 3d-century circles with which he was associated. See the full passage, above, n. 46.

the rabbis resided.[60] Thus our *bouleutai* are simply an example of leadership that did not deserve greater honor than the more learned, here represented by the *pagani*, among whom the rabbis wished to foster Torah study.

Still, the *bouleutai* of Sepphoris are not merely a foil to the interests of the rabbis. Elsewhere we do in fact hear of the power wielded by these councilors. Thus *y. Pe'a* 1.16a has the councillors (Aramaic: *bulevatayyah*) of Sepphoris meet for the purposes of distributing the *leitourgiai.*[61] When one Yoḥanan failed to come, he was denounced by a fellow councillor, who inquired, "Are we not going to visit Yoḥanan today?" Decurions were only granted exemptions from liturgies when they were ill, so it is possible that Yoḥanan was perceived by his denouncer as feigning sickness.[62] In any event, the denunciation is characterized as *lashon ha-ra' be-ṣedeq*, that is, 'evil tongue' of one who plays the higher moral ground. Evidently, the decurions who served on the *boulē* at Sepphoris were seen by the rabbis as less-than-ideal personalities and were known for their abusive use of power. This would, however, fit the general perception of such councillors, not merely those of Sepphoris. Thus *Sipre Deut.* 309 suggests that only a fool would insult a *bouleutēs* in the marketplace, since he could easily strike, imprison, or restrain whomever he wanted.[63]

The Priests and the People

We should not, however, be too quick to dispense with our discussion of the priests of Sepphoris. In *Studies in the History and Traditions of Sepphoris*, I discussed two traditions that cast individual priests who reportedly once served at the Temple in a poor light. Thus we hear of Joseph ben Elim, a priest who both Josephus and rabbinic sources tell us substituted for the official high priest one Yom Kippur. From Josephus we know that the event described occurred during the last years of Herod.[64] According to *t. Yoma* 1.4, ben Elim tried to usurp the high priesthood.[65] The other tradition, *t. Soṭa*

60. Contra Kimelman, "*Ha-'Oliga'rkiyah Ha-Kohanit*," 143 n. 56. On the *boulē* of Tiberias, see *y. Šeqal.* 7.50c and *y. Ta'an.* 1.64a. Cf. S. Klein, *'Ereṣ Ha-Galil* (Jerusalem: Mossad Ha-Rav Kook, 1967) 99, 105 [Heb.].

61. See S. Lieberman, "Palestine," 130 n. 132, where the meaning of *ṣomot* is discussed.

62. See P. Garnsey, "Aspects of the Decline of the Urban Aristocracy in the Empire," ANRW II:1 (1974) 236. Cf. Lieberman, "Palestine," 131 n. 135. On the pressures on the *curiales* in the 3d century, see G. E. M. de ste. Croix, *The Class Struggle in the Ancient Greek World* (Ithaca, N.Y.: Cornell University Press, 1981) 465–74.

63. Cf. the ruthless behavior of the *curiales* in a somewhat later period discussed by P. Brown, *Power and Persuasion in Late Antiquity: Towards a Christian Empire* (Madison: University of Wisconsin Press, 1992) 27.

64. Josephus *Ant.* 17.165–68.

65. *T. Yoma* 1.4; *y. Yoma* 1.38c–d; *b. Yoma* 12b–13a and parallels. See my *Studies*, 63–87.

13.7, concerns a priest who was dubbed *ben Ḥamsan* ('the violent one') because he snatched more than his fair share of the Showbread and Two Loaves.[66] The *maʿaseh* involving ben Elim is attributed to R. Yose ben Ḥalafta; the *maʿaseh* concerning ben Ḥamsan is also traceable to a 2d-century circle.[67] Aside from these accounts, *y. Taʿan.* 4.68d preserves the allusion of the late 4th-century Palestinian sage, R. Berakhiah, to the priests of the *mishmar* of *Yedaʿyah*, who reportedly were "exiled to Sepphoris" because "God (*yah*) knew (*yadaʿ*) the profound design in their heart." Berakhiah connects the departure of the priestly course for Sepphoris with the destruction of the Temple. Earlier in the passage, R. Levi, a late 3d-century Palestinian *amora*, provides an equally disparaging interpretation of *Yehoyariv*, the priestly course that ends up at Meron, since it was the *mishmar* that was thought to be officiating at the time of the Destruction. Perhaps the "profound design" of the priests of *Yedaʿyah* is an allusion to the pro-Roman stand that Sepphoris eventually assumed in the First Revolt.[68] In any event, these allusions most certainly were preserved by circles who did not flinch from viewing the priests, at least the priests of Temple times, with aspersions.

We must, however, be careful. The fact that there are negative reports preserved in tannaitic and amoraic sources does not necessarily mean that the rabbis *of Sepphoris* were especially at odds with the priests *of their times*.[69] Büchler, nevertheless, has so argued,[70] relying on an array of sources that point to the disdain of the sages for priests who do not study Torah. Thus the sages repeatedly exhort that *terumah* be given only to learned priests and may even have suggested that tithes should be presented to the rabbis instead.[71] But here again, there are no specific allusions to Sepphoris among these sources, and these sentiments are not exclusively attributed to Sepphorean sages.[72] Furthermore, the misdemeanors of pre-70 priests are alluded to by

66. *T. Soṭa* 13.7; *b. Yoma* 39a–b; and *b. Qidd.* 53a. *Y. Yoma* 6.43c has ben Ha-ʾAfun for ben Ḥamsan. For a full discussion, see my *Studies*, 88–102.

67. See ibid., 89–90.

68. Cf. ibid., 124.

69. Note how the Palestinian versions of the ben Ḥamsan story says he was remembered by this sobriquet 'until today' (*ʿad ha-yom*). Contrast the Babylonian Talmud, which reads 'until his death' (*ʿad yom moto*)!

70. Cf. also Lieberman, discussed above, and Kimelman, "*Ha-ʾOligaʾrkiyah Ha-Kohanit*," 140–42.

71. For the emphasis regarding learned priests, see especially, *Sipre Num.* 119 (ed. H. S. Horovitz, p. 143), *y. Maʿaś. Š.* 5.56b and *b. Sanh.* 90b. For the provision of tithes (*maʿaśerot*) to the *kohanim*, see *b. Yebam.* 86a. Cf. Levine, *Rabbinic Class*, 71; and A. Oppenheimer, "*Hafrashat Maʿaśer Riʾshon Ba-Meṣiʾut She-Le-ʾAḥar Ḥurban Ha-Bayit Ha-Sheni*," *Sinai* 83 (1978) 284–85 [Heb.].

72. See Büchler, *Political and Social Leaders*, 69–70. Büchler includes a saying of R. Yoḥanan, who lived at one point at Sepphoris but also became the head of an academy at Tiberias. He also points to a statement attributed to R. Yonatan, whose

others, and the moral shortcomings of priests of the biblical period are a recurring theme of the *aggadah.*[73] At the same time, the priestly class should not be regarded as monolithic, when in reality it was considerably stratified. Not all priests belonged to the aristocracy, nor did they necessarily gravitate toward positions in the city administration, at Sepphoris or elsewhere. Indeed, there were priests who also happened to become prominent rabbis, that is, some did in fact acquire knowledge of Torah and *halakhah.*[74]

Thus there is no reason to suppose that there was any extraordinary tension between the priests of tannaitic and amoraic Sepphoris and the rabbis. The 2d-century *tannaim* who depict ben Elim and ben Ḥamsan in rather ignoble terms cannot be said with certainty to have harbored any ill feelings toward the priests of Sepphoris of their time.[75] To be sure, 2d-century

---

connection with Sepphoris is questionable. See above, n. 39. Finally, Büchler's assumption that R. Yannai was from Sepphoris is clearly incorrect, since he is more likely to have been from Akhbara. See my *Studies*, 118 n. 316.

73. This is especially true of tannaitic *aggadah*. Although negative views of the priests, as we have seen, persist into the amoraic period, other voices begin to be heard at this time. See M. Beer ("*Banav shel ʾEli be-ʾAggadot Ḥazal*," *Bar-Ilan Annual* 14 [1977] 79–93 [Heb.]), who detects a change in attitude toward the priests and other leaders of the biblical period by the 3d century, when at least some elements of the scholarly class, particularly among the circle of the *Nasi*, began to promote the notion of dynastic and nepotistic succession in emulation of succession practices found among the priests, prophets, and rulers of earlier times. Also see, S. A. Cohen, *The Three Crowns: Structures of Communal Politics in Early Rabbinic Jewry* (Cambridge: Cambridge University Press,1990) 167, 243.

74. For a recent discussion of priests in rabbinic literature, see S. Schwartz, *Josephus and Judaean Politics* (Leiden: Brill, 1990) 96–107. Cf. A. Aderet, "*Masekhet ʿEduyot Ke-ʿEdut Le-Darkhei Ha-Shiqqum Ve-Ha-Tequmah Le-ʾAḥar Ḥurban Bayit Sheni*," in *Yehudim Ve-Yahadut Bi-Yemei Bayit Sheni, Ha-Mishnah Ve-Ha-Talmud: Meḥqarim Li-Khevodo shel Shmuel Safrai* (ed. A. Oppenheimer, I. Gafni, and M. Stern; Jerusalem: Yad ben-Zvi, 1993) 260–63 [Heb.]. Kimelman's suggestion that a priestly "oligarchy" at Sepphoris was the brunt of much of the rabbis' criticism is highly unlikely. See above discussion of *y. Šabb.* 12.13c and of the *boulē* at Sepphoris. In addition, Kimelman relies on *Qoh. Rab.* 7:11 where the *Ṣipporaʾe* seem to be equated with the *bene Yedaʿyah*. The parallel texts do not have the allusion to the *bene Yedaʿyah*, which can be shown to be a later interpolation. See my *Studies*, 120–23; and D. Trifon, "*Ha-ʾIm ʿAvru Ha-Kohanim Mi-Yehudah La-Galil ʾAḥarei Mered Bar Kokhba?*" *Tarbiz* 59 (1989–90) 80–81 [Heb.], where my argument is repeated. On the meager evidence for a priestly oligarchy at Sepphoris, also see Schwartz, *Studies in the Jewish Background of Christianity*, 54–55 n. 49.

75. Actually, Büchler's collection of sources that refer to the presence of lawless *ḥamsanim* in the 2d century (*Political and Social Leaders*, 43–44) may help us to appreciate why the *tannaim* of that period would have preserved the story of an avaricious priest from Sepphoris who was dubbed ben *Ḥamsan*. His behavior may have been of greater interest than the fact that he was a priest. See my *Studies*, 91–92, esp. n. 167. Cf. above, n. 69.

contention with an alternate, priestly court system may be indicated in *m. Roš Haš.* 1:7, where R. Yose (ben Ḥalafta) relates that a rabbinic court once rejected a view of the priests in Jerusalem pertaining to valid witnesses for the sighting of the new moon. This source may reflect the ongoing struggle for control that followed the Destruction,[76] but this kind of competition is unlikely to have been an issue at Sepphoris alone, and, in any event, is likely to have receded with time.[77] As for R. Berakhiah's allusion to *Yedaʿyah*'s "exile," he, like R. Levi, may merely have associated the departure of the priestly courses from Jerusalem with the overall shame of the Destruction. There simply is no other evidence for difficult relations with the descendants of *Yedaʿyah* who, for that matter, did not settle at Sepphoris until sometime in the 3d century.[78]

The Ṣippora'e Criticize R. Meir and R. Ḥanina bar Ḥama

Next we turn to the relationship of the Sepphoreans to the 2d-century *tanna* R. Meir and the 3d-century sage Ḥanina bar Ḥama. In *y. Ber.* 2.5b (*y. Moʿed Qaṭ.* 3.82d) the *Ṣippora'e* take exception to R. Yose ben Ḥalafta's assertion that R. Meir was a "great," "holy," and "humble" man, which is how Yose commends (*meshabaḥ be-*) his colleague upon introducing him to his fellow residents of Sepphoris.[79] The *Ṣippora'e* deemed it inappropriate to welcome mourners on the Sabbath, so when they witnessed Meir do so at Sepphoris, they expressed their indignation to Yose and questioned his assessment of Meir. Yose in turn defended Meir by asserting that Meir's intention was to teach them the *halakhah* that there is no mourning on the Sabbath.

Büchler contends that there is more to this story because the tension between the *Ṣippora'e* and Meir "can hardly have been more than the occasion for criticizing."[80] Accordingly, a deep-seated contempt for scholars among

76. Cf. Schwartz, *Josephus and Judaean Politics*, 106.

77. Note how priestly courts are not even considered by Goodman (*State and Society*, 155–71) in his discussion of "conflicts of jursidiction" in the 2d century. They seem no longer to have been a factor.

78. See my *Studies*, 119–27; and Trifon, "*Ha-'Im ʿAvru Ha-Kohanim Mi-Yehudah La-Galil 'Aḥarei Mered Bar Kokhba?*" 77–93. For a different view, see Z. Safrai's response to Trifon, "*Matai ʿAvru Ha-Kohanim La-Galil?*" *Tarbiz* 62 (1993) 287–92 [Heb.].

79. G. Alon (*Toledot Ha-Yehudim Be-'Ereṣ Yisra'el Bi-Tequfat Ha-Mishnah Ve-Ha-Talmud* [Tel Aviv: Hakibutz Hameukhad, 1961] 2.72–73 [Heb.]) claims that R. Yose was promoting R. Meir as *'ab bet din* at Sepphoris. (Alon's discussion is not reproduced in the English-language version of his work.) Cf. Klein, "*Ṣippori*," 58; and see my "*Ṣippori Ve-Ha-Tefuṣot: Ha-Hashpaʿah Ha-Mitmashekhet shel Merkaz Talmudi Ba-Galil*," in *'Ereṣ Yisra'el and the Diaspora in the Time of the Mishnah and Talmud* (tentative title; ed. A. Baumgarten, S. Gafni, and L. H. Schiffman; Jerusalem: Shazar, forthcoming).

80. Büchler, *Political and Social Leaders*, 57 n. 1.

the people of Sepphoris underlies the criticism aimed at Meir. However, a close look at the use of the form *meshabaḥ be-/le-* in the Jerusalem Talmud and of the equivalent *mishtabaḥ be-* in the Babylonian Talmud indicates that our story is similar to other accounts in which one sage commends another sage before a third *colleague*.[81] The latter then finds fault with the commended sage because of a faulty understanding of a particular *halakhah* or other matter, and the sage's behavior is then defended by the original commender. Especially noteworthy is the usage at *y. Nid.* 2.49d, where Rabbi commends R. Ḥama, the father of R. Hoshaya, to R. Ishmael ben Yose (ben Ḥalafta). In this instance R. Ishmael questions the approbation because R. Ḥama was willing to give priority to a view of Rabbi over that of the patriarch's master (and Ishmael's father!) R. Yose, thereby violating the principle that the opinion of a master always comes before that of a disciple. R. Ḥama was actually correct, however, since Rabbi was *his* master.

Thus the criticism of the *Ṣippora'e* appears within a conventional rabbinic form used by both gemarot to present instances in which, most often, rabbis criticized their colleagues. Our passage in no way suggests that weightier differences between the masses and the rabbis were at stake. In fact, the term *Ṣippora'e* is frequently used to designate persons who associated with the rabbis in a somewhat informal way, or even to refer to the members of certain rabbinic circles at Sepphoris. The Jewish masses in general are very likely not intended, at least not here.[82]

Accounts concerning R. Ḥanina bar Ḥama have perhaps contributed more than any others to the negative portrayal of the Sepphoreans and their relationship with the sages. At *y. Ta'an.* 3.66c the *Ṣippora'e* confront Ḥanina during a pestilence and charge him with indifference to their plight, since his neighborhood has remained unaffected. Ḥanina replies with a rebuke: "There was one Zimri in his generation but twenty-four thousand fell of Israel. And among us, how many Zimris are there in our generation, and you grumble?" This is followed with another confrontation, this time during a series of droughts when the fasting *Ṣippora'e* charged that Ḥanina's prayers were ineffectual. When R. Joshua ben Levi is summoned from the South, he too is unable to bring the rains despite his reputation for having done so for the *Deroma'e* (Southerners). Ḥanina takes this opportunity to rebuke his neighbors further: "The hearts of the *Deroma'e* are soft and when they hear a word of the Torah they humble themselves. But the hearts of the *Ṣippora'e* are obstinate and when they hear a word of the Torah they do not humble

81. For an exception, see *b. 'Abod. Zar.* 4a, where R. Abbahu commends R. Safra in front of some *minim*. The usage in the Jerusalem Talmud, however, is consistent.

82. Note how R. Yose utilizes biblical exegesis to prove to the *Ṣippora'e* the correctness of Meir's behavior and how the mourning customs among the *rabbanan deroma'e* ('Southern masters') are discussed earlier in the *sugia'*. See my "*Ẓippora'ei, Tibera'ei* and *Deroma'ei*," 15–22; and idem, "R. Ḥanina bar Ḥama at Sepphoris," 175–200.

themselves." Remarks attributed to both Ḥanina and Joshua follow, which make the point that the *gedole ha-dor*, that is, the pious of the generation,[83] could not always ward off catastrophe, since a community is judged by the character of the majority of its residents.

Elsewhere in *y. Taʿan.* (4.68a) we learn that when Rabbi was on his deathbed, he instructed his son to make all the appointments (*minnuyin*) at once, rather than two annually, and to appoint R. Ḥanina "at the head."[84] The *gemara* explains that in Judah's day, appointees who would prove to be unworthy would not continue in office. The obvious question is why the prestigious appointment intended for Ḥanina was not awarded altogether during the *Nasi*'s lifetime. Two reasons are attributed to *amoraim* who lived approximately a century later. R. Derosa contended that the *Ṣippora'e* "shouted" against Ḥanina. Why the *Ṣippora'e* protested Ḥanina's appointment is not evident, despite the attempt of S. Lieberman to read into their "shout" resentment of the masses for the tax exemptions that this wealthy sage would gain with his promotion.[85] Skepticism is already expressed in the text that asks, "Because of a shout do we act? (that is, what difference should that make)?" R. Eleazar ben Yose's explanation that Ḥanina had once publicly

83. Rashi to *b. Pesaḥ.* 49b defines *gedole ha-dor* as 'men of deeds and righteous ones' (*'anshe maʿaśeh ve-ṣadiqim*). Büchler (*Political and Social Leaders*, 8–10) says that the phrase can refer to civic leaders in general, that is, of no specific locale, and that scholars are not necessarily implied. In fact, he claims, the term can be used to refer to non-Jews as well. Büchler believes, however, that the *gedole ha-dor* of our passage are scholars, since he connects the statement attributed to Ḥanina about the character of a community with the previous story of the droughts at Sepphoris, in which the rebuke by Ḥanina (according to Büchler, a rebuke by *Joshua*!) seems to differentiate between people ignorant of Torah (that is, the *Ṣippora'e*) and the learned. *Gedol/ Gedole ha-dor* can refer to scholars, for example at *b. Moʿed Qaṭ.* 22b, but this is not necessarily the case here. The Jerusalem Talmud seems to use the phrase to refer to pious leaders in general. See *y. Pe'a* 8.21a (= *y. Šeqal.* 5.48d); and *y. Yebam.* 8.9d (= *y. Qidd.* 3.65c). Büchler's reading (p. 8) of *b. Ḥul.* 87a, which he believes names a family of *gedole ha-'areṣ* ('the great ones of the land') at Sepphoris, is faulty. The passage does not mention Sepphoris, and MS Munich has *gedole rom* ('the great ones of Rome'). Cf. W. Bacher's review of Büchler's *Political and Social Leaders* in *OLZ* 12 (1909) 545. There is also no basis for Büchler's claim that the family intended is to be identified with the *bouleutai* of *y. Šabb.* 12.13c.

84. For the possible meanings of *be-re'shah*, see my "R. Ḥanina bar Ḥama at Sepphoris," 195 n. 85. The term *minnuy*, which is often translated 'ordination', can refer to various types of teaching and judicial appointments, the precise nature of which is often too difficult to determine. See I. Gafni, "Yeshiva and Metivta," *Zion* 43 (1978) 19–20; Levine, *Rabbinic Class*, 141 n. 33: and H. Mantel, *Studies in the History of the Sanhedrin* (Cambridge: Harvard University Press, 1961) 211–12.

85. See Lieberman, "Palestine," 146–47.

disagreed with his teacher Rabbi over the rendering of Ezek 7:16 is then offered as an alternative.[86]

A. Baumgarten has maintained that behind Rabbi's deathbed pronouncement is an attempt by the sages to weaken the prerogatives of the patriarch, who normally used his right to make appointments as a means of controlling the sages and ensuring their loyalty.[87] Appointments made "all at once" would limit the patriarch's authority, since he would now have to wait for a vacancy, presumably through death, to place another sage in office;[88] important positions could no longer be assigned at will. If Baumgarten is correct, the opinions of Derosa and Eleazar may also mirror different perceptions of the role of the *Nasi*. That is, the shout of the *Ṣippora'e* could reflect the determination of a (later) rabbinic opposition group who sought to lessen the authority of the patriarchs to assign appointments. Eleazar's view that Ḥanina was disrespectful toward the *Nasi* may have originated among those who supported the prerogative of the patriarch "to rule with *hauteur*."[89] In either case, the passage may simply mask *later* perceptions of patriarchal authority behind some popular accounts of the colorful but otherwise highly regarded Ḥanina. Tensions between Ḥanina/the rabbis and the people may not at all have been the central issue.

In any event, the sages were conscious of the fact that their role in society as holy men was one that cut both ways in the eyes of the public. That is, Ḥanina was indeed thought of as a wonder-worker who could, if not at this time, at others, bring rain and who, as a leading sage, deserved a prominent appointment regardless of whether he was ultimately to receive one. His stinging rebukes of the *Ṣippora'e* and the later contention of Derosa that the *Ṣippora'e* protested his appointment imply that there were tensions with the people that surfaced from time to time. Nevertheless, not all *Ṣippora'e* should be thought of as detractors of the rabbis because it can be shown that others designated by this term were actually members of Ḥanina's circle who passed on his traditions. Indeed, the overall impression one gets in the sources is that Ḥanina was an acclaimed scholar who often was supportive of the masses but who, precisely because of his status, had to endure their criticism.[90] Moreover, the reproach he levels at the *Ṣippora'e* is similar to the

86. For a fuller discussion, including an assessment of Lieberman's view, see my "R. Ḥanina bar Ḥama at Sepphoris," 194–97.

87. See A. Baumgarten, "Rabbi Judah I and His Opponents," *JSJ* 12 (1981) 142–45.

88. So the *gemara* seems to imply. See *Qorban Ha'Edah*, ad loc. Cf. Lieberman, "Palestine," 145 nn. 231–32.

89. Cf. the views attributed to the dying patriarch at *b. Ketub.* 103b. There Rabbi instructs his son, Gamaliel, נהוג נשיאותך ברמים. See Baumgarten, "Rabbi Judah I and His Opponents," 142–43, who translates 'Rule with *hauteur*'.

90. On Ḥanina's circle and his overall reputation, see my discussion in "R. Ḥanina bar Ḥama at Sepphoris," 185–90, 199.

criticism aimed at others living in different places by the sages, who undoubtedly did not view the situation at Sepphoris as unique. Thus the *Deroma'e* may come off swell here in comparison to the *Ṣippora'e* since they are receptive to the words of Torah, but in other 3d-century contexts, the Southerners as well as the Babylonians are regarded as *gasse ruaḥ u-me'ute Torah*, that is, 'haughty and ignorant of Scripture!'[91]

Other "Families" at Sepphoris

Aside from the opposition between the *zar'iyan* of *bouleutai* and *pagani* at Sepphoris, we also hear of rivalry among other 'families' (*mishpaḥot*) at Sepphoris. *Y. Ber.* 3.6b reports that it was originally the custom for the *mishpaḥot* to stand while mourners passed before them, but once contention (*taḥarut*) broke out at Sepphoris, R. Yose decreed (*hitqin*) that the mourners should remain in place as the families passed before them. Obviously, the urgent desire to be among the first to comfort the mourners created disorder. Remarkably, the Babylonian Talmud preserves a somewhat differrent version. *B. Sanh.* 19a states that "two families were envious of each other (*mitgarot*) *in Jerusalem*," each wanting to be first to pass before the mourners. It was therefore decreed that the people (*kol ha-'am*) should stand as the mourners passed before them. R. Yose subsequently issued a *taqqanah* at Sepphoris whereby the procedure reverted to its original form.[92]

The "families" in these instances are not specified, so the contention alluded to should best be understood as representative of the general situation: Funeral processions at Sepphoris, Jerusalem, and elsewhere at times led to unruly circumstances among the relatives and others who participated. These families, unlike the families of Hoshaya and Pazi, do not represent specific circles of scholars or patriarchs or, in the case of the *bouleutai* and the *pagani*, councillors and commoners. No social conflict is evident. Instead what we are treated to is a glimpse of human nature and the resulting, perhaps real life circumstances, that led to halakhic change.

The Burglars of Sepphoris

Y. Ma'aś. Š. 5.55d includes a curious incident that seems to reflect upon the character of at least some Sepphoreans. Here R. Ḥanina (bar Ḥama) re-

91. See *y. Pesaḥ.* 5.32a and *y. Sanh.* 1.18c. Cf. Levine, *Rabbinic Class*, 93; A. Oppenheimer, *Ha-Galil Bi-Tequfat Ha-Mishnah* (Jerusalem: Zalman Shazar, 1991) 130 [Heb.]; and Schwartz, *Lod*, 103–5. On the arrogance implied by *gassut ruaḥ*, see above, n. 8.

92. In the Babylonian Talmud, Rammi bar Abba (late 3d–early 4th century) reports the *taqqanah* of R. Yose. In the Jerusalem Talmud, the Sepphorean R. Ḥanina bar Ḥama does so. For a clever harmonizing of the Babylonian and Jerusalem Talmud versions, see L. Ginzberg, *Perushim Ve-Ḥiddushim Ba-Yerushalmi* (New York: Jewish Theological Seminary, 1941) 2.131–32 [Heb.].

sorts to Job 24:16, "In the dark they break into houses; By day they shut themselves in; They do not know the light," to explain the sin of the generation of the flood *(dor ha-mabul)*. Ḥanina states that *dor ha-mabul* would apply balsam during the daytime to objects they sought to steal in order to be able to locate them under the cover of night using their sense of smell.[93] The *gemara* then relates that Ḥanina once explicated Job 24:16 in this fashion at Sepphoris and some 300 homes were broken into![94]

The version at *b. Sanh.* 109a introduces other verses from Job (24:2, 3, 7, 10, and 21:32) to demonstrate the lengths to which *dor ha-mabul* would go to steal. Here, however, a *derashah* concerning the use of balsam in thefts is attributed to the 4th-century Babylonian *amora* Rava, and it is simply reported that *Yose ben Ḥalafta* once taught (*derash*) a similar understanding of Job 24:16 at Sepphoris.[95] This time, however, the burglars went into action and the people subsequently taunted Yose (*meṣaʿare leh*) with the words, "You have shown the thieves the way!" to which he protested, "Could I have known that *you* are thieves?"[96] So, in this version, the Jewish residents of Sepphoris come off poorly because they include not only thieves but others who are disrespectful to the Sages, in this case Yose, whom they hold accountable for the robberies. Yose's retort only serves to highlight the tension between his accusers and the sage. The *sugiaʾ* closes with an allusion to the loss

93. The exegesis is presented in the name of R. Ḥanina by the 4th-century Sepphorean *amora* R. Mana. It is part of a larger discussion of whether a demarcation is necessary in the case of *kerem revaʿi* (see Lev 19:23–25) in years other than the sabbatical year. During the seventh year, the fields were pronounced ownerless (*hefqer*). Therefore, people might mistakenly take produce that in fact was prohibited because it belonged to *kerem revaʿi*. The *rabbanan*, as opposed to R. Simeon ben Gamliel (see *m. Maʿaś. Š.* 5:1), thought this produce should also be marked in all other years. But why? It would seem markings are not necessary, since thieves only operate at night. The exegesis attributed to R. Ḥanina is then introduced to clarify the actions of thieves, who arrange for their nocturnal thefts during the daytime. See *Beʾure Ha-Graʾ*, ad loc., where it is assumed that the thief will not take of the *kerem revaʿi*. Cf. Ridbaz, ad loc., and see the somewhat different understanding of *Pene Mosheh*.

94. The point is that thieves do indeed prepare during the daytime (see previous note). The elucidation of Gen 6:5 at *Gen. Rab.* 27:2 includes the same exegesis and story and is essentially identical except for a cryptic allusion to the Sepphoreans (*Ṣipporaʾe*) at the conclusion of the excerpt. Cf. the parallel at *Yal.* 909 to Job 24:16.

95. Contrast the Palestinian versions which attribute the exegesis directly to Ḥanina and then relate that he once taught accordingly at Sepphoris. The Babylonian Talmud produces the account concerning Yose only after the exegesis is introduced by Rava. This points to the lateness and composite nature of the Babylonian account. See below, n. 98.

96. Alternatively, "Could I have known that thieves would come?" Cf. Rashi, ad loc. For the rendering here, which implies that Yose regarded his larger audience at Sepphoris as including a great many thieves, see Y. N. Epstein, *Diqduq ʾAramit Bavlit* (Jerusalem: Magnes, 1960) 21 [Heb.]. Cf. *Yalquṭ* 909 to Job 24:16.

that was felt at Yose's death,[97] which effectively drives home the greatness of Yose, thereby further emphasizing the audacity of those who had harassed him. The Babylonian Talmud account is obviously an embellished version of a tradition that had originally been associated with Ḥanina, as in the Palestinian versions.[98] Thus, this extreme characterization of the residents of Sepphoris in the Babylonian Talmud should not be allowed to color our overall assessment of the Sepphoreans.[99]

The Snub of the Cappadocians

Y. Šeb. 9.39a has the Cappadocians of Sepphoris (*qapodqa'e de-Ṣipporin*) inquire of the late-3d-century sage R. Immi (Ammi) concerning the mechanism for annuling 7th-year produce. The idea was to declare the produce ownerless so that the original owner could eat it, should no one else claim it. The Cappadocians were concerned that "because this people (that is, the Cappadocians) has no friend or anybody to greet them, what should they do?" R. Immi (Ammi) suggests that the Cappadocians declare their produce ownerless when the "foot is clear," that is, when fewest people are in the public way.

This notice is quite curious. S. Lieberman suggested that behind the seeming antipathy of the people of Sepphoris toward the Cappadocians is the fact that Cappadocia was pro-Roman in the conflict with Persia. Thus, he says, "the blameworthy behavior of the Sepphoreans is at least partly extenuated by their hatred of Rome."[100] Lieberman appears to be alluding to the fact that by the mid–4th century, Sepphoris seems to have become the center of a revolt against Rome, one that he believes was rather limited in

97. More specifically, to the fact that the gutters (*marzave-*) of Sepphoris flowed with blood, apparently an allusion to the great loss that was perceived. Cf. Rashi, ad loc., and see *b. Mo'ed Qaṭ.* 25b and *y. 'Abod. Zar.* 3.42c. See especially the comments of S. Lieberman, "The Martyrs of Caesarea," *Annuaire de l'Institute de Philologie et d'Histoire Orientales et Slaves* 7 (1939–44) 401 n. 33.

98. Note how *Yal.* 909 to Job 24:16 connects the *derashah* of R. Ḥanina and that of Yose resulting in a version that clearly combines the Jerusalem Talmud / *Genesis Rabbah* and Babylonian Talmud accounts. The fact that the notice concerning Yose's death also appears at *b. Mo'ed Qaṭ.* 25b and, in somewhat different form, at *y. 'Abod. Zar.* 3.42c, indicates that it circulated as a separate tradition and further testifies to the composite structure of the account at *b. Sanh.* 109a.

99. Interestingly, Roman writers tended to exaggerate the extent of crime in the villages of Roman Egypt, but this crime is at least well documented by the evidence of the papyri. N. Lewis (*Life in Egypt under Roman Rule* [Oxford: Clarendon, 1985] 77–78) comments, "The normal quota of human greed, especially when intensified by the pinch of poverty, constitutes a fairly universal stimulus to illicit actions." Also, see Juvenal's third satire for crime, including burglary, at Rome.

100. Lieberman, "Palestine," 159–60.

scope.[101] Even if the so-called Gallus Revolt of ca. 352 C.E. is alluded to in rabbinic sources,[102] it is equally clear that relations between Rome and the Jews of *ʾEreṣ Yisraʾel*, particularly the patriarchal house that was located at Sepphoris during the 3d century, were quite good for the better part of the amoraic period. In fact, the positive relationship of Sepphoris and Rome seems to have been longstanding, reaching back to the First Revolt.[103]

Moreover, as a rule, Cappadocians are regarded rather favorably in rabbinic literature.[104] Sensitivity toward the needs of Jews living in Cappadocia was expressed in the tannaitic period, when the sages permitted these Jews to use naphtha for their sabbath lights, since it was the only oil available.[105] Two Palestinian *amoraim* of roughly the time of R. Immi (Ammi) were known to have come from Cappadocia, R. Samuel *Qappodqayaʾ* and R. Yannai *Qappodqayaʾ*. In addition, there is R. Yudan *Qappodqayaʾ* of the early to mid–4th century.[106] As for our passage, it would seem that the number of Cappadocians at Sepphoris was insignificant, since otherwise it is difficult to understand why the possibility of annulling their ownership before the compatriots was not considered. Alternatively, as Y. Feliks suggests, relations among the very Cappadocians intended may not have been all that great; native residents of Sepphoris may not have been those who were unwilling to greet the Cappadocians.[107] The *gemara* simply does not allow for any generalizations about xenophobia or antagonism on the part of the Sepphoreans at large. The sentiment here is nothing like the frequent taunts we hear of Babylonians who resided in *ʾEreṣ Yisraʾel*, and even where these foreigners are concerned, there are occasional admissions that even they have positive attributes.[108]

101. Ibid., 124.

102. See B. G. Nathanson, "Jews, Christians, and the Gallus Revolt in Fourth Century Palestine," *BA* 49 (1986) 26–36.

103. See my "Intercity Relations," 7.

104. In general, see S. Safrai, *Ha-ʿAliyah Le-Regel Bi-Yeme Ha-Bayit Ha-Sheni* (Jerusalem: Akademon, 1965) 69 [Heb.]. There is epigraphic evidence for a Jew of Cappadocia in Jaffa. See p. 86 n. 266.

105. Interestingly, R. Yoḥanan ben Nuri, who is associated with Sepphoris in at least a couple of traditions (*t. Meg.* 2.4; *t. Kelim B. Bat.* 2.2), supports the Cappadocians' right to use naphtha at *y. Šabb.* 2.4d. Büchler ("Familienreinheit," 185) suggests that Yoḥanan may have been at Sepphoris following the Bar Kokhba revolt. Also, see E. E. Urbach, "*Mi-Yehudah La-Galil*," in *Sefer Zikaron Le-Yaʿaqov Fridman* (ed. S. Pines; Jerusalem, 1974) 64 [Heb.].

106. On a number of occasions, R. Yudan *Qappodqayaʾ* quotes R. Yehudah ben Pazi, on whom see *Esth. Rab.* 4:4 and above, nn. 53 and 55. See *y. Ber.* 4.7c; *y. Taʿan.* 2.66a and 4.67c. Yannai *Qappodqayaʾ* is the most obscure, appearing only at *y. B. Bat.* 8.16a.

107. See Y. Feliks, *Talmud Yerushalmi, Masekhet Sheviʿit* (Jerusalem: Rubin Mass, 1986) 2.264.

108. See J. Schwartz, "Tensions between Palestinian Scholars and Babylonian Olim in Amoraic Palestine," *JSJ* 11 (1980) 78–94.

The Butchers of Sepphoris

Two traditions cast aspersions on the butchers of the city. Y. *Šeqal.* 7.50c reports an incident in which a butcher who was unwilling to sell meat to a Jew is suspected of dealing in *nevelot.*[109] A *maʿaseh* then has Rabbi declare the Jewish *macellum* of Sepphoris permitted, nonetheless.[110] Another *maʿaseh* reported in *Lev. Rab.* 5:6 in the name of R. Aibo,[111] a 4th-century Palestinian *amora*, reports that a butcher who had sold *nevelot* and *ṭerefot*[112] to his fellow Jews in Sepphoris got drunk on the eve of Yom Kippur[113] and fell to his death from a rooftop; whereupon, Ḥanina bar Ḥama was asked whether it was permissible to move the corpse on the holiday. In response, Ḥanina quotes Exod 22:30, "You shall be holy people to Me; you must not eat flesh torn by beasts in the field; you shall cast it to the dogs," and comments: "This one who stole dogs and fed Israel *nevelot* and *ṭerefot*—allow them (the dogs) to eat of him as if they are eating one of their own."

That there would be untrustworthy Jewish butchers in Sepphoris would be remarkable if indeed there were no other types. In point of fact, there are a number of recollections that portray highly reputable Sepphorean butchers who were noted for their abilities. Thus *t. Ḥul.* 3.2 names the head butcher (*r'osh ṭabaḥim*) of Sepphoris, ben Shila, who testifies on behalf of R. Natan, a contemporary of Rabbi, about the anatomy of cattle. The parallel version in the Babylonian Talmud (*b. Ḥul.* 50b) actually has Natan bar (*sic*) Shila offer his testimony in the presence of Rabbi at Sepphoris.[114] Evidently he is regarded as an expert who can quote sages. The Babylonian Talmud (*b. B. Qam.* 99b) also preserves a report attributed to Rabbah b. bar Ḥanah, a 4th-

109. That is, meat of an improperly slaughtered animal or of one that met a violent death, both of which are rendered carrion. Actually the concern here is whether meat found in the hands of a Gentile is permissible to a Jew. In the present case, the Jew eventually sends a Roman to purchase meat for him from the unwilling butcher, who either provides him with *nevelot* (*Qorban Ha-ʿEdah*, ad loc.) or is willing to sell the meat only after the Roman provides him with *nevelot* (*Pene Mosheh*, ad loc.) in return. Also see B. Ratner, *Sefer 'Ahavat Ṣiyyon Vi-Yerushalyim: Sheqalim* (10 vols.; reprinted, Jerusalem, 1967) 48 [Heb.].

110. Cf. the ruling attributed to Rabbi at *b. Ḥul.* 95a, which appears to be derived from this incident.

111. The parallels in *y. Ter.* 8.45c and *y. ʿAbod. Zar.* 2.41a are unattributed.

112. Meat of an animal that is discovered, once slaughtered, to have had a fatal disease or injury.

113. The version in *y. Terumot* has 'the eve of the Sabbath' (*ʿerev shabbat*), but see the comments of M. Margaliot, *Midrash Vayiqra' Rabbah* (5 vols. in 3; Jerusalem: Wahrmann, 1972) 1.119–20.

114. Note that the Babylonian Talmud uses *bar* instead of *ben* and provides ben Shila with the name *Natan*, which may be a carry-over from R. Natan, in whose name the butcher reports. The same is true at *b. Ḥul.* 58b, where a different aspect of the anatomy of cattle is reported by bar Shila in R. Natan's name.

century Babylonian *amora*, that R. Yoḥanan once stated that a ritual slaughterer who did not properly perform his skill was obliged to pay the owner of the animal, "even if he was as skillful as the slaughterers of Sepphoris!"[115]

Summary and Conclusions

Our analysis does not allow for any broad generalizations about the character of the Sepphoreans or, for that matter, how they are depicted in rabbinic sources. The rivalry we hear of between the councillors and commoners in 3d-century Sepphoris afforded the opportunity for the rabbis to foster the notion that the acquisition of Torah knowledge entitled even the *pagani* to respect and honor. Along the same lines, it is unlikely that the 2d- and 3d-century circles responsible for negative reports concerning the priests of Sepphoris who once served at the Temple harbored especially ill feelings toward the priests who lived in the city during their day. These circles probably shared the overall rabbinic view that men born into the priestly class, as with other *honestiores*, deserved honor only when they applied themselves to the teachings of the Torah.

115. אפילו הוא אומן כטבחי ציפורי. Cf. Z. Safrai (*The Economy of Roman Palestine* [London: Routledge, 1994] 217), who suggests that the ritual slaughterers in larger towns had greater expertise. For a remarkable passage that has a butcher strike the 3d-century sage R. Zeira upon his arrival from Babylonia, see, *y. Ber.* 2.5c. This source may reflect tensions between Babylonian emigrants and Tiberian locals. See Levine, *Rabbinic Class*, 125; and cf. Schwartz, "Tension between Palestinian Scholars and Babylonian Olim," 91–92. Butchers, tanners, smiths, craftsmen, shopkeepers, and others who belonged to similar occupations were despised by the upper classes in the Roman Empire. This attitude does not, however, appear to have been shared by the rabbis, at least not to the same extent. See R. MacMullen, *Roman Social Relations: 50 B.C. to A.D. 284* (New Haven: Yale University Press, 1974) 114–15, 120; and S. Baron, *A Social and Religious History of the Jews* (New York: Columbia University / Philadelphia: Jewish Publication Society, 1952) 2.256. The rabbis, as opposed to the Roman intelligentsia, had a general appreciation for labor. See M. Aberbach, *Labor, Crafts and Commerce in Ancient Israel* (Jerusalem: Magnes, 1994) 91–125. At times, however, their comments reflect the animosity *of the masses* toward certain occupations. See M. Ayyali, *Poʿalim Ve-ʾOmanim: Melaʾkhtam U-Maʿamadam Be-Sifrut Ḥazal* (Givatayim: Masada, 1987) 79–101 [Heb.]. In view of these varied assessments, it is difficult to ascertain the attitude at Sepphoris toward any particular profession. Gristmakers of Sepphoris are singled out for a halakhic stringency at *y. Moʿed Qaṭ.* 2.81b and *b. Moʿed Qaṭ.* 13b. Similarly, the behavior of Sepphorean weavers seems to be regarded positively at *y. B. Bat.* 2.13b, at least according to most commentators. See, for example, H. Daiches, *Netivot Yerushalayim, Babaʾ Batraʾ* (London, 1927) ad loc. Contrast, however, the comments of S. Lieberman, in *Yerushalmi Neziqin* (ed. E. S. Rosenthal; Jerusalem: Israel Academy of Arts and Sciences, 1983) 181. Other interesting portrayals of workers at Sepphoris include a fuller at *y. Kil.* 9.32b, bakers at *y. Sanh.* 3.21b, and a tailor at *Cant. Rab.* 6:12. All of these characterizations are either neutral or positive.

As for the attacks on the dignity of the rabbis of Sepphoris, these too are hardly exceptional. The objection of the *Ṣippora'e* who contest R. Yose's commendation of R. Meir is framed in a stock rabbinic literary formula for presenting the ultimate virtues and/or abilities of a scholar whose opinions or behavior are seemingly objectionable. The rabbis involved in these episodes may criticize one another, but the outcome is usually the same; the reputation of the sage whose abilities are questioned is upheld. In any event, such criticism is similarly presented with respect to rabbis who lived elsewhere. At the same time, Ḥanina bar Ḥama's acerbic counter assertion that the *Ṣippora'e* were not receptive to Torah, resembles charges leveled by rabbis at other people in other towns and places. Holy men at Sepphoris *and elsewhere* received not only acclaim but also the abuse that went along with their charisma and status, and they no doubt knew how to respond in kind.[116]

The remaining traditions only confirm just how ordinary life at Sepphoris must have been. People attending funerals at Sepphoris were probably no more unruly than people anywhere else; the desire to be among the first to greet the mourners could hardly have been peculiar to the Sepphoreans. Some crafty Sepphoreans attending Ḥanina's *derashah* on the generation of the flood may have learned a lesson in thievery, but the more likely point of the exegesis is that human nature is often resistant to change—each generation has its thieves. The butchers of 2d- and 3d-century Sepphoris included dishonest dealers in *nevelot* and *ṭerefot*, for whom the rabbis everywhere were on the lookout, but more remarkable is the way in which Sepphorean *ṭabaḥim* are singled out for their abilities and knowledge. Cappadocians of the 3d century could very well have found that their minority status at Sepphoris set them apart, but they in no way met with the kind of opposition that the Babylonians and Southerners often faced in *'Ereṣ Yisra'el*. Moreover, the rabbis were at least sympathetic to the plight of the Cappadocians.

Classical sources abound in negative characterizations of residents of some of the well-known cities of the Roman Empire. Dio Chrysostom, writing in the late first–early 2d centuries, in fact provides us with the etiology of a city's reputation:[117]

> . . . all varieties of human weakness might be discovered anywhere at all, and drunkards, perverts, and woman-crazed wretches are present in every city; and

116. Note *t. Soṭa* 3.16, where R. Yose (MS Erfurt: R. Nehora'i, also a 2d-century *tanna*) criticizes both the *bene Teveryah* ('sons of Tiberias') and the *bene Ṣippori* for not cutting their hair in honor of the Sabbath, something that even Absalom was said to have done! See Lieberman, *Tosepta' Ki-Feshutah*, 8.643. For other traditions in which the Tiberians and Sepphoreans are compared or contrasted, see my "Intercity Relations," 10–11.

117. Chrysostom *Or.* 32.91. All translations of Dio Chrysostom follow J. W. Cohoon and H. L. Crosby (trans.), *Dio Chrysostom* (5 vols.; LCL; London: Heinemann / Cambridge: Harvard University Press, 1961 reprint) 3.261.

> yet not even that condition is disturbing or beyond endurance; but when the malady becomes prevalent and a common spectacle, then it becomes noteworthy and serious and a civic issue.

Residents of cities could also gain good reputations. Thus Dio comments that the Athenians were admired because of their devotion to speech, poetry, choral song, and dance, and the Spartans acquired a love of honor. Dio warns residents of cities to "take care lest the reputation that you gain resemble not that of the Athenians and the Spartans, but rather that of certain others—for I do not care to name them."[118]

Dio in fact *does* name "them." Thus he describes the contemptible behavior of the Alexandrians, who behave poorly in the theater and stadium where they are uninhibited, saying and doing anything they like; they are oblivious to the show and act "out of their senses, deranged, not only for men, but even women and children."[119] Indeed, the Alexandrians are "not sensible, temperate or just," and life with them has become a continuous "revel of dancers, whistlers, and murderers."[120] Confusion in general rules the lives of the Alexandrians who lack self-control and are known for their frivolity.[121] Dio's summation of the reputation of the Alexandrians is worth quoting in full:[122]

> And certainly it is disgraceful, men of Alexandria, that those who inquire about your city are told how wonderful everything else is here, but that with respect to yourselves nothing is mentioned of which to be proud or fit to emulate, but that, on the contrary, you are given a bad name as being worthless fellows, mere mimes and buffoons instead of men of real valour, as one of the comic poets said of people like yourselves, "An unbridled mob, a disorderly gang of tars."[123]

Dio is not alone in his assessment of the Alexandrians. Philo also spoke of the "lazy and unoccupied mob" of Alexandria as "a multitude well practiced in idle talk, who devote their leisure to slandering and evil speaking."[124] Nor are Alexandians the only city dwellers to have gained notoriety.[125] Philostratus, writing in the late 2d–early 3d century, relates how Apollonius of Tyana urged the Ephesians to pursue philosophy rather than idleness and revelry. The city

118. *Or.* 32.93 (Cohoon and Crosby, 3.261–63).
119. *Or.* 32.41–42 (Cohoon and Crosby, 3.213).
120. *Or.* 32.69 (Cohoon and Crosby, 3.239–41).
121. *Or.* 32.73 (Cohoon and Crosby, 3. 243–45).
122. *Or.* 32.86 (Cohoon and Crosby, 3.255).
123. See Euripides *Hecuba* 607, which has ἀναρχία instead of ἀταξία. See Cohoon and Crosby, *Dio Chrysostom*, 3.254–55 n. 2.
124. Philo *Flaccum* 33. For the rendering presented here, see F. H. Colson and G. H. Whitaker (trans.), *Philo* (10 vols.; LCL; London: Heinemann / Cambridge: Harvard University Press, 1929–68) 9.321.
125. Cf. above, n. 99, on crime in the villages of Roman Egypt.

of Ephesus was "full of pipers, effeminate rascals and noise."[126] Apollonius, Philostratus says, was forced at one point to sail from Seleucia rather than from Antioch, where the people "displayed their customary insolence and took no interest in any affairs of the Hellenes." Indeed, it took an earthquake to reconcile the various feuding factions of Antioch![127]

Neither the residents of Sepphoris nor, for that matter, residents of any other major town of *ʾEreṣ Yisraʾel*, are consistently vilified in such vivid terms in rabbinic sources. Aside from an occasional report that reflects poorly on some Sepphoreans, there are also allusions to the exemplary behavior of other elements and to the positive relationships that were engendered within the city. Thus the judges of Sepphoris (*dayyane Ṣippori*) are singled out for a legal opinion in the Mishnah,[128] the *benot Ṣippori* were remembered for their devotion to the Temple,[129] and the *gedole Ṣippori* seek out the advice of the sages who honor them.[130]

In the final analysis, the enduring, negative portrayal of the Sepphoreans is ultimately the creation of scholars, à la Büchler, who took a few juicy reports and distorted the entire picture.[131] Talmudic Sepphoris was undoubtedly a vibrant urban center in which rich and poor, aristocrat and commoner, city dweller and peasant, priest and nonpriest, foreigner and native, and, as the rabbis were acutely aware, learned and unlearned came into contact. Perhaps as they moved to the larger towns in the 3d century and beyond, the rabbis' perceptions of these contacts and of city folk in general continued to be shaped by the well-documented rural bias of antiquity.[132] Our inquiry, how-

126. Philostratus *Life of Apollonius of Tyana* 4.2; F. C. Conybeare (trans.), *Philostratus: The Life of Apollonius of Tyana, The Epistles of Apollonius and the Treatise of Eusebius* (2 vols.; LCL; London: Heinemann / New York: Macmillan, 1912) 1.351.

127. Philostratus *Life of Apollonius of Tyana* 3.58, 6.38 (Conybeare, *Philostratus*, 1.345). Philostratus also has Apollonius rebuke the Alexandrians, but here he may be mimicking Dio. See C. P. Jones, *The Roman World of Dio Chrysostom* (Cambridge: Harvard University Press, 1978) 43.

128. M. *B. Bat.* 6:7. Cf. *b. B. Bat.* 100b. See G. Alon, "Those Appointed for Money: On the History of the Various Juridical Authorities in Eretz-Israel in the Talmudic Period," *Jews, Judaism and the Classical World: Studies in Jewish History in the Time of the Second Temple and Talmud* (Jerusalem: Magnes, 1977) 384 n. 35. Also see *m. Qidd.* 4:5, where R. Yose mentions the 'old archives of Sepphoris' (ערכי הישנה של צפורי), which were regarded a reliable source for information about genealogies. See Zuri, *Toledot Ha-Mishpaṭ Ha-Ṣibburi Ha-ʿIvri*, 119; and cf. my discussion, *Studies*, 46–55.

129. *y. Maʿaś. Š.* 5.56a (= *Lam. Rab.* 3:9).

130. See above. Also n. 115, where various workers at Sepphoris whose practices were regarded in a positive light by the rabbis are noted.

131. To be sure, the negative reports found in the Jerusalem Talmud were already noted by Z. Fraenkel (*Mevoʾ Ha-Yerushalmi* [Breslau, 1870] 4b [Heb.]), but Büchler's work has been most influential.

132. See especially, MacMullen, *Roman Social Relations*, 32. On the rural framework of much of the rabbis' mindset, see J. Neusner, "The Experience of the City in

ever, suggests that their determination to promote the *keter* ('crown') of *Torah* over *kehunah* ('priesthood') and *malkhut* ('royalty') prompted many if not most of their observations.[133] The residents of Sepphoris, therefore, should hardly be seen as an unusually reprehensible lot.

Late Antique Judaism," in *Approaches to Ancient Judaism*, vol. 5: *Studies in Judaism and Its Greco-Roman Context* (ed. W. S. Green; Atlanta: Scholars Press, 1985) 37–52.

133. Cf. Cohen, *The Three Crowns*, 147–212. By the 3d century, the rabbis regarded the true guardians of a town (*neture qarta'*) to be its Bible teachers and instructors of tannaitic tradition (*safrin u-matnayynin*), not its 'watchmen' (*santure qarta'*). See *y. Ḥag.* 1.76c.

The Sukkot Wine Libation

Jeffrey L. Rubenstein
New York University

Sukkot was the leading cultic festival throughout the Second Temple Period. After the autumnal harvest brought the agricultural year to its close, vast crowds made the pilgrimage to the Jerusalem Temple to celebrate and give thanks. The beginning of the rainy season, Sukkot was also the festival at which the cult sought to ensure ample rain for the coming year. Elaborate rituals including processions, vigils, fertility rites, and prayers were directed to this end. Each day a priest poured a double libation of water and wine upon the altar. Water was drawn from the Siloam Pool, carried with great fanfare in a formal procession to the Temple, and placed in a bowl set on the south-western corner of the altar.[1] The priest poured a libation of wine into a second bowl in such a way that the two libations flowed onto the altar simultaneously. Rabbinic descriptions of the libation procession, its preparatory all-night celebration, the great joy experienced, and the crowds in attendance make it clear that the ceremony was of great significance.[2] The

Author's note: Our teacher Baruch Levine has contributed a great deal to our knowledge of the cult, and it is an honor to dedicate this study of a cultic ritual to him.

1. M. *Sukk.* 4:9–10. The procession did not take place on the Sabbath.

2. M. *Sukk.* 4:9–10; *t. Sukk.* 3.3, 14–16; *b. Sukk.* 48b, *y. Sukk.* 4.8, 54d. The importance of the rite is seen in the Mishnaic tradition that a priest who performed the libation incorrectly was pelted with citrons by the incensed crowd (*m. Sukk.* 4:8). This tradition is generally interpreted as evidence of a conflict between the Pharisees and Sadducees concerning the oral law, since the libation is not explicitly mentioned in scripture. Elsewhere I have questioned this interpretation ("The Sadducees and the Water Libation," *JQR* 84 [1994] 413–40), but the pelting demonstrates that the people considered the libation of such importance that they took drastic action when some aspect of the rite was not performed properly. Improper performance of the ritual jeopardized the expected effect—the production of copious rain—which would have disastrous consequences. In what may be a parallel tradition, the historian Josephus reports that Alexander Janneus was pelted by citrons when he stood to sacrifice

water libation was a rain-making ritual, as both rabbinic sources and the comparative study of religion attest[3] and has merited a great deal of scholarly interest.[4] The background and function of the wine libation is less clear, and it is rarely mentioned either in studies of the water libation or in general treatments of the Sukkot rituals.[5] This study attempts to fill this lacuna by investigating the origin and function of the Sukkot wine libation.

---

at the altar, although he does not mention the libation specifically (*Ant.* 13.372). This account also reflects the large crowds in attendance and the great importance associated with the festival rituals.

3. Rabbinic sources: *t. Roš Haš.* 1.12; *t. Sukk.* 3.18; *Sipre Bemidbar* (ed. S. Horovitz; Jerusalem: Wahrmann, 1966) 196, §150. Comparative studies: G. Frazier, *The Golden Bough* (3d ed.; New York: Macmillan, 1935) 1.248ff.; M. Grunwald, "Zur Vorgeschichte des Sukkothrituals," *Jahrbuch für jüdische Volkskunde* 25 (1923) 50; J. Jeremias, "Golgotha und der Heilige Felsen," *Angelos* 2 (1926) 74–128; R. Patai, *Man and Temple* (New York: Ktav, 1947) 35–36.

4. L. Herzfeld, *Geschichte des Volkes Israel* (Braunschweig: Westermann, 1847–63) 3.124–25; H. Graetz, *Geschichte der Juden* (5th ed.; ed. M. Brann; Leipzig: Leiner, 1905) 3.140–43; A. Geiger, "Biblische und thalmudische Miscellen," *Jüdische Zeitschrift* 5 (1867) 108–9; J. Hochman, *Jerusalem Temple Festivities* (London: Routledge, 1911); L. Finkelstein, *The Pharisees: The Sociological Background of Their Faith* (3d ed.; Philadelphia: Jewish Publication Society, 1962) civ–cxii, 102–15; S. Zeitlin, *Studies in the Early History of Judaism* (3 vols.; New York: Ktav, 1973–78) 2.276–77; J. le Moyne, *Les Sadducéens* (Paris: Gabalda, 1972) 285–87; A. Rofé, "The Onset of Sects in Postexilic Judaism," in *The Social World of Formative Christianity and Judaism* (ed. J. Neusner; Philadelphia: Fortress, 1988) 40–41; R. Patai, *Hamayim* (Tel Aviv: Dvir, 1936) 52–63; idem, *Man and Temple*, 23–52; W. Oesterly, "Early Hebrew Festival Rituals," in *Myth and Ritual* (ed. S. Hooke; London: Oxford University Press, 1933) 111–46; D. Feuchtwang, "Das Wasseropfer und die Damit Verbundenen Zeremonien," *MGWJ* 54 (1910) 535–52, 713–29; 55 (1911) 43–63; Jeremias, "Golgotha," 100–104.

5. J. Licht, "Sukkot," *Encyclopaedia Biblica* 5.1037–44; S. Safrai, *ʿAliyah Laregel Biyeme Bayit Šeni* (Tel-Aviv: ʿAm Hasefer, 1965); A. J. Wensinck, *Arabic New Year and the Feast of Tabernacles* (Amsterdam: Uitgave van de Koninklijke Academie van Wetenschappen te Amsterdam, 1925); H. Riesenfeld, *Jésus Transfiguré* (Copenhagen: Munksgaard, 1947); H. Ulfgard, *Feast and Future: Revelation 7:9–17 and the Feast of Tabernacles* (Stockholm: Almqvist & Wiksell, 1989); Patai, *Man and Temple*, 24–104. The lack of attention to the wine libation is perhaps explained by the fact that wine libations typically accompanied animal sacrifices throughout the year. A wine libation on Sukkot was routine. However the mixing of the wine and water libations on Sukkot is an independent ritual that points to the special importance of the Sukkot wine libation. In addition, ordinary wine libations were probably poured on the base of the altar. Only on Sukkot were wine libations poured together with the water libation into bowls perched on the corner of the altar. See Maimonides, *Mishneh Torah*, Laws of Daily and Additional Offerings 10:6–9, Laws of Sacrifices 2:1 and *Kesep Mishneh*, ad loc. This is confirmed by the eyewitness testimony of Sir 50:14–15: "He stretched out his hand to the cup, and poured out some of the blood of the grape. He poured it out at the foot or the altar, a pleasing odor unto the Most High, the King

Wine in Biblical Religion

A vintage festival followed the autumnal harvest throughout biblical times.[6] In Judg 9:27 the Shechemites gather to tread their grapes and celebrate a festival of jubilation (*hillûlîm*). They then return to their temple and enjoy a sacred feast. Judg 21:19 reports of an annual pilgrimage festival celebrated at Shiloh. That the Benjaminites hide in the vineyards to carry off the women dancing there points to a vintage celebration.[7] In Israel grapes ripen in August and September and are harvested at this time, so the festivals at Shechem and Shiloh were undoubtedly celebrated then.[8] The dancing, feasting, and ecstatic celebration of the *hillûlîm* are typical elements of harvest festivals and recall the rejoicing characteristic of Sukkot. Moreover, the origin of the custom of residing in festival booths probably derives from the shady booths erected for watchmen in vineyards and used as shelters by the workers during their arduous vintage labors. Thus the origin of the central festival rite reveals a strong connection to vintage celebrations.

The Covenant Code refers to the autumnal festival as the 'festival of ingathering' (*ʾasip*), without specifying the object of the harvest (Exod 23:16). Lev 23:39 also mentions the gathering of the fruit of the land in general terms. Deut 16:13–15, however, the first source to call the autumnal festival Sukkot, explicitly mentions the "ingathering from the threshing places and wine-press." The background is again the vintage, while the emphasis on rejoicing echoes the *hillûlîm* of Judges 9. Thus both narrative and legal traditions

---

of All." (So the Greek. The Hebrew preserves essentially the same reading.) I say "probably" (and cite Maimonides' interpretation) because the rabbinic sources are ambiguous; see *Sipre Num.* 110, §107; *m. Zebaḥ.* 6:2; and *b. Zebaḥ.* 91b. In any case, the use of wine in the cult antedates the libations prescribed by the Priestly Code to accompany animal sacrifices.

6. J. Pedersen, *Israel: Its Life and Culture* (London: Oxford University Press, 1926–40) 2.418; J. Wellhausen, *Prolegomena to the History of Ancient Israel* (New York: Meridian, 1878) 94.

7. R. de Vaux, *Ancient Israel: Its Life and Institutions* (trans. J. McHugh; New York: McGraw-Hill, 1961) 495.

8. Wellhausen, *Prolegomena*, 93–94; de Vaux, *Ancient Israel*, 495, 501–2; Pedersen, *Israel*, 2.418–19; G. W. MacRae, "The Meaning and Evolution of the Feast of Tabernacles," *CBQ* 22 (1960) 251–76; J. Döller, "Der Wein im Bibel und Talmud," *Bib* 4 (1923) 157–58; W. Dommershausen, "Yayin," *TDOT* 6.60. However, Y. Kaufmann (*Toledot Haʿemunah Hayiśreʾelit* [4 vols.; Jerusalem: Bialik, 1937–56] 2.135–56) and M. Haran (*Temples and Temple-Service in Ancient Israel* [Oxford: Clarendon, 1978; reprinted Winona Lake, Ind.: Eisenbrauns, 1985] 299) do not associate these celebrations with the autumnal festival. Wellhausen (*Prolegomena*, 94–95), de Vaux (*Ancient Israel*, 496), and others suggest that the autumnal festival is the annual pilgrimage to which 1 Sam 1:3 alludes. Eli may have assumed that Hannah was drunk from the wine typically consumed at such vintage festivals (1 Sam 1:14). As in Judg 21:19, the festival took place at Shiloh.

testify that the autumnal festival included a vintage celebration. In most agricultural societies wine has great importance, both for cultic and popular use, and popular vintage celebrations are almost universal.[9]

The wine or vintage celebration associated with the autumnal festival may have been a firstfruit festival in part. In the early period of Israelite worship the three annual harvest festivals were occasions for bringing firstfruits,[10] which biblical legislation required from all crops.[11] Before its linkage to the Pesaḥ sacrifice, the *maṣṣôt* festival was a ritual feast of the firstfruits of the harvest hastily baked into coarse bread.[12] The communal counterpart to the *maṣṣôt* was the sheaf (*ʿōmer*), the first of the new crop presented at the Temple (Lev 23:9–14). On the second pilgrimage festival, which celebrates the completion of the grain harvest (the *ḥag haqqāṣîr*; Exod 23:16), two loaves of bread served as an offering of the firstfruits of grain in mature form (Lev 23:15–21).[13] The name of the festival, *yōm habbikkurîm* 'the Day of Firstfruits', expresses this understanding of the loaves (Num 28:26).[14] On Sukkot, the final harvest of the year, grapes and olives were the chief firstfruit offerings, as the vintage and olive-harvest took place at this time.[15] These may have been brought in the form of wine and oil, the completed products of the vat and winepress.[16] It is also possible that the commandment of Lev 23:40 to bring the "fruit of goodly trees," later interpreted as the citron, originally instructed the Israelite to bring the most beautiful firstfruits of his trees.

9. See the bibliography in H. Seeseman, "OINOS," *TDNT* 5.162; and C. Seltman, *Wine in the Ancient World* (London: Routledge & Kegan Paul, 1957) 3.

10. Exod 23:17–19, 34:23–6. Wellhausen, *Prolegomena*, 89; Pedersen, *Israel*, 3.305–6. Deut 16:13–17 commands that when pilgrims come to celebrate the three annual festivals they must bring gifts, a later reflex of the common practice of bringing firstfruits at these times. The elaborate description of the ritual in Deuteronomy 26, however, does not link the firstfruits to any particular time of year. See Philo *Special Laws* 2.220–22.

11. Exod 23:19, 34:26; Deut 26:2; Ezek 44:30; Neh 10:36. Thus Philo (*Special Laws* 2.216) writes that firstfruits come from every fruit. On the rabbinic law, see p. 587.

12. De Vaux, *Ancient Israel*, 490; Wellhausen, *Prolegomena*, 87.

13. Deut 16:9–12 calls it "the Festival of Weeks" and does not mention the loaves.

14. Assuming that Num 28:26 refers to the same festival as Lev 23:15–21. On the differences between P (Num 28:26) and H (Lev 23:17), see I. Knohl, "The Priestly Torah versus the Holiness School: Sabbath and the Festivals," *HUCA* 58 (1987) 81–85.

15. See n. 8. Num 13:20 notes that the spies entered Israel at the "season of the firstfruits of grapes."

16. The LXX translates Exod 22:28, מלאתך ודמעך לא תאחר 'You shall not hold back the firstfruits of your threshing-floor and press' (NJPSV = 'you shall not put off the skimming of the first yield of your vats'). Also see Pedersen, *Israel*, 2.301; and Wellhausen, *Prolegomena*, 92–99.

Beyond the role of wine in the autumnal festival and as firstfruit offerings, wine libations came to play a wider role in temple worship. Hosea warns the Northern tribes that, because of their corruption, God finds their wine libations and sacrifices unacceptable.[17] Joel laments that "offering and libation have ceased from the House of the Lord."[18] The Psalms, many of which served as cultic liturgy, imply that libations were regular rituals.[19] Libations of wine are prevalent in the Priestly Code, although these libations generally accompany the sacrifices and do not comprise independent rites.[20] Of course the practice of wine libations suggests that wine was regularly consumed in the context of cultic worship. Libations were a tribute to God, but humans enjoyed the bulk of the wine. Thus Amos 2:8 protests those who "drink in the House of their God wine bought with fines they imposed."[21] Drinking wine in the Temple is fine, but the wine must not be purchased with ill-gotten funds. Isa 62:8–9 may even point to a wine festival within the Temple precincts: "Strangers shall not drink your wine for which you have labored; rather, they who have gathered it shall eat it and praise (*hillēlû*) the Lord, and those who have collected it shall drink it in the courts of my sanctuary."[22] Sacrificial feasts probably included wine, although the first explicit testimony to this practice is late.[23]

Libations and vintage celebrations were also prominent in "popular religion." Wine "gladdens God and men" and was considered a cherished

17. Hos 9:4. These libations were brought on the "feast days" and "festivals" mentioned in the next verse. See F. I. Andersen and D. N. Freedman, *Hosea* (AB 24; Garden City, N.Y.: Doubleday, 1980) 529.

18. Joel 1:9. See also 1:4–8, 2:14, 2:19, 2:24, 4:14, 4:18.

19. A. Weiser, *The Psalms* (trans. H. Hartwell; Philadelphia: Westminster, 1959) 175, ad Ps 16:5; H. J. Kraus, *Worship in Israel* (Oxford: Blackwell, 1966) 22; R. Kittel, *Die Psalmen* (Leipzig: Deichert, 1914) 413. Josephus and the Mishnah report that a golden vine hung above the entrance to the temple, and it is likely that such a prominent icon had more than symbolic significance; see *m. Mid.* 3:8; Josephus *Ant.* 15.394; *J.W.* 5.210–11 (with grape clusters as tall as a man!).

20. Exod 29:40; Num 28:7ff.; 15:5, 7, 10, 24; 6:15, 17; Lev 23:13, 18, 37.

21. Cf. Isa 28:7, Lev 10:9, and Ezek 44:21.

22. The background of this prophecy is obscure. Medieval Jewish exegetes see a reference to second tithe or the fourth-year grapes (*kerem rivʿai*; Lev 19:23–25), which rabbinic law mandates be taken to Jerusalem and consumed there (see below). Yet the term "courts of the sanctuary" refers to the Temple courtyards, not simply to Jerusalem. A. Ehrlich (*Hamiqra Ki-fshuṭo* [reprinted New York: Ktav, 1969] 3.151) explains the allusion as wine consumed with animal sacrifices. C. Westermann (*Isaiah 40–66* [London: SCM, 1969] 378) suggests that the prophet speaks of the three pilgrimage festivals. Similarly, P. Volz (*Jesaiah II* [KAT 9; Leipzig: Scholl, 1932] ad loc.), taking note of the 'praise' (*hillĕlû*), connects the prophecy to the *hillûlîm* celebration of Judg 9:27 and to Sukkot. This accords nicely with my conclusions below.

23. *Jub.* 49:6 mentions that wine should be consumed together with the Pesaḥ offering.

blessing of God, so the Israelite could be expected to show his appreciation whenever he drank.[24] Indeed, wine libations were so pervasive that the prophets lament that they occur on the "rooftops and in the streets of Jerusalem," and "by every high hill and leafy tree."[25] The prophets rebuke the people for pouring such libations to foreign gods, not to YHWH, but we can be sure that YHWH received his due share as well.[26] Hosea castigates the deviant forms of behavior at harvest and vintage festivals: "You have loved fornication by every threshing floor and winepress; the new grain shall not join them, and the new wine shall fail them."[27] Jer 31:12–13 prophesies bounteous "new grain and wine and oil," at which time "maidens shall dance gaily, young men and old alike." The prophet probably has popular vintage celebrations in mind. Traces of such celebrations persist in rabbinic sources.[28]

Thus evidence of wine libations in both cultic and popular celebrations is ample. The ceremonial wine libation on Sukkot, poured together with the water as the culmination of the splendid procession, must have had great significance. But what was its specific nature and purpose? Only a few scholars have considered this question. R. Patai considers the wine libation to have been a rain-making ritual.[29] S. Mowinckel suggests that the wine libation served to ensure a successful grape harvest.[30] Both conjectures attempt to

24. Judg 9:13 (cf. Ps 104:15). Wine as blessing: Gen 27:28, 37; Amos 5:11; 9:14; Isa 16:10; 24:11; Jer 13:12; 40:10, 12; 48:33; Zeph 1:13; Mic 6:15; Joel 2:23. See also Gen 49:11; Exod 23:11; Lev 25:3; 26:5; Num 13:23; Deut 20:6; 28:39; Joel 4:18; Isa 25:6; Zech 3:10; Amos 9:13; 2 Chr 2:9.

25. Jer 19:13, Ezek 20:28. See also Jer 7:18, 32:29, 44:15–19; Isa 57:5, 65:11; Deut 32:38.

26. For meals with wine, see Deut 32:14, 1 Sam 25:36, 2 Sam 13:23, Isa 5:12, Qoh 9:7, etc. The tithe that must be brought to Jerusalem included wine, Deut 12:17; 14:23; Neh 13:5, 12.

27. Hos 9:2, as emended in the NJPSV translation. See Andersen and Freedman, *Hosea*, 515, 523.

28. The open space between adjacent vineyards, the *meḥol* (*m. Kil.* 4:2–3; *t. Kil.* 3.1), was a place for the dancing of vintage celebrations. See *Heʿarukh* (ed. A. Kohut; Vienna, 1878–92) 3.391–92, s.v. *ḥl.* M. *Taʿan.* 4:8 describes the halcyon days of Israel when the women danced in the vineyards while the men selected their brides. The purported dates are Yom Kippur (the tenth of Tishrei) and the fifteenth of Av. The tenth of Tishrei, five days before Sukkot, corresponds to the time of the vintage. (Should the fifteenth of Av be emended to the fifteenth of Tishrei?) And see J. Morgenstern, "Two Ancient Israelite Agricultural Festivals," *JQR* n.s. 8 (1917) 31–54.

29. Patai, *Man and Temple*, 36–37. Patai cites a few examples from Frazier (*Golden Bough*, 1.250; 2.367, 370), in which wine (and other liquids) is used in various rainmaking ceremonies. But the parallels are not convincing, and it is clear that the use of wine in this context is extremely rare.

30. S. Mowinckel, *Psalmen-studien II: Das Thronbesteigungsfest Jahwes und der Ursprung des Eschatologie* (reprinted Amsterdam: Schippers, 1961) 106; idem, *The Psalms in Israel's Worship* (trans. D. R. Ap-Thomas; Oxford: Blackwell, 1962) 1.131.

draw parallels between the two libations and interpret the wine in terms of the water: just as the water libation caused rain, so too the wine libation produced rain or produced its own source. G. W. MacRae is more on target when he suggests: "About the wine-pouring and its significance we know very little; perhaps it reflected an offering of the fruits of the grape-harvest."[31] This suggestion derives from general biblical legislation requiring firstfruit offerings from all fruits, including grapes.[32] Is there evidence of a ceremonial firstfruit offering of wine or an independent wine festival in post-biblical sources?

Postbiblical and Rabbinic Literature

The Qumran Scrolls describe in detail a festival of "new wine."[33] This festival is part of the series of firstfruit festivals occurring at fifty-day intervals. The feast of firstfruits of barley occurs on the first Sunday after Pesaḥ while Shavuot, the feast of firstfruits of wheat, takes place fifty days later, as prescribed by Lev 23:16–17. Fifty days later, on the third of the fifth month, the feast of firstfruits of new wine (*moʿēd hattîrōš*) occurs, and finally the feast of first fruits of oil takes place fifty days later on the twenty-second of the sixth month. Here the Qumran texts have preserved from ancient times observances that mark the importance of firstfruit offerings. Rabbinic tradition knows only of the new barley offering (the *ʿōmer*), brought on the second day of Pesaḥ, and the first wheat offering, brought in the form of two loaves on Shavuot, as spelled out in Lev 23:9–21.[34] For the rabbis the barley offering

31. G. W. MacRae, "The Meaning and Evolution of the Feast of Tabernacles," CBQ 22 (1960) 273. See also P. Volz, *Das Neujahrsfest Jahwes* (Tübingen: Mohr, 1912) 37. L. Venetianer ("Die eleusinische Mysterien im Tempel zu Jerusalem," *Populär wissenschaftliche Monatsblätter* 17 [1897] 170–81) exlains the wine as a reflex of a Dionysian festival imposed on the Jerusalem cult by the radical Hellenizers in pre-Maccabean times.

32. See n. 11.

33. J. M. Baumgarten ("The Laws of Orlah and First Fruits in Light of Jubilees, the Qumran Writings, and the Targum Ps.-Jonathan," *JJS* 38 [1987] 195–202 = *Studies in Qumran Law* [Leiden: Brill, 1977] 133–42) first reconstructed the festival on the basis of various fragments. The festival is explicitly mentioned in the Temple Scroll; see Y. Yadin, *The Temple Scroll* (Jerusalem: Israel Exploration Society, 1983) 1.108–11, 2.80–96, columns XIX–XXI. (The fragments are cited by Yadin, 2.80–81, 84–85.) The (reconstructed) calendar of 4QMMT also mentions these festivals. See Y. Sussmann, "The History of Halakha and the Dead Sea Scrolls: Preliminary Observations on Miqṣat Maʿaśe Ha-torah (4QMMT)," *Tarbiz* 59 (1989–90) 30 [Heb.]; and E. Qimron and J. Strugnell, *Qumran Cave 4*, vol. 5: *Miqṣat Maʿaśe Ha-Torah* (DJD 10; Oxford, Clarendon, 1994) 44.

34. Leviticus 23 does not specify that the *ʿōmer* is to be brought from barley, but that was the consensus of the rabbis (*b. Menaḥ*. 68b), Philo (*Special Laws* 2.17), Josephus (*Ant*. 3.250), and the *Temple Scroll* (although this part of the text is lost; see Yadin, *Temple Scroll*, 2.102).

permitted all grains—including wheat—for secular use. All grains, including barley, were proscribed from cultic use until after the Shavuot wheat offering.[35] The Mishnah also prohibits general firstfruit offerings and libations from the new wine before the barley offering but does not prohibit any secular consumption of wine or fruit.[36] In Qumran law, each firstfruit festival sanctioned use of its kind for both cultic and private use.[37] Hence consumption of new wine and oil could not precede the firstfruit offerings on the third of the fifth month, nor could libations of new wine be poured on the altar.[38] This conception of the festivals was apparently derived exegetically from Num 18:12, "All the best of the new oil, wine and grain—the choice parts (*rēʾšîtām*) that they present to the Lord—I give to you (the priests)," in combination with Lev 23:9–21.[39] Grain had its firstfruit festivals described in Leviticus 23, so wine and oil, grouped with grain in Numbers 18, deserved parallel festivals. And just as Lev 23:15–17 ordained a fifty-day interval between the firstfruit festivals of barley and wheat, so too the wine and oil festivals should come at fifty-day intervals.

In Qumran law the new wine offering consists of four *hîn* of wine, one-third of a *hîn* from each tribe.[40] Cereal offerings and twelve rams as burnt offerings accompany the libation, and other sacrifices are brought as well, based on Num 28:26. The ceremony takes place during the first quarter of the day. After the priests sacrifice the wine, "all the people both great and small" eat a feast in the outer courtyard and drink the new wine.[41] The scroll repeatedly stresses that it is a time of rejoicing and celebration.[42]

35. M. *Menaḥ.* 10:6.

36. Ibid.

37. See the fragment discussed by Baumgarten (*Studies*, 133–35) for prohibition against secular use. See 11QTemple XXI 7–8 (Yadin, *Temple Scroll*, 2.94) and Yadin's reconstruction of XXII 02–03 (2.98) for prohibition against cultic use. And see Baumgarten's review of Yadin, *JBL* 97 (108) 584–85.

38. Philo *Special Laws* 2.179–80, like the Qumran sect and against the rabbis, understood the Bible to prohibit use of new wheat until Shavuot. See also the sectarian tradition cited by Saadia, ascribed to "Judah the Alexandrian" (probably a medieval appellation for Philo) but almost identical to the Qumran tradition (cited in Baumgarten, *Studies*, 136 n. 21).

39. 'Grain, new wine and oil' (*dāgān tîrōš wĕyiṣhār*) is a Deuteronomic favorite (Deut 7:13, 11:14, 12:17, 14:23, 18:4, 28:51) and quite routine in the rest of the Bible as well (Jer 31:11; Hos 2:10; Joel 1:10; 2 Chr 31:5, 32:28; Neh 5:11, 10:40, 13:5, 13:12). Baumgarten (*Studies*, 142) suggests that the Qumran exegetes understood from Exod 22:28 that an offering from each major species was required.

40. In Num 15:7 one-third of a *hîn* of wine accompanies a ram offered as a *neder* or *nĕdābâ*.

41. Surprisingly the raison d'être of this feast seems to contradict other sources which suggest that the sect abstained from wine. Josephus, for example, omits wine in his description of Essene meals and stresses that they are always sober (*J.W.* 2.303). Yadin (*Temple Scroll*, 1.140, 142) resolved this contradiction by arguing that the sect

The Qumran wine festival recalls the account of the first vintage celebration, observed by Noah and his family, found in *Jub.* 7:1–6:

> (1) And in the seventh week in the first year in that Jubilee, Noah planted a vine on the mountain on which the ark rested, whose name is Lubar, (one) of the mountains of Ararat. And it produced fruit in the fourth year, and he guarded its fruit; and he picked it in that year in the seventh month, (2) and he made wine from it, and he put it in a vessel, and he guarded it until the fifth year, until the first day on the first of the first month. (3) And on that day he made a feast with rejoicing. And he made a burnt offering. . . . (5) And after that, he sprinkled wine in the fire which he had placed on the altar. And he presented frankincense upon the altar, and offered up a sweet odor which is pleasing before the Lord his God, (6) and rejoiced. And he drank some of that wine, he and his sons, with rejoicing.[43]

This festival is not an annual festival of the new wine, as in the Qumran scrolls, but relates to the first permitted consumption of fruit of a newly planted tree or vine (the law of *ʿorlâ*). Lev 19:23–25 prohibits consumption of the fruit during the first three years and enjoins "on the fourth year, all of its fruit shall be set aside for jubilation before the Lord. On the fifth year, you shall eat its fruit, that it may yield increased produce for you." Exactly what should be done with it in the fourth year and what "set aside for jubilation"

---

drank no wine at secular banquets but imbibed at the meals of Temple feasts. He eventually concluded that this was the only day of the year on which the sect drank wine. Yadin has probably overinterpreted Josephus here, who only means to portray the Essenes as highly disciplined religious virtuosi. See 1QS II 17–22, VI 4–5 (cited by Yadin himself, *Temple Scroll*, 2.140) and 1QH X 24, which prove that the sect did drink wine regularly. See also Baumgarten's review of Yadin, *JBL* 97 (108) 588. But if Yadin is correct, then the wine feast must have been of great importance. On this day alone even members of the sect renounced their usual abstinence, drank copiously of the new wine, and celebrated joyfully.

42. 11QTemple XXI 9–10 (Yadin, *Temple Scroll*, 2.95): "And they shall rejoice on [this da]y, [for they began] to pour out a strong drink offering, a new wine on the altar of the Lord, year by year." So the Rockefeller fragment (PAM 43.975, cited in Yadin, *Temple Scroll*, 2.91), lines 13–14. According to cols. XLIII–XLIV and *Jub.* 32:11–14, the consumption of the second tithe depends on the firstfruit festivals. Each year the tithes of oil, wine, and grain may only be consumed until the appropriate firstfruit festival of the coming year. Thus the tithes of wine had to be drunk prior to the third of the fifth month, the festival of the firstfruits of wine. Tithes not consumed by the deadlines were to be burned. This interpretation was far more strict than the rabbinic law, by which tithes could be stored until the "time of removal" (*m. Maʿaś. Š.* 5:6) every fourth year at Pesaḥ (based on Deut 26:12). Moreover, the *Temple Scroll* restricts consumption of tithes to the festivals and prohibits their consumption on "working days" (XLIV 16). It is likely that the tithes of wine were consumed at the wine feast, since they would have to be burned if retained after this date. See Baumgarten, *Studies*, 141–42; Yadin, *Temple Scroll*, 1.114–16; 2.181–84.

43. Translation from O. S. Wintermute, "Jubilees," in *OTP*, 2.68–69.

designates was disputed.[44] In rabbinic law these fruits (*ʿorlâ*) are brought to the temple and eaten there by the owner.[45] From Noah's actions it appears that the author of the *Jubilees* passage envisioned a popular festival at which the wine from the fourth year is consumed, although the festival only takes place on the first day of the fifth year. He interpreted the direction that the fruit be "set aside for jubilation" to mean that wine be set aside during that year and then used "for jubilation" at a later time. The festival must be deferred until the fifth year, for the verse only permits the owner to eat the fruits then.[46] Whether this protocol should be maintained with all fruits, as Leviticus implies, or grapes alone, is uncertain.[47] In any case, the vivid description of Noah's festival points to a wine festival of great joy, like that in the Qumran scrolls. Noah both sprinkles wine as a libation on the altar and then drinks from that wine. Note too that Noah picks the grapes in the seventh month, when Sukkot occurs, although he only celebrates the festival in the first month of the following year.

A similar tradition appears in several lines of the *Genesis Apocryphon* recently published by Menahem Kister, which the editors of the initial publication, N. Avigad and Y. Yadin, were not able to read.[48] The passage is an account of Noah's wine festival parallel to that of *Jub.* 7:1–7. Kister supplies the following translation:

> 13. [And] I and all my sons began to till the soil, and I planted a large vineyard in Mount Lubar. After four years it yielded wine for me.

44. Part of the dispute may derive from a textual variant, whether to read *hillûlîm* ('jubilation') or *ḥilûlîm* ('redemption'). See Kister, "Qumranic Halakhah" (see below, n. 48), 577 and the references in n. 21. The view of this passage contradicts the law of *Jub.* 7:36, cited below, in which the priests receive the fruit of the fourth year.

45. M. *Maʿaś. Š.* 5:1–5. Josephus also asserts that the produce of the fourth year must be taken to the holy city and spent "along with the tithe of his other fruits, in feasting with his friends, as also with orphans and widows" (*Ant.* 4.226).

46. See the remarkable parallel attributed (and dismissed as a corruption) by Tosafot, *b. Roš Haš.* 10a, s.v. *uperot* to *Halakhot Gedolot*: "And there are [versions of] *Halakhot Gedolot* in which it is written, 'The fruits of the fourth year, after they have been redeemed, are forbidden until [the fourth year] ends and the fifth begins.'" (In *Jubilees*, however, Noah merely sets aside the fruit; he does not redeem it.) Maimonides, *Mishneh Torah*, Laws of Forbidden Foods 10:18 attributes this ruling to the Geonim, and rejects it.

47. See M. Kasher, *Tirgume Hatorah*, part 1: *Torah Shelemah* (Jerusalem: American Biblical Encyclopedia Society, 1974) 24.150. Deut 20:6 singles out one who has planted a new vineyard, not any type of orchard, for exemption from battle.

48. Menahem Kister, "Some Aspects of Qumranic Halakhah," *The Madrid Qumran Congress* (ed. J. Trebolle Barrera and L. Vegas Montaner; Leiden: Brill, 1992) 2.576–88. The passage is from col. xii, and Kister has now added lines 14 and part of 15. Cf. N. Avigad and Y. Yadin, *A Genesis Apocryphon* (Jerusalem: Magnes / Shrine of the Book, 1956) 21.

14. _____ all _____ vac and when the first festival (*rigla'*) arrived, on the first day of the first festival of month
15. [____] __________ my vineyard, this *kumara'* I opened, and I began drinking it on the first day of the fifth year
16. [______]_____ on this day I called my sons and my sons' sons and the wives of all of us, and their daughters, and we met together and went
17. [____________]__ and I blessed the Lord of heaven, the Most High God, the Great Holy One, who saved us from destruction.

The "first festival" is apparently Sukkot, and it is on the first day of the festival that the *kumara'*, which Kister suggests is a type of vessel, is opened.[49] Kister takes this to mean that the vessel was opened and filled with wine and that the wine was "gathered in," which would parallel *Jub.* 7:1–3. But *Jubilees* refers to the seventh month, and the *Genesis Apocryphon* speaks of the first day of the festival. It cannot be that the labor of gathering in wine was conducted on the festival day. Rather, the text probably means that the vessel was opened and the wine used for a cultic ceremony on the festival. As in *Jubilees*, secular consumption of the wine was deferred until the beginning of the fifth year, when Noah and his family drink, to conform with Lev 19:25. Kister also mentions that Qimron deciphered the words "And I poured out . . . wine" in lines 18 and 19, which allude to a libation. That libation was presumably performed by Noah at his festival in the fifth year. Could the vessel have been opened and the wine used as a libation on Sukkot in the fourth year as well?

A second passage from *Jubilees* in fact describes a wine offering in the fourth year (*Jub.* 7:35–36):

49. The designation of Sukkot as the "first festival" or "first pilgrimage" is rare. Sukkot is the first pilgrimage festival after Rosh Hashanah, the New Year, and certainly could be designated the "first festival" on this basis. But Rosh Hashanah and Sukkot occur in the seventh month, and Pesaḥ is the first festival according to the cycle of months. *T. Roš Haš.* 1.2 (= *b. Roš Haš.* 4a–b) and *t. ʿArak.* 3.17–18 indeed designate Pesaḥ the first of the pilgrimage festivals. See also the references cited in S. Lieberman, *Tosefta Ki-fshutah* (Jerusalem: Jewish Theological Society, 1992) 5.1017–18. Moreover, Sukkot is the final harvest festival of the agricultural cycle. However, *Midraš ha-Gadol* to Lev 23:43 ([ed. A. Steinsalz; Jerusalem: Mosad Harav Kook, 1975] 657–58) contains a series of *derashot* that designate Sukkot as "the first." The exegetical difficulty is that the festival falls on the fifteenth day of the month, but Lev 23:43 instructs "you shall take on the first day." The *derashot* explain that the verse does not mean the first day of the month, but that Sukkot is called "first," either because it is the first time that rains should fall or the first opportunity to study Torah since the harvest labors have been completed or the beginning of a new reckoning of merit and sin. See too the fragments published by L. Ginzberg ("Three Incomplete Homilies from an Unknown Midrash," *Tarbiz* 4 [1933] 328 [Heb.]), which contain a similar tradition, and *Pesiqta de Rab Kahana* ([ed. B. Mandelbaum; New York: Jewish Theological Seminary, 1987] 412–13 ad 27:7). I am not sure, however, that these midrashic explanations of the meaning of "first day" shed light on Sukkot as the "first festival."

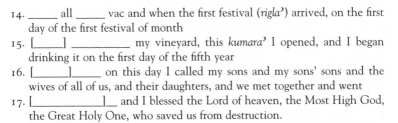

> You will plant in them (your cities) every plant which is upon earth and every tree, moreover, which bears fruit. For three years its fruit will not be gathered from everything which may be eaten, but in the fourth year its fruit will be gathered. And let one offer up the firstfruits which are acceptable before the Lord Most High, who made heaven and earth and everything, so that they might offer up in the juice the first of the wine and the oil as firstfruits upon the altar of the Lord, who will accept it. And that which is left the servants of the house of the Lord will eat before the altar which receives (it).[50]

In this passage a portion of the wine of the fourth year is offered on the altar as a firstfruit offering.[51] The remainder is eaten by the "servants of the house of the Lord," that is, the priests.[52] This contradicts in part *Jubilees*' account of Noah's celebration, for Noah sets aside the wine and then consumes it in the fifth year. So too in the *Genesis Apocryphon* Noah, not the priests, ultimately consumes the wine in the fifth year. But perhaps it is a firstfruit offering such as this for which the *Genesis Apocryphon* dictates that the vessel be opened on the first day of Sukkot.

The *Testament of Levi*, generally dated to the 2d century B.C.E. and thus roughly contemporaneous with *Jubilees*, also mentions a firstfruit offering of wine: "And of all your firstfruits and wine bring the very first as a sacrifice to the Lord God."[53] As in the Qumran texts, the firstfruit sacrifice is an annual offering. Now in this section of the *Testament*, Levi relates what his grand-

50. Wintermute (trans.), "Jubilees," 71.

51. Kister ("Qumranic Halakhah," 582) suggests that the firstfruits of the fourth-year wine were offered on the altar, and the priests received the rest.

52. This tradition interpreted *qōdeš* of Lev 19:24 as 'set aside' for the priests. Kister ("Qumranic Halakhah," 578) points out that this interpretation (probably the *pešaṭ*; see Ibn Ezra and Abravanel, ad loc.) follows from the promise of Lev 19:25, "that its yield may increase for you." The yield will increase in the fifth year as compensation for giving the fruits of the fourth year to the priests. *Jub.* 7:36 accordingly interpreted that the owner does not enjoy any of the fruit until then. 11QTemple LX 3–4 also rules that the fruit of the fourth year belongs to the priests; see Yadin, *Temple Scroll*, 1.162–3, 2.271–72. 4QMMT seems to contain a similar ruling. See Sussmann, "The History of Halakhah," 33; and Qimron and Strugnell, DJD 10, B 62–63, pp. 52–53, 164–65: "And concerning (the fruits of) the trees for food planted in the Land of Israel: they are to be dealt with like first fruits belonging to the priests." The Samaritans, Karaites, and *Tg. Ps.-J.* to Lev 19:24 rule that the fruit belongs to the priests; see C. Albeck, *Das Buch der Jubiläen und die Halakha* (Berlin, 1930) 32; and M. Kasher, *Tirgume Hatorah*, part 2: *Torah Shelemah* (Jerusalem: American Biblical Encyclopedia Society, 1982) 35.81–84. *Sipre Bemidbar*, 9–10, §6 is aware of this interpretation but rejects it.

53. *T. Levi* 9:14. Some textual witnesses omit the words "a sacrifice," leaving "bring the very first to the Lord God." The context, in any event, makes it clear that a sacrifice is intended. See R. H. Charles, "Testaments of the Twelve Patriarchs," *APOT*, 2.48. Charles reconstructs the original Hebrew as ראשית . . . בכוריך, as in Ezek 44:30 and Sir 45:20.

father Isaac admonished him concerning his future duties as priest. Isaac's injunctions consist of laws that apply exclusively to priests: for example, to wash before and after sacrificing, to bring sacrifices from every clean living animal and bird, and to salt every sacrificial offering. It is likely, then, that the commandment to bring the first of the firstfruits and wine as a sacrifice is directed to the priests. Of course the priests would have had to receive such gifts from the people, as in fact Num 18:12–13 prescribes.[54] The *Testament* accordingly adds that the priests do not gain absolute possession of all the firstfruits but must offer a portion as a sacrifice to God, to whom the firstfruits belong.[55] If this analysis is correct, then the *Testament of Levi* is consistent with *Jub.* 7:36. It differs from the *Temple Scroll* in which new wine serves as a corporate offering and is subsequently consumed by all the people in a festive meal.[56] In any case, like the Qumran texts and *Jub.* 7:36, the *Testament* prescribes a sacrifice of firstfruits of wine.[57]

Rabbinic *halakhah* limited the comprehensive biblical requirement to bring firstfruits from all agricultural products.[58] Firstfruits were restricted to the "seven species": wheat, barley, grape, fig, pomegranate, olive, and date.[59] Tannaitic sources dispute whether liquids, including wine and oil, are admissible as firstfruit offerings. M. *Ter.* 11:3 ordains that no liquids may be brought as firstfruits except olive and grape derivatives. Wine, accordingly, is eligible as a firstfruit offering. Similarly, *Mekilta de Rabbi Ishmael, Kaspa* §20 rules:

> *The choicest first fruits of your land (Exod 23:19).* Why is this section said? Because it says: *You shall take some of every first fruit of the soil (Deut 26:2).* I know only that fruits are to be brought as the first-fruit offering. Whence [do I know about] liquids? It teaches: *You shall bring into the house of the Lord your God*—in

54. So too Ezek 44:30, *Jub.* 7:36.

55. The older legislation does not make clear what happens to the firstfruits. Exod 23:19 and 34:26 (so Neh 10:36) instruct the firstfruits to be taken to the "House of the Lord your God," while Deut 26:4 and 26:14 have the pilgrim place the basket before the altar. In both cases the priests probably took possession of the gifts. Deut 18:4 rules that *rēʾšît* of grain, wine, and oil must be given to the priest, but it is unclear whether the same applied to the *bikkûrîm*, the firstfruits.

56. It is possible, however, that the *Testament* author omitted these details of the festival, focusing exclusively on priestly concerns.

57. C. Albeck (*Šišah Sidre Mišnah* [6 vols; Jerusalem: Bialik / Tel Aviv: Dvir, 1954–59] 1.411) claims that the passage is to be interpreted in light of Lev 2:12. The offering of wine is not a firstfruit offering but a sacrifice upon the altar. Albeck here struggles with the contradiction between this passage and rabbinic *halakhah*, which frowns upon wine as a firstfruit offering (see below). Baumgarten (*Studies*, 140), on the basis of the Qumran texts, points out that Albeck's distinction is unnecessary. Wine was brought both as firstfruit offering and as sacrifice. See also Kister's suggestion (above, n. 51).

58. See n. 11.

59. M. *Bik.* 1:3, 3:9; *t. Bik.* 2.8. Further restrictions appear in a series of baraitot, *y. Bik.* 1.3, 63d. The seven species are listed in Deut 8:8.

any form. And what is the difference between these? Those [who bring fruits] bring and recite,[60] while those [who bring liquids] bring and do not recite.[61]

Although liquids are legitimate firstfruit offerings, they are somewhat less "appropriate" than full-fledged fruit, so one who brings liquids may not recite the liturgical formula that generally accompanies the offerings. Similarly, *Tg. Ps.-J.* to Exod 22:28 enjoins that "the firstfruits of your fruits and the firstfruits of the wine of your vat you shall not delay." However, *Sipre Deut.* §297 rules that wine and oil may not be brought as firstfruits,[62] and *m. Ḥal.* 4:11 reports that when Joseph the Priest brought wine and oil as firstfruits, his offering was not accepted.[63] Given the nonrabbinic sources and the comprehensive biblical requirement to bring firstfruits from all produce, the opinion that wine and oil may be brought as firstfruits seems to represent an earlier *halakhah*. Later the obligation was limited to the seven species and to dry fruits, and other restrictions were promulgated as well.[64]

The Wine Libation as Firstfruit Ritual

Five distinct sources—the Qumran Scrolls, *Jubilees*, *Testament of Levi*, the *Genesis Apocryphon*, and rabbinic texts—relate that new wine featured in some form at a firstfruit festival or as a firstfruit offering. In (most) rabbinic traditions the wine is brought with other firstfruits and left at the base of the altar; in the *Temple Scroll* and the *Testament of Levi* it is offered upon the altar. The Qumran scrolls, *Jub.* 7:1–6, and the *Genesis Apocryphon* have the people participate in the festival by drinking the new wine.[65] The sample

60. The prescribed liturgy, Deut 26:5–10.

61. H. Horovitz (ed.), *Mekilta de Rabbi Ishmael* (Jerusalem: Wahrmann, 1960) 335.

62. "*You shall take some of every firstfruit of the soil (Deut 26:2)*—fruit. You are to bring fruit as firstfruits, but you are not to bring wine and oil as firstfruits"; L. Finkelstein (ed.), *Sipre Debarim* (New York: Jewish Theological Seminary, 1979) 317. A similar baraita is cited in *b. ʿArak.* 11a (= *b. Ḥul.* 120b) and attributed to R. Yose. However, that baraita concludes that one may indeed bring wine as a firstfruit offering.

63. *Y. Ḥal.* 4.11, 60b resolves the contradictory sources by ruling that if one gathered grapes with the intention that they be made into wine and brought as firstfruits in that state, it is permitted, but if one did not have that intention when the grapes were harvested and subsequently made into wine, that wine is inadmissible as a firstfruit offering. *B. Ḥul.* 120b offers a different resolution. See Y. N. Epstein, *Mavo Lenusaḥ Hamišnah* (2d ed.; Jerusalem: Magnes / Tel Aviv: Dvir, 1964) 304 n. 2.

64. *Sipre Deut.* 299, §301; *m. Bik.* 1:10 and *m. Ḥal.* 4:11 limit the area from which firstfruits may be brought. But Josephus *Ant.* 16.172 reports that the Jews of Asia Minor brought firstfruits to Jerusalem. *M. Bik.* 1:10 and *Sipre Deut.* 317, §297 rule that those who bring firstfruits before Shavuot or after Sukkot may not recite the Deuteronomic liturgy. However, Philo *Special Laws* 2.220–22 knows of no such restriction. See *Sipre Debarim*, 299, §301 and *m. Bik.* 1:10 for other limitations.

65. Assuming that Noah's festival in *Jub.* 7:1–6 and in the *Genesis Apocryphon* is paradigmatic.

includes both prescriptive legal texts (*Temple Scroll*, *Jub.* 7:36, most rabbinic sources) and narrative accounts (Noah in *Jub.* 7:1–6 and the *Genesis Apocryphon*, and the account of Joseph the High Priest in *m. Ḥal.* 4:11), and thus points to a real practice. Even if we consider the rigid pentacontad structure of the *Temple Scroll* a hypothetical construction of the utopian calendar, the legislation stemmed from a popular practice of bringing new wine to the Temple and offering it as a sacrifice. Indeed, it is precisely because of disputes over the calendar that the different sources prescribe the festival for different times. Each placed the wine festival at the appropriate time for its calendrical scheme.

These sources suggest that the Sukkot wine libation may have originated as the firstfruit offering of the new wine consumed at a wine festival. On the autumnal festival the people gave thanks to God for the grapes and wine by offering new wine as a libation. By Sukkot the vintage was generally over. The grapes, having been placed in wineskins or vats, ferment in a matter of hours, so there was ample time to make wine before the festival.[66] The celebrations described in Judges suggest that the autumnal festival celebrated the vintage specifically, so the wine libation may go back to the earliest strata of the festival.[67]

That a firstfruit offering of wine was brought on Sukkot also makes sense from a logistical point of view. The people aspired to come up to Jerusalem for Pesaḥ, Shavuot, and Sukkot, so to make an additional pilgrimage specifically to present firstfruits was undoubtedly a hardship. Albeck cites Tob 1:6–7 as evidence that rural residents brought their firstfruits on the pilgrimage festivals when they would travel to Jerusalem to celebrate:[68]

66. Grapes were sometimes crushed in the hand into a cup and immediately drunk, as in the dream of Pharaoh's cupbearer, Gen 40:10–11. See S. Krauss, *Talmudische Archäologie* (3 vols.; Leipzig: Fock, 1910–12) 2.233.

67. It is true that *Jub.* 7:1–6 and the *Genesis Apocryphon* have Noah drink on the first day of the first month, not on Sukkot. But they are motivated by the constraint placed by Lev 19:25 that the fruit may not be consumed until the fifth year. So they allow Noah to consume the fruit at the earliest possible point, the first day of the first month. Rabbinic *halakhah*, we noted, treated the fruits as second tithe and allowed the owner to consume them in Jerusalem, so there was no need to defer the celebration to the first of the fifth year. The associated festival could be observed on Sukkot of the fourth year, where indeed the *Genesis Apocryphon* mentions that something took place. Similarly, the new wine festival of the Qumran scrolls occurs on the third of the fifth month because of the pentacontad structure of its solar calendar. The rabbinic or protorabbinic calendar was not governed by that concern. Thus the fact that the dates of the festivals of new wine or firstfruit are not associated specifically with Sukkot does not militate against my hypothesis. The sources are trying to fit the wine festival into their calendars.

68. Albeck, *Mišnah*, 1.307. See above, p. 578, on the pilgrimage festivals as firstfruit celebrations in ancient times. According to rabbinic *halakhah*, firstfruits may be brought only from Shavuot to Sukkot. Philo (*Special Laws* 2.216) relates that the season

> I alone used often to journey to Jerusalem at the feasts, as it had been ordained in all Israel by an everlasting decree. I used to go to Jerusalem with the firstfruits and the firstlings and the tenths of the cattle and the first shearings of the sheep, and give them to the priests, the sons of Aaron, for the altar. . . .

Since grapes only ripened in August and September, there was little opportunity prior to Sukkot to bring firstfruits of grapes or wine. Peasants were preoccupied with the arduous vintage labors in any case. After the vintage, on Sukkot, when the farmers made their way to Jerusalem for the festival, it was the perfect time to bring a firstfruit offering of new wine as well.

If a wine-feast accompanied the libation, as in Qumran law, we may also have a component of *Śimḥat bêt haššōʾēvâ* ('rejoicing at the place of water-drawing'), the all-night festival celebrated in the Temple courtyard.[69] Both the Qumran account of the wine feast and the description of *Śimḥat bêt haššōʾēvâ* emphasize joy and rejoicing. The dancing, singing, joy, and general gaiety that the Mishnah associates with this nocturnal ritual are perfectly understandable as repercussions of rejoicing with wine.[70] If not *Śimḥat bêt haššōʾēvâ* specifically, then the emphasis on cultic *śimḥâ* ('rejoicing') in connection with Sukkot may reflect a wine feast. True, *śimḥâ* is associated with sacrificial meat and hence with the other pilgrimage festivals as well.[71] And the elation at the completed autumn harvest and vintage helps to explain the emphasis on festal joy. But wine, as divine gift, the drink that "gladdens God and men," bears a special association with joy and *śimḥâ*.[72] Against this background the exhortation to be *ʾak śamēaḥ* 'to have nothing but joy' (Deut 16:16) is fully understandable. It should also be noted that Plutarch associated Sukkot with the vintage, Dionysian rites (which included wine-drink-

---

for bringing firstfruits (the "basket") lasted from the beginning of summer until the end of autumn. See Josephus *Ant.* 4.240; and Safrai, *ʿAliya*, 226 and nn. 80–82.

69. M. *Sukk.* 5:1–5.

70. As are the rabbinic traditions concerning lewd behavior and wildness that occurred during the night; *t. Sukk.* 4.1, *y. Sukk.* 5.4, 55b. Songs and music accompanied the pressing of grapes, Isa 5:12, and enhanced drinking parties, Isa 24:9, Amos 6:5–6, Ps 69:13, Sir 40:20. Note that Psalms 8, 81, and 84 are preceded by the superscription *ʿal haggitît*. While most modern scholars generally concede that the meaning is unknown, some derive *gitit* from *gat* 'winepress' and interpret the phrase as 'for the winepress', perhaps alluding to the instruments used during vintage celebrations. The term is understood in this sense by the LXX, the Vulgate, and *Midraš Tehillim* to Ps 8:1 and 84:1. Ps 81:1–6, moreover, is clearly intended for Sukkot, the festival alluded to in v. 4. See Kittel, *Psalmen*, 299–301.

71. Deut 27:7. Cf. *b. Pesaḥ.* 119b.

72. Prov 31:6–7; Ps 104:14–15; Jer 25:20, 48:33; Isa 16:10, 22:13; Sir 31:27–28, 40:20. Cant 1:4, 4:10, and 7:9 connect joy, love, and wine. See also *b. Pesaḥ.* 109a: "A man is obligated to make his children and household rejoice on a festival. . . . How does he make them rejoice? With wine." See also *b. ʿArak.* 11a and *y. Ber.* 6.8, 10b.

ing) and revelry.[73] Of course his evidence cannot be taken as decisive, but his source does have quite accurate information on the building of booths, the taking of the *lulav*, the dress of the High Priest, and some details of sacrificial legislation. A wine festival would explain why Plutarch pictured Dionysian rites.[74] The wine libation was probably a firstfruit offering, and may have been accompanied by a feast and imbibation. Like the water-libation, it points to an important dimension of the ancient festival of Sukkot.[75]

73. *Quaes. Conv.* 6.6.2. See M. Stern (ed.), *Greek and Latin Authors on Jews and Judaism* (3 vols.; Jerusalem: Israel Academy of Sciences, 1974–84) 2.553–62.

74. M. Smith ("On the Wine God in Palestine [Gen. 18, Jn. 2, and Achilles Tatius]," in *Salo Wittmayer Baron Jubilee Volume* [Jerusalem and New York: American Academy for Jewish Research, 1974] 815–29) has argued that YHWH was conceived as a wine-God in Jewish-Hellenistic circles.

75. An earlier version of this paper appears in my *History of Sukkot during the Second Temple and Rabbinic Periods* (Ph.D. dissertation, Columbia University, 1991) 229–46.

Sacred Space and Mental Iconography: *Imago Templi* and Contemplation in Rhineland Jewish Pietism

Elliot R. Wolfson
New York University

Temple as the Site of Contemplation

Historians of religion have long noted that a central component in the phenomenological constitution of religious belief is the notion of sacred space.[1] Together with sacred time, the idea of sacred space orients *homo*

Author's note: I offer this study on the role of sacred space in a later phase of Jewish spirituality as a token of admiration and friendship for my esteemed colleague with whom I share a deep and abiding interest in exploring the phenomenological texture of religious experience.

1. See G. van der Leeuw, *Religion in Essence and Manifestation* (London: Allen & Unwin, 1938) 393–402. The role of sacred space in the phenomenology of comparative religion has been featured prominently in the work of Mircea Eliade. In particular, Eliade has focused on the notion of sacred space as the *omphalos* or *umbilicus terrae*, the navel of the earth, which is the *axis mundi*, the cosmic center that connects heaven and earth. I here mention a representative sampling of Eliade's writings on this subject: *Patterns in Comparative Religion* (New York: Sheed & Ward, 1958) 367–87; *The Sacred and the Profane: The Nature of Religion* (New York: Harcourt, Brace, Jovanovich, 1959) 20–65; *Images and Symbols: Studies in Religious Symbolism* (Kansas City: Andrews and McMeel, 1961) 27–56; *A History of Religious Ideas* (3 vols.; Chicago: University of Chicago Press, 1978) 1.42–43; *Symbolism, the Sacred, and the Arts* (ed. D. Apostolos-Cappadona; New York: Crossroad, 1985) 105–29. For a relatively brief study of sacred space in Jewish sources, discussed from the particular vantage point of the mythology of exile and the homeland, see J. Z. Smith, "Earth and Gods," *Map Is Not Territory: Studies in the History of Religions* (Leiden: Brill, 1978) 104–28. For a more extensive discussion of the notion of sacred space, particularly as it relates to ritual, see idem, *To Take Place: Toward Theory in Ritual* (Chicago: University of Chicago Press, 1987). Also noteworthy are the studies on the transformation of the biblical notion of a sacred center in early rabbinic Judaism by J. Neusner, "Map Is without Territory: Mishnah's System of Sacrifice and Sanctuary," *HR* 19 (1979) 103–27, and B. M. Bokser, "Approaching Sacred Space," *HTR* 78 (1985) 279–99.

religiosus in the world both vertically and horizontally. This orienting tendency plays an especially significant role in terms of cultic activity, manifest primarily in the sacrificial rite or liturgical order, for the particular time and place of worship inform the mentality of the religious person and shape his or her lived experience of the sensible plane.[2] The life-world of the practioner is conditioned by the phenomenal structures of sacred space and sacred time; indeed, the convergence of these two categories is characteristic of religious intentionality, for the space that is perceived as sacred is so perceived on account of the designated times wherein that space is inhabited and consecrated, and, conversely, the designated times are perceived as sacred inasmuch as during those times one inhabits the particular space that is considered sacred.[3] It goes without saying that time and space can function independently, but from the perspective of ritual behavior the one is dependent on the other. A space can be deemed sacred even at times that are not designated as official moments of religious practice or devotion, just as the gravity of time may be sensed outside the boundaries of an accepted place. Nevertheless, the sacrality of space and time is derived from the coincidence of the two phenomenal structures in the lived experience of holiness that is central to religious consciousness. As Ernst Cassirer put it,

2. The significance of sacred space in ancient Israelite religion has been an ongoing concern in the scholarly work of Baruch Levine, to whom this collection of studies is dedicated. In this context I will mention only some of the more salient examples from Baruch Levine's *ouevre*: "On the Presence of God in Biblical Religion," in *Religions in Antiquity: Essays in Memory of Erwin Ramsdell Goodenough* (ed. J. Neusner; Leiden: Brill, 1970) 71–87; *In the Presence of the Lord: A Study of Cult and Some Cultic Terms in Ancient Israel* (Leiden: Brill, 1974); "Biblical Temple," *Encyclopedia of Religion* (ed. M. Eliade; New York, 1986) 2.202–17; "An Essay on Prophetic Attitudes toward Temple and Cult in Biblical Israel," in *Minḥah le-Naḥum: Biblical and Other Studies Presented to Nahum M. Sarna in Honour of His Seventieth Birthday* (ed. M. Brettler and M. Fishbane; Sheffield: Sheffield Academic Press, 1993) 202–25; "*Lpny* YHWH: Phenomenology of the Open-Air Altar in Biblical Israel," *Biblical Archaeology Today* 2 (Jerusalem: Israel Exploration Society, 1994) 196–205; "'The Lord Your God Accept You' (2 Samuel 24.13): The Altar Erected by David on the Threshing Floor of Araunah," *ErIsr* 24 (1994) 122–29 [Heb.]; "The Next Phase in Jewish Religion: The Land of Israel as Sacred Space," in *Tehillah le-Moshe: Biblical and Judaic Studies in Honor of Moshe Greenberg* (ed. M. Cogan, B. L. Eichler, and J. H. Tigay; Winona Lake, Ind.: Eisenbrauns, 1997) 245–57; and "Mythic and Ritual Projections of Sacred Space in Biblical Literature," *Journal of Jewish Thought and Philosophy* 6 (1997) 59–70.

3. See D. M. Knipe, "The Temple in Image and Reality," in *Temple in Society* (ed. M. V. Fox; Winona Lake, Ind.: Eisenbrauns, 1988) 105–38, esp. 107–8, 112–17. Knipe correctly notes that the intersection of sacred space and sacred time is a prominent feature of Eliade's work (see references above in n. 1). See also S. Cucchiari, "The Lords of the Culto: Transcending Time through Place in Sicilian Pentecostal Ritual," *JRelS* 4 (1990) 1–14; and M. Barker, *The Gate of Heaven: The History and Symbolism of the Temple in Jerusalem* (London: SPCK, 1991) 58–65.

> the expression of temporal relations develops only through that of spatial relations. . . . All orientation in time presupposes orientation in space, and only as the latter develops and creates definite means of expression are temporal specifications distinguishable to feeling and consciousness.[4]

Basing himself on the philological insight of Hermann Usener, Cassirer goes on to say that the intersection of space and time is disclosed especially in the symbol of the temple, for the word *templum* is derived from *tempus*, which connotes a section of space or a section of time that is marked off.

In this study I will explore the motif of sacred space in the mystical theosophy of the Rhineland Jewish Pietists of the 12th and 13th centuries as it relates specifically to their discussions of the proper liturgical intention.[5] A number of scholars have discussed the mystical nature of the Pietistic treatment of prayer, noting in particular the relationship to parallel discussions in the emerging theosophy of kabbalistic literature.[6] I myself have addressed

4. E. Cassirer, *The Philosophy of Symbolic Forms* (3 vols.; New Haven: Yale University Press, 1955) 2.107.

5. I have discussed the German Pietists' attitude on prayer and the visualization of the glory in *Through a Speculum That Shines: Vision and Imagination in Medieval Jewish Mysticism* (Princeton: Princeton University Press, 1994) 188–269, esp. 195–214. The impetus to study anew the German Pietists' religious orientation from the perspective of sacred space came from a question addressed to me by Geoffrey Hartman when I delivered a lecture entitled "Worshiping Mental Icons: The Impact of Christian Culture on the Rhineland Jewish Pietists" at the Yale University Seminar on Jewish Studies on March 2, 1994. On that occasion I summarized my discussion of the mental iconization of God in German Pietistic sources, and I elaborated on possible links connecting Ḥaside Ashkenaz and Byzantine Christian theologians (discussed briefly in *Through a Speculum That Shines*, 199 n. 43). Hartman expressed interest in the restriction of the contemplative exercise to a particular place as it emerged from some of the Pietistic texts that I had distributed on that occasion. His remarks prompted me to explore in more detail this dimension of the mental iconography in the relevant material.

6. See I. Elbogen, *Jewish Liturgy: A Comprehensive History* (Philadelphia: Jewish Publication Society of America, 1993) 288–90; H. G. Enelow, "Kawwana: The Struggle for Inwardness in Judaism," in *Studies in Jewish Literature Issued in Honor of Professor Kaufmann Kohler on the Occasion of His Seventieth Birthday* (ed. D. Philipson, D. Neumark, and J. Morgenstern; Berlin: Reimer, 1913) 97–100; G. Scholem, *Major Trends in Jewish Mysticism* (New York: Schocken, 1956) 100–103, 116; idem, "The Concept of Kavvanah in the Early Kabbalah," in *Studies in Jewish Thought: An Anthology of German Jewish Scholarship* (ed. A. Jospe; Detroit: Wayne State University Press, 1981) 163–64; idem, *Origins of the Kabbalah* (Princeton: Princeton University Press, 1987) 195–96; G. Vajda, *L'Amour de Dieu dans la théologie juive du moyen age* (Paris: Librairie Philosophique J. Vrin, 1957) 154–55; J. Dan, *The Esoteric Theology of Ashkenazi Ḥasidism* (Jerusalem: Bialik, 1968) 140–41, 182–83 [Heb.]; idem, "The Emergence of Mystical Prayer," in *Studies in Jewish Mysticism* (ed. J. Dan and F. Talmage; Cambridge, Mass.: Association for Jewish Studies, 1982) 85–120; idem, "The Intention of Prayer from the Tradition of R. Judah the Pious," *Daʿat* 10 (1983) 47–56 [Heb.]; idem,

this topic as part of my treatment of the role of visionary experience in the Pietists' theological treatises.[7] The present study builds upon and further elaborates some points that I only discussed tangentially in my previous work. In particular, I will focus on the role of sacred space in the imaginative visualization of the enthroned glory that figures as a prominent feature of the Pietistic ideal of intention in prayer. Moreover, as I shall argue, the visionary praxis cultivated by the Pietists is predicated on the *imago templi*, the imaginal symbol of the transcendental reality (the celestial Temple) experienced concretely in the heart of the worshiper.[8]

Prayer (in the classical form inherited by medieval poets, mystics, and rabbis) necessitates conjuring an image of the glory sitting upon the throne in the heavenly abode, but the locus of that image is in the human imagination. From that vantage point there is an indisputable connection between the process of contemplation and the image of the Temple. Here it is in order to recall that the Latin *contemplari* is etymologically derived from the word *templum* (Greek τέμενος from the root τεμ 'to cut'), the space in heaven marked off for augural observation.[9] The Temple, therefore, is the

---

"Pesaq ha-Yirah veha-Emunah and the Intention of Prayer in Ashkenazi Hasidic Esotericism," *Frankfurter judaistische Beiträge* 19 (1991–92) 185–215; idem, "Prayer as Text and Prayer as Mystical Experience," in *Torah and Wisdom: Essays in Honor of Arthur Hyman* (ed. R. Link-Salinger; New York: Shengold, 1992) 33–47; I. G. Marcus, *Piety and Society: The Jewish Pietists of Medieval Germany* (Leiden: Brill, 1981) 98–100, 117–18; idem, "The Devotional Ideals of Ashkenazic Pietism," in *Jewish Spirituality from the Bible through the Middle Ages* (ed. A. Green; New York: Crossroad, 1986) 356–66, esp. 360–64; idem, "Prayer Gestures in German Hasidism," in *Mysticism, Magic, and Kabbalah in Ashkenazi Judaism: International Symposium Held in Frankfurt a.M. 1991* (ed. K. E. Grözinger and J. Dan; Berlin: de Gruyter, 1995) 44–59; A. Farber, *The Concept of the Merkabah in Thirteenth-Century Jewish Esotericism: 'Sod ha-ʾEgoz' and Its Development* (Ph.D. dissertation, Hebrew University, 1986) 237–44 [Heb.]; M. Idel, "Intention in Prayer in the Beginning of Kabbalah: Between Germany and Provence," in *Ben Porat Yosef: Studies Presented to Rabbi Dr. Joseph Safran* (ed. B. Safran and E. Safran; Hoboken, N.J.: Ktav, 1992) 5–14 [Heb.]; idem, "Prayer in the Provençal Kabbalah," *Tarbiz* 62 (1993) 265–86, esp. 270–72 [Heb.]; D. Abrams, "'The Secret of Secrets': The Concept of the Divine Glory and the Intention of Prayer in the Writings of R. Eleazar of Worms," *Daʿat* 34 (1995) 61–81 [Heb.]. See also G. D. Cohen, "The Hebrew Crusade Chronicles and the Ashkenazic Tradition," in *Minḥah le-Naḥum: Biblical and Other Studies Presented to Nahum M. Sarna in Honour of His Seventieth Birthday* (ed. M. Brettler and M. Fishbane; Sheffield: Sheffield Academic Press, 1993) 36–53.

7. See my study *Through a Speculum That Shines*.

8. My use of the term *imago templi* and the description of its phenomenological content are indebted to the discussion in H. Corbin, "The *Imago Templi* in Confrontation with Secular Norms," *Temple and Contemplation* (London: Routledge & Kegan Paul, 1986) 263–390.

9. Cassirer, *The Philosophy of Symbolic Forms*, 2.99–102.

sacred precinct consecrated to a divine being. In Jewish sources as well there is an inextricable nexus between visual contemplation of the enthroned glory and the Temple. With the gradual decline of the earthly Temple and the ascendancy of the celestial Temple, the focus of that contemplative vision changes accordingly. To contemplate is to set one's sight on the Temple in heaven, the place that determines the field of one's spiritual vision. The heavenly Temple, however, is visible only through the mirror of the imagination. Hence, one may speak of the human imagination (typically located in the heart) as the sacred site of vision, as the consecrated space of contemplation. God and human are united and mutually transformed through the symbol of the *imago templi*, for the divine is rendered accessible to human imagination in anthropomorphic form and the human imagination is sacralized as the prism through which the divine is manifest. In the *imago templi*, therefore, the divine becomes human and the human divine.

The imaginal representation of God in the *imago templi* embraces the realm of myth, which I relate to a symbolic form that overcomes the epistemic binaries reified by rational discourse, real versus imagined, somatic versus psychic, external versus internal, experienced versus interpreted.[10]

10. My understanding of myth and symbol as a unitary consciousness that overcomes the dualism between inside and outside, subjective and objective, reflects the thought of Cassirer. See *The Philosophy of Symbolic Forms*, 1.178; 2.20, 23, 99. Following Cassirer, moreover, I use the word "symbol" to refer to a "structural form" that articulates the experience of mythical consciousness in terms of distinctive cultural configurations. In my view, therefore, it is incorrect to set up a dichotomy between myth and symbol. On the contrary, the symbol, which is an imaginative construct, is the linguistic expression of that which is experienced ontically as myth. In contrast to the Romantic notion of symbol, to which Scholem was indebted, I do not posit an unbridgeable chasm separating the symbol and that which is symbolized, for the latter can be experienced and expressed only through the former, even if the symbolic characterization of the one reality is multivalent. See my discussion in *Through a Speculum That Shines*, pp. 61–67. For a recent attempt to distinguish myth and symbol in kabbalistic literature, see Y. Liebes, "Myth vs. Symbol in the Zohar and in Lurianic Kabbalah," in *Essential Papers on Kabbalah* (ed. L. Fine; New York: New York University Press, 1995) 212–42. Liebes's distinction between *symbolic* and *mythic* is rooted in a misconception about the symbol as distinct from the *real*. In his view, the *mythic* signifies an actual event, something ontically real, whereas the *symbolic* is a formal representation of that reality. In his effort to respond to the dominance of the use of symbol to characterize kabbalistic hermeneutics, Liebes has dichotomized symbol and myth in a way that, I believe, is inappropriate. The examples he adduces of what he calls the *symbolic* (as opposed to the *mythic*) also embrace an ontic reality, actualized in the imagination, that would justify the use of the term *mythic*. The inherent nexus of myth and symbol has also been affirmed by Paul Ricoeur, who has influenced my own thinking. See P. Ricoeur, *The Symbolism of Evil* (Boston: Beacon, 1967) 18; idem, *The Conflict of Interpretations* (Evanston: Northwestern University Press, 1974) 28; R. Kearney, "Paul Ricoeur and the Hermeneutic Imagination," in *The Narrative*

With respect to the particular case that I am discussing here, liturgical worship in a theistic context is impossible without an image of God, but God has no image. To pass from the theological presumption of an imageless God to the phenomenological configuration of an imagined God, it is necessary to posit the symbol of the *imago templi*. That is, within the imaginary edifice of the celestial Temple, which conforms to the structure of the imagination, the incorporeal God assumes the shape of the imaginal body. The imaging of the celestial Temple, however, occurs only in the spatial delimitation of the synagogue. The visualization of God as the glory enthroned in the heavenly realm takes place in the sacred space woven by the words of prayer.

Intentionality in Prayer and the Visual Imaging of Šekhinah

The symbolic notion of *imago templi* that evolved in the theosophy of the Rhineland Jewish Pietists is in great measure presaged in rabbinic statements on the nature of intention (*kawwanah*) in prayer. Inasmuch as my theoretical assumption is that the gap separating the rabbinic and the medieval mystical conceptions of *kawwanah* should be substantially narrowed, it is in order to begin with a very brief review of the analysis of the relevant rabbinic materials that I have given in great detail elsewhere.[11] To cast my own view in bold relief, let me note that various scholars, most notably Joshua Abelson, have previously argued that the medieval kabbalistic notion of *kawwanah* made explicit what was implied in the classical rabbinic sources. More specifically, according to Abelson, the common element in the rabbinic and the kabbalistic discussions on *kawwanah* is the presumption that the latter entails the "abandonment . . . of all mundane thoughts and of all physical necessities, in the unalloyed consciousness of a union with God."[12] While I,

---

Path: The Later Works of Paul Ricoeur (ed. T. P. Kemp and D. Rasmussen; Cambridge: Massachusetts Institute of Technology Press, 1989) 1–31; R. A. Champagne, *The Structuralists on Myth: An Introduction* (New York: Garland, 1992) 13, 46–47, 75; E. Deutsch, "Truth and Mythology," in *Myths and Fictions* (ed. S. Biderman and B.-A. Scharfstein; Leiden: Brill, 1993) 46–47.

11. See my "Iconic Visualization and the Imaginal Body of God: The Role of Intention in the Rabbinic Conception of Prayer," *Modern Theology* 12 (1996) 137–62. The reader interested in the fuller philological and textual support of my argument presented very briefly here should consult this study.

12. J. Abelson, *The Immanence of God in Rabbinical Literature* (London: Macmillan, 1912) 327–28. Enelow ("Kawwana," 87) suggests that the rabbinic comments regarding the practice of lingering on the word *ʾeḥad* in the *Šemaʿ* (*y. Ber.* 2.1, 4a; *b. Ber.* 13b) "offers a glimpse of another aspect of the idea of kawwana and of a later stage of its evolution: intense pondering of the words of prayer and of their mystic content." See also D. Hedegård, *Seder R. Amram Gaon: Hebrew Text with Critical Apparatus, Translation with Notes and Introduction* (Lund: Lindstedts Universitetsbokhandel, 1951) xxxix–xl.

too, assume that the rabbinic and the kabbalistic conceptions of *kawwanah* reflect a continuity of tradition,[13] the shared element in my opinion is not union with God but the iconic visualization of the immediate or direct presence of God.[14] With respect to this issue I posit a phenomenological affinity between the writings of the German Pietists, the theosophic kabbalists, and the prophetic kabbalists.[15] I am not denying that unitive experiences were

13. My approach should be contrasted with that of Scholem, who assumed that the kabbalistic notion of *kawwanah* was an innovation imposed upon the rabbinic texts. See Scholem, "Concept of Kavvanah," 163; idem, *Major Trends*, 34; idem, *On the Kabbalah and Its Symbolism* (New York: Schocken, 1965) 126, 133; idem, *Kabbalah* (Jerusalem: Keter, 1974) 176. For a critique of the Scholemian position, see also I. Gruenwald, "Writing, Script, and the Explicit Name: Magic, Spirituality, and Mysticism," in *Massu'ot: Studies in Kabbalistic Literature and Jewish Philosophy in Memory of Prof. Ephraim Gottlieb* (ed. M. Oron and A. Goldreich; Jerusalem: Bialik, 1994) 75–98 [Heb.].

14. M. Kadushin (*The Rabbinic Mind* [New York: Jewish Theological Seminary of America, 1952] 208–9 and 226–27) remarks that the statements in rabbinic literature that correlate the presence of God and the recitation of prayer are indicative of a "normal mysticism," which is defined by Kadushin as the "experience of God's nearness." See idem, *Worship and Ethics* (Evanston, Ill.: Northwestern University Press, 1964). For a critique of Kadushin's position, see E. Schweid, *Judaism and Mysticism according to Gershom Scholem: A Critical Analysis and Programmatic Discussion* (Atlanta: Scholars Press, 1985) 101. Schweid concedes that the prayer regulated by early rabbinic sages contained the experience of the presence of God, but he rejects labeling this mysticism. See, by contrast, A. Goldberg, "Service of the Heart: Liturgical Aspects of Synagogue Worship," in *Standing before God: Studies on Prayer in Scriptures and in Tradition with Essays in Honor of John M. Oesterreicher* (ed. A. Finkel and L. Frizzell; New York: Ktav, 1981) 195–211, esp. 201–4. Although Goldberg argues that the synagogue did not replace the Temple as the "visible sacred center" of God's presence (p. 201), he does acknowledge that worshipers "prepare a throne for God in their midst" and that prayer inculcates the "reality of faith in, or the mystical experience of, God's presence" (p. 203). In another passage, however, Goldberg differentiates the face-to-face encounter presupposed by liturgy and the mystical withdrawal entailed by internalization (p. 209). My own analysis agrees with Goldberg's former characterization, but I have attributed a more significant role to iconic visualization in the encountering of the divine presence.

15. On the visualization of the divine form in the German Pietistic literature, see my *Through a Speculum That Shines*, 195–214. On the theosophic kabbalah, see ibid., pp. 288–306, 317–25. In the ecstatic kabbalah as well, the meditative path leads to a visualization of God in anthropomorphic form. Two striking examples of this phenomenon from the writings of Abraham Abulafia may be found in *Ḥayye ha-ʿOlam ha-Baʾ*, MS Oxford, Bodleian Library 1582, fol. 52a, and *Sefer ha-Ḥesheq*, MS New York, Jewish Theological Seminary of America Mic. 1801, fol. 9a. In the ecstatic treatise by Judah Alboṭini (*Sullam ha-ʿAliyyah* [ed. J. E. Parush: Jerusalem: Shaare Ziv, 1989] 73), the disembodied soul is instructed to imagine sitting in heaven before God's splendor and to imagine God sitting before it in the image of an enthroned king. Mention

cultivated by medieval Jewish mystics. My point is, rather, that the experiences of union served the ultimate aim of facilitating the visual apprehension of God as an imaginal body.[16] The mindfulness achieved by the meditative practices affirmed in pietistic and kabbalistic texts is not a state of abstract emptiness, a peeling away of all material form from consciousness to attain the illumination of formless absorption.[17] It is quite the opposite: contemplation eventuates in the polishing of the mind so that reflected in the mirror of the imagination is the concrete image of the divine anthropos.[18]

---

should also be made of Ḥayyim Vital, *Shaʿare Qedushah*, IV.2 (*Ketavim Ḥadashim le-Rabbenu Ḥayyim Vital* [Jerusalem: Ahavat Shalom, 1988] 12), which reflects a synthesis of the ecstatic and the theosophic traditions. After Vital characterizes *hitbodedut* as the radical stripping away of all things corporeal, he cites a passage from the anonymous kabbalistic treatise, *Maʿarekhet ha-ʾElohut*, which deals with the esoteric gnosis of the *Šiʿur Qomah*. The ultimate secret of the prophetic experience, therefore, is the imaginative representation of the divine as an anthropos. On the role of the anthropomorphic image in the visual technique of the ecstatic kabbalah, see M. Idel, *The Mystical Experience in Abraham Abulafia* (Albany: State University of New York Press, 1988) 95–100.

16. My understanding contrasts sharply with Scholem's characterization of meditation as it appears in kabbalistic literature from the middle of the 13th century as "contemplation by the intellect, whose objects are neither images nor visions, but non-sensual matters such as words, names, or thoughts" (*Kabbalah*, 369). See also Scholem's characterization in *Major Trends*, 276–78; *Origins of the Kabbalah*, 243–44, 414–19; and *The Messianic Idea in Judaism* (New York: Schocken, 1971) 217–18.

17. Compare the description of Buddhist meditation in S. W. Laycock, *Mind as Mirror and the Mirroring of Mind: Buddhist Reflections on Western Phenomenology* (Albany: State University of New York Press, 1994) 76–78. For an approach to Jewish mystical texts more congenial to the model that I am rejecting, see D. C. Matt, "Ayin: The Concept of Nothingness in Jewish Mysticism," in *The Problem of Pure Consciousness: Mysticism and Philosophy* (ed. R. K. C. Forman; New York: Oxford University Press, 1990) 121–59. I, of course, recognize that there are apophatic statements in Jewish mystical literature, but I would argue that the encounter with the divine nothing is an experience of God's presence as absence rather than an experience of the absence of God's presence. See my "Negative Theology and Positive Assertion in the Early Kabbalah," *Daʿat* 32–33 (1994) v–xxii. A similar argument has been made by Bernard McGinn for the apophatic mystics in the history of Western Christianity; see following note.

18. My orientation to the history of Jewish mysticism bears a close resemblance to Bernard McGinn's approach to the history of Western Christian mysticism, which he has aptly called *The Presence of God*. Contrary to a widely held view, McGinn argues that "union with God" is not the most central category for understanding mysticism. The mystical element in Christianity relates to the "belief and practices that concerns the preparation for, the consciousness of, and the reaction to what can be described as the immediate or direct presence of God." See *The Foundations of Mysticism: Origins to the Fifth Century* (New York: Crossroad, 1991) xvii and xix; idem, *The*

In my study of the rabbinic idea of *kawwanah*, I have argued that the intention implied by this technical term in several key passages involves the formation of an iconic image of God within the mind (or heart). The term *kawwanah*, therefore, can refer to an internal state of consciousness by means of which the worshiper creates a mental icon of God, the function of which is to locate the divine presence in space. The rabbinic ideal is captured in the dictum of Simeon the Pious reported by Ḥana ben Bizna:

> The one who prays must see himself as if the *Šekhinah* were opposite him, as it says, "I have set the Lord always before me" (Ps 16:8).[19]

Even though the term *kawwanah* is not used in this dictum, it is reasonable to conclude that the process described by Simeon the Pious is related to the intention required by one who prays. This conjecture is borne out by an examination of the medieval codes of Jewish law and ritual, which demonstrate that various rabbinic commentators interpreted the term *kawwanah* (when applied to prayer) in light of the teaching of Simeon the Pious. Thus, for example, in the halakhic code of Isaac Alfasi and in the *Sefer ha-ʾEshkol* of Abraham ben Isaac of Narbonne, the dictum that the worshiper must direct his heart to heaven[20] is followed by the dictum that the worshiper must see himself as if the *Šekhinah* were facing him.[21] The juxtaposition of these two dicta implies that the one illumines the other, i.e., the directing of the heart to God entails the conjuring of an anthropomorphic image of the *Šekhinah*. Further evidence for this is found in the paraphrase of the words of Simeon the Pious by Rashi, who explains the opinion attributed to Rava that at the conclusion of the *ʿamidah* one must bow first to his left. Since the worshiper is standing opposite the divine Presence, his left side is the right side of God. Rashi comments:

> He who prays must see himself as if the *Šekhinah* were facing him, as it says, "I have set the Lord always before me" (Ps 16:8).[22]

Interestingly enough, even Maimonides, the philosopher who unequivocally and repeatedly denied the morphic nature of God, defined *kawwanah* in part on the basis of the dictum of Simeon the Pious:

> A person should empty his heart from all thoughts and look upon himself as if he were standing before the *Šekhinah*.[23]

Growth of Mysticism: Gregory the Great through the 12th Century (New York: Crossroad, 1994) x–xi.

19. *B. Sanh.* 22a.

20. *B. Ber.* 31a.

21. *Hilkhot Rav Alfasi*, printed in standard editions of the Babylonian Talmud, *Ber.* 22b; *Sefer ha-ʾEshkol* (ed. S. Albeck and C. Albeck; 2d ed.; Jerusalem: n.p., 1984) 33.

22. Rashi's commentary to *b. Yoma* 53b, s.v. *la-śemoʾl didakh*.

23. *Mishneh Torah*, Hilkhot Tefillah 4.16. Cf. ibid. 5.4, where Maimonides paraphrases the teaching attributed to R. Yose in *b. Yebam.* 105b in the following words: "When a person rises to pray . . . he should cast his eyes below as if he were looking at

Elaborating this line of interpretation, Jacob ben Asher codified the requirement to pray with proper intention in the following way:

> It has been taught, "he who prays should direct his heart, as it says, 'You will make their hearts firm, You will incline Your ear' (Ps 10:17)." The explanation of this is that he should concentrate on the meaning of the words that he brings out with his lips, and he should contemplate as if the *Šekhinah* were facing him, as it says, "I have set the Lord always before me" (Ps 16:8). He should arouse the intention and remove all the thoughts that burden him until the point that his mind and his intention are pure in his worship. . . . Thus the pietists and men of action would concentrate and intend in their prayer until they attained the stripping away of corporeality and the augmentation of the rational spirit, thereby proximating the level of prophecy.[24]

---

the ground and his heart should be turned above as if he were standing in heaven." Maimonides' acquiescence to the psychological necessity of iconic representation in theistic worship is implied in his remark in the *Guide of the Perplexed* III:32, that the demand to abolish the cult of sacrifices entirely in the time of Moses would be equivalent to the appearance of a prophet in his own time who would call upon the Jewish people to worship God solely in meditation. Such silent meditation is, of course, the ideal of intellectual worship that Maimonides sets forth in *Guide* III:51. He describes such worship in a mystical-pietistic vein as emptying the mind of everything but the contemplation of the intellectual bond that connects the human soul and God. (Cf. Maimonides' description of the prophet in *Mishneh Torah*, Hilkhot Yesode Torah 7.1 and 4.) Although Maimonides characterizes this state of intellectual apprehension, which is best attained in seclusion, as an intense and passionate love (*ʿishq*), and he utilizes the erotic language of the kiss (derived from Cant 1:2) to describe it, he is clear that this language is merely figurative and does not relate in any way to the body or the senses. See S. Rawidowicz, *Studies in Jewish Thought* (ed. N. N. Glatzer; Philadelphia: Jewish Publication Society of America, 1974) 295–96; R. J. Zwi Werblowsky, *Joseph Karo: Lawyer and Mystic* (Philadelphia: Jewish Publication Society of America, 1977) 57 n. 1; D. R. Blumenthal, "Maimonides: Prayer, Worship, and Mysticism," in *Approaches to Judaism in Medieval Times* (ed. D. R. Blumenthal; Atlanta: Scholars Press, 1988) 3.1–16. The lofty philosophical notion of contemplation may be a truly aniconic form of worship, but normative theistic worship is decidedly iconic inasmuch as it is predicated on forming an anthropomorphic image of God. See M. Fox, *Interpreting Maimonides: Studies in Methodology, Metaphysics, and Moral Philosophy* (Chicago: University of Chicago Press, 1990) 297–321; G. J. Blidstein, *Prayer in Maimonidean Halakha* (Jerusalem: Bialik, 1994) 77–86 [Heb.]; and I. Twersky, "'And One Should Regard Oneself as if Facing the Lord': Intention in Prayer according to Maimonides," in *Knesset Ezra: Literature and Life in the Synagogue: Studies Presented to Ezra Fleischer* (ed. S. Elizur et al.; Jerusalem: Yad Yitzhak Ben-Zvi, 1994) 47–67 [Heb.].

24. *Ṭur*, ʿOraḥ Ḥayyim §98; cf. *Shulḥan ʿArukh*, ʿOraḥ Ḥayyim, §98.1; Israel ibn al-Nakawa, *Menorat ha-Maʾor* (ed. H. G. Enelow; New York: Bloch, 1930) 2.116–17. Al-Nakawa emphasizes the semantic aspect of *kawwanah*, that is, the need to concentrate on the meaning of the words that one utters, and he refers to this intentionality as the 'foundation of faith' *yesod ha-ʾemunah*. On the need to focus on the meaning of

In the above passage, Jacob ben Asher translates the implications of the earlier discussions on *kawwanah* in talmudic literature into the idiom of medieval spirituality, reflecting a synthesis of scriptural and philosophical pietism. Thus the traditional idea of *kawwanah* is linked with the technical term *hitbodedut*, which connotes both physical seclusion and mental concentration.[25] Moreover, the placing of the obligation to concentrate on the meaning of the words that one utters right next to the need to contemplate the visual presence of the *Šekhinah* suggests that the former involves a technical praxis that results in the latter. According to this reading, the citation of Ps 16:8 takes on new significance: *šiwwiti yhwh lenegddi tamid* means that one should concentrate on the letters of the Tetragrammaton, and this contemplation causes the formation of an anthropomorphic image of the *Šekhinah* before one's eyes.[26] Support for my interpretation may be gathered from another comment of Jacob ben Asher:

> One should intend in one's blessings the meaning of the words that he brings out from his mouth. When he mentions the [divine] name he should concentrate on the meaning of its pronunciation with *ʾalef dalet* [i.e., Adonai], from

---

words as part of the proper *kawwanah* in prayer, cf. *Sefer Ḥasidim* (ed. J. Wistinetzki; Frankfurt a.M.: Mekize Nirdamim, 1924) §1590. The importance of comprehension to intentionality is underscored by the position affirmed by the author of *Sefer Ḥasidim* that it is preferrable for one who does not comprehend Hebrew to say the *Šemaʿ* and its blessings in a language that he comprehends. For a similar position, see ibid., 11 (this passage is from *Sefer ha-Yirʾah*, the section of *Sefer Ḥasidim* assumed to have been written by Samuel the Pious). The value of intentionality is emphasized time and again in the Pietistic writings, and it is the moral of the well-known exemplum concerning the nontraditional prayer of the herdsman (*roʿeh behemot*) in *Sefer Ḥasidim*, §§5–6 (again part of *Sefer ha-Yirʾah*). For a detailed analysis of this tale, see T. Alexander-Frizer, *The Pious Sinner: Ethics amd Aesthetics in the Medieval Hasidic Narrative* (Tübingen: Mohr, 1991) 58–86.

25. See M. Idel, *Studies in Ecstatic Kabbalah* (Albany: State University of New York Press, 1988) 103–69; idem, "*Hitbodedut* as Concentration in Jewish Philosophy," *Jerusalem Studies in Jewish Thought* 7 (1988) 39–60 [Heb.]; P. Fenton, "La 'Hitbodedut' chez les premiers Qabbalists en Orient et chez les Soufis," in *Prière, mystique et Judaïsme* (ed. R. Goetschel; Paris: Presses Universitaires de France, 1987) 133–57. On the ecstatic element implicit in the passage from Jacob ben Asher and its important influence on subsequent Jewish mysticism, including Beshtian Hasidism, see G. Scholem, *On the Mystical Shape of the Godhead: Basic Concepts of the Kabbalah* (New York: Schocken, 1991) 291 n. 91; Idel, *Studies in Ecstatic Kabbalah*, 163 n. 136; idem, *Hasidism: Between Ecstasy and Magic* (Albany: State University of New York Press, 1995) 64 and 281–82 n. 109.

26. A similar application of Ps 16:8 is well attested in kabbalistic literature. See my *Through a Speculum That Shines*, 199 n. 42. Needless to say, the number of textual examples that illustrate the point could have been greatly multiplied. I hope to elaborate on this point in a monograph on incarnation and the imaginal body in Jewish sources, which will be an expanded version of my study referred to above, n. 11.

the expression *ʾadnut* ('lordship'), for He is the lord of everything (*ʾadon ha-kol*), and he should also concentrate on how it is written with *yod heʾ* [i.e., YHWH], from the expression *hawwayah*, for He is, was, and will be. And when he mentions [the name] *ʾelohim* he should intend that He is powerfully strong for He has power in the upper and the lower realms. The expression *ʾel* has the meaning of power and strength as [in the verse] 'he carried away the nobles of the land' *we-ʾet ʾele ha-ʾāreṣ lāqaḥ* (Ezek 17:13).[27]

The likelihood that Jacob ben Asher is drawing upon a mystical praxis, based on the notion that proper concentration is linked to the different names of God, is enhanced by a comment in Abraham ben Nathan of Lunel:

I have found in the esoteric books (*sefarim penimiyyim*) that when one blesses the Lord he should concentrate in his heart on the present, past, and future, just as it says,[28] 'the Lord reigns, the Lord reigned, and the Lord will reign forever' *yhwh melekh yhwh malakh yhwh yimlokh leʿolam waʿed*. Through the [letter technique of] *a"t ba"sh*[29] [the three occurrences of the Tetragrammaton] are *mṣp"ṣ mṣp"ṣ mṣp"ṣ*, but the matter is only transmitted to the humble.[30]

Further evidence for such an understanding of the concept of *kawwanah* may be gathered from the writings of the Rhineland Jewish Pietists. One passage in particular from the classical work of pietistic ethics and religious devotion, *Sefer Ḥasidim*, is worthy of note. Reflecting on why there are three divine names mentioned in the *Šĕmaʿ*, *yhwh ʾĕlohênû yhwh*, preceded by one name in the introductory remark *ʾel melek neʾeman*,[31] Judah the Pious comments:

There are four names because when people sit in the four corners of the synagogue each one must intend as if the face of the *Šekhinah* were facing him, so that a person will not say since it is facing me and I am in the east and it is in the west, how can it face every side in one moment? It is written, "I will look upon you" (Lev 26:9), each and every person must direct his heart as if the

27. *Ṭur*, ʿOraḥ Ḥayyim, §5.

28. This liturgical expression (cf. *Maḥzor la-Yamim Noraʾim* [2 vols.; ed. D. S. Goldschmidt; Jerusalem: Koren, 1970] 1.77–78 and 199–202) is based on different biblical verses. Cf. Ps 10:16 (*yhwh melek*); Ps 93:1 (*yhwh mālāk*; cf. 1 Chr 16:31); and Exod 15:18 (*yhwh yimlōk lĕʿōlām wāʿed*; cf. Ps 146:10).

29. This is an ancient hermeneutical technique of letter substitution, which became especially popular in medieval pietistic and mystical groups. The first letter, *ʾalep*, corresponds to the last letter, *taw*, and so on. According to this technique, the letters of the Tetragrammaton, *yhwh*, correspond to *mṣp"ṣ*.

30. *Sefer ha-Manhig* (2 vols.; ed. Y. Raphael; Jerusalem: Mosad ha-Rav Kook, 1978) 1.85. Cf. Aaron ha-Kohen of Lunel, *ʾOrḥot Ḥayyim* (2 vols.; Florence, 1750) 1.4d; *Perushe Siddur ha-Tefillah la-Roqeaḥ* (ed. M. Hershler and Y. A. Hershler; Jerusalem: Machon ha-Rav Hershler, 1992) 131.

31. On the historical development of the saying of this expression as an introduction to the *Šemaʿ*, see I. Ta-Shema, *Early Franco-German Ritual and Custom* (Jerusalem: Magnes, 1992) 285–98 [Heb.].

> *Šekhinah* were facing him, and with respect to the *Šekhinah* it is not appropriate to say, how is it possible for it to turn to four directions at once?[32]

At work in this passage is a central idea that informs the mystical theosophy of the Pietists: utterance of the divine names results in the visual manifestation of the divine glory.[33] In this particular context, this praxis is related more specifically to the *kawwanah* that the worshiper must have in the synagogue. This *kawwanah* brings about the optical representation of the *Šekhinah*.[34] Every worshiper must imagine that the *Šekhinah* is facing him within the sacred space of the synagogue when he stands to pray, a central motif in the writings of Ḥaside Ashkenaz to which I shall return.

I surmise that Jacob ben Asher, like Abraham ben Nathan, derived his understanding of *kawwanah* related to the divine names from esoteric works such as those transmitted and/or composed by the German Pietists.[35] Whatever the direct source, it may be concluded that, according to Jacob ben Asher, the meditational praxis of *kawwanah* involves concentration on the names of God that results in a state of disembodiment and the concomitant intensification of the rational spirit, which proximates the experience of prophecy. Jacob ben Asher astutely understood the morphological nature of *kawwanah* implied by the dictum of Simeon the Pious. The ultimate goal of contemplation may be the separation of the intellect from the body, but the consciousness fostered by intention in prayer is predicated on the iconic visualization of the divine Presence in bodily terms. The ascetic negation of the physical body allows for the ocular apprehension of God's imaginal body.[36]

32. *Sefer Ḥasidim*, §512. For a slightly different version of the text, cf. *Sefer Ḥasidim* (ed. R. Margaliot; Jerusalem: Mosad ha-Rav Kook, 1957) §808. Cf. *Perushe Siddur ha-Tefillah la-Roqeaḥ*, 362: "The face of the *Šekhinah* is in all four directions of the world at one time."

33. See my *Through a Speculum That Shines*, 234–54. The divine names are identified as the visions of the glory in Eleazar of Worms, *Sode Razayya* (ed. I. Kamelhar; Bilgoraj, 1936) 35. Cf. ibid., 60:

> Everything is sealed with His name. Therefore the beginning [of the words] *yiśmĕḥû haššāmayim wĕ-tāgēl hā-ʾāreṣ* (Ps 96:11) [spells] the name [*yhwh*], for the [name of the] Creator is written *yhwh*, His name is present in everything and He manifests His glory as it seems appropriate before Him, "It is I, the Lord, who made everything" (Isa 44:24).

34. In other passages the ideal of *kawwanah* is upheld, but there is no specific indication that the term implies a visualization of the *Šekhinah*. Cf. *Sefer Ḥasidim*, §§441–43, 445–46, 451, 456, 466, 475–76, 481, 1577, 1587.

35. On the development of this technique in early theosophic kabbalah, see M. Idel, "On the Intention of the Eighteen Benedictions according to R. Isaac the Blind," in *Massuʾot*, 25–52 [Heb.]. Idel mentions the passage from *Sefer ha-Manhig* on p. 32, and in n. 50 he lists various scholars who have considered the mystical element in Abraham ben Nathan.

36. A similar argument can be made for the history of Christianity: the theological doctrine of incarnation provided the psychological impetus for the divinization of

Iconic Visualization of the Imageless Creator in Ḥaside Ashkenaz

The Kalonymide Pietists developed an intriguing and rather sophisticated phenomenology of liturgical worship based on the idea that the imageless and formless Creator takes shape through the image that is placed by the divine will in the human imagination. The imagination is thus comparable to a mirror that reflects in its ideal transparency the form that manifests itself. The radiance of the glory can shine only within the pure heart in the same manner that the face of a person will be clear only in a mirror that is luminously bright.[37] Given the identification of the imagination as the heart, the Pietists assign esoteric significance to the rabbinic idiom for prayer, *ʿavodah she-ba-lev,* that is, worship through the heart is worship by means of the imagination. The point is underscored in the following observation of Eleazar of Worms:

---

the human body, for just as the divine miracuously became human, the human could become divine, particularly through renunciation of the physical or the transfiguration of the carnal body into a psychic or spiritual body. Ascetism, therefore, sanctifies the coarse body, transforming it into a temple of God or a limb of Christ's body. Subjugation of the human body allowed for the symbolic retrieval of the body to characterize spiritual realities. See J. Gager, "Body-Symbols and Social Reality: Resurrection, Incarnation, and Asceticism in Early Christianity," *Religion* 12 (1982) 345–64; P. Brown, *The Body and Society: Men, Women, and Sexual Renunciation in Early Christianity* (New York: Columbia University Press, 1988) 31, 174–77, 235–37; A. Cameron, *Christianity and the Rhetoric of Empire: The Development of Christian Discourse* (Berkeley: University of California Press, 1991) 68–69; C. Walker Bynum, *Holy Feast and Holy Fast: The Religious Significance of Food to Medieval Women* (Berkeley: University of California Press, 1987) 31–69; idem, *Fragmentation and Redemption: Essays on Gender and the Human Body in Medieval Religion* (New York: Zone, 1991) 119–50; idem, *The Resurrection of the Body in Western Christianity, 200–1336* (New York: Columbia University Press, 1995) 59–114; D. Elliott, *Spiritual Marriage: Sexual Abstinence in Medieval Wedlock* (Princeton: Princeton University Press, 1993). On sexual asceticism and erotic spirituality in theosophic kabbalistic literature, see Scholem, *Major Trends,* 235; G. Vajda, "Continence, mariage et vie mystique selon la doctrine du judaïsme," *Mystique et continence: Travaux scientifiques du VIIe Congrès International d'Avon* (Bruges: Desclee, 1952) 82–92; Werblowsky, *Joseph Karo,* 38–83, 113–18, 133–39, 149–52, 161–65; M. Pachter, "The Concept of *Devekut* in the Homiletical Ethical Writings of 16th Century Safed," *Studies in Medieval Jewish History and Literature* (2 vols.; ed. I. Twersky; Cambridge: Harvard University Press, 1984) 2.200–210; L. Fine, "Purifying the Body in the Name of the Soul: The Problem of the Body in Sixteenth-Century Kabbalah," in *People of the Body: Jews and Judaism from an Embodied Perspective* (ed. H. Eilberg-Schwartz; Albany: State University of New York Press, 1992) 117–42; D. Biale, *Eros and the Jews: From Biblical Israel to Contemporary America* (New York: Basic Books, 1992) 113–18. Regarding asceticism in the ecstatic kabbalah, see Idel, *Mystical Experience in Abraham Abulafia,* 143–44.

37. The analogy is used explicitly in *Sefer ha-Kavod,* MS Oxford, Bodleian Library 1566, fol. 30a. Cf. *Perushe Siddur ha-Tefillah la-Roqeaḥ,* 713.

> One must concentrate on prayer with a complete heart, as it is written, "[loving the Lord your God] and serving Him with all your heart" (Deut 11:13), this refers to prayer, as it is written in Daniel, "[Your God] whom you serve so regularly" (6:17). This is to inform you that for this everything was created, for the sake of this every man has been created, for the eyes of the worshiper are on earth and his heart is toward heaven.[38]

The conclusion of this statement is a paraphrase of the saying attributed to R. Yose, "the one who prays should cast his eyes below and his heart above."[39] I shall return to the use of this talmudic dictum in the Pietistic sources at a later stage of my analysis, but at this juncture it is important to note that, phenomenologically, the Pietists discerned that a theistic conception of prayer necessitated endowing the formless God with form. Prayer is, after all, dwelling in the presence of the divine glory.[40] Thus, in the opening section of his commentary on the liturgy, Eleazar reflects on the change in tense in the traditional formula of a blessing from the second to the third person:

> It is necessary to explain that at the beginning of the prayer of every person the Holy One, blessed be He, is found, as it says, "I have set the Lord always before me" (Ps 16:8), and another verse says, "in every place where I cause My name to be mentioned I will come to you and bless you" (Exod 20:21). . . . It

38. *Perushe Siddur ha-Tefillah la-Roqeaḥ*, 483.

39. *B. Yebam.* 105b. I would like to take this opportunity to correct two errors that I made with respect to this talmudic passage in *Through a Speculum That Shines*, 202 n. 53. First, I inadvertently cited the source as *b. Yebam.* 108b instead of 105b. Second, I mistakenly attributed the dictum to Abba instead of R. Yose. The latter is indeed referred to as *ʾabbaʾ* in that context, for Ishmael ben Yose is the one who transmits the dictum in the name of his father.

40. It is precisely this phenomenological aspect of prayer that underlies Gerson Cohen's attempt to view the Hebrew Crusade chronicles as part of the genre of Ashkenazic liturgical commentary. That is, the chronicles reflect this literary genre because their authors wished to convey the idea that the martyrs occupied a place in the inner sanctum of the divine glory. See Cohen, "The Hebrew Crusade Chronicles and the Ashkenazic Tradition," 36–53. Cf. the passages translated in R. Chazan, *European Jewry and the First Crusade* (Berkeley: University of California Press, 1987) 281–82 and 286. On the coronation of Jewish martyrs, which I assume implies a form of angelification, cf. the description in the addition of Eleazar of Worms to the dirge composed by Qalonymous ben Judah of Mainz, *mî yittēn rōʾšî mayim, Seder ha-Qinnot ha-Meforash le-Tishʿah be-ʾAv* (Jerusalem: Gefen, 1988) 230: *kelule keter ʿal roʾšam leʿaṭṭerah we-ʿal ʾaddire qehal maggenṣaʾ ha-hadurah.* The additional part is published with the title *qehillot ha-qodesh* in *Shirat ha-Rokeaḥ: The Poems of Rabbi Eleazar ben Yehudah of Worms* (ed. I. Meiseles; Jerusalem, 1993) 268–70 [Heb.]; the afore-cited passage occurs on p. 269. On the relationship between the behavioral patterns exemplified by Jewish martyrs in 1096 and the attitudes toward the divine will expressed by Ḥaside Ashkenaz, see Chazan, *European Jewry*, 214–16. Regarding the impact of the First Crusade on Ḥaside Ashkenaz, see also the discussion in ibid., 143–47, and references to the studies of Dan and Marcus cited on pp. 325–26 n. 14.

is appropriate that the *Šekhinah* will be seen by a person in the beginning but more than that would be a disgrace for the *Šekhinah*.[41]

Similarly, in *Sod Maʿaseh Bereʾshit*, Eleazar writes:

When a person makes a blessing he should intend with his heart, as it written, "I have set the Lord always before me" (Ps 16:8). Therefore, they established [the liturgical formula] "blessed are You, O Lord," in the manner of someone talking to his friend.[42]

Eleazar repeats this theme in slightly different terms in *Shaʿare ha-Sod ha-Yiḥud we-ha-ʾEmunah*:

When you rise to pray, know before whom you stand, and your thoughts should only be about the Creator of the world who is standing opposite you. . . . When you say, "blessed are You," do not think about the glory but only about the Creator, blessed be He;[43] you will come to see, and to discern Him and to attest to Him through His glorious name . . . through His name you will know His unity, His actions, and the desire of His will, and then you will know how to worship Him.[44]

The grammatical syntax of the blessing reveals a more general secret about liturgy: worship is predicated on the very possibility of standing visually in the presence of God, if only for a limited duration. From that vantage point idolatry—the attribution of visible form to the divine—is an inevitable consequence of theistic worship.[45] Significantly, according to the conclusion of

41. *Perushe Siddur ha-Tefillah la-Roqeaḥ*, 2. Similar language is used by Eleazar in a liturgical commentary extant in MS Munich, Bayerische Staatsbibliothek 232, fol. 2a.

42. *Sefer Raziʾel* (Amsterdam, 1701) 8b. Cf. *Perushe Siddur ha-Tefillah la-Roqeaḥ*, 143: "'I will extol You' (Ps 145:1), as if he were speaking to Him, for he is facing Him, 'I have set the Lord always before me' (Ps 16:8)." Ibid., 156–57: "Therefore they established [the liturgical formulas as] 'blessed are You, O Lord,' as if he were speaking to Him mouth to mouth, 'I have set the Lord always before me' (Ps 16:8)." Cf. ibid., 157, 195, 315, 401.

43. This is a theme repeated many times in Eleazar's writings and in the works of other Pietists. Cf. *Sefer ha-Roqeaḥ* (Jerusalem, 1961) 9. See Scholem, *Major Trends*, 107; Dan, *Esoteric Theology*, 167, 182–83. I have translated and discussed some of the relevant sources in *Through a Speculum That Shines*, 201–4.

44. J. Dan (ed.), "*Sefer Shaʿare ha-Sod ha-Yiḥud we-ha-ʾEmunah*," in *Temirin: Texts and Studies in Kabbala and Hasidism* (2 vols.; ed. I. Weinstock; Jerusalem: Mosad ha-Rav Kook, 1972–81) 1.153.

45. Several recent studies have reconsidered the significance of idolatry, related specifically to anthropomorphism and iconic representation, to the monotheistic faith of Judaism. See, for example, R. M. Adams, "Idolatry and the Invisibility of God," in *Interpretation in Religion* (ed. S. Biderman and B. Scharfstein; Leiden: Brill, 1992) 39–52; M. Halbertal and A. Margalit, *Idolatry* (Cambridge: Harvard University Press, 1992); E. N. Dorff, "In Defense of Images," *Proceedings of the Academy for Jewish Philosophy* (ed. D. Novak and N. M. Samuelson; Lanham: University Press of America,

the first passage cited above, the imaginative visualization of the *Šekhinah* is limited by the moralistic demand that overexposure would be a disgrace for the divine presence, *hayah genai li-šekhinah*. This remark, I surmise, is related to a larger motif (to be discussed more fully below) regarding the gender of the *Šekhinah* and the consequent nexus between eros and vision.

On the other hand, the Pietists were, of course, committed to the philosophical claim that the Creator is incorporeal and thus beyond imaginative representation. From that vantage point it is strictly forbidden to conjure an image of God. As may be deduced from a passage in *Sefer Ḥasidim*, living in a Christian environment sensitized Ḥaside Ashkenaz to this issue, and they thus prohibited the presence of any image of living beings in the synagogue. Even though there were cherubim and images of cattle and lions in the Temple, no image was allowed in the synagogue, especially before the Ark that contained the Torah scrolls, lest the Christians say that the Jews believe in and bow down to icons (*demuyot*).[46] The clash of the aniconic and the iconic tendencies is evident already in the following passage from *Shir ha-Kavod*, a liturgical composition most probably stemming from an early stage of Rhineland Pietism:[47]

> I will speak of Your glory,
> but I have not seen You,
> I will image and name You,
> but I have not known You;
> Through Your prophets, the counsel of Your servants,
> You made the splendor of the glory of Your majesty appear.
> Your greatness and Your power they named
> according to the strength of Your actions,
> They imagined You,
> but not as You are,

1992) 129–54; A. L. Ivry, "The Inevitability of Idolatry," also in *Proceedings*, ibid., 195–211. For a different assessment, one more congenial to the medieval philosophical orientation, see the essays in the same volume by B. S. Kogan, "Judaism and the Varieties of Idolatrous Experience," 169–93; and S. S. Schwarzschild, "De Idololatria," 213–42.

46. *Sefer Ḥasidim*, §1625. From §1626 it may be deduced that pictorial images for decorative purposes were allowed on the inside and the outside of the synagogue. On decorating the Ark in order to honor the Torah, cf. §648.

47. The poem, which is the concluding part of the *Shir ha-Yiḥud*, was attributed in the 13th century by Moses Taku to R. Bezalel and R. Samuel, the latter perhaps referring to Samuel ben Qalonymous. In some editions the composition is ascribed to Judah ben Samuel the Pious. For a review of the problem of authorship, see A. M. Haberman, *Shire ha-Yiḥud we-ha-Kavod* (Jerusalem: Mosad ha-Rav Kook, 1948) 11; see also J. Dan's introduction to *Shir ha-Yiḥud: The Hymn of Divine Unity with the Kabbalistic Commentary of R. Yom Tov Lipmann Muelhausen, Thiengen 1560* (Jerusalem: Magnes, 1981) 7–15 [Heb.].

they compared You according to Your actions.
They configured You in many forms,
but You are one in all the images.[48]

One might be tempted to resolve the tension between the philosophical conception of the invisible deity and the anthropomorphic conception by noting that the latter applies to the glory and not to the Creator. The glory, it may be further assumed, is ontologically inferior to the Creator, and thus anthropomorphic characterizations of the glory do not impinge on rationalist theology.[49] Upon closer reflection, however, it becomes apparent that in this text the glorious form is not depicted as ontically distinct from God. On the contrary, as the above stanza concludes, "They configured You in many forms, but You are one in all the images," that is, it is the invisible Creator who is imaged by the prophets in a multiplicity of anthropomorphic forms, many of which are mentioned explicitly in the continuation of the poem. The statement 'Through Your prophets and the counsel of Your servants, You made the splendor of the glory of Your majesty appear' *be-yad nebi'eka be-sod ʿabadeka dimita hadar kebod hodeka* is particularly significant, for the first part is a conflation of two biblical verses: 'and through the prophets I was imaged' *û-wĕ-yad hā-nĕbî'îm 'ădammeh* (Hos 12:11) and 'He revealed His design to His servants the prophets' *gālah sōdô 'el ʿăbādāyw hā-nĕbî'îm* (Amos 3:7).[50] Clearly, the author of *Shir ha-Kavod* is referring to ancient times when he claims that the prophets, who are the servants of God, merited an epiphany of the divine splendor. I surmise, however, that the servants here may also re-

48. I have translated from the Hebrew text as it appears in Haberman, *Shire ha-Yiḥud we-ha-Kavod*, 47–48.

49. This is the position articulated by J. Petuchowski, *Theology and Poetry: Studies in Medieval Piyyut* (London: Routledge & Kegan Paul, 1978) 37. Petuchowski, basing himself largely on the scholarship of Scholem and Dan, acknowledges that the works of the German Pietists represent a "rather unusual mixture of mysticim and rationalism," the concomitant denial and affirmation of anthropomorphism. He argues, however, that there is no contradiction because the mythological and anthropomorphic images are not attributed to the Creator, or the "philosophical God-concept," but to the glory, or the "God of religious experience." The situation, in my opinion, is more complex insofar as the anthropomorphic characteristics are on some occasions related directly to the Creator. Moreover, I am reluctant to view Pietistic theology as radically dualistic. Although there is clearly a distinction between the hidden God and the revealed glory, the two aspects are interrelated and it is not adequate to differentiate in such stark terms between the Creator and the God of religion. The complex interrelationship between the two can be seen in the particular case of visionary experience, for it is the hidden God who takes shape through the visible glory. On the role of anthropomorphism in the German Pietists, see my *Through a Speculum That Shines*, 192–95.

50. In *Sode Razayya*, 46, Eleazar cites these two verses together in an attempt to characterize the nature of prophetic experience. Regarding the Pietists' application of Amos 3:7 to themselves, see the comments of Marcus, *Piety and Society*, 70.

fer to the Pietists themselves who are capable of having visionary experience on a par with prophecy, and the object of that experience is the majestic and splendid image assumed by the imageless Creator.[51]

What is expressed poetically in the *Shir ha-Kavod* is reiterated in a more speculative and discursive tone in a Pietistic commentary on *ʿAleynu* attributed to Judah the Pious. According to that text, the Creator places an image in the heart of the prophet, which he governs, so that the prophet can bow down to it and thereby worship God.[52] The view articulated here stands in marked contrast to, indeed is a polemical rejection of, two theological positions articulated in other Pietistic works to explain the ontic status of the glory and the nature of visionary experience. The first position is the Saadianic doctrine of the created glory and the second the idea, ultimately traceable to Hai Gaon,[53] that the image of the glory is a mental construct, akin to magical delusion (*ʾaḥizat ʿeinayim*), which has no objective correlate in the sensible world.[54] The paradox generated by the Pietistic theology is well captured in a statement from this composition, which appears with slight variations in a number of other esoteric Ashkenazi sources, including works

51. The nexus between prayer and prophecy is established in *Sefer Ḥasidim*, §425. In that context the worshiper is described as being rapt in the love of God in a way comparable to the prophet whose soul is bound in love to God. On the erotic and all-consuming quality of a pietist's love for God, cf. ibid., §815, and parallel in Eleazar's *Sod Maʿaseh Bereʾšit*, in *Sefer Raziʾel*, 9a. Cf. the erotic description of the relationship of the righteous and the *Šekhinah* in *Sode Razayya*, 6. In that context Eleazar uses the expression *šaʿašuʿa le-ṣaddiqim* '(sexual) delight for the righteous'. The word *yešaʿašeʿa* is used to connote sexual activity between a man and his wife in one of the responsa attributed to Judah the Pious, MS Munich, Bayerische Staatsbibliothek 232, fol. 18b. The word also connotes vision; cf. *Perushe Siddur ha-Tefillah la-Roqeaḥ*, 671. The love of God in the writings of the German Pietists has been discussed by a number of scholars. See Scholem, *Major Trends*, 95–96, 226; Vajda, *L'Amour de dieu*, 149–62; Marcus, *Piety and Society*, 36; J. Dan, *Jewish Mysticism and Jewish Ethics* (Seattle: University of Washington Press, 1986) 74–75; idem, "A Re-evaluation of the 'Ashkenazi Kabbalah,'" *Jerusalem Studies in Jewish Thought* 6/3–4 (1987) 136–37 [Heb.]. On the love between man and woman, see M. Harris, "The Concept of Love in Sepher Hassidim," *JQR* 50 (1959) 13–44.

52. The text is published by J. Dan, *Studies in Ashkenazi-Hasidic Literature* (Ramat-Gan: Massada, 1975) 82–84 [Heb.]. The relevant passage occurs on 83; for partial translation and discussion, see *Through a Speculum That Shines*, 197–98.

53. An early attestation of the influence of Geonic doceticism in an Ashkenazic text is found in the citation of Ḥananel ben Ḥushiel's explanation of the talmudic aggadah that God wears phylacteries (*b. Ber.* 6a) in Eliezer ben Nathan of Mainz, *Sefer Raban* (ed. S. Albeck; Warsaw, 1904) §127, 50a–b. Ḥananel, following the lead of Hai, explains this passage by saying that God is seen by a 'vision of the heart' (*reʾiyat lev*) and not a 'physical vision' (*reʾiyat ʿayin*).

54. See Dan, *Esoteric Theology*, 165–66. For discussion of the various opinions on the nature of the glory found in Pietistic sources, see ibid., 129–43.

of Eleazar of Worms, that the "Creator is within the image and outside it."[55] Insofar as the Creator is imageless, he is obviously outside the visible image of the glory; yet, to the degree that the image represents the will of the Creator, he is within the image in the manner that a face is reflected in a mirror. As Eleazar expressed it, "in the glory is manifest the will of the Creator, blessed be He, as in a speculum, and this is [the meaning of] 'the glorious majesty of Your splendor' (Ps 145:5)."[56] The glorious image is the configuration of God's thoughts or decrees, which are identified as the archetypal forms or angels.[57] To cite one of many texts that articulate this idea:

> The prophet sees in a vision all the decrees. . . . "When I spoke concerning the prophets" (Hos 12:11), it does not say 'to the prophets' (*ʾel ha-neviʾim*) but 'concerning the prophets' (*ʿal ha-neviʾim*). I spoke to the angels so that they will show you everything and they will speak of everything. "For I granted many visions" (Hos 12:11). . . . Initially the glory speaks to the prophets and afterwards they see visions in order that they will know everything. . . . And this is [the import of] "Words of him who hears God's speech . . . and beholds visions [from the Almighty]" (Num 24:16). By means of this "he obtains knowledge from the Most High" (ibid.), for the Creator manifests and images His thoughts that He wills to accomplish. . . . And this is [the meaning of] "When I spoke concerning the prophets" and afterward "I granted many visions," for he knows by means of the visions the supernal mind, and afterward "and through the prophets I was imaged." . . . All that which He shows to the prophets is assimilated by their minds and He shows to their minds His will

55. Dan, *Studies in Ashkenazi-Hasidic Literature*, 83. Cf. Eleazar of Worms, *Sefer ha-Shem*, MS London, British Museum 737, fol. 320b: "The Creator is outside the images and within them." And idem, *Ḥokhmat ha-Nefesh* (Bene-Beraq, 1987) 90: "The Creator is outside the images and within them." These three sources have been previously cited in my *Through a Speculum That Shines*, 198 and 200.

56. *Perushe Siddur ha-Tefillah la-Roqeaḥ*, 146.

57. See my *Through a Speculum That Shines*, 205–6. Underlying the identification of the angels as the divine thoughts is the idea that the angels are constituted by the Hebrew letters. I have cited some illustrations of this motif in the writings of Ḥaside Ashkenaz and Abraham Abulafia, in ibid., 245 n. 235. This idea is also attested in medieval magical sources, as may be gathered from the Genizah fragments published by J. Naveh and S. Shaked, *Magic Spells and Formulae: Aramaic Incantations of Late Antiquity* (Jerusalem: Magnes, 1993) 196 (translation on p. 202) and 239 (translation on p. 240). In both contexts the "holy letters," which refer to the magical signs, are identified as angels. Consider also the linkage of angels and magical symbols of a linguistic nature called *karaqtirim* or *kalaqtirim* (from the Greek χαρακτῆρες) in *Sefer ha-Razim: A Newly Recovered Book of Magic from the Talmudic Period* (ed. M. Margaliot; Tel-Aviv: Yediot Achronot, 1966) 84 and 87; for further discussion, see ibid., 4, 83 n. 40, and 94 n. 35; and *Sepher ha-Razim: The Book of Mysteries* (trans. M. A. Morgan; Chico, Calif.: Scholars Press, 1983) 46 n. 14. This correlation later developed into the idea of the angelic alphabets. See, e.g., I. Weinstock, "The Alphabet of Meṭaṭron and Its Commentary," in *Temirin: Texts and Studies in Kabbala and Hasidism* (2 vols.; ed. I. Weinstock; Jerusalem: Mosad ha-Rav Kook, 1972–81) 2.51–76 [Heb.].

through speech, in a vision, and by means of an angel. . . . He manifests to the prophets the matter of the purpose that He wills to accomplish, "He revealed His design to His servants the prophets" (Amos 3:7).[58]

Sacred Space and the Imago Templi

The mental iconization of the divine must occur, according to the Pietistic sources, within the confines of a specific place chosen by the will of God. In classical Jewish sources, the notion of sacred space, *maqom qadosh*, entailed the sense of liminality, demarcation, and separation. Within the community of Ḥaside Ashkenaz this traditional sense of holiness, linked to a ritual site of exclusivity, was most probably enhanced by socioeconomic and political factors that led to their spatial confinement.[59] More specifically, in terms of the synagogue, the Pietists accepted and elaborated the halakhic regulations regarding the appropriate place wherein one might pray and the precautions one must take to preserve the sanctity of that place.[60] The sacred space of the synagogue is even further restricted by the fact that in the idealized world of the Pietists, especially as expressed by Judah the Pious, proper boundaries must be set between Pietist and non-Pietist, whether Jew or Christian.[61] Indeed, if the space of the believer is invaded by the non-Pietist, it is desecrated. The point is epitomized in the following passage:

> When he who fears God prays, he should not stand or sit near a wicked person, for when in worship he stands near a wicked person he will think bad thoughts and the *Šekhinah* will be distanced from him.[62]

So strong is the potential of the non-Pietist to defile the space of the Pietist that it is related in another passage that a particular sage (*ḥakham*) refused to sit on the chair or even to use the ink and pen of a wicked scribe who pretended to be righteous.[63]

In light of this obsession with determining social and religious boundaries to foster segregation and isolation, one could well understand that the notion of sacred space occupied a prominent place in the theological ruminations

58. MS Oxford, Bodleian Library 1566, fols. 45a–b.

59. See K. R. Stow, "Sanctity and the Construction of Space: The Roman Ghetto as Sacred Space," in *Jewish Assimilation, Acculturation and Accommodation: Past Traditions, Current Issues and Future Prospects* (ed. M. Mor; Lanham: University Press of America, 1992) 54–76, esp. 54–58.

60. Cf. *Sefer Ḥasidim*, §§419–21, 432, 440, 442, 1606–8, 1612–13, 1627.

61. See H. Soloveitchik, "Three Themes in the *Sefer Ḥasidim*," *AJS Review* 1 (1976) 330–35; Marcus, *Piety and Society*, 99–100; idem, "Hierarchies, Religious Boundaries and Jewish Spirituality in Medieval Germany," *Jewish History* 1 (1986) 7–25.

62. *Sefer Ḥasidim*, §403.

63. Ibid., §404. In §405, it is related that a prayer book written by a wicked person is ineffectual even when used by righteous people. A similar point is made in §1621.

of Ḥaside Ashkenaz. One particular aspect of this phenomenon involves the function of sacred space in the contemplative visualization of the glory through prayer. In the Pietistic commentary on *ʿAleynu*, to which I referred above, the author raises an obvious philosophical question: if the object of one's worship is the mental image, and God is within that image to the degree that no prophet could distinguish between the image and God, then it is conceivable that one could worship in any place that one wants provided that in that place one conjures the mental image of God. The response to this question makes it clear that God places the image in the mind of the worshiper only in the place that God deems to be worthy:

> He desires to be in the place of His glory and to fulfill the will of the worshiper. . . . And, in the place in which He was made visible to David, there the Temple had to be built, for there He was occupied with hearing prayers, and this is [the import of] "My eyes and My heart shall ever be there" (1 Kgs 9:3); there He is occupied with fulfilling the needs of the worshipers . . . but in other places it is not known what is His occupation. Therefore, it is necessary to pray in the place wherein He is occupied with fulfilling the will of the worshiper.[64]

The mental visualization of God can occur only within the place that God selects, for in that place He desires to fulfill the will of the worshiper. What once applied to the Temple was transferred to the synagogue in the time since the Temple was destroyed. Indeed, the sacredness of the synagogue is related to the Temple, which is described as the place that God selected in which to heed prayer.[65] What is implied in this text is spelled out in more detail in one of the compositions of Eleazar of Worms in which he raises the apparent textual discrepancies between the verses that emphasize God's omnipresence on earth and those that stress that one direct one's prayers to heaven. Moreover, the claim to God's omnipresence seemingly challenges the rabbinic notion that one must have a set place for prayer in

64. Dan, *Studies in Ashkenazi-Hasidic Literature*, 83–84.

65. The function of the Temple as the place where God receives the prayers of Israel is emphasized in the Pietistic composition *Sefer ha-Neʿelam*, MS Oxford, Bodleian Library 1566, fol. 163a. Cf. *Ḥokhmat ha-Nefesh*, 92, cited in my *Through a Speculum That Shines*, 203 n. 54. On the description of the Jerusalem Temple as the place where God will cause the splendor of His presence to dwell, *yaškken šam hod šekhinato*, see the *ʾofan* attributed to Judah the Pious, *ʾelohekhem yašiv be-šalem sukko u-meʿonato*, in *Seder ʿAvodat Yisraʾel* (ed. S. Baer; Roedelheim, 1868) 243. Cf. *Perushe Siddur ha-Tefillah la-Roqeaḥ*, 191, 548, 646, 655–56. The description of the Temple in Jerusalem as the locus of God's appearance or the place to which prayers are directed recurs in many of Eleazar's poems. Cf. *Shirat ha-Rokeaḥ*, 87, 95, 98, 170, 249, 251, 256. It is also relevant to note that Ḥaside Ashkenaz, elaborating on a point emphasized in rabbinic texts, view the land of Israel as the most appropriate place for the epiphany of the divine glory to the prophets. Cf. *Sode Razayya*, 33. The opinion expressed by Eleazar closely resembles the mystical orientation of Judah Halevi and Naḥmanides.

the synagogue; on the contrary, one should be able to pray wherever one desires, since the divine glory fills the whole earth:

> When the Temple stood He would show the place of His glory in His holy palace corresponding to the Temple . . . there is the assembly of angels who ascend and descend within it. And this is the gate of heaven. Thus the cherubim spread their wings above . . . facing the eyes of the king, for there He shows His glory to the angels. Similarly, the Temple in a state of our destruction is built to hold weapons and prayers.[66] "My eyes and My heart shall ever be there" (1 Kgs 9:3), for the angels who are appointed need a holy place, for according to them He decrees what is to be done. In the place that He discloses His glory, there He desires the will of the worshiper to be. Therefore, one must fix a place for one's prayer. When a person bows down in the place where His glory is, the Creator is in His glory and He governs it according to His will to instruct the prophet about the will of the Creator. . . . Within the image is the Creator who governs it. . . . In the place where David knew that He was occupied with hearing prayers, he said that the Temple should be built.[67]

Prayer is restricted to the synagogue because only within that place can the person conjure a mental image from which God's presence is, paradoxically, both absent and present. The iconographic function endows the space of the synagogue with a sacredness that was characteristic of the Temple. Indeed, the role of the latter in this process is still much in evidence even after it has been physically destroyed. Ḥaside Ashkenaz follow the talmudic injunction that prayers must be directed to the Temple in Jerusalem, and in that regard it remains the locus of visionary experience.[68] In the absence of the Temple, however, the focus shifts from the physical locality of the earthly Temple to the imaginal space of the heavenly Temple.[69] But, just as

66. The Hebrew reads *banuy le-talpiyyot u-li-tefillot*, based on Cant 4:4. Eleazar's rendering of this verse reflects the rabbinic reading attested in a number of sources. Cf. *y. Ber.* 4.5, 8c; *b. Ber.* 30a; *Pesiqta Rabbati* (ed. M. Friedmann; Vienna: Selbstverlag des Herausgebers, 1880) 33, 149b; *Canticles Rabbah* (ed. S. Dunansky; Jerusalem and Tel-Aviv: Dvir, 1980) 4:11, 110.

67. "*Sefer Shaʿare ha-Sod*," 154–55. This passage of Eleazar's parallels the text attributed to Judah the Pious published in Dan, *Studies in Ashkenazi-Hasidic Literature*, 83. On the notion of the sacred place in the heavenly realm, connected to the throne, and in the earthly Temple, cf. MS Oxford, Bodleian Library 1566, fols. 89b–90a.

68. I have discussed many of the relevant rabbinic passages in "Iconic Visualization and the Imaginal Body of God."

69. Cf. *Perush Siddur ha-Tefillah la-Roqeaḥ*, 289. Cf. commentary on the 42-letter name of God in Eleazar's *Sefer ha-Ḥokhmah*, MS Oxford, Bodleian Library 1568, fol. 3a: "[The name] *qrʿ* is numerically equal to *šakhan* [i.e., both words equal 370] for He caused His presence to dwell (*šikken šekhinato*) in the Temple, and when it was destroyed He departed (*qaraʿ*) and ascended." With respect to this issue one should mention the fact that in the Hebrew crusade chronicles the martyrs are depicted as standing in the celestial Temple. They are symbolized, alternatively, as sacrifical animals and as the priests who officiate before the glory. In the latter instance there is

in the time that the Temple stood there was a parallelism between the earthly and the heavenly chambers, so at present there is a parallelism between the synagogue and the supernal Temple. By bowing down to the anthropomorphic image of the glory in the synagogue, one triggers a reaction on the part of God, which Eleazar boldly characterizes as 'the Creator is in His glory' *ha-bore᾽ bi-khevodo*. Given the presumed ontological parallelism, the act of the worshiper triggers a corresponding event above, and thus the focal point of the imaginative visualization is the celestial throne of glory. As Eleazar writes,

> Since He created all the [archetypal] images (*temunot*) above, He created the throne so that it would be known toward what one should bow down. The presence of His glory is above, and He places His presence below in the Temple, which corresponds to that which is above [as it says], "The place You made to dwell in, O Lord, the sanctuary [O Lord, which Your hands established]" (Exod 15:17). And, similarly, the phylacteries correspond to the soul in the head.[70]

The presence of the glory in the earthly Temple corresponds to the enthroned glory above, which is the real abode of the divine.[71] At the end of the passage the reader is provided with a hint regarding the mystical significance of the phylacteries: just as the throne is the seat upon which the *Šekhinah* dwells, so the phylacteries, which correspond the soul in the head (that is, the rational faculty[72]), are like a throne upon which the *Šekhinah* dwells. The phylacteries of the head, therefore, assume the symbolic function of the glorious throne.[73] Accordingly, in a number of places in the writings of

obviously a transformation of the human into an angel. See Cohen, "Hebrew Crusade Chronicles," 40–41; and I. G. Marcus, "From Politics to Martyrdom: Shifting Paradigms in the Hebrew Narratives of the 1096 Crusade Riots," *Prooftexts* 2 (1982) 40–52.

70. Eleazar, *Ḥokhmat ha-Nefesh*, 70.

71. The parallelism between the heavenly throne and the Jerusalem Temple is emphasized recurringly in the Pietistic writings, based on earlier biblical and rabbinic texts. See, for example, the *'ofan* attributed to Judah the Pious, *᾽elohekhem šikhno śam kes ῾elamo*, in *Seder ῾Avodat Yisra᾽el*, 244, which ends with the words, *qero᾽ lirušalayim kisse᾽ meqomo*. Cf. *Shirat ha-Rokeaḥ*, 105, 217; *Perushe Siddur ha-Tefillah la-Roqeaḥ*, 55–56, 68, 134–35, 197, 200, 221, 346, 680.

72. In the Pietistic sources, the soul (referred to by the technical term *nešamah*) is said to be located in either the head, the brain, or the heart. Cf. *Sode Razayya*, 31; *Ḥokhmat ha-Nefesh*, 17, 96, 116, 144; *Perushe Siddur ha-Tefillah la-Roqeaḥ*, 6, 98, 377–78, 711.

73. The identification of the head phylacteries (which correspond symbolically to the crown) as the throne is a motif found in the German Pietistic and theosophic kabbalistic literature, already attested in *Sefer ha-Bahir*. For references, see my *Along the Path: Studies in Kabbalistic Myth, Symbolism, and Hermeneutics* (Albany: State University of New York Press, 1995) 158–59 n. 234, 166 n. 279, 221 n. 167. To the sources mentioned in those contexts, one might add *Sode Razayya*, 17; *Perushe Siddur*

Ḥaside Ashkenaz, the phylacteries (or the letter *šin* on the head phylacteries, which stands for the name of God[74]) are identified as the object of visual meditation on a par with the throne of glory.[75] The symbolic valence accorded the phylacteries displaces both the earthly and the heavenly Temples as the locus of intentionality, for by donning the phylacteries one can visualize the divine glory that rests between the eyes, which are therefore compared to the cherubim.[76] To cite one textual example from Eleazar's commentary on the prayers in which all the relevant themes are mentioned:

> Why did He command the phylacteries [to be worn] over the heart and between the eyes? This is a reminder of the ark, which is in the middle like the heart, and of the cherubim between whom [speaks] the voice [of God].[77] The phylacteries between the eyes, the countenance of the human,[78] and this is [the import of] "the Lord's name is proclaimed over you" (Deut 28:10).[79] Every

---

ha-Tefillah la-Roqeaḥ, 547. The convergence of the symbols of the crown and of the throne underlies another motif that appears frequently in the Pietistic literature: the mutual elevation and augmentation of the crown and the throne. Cf. *Perushe Siddur ha-Tefillah la-Roqeaḥ*, 245:

> The praise of the glory (*pe'er*) is the praise of Israel, His glorious diadem is glorified in the effulgent splendor, the illumination of the face. . . . When the crown is glorified, the throne of glory is elevated . . . with the elevation of His throne the majesty of His kingship is glorified.

For other sources, see *Along the Path*, 170–71 n. 307.

74. That is, the letter *šin* has the numerical value of 300, which is also the value of the letters *mṣp"ṣ*, the *a"t ba"š* of *yhwh*. Hence, the *šin* stands for the Tetragrammaton.

75. See my *Through a Speculum That Shines*, 229 n. 166; idem, *Along the Path*, 37–39, 159 n. 234.

76. See ibid., 39 and 162 n. 247.

77. Num 7:89; cf. Exod 25:22.

78. In Hebrew, *parṣuf 'adam*. The meaning of Eleazar's remark may be gathered from a parallel to this passage in *Sode Razayya* (ed. S. Weiss; Jerusalem: Shaarey Ziv Institute, 1991) 167:

> When Israel are righteous and they have phylacteries on their heads, the name is upon them, and thus the explicit name is on the forehead of the cherubim. . . . Thus, the phylacteries are placed opposite the hand and in between the eyes for in them is the countenance of the cherubim, and the cherubim have the face of a human.

Hence, what Eleazar intends by speaking of the human countenance in conjunction with the eyes is that the latter correspond to the cherubim, which have a human visage. On the relationship of the face of the cherub and the face of a human in the esoteric thought of Ḥaside Ashkenaz, see my *Along the Path*, 9–10, 121 n. 66. On the tradition of the divine names inscribed upon the forehead of the cherubim, see ibid., 39, 45–46, 49–50, and relevant notes.

79. This part of the biblical verse was interpreted as a reference to the phylacteries in targumic and rabbinic sources. Cf. *Targum Pseudo-Jonathan of the Pentateuch: Text*

> person upon whose head are the phylacteries should consider it as if the *Šekhinah* were upon his head, for just as it is written by the phylacteries, "the Lord's name is proclaimed over you," it is written, "[the ark of God] to which the name was attached, the name Lord of Hosts enthroned on the cherubim" (2 Sam 6:2). Therefore, the phylacteries are on the head for "such a one shall dwell in the lofty heights"[80] (Isa 33:16).[81]

For Ḥaside Ashkenaz, Jerusalem and the Temple are transformed into symbols of the phylacteries that are placed on the head of God through the theurgical efficacy of Israel's prayer.[82] The mystical interpretation of the ritual of putting on the phylacteries as a means to facilitate the indwelling of the *Šekhinah* atop the head of the worshiper reflects the theosophic symbolization of the phylacteries on God's head (which are interchangeable with

---

and Concordance (ed. E. G. Clarke; Hoboken, N.J.: Ktav, 1984) 241 (ad Deut 28:10); *b. Ber.* 6a, *b. Menaḥ.* 35b. In the Ashkenazi sources, the first letters of the expression *šem yhwh niqra'* spell *šin*, which is associated with the *šin* of the phylacteries and the name *mṣp"ṣ*, the *a"t ba"š* permutation of *yhwh*. See my *Along the Path*, 39, 161–62 n. 246. To the sources mentioned there one could add Meir ben Baruch of Rothenburg, *Ṭaʿame Mesoret ha-Miqra'*, cited in *Torat Ḥayyim: Ḥamishah Ḥumshe Torah* (5 vols; Jerusalem: Mosad ha-Rav Kook, 1986–93) 5.233.

80. The verse reads *hû' mĕrōmîm yiškōn*, but Eleazar cites it as *hû' bĕ-rō'š mĕrōmîm yiškōn*, to underscore the significance of the head on which the phylacteries are placed.

81. *Perushe Siddur ha-Tefillah la-Roqeaḥ*, 287. My translation reflects a slight modification of the text according to MS Paris, Bibliothèque Nationale héb. 772, fol. 67b. Cf. the passage from Eleazar's *Perush ha-Merkavah*, MS Paris, Bibliothèque Nationale héb. 850, fol. 74b, translated in my *Along the Path*, 39, and the passage from *Sefer Ṣiyyoni* cited on 162–63 n. 248. See also *Sode Razayya* (ed. Weiss), 91. It is of interest to note in this connection that in *Sefer Ḥasidim*, §1669, the straps of the phylacteries are linked exegetically to the description of the hair of the beloved in Cant 4:1 and the curls of the lover in Cant 5:11. The exegesis may presuppose some mythical notion of the phylacteries as the hypostasis of the divine glory. The ritual of the fringe garment (*ṣiṣit*) is treated in a similar way by Eleazar. Cf. *Sefer ha-Shem*, MS London, British Museum 737, fols. 261b–262a:

> Concerning he who is careful with respect to the *ṣiṣit*, the *Šekhinah* is upon him just as [it is] upon the celestial creatures. This is [the import of the verse] *ʿōṭeh 'ôr kaśśalmâ* (Ps 104:2) [the words *'ôr kaśśalmâ*] are numerically equivalent to *be-ṣiṣit* [that is, both equal 602]. Therefore the ancient elders (*zeqenim ha-ri'šonim*) in the morning would look at their fringes and would say, "O Lord, my God, You are very great, You are clothed in glory and majesty, wrapped in a robe of light; You spread the heavens like a tent of cloth" (Ps 104:1–2).

A similar custom is attributed to the 'older generations' *dorot ha-ri'šonim*, in *Perushe Siddur ha-Tefillah la-Roqeaḥ*, 272. For other relevant references to this ritual reflecting the Pietistic interpretation, see my *Along the Path*, 183 n. 358; and cf. *Sefer Ḥasidim*, §1668. On the importance of wearing a *tallit qaṭan*, cf. the responsum attributed to Judah the Pious, MS Munich, Bayerische Staatsbibliothek 232, fol. 23a.

82. See my *Along the Path*, 37, 118 n. 40, 158 n. 234.

the image of the crown) as the hypostatic manifestation of the *Šekhinah*.[83] This complex of symbols is implicit already in *Shir ha-Kavod*:[84]

> Abode of righteousness,[85]
> house of His splendor,[86]
> shall He raise above His joyous head.[87]
> His treasured possession[88] shall be a crown in His hand,
> a royal diadem,[89] glorious beauty.[90]
> He uplifted the ones who have been supported,[91]
> He bound them with a crown.[92]

83. See ibid., 40–43, and relevant notes wherein I have referred to other scholars, notably Farber and Idel, who have also noted this symbolic nexus.

84. Haberman, *Shir ha-Yiḥud we-ha-Kavod*, 49.

85. That is, Jerusalem or the Temple Mount; cf. Jer 31:22.

86. That is, the Temple; cf. Isa 60:7.

87. Based on Ps 137:6. In the biblical context, *ʿim lōʾ ʾaʿāleh ʾet yĕrûšālayim ʿal rōʾš śimḥātî* means 'If I shall not elevate Jerusalem above my chief delight'. I have translated the expression in *Shir ha-Yiḥud* based on these words, *yaʿaleh nāʾ ʿal rōʾš śimḥatô*, in a hyperliteral way, 'shall He raise above His joyous head', to convey the sense of the poem. It seems to me that the issue here is the elevation of the hypostatic Jerusalem (or the Temple) to the head of the divine, which may very well be a symbolic displacement for the phallus. Regarding this symbolic usage, see my *Through a Speculum That Shines*, 43, 103, idem, *Circle in the Square: Studies in the Use of Gender in Kabbalistic Symbolism* (Albany: State University of New York Press, 1995) 154 n. 91. A similar suggestion regarding the preoccupation with the image of the head in *Shir ha-Kavod* has been made independently by Arthur Green, *Keter: The Crown of God in Early Jewish Mysticism* (Princeton: Princeton University Press, 1996). I thank the author for providing me with a copy of his manuscript prior to its publication. I note, parenthetically, that the main biblical verses in which are found the image of the head that influenced the author of *Shir ha-Kavod* are cited by Eleazar, *Perushe Siddur ha-Tefillah la-Roqeaḥ*, 362. Marcus ("Prayer Gestures," 58–59) also notes the special emphasis on the head, but he does not opt for a sexual interpretation. On the contrary, on p. 53 n. 55, he suggests (interpreting the parable of the giant in *Sefer Ḥasidim*, §1585) the possibility that looking at the trunk of the body, as opposed to the head, may have the sexual connotation of looking at the male organ. (I would add that it is not impossible that the word *gup* in that context refers primarily to the penis.) The phallic interpretation of the head actually supports Marcus's reading, for gazing at the head symbolically displaces looking at the trunk. On the association of joy, the land of Israel, and the head, see *Perushe Siddur ha-Tefillah la-Roqeaḥ*, 564: "Thus we say [in the *musaf* prayer on Sabbath] 'may He take us up in joy to our land,' as it is written, 'everlasting joy is upon their heads' (Isa 35:10)." Cf. ibid., 632–33, 650.

88. That is, the people of Israel, based on Ps 135:4; cf. Exod 19:5; Deut 7:6, 14:2, and 26:18.

89. Cf. Isa 62:3.

90. Isa 28:1, 4.

91. That is, Israel, based on Isa 46:3.

92. Cf. Job 31:36.

> Because they were precious in His eyes,[93]
> He honored them.
> His glory is upon me and my glory is upon Him,
> and He is near me when I call to Him.[94]

In this web of skillfully crafted biblical images, the author of *Shir ha-Kavod* has alluded to one of the basic mythic ideas later expressed in the more fully developed theosophic treatises composed by Ḥaside Ashkenaz, namely, the reciprocal coronation of God and the Jewish people: God is crowned by Israel's prayers and Israel is crowned by the divine efflugence.[95] The crown on God's head is identified further as Jerusalem (the 'abode of righteousness' *neweh ha-ṣedeq*), the Temple (the 'house of His splendor' *bet tip'arto*), and the people of Israel ('His treasured possession' *segullato*). It is reasonable to conclude, moreover, that the crowns may refer to the phylacteries worn by God and man. This is implied in the statement *pe'ero ʿalay u-pe'eri ʿalayw* 'His glory is upon me and my glory is upon Him', for the word *pe'er* is interpreted in rabbinic sources as a reference to the phylacteries, sometimes connected exegetically with the verse *pe'erkha ḥavosh ʿaleka* 'put on your turban' (Ezek 24:17).[96] The donning of the phylacteries serves as a catalyst for the mutual crowning of God by Israel and Israel by God, which results in the visionary encounter.

In another composition, *Sod ha-Merkavah*, Eleazar elaborates on the idea that *kawwanah* in prayer essentially involves an imaginary representation of God upon the throne of glory:

> "The throne of His glory is in heaven above."[97] Therefore, we direct our hearts to our Father in heaven. If the world had not been created, the throne would

93. Cf. Isa 43:4.

94. Cf. Ps 145:18.

95. See my *Through a Speculum That Shines*, 264–65. This point is also emphasized in the monograph of Green referred to above in n. 87. The image of God's crown being woven from the words of Israel's prayer is repeated on many occasions in the Pietistic compositions. See Farber, "Concept of the Merkavah," 231–42; M. Idel, *Kabbalah: New Perspectives* (New Haven: Yale University Press, 1988) 193–96; and my *Along the Path*, 37, 118 n. 40, 158 n. 234.

96. *B. Ber.* 11a, 16b; *b. Sukk.* 25a, 25b; *b. Taʿan.* 16a; *b. Ketub.* 6b; *b. B. Bat.* 60b; *Midr. Pss.* 137:6; Targum to Ezek 24:17. Cf. the text of Eleazar of Worms (translated in my *Along the Path*, 37; and see the other references cited on p. 161 n. 240). It is likely that the head phylacteries of God are referred to in another passage in *Shir ha-Kavod*, derived from Isa 59:17, *ḥabuš kobaʿ yešuʿa bero'šo*, in Haberman, *Shir ha-Yiḥud we-ha-Kavod*, 48. Regarding this image, see the commentary on the 42-letter name in Eleazar's *Sefer ha-Ḥokhmah*, MS Oxford, Bodleian Library 1568, fol. 4a. Cf. *Shir ha-Yiḥud we-ha-Kavod*, 50: *qešer tefillin her'ah le-ʿanaw temunat yhwh leneged ʿenaw*, which reflects a combination of the aggadic reading of Exod 33:23 in *b. Ber.* 7a and Num 12:8. The composition of the divine crown from prayer is affirmed as well in another passage from *Shir ha-Kavod: tehillati tehi le-ro'šeka ʿaṭeret.*

97. This sentence is taken from the *ʿAleynu* prayer. A similar explanation of this text is found in *Perushe Siddur ha-Tefillah la-Roqeaḥ*, 658. For a slightly different version

not have been possible nor would the presence of His strength in the exalted heights have been possible. Without human beings there would be no throne, for the throne of glory has a circumference and boundary, but the Creator, blessed be He, has no boundary or limit, and the throne has a surrounding limit. Since He desired to create human beings, it was necessary to create the world, and since it was necessary to create the world, the heaven was necessary and upon it was His throne of glory, that is, so that they would bow down toward heaven. The Creator is in one place just as He is another, He is below just as He is above. . . . If this is so, then why should one direct one's heart to heaven? In order to show His creatures to which place their hearts should be directed, when He created the world it was necessary to set up a throne in heaven.[98]

The imaging of God that occurs in conjunction with prayer is thus connected to the heavenly throne.[99] Yet the latter can only be visualized within the human imagination. The point is underscored in two passages in Eleazar's *Sefer ha-Shem.*

If the heart begins to contemplate,[100] he should rush and quickly place his heart as if the throne of glory above were facing him and the supernal God sitting on it, and he should bow down to Him, and he will remember the One.[101]

The realization of divine oneness is here connected to the enthronement of God, which is actualized only through the imaginative visualization, since the One is not a body that occupies a throne. Similarly, in a second passage from this work, Eleazar comments:

---

version from MS Oxford, Bodleian Library 1204, cf. G. Hasidah, "Some Supplements to the Commentary on the Prayers by the Author of the *Roqeaḥ*," *Tzfunot* 19 (1994) 7 [Heb.].

98. *Sode Razzaya*, 19. Cf. p. 58:

Know that the Creator has no need for a throne for He has no limit, but the glory is seen opposite the throne and the throne is limited, as it is written, "The heaven is My throne and the earth is My footstool" (Isa 66:1).

Cf. also *Ḥokhmat ha-Nefesh*, 91. It is of interest to note that Moses Taku, as part of his polemic against an overly rationalist interpretation of Jewish sources, emphasizes that passages describing the throne must be taken in a literal fashion. Cf. *Ketav Tamim*, ed. R. Kirchheim, *Ozar Nechmad* 3 (1860) 85–86.

99. Cf. *Sode Razzaya*, 31: "the Holy One, blessed be He, sits in the innermost chambers in the exalted heights of His glory, and all of Israel concentrate on their Father in heaven." Cf. the poem *ʾelohekhem tifʾarto mi-maʿal we-ʾein bilʿado*, in *Shirat ha-Rokeaḥ*, 72; and *Perushe Siddur ha-Tefillah la-Roqeaḥ*, 114, 128, 130, 326, 540, 547.

100. Eleazar's comment is an interpretation of *Sefer Yeṣirah* 1:8.

101. Eleazar, *Sefer ha-Shem*, MS London, British Museum 737, fol. 280a. Cf. *Perush ha-Rav ʾEleʿazar Mi-Germaizaʾ ʿal Sefer Yeṣirah* (Przemysl, 1883) 2c: "Remove that thought [about God] from your heart and close your mouth from speaking, and if your heart runs to that thought remove it from your heart and return to the unity of God, to worship Him and to fear Him." And ibid., 3a: "If your heart entices you into thinking about all these things, immediately remove all thought from your heart and bow down to the Holy One, blessed be He."

> The One has no limit for He is everything, and if not for the fact that "through the prophets [God] was imaged" (Hos 12:11) as a king sitting upon a throne, they would not have known to whom to pray. . . . This is what is said in *Sefer Yeṣirah* (1:4), "and set the Creator on His place."[102]

According to these passages, the object of intentionality in worship is the Creator and not the glory, a point emphasized on a number of occasions in the writings of Eleazar and other Pietists.[103] Thus we read in one of the earlier speculative works written by Judah the Pious or one of his disciples:

> The heart of the worshiper: With regard to everything his heart must think about the One who is supernal to all, and he should not think or imagine any vision in his heart. It is written, "I will extol You, my God and king" (Ps 145:1), and the Creator is above, as it is written, "His glory is above the heavens" (Ps 113:4), so that the contemplation of the heart will be [directed] towards what is above.[104]

On the surface it would appear that this position is contradicted by other texts that explicitly state that the object visualized through worship is the glory and not the Creator. In one context, for instance, Eleazar remarks,

> Therefore, the name of the Creator is YHWH and to Him they pray. Thus the rabbis, blessed be their memory, said in Yevamot [105b] the eyes of a person should be below during his prayer but his heart should be above, for the essence of the glory is seen above, and an unfathomable, resplendent fire is above opposite the throne of glory and in it is seen the glory according to the will of the Creator, sometimes as an elder and sometimes as a youth.[105]

Similarly, Eleazar comments in another passage:

> The Creator is close to you in actuality, that is, He fills everything and there is nothing hidden from Him, and regarding what is written, "For God is in heaven" (Qoh 5:1), for He manifests the essence of His glory above. . . . There-

102. Eleazar, *Sefer ha-Shem*, MS London, British Museum 737, fol. 288b. A parallel to this passage is found in *Sode Razayya*, 32, cited by Scholem, *Major Trends*, 116. I have previously cited the two passages from *Sefer ha-Shem* in *Along the Path*, 180–81 n. 352. See also the version of Eleazar's *Hilkhot ha-Kavod* published in Abrams, "The Secret of the Secrets," 79.

103. See above, n. 43.

104. Dan, *Studies in Ashkenazi-Hasidic Literature*, 171. My translation reflects some slight corrections to the Hebrew text made on the basis of MS Oxford, Bodleian Library 1566, fol. 9b. In another passage from this same work (*Studies in Ashkenazi-Hasidic Literature*, 169), the point is made in the following way: "Therefore the heart of a man in worship turns above as one who stands and speaks to his friend face to face."

105. *Sode Razayya*, 31. Cf. ibid., 41: "Regarding the changes that we have found in the *Šekhinah*, sometimes as a youth and sometimes as an elder: Know that the reason is that the glory appears to the prophets in accordance with the need of the hour. . . . The glory appears to the heart." Cf. ibid., 57–58, and *Perushe Siddur ha-Tefillah la-Roqeaḥ*, 401.

> fore, the sages said in Yevamot, "the worshiper should cast his eyes below and his heart above," for the Creator is near him but His glory is opposite the high and exalted throne above.[106]

The contradiction is merely apparent, however, for the worshiper must direct his intention in prayer to the Creator, but the latter is phenomenally accessible only through the image of the glory that is conjured in the imagination. Moreover, as I have already emphasized, even though the object of imaginary visualization is the glorious and luminous form upon the celestial throne, that visualization can occur only within the sacred space of the synagogue.[107] The point is expressed in the following passage in *Sefer Ḥasidim*, which may be viewed as a synthesis of the dictum of Simeon the Pious, the "one who prays must see himself as if the *Šekhinah* were opposite him," and that of R. Yose, the "one who prays should cast his eyes below and his heart above":

> When a person prays the *Šekhinah* is opposite him, as it says, "I have set the Lord always before me" (Ps 16:8). Even though it is written that the Lord is opposite him, he should not direct [his intention] except above to heaven. Since he does not know where the Temple is, he should think in his heart that through his prayer it is, as if, the glory were opposite him within four cubits, and its height extends above to heaven . . . even though the Creator is in everything, [the worshiper] must fulfill [the obligation by turning] toward His face, as it says, "Pour out your heart like water before the face of the Lord" (Lam 2:19), for the creatures below must lift their souls and their hearts to heaven. Therefore, the heart of the worshiper faces above.[108]

The one who prays must, simultaneously, imagine that the *Šekhinah* is opposite him in the synagogue and sitting above on the celestial throne. This is achieved by imagining that the form of the *Šekhinah* extends from his space of four cubits in the synagogue to heaven. We clearly have here an innovative application of the older *Shiʿur Qomah* speculation, for attributed to the *Šekhinah* is an enormous stature spanning the whole universe.[109] The intention in prayer is fulfilled when the worshiper looks at God's face, *keneged panaw*. This is realized by an imaginal flight to the celestial abode. One directs the imaginary gaze above to the heavenly throne and thereby faces

106. *Sode Razayya*, 37.

107. On occasion the Pietist authors also recommend the specific gesture of looking at the Ark that contains the Torah scrolls in order to visualize the glory. Underlying this gesture is the presumption that the Ark in the synagogue corresponds to the throne in heaven. I have translated and analyzed some of the relevant sources in *Through a Speculum That Shines*, 248–52.

108. *Sefer Ḥasidim*, §1585. Cf. §1605.

109. Cf. *Perushe Siddur ha-Tefillah la-Roqeaḥ*, 144. On the role of *Šiʿur Qomah* speculation in the theosophy of the German Pietists, see my "Meṭaṭron and Shiʿur Qomah in the Writings of Ḥaside Ashkenaz," *Mysticism, Magic, and Kabbalah in Ashkenazi Judaism*, 60–92, and reference in 62–63 n. 10 to other scholars who have dealt with this issue. My discussion is reworked in *Through a Speculum That Shines*, 214–34.

God. Although the locus of the visionary encounter is the imaginative faculty, the vision is restricted to the synagogue, for only within the physical boundaries of the synagogue can the heart imagine the *imago templi*.[110] As Eleazar puts it:

> The prophet sees the glory created so that he may envision the will of the Creator, for the Creator is in everything. . . . But [He does not appear] to the heart of the worshiper in a place that is not honorable, and according to the contemplation of the heart he must raise his heart toward heaven. It is written, "I have set the Lord always before me" (Ps 16:8), but he should direct his heart above to that which is exalted over everything.[111]

It is mandatory that the worshiper have an image of God opposite him constantly, but that image appears in the heart of the worshiper only in the 'honorable place' (*maqom nikhbad*) of the synagogue; within that space the heart must be directed to heaven, for the image of God that one has is of the glorious form seated upon the throne.

Unveiling the Veil: Eros and the Vision of the Glory

This shift from physical to imaginal space is linked frequently by Pietistic authors to the teaching of R. Yose, which has been mentioned several times in this study. The utilization of this statement in the Pietistic sources has been noted by various scholars, but its eidetic function in the meditational practice has not been adequately addressed. To appreciate the meaning of this dictum in the world view of the Pietists, it is necessary to bear in mind that the "heart," which is contrasted with the "eyes," designates the imaginative faculty. The casting of the eyes below signifies that the Creator is not physically visible, whereas the directing of the heart above indicates that within the imagination the glory is visualized as an anthropomorphic form

110. The orientation of Ḥaside Ashkenaz is attested in the following words from the poem "*ʾorot me-ʾofel hiẓriaḥ me-hodo*," by Meir ben Baruch of Rothenburg, published in *Seder ʿAvodat Yisraʾel*, 686:

> *pinniti ha-bayit le-ḥešeq nešeq tešeq tešuqatekha we-ʾani be-rov ḥasddekha ʾavoʾ vetekha reʾut ʿayin loʾnirʾatah li-veriyyotekha ṣefiyyat lev be-miqṣat himšalta. . . . šiwwitikha lenegddi hineni ʿomed lefanekha leromamekha . . . ʾeštaḥaweh ʾel hekhal qodšekha we-ʾodeh ʾet šemekha.*

111. *Sode Raẓayya*, 49. Cf. *Perushe Siddur ha-Tefillah la-Roqeaḥ*, 157:

> Therefore it is said in every blessing, "blessed are You, O Lord," as if the *Šekhinah* were opposite him, as it is written, "I have set the Lord always before me" (Ps 16:8). Therefore our rabbis said [*b. Yebam.* 105b], "the one who prays must cast his eyes below and his heart above" with intention, and this is [the meaning of "The Lord is near to all who call Him] to all who call Him with sincerity" (Ps 145:18).

Cf. *Perushe Siddur ha-Tefillah la-Roqeaḥ*, 164: "He manifests His kingship (*malkhuto*) above and below."

enthroned in the heavenly chamber. Bearing this in mind, we can understand the comment in *Sefer Ḥasidim* that "when a person prays he does not have to shut his eyes because his eyes are below and his heart is above."[112] On the most basic level, the shutting of the eyes enhances mental concentration by blocking out external stimuli.[113] Thus, in another passage in *Sefer Ḥasidim* the gesture of covering the face during the supplication prayer (*taḥanun*) is explained as an effort to focus the intention of the heart.[114] If the eyes are cast below, however, they do not have to be shut in order to increase the concentration. It is thus recommended that during the morning prayers one can place the prayer shawl over one's eyes in order to avoid distracting objects in one's visual field, whereas at night, when one is not normally wearing the prayer shawl, it is necessary to cast one's eyes downward or to shut one's eyes tightly.[115]

Viewed from a more esoteric vantage point, the gestures of shutting the eyes or casting the eyes downward are not principally concerned with intensifying concentration; they are external acts that express the appropriate response to seeing the *Šekhinah*. Indeed, obstructing the vision dialectically represents the highest form of seeing.[116] Precisely such a viewpoint is conveyed in another passage in *Sefer Ḥasidim*, in which it is reported that when the priests uttered their blessing they would

> close their eyes on account of the fact that, when the Temple stood, they would mention the explicit name.[117] . . . and the *Šekhinah* was upon their

112. *Sefer Ḥasidim*, §1583.

113. Cf. ibid., §1582: "Whoever prays in a synagogue should close his eyes so that he will not see those who exit and those who enter, and he will not disturb his intention." In the continuation of this passage, it is recommended that one open one's eyes and look heavenward when the blessings *yoṣer ʾor* and *maʿariv ʿaravim* are recited, since both deal with the celestial luminaries. The instruction to cast the eyes toward heaven is upheld even though the talmudic dictum emphasized that the worshiper's eyes should be below and his heart above.

114. Ibid., §455. Cf. *Perushe Siddur ha-Tefillah la-Roqeaḥ*, 412.

115. *Sefer Ḥasidim*, §1584.

116. One finds a similar motif in both theosophic and ecstatic kabbalah. Regarding the former, see my *Through a Speculum That Shines*, 339–40, and regarding the latter, idem, "Mystical Rationalization of the Commandments in the Prophetic Kabbalah of Abraham Abulafia," n. 121, to be published in the proceedings of the conference in memory of Alexander Altmann held at University College, London, June 1994.

117. On the various traditions regarding the pronounciation of the divine name in the Temple, see G. Alon, *Jews, Judaism and the Classical World: Studies in Jewish History in the Times of the Second Temple and Talmud* (Jerusalem: Magnes, 1977) 241–43. On the evolution of the progressive restriction on the use of the Tetragrammaton in the Second Temple period, see E. J. Bickerman, *The Jews in the Greek Age* (Cambridge: Harvard University Press, 1988) 263–66.

> eyes[118] and thus they closed them. As it is written, "This shall be My name forever" (Exod 3:15), [the word *le-ʿolam*] is written *leʿalem*,[119] to hide the eyes from [seeing] Him when the priests place His name upon Israel, as it is written, "Thus they shall place My name upon the people of Israel, and I will bless them" (Num 6:27), and it is written, "And when you lift up your hands, I will turn My eyes away from you" (Isa 1:15), and the essence of the blessing is to direct one's heart to heaven.[120]

The closing of the eyes on the part of the priests is due to the fact that the *Šekhinah* rests upon their eyes when they mention the divine name. That the author of *Sefer Ḥasidim* considered this particular example instructive of blessing in general is evident from the concluding remark, "the essence of the blessing is to direct one's heart to heaven." Also relevant to this discussion is another passage in *Sefer Ḥasidim*, in which mention again is made of the gesture of covering the face, which I relate to the shutting of the eyes. This section concerns the 'ancient elders' (*ha-zeqenim ha-riʾšonim*)[121] who "would sit and cover their faces" after having returned from reading the Torah. The reason given for this gesture is that the "one who hears [the Torah] from the one who reads is like the one who heard it from Moses."[122] Underlying this comment is the assumption that the one who reads from the Torah scroll is illuminated from the light of its letters, which represent the material concretization of the divine glory.[123] As may be deduced from the first prooftext that is cited, Exod 34:34–35, the covering of the face is a ritualistic emulation of Moses who covered his face with a veil so that the Israelites could hear the command of God that he had received. Similarly, the one who reads the Torah must cover his face so that others will not be harmed by the radiance that issues from his countenance. There are, however, two additional prooftexts, one regarding Moses' hiding his face in order not to gaze upon God (Exod 3:6) and the other concerning Elijah's covering his face after hav-

118. According to a passage in *b. Ḥag.* 16a, it was recommended that one not look at the priests when they blessed the people of Israel and uttered the explicit name. In his commentary on the passage, Rashi remarks that "the *Šekhinah* dwelt in the joints of their fingers." A similar approach is elaborated in kabbalistic literature. See my *Through a Speculum That Shines*, 336–39. Compare the Ashkenazi text in *Synopse zur Hekhalot-Literatur* (ed. P. Schäfer; Tübingen: Mohr, 1981) §982.

119. Cf. *b. Pesaḥ.* 50a; *b. Qidd.* 71a.

120. *Sefer Ḥasidim*, §1588.

121. Cf. the passage from Eleazar cited above, n. 81, and *Perushe Siddur ha-Tefillah la-Roqeaḥ*, 312.

122. Ibid., §1597. In *Through a Speculum That Shines*, 251–52, I discussed a passage from Isaac ben Judah ha-Levi's *Paʿaneaḥ Raza* that makes a similar point regarding the gesture of covering the face after hearing the Torah. Unfortunately, I neglected to note the relevant passage from *Sefer Ḥasidim* in that context.

123. See my "Mystical Significance of Torah Study in German Pietism," *JQR* 84 (1993) 43–78, esp. 62ff.

ing experienced the theophany on the mountain (1 Kgs 19:13). These verses add another dimension to the ritual of covering the face: it is not only an act of altruism to protect others from potential harm; it is an expression of humility that is appropriate to one who has visually encountered the divine.[124] The downward casting of the eyes, I submit, fulfills the same function.[125]

This leads me to the final point. The directing of the heart above fosters the imaginative visualization of the divine enthronement, for what is chiefly seen in the heart of the worshiper is an anthropomorphic form seated upon the throne of glory. As I have discussed elsewhere, the moment of enthronement in the German Pietistic sources, based on much older esoteric texts, is treated as a sacred union between the upper and the lower glories, or the glory and the cherub, which is identified as the throne upon which the glory sits.[126] I suggest that this dimension of Ashkenazi esotericism is essential for

124. Relevant to this discussion is the passage from the 13th-century anonymous collection, *Sefer Minhag Ṭov*, cited by Marcus, "Prayer Gestures," 51. According to that text, since the *Šekhinah* is above the cantor's head when he recites *barekhu*, the custom is not to raise one's eyes at that point of the service. The gesture thus reflects an appropriate pietistic response to the visible presence of God. The nexus between humility and visionary experience is evident in Eleazar's remark in *Perushe Siddur ha-Tefillah la-Roqeaḥ*, 95: "The one who lowers himself like a bent *yod* merits prophecy." Cf. ibid., 153, 188, 239, 526–27. The virtue of submissiveness is emphasized as an essential component of *kawwanah* in the responsa attributed to Judah the Pious, MS Munich, Bayerische Staatsbibliothek 232, fols. 21b and 24a; cf. *Perushe Siddur ha-Tefillah la-Roqeaḥ*, 88. Finally, it is important to note the description of the angels who serve before the throne given by Eleazar, ibid., 206: "All the heavenly hosts that stand before Him are bent over, and they are all garbed in white fire, and they bow down to Him and cover their faces." Cf. commentary on the 42-letter name in Eleazar's *Sefer ha-Ḥokhmah*, MS Oxford, Bodleian Library 1568, fol. 6b. The notion that the angels before the throne cover their faces in order not to see the image of the glory is expressed in earlier mystical literature. Cf. *Synopse zur Hekhalot-Literatur* (ed. Schäfer) §§183, 793, 813; and see my *Through a Speculum That Shines*, 102–3.

125. A similar explanation can be found in kabbalistic texts. For example, cf. *Maʿarekhet ha-ʾElohut* (Mantua, 1558), chap. 9, 132a–b:

> We have already mentioned above that the worshiper must cast his eyes below and place his heart above for it is as if the worshiper were standing before the *Šekhinah* and it is necessary that his eyes not be nourished from that place. . . . We also mentioned the matter of one who looks at the rainbow and the matter of one who sees his genitals.

Cf. ibid., 113b–114a. In this text the erotic element of the visual encounter is made explicit. Hence, the rabbinic recommendation of casting the eyes below is associated with the taboo of looking at the genitals, also symbolized by the rainbow. Regarding the use of this symbolism in kabbalistic literature, see my *Through a Speculum That Shines*, 334 n. 30 and 340–41 n. 48. Cf. MS Moscow, Günzberg 1302, fol. 17a: "The worshiper must cast his eyes below in [the emanation that is called] ʿ*Aṭarah*."

126. See my *Through a Speculum That Shines*, 246; idem, *Along the Path*, 54–56, 180–81 n. 352.

a proper understanding of the Pietists' use of R. Yose's dictum. In order to pray it is necessary for the worshiper to conjure a visual image of the *Šekhinah* opposite him in the synagogue. At the same time, however, the worshiper is obligated to cast his eyes below so that he does not gaze directly upon the *Šekhinah*. The visual aspect is retrieved by the heart that is cast above so that it may imagine the *hieros gamos* between the glory and the throne in the *imago templi*. One of the most important liturgical settings in which this erotic drama unfolds is the *qedushah*, for, according to a highly influential passage from *Hekhalot Rabbati*, when Israel utter the *qedushah* below, the glory bows down to caress, embrace, and kiss the icon of Jacob engraved on the throne.[127] The Ashkenazi custom, followed by the Pietists, is to cast the eyes above when the *qedushah* is recited.[128] Through the ocular gaze, the worshiper is witness to sexual play in the divine realm, a motif that assumes a central role in the esoteric teaching of Ḥaside Ashkenaz, especially Eleazar.[129] I surmise that the recommendation to cast the eyes below and to direct the heart above is also related to the erotic drama unfolding in heaven, even though on the surface there is a blatant contradiction between the two gestures of looking down and looking up.

It is critical to emphasize, however, that Ḥaside Ashkenaz understood prayer in general, and not specifically the recitation of the *qedushah*, in light of the aforementioned text from *Hekhalot Rabbati*. That is, the purpose of prayer is to promote the sacred union in the divine realm, which is depicted mythically in terms of the image of God erotically embracing the icon of Jacob.[130] Thus, we find the following remark in some of the manuscript versions of Eleazar's commentary on the prayers:

127. *Synopse zur Hekhalot-Literatur* (ed. Schäfer)§164. The passage is translated and analyzed in my *Through a Speculum That Shines*, 101–2; and idem, *Along the Path*, 25–26.

128. See the concluding part of *ʾofan* that begins *kevodo ʾot* by Meir ben Isaac Sheliaḥ Ṣibbur in *Seder ʾOṣar ha-Tefillot* (2 vols; New York: Otzar ha-Sefarim, 1966) 2.35 (section on *yoṣerot*); Jacob ben Asher, *Ṭur*, ʾOraḥ Ḥayyim §125, and the comment of Jacob Karo in the *Bet Yosef*, ad loc.; Ṣedekiah ben Abraham ha-Rofe, *Shibbole ha-Leqeṭ ha-Shalem* (ed. S. Mirsky; Jerusalem: Sura, 1966) §20; Abraham bar Azriel, *ʿArugat ha-Bosem* (4 vols., ed. E. E. Urbach; Jerusalem: Mekize Nirdamim, 1939) 1.214. Some of these sources have been noted by E. Zimmer, "Poses and Postures during Prayer," *Sidra* 5 (1989) 89–95 [Heb.]; and Marcus, "Prayer Gestures," 52.

129. See my *Along the Path*, 56–59, and references to Eleazar's citation or paraphrase of the key passage from *Hekhalot Rabbati*, on pp. 111 nn. 2–3, and 186 n. 366. Needless to say, many more textual examples could have been added. Cf. *Perushe Siddur ha-Tefillah la-Roqeaḥ*, 235, and references in the following note.

130. The sacred union is also expressed through images of enthronement, coronation, and robing. Cf. *Perushe Siddur ha-Tefillah la-Roqeaḥ*, 239–40: "'Blessed are You, O Lord.' . . . When they bless the Holy One and they praise Him, He appears as one who is elevated and exalted." The very purpose of prayer is to elevate and to exalt God upon the throne. This is also expressed in terms of the biblical motif of God's

"Israel, as His treasured possession" (Ps 135:4): When Israel pray before the Holy One, blessed be He, He embraces Jacob, our patriarch, who is engraved on the throne of glory, like a man who kisses and loves his wife.[131]

Note how the homoerotic relationship between God and the engraved image of Jacob is transmuted into the heterosexual terms of a man's physical embrace of his wife. Further support for my contention may be found in the juxtaposition of two comments in another one of Eleazar's liturgical commentaries:

Thus the poet said, "I have set the Lord always before me" (Ps 16:8), for the *Šekhinah* fills everything, and those who fear His name know the essence of the matter, but "the secret of the Lord is with those who fear Him" (ibid. 25:14), (and only) "a base fellow gives away secrets" (Prov 11:13), (so) I will place my hand on my mouth.[132] In the Trisagion (Isa 6:3) are nine words corresponding to the nine theophanic forms (*mar'ot*) before the great glory[133] . . . for the throne is engraved with the image of Jacob, but this whole matter cannot be explained except orally to the one who fears his Creator at all times.[134]

The appearance of the *Šekhinah* below parallels the manifestation of the enthroned glory above. Moreover, there is an element of concealment that pertains to the lower and the upper manifestations of the divine glory, an element that is related in both cases to the erotic nature of the visual object.

The nexus between eros and vision, a motif well attested in older Jewish sources, is confirmed in a number of passages in the writings of Ḥaside Ashkenaz.[135] This nexus, for instance, underlies the connection between the

---

mounting a cherub. Of the many texts that could have been cited in support of this idea, I here mention a passage from the Pietistic *Perush Hafṭarah*, MS Berlin Or. 942, fol. 155a:

[The word] *keruv* [has the same] letters [as the word] *barukh* and also [as the word] *rokhev*, for when the Holy One, blessed be He, rides upon the cherub, they bless Him, and the seraphim and ophanim say, "Blessed is the name of the glory of His kingdom forever."

For other Pietistic sources in which the word *keruv* is related to *barukh* or *barekhu*, see my *Along the Path*, 156 n. 226.

131. *Perushe Siddur ha-Tefillah la-Roqeaḥ*, 108. Cf. ibid., 135.

132. Cf. Job 40:4.

133. Regarding this central motif in the German Pietistic theosophy, see my *Along the Path*, 153–55 n. 219.

134. MS Munich, Bayerische Staatsbibliothek 232, fol. 7b.

135. Cf. *Sefer Ḥasidim*, §§59, 978, 979, 986; *Sefer ha-Roqeaḥ*, 26, 30. I have discussed these and some other relevant texts in "The Face of Jacob in the Moon: Mystical Transformations of an Aggadic Myth," in *The Seductiveness of Jewish Myth: Challenge or Response?* (ed. S. Daniel Breslauer; Albany: State University of New York Press, 1996) 243–44, 264–66 nn. 51–52. To the sources mentioned there, one might add the statement in *Massekhet Kallah*, chap. 1, "he who gazes intentionally upon a woman it is as if he has [sexually] come upon her." The underlying assumption here is clearly that vision is ejaculatory, and thus looking at a woman is equivalent to having intercourse with her. In the same text, the voyeuristic act of gazing at a woman's

rite of circumcision and the vision of the glory that one finds in Pietistic literature, a theme expressed in midrashic texts and further developed in kabbalistic works.[136] Indeed, in a manner consonant with the kabbalists, Ḥaside Ashkenaz maintain that the aspect of the Šekhinah revealed in the theophanous moment is the crown, which, I contend, symbolically represents the corona of the *membrum virile*. It follows that what is visually apprehended by the prophet or the mystic is the most concealed element of God. An especially important passage in which the inherent hiddenness of the crown is affirmed is found in the pseudo-Hai commentary on the 42-letter name of God included in the introductory section of Eleazar's *Sefer ha-Ḥokhmah*:

> When the diadem is on the head of the Creator, the diadem is called Akatriel, and then the crown is concealed from all the holy angels, and it is hidden in 500 myriad parasangs. Then they ask one another, "where is the place of His glory?" Concerning it David said, "O you who dwell in the shelter of the Most High and abide in the protection of Shaddai" (Ps 91:1), [the word] *be-seter* has the numerical value of Akatriel.[137]

---

vagina (euphemistically referred to as 'that place' *ʾoto maqom*) is offered as an explanation for blindness. This explanation is presented as part of an angelic revelation to R. Yoḥanan in which he learned the reasons for the physical defects of lameness, deafness, dumbness, and blindness. All four handicaps are related to sexual misconduct. Cf. *b. Ned.* 20a. I have noted some other examples of the eroticization of vision in rabbinic sources in *Through a Speculum That Shines*, 43 n. 130, 85–86 n. 50. In the Jewish mystical tradition, blindness is viewed primarily as punishment for masturbation rather than for the sexual trespass of voyeurism. Underlying this motif is the symbolic association of the eye and the male organ. See my "Weeping, Death, and Spiritual Ascent in Sixteenth-Century Jewish Mysticism," in *Death, Ecstasy, and Other Worldly Journeys* (ed. J. J. Collins and M. Fishbane; Albany: State University of New York Press, 1995) 220–22. On the linkage of blindness and sexual transgressions in ancient Greek mythology, see E. A. Bernidaki-Aldous, *Blindness in a Culture of Light: Especially the Case of Oedipus at Colonus of Sophocles* (New York: Peter Lang, 1990) 57–93.

136. On the correlation of circumcision and visionary experience in Ḥaside Ashkenaz, see my *Through a Speculum That Shines*, 249 n. 251 and 343 n. 53; idem, *Along the Path*, 142 n. 183. Cf. *Perush ha-Roqeaḥ ʿal ha-Torah* (3 vols., ed. C. Konyevsky; Benei Berak: Yeshivat Ohel Yosef, 1986) 1.157, 3.101. On the dwelling of the Šekhinah and circumcision, cf. *Perushe Siddur ha-Tefillah la-Roqeaḥ*, 104. Regarding this motif in midrashic and kabbalistic sources, see my "Circumcision, Vision of God, and Textual Interpretation: From Midrashic Trope to Mystical Symbol," *HR* 27 (1987) 189–215; revised version in *Circle in the Square*, 29–48, and notes on pp. 140–55.

137. Cited in Dan, *Esoteric Theology*, 120. My translation is based on the version of the text extant in MSS Oxford, Bodleian 1568, fol. 5a and 1812, fol. 61a, which differs slightly from the version presented by Dan. A parallel to this passage is found in another part of the introduction to Eleazar's *Sefer ha-Ḥokhmah*, MS Oxford, Bodleian 1568, fol. 23a, which in turn parallels the Ashkenazi source in MS New York, Jewish Theological Seminary of America Mic. 1786, fol. 43a, cited by Idel, *Kabbalah:*

In the continuation of this passage, which has been commented on by a number of scholars, the hypostatic crown is identified further as the prayer that sits to the left of God like a bride near the bridegroom, the princess, the voice of revelation, the *Šekhinah*, the angel of the Lord, and the tenth kingship. For my purposes the description of the last image is critical:

> And she is the tenth kingship (*malkhut ʿasirit*) and she is the secret of all secrets (*sod kol ha-sodot*). Know that the hidden [letters] of [the word] *sod* are *mem*, *kaf*, *waw*, *lamed*, *taw*, the letters of *malkhut*.[138]

The hidden letters refer to the consonants that are necessary to spell the letters of a given word phonetically. In the particular case of the word *sod*, the hidden letters consist of *mem*, *kap*, *waw*, *lamed*, and *taw*, which spell *malkhut*. The concealed aspect of the 'secret', the *sod kol ha-sodot*, is the "kingship," which is the crown on the head of God. The secrecy ascribed to the crown is also expressed by the numerical equivalence of *be-seter* and Akatriel.[139] I note, parenthetically, that the citation of Ps 91:1 in this context reflects the influence of the targumic translation of the expression *yoshev be-seter ʿelyon* as *de-ʾashre shekhinteih be-raza ʾ ʿilaʾah* 'He placed His presence in the supernal mystery'.[140] For the Ashkenazi author, this image is applied to the ascent of the *Šekhinah* as the crown on the head of God. Encoded here is a primary esoteric doctrine—or what may be called a ground concept—that has also informed the theosophic kabbalah: the head is a symbolic displacement of the phallus, and thus the crown on the head is the corona.[141] The change in

---

New Perspectives, 195. For a different translation, see my *Along the Path*, 42. See also the passage from *Sefer ha-Ḥokhmah*, printed in *Perush ha-Roqeaḥ ʿal ha-Torah*, 1.15–16. On the hiddenness of the crown when it sits on the head of the glory, cf. *Perushe Siddur ha-Tefillah la-Roqeaḥ*, 203.

138. Dan, *Esoteric Theology*, 120–21.

139. That is, both equal 662. For other examples of this numerology in Pietistic sources, see my *Through a Speculum That Shines*, 262 n. 315. And cf. *Sefer ha-Ḥokhmah*, 25:

> [The first and last letters of] *bereʾšit* are the letters *ba"t*, and this refers to community of Israel, which is called *bat* . . . and, similarly, *bat qol*, for the voice of the prayers of the daughter of Israel (*qol tefillat bat yiśraʾel*) rises to the head of the Creator and sits next to him like the daughter (*bat*) that is called *Šekhinah*, and this is what is written, "O you who dwell in the shelter of the Most High" (Ps 91:1), [the word] *be-seter* [is made up of] the letters *bt sr* [which can be vocalized as *bat sar*], for He is the archon (*sar*) who receives the daughter (*bat*).

140. Cf. the exegesis on the targumic rendering of Ps 91:1 in *ʿArugat ha-Bośem*, 2.11.

141. See my *Through a Speculum That Shines*, 342, 357–68. On the phallic constitution of maculinity and femininity in kabbalistic symbolism, see my "Woman—The Feminine as Other in Theosophic Kabbalah: Some Philosophical Observations on the Divine Androgyne," in *The Other in Jewish Thought and History: Constructions of Jewish Culture and Identity* (ed. L. J. Silberstein and R. L. Cohn; New York: New York

position of the *Šekhinah* from being the bride or the princess sitting alongside God to being the crown on the head of God signifies the gender transformation of the *Šekhinah* from an autonomous feminine into the feminine that is reintegrated into the masculine. In the transformed state, the *Šekhinah* is designated by the technical term *malkhut*, the inner dimension of *sod.*[142] In the final analysis, the mythic symbol of the elevation of the crown indicates that the *Šekhinah*, which is characterized in feminine terms, is ontically part of the phallus (*malkhut* within *sod*), indeed the disclosed part that must be concealed in the visionary encounter.

It will be recalled that in a passage from Eleazar cited above, the *Šekhinah* is said to be revealed only momentarily to the worshiper, for if it were displayed for a longer duration it would be a "disgrace for the *Šekhinah*." We can now propose an interpretation of Eleazar's comment: it is a disgrace for the *Šekhinah* to be revealed, for the aspect that is disclosed is related to the male organ, which by nature must be concealed. The visionary encounter, therefore, is marked by the appearance of that which conceals itself. Consequently, the exposure of the *Šekhinah* elicits disgrace on the part of the *Šekhinah* and shame on the part of the worshiper. A similar explanation can be applied to Eleazar's statement that when the glory spoke to the prophet it would surround him in a cloud, a matter that is not to be transmitted in writing but only orally.[143] The esoteric element in this case as well is linked to the erotic nature of the visible aspect of the *Šekhinah.*[144] Confirmation of my interpretation can be found in Eleazar's commentary to the passage in the *musaf* service for Rosh ha-Shanah, "You were revealed in the cloud of Your glory upon Your holy people to speak to them": "Thus He was revealed in the cloud surrounding the glory just as above 'dark thunderheads, dense clouds of the sky [were His pavilion round about Him]' (Ps 18:12). 'Upon Your holy people,' then Israel were holy . . . for they separated from their wives for three days and they were like ministering angels. Therefore, His glory was revealed 'to speak to them.'"[145] As a result of abstaining from sex-

University Press, 1994) 166–204; idem, "Crossing Gender Boundaries in Kabbalistic Ritual and Myth," *Circle in the Square*, 79–121, and notes on 195–232.

142. The elevation of the crown functions in a similar way in kabbalistic sources. See my *Through a Speculum That Shines*, 275 n. 14, 362 n. 123, 363; idem, *Circle in the Square*, 116–20, 231–32 n. 198. The gender transformation is also expressed in Pietistic sources in terms of the transition from Jacob, which is related to the heel that symbolizes the feminine, to Israel, which is the head that symbolizes the masculine. Cf. *Perushe Siddur ha-Tefillah la-Roqeaḥ*, 536, translated in my *Along the Path*, 58–59.

143. *Perushe Siddur ha-Tefillah la-Roqeaḥ*, 195. The text is translated in my *Through a Speculum That Shines*, 203. Consider also Eleazar's interpretation of Exod 33:22–23 cited in *ʿArugat ha-Bośem*, 1.198, which more or less parallels *Perushe Siddur ha-Tefillah la-Roqeaḥ*, 388.

144. See my *Along the Path*, 182 n. 353.

145. *Perushe Siddur ha-Tefillah la-Roqeaḥ*, 674. Cf. ibid., 712–13.

ual intercourse with their wives for three days,[146] the male Israelites were transformed into angels and they thus merited to see the glory of God who appeared from within the covering of the cloud. In the mystical theosophy of the Pietists, the disclosure of that which is concealed results in the concealment of that which is disclosed.

In light of the identification of the *Šekhinah* as the crown and the symbolic decoding of that image as the corona of the phallus, we can better understand the repeated prohibition (based on earlier rabbinic sources) in Pietistic literature of looking at women and the promise that one who shuts his eyes to avoid staring at women's physical beauty will be nourished by the visible splendor of the *Šekhinah*.[147] By withstanding sexual temptation, one is granted a vision of the *Šekhinah* in the form of the phallic crown. The link between the visual manifestation of the *Šekhinah* and the abrogation of sexual desire parallels the connection made in Pietistic sources between transmission of the divine name and sexual abstinence: just as only one who is sexually abstinent can receive the name, a reception that involes esoteric gnosis and mystical praxis, so only one who has mastered the sexual passions

146. Cf. Exod 19:15; *b. Šabb.* 86a and 87a.

147. Cf. *Sefer Ḥasidim* §59, 978–79; *Sefer ha-Roqeaḥ*, 26, 30. I have translated and discussed these passages in "Face of Jacob in the Moon," 243–44. See also the responsum on illicit sexual relations (*ʿarayot*) attributed to Judah the Pious in MS Munich, Bayerische Staatsbibliothek 232, fols. 10b–11a, and cf. ibid., fols. 16a and 29a; *Perushe Siddur ha-Tefillah la-Roqeaḥ*, 296, 725 (in that context Abraham's perfection is linked to his circumcision, which is connected to the aggadic motif that he did not gaze upon women). And cf. ibid., 151:

> Twenty-three matters correspond numerically to *û-bĕ-tôrātô yehggĕh* (Ps 1:2) [i.e., the word *yehggĕh* equals twenty-three]. . . . twenty-two letters and one below, which is the sexual desire (*taʿawat ʿerwah*), [to signify that there are] twenty-two forbidden sexual relations. Therefore a person must study (*yehggĕh*) the twenty-two letters [of the Torah] to remove from himself the twenty-two types of desire, and his desire should only be for his wife. Thus the Torah is compared to a woman.

According to this text, engagement in Torah serves as a substitute for the pursuit of sexual pleasure, which is related to the aggadic motif of the Torah as a feminine persona. On the application of this motif in German Pietistic sources, see my *Circle in the Square*, 133–34 n. 60. Finally, it is worth mentioning that preserved in the Genizah is a magical recipe attributed to Simeon ben Yoḥai and his disciples that includes the prohibition of looking at women. This is immediately followed by the liturgical expression "Blessed be the name of the glory of His kingdom forever and ever" and the mishnah in *m. Ḥag.* 2:1 regarding the three subjects considered by the rabbis to be esoteric. The text and translation may be found in Naveh and Shaked, *Magic Spells and Formulae*, 216–18. Sexual abstinence as a prerequisite for undertaking magical rites, usually connected with other forms of physical ascetism, is not an uncommon feature of Jewish magic. Cf. *Sefer ha-Razim*, 9, 83, 89, 90, 103; and see discussion in M. D. Swartz, "Ritual and Purity in Early Jewish Mysticism and Magic," *AJS Review* 19 (1994) 153–57.

is capable of visually contemplating the *Šekhinah* as the expanded crown[148] exposed on the head of God.[149] But even such a person cannot gaze with his eyes opened; the heart alone is the instrument of the visualization. The mental confronting of God's face in the imagination takes the place of facing the *Šekhinah* in the physical space of the synagogue.

148. On the motif of the expansion of the crown in the religious thought of Ḥaside Ashkenaz, see my *Along the Path*, 185 n. 363. To the sources mentioned there, one might add *ʿArugat ha-Bośem*, 3.481–82.

149. I have noted some of the relevant sources in *Along the Path*, 113–14 n. 20; see also my "Face of Jacob in the Moon," 265 n. 52.

Abstracts of Hebrew Essays

The Archaeological Background of the History of Southern Phoenicia and the Coastal Plain in the Assyrian Period

Ephraim Stern

This essay deals with the image of the Assyrian domination of the large harbor towns along the southern Phoenician and northern Israelite coast that emerges from the known Assyrian and local documents. These sources indicate direct Assyrian rule over the major maritime centers, implemented by Assyrian officials who were sent to inspect the Phoenician harbors and to look out for the interests of the Assyrian treasury.

In the second part of the discussion, the archaeological finds from this period in each of the harbor towns of the region are described: Achzib, Acco, Tell Keisan, Tell Abu-Hawam, Shiqmona, and especially the rich finds recently discovered by the writer in excavations at the site of Tell Dor. In this large harbor city the Assyrian-destruction layer of the year 734 B.C.E. has been detected, followed by a stratum of comprehensive rebuilding that included a new fortification system and a gate, and many small finds such as Assyrian "palace ware," Assyrian clay coffins, Assyrian imported seals, and so forth. However, south of Dor, down to Jaffa, in all excavated sites no Assyrian period strata have been uncovered, and it seems that this region was still abandoned during this age. The conclusions drawn from the combined historical and archaeological results are that the northern coastal region of Palestine passed through two stages during the short Assyrian period: in the first (probably in the days of Tiglath-pileser III), the Assyrians destroyed all of its important towns, while during the second (from the days of Sargon II on), most of them were rebuilt, and Dor became the most important among them. Dor was not just another Assyrian Karum, as was recently suggested by A. Gilboa, but the capital of a newly established Assyrian province, besides the older Megiddo and Samaria. This city was probably directly ruled by an Assyrian official who was located at the court of the king of Tyre.

Nomads in the Desert in Egyptian Sources

Shmuel Aḥituv

The existence of nomads in the outer regions of Egypt is well attested in Egyptian literature and topographical lists of the New Kingdom Period (16th–12th centuries B.C.E.); however, several names are used to identify these people. This essay focuses on nomads that were called Šosu. It may appear that this name refers to a geographical area; however, according to certain sources, the term refers to a socioethnic group. Although in some of the material one finds the term "the land of the Šosu," these sources simply treat the area in which the Šosu roamed as being the land of the Šosu. The Šosu were found throughout southern and southeastern Israel because the area supported a seminomadic existence. There are also sources that testify to the existence of Šosu in the areas of Seir and Edom. The Egyptian sources do not offer detailed descriptions of the social structure of the Šosu. However, they do supply some information indirectly. The sources describe the Šosu's social structure as tribal, with the various tribes headed by a chief. They lived in tents and their economy was pastoral. Their tribal social organization facilitated their employment as soldiers in the Egyptian or Hittite armies. They did not shy away from robbery and theft. In the eyes of city dwellers, they were ruthless and merciless enemies. The Šosu show parallels to the Israelites, and it may be that the Israelites and their kinfolk belonged to the Šosu socioethnic groups.

On the Explanation of First Mishna in Tractate Baba Meṣiʿa

David Halivni

This essay analyzes the Babylonian Talmud's commentary to the first Mishna in Tractate *Baba Meṣiʿa*. The talmud begins with an Amoraic comment that, in its present context, explains the force of a superfluous clause of the Mishna. However, since the clause is not necessarily superfluous, it is likely that the Amoraic comment originally was motivated by other legal considerations. Indeed, it is related to a wide-ranging Amoraic debate attested in several other talmudic passages. By the time of the post-Amoraic redactors (*setam hatalmud*), a different legal consensus had emerged that clashed with the assumptions of the Amoraic comment. The redactors could find no other explanation for the comment than to present it as an explanation of superfluous language.

The Flow of Cultural Influences from Syria and the Land of Israel to Mesopotamia in the Old Babylonian Period

ABRAHAM MALAMAT

Much has been written about the political and economic ties between the east and the west in the Near East. However, little has been written about the cultural ties between the two. This essay attempts to correct this lack, based on material found at Mari. There are three areas of focus: diplomatic marriages, literature, and law. One finds that many rulers of Mari arranged diplomatic marriages with the cities of western Syria. These marriages, the purpose of which was to strengthen relations between east and west, also brought about exchange of customs, behavior patterns, and life-styles. Moreover, one finds some evidence of visits to Mari by eastern upper-class personages. These visitors assimilated some local customs, which were then transported back to the east.

The literature also reflects cultural connections between east and west. For instance, one finds the motif of the storm-god defeating the sea-god in one document found at Mari. This refutes the view that the motif is of eastern origin and migrated westward and supports the view that the stories originated in the west and moved eastward. Moreover, there is a "prophetic" document that exhibits differences in conceptions of prophecy in the west and the east. In the west one finds intuitive prophecy, while in the east there is mantic prophecy. Therefore, it is possible that intuitive prophecy is a western development that migrated eastward. In comparing the law codes of east and west, we find major similarities between the codes of Hammurabi and the Bible, for example. The idea of *lex talionis* found in the Code of Hammurabi is an innovation that is based on Amorite and other western legal codes. Influence of the western legal codes on the eastern is just one more indication of the ancient cultural ties that existed between east and west.

Tannaitic Disputes in Light of the Dead Sea Scrolls

LAWRENCE H. SCHIFFMAN

Reliance on tannaitic material for historical information should be reevaluated in light of the material discovered in the Judean Desert. Halakot and the tannaitic debates are found in the material discovered at Qumran. For example, the tannaitic sources differ as to whether proselytes are a separate community or a part of the Jewish community. Rabbi Judah argues that they are indeed distinct, whereas Rabbi Meir contends that they are not. In the Qumran material, one finds two approaches to proselytes. Some sources see them as a separate group similar to the other three groups (Priests, Levites, Israel) within Israel. However, other texts do not view proselytes as a part of Israel but as a separate and distinct group.

Another example in the issue of an idolatrous city. Does one kill children and beasts found in an idolatrous city? The tannaitic material gives two opinions: some sources content that they are to be killed, while other sources argue the contrary. The *Temple Scroll* argues that one must kill both children and beasts found in an idolatrous city. Thus one finds a document from the beginning of the Hasmonean period dealing with the same issue that occupied the tannaim later.

Last, there is a debate in the tannaitic material with regard to the prohibition against slaughtering a beast and its offspring. Some rabbinic sources argue that the prohibition relates only to female beasts and their offspring, while other sources contend that the prohibition extends to both males and females. Again, one finds both opinions in the sources found at Qumran.

Index of Authors

Classical and Premodern Authors and Authorities

Index of Scripture

Hebrew Canon

The Hebrew Bible is indexed according to Hebrew chapter and verse divisions; where the English versification differs, English chapter and verse are supplied in brackets.

Deuterocanonical and Pseudepigraphical Works

New Testament

Index of Ancient and Premodern Sources

Ancient Near Eastern Sources

Classical Sources

Qumran Scrolls

1QDan[b] 380
1QH X 24 583
1QS II 17–22 583
1QS VI 4–5 583
4Q180 342
4Q181 342
4QEnGiants[a] 7 342
4QEnoch[a] 1 ii 11–12 336
4QEnoch[b] 1 ii 26–29 343
4QMMT 586
4QSam[a] 353
11QPs[a] 203
11QTemple LX 3–4 586
11QTemple XXI 9–10 583
Genesis Apocryphon 584, 585, 586, 588, 589
PAM 43.975, lines13–14 583

Bible Translations and Manuscripts

Peshiṭta
  Exod 28:42 376
Samaritan Pentateuch 429–31
Septuagint 402, 437
  Exod 28:42 376
  Exod 22:28 578
  Ezek 45:1 252
  Isa 27:9 195, 200
  Isa 28:18 194–95, 198
  Josh 13:6 252
  Josh 23:4 252
  Nah 3:14 382
  Ps 8:1 590
Targum
  Ezek 24:17 620
Targum Esther II 3:7 335
Targum Jonathan 198
  Isa 27:9 200
  Isa 28:18 194, 198
Targum Neofiti
  Exod 28:42 376
Targum Onqelos 541
  Exod 28:42 376
  Exod 32:13 195
Targum Pseudo-Jonathan 344
  Exod 22:28 588
  Gen 6:4 341
  Lev 16:21–22 343
  Lev 19:24 586
Vulgate 402
  Ps 8:1 590

Rabbinic Sources

Mishna
  ʾAbot
    6:1 543
    6:9 545
  Baba Batra
    6:7 572
  Bikkurim
    1:3 587
    1:10 588
    3:9 587
  Ḥagiga
    2:1 633
  Ḥalla
    4:11 588–89
  Horayot
    3:8 551–553, 555
  Kelim
    27:6 377
  Ketubot
    5:7 253
    8:1, 3, 5 253
    13:6 252
  Kilʾayim
    4:2–3 580
  Maʿaśer Šeni
    5:1 565
    5:1–5 584
    5:6 583
  Menaḥot
    10:6 582
  Middot
    3:8 579
  Pesaḥim
    10:9 412
  Qiddušin
    4:5 572

Miscellaneous Sources

כי ברוך הוא

מחקרים במזרח הקדמון, המקרא, ומדעי היהדות לכבוד ברוך אברהם לוין

בעריכת

וויליאם וו. האלו
רוברט חזן
יהודה שיפמן

אייזנבראונס
וינונה לייק, אינדיאנה תשנ״ט

כי ברוך הוא

מחקרים במזרח הקדמון, המקרא, ומדעי היהדות לכבוד ברוך אברהם לוין

תוכן העניינים של החלק העברי

רקע ארכיאולוגי לתולדות דרום פיניקיה וחוף השרון בתקופה האשורית

אפרים שטרן
האוניברסיטה העברית בירושלים

העדות ההסטורית

בשנת 743–738 לפנה״ס עלה הצבא האשורי בהנהגת תגלת פלאסר הגי על מדינות סוריה וכבשן. הוא ארגן כבר בשלב זה את החוף הצפוני של פיניקיה עם העיר צמר בראשה לפחווה אשורית.[1] זמן קצר אחר-כך, בשנת 734 לפנה״ס, יצא שוב למסע לאורך החוף הפיניקי הדרומי, הכניע את כל ערי החוף בדרכו, והרחיק עד לעזה.[2] במסע זה נכנע לפניו חירם מלך צור אלא שחזר ומרד תוך זמן קצר. תגלת פלאסר הגי היכה את הצורים מחדש והרחיב את גבולות הפחווה הפיניקית צמר כלפי דרום וכן צמצם את האוטונומיה שהתיר לערי פיניקיה בשלב קודם. הוא גם הושיב בממלכת צור פקיד אשורי בראש יחידת צבא שתפקידו היה לפקח על המסחר הימי שהתנהל בנמל, כולל הסחר החשוב בעצי ארז. עדות זו מצויה במכתב של קרדי אשור למור ששירת בימי תגלת פלאסר הג׳ וסרגון השני בלבנט. במכתב זה, מראשית השלטון האשורי בפיניקיה, דווח הכותב לתגלת פלאסר הג׳, כיצד הסדיר את היחסים עם שליטה של צור ועל המאורעות שקדמו להסדר זה. לדבריו הוא הודיע לשליט הצורי:

> כל הרציפים פתוחים לפניו. עבדיו נכנסים ויוצאים לבית הרציפים כרצונם (ו)סוחרים; הר הלבנון לרשותו, כרצונם הם עולים ויורדים ומורידים עצים. אני גובה מכס מכל אחד שמוריד עצים ומניתי גובה מכס על רציפי הר הלבנון כולו (שורות 5–12).

הוא גם דיווח, שמינה מוכסים ברציפים שבצידון (שורות 14–19), ומסיים את דיווחו על ההסדר שקבע בהצהרה, שהעניק לצידונים חופש פעולה במסחרים: ״הם רשאים להוריד עצים

1. ראה ב. עודד, ״אשור וערי פיניקיה בזמן האימפריה האשורית,״ באר-שבע א׳ (1973) 139–149; וכן מ. אילת, ״המסחר הבינלאומי בארץ ישראל תחת שלטון אשור,״ בתוך ב.ז. קדר ואחרים (עורכים), פרקים בתולדות המסחר בארץ ישראל (ירושלים: יד בן צבי, 1990) 67–88.

2. ח. תדמור, ״מסעות המלחמה האשוריים לפלשת,״ בתוך י. ליור (עורך), הסטוריה צבאית של ארץ-ישראל (תל-אביב: מערכות, 1964) 263–269.

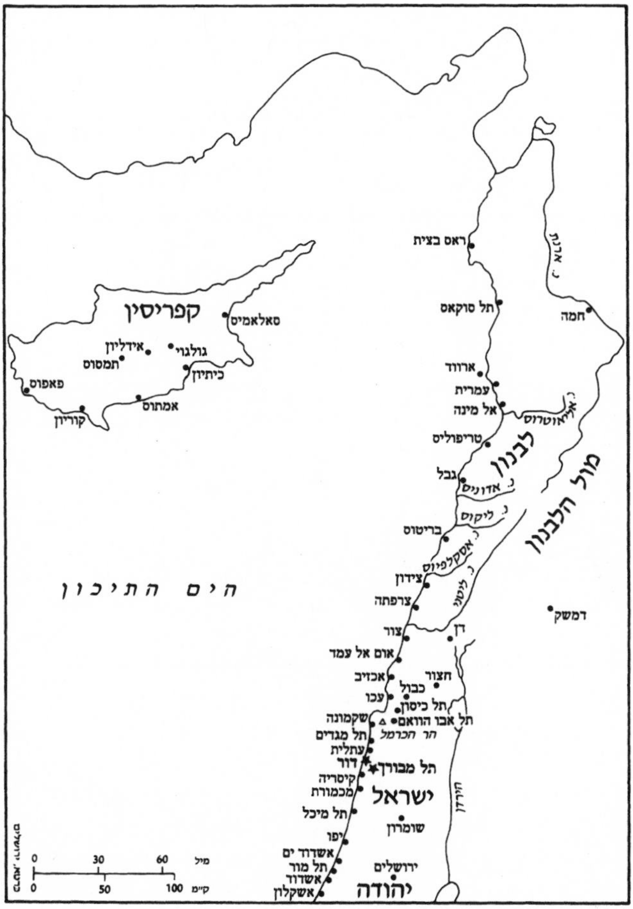

ציור 1. מפת ערי החוף של הים התיכון המזרחי.

ולעבוד בו כרצונם,״ אבל הגביל את שיווקו באיסור מכירתו למצרים ולפלישתים (שורות 23–29).[3]

כלומר, במגמה לזכות בחלק מרווחי המסחר הימי של הפיניקים, פעלו האשורים בממלכת פיניקיה תוך התאמת שיטותיהם לתנאים הפוליטים, החברתים והכלכליים ששררו בממלכה זו. מאחר שממלכה זו שכנה בארץ מיושבת, והנמלים שדרכם זרם המסחר הימי היו קיימים ופעילים, לא היה מקום לפתיחת תחנות מסחר וייסוד יישובים חדשים. לפיכך, כאן ניסו האשורים להשיג את מטרותיהם על-ידי היאחזותם בתוך נמלי ממלכות אלה, ע״י שמינו פקידי

3. עפ״י אילת, ״המסחר הבינלאומי,״ 84; והערות 101–102.

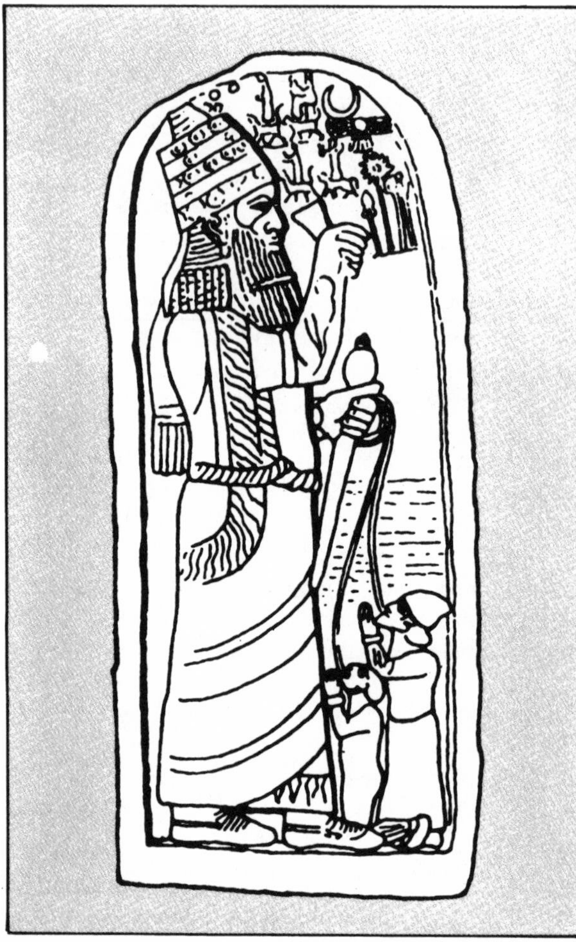

ציור 2. ציור של אסטילת אסרחדון מלך אשור מ-677 לפנה״ס, המתואר כשהוא מוביל את מלכי צור ומצרים בחח.

מכס בתוך הנמלים של הממלכות הוואסליות בפלשת ובפיניקיה. באמצעותן הטילו את פיקוחם על סחר החוץ וגבו בהן מכסים על הסחורות שעברו בהן, וכך נטלו חלק ברווחים ממסחר זה, מבלי לקחת בו חלק פעיל. לכך כלל לא היו מסוגלים, כי לא ידעו לבנות אוניות ולהשיטן בים ובכל המקרים עשו זאת עבורם הפיניקים.[4]

על פי קדמוניות (א׳ יד, ב) מרדו ערי פיניקיה שוב בימי שלמנאסר הה׳ (727–722 לפנה״ס) והאחרון צר במשך חמש שנים על העיר צור. המצור נעשה גם בעזרת צי שהעמידו לרשותו ערים פיניקיות אחרות ממתנגדיה של צור.

4. אילת, ״המסחר הבינלאומי,״ 83.

בימי סרגון הב׳ (722–705 לפנה״ס), הושלם תהליך יצירת הפחוות האשוריות בחוף הפיניקי, ובצידן הושארו על כנן ערי מלוכה אחרות בהן ארווד, גבל, צידון וצור. בימיו הגיע השלטון האשורי בפיניקיה ליציבות מה. בעזרת הצי הפיניקי השתלטו האשורים גם על חלק מהאי קפריסין. מכל מקום, מצבת סרגון נמצאה באי.

בעצם, המבנה המדיני הזה של החוף הסורי והארץ-ישראלי שעצבו תגלת פלאסר הג׳, שלמנאסר ה׳ וסרגון הב׳ התקיים גם בימי יורשי סרגון, עד סוף השלטון האשורי בארצות אלה. רק אסרחדון ביטל את עצמאותה של ממלכת צידון לאחר מרידתה וייסד תחתיה את העיר האשורית כר אסרחדון שאותה סיפח לממלכתו.

מרידות פרצו שוב בימי סנחריב (705–681 לפנה״ס). בשנת 701 יצא מלך אשור לדכא את המרידה הזו, מלך צידון נמלט לקפריסין, וסנחריב חזר להכניע את ארבע ערי פיניקיה העיקריות: ארווד, גבל, צידון וצור וכן את הערים שסביבן כגון בית זית, צרפת, אחלב, אכזיב ועכו.

גם בימי שני מלכי אשור האחרונים, אסרחדון ואשורבנפל, ניסו הפיניקים למרוד. כך מרדו צור וצידון באסרחדון בשנתו הרביעית (677). אסרחדון הרס את צידון והפכה לפחווה אשורית ואילו את שטחה הדרומי העביר לשליטת צור. במקום העיר הפיניקית ובסמוך לה בנה עיר חדשה אותה כינה ״כר אסרחדון.״ לדעת מ. אילת,[5] ייסוד מושבת המסחר הזו, בנוסף ל-Karum אשורי שהיה קיים אותה עת בארווד, ובעיקר החוזה של אסרחדון שנעשה אותה עת עם בעל מלך צור, מעידים על העניין שהיה לאשורים בחוף המזרחי של הים התיכון. לדעתו, מסתבר כי ערי הנמל שלחופי פיניקיה וארץ ישראל, כמו עכו, דור וערי חוף פלשת, נחשבו על ״תחום ארץ אשור.״ בעל מלך צור קיבל אומנם זכויות מסחריות בערים אלה, אך בד בבד נזכר בחוזה פקיד אשורי היושב בצור, נוכח באסיפת זקני העיר ומפקח על מעשיו של המלך הוואסל.

אכן מדיניותם זו של מלכי אשור הכתיבה גם את התנאים בחוזה שכרת אסרחדון מלך אשור לבעל מלך צור, כנראה בשנת 677 לפנה״ס. החוזה שנשתמר רק בחלקו מכיל שני קטעים הנוגעים לספנות הצורית, והוא מהווה לפי שעה המסמך העיקרי ללימוד יחסי אשור ופיניקיה בפרק זמן זה.

בקטע הראשון (טור 3 שורות 13–17; תרגום עברי עפ״י אילת) נאמר:[6]

> אם אוניה של בעל או של אנשי צור אשר בפלשת או בתחום אשור טובעת, כל אשר בתוך האוניה לאסרחדון מלך אשור (יהיה) אבל האנשים כולם אשר באוניה לא יפגעו ויש להחזירם לארצם.

בהמשך (שורות 18–22) נאמר:

> אלה הנמלים ודרכי המסחר אשר אסרחדון מלך אשור לעבדו בעל (נתן) לעכו דור למחוז פלשת כולה בכל הערים בתחום אשור על כל חוף הים בגבל, בלבנון, הערים אשר בהר—כולו, כל הערים של אסרחדון מלך אשור. . . .

לפי תנאי חוזה זה התיר איפוא אסרחדון לאוניות הצוריות לעגון בכל הנמלים שלחוף הים התיכון אשר היו נתונות לשליטתו הישירה או העקיפה. אבל אוניה צורית שנפגעה סמוך לחוף זה ולא יכלה עוד להמשיך בדרכה בכוחות עצמה, מטענה הוחרם לטובת מלך אשור

5. אילת, ״המסחר הבינלאומי,״ 83-86.

6. אילת, ״המסחר הבינלאומי,״ 85–86.

ואנשיה שוחררו. דומה איפוא שתעודה זו מעידה כי התנאים שקבע אסרחדון לבעל היו חריגים למדי אבל שיקפו וודאי את מדיניותם הכלכלית הכללית של האשורים כלפי ממלכות ואסליות ששכנו לחוף הים שבהם האשורים לא יכלו לשלוט בכוחות עצמם.

אבל גם אסרחדון עצמו נאלץ לדכא מרידות פיניקיות שנעשו ככל הנראה בתמיכה מצרית. באחת הפעמים נכבשו כל ערי הלווין של צור ולמלך צור הותר לשלוט רק בעירו על האי.

אשורבניפל שמלך אחריו מונה את מלכי צור, גבל וארווד בכלל המלכים שנשתעבדו לו וסייעו לו במלחמתו במצרים (666/667 לפנה״ס). בשלב מאוחר יותר מרדו הפיניקים גם בו והוא כבש מחדש את אוסו (צור היבשתית) ואת עכו והגלה חלק מתושביהן.

מאותו זמן קיימת בידנו תעודה אשורית של פקיד אשורי בשם אתישמש בלטו שכתב לאשורבניפל בראשית מלכותו. עפ״י מ. אילת[7] נאמר בו כי אכלו, הזהה עם יכנלו מלך ארווד, נוהג באיבה נגד האינטרסים האשוריים בנמלו. במכתבו מבחין הכותב בין ׳הנמל כולו׳ (*karu gabbu*—שורה 17) שבשליטת אכלו, ובין חלק מנמל זה הקרוי *karu ša šarri* (שורה 16) או *karu ša Assur* (שורה 20); ולכן עדיף לתרגם בשני המקרים במלה ׳רציף׳, היינו ׳הרציף של מלך אשור׳ או הרציף האשורי׳, שהיה בפיקוחם של נציגים אשוריים במקום. אתי שמש בלטו דיווח למלכו, שאכלו מנע מאוניות שנכנסו לנמל לעגון ברציף האשורי.

לא ברור מתי הסתיים השלטון האשורי על אזור זה בפרט, ועל ארץ-ישראל בכלל. העדות האחרונה לנוכחותם של האשורים בארץ היא בכתובת אנאלים של אשורבניפל (669–627 לפנה״ס), שלפיה ערך מסע נגד אוסו, היא צור היבשתית, הזהה עם פלייטרוס של המקורות היוונים, ונגד עכו שתושביה מרדו בשלטונו והוא הענישם.

מכל מקום, לאחר ימי אשורבניפל נסוגו ככל הנראה הצבאות האשוריים מכל האזור והשאירו אותו למשך כ-40 שנים, עד בוא הבבלים, בידי הפיניקים. תקופה זו היתה עת של פריחה כלכלית. הופעת הבבלים היתה הרסנית. תחילתה במצור הממושך מאוד על צור והמשכה בפגיעה אנושה בכל אתרי חוף הים הפיניקי והארץ-ישראלי כאחד. פגיעה שהותירה אותו שומם למחצה עד בוא הפרסים.

על רקע הפעילות האשורית הכללית לאורך חופי פיניקיה וארץ-ישראל שתוארה לעיל, נותר לנו עוד לדון במבנה המדיני של חופיה הצפוניים של ארץ-ישראל.

אכן, כיבושיה של האימפריה האשורית היו כרוכים, כאמור, בביטול המעמד המדיני והעצמאי של הארצות הכבושות ובסיפוחן לתחומי המנהל האשורי. עפ״י י׳ אפעל[8] נתכוננו בארצות אלה: ״מחוזות-מנהל חדשים ובראשם הוצבו מושלים אשוריים, שנתמנו בדרך-כלל, מבין סריסי המלך וקציניו (השם האשורי ליחידת מנהל כזו הוא *pihatu* = פחווה). מעמדם האזרחי של אוכלוסי הפחוות, הן המקומיים והן גולים שהובאו זה מקרוב, על חובותיהם כלפי המלכות, הושוו לאלו של תושבי ארץ אשור. בדרך-כלל היתה רציפות טריטוריאלית בין תחום אשור ובין הפחוות, ורק לעיתים רחוקות מצינו פחווה מבודדת.

תוארו של מושל הפחווה הוא *bel piḫati* (= פחה) או *šaknu* (= סגן, השווה ירמי׳ נא:כג, כח, נז). שני התארים משמשים בעירבוביה ומיוחסים בתעודות האשוריות לאותם אישים, מבלי שנוכל לקבוע בברור את ההבדל הפונקציונלי ביניהם במצב הנוכחי של מחקר מבנהו של המנהל האשורי. תוארי מינהל אחרים, הבאים בכתובות אשוריות שנמצאו בתחומה של פחוות שומרון, הם *rab alani*, שהוא פקיד הממונה על קבוצת יישובים (מושל מחוז); וכן *ḫazannu*, מעין ׳שר העיר׳ (השווה שופ׳ ט:ל; מל״א כב:כו; דה״ב לד:ח).

7. אילת, ״המסחר הבינלאומי,״ 70.

8. י. אפעל, ״השלטון האשורי בארץ-ישראל,״ בתוך א. מלמט (עורך), ההסטוריה של עם ישראל, ימי המלוכה, הסטוריה מדינית (ירושלים: מסדה, 1982) 191–201.

כינון הפחוות האשוריות היה מלווה בעקירת אוכלוסין רבים ממולדתם ושילובם מחדש במסגרת האימפריה. המערכת האירגונית של הגליית ההמונים פותחה ושוכללה במיוחד בימי תגלת פלאסר ג' ויורשיו, ששקדו על תנועה דו-סיטרית של גולים, כדי למנוע פגיעה בפוטנציאל הכלכלי של חבלים שנתרוקנו מיושביהם."

א. פורר, במחקרו המקיף,[9] הוא שהעלה לראשונה את ההנחה שהאשורים הקימו בשטחה של ממלכת ישראל שלוש פחוות: מגידו ודור (בימי תגלת פלאסר) ושומרון (בימי סרגון). בהסתמכו על הזכרת דור בשתי רשימות טופונומיות אשוריות מקוטעות מנינוה. החזיקו אחריו חוקרים רבים כגון אולברייט, אלט, נות, ולאחרונה גם אילת ועוד.[10] לדעת אלה המשיכה מסגרת מינהלית זו להתקיים עד סוף התקופה הפרסית.[11]

לעומת זאת, העלו אהרוני ואפעל[12] השערה אחרת: אהרוני סבר שגם אם היתה דור תחילה פחווה אשורית בימי תגלת פלאסר ג', הרי לאחר כיבוש שומרון נכללה פחוות דור בתוך הפחווה החדשה של שומרון, שכן למרות שדור נזכרת ברשימת ערים אשוריות, הכוללות בעיקר את בירות הפחוות, אין היא מופיעה ברשימות האפונימים האשוריות, כפי שמופיעים בהן שמות הפחוות של שומרון ומגידו. לדעת אהרוני, מכריעה בעניין זה עדותו של אסרחדון מלך אשור, המספר באחת מכתובותיו (משנת 671 לפנה"ס) שאיש לא עמד נגדו במסעו מאפק "שבאזור שומרון" ועד רפיח.[13]

אהרוני סבור שיצירת פחווה על חוף הים היתה מוצדקת רק קודם לחורבן שומרון, כל עוד עבר גבול הפחוות האשוריות באזור זה. אולם עם סיפוח שומרון, חידשו האשורים את הקשר המינהלי בין השרון להר שומרון. מכל עדויות אלה ניתן לדעתו להסיק, כי נפת דור נשארה בתקופה האשורית חטיבה מינהלית משנית במסגרת פחוות שומרון וכי התפתחות זו מסבירה את הופעתה ברשימת הערים האשוריות שנזכרה למעלה.[14]

גם אפעל סובר כאהרוני, ובניגוד לפורר, כי לאור כתובותיו של תגלת פלאסר הג' שנתגלו בעשרות השנים האחרונות, ולאור השימוש בהן לתיקונן של קריאות משוערות בכתובות שפורסמו קודם לכן, משתנות האינטרפרטציה ההיסטורית והתמונה הגיאוגרפית-מינהלית שהיתווה פורר: שיחזורם של קטעי "כתובות ראווה" של תגלת פלאסר מעלה, שאין בכתובות אלו מילה אודות ייסודן של פחוות אשוריות בשטחה של ממלכת ישראל. אף זאת, מציאות השם *Ka-as-pu-na* באחת מכתובות תגלת פלאסר, לציון עיר בחוף פיניקיה, בגבול האזור שסופח לתחום פחוות צ[מר], מבטלת את ההשלמה *[Ra]-as-pu-na* שהציע פורר בקטע מקביל, יחד עם זיהויה של רשפון-ארסוף-אפולוניה; וממילא מתבטל הצורך להניח, כי תחום הפחוות האשוריות השתרע עד אזור הירקון כבר בימי תגלת פלאסר. לבד מן האמור

9. E. Forrer, *Die Provinzeinteilung des assyrischen Reiches* (Leipzig: Hinrichs, 1920) 52ff.

10. אילת, "המסחר הבינלאומי," 67–88.

11. א. מלמט, "מלחמות ישראל ואשור," בתוך י' ליור, הסטוריה צבאית, 241–256; א. שטרן, דור המושלת בימים (ירושלים: מוסד ביאליק והחברה לחקירת א"י, 1992) 73.

12. Y. Aharoni, *The Land of the Bible: A Historical Geography* (Philadelphia: Westminster, 1979) 377; אפעל, "השלטון האשורי," 191–201.

13. A. L. Oppenheim, "Babylonian and Assyrian Historical Texts," *ANET*, 292–294

14. שטרן, דור המושלת בימים, 68-69.

בכתובות סרגון על כיבוש שומרון וסיפוחה למערכת הפחוות האשוריות, אין בידינו ידיעות מפורשות על תהליך התארגנותו של השלטון האשורי בשטחה של ממלכת ישראל. יתר-על-כן גם אפעל סבור שעלפי תואריהם של פחות (שהיו אפונימים בשנים 690, 679, 640) וכן מרשימות מיסים, ידוע על קיומן של הפחוות מגידו ושומרון בארץ-ישראל המערבית. לעומת זאת, מהזכרות דור במקורות האשוריים לא ניתן ללמוד בודאות אם אמנם היתה קיימת פחווה מיוחדת לאורך החוף שנקראה בשם זה או שמא שמשה העיר מרכז מינהלי אשורי ותו לא. כלומר, שלדור לא היה קיום עצמאי משלה והיא היתה כפופה לפחוות שומרון או, לחילופין, למלך צור.

בעניין זה ניתן אולי להסתמך על החוזה של אסרחדון עם בעל מלך צור (לעיל) שבו נזכרת דור, כעיר הגבול הדרומית בתחום הטריטוריה שהוענקה לאחרון. אכן, לאחרונה העלתה א. גלבוע השערה נוספת, המבוססת על הממצא הארכיאולוגי בדור, כי העיר לא שמשה כבירת פחווה אלא כנמל (*karu*) אשורי, לאמור בשלטון אשורי ישיר בדומה לנמלים האשוריים שהוקמו ליד ארווד וליד צידון.[15]

העדות הארכיאולוגית

נעבור עתה לדון בעדות הארכיאולוגית העולה מתוצאות החפירות, ובעניין זה נתרכז בחפירות בחוף הארץ-ישראלי מאכזיב ועד יפו. בטריטוריה הפיניקית שמדרום לצור, לאמור: בחוף הגליל המערבי ובעמק עכו, נחפרו עד כה ארבעה אתרים שהכילו שכבות מימי השלטון האשורי והם אכזיב, כברי, עכו ותל כיסון. בהמשך ודרומה לאורך חופי הכרמל, בשטח שהיה עד לכיבוש האשורי בתחום ממלכת ישראל ולאחריו הפך לפחוות דור (*Duru*), נחפרו שקמונה ודור עצמה שאכן הכילו שרידים מתקופה זו. לעומת זאת, כל יישובי החלק הדרומי של הפחווה, "למן דור ועד יפו," שנחפרו עד כה, והם תל-מבורך, מכמורת, תל חפר, תל מיכל ואפולוניה, כמעט ולא הכילו שרידים של ממש להוציא שנים שלושה ממצאי אקראי. יפו וסביבותיה כבר היו שייכות בפרק זמן זה למובלעת האשקלונית הפלישתית ולא נכללו בתחום הפחווה הפיניקית. בשלהי התקופה, ככל הנראה מימי יאשיהו ואילך, חדרה גם ממלכת יהודה לגבול הדרומי של השטח וממצאים מפרק זמן זה השייכים כנראה אליה נתגלו בקסילה ואולי גם בתל כודאדי.

נסקור עתה את תוצאות החפירות באתרים שנמנו לעיל המתיחסות לפרק הזמן של הכיבוש האשורי.

מאכזיב שרדו אלינו בעיקר בתי הקברות, מהם עשירים בממצאים המעידים שאותו זמן נתקיים בעיר יישוב פורח.[16]

בחפירות החדשות בכברי שנערכו בצידו הצפוני של התל הקדום נתגלתה מערכת ביצורים איתנה, הכוללת חומה ומגדל הבנוי בבנייה פיניקית טיפוסית. מגדל זה נהרס בשלהי המאה ה-8 לפנה״ס, ככל הנראה בידי האשורים. על היישוב שנתחדש בתקופת הברזל המאוחרת (מאה ה-7 לפנה״ס), ככל הנראה תחת מרותה של צור, מעידים שרידי רצפות שנמצאו על-גבי הריסות המגדל. לפי שעה נגלו ממנו רק ממצאים מעטים. מכל מקום, לדעת החופרים היה

15. א. גלבוע, "קרמיקה אשורית בדור והערות למעמדה של העיר בתקופת הכיבוש האשורי," ארץ-ישראל כ״ה (ספר י. אבירם, ירושלים החברה לחקירת א״י 1996) 122-135.

16. א. שטרן (עורך), האנציקלופדיה החדשה לחפירות ארכיאולוגיות בארץ-ישראל (ירושלים: החברה לחקירת א״י וכרטא, 1992) 27–33.

שטחה של העיר בתקופה זו קרוב ל-20 דונם. לדעתם, יש לזהותה עם העיר רחוב. רחוב ואכזיב, ביחד היו הערים החשובות בצפון עמק עכו.[17]

בתל פ׳וחאר, הוא תלה של עכו הקדומה, העלו החפירות כי בשלהי תקופת הברזל, לאמור במאות 8–7 לפנה״ס, החלה בניה אינטנסיבית בתוך העיר. לראשונה הופיעה בניית גזית של מבני ציבור, נוסף על בנייה רגילה באבן ובלבנים. באחד הבניינים בשטח זה, נמצא קיר לבנים מוצק, שנשתמרו ממנו שבעה נדבכים. בבניין זה שנשרף באחד החורבנות הנזכרים במקורות האשוריים, כנראה בימי סנחריב, נמצא, בין היתר, מטמון של גושי כסף קטנים, שעוצבו בצורות גאומטריות. באחד המבנים האחרים נתגלתה קבוצה של חדרים שקירותיהם נשתמרו לכדי גובה של ארבעה נדבכים. גם קבוצה זו חרבה בשריפה, אולי בעת חורבנה של עכו בידי אשורבניפל. בשכבות אלו נחשפו עקבות של חרושת מתכת. כן נמצאו יסודות של בניני אבן, אולי של חומת סוגרים. ייתכן, כי זו החומה המופיעה בתיאור החורבן האשורי בימי אשורבניפל. בשטחים אחרים נחשפו יסודות מוצקים של מבנים רחבי ידים. חשובה בעיקר שכונה שנחשפה ובה בתי לבנים בעלי יסודות אבן. בשכונה זו, ששימשה למגורים ולמלאכה כאחת, נתגלה בין היתר, כבשן יוצרים מטוייח, הוא בעל צורה סגלגלה, ובו תמיכה מרכזית של עמוד לבנים. נוסף על שפע כלי החרס המקומיים נתגלו כלים מטיפוס פיניקי וקיפרי וצלמיות חרס.[18] מן הממצא הזעיר ראוי להזכיר חותם גליל שטרם פורסם, בסגנון אשורי. על-פי הדגם והסגנון שייך לראשית התקופה.[19]

בסמוך וממזרח לעכו ובעמק הצמוד אליה נערכו חפירות אינטנסיביות בתל כיסון שגם בו נתגלו שרידי עיר פורחת מפרק זמן זה. עיר 5 שקדמה לכיבוש האשורי נהרסה ככל הנראה על-ידם כאשר הגיעו לאזור צבאותיו של תגלת פלאסר ג׳.[20]

תקופת הכיבוש האשורי מיוצגת באתר זה היטב בשכבה 4. בשכבה זו יש עדויות לתכנון עירוני חדש, השונה לגמרי ממסורות תקופות הברונזה והברזל, וכיוונם של קירות הבתים אינו נקבע עוד על-פי קו המתאר של החומה. בשכבה 4 נמצאו שני שלבי יישוב שביניהם מפריד כנראה רובד של הרס וחורבן. שלב היישוב הקדום (4B) הוא זה שבו ניכרת ביותר ההשפעה האשורית: גביעים אשוריים, ״קרמיקת ארמון״ אשורית בצבע בז׳ ולבן, וחותמות המעוטרים בדגמים פולחניים כגון סהר על- גבי מטה אנכי, החרט של האל מרדוך. בולט ביניהם הוא חותם טביעה שמתוארת בו שלוש סצינות פולחן אשוריות (ציור 3). א. קיל שדן בחותם זה קבע את זמנו ל-700 לפנה״ס.[21] וככל הנראה היה זה חותמו של פקיד באדמיניסטרציה המקומית הקשור בהתישבות החדשה באתר שנעשתה לאחר 720 לפנה״ס כבכל אזור החוף.

יש לציין כי בדו״ח החפירה שוייך חלק הארי של הממצאים האלה לשכבה 5. כיסון נהנתה, ועמה כל סביבותיה, מן הפיתוח הכלכלי שהביא עמו השלטון האשורי. על-כך מעידה כאמור התעשייה הקירמית המשגשת, שהיא פיניקית מובהקת, אך משולבים בה יסודות ודגמים אשורים. הבקבוקים הגבוהים— צורתם אשורית, אך צווארם ובסיס האומפלוס

17. א. קמפינסקי וו. ד. נימאייר, ״כברי 1992–1993,״ חדשות ארכיאולוגיות ק״א–ק״ב (1994) 14–17.

18. M. Dothan, “Akko Interim Excavation Report, First Season 1973/4,” *BASOR* 224 (1976) 1–48; הנ״ל אצל שטרן, האנציקלופדיה, 1228–1229.

19. ט. אורנן, עיונים בממצא הגליפטי מארץ-ישראל ומעבר הירדן: חותמות גליל אשוריים, בבליים ואחמניים מן המחצית הראשונה של האלף הראשון לפנה״ס, עבודת גמר לתואר מוסמך, (ירושלים: האוניברסיטה העברית, 1990) 28.

20. J. Briend and J. B. Humbert, *Tell Keisan (1970–1976)* (Paris: Gabalda, 1980)

21. שם; 279-280; לוח 4:89.

ציור 3. חותם-טביעה אשורי מתל כיסון.

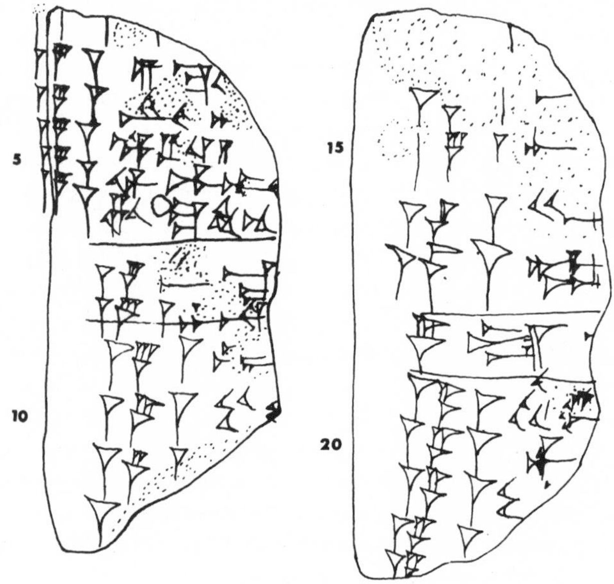

ציור 4. טבלת טין בכתב יתדות אשורי מתל-כיסון.

שלהם הם פיניקים טיפוסיים, והוא הדין גם בעיטור ובמירוק. דומה כי בתל כיסון נתקיים בתקופה האשורית מרכז מינהלי כלשהו, שכן, לבד מן החותמות שנמנו לעיל ושחלקם לפחות קשורים כנראה בפולחן סין מחרן,[22] מאותה שכבה (5) בא גם לוח טין כתוב אשורית ובו רשימה של מידות ומשקולות (ציור 4).[23] אל אלה יש להוסיף שבר של צלמית טין בסגנון אשורי

22. A. Spycket, "Le culte du Dieu-Lune à Tell Keisan," *RB* 80 (1973) 384–385

23. M. Sigrist, "Une tablette cunéiforme de Tell Keisan," *IEJ* 32 (1982) 32–35

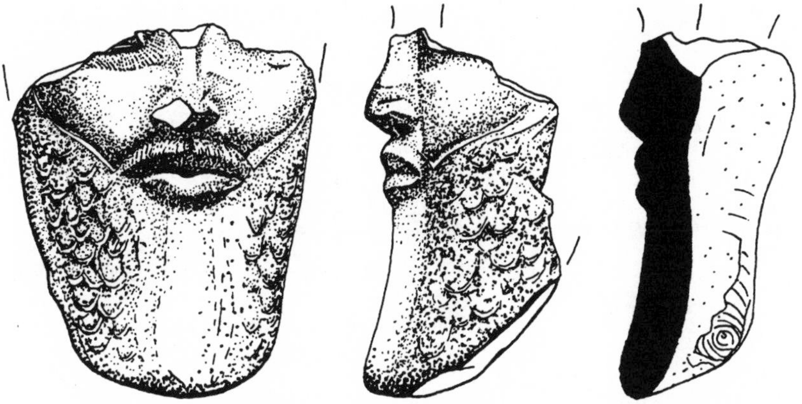

ציור 5. קטע מראש של צלמות-טין בסגנון אשורי מתל-כיסון.

טהור שאפשר שהיא מייצגת את דמותו של אחד ממלכי אשור (ציור 5).[24] זמנו של שלב זה צריך להקבע—לדעת כותב שורות אלה—למן הכיבוש האשורי בימי תגלת פלאסר ג׳ (733/732 לפנה״ס) ועד לערך 640 לפנה״ס עם פינוי כל שטחה של א״י ופיניקיה ע״י צבאות אשור. אבל אפשר גם שנהרס, כדעת החופרים, כמה שנים קודם לכן בעת מסע עונשין שערך אשורבניפל ב-643 לפנה״ס, מסע הנזכר באנאלים שלו ואשר בו חרבה גם עכו.

השכבה הבאה בתל כיסון היא שכבה 4 והיא מאופיינת כבר ע״י השפעות יוונית-מזרחית וקיפרית חזקות. היא מכילה כלי חרס רבים המיובאים ממקומות אלה בהם קנקני סל, קערות מורטריה, אמפורות יווניות, ובעיקר קבוצה של כלים מעוטרים בסגנון ה-Wild Goat, מכלול הקרוב מאוד לזה שנתגלה במצד חשביהו שליד יבנה ים[25] ואשר מספק את התאריך המדוייק לשכבה. לדעת כותב שורות אלה שלב זה זמנו למן 640 לפנה״ס בקירוב ועד לכיבוש הבבלי שסביב 600 לפנה״ס.[26] גם שכבה זו חרבה בשריפה, ככל הנראה בהקשר עם המצור הבבלי הממושך על צור ובנותיה.

אין בידינו עדויות על שכבת ישוב מן התקופה האשורית בתל אבו-הוואם שבקצהו הדרומי על עמק עכו.[27] וסביר להניח גם עפ״י המחקרים החדשים שלא היה בה כלל יישוב בפרק זמן זה. כשאנו עוברים לחוף הכרמל, יש בידינו עדות ראשונה משקמונה, אשר לדעת חופרה נכללה בתחום הפיניקי הקשור בצור, ולא בפחוות דור שלפני הכיבוש האשורי היה בתחום ממלכת ישראל. מחפירות אלה אין בידינו דו״ח סופי לשכבות מתקופת הברזל. לפי הדו״חות הזמניים שפורסמו עד כה נראה שמספרי השכבות ותקופות היישוב עברו כמה וכמה גלגולים. בספר מסכם שפורסם זה לא מכבר[28] נאמר כי שכבה 9 היא העיר שחרבה בידי תגלת פלאסר ג׳ בשנת 733/732 לפנה״ס. שכבה 8 היא העיר שמימי הפחווה האשורית. החופר מציין כי למרות דלותם של שרידי הבנייה, הניבה שכבה זו קבוצות של כלי חרס

24. בריינד והומבר, תל כיסון, לוח 102:10.

25. בריינד והומבר, תל כיסון.

26. F. J. Salles, "A propos du Niveau 4 de Tell Keisan," *Levant* 17 (1985) 203–204

27. R. W. Hamilton, "Excavations at Tel Abu Hawam," *QDAP* 4 (1934) 1–69

28. י. אלגביש, שקמונה לחוף הכרמל (ירושלים: החברה לחקירת א״י ועתיקותיה והוצאת הקבוץ המאוחד, 1994) 69–73.

שלמים וכן כמה חותמות שבאחד מהם מתואר כהן עומד בתפילה לפני סמלי אל הירח בדומה לחותמות תל כיסון.[29] יתר על-כן, בפינת אחד החדרים ועל רצפתו נתגלה ראש אלה מן הטיפוס—לדעת החופר—שהיה רווח בשימושו של הצבא האשורי.

בשקמונה לא הבחין החופר בין שני שלבים של העיר מן המאה ה-7, דהיינו זו שהיתה תחת כיבוש ישיר של האשורים לזו שנתקיימה בשלהי המאה בין 640 ועד בוא הבבלים. מכל מקום, ייחוסם של קנקני סל רבים וכלי חרס יוונים מזרחיים רבים לשכבה זו מאפשר לנו לשער שהיא נתקיימה לכל אורכה של המאה ה-7 ונחרבה בידי הבבלים.

החפירות המרכזיות בחוף הכרמל הן אלה שנערכו בתל דור, בירת האזור והפחווה, ששרידיה הארכיטקטוניים נשתמרו במידה טובה ורבים גם הממצאים מפרק זמן זה.[30] כאן חרבה שכבת הישוב מימי הממלכה המפולגת על ביצוריה המשוכללים ושערה בן ארבעת התאים—בשריפה עזה—ולא היה ספק לפי עדות החרסים (כולל החרסים המיובאים מיוון), שחורבן זה נעשה בידי צבאות אשור בשלהי המאה השמינית לפנה״ס, דהיינו במסע תגלת פלאסר הגי. מכאן ואילך אין בידינו למעשה כל מקורות כתובים שיעידו כמה זמן עמדה העיר בשממונה ואימתי נושבה מחדש.

לעומת זאת, תוצאות החפירות מורות עתה בבירור כי חורבן זה, שאולי קשור גם בהגליות בהיקף רחב כדרכם של האשורים, לא נמשך זמן רב. דומה כי האשורים, אשר לא היה להם צי משלהם או ידע כיצד להפעילו, נזקקו כל העת לשירותיהם הטובים של הפיניקים לשם פיתוח סחרם עם מדינות הים. יתר על-כן, יש לזכור כי זמן מה שלטו האשורים אף בקפריסין, לפי עדותם שלהם ולפי עדות הממצא הארכיאולוגי באי. אין ספק שהגיעו אל האי בעזרתם הפעילה של הפיניקים, וקיום שלטונם שם נשען אף הוא על הצי הפיניקי. מן הסתם היה דחוף להם לחדש את ערי הנמל בשטחים שהיו בשלטונם הישיר, אם לצורך פיתוח הסחר הימי בכלל וגביית מיסים ממנו, ואם לצורך סיוע בהחזקת השטחים שמעבר לים. לא פחות מכן נזקקו לנמלים אלה לצורר סיוע באספקת מזון וציוד לצבאותיהם בדרום הארץ, ולאחר מכן, לצבאות ולצוות המנהל שישבו במצרים; שכן כיבוש ארץ זו נעשה לאחת המטרות העיקריות של אשור. בתוך כך נהפך החוף הארץ-ישראלי לאיזור מעבר, ונמליו, וביניהם דור, שימשו מחסני-אספקה.

אכן, תוצאות החפירות בדור של פרק-זמן זה מורות שוב ובבירור כי העיר חזרה ושוקמה מחורבנה בתוך זמן קצר. החפירות במזרח התל גילו מערכת ביצורים חדשה, חזקה מאוד, שהקיפה את העיר. הביצורים כללו חומה מטיפוס ״קדמות ונסגות,״ לאמור: שקטעים ממנה בולטים לסירוגין כלפי חוץ (קדמות) וקטעים אחרים שביניהם ״נסוגים״ פנימה כדי לאפשר למגינים לפגוע בתוקפי החומה מן הצד גם בהיותם כבר סמוך לחומה ולרגליה בשטח מת. השימוש בחומה זו החל כבר בשלב הקודם, לאמור: מימי הממלכה המפולגת (אחאב), ונמשך לכאן. מן החומה נותר בעיקר בסיסה האיתן, שחלקו היה מורכב מתשתית אבן מוצקה שבפינותיה אבני גזית (אפשר שכמה מהן היו בשימוש משני מהשכבה הקודמת ובאחת אף שרד סימן סתתים בצורת +, הזהה בצורתו עם סימן סתתים ממגידו; ציור 6).

מעל מסד אבן זה, שרוחבו כשני מטרים, נבנתה ודאי חומת לבנים, ומן הסתם—אם לשפוט לפי חומות אחרות שנתגלו בארץ—היתה גבוהה למדי וטוייחה בטיח טין. בקטעים אחרים השתנה בסיס החומה ונבנה אף הוא מגוש לבנים מוצק שהונח על רובד דק של חצצי אבן וחוזק במרכזו בקיר של אבן שנבלע בתוך גוש הלבנים. כמו כן חוזקה החומה לכל

29. אלגביש, שקמונה חוף הכרמל, 70.

30. א. שטרן, ״חצור, דור ומגידו בימי אחאב ואשור,״ ארץ-ישראל כ (1985) 233–248; הנ״ל, דור המושלת בימים, 62–70.

ציור 6. חומת הקדמות ונסגות מן התקופה האשורית בדור; מבט למערב.

אורכה גם בחלקלקת-טין משופעת, שעליה נמרח לעתים מזומנות טיח-גיר כדי להגן עליה מפני הגשמים. ואכן, שרידים של טיח גירי זה, לעתים בעובי ניכר, נתגלו בכל החפירה. מן הסתם טיח גירי דומה ציפה את כל החומה לכל גובהה, אלא שלכך לא היתה בידינו עדות מן השטח.

מחובר לחומה זו נחשף בשטח ב׳ שער מזרחי חדש אשר נבנה בדיוק במקומו ועל גביו של שער ׳ארבעת התאים׳ שמתקופת הממלכה הישראלית. אמנהם תוכניתו של שער זה היתה שונה; הוא היה מורכב משני תאים בלבד, כלומר: תא אחד מכל צד של מבוא השער. תאים אלה הם רחבים ביותר ובולטים ביותר (כדי כפלים) לדרום ולצפון מן השער הקודם. לעומת זאת, עומקו של בית השער עצמו קטן כמעט בחצי משל שער ׳ארבעת התאים׳, ולמעשה בנויים קירותיו הפנימיים על גבי המחיצה המפרידה בין שני תאי השער הקודם ועל גבי שני התאים הקדמיים. גם אבניו, אף שהיה בנוי אבני גיר גדולות למדי, אינן מגיעות לכדי מידות אבני השער הקודם (ציור 7).

לפני השער נחשפה רחבה גדולה מרוצפת אבנים גדולות שטוחות ומיושרות. רחבה זו הובילה—כפי שאנו יודעים היום—אל שער חיצון, שטרם נחפר, אשר נמצא מצפון לשער הפנימי ומחוצה לו. עד עתה נחשפו קטעים נרחבים של דרך הגישה אל שער שני התאים. הדרך רוצפה באבני שדה שהודקו היטב זו לזו והיא שמורה להפליא. היא עולה בשיפוע מתון מצפון לדרום לאורך חומת העיר. עד עתה נחשפו ממנה למעלה ממאה מ״ר. מבוא השער עצמו, כלומר: השטח שבין הכניסה אליו והיציאה ממנו, היה מרוצף באבני גזית מעובדות היטב. מפתח השער פנימה לעיר הוליכה דרך מרוצפת אבן, ועליה נוסף—אם מיד, אם בהמשך הזמן—רובד של כורכר כתוש.

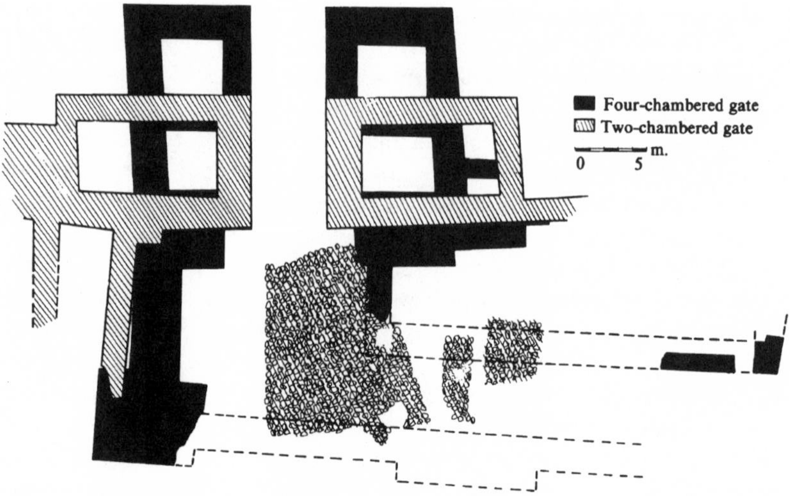

ציור 7. תל דור; תכנית של שער התאים מן התקופה האשורית בנוי על-גבי שער ארבעה תאים מתקופת המלוכה.

הכלים שנתגלו על-גבי ריצוף השער היו מאוחרים למדי. זמנם הגיע עד לראשית המאה הרביעית לפנה״ס, כלומר: עד לחלקה המאוחר של התקופה הפרסית, והם שקבעו את זמן שימושו האחרון וחורבנו (ככל הנראה בימי המרידות הגדולות של ערי פיניקיה בשלטון פרס; וראה עוד להלן). השאלה היתה אימתי נבנה השער? לכך היה ניתן למצוא פתרון בממצא: עניין אחד היה זמן חורבנו של השער הקודם—שער 'ארבעת התאים'. ובכן, ראינו כבר, כי לפי כל הסימנים חרב שער זה בשריפה בזמן כיבושה של דור בידי צבא אשור בימי תגלת פלאסר ג' (733 לפנה״ס). שערנו חייב אפוא להיות מאוחר מכך; ואכן, תוך כדי חפירת מבוא השער (שמטעמים של שימור השערים העליונים חפרנוהו רק במחציתו הדרומית), נתגלתה כשהיא צמודה למשקוף הדרומי, 'אבן פותה' מבזלת, כלומר: אבן שבמרכזה שקערורית עגולה משופשפת ומוחלקת היטב מרוב שימוש, אשר שימשה בסיס לציר הדלת הדרומית שהסתובבה בתוכה. אפילו נשתמר במרכז השער חריץ עמוק ומסותת היטב אשר לתוכו החדירו את בריח המתכת שנעל את הדלתיים במרכזן כלפי מטה. עוד נתברר, שאבן הפותה מבזלת כוסתה בחלקה העליון באבן גיר שבוודאי הגנה עליה מפני כניסת בוץ או לכלוך העשויים להקשות על סיבוב הציר. אכן, לאבן כיסוי זו יש צורה בלתי שכיחה: היא מסותתת, בצורת חצי-סהר ונתגלו עליה, דרך אגב, סימני חריצים שהותורו בה ציר הדלת ותחתיתה בהסתובבה. במשך הזמן העמידני רוני רייך, שהתמחה בסוגיה זו,[31] על כך, שטיפוס זה של אבן כיסוי לאבני פותה מצוי בארץ וברחבי המזרח הקדמון כולו תמיד בהקשר למבנים אשוריים. בארץ נתגלו כבר דוגמאות אחדות של אבני כיסוי דומות, כולן אכן במבנים אשוריים. מאוחר יותר התברר עוד, כי לכשהסרנו קורות ומילויים מאוחרים וחשפנו את הפינה הדרומית-מערבית של שער שני התאים, פגענו ברצפה הניגשת אל הקיר החיצוני של התא ועליה כלים משלהי תקופת הברזל. ובכן, היתה זו הבחנה חשובה, שכן

31. R. Reich and B. Brandel, "Gezer under Assyrian Rule," *PEQ* 117 (1985) 41–45

השלימה היטב עם תולדות דור כפי שהיו מוכרים לנו מן המקורות הכתובים. חיזוק נוסף בא לנו בעניין זה גם מהשוואת ביצורי דור כפי שנתבררו בחפירותינו, עם ביצורי העיר הסמוכה מגידו, שנחפרה לפני שנים רבות ואשר גם אותה בנו האשורים כבירה של פחווה; שכן גם במגידו נבנה מעל שער 'ארבעת התאים' מימי אחאב, שער של שני תאים בתוכנית דומה מאוד לזו של דור, אם כי אולי במידות שונות במקצת. גם השער במגידו מהווה רק שער פנימי, ויש לו מערכת נוספת של שער חיצון. שער שני התאים במגידו מיוחס ללא עוררין, ועל דעת כל החוקרים כולם, לשכבה III שם, שהיא היא העיר שבנוה האשורים במקומה של עיר אחאב. ליד שער זה נבנו ונחשפו במגידו גם מבני ציבור גדולים מטיפוס 'אשורי', לאמור: בתים בתוכנית 'בית החצר הפתוחה' בעלי חצר מרכזית המוקפת חדרים מכל עבריה.[32] בסמוך גם רובעי מגורים רבועים, מתוכננים היטב על-פי תוכנית בנייה זהה וכן אסם תבואה מעוגל וגדול-ממדים; שכן במגידו, שלא כבדור, הספיקו לחשוף שטחים גדולים בתוך העיר של פרק זמן זה.[33]

לסיכום נראה לנו, שמערכת הביצורים בדור, הכוללת שער של שני תאים וחומת קדמות ונסגות, נבנתה בידי האשורים זמן קצר לאחר שהחריבו את קודמתה, בעת שעשאוה לבירה של פחווה—היא 'פחוות דורו'. הדמיון בין ביצורי דור ומגידו בפרק זמן זה נובע ככל הנראה מן התפקיד הזהה שהועידו להם האשוריים: בירה של פחווה ומקום מושבו של מושל אשורי (פחה).

ימי השלטון האשורי בארץ-ישראל היו קצרי זמן. כאמור, דור הישראלית נכבשה ונהרסה כבר בימי תגלת פלאסר ג' בשנת 733 לפנה"ס, אולם כפי ששיערנו קודם, לא נעשתה בנייתה מחדש קודם לחורבנה של שומרון, בירתה של הממלכה הישראלית בשנת 720 לפנה"ס, כלומר: כ-13 שנים לאחר מכן.

מבחינה הסטורית הגיע השלטון האשורי לקצו קצת יותר ממאה שנים לאחר מכן, עם מפלתם הסופית של צבאות אשור בכרכמיש, בשנת 605 לפנה"ס. אולם, ככל הידוע לנו כיום, נסתיים שלטונם המעשי בארץ כבר שנים רבות קודם לכן, בראשיתם של ימי יאשיהו מלך יהודה (לערך 640 לפנה"ס), כאשר החלו מהומות פנימיות והפיכות-חצר בתוך בית-המלוכה האשורי, ושליטים חלשים וקצרי זמן החליפו זה את זה במהירות רבה. אחיזתה של האימפריה בפרובינציות המרוחקות נחלשה אותה עת עד למאוד.

ימי השלטון האשורי בעיר דור, שאותה בנו מחדש, לא ארכו, לפיכך, אלא כ-80 שנה. אולם למרות פרק זמן קצר יחסית זה, ועל-אף שחפרנו רק שטח מצומצם בפנים העיר, נתגלו בחפירתנו כמה ממצאים שיש בהם עדות חשובה ביותר. בתוך רובד המגורים שבתוך העיר גילינו שני סוגים של ממצאים שיש בהם השפעה אשורית ישירה: (א) חותמות; (ב) כלי חרס.

חותם גליל אחד, (ציור 7) המשקף השפעה אשורית פרובינציאלית. החותם נתגלה בשטח B1 בלוקוס שכלל ממצאים מסוף תקופת הברזל ומהתקופה הפרסית ומיוחס לפאזה 5 שטח B1 הוא החלק הצפוני של שער העיר במזרח התל ופאזה 5 היא השלב שבו נבנה שער שני התאים המיוחס לתקופה האשורית. חותם אשורי נוסף, שצורתו חביתית עשוי אגאט, נתגלה לא הרחק, בחלק הדרומי של השער (שטח B2) בתוך מכלול מעורב (ציור 8).[34]

32. R. Amiran and I. Dunayevsky, "The Assyrian Open Court Building and Its Derivatives," *BASOR* 149 (1958) 25–32

33. R. S. Lomon and G. M. Shipton, *MEGIDDO I, Seasons of 1925–34, Strata I–V* (Chicago: University of Chicago Press, 1939) 62–83

34. שטרן, דור המושלת בימים 67-68; שני חותמות אלו מדור מצטרפים לחותמות-גליל אשוריים נוספים שנתגלו בתחומי פחוות דור. האחד נתגלה זה לא מכבר בקיסריה וטרם פורסם (כאן ציור 9;

ציור 8. תל דור; חותמות אשוריים: למעלה חותם-גליל;
למטה: חותם-טביעה.

בדור נתגלו גם כלי חרס אשוריים רבים מטיפוס 'כלי הארמון' וכן חיקויים מקומיים לכלים אלה. רוב הכלים שנתגלו בדור, כמו במקומות אחרים, הן קערות (או שברי קערות), מזוות בזיווי חד ובעלות דפנות דקות וגבוהות שצבע החרס שלהן בהיר מאוד; ודומה כי אינם

הנני מודה לד"ר י. פטריך על שנתן לי רשות להביאו כאן). זהו חותם גליל שחקוקה בו סצינה שכיחה למדי: סצינת המשתה, לאמור המלך עומד בצידו האחד של שולחן עמוס מנחות כאשר מצידו השני יושב האל אשור על כסאו. זהו חותם שעשו בסגנון הקידוח וזמנו משלהי המאה השמינית לפנה"ס או מראשית המאה השביעית. חותם גליל אשורי נוסף נתגלה הלאה דרומה ליד מכון וינגייט של היום (מדרום לנתניה על שפת נחל פולג; ציור 10). על חותם זה — שלא כבחותמות שלנו — נמנו שמו ותוארו של בעל החותם: "בל אַשַרֵד שר הארמון," שעל פי מסקנתם של מפרסמיו מרים וחיים תדמור, הוא תוארו של פקיד רם דרג בהיררכיה האשורית. דומה איפוא, ששני החותמות מקיסריה ואיזור מכון וינגייט השתייכו אף הם לפקידים של פחוות דור, אשר הביאום עימהם מאשור למקום כהונתם, ויש באלה כדי להעיד על חשיבותה של העיר. ככל הנראה אבדו שני החותמות מקיסריה ומנחל פולג לפקידים אשוריים שעשו את דרכם בתחומי הפחווה בדרך הים מדור ליפו. והשווה: ח. ומ. תדמור, "חותם בל אשרדו שר הארמון," ידיעות החברה לחקירת ארץ-ישראל ועתיקותיה ל"א (1957) 68—79.

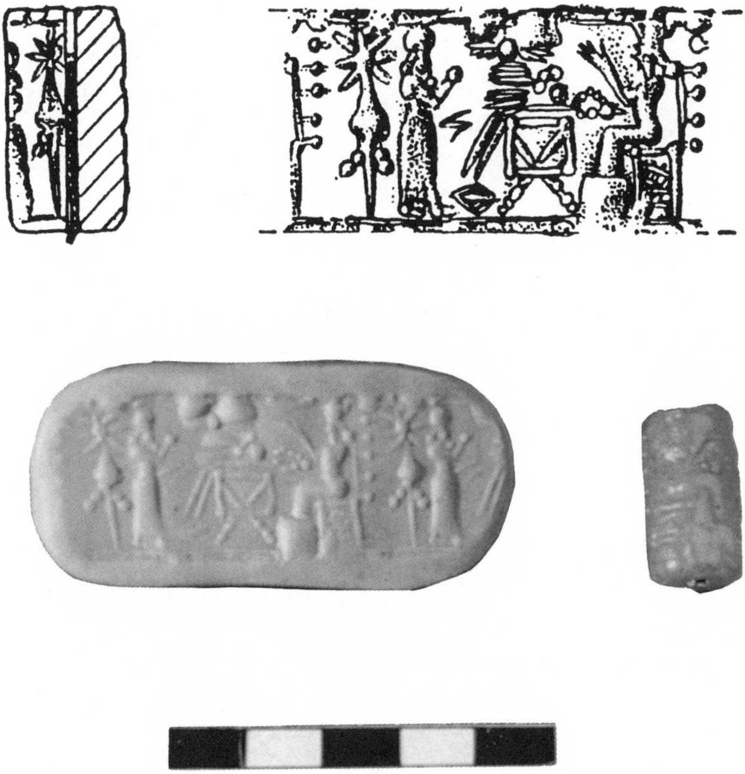

ציור 9. תצלום וציור של חותם-גליל אשורי שנתגלה לאחרונה בקיסריה.

ציור 10. חותם-גליל אשורי ממכון וינגיט (עפ״י תדמור).

אלא חיקויים לקערות-המתכת האשורית הנודעת. בדיון טיפולוגי ממצה שערכה לאחרונה איילת גלבוע בממצא זה, נתברר שהמכלול מורכב בעיקרו משבעה טיפוסים של קערות וכן בקבוקים מחודדים, אמפוריסקוי ואגני חרס.[35]

מן הראוי לציין כי על סמך הממצא האשורי העשיר בדור, דהיינו הביצורים והשער, הקרמיקה, והחותמות סוברת איילת גלבוע כי האשורים הקימו במקום Karum, דהיינו נמל מסחרי בפיקוח אשורי ישיר שבאמצעותו נגבו מיסים מן הסחר הימי הישר לאוצר המלוכה. היא מבכרת פירוש זה על הפירוש המסורתי המצדד בקיומה של פחווה פיניקית נפרדת שבירתה דור, ואין הדברים נראים לנו.

השלטון האשורי בדור היה, כאמור, קצר-זמן והוא פסק למעשה בקירוב בשנת 640 לפנה״ס. ב-40 השנים הבאות, עד בוא צבאות בבל לדור, לא ברור מה עלה בגורלה, ובעניין זה יש להודות, כי לפי שעה גם החפירות לא הבהירו הרבה את התמונה. אמנם אפשר שהעיר היתה נתונה ישירות לזמן מה בידי מלך צור והיתה מעין עיר נמל אוטונומית למחצה. אבל אפשר מאוד שלפרק זמן קצר מאוד, בשנים 610–609 לפנה״ס בקירוב, החזיק בה שוב מלך יהודי—הוא יאשיהו מלך יהודה—בעת שבא למגידו כדי לעצור בעד צבאות פרעה נכה מלך מצרים, שיצא לכרכמיש לסייע בידי צבא אשור (מל״ב כג:כט-ל). כידוע, נהרג יאשיהו במערכה זו.

אולם, בין אם היתה דור בידו ממש ובין אם היתה עיר פיניקית אשר רק סייעה לו במלחמתו במצרים, הרי זכר אחד לימים סוערים אלה בדור שרד לנו בדמותה של משקולת אבן קטנה (בת שקל אחד, דהיינו: כ-11.4 גרם), שעליה טבוע סמל בית המלוכה היהודאי מימיו, שנתגלתה בתוך בור סמוך לשער העיר.

עיר זו היא שנפלה בידי הבבלים בסוף המאה. הכיבוש הבבלי של דור הביא, כמו בכל יישובי החוף הפיניקי (ולמעשה בארץ-ישראל כולה), לחורבן כללי שלא נרפא אלא בהתחדש היישוב באזור זה בראשית התקופה הפרסית.[36]

אשר ליישובים שמדרום לדור בשטח שממנה ועד יפו, כאן מתבררת תמונה שונה.[37] בתל מבורך לא היה קיים כלל יישוב בפרק זמן זה. הוא חרב בשלהי המאה העשירית ויישובו חודש רק בתקופה הפרסית.[38] גם בתל מיכל נחרב היישוב במאה העשירית. שרידים דלים ביותר נתגלו מהמאה השמינית ואילו מן התקופה האשורית לא נתגלה דבר. היישוב חודש במקום רק בתקופה הפרסית.[39] תמונה דומה עולה גם מתל חפר שנתקיים בו יישוב דל מסוף המאה השמינית שחרב ולא חודש עד לתקופה הפרסית.

35. והשווה גלבוע, ״קרמיקה אשורית.״ בעונות החפירה האחרונות בדור (1994–95) נתגלה באחד השטחים שמדרום התל (שטח ד׳ 2) מכלול גדול מאוד של כלי חרס מהמאה ה-7 לפנה״ס. המכלול נתגלה בקבוצה של בורות חפורים וטרם טופל או פורסם. אבל כבר עתה ברור כי הכיל כלי חרס אשוריים רבים מהם מטיפוסים שלא נכללו בדיונה של גלבוע. ככל הנראה זהו מכלול הכלים השלם והמקיף ביותר מפרק זמן זה שנתגלה עד היום בצפון הארץ.

36. א. שטרן, התרבות החומרית של ארץ-ישראל בתקופה הפרסית, 538–332 לפנה״ס (ירושלים: מוסד ביאליק והחברה לחקירת א״י, 1973).

37. א. שטרן, ״מערך יישובי השרון בתקופה הישראלית ובתקופה הפרסית,״ בתוך א. דגני ואחרים (עורכים), השרון בין ירקון וכרמל (תל אביב: משרד הבטחון / ההוצאה לאור, 1990) 167–173.

38. E. Stern, "Excavation at Tel Mevorakh (1973–1976), Part One: From the Iron Age to the Roman Period," *Qedem* 18 (1978)

39. Z. Herzog et al., *Excavations at Tel Michal, Israel* (Minneapolis: University of Minnesota Press, 1989)

גם במכמורת לא נתגלו שום שרידים של יישוב מפרק זמן זה, אבל כאן נתגלה שבר של כתובת בכתב יתדות אשר מאוחר יותר נתברר כי הובאה אמנם מבבל. אולם, זמנה מן התקופה הפרסית, מימי כנבוזי מלך פרס, ואף הוא שייך ליישוב מן התקופה הפרסית שחודש במקום אשר לאפולוניה יישוב זה הוקם למעשה בתקופה הפרסית ולא נתקיים קודם לכן.[40]

גם בתל קסילה שבקצהו הדרומי של השטח לחוף הירקון נתברר כי העיר חרבה במאה העשירית והאתר עמד בשממונו עד לתקופה הפרסית. רק במקום אחד נתגלה רובד עפר סמוך לפני השטח ובו חרסים משלהי המאה השביעית שרובם אופייניים לממלכת יהודה. בהם נרות בעלי בסיס גבוה וכיו״ב, אבל גם כלים אשוריים. יתכן שממצא זה מיצג יישוב קצר ימים בשלהי המאה השביעית שקשור היה ככל הנראה לממלכת יהודה, אולי בימי יאשיהו.[41]

לאור כל זאת ניתן לשחזר את תולדות חוף הים שבין דור ליפו בשטחה של פחוות דור האשורית כשטח שלא היה מיושב בעיקרו של דבר למן המאה העשירית ועד לתקופה הפרסית, שרק אז חודש בו היישוב בהיקף רחב כחלק מגל ההתישבות הפיניקי הגדול שהציף את כל איזור החוף של מרכז הארץ.[42] דומה כי בימי הכיבוש האשורי היה שטח זה עזוב בעיקרו ונוצל כדרך מעבר מיפו לדור. לרשימה זו כדאי אולי להוסיף ממצאים של שתי כתובות מונומנטליות אשוריות, האחת מחורבות הכפר קאקון שבמרכז השרון והשנייה באיזור בן שמן. שתי הכתובות הן כנראה מימי סרגון.[43]

סיכום

השילוב בין המקורות ההיסטורים ותוצאות החפירות הארכיאולוגיות באתרי החוף של דרום פיניקיה וצפון ארץ-ישראל מורה כי הופעת האשורים באיזור עברה שני שלבים מנוגדים. בשלב הראשון עבר האיזור תקופות כיבוש מלווה בהרס אינטנסיבי של כל מרכזי ערי דרום פיניקיה והמרכזים העירוניים של ממלכת ישראל בגליל, שומרון וחוף הים. שלב זה נמשך ככל הנראה מימיו של תגלת פלאסר ג׳ ועד לחורבנה הסופי של שומרון בשנת 720 לפנה״ס בידי סרגון ב׳. בשלב השני, עוד בימיו של סרגון, נתייצב האיזור ועבר מהפך מוחלט, ככל הנראה בעקבות שינוי במדיניות האימפריאלית האשורית. סרגון ששהה באיזור לעיתים מזומנות, הוא שהבחין ביתרונות הכלכליים העצומים שניתן להפיק מערי הנמל הפיניקיות והוא זה שפנה ליישב מחדש ולבנות מחדש את כל הערים ההרוסות הן באוכלוסיה שהובאה ממקומות רחוקים אבל בעיקר ע״י מתן הרשאה לאוכלוסי הערים הפיניקיות הותיקות והגדולות להתיישב בשטחים שדרומה ומזרחה להם, בהם כל יישובי רצועת החוף מצור ואכזיב, דרך כברי, עכו, תל כיסון, מגידו שקמונה ודור. בכל המקומות הללו נבנו ערים חדשות מבוצרות, שתוך זמן קצר הגיעו לפריחה של ממש. ערים אלה הן בעלות ייחוד ארכיטקטוני, הן במה שנוגע לביצורים והן בתוכניות המבנים, וכן בתרבות החומרית הקשורה באשור והבאה לידי ביטוי בכל מרכיבי התרבות החומרית: כתובות, נוהגי-קבורה, קרמיקה,

40. שטרן, האנציקלופדיה, 943–947; י. רול וא. איילון, אפולוניה ודרום השרון (ירושלים: החברה לחקירת א״י ועתיקותיה והוצאת הקיבוץ המאוחד, 1989).

41. A. Mazar, "Excavations at Tel Qasile, Part Two: The Philistine Sanctuary," *Qedem* 20 (1985) 12–120

42. שטרן, התרבות החומרית, 237–239.

43. י. פורת, ש. דר וש. אפלבאום, קדמוניות עמק חפר (תל אביב: הוצאת הקבוץ המאוחד, 1985) 59.

פיסול, חותמות, כלי אבן וכיו״ב שבהתחשב בפרק הזמן הקצר של התקופה האשורית (כ-60–70 שנים בלבד) מעוררת השתאות.

ייחוס השלב הזה דווקא לימי סרגון המאוחרים ניתן להעשות גם על-סמך ממצא הכתובות המונומנטליות בארץ שכולן יוחסו אליו (באשדוד, בן-שמן, קאקון, ושומרון).[44] אופייני הדבר שבימיו הגיעו האשורים גם לקפריסין, כפי שמעידה לטובתו שם.[45] עובדה נוספת שניתן ללמוד מן הממצא הארכיאולוגי היא שהאשורים לא טרחו לבנות מחדש ערים שהיו בלתי מיושבות כבר קודם לבואם לחוף הארץ-ישראלי, כגון תל אבו הוואם שבעמק עכו וכל יישובי השרון הדרומי מתל מבורך ועד יפו.

אשר למבנה השלטון, דומה, שלאחר שנקבע בימי סרגון שוב לא נשתנה בימי יורשיו עד תום השלטון האשורי הממשי בחוף סביב שנת 640 לפנה״ס. שלטון זה היה מורכב משני סוגי מערכות: האחת היתה מערכת של שלטון ישיר דהיינו של פחוות בראשות פחה אשורי כגון פחווה צמר ולפרק זמן קצר גם אולי פחוות צידון. והמערכת האחרת העיקרית באיזור זה היתה של שלטון עקיף בערי החוף הפיניקיות העיקריות, ארווד, גבל, צידון וצור, שנעשה בעזרת פקידים ממונים ויחידות צבא קטנות שנשתכנו בערים ופיקחו על תנועת הסחורות ותשלום המיסים. סדר זה הופרע רק כתוצאה ממרידות והצורך בהענשת המורדים ובהגלייתם, שאז גם נבנו ״ערי נמל אשוריות״ בשלטון ישיר לפרקי זמן קצרים כגון ״כר אסרחדון״ שנזכרה לעיל.

באיזור החוף הארץ-ישראלי אין ספק שבפרק זמן זה היו ערי החוף של הגליל המערבי ועמק עכו מנוהלות על-ידי צור, שמלכיה קיבלו לשם כך רשות ממלך אשור. עדות לכך מצויה כנראה ב״חוזה אסרחדון״ שנדון לעיל, שבו נקבעו הכללים לגבי אוניות טרופות של צור ושבו נמנה גם התחום מעכו עד דור. אשר לרצועת חוף הכרמל והשרון מ״דור ועד יפו,״ אף על-פי שהמקורות ההיסטורים המעידים בהחלט על חשיבותה של העיר אינם מונים אותה בבירור כבירה של פחווה כדעת א. פורר (או לפחות בחלק מפרק הזמן הזה--כדעת אהרוני ואפעל), הרי דווקא הממצאים הארכיאולוגים הרבים מעיר זו הם התומכים בפירוש זה, שכן ביצוריה וממצאיה עשירים מאוד.

פיזור החותמות על-פני כל שטח הפחווה, מדור, דרך קיסריה, ועד נחל פולג, מעיד גם שדרך הים לפחות היתה בשימוש רווח בפרק זמן זה. ממצאים רבים אלה (עליהם נוספו עוד בעונות החפירה האחרונות) הם שהביאו את גלבוע[46] לסברה שדור היתה ׳כרום׳ לאמור: עיר נמל בשלטון אשורי ישיר. אולם לנו נראה שלעניין זה אין כלל סימוכין היסטורים מספיקים, ולעומת זאת מרכזיותה של העיר הן במקורות ההיסטורים והן בממצא הארכיאולוגי מצביעים על היותה הנמל החשוב של האיזור וככל הנראה תומכים גם במעמדה כבירה של פחוות איזור החוף של ממלכת ישראל לשעבר. בדומה למעמדה כבירת נציבות בימי הממלכה המאוחדת ונמל ראשי של ממלכת ישראל בימי הממלכה המפולגת, אגב כך ניתן היום לאמר בבטחון שמעמד זה חזר אליה בתקופה הפרסית. שכן גם שליטיה של אימפריה זו—כאשורים לפניהם ושלא כבבלים—אימצו לעצמם מדיניות דומה של ניצול הסחר הימי של הפיניקים.

יש עניין נוסף שצריך ליתן עליו את הדעת. הוא שאלת מי היו האוכלוסין שהתיישבו בדור וסביבותיה לאחר שחזר סרגון ובנאה. דומה, כי פרט למעט אשורים (חילים, פקידים וכיו״ב) נבנתה העיר בידי הפיניקים, שהיו ללא ספק מרכיב עיקרי מכאן ועד התקופה ההלניסטית.

44. ח. תדמור בתוך י. אבירם (עורך), ארץ שומרון (ירושלים: החברה לחקירת א״י ועתיקותיה, 1974) 71.

45. *ANET*, 284

46. גלבוע, ״קרמיקה אשורית.״

נוודים בנגב במקורות מצריים

שמואל אחיטוב
אוניברסיטה בן-גוריון בנגב

על השם ועל תולדות המחקר

נוכחותם של נוודים באזורים הצחיחים-למחצה הגובלים במצרים היתה תופעה של קבע בתולדות מצרים. מציאות זו משתקפת בתעודות מצריות למן ימי הממלכה הקדומה, ואולי כבר בימי השושלת הראשונה של מצרים, כלומר למן תחילת האלף השלישי לפני סה״נ בקירוב. המצרים קראו לנוודים אלה בשמות שונים, לא תמיד מדויקים. פעמים שהם משתמשים לגביהם בשמות הכלליים לזרים, או לתושבי אסיה, ורק לפי תיאורם אנו למדים שהכוונה לנוודים. במשך ההיסטוריה הארוכה של מצרים שמות איבדו את משמעותם הייחודית, אבל משום שבמצרים השמרנית שום דבר אינו הולך לאיבוד, גם השמות הללו ממשיכים להופיע בתעודות, תופעה אופיינית של ארכאיזם.

בתקופת הממלכה החדשה של מצרים (מאות ט״ז–י״ב לפני סה״נ בקירוב), נתפשט השם שאסו לציין בו את נודדי אסיה. אף שהשם הופיע לראשונה כנראה כבר בפירמידה של וניס (השושלת החמישית, 2350 לפני סה״נ בקירוב), הרי זו הופעה יחידה, בודדת. השם שאסו הוסיף לשמש גם בתקופות מאוחרות, כולל התקופה התלמית, אבל אז כבר יצא משימושו המדויק ואינו מעניננו כאן. נראה שהשם נגזר משורש *šꜣs* = נסע, ומכאן בקופטית *šos* = רועה. השם דומה אפוא לשם *nmyw-šꜥ* = נודדי החולות, משורש *nmi* = לעבור, לחצות.

עניננו לתאר כאן את הנודדים המצוינים דרך כלל בשם שאסו. המחקר המקיף ביותר הוא ספרו של רפאל גבעון ז״ל: *Les bédouins shosou des documents égyptiens*,[1] והוא האוסף הכולל של התעודות המצריות הדנות בשאסו. עליו יש להוסיף את שני מאמרי הביקורת החשובים שנכתבו על ספרו של גבעון.[2] התיאור הבא יצטמצם למקורות שבכתב ולא יתייחס למקורות שבציור ותבליט שהם בעייתיים ביותר.

1. Raphael Giveon, *Les bédouins shosou des documents égyptiens* (Leiden: Brill, 1971)

2. W. A. Ward, "The Shasu 'Beduins,' " *JESHO* 15 (1972) 35–60; M. Weippert, "Semitische Nomaden des zweiten Jahrtausends: Über die *šꜣsw* der ägyptischen Quellen," *Bib* 55 (1974) 256–280, 427–433. לנוחיותם של הקוראים סימנתי את המובאות במספרי התעודות שבספרו של גבעון, הכולל גם את תרגום התעודות לצרפתית. בסוגרים ציינתי את מראי המקומות לתעודות מהתקופה הרעמססית, לפי האוסף העדכני (בהירוגליפים) של קיצ׳ן: K. A. Kitchen, *Ramesside Inscriptions* (= KRI), vols. 1–8 (Oxford: Blackwell, 1975–1990)

שאסו-ציון גיאוגרפי או סוציואתני?

אחת השאלות הראויות לציון היא האם המונח שאסו מתכוון לציון גיאוגרפי או לקבוצת אנשים. מי שיבקש לתלות ישועתו במגדירים המלווים את השם שאסו יתאכזב. לא זו בלבד שפעמים הרבה המגדיר של ארץ-נכר בא במקום שמדובר בקיבוץ של אנשים, אלא שהשימוש במגדירים נעשה מאוד לא מדויק בתקופה שאנו עוסקים בה. אם נתעקש להסתמך על המגדירים יתברר לנו כי שאסו הוא שמה של כל הארץ המשתרעת מסילו שבאזור קנטרה של מצרים ועד קדש שעל הארנת (אורונטס), ולא נשתייר אפוא מקום לרתנו-חיורו-כנען.

הזכרתו של השם שאסו ברשימות הטופוגרפיות המצריות אינו מסייע בידנו, שכן הוא בא ברשימות סטריאוטיפיות, שלא בהקשרים גיאוגרפיים מוגדרים. כך הוא יכול לבוא ליד קדש שעל נהר ארנת, שבבקעת הלבנון הצפונית, ליד אַרזַוַה שבמערב אסיה הקטנה, בין מצרים התחתונה לארץ חת, או כאחד מתשעה שמות-תחליף ל״תשע הקשתות,״ תשעת אויביה המסורתיים של מצרים.

על מהותו של השם שאסו יש ללמוד רק לפי ההקשר בו הוא מופיע. כך למשל בטקסט סטריאוטיפי, במקדש הגדול של פרעה רעמסס השני (1279–1213 לפני סה״נ) באבו-סִמבל, בכתובת-לוואי לתיאור של פרעה המכה את הלובים, נאמר: ״המביא את נוביה (*tꜣ nḥsy*) לארץ הצפון, את העאמו (*ꜥꜣmw*) לנוביה (*tꜣ sty*). הוא הניח את השאסו בארץ המערב. הוא יסד את לוב (*tḥnw*) על ההרים. המבצרים אשר בנה מלאים בשלל זרועו החזקה. הורג את חיורו בחרבו, רתנו נפלה בגלל ההרג שלו.״[3]

בטקסט של תהילה למלך שנמצא בסַוֵיס העתיקה (כּוֹם אל-קֻלְזֻם) ושנפגם מאוד, נאמר על רעמסס השני כי ״[הושיב] את לוב (*tḥnw*) בערים בשמו . . . [. . .] חת כלא היתה . . . [. . .] השאסו הובאו בכוחו למצרים.״[4]

בשתי התעודות מופיעים שמות של ארצות ועמים ביחד, וההחלטה אם מדובר או בארץ או בתושביה תלויה רק בהקשר. ברור כי במקום שנאמר ״המביא את נוביה לארץ הצפון״ הכוונה לנובים, וכשנאמר ״את העאמו לנוביה,״ הכוונה לארץ נוביה. מתוך ההקשר עולה שאין שאסו שם של ארץ, אלא ציבור של אנשים.

רעמסס השני מזכיר בכתובותיו ניצחון על ארץ השאסו (*tꜣ šꜣsw*). רוב הכתובות הסטריאוטיפיות הללו, המזכירות את ארץ השאסו באו מאזור הדלתה: מצוען (מקורן כנראה בעיר רעמסס הסמוכה),[5] פי-בסת,[6] תל א-רטאבה,[7] תל אל-מסחוטה,[8] גבל א-שאלוף שבאזור התעלה,[9] וכן ברשימה טופוגרפית ממוף.[10]

נראה שבעיקרו של דבר הכינוי שאסו מתייחס לישות סוציואתנית, ולכן כשבימי רעמסס השני ביקשו לדייק רשמו 'ארץ השאסו', אבל לא תמיד הקפידו בכך.

3. מסי 16 (KRI 2.206–207)
4. מסי 34 (KRI 2.304)
5. מסי 25–29 (KRI 2.408–409, 408 [obelisk 9!], 289–290, 294, 300)
6. מסי 24 (KRI 2.465)
7. מסי 32 (KRI 2.304)
8. מסי 31 (KRI 2.404), מתל אל-מסחוטה.
9. מסי 33 (KRI 2.304)
10. מסי 23 (KRI 2.194)

היכן ישבו שאסו ואיפה היא ארץ השאסו?

תפוצתם של השאסו היתה רחבה ביותר וחפפה כנראה את כל תחום השלטון המצרי באסיה. בימי סתי הראשון (1294—1279 לפני סה״נ) אנו מוצאים שאסו בדרומה של ארץ-ישראל. בכתובות שבמקדש אמון בכרנך המלוות את תיאורי מלחמותיו, כולל המפה הריאלית המתארת את הדרך מסילו ועד ״הכנען,״ מתוארים השאסו כתושבי ארץ חורו, היא כנען. נאמר עליהם ש״הם ניצבים על ראשי ההרים של חורו.״[11] בכתובת אחרת מכתובות-לוואי אלה נאמר: ״ההרג אשר עשתה זרועו החזקה של פרעה—חיים, שפע, בריאות!—בשאסו האויבים למן מבצר סילו ועד הכנען, כאשר הוד מלכותו התגבר עליהם כמו אריה זועם. גוויותיהם מוטלות בעמקיהם, הם מתבוססים בדמם כלא היו.״[12] בין שהתיבה ״פ-כנען״ = הכנען, האמורה כאן מכוונת לארץ כנען, בין שהכוונה ״לעיר הכנען״ המזוהה בעזה, שתוארה במפת הדרך מסילו לכנען, ברור שיש לבקש את מקומם של השאסו לאורך הדרך המתוארת. הרי שמקום מושבם של השאסו היה בצפון סיני ובקצהו הדרומי של מישור החוף הדרומי של ארץ-ישראל.

לעומת מיקום דרומי זה של השאסו בכתובותיו של סתי הראשון, בכתובות קרב קדש של רעמסס השני אנו מוצאים שאסו בבקעת הלבנון הצפונית. לפי המסופר שם, בהתקרב פרעה וחילו לקדש שעל נהר ארנת, נלכדו שני שאסו והובאו לחקירה לפני פרעה. שני אלה, שנפלו במתכוון לידי המצרים כדי להלעיטם במידע כוזב, נמנו של חילות העזר של המלך החתי שחנה עם צבאו בקדש.

נראה שלמיקום צפוני זה מכוון גם הסיפור באוטוביוגרפיה של החייל יעחמס פן-נחבת, על ימי פרעה תחותימס השני (1492—1479 לפני סה״נ): ״ליוויתי את הוד-מלכותו מלך מצרים העליונה והתחתונה עא-חפר-רע. אשר הבאתי משאסו—שבויים רבים עד אין מספר.״[13] המלחמה היחידה בימי תחותימס השני שעליה נודע לנו—ואולי המדובר בקוצר ידיעותינו בלבד—היתה בצפון, בתחום ניא, שלפי הנראה שכנה באזור חמץ שבסוריה. האם שם שבה יעחמס פן-נחבת שאסו, או אולי אין קשר בין שני המאורעות, ולפנינו שני מקרים שונים מימי תחותימס השני שאינם קשורים זה בזה.

מקור לא ברור אחר מצוי באנלים של תחותימס השלישי (1479—1425 לפני סה״נ), משנתו ה-39: ״הנה הוד-מלכותו בארץ-הנכר רתנו במסע הניצחון הארבעה-עשר אחרי שהלך [להכות] את השאסו האויבים.״[14] מאחר שהשם רתנו הוא שם כללי לתחום השלטון המצרי באסיה בכתובותיו של תחותימס השלישי, אין להוציא ממובאה זו שום מידע גיאוגרפי מוגדר.

תופעת השאסו היתה כנראה נפוצה בכל האזור, בחבלים שאופיים התאים לכלכלה של נוודים-למחצה, שבסיסה גידול מקנה. אם כן הוא, סביר שנמצא שאסו באזורי המדבר של דרום ארץ-ישראל ודרום מזרחה. ואכן, יש עדויות מספיקות על שאסו באזורים אלה.

לעיל כבר נדונו כתובות-הלוואי של תבליטי כרנך של סתי הראשון, המזכירות שאסו בצפון סיני ובדרום מישור החוף של ארץ-ישראל. לכאן מצטרפות ידיעותינו על זיקתם של שאסו לשעיר ולאדום. והתעודות מדברות בעד עצמן:

במצבה של רעמסס השני שנמצאה בצוען (צאן אל-חַגַר שבצפון מזרח הדלתה), ומקורה כרוב המצבות מצוען בעיר רעמסס, נאמר: ״האריה האכזר . . . ההורס את ארץ השאסו,

11. מסי "A" 11 (KRI 1.9)
12. מסי "C" 11 (KRI 1.7)
13. מסי 1.
14. מסי 2.

שולל את הר שעיר בזרועו החזקה"[15] אפשר שלכאן יש לצרף גם את המצבה מתל א-רטאבה האומרת על רעמסס השני: "העושה הרג רב בארץ השאסו, הוא בזז את הריהם, ההורג אותם ובונה ערים בשמו, לנצח!"[16] תעודות אחרות של רעמסס השני מזכירות את ארץ השאסו בצורה כללית יותר ואינן תורמות להבנתנו את הנושא.

תעודה מאוחרת יותר, מסוף ימי רעמסס השלישי (1184–1153 לפני סה"נ), או מימי יורשו רעמסס הרביעי (1153–1147 לפני סה"נ) מפרשת יותר את זיקת השאסו לשעיר. המדובר בפפירוס האריס א (פפירוס האריס הגדול, עשרים מ' אורכו), שעיקרו רשימת מענקים ומתנות של רעמסס השלישי למקדשי מצרים. אבל בחלק ההיסטורי שלו נאמר כי רעמסס השלישי עשה הרג רב בשעיר, שבטי השאסו והיכה את אוהליהם.[17] עוד תזכר כאן תעודה ספרותית-למחצה, פפירוס אנסטזי ו מסוף ימי שושלת י"ט (1200 לפני סה"נ בקירוב) המזכירה את שבטי השאסו של אדום (ראה לקמן), שעוד ידובר בהם בפירוט.

עתה, משסקרנו את התעודות הספרותיות יותר, ניתן לגשת לעדות מעניינת ברשימות הטופוגרפיות. המדובר ברשימה טופוגרפית ממקדשו של אמנחתפ השלישי (1279–1213 לפני סה"נ) בצלב (סולב) שבנוביה (סודאן).[18] שהועתקה על ידי האומנים של רעמסס השני במקדשו שבעמארה המערבית הסמוכה לצלב, מעברו השני של היאור[19] ברשימה הרעמססית שני שמות שלא נמצאו ברשימה שבמקדש בצלב, אם מפני שאבדו או שיש לראות בהם תוספת, וכנראה האפשרות הראשונה תקפה יותר.

ואלה השמות שאמנו שם:

ארץ השאסו סמת
ארץ השאסו יהוא
ארץ השאסו תרבר
ארץ השאסו פספס

הרשימה הרעמססית מוסיפה:

ארץ השאסו שעיר
ארץ השאסו לבן

מבין השמות הנמנים כאן לפחות שניים זרים לאוזן השמית: תרבר ופספס.

לבן היא אותה לבן הידועה מסופה של רשימת ערי ישראל והנגב שכבש שישק מלך מצרים, בקצה הדרומי של ארץ-ישראל,[20] ומכתובותיו של סרגון השני מלך אשור בזיקה לנחל מצרים.[21] נראה שיש לזהות את לבן בתל אבו-סלֵימה שליד א-שיח' זויד בצפון סיני.[22] אין צורך להרבות דברים על שעיר, רק יש לזכור כי שעיר אינה בהכרח ממזרח לערבה. השם שעיר נופל גם על הרי סיני והנגב הרחוק. ראה למשל: "אחד עשר יום מחורב דרך הר שעיר עד קדש ברנע" (דברים א, ב). או הסיפור על תבוסת ישראל בחרמה שבנגב: "ויצא האמורי היושב בהר ההוא לקראתכם וירדפו אתכם בשעיר עד חרמה" (שם, פס' מד).

15. מס' 25 (KRI 2.408–409)
16. ראה לעיל הע' 7.
17. מס' 38.
18. מס' 6a.
19. מס' 16a (KRI 2.217 nos. 92–97)
20. ראה S. Aḥituv, *Canaanite Toponyms in Ancient Egyptian Documents* (Jerusalem: Magnes / Leiden: Brill, 1984) 129
21. *ANET*, 286
22. ראה Aḥituv, *Canaanite Toponyms*, 149–150

לשעיר של צפון סיני מתייחסים גם התיאורים של התגלות ה׳:

ה׳ מסיני בא / וזרח משעיר למו
הופיע מהר פארן / ואתה ממריבת קָדֵש

(דברים לג, ב; כך יש לגרוס תחת מֵרִבבות קֹדֶש).

ה׳ בצאתך משעיר / בצעדך משדה אדום
ארץ רעשה / גם שמים נטפו
גם הרים נטפו מים / הרים נזלו
מפני ה׳ זה סיני / מפני ה׳ אלהי ישראל

(שופטים ה, ד)

לכאן מתקשרת בבירור הזכרת ארץ השאסו יהוא, הנושאת את שמו של ה׳ אלהי ישראל. וקשה להפריז בערכה וחשיבותה של הזכרה זו לתולדות ישראל. כאן עלי להסתפק בקביעה הגיאוגרפית.

מה פשר ארצות שאסו אלה? ברור שהמדובר בתחומים מצומצמים לערך, ונכון להשוותם לינגבים המוזכרים במקרא (נגב יהודה, נגב הירחמאלי ונגב הקיני של שמואל א כז, יח) או בכתובת שישק (נגב עצחת, נגב אשחת ונגב ׳והתורד׳)[23] שאינם אלא ארצותיהם-נחלותיהם, תחומי נדודיהם, של השבטים ששמם נקרא עליהן. גם המדבר אינו שטח הפקר ולכל שבט תחום נדודים משלו.

המבנה החברתי של השאסו

אמנם בתעודות המצריות אין הרבה פרטים על המבנה החברתי של השאסו, שהרי אין להן עניין בכך. אבל גם מן הדברים שנאמרו בהן באקראי ניתן ללמוד משהו. גם ניתן לנצל תעודות המזכירות אסייתים שלא בשם שאסו להשלמת ידיעותינו. תספרנה התעודות את סיפורן:

בכתובת-לוואי בתבליטים של סתי הראשון בכרנך שנזכרה למעלה נאמר: ״הנה באו לומר להוד-מלכותו. השאסו האויבים קשרו קשר. ראשי שבטיהם נאספו במקום אחד כשהם ניצבים על ההרים של חורו. הם התחילו במהומות וריב. איש הורג את רעהו.״[24] המאורע המרומז בכתובת אינו ידוע, וכנראה גם אינו חשוב ביותר. באופיו הוא דומה למאורע אחר המסופר במצבה הקטנה של סתי הראשון בבית שאן, משנתו הראשונה. כלומר שני המאורעות אירעו באותה שנה עצמה. במצבה מסופר כי ״העפירו של הר ירמות עם התיר/לו תוקפים את העאמו של רוהם.״[25] המצבה מבית שאן מספרת על מהומות בין יסודות שונים באוכלוסיה המקומית בסביבות בית שאן, כנראה באזור רמת יששכר של ימינו. שם הותקפו תושבי הקבע—העאמו—של מקום (?) בשם רוהם על ידי העפירו של הר ירמות ועל ידי גוף לא ידוע בשם תיר/לו, שאולי אפשר למנותו על השאסו. אבל בכתובת מכרנך מסופר על מלחמות שבטיות בין השאסו עצמם, סכסוך שפרץ אולי במהלך התכנסות של ראשי השבטים, אם נדייק מלשון הכתובת מכרנך.

מקור חשוב אחר להכרת המבנה החברתי של השאסו הוא הסיפור על שליחי מלך החתים שנפלו אל רעמסס השני בקרב קדש כדי להטעותו על ידי מסירת מידע כוזב, תכסיס של דיסאינפורמציה. וזה לשונו: ״בוא שני שאסו משבטי השאסו לומר להוד-מלכותו: ׳אלו הם

23. שם.
24. ראה לעיל הע׳ 10.
25. *ANET*, 255

אחינו אשר הם ראשי השבטים אצל האויב החתי אשר שלחונו.׳ ״[26] המונחים המעניינים בהקשר זה הם ׳שבטים׳ (מצרית *mhwt*) ו׳ראשי שבטים׳. המונח *mhwt* שהמצרים השתמשו בו לציין שבטים הוא אותו מונח לציון משפחה. המצרים הבחינו יפה שהמושג המתאים ביותו להגדיר את השבט הוא משפחה (גם במקרא המונחים שבט ומשפחה מתחלפים). אשר למונח ראש שבט, המצרים הבחינו יפה בין מלכי המעצמות הגדולות (*wr ꜥ3*), לשאר מלכים כולל מלכי ממלכות העיר הכנעניות (*wr*) ולראשי שבטים (*ꜥ3*), כולן מלים שפירושן המילולי ׳גדול׳.

תעודה המלמדת על כלכלתם של השאסו ואורח חייהם היא הדו״ח על מתן רשות כניסה למצרים לשבט אדומי. זו תעודה מהימנה, או אמיתית-למחצה, ששימשה כמכתב דוגמה לפרחי סופרים במצרים. בתעודה, מובאה מפפירוס אנסטזי ו מסוף ימי שושלת י״ט נאמר: ״אשר סיימנו להניח למשפחות (*mhwt*) השאסו של אדום לעבור את מבצר מרנפתח . . . אשר {ב}ת׳כו, אל הבריכות של פיתום [של] מרנפתח אשר {ב}ת׳כו להחיות את עצמם ולהחיות את מקניהם, על ידי היכא׳ הגדול של פרעה . . . השמש הטוב של כל הארץ . . .״[27] הרי לנו שבט אדומי המוגדר כשאסו שפרנסתו על המרעה והוא יורד לאזור המרעה של ואדי תֻמילאת להחיות את בעירו. מעין זה נמצא גם ב׳נבואת נפרתי׳, יצירה ספרותית-פוליטית מימי שושלת י״ב. שם נאמר כי המלך שיקום יבנה את ״חומות המושל״ כדי למנוע את האסייתים מלהיכנס למצרים. הם יתחננו למים כדי להשקות את צאנם.[28] שימו במקום השם אדום את השם ישראל, והרי לכם תמונת יעקב ובניו היורדים מצרימה.

בקטע מפפירוס האריס א שנזכר למעלה, נאמר על רעמסס השלישי: ״העושה הרג גדול בשעיר, שבטי (*mhwt*) שאסו. מכה את אוהליהם. אנשיהם, רכושם וצאנם לאין מספר אסורים ומובאים למצרים כשלל וכמס. נתתים לתשעת-האלים כעבדיהם, למקדשיהם.״[29] החידוש שבתעודה זו—בתיאור משכנותיהם של השאסו בשם אוהל. ומעניין שהסופר לא השתמש במלה המצרית *ỉm(3)w* אלא במלה השמית אוהל.

השאסו הנודדים המאורגנים בחברה שבטית שאפשר היה לגייסם לצבא, אם לצבא החתי או לצבא המצרי—כתיאורי התבליטים עצמם—חיו בעיקר בשולי היישוב והיוו סכנה לעוברי דרכים. כך תוארו בפפירוס אנסטזי א, סטירה ספרותית של מעמד הסופרים המצרי, כנראה מימי רעמסס השני. השאסו מתוארים שם כאורבים לצבא המצרי וצופים לעברו בסתר (השווה לתיאורו של האסייתי בצוואת מריכּארע, שמימי הממלכה הקדומה: ״כמו גנב המתרוצץ סביב לחבורה״ [שורה 94]).[30] הם אימת הסופר הצבאי המצרי, ה׳מהר׳, ביער של בקעת הלבנון(?), כמותם כאריות, ברדלסים וצבועים. הם אויב אכזר הנחבא בין השיחים בערוץ העמוק שבו עובר הסופר. השאסו הללו האורבים לעוברי אורח מנצלים את חשכת הלילה למעשיהם. בלילה גנבו את סוסו ובגדיו של הסופר. הרכּב שלו התעורר בלילה וראה את שאירע, גנב את הנותר והצטרף אל הרשעים, התערב במשפחות (*mhwt*) השאסו, ונהפך לאסייתי (*ꜥ3mw*).[31]

אם נסכם את התמונה החברתית של השאסו, הרי הם מאורגנים בחברה שבטית שבראשה ראשי שבטים. הם שוכני אוהלים המתפרנסים על מרעה צאן, שהרעב דוחפם לנדוד ולהגיע

26. מס׳ 14 (KRI 2.103–107)

27. מס׳ 37.

28. *ANET*, 446

29. ראה לעיל הע׳ 17.

30. M. Lichtheim, *Ancient Egyptian Literature* (Berkeley: University of California Press, 1973) 1.104.

31. מס׳ 36.

עד מצרים. יש שהם מתגייסים לשרת בצבא. הם לא מושכים ידם משוד וגניבה, הם חיים בשולי הישוב וקולטים לתוכם פליטים המתערים בתוכם ונעשים כמותם. לתושבי הקבע הם נדמים כאויב אכזרי וחסר רחמים, אימת כל עוברי דרך.

השאסו ובני ישראל

יש בתיאורם של השאסו קווים המתאימים לבני ישראל לפני היאחזותם בקרקע. בראש וראשונה החברה השבטית של משפחות ושבטים המונהגים על ידי ראשים. הם חיים על מרעה צאן. זיקתם לנגב ולצפון סיני ובפרט לארץ השאסו יהוא. הגדרת משפחות אדום ושעיר 'אחיהם' של בני ישראל כשאסו, וכמובן הסיפור של פפירוס אנסטזי ו על ירידת משפחות שאסו מאדום למצרים, הדומה כל כך למסופר על ירידת יעקב ובניו מצרימה.

אמנם איו מקום למשוואה שאסו = בני ישראל. תחום תפוצתם של השאסו רחב ביותר. אבל סביר להניח שלו נתבקש איש מצרי להגדיר איש ישראלי לא היה מוצא לו הגדרה טובה יותר משאסו. אבל כמובן יש בכינוי שאסו יותר משמץ של גנאי. אף לא אחד מבני משפחת עמי עבר, מבני אדום או מישראל, היה מכנה עצמו בשם זה. בירור מעמדם החברתי של בני ישראל בתקופה שקדמה להיותם תושבי קבע גמורים חורג ממסגרתה של סקירה זו.

לפירושה של המשנה הראשונה בבבא מציעא

דוד הלבני
אוניברסיטה קולומביה

שנינו במשנה בבא מציעא א:א–ב:

שנים אוחזין בטלית זה אומר אני מצאתיה וזה אומר אני מצאתיה זה אומר כולה שלי וזה אומר כולה שלי זה ישבע שאין לו בה פחות מחציה וזה ישבע שאין לו בה פחות מחציה ויחלוקו. זה אומר כולה שלי וזה אומר חציה שלי האומר כולה שלי ישבע שאין לו בה פחות משלשה חלקים והאומר חציה שלי ישבע שאין לו בה פחות מרביע[1] זה נוטל שלשה חלקים וזה נוטל רביע. היו שנים רוכבין ע״ג בהמה . . .[2] זה אומר כולה שלי וזה אומר כולה שלי . . . בזמן שהם מודים או שיש להן עדים חולקין בלא שבועה.

ושואלת הגמרא: למה לי למתנא ״זה אומר אני מצאתיה וזה אומר אני מצאתיה זה אומר כולה שלי וזה אומר כולה שלי״ ליתנא חדא חדא? קתני זה אומר אני מצאתיה וכולה שלי וזה אומר אני מצאתיה וכולה שלי . . . והא זה וזה קתני?[3] . . . אמר רב פפא ואיתימא רב שימי בר

1. בכת״י פירנצה: ״פחות מחלק אחד.״ על גירסה זו אומר בעל דק״ס אות א׳: ומסתבר שהיא ט״ס דכיון דמיירי נמי במקח וממכר אפשר שיש לו בה רק חלק קטן והוא טוען שיש לו מחצה. ועיין ב״ב סג, א.״ לא ברור לי למה דוקא במקח וממכר שייך לומר שהיה לו בה רק חלק קטן ״והוא טוען שיש לו מחצה״ ולא במציאה. וודאי לא חשב שבמציאה או שיש לו כולה או שיש לו חציה (״תרוייהו בהדי הדדי אגבהוה״) אבל לא פחות. ראה תוספתא וירושלמי ראש המסכת: ״זה אומר כולה שלי וזה אומר שלשה שלי וכו׳ האומר שלושה שלי ישבע שאין לו בה פחות משתות.״ בכל אופן איך לומר על גירסה שהיא ט״ס אך ורק משום שהיא מתנגדת לגמרא.

2. ראה מ״ש במקורות ומסורות לבבא מציעא ח,א בסוגית הגמרא שם בפירוש המשנה כאן.

3. התוס׳ ועוד: ״איכא דוכתי דפריך כי האי גוונא ואיכא דוכתי דלא פריך.״ זאת אומרת, גמרות חלוקות הן, יש מי שפריך כי האי גוונא ויש מי שלא פריך. א״כ צ״ל שרב פפא ואיתימא רב שימי בר אשי היו בין אלה שהקשו כי האי גוונא. ואילו אלה שאינם מקשים כי האי גוונא אינם מעמידים את המשנה ״רישא במציאה וסיפא במקח וממכר.״ אבל מפרשי המשנה המסורתיים כולם מפרשים את המשנה כן. ובאמת אפילו אלה שמקשים על ״פירושי קא מפרש״ (ראה תוס׳ בכורות לא, ב ד״ה א״כ) יתכן שלא יקשו כאן. כאן יש פחות קושי לומר שבבא אחת היא וכופל את הלשון משום שכל אחד טוען שני דברים, שהוא מצא את האבידה ולכן כולה שלו.

אשי[4] ואמרי לה כדי רישא במציאה וסיפא במקח וממכר. וצריכא . . .[5] ולחזי זוזא ממאן נקיט? לא צריכא דנקיט מתרוייהו . . . ממון המוטל בספק חולקין[6] וכו׳.[7]

ידוע הוא פירושו של ר׳ מנשה מאיליא[8] (הובא גם בתפארת ישראל כאן) שגם הרישא וגם הסיפא מיירי במציאה אלא ש״זה אומר אני מצאתיה וכו׳״ הוא הכלל ו״זה אומר כולה שלי וזה אומר כולה שלי״ ו״זה אומר כולה שלי וזה אומר חציה שלי״ הם הפרטים. וכך הוא הפירוש במשנה: ״שנים אוחזין בטלית, זה אומר אני מצאתיה וזה אומר אני מצאתיה (הדין הוא; אם) זה אומר כולה שלי וזה אומר כולה שלי (אז) זה ישבע שאין לו בה פחות מחציה וזה ישבע שאין לו בה פחות מחציה ויחלקו. (ואם) זה אומר כולה שלי וזה אומר חציה שלי,[9] (אז) זה ישבע שאין לו בה פחות משלשה חלקים וזה ישבע שאין לו בה פחות מרביע. זה נוטל שלשה חלקים וזה נוטל רביע.״ המשנה כולה מדברת במציאה. ואולי הוא הדין במקח וממכר.[10] אבל במשנה עצמה לא נזכר מקח וממכר.

ר׳ מנשה לא הפריד בין סתמא דגמרא ובין האמוראים ולא פיקפק שרב פפא ואיתימא רב שימי בר אשי העמיד את המשנה רישא במציאה וסיפא במקח וממכר מטעם קושית הגמרא, ״למה לי למתנא זה אומר אני מצאתיה וכו׳ זה אומר כולה שלי וכו׳ ליתני חדא.״ הואיל ולדעתו קושיה זו אינה קושיה, לא ראה שום צורך לפירושם של האמוראים במשנה. ועליו לומר שהאמוראים נדחקו לתרץ קושיה זו משום שלא עלה על דעתם שיש לתרץ אותה כמו שתירץ הוא. אבל אנו מפרידים בין סתמא דגמרא ובין האמוראים ומניחים הרבה פעמים בש״ס נימוקים אחרים לדברי האמוראים מאלה שהסתמא דגמרא נותנת, אך משתדלים להסביר למה הסתמא דגמרא מיאנה לפרש כמו שפירשנו אנו ואינם מסתפקים לומר שלא עלה על דעתה. ולכן עלנו לחפש גם כאן הסבר אחר למה האמוראים פירשו את המשנה כן, הסבר שסתמא דגמרא לא יכלה לקבל ומשום כך נתנה הסבר אחר, לקושית

4. בכת״י מינכן (בר״ז אגמתי בשם ר׳ ברוך הספרדי) ועוד: רב אשי. ומעיר על זה בעל דק״ס אות י׳: ״ומסתבר שנשמט (שימי בר) בט״ס כי ר״ש ב״א תלמידיה דרב פפא הוה כדאמר בתענית ט׳ ב׳ ומחלפין ביה שמועתא דר״פ.״ הוא מניח שכל ״ואיתימא ר״פ״ הוא חילוף שמועה בין רב ותלמיד או בין אמוראים בני דור אחד. וכבר השגתי על דעה דומה במקורות ומסורות עירובין עמ׳ סג, הערה 5 וציינתי לגמרא גיטין נו, ב: קרי עליה רב יוסף ואיתימא ר׳ עקיבא.״

5. מסתבר שוצריכא וכו׳ הוא מסתמא דגמרא. אבל הראשונים (רמב״ן, רשב״א, ר״ן, ריצב״ש (בשטמ״ק), ריטב״א ועוד תפסו שוצריכא וכו׳ הוא מרב פפא (ואיתימא רב שימי בר אשי ואמרי לה כדי). ומפני שרב פפא נזכר ראשון, מייחסים לו. ע״ש.

6. ראה מ״ש בב״ק מו, ע״א בשאלת ניסוח דיבור זה בשם סומכוס.

7. יכול היה לתרץ, כמו שהעירו כבר הראשונים, שאין המוכר לפנינו לישאול. אלא שכנראה השאלה והתשובה כאן העברות הן מקידושין עד,א: ״נאמן בעל המקח לומר וכו׳.״ וכבר נאמר דבר זה על ידי רי״צ דינר ואחרים. לפי בעל העיטור, מאה שערים על הרי״ף, ״גירסא דרבנן סבוראי מרישא דפרקין״ [ומה יעשה עם ״אמר רב פפא וכו׳״? ״כדי,״ סתמא, יכול להיות מרבנן סבוראי] ״עד לימא מתניתין.״ ואילו בקטע גאוני, אוצה״ג, פירושים, סי׳ ג׳ ״שמה שאמרו מקח וממכר ניחזי זוזי וכו׳ כל הדברים האלה הם דברי רבנן סבוראי וכו׳.״ חולקים היכן מתחילים דברי רבנן סבוראי כאן. בראש קידושין חולקים הראשונים היכן מסתיימים דברי רבנן סבוראי שם. ראה מה שכתבנו במקורות ומסורות, קידושין, עמ׳ תרכח הערה 6.

8. ראה גם מ״ש ר״י בקון בתרביץ, שנה לב עמ׳ 298–296. ואין בדבריו כדי לערער את פירושו של ר״מ מאליא. ״זה אומר כולה שלי״ אצל ״היו שנים רוכבין,״ על כרחך מיירי במציאה.

9. כלומר, זה אומר אני מצאתיה כולה וזה אומר אני מצאתיה חציה.

10. השוה דברי הגמרא: וצריכא, דאי תנא מציאה וכו׳.

"למה לי למתנא" וכו' שהיא לגמרי אינה הכרחית ואפשר לתרצה כמו שתירץ אותה ר' מנשה. והנה הסברנו:

גם הבבלי לקמן ח,א וי,א[11] וגם הירושלמי פיאה ד, ו (יח, ב) מביאים מחלוקת אמוראים אם המגביה מציאה בשביל חבירו קנה חבירו או לא קנה חבירו (בלשון הירושלמי אם "אדם זוכה לחבירו במציאה" או לא). בח,א המחלוקת היא בין רמי בר חמא המדייק מן המשנה (על הדיוק, ראה להלן) שקנה חבירו ובין רבא הדוחה את דיוקו של רמי בר חמא ואומר, "לעולם אימא לך המגביה מציאה לחבירו לא קנה חבירו והכא היינו טעמא, משום דאמרינן מיגו דזכי לנפשיה זכי נמי לחבריה." אמוראים אלה חולקים כשהמוצא אינו זוכה כלל לעצמו ואין לומר בו, "מיגו דזכי לנפשיה זכי נמי לחבריה," אלא מיגו "דאי בעי" זכי לנפשיה זכי נמי לחבריה. לרמי בר חמא אין הבדל בין "מיגו דזכי לנפשיה," והמשנה, אע"פ שמיירי ב"מיגו דזכי לנפשיה," אפשר ללמוד ממנה גם "מיגו דאי בעי זכי לנפשיה." ולרבא יש הבדל ביניהם. מיגו דזכי לנפשיה וכו' אמרינן ומיגו דאי בעי זכי לנפשיה וכו' לא אמרינן. משתיקת הגמרא משמע, וכן הבינו הראשונים,[12] שכך חלקו גם האמוראים בי,א. כשהמוצא זוכה לעצמו כולם מודים—אפילו רב נחמן ורב חסדא—שקנה חבירו. אין מי שחולק על העיקרון של "מיגו דזכי לנפשיה זכי נמי לחבריה." ובהתאם לשיטה זו לא מצאה סתמא דגמרא הסבר אחר לאוקימתא של רב פפא ואיתימא רב שימי בר אשי, "רישא במציאה וסיפא במקח וממכר," מלבד לומר שבאו לתרץ את יתור לשון של" זה אומר אני מצאתיה וזה אומר כולה שלי."

ברם מטעמם של רב נחמן ורב חסדא (למה המגביה מציאה לחבירו לא קנה חבירו), משום "דהוי תופס לבעל חוב במקום שחב לאחרים והתופס לבעל חוב במקום שחב לאחרים לא קנה," יוצא שאפילו במקום שיש לומר בו "מיגו דזכי לנפשיה," לא קנה. הם חולקים על רמי בר חמא ורבא בח,א וסוברים שגם "מיגו דזכי לנפשיה וכו'" לא אמרינן. העניינים של מי שליקט את הפיאה וכו' לקמן ט,ב ומילא מים ונתן לחבירו וכו' בביצה לט,א–ב (וכן בירושלמי שם) הם עניינים של מיגו "דאי בעי." אבל הלשון הוא מיגו דזכי וכו'. האמוראים לא חילקו ביניהם. מי שסובר קנה סובר בשניהם קנה ומי שסובר לא קנה סובר בשניהם לא קנה מלבד רבא שהוא, כנראה, הראשון שחילק ביניהם. וגם הוא לא אמר כן בפירוש. ורק מתוך דחייתו את דיוקו של רמי בר חמא אנו לומדים כן. ובאמת מיגו "דאי בעי" לא נזכר כלל בגמרא, לא בבבלי ולא בירושלמי. גם ר' יוחנן לא חילק ביניהם. ואע"פ שסובר בכתובות פד,ב ובגיטין יא,ב "תופס לבע"ח במקום שחב לאחרים לא קנה," פסק (לקמן י,א) "המגביה מציאה לחבירו קנה חבירו" לא מטעם מיגו דאי בעי וכו' (תוס' ועוד) אלא כמ"ש הרמב"ן שלר' יוחנן מציאה אינה נחשבת לחב לאחרים. "דכיון דלא זכה בה אדם לאו חובה היא לו אם אינו מוצא וכו' ובעל אבידה גופיה הואיל וכו' שהרי נתייאש ויצאה מרשותו ביאוש." על פירוש זה של הרמב"ן אומר הר"ן (הובא בשטמ"ק), "ואין צריך לפנים."

והנה לרב נחמן ורב חסדא, הסוברים "המגביה מציאה לחבירו לא קנה חבירו" אפילו במקום שיש לומר בו "מיגו דזכי לנפשיה זכי נמי לחבריה," קשה דיוקו של רמי בר חמא מן המשנה. דיוק זה מתנגד לדעתם. הם הרי אינם יכולים לדחות את דיוק זה כמו שדחה אותו רבא. ותרצו רב פפא ואיתימא רב שימי בר אשי שהם מעמידים את הבבא שממנה דייק רמי

11. ועיין גם ביצה לט, א–ב בראשונים שם וכאן וירושלמי כאן הלכה ג': "אמר ר' יצחק הדא הילכתא לית שמע מינה כלום לא מראשה ולא מסי פא וכו'." ראה נתיבות ירושלים לרי"ח דייכעס שם ויפה עינים כאן (בהקדמה, "דברים אחדים," מתלונן רי"ח דייכעס "כי במקומות הרבה נמצאו [ביפה עינים] מביאורי מבלי הזכיר שם ספרי"). לפירושנו להלן בפנים, י"ל "ראשה" היא הבבא "וזה אומר חציה שלי").

12. ראה, למשל, רש"י ט, סע"ב ד"ה אי.

בר חמא, "המגביה מציאה לחבירו קנה חבירו," במקח וממכר. נמצא שנימוקם של רב פפא ואיתימא רב שימי בר אשי להעמיד את המשנה במקח וממכר הוא לא יתור לשון של "זה אומר אני מצאתיה וזה אומר כולה שלי," כמו שהבין אותו סתמא דגמרא (בלשוננו, הסתם. יתור זה אפשר להסביר כפי שהסבירו ר' מנשה מאיליא), אלא הצורך לתרץ את דברי רב נחמן ורב חסדא שלא יקשה עליהם מן המשנה. ואילו הסתמא דגמרא שתפסה, כמו שתפסו הראשונים, שאין מי שחולק על "מיגו דזכי לנפשיה זכי נמי לחבריה," הוכרחה למצוא נימוק אחר לאוקימתא של רב פפא ואיתימא רב שימי בר אשי ולא מצאה אלא יתור לשון.

מאיזו בבא במשנה דייק רמי בר חמא את דיוקו לא ברור. לא היתה להם מסורת מדויקת בזה לכן שאל רב אחא בריה דרב אדא (או אויא[13]) לרב אשי (דור אחד אחרי רמי בר חמא) לקמן ח,א: "דיוקיה דרמי בר חמא מהיכא." גם תשובתו של רב אשי שם לא בטוחה. דבריו שם מעורבים בדברי הסתם. מסידור הדברים נראה לכאורה כאילו רב אשי ורב אחא התווכחו על כל בבא ובבא שבמשנה. רב אשי התחיל עם הרישא, "שנים אוחזין בטלית" וכו' והציע אותה כמקור לדיוקו של רמי בר חמא. רב אחא דחה אותה. חזר רב אשי והציע את הבבא שלאחריה "זה אומר כולה שלי" וכו' כמקור לדיוקו של רמי בר חמא וגם אותה דחה רב אחא. וכך היה עם כל הבבות שבמשנה עד שהגיע רב אשי לסוף המשנה, "בזמן שהם מודים או שיש להן עדים, חולקין בלא שבועה," והסיק שממנה דייק רמי בר חמא. (והדיוק הוא: "במאי, אי במקח וממכר צריכה למימר? אלא לאו במציאה, ושמע מינה, המגביה מציאה לחבירו קנה חבירו"). עליה לא היתה לרב אחא תשובה ונגמרה הסוגיא. אמנם קרוב לודאי שרב אשי לא חזר על כל הבבות אלא נתן את תשובתו פעם אחת, והסתם כבר לא ידע בדיוק מה היתה והוא (מטעמים ספרותיים), ולא רב אשי, חזר על כל הבבות. גם מסתבר שרב אשי לא היה משיב שדיוקו של רמי בר חמא הוא מ"משנה יתירה" (כי אין קשר פנימי בין משנה יתירה ובין מגביה מציאה לחבירו) אלא או שהשיב שהדיוק הוא מן הבבא "זה אומר כולה שלי וזה אומר חציה שלי"[14] או שהדיוק הוא מן סיפא דסיפא "בזמן שהם מודים" וכו'. הדיוק הוא אותו הדיוק. כשטוען חציה שלי, או כשהם מודים ששניהם "בהדי הדדי אגבוה," אם המגביה מציאה לחבירו לא קנה חבירו אף אחד לא קנה. "תיעשה זו כמי שמונחת על גבי קרקע וזו כמי שמונחת ע"ג קרקע ולא יקנה לא זה ולא זה." רב אשי או הסתם הסיק שהדיוק הוא מסיפא דסיפא משום שהבבא "וזה אומר חציה שלי" אפשר להעמיד בממקח וממכר. ואילו הסיפא דסיפא, "אי במקח וממכר צריכא למימר?" אם מסכימים ששניהם קנו אותו אין סכסוך ביניהם ולא היו באים לדין. אבל כהסבר בדברי רב פפא ואיתימא רב שימי בר אשי מסתבר יותר לומר שהם התכוונו לבבא "וזה אומר חציה שלי" ששם כמעט נאמר בפירוש "המגביה מציאה לחבירו קנה חבירו" מאשר הסיפא דסיפא ששם הוא דיוק בתוך דיוק. (הרמב"ם והרע"ב באמת פירשו את הסיפא דסיפא באופן אחר, ראה להלן.) הם באו לתרץ את דעת רב נחמן ורב חסדא מדיוקו של רמי בר חמא והעמידו את המשנה "רישא (זה אומר כולה שלי וזה אומר כולה שלי[15]) במציאה וסיפא (זה אומר כולה שלי וזה אומר חציה שלי) בממקח וממכר."

13. כמו שהוא בכת"י. ראה דק"ס שם אות ת'.

14. בגירסותנו נאמר גם שם "הא תו למה לי?" וגם שם הדיוק הוא ממשנה יתירא. אלא שכבר מחקר אותו רוב ראשונים.

15. השוה גם מ"ש ר"ח אלבק בהשלמותיו למשנה כאן. הוא מציע ש"הסיפא היא משנה ב: היו שנים רוכבים ע"ג בהמה" ומטעם יתור לשון. עיין גם תוס' דרעק"א ד"ה בזמן.

* * *

לעיל הבאנו את פירוש הגמרא בסיפא דסיפא, "בזמן שהם מודים או שיש להן עדים, חולקים בלא שבועה," שהרישא "בזמן שהם מודים" מיירי במציאה (במקח וממכר "צריכא למימר?") והמשנה משמיעה "המגביה מציאה לחבירו קנה חבירו" (אבל הסיפא "או שיש להן עדים" מיירי גם במקח וממכר וכגון שיש עדים לזה ועדים לזה. ואע"פ שהעדויות מבטלות זו את זו, פטורים משבועה, "דכל שבועה זו תקנת חכמים היא וכו' ובמידי דלא שכיח כהאי וכו' לא תקנו חכמים"[16]). "והדברים (קצת) דחוקים שתרמוז המשנה בזה באמרה חולקין בלא שבועה."[17] למה לא אמרה כן בפירוש? הרמב"ם והרע"ב סטו כאן מפירוש הגמרא ופירשו שהמשנה משמיעה שאם הודו או באו עדים אפילו לאחר שנפסק הדין, חולקים בלא שבועה. ותמה עליהם בעל תוס' יו"ט כאן, ד"ה בזמן, "מאי רבותא היא לאחר שנפסק הדין?" הודאתם ועדותם של העדים מבטלות את הפסק דין.[18] וגם יכולה היתה המשנה להשמיע דין זה במקום אחר שלא בקשר ל"שנים אוחזין בטלית."

לכן נראה לנו לפרש את "בזמן שהם מודים" כאן לא במובן וידוי, כאילו הם מתוודים ששקר טענו מקודם כשזה אמר "כולה שלי" וזה אמר "כולה שלי" ומודים ששניהם מצאוה, אלא שעדיין מחזיקים בטענותיהם הראשונות אך מסכימים (זה הוא המובן של "ומודים" כאן[19]) לוותר על השבועה ויגבה כל אחד חציה בלי שבועה (הרי בין כך ובין כך אין להם בה יותר מחציה). לפעמים צד אחד דורש שבועה משום שמשוכנע שהשני לא ישבע לשקר ויודה. או נשבעים. אבל אם מסכימים לחלק ביניהם בלא שבועה, הרשות בידם. דין זה לא יתכן אלא במקום ששניהם נשבעים וחולקים. במקום שרק אחד נשבע ונוטל את הכל (והוא רוב המקרים) אין מקום לויתור. לכן נמצאת הלכה זו כאן.

16. הגהות רש"ש ראש המסכת. השוה תפארת ישראל כאן.

17. רצ"מ פיניליש, דרכה של תורה ס' צה, עמ' 114.

18. בעל דרכה של תורה שם מציין למכילתא משפטים פרשה טז: "שבועת ה' תהיה בין שניהם, להוציא את הדיין שלא ישביענו בע"כ. והמשנה כאן באה "להזהיר לב"ד שלא יכפו אותן לישבע וכו' בזמן שהודו או באו עדים." גם דין זה אינו קשור דוקא בענין שנים אוחזין בטלית.

19. המלונים מייחסים שימוש זה לתקופה של אחר התלמוד.

זרימת השפעות תרבותיות מסוריה וארץ ישראל למיסופוטמיה בתקופה הבבלית העתיקה

אברהם מלמט
האוניברסיטה העברית בירושלים

הקשרים המדיניים והכלכליים בין מזרח ומערב בקדמת אסיה בשליש הראשון של האלף השני לפה״ס זכו במחקר למקום נכבד ולסקירה שקולה וממצה. נדמה, שאין הדבר כן ביחס לתחומי התרבות למיניהם, כגון דת ופולחן, אפשר משום שהם תופעות שאינן גלויות לעין ואינן ניתנות להשגה על נקלה. על חלק מן המגוון של התרבות הרוחנית נדון במאמר זה. אחד המקורות הנודעים, ואולי המקור הראשי, שיש בו כדי ללבן את הבעיה הנדונה כאן, הן התעודות מן הארכיונים המלכותיים של מארי, ביחוד תעודות שנתפרסמו בשנים האחרונות. יש להצטער, שעדין אינו עומד לרשותנו קובץ תעודות מארי על המערב, שעתיד לפרסם ז׳.מ. דיראן, בכרך כ״ו, ג שבסידרת התעודות של הארכיונים המלכותיים ממארי (להלן אמ״מ).[1] אמנם כמה מן התעודות שנועדו להיכלל בכרך זה ראו אור בעשור השנים האחרון והן תשרתנה אותנו להלן.

נסיכות מן המערב

אפתח בנושא, שהוא ברור וגלוי די הצורך מבחינה היסטורית, כלומר בנישואים הדיפלומטיים של שליטי מארי עם ערי המטרופולין שבסוריה המערבית, בצפון ובמרכז.[2] בתעודות מארי עולה שרשרת של נישואים מסוג זה, שאפשר הם מלווים גם תופעות תרבותיות שונות. המלך הראשון של מארי בתקופה הבבלית העתיקה, יחדון-לים, שהיה שליט דגול והעלה את מארי (העיר והממלכה) לדרגת גורם בכיר באיזור הפרת התיכון, נשא כאחת מנשותיו נסיכה מחלב,

Author's note: המחקר הזה נתמך ע״י הקרן הלאומית למדע בניהול האקדמיה הלאומית הישראלית למדעים.

1. ראה J.-M. Durand, *Archive épistolaire de Mari* 1/3 (Paris: forthcoming) [= ARM 26/3]

2. ראה את הקובץ J.-M. Durand (ed.), *La femme dans le Proche-Orient antique* (Paris: Éditions Recherche sur le Civilisations, 1987). על הנסיכה מחלב ראה מאמרו של F. Abdallah. והשווה ביחוד J.-M. Durand, ARM 26/1, pp. 95–117; B. F. Batto, *Studies on Women at Mari* (Baltimore: Johns Hopkins University Press, 1974)

ששמה אינו ידוע.[3] אחריו כבש את מארי המלך שמשי-אד (שבסיסו היה בעיר אשור), שמינה את בנו הצעיר ישמח-אד למשנה המלך במארי. זה מכבר היה ידוע ששמשי-אד למעשה אילץ את בנו, לשאת נסיכה מן העיר קטנה שבסוריה המרכזית. הנסיכה כונתה בכינוי Bēltum, היינו בעלת, היא הגבירה לעתיד לבוא בחצר מארי.[4] ושוב עם מעבר השלטון אל שושלת המלכים המקומית במארי ועלייתו של זמרי-לים, המלך האחרון במארי, לכס המלוכה, נשא מלך בראשונה, כפי שמסתבר היום, נשא סמוך להתמלכותו נסיכה מקטנה בשם Dam-huraṣi,[5] ובשנת ג׳ או ד׳ למלכו נשא, בנוסף לה, את הנסיכה המהוללה שיבתו (גירסת קריאה אחרת: שיפטו וכדומה) מחצר המלכות בחלב. אשת חיל זו היתה בת ירים-לים, המלך התקיף מארץ ימחד, היא ארץ שבירתה חלב בצפון סוריה.[6] אפשר שזמרי-לים נשא נסיכה נוספת מן המערב, היא אַתַּר-אַיַּה, האישה שליוותה את המלך בסיורו הגדול לסוריה עד לעבר חוף הים התיכון, בשנת מלכותו ה״תשיעית.״ מוצאה של אישה זו היה לדעת המהדיר מן העיר אוגרית ואילו לדעת ז׳.מ. דיראן היה אפילו מן העיר חצור, על סמך תעודות שטרם פורסמו.[7]

הנישואים הנזכרים עם נשים מן האצולה בסוריה, שבאו להדק את היחסים בין הפרת התיכון והמערב, היו מלווים, בלי ספק, בחדירה כלשהי של מנהגים ונימוסים, טקסים ואורח חיים אשר רווחו במערב והבנות האמוריות נתחנכו עליהם, לתוך חיי החצר של מארי. אגב, מעין תמונת ראי לנישואים אלה, על פי ראייה גסה, קיימת בסיפורי האבות שבס׳ בראשית. ״כיוון״ הנישואים שם הוא הפוך—ממזרח למערב. נשים מכבדות בעיר נחור (שעל הזרוע הצפונית מערבית של נהר חבור) הושאו ליצחק וליעקוב, אבותיהם של עם ישראל. כמו במקרא יש לשער שאף בין מארי וסוריה המערבית היתה קיימת קרבה משפחתית-שבטית כלשהי. בכל האתרים הנזכרים התמקדו שבטים שמיים- מערביים, או במלים אחרות שבטים אמוריים, כבר בראשית האלף השני לפה״ס,[8] והללו טיפחו ביניהם קשרי נישואים. מנהג מלכותי זה ליטול בנות זוג מן המערב היה מקובל אף בתקופה הניאו-אשורית, דוגמת המלך סנחריב, שאחת מנשותיו היתה נקיה—זכותו, אישה מסוריה או אפילו ארץ-ישראל. כן אפשר שאחת מנשי אשורנצירפל ב׳, וכנראה אמו של המלך שלמנאסר ג׳, שקִיבְּרָה

3. ראה J.-M. Durand, *M.A.R.I.* 6 (1990) 291; idem, *La circulation . . . Actes 38e RAI* (Paris: Éditions Recherche sur le Civilisations, 1992) 108

4. הנסיכה באה בליווי אמתה; ראה D. Charpin, ARM 26/2, p. 11; no. 298: 29–30. היא בתו של מלך קטנה בשם יִשְׁחִ־אַדֻּ והתעודה, שבה נמנו המתנות שאמורות להישלח ממארי אל הנסיכה, היא ARM 1, no. 77.

5. ראה באחרונה B. Gronenberg, "Dam-hurasim: Prinzessin aus Qatna und ihr *nūbalum*," *Mém. de* N.A.B.U. 3 (*Mém.* M. *Birot*; Paris, 1994) 132ff.

6. ראה אחד הדיונים המוקדמים שהוקדשו לנסיכה זו P. Artzi and A. Malamat, "The Correspondence of Shibtu, Queen of Mari," *Or* 40 (1971) 75–87. וראה עתה P. Villard, *M.A.R.I.* 7 (1993) 318ff.

7. השווה J.-M. Durand, ARM 23, p. 475 n. 52.

8. על שבטי האמורים בתקופת מארי ראה, דרך משל, M. Anbar, *Les tribus amurrites de Mari* (Freiburg: Universitätsverlag / Göttingen: Vandenhoeck & Ruprecht, 1991) ושם ספרות קודמת.

המלכותי נתגלה זה לא מכבר בכלח, היתה מן המערב[9] והוא הדין, כנראה, של אחת מנשות המלך סרגון ב׳ בשם עתל(יה).

נעבור לסוגיה אחרת שבה הקשר בין מערב למזרח גלוי פחות או יותר: ביקור אפשרי של בני אצולה ממיסופוטמיה במארי וכנראה בערי המערב, שם בוודאי קלטו השפעות תרבותיות מקומיות והעבירון אל ארץ מוצאם במזרח. בנדון זה רילוונטית תעודה מס׳ 375 באמ״מ כו, ב,[10] שהיא איגרת של ירים-אד, שליח מארי בבבל, שנועדה למלך זמרי-לים. הכותב מדווח לאדוניו שחמורבי, מלך בבל, שלח את בנו (בשם Mutu-Numaha) למארי, לאחר שכבר קודם לכן שלח לשם את בנו בכורו. בהמשך מציע חמורבי: ״שלח נער זה (היינו את הבן הצעיר) אם לימחד, אם לקטנה, כטוב בעיניך!״ נזכר גם איש ליווי מבבל שילווה אל הנער במסעו ממולדתו לניכר. כן נזכרות משלחות מערים שונות, ובכללן קטנה וחצור, הנאספות סביב ירים-אד כדי להאזין להוראותיו. השאלה היא אם יש קשר כלשהו בין חלק מן המשלחות והביקור העתידי של בן חמורבי במערב, היינו אם עליו לבקר רק בימחד או קטנה, או שמא גם בחצור? על שיגורם של שניים מבני חמורבי, בכורו ואח צעיר, למארי ושהותם במקום פורסמו עתה תעודות נוספות הנוגעות בחלקן בעקיפין בתעודה שבה דנו לעיל.[11] ושוב, כמו ביחס לנישואים לעיל, נוכל להביא תמונת ראי לסוגיה זו, היינו של ביקור מלכותי מתוכנן, מן המערב בפרת התיכון. הכוונה לביקורו של בנו או שליחו של מלך אוגרית בארמון מארי בימי המלך זמרי-לים, כדי לחזות בתפארתו, כוונה המתועדת בתעודה שפורסמה לפני כ 55 שנה.[12] בהקשר זה מאלף לשים לב לעובדה שכמה וכמה אנשים מסוריה נזכרים קודם לכן בתעודות מתקופת אור ג׳.[13]

ספרות ונבואה

נפנה עתה לעניינים שברוח—ספרות, נבואה וחוק—אך קודם לכן נזכיר דיון קצר ונועז של ת. יקובסן, שהוא רלוונטי לנושא שלנו, מאמר שלא זכה לתשומת הלב הראויה לו.[14] יקובסן העלה השערה יוצאת דופן ביחס למוצאה של עלילת הבריאה הבבלית הנודעת, הידועה בשם Enuma Eliš, וביחוד בנוגע לקטע המתאר את המאבק בין אל הסער מרדוך והים הקדמון תיאמת (מלה הזהה בעברית ל״תהום״). לפי יקובסן מקורו של מוטיב זה ושל העלילה בכללה אינם במזרח (במיסופוטמיה המזרחית-הדרומית), כפי שמניחה הדעה

9. מעיד על כך, כנראה, שמה שניתן לגרוס *la-pa-a* ופירושו אפשר הוא ׳יפה׳, אם כי המחבר שוקל, בין השאר, גיזרון שמי-מערבי מהשורש *nby* וגורס את שמה *la-ba-a*; ראה A. Fadhil, *BaM* 21 (1990) 461–470, esp. p. 466. על המלכה עתל(יה) אשתו של תגלת-פלאסר ג׳ או סרגון ב׳ ראה Amir Harrak, "The Royal Tombs of Nimrud and Their Jewellery," *Bulletin of the Canadian Society for Mesopotamian Studies* 20 (1990) 5–13

10. D. Charpin, ARM 26/2, no. 375

11. B. Lion, "Des princes de Babylone à Mari," *Mém. de N.A.B.U.* 3 (*Mém. M. Birot*; Paris, 1994) 221–234

12. ראה א. מלמט, מארי וישראל: ירושלים תשנ״א, עמ׳ 46; שם בהערה 56; השווה את ההפנייה על פרסום התעודה.

13. ראה D. I. Owen, "Syrians in Sumerian Sources from the Ur III Period," in *New Horizons in the Study of Ancient Syria* (ed. M. W. Chavalas and J. H. Hayes; Bibliotheca Mesopotamica 25; Malibu: Undena, 1992) 107–176

14. T. Jacobsen, "The Battle between Marduk and Tiamat," *JAOS* 88 (1968) 104–108

המקובלת, אלא הם נוצרו במערב, בחוף הסורי ובתקופה האמורית. אז הובאו בידי השבטים האמוריים מזרחה. הואיל ויקובסן לא הביא להשערתו עדויות של ממש נותרה גישתו בגדר ספיקולציה גרידא. מצד אחר סובר באחרונה ו.ג. למברט שהן הגירסה המערבית של הקרב עם הים והן העלילה המזרחית Enuma Eliš מוצאן ממקור משותף, הפרוס בין הודו והים האגיאי.[15] שמא אחד הנימוקים לאבת התיזה של יקובסן גלום בעלילת הבריאה הבבלית גופה, הלוא הוא אחד מ-50 השמות התיאופוריים שבהם עוטר האל מרדוך על פי לוח ז׳ של היצירה (אמנם יתכן שקטע זה סופח לעלילה בזמן מאוחר). הכוונה לשם האל אד, שנכתב בעלילה בכתיב המערבי AD.DU (אדד הוא הכתיב האכדי המזרחי). אל זה זהה ללא ספק, לאל הגדול של חלב המכונה באותו שם.[16]

עדות ממשית לקרב שבין אלוהי הסער אד מחלב ואלהי הים (הכוונה כנראה במקורה לים התיכון כפי שטען כבר יקובסן) מובאת באופן בלתי צפוי באחת האיגרות ממארי, שפירסם דיראן לא מכבר ושעתידה להיכלל בתעודות מארי כו, ג.[17] האיגרת היא בחזקת "תעודה נבואית," היינו מכתב ששיגר נור-סין, שהיה שגריר מארי בחצר חלב, לזמרי-לים ובה העלו דברי נבואה מפי האל אד המכוונים למלך מארי. הנביא או מתנבא, ששמו אביה, נושא את התואר *āpilum*, היינו "העונה,"[18] טיפוס מיוחד של מתנבא שהוא רווח בתעודות מארי. הנביא מנבא בשם האל אד. לאחר שהאל סוקר את קורות ממלכת מארי ואת חילופי השושלות בה והוא מכריז: "השיבותיך (את זמרי-לים) לכס אביך ואת כלי הנשק אשר בעזרתם היכיתי את הים (*tâmtum/temtum*, המציין כאן את הים המיתי, האוקיאנוס) נתתי לך." להלן מוזכרות תביעות שונות שתובע האל אד מזמרי-לים.

התעודה הנ״ל היא בחזקת פרוטו-טיפ של מוטיב הרווח בקדמת אסיה בדבר מאבקו של אלוהי הסער עם הים. מוטיב זה נודע קודם לכל במערב, ביחוד באוגרית כ-400 שנה לאחר תקופת מארי, ומעבר לאוגרית עולים הדיו במקרא ואפילו בספרות חז״ל.[19] יתרה מזאת, בעלילות אוגרית נזכר גם טיבם של כלי הנשק שבידי האל, שבהם הכניע את אלוהי הים (באוגרית אל הסער הוא בעל ולא אד, הדד). כלי הנשק הם אלה וחנית. כאמור, לפי התעודה

15. W. G. Lambert, "Second Postscript (September, 1994)" in "A New Look at the Babylonian Background of Genesis," in *"I Studied Inscriptions from before the Flood": Ancient Near Eastern, Literary, and Linguistic Approaches to Genesis 1–11* (ed. R. S. Hess and D. T. Tsumura; SBTS 4; Winona Lake, Ind.: Eisenbrauns, 1994) 111

16. ראה באחרונה S. Dalley, *Myths from Mesopotamia* (Oxford, 1989 [1991]) 230, 272, 277

17. התעודה פורסמה על ידי J.-M. Durand, "Le mythologème du combat entre le dieu de l'orage et la mer en Mésopotamie," *M.A.R.I.* 7 (1993) 41ff. על תעודה זו והשוואתה למקרא ראה A. Malamat, "A New Prophetic Message from Aleppo and Its Biblical Counterparts," in *Understanding Poets and Prophets: Essays in Honour of George Wishart Anderson* (ed. A. G. Auld; JSOTSup 152; Sheffield: JSOT Press, 1993) 236–241; וגירסה עברית קדמוניות, 105–106; כ״ז תשנ״ד, עמ׳ 44-46.

18. על משמעות תואר זה וטיבו של הטיפוס המתנבא רבו הדיונים; ראה סיכום A. Malamat, *Mari and the Early Israelite Experience* (London: British Academy / Oxford: Oxford University Press, 1989 [1992]) 86–87. מעניין לציין שמתנבא מסוג זה נזכר גם פעם אחת בעיר בבל.

19. השווה א. מלמט, אלהותו של הים התיכון בטקסט פרה-אוגריתי, מחקרים במקרא לזכר מ.ד. קאסוטו, ירושלים תשמ״ז, עמ׳ 184–188; וכן מאמרי המסכם, Das heilige Meer, *Wer ist wie du. Herr. unter den Göttern?* (Festschrift O. Kaiser; ed. I Kottsieper et al.; Göttingen: Vandenhoeck & Ruprecht, 1994) 65–74

הנ״ל ממארי נמסרו כלי הנשק, שאותם בוודאי יצרו בחלב בהתאם לתאור המיתי של העלילה, על ידי מלך חלב לזמרי-לים. ושמא יצרו מספר דגמים של כלי הנשק שאולי נמסרו גם לידי ואסלים אחרים של מלך חלב. מאלפת תעודה קצרה חדשה שמביא דיראן במאמרו, שכנראה כרוכה בתעודה הנבואית הנ״ל, לפיה הפקיד זמרי-לים את כלי הנשק של האל אד במקדש האל דגן שבעיר תרקה השוכנת מערבית למארי.[20] קרוב לשער שיחד עם כלי הנשק שהובאו מחלב שבמערב לאזור הפרת התיכון עבר גם סיפור העלילה גופה לשם אלא שלפי שעה לא נמצא לו זכר במארי.

התעודה ה״נבואית,״ שבה דנו, מעבירה אותנו לתופעה נוספת בקדמת אסיה, שכנראה עיקר צמיחתה במערב וכי עברה ברבות הימים מזרחה, הוא החיזיון המרטיט של עצם ההתנבאות והשמעת דברי חזון. במרחב המזרחי, כגון בבל, אך גם במערב, אם כי במידה מעטה יותר, ההתנבאות היתה דרך כלל בעלת אופי מאנטי; זאת אומרת דרישת דבר האל היתה כרוכה במיכשור מיוחד ובטכניקה כלשהי והמתנבא הראשי נשא את התואר *bārû*, ״הרואה.״ הלה מגיד עתידות לפי בדיקת הקרביים של חיות וביחוד לפי כבד של כבש. אכן, טיפוס זה של דרישת דבר האל היה רווח גם במארי. אולם שם,[21] ובארצות המערב, ביחוד במקרא עולה ובולט גם טיפוס אחר של התנבאות. טיפוס זה נוכל לכנות בשם הנבואה האינטואיטיבית (ומשמשים גם מונחים אחרים להגדרת התופעה) מכיוון שהיא מופיעה ללא טכניקה מאנטית או מאגית אלא נובעת מהשראה אלוהית (היינו לפי תפיסת הקדמונים התופעה נוחתת מ״בחוץ״ ואילו היום היינו אומרים כי היא פורצת מ״בפנים״).

במקום אחר שבנו ודנו בפירוט בנבואת מארי תוך השוואה לנבואת המקרא.[22] כאן נעמוד על האפשרות שהנבואה האינטואיטיבית היא תופעה מערבית[23] ולא מזרחית, כדעת כמה חוקרים.[24] מאחר שהתנבאות זו כרוכה לעתים גם ביסוד אכסטאטי, כמו בתעודות מארי ובמקרא, הרי ניתן למצוא במרווח הכרונולוגי שבין שני הקורפוסים הללו דווקא מתנבאים אכסטאטיים במערב, כגון הנביא מגבל, המתואר במגילת ון אמון המצרית מן המאה הי״א לפה״ס. אמת, מצויים מתנבאים ״אינטואיטיביים״ בתקופת מארי גם בעיר בבל (המתנבא הנזכר שם על פי תעודות מארי מכונה *āpilum*) (אמ״מ כו, ב, מס׳ 371) ואף תעודות מחוץ למארי מכירות את ההתנבאות מסוג זה במזרח ובדרום. יש להזכיר כאן בראש וראשונה את החפירות באִישְׁחַלִי שמעבר לחידקל. שם האלה כִּיתִתּוּם משדרת נבואות לאִבַל-פִּי-אֵל, מלך אשנונה.[25] אולם אין הדוגמאות האלה מוכיחות שטיפוס נבואה זה מקורו באזורים הנ״ל

20. ראה (A. 1858) Durand, "Le mythologème du combat," 53

21. ראה Durand, *Archive épistolaire de Mari*, 377–453. שם קובצו מכלול הנבואות של מארי, פרט לאחדות שתובאנה בכרך כו, ג. תעודות המכילות חלומות ״נבואיים״ הובאו גם כן בכרך כו, א, עמ׳ 455–483.

22. ראה א. מלמט, מארי וישראל, עמ׳ 123–145. הכרך האנגלי (לעיל, הערה 18) יצא בשנת 1989 ואיננו דן בנבואות שהובאו לראשונה בכרך כו, א של תעודות מארי. ראוי להזכיר כאן שני ניתוחים נוספים של נבואות מארי D. Charpin, "Le contexte historique . . . des prophéties . . . à Mari," SCM *Bulletin* 23, May 1992; J. M. Sasson, "The Posting of Letters with Divine Messages," *Mém. de N.A.B.U.* 3 (*Mém. M. Birot*; Paris, 1994) 299–317

23. השווה דיראן (לעיל הערה 15), ביחוד עמ׳ 408, 411–412.

24. בדעה זו מחזיק כנראה A. R. Millard, "La prophétie et l'écriture . . . ," *RHR* 202 (1985) 125–145; וראה דברי ההסתיגות מעמדה זו אצל שרפין (לעיל הערה 22), עמ׳ 30 והערה 36.

25. ראה M. de Jong Ellis, *JCS* 37 (1985) 61–85; eadem, *M.A.R.I.* 5 (1987) 235–266. המחברת מסכמת את מחקרה בהנחה שטיפוס נבואה זה הובא לאשנונה באמצעות יסודות שמיים מערביים או אמוריים שהיגרו בתקופה הבבלית העתיקה למיסופוטמיה.

אלא מתקבלת על הדעת יותר הסברה כי עבר לשם מן המערב בעקבות התנועה האמורית רבתי שהתנהלה מן המערב למיסופוטמיה הדרומית. דווקא ביחס לבבל, והן ביחס לאשנונה, יש שהעלו את הסברה שהיו כעין מובלעות אמוריות או שלפחות היסודות האמוריים ששכנו בהן היו חזקים.[26]

חוק

מכאן אפשר יסתבר גם הדמיון המפתיע בין החוקה של חמורבי, ואפשר במידה עוד יתרה, חוקי אשנונה עם חוקי המקרא. בכך אנו פונים לתחום חוקי המזרח הקדמון באיזורי מיסופוטמיה. ברובם קובצי החוקים אינם מעלים דמיון למקרא פרט לשתי החוקות שהזכרנו (לא נמצאו עד כה כל שרידים של חוקות אמוריות אפשריות). חוקת חמורבי וחוקת אשנונה, שנתחברו פחות או יותר באותו פרק זמן, מראות בכמה וכמה סעיפים דמיון רב למקרא, ביחוד לחוקים הכלולים בספר שמות. על בעייה זו נתחברה ספרות ענפה. נזכיר כאן רק דעה מן הזמן האחרון, של ו.ג. לאמברט,[27] כי החוקים ״עין תחת עין, שן תחת שן״ וכו׳ (היינו *lex talionis*), הכלולים גם במקרא (שמ׳ כא, כג–כה) וגם בחוקי חמורבי (סעיפים 196–200), ששם הם בחזקת חידוש. משפטים מסוג זה מתועדים גם במקורות שמחוץ לחוקה, הן בנהלים שרווחו בחוגים אמוריים והן בספרות המקרא. אבל הם אינם מצויים בשאר חוקי המזרח הקדמון. בלי ספק יש לייחסם למורשת התרבות האמורית, היינו הם הגיעו לבבל מן המערב. אשר לחוקי אשנונה[28] מפתיע דמיונם הרב למקרא החוק בדבר ״שור נגח״ (אשנונה, מס׳ 53–55; שמ׳ כא, כח–לב) וכן ההבחנה בענישה שבין גנב השודד לאור יום, שענשו דמים בלבד, והשודד בלילה שדינו מות (סעיפים 12–13). לכך יש להשוות במקרא את הגנב שזורחת עליו השמש והגנב במחתרת (היינו בחשכה והלילה) (שמ׳ כב, א–ב). בתחום זה אין ספק שקיימת זיקה הדוקה בין מערב ומזרח ויש לשער שבחוקים ה״פרימיטיביים״ יש לראות תוצר אמורי וכי הם נדדו מן המערב למזרח ולדרום-מזרח.

פחות ברורות וודאיות הן הסוגיות הבאות, המחזירות אותנו שוב אל הדת ואל ספור העלילה, והפעם לעלילת גילגמש. כידוע, נתפרסמה גירסה של העלילה מן התקופה הבבלית העתיקה המכונה על שם מפרסמה הפראגמנט של Bauer, המתארת את מסעם של גלגמש ובן זוגו אנקידו ליער הארזים שעל שמירתו הופקדה המפלצת חֻוָוה.[29] בניגוד לשאר הגירסאות

26. בנוגע לבבל ראה השערתו הנועזת של אולברייט הטוען שהעברים הקדמונים הם שייסדו את השושלת הראשונה של בבל; W. F. Albright, *Yahweh and the Gods of Canaan* (London: Athlone, 1968) 71

27. W. G. Lambert, "Interchange of Ideas between Southern Mesopotamia and Syria–Palestine . . . ," in *Mesopotamien und seine Nachbarn* (ed. H. J. Nissen and J. Renger; Berliner Beiträge zum Vord. Orient 1; Berlin, 1982) 312–313. ראה גם T. Frymer-Kenski, "Tit for Tat: The Principle of Equal Retribution in Near Eastern and Biblical Law," *BA* 43 (1980) 230–234

28. השווה המהדורה של חוקי אשנונה R. Yaron, *The Laws of Eshnunna* (2d ed.; Jerusalem and Leiden, 1988) 51, 77

29. לפרסום השווה T. Bauer, "Ein viertes altbabylonisches Fragment des Gilgameš-Epos," *JNES* 16 (1957) 254–262. על חשיבותו לתעודות מארי (ביחוד כתובת יחדון-לים) ולמקרא ראה א. מלמט (לעיל, הערה 22), עמ׳ 172–180 (״מסעות ללבנון, גילגמש ומזמור מקראי״). תרגום וקולאציה חדשים ראה K. Hecker in "Mythen und Epen II," *Texte aus der Umwelt des Alten Testaments* 3/4 (Gütersloh: Mohn, 1994) 612–613 וראה כעת המהדורה החדשה של עלילת גילגמש R. J. Tournay and A. Shaffer, *L'épopée de Gilgameš* (Paris: du Cerf,

של עלילת גלגמש נזכר כאן במפורש מקומו של יער הארזים, שכן בשעת ההיאבקות לחיים ומות בין הגבורים והמפלצת רעדו הרי שריון ולבנון. לאמור, הזירה היא יער הארזים הגדול שבהרים אלה ובבקעת הלבנון. אנו נמצאים אפוא בתוך תוכי האזור האמורי. אך אין זו ראיה שאף עלילת גלגמש, או חלק ממנה, נוצרה בהשפעה אמורית והעברה משם למיסופוטמיה הדרומית. אולם דווקא לאמברט סבור שקיים קו מערבי ברור אחר בעלילת גלגמש, שחדר מן המערב לספור זה. הכוונה ללוח ה, טור 1, שורה 6, של הגירסה הרשמית המאוחרת, שמזכירה שיער הארזים שימש מושב לאלים (*mušab ilāni*), היינו שימש מעין הר מועד או אולימפוס לפנתיאון. לאמברט רואה כאן קו אמורי מובהק, שכן הרי אלים מעין זה מצויים דווקא באוגרית, במקרא וביוון ואילו הם אינם קיימים בשומר ובבל.[30]

הסתפקנו להביא לעניינו נקודות ספורות בלבד, שאפשר מוכיחות את חדירתה של השפעה מערבית-אמורית למזרח מיסופוטמיה ולדרומה וניתן בוודאי להביא נקודות נוספות.[31] אחת הנקודות העיקריות היא בתחום הלשוני שהן במארי והן בערים נוספות במיסופוטמיה נתגלו שימושי לשון למכביר מן הלשון האמורית, או ביתר דיוק, מן הדיאלקטים האמוריים, שמצד אחר חדרו לכנענית ולעברית המקראית.[32] אך נקודה זו מחייבת דיון בפני עצמו. מכל מקום מסתבר שאת הראייה המקובלת במחקר לראות בבבל חזות הכל יש כיום להגמיש לטובת הפריפריה המערבית.[33]

124ff. (1994). הר הלבנון נזכר גם בגירסה מאוחרת של גילגמש מן העיר אורוך. מקום היער בלבנון כבר הוצע על ידי חוקרים בראשית המאה העשרים, דוגמת A. T. Clay, *The Empire of the Amorites* (New Haven: Yale University Press, 1919) 87–88

30. Lambert, "Interchange of Ideas," 313–314; idem, *Babylonien und Israel* (ed. H. P. Müller; Darmstadt: Wissenschaftliche Buchgesellschaft, 1991) 112. אולם דווקא נקודה זו כראיה להשפעה אמורית מוטלת בספק, שכן המקדשים בספרות השומרית היו באותו זמן גם בחזקת הרים ובהם מכונסים האלים. ראה, למשל, את מקדש האל אנליל בעיר ניפור ושמו Ekur (אני מודה על הערה זו לפרופ׳ א. שפר).

31. ראה בנדון זה את מאמרו המאלף של דיראן *La circulation* . . . (לעיל, הערה 3) ושם מובאות שונות מתעודות מארי בדבר כפילות תארו של פלוני כאיש אכד ובאותו זמן כאיש אמורו וכן זמרי-לים המכונה גם מלך אכד ואף מלך אמורו (עמ׳ 113). כן קיים דו-קיום בין הלשון האכדית (או השומרית) ולשון הדבור האמורית (עמ׳ 124–125). לאלה מוסיף דיראן מקצועות ומלאכות שהם ייחודיים לאמורים בקרב ממלכת מארי (עמ׳ 126 ואילך). על נהלים ייחודיים במערב מזה ובמזרח מזה עמד גם Charpin, "Mari entre l'est et l'ouest . . . ," *Akkadica* 78 (1992) 1–10 אלא שהמחבר מפחית במשמעותם של הבדלים אלה בתוך המסגרת של קדמת אסיה.

32. ראה, דרך משל, אוסף מטבעות הלשון האמוריים ממארי, מלמט (לעיל הערה 18), עמ׳ 57–58.

33. ראה, דרך משל, את דברי דיראן *La circulation*, 128

מחלוקות בספרות התנאים לאור מגילות מדבר יהודה

יהודה שיפמן
אוניברסיטת ניו יורק

בשלושים השנים האחרונות עסקו חוקרי ספרות התנאים ותולדות תקופתם בשאלת אמינות החומר התנאי כמקור היסטורי. לבעיה זאת יש מספר הביטים: אחד מהם, שעליו לא נדון היום, היא מהמנותם של מקורות אלו לשחזור ההיסטוריה של תקופת התנאים וספרותם. שני, שהוא מהווה בעיה עוד יותר מסובכת, הוא השימוש בחומר זה למחקר ההיסטוריה של תקופת הבית השני ומגוון הזרמים והכיתות שהציגו איש את יהדותו בימים ההם. ומהרבה סיבות, עוד יותר קשה היא שאלת ניצול החומר התנאי למחקר תולדות ההלכה בתקופה זו.

אלה שטענו שאסור לנו לסמוך על מקורות אלו למחקר היסטורי הצביעו על הפער הכרונולוגי והדתי בין התקופה שלפני החורבן לבין זו שלאחריה. ובמיוחד, ציינו את מגמתם של חז״ל להציג את הרצף ההיסטורי של מסורותם ויחוסן לסיני. טענו שכל מה שאפשר ללמוד מספרות התנאים הוא איך שהתיחסו התנאים לתקופה שקדמה להן. הבסיס האיתן לכל גישתם של חוקרים אלו היתה הטענה שלגמרי חסרות לנו עדויות בנות הזמן להלכות הפרושים ולדעותיהם. ובכן, הציגו כמה חוקרים את מקורות חז״ל כחסרי ערך היסטורי לחקר התקופה שקדמה לחורבן.

חוקרים אלו התעלמו מכל וכל מן החומר שכן עומד לפנינו ושללו את השתייכות החומר הזה לעניינם. אבל באמת, בדיקת הספרים החיצוניים מתקופת הבית השני מספיקה להראות את הטעות בגישה זאת.[1] היום, לאחר שנתעשרנו על ידי הגילויים במדבר יהודה—מגילות קומראן ומצדה ומסמכי תקופת בר כוכבא—קיימת אפשרות להעריך מחדש את המידה שבה אפשר לסמוך על מקורות חז״ל לחקר היסטוריית ההלכה בתקופת הבית השני.

לאור בדיקת מגילות מדבר יהודה בהתיחסות לספרות חז״ל ברור שבהרבה מקרים אפשר להוכיח בלי ספק את קדמותם של הלכות, ואפילו מחלוקות, המובאות בספרות התנאים. ננסה להדגים תופעה זו.

1. לדוגמא, ראה C. Albeck, *Das Buch der Jubiläen und die Halacha* (Siebenundvierzigster Bericht der Hochschule für die Wissenschaft des Judentums in Berlin; Berlin, 1930); R. Marcus, *Law in the Apocrypha* (Columbia University Oriental Studies 26; New York: Columbia University Press, 1927)

מעמד הגרים

נתחיל במחלוקת תנאים בעניין מעמד הגרים. שנינו בתוספתא קידושין ה:א:

> גירי . . . וכל האסורים לבא בקהל, מותרין לבא זה בזה, דברי ר׳ מאיר. ר׳ יהודה אומ׳: ארבעה קהלות הן, קהל כהנים, קהל לוים, קהל ישראל, קהל גרים, והשאר מותרין לבא זה בזה. וחכמים אומ׳: שלש קהלות הן, קהל כהנים, קהל לוים, קהל ישראל.[2]

יש כאן רק שתי דעות. דעתו של ר׳ מאיר היא שהקבוצות הנרשמות כאסורות לבוא בקהל, כולל הגרים, מותרות להתחתן זו בזו מכיוון שכולן הן פסולות. רבי יהודה אוסר על הגרים להתערב עם הפסולים האחרים. הוא רואה בהם קהל ה׳, דהיינו קבוצה של ״עולים בקודש״ שנכנסו מרצונם תחת כנפי השכינה. דעת החכמים באה, בהקשר התוספתא כפי שהיא ערוכה, לפסוק את ההלכה כדברי רבי מאיר ואינה מהווה דעה שלישית.[3] מבחינת ההיסטוריה הספרותית של הקטע, ברור שדברי רבי מאיר אמורים להרחיב את רשימת הפסולים המופיעה במשנה קידושין ד:יא. לעומת זאת, דעות רבי יהודה והחכמים מנוסחות בצורה אחידה, כך שכנראה היוו ברייתא בשלעצמה כבר לפני שסודרו בתוספתא מיד לאחר הרחבת הכלל ההלכתי של המשנה.

ברייתא כזאת, עם שתי דעות אלה, אכן מופיעה בספרי דברים רמ״ז:

> רבי יהודה אומר: ארבע קהלות הן, קהל כהנים, קהל לויים, קהל ישראל, קהל גרים. וחכמים אומרים: שלש.[4]

תוספתא זו, כפי שאמרנו, מבארת את משנה קידושין ד:א:

> לויי, ישראלי, חללי, גרי, וחרורי—מותרים לבא זה בזה. גרי, וחרורי, ממזרי, ונתיני, שתוקי, ואסופי— מותרין לבא זה בזה.

לפי משנה זאת, הגרים, על אף שמותרים להתחתן עם לויים וישראלים (הגרים אסורים עם כהן), מותרים כמו כן להתחתן עם מספר קבוצות של פסולים. לפשוטה של משנה זו, גרים ועבדים משוחררים מהווים מעין מעמד בינוני בעניין זה. וכדאי לזכור שהעבד הכנעני (ז.א. הלא-יהודי) המשוחרר בעצם עובר גם הוא תהליך של העברה מגויות ליהדות—מעין גיור. שרבי יהודה חולק על דעה זו משמע גם כן ממשנה ג:

> כל האסורים לבא בקהל, מותרים לבא זה בזה; רבי יהודה אוסר.

דעתו של רבי מאיר מופיעה גם כן בברייתא מובאת בתוספתא קידושין ה:ב, לפי גירסת הדפוס הראשון, ובבלי קידושין סז עמ׳ א ועב עמ׳ ב:

> רבי יהודה אומר: גר לא ישא את הממזרת. (גירסת כתבי היד של התוספתא: ״הגיורת.״)

כללו של דבר, שלפי מקורות התנאים, נחלקו רבי מאיר ורבי יהודה אם הגרים מהווים קהל נפרד. פסקו החכמים לפי רבי מאיר, כנראה בדור שלאחריו.

2. מהדורת ש׳ ליברמן, תוספתא (נויארק: בית המדרש לרבנים באמריקה, תשל״ג) 293.

3. ד׳ פארדו, ס׳ חסדי דוד, סדר נשים (ירושלים: ח. וגשל, תשג״ד) רפב; י׳ הכהן שבדרן, ס׳ עטרת יצחק על תוספתא, סדר נשים (ירושלים: מכון דעת תורה, תשמ״ב) רעט; ראה ש׳ ליברמן, תוספתא כפשוטה ח׳ (נויארק: בית המדרש לרבנים שבאמריקה, תשל״ג) 963–964; ד׳ הלבני, מקורות ומסורות, באורים לתלמוד על סדר נשים (תל-אביב: דביר, תשכ״ט) תשז-תשי.

4. מהדורת א״א פינקלשטין, ספרי על ספר דברים (ניו-יורק: בית המדרש לרבנים באמריקה, תשכ״ט) 276.

כשנעיין במגילות מדבר יהודה מוצאים שבתקופת החשמונאים היו קבוצות שנהגו לפי הדעה שאנו מכירים אותה כדעת רבי יהודה. בברית דמשק יד:3–6, לפי נוסח הגניזה מתוקן על פי כתבי היד מקומראן, אנו קוראים:

> וסרך מושב כל המחנות. יפקדו כולם בשמותיהם, הכ[הני]ם לראשונה והלוים שניים ובני ישראל שלישיים והגר רביעי. ויכתבו בש[מות]יהם, איש אחר אחיהו, הכהנים לראשונה והלוים שניים ובני ישראל שלישיים והגר רביעי. וכן ישבו וכן ישאלו לכל.[5]

המדובר כאן במושב הרבים, האספה הכללית של כל בני הכת, כולל אלו שגרו ב"מחנות," דהיינו המושבות הכיתתיות שהיו מחוץ למרכז הראשי בקומראן.[6] כדי לנהל את ישיבות האספה, היו פוקדים את כל אנשי הכת ורושמים אותם לפי מעמדם.[7] בישיבה היו אמורים החברים לדבר ולהצביע לפי סדר זה.

מבחינתנו, החשוב כאן הוא שחילקו את החברים לארבע קבוצות, כך שהגרים היוו קבוצה נפרדת בצדם של האחרים. ידוע שמחברי מספר טקסטים כיתתיים ציפו לנוכחותם של גרים בכת, אף שאין לנו שום עדות היסטורית המאפשרת לנו לקבוע אם אכן נלוו אליה.

למרות כך, כנראה מחבר סרך היחד לא כלל את הגרים בכת. בקשר למפקד אנשי היחד הוא כותב (סרך היחד ב:19–22):

> הכוהנים יעבורו ברשונה בסרך כפי רוחותם, זה אחר זה. והלויים יעבורו אחריהם. וכול העם יעבורו בשלישית בסרך, זה אחר זה, לאלפים ומאות וחמשים ועשרות.

וכן מחבר סרך העדה לא הניח שישתתפו גרים במושב הרבים או בסעודה המשיחית של אחרית הימים ולכן לא הזכיר אותם.[8]

כניסת הגרים לבית המקדש נדונה במגילות בשני חיבורים, בפלורולגיום (רשימה) של פשרים ממערה ד' ובמגילת המקדש. בפלורולגיום אנחנו קוראים:

> הוא הבית אשר לוא יבוא שמה [עד ע]ולם, ועמוני ומואבי וממזר ובן נכר וגר עד עולם.[9]

5. ראה E. Qimron, "The Text of CDC," *The Damascus Document Reconsidered* (ed. M. Broshi; Jerusalem: Israel Exploration Society / Shrine of the Book, Israel Museum, 1992) 37. קימרון ההדיר שם את נוסח הגניזה וערך את נוסחאות כתבי היד ממערות קומראן כשינויי נוסחאות. אנו הצגנו כאן נוסח אקלקטי המהווה לדעתנו את הנוסח המקורי. למהדורה פרלימינרית של כתבי היד מקומראן, ראה B. Z. Wacholder and M. G. Abegg, *A Preliminary Edition of the Unpublished Dead Sea Scrolls: The Hebrew and Aramaic Texts from Cave Four*, Fascicle One (Washington, D.C.: Biblical Archaeology Society, 1991) 2 (4Q266 2 3–5), 34 (4Q267 11 ii 7–10)

6. על מושב הרבים, ראה י' שיפמן, הלכה, הליכה ומשיחיות בכת מדבר יהודה (תרגום ועריכה, טל אילן; ירושלים: מרכז זלמן שזר, 1993) 81–84.

7. ראה שיפמן, 79–81.

8. על החברה המשיחית בתפיסת כת קומראן, ראה שיפמן, 268–311.

9. הטקסט במלואו פורסם ב-DJD (J. M. Allegro, *Qumrân Cave 4, I: (4Q158–4Q186)* 5; Oxford: Clarendon, 1968) 53–57. הרבה תיקוני קריאה הוצעו בביקורת חריפה של J. Strugnell, "Notes en marge du volume V des 'Discoveries in the Judaean Desert of Jordan,'" *RevQ* 7 (1970) 220–225. מהדורה חדשה עם סקירת כל השיחזורים והקריאות נמצאת ב- G. J. Brooke, *Exegesis at Qumran: 4QFlorilegium and Its Jewish Context* (JSOTSup 29; Sheffield: JSOT Press, 1985) 86–91, 100–103

קטע זה אוסר על הגר, בין רשימת פסולים אחרים, מלהכנס לבית המקדש של אחרית הימים, הנזכר למעלה בעמוד זה של המגילה.[10] ברור שלפי תפיסה זאת הגר שייך בין הפסולים האלו.

איסור דומה מופיע בחלק מקוטע במגילת המקדש מ:5–7:

]ועשיתה חצר שליש[י]ת [סובבת את החצר התיכונה . . .]ולבנותיהמה ולגרים אשר נולד[ו] בישראל [עד הדור השלישי.[11]

בעל המגילה (או מקורו) ציפה למקדש בן שלוש חצרות[12] ובדרך כלל הרחיק את כל הספקות לחצר החיצונה.[13] כאן הוא קובע שהגרים עד דור שלישי עומדים במצב בינוני ומותרים להכנס רק לחצר החיצונה.[14] אבל מקטע שני בלט:5–6 אנו לומדים שמדור רביעי והלאה מותר לגרים להכנס לחצר התיכונה עם אחיהם בני ישראל:

[יבואו אל] החצר הזואת כול קהל עדת [ישראל והגר אשר יולד בתו]כמה דור רביעי.[15]

אין ספק שדעת מגילת המקדש קשורה לפירוש דב׳ כג:א-ט. פסוקים אלו שמשו מקור למחברי מגילות אלו לקביעת היתר הכניסה לבית המקדש. זאת אומרת, הביטוי ״בוא בקהל ה׳״ הובן כמצביע על ביאת המקדש. שם קובעת התורה שממזר, עמוני, ומואבי אסורים עד הדור העשירי. האדומי והמואבי נאסרו שם רק עד הדור השלישי. המגילה הבינה את האיסור גם כן כהיתר. מהדור הרביעי והלאה מותרים בני עמים אלו שנתגיירו, וכן כל הגרים, להכנס לתוך החצר התיכונה כיהודים שלמים. עד דור שלישי של ילדיהם—הדור הרביעי אם כוללים אותם—צריכים להשאר בחצר החיצונה עם הספקות והפסולים. בעל הפלורולגיום כנראה חלם, כמו מגילת הסרכים, ליום שלא יכנסו גרים לתוך המקדש.

עניין זה נדון גם כן, כנראה אחרת, באיגרת ההלכתית. מקצת מעשי התורה מתלוננת, כפי שיחזורם של העורכים (B39–49):[16]

10. ראה J. M. Baumgarten, *Studies in Qumran Law* (SJLA 24; Leiden: Brill, 1977) 75–87; G. Blidstein, "4QFlorilegium and Rabbinic Sources on Bastard and Proselyte," *RevQ* 8 (1974) 431–435

11. לפי קריאת E. Qimron, *The Temple Scroll: A Critical Edition with Extensive Reconstructions* (Beer Sheva: Ben-Gurion University of the Negev / Jerusalem: Israel Exploration Society, 1995) 57. השווה י׳ ידין, מגילת המקדש (ירושלים: החברה לחקר א״י ועתיקותיה, תשל״ז) ב׳, 120.

12. על תוכנית המקדש בן שלוש חצרות, ראה ידין א׳, 154–163, 186–200; L. H. Schiffman, "Architecture and Law: The Temple and Its Courtyards in the *Temple Scroll*," in *From Ancient Israel to Modern Judaism—Intellect in Quest of Understanding: Essays in Honor of Marvin Fox* (2 vols.; ed. J. Neusner, E. S. Frerichs, and N. M. Sarna; BJS 159; Atlanta: Scholars Press, 1989) 1.267–284

13. L. H. Schiffman, "Exclusion from the Sanctuary and the City of the Sanctuary in the Temple Scroll," *HAR* 9 (1985) 315

14. ראה שם, 303–305.

15. לפי מהדורת קימרון, 56; קריאותיו בעמוד זה שונות הרבה מאלה של ידין ב׳, 117.

16. E. Qimron and J. Strugnell, *Qumran Cave 4, V: Miqsat Ma'ase Ha-Torah* (DJD 10; Oxford: Clarendon, 1994) 50. מהדורתם מצביעה כשיחזור (על ידי סוגריים מרובעים) אף על קריאות המבוססות על כתבי יד אחרים. בעקבות התעתיק המופיע בעמ׳ 158, אנו השתמשנו

[על העמונ]י והמואבי [ו]הממזר ופ[צוע הדכה וכרו]ת השפכת שהם באים בקהל. [. . . ונשים]
ל[ו]קחים [לעשו]תם עצם אחת, [ובאים למקדש . . .] טמאות. ואף חושבים אנחנו [שאין . . .
ואין לבו]א עליהם. [. . . וא]ין להתיכם ולעשותם [עצם אחת . . . ואין להבי]אם [למקדש . . .
ואתם יודעים שמק]צת העם [. . . מתוכ]כים [כי לכול בני ישראל ראוי להזהר] מכול תערובת
[ה]גבר ולהיות יראים מהמקדש.[17]

לפי קטע זה אין שום איסור על הגר מלהכנס למקדש ואין שום הגבלות על גרים בקשר לחיתון. איסורים כאלה חלים רק על הפסולים הנרשמים כאן. על אף הקירבה בין מקצת מעשה התורה לבין מגילת המקדש,[18] בעניין זה עומדות שני הטקסטים בניגוד.

במגילות מדבר יהודה מצאנו, איפוא, שתי גישות לגרים. גישת ברית דמשק רואה בהם קבוצה נפרדת, ביחד עם שלוש הקבוצות האחרות, וחלק אינטגרלי של עם ישראל. מגילת המקדש רואה את הגר עצמו כפסול עד דור שלישי, ורק אחר כך, כישראל לכל דבריו. הפלורולגיום מסתכל על הגר כפסול לעולם כממזרים והפסולים האחרים. מקצת מעשה התורה אינה אוסרת על הגר לא הכניסה למקדש ולא החיתון עם כלל ישראל. בדרך כלל, אפשר להצביע על ברית דמשק ומקצת מעשה התורה מצד אחד, ועל מגילת המקדש והפלורולגיום מצד שני.

לדעתינו, מחלוקת זאת היא בעלת אותן המגמות שהבחנו אצל חז״ל. ההבדל העיקרי הוא בהבנת דב׳ כג:א-י. המגילות מבינות את המלים ״בוא בקהל ה׳״ כמתיחסות לביאת המקדש (או במקרה של ממ״ת כמתיחסות גם לביאת המקדש וגם לחיתון). חז״ל מפרשים את אותן המלים כמצביעות רק על איסורי חיתון. רבי יהודה פוסק כמו ברית דמשק (וכנראה מקצת מעשה התורה) שהגרים הם קהל בתוך בני ישראל ואסורים להתחתן עם פסולים. רבי מאיר, ובעקבותיו החכמים, רואים את הגרים כפסולים המותרים להתחתן עם פסולים אחרים. שיטה זאת הולמת את זו של מגילת המקדש המסווגת את הגרים עם הספקות והפסולים. החלום של הפלורולגיום, דהיינו איסור גמור על כניסת גרים למקדש, גם כן נובע מתפיסת המחבר שהגר הוא פסול, אלא שלדעתו פסול זה הוא קבוע ותמידי. כנראה בעלי סרך היחד וסרך העדה גם נקטו בדעה זו.

המשכיות מחלוקת זאת מימי הבית השני ועד תקופת התנאים איננה רק מקרה. המדובר כאן בשאלה שהיתה על סדר היום בתקופה החשמונאית מהרבה סיבות היסטוריות. אין ספק שהגישות שאפשר להבחין בהן אצל התנאים מקורן כבר בוויכוחים ומחלוקות הרבה יותר קדומים.

עיר הנדחת

בדוגמא הראשונה ראינו שלשתי הדעות במחלוקת התנאים היו תקדימים במגילות. נעבור עכשיו לעניין שבו, בשתי הלכות, רק דעת המיעוט בספרות התנאים קיימת במגילות. אף על פי כן, נראה שהמגילה מתפלמסת נגד השיטה המוכרת לנו כדעת הרוב בספרות חז״ל. נציג את שתי המחלוקות של חז״ל ואחר כך נעבור לחומר המשתמר במגילות.

בסוגריים המרובעים להבליט רק את המילים שאינן מופיעות בשום כתב יד וששוחזרו על ידי קימרון וסטרוגנל.

17. לדיון הלכתי, ראה קימרון וסטרוגנל, 158–160.

18. ראה L. H. Schiffman, "*Miqsat Ma'ase ha-Torah* and the *Temple Scroll*," *RevQ* 14 (1990) 435–437

בתוספתא סנהדרין יד:ג שנינו:

קטני בני אנשי עיר הנידחת שהודחו עמה אין נהרגין. ר׳ אליעזר אומר: נהרגין. אמ׳ לו ר׳ עקיבא: . . . ומה אני מקיים ״ונתן לך רחמים,״ אילו קטנים שבתוכה. . . .

התוספתא פוסקת עם הסתם שהילדים בעיר הנדחת, אף על פי שהשתתפו בעבודה זרה, אינם נהרגין; ומביאה את דברי רבי עקיבא הלומד הלכה זאת מדב׳ יג:יח. לעומת זאת, דעתו של רבי אליעזר (בן הורקנוס) היא שכן נהרגים הילדים. אפשר לדייק מדברי הסתם (״שהודחו עמה״) שלפי רבי אליעזר אין להרוג את הילדים אם לא עבדו עבודה זרה.

אותה מחלוקת קיימת בשרידי המכילתא לדב׳ יג, סימן כט,[19] ובכחצי כתבי היד של ספרי דברים. וזה לשונו לפי ספרי דברים צג:

״את יושבי העיר ההיא,״ מיכן אמרו: אין מקיימים את הטפלים. אבא חנן אומר: ״לא יומתו אבות על בנים,״ בעיר הנדחת הכתוב מדבר.[20]

מהשימוש ב״מכאן אמרו,״ ומהעובדה שמקומה של ברייתא זאת במספר כתבי יד של הספרי ובשרידי המכילתא לדברים הוא בפסוק יח, נראה שהמדובר כאן בברייתא שבמקורה לא היתה קשורה להקשר מקראי-מדרשי. הברייתא כללה את פסק הסתם שאין מקיימים את הטפלים (היינו הילדים) ואחר כך את דעתו הסותרת של אבא חנן עם הבסיס המקראי שלו. ובנוסף, ברור שמקורו של ברייתא זאת אינה בספרי מאחר והיא לגמרי סותרת את הבנת הספרי לדב׳ כד:טז (״לא יומתו אבות על בנים״) בסימן רפ.[21] שם נדרש הפסוק כאוסר עדות בנים על אבות ואבות על בנים. נדמה לנו מהפסוק שהביא (״לא יומתו אבות על בנים״) שלדעתו של אבא חנן עוסקים כאן בילדים שלא עבדו עבודה זרה, דלא כמו בתוספתא המניחה שכן חטאו אף הילדים.

כללו של דבר הוא, שלפי הסתם ורבי עקיבא בתוספתא, ולפי אבא חנן במכילתא דברים-ספרי, הילדים אינם נהרגים. לפי ר׳ אליעזר בתוספתא ולפי הסתם במכילתא דברים-ספרי כן נהרגים.

המחלוקת השניה בעניין זה מתיחסת לבהמת עיר הנדחת. בתוספתא סנהדרין יד:ה שנינו:[22]

קדשי מזבח ימותו; קדשי בדק הבית יפדו. ר׳ שמעון אומ׳: ״בהמתה,״ פרט לבכורות ולמעשרות.

דעת הסתם היא שכשקבעה התורה שחייבים להחרים את בהמת עיר הנדחת לפי חרב (דב׳ יג:טז) כללה התורה את קדשי המזבח שהיו בתוך העיר, דהיינו בהמות שכבר הוקצו לקרבנות. אם הוקדשו בהמות לבדק הבית, לצרכי בית המקדש ולתיקונו, בהמות אלו היו חייבים להחרים אלא שגם פודים אותן על כסף ומשתמשים בכסף למקדש. רבי שמעון חולק על דעה זאת.[23] לדעתו, על אף שמקריבים את חלב ודם בכורות ובהמות מעשר שני על המזבח, אין מחרימים אותם כשאר הקורבנות. המחלוקת היא בדיוק בפרט זה. הסתם כולל אותם עם קדשים אחרים ודורש החרמתם, ורבי שמעון אינו מחייב החרמתם. במלים

19. מובא במדרש תנאים לספר דברים, מהדורת ד״צ האפפמאנן (ברלין: איטצקאווסקי, 1900) 71.

20. מהדורת פינקלשטין, 155. ועיין בחילופי נוסחאות. בכתבי יד של הספרי שבהם קיימת הוספה זאת, הגירסא היא ״מקיימים.״ הגירסא ״אין מקיימים״ מופיעה בראשונים ונתמכת על ידי הקונטקסט, כי אין ספק שאבא חנן חולק על הסתם. עיין בפירושו של פינקלשטין.

21. שם, 297.

22. עיין בבלי סנהדרין קיב עמ׳ ב.

23. ד׳ פארדו, ס׳ חסדי דוד, סדר נזיקין ב׳, תרלד-תרלה (ושם מספר ההלכה הוא ב).

אחרות: בזמן שהסתם קובע את החרמת כל בהמת עיר הנדחת, לרבי שמעון יש יוצאים מן הכלל שאינם נהרגים.

פעמיים, פוסק סתם ספרי דברים לפי הסתם תוספתא. בסוף סימן צד קוראים:

"ואת בהמתה," ולא בהמת הקדש.[24]

פרוש זה אומר שאין מחרימים את ההקדש, דהיינו קדשי בדק הבית. לפי פשוטו היה נראה שמשאירים בהמות אלו בחיים, דבר שהיה סותר את הסתם בתוספתא הדורש פדיון והמתה.[25] אבל למטה בסימן צה פוסק עוד פעם הסתם ספרי:

"ואת כל שללה," ולא שלל שמים. מיכן אמרו: ההקדשות שבתוכה יפדו. . . .[26]

כנראה, למד הספרי מ"ואת בהמתה" (דב' יג:טז) שבהמות הקדש לבדק הבית אינם בכלל בהמת העיר. אבל רק מ"ואת כל שללה" (פסוק יז) למד שפודים אותן וממיתים אותן. אבל אין להתעלם מהקושי בפירוש זה. לכן יש שרוצה למחוק את המאמר הראשון.[27]

מן הראוי להעיר שדברי הספרי דברים בסימן זה מופיעים כמות שהם במשנה סנהדרין י:ו.[28] אין ספק שמשנה זאת שאובה ממדרש הלכה. המדרש הזה עצמו שאב ממסורת יותר עתיקה, ובכן נקט בלשון, "מכאן אמרו." אבל "משנה" אפודיקטית זו לא נשתמרה אלא בהקשר מדרשי.

יוצא לנו שיש מחלוקת תנאים בשאלת בהמות קרבנות בעיר הנדחת. לפי סתם תוספתא והספרי—הרוב בין התנאים—כל בהמות עיר הנדחת יוצאות להורג. לדעתו של רבי שמעון יש יוצאות מהכלל.

סקרנו כאן שתי מחלוקות תנאים בקשר לעיר הנדחת. נראה עתה ששתיהן הן נושאום לפולמוס במגילת המקדש. מגילת המקדש נה:2—14 מביאה את דין עיר הנדחת מדב' יג:יג-יט. בשורות 6—8 קובעת המגילה:

הכה תכה את כול יושבי העיר ההיא לפי חרב. החרם אותה ואת כול אשר בה ואת כול בהמתה תכה לפי חרב.[29]

השואה לנסח המסורה מראה שהמגילה, לדעתנו בכוונה, הוסיפה פעמיים את המילה "כול." בעל המגילה רצה להדגיש שכל תושבי העיר היו חייבים למות. בזה יצא נגד הדעה שהילדים אינם נהרגים, הדעה המופיעה בזמן התנאים בפיהם של סתם תוספתא, רבי עקיבא ואבא חנן. בקביעתו פסק כדעה המופיעה אחר כך כשיטת רבי אליעזר והסתם במכילתא דברים-ספרי. מכיוון שהמגילה רק דורשת החרמת העיר כשכל התושבים עבדו עבודה זרה (לא רק הרוב כפי שקבעו חז"ל) אינה חוששת מהריגת הילדים שוודאי נמשכו אחרי עבודת

24. מהדורת פינקלשטין, 156.

25. לפי הרמב"ם, הל' ע"ז ד:יג, שחולק עליו הראב"ד.

26. מהדורת פינקלשטין, 156.

27. פינקלשטין, שם, הערה לשורה 2.

28. השווה אלבק, נזיקין, 456.

29. ידין, מגילת המקדש ב', 174. ועיין L. H. Schiffman, "Laws concerning Idolatry in the *Temple Scroll*," *Uncovering Ancient Stones: Essays in Memory of H. Neil Richardson* (ed. L. M. Hopfe; Eisenbrauns: Winona Lake, Ind., 1994) 168–171; idem, "The Septuagint and the Temple Scroll: Shared 'Halakhic' Variants," *Septuagint, Scrolls and Cognate Writings* (Septuagint and Cognate Studies 33; ed. G. J. Brooke and B. Lindars; Atlanta: Scholars Press, 1992) 283–284

אלילים. גם כן דורשת המגילה הריגת כל הבהמות, אפילו המיועדות לקרבנות, בכורות ומעשרות. כאן דעת בעל המגילה הולמת את הסתם בתוספתא ולא את דעת רבי שמעון שהיא דעת מיעוט בין החכמים. בדוגמא זאת ראינו שמגילת המקדש, בתחילת תקופת החשמונאים, כבר דנתה באותן המחלוקות שהעסיקו את התנאים אחר כך. פעם הסכים המחבר עם סתם תוספתא ופעם לא הסכים. אבל אין ספק שדעות כאלו כבר היו ידועות בימיו.

״אותו ואת בנו״

נעבור עכשיו למחלוקת בעניין האיסור לשחוט בהמה וולדה. בדוגמא זאת נראה שדעה תנאית אחת הולמת את זו של מגילת המקדש ודעה שניה את זו של מקצת מעשה התורה. ברייתא בבבלי חולין עח עמ׳ ב אומרת:[30]

״אותו ואת בנו״ נוהג בנקבות ואינו נוהג בזכרים. חנניה אומר: נוהג בין בזכרים ובין בנקבות.

המדובר כאן במצות לא תעשה בויק׳ כב:כח, ״ושור או שה, אתו ואת בנו לא תשחטו ביום אחד.״ למרות הניסוח בלשון זכר, קובע הסתם שמצוה זאת נוהגת רק בנקבות, זאת אומרת באם וולדה. חנניה פוסק שנוהגת גם בזכרים (אב וולדו) וגם בנקבות. ברור מהשקלא וטריא הארוך בברייתא בספרא אמור שהיו הרבה שהקשו על פירוש הסתם. ברייתא זאת אינה מזכירה את דעתו של חנניה אף על פי שמתפלמסת נגד אותה שיטה שנקט בה. וזה לשון הספרא בתוספת באור:[31]

יכול יהא ״אותו ואת בנו״ נוהג בזכרים כנקיבות? ודין הוא: חייב כאן וחייב ב״אם על הבנים.״ מה אם על הבן (ז.א. ב״אם על הבנים״) לא עשה בו את הזכרים כנקיבות, אף כאן (ב״אותו ואת בנו״) לא נעשה את הזכרים כנקיבות. לא! אם אמרת ב״אם על הבנים״ שלא עשה בו את המזומן כשאינו מזומן (שבהלכה זו אין איסור ברשות בעלים), תאמר כאן (ב״אותו ואת בנו״) שעשה את המזומן כשאינו מזומן (שיש איסור גם ברשות בעלים וגם בהפקר)? הואיל ועשה בו (ב״אותו ואת בנו״) את המזומן כשאינו מזומן, יהא ״אותו ואת בנו״ נוהג בזכרים כנקיבות? תלמוד לומר, ״אותו.״ על אחד (האם) הוא חייב ואינו חייב על שנים (ז.א. גם על האב). אחר שריבה הכתוב (חילק, כגירסת הבבלי) זכיתי לדין: חייב כאן (ב״אותו ואת בנו״) וחייב ב״אם על הבנים.״ מה אם על הבן לא עשה בו את הזכרים כנקיבות, אף כאן (ב״אותו ואת בנו״) לא נעשה בו את הזכרים כנקיבות. אם נפשך לומר: ״אותו ואת בנו,״ את שבנו כרוך אחריו, יצא זכר שאין בנו כרוך אחריו.

הספרא לומדת מהשוואה למצות שילוח הקן (דב׳ כב:ו-ז) שמצות ״אותו ואת בנו״ גם כן נוהגת רק בנקבות. השוואה זו תקיפה אף שקיים הבדל אחד. בשילוח הקן אין מצוה במזומן, דהיינו כשהעוף שייך לו. ובאותו ואת בנו חייב אף על בהמתו. השימוש ב״אותו״ בלשון יחיד מראה שרק באחד (האם) חייב ולא בשנים (האב והאם). אז מוסיפה הספרא טעם שני, שהמלים ״אותו ואת בנו״ מצביעים על האם שאליה מתקרב הבן באופן טבעי.

למרות שאין זכר בספרא לדעתו של חנניה, דעה זאת מופיעה לפי האמוראים במשנה בכורות ז:ז:

אלו כשרין באדם ופסולין בבהמה: ״אותו ואת בנו. . . .״

30. מובאת גם בבבלי בכורות מה עמ׳ ב.

31. ספרא אמור, פרשה ח:יא-פרק ח:ב (צט עמ׳ ב), מובאת גם בבבלי חולין, שם ובמדרש תנאים לדב׳ כב:ז (עמ׳ 135–136).

על משנה זאת מדייקת הבבלי בכורות מה עמ׳ ב וזה לשונו בתוספת באור:

> לעולם אהרן ובניו (ז.א. אב ובנו מותרים לשרת בקודש בבת אחת), דכוותה הכא תייש (עז) ובנו (כמו כן כאן, אסור לשחוט אב ובנו ביום אחד). אמרי במערבא (בארץ ישראל) משמיה דר׳ יוסי בר אבין: עדא אמרה (זאת אומרת) חנניה היא. . . .

ומביאה הגמרא את הברייתא מחולין עם שיטות הסתם וחנניה. הדיוק האמוראי הוא הגיוני. לפי שהמשנה משווה בין כוהנים בעבודתם וקרבנות, ורק בני אהרן הזכרים עוסקים בקרבנות, זכרים צריכים להיות כלולים במצות ״אותו ואת בנו.״ אם כן, המשנה בבכורות נוקטת בשיטת חנניה.

ראינו מחלוקת תנאים בעניין ״אותו ואת בנו.״ הסתם בברייתא מחולין והספרא פוסקים שמצוה זאת נוהגת רק בנקיבות. חנניה בברייתא והסתם משנה בבכורות, כנראה, קובעים שמצוה זו נוהגת גם בזכרים.

שאלה זאת נדונה במגילת המקדש נב:5–7 בקשר להקרבת בהמה מעוברת. המגילה כותבת:

> ולוא תזבח לי שור ושה ועז והמה מלאות, כי תועבה המה לי. ושור ושה, אותו ואת בנו לוא תזבח ביום אחד. ולוא תכה אם על בנים.[32]

כאן אוסרת המגילה זביחת בהמה מעוברת ואחר כך מביאה את איסור ״אותו ואת בנו.״ הוספת המלים ״ולוא תכה אם על בנים״ מדב׳ כב:ו (מצות שילוח הקן, ״לא תקח האם על הבנים״) מראה שלפי בעל הקטע, ״אותו ואת בנו״ אינו די ברור. ההוספה היא אמורה לרבות את הנקבות בפסוק המדבר לכאורה רק על הזכרים. פירוש אחר כבר הועלה על ידי החוקרים.[33] לפי דעה זאת בעל המגילה הוסיף את המלים מספר דברים כדי לפרש את מצות ״אותו ואת בנו״ כמתיחסת אך ורק לנקיבות. הם מסבירים את ״וו״ החיבור (״ולוא תכה״) במשמעות ״כי״ או ״כדי ש-.״ פירוש זה אינו מקובל עלינו, כי דרך המגילה במקרים כאלו היא לנסח מחדש את החומר, ולכן היינו מצפים להעברת הכל ללשון נקבה. נראה להלן שיש סמוכין לפירושנו מקטע במקצת מעשה התורה.

היוצא לנו הוא ששיטת חנניה, וכנראה הסתם משנה בבכורות, הולמת את זו של מגילת המקדש. מאידך גיסא, המגילה מתפלמסת נגד דעה כמו זו של הסתם בחולין ובספרא המיחסת מצוה זו רק לנקבות, בניגוד לדברי התורה עצמה הכתובים בלשון זכר. גם הספרא וגם מגילת המקדש רואים במצות שילוח הקן חומר להקיש. לפי הספרא, השוואה זו מלמדת אותנו שכשם שמצות שילוח הקן נוהגת רק בנקבות, כן הוא במצות ״אותו ואת בנו.״ אולם מגילת המקדש לומדת מהשוואה זו שצריכים להוסיף את הנקבות למצות ״אותו ואת בנו,״ המתיחסת לפי עצם לשונה רק לזכרים.

מן הראוי להעיר כאן שלדעתם של חז״ל במשנה חולין ד:ה לא היה שום איסור בהקרבת או שחיטת בהמה מעוברת. אלא שהיתה מחלוקת בקשר לבן תשעה חודשים, דהיינו שליל בהמה שהגיע להתפתחותו המלאה:

> מצא בן תשעה חי, טעון שחיטה וחיב ב״אותו ואת בנו,״ דברי רבי מאיר. וחכמים אומרים: שחיטת אמו מטהרתו.

לפי שיטת רבי מאיר, אם מוצאים בתוך בהמה שחוטה שליל של בהמה שהגיע להתפתחות מלאה, צריך שחיטה. אם שחטו באותו יום ששחט בו אמו, עבר על מצות ״אותו ואת בנו.״ אולם, לפי שיטת החכמים, כל זמן שלא נולד הוולד אין צריך שחיטה ואינו בגדר מצות

32. ידין ב׳, 164. השווה א׳, 242–243.

33. קימרון וסטרוגנל, 158 הערה 117.

"אותו ואת בנו." ברור גם כן ממשנה זאת שהחכמים אינם רואים שום איסור בשחיטת בהמה מעוברת. לרבי מאיר יש איסור בחודש האחרון של ההריון.

למרות שמצאנו שבמצות "אותו ואת בנו" נקטה מגילת המקדש בשיטה דומה לזו של חנניה, בשאלת שחיטת בהמה מעוברת אין שום דמיון בין דעת המגילה לגישת שום תנא. אולם ידוע לנו שלאלו שייסדו את כת קומראן שאלה זאת היתה חיונית, שכן הכניסו אותה לתוך אגרת התירוכין שכתבו למנהיגי המקדש בירושלים, מקצת מעשי התורה. שם אנו קוראים (לפי שיחזור העורכים):

> [ועל העברות א]נחנו חו[שבים שאין לזבוח את] האם ואת הולד ביום אחד. [ועל] האוכל [אנח]נו חושבים שיאכל את הולד [לאחר שחיטתו. ואתם יודעים שהו]א כן והדבר כתוב עברה.[34]

כאן מוצאים את האיסור להקריב בהמות מעוברות. גם טוענים בעלי האיגרת שאין להתיר את השליל על ידי שחיטת אמו. הכי מעניין הוא שמקצת מעשה התורה נוקטת כאן בשיטת הסתם בחולין והספרא, שמצות "אותו ואת בנו" מתיחסת רק לנקבות, לעומת מגילת המקדש הנוקטת בשיטת חנניה המיחס מצוה זו גם לזכרים. פעם נוספת מצאנו שאותה מחלוקת שהיתה קיימת בתקופת התנאים כבר רווחה בתקופת החשמונאים.

מסקנות

בדקנו כאן מספר מחלוקות בספרות התנאים שלהם קיימים תקדימים ומקבילות במגילות מדבר יהודה. בכולם מצאנו שמשא ומתן באותם העניינים שהעסיקו את חז"ל כבר היה חלק מהתסיסה הדתית וההלכתית של ימי הבית השני. אין ספק שמאחרי הרבה מחלוקות המשתמרות לנו בספרות התנאים יש היסטוריה ארוכה ומסובכת. חקר מגילות מדבר יהודה אמור להסיר את קצת מערפלי הזמן מעל ההלכה בתקופה זאת. אפשר להוסיף גם מבדיקת הספרים החיצוניים, יוסיפוס והממצא הארכיולוגי. וככל שחוקרים חומר זה, מספר המקבילות הולך וגדל. אפילו ממקצת הדוגמאות שהצענו, ברור שאסור לנו להתחיל את תולדות ההלכה של חז"ל רק אחרי החורבן. היסודות להרבה הלכות ואפילו מחלוקות כבר היו קיימים בתקופת החשמונאים.

34. MMT B 36; קימרון וסטרוגנל, 50–51. וראה שיפמן, "Miqsat Ma'ase Ha-Torah," 448–451